# ENCYCLOPEDIA OF

# Consumer Brands

# ENCYCLOPEDIA OF CONSUMER BRANDS

## VOLUME I
## CONSUMABLE PRODUCTS

## VOLUME II
## PERSONAL PRODUCTS

## VOLUME III
## DURABLE GOODS

# ENCYCLOPEDIA OF
# Consumer
# Brands

**VOLUME 2**

*Personal*

*Products*

*Editor*   JANICE  JORGENSEN

St. James Press

Detroit    London    Washington D.C.

## STAFF

Janice Jorgensen, *Editor*

Sonia Benson, Nicolet V. Elert, L. Mpho Mabunda, Mary Ruby, *Associate Editors*
Kathleen Wilson, *Assistant Editor*
Suzanne M. Bourgoin, Kevin Hillstrom, Paula Kepos, *Contributing Editors*
Marilyn Allen, *Editorial Associate*

Peter M. Gareffa, *Senior Editor*

Mary Beth Trimper, *Production Director*
Shanna Heilveil, *Production Assistant*
Cynthia Baldwin, *Art Director*
Mark C. Howell, *Graphic Designer*

Victoria B. Cariappa, *Research Manager*
Jeanne Gough, *Permissions Manager*

∞™ This book is printed on acid-free paper that meets the minimum requirements of American National Standard for Information Sciences—Permanence Paper for Printed Library Materials, ANSI Z39.48-1984.

Brand logos appearing inside this publication are trademarks or registered trademarks of their respective parent companies. The presence of these logos does not imply endorsement from the brands' companies; they are featured for identification purposes only. Brand logos appearing on the cover have been reproduced with permission.

Library of Congress Catalog Card Number 93-37940
ISBN 1-55862-337-X
Printed in the United States of America
Published simultaneously in the United Kingdom

I(T)P

The trademark **ITP** is used under license.

10 9 8 7 6 5 4 3 2 1

# ADVISERS

**Martin Boddy**
Information Officer
ICI Group Headquarters, London, England

**Linda Golden**
Professor of Marketing
University of Texas, Austin

**Pamela K. Jenkins**
Librarian/Business Specialist
Kansas City Public Library, Kansas City, Missouri

**Paul Kirner**
Vice President/Executive Art Director
J. Walter Thompson, Detroit, Michigan

**Jeanette M. Mueller-Alexander**
Reference Librarian/Business Subject Specialist
Hayden Library, Arizona State University, Tempe

# BRAND CATEGORIES COVERED IN THE ENCYCLOPEDIA

## VOLUME I: CONSUMABLE PRODUCTS
Food
Pet Food
Non-Alcoholic Beverages
Alcoholic Beverages
Tobacco

## VOLUME II: PERSONAL PRODUCTS
Apparel and Accessories
Cosmetics and Fragrances
Health and Beauty Aids
Household Cleaning and Paper Products
Miscellaneous Household Products
Over-the-Counter Drugs
Stationery and Office Supply

## VOLUME III: DURABLE GOODS
Appliances
Automobiles and Related Products
Computers, Electronics, and Office Equipment
Home Furnishings and Building Supplies
Musical Instruments
Photographic Equipment
Sporting Goods
Toys

# CONTENTS

## *Volume II: Personal Products*

# PREFACE

*Encyclopedia of Consumer Brands* provides substantive information on products that have been leaders in their respective brand categories and have had decided impact on American business or popular culture. Often considered "household words," the featured products have become integral parts of the lives of American consumers, and many have gone on to achieve international recognition.

The *Encyclopedia*'s three volumes highlight approximately 600 of the most popular brands in America. Coverage in each book emphasizes brands that have been prominent since 1950 and are now on the market, with a few inclusions of instructive debacles such as the Edsel. Younger products that have experienced profound success or have notably influenced their industry are also included. With thousands of new products being introduced to the market each year—and only a handful of them still in existence five years after their launch—much can be learned from the stories behind prominent brands, whose success depends on an elusive combination of careful research, quality development, market savvy, advertising prowess, and precise timing. The *Encyclopedia* is intended for use by students, librarians, job seekers, advertising and business people, and others who want to learn more about the historical and modern development of brands most significant to American culture.

## Inclusion Criteria

Brands included in the series were selected by the editor and advisory board members, who chose brands possessing a combination of elements: top sales and leading market share in their field, strong public recognition, and longevity. Many top selling brands and market share leaders were discovered through listings found in trade journals, advertising periodicals, and industry and business publications; Gale Research's *Market Share Reporter* and *Business Rankings Annual* also aided in identifying leading brands. The editor and advisory panel selected brands from a wide range of categories, but because of the increasingly vast number of brand names on the market, some significant products inevitably were left out.

St. James Press does not endorse any of the brand names or companies mentioned in this book. Brands that appear in the *Encyclopedia* were selected without reference to the wishes of their parent companies, who have in no way endorsed their brands' entries. Parent companies were given the opportunity to participate in the compilation of the articles by providing first-hand research and reading their entries for factual inaccuracies. We are indebted to many of these companies for their comments and corrections; we also thank many of the companies for providing logos and other art work for identification purposes. All brand names mentioned in the *Encyclopedia* are trademarks or registered trademarks of their respective parent companies.

## Focus

The focus regarding a particular brand name varies from entry to entry. When an individual *product* has found significant success in the market place, that one product is featured in its own entry (e.g. Twinkies, Scotch Tape, or Mustang). When a *brand name* or *trademark* is placed on a wide range of products in different brand categories (e.g. Pillsbury, Calvin Klein, or Sony), that brand name or trademark is the focus of the entry, and discussion of most or all of the products on which that brand name appears will ensue.

Because companies choose to market their products using a variety of tactics—which can include capitalizing on an existing brand name by placing it on new products, or creating new brand names while still emphasizing the company name a consistent rule of thumb for determining the focus of each of the *Encyclopedia*'s entries was sometimes challenging to establish. The responsibility of deciding the focus of each article rested with the editor, advisory board members, and writers and researchers. Please refer to the Index to Brand Names to identify products that have been either historically chronicled in full or merely mentioned within the series.

## Entry Format

An array of special features is included in the entries, which have been designed for quick research and interesting reading.

● **Attractive page design** incorporates textual subheads, making it easy to pinpoint specific information.

● **Easy-to-locate data sections** provide an "At a Glance" overview of brand history, sales and market share (when available), major competitors to the brand, advertising information, and the address and phone number of the brand's parent company.

● **Informative essays** trace how a product originated and was first marketed, how it evolved as a product and developed commercially, and how it fares today compared with its competitors and its own past history. Current coverage encompasses today's changing markets and marketing strategies, the impact of a global economy, and future projections, as well as any controversies associated with the product such as trade name disputes, false advertising claims, and safety, ethical, and environmental issues.

● **Current brand logos or photos** have been included with most entries to further enhance your appreciation of the brand; some entries include historical illustrations as well.

● **Sources for additional information** provide the reader with suggested further reading on the brand; these sources, also used to compile the entries, are publicly accessible materials such as magazines, general and academic periodicals, books, and annual reports, as well as material supplied by the brands' companies.

## Helpful Indexes

*Encyclopedia of Consumer Brands* includes cumulative indexes to Brand Names, Companies and Persons, Advertising Agencies, and Brand Categories that make it easy to locate not only featured brand names but pertinent brand names, companies, people, and advertising agencies mentioned within each article.

# ACE®

ACE brand products, manufactured by Becton Dickinson and Company, have been the nation's top-selling elastic support products since the early 1920s. Providing compressive support and therapy for acute injuries are such products as the elastic bandage—for which ACE is so well known—preformed supports (braces) and cold therapy products, including instant cold compresses, reusable cold compresses, and cold compression wraps. Protection against injuries is also made available through the use of athletic bandages and supporters.

ACE brand products are marketed for consumers in need of first aid as well as to meet the needs of an active lifestyle. Two consumer trends that began in the 1980s have heightened these needs and boosted sales of ACE products. First, more people are trying to maintain good health through physical activity and exercise. An estimated 100 million Americans exercise regularly. This group includes people in the baby boomer generation as well as people over 50. A report by the Simmons/MRS Group found that 69 percent of the consumers in the latter group reported that they had participated in a sport in the previous year.

In addition, due to escalating health costs, consumers put more emphasis on preventive medicine and self-medication. The more activity in which a person engages, the greater the chance for injury and the higher the likelihood that the injury will be self-medicated. The National Institute of Health estimated that 17 million sports injuries occur among amateur athletes annually, and the number is increasing at the rate of eight percent each year.

Consumers spend about $250 million every year on first-aid products. Market research has revealed four reasons that consumers use these products. Consumers want to treat an injury, such as a sprain or strain, that requires immediate attention. They also want to prevent an old injury from recurring, or avoid a new injury, while taking part in a strenuous sports activity. Finally, they want to protect a physical weakness that might result in an injury if subjected to too much stress.

Throughout the years the company has developed different versions of ACE brand products to provide greater ease and convenience of use to consumers, and thus enhance their comfort during a period of injury. In addition, market research has enabled the company to identify how ACE brand products should be positioned in the marketplace, which retailing outlets best fit consumer needs, and how both consumers and retailers should be educated about ACE brand products.

## Brand Origins

Becton Dickinson and Company was founded in New York City by Maxwell W. Becton and Fairleigh S. Dickinson in 1897. Among the first of the company's acquisitions was the Surgical Supply Import Company, purchased in 1913. One of Surgical Supply's products, a German import, was Bender's Ideal Elastic Bandages, made of long-staple Egyptian cotton with warp threads twisted 30 or 40 times per inch. The bandages could be stretched and still regain their original shape.

About a year after the acquisition, however, World War I began and all importing from Germany had to cease. In 1921 the decision was made at Becton Dickinson to begin manufacturing their own elastic bandages. The name ACE was selected from 3,000 entries in a contest sponsored by the company to develop "a suitable name for a new and superior elastic bandage." The winner of the $200 prize was a group of 48 physicians who used ACE as an acronym for "all cotton elastic." The company's sales force chose ACE because it was easy to remember and had a connotation of excellence.

## Brand Development

The ACE brand is composed of a complete line of products that help consumers to self-medicate at each stage, from the time of injury through recuperation. The first products that are recommended for use after the injury occurs are the cold therapy products, used to reduce swelling and pain. Cold compresses have been the recommended treatment for many injuries and can be easily administered on the playing field as well as in the home. Consumers have become increasingly aware of proper cold therapy through messages in the media, and from specialized sports books and magazines. The cold therapy products are part of RICE strategy for treatment of injuries, which stands for Rest, Ice, Compression, Elevation.

ACE brand elastic and athletic bandages—considered staple items for people with active lifestyles—have been made easier to

## AT A GLANCE

ACE brand of elastic bandages founded by Becton Dickinson and Company, 1921; brand has been expanded to include braces, athletic supporters, and cold therapy products.

**Performance:** *Market share*—78% (top share) of elastic health support products. *Sales*—$225.6 million (1991) for ACE brand bandages, braces, supporters and cold therapy products.

**Major competitor:** Futuro brand.

**Addresses:** *Parent company*—Becton Dickinson and Company, 1 Becton Drive, Franklin Lakes, NJ 07417-1880; phone: (201) 847-6800; fax: (201) 847-6475.

use with new methods of closure. The elastic bandages are available with either the clip version or a Velcro closing, while the athletic bandages are self-adhesive, requiring no other form of closure. High acceptability from health professionals and consumers alike has made ACE brand a household name with 99 percent awareness. In fact, in 1991 the sales for ACE bandages were almost 16 times those of the brand's closest competitor, and slightly more than 7 times those of all other competitors combined.

Another product is designed specifically for the needs of the active male. The ACE brand includes a complete line of men's and boys' athletic supporters for use during sports and recreational activities. The athletic supporters are designed and built to prevent injury, while simultaneously providing comfort.

ACE brand preformed elastic braces are needed to give extra support for an injury or weakened area of the body. In addition, the braces help prevent injury during activities. The form-fitted braces provide consumers with support, comfort, convenience, and durability.

## Marketing Strategies

The special nature, purpose, and usage of these products required specially-designed marketing strategies. The development of such strategies was based on extensive market research. Taking this data into consideration, marketing efforts focused on consumer needs during times of physical activity, the way in which products for self-medication were selected when an injury occurred, the retailing outlets deemed most effective in bringing these products to consumers, the way such products could best be promoted and advertised during a time of injury and treatment, and how both consumers and retailers could most effectively be educated about the products.

According to the company's research, when consumers need products to enhance their active lifestyles, they first visit drug stores. The highest number of unit sales as well as dollar volume has been found to take place in drug stores. In fact, these stores accounted for more than 60 percent of unit sales, and almost 55 percent of dollar sales, of total bandages and braces sold in all types of retail outlets. The type of product sold is also influenced by the type of drug store, whether it is part of a drug chain or an independently owned store. In 1991, bandages, braces, supporters, and cold therapy products had the highest sales volume in drug

chains, where consumers could make their own selection of products and were less likely to ask for personal attention or service.

According to A.C. Nielsen's 1991 data for dollar sales, 68 percent of total bandage sales took place in drug chains compared to 32 percent at independents; 63 percent of the sales for braces took place in drug chains compared to 37 percent at independents; 58 percent of the sales of athletic supporters were sold in chain stores compared to 42 percent at independents; and 68 percent of sales of cold therapy products took place in drug chains compared to 32 percent at independent stores.

It is this self-selection process that has shaped the company's marketing strategy. ACE brand products are not advertised in the same way as other consumer products, using print ads or TV commercials, because most consumers buy them only as they need them. Instead, the strategy has been for the company's sales force to acquaint drug store personnel with ACE brand items, then educate them about the products so that they can recommend usage when consumers inquire about them. The sales force plays a consultive role with the retailers that are called upon. In addition, point-of-purchase materials are used to promote the products so that the consumer can easily see the name ACE when a product selection needs to be made.

As a global medical technology company, Becton Dickinson has overseas manufacturing plants located in Singapore, Canada, France, Brazil, Japan, and Mexico. Many of the ACE brand products familiar to Americans are also familiar to active persons living in other countries. As these nations become more affluent, there is the likelihood that people will become more health and fitness conscious. Exercise and sports activities will increase, likely meaning a rise in injuries that would require ACE products.

## Performance Appraisal

ACE brand products have more than three-quarters of the market for such items. According to A.C. Nielsen data for 1991, total unit sales for bandages, braces, supporters, and cold therapy products were 229.8 million for sales of $225.6 million. The data showed that in comparison to unit sales of the company's closest competitor, Kendall Company's Futuro brand, almost 15 times more ACE brand bandages were sold; about 8 percent more ACE brand braces were sold; and nearly 67 percent more athletic supporters were sold. Kendall did not market cold therapy products.

ACE brand products also outpaced all other competing brands combined, according to the data. Unit sales for ACE brand bandages were almost 6 times greater; braces almost 7 times greater; and athletic supporters almost a whopping 18 times higher. As the fitness trend continues to take hold among new types of consumers, and strengthens among current participants, the company is expected to reap further success.

## Further Reading:

''ACE Brand Products,'' Franklin Lakes, NJ: Becton Dickinson and Company.

Becton Dickinson and Company Annual Report, Franklin Lakes, NJ: Becton Dickinson and Company, 1992.

*The Elastic Health Support Category Expert,* section 2, Franklin Lakes, NJ: Becton Dickinson and Company.

—*Dorothy Kroll*

# ADIDAS®

# adidas®

Adidas is the world's largest manufacturer of sporting goods. The branded athletic equipment is supplied to more than 160 countries, and the company produces 180,000 pairs of shoes and 50,000 meters of fabric each day. The Adidas brand is applied to equipment in practically every sport except equestrianism and downhill skiing and is especially well established in soccer, tennis, basketball, and track and field events. The brand's parent, Adidas AG, has subsidiaries, licensees, or subcontractors in approximately 50 countries. The Adidas museum's acclaimed collection of track and field footwear dating from 1924 is located at the company headquarters in Herzogenaurach, near Neuremberg, Germany. Adidas has been outfitting the world's best athletes, from Jesse Owens (1936) to Florence Griffith-Joyner (1992), for over 60 years. It is also one of the top ten sporting goods and activewear brands. The brand's sales and market share have declined since the early 1970s, however, due to competition from such formidable adversaries as Nike, Inc., and Reebok International Ltd.

## Brand Origins

The genesis of Adidas footwear occurred in 1920, when brand founder Adolf Dassler made his first pair of sport shoes. At just 20 years old, Dassler had made slippers and dress shoes, but his personal interest in athletics lead him to design specialized shoes for sport. Adolf and his brother, Rudolph, made their first pair of running shoes in 1925. From the beginning, Dassler shoes established the vanguard of athletic shoe design and market segmentation by sport. The brothers brought out soccer shoes with nailed studs and track shoes with hand-forged spikes that year; within about a decade, Dassler Brothers shoes had earned an international reputation for quality. In 1931 the Dasslers brought their first tennis shoes onto the market. By the end of 1937, the line of Dassler shoes included styles designed for eleven specific sports.

Adolf Dassler enrolled in a professional shoe-design school in Pirmasens and completed a two-year educational program in just 12 months. His classes at Pirmasens gave Dassler the total stock of knowledge available at that time on shoe planning and shoe manufacture. He augmented this formal education with advice and input from athletes, trainers, doctors, and materials specialists.

Adolf used his findings to continuously improve athletic shoes with innovations like arch support lacing and an early type of speed lacing in the early 1940s. The now-trademark three-stripe design of Adidas shoes was introduced in 1941 as part of the

shoes' support structure. The three-stripe device was not registered as a trademark until 1949. By the time Adolph "Adi" Dassler died in 1978, he had earned more than 700 patents and other industrial property rights worldwide for innovations that became industry standards. That year, Dassler became the first non-American to be inducted into the American Sporting Goods Industry Hall of Fame.

The Dassler brothers' partnership ended in 1948. The two brothers had fought bitterly and often, and formed two separate companies that year. Adolf first named his venture "Addas," then changed the name to "Adidas," a combination of his nickname, Adi, and a shortened form of Dassler. The brand founder adopted the lowercase "a" to further distinguish his brand. Rudolph created the Puma Company, and the familial rivalry continued throughout the 20th century. Sadly, some have said that Adi and Rudi never spoke again.

## Early Marketing Strategy

Dassler was one of the first shoe manufacturers to use athletic promotions and endorsements to make Adidas synonymous with serious, successful athletes. He started giving free shoes to athletes and made it a principle to launch a product innovation at every major sports event. Olympic athletes at the 1928 Amsterdam Games were the first to wear Adi Dassler's shoes. Four years later, Arthur Jonath wore Dassler track shoes when he won a bronze medal at the Los Angeles Olympic Games. His was the first in a long line of Dassler-shoe medals. Jesse Owens wore Dassler shoes when he won Olympic Golds and crossed color barriers at the 1936 Berlin Games. Adidas continued to use promotions at major sporting events as primary advertising vehicles throughout the 20th century.

After the 1948 breakup, competition between the Dassler brothers heightened every four years at the Olympic Games, where Adidas and Puma fought to equip more athletes. The trademark three-stripe device made Adidas shoes stand out from others, a feature that became increasingly important as media attention focused on sporting events beginning in the 1950s. Adidas became the most-worn German sports shoe brand at the 1952 Helsinki Olympic Games. That year, the brand introduced track shoes with changeable spikes and its first accessory, sport bags.

## AT A GLANCE

**A**didas brand shoes founded in 1948 in Herzogenaurach, Germany, by Adolf Dassler, whose company was family owned until 1989 when it was formed into an "Aktiengesellschaft" (AG), or public German corporation; company/brand acquired by Bernard Tapie Finances G.m.b.H. in 1991; purchased by Robert Louis-Dreyfus and a group of institutional investors in February, 1993.

**Performance:** *Market share*—15% of global athletic shoe market (1989); 2% of U.S. athletic shoe market (1993). *Sales*—DM 3.35 billion (1992).

**Major competitor:** Nike (with 17% of global athletic shoe market; 1989); also, Reebok.

**Addresses:** *Parent company*—Adidas AG, Adi-Dassler-Str. 1, 8522 Herzogenaurach, Germany; phone: 9132/840; fax: 9132/842027. *Ultimate parent company*—Adidas G.m.b.H, Adi-Dassler-Str. 1, 8522 Herzogenaurach, Germany; phone: 9132/840; fax: 9132/842027.

In addition to the Olympics, other major sports competitions helped Adidas shoes gain fame: in 1954 the German soccer team won the world championship wearing Adidas shoes. The team wore the first shoes with screw-in soccer studs. Two years later, Adidas revolutionized the game of soccer with the introduction of nylon soles. Soccer quickly became one of Adidas' fortes: in 1958 the majority of soccer players at the World Cup in Sweden wore the brand; they were worn in all 32 games of the 1962 Soccer World Cup in Chile; in 1966 75 percent of soccer's best athletes played in Adidas at the World Cup in England; and that figure rose to 85 percent by the time the 1970 championship matches were played in Mexico. The Adidas brand was extended to sporting equipment in 1963, when soccer balls were introduced under the trademark. By 1970, the brand's balls were accepted as the official soccer ball of the World Cup.

At the same time, Adidas' technological innovations made their mark on track and field. In 1956 many of the medal winners at the Melbourne summer Olympic Games wore the three-striped shoes. The brand introduced the first nylon half-sole for track shoes in 1957, and added a rubber protector for the toe in 1960. That year, 75 percent of the track and field competitors at the Summer Olympic Games in Rome wore Adidas shoes. Four years later, that number had risen to 80 percent on the introduction of Adidas' 140-gram track shoes, then the lightest in the world. Adidas "stretched out" into the world of sportswear during the 1960s, launching its first training suit in 1967. It was then that the brand adopted the trefoil device with three stripes running through it to distinguish the branded sportswear. The clothing was often decorated with three stripes extending down the arms or legs as well.

### The American Introduction

Adidas shoes were launched in the United States in conjunction with the 1968 Mexico City Olympics, where athletes wearing the branded footwear won 85 percent of all track and field medals. The brand used its standard athletic promotions to impress its new American customers: in 1971 both Muhammad Ali and Joe Frazier wore Adidas in their "fight of the century." By 1972, Adidas had captured such a large portion of the American sports

shoe market that Brunswick's Mac-Gregor Division and Pepsico's Wilson subsidiary dropped out of track shoes.

Adidas introduced segmentation by sport, modern styling, and technology to the American sports shoe market. Its technological improvements, like interchangeable spikes and sharkskin soles for traction, drew many amateur athletes who were caught up in the running craze of the 1970s. Adidas claimed that its production of eight million pairs of sports shoes made it the world's largest brand in 1972. By that time, the shoes were marketed through four distributors in the United States.

By the end of the decade, Adidas led the industry in sales, and worked hard to maintain that lead by expanding into more sports. As competition in running shoes intensified, the brand's advertising budget was doubled, from $500,000 to almost $1 million, and Adidas added more television and consumer magazines to its normal schedule of specialty sports publications. The brand also employed its first professional ad agency, F. William Free & Co. from New York, in 1978. Prior to that time, American ads had been generated in-house at Adidas world headquarters in Herzogenaurach. New ads emphasized Adidas's worldwide reputation and its extensive research in product development. Even with the media increases, the brand concentrated most of its ad budget on endorsement and promotional contracts with famous athletes.

By 1979, 25 million Americans were involved in the jogging and running boom, double the number of runners in 1977. The trend helped triple Adidas' sales from 1976 to 1979 to over $500 million. At the height of its popularity, Adidas had 100 different shoe styles and between 30 percent and 40 percent of the sports shoe market. Throughout its first decade in the American market, the brand was the undisputed leader in running shoes.

### Decline in America

But 1979 marked the apogee of Adidas's dominance of the United States' almost $7 billion footwear market. The brand's share took a hard fall that year to 20 percent, down from 25 percent in 1978. An American-made threat had been gaining momentum since the early 1970s: Oregon-based Nike shoes were leading the passel of newer brands sold in the United States. In 1979 Nike captured a full third of the market with its modern, colorful styling, aggressive advertising, and high-tech innovations. A year later, it had surpassed Adidas, garnering more than half of the American shoe market. In 1982 the jogging craze started to wane.

Adidas had introduced its line of "action clothes" and, with over $1 billion in global sales, was still the worldwide leader. The brand completely dominated the German market, with 75 percent, but even faced challenges on its home front from Nike and Pony International, the number one and number four U.S. sport shoe brands, respectively.

One of the brand's own athletes struck a blow to Adidas in the mid-1980s. Joe Montana, the Super Bowl-winning San Francisco 49ers' quarterback, had signed a promotional contract with Adidas for $25,000 per year from 1981 to 1983. Montana was required by the contract to wear Adidas footwear during games, appear in ads, make personal appearances, and be featured on a poster. The pay was reasonable when Montana was a relative unknown, but after the quarterback led his team to the 1982 Super Bowl championship, Adidas was quick to take advantage of the marketing opportunity. The brand took out major-market newspaper ads that declared, "We've been with you all the way," in reference to Montana. Adidas also started marketing a "Montana" shoe. In 1984, when the football player sued the brand's parent for using his name without permission, Adidas claimed the shoe was named for the state, not the football star. The negative publicity surrounding the incident could not have helped the brand's declining fortunes.

Adidas consolidated all of its worldwide advertising under one agency, Young & Rubicam (Y&R), in 1985. Y&R beat out BBDO, McCann-Erickson, and 20 other agencies for the global account that tried to combine Adidas footwear and clothing lines for a global advertising campaign. Some industry observers noted that a single-athlete worldwide campaign could backfire on Adidas, since many sports stars were country-specific. Adidas pressed on with a prestige positioning of the branded shoes and clothing featuring Ivan Lendl. The $22 million campaign put the tennis star in branded apparel and footwear against a sky background and the Adidas logo.

But after having led a revolution in athletic footwear, Adidas missed such major American sporting trends as aerobics, basketball, and cross-training. At the same time, the market shifted to an emphasis on "image-conscious" shoes and apparel, rather than purely athletic gear.

## Corporate Distractions

In 1990 Bernard Tapie, a French Socialist politician and businessman, purchased 80 percent of Adidas for DM700 million (US$425 million). Adi Dassler's son, Horst, had run the family-owned company since his father's death in 1978, but when Horst died in 1987, family turmoil had put the future of the brand's parent in question. Many hoped that the change in ownership would reverse Adidas's downward spiral. Tapie slashed Adidas's strung-out product line, which had swelled to 2,500 items, down to several hundred choices. He also sold off Adidas A.G.'s Pony, Le Coq Sportif, and Arena brands to focus on the core label.

But Tapie's efforts were nullified by Adidas's unfocused marketing efforts, consistently poor distribution practices, and increased competition from Nike and Reebok in European markets. In 1991 the brand's pre-tax profits were cut in half, to DM5 million on nearly flat sales of DM996.

The news that Great Britain's Pentland Group planned to acquire Adidas was greeted with relief by brand management and retailers alike. By July of 1992, when the announcement was made, the brand's share of America's sports shoe market had plunged to three percent. Morale at Adidas had plummeted during Tapie's brief ownership, due to allegations of fraud and poor fiscal management of the ultimate parent, Bernard Tapie Finances G.m.b.H. Even in its single largest market, Germany, Adidas's share had fallen ten percentage points to 40 percent from 1990 to 1992 in the face of competition from Nike and Reebok, with 28 percent and 23 percent, respectively. The two rivals also started to erode Adidas's exclusive endorsement contracts with athletes in Eastern Europe and the former Soviet Union.

Many expected Pentland to use its vast financial resources to match competitor's seemingly limitless advertising budgets, update merchandise, improve distribution, and sign up more prominent endorsers. But those hopes were dashed when the British conglomerate pulled out of acquisition negotiations in October of 1992. The brand lost DM76 million (US$47.2 million) in 1992 on an 18 percent decline in sales, to DM922 million (US$572.67 million).

Adidas's roller-coaster ride climbed again in the spring of 1993, when a group of investors lead by the former head of British advertising group Saatchi & Saatchi P.L.C. acquired control of Adidas A.G. Robert Louis-Dreyfus, a member of one of France's wealthiest families, was expected to repeat the turnaround strategy he had used at Saatchi: cost-cutting, debt reduction, and increased profit margins. It was also hoped that Louis-Dreyfus's presence would energize Adidas's marketing strategy.

## Future Activity

Several factors evident in the early 1990s promised to positively affect the brand's future. Early in 1993, Adidas A.G. formed a new American subsidiary through the acquisition of Sports Inc., a Portland-based marketing firm. Sports Inc. was transformed into Adidas America, which superseded, but did not replace, the brand's other U.S. subsidiaries. Robert J. Strasser, a former vice president of marketing with Nike, Inc., was named chief executive of the organization. While with Nike, Strasser had developed the famous Air Jordan line of basketball shoes. The move drastically transformed Adidas's American marketing strategy, which had been developed in Germany since the brand was introduced to the United States in 1968. Strasser hoped to be more able to react to the "fickle" American market, and planned to aim future advertising campaigns at urban youth.

Adidas's Equipment line of footwear and apparel was also considered a positive aspect of the brand's business. Some retailers polled in *Footwear News* claimed that Adidas had brought "the technology of an athletic brand into the outdoor area" with the category, which was introduced in 1991. Others noted that the brand had "made something of a comeback" in tennis and soccer. But according to the fall, 1992, article, most retailers did not think that Adidas could regain the top spot it held in the 1960s and early 1970s, or even compete with Nike and Reebok in the first tier of athletic footwear. However, many thought Adidas could be a strong second-tier brand.

## Further Reading:

"Adidas A.G.: The World's Largest Manufacturer of Sporting Goods," Portland, OR: Adidas America, 1988.

"Adidas' Olympic Shoe-in," *Sales Management,* September 4, 1972, pp. 3, 4.

"The Adidas Story," Herzogenaurach, Germany: Adidas A.G., 1982.

Bannon, Lisa, "Pentland Drops Plan to Acquire Control of Adidas," *Wall Street Journal,* October 16, 1992, pp. B3A, c.3.

Chase, Dennis and Julia Michaels, "Adidas Czechs in with Global Ad Pitch," *Advertising Age,* November 4, 1985, p. 10.

Fallon, James, "Adidas Pre-tax Net Tumbles 51% in 1991," *Footwear News,* May 25, 1992, p. 21.

"France 1; West Germany Nil," *The Economist,* July 14, 1990, p. 66.

"The Jogging-Shoe Race Heats Up," *Business Week,* April 9, 1979, pp. 124–25.

Melcher, Richard A. and Ann Hollifield, "Now, This Should Get Adidas on Its Feet," *Business Week,* July 20, 1992, p. 42.

Raissman, Robert, "Montana Goes on Offensive," *Advertising Age,* September 24, 1984, pp. 1, 104.

Raissman, and Dagmar Mussey, ''Y&R Wins Race for Adidas,'' *Advertising Age,* July 22, 1985, p. 60.

Reichlin, Igor, ''Where Nike and Reebok Have Plenty of Running Room,'' *Business Week,* March 11, 1991, pp. 56, 60.

Revett, John, ''Adidas Joins More Sports to Secure Footwear Hold,'' *Advertising Age,* September 4, 1978, pp. 2, 66.

Schwartz, Jerry, ''Adidas Hires Former Nike Executive,'' *New York Times,* February 6, 1993, pp. 37(L), c.3.

''Two U.S. Rivals Give Adidas a Run for Its Money,'' *Business Week,* July 18, 1983, p. 69.

Wilner, Rich, ''Retailers' Hopes Wilt as Adidas Turns into a Wall Flower Again,'' *Footwear News,* October 26, 1992, pp. 1, 22.

*—April S. Dougal*

# ADVIL®

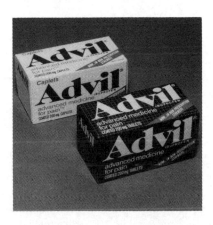

Introduced in 1984, Advil was the first nonprescription brand of ibuprofen in the United States. It has since remained the top-selling ibuprofen brand, and by the early 1990s it had become a dominant force in the over-the-counter (OTC) analgesics market, with sales second only to those of Tylenol (acetaminophen). Approved by the U.S. Food and Drug Administration (FDA) as an all-purpose pain reliever and fever reducer, Advil was recommended for the temporary relief of minor aches and pains associated with headaches, toothaches, backaches, musculoskeletal injuries, arthritis, and menstrual cramps.

American Home Products Corporation, the brand's parent company, purchased the license to market ibuprofen as an OTC drug in 1983 from the British firm Boots Pharmaceutical Company, which held the drug's worldwide patent. When the license was acquired, John Bryer, president of the U.S. subsidiary of Boots, told *Advertising Age* that American Home Products was chosen because it had "the sort of operation that can take on Tylenol eyeball to eyeball." Advil, in fact, quickly became an aggressive competitor in the lucrative pain-reliever market. According to the *Wall Street Journal,* Advil accounted for 52.3 percent of all over-the-counter ibuprofen sales by the early 1990s, with sales growing at an annual rate of about 15 percent. By this time ibuprofen had become the fastest-growing segment of the pain-reliever market. Aspirin sales were on a steady decline, and sales growth of the country's top-selling analgesic, acetaminophen, had slowed to a near halt.

Advil was just one of many brands owned by American Home Products, which had sales surpassing $7 billion in the early 1990s. Among its other successful OTC medicines, produced under its Whitehall and A.H. Robins divisions, were Anacin, Robitussin, Preparation H, Dristan, and Dimetapp. It also produced a variety of prescription drugs, including Inderal-LA, a once-a-day, long-acting beta-blocker for the treatment of angina and hypertension; Ativan, a tranquilizer; Premarin, the leading estrogen replacement therapy in the United States; Triphasil, the second-leading oral contraceptive; and Lo/Ovral and Nordette, which were other widely used oral contraceptives. New prescription drugs introduced by American Home Products in the early 1990s included the Norplant System, a reversible five-year contraceptive; and Lodine, a nonsteroidal anti-infammatory drug (NSAID).

## Brand Origins

Ibuprofen, also classified as an NSAID, was developed in the 1960s by chemists of the Boots Pharmaceutical Company. Based on carboxylic acid derivatives, ibuprofen (Brufen) was introduced by Boots in 1964, and the company held its worldwide patent until May 28, 1985. Ibuprofen, like aspirin, worked by inhibiting the production and concentration of prostaglandins, hormone-like chemicals thought to provoke pain receptors, cause fever, and generate an inflammatory response. A peripherally acting analgesic, ibuprofen reduced inflammation at the site of injury.

Ibuprofen first appeared in the United States in 1974 as a prescription pain reliever (in a 400 mg. dose) under the brand name Motrin. The brand was marketed by Upjohn Company, which had acquired nonexclusive rights from Boots. Motrin was prescribed for pain and inflammation associated with such conditions as arthritis, soft-tissue injuries, and menstrual cramps.

In 1984 Whitehall Laboratories, a division of American Home Products, gained approval from the FDA to market an OTC ibuprofen in a 200 mg. dose, or half the prescription strength. Introduced that year, the new product was called Advil, which would benefit greatly from being the first such OTC product in the United States. Upjohn chose not to respond with its own nonprescription ibuprofen, but it later sold the marketing and distribution rights for OTC Motrin to Bristol-Myers, which in 1985 introduced a 200 mg. formulation under the name Nuprin, an acronym for new aspirin. Nuprin, however, would never seriously challenge Advil. American Home Products would use its large direct-sales force and its ability to garner maximum shelf space in chain stores to help Advil stand out early in the ibuprofen stakes.

By 1987, just two years after the Boots patent on ibuprofen expired, several generic brands of ibuprofen flooded the market, and ibuprofen quickly became the fastest-growing segment of the painkiller market. Despite the new competition, Advil continued to be the category leader, capturing about 50 percent of ibuprofen sales by the early 1990s.

## Sales Trends

Introduced with the slogan "advanced medicine for pain," Advil entered the United States well positioned to gain a substan-

## AT A GLANCE

**A**dvil brand of ibuprofen introduced in 1984 in 200 mg. tablets by American Home Products Corporation; at that time prescription ibuprofen, in 400 mg. tablets, was the best-selling remedy for arthritis; Advil has remained the category leader of nonprescription ibuprofen since its introduction.

**Performance:** *Market share*—52% (top share) of ibuprofen category; second-largest share of analgesics category. *Sales*—$285 million (1991).

**Major competitor:** Johnson and Johnson's Tylenol; also Motrin.

**Advertising:** *Agency*—Young and Rubicam, 1984—. *Major campaign*—Television commercials featuring Nolan Ryan, a record-holding major league pitcher.

**Addresses:** *Parent company*—American Home Products Corporation, 685 Third Avenue, New York, NY 10017-4085; phone: (212) 878-5000; fax: (212) 286-9746.

tial share of the analgesics market. According to *Progressive Grocer,* in 1984, when the brand entered the country's $1.5 billion analgesics market, more than 80 percent of all adults were estimated to use some type of pain reliever; aspirin consumption was on the wane because of bad publicity about adverse gastrointestinal complications; and prescription ibuprofen had been used by more than seven million Americans. It was aspirin's declining market share that posed the best opportunity, and Advil was promoted as an advanced anti-inflammatory medicine with a better safety record than aspirin.

Advil's entry into the market coincided with a shifting view on pain and the consumption of pain-relief drugs. Both doctors and the general public agreed that everyday maladies need not cause pain, and drugs increasingly promised relief from not only headaches and fever but also a broad range of other problems, including colds and flu, allergies, muscle and body aches, menstrual pain, arthritis, and insomnia. By 1990 Simmons Market Research data revealed that 87.3 percent of those surveyed used some type of pain reliever, compared with 80 percent reported by *Progressive Grocer* in 1984. This trend toward increasing self-medication also may have helped boost sales of a new pain reliever.

By the early 1990s Advil had become the number-two analgesic brand, second only to Tylenol, leaving both the long-trusted aspirin brands and the newer ibuprofens far behind. According to *Supermarket News,* Advil's sales had reached $285 million in 1991. Even Nuprin did not succeed in capturing much of the ibuprofen market. In 1986 *Fortune* reported that Advil sales were three times greater than Nuprin, and by 1993, with just 8.8 percent of the ibuprofen category, Nuprin posed little threat to Advil's dominance. All ibuprofen brands, however, benefited from the trend toward long-term use of the drug, notably for the chronic pain of arthritis, which led to demand for packs of 100 tablets or more. Arthritics, representing just 22 percent of analgesic users, accounted for some 50 percent of unit sales.

Advil and other ibuprofen products have been especially popular with younger adults and women. In 1992 *BrandAdvantage* revealed that 45.4 percent of Advil users were 18 to 34 years old, compared with 36.6 percent in the 35 to 54 age group and 18 percent among those 55 years and older. Moreover, women made up 57.5 percent of its customers, a higher level than found in the

other top-selling analgesics—54.8 percent for Tylenol and 48.6 percent for Bayer aspirin.

### Brand Extensions

Advil was available in coated caplet and tablet forms. American Home Products would also use the Advil name on the industry's first ibuprofen-based cold remedy, CoAdvil, made of ibuprofen and pseudoephedrine. Introduced in 1989, CoAdvil was later renamed Advil Cold and Sinus. Procter & Gamble filed a suit in 1992 charging that American Home Products' cold remedies containing ibuprofen—Advil Cold and Sinus, as well as Dristan Sinus and Dimutab Sinus—infringed upon its patents.

Advil entered the children's analgesics market in 1989 with its launch of Children's Advil Suspension, a nonsteroidal, sucrose-sweetened, fruit-flavored "liquid suspension" containing 100 mg. of ibuprofen per milliliter. Approved as a prescription drug, Children's Advil Suspension was indicated for fever reduction in children, as well as relief of the signs and symptoms of juvenile arthritis, rheumatoid arthritis, osteoarthritis, and primary dysmenorrhea. It was also indicated for the relief of mild to moderate pain in adults.

In the 1990s many analysts predicted the pain-reliever market would soon become further segmented by new products targeted to specific pains, ailments, and discomforts. As a result, further diversification of the Advil line seemed likely. By 1991 sales of all products in the Advil line had reached $305 million, second only to those of the Tylenol line.

### Controversies

Advil's rising sales in the late 1980s and early 1990s came largely on the heels of bad publicity about the potential adverse side effects of aspirin, notably internal bleeding. Ironically, by 1990 there were reports of ibuprofen-related side effects—including kidney complications and gastrointestinal pain, ulceration, and bleeding—and that year the FDA began considering changes in the label requirements for all ibuprofen products. Opposed to any label changes, American Home Products fought back, claiming that nonprescription doses were safe for patients without preexisting or complicating conditions. The FDA eventually ruled that specific side effects would not need to be mentioned on the labels of ibuprofen products, but it did propose a minor addition to the labels—a statement warning consumers to consult a physician if they experienced any symptoms that were unusual or seemed unrelated to the condition for which they were using ibuprofen.

Advil was not particularly damaged by the debate about its safety. Its market share continued to climb, and the product's image remained positive. When the label changes were being considered, American Home Products filed suit to require similar changes on acetaminophen products so that arch-rival Tylenol would not gain a competitive advantage.

### Advertising

In its first ten years on the market, Advil's essential pitch was underlined by the slogan "advanced medicine for pain," which promoted the brand as the newest, most advanced pain-relief formula. Early Advil advertisements emphasized its origins as a prescription drug and touted its image of superior painkilling capability. Comparative advertising was used widely, with many ads featuring the claim that one Advil works as well as two regular-strength aspirin or Tylenol.

Advertising for Advil and other ibuprofen brands has been aggressively directed toward the young, the physically fit, and women and has used professional athletes in promotions. In 1993 Nolan Ryan—a record-holding major league pitcher, a successful executive, and a father of three children—appeared repeatedly in Advil's highly visible television ads. Ryan's appeal was that he was an aging though still successful athlete who needed Advil to cope with the aches and pains of continuing competition, a quite different pitch from that used in aspirin advertising.

American Home Products, which had vigorously propelled Preparation H and Anacin into prominent market positions by outspending the competition, did the same for Advil. Data from Leading National Advertisers Inc. (LNA) reveals steady yearly increases in advertising expenditures for Advil, with no other ibuprofen brand coming anywhere close to its advertising budget. According to LNA, in 1991 Advil's advertising expenditures totaled $54.1 million; in 1992 $68.2 million was spent. More money, in fact, was spent on promoting Advil than on any other analgesic brand except Tylenol.

Randall Yates, president of Whitehall Laboratories, told the *Wall Street Journal* in 1993, "We believe that we have a lot of growth potential left. We'd love to be No. 1." He also indicated that the company would continue to spend at least as much, if not more, on advertising, depending on the competition.

## Brand Outlook

In the early 1990s Advil was the second-leading nonprescription analgesic on the U.S. market and the top-ranking ibuprofen, with 52.3 percent of the ibuprofen category. Although competition was anticipated from new anti-inflammatory drugs poised to enter the OTC analgesics market, American Home Products was expected to protect Advil's strong market position through continuing escalation of advertising expenditures, high visibility promotions, and aggressive comparative advertising. Barring entry of a new wonder drug for pain or new questions about the safety of Advil, the brand was likely to remain in the forefront of the U.S. analgesics market, which by the early 1990s had grown to some $3.5 billion.

**Further Reading:**

*Ad $ Summary, January-December 1992*, New York: Leading National Advertisers Inc., 1992.

"The Analgesics Explosion," *Progressive Grocer*, December 1984, pp. 87–88.

"Big Growth Expected from Switches to OTC: Over-the-Counter Drug Sales Projected to Rise to $40 Billion by 2000," *Supermarket News*, September 28, 1992, p. 23.

"Consumer Use of Ibuprofen Safe, Whitehall Asserts," *Drug Topics*, October 22, 1990, p. 28.

Deveny, Kathleen, "Marketscan: Ibuprofen's Success Pains Aspirin Makers," *Wall Street Journal*, January 12, 1993, p. B1.

Gannon, Kathi, "Drug Makers, FDA Spring to Defense of OTC Ibuprofen," *Drug Topics*, May 21, 1990, pp. 29–30.

Giges, Nancy, "Whitehall Labs Plans Major Painkiller Effort (Ibuprofen), *Advertising Age*, July 25, 1983, p. 1.

"Headache and Pain Relievers," *1990 Study of Media and Markets*, Simmons Market Research Bureau, 1990.

"Headache and Pain Relievers Brand Profile," *BrandAdvantage*, Wilmette, IL: Standard Rate and Data Service, 1992.

"How Safe Is Ibuprofen?" *Patient Care*, July 15, 1991, p. 138.

"Ibuprofen Carries a Risk for Some Users, Study Says," *Wall Street Journal*, April 17, 1990, p. B10.

"Ibuprofen Field Gets Bigger and Bigger," *Chemical Marketing Reporter*, January 19, 1987, p. 3.

"Internal Remedies Market Shifts," *Chain Drug Review*, January 4, 1993, p. B17.

Janofsky, Michael, "Nolan Ryan's Other Pitching Career," *New York Times*, March 28, 1993, business section, p. 5.

Nicholson, J.S., "Ibuprofen," *Chronicles of Drug Discovery*, volume 1, Chichester, England: John Wiley, 1988, pp. 149–172.

"Pills with a Purpose: Symptom-Specific Analgesics a Growing Category for Retailers," *Supermarket News*, January 18, 1993, p. 56.

"The Politics of Pain: A New Attitude toward Treatment," *Drug Topics*, September 21, 1992, pp. 60–62.

"Prescription O-T-C Switches Hike Category Volume," *Chain Drug Review*, April 20, 1992, p. 156.

"Segmentation in Analgesics Spurs Growth," *Drug Store News*, March 16, 1992, p. 34A.

Squires, Sally, "Painkiller Safety Questioned: High Doses of Ibuprofen Linked to Kidney Damage, New Studies Say," *Washington Post*, March 2, 1993, p. WH7.

"Strong Medicine: Ibuprofen Products are Gaining Strength in the Competitive Analgesics Market," *Supermarket News*, August 31, 1992, p. 21.

*—Laura Newman*

# AJAX®

In 1946 Colgate-Palmolive Company emerged from World War II with a booming international franchise in soaps, foods, and other consumer products. However, there was much stiffer competition at home, where the industry was dominated by Procter & Gamble and Lever Brothers. In was in that year that Colgate-Palmolive, an enterprise built on toothpaste, shaving cream, and floating soap broadened its product line with a new scouring powder called Ajax.

## Brand Origins

Named for the warrior in Greek mythology who fought at the battle of Troy, Ajax scouring powder was the first of several new Colgate-Palmolive products that were developed to get money flowing through the financially anemic organization. The Ajax brand entered the market as an upstart competitor of Dutch, Bab-O, and Bon Ami cleansers. Supported by good promotion and an excellent distribution network, particularly in the northeastern United States, Ajax cleanser quickly became the nation's top selling scouring powder.

However, Procter & Gamble, having launched a successful assault on Colgate toothpaste in 1955, targeted Ajax two years later when it put its Comet cleanser into national distribution. Noting that the Comet brand contained bleach, advertisements showed the new brand winning a series of scrub-off contests. Colgate-Palmolive unfortunately took too long to respond that Ajax scouring powder, known simply as a "foaming cleanser," also contained bleach, and sales of the brand plunged.

## Brand Development

George Lesch, the architect of Colgate-Palmolive's huge foreign operations, was recalled to New York to fix the company's faltering domestic business. Lesch slashed costs by developing more efficient manufacturing processes for Ajax and other Colgate-Palmolive brands and loaded the savings into new product development.

Lesch noted that Procter & Gamble had built up a sizeable stable of completely unrelated brands, each of which had to be independently promoted at a great cost. He proposed that Colgate-Palmolive create extensions of its existing products—in effect, giving a new product an old name—to economize on the promotional expense. In search of a new product that would knock P&G

from the top spot, the company sent a handful of product development managers out to knock on doors and query housewives on their cleaning needs. They found ammonia widely in use as a complementary cleaning agent. They also learned that powdered cleansers were messy and their dust caused women to sneeze.

In October of 1961 the company rolled out a companion to its existing cleanser, a liquid called Ajax All-Purpose Cleaner with Ammonia. Advertising for the new brand was designed specifically to avoid cannibalizing sales of the scouring powder, proclaiming that the new brand "cleans everything from the floor up without rinsing." The brand surged to first place in its category only nine months after it was introduced, surpassing Lestoil, Handy Andy, and even Mr. Clean.

On the strength of the rejuvenated Ajax name, a second extension was quickly developed, a powdered floor and wall cleaner. Promoted with the tagline, "It gives you a bucket of power," the ammoniated cleaner struck right at the heart of P&G's Spic & Span franchise. The fourth product in the Ajax line was a heavy-duty laundry detergent, aimed at P&G's market leader Tide as well as Cheer, Dash, and Oxydol. Containing the mystery ingredient "ultramarine-plus," the new Ajax brand was advertised as a "safe suds" detergent that wouldn't choke up washer pipes or emerge from the wash cycle as a soapy clump.

Lesch's extension scheme was a fabulous success. It made maximum use of the Ajax name in superior new formulations, introduced memorable commercial themes, and pounded those themes home on the most effective wide target medium: television. In addition, the new versions of Ajax as well as the flagship cleanser all benefitted from the others' advertising. The consumer was left with the impression that Ajax—in any formula—was so good that it could clean anything. Colgate-Palmolive considered several other extensions, but an Ajax bleach was the only product ever test marketed.

In 1964 Colgate-Palmolive added a powdered chlorine bleach, superseding its Action brand, called Ajax Bleach Lightning. The new product was introduced with an unusual TV ad campaign, featuring, for that time, a high-tech graphic: an actual lightning bolt. Ajax bleach went up against conventional bleaches, including Clorox, then a P&G brand, as well as Snowy, Fleecy, and Purex.

## AT A GLANCE

**A**jax brand introduced as a cleanser by Colgate-Palmolive Company, 1945; Ajax liquid all-purpose cleaner with ammonia introduced in 1961; laundry detergent and White Knight campaign developed, 1962; Ajax Dishwashing Liquid introduced in 1963; Ajax scouring powder reformulated as Blue-Dot Cleanser, 1965; Ajax 2 detergent introduced, 1966; Gene the dishwasher featured in advertising beginning in 1969.

**Performance:** *Market share*—14.5% of the cleanser market; 0.8% of the cleaning solution market; 5.4% of the dishwashing liquid market; 2% of the laundry detergent market.

**Major competitor:** (For cleaning solutions) Procter & Gamble Company's Comet; (for dishwashing liquid) P&G's Dawn; (for laundry detergent) P&G's Tide.

**Advertising:** *Agency*—Foote, Cone & Belding. *Major campaign*—(for Ajax liquid) "Cleans Like a White Tornado"; (for laundry detergent) "Stronger than Dirt"; (for dishwashing liquid) "Squeaky Clean."

**Addresses:** *Parent company*—Colgate-Palmolive Company, 300 Park Avenue, New York, NY 10022; phone: (212) 310-2000.

A sixth Ajax product, a spray cleaner, was introduced in 1965. The spray was aimed at Bristol-Myers's Windex brand with the claim, "You can see one hundred miles." The product rocketed to a 20 percent market share. A year later the company marketed Ajax Power Pads, disposable scrub pads that contained a dollop of Ajax soap.

Ajax Cleanser was reintroduced in 1965 with the old "Ajax, the foaming cleanser" jingle of the 1950s. However, the product was repackaged in order to incorporate a distinctive blue dot which denoted that the cleanser was fortified with blue chlorine bleach, and the words to the jingle were changed to "Ajax, the Blue-Dot cleanser."

P&G battled the loss of its Mr. Clean business to Ajax not by relaunching the product, but by introducing an entirely new all-purpose cleaner with ammonia called Top Job. True to form, Procter & Gamble supported its introduction with a massive—and extremely costly—campaign that wrested market leadership away from Ajax. Colgate-Palmolive responded with a separate brand, Big Leo, colored green like Top Job, but with no enduring success.

## Advertising

Procter & Gamble's style of advertising was typified by its response to the sudden rise of Ajax. The company portrayed people in slightly goofy, but believable situations to demonstrate exactly how its products worked. Comedienne Jane Withers played Josephine, the happy lady plumber who bolted into the kitchens of distressed homemakers with a can of Comet. To advertise Ajax in a similar way, Colgate-Palmolive would have completely diluted the differentiation from P&G products it worked so hard to build. Instead, Colgate-Palmolive advertising focused on the House of Ajax concept.

Norman, Craig & Kummel, the advertising agency in charge of Ajax, focused its pitch on the housewife, whose days were spent near, if not watching, a television. Rather than show exactly how the product worked, the agency appealed to the fantasies of house-wives through their daydreams. Taking an empathetic stance, ads characterized housework as a boring, unappreciated and never-ending task. But the housewife using Ajax brand products cleaned with such ease that she could fly from her kitchen and out of the house. "Ajax," said the ad, "gets you out of the house fast."

Even more renowned was the campaign for Ajax liquid. In these ads, when a housewife screws the top off a bottle of Ajax, a small swirling tornado emerges to clean the home. The tiny animated white twister created a powerfully memorable visual that made the slogan, "It cleans like a white tornado," unforgettable. The ad was widely mocked on comedy shows, where white tornadoes spun out of their bottles and completely destroyed the kitchen. But these satires only helped to propel the tongue-in-cheek campaign to even greater fame.

Adman Joe Sacco created the idea of a vernacular woman—in contrast to the seemingly perfect housewives in P&G ads—who proclaimed to the camera, "I hate dirt." Suddenly, there appeared a knight in white armor, riding a white horse, who pierced the woman's dirty laundry with a long white lance. "New Ajax laundry detergent," she states, "is stronger than dirt." Although *Madison Avenue* magazine awarded the ad "Worst Campaign of 1963," the White Knight went on to eclipse even the White Tornado, both in sales generated and comedic parodies spawned.

By 1966 the Ajax extension formula had nearly run its course. Colgate-Palmolive had taken on so many competitors with the Ajax name that the brand had begun to lose its impact. In time, Colgate-Palmolive was forced to scale back the line of products—which the company called the House of Ajax—dropping the limited distribution of its new Ajax Dishwashing Liquid, choosing instead to focus on Palmolive.

It was at this time, while Ajax was still an extremely profitable brand family, that Colgate-Palmolive turned away from the advertising formulas that had so successfully revived the brand name. After four years, and an unsuccessful promotion to name the White Knight, the campaign was dropped because too many viewers were thought to "tune out" the commercial. Knowing exactly what to expect from the ad as soon as they spotted the knight, viewers simply ignored the message. The target audience, women, were known to grow dissatisfied with their detergents, and the loss of impact from the White Knight only heightened their eagerness for a new message, one that could come from a competing brand. In order to avoid such a situation, Colgate-Palmolive introduced a reformulated laundry detergent called Ajax 2.

Ajax Dishwashing Liquid made a return by this period with its own spokesman, a professional dishwasher named Gene. For this campaign, Colgate-Palmolive adopted the P&G ad format. Gene spoke directly to the audience, testifying how effectively Ajax cut grease and left dishes "squeaky clean," as he rubbed his finger across a plate fresh from his dishwater in order to prove it. Through relentless advertising, Gene became as familiar to consumers as the tornado and the knight.

Sensing skepticism with its claims for Ajax Liquid, Colgate-Palmolive offered consumers a free 43-page report from the Nationwide Consumer Testing Institute which concluded that Ajax was superior to 17 competing brands, including Palmolive. Despite an ad campaign featuring the now well-known Gene, only 300 people requested the report.

## Performance Evaluation

Procter & Gamble and other competitors to the House of Ajax gradually rebuilt their brand franchises, mostly at the expense of such Ajax extensions as the bleach, window cleaner, and power pads. The Ajax family retained an immensely strong aggregate identity, but lost much of the momentum of its earlier growth. Entering the 1980s, the House of Ajax concept had shrunk to include just three flagship products, the cleanser, dishwashing liquid, and detergent. This mix, where each Ajax brand continues to dominate its respective market, has remained basically unchanged.

## Further Reading:

"Ajax Market Share Improves, but White Knight Turns in His Tin Suit," *Advertising Age,* December 25, 1967, p. 3.

"Ajax—Story of Colgate's White Knight," *Advertising Age,* February 17, 1975, pp. 35–36.

"Any Number Can Play," *Sponsor,* March 15, 1965, pp. 31–33.

"Colgate Offers Proof of Ajax Claim, but Consumers Show Little Interest," *Advertising Age,* September 11, 1972, p. 72.

"Colgate Tests Ajax Power Pads; Drops Dish Liquid," *Advertising Age,* July 18, 1966, p. 1.

"Colgate vs. P&G," *Forbes,* February 1, 1966, pp. 26–35.

"Comet Leads Ajax in Hot Cleanser Clash," *Printers' Ink,* March 18, 1960, pp. 11–12.

"Does Ajax Surge Mean Closer Race Between Colgate and P&G?," *Printers' Ink,* September 28, 1962, p. 24.

"A Name for the White Knight," *Broadcasting,* August 22, 1966, p. 44.

"Why Ajax Vanquished Mr. Clean," *Broadcasting,* January 31, 1966, pp. 48–49.

—*John Simley*

# ALKA-SELTZER®

# Alka-Seltzer.

Not many remedies could claim they provided relief from concurrent symptoms, but effervescing Alka-Seltzer Original, owned by Miles Inc., gave relief to headache and stomach upset since it went on the market in 1931. Alka-Seltzer tablets effervesced and dissolved into a solution of sodium acetylsalicylate (salt of aspirin) when dropped into a glass of water and could help headache. Because the solution also was highly buffered, it was absorbed more quickly into the blood. The buffer, sodium citrate with residual sodium bicarbonate and carbon dioxide, handled excess stomach acid. Thus, Alka-Seltzer was both an analgesic and antacid. The Alka-Seltzer name derived from the alkaline nature of the product and from its resemblance to seltzer water when it effervesced. (Seltzer was an artificially prepared carbonated mineral water from Nieder-Selters in Germany that supposedly was medicinal.)

## Brand Origins

Dr. Franklin L. Miles founded the Miles Medical Company (later Dr. Miles Laboratories, then Miles Inc.) in 1884 in Elkhart, Indiana, to bottle proprietary medicines. The company's prime product and main source of growth was Restorative Nervine, which was used in the treatment of a number of chronic illnesses. Although the company's sales were strong, profits began to fall during the 1920s. Andrew "Hub" Beardsley, the first corporate chairman of Miles, and Charles Beardsley knew the company needed to diversify, and they thought effervescence was an area ripe for new products. At the time, people used powdered remedies for headaches and colds, and they found effervescent products to be faster-acting than plain powders. The company's first effervescent product, brought out in 1925, was Pura-Lax.

Dr. Miles Laboratories hired a British chemist and effervescence technologist in 1927 to develop other products. Maurice Treneer, who described himself as "a pioneer of the effervescent tablet business in the United States," put Nervine into effervescent form (for a time called Bromo-Vess) and developed Aspir-Vess, which eventually became Alka-Seltzer.

The idea for Alka-Seltzer was first conceived in December 1928, when an estimated half of the population of the United States was down with colds and influenza. Dr. Miles Laboratories had twenty-five percent of its employees out at one time or another during the epidemic. Imagine Hub Beardsley's surprise when he went to the office of the *Elkhart Truth* and heard that its managing editor, Tom Keene, was sending two employees out to help the illness-ridden *News-Times* of Goshen. Keene had come up with a concoction that kept his employees from losing any time because of colds and flu. Whenever an employee showed signs of becoming ill, he took them into his office and gave them aspirin and bicarbonate of soda and instructions to continue the doses until they were free of symptoms.

Beardsley went to Treneer and asked him if he could make an effervescent tablet containing aspirin and bicarbonate of soda. In roughly a week, Treneer produced some samples that approximated the formula of Upjohn's Citro-carbonate formula. The Miles office successfully "tested" the tablets in January, and when Beardsley and his family went on a Mediterranean cruise they took a gross of the tablets along and gave them to other passengers. The tablets received compliments for their effectiveness in providing relief from seasickness, colds, and flu.

The company apparently had a good idea, but production and packaging problems proved difficult to overcome. Nearly two years passed before they could produce a product that was stable enough to market. Fred Lobley, the chief engineer in charge of the company's new modern multicolor printing press, solved the problem of heat and humidity controls in the production area by experimenting until they were right for manufacturing the new product.

Finally, in 1931 Alka-Seltzer was ready to be launched. Hub Beardsley thought it would be a huge success, but Harry Beaver worried the five pounds of cotton he ordered to stuff into the tops of the Alka-Seltzer bottles was too much. Originally positioned as a cold remedy, Miles invited consumers in eight test markets in Indiana and Michigan through newspaper ads to visit a local drugstore for a free drink of the product. The ads were crammed with information typical of advertising for patent medicine. William C. Cray wrote in *Miles: A Centennial History* that "the ads presented Alka-Seltzer as the 'New Effervescent Alkaline Tablets' that 'Make a Harmless Anti-Acid Drink for Headache, Colds, Indigestion and Most Everyday Ailments.' Beneath a hand holding a bubbling glass appeared the legend, 'Here's to Your Health.' Another early theme was, 'Good for What Ails You.' " Later, after users wrote to Miles about the symptoms for which they used Alka-Seltzer, the company suggested the product's use as a remedy for the concurrent symptoms of headache and upset stomach.

## AT A GLANCE

**A**lka-Seltzer brand of effervescent antacid and analgesic developed as Aspir-Vess in the late 1920s by chemist Maurice Treneer of Dr. Miles Laboratories; became a registered trademark, 1931; company renamed Miles Inc. when merged with Bayer AG in 1978.

*Performance:* *Market share*—(Alka-Seltzer Plus Cold Medicine) 6.3% (fifth-largest share) of cough and cold remedies category.

*Major competitor:* (To Alka-Seltzer Plus Cold Medicine) Robitussin; (to Extra-Strength Alka-Seltzer) Extra-Strength Tylenol Headache Plus Caplets.

*Advertising:* *Agency*—(For Alka-Seltzer Original) McCann-Erickson, New York, NY, beginning in 1973; (for Alka-Seltzer Plus Cold Medicine) Foote Cone & Belding Communications, Chicago, IL, 1993—. *Major campaign*—(For Alka-Seltzer Plus Cold Medicine) "Tough medicine for tough winter colds."

*Addresses:* *Parent company*—Miles Inc., P.O. Box 340, 1127 Myrtle St., Elkhart, IN 46515-0340; phone: (219) 264-8111; fax: (219) 262-7427. *Ultimate parent company*—Bayer AG, Germany.

## A Remedy for the Times

Being introduced during the Depression could have spelled doom for Alka-Seltzer, but the product had two things in its favor: it worked and Miles did not stint on advertising. Among the first promotions were advertisements in Miles's popular almanacs, which included a coupon that offered a 25-cent package of Alka-Seltzer for 10 cents, and newspaper ads that offered readers a free drink of Alka-Seltzer at their favorite drugstore. The first printed ads stated that it was "a new drink for health. The new alkaline way to relieve sour stomach, colds, headaches, gas on stomach, neuralgia, rheumatism, and that tired run-down feeling." The theme that excess stomach acid caused colds, respiratory ailments, and other problems was expanded in the 1930s. An ad had the lines "They've had a terrible fight. He snapped at her and left. . . . It's all lovely now. . . . What caused it? Too much acidity in the body."

Alka-Seltzer had sales of $112,330 in the year it was launched; $400,000 in 1933, its second full year on the market; and shot up to $2.1 million in 1934. Innovative advertising might be an explanation for the huge increase in 1934. The public looked forward to the next installment of streetcar cards and subway signs featuring distinctively drawn cartoonlike characters by George French and colloquial rhymes. Announcers told radio listeners to "Listen to it fizz!" as two tablets dropped into a glass of water held near the microphone. Charles Beardsley coined the predominant slogan used in the early years, "Be Wise, Alkalize with Alka-Seltzer." *Miles: A Centennial History* says that the slogan "summarized medical opinions of the day suggesting that excess acid in the blood was associated with many common complaints and that alkaline medicines 'corrected' this 'systemic acidity.' "

Perhaps the biggest reason for the 1934 spike in sales was the repeal of Prohibition in 1933. Alka-Seltzer gained a reputation for being the best possible cure for hangovers. A slogan used in the 1935 almanac was "You wouldn't dread the morning after if you take Alka-Seltzer the night before." However, Alka-Seltzer could be an annoyance to those who imbibed. An anecdote relates how

W. C. Fields, after a night of overindulgence, once complained about an Alka-Seltzer fizzing in a glass of water, "Can't anyone do something about that racket!"

Alka-Seltzer had a big impact on Miles's sales, finances, and growth. The company paid tribute to the brand's contribution by painting its Franklin Street plant water tower with the Alka-Seltzer logo. Sales continued to grow, reaching $8.7 million in 1937 and $9.0 million in 1943, and extended into numerous countries. The Latin America sales and advertising director, Herbert C. Beulke, is said to be the one who went the farthest out for sales. *Miles: A Centennial History* tells how, in 1959, Beulke "ventured into the Peruvian part of the Upper Amazon—to what *The Alkalizer* called 'the most uncivilized outpost of Alka-Seltzer.' Beulke got the witch doctor of a local tribe to try the tablets. When they saw the bubbles, the natives got a bit restless, and Beulke feared for a moment that they might resort to their blow guns. At any rate, he never went back!"

## Broadcast Sponsorship

Charles Beardsley was the impetus behind the creative promotion for Alka-Seltzer. He and Albert Wade of Wade Advertising (the company's agency) believed one had to spend money to make money. Miles spent $4 to $5 million a year on advertising before World War II, most of it on Alka-Seltzer. Alka-Seltzer advertising broke into the new medium of radio on January 12, 1932, when its first commercials aired on Chicago's WLS radio during a program called *The Songs of Home Sweet Home.*

Although the success of the first ads was not repeated when Alka-Seltzer advertised for thirteen weeks on a national program, Miles decided to sponsor another WLS program in 1933, the *Saturday Night Barn Dance.* Four weeks into the sponsorship banks closed and the nation began experiencing a severe economic emergency; however, Miles continued its sponsorship, cut Alka-Seltzer prices, and sales rocketed. *Barn Dance* eventually aired on 200 stations of NBC's Blue Network, and listeners heard the announcement "There's nothing quite like Alka-Seltzer" for over fourteen years. Alka-Seltzer also sponsored pianist Alec Templeton and the *Quiz Kids,* the summer replacement for *Barn Dance.* In fact, ads for Alka-Seltzer and other Miles products were on practically every highly rated radio show, including *One Man's Family* and *News of the World,* as well as the "potted-palm-type" radio shows, *Comedy Stars of Broadway* and *Comedy Stars of Hollywood,* for sophisticated city audiences.

Between 1951 and 1952, Miles edged into television sponsorship with *One Man's Family, Garry Moore, Ernie Ford,* and news telecasts. Alka-Seltzer became the sponsor of a variety of shows: *Broken Arrow, Wednesday Night Fights, The Rifleman, Bonanza, Laramie, Andy Williams, Hawaiian Eye, Jack Paar, Combat, The Naked City, Break the Bank, Hootenanny, The Virginian,* and *The Flintstones.* Early radio and television broadcast sponsors and their advertising agencies developed and produced network programs. In the 1960s, Miles was the last corporate sponsor to relinquish control of its television time to network ownership. It remained active in popular programming as late as 1972, through the J. Walter Thompson agency, with *The World of Survival* with John Forsythe.

Not all television broadcast networks welcomed Alka-Seltzer advertising; CBS would not accept ads for proprietary medicine. Charles Beardsley went to New York to talk with the head of CBS, William S. Paley, about the policy. After waiting two hours in an outer office to see Paley, he stomped out and issued an order that stood for a long time—no one was ever to approach CBS again.

## Award-Winning Ads

Alka-Seltzer advertising innovation extended beyond an enthusiasm for trying new mediums. Instead of competitive, forceful copy, Alka-Seltzer commercials were entertaining as they subtly pursued general symptomatology. The original Alka-Seltzer entertainer was Speedy Alka-Seltzer, an elfin puppet who represented the product for almost a decade. In 1951, Robert Watkins, a St. Louis-based advertising artist created the "red-haired, blue-eyed, pink-cheeked sprite sporting a toothy grin and a magic wand, who wore an Alka-Seltzer tablet on his head. Another tablet made up his body." Watkins suggested the name Sparky, but Miles sales manager Perry Shupert changed it to Speedy. (In Latin America, Speedy became Pron-tito.) The slogan attached to the character was "Speedy is its middle name."

Speedy first appeared in magazines and drug trade promotions. The Wade Agency commissioned Jack Shafton Puppets of Hollywood in late 1951 to carve a five-inch-high model for commercials and auditioned over 400 voices to be Speedy. Richard Beals, a four-and-a-half foot tall, 24-year-old voice actor, read only once and became the only voice for more than 200 Speedy Alka-Seltzer commercials.

Speedy began waving his magic wand over a fizzing glass in television commercials in 1954, but he appeared in only about half of the Alka-Seltzer commercials for fear of overkill. Buster Keaton abandoned silent acting for a speaking role when he appeared in "Speedy and the Mountie," part of a wryly humorous 1958 series of ads. A Speedy Alka-Seltzer commercial won an award for the top commercial of the entire decade of the 1950s. Miles brought Speedy back in 1976 for the American Bicentennial and for the ill-fated 1980 Olympics, from which the United States withdrew.

"Stomachs" replaced Speedy in 1964. The campaign featured funny, artful close-up shots of stomachs accompanied by a catchy sound track, "No Matter What Shape (Your Stomach's In)," but no dialogue. The commercials ran for more than three years, appearing in French, British, Spanish, and other versions. The tune became a No. 13 record on the *Billboard* chart. Because the campaign started a trend to use humor for a hard sell and took spunk to put on television, *Advertising Age* selected a "Stomachs" commercial as one of the best of 1964.

Alka-Seltzer advertising was possibly the winner of more awards than any other single product in the history of advertising in the United States and overseas. Consumers consistently placed Alka-Seltzer ads in the top ten of the *New York Times'* annual poll of popular commercials. "Magadini's Meatballs," a 1969-1970 commercial about making a commercial with the tagline "That's a spicy meatball," was acclaimed the world's best-written commercial in the International Broadcast Awards of 1980 and voted the best in twenty years by the Hollywood Radio and Television Society. From the "Personality Series" of commercials came "Restaurant," with the tagline "Try It, You'll Like It," and "Whole Thing," with the tagline "I can't believe I ate the whole thing." These lines were so parodied that George McGovern said "I can't believe I won the whole thing" when he won the 1972 Democratic nomination for president. *Newsweek* picked "I can't believe I ate the whole thing" as one of the ten best quotes of decade.

"Stomach Talk," an ad featuring a man in therapy with his stomach, preceded commercials showing a new bride cooking indigestible meals of marshmallowed meatballs and poached oysters for her husband, causing him to reach for the Alka-Seltzer. *Advertising Age* in 1980 selected "Groom's First Meal" as one of the ten best ads ever. Singer/entertainer Sammy Davis, Jr., was featured in a 1970s campaign that used the line "Plop, plop! Fizz, fizz! Oh, What a relief it is!" In the 1980s, the "Alka-Seltzer to the Rescue" campaign promoted Alka-Seltzer as the product "For these symptoms of stress that can come from success."

## Brand "Flattery"

The success of Alka-Seltzer led several commercial enterprises to attempt to cash in on the brand's name recognition. Miles won infringement cases in 1935 against firms using Premo-Seltzer, Foamo-Seltzer, and Healtho-Seltzer; in 1943 against Vita-Seltzer; in 1953 against Aphco-Alkaline-Seltzer; and in 1955 against Carba-Seltzer.

Many entrepreneurs sought permission to use Speedy Alka-Seltzer on items as diverse as racing motorcycles, Mexican food, dog food, hair-thinning shears, helmets, shirts, utility masks, belt buckles, race horses, and carpet cleaners. Miles denied all the requests except one: Speedy was allowed to appear in a television spot when Standard Oil changed its name to Exxon.

Sometimes the permission denials included humor. In 1966, corporate attorney John Gildea wrote to a musical trio wanting to call themselves "Speedy and the Alka-Seltzers" that "since we know that any venture of this sort encounters some headaches, we are enclosing an Alka-Seltzer credit card to assist in alleviating these difficulties." Similarly, attorney Mel Silver responded to a dancer in Philadelphia known as "Elke Seltzer" who was "bubbling over with sex" that "she is in a line of business so unrelated to ours that no confusion is likely. On the other hand, her stage name might be considered disparaging to our trade reputation, and thus actionable under a state's unfair competition laws."

Alka-Seltzer was also well-known in Latin America. Parts of the Pan-American Highway were referred to as Alka-Seltzer Canyon because they looked as if the sandy terrain was bubbling. Pron-tito became a mascot for a soccer team in Ecuador, parents named their children for Pron-tito, and bars were called Pron-tito. Alka-Seltzer also became contraband in countries where the price was higher than in neighboring countries.

The Miles files contain records of some unusual uses of Alka-Seltzer. A writer suggested seeding clouds to produce acid-free rain. A divorce kit included two Alka-Seltzer tablets. A fisherman used Alka-Seltzer to catch bass; he attached a tablet to the line with a clothespin and pulled the fish in as it went for the fizz.

## The Stipulation

Early advertising copy for Alka-Seltzer had few legal or medical constraints, except to be in good taste and show reasonable discretion, although Charles Beardsley insisted the messages comply with "pharmaceutical elegance." The company voluntarily toned down advertising in the 1930s, deciding not to claim Alka-Seltzer helped neuritis and rheumatism much, although it continued to stress the excess systemic acid theme. Then the Federal Trade Commission (FTC) dropped a bombshell on Miles in 1939. The FTC described Alka-Seltzer advertising as "false, misleading, and deceptive" because of its claims "that systemic acidity caused various bodily disturbances and that Alka-Seltzer, by correcting this acidity, could relieve symptoms.'' Dr. Walter Ames Compton, Miles's first research and medical director, knew that neither the medical world nor Miles's laboratories had found any evidence to support the brand's medical claims. He went to the FTC and worked out a compromise that became known as ''The Stipulation.'' Alka-Seltzer advertising would drop claims involving systemic acidity, stipulating that they were false and misleading except where subsequent research might support them. In addition, Miles would submit all advertising copy and claims for review and approval by licensed physicians.

The stipulation did not force Miles to abandon all of its Alka-Seltzer slogans. Listeners heard ''Be Wise—Alkalize with Alka-Seltzer'' on radio until the late 1950s. However, *Miles: A Centennial History* states that the Miles Medical Department became ''a stern monitor of promotional copy. It did not like the word 'stop' in advertising copy, since that implied complete relief; neither was 'treatment' considered suitable. It insisted that 'suffer' be eliminated and that 'misery' and 'distress' be used with caution. It did approve of 'soothe' for acid indigestion claims.''

Advertising that met the approval of the Medical Department and the stipulation included the rhyme, ''When your tablets get down to four, that's the time to buy some more'' (used until 1954) and the jingles ''an extra package in the grip can come in handy on a trip'' and ''an extra package in the car can act just like a spare; you may not need to use it, but it's wise to have it there.''

In 1949, Alka-Seltzer adopted a ''first-aid'' theme. The slogans ''feel better while you're getting better'' (used for nine years) and ''Alka-Seltzer—for that feel-better feeling'' were introduced in 1952. The tagline ''triple comfort relief,'' introduced in 1955, referred to the product's use for upset stomach symptoms, as did the later slogans ''action in the glass'' and ''relief is just a swallow away.''

## Brand Defense

The stipulation was only the beginning of a regulatory, legal, medical, and public relations story of substantial proportions. Miles had presented a medical defense of Alka-Seltzer practically since its founding; the first recorded Alka-Seltzer studies were done in 1935. By the early 1960s, Miles had completed 45 investigations, and experts in 15 medical specialties had contributed to the voluminous medical profile of Alka-Seltzer. The brand would need that research.

After the Food, Drug, and Cosmetic Act strengthened federal regulation of drug labeling practices in 1938, drugs had to be reviewed for safety before marketing. That act did not apply to older drugs such as Alka-Seltzer, which were generally recognized as safe, nor did a 1962 amendment that required ''substantial evidence of effectiveness.'' But in 1972 the Food and Drug Administration (FDA) began a review of the safety and effectiveness of all over-the-counter products. Alka-Seltzer, because of its unique composition, faced three FDA Advisory Review Panels: Antacids, Analgesics, and Miscellaneous Internal Drug Products. The FDA had a ruling that each ingredient in a product had to contribute to the claimed effect; Miles had to prove that the separate symptoms of headache and upset stomach were treated by the two types of ingredients in Alka-Seltzer, analgesic and antacid. Under the direction of general counsel Adrien Ringuette, the Alka-Seltzer Research Committee of Miles scientists and consultants arranged submissions and prepared for hearings. Miles submitted

to the Antacid Panel eight volumes of material, covering some 50 studies and 169 references. The panel rejected Miles's claim that Alka-Seltzer could be used as an antacid only, but did conclude it was rational to combine antacid with analgesic for concurrent symptoms of headache and acid indigestion.

On April 4, 1973, the FDA called a press conference to summarize and praise the findings of the Antacid Panel. Representatives of Ralph Nader's Health Research Group, including Dr. Sidney Wolfe, showed up, and they were not there to give praise. They said Miles used ''undue influence'' to obtain ''favored treatment'' for Alka-Seltzer, which they said was ''unsafe and ineffective.'' Miles and the FDA denied the accusations, but that did not stop Dr. Wolfe from filing a formal statement. Miles spent the next year rebutting accusations and countering testimony made before the Subcommittee on Monopoly of the Senate Select Committee on Small Business, chaired by Senator Gaylord Nelson, an avowed critic of the drug industry. The Nelson Hearings generated negative publicity on drugs, pharmaceutical companies, doctors, and the government's handling of health matters. The FDA found one last charge against the product baseless—that Miles had withheld data showing that Alka-Seltzer caused bleeding in normal people—before issuing its final order for antacids on June 4, 1974. The order cleared Alka-Seltzer for use in relieving acid indigestion when it occurred concurrently with headache or other pain. However, the Nader-Wolfe-Nelson assaults raised consumer doubts and years passed before sales recovered.

Miles presented voluminous evidence and testimony to the other two FDA panels reviewing Alka-Seltzer from the mid-1970s through the early 1980s. Before the Analgesics Panel, Miles built a case that Alka-Seltzer did not cause bleeding and attempted to counter the panel's position that aspirin should not be taken when there is upset stomach (a contradiction to the Antacid Panel's approval for use with concurrent symptoms). In 1980, Miles delivered to the Miscellaneous Internal Drug Products Panel over 9 sets of 400 scientific papers bound into 16 books, weighing 650 pounds. The statement and argument alone was 160 single-spaced pages. On October 1, 1982, the panel recommended that the FDA approve Alka-Seltzer as safe and effective for the concurrent symptoms of headache and upset stomach associated with overindulgence.

## Packaging Challenges

Miles Laboratories overcame its first major quality control problem when it developed packaging that provided critical moisture protection, thus assuring that moisture in the bottle would not destroy the product's effervescence. Originally, Alka-Seltzer bottles were stuffed with cotton, corked, and sealed in paraffin. Screw caps were adopted in 1935.

The next production innovation was a Colton rotary press, which accurately pressed tablets without letting powder stick to the punches. The new machine, for which Miles perfected a central lubrication system, made possible the high-speed compression of up to 2,600 tablets a minute. Before this 1953 innovation, single-punch presses compressed Alka-Seltzer tablets at the rate of about 200 a minute. The production volume required 85 such machines, each operated by one person.

Although Miles devised hermetic packaging to seal Alka-Seltzer before World War II, the company did not switch from bottles to foil pouches until the 1960s. (Maurice Treneer adapted the hermetic packaging to seal five grams of powdered coffee to go with K-rations for servicemen during the war. The packaging kept the coffee soluble and flavorful, unlike coffee packed in tin containers, which became hard and resinous. For four years during the 1940s, Miles produced 384 million packages of soluble coffee.) After DuPont created a better substance for sealing materials, Miles devised a megapack sealer that took Alka-Seltzer tablets from the Colton machine and sealed them in foil. The apparatus made Miles a leader in high-speed tablet production lines.

## Flanker Products

Alka-Seltzer was a unique product that consumers turned to when they felt really sick. Miles leveraged its brand equity by introducing several flanker products. The first new product was Alka-Seltzer Plus, an extra-strength version of the antacid that came out in 1969. It did not spur growth until it was reformulated as Alka-Seltzer Plus Cold Medicine (originally Alka Seltzer Plus Cold Tablets) in 1976. In 1990 Alka-Seltzer Plus became the country's leading cold remedy by unit sales and overtook Alka-Seltzer Original in dollar sales. Alka-Seltzer Plus had an antihistamine, a decongestant, and an analgesic. It was positioned as the brand for "major league" colds. Commercials featured a Green Bay Packer football crowd calling it "Fast, effective relief for tough winter colds." The tagline was later modified to "Tough medicine for tough winter colds." The company launched Alka-Seltzer Plus Night-Time Cold Medicine in 1987.

Although the company experimented with lemon and mint flavors, and tested a citrus-flavored formula as early as 1960, it did not put Flavored Alka-Seltzer on the market until 1985. Described as having "a sparkling fresh lemon-lime taste," the product was a remedy for concurrent symptoms. In 1981, Miles introduced ginger-lime flavored Extra-Strength Alka-Seltzer, which also had increased levels of medication. The company introduced Alka-2 chewable antacid tablets in 1976 to compete against Tums, Rolaids, and other antacids. The product did not catch on with consumers. Later, Miles marketed Alka-Mints chewable tablets. Other flanker product introductions were Alka-Seltzer Gold, an antacid without aspirin, launched in 1974; Alka-Seltzer Advanced Formula, launched in 1989 and discontinued in 1992; Alka-Seltzer Plus Sinus Allergy Medicine, launched in 1990; and Alka-Seltzer Plus Cold & Cough Medicine, launched in 1991.

## Brand Outlook

Alka-Seltzer was the foundation for the modern Miles company, funding research for other products and leading to the company's diversification. Miles started production of citric acid in 1952 to have its own source of the ingredient for manufacture of Alka-Seltzer; citric acid in turn became an important, profitable product. However, marketed in more than 100 countries, Alka-Seltzer remained Miles's number one brand.

Sales remained strong through the early 1990s. The 100 billionth Alka-Seltzer tablet rolled off the line in 1981, the product's 50th year. Alka-Seltzer withstood direct challenges from Johnson & Johnson, which introduced effervescent Tylenol products, and from Johnson & Johnson, Sandoz Corp., and SmithKline Beecham, which came out with powdered medicines to be mixed with hot water. Miles defended the brand with increased marketing budgets.

Although Miles considered licensing its effervescent technology so other products could be reintroduced in effervescent form (the packages would carry the line "from the makers of Alka-Seltzer"), the company was expected to continue its support of consumers' favorite Alka-Seltzer products.

## Further Reading:

"Alka-Seltzer Special Antacid Formula (Gold)," Elkhart, IN: Miles Inc., October 1991.

Bird, Laura, "Foote Cone Takes Over Alka-Seltzer Plus," *Wall Street Journal,* February 25, 1993, B6.

Cray, William C., *Miles: A Centennial History,* Englewood Cliffs, NJ: Prentice-Hall, Inc., 1984.

"Extra Strength Alka-Seltzer," Elkhart, IN: Miles Inc., October 1991.

Fox, Stephen, *The Mirror Makers: A History of American Advertising and Its Creators,* New York: Vintage Books, 1985, pp. 268–69, 314.

Kiley, David, "Oh, What a Success It Is," *Adweek's Marketing Week,* September 16, 1991, pp. 16–17.

McGrath, Molly Wade, *Top Sellers, U.S.A.: Success Stories Behind America's Best-Selling Products From Alka-Seltzer to Zippo,* New York: William Morrow and Company, Inc., 1983, pp. 163–65.

Moskowitz, Milton, Robert Levering, and Michael Katz, eds., *Everybody's Business: A Field Guide to the 400 Leading Companies in America,* New York: Doubleday, 1990, pp. 175–76.

"Original Alka-Seltzer and Flavored Alka-Seltzer," Elkhart, IN: Miles Inc., October 1991.

Room, Adrian, *NTC's Dictionary of Trade Name Origins,* Lincolnwood, IL: NTC Business Books, 1991, pp. 25–26.

Sharp, Harold S., *Advertising Slogans of America,* Metuchen, NJ: The Scarecrow Press, 1984, p. 8.

Urdang, Laurance, and Ceila Dame Robbins, eds., *Slogans: A Collection of More Than 6,000 Slogans, Rallying Cries, and Other Exhortations,* Detroit: Gale Research Company, 1984, pp. 123, 125, 126.

Yates, Donald N., "Advertising with Effervescence," *Pharmaceutical Executive,* May 1985.

*—Doris Morris Maxfield*

# ALL®

The laundry detergent "all" was one of the earliest synthetic detergents on the U.S. market after World War II, and the first low-sudsing detergent for automatic washing machines in the world. Ever since, "all" has remained among the top five of the most popular laundry detergents in the United States. Manufactured by the Lever Brothers Company, "all" is marketed along with two other popular Lever Brothers' brands, Wisk and Surf.

## Brand Origins

Detergent specifically for laundry was almost unknown to consumers prior to World War II. Soap flakes, without bleaches or whiteners, were in general use as a cleaning agent for clothing, and these could turn into harsh substances in hard water regions. During the Allied blockade of Germany during the First World War, German chemists developed synthetic soaps, substituting chemicals derived from coal tar for natural fats. After the war, perhaps because the need for synthetic detergents and soaps was no longer felt, their production was limited to industrial uses. World War II, however, once again prompted the use of synthetic substances to replace scarce natural substances. Cheaper methods had been developed to create products—from lingerie to soaps—out of synthetic materials.

The years following the end of the war saw both the baby boom and a boom in automatic washing machines. Synthetic detergents cleaned more thoroughly than the old soap flakes, largely because the addition of phosphates enabled clothes to be washed easily in the hardest water. However, the resulting suds caused problems when they spilled out of the machines, a problem which was magnified in front loading washing machines. Most of these were manufactured by the Westinghouse Electric Company of Pittsburgh.

As early as 1945, Westinghouse turned to the Monsanto Chemical Corporation for help in developing a detergent that cleaned well but sudsed minimally. The product, dubbed "Sterox," was developed in 1946. Developing a product for mass consumer use was something new for Monsanto, whose managers determined as a result of their experience that the company should branch into consumer goods. Meanwhile, an executive at Westinghouse suggested a more punchy, attractive name for the low sudsing product: "all." In 1948 full production of "all" began in Monsanto's new factory in Trenton, Michigan.

## First Commercial Success

Westinghouse was delighted with this new, low-sudsing detergent, which solved forever the problem of suds spilling out of their front loading washing machines. To ensure that homemakers got the message, the company began placing a box of "all" in every new front loading machine. By 1951 demand exceeded supply.

In 1953 Monsanto acquired a new subsidiary, Detergents, Inc., that would market and distribute the detergent to store shelves. To Monsanto executives, their new subsidiary's proposal to launch an advertising blitz of "all" in 100 cities across America was a novelty, and it worked. "All" became a leading brand of detergent, joined in 1955 by its dish washing counterpart, Dishwasher "all." In a surprise about face, Monsanto sold its detergent trademark and franchise in 1957 to the giant consumer products company Lever Brothers, which up to that point had not produced a detergent of its own.

## Product Development

Lever Brothers Company would develop "all" significantly, as well as introducing its own new detergent brands. By 1960, besides the low sudsing detergent "all" and Dishwasher "all," there was also Fluffy "all," followed by one of the first liquid detergents on the market, Liquid "all," and by reformulated Active Condensed "all." In 1963 product development was carried a step further with the revolutionary Cold Water "all."

Just when one would have thought that all possible detergent variants had been conceived, the late 1980s witnessed the development of the first-ever detergent with bleach, the new Triple Action "all." Besides containing color-safe bleach, the new "all" featured brighteners and enzymes that acted as more effective stain removers. On the market in 1990, Triple Action "all" diverted consumers from other detergent brands, with Lever Brothers capturing a quarter of the fiercely competitive laundry detergent market.

At around this time, demand for environmentally safe consumer products increased sharply. Lever Brothers responded with Double Power "all" Free Clear, the only brand that was free of all dyes and chemical fragrances. Smaller package sizes of powdered "all" were followed in 1993 by the introduction of superconcentrated liquid and powder. Double Power "all," for example, contains a recyclable plastic scoop in a recyclable package that holds 25 percent less detergent than regular "all," but with even greater cleaning power. The superconcentrated liquid "all" comes in not only recyclable but also reusable plastic containers.

## Environmental Controversy

During the 1960s, sudsy foam that was observed in many lakes and streams was traced to detergent waste. By 1965 the biggest detergent makers, which included Lever Brothers, had come out with biodegradable detergents, which solved the foaming problem. Another environmental concern had surfaced by 1970: streams and rivers were suffering from eutrophication, a problem in which algae proliferated by feeding on the phosphates that were deposited from sewage treatment plants, choking off fish and other marine life. The problem was attributed to the phosphate content of powdered detergents, and a congressional subcommittee recommended a federal ban on the use of phosphates. Under pressure from the public and from local governments, detergent manufacturers reduced or eliminated the phosphate content in their products. There is at present still no federal ban on phosphates, although local regulations are in effect throughout the United States. The widespread use of liquid detergents, which contain no phosphates, has further reduced this environmental problem.

## Advertising

Lever Brothers is one of the top five advertisers in the United States, and ever since the advertising blitz in the early 1950s recommended by Detergents, Inc., "all" has been heavily promoted via television commercials and in-store promotions. With so much competition in the detergent market, Lever spent over $100 million in 1993 alone to advertise its superconcentrated "all," Wisk, and Surf.

Unconventional marketing initiatives have included a 1989 sing-along in which the company invited the public at New York's Grand Central Station to join in singing the praises of "all" and other detergent brands. A particularly well received TV commercial depicted a new "all" product (Triple Action "all"), in which three small children are attracted to the laundry room by a strange light that is being emitted by the new laundry detergent. They watch in awe as a shirt turns whiter before their eyes.

## Further Reading:

Bird, Laura, "Detergent Industry Spins into New Cycle," *Wall Street Journal,* January 5, 1993, p. B1(W), B1(E).

DeNitto, Emily, "Lever Brothers Test-Marketing New Recyclable Packaging," *Supermarket News,* May 21, 1990, p. 8(1).

Elliott, Stuart, "Lever Brothers' Latest Soap Blitz (Advertising Campaign for Super-Concentrated Versions of Wisk, Surf and All Detergents)," *New York Times,* May 25, 1993, p. C1(N), D1(L).

Forrestal, Dan J., *Faith, Hope & $5,000: The Story of Monsanto,* New York, 1977.

Freeman, Laurie, "Lever Tests Reformulated All," *Advertising Age,* October 30, 1990.

Gerry, Roberta, "Ultra Detergents Continue Very Big," *Chemical Business,* January 1993, pp. 6–8.

McCoy, Michael, "Environmental Issues Challenge Detergents," *Chemical Marketing Reporter,* February 22, 1993, p. 23.

Price, Donald, *Detergents, What They Are and What They Do,* New York, 1952.

Rukeyser, William Simon, "Fact and Foam in the Row Over Phosphates," *Fortune,* January 1972, pp. 71–74, 168–171.

*—Sina Dubovoj*

# ANACIN®

Providing "fast pain relief" from headaches, arthritis, and other ailments, Anacin is one of the best-known analgesics in the United States. Developed in 1915 as a mixture of four drugs—aspirin, acetanilid, caffeine, and quinine sulfate—it was reformulated a number of times, eventually becoming just aspirin and caffeine. Some clinical studies have shown caffeine to increase the potency of aspirin.

American Home Products Corporation, since 1930 the parent company of Anacin, owns a variety of other consumer brands, such as Advil, Robitussin, Preparation H, Chap Stick, Chef Boyardee, and Jiffy Pop. Its Anacin line includes regular Anacin (400 mg aspirin, 32 mg caffeine); Anacin Maximum Strength (500 mg aspirin, 32 mg caffeine); Aspirin Free Anacin, Maximum Strength (500 mg acetaminophen); and, for both pain and sleeplessness, Aspirin Free Anacin P.M. (500 mg acetaminophen and 25 mg diphenhydramine hcl). Because of a trademark conflict, the brand was renamed Anadin in its two foreign markets, Canada and the United Kingdom.

## Brand Origin

The original Anacin formula was a mixture of four drugs widely used in the early 20th century. The best known among these were caffeine and aspirin. Caffeine, discovered in 1820 in green (unroasted) coffee beans, was commonly consumed in not only coffee but also tea and chocolate. Medicinally, it was used as a stimulant and diuretic. Aspirin, an analgesic known scientifically as acetylsalicylic acid, was synthesized in a crude form as early as 1853, but it became a commercial drug only after Felix Hoffmann, a chemist at the German firm Farbenfabriken vormals Friedrich Bayer & Company, improved the process in 1897. The result, introduced in 1899, was Bayer aspirin, a patented drug and thus until 1916 the only aspirin legally sold in the United States.

The two other original ingredients, quinine sulfate and acetanilid, were also standard drugs in the pharmacoepia. Quinine, from which quinine sulfate is produced, was used as early as the 1600s for treating malaria. Extracted from the Peruvian cinchona tree, quinine was also prescribed as an antipyretic, or fever reducer. Acetanilid, initially used in the dye industry, was a chemical derived from coal tar, a gooey residue left over after the production of gas from coal (mostly for lanterns). It was discovered to be an effective antipyretic in 1886, when, because of a mix-up at a

pharmacy, two Strasbourg doctors accidentally gave the chemical to a patient.

William M. Knight, a pharmacist living in Minneapolis, was the man responsible for putting together the Anacin formula. At the time, the U.S. market was glutted with pain- and fever-reducing products, and because there was little regulation, the safety and efficacy of these products varied considerably. It was in 1915 that Knight invented his own analgesic brand, called An-A-Cin, a capsule made of aspirin, acetanilid, quinine sulfate, and caffeine. Three years later, on November 19, 1918, he received a trademark for the brand under the modified spelling Anacin. Sold by his Anacin Chemical Company, the capsules were initially marketed to dentists for the relief of pain and inflammation resulting from tooth extractions. It was also sold as a remedy for headaches and neuralgia.

## Changes in Brand Ownership

Despite its promise, Knight sold the Anacin brand in 1919, and over the next several years it was owned by a number of firms, finally coming under the control of Van Ess Laboratories, Inc., of Delaware on November 17, 1926. A producer of nostrums, including Liquid Scalp Massage, Van Ess also peddled Anacin to dentists, but the company soon found the American Dental Association less than pleased with its advertisements. At issue was the company's claim that Anacin, because of its special mixture of ingredients, was more effective than aspirin. Not only was there no clinical evidence to support the assertion but it played upon a popular, though mistaken, notion that several medicinal ingredients were always better than one. It was this claim, however, that would dominate much of the brand's advertising over the next half century.

The scorn of the association, in fact, had little if any effect on sales, which jumped from a mere $20,000 in 1926 to nearly $700,000 in 1930. It was in 1930 that Van Ess itself was purchased by a large holding company, American Home Products, which despite its size had been established only four years earlier by a group of prominent businessmen. Ironically, one of these men, Albert Diebold, had also cofounded Sterling Products, Inc., since 1918 the U.S. owner of Bayer. At the time, Bayer was by far the best-selling aspirin product, partially because of its earlier patent on aspirin sales but also because of its then extraordinary advertising budget. In 1935, when more than $750,000 was spent on Bayer

## AT A GLANCE

**A**nacin brand of aspirin founded in 1915 by William M. Knight, a Minneapolis pharmacist; became a registered trademark of Knight's Anacin Chemical Company in 1918; brand sold to Van Ess Laboratories, Inc., of Delaware in 1926 and to American Home Products Corporation of New York City in 1930.

**Performance:** *Market share*—14% of the aspirin category; 5% of the analgesics category. *Sales*—$100 million.

**Major competitor:** Bayer (aspirin), by Sterling Winthrop, Inc.; also, Tylenol (acetaminophen), by Johnson & Johnson; Advil (ibuprofen), by American Home Products Corporation; Excedrin (acetaminophen, aspirin, and caffeine) and Bufferin (aspirin, calcium carbonate, magnesium oxide, and magnesium carbonate), by Bristol-Myers Squibb Company.

**Advertising:** *Agency*—McCann-Erickson Worldwide, New York, NY, 1992—. *Major campaign*—"Daytime or Nighttime Headache Relief," recommending regular Anacin for headaches at work and Aspirin Free Anacin P.M., with "a gentle ingredient to help you fall asleep," for "nighttime headaches."

**Addresses:** *Parent company*—American Home Products Corporation, A.H. Robins Division, 685 Third Avenue, New York, NY 10017-4076; phone: (212) 878-5500; fax: (212) 878-6048.

advertisements, American Home Products budgeted just $200,000 for all of its numerous products. This budget would soon skyrocket, thus beginning the long battle between Bayer and Anacin.

## Advertising

Anacin's advertising dollars grew fourfold between 1935 and 1937, and with continued increases, especially for radio advertisements, its budget exceeded even Bayer's by 1941. The advertising strategy, however, remained the same. "Anacin is compounded on the prescription principle," customers were reminded in one radio spot, "meaning it is a combination of medically proven and tested ingredients—not just one." "Like a doctor's prescription," another ad emphasized, "not one but a combination of ingredients." Such advertisements were reinforced by other marketing techniques. Anacin representatives, for example, visited more than 500 doctors each day, and some 65,000 samples were sent out monthly to physicians and dentists.

Though great sums of money were spent on spreading the Anacin name, advertisements never revealed the brand's owner, American Home Products, nor the division that made it, Whitehall Pharmacal (later renamed Whitehall Laboratories). Moreover, in its claims of superiority over aspirin, the special Anacin formula was never disclosed, even when the formula itself was changed. Acetophenetidin, for example, eventually took the place of acetanilid, and in 1963, after reports that acetophenetidin might cause kidney damage, the ingredients were pared down to simply aspirin and caffeine.

The ads, however, effectively chipped away into Bayer's formidable lead in market share. By the early 1950s Bayer had slipped to roughly 25 percent of the analgesics market, with Anacin just behind at some 20 percent. Meanwhile, a new analgesic, Bufferin (aspirin "buffered" with antacids), was making its own run against top-ranked Bayer.

In the 1950s Anacin also began an advertising crusade on television, the country's new entertainment medium. Like its radio advertisements, Anacin commercials were simple but extremely effective. The most famous began with a silhouette of a human head containing three boxes. In the first was a pounding hammer; in the second, a spring compressing and extending; and in the third, flickering between two terminals, a lightning bolt. An announcer shouted, "stops headaches" (the hammer would then stop pounding), "relieves tension" (the spring would relax), "calms jittery nerves" (the lightning would be grounded). Appearing next on the screen were two heads, each containing three boxes and each connected to an outline of a stomach. In one stomach was aspirin, which, bubbling up to the head, stopped only the pounding hammers. Rising up from the other stomach was Anacin, which again relieved all three problems. The announcer concluded with the tag line, "For fast, *fast, FAST* relief, take Anacin!"

Customers apparently got the message, as Anacin managed to hold onto its market share throughout the 1950s, despite a remarkable rise in Bufferin sales, which cut instead into Bayer's dwindling lead. Finally, with 18 percent of the market in 1957, Anacin was able to squeak by Bayer to become the country's best-selling analgesic. Over the next decade, in order to bolster the brand's new position, American Home Products would invest an increasing amount of money in radio and television advertising, which in 1971 alone would cost some $1.5 million and $25 million, respectively.

## Advertising Restrictions

Soon after it reached the top, Anacin began facing a challenge from a new source, the U.S. Federal Trade Commission (FTC), which had long been charged with regulating advertisements of over-the-counter (nonprescription) drugs. Traditionally the FTC targeted only drug companies whose advertising claims conflicted with known clinical studies. Because pain relief was hard to measure, it was correspondingly difficult for the FTC to dispute claims made by the country's analgesics manufacturers. In fact, the commission attempted and failed to do just that in the early 1960s.

In what would produce a migraine for American Home Products, Sterling (maker of Bayer), and Bristol-Myers (Bufferin and Excedrin), the FTC shifted the burden of proof in the early 1970s. Drug companies would now be required to show a "reasonable basis"—that is, the support of clinical studies—for their claims. In 1973 all three companies were formally charged with misleading or unsubstantiated advertising, and by the early 1980s each had lost its case. American Home Products was unable to support (and thus ordered not to advertise) a number of claims, including the longtime assertion that Anacin (400 mg of aspirin with a small amount of caffeine) was more effective than regular strength (325 mg) aspirin. Through appeals, however, American Home Products was able to avoid the worst of the sanctions—an order to spend $24 million advertising that Anacin did not relieve tension.

## Nonaspirin Competition

While Anacin was busy battling the federal government, the analgesics market was being redefined by a single nonaspirin product, Tylenol (acetaminophen), made by Johnson & Johnson. Initially marketed in the early 1960s to doctors and hospitals, the brand took off in 1976 with the introduction of Extra Strength

Tylenol, supported by the advertising claim, "You can't buy a more potent pain reliever without a prescription" (the claim, though true, failed to mention that customers could buy an equally effective analgesic—aspirin). By 1977 its market share had reached 15 percent, a figure that would double in the next decade.

Like other aspirin makers, American Home Products responded first by attacking Tylenol's inability to reduce inflammation. When that did not work, it introduced its own acetaminophen product, Trilium, soon renamed Extranol and then Extramed. When Extramed failed, it, too, was replaced, this time by Anacin-3, a mixture of acetaminophen and caffeine, introduced in 1977. Although American Home Products was unable to threaten Tylenol with Anacin-3, in 1984 it would introduce its own successful aspirin substitute, Advil (ibuprofen), which would gain well over ten percent of the analgesics market by the early 1990s. By then the share of Anacin, squeezed by the major brands of acetaminophen and ibuprofen, would sink to some five percent. Anacin-3, moreover, would be replaced by Aspirin Free Anacin, Maximum Strength (acetaminophen without caffeine), and Aspirin Free Anacin P.M. (acetaminophen with diphenhydramine, a drug causing drowsiness).

## Brand Outlook

Although Anacin has remained one of the best-selling aspirin brands, the demand for aspirin has experienced a near free-fall. From 1984 to 1993 aspirin's share of the analgesics market declined from 48 to 26 percent, while ibuprofen grew from 5 to 29 percent. During the same period acetaminophen's share changed only slightly, from 47 to 45 percent. With its acetaminophen-based products, the Anacin line was better positioned to adjust to the changing consumer preferences.

Aspirin products, however, still formed a major part of the analgesics market, and their growth potential was being enhanced by the discovery of new indications for the drug. Most important have been clinical studies suggesting that aspirin can reduce the risk of second heart attacks and recurrent transient ischemic attacks (ministrokes). Perhaps especially satisfying to American Home products, though, have been clinical studies supporting Anacin's claim that caffeine increases the potency of aspirin. In a 1984 issue of the *Journal of the American Medical Association,* a report of 30 studies on the efficacy of caffeine concluded that "the addition of caffeine, 65 mg, to an analgesic tablet taken in a two-tablet dose results in a more effective analgesic. Mood enhancement may result as well." Nine years later, in 1993, an advisory commission of the U.S. Food and Drug Administration reported a similar conclusion, suggesting that caffeine was an "effective analgesic adjuvant" to aspirin. In an apparent response to these studies, American Home Products began for the first time to advertise the ingredients of the Anacin formula. As one commercial boasted in the early 1990s, "Caffeine energizes the aspirin . . . to work better on your headache . . . so you can work better."

## Further Reading:

"Aspirin Makers Dispute Charges: They Assail F.T.C. Plan for Reports on Ad 'Mistakes,' " *New York Times,* June 15, 1973, p. 14.

Beaver, William T., "Caffeine Revisited," *Journal of the American Medical Association,* April 6, 1984, pp. 1732–33.

"Caffeine Is Effective as Analgesic Adjuvant in Aspirin Products," *F-D-C Reports,* April 12, 1993, pp. 3–4.

"Formula for Anacin, Excedrin Changed; No Reasons Are Given," *Wall Street Journal,* March 14, 1963, p. 11.

"FTC Plans Ad Suit Charging Deception by Makers of Aspirin," *New York Times,* March 13, 1973, p. 24.

Lafayette, Jon and Pat Sloan, "$28M Anacin Headache: Other Shops Asked to Work on Alternate Campaign," *Advertising Age,* January 6, 1992, p. 1.

Lafayette, Jon and Patricia Winters, "Y & R in Trouble on $17M Anacin?," *Advertising Age,* July 2, 1990, pp. 3, 29.

Laska, Eugene M., et al., "Caffeine as an Analgesic Adjuvant," *Journal of the American Medical Association,* April 6, 1984, pp. 1711–18.

Mann, Charles C. and Mark L. Plummer, *The Aspirin Wars,* New York: Alfred A. Knopf, 1991.

"Study Says Caffeine Increases Potency of Pain Relievers," *New York Times,* April 6, 1984, p. 18.

—*Thomas Riggs*

# AQUAFRESH®

Aquafresh was the fourth-best-selling brand of toothpaste in the United States in the early 1990s. Since being introduced to the market in 1979 by SmithKline Beecham, it has remained one of the nation's leading brands. Aquafresh is a full line of toothpaste products easily recognized by its exclusive striped gel and paste combination, the first of its kind. Aquafresh is flavored, therapeutically effective because it contains fluoride to protect against cavities, and approved by the American Dental Association (ADA).

The toothpaste marketplace is a highly competitive one, crowded with marketers that include consumer product manufacturers, pharmaceutical companies, and private label brands from stores and discount chains. Toothpastes are offered in different flavors, forms, packages, and with varying claims of benefits. Total toothpaste sales for 1993 were estimated at $1.4 billion, and sales were expected to grow about three percent over 1992.

The requirements for any brand of toothpaste are essentially the same. Toothpastes must have detergents, abrasives, and fluoride to help prevent cavities. Detergents help clear away plaque and other debris. Fine abrasives help scour plaque and stains from tooth surfaces and polish teeth. Typical abrasives are minerals and various synthetic compounds. Throughout the years, Aquafresh has been successful in attracting and retaining consumers because its products have satisfied these basic requirements as well as provided specific rewards for consumers in certain age or population groups.

Aquafresh products also have been innovative. Kid's Aquafresh pioneered the kid's toothpaste segment, and Aquafresh Sensitive was the first sensitive teeth toothpaste to contain fluoride. In addition, the company's success has been due to such marketing strategies as market research, packaging, merchandising, advertising, and promotion.

## Brand Development

Aquafresh made its debut in 1979 when it was introduced as Double Protection Aquafresh. The double-striped toothpaste was the first one to combine gel and paste and still provide a refreshing peppermint flavor while brushing and as an aftertaste.

Throughout the years, Aquafresh improved existing products and introduced new products. The improvements were in the ability to fight cavities or to deliver more flavor. The new products were meant to provide certain therapeutic benefits to specific target groups.

All Aquafresh toothpastes are promoted to freshen breath and fight cavities. Some products also are promoted to fight plaque buildup that can cause gingivitis, an inflammation of the gums due to a plaque accumulation along the gumline. Red swollen gums that bleed when brushed are an indication of the early stage of gingivitis. Another product is promoted as helping to ease the pain of sensitive teeth.

In 1981 Double Protection Aquafresh with two stripes became Triple Protection Aquafresh with three stripes. This product was clinically proven to help remove plaque. The actual level of abrasion falls well within the range of that in the leading fluoride dentrifices accepted by the ADA. The Triple Protection Aquafresh formula contains a calcium carbonate cleaning system.

In 1985 Aquafresh became the first toothpaste marketed specifically for the needs of children. Called Kid's Aquafresh, it provides gentle cleaners for young teeth and maximum fluoride protection to fight cavities. Clinical testing confirmed that the abrasive system used was both safe and gentle. Kid's Aquafresh was formulated with calcium carbonate as a polishing and cleaning agent suitable for a child's developing tooth enamel.

In 1988 a different type of plaque-fighting product was introduced as Tartar Control Aquafresh. This product was clinically proven to help remove plaque, and contains ingredients that block the tendency of plaque to bond with minerals in saliva to form tartar. In 1989 Aquafresh Extra Fresh with a high impact flavor was first marketed, and in 1992 Aquafresh Sensitive was introduced. While there were other toothpastes promoted for sensitive teeth, this Aquafresh product was the first sensitive teeth toothpaste that contained fluoride. Desensitizing toothpastes are designed for people who experience pain while brushing their teeth because of receding gums. Receding gums expose softer tissues that can make teeth sensitive to heat, cold, or pressure. Sensitive toothpastes can dull the pain by sealing tiny tubules in teeth or disrupting nerve impulses.

## AT A GLANCE

**A**quafresh brand toothpaste manufactured by SmithKline Beecham Consumer Brands, a division of the pharmaceutical company SmithKline Beecham that was founded in 1989 and is involved in manufacturing over-the-counter health care products; SmithKline traces its history to 1830, and in ensuing years was associated with various companies that were ultimately divested; in 1989 SmithKline merged with the British pharmaceutical company Beecham to form SmithKline Beecham and to become part of Beecham Group PLC.

**Performance:** *Market share*—9.5% of toothpaste category. *Sales*—Estimated $120 million.

**Advertising:** *Agency*—Grey Advertising, New York, NY, 1977—. *Major campaign*—Situations discussing the importance and length of brushing, and the American Dental Association (ADA) Seal; the tag line reads, "Striped to Fight." Also, situations showing kids who would rather brush their teeth with Kid's Aquafresh than play with their dog or with their friends; the tag line reads, "Gets them brushing. Helps keep them brushing."

**Major competitor:** Procter & Gamble Company's Crest; also, Colgate-Palmolive Company's Colgate and Block Drug & Co.'s Sensodyne.

**Addresses:** *Parent company*—SmithKline Beecham Consumer Brands, P.O. Box 1467, Pittsburgh, PA 15230; phone: (412) 928-1105. *Ultimate parent company*—SmithKline Beecham, P.O. Box 7929, Philadelphia, PA 19101; phone: (215) 751-4000; fax (215) 751-3400. *Ultimate parent company*—Beecham Group PLC.

Mark Prus, Aquafresh toothpaste senior brand manager, told *Advertising Age* why the company chose to market the sensitive toothpaste in the Aquafresh line. "SmithKline Beecham chose to use the Aquafresh label because of the product's good taste, an especially important attribute for a sensitive toothpaste." Potassium nitrate, the ingredient that relieves the pain of sensitive teeth, has a distinctive, unpleasant taste that can be difficult to disguise, so a pleasant flavor was needed to overcome it.

All Aquafresh products are peppermint-flavored except for Kid's Aquafresh, which has a "bubble mint" flavor. Research suggested that kids preferred this type of flavor. The flavors that contain sodium monofluorophosphate that provides cavity prevention are in Triple Protection, Extra Fresh, and Kid's toothpastes. Tartar Control Aquafresh contains sodium fluoride, which provides cavity prevention plus pyrophosphates that help to reduce tartar buildup.

### Packaging

For consumer convenience, Aquafresh toothpastes are packaged in tubes and/or pumps. Aquafresh pumps were introduced in 1985. Originally, the pump varieties were more expensive than tube varieties, but in 1992 pump prices were lowered to match tube prices. An estimated 7.5 percent of the households bought Aquafresh pumps each year, and lower prices were expected to increase sales.

Triple Protection Aquafresh and Tartar Control Aquafresh are packaged in tubes and stand-up pumps. Kid's Aquafresh is packaged in a pump, and Aquafresh Extra Fresh and Sensitive are both packaged in tubes.

### Marketing and Advertising

Aquafresh products are promoted through various advertising and promotions. The company, however, found that the products sell three to seven times better when they are featured and displayed in stores. Other promotional efforts include incentives for consumers to enjoy greater value with cost savings, such as special packs and coupons. A 1992 promotion for pumps was, "Buy any 2 pumps and get a third pump free." Taking another route, when Aquafresh Sensitive was first introduced, the company sent samples to dentists for them to give to their patients.

Advertising in print and television commercials seeks to convey the message to consumers that Aquafresh can improve some aspect of their daily oral care. A different message is developed for each type of toothpaste and directed toward potential consumers in each target group. For example, two 15-second commercials for Kids Aquafresh showed how enjoyable brushing teeth could be if it is was done with Aquafresh. In one commercial, viewers saw a young boy with his dog watching him brush his teeth. The boy was so engrossed in brushing that the dog felt neglected by the lack of attention, his barks ignored.

Another 15-second commercial showed a young boy happily brushing his teeth with Kids Aquafresh while his friends, who have called for him to come out and play, watch him in amazement through a window. The tag line for both of these Kids Aquafresh commercials was, "Gets them brushing. Helps keep them brushing."

An example of a 30-second commercial for Tartar Control Aquafresh was a women showing the TV viewers pictures of what tartar can do to a family's teeth before and after regular visits to a dentist. A further message from the announcer conveys that Aquafresh Tartar Control toothpaste can also help to fight cavities and tartar buildup, and to freshen breath with a good taste that the whole family loves. The tag line was, "It's striped to fight."

An example of advertising for Aquafresh Sensitive was a 30-second commercial that showed a few men and women eating or touching their teeth and wincing in pain. Aquafresh Sensitive was introduced as a solution, because it comforts the nerves that have been hit by hot or cold. The tag line was, "Soothes the nerve. Stops the pain."

### International Market

Overseas markets for Aquafresh are important to the company. Worldwide sales in 1992 grew 17 percent over the previous year. Most of the products are marketed in the same package forms as in the United States.

International marketing of Aquafresh toothpastes began in 1978 with the first product, Double Protection. Then Triple Protection Aquafresh was marketed in a stain tube in 1982, in pump form in 1985, and in plaque tube in 1986. Kid's Aquafresh was marketed in pump form in 1985 and in tube form in 1987. Tartar Control Aquafresh was introduced in both tube and pump form in 1988. Triple Protection Extra Fresh Aquafresh was marketed in 1989, followed by Aquafresh Sensitive in 1992.

### Performance Appraisal

Aquafresh is approved by the ADA. Approval by the Association is given after a company has submitted convincing research that shows the product is safe, effective, does what it should, and follows certain criteria for abrasives and fluoride. For its part, the company must agree to follow the ADA's rules for advertising and packaging.

Aquafresh toothpastes have remained one of the nation's leading brands because they satisfy certain needs and preferences. There is always the question, however, if sales are from new users or consumers who switched from a regular type of toothpaste. The increasing sales for Aquafresh Sensitive, for example, were attributed to consumers switching from regular Aquafresh products. The target group is composed of people aged 35 and over who suffer from sensitive teeth but use regular brands.

Nevertheless, growth for this type of product is expected in the future, because only about ten percent of the people with sensitive teeth regularly use a sensitive teeth toothpaste. Typically, sensitive teeth affect people as they get older, and since the U.S. population is aging, there will be higher numbers of people with sensitive teeth as potential consumers. About 18 percent of the adult population in the United States, or 34 million people, are estimated to have sensitive teeth.

## Future Products

It can be expected that Aquafresh products will continue to follow two trends when developing future products. One trend is marketing different types of therapeutic toothpastes, and the other is marketing premium-priced products. Generally, these trends coincide because therapeutic products are higher-priced than regular toothpastes. Premium-priced toothpastes bring higher profits for toothpaste makers; some makers charge twice as much for their sensitive toothpastes as for their regular brands. Aquafresh priced its Sensitive product 30 percent higher.

One future type of therapeutic product would be anti-microbial toothpastes that contain triclosan, which are pending approval by the Food and Drug Administration (FDA). Triclosan is used in anti-microbial toothpastes sold in some foreign countries, and used in deodorants in the United States. Triclosan, however, has not been approved for use in U.S. toothpastes as of late 1993. The combination of triclosan, fluoride, and antitartar agents curbs plaque and gingivitis, according to toothpaste manufacturers.

## Further Reading:

Smithkline Beecham Consumer Brands company materials.

"Toothpastes," *Consumer Reports,* September 1992, pp. 602–06.

Winters, Patricia, "AquaFresh Gets Sensitive about Baby Boomer Teeth," *Advertising Age,* October 12, 1992, p. 4.

*—Dorothy Kroll*

# ARAMIS®

Aramis is the U.S. and worldwide leader in men's prestige fragrance and grooming products, and has held that position since its launching in 1964. Aramis, manufactured by Aramis Inc., a wholly owned subsidiary of Estee Lauder Inc., was the first brand to offer a full line of grooming products for men, and revolutionized the fragrance industry in the process. About 25 years later, Aramis again created a "first" for the industry by introducing a fragrance for women in a men's line.

Since its inception, the name Aramis has become synonymous with luxury, quality, and prestige throughout the world. The brand is sold in 128 countries, in a total of 2,300 "doors" in the United States and over 4,000 others in foreign nations.

The Aramis brand actually encompasses four product lines that include fragrance and grooming products imbued with the Aramis scent. New product development for each of the four lines has been based on the unique needs of a target market, needs that differentiate it from other markets targeted by the brand's other product lines.

The target markets reflect different consumer interests, preferences, age groups, levels of sophistication, and lifestyles. Marketing strategies, packaging, design, and advertising are developed according to the individual needs of each target group.

The market for men's fragrances is much smaller than that for women. While there are fewer product introductions each year for men than for women, the men's fragrance marketplace is global and crowded with U.S. and foreign manufacturers. Sales for the total fragrance market were estimated at $4.7 billion in 1992, and men's fragrances were estimated at 15 percent or $750 million.

Economic and social factors are two of the strongest influences on sales for men's fragrances. During the early 1990s product introduction by many global fragrance makers slowed down because of the economic recessions in Europe and America. The cost of launching a product continued to escalate even as demand slowed down. Sales growth was also slight as consumers had less disposable income for luxuries.

Nevertheless, the total fragrance market for men has grown as men have become increasingly comfortable with the idea that they can wear fragrances. They still resist, however, any products that are considered to be unmanly or feminine. The reason that demand has increased is that more men are interested in appearing younger, are more willing to try new products, and have more choices available from so many different domestic and European makers of either prestige or mass market fragrance products.

In such a highly competitive industry environment, marketing strategy is key. The ability of Aramis to adapt to changing consumer needs has been the chief reason for its market leadership throughout the years. In addition to developing new products for new types of consumers and looking for new markets to sell them in both in the United States and abroad, Aramis changed its merchandising methods to fit changing shopping patterns, and developed new advertising and promotional efforts to ensure the brand's continued success with consumers.

## Brand Origins and Development

The Aramis line was launched by Estee Lauder in September of 1964. In addition to the Aramis fragrance, the original line included aftershave, soap, and 17 other products that were designed to enhance a man's appearance and self-image.

In ensuing years, the classic Aramis scent was used in a variety of fragrance and grooming products. By the early 1990s, the Aramis line had grown to four different product lines that included more than 130 products. In addition to fragrances, there were products for hair, skin, and shaving. In 1992 the original Aramis Classic Brand was relaunched with an enhanced formula, new packaging, and new advertising.

The first new line to be introduced within the Aramis family was Tuscany, in 1984. Tuscany was Aramis's first European-inspired fragrance and grooming line. Within five years, it became the top-selling men's fragrance at Bloomingdale's, one of New York City's upscale department stores. The Tuscany line was meant to reflect the sophistication and spirit of Italy and was, in fact, developed in Italy. It is made of a blend of exotic spices, herbs, lavender, and fresh citrus. The line is meant to reflect the soothing and reviving pleasures of the Italian spa. Its design reflects the classic Italian motifs and materials.

The next Aramis product line to be introduced was in 1987 and called Aramis Lab Series. This line offered high-tech, advanced products for a man's skin and hair. The products were promoted as problem-solvers for the busy, modern man. Within a few years the series ranked as the nation's top-selling men's treatment line.

The next Aramis introduction focused on a uniquely American lifestyle. Called New West, the product line reflected the California/American West lifestyle. Introduced in 1989, it used natural ingredients and was targeted to the contemporary, fitness-minded consumer. This new product was set apart from other Aramis products by its bold packaging and unique image. And in 1993 a new fragrance called Havana was introduced. This line was targeted toward the needs and interests of young men.

## Marketing Strategy

The company reports that its marketing strategy includes a commitment to excellence and innovation, and therefore focuses on merchandising and sales training; product packaging, design, and advertising; sales education and service; and distribution. Distribution is a key factor because the Aramis line is a prestige line geared to men of affluence, sophistication, and wealth. In order to maintain this image, the Aramis brand is distributed and sold only in exclusive, upscale department stores in the United States and overseas. The Aramis brand commands the largest and choicest counter spaces in these stores, according to the company.

## AT A GLANCE

**A**ramis brand men's cologne manufactured by Aramis Inc., a wholly owned subsidiary of the privately held, family-owned company Estee Lauder Inc.; Estee Lauder opened an office in New York City in 1944 to sell skin care products and cosmetics to department stores and beauty salons; her Aramis fragrance line was introduced in 1964.

**Performance:** *Market share*—18.9% of men's fragrance and grooming market. *Sales*—Estimated $70 million (1992).

**Major competitor:** Men's fragrances marketed by leading American and foreign fashion designers, such as Kouros by French designer Yves St. Laurent, and Polo by American designer Ralph Lauren.

**Advertising:** *Agency*—AC&R, New York, NY, 1968—.

**Addresses:** *Parent company*—Aramis Inc., 767 5th. Ave., New York, NY 10153; phone: (212) 572-3700; fax: (212) 572-4292. *Ultimate parent company*—Estee Lauder Inc., 767 5th. Ave., New York, NY 10153; phone: (212)-572-4600; fax: (212) 572-3941.

Sales education and training is another key component. This marketing strategy traces its beginnings to Estee Lauder personally travelling around the country during the 1950s to sell her line of cosmetics to high profile department stores. Mrs. Lauder trained the saleswomen herself to properly market her products.

In addition, sales personnel serve as an educational source for the company. A worldwide network of sales specialists and marketers give the company feedback about consumer needs and desires, and how those needs might be changing. New trends can then be discerned by the company, and new products can be developed to fit these trends.

Just as Aramis products might be developed to fit changing consumer needs, marketing strategies must be continually evaluated and adapted. In 1993 the company decided to change its marketing focus from advertising to sampling. "Sampling will be our No. 1 priority," said Sharon Le Van, senior vice president of marketing and creative services. "Advertising will still be needed to establish an image, but we've found the most important thing we can do for a fragrance is to get it into the hands of the consumer."

This shift in marketing emphasis was due to a noticeable change in consumer shopping patterns. It was learned that consumer brand loyalty was on the decline. Instead, consumers were more apt to select a brand that appealed to them after sampling it, either while shopping in a store or, perhaps, receiving something in the mail. The technique of sampling also allows men to make their own fragrance selections rather than the traditional advertising approach of convincing women to buy fragrances for men.

As a result, Aramis shifted to more in-store, direct mail, and off-site sampling instead of advertising, which was largely directed toward gift-givers. Previously, there was heavy promotion on gifts-with-purchase. Aramis's vice president of marketing, Pamela Baxter, told *Brandweek* magazine, "We have to keep up with what the consumer is asking for at the counter. In the 1980s gifts meant something to consumers. But in the 1990s we found them shopping from counter to counter, not having any brand loyalty." Eventually gift promotions could be phased out.

Searching for new markets is another aspect of the new marketing strategy. One new market was men attending health clubs. Said Baxter, "If you're sold in department stores and the department store consumer is declining, you have to look for other avenues. Your advertising isn't the only thing you can rely on to get that consumer into the department store. If it was, they would be coming. But they're not. We've increased not only the variety of our sampling but the quantity of the varieties."

### Advertising and International Markets

Aramis has always tried to create an image of prestige, status, wealth, and savvy through its advertising. Advertising, packaging, and promotional activities emphasized the Aramis connection and parentage. For example, when Tuscany was launched, packaging and ads had the tag line, "Created by Aramis Firenze Italia." When New West was introduced, packaging and advertising had the tag line, "Created by Aramis, Los Angeles, California."

The same marketing strategies employed for Aramis sold in the United States apply to the brand sold around the world. To maintain its prestigious image, the same selectivity of retailers is made. Aramis Inc. has chosen to sell its fragrance line in only about 50 percent of the international retailing outlets available, and the scent can be found only in the world's finest stores such as London's Harrods and Selfridges and Galleries Lafayette in Paris. In addition, Aramis advertising, packaging, logo, and designs are exactly the same in each country, easily recognized by a traveller from Europe, Asia, or South America.

Facilitating this global distribution is Aramis's parent company, Estee Lauder Inc., which has wholly owned affiliates in 28 countries; it has distribution in 100 more countries and manufacturing plants in Australia, Belgium, Canada, Spain, Switzerland, the United Kingdom, and Venezuela. Europe is a particularly strong market because the continent has a tradition of fine fragrances. Developing countries are emerging markets, because as nations gain in affluence, consumers have more money to spend and reportedly take a greater interest in self-care.

### Performance Appraisal and Future Products

Aramis ranks as number one in "sales per door" in the men's fragrance industry. In the United States in 1992, its share, according to the company, was 18.9 percent of the men's fragrance and grooming market. The share is higher in some overseas countries, such as Japan where Aramis enjoys a whopping 90 percent market share. In some U.S. department stores, the Aramis line of products accounts for 50 percent to 80 percent of total men's fragrance sales. Sales are especially strong for the products that combine fragrance with grooming.

The parent company of Aramis has a reputation for marketing innovative brands with product lines that fit the needs and interests of special niche groups. It can be expected that both the parent company and Aramis unit will continue this pattern in the future. For example, Estee Lauder Inc. launched Clinique in 1968, a line of hypoallergenic cosmetics for women that were the first of its kind. The line includes skin care and makeup for women and skin products for men. In 1979 the company introduced Prescriptives, a skin care, cosmetics, and fragrance line targeted to young professional women. In the 1990s the Origins line of environmentally safe cosmetics was first marketed. The line brandishes environmentally safe packaging, and none of the products are tested on animals. Origins products are sold in special Origins stores.

The Aramis line also expanded into new, uncharted territories for men's fragrances. In the fall of 1990 Aramis introduced New West Her; geared for young women, the scent was the first women's fragrance to be marketed by a men's line. Two years later, in 1992, the Aramis Tuscany line followed suit and introduced Tuscany Per Donna, targeted "to the modern woman who doesn't fit into an age bracket." The scent is "more of a lifestyle statement," said Amy Mayfield, public relations director of Aramis. In keeping with Aramis's new marketing strategy of sampling, 78 million scented impressions of Tuscany Per Donna were delivered to consumers through magazines and direct mail, as well as in stores.

**Further Reading:**

Nayyar, Seema, "Aramis Shifts from Gifts to Sampling," *Brandweek,* January 18, 1993, p. 5.

Omelia, Johanna, "More Scents," *Drug and Cosmetic Industry,* March 1993, pp. 31–36.

Parson, Stephen F., "Cosmetic Chemicals '92 - Men's Toiletries: Perennially Poised," *Chemical Marketing Reporter,* August 10, 1992, pp. SR16–20.

*Press Release,* New York: Aramis Inc.

Sloan, Pat and Scott Donaton, "Sampling Smells Sweet for Scent Biz," *Advertising Age,* August 3, 1992, p. 17.

Topfer, Kurt, "Prestige Fragrances a Draw with Men in US Marketplace," *Chemical Marketing Reporter,* August 10, 1992, p. 5, 23.

*—Dorothy Kroll*

# ARRID®

Arrid brand deodorants and antiperspirants, marketed by pharmaceutical and consumer product manufacturer Carter-Wallace, Inc., boast of one of the oldest names in their market. Arrid products, led by Arrid Extra Dry antiperspirant, held a leading share in the U.S. deodorant and antiperspirant market until the early 1970s, when heightened competition, changing technology, and increased government regulation contributed to Arrid's fall to the second tier of products. In 1972, Arrid products held a 14.8 percent share of the market, but the share had plunged below 10 percent just a few years later and since that time has remained in the 8-10 percent range. Industry analysts blame Arrid's decline on poor marketing decisions and on the competition of huge firms such as the Procter & Gamble Company, maker of Secret and Sure brands, and the Gillette Company, maker of Right Guard, Soft & Dri, and Dry Idea.

## Early Success

In the early 1950s, Carter-Wallace chemist John Wallace introduced to the consumer market one of the many new products he engineered: Arrid cream deodorant. Arrid took advantage of the boom in the personal products industry, which had benefitted from the rise in U.S. consumer's purchasing power after World War II. More and more Americans were convinced of the need to keep themselves smelling fresh all day long, and only a few products had yet been designed to meet that need. By 1960 Arrid cream deodorant held the top share in the U.S. deodorant market, leading competitors such as Mennen and Mum.

The entire Carter-Wallace organization was boosted by the postwar boom. In 1930 Henry Hoyt bought the Carter Medicine Company from his father-in-law and pursued an aggressively entrepreneurial strategy that placed the once-tiny company on *Fortune* magazine's list of the second 500 largest industrial companies in the United States by 1976. The company's early growth rested on sales of the popular Carter's Little Liver Pills, but by the 1950s the company had introduced a number of new products that guaranteed continued success. Wallace, the chemist responsible for the creation of Arrid cream deodorant, invented consumer products categories with Nair hair remover and Rise shaving cream. His contributions were recognized in 1965, when the company became Carter-Wallace, Inc.

Carter-Wallace sought to continue its success in the personal products industry, and introduced numerous new products, many of which failed. Attempts to bolster the Arrid line included Arrid Whirl-in roll-on deodorant, Arrid deodorant bath oil, Arrid Extra foot spray, and Lady Arrid feminine deodorant spray. None of these met with the success of the first Arrid product, but in 1968 the company achieved dramatic success with the introduction of Arrid Extra Dry spray, the first aerosol antiperspirant to be introduced in the United States. According to *Advertising Age* contributor Nancy Giges, the new product "zoomed up to share first place with Gillette Co.'s Right Guard aerosol, a deodorant that lacked antiperspirant benefits at the time." A heavy advertising campaign helped sales of Arrid. The campaign, designed by the Sullivan, Stauffer, Colwell & Bayles agency, featured consumer testimonials. In addition, Carter-Wallace designed incentive plans that were tied to distribution, sales, and promotional campaigns, according to *Advertising Age* contributor Fred Danzig. One Carter-Wallace executive told Danzig that field sales representatives "can pitch right in with enthusiasm because they know exactly what's behind the product that has the incentive schedule." Although Arrid Extra Dry spray was Carter-Wallace's biggest achievement, Giges notes that it was the company's last triumph for many years.

## Surviving the Seventies

Although Arrid had been one of the big success stories of the 1950s and 1960s, the brand struggled to maintain market share in the 1970s. After battling for the leading market share for nearly twenty years, Arrid became just one of many brands competing for a piece of the still-growing deodorant and antiperspirant market. *Adveritising Age*'s Giges held upper management at Carter-Wallace responsible for Arrid's decline: "If Carter-Wallace's present day misfortunes can be traced to a single origin," she wrote in 1977, "it is the dictatorial presence of the Hoyt family, which has run the drug and toiletries marketer for nearly five decades." Carter-Wallace succeeded when Henry Hoyt, Sr., ran the company, Giges charged, but a "genius system" can't succeed when the genius is on the sidelines and his son is running the company. Hoyt's son, Henry Hoyt, Jr., had taken over the management of the company in the early 1970s. Under Hoyt Jr.'s leadership, new product development and research declined dramatically, and promotional spending was frozen. Giges claimed in 1977 that "the company is one of the most poorly managed of its size in the country today."

## AT A GLANCE

**A**rrid brand of cream deodorant introduced in the early 1950s by John Wallace of the Carter Medicine Co., which became Carter-Wallace, Inc., in 1965; Arrid Extra Dry antiperspirant spray, introduced in 1968, was the first aerosol antiperspirant in the United States.

*Performance:* *Market share*—8.4% (seventh place) of the deodorant and antiperspirant category. *Sales*—Approximately $122 million.

*Major competitor:* Procter & Gamble's Secret, Sure, and Old Spice; also Colgate-Palmolive's Mennen, Gillette Company's Right Guard and Bristol-Myers Squibb's Ban.

*Advertising:* *Agency*—Backer Spielvogel Bates, New York, NY. *Major campaign*—"It's there when you need it most."

*Addresses:* *Parent company*—Carter-Wallace, Inc., 1345 Avenue of the Americas, New York, NY 10105; phone: (212) 339-5000; fax: (212) 715-1660.

Arrid's fortunes in the 1970s reflected the problems within Carter-Wallace. Although Arrid products maintained the second leading market share among deodorants and antiperspirants in 1973 (directly behind Right Guard), Procter & Gamble's new Sure brand was stealing market share at an alarming rate and threatened to overtake the much older Arrid. Carter-Wallace rushed to counter advertisements that demonstrated Sure antiperspirant's superiority at maintaining underarm dryness. Unable to obtain tests indicating Arrid's greater effectiveness, Carter-Wallace still ran ads that demonstrated its product's dryness. But in such a competitive market, merely being dry was not enough. To capture market or maintain share, a product had to be able to claim it was the driest. Arrid could no longer do so.

Seeking to recover from what *Advertising Age*'s Giges called "a critical marketing error," Carter-Wallace rushed to introduce its new product, Arrid XX antiperspirant spray, by Labor Day, 1974. The new product had fared well in the test market of Omaha, Nebraska, behind a Sullivan, Stauffer, Colwell & Bayles advertisement that promised "50 percent more wetness-stopping power than any spray we've ever made, to help X out wet spots." Carter-Wallace was expected to channel much of its $15 million dollar advertising budget into promoting the line extension, and retailers were awaiting the anticipated promotional push. Just as the new product was introduced, however, Carter-Wallace was hit by two major regulatory challenges to its product line.

In 1974, according to the *Wall Street Journal*, researchers reported that "the fluorocarbon gases used in aerosol sprays could impair the atmosphere's ability to screen out excess ultraviolet radiation." As the Food and Drug Administration (FDA) moved to eliminate fluorocarbon aerosols, consumers looked for alternative deodorant and antiperspirant applications. Moreover, the FDA was rumored to be contemplating a ban on the marketing of antiperspirants that contained zirconium. Particles of the antiperspirant ingredient "had been shown to cause lung disease when inhaled by test animals and can cause an inflammatory reaction on human skin," according to a *Wall Street Journal* article. Arrid XX antiperspirant spray, a fluorocarbon-propelled aerosol with zirconium as its active ingredient, was in trouble on both counts, but Carter-Wallace executives announced in 1975 their determination to continue marketing the product. "The product was subjected to the most sophisticated and intensive research in the history of the antiperspirant industry," they asserted. "Because of this research, the company believes—and continues to believe—that the product can be used safely. Otherwise, the company would not have sold it." Less than a year later, however, Carter-Wallace withdrew its product from the market, telling the *Wall Street Journal*, "there's no sense in continuing the battle."

### Recovery and Recommitment

Given the troubles of the mid-1970s, it is surprising that Arrid products fared as well as they did in the late 1970s and 1980s. Arrid introduced a hydrocarbon-propelled pump spray in 1977, and boosted promotional spending on its roll-on application. According to *Media Decisions*, Carter-Wallace spent $12.8 million advertising Arrid in 1976, 90 percent of which went into network television ads. The magazine noted, "Observers suggest that Carter-Wallace management has realized that it will take at least $12 million annually in media to continue a competitive stance in the marketplace." In 1980 *Marketing & Media Decisions* reported that Arrid had been able to take advantage of other manufacturer's abandonment of the aerosol category by cornering 12 percent of all aerosol sales. Carter-Wallace used the "Get a little closer" theme to promote all of its Arrid products in 1980, when the product line had over thirty different varieties.

The 1980s saw no major changes in Arrid's positioning or its product line. Like most other deodorant and antiperspirant manufacturers, Carter-Wallace introduced Arrid versions of the newly popular stick and solid applications and experimented with different scents, adding a sport scent in the late 1980s when sport scents were quite popular. Arrid did experience significant growth overseas, since Carter-Wallace invested heavily in promoting its products in the United Kingdom. The British market had been slow to follow the U.S. trend towards increasing usage of deodorant and antiperspirant products, but *Chemist & Druggist* reported that the value of that market had increased by more than 70 percent between 1987 and 1992. Arrid had been launched in the United Kingdom in 1970 and received consistent product support through the 1980s, but in 1992 Carter-Wallace decided to repackage Arrid Extra Dry in a new range of six aerosols and five roll-ons. Carter-Wallace product manager Janette Scott told *Chemist & Druggist* that "the antiperspirant/deodorant sector is one of the most buoyant in the whole of this vast market, and we are convinced that Arrid Extra Dry's repackaging puts it well ahead of the competition." The new line was backed by television advertising, sales promotions, and public relations.

Arrid products have long been the top sellers among Carter-Wallace's many products. According to the 1992 annual report, antiperspirant and deodorant sales accounted for 19.5 percent of the company's $673.4 million in sales. Carter-Wallace manufactures products in two broad categories: consumer products and health care. Its Consumer Products Division includes Arrid, Nair, Rise, Pearl Drops tooth polish, Sea & Ski suncare products, Trojan condoms, and a variety of pet products. The Health Care Division markets prescription pharmaceutical products to trained professionals and hospitals and a limited number of over-the-counter drugs and home pregnancy tests.

### Future Prospects

Carter-Wallace took steps to reinvigorate its Arrid line in the early 1990s, reformulating and repackaging old products and introducing new ones. Arrid Extra Dry Anti-Perspirant Deodorant Spray was reformulated to offer "sustained action" and promoted with the tagline "It's there when you need it most." Arrid Extra Dry Anti-Perspirant & Deodorant Cream was repackaged in a new "no mess applicator," which was promised to feel smooth and comfortable under the arm. In 1993, Carter-Wallace announced the introduction of its Arrid Teen Image line of products, aimed at a market that is expected to grow to $55 million by 1995, according to *Brandweek.* Arrid Teen Image was backed with an estimated $5.3 million in advertising. Although Carter-Wallace made each of these line improvements hoping to retain Arrid's share of the deodorant and antiperspirant market, the improvements were a reaction to shifts within the market instigated by market leaders. The "sustained action" reformulation represents an attempt to keep up with the Degree brand's innovation in body-heat activated antiperspirant protection, and Teen Image was an attempt to capture some of the market created by the introduction of Mennen's Teen Spirit line. Market share gains within the U.S. deodorant and antiperspirant market have traditionally gone to innovators, as Carter-Wallace learned in 1968. Carter-Wallace's strategy of developing new products only in reaction to changes within the market seems to promise Arrid a respectable but secondary portion in a growing market.

## Further Reading:

"Arrid Extra Dry Spearheads Growth of the Anti-Perspirant Deodorant Market," *Chemist & Druggist,* April 18, 1992, p. 644.

"Brand Report 35: Deodorants and Anti-perspirants," *Media Decisions,* November 1978.

Carter-Wallace, Inc., *Annual Report,* New York: Carter Wallace, Inc., 1977–1988.

"C-W Says Double X Ads Will Continue as Ingredient Ban Looms," *Advertising Age,* June 2, 1975, pp. 1, 55.

Danzig, Fred, "Carter's 'Particularized' Incentive Drive Booms Arrid," *Advertising Age,* June 23, 1969, pp. 35, 58.

Fannin, Rebecca, "Brand Report 62: Deodorants," *Marketing & Media Decisions,* February 1981.

"FDA Proposes to Ban Zirconium-Containing Antiperspirant Sprays," *Wall Street Journal,* May 30, 1975.

Giges, Nancy, "Carter Seeking to Regain Shares with Arrid's Double X," *Advertising Age,* July 22, 1974, pp. 1, 78; "Arrid Double X Roll Continues, But Ad Support Backs Roll-on," *Advertising Age,* May 5, 1975, pp. 1, 57; "Carter-Wallace Woes Are a Family Affair," *Advertising Age,* July 11, 1977, pp. 3, 169–70.

"Hoyt," *Forbes,* October 22, 1990, p. 294.

Riddle, Judith S., "Arrid's Teen Image Will Get $5.3M to Take On Teen Spirit," *Brandweek,* March 29, 1993, pp. 1, 6.

Rosendahl, Iris, "Drugstores Meeting Tougher Competition for Deodorants," *Drug Topics,* August 19, 1991, pp. 65–66.

Shore, A., "Cosmetics and Household Products Industry Report," Paine-Webber, Inc., April 8, 1993.

Sloan, Pat, and Laurie Freeman, "Degree Makes Leaders Sweat," *Advertising Age,* December 10, 1990.

"Zirconium Dispute Prompts Its Removal from Antiperspirants," *Wall Street Journal,* May 4, 1976.

—*Tom Pendergast*

# ARROW®

The Arrow brand, managed since 1990 by Bidermann Industries, Corp., has been a leader in the realm of quality men's shirts for well over one hundred years. Until 1992 it was the foremost player in the $2.4 billion men's dress shirt market. During that year Van Heusen slid past Arrow in total market share. Today Van Heusen boasts an overall share of 11 percent, while Arrow now hovers beneath ten percent—a striking decline for the longtime leader considering that it once commanded a nearly 20 percent share. Yet these numbers are at least partially deceiving, for Arrow still retains sizable leads in both medium-price range department store sales (45 percent of market share) and overall department store sales (26 percent).

Manhattan-based Bidermann Industries purchased the Arrow brand in 1990 from financially imperiled William Farley and his hastily built textile and apparel empire, Farley Industries. At the time, the $410 million purchase price of Arrow's immediate parent, Cluett, Peabody & Co., was considered a steal by many. But by September 1993 *Forbes* was declaring it an acquisition of the "wrong company" at the "wrong time." Competition in the industry was intense and Bidermann took on Arrow at a dangerous crossroads in men's fashions, when sales of branded dress shirts were declining. Despite clothier Maurice Bidermann's filing of personal bankruptcy in 1993, attempts to spark new life into the Arrow brand continue. The naming of Mandelbaum Mooney Ashley as the shirt manufacturer's new advertising agency, the targeting of female buyers, and the Fall 1993 debut of the Arrow sportsman collection are just some of the measures being taken to revitalize Arrow.

## Brand History

According to Molly Wade McGrath's *Top Sellers, U.S.A.,* "The history of the Arrow shirt dates back to the invention of the detached collar at Troy, New York, in 1820." Some 30 years later collar manufacturing was a thriving industry in Troy. The predecessor of Cluett, Peabody & Co., was among the cottage businesses headquartered there and soon proved itself to be one of the most promising. In 1889, with 400 collar styles to its credit, Cluett merged with Loon & Company, which brought to the new corporation the Arrow brand name. Another valuable addition was salesman Frederick F. Peabody, who quickly became a partner in the expanded company. In 1905 Peabody teamed with commercial artist J. C. Leyendecker to create the "Arrow Collar Man." A

widely recognized symbol that kept pace with changing fashions, the Arrow Collar Man, designed to appeal to both women and men, exemplified the ideal American male.

Arrow was already a classic by the end of World War I, and was clearly the driving force behind a company that employed 6,000 people and posted sales of more than $32 million. During the 1920s Arrow made two significant advances. In 1927 it introduced the industry's first soft collar attached shirt, the Trump. The successful transition from a starched collar to a dress shirt business for Cluett was hastened by the power and prestige of the Arrow brand name. In 1928 Sanford L. Cluett, then a vice-president of research and development, invented and patented for the company the "Sanforized" anti-shrinkage process. Excess cotton shrinkage was the chief complaint among Arrow customers; this development not only corrected the problem but became a standard technique in the industry, used by cotton finishers around the world.

During the Great Depression, the New York-based Young & Rubicam ad agency made a name for itself, and an even larger name for its client, with a series of stylish Arrow shirt ads. By the end of the decade Arrow controlled the world's largest shirt factory, which would soon be converted to aid the war effort. During the early 1950s Arrow prepared for global expansion through its creation of the Cluett International division. Interested not simply in shirts but all men's apparel, Cluett acquired menswear manufacturer J. Schoeneman in 1955 and then launched the Cluett Suit Group. The company capped the decade by introducing Dectolene, which made for the first authentic wash-and-wear shirt on the market. Despite an ongoing program to diversify in men's apparel, Cluett announced in 1964 that it would discontinue its tie-making business; a company spokesperson declared to *Wall Street Journal*: "We are the last of the major shirt manufacturers to go out of the tie business; the company is proud it was able to hold out so long." The move, in fact, underscored a double-edged consumer trend, that shoppers were now buying twice as many sports shirts as business shirts. For a shirtmaker willing and able to adapt, this news spelled opportunity rather than demise. Arrow's parent remained healthy by purchasing Great American Knitting Mills—the producer of Gold Toe, the nation's largest-selling branded men's socks—in 1968. The solid move into hosiery served to anchor Cluett and, coupled with Arrow, provided for a more dominant stake in department store sales.

## AT A GLANCE

**A**rrow brand founded in 1851 in Troy, NY, by The Cluett Company founders Maullin & Blanchard; The Cluett Company merged with Loon & Company, 1889; Cluett was later renamed Cluett, Peabody & Co., Inc.; later developers include J. C. Leyendecker, Frederick F. Peabody, and Sanford L. Cluett; Cluett, Peabody & Co. was acquired by West Point-Pepperell, 1986; West Point-Pepperell acquired by Farley Industries, 1989; Cluett, Peabody subsidiary acquired by Bidermann Industries, Corp., 1990.

**Performance:** *Market share*—9.2% (No. 2) of all U.S. shirt sales; 26% (top share) of all department store sales; 45% (top share) of medium-price range department store sales.

**Major competitor:** Phillips-Van Heusen Corp.'s Van Heusen.

**Advertising:** *Agency*—Mandelbaum Mooney Ashley, 1993—.

**Addresses:** *Parent company*—Bidermann Industries, Corp., 575 Fifth Avenue, New York, NY 10017; phone: (212) 984-8900; fax: (212) 984-8938. *Ultimate parent company*—Bidermann International S.A., 14 Rue de Turenne, 75003 Paris, France; phone: 42-77-15-20; fax: 42-77-95-99.

In 1971 Cluett backed its foremost brand with an unprecedented preemptive purchase of network television time. On Thursday, October 23, Arrow shirt ads were everywhere; Cluett bought up all the available national time on the three major networks during the airing of the Johnny Carson, Dick Cavett, and Merv Griffin shows. In addition, it asked its regional dealers to buy whatever local television time they could. At the time the president of the Television Bureau of Advertising declared the Cluett-Arrow media blitz "the biggest blast ever in the men's wear industry," according to the *Wall Street Journal.* High-profile campaigns were the norm for Arrow during the 1970s. In 1972 scrambling Vikings quarterback Fran Tarkenton became a pitchman for Arrow. Three years later, New York Jets quarterback "Broadway" Joe Namath joined the Arrow celebrity team. Meanwhile, research and development efforts kept Arrow on top in style and design with the introduction of Brigade, touted by the company as "the first true fitted shirt."

As Arrow entered the 1980s it was the clear frontrunner in the men's dress shirt category with a 20 percent market share; Arrow's rival Van Heusen held just a two percent share. Ten years later Van Heusen's parent, Phillips-Van Heusen Corp., would be able to lay claim to the title of the country's largest shirt manufacturer. What precipitated the turnaround? No doubt the biggest reason was the fact that from 1986 to 1990, Cluett and Arrow were subject to a dizzying acquisition, takeover, and divestment drama.

### Advertising Efforts

In January 1986 Georgia-based textile conglomerate West Point-Pepperell purchased Cluett, Peabody & Co. Cluett was allowed to run autonomously and continue its successful product line growth. The Arrow brand's share of the market began to drop, however, despite the company's efforts. In 1987 the Chiat/Day agency put together a brilliant commercial spot intended to stress Arrow's rebirth as a shirt with color and pizazz. The spot began with a shot of an all-male choir dressed in traditional white shirts and singing a subdued, a capella version of the Jackie Wilson-Rita Coolidge hit "(Your Love Keeps Lifting Me) Higher and

Higher." Suddenly choir members began breaking tempo, shouting out lyrics, snapping fingers, and dancing; as they transformed, so did their attire, from plain white to a vivid array of styles and colors. The CLEO-winning commercial, according to Debbie Seaman, was inspired by the agency's " 'The Men's Club' print ad, which juxtaposed the members of The University Glee Club of New York City, all dressed in traditional white shirts, with the same group on the other side of the spread, dressed in an array of colorful Arrows." The good news was that a marketing high point had been reached. The bad news was that it mattered not in terms of total U.S. shirt sales.

By 1988 Van Heusen had captured a 6.4 percent market share, while Arrow had slipped to 11.6 percent. A year later Arrow was at 11.2 percent and its savvy competitor had gained another point. In 1990 Arrow teetered at 10.5 percent, poised to topple. During this market upheaval Arrow was unfortunately sidetracked. In March 1989 Chicago financier William Farley acquired a majority stake in West Point. Arrow appeared to have a new owner and, because Farley had already acquired Fruit of the Loom, the matchup made sense on the surface. However, Farley's leveraged takeover had left him vulnerable to massive interest payments and so, by late 1989, Cluett and Arrow were again up for grabs. This time the buyer was Bidermann, a Paris-headquartered menswear manufacturer founded in the mid-1920s. The U.S. branch of Bidermann was founded in 1973. According to "Bidermann: A Chronicle of Innovation in the World of Fashion," Bidermann Industries "soon became an 'insider' and key player in the American fashion realm. The company shortly thereafter developed and implemented a variety of innovations that have since revolutionized the industry. Foremost among these was Bidermann's early licensing agreements with several of the most respected designers of the time." Such licensees include Yves Saint Laurent (1975), Calvin Klein (1977), Daniel Hechter (1978), Ralph Lauren (1979), and Bill Robinson (1986).

The addition of Arrow to this elite cast was calculated to smooth out fluctuations in Bidermann's high-end sales while providing a brand worthy of worldwide expansion. At the time, Arrow was already recognized as an upscale brand in 35 European countries. Bidermann intended to propel it into perhaps 40 more. The Cluett-Arrow purchase also had the welcome effect of more than doubling Bidermann's size, for Cluett's annual sales were now approaching $750 million. Arrow's principal handicap, according to Katherine Weisman, was that it needed to "change its white-bread image. Few people know it sells more than polyester-cotton blend shirts." With 45 percent of the men's shirt market in the $20-$25 range, it would seem that little change was in order, but Weisman was right. Consumer spending slowed beginning in 1990 and Cluett was forced to lay off some 2,000 workers. Meanwhile, Van Heusen's sales and share continued to climb because of its flashier, more contemporary image. The primary reason for the reversal was that Van Heusen, according to a 1993 *Forbes* article, "targets its advertising to women, who buy an estimated 60% to 70% of men's shirts. Arrow's image, by contrast, has lacked sex appeal."

Although Arrow has taken a page from Van Heusen's marketing, its overall advertising thrust has been less than successful. Arrow's most recent slogan, under Ammirati & Puris, was the staid "America's shirtmakers since 1851." Ammirati resigned the account in 1991. The following year Arrow's total ad outlay was less than $500,000. Arrow did not sign an agency replacement until July 1993. As Kevin Goldman explained in the *Wall Street*

*Journal,* "Arrow is facing the same dilemma confronting many brands that established their reputations long ago and need to make a generational transition. But coming up with the right campaign to do that is a tough challenge." The new agency, Mandelbaum Mooney Ashley, may have the answer. This time the money is right: $10 million for television and print ads through 1994. The campaign by Mandelbaum Mooney, a small upstart agency that made a name for itself with its model-free Bugle Boy ads, is expected to debut by early 1994. Until then, Arrow will have to rely on its tried-and-true shirt collection (Bradstreet, Brigade, Dover, Fairfield, and Kent) as well as new point-of-sale merchandise, including the Fall 1993 Arrow Sportsman series. Although it may be true that "today more than ever, Arrow remains the world's most recognized shirt label in terms of style, quality, comfort, and value," Arrow is nonetheless a brand searching for direction. Moreover, the ultimate fallout from Maurice Bidermann's bankruptcy has yet to be evaluated.

## Further Reading:

Agins, Teri, "Women Help Van Heusen Collar Arrow," *Wall Street Journal,* May 22, 1992, pp. B1, B5.

"Arrow Ends Tie Output: Sports Shirt Boom Blamed," *Wall Street Journal,* February 17, 1964, p. 7.

"Arrow Shirt Chooses San Francisco Shop," *New York Times,* July 19, 1993, p. D6.

Banerjee, Neela, "Van Heusen Ends Tradition with New Chief," *Wall Street Journal,* May 21, 1993, p. B9.

*Bidermann: A Chronicle of Innovation in the World of Fashion,* New York: Bidermann Industries, 1993.

*Bidermann Industries Corp.: The Company & Its Products,* New York: Bidermann Industries, 1993.

"Carson, Cavett, Griffin: It's Arrow, Arrow, Arrow," *Wall Street Journal,* February 8, 1971, p. 5.

*Cluett Peabody & Co., Inc.: A Tradition in Men's Apparel For Over 125 Years,* New York: Bidermann, 1993.

Elsworth, Peter C. T., "Can Colors and Stripes Rescue Shirt Makers from a Slump?" *New York Times,* March 17, 1991, p. F5.

Furman, Phyllis, "Trying to Collar a Niche: Shirt Makers Find Market Is Shrinking," *Crain's New York Business,* November 26, 1990, pp. 3, 42.

Johnson, Robert, and Rick Christie, "Farley Lags in His Plans to Pay Debt as Cluett Is Sold for a Low-End Price," *Wall Street Journal,* March 19, 1990, p. A4.

McGrath, Molly Wade, "Arrow Shirt," *Top Sellers, U.S.A.: Success Stories Behind America's Best-Selling Products from Alka-Seltzer to Zippo,* New York: William Morrow and Company, 1983, pp. 26–7.

Morgenson, Gretchen, " 'We're Still Hungry,' " *Forbes,* October 14, 1991, pp. 60, 62.

Seaman, Debbie, "Arrow Scores Bull's-Eye with Soul Classic," *Adweek's Marketing Week,* October 26, 1987, p. 46.

"A Shirty Tale," *Forbes,* September 27, 1993, pp. 14, 19.

Weisman, Katherine, "Mass Meets Class," *Forbes,* September 17, 1990, pp. 108, 112.

Zeitz, Baila, and Lorraine Dusky, "Bidermann Industries," *The Best Companies for Women,* New York: Simon and Schuster, 1988, pp. 50–6.

*—Jay P. Pederson*

# ASICS®

ASICS was the fifth-best-selling brand of athletic footwear in the United States in 1992, with three percent of the market, and the fourth-best selling brand worldwide. ASICS TIGER Corporation, the U.S. subsidiary of ASICS Corporation Japan, also marketed a line of athletic apparel and accessories in addition to athletic footwear. Most ASICS brand shoes featured gel-filled pads in the arch and heel, introduced in 1986, that cushioned the feet and helped dissipate the shock of running on hard surfaces. ASICS shoes were also popular with wrestlers and volleyball players.

## Brand Origins

Kihachiro Onitsuka founded the Onitsuka Corporation in Japan in 1949. He chose "Tiger" as the brand name for his basketball shoes because the tiger was considered the strongest animal in Asia. Onitsuka introduced a Tiger wrestling shoe with a lightweight upper made of nylon in 1956. In 1967 he produced the first running shoes to use nylon uppers.

The Onitsuka Corporation concentrated on producing high quality athletic footwear until 1976, when the Olympic Games provided Onitsuka with a lesson in sports marketing. Although Tiger was the official shoe of the Polish volleyball team, a competitor grained more exposure by providing uniforms and other equipment that featured an easily recognizable trademark. The next year the Onitsuka Corporation merged with two other Japanese companies, GTO, a maker of volleyball and tennis nets, and Jelenk, a sportswear company, to form ASICS Corporation.

ASICS was an acronym for the Latin phrase "anima sana in corpore sano," which means "a sound mind in a sound body." The company took the acronym for its name because Onitsuka felt it "echoed the philosophy he had worked toward his entire life," according to a press release. Over the next 15 years, ASICS Corporation became a $1.4 billion manufacturer of athletic footwear, apparel, and accessories.

## ASICS Logo

The original ASICS logo consisted of two pairs of stripes that crossed to form what was once described by the *Los Angeles Times* as a stylized game of tic-tac-toe. The cross-hatched stripes remained an integral part of ASICS shoe design, but in 1993 the company adopted a new logo for all its advertising. Described as a "spiral design motif," the new logo was a uniquely styled "a" that preceded the corporate name. ASICS said the logo, created by Masashi Uehara of the Japan Design Center, "serves as an interpretation and inspiration to the speed and motion inherent in all sports."

## Marketing

After many years of being a relatively quiet player in the competitive U.S. athletic shoe market, ASICS TIGER Corp. launched a multi-year marketing plan in 1990 designed to boost the company's presence in five categories: running, cross training, basketball, volleyball, and wrestling. The marketing campaign included a series of offbeat television commercials that poked fun at the company's two biggest competitors, Nike and Reebok. In one commercial, a basketball player wearing ASICS shoes was shown scoring repeatedly while another player stood helplessly on the sidelines trying to inflate his own air-cushioned shoes with everything from a bicycle pump to an air compressor. The commercials closed with the tag line, "Anything more is a lot of hot air."

Although neither Nike nor Reebok were mentioned by name, both marketed basketball shoes that featured built-in pumps that provided stability and cushioning. ABC refused to run the commercials, which it said was "disparaging to the competition." The commercials aired on the NBC and Fox television networks. The company also signed all-star guard Isiah Thomas of the NBA's Detroit Pistons to endorse its products.

## Night Running

In 1992 ASICS introduced running shoes with small lights built into the heels to provide additional safety for joggers running at night. Called the Gel-Nite Lyte and the Gel-Twilyte, these introductions played off the company's popular gel-cushioned lightweight running shoes. The shoes incorporated a piece of piezo film, a lightweight material that generated a small electrical pulse when compressed. Whenever the heel of the shoe struck the ground, the piezo strip sent a triggering impulse to a tiny battery that lit up an LED (light emitting diode) for about 10 milliseconds. The shoes also sported reflective strips for added visibility.

## AT A GLANCE

ASICS brand athletic shoes (originally Tiger brand) developed by Kihachiro Onitsuka of Onitsuka Corporation in Japan in 1949; name changed from Tiger brand to ASICS brand in 1977, when Onitsuka Corporation merged with GTO and Jelenk to form ASICS Corporation; name is an acronym for the Latin phrase "anima sana in corpore sano," which means "a sound mind in a sound body."

*Performance:* Market share—3% of U.S. athletic footwear market; 5.3% of international market. *Sales*—$247 million U.S. sales; $1.4 billion worldwide sales (all products).

*Major competitor:* Nike.

*Advertising:* Agency—Bozell, Inc., Los Angeles.

*Addresses:* Parent company—ASICS TIGER Corporation, 10540 Talbert Ave., Fountain Valley, CA 92708; phone: (714) 962-7654. Ultimate parent company—ASICS Corporation Japan, 7-1-1, Minatojima-Nakamachi Chuo-ku, Kobe 650, Japan; phone: (078) 303-3333.

## Trends

ASICS was among the fastest growing brands of athletic footwear in the early 1990s. Between 1990 and 1992, the company's market share grew from less than two percent to three percent. Sales in the United States more than doubled during the same period, from $110 to $225 million, despite a U.S. market for athletic shoes that increased less than ten percent. ASICS passed LA Gear and Puma to become the fourth-best-selling brand worldwide behind Nike, Reebok, and Adidas.

While running shoes were the most popular category of ASICS athletic footwear, with cross-training shoes in second place and basketball third, ASICS also continued to expand its line of athletic footwear for specialty markets, such as wrestling, volleyball, and baseball. In 1987 ASICS introduced the first split-sole wrestling shoes for increased flexibility, and in 1990 introduced the ASICS PurpleLyte, a wrestling shoe with a super thin sole. ASICS also began placing more emphasis on its basketball shoes in 1992, including the signing of Calbert Cheaney to a five-year endorsement contract in 1993. Cheaney, college basketball player of the year with Indiana University in the 1992–93 season, was a rookie with the Washington Bullets in the 1993–94 season.

In 1994 the company introduced its first shoes designed specifically for the women's aerobics market. The company also re-entered the market for tennis shoes in 1994 after a four-year absence. Included in the new line was an "entry-level" tennis shoe for the consumer attracted to the ASICS reputation for quality but put off by the cost of top-of-the-line models.

In athletic wear, ASICS continued to promote an extensive line of clothing for skiers as well as shorts, shirts, and warm-up apparel made from high-performance synthetic fabrics for runners and other athletes. In 1994 the ASICS line of apparel for runners alone included more than 50 different styles. ASICS apparel also was popular with high school and college volleyball and wrestling teams. In 1994 the company introduced a line of sunglasses for sports enthusiasts.

One problem looming for ASICS was the possibility that the United States would cancel Most Favored Nation status for trade with China because of human rights violations. A substantial number of ASICS shoes were made in China.

## Further Reading:

"Asics Boosts Marketing, Focuses on 5 Categories," *Sporting Goods Business,* July 1990, p. 129.

"ASICS TIGER Corporation: From a Soldier's Dream to Corporate Success," ASICS TIGER Corporation, July 15, 1991.

Magiera, Marcy, "Rivals' Ads Hammer Nike," *Advertising Age,* February 25, 1991, p. 3.

"Running Shoe Lights the Night," *Machine Design,* October 8, 1992, p. 12.

Woodyard, Chris, "Asics Secures Foothold in the U.S.," *Los Angeles Times,* Sept. 4, 1991, p. D5.

*—Dean Boyer*

# AVIA®

Avia was the ninth most popular brand of athletic shoes in the United States in 1992, and the top brand in the niche market of aerobics footwear. Avia shoes were best known for their Cantilever technology, a concave sole developed by founder Jerry Stubblefield that helped cushion the feet and disperse the pounding shock of running or high-impact aerobics. Avia brand shoes were available in more than 40 countries. Avia also marketed a line of apparel, including men's and women's shorts, tee shirts, sweat clothes, fanny packs, and caps. The Avia brand was owned by the Avia Group International Inc. of Beaverton, Oregon, a subsidiary of athletic footwear industry giant Reebok International Ltd.

## Brand Origins

Jerry Stubblefield was a former track coach at Montana State University and a part-time inventor who licensed the cushioning technology he developed for athletic shoes to Osaga Inc., a small footwear company in Eugene, Oregon. When Osaga was sold in 1980, Stubblefield teamed up with William Toney, a sporting goods store owner, and Rick Kriss, a former Osaga employee, to form Pensa Inc. Using Cantilever technology, Pensa introduced a running shoe known as the Avia, a make-believe word that Stubblefield thought sounded classical. Avia later became the brand name for the entire line of Pensa shoes. The company's name was then changed to Avia International Group in 1987, less than a year before being sold to Reebok.

## Aerobics

Avia's reputation in the early 1980s was anchored firmly in aerobics. Pensa introduced its first shoes designed for women's aerobics in 1984, about the time that Reebok, not yet Avia's parent corporation, was pushing aerobics as a separate category for athletic footwear. Pensa, whose corporate mission statement stressed the prevention of injuries, positioned Avia, with its shock-absorbing sole, as the shoes scientifically engineered for the stressful demands of aerobics. Reebok's advertising helped focus attention on aerobics in general, while Pensa's advertising, created around the slogan "Built for Your Body," focused attention on the distinctive advantages of Avia.

When Reebok purchased Avia Group International in 1987, *Advertising Age* said, "Avia's main customers, the hard-core aerobic sports participant, represents a virtually untapped market for Reebok. Although it also sells to the aerobics market, Reebok's products appeal mainly to fashion rather than fitness-conscious customers." James Solomon, then Avia's vice-president for marketing, said, "Avia is concerned with technology first, fashion second." There was speculation in the late 1980s that Reebok would eliminate Avia to strengthen its own position in the aerobics market, but Avia continued to operate as an independent business in the early 1990s.

In 1988 Avia introduced the Model 600, then the most expensive aerobics shoe on the market. Although men's athletic shoes often topped $100, most marketers believed that women were more price sensitive and top-of-the-line aerobics shoes had cost about $60. Avia's Model 600 cost $80, and even Kate Bednarski, then Avia's marketing director, admitted to *Savvy*, a women's fashion magazine, that she had been "uptight" about the high price. However, the Model 600 caught on quickly and became one of Avia's best-selling shoes. "If you're looking for leading edge technology and high performance, you're going to have to shell out the bucks," Bednarski said.

Women's aerobics shoes remained Avia's strongest market niche, accounting for about 45 percent of the company's revenues in the early 1990s. A print ad in 1993 declared, "Only a woman could think of a sport where no one loses." The ad went on to explain the essence of aerobics: "This is a sport? Where are the trophies, and the medals, and the instant replays? How do you know who wins without the instant replays? Easy, just look around you. Can't you see the sweat and muscle? Can't you feel the commitment and determination? Don't you get it? On this floor, everybody's a winner. And you don't need a score board to tell you that."

## Litigation

Avia International was aggressive in defending its shoe designs and patents against infringement by other manufacturers in the highly competitive market for athletic footwear. In a landmark case filed in 1986, Pensa accused LA Gear Inc., then the third-largest maker of athletic shoes in the United States, of copying an Avia shoe design. Making "knock-offs" of popular designs was a common practice in the athletic shoe industry, until Avia won its case in a summary U.S. District Court judgment that was later upheld by the U.S. Court of Appeals.

## AT A GLANCE

**A**via brand athletic shoes introduced by Pensa Inc. in 1980; company name changed to Avia Group International Inc. in 1986; company purchased by Reebok International Ltd. in 1987.

**Performance:** *Market share*—1.8% of athletic footwear category in United States. *Sales*—$100 million.

**Major competitor:** Nike Inc.

**Addresses:** *Parent company*—Avia Group International Inc., 9605 SW Nimbus Avenue, Beaverton, OR 97224; phone: (503) 520-1500. *Ultimate parent company*—Reebok International Ltd., 100 Technology Ctr. Dr., Stoughton, MA 02072; phone: (617) 341-5000; fax: (617) 341-5087.

Pensa vs. LA Gear was the first time a design patent was used successfully to stop knock-offs in the athletic shoe industry. Perry J. Saidman, a patent attorney who argued the case for Avia, told the *Los Angeles Times,* "The culture in the footwear industry is it's okay to do this, it's okay to copy the popular styles. We wanted to make it very clear to LA Gear that it would be very expensive for them to do this in the future. We wanted to teach them a lesson that they should not [copy] Avia designs." LA Gear eventually paid $450,000 to settle the suit.

In 1991 Avia International took on Nike, then the best-known brand name in the athletic shoe industry. Avia charged Nike Inc. with pirating its shock-absorbing Cantilever sole design for its Air 180 basketball shoes. Richard Donahue, then president of Nike, issued a statement claiming the suit was "clearly another attempt by Reebok to discredit Nike. This time they are simply using Avia as a cover." Nike also retaliated by claiming that Avia had copied its "center of pressure" heel design. Nike later withdrew the counter suit, and the two companies settled out of court in late 1992, with Nike agreeing to pull its Air 180 shoes off the market. Bill Dragon, then president of Avia, told *Sporting Goods Business* that the Cantilever technology "has been the technical foundation of all our footwear since the company was founded in 1980. We will continue to do what it takes to enforce the patents that cover our Cantilever technology."

In 1993 *Consumer Reports* rated Avia's Archrocker 382 top among women's athletic shoes designed for walking and second to Nike' s Air Essential in the men's category. When Hyde Athletic Industries, Inc., ran advertisements in *USA Today* claiming that *Consumer Reports* rated its Saucony brand shoes best in the women's category, Avia sued. Saucony, although "recommended" by *Consumer Reports,* was actually rated below Avia. Hyde pulled the ads and settled the suit within a month. Although details of the settlement were not released, Harry de Boer, then Avia president, said in a press release, "We filed our lawsuit against Hyde in order to set the record straight on which company has the number one rated women's walking shoe. We have achieved that objective, plus a lot more, and are thrilled that our rights have been vindicated in a such a decisive manner."

## Marketing

Avia changed slogans, market thrusts, and advertising agencies several times in the late 1980s and early 1990s as it attempted to clearly establish a market identity. "Innovative by Design," the advertising tag line adopted in 1983, was dropped in 1985 in favor

of "Built for Your Body," which played off Avia's reputation as a scientifically engineered shoe. However, the company's first television commercials, launched less than two years later, attempted to give Avia a fashion image. One unusual commercial contrasted the National Football League's Los Angeles Raiders, wearing Avia shoes and dancing to ballet music, with the Joffrey Ballet, also in Avia shoes, doing aerobic exercises to a hard rock beat.

In 1989 Avia abandoned the trendy image commercials to focus again on people who take fitness seriously. Using the slogan "For Athletes Only," an aggressive advertising campaign appealed to the self-image of real and would-be athletes by knocking smokers, heavy drinkers, and the overweight. One commercial opened by showing a young man playing a hand-held video game, then faded to a sweaty basketball player who told viewers, "If this is the only basketball you want to play, Avia doesn't want you buying their shoes." Brian Bosworth, then a linebacker with the NFL's Seattle Seahawks, delivered the same message to people who never got closer to real sports than their living room couches.

A memorable print ad in the "For Athletes Only" campaign showed a cigarette smoldering in an ashtray with the headline, "If this is the only thing that gives your lungs a workout, don't buy our shoes." The ads drew praise from anti-smoking groups, but was panned by the American Smokers Alliance.

Patrick Kipisz, then director of advertising at Avia, told the *Los Angeles Times* that the health-conscious ads helped define Avia's market. "We're saying Avia designs shoes for active, vibrant people. We're not a shoe for everyone. We produce a shoe for people who take exercise and sports seriously." But Bill Borders, then president of Borders, Perrin & Norrander, the Portland-based advertising agency that created the "For Athletes Only" campaign, told the *New York Times* that the campaign was also "a little bit of reverse psychology. Ever since you were a kid and were told not to do something, what did you do? You went out and did it. So we designed the ads to talk to athletes. But it will also appeal to you if you're a poser."

## Trends

After topping the $200 million mark in 1988, Avia's sales slumped in 1989. Sales then fell precipitously in 1990 to about $150 million, forcing Avia to lay off staff. By 1992 sales had fallen to about $129 million. *Sporting Goods Intelligence,* an industry newsletter, estimated that Avia's share of the U.S. athletic footwear market fell from about 4.3 percent in 1988 to 1.8 percent in 1992. The decline came despite the fact that *Shape,* a fitness magazine, named Avia as the best brand of athletic shoes in four out of five major exercise categories in 1990.

The company blamed the drop in sales on a decision to pull out of the market for children's shoes, where the company's high-tech image was less of a selling point. Avia had also pulled out of the market for cleated shoes. Avia further blamed a trend by retailers to cut back on the number of brands and to sell cross-training shoes as all-purpose athletic footwear rather than selling shoes designed for a special purpose, such as Avia's aerobics models.

However, media reports questioned Avia's advertising budget and Reebok's commitment to its newly acquired brand. Avia's advertising budget in 1991 was about $10 million, less than a tenth of Reebok's budget. John Horan, then publisher of *Sporting Goods Intelligence,* declared flatly that "Avia's chief competitor is its parent." But Paul Fireman, then chief executive officer at

Reebok, told the Associated Press, "Avia's sales aren't being held back because of a lack of advertising spending."

In 1993 Avia announced that it had redesigned almost its entire line of shoes, adding new models and colors, but retaining the line's performance engineering. The company also redesigned its sports apparel, initially introduced in 1988, again focusing on function rather than fashion. Avia claimed that every item in its solid black, no nonsense Fitness Training line of women's clothing was "technically correct, engineered for fit, comfort and movement" in fabrics that "move, breathe and support your body."

Avia also expanded its line of running shoes in 1993 and planned to focus on basketball in 1994. In a press release, then-president de Boer explained, "With our solid technical history, running and basketball are the next steps in building our domestic business and strengthening our position with the male consumer." Clyde Drexler of the NBA's Portland Trailblazers, was signed to star in television commercials for Avia basketball shoes.

**Further Reading:**

"Avia Charges Nike With Patent Suit," *Sporting Goods Business,* May 1991, p. 7.

"Avia Taking Steps To Find Market Niche," *Seattle Times,* May 20, 1991, p. E6.

"Avia Unit Sues Rival Hyde Over No. 1 Footwear Title," *Wall Street Journal,* July 16, 1993, p. B6B.

Gillman, Todd J., "Attorney Puts Foot Down About Sneaker Patents," *Washington Post,* July 20, 1987, p. WB3.

Groves, Martha, "Reebok Agrees to Buy Its Fastest-Growing Rival Avia for $180 Million," *Los Angeles Times,* March 11, 1987, p. IV-1.

Kort, Michele, "The Selling Of Soles," *Savvy,* September 1988, p. 12.

Magiera, Marcy, "Avia Buy Puts Reebok on Nike Turf," *Advertising Age,* March 16, 1987, p. 12.

Rothenberg, Randall, "Second Shoe Drops for Image Ads," *New York Times,* February 10, 1989, p. D17.

Smith, Matthew, "Avia Retreads Thin Sales Figures with Focused Marketing," *Portland Business Journal,* July 29, 1991, p. 4.

White, George, "New Avia Ads Put Smokers on the Run," *Los Angeles Times,* Feb. 17, 1989, p. IV-2.

*—Dean Boyer*

# AVON®

One of the world's largest and best-known brands of fragrances, make-up, and personal care products, Avon has achieved its success as much because of its unique marketing and distribution system as its quality products. Avon grew to become one of the world's largest beauty companies through direct selling utilizing women representatives. With almost 1.7 million sales associates worldwide, the company offers earnings opportunities to women in more than 100 countries.

## Brand Origins

The Avon name was introduced in 1928 to represent the California Perfume Company's products, which had been offered since 1886. Founder David H. Mc Connell sold books door-to-door in Brooklyn, and used tiny perfume samples to capture the interest of the homemakers who were his primary customers. When he realized that customers were more interested in the perfume than the books, McConnell started the California Perfume Company, a name that conjured up images of fresh air to his city-bound customers. The company's first product was manufactured, as McConnell put it, "in a space scarcely larger than an ordinary kitchen pantry." The Little Dot Perfume Set contained five different perfumes—heliotrope, violet, white rose, lily of the valley, and hyacinth. Later, the line was extended to include shampoo, Witch Hazel Cream, Almond Cream Balm, and a "Tooth Tablet."

McConnell's experience with door-to-door selling, or canvassing, led him to believe that personal contact was the best and most efficient sales method. He employed Mrs. P.F.E. Albee, the first Avon lady, to sell cosmetics to friends and neighbors in her community. In now-classic fashion, she soon convinced several friends to help her sell the popular products. The direct sales system developed by Avon would prove remarkably successful in the United States and around the world.

By 1896 McConnell felt confident enough in his new business to engage renowned perfumer Adolf Goetting. The following year, the businessman built a manufacturing laboratory in Suffern, New York. McConnell also distributed Avon's first text-only catalog in 1896, launching a promotional tool that was used throughout the twentieth century. Avon began advertising its burgeoning line of over a hundred products in the first decade of the century. For example, the brand's Roses Perfume was promoted in *Good Housekeeping* magazine as early as 1906. That same year Avon published its first color catalog.

By 1920 the California Perfume Company had topped the $1 million annual sales mark and had reached national distribution. When founder David McConnell visited England, he saw a resemblance between the site of his Suffern, New York, laboratory and William Shakespeare's birthplace, Stratford-on-Avon. The Avon brand name was first applied to products in 1928, and the official corporate title was changed to Avon Products, Inc., in 1939. Dreher Advertising won the Avon advertising account in 1938 and produced Avon promotions until the early 1970s. Avon went public in 1946, and the brand's annual sales reached $25 million in 1949.

## Commercial Success

In the post-World War II era, increasing numbers of American women expanded their world of work to include jobs outside the home. Jobs as "Avon Ladies" were ideal part-time earnings opportunities for many women. With more representatives and the general air of prosperity in the country, Avon achieved phenomenal growth. In 1954 Avon inaugurated its long-running slogan, "Ding-Dong, Avon Calling!" Sales and earnings gains consistently ran in the 17 to 19 percent range during the 1950s, and could be attributed, in part, to the decorative perfume decanters the brand promoted. The items soon became kitschy collectors' items.

The growth continued during the 1960s: from 1961 to 1971, the brand's sales experienced double-digit increases, and topped $1 billion in 1972. Avon's market share grew from 30.5 percent in 1969 to 33.2 percent in 1972. The brand's sales made Avon the most consistently profitable company in the country, and a darling of Wall Street; in 1973 Avon's shares peaked at $140.

By the mid-1970s, Avon had become the world's largest cosmetics and toiletries company, and had expanded into Canada and sixteen other foreign countries, including Mexico, Brazil, Australia, Germany, Italy, Sweden, Great Britain, and Japan. But early international operations had a halting start; sales productivity was half the American rate. Part of the problem stemmed from a the fact that Avon was not yet a well-known brand. In some countries, like Germany and Sweden, door-to-door selling held inherently bad connotations. In Japan competition from four established cosmetics companies held Avon to less than one percent of the market, even though Japanese operations had been established in 1969.

## AT A GLANCE

**A**von brand of fragrances, make-up, and personal care products established in 1928 in New York City, by David H. Mc-Connell as a brand of the California Perfume Company; company changed name to Avon Products, Inc., in 1939.

*Performance:* *Sales*—$3.8 billion worldwide.

*Major competitor:* Cover Girl; also L'Oréal and Maybelline.

*Advertising:* Agency—FCB/Leber Katz Partners, 1990—. Major campaign—"Smartest Shop in Town" and "Women Are Beautiful."

*Addresses:* Parent company—Avon Products, Inc., 9 West 57th Street, New York, NY 10019; phone: (212) 546-6015; fax: (212) 546-6136.

## A Rapid Fall from Grace

Avon's fabulous growth in the early 1970s slowed to a more mediocre performance in the last half of the decade. High inflation fueled rising manufacturing costs and raw material shortages and simultaneously squeezed the cosmetic dollar. The wildly popular decorative decanters of the 1960s had become a pricey extravagance to many people, and the rapid expansion of Avon's sales force had actually lowered profit margins. By 1974 the brand's market share dropped to 20 percent of the overall cosmetics and toiletries market, and 85 percent of the door-to-door trade. Although the brand still held the top position, it was not as profitable as it had been the previous decade.

Brand management recognized that Avon was not effectively targeting its most receptive customers, but its primary reaction to the crisis was to slash prices by as much as 50 percent in an "inflation fighter" campaign. The price cutting continued through the end of the decade with the "Avon, you make me smile," multi-media campaign. Prepared by N.W. Ayer ABH, the promotion included bus posters and television, radio, and print ads. Avon's $2.25 lipsticks were sold for 35 cents during the publicity drive to any customer who traded in a competitor's lipstick. Dubbed "Operation Smile," the campaign helped bring Avon's sales back above $1 billion by the end of the year.

## "Avon Fashions" Extends Product Line

The "Avon Fashions" catalog was introduced in 1973 to sell low- to medium-priced clothing to working women. Initially titled "Family Fashions," the venture lost $4 million in its first year. Family Fashions went through four different presidents within the next three years and never achieved a profit. In 1977 the vice president of marketing, Bill Willett, took over the top spot and was initially asked to carefully and quietly close the business down. Instead, he asked for one year to turn the catalog around. After eliminating one-third of the staff, the renamed "Avon Fashions" had its first profitable year in 1978 and had become a top direct response marketer by the mid-1980s.

During the 1970s and early 1980s, Avon began a diversification program into non-beauty business involving direct mail clothing catalogs, jewelry retailing, magazine subscriptions, and health care. However, with the unsuccessful venture into the health care industry, Avon refocused its strategic direction and returned to its original core beauty business.

By mid-1989, Avon had sold the last of its non-beauty businesses and was once again focused solely on beauty products for the first time in more than 15 years. Willett purchased the catalog business through a new company, New Hampton Inc., and arranged a ten-year licensing agreement with Avon for rights to the Avon Fashions name. He targeted the catalog's 20 different mailings each year to young, working women. The catalog posted $210 million in 1989 sales.

## New Sales Techniques

Avon's direct selling strategy began to show signs of age in 1979, when cultural changes, a wrinkled image, and high turnover among the sales associates caught up with the strategy. As an estimated 32 million American women moved into the workplace, "Avon Ladies" found fewer potential customers at home during the day. Fewer homemakers meant fewer answered doorbells when Avon came calling—and fewer sales representatives to ring those bells.

The brand was also suffering something of an identity crisis: an increasingly far-flung product line that offered everything from makeup to gifts to jewelry made customers feel Avon had no area of expertise. Avon was further undermined by its 1970s bargain-basement cosmetics prices, which cheapened the brand's image.

Turnover rates for sales representatives soared as high as 150 percent, and sales representatives made an average of less than $2,000 annually. From 1980 to 1984, the sales force declined from 425,000 to 400,000.

These setbacks showed on Avon's balance sheet as well. Profits declined 12 percent annually from 1979 until 1984, and sales plateaued at $2.2 billion. In 1983 alone corporate profits declined 16 percent to $164.4 million, and 1985's profits were half those of 1979. By the mid-1980s, Avon's direct selling division, which still generated about two-thirds of the company's $2.9 billion in sales, was ripe for reorganization. Although the brand's distribution had grown proportionately with the number of sales representatives in the past, chairman and CEO Hicks Waldron told *Marketing & Media Decisions* magazine in 1984 that "beginning in 1979 and 1980, you couldn't just add 10,000 or 20,000 salespersons. The old system that had worked for 96 years failed to work."

Waldron worked to transform the company by focusing on Avon's brand power. In 1984, the man known for his marketing wizardry planned to increase the brand's $20 million advertising budget by one-fourth for 1985. Proposed marketing strategies included targeted marketing, direct response, direct mail, electronic shopping, and pinpointed retailing. Avon worked to capture more senior citizens and college students and sharpened its focus on Hispanics by offering sales brochures in Spanish. In 1987 Avon chose UniWorld Group Inc. to advertise its products to minority consumers. Consumer marketing schemes included offering trial sizes, gifts with purchases, and coupons.

A pared-down product line brought the brand identity back to a focus on beauty products (most of the old-style decanter items were already gone), and new offerings in the growing area of skin care kept Avon abreast of beauty trends. The cosmetics color palette was increased in 1988 to compete with Maybelline and the Noxell Corporation, which produces Cover Girl. The line was called Avon Color, and replaced the company's Color Coordinates and Ultra Wear brands, bringing together 350 versatile shades for lips, cheeks, eyes, and nails. Pricing was also a part of Avon's redirected marketing focus. Deep discounting was eliminated to raise profits and the perception of quality. To motivate its sales force, Avon raised commissions as a percentage of pay for its district managers from five percent to 20 percent. The changes helped raise average sales of the 78,000 highest-volume sales representatives from $12,818 in 1982 to $15,000.

But with all of the innovations, Avon did not drop the direct selling strategy, and instead updated the method to match the times. Increasingly, Avon representatives made appointments, dropped off brochures, and followed up with phone calls. The revision of an age-old policy also allowed women to sell in offices, factories, hospitals, schools, and anywhere else women worked.

## International Success

Avon's overseas operations began to improve and take on increased importance for the brand in the late 1970s. The 1980s saw Avon expand rapidly in Latin America, Asia, and Eastern Europe. By 1990, international sales contributed 56 percent of Avon's product turnover.

After a troubled start in Japan, the brand began to gain momentum in 1978 when it overtook rival Revlon. Ten years of experience in the country led Avon to adapt its marketing and sales management techniques to more closely fit Japanese culture. Upon learning that Japanese women use significantly more skin care products than their American counterparts, for example, Avon expanded its line of products to meet the demand. District sales managers held meetings with sales representatives more frequently, in order to conform to common practice. By 1989 Avon had become the leading seller of cosmetics in Asia in terms of rate of growth and earnings. Regional sales in 1989 topped $400 million, or 13 percent of the company's total revenue.

Activities undertaken in China in November of 1990 were especially promising. The region was projected to have two-thirds of the world's population and a gross national product exceeding that of North America and Europe combined by the turn of the twentieth century. The Chinese operation was a joint venture with the Guangzhou Cosmetics Factory, named for the region that includes the city of Guangdong. By 1992, 25,000 sales representatives employed the tried-and-true direct sales method and helped Avon meet its six month sales goals within its first two months. Avon became the first brand authorized to be sold directly to the Chinese consumer and the largest cosmetics line in the country.

## Continued Difficulties

In 1989 in an effort to cut costs while the company struggled under $1 billion in debt, Avon dropped both N.W. Ayer and UniWorld Group, Inc. in favor of its in-house advertising and promotional group. The split came on the heels of a decision to cut advertising spending from an estimated $16 million in 1988 to $4.6 million for 1990. In September of 1990 Avon hired FCB/Leber Katz Partners to manage its account.

Direct selling continued to drive Avon in the early 1990s. The beginning of the decade saw Avon expand and update its direct marketing through its Avon Select program. This strategy was started in Japan, and had grown to contribute 25 percent of sales there by the end of 1990. The service offered the option of traditional ordering through the local sales representative, or ordering through an 800 number and mail delivery. Avon also

expanded its line of catalogs and brochures to target specific market segments. A new corporate logo and revamped basic catalog were introduced in 1991 to graphically represent Avon's new positioning. Two-page print ads released in April touted Avon Select and positioned the brand's products in competition with department store cosmetics.

Despite continuing innovations, Avon's U.S. sales slipped to the number two position behind Estée Lauder. Consolidation in the cosmetics industry had relegated Avon to the third rank in sales, behind Cosmair Inc.'s L'Oréal and Procter & Gamble Co.'s combined Cover Girl and Max Factor lines. The acquisitions and subsequent divestitures of the 1970s and 1980s left Avon with a staggering debt and a financial situation that made it vulnerable to potential raiders. From May of 1989 to May of 1991, Avon successfully maintained its independence from hostile overtures from Amway; Minneapolis investor Irwin Jacobs; Chartwell Associates, a limited partnership consisting of the Fisher real estate family; Argonaut Partners, headed by John Rochon, an officer of Mary Kay Cosmetics; and the Getty Family Trust. Perhaps most ominous were Avon's flagging overseas sales; although they constituted 60 percent of the brand's total, they only inched ahead in the early 1990s.

## Further Reading:

Appelbaum, Cara, "Avon's Calling on Retail Customers," *Adweek's Marketing Week,* March 25, 1991, p. 8.

Bencivenga, Dan, "Avon Fashions Alive and Kicking," *Target Marketing,* May 1989, pp. 29–31.

Blesky, Gary, "Avon Dingdongs for Profits Overseas," *Money,* June 1991, pp. 74–75.

Dunkin, Amy, "Big Names Are Opening Doors for Avon" *Business Week,* June 1, 1987, pp. 96–97.

"From Direct Sales to Direct Mail," *Catalog Age,* February 1992, p. 7.

Giges, Nancy, "Swiss Bell Ringers No Match for U.S. Marketers," *Advertising Age,* January 11, 1971, pp. 1, 79.

Hager, Bruce, "Despite the Face-lift, Avon Is Sagging," *Business Week,* December 2, 1991, 101–2.

Konrad, Walecia, "For Avon, Rodeo Drive Is No Easy Street," *Business Week,* December 28, 1987, p. 78.

Nelson, Kelly, "Avon Plan Calling on Leaner Lines, Ad Boost," *Advertising Age,* October 4, 1984, pp. 2, 29; "Avon Plans Mass-Retail Expansions," *Advertising Age,* October 26, 1987, p. 2; "Avon Drops Ayer with In-house Shift," *Advertising Age,* September 18, 1989, p. 2; "Avon Is Calling on New Tactics, FCB," *Advertising Age,* January 7, 1991, pp. 3, 41; "Door-to-Door in Guangzhou," *China Business Review,* March/April 1991, pp. 40–41.

Salmans, Sandra, "Japan Changes Avon's Make-up," *International Management,* July 1979, pp. 42–43.

Sloan, Pat, "Record Sales, Earnings Have Avon 'Smiling' Again," *Advertising Age,* February 26, 1979, p. 21.

Smikle, Ken, "Avon Picks UniWorld," *Black Enterprise,* February 1987, p. 24.

Tanzer, Andrew, "Ding-dong, Capitalism Calling," *Forbes,* October 14, 1991, p. 184.

"Tracking Leading Marketers Becomes More Complicated," *Drug & Cosmetic Industry,* June 1992, pp. 30–35.

"Troubled Avon," *Business Week,* May 11, 1974, pp. 98–101.

"A Troubled Avon Knocks at Several New Doors," *Marketing & Media Decisions,* November 1984, pp. 68–70, 122–24.

Zellner, Wendy, and Bruce Hagler, "Dumpster Raids? That's Not Very Ladylike, Avon," *Business Week,* April 1, 1991, p. 32.

—*April S. Dougal*

# BAIN DE SOLEIL®

The Bain de Soleil brand of suncare products, in its original orange gelee formula, is one of the most enduring sunscreens in the United States. Packaged in the trademark pale orange box with colors in the logo ranging from light orange on the left to brown on the right, Bain de Soleil has been offering sunbathers a silky sunshield to allow gradual tanning for over 65 years. When fears about skin cancer arose in the 1970s and 1980s because of the earth's thinning ozone layer, Bain de Soleil was reformulated in Sun Protection Factor (SBF) formulas to protect against overexposure to ultraviolet rays.

## Brand Origins

In 1925 vacationers on the beaches of St. Tropez on the French Riviera were sunning not only their faces, necks, arms, and legs, but other parts of their bodies as well. Not just any suntan lotion would suffice to protect those delicate areas of the body from the sun's harmful ultraviolet rays. These sunbathers wanted a specialty suntan product designed exclusively for their type of sunbathing. In France, Monsieur Antoine de Paris created such a product—an orange gelee for women to apply to their skin while sunbathing that contained a classic formula for skin that tanned easily.

Formulated to help shield the skin from the sun's burning rays while allowing gradual tanning, this gelee was enriched with moisturizers that enabled sunbathers to achieve a golden, silky tan. Women who had previously shied away from the sun under broad-brimmed hats and parasols were now free to enjoy sunbathing without fear. Called "Antoine de Paris," the product was designed to encourage rapid and even bronzing while moisturizing and protecting the skin. The advertising proclaimed that liberal and regular use of the product over the years would help to reduce the chance of premature aging of the skin due to overexposure to the sun. Tanning quickly became trendy in Europe.

## Early Marketing Strategy

Buoyed by the brand's success in Europe, Monsieur Antoine de Paris's company brought the orange gelee to New York City. Here it was marketed in the 1940s as "Antoine de Paris's 'Bain de Soleil,'" (french for "bath of the sun,") by the Charles of the Ritz Division of The Revlon Company. During the 1960s, tans became an international symbol of prestige, prosperity, and good health. By this time, the orange bronzing gelee had become so

well-known that it was simply called Bain de Soleil. The best advertisements for the product were the people who used it. During the 1970s, the deep, magnificent tan commonly associated with exotic beach resorts became popular, spurring the introduction of Bain de Soleil's "St. Tropez tan," an image which enhanced the brand's reputation as the pre-eminent tanning authority.

## Brand Development

In the early 1980s, as the dark tanning trend began to fade and clinical studies indicated that overexposure to the sun's damaging rays could lead to premature aging and skin cancer, Bain de Soleil developed products with Sun Protection Factors (SPFs) for different parts of the body which required unique protection. In 1983 Bain de Soleil introduced products that were cosmetically formulated for the face. Also during the 1980s, scientific research found that there were two types of ultraviolet rays—UVA, which broke down the skin's natural elasticity, hastening wrinkling and toughening, and UVB, the burning rays, which caused the skin to redden, dry, and peel. Bain de Soleil products subsequently offered consumers protection from both UVA and UVB rays. SPF numbers on the bottles and tubes informed the user of the amount of time she or he could stay in the sun without burning—the higher the SPF number, the more protection the product afforded the user.

In 1987 Bain de Soleil was acquired by The Procter & Gamble Company subsidiary RVI. In 1989 Bain de Soleil launched Protecteur Gentil, a new ultra protection suncare line for the body and face which offered a gentle suncare system for those individuals who desired or required a high level of sun protection. The products available in this line included body silkening spray SPF 20; body silkening stick SPF 25; body silkening creme SPF 25; face creme SPF 25; lip protecteur SPF 30; and under eye protecteur SPF 30.

Bain de Soleil light-weight cremes for the body included deep tanning creme SPF 2, suntan creme SPF 6, and sunblock creme SPF 15. Fragrance-free, nonstinging, and noncomedogenic, Bain de Soleil face creme fluide selections available were face creme fluide sunfilter SPF 6 and face creme fluide sunblock SPF 15. In oil and lotion formulations, dark tanning spray oil, golden tanning spray oil SPF 4, and protectif spray lotion SPF 15 were on the market. Specially created for tanning with sun protection,

## AT A GLANCE

The Bain de Soleil brand of suntan products was founded in 1925 by Monsieur Antoine de Paris in France; brand first marketed in the United States in the 1940s by The Charles of the Ritz Division of The Revlon Company, New York City; brand acquired by the Procter & Gamble Company, of Cincinnati, Ohio, in 1987.

*Major competitor:* Coppertone; also Banana Boat and Hawaiian Tropic.

*Advertising:* Agency—Ayer, New York, NY. *Major campaign*—"Discover Bain de Soleil for: beautiful color today, beautiful skin tomorrow."

*Addresses:* Parent company—Procter & Gamble Company, One Procter & Gamble Plaza, Cincinnati, Ohio 45202; phone: (513) 983-1100; fax: (513) 983-7847.

classique gelee orange, Bain de Soleil's original and most popular suncare product, provided smooth application on all areas of the body and was available with SPFs ranging from 4 to 15 and in an innovative glide-on stick. Emollient-rich tropical deluxe formulas contained no sunscreens, only the finest natural oils and tropical-moisturizers, which encouraged a deep, dark St. Tropez tan while saturating the body with skin conditioners. Pre- and after-sun products included bikini and leg hair remover creme, tan accelerator, and tan-extending body lotion.

In the 1990s, as the vogue toward lighter tanning became more vigorous, Bain de Soleil offered more than 20 products expertly formulated for different parts of the body to achieve desired gradations of sun protection and safer, lighter tanning. In 1993 all Bain de Soleil products were dermatologist- and allergy-tested and free of fragrance and PABA (para-aminobenzoic acid), a potent chemical in sunscreens that could irritate some people's skin. All-Day Sunblock with SPFs of 4, 8, 15, and 30 offered a water-proof, nongreasy formula; one application lasted six hours. All-Day Sunblock for Kids SPF 30, a special gentle, waterproof formula for children, was pediatrician-tested; one application lasted eight hours. For a faster, darker, more enduring tan than the leading sunscreens or tan magnifiers could provide, Megatan Waterproof Lotion SPF 4 was available, containing a natural self-tanner which

brought out the color in an individual's skin. For tanning without the sun, Bain de Soleil sunless dark tanning creme and sunless light tanning creme offered the user a healthy-looking, even tan in only two to three hours.

### Performance Appraisal

In 1988 Consumers Union in New York performed a battery of tests on America's leading sunscreen products. Bain de Soleil Supreme, a cream which had a SPF of 15, ranked in the top 20. Debuting as a simple orange gelee suncare preparation for the residents of St. Tropez who liked to sunbathe *au naturel*, Bain de Soleil has remained a market share leader in the volatile suntan lotion category.

### Further Reading:

*Answers About Marketing,* Cincinnati: The Procter & Gamble Company, 1993.

"Bain de Soleil Goes to Ayer," *Advertising Age,* September 16, 1991, p. 1.

"Don't Let the Sun Catch You Frying: Bain de Soleil's Quick Response to Fears of Skin Cancer Established It As a Leader in Healthy Tanning," *Adweek's Marketing Week,* July 31, 1989, p. R8.

*Facts About Procter & Gamble,* Cincinnati: The Procter & Gamble Company, 1993.

Lawrence, Jennifer, "P&G Hooks Up Interactive Product-Sampling Hot Line," *Advertising Age,* October 5, 1992, p. 3.

Lief, Alfred, *"It Floats"; The Story of Procter & Gamble,* New York: Rinehart, 1958.

*The Procter & Gamble Company Annual Report,* Cincinnati: The Procter & Gamble Company, 1993.

*Procter & Gamble: The House That Ivory Built,* Lincolnwood, Illinois: NTC Business Books, 1988.

Schisgall, Oscar, *Eyes on Tomorrow: The Evolution of Procter & Gamble,* Chicago: J. G. Ferguson Publishing Company, 1981.

Starkman, Jesse Howard, *A Study of the Functional Stability of Suncreen Compounds,* Newark, New Jersey: Newark College of Engineering, 1956.

"Sunscreens," *Consumer Reports 1993 Buying Guide,* December 1992, pp. 173–74.

Torbet, Laura, ed., *Helena Rubinstein's Book of the Sun,* New York: Times Books, 1979.

Vogel, Jason, *The Official Suntanner's Bible: The Lighter Side of Dark,* New York: Acropolis Books, 1987.

*—Virginia Barnstorff*

# BAN®

Ban deodorants and antiperspirants, marketed by pharmaceutical giant Bristol-Myers Squibb Company, have played a major role in the highly competitive U.S. deodorant and antiperspirant market since the introduction of Ban roll-on antiperspirant in 1955. The first Ban product was nearly an overnight success, and it led category sales for the remainder of the decade. The surging popularity of aerosol applications pushed Ban out of its lead among deodorant and antiperspirant products, but aggressive advertising and numerous line extensions over the years have guaranteed Ban products a significant share of a market worth $1.4 billion in 1992.

## Rolling to Success

Bristol-Myers Company (now Bristol-Myers Squibb) had been a major participant in the post-World War II boom in consumption of personal products, reported *Printers' Ink,* but by the late 1940s its lone deodorant offering, Mum cream, had fallen behind Carter Products' Arrid as the leader in the increasingly competitive deodorant and antiperspirant market. Product planners at Bristol-Myers, noting the rapid growth of the market and a growing consumer preference for antiperspirant over deodorant products, decided that it was time for Bristol-Myers to develop an antiperspirant of their own. Little did they realize that it would take six years before their new product was ready for the market. In that long developmental stage, Bristol-Myers not only created a new brand name, Ban, but an entirely new way of applying underarm protection.

The makers of Ban wanted to offer the consumer a more convenient way of applying deodorants and antiperspirants than the existing creams, lotions, and sprays. But developing a new application proved quite difficult. When an outside inventor helped Bristol-Myers create the roll-on applicator, the company tested the product in six major markets in 1951, under the name Mum Rollette. Rollette was unsuccessful—as it sat on the shelves, ingredients in the lotion damaged the rolling ball, rendering it unusable—but Bristol-Myers thought the roll-on application important enough to continue testing. After experimenting with 480 different combinations of plastics, another company offered the advice and the "plastic marble" that made the roll-on feasible. After strenuous product testing, consumer input, and careful testing, Ban was released for national distribution on February 15, 1955.

## Early Advertising

Ban roll-on antiperspirant met with immediate success, due to aggressive distribution strategies that placed the product in 89 percent of U.S. drug stores within nine months of release and a strong advertising effort lead by the Batten, Barton, Durstine and Osborn (BBDO) agency. Within eight months, Ban was the number three selling product on the market, and three straight years of 30 percent growth made Ban the undisputed sales leader by 1957. In that year, Ban's sales topped $5 million, or 15 percent of the retail deodorant and antiperspirant market, according to *Advertising Age.* When Ban's sales flattened out in 1957, however, Bristol-Myers quickly moved the Ban advertising account, which was estimated at over $4 million in billings in 1957, to Ogilvy, Benson & Mather (later Ogilvy & Mather), *Printers' Ink* reported that the majority of Ban's advertising was on television, in "live action commercials, with a girl demonstrating the roll-on feature while a man's voice delivered the sales message."

Bristol-Myers wasted no time marketing its new product overseas, introducing their new Ban roll-on as Mum Rollette in Britain shortly after it was introduced in the United States. Advertising took a slightly different approach overseas, since Europeans were unaccustomed to using deodorant and antiperspirant products, and the British had only recently allowed advertising on commercial television. Consequently, Mum Rollette's advertisements were more discreet—the female demonstrator rolled the product on her arm rather than her underarm—and emphasized the product's long-lasting deodorant protection. Mum Rollette captured ten percent of the British market in its first year of distribution.

## Competition and Regulation: Twin Challenges

Ban's success bred imitation: by 1960 there were more than 40 entries in the roll-on category. But a more significant challenge came from yet another new form of deodorant and antiperspirant application: aerosol sprays. Right Guard spray, manufactured by shaving giant Gillette, soon dominated the deodorant and antiperspirant market with over 20 percent of the market. In the 1960s and early 1970s, Bristol-Myers introduced a number of extensions to the Ban line—including Dry Ban, Ban Basic, Ultra-Ban, Ultra-Ban II, and Ultra-Ban 5000—but it had to wait until the late 1970s, when aerosols fell into disrepute among consumers concerned with the effect of fluorocarbon propellants on the environment, to regain its early prominence. Until that time, Ban faced many of the difficulties involved in competing in an increasingly regulated market.

In 1969 and 1970, Bristol-Myers and its advertising agency, Ogilvy & Mather, aired television commercials for Dry Ban spray which were designed to promote the benefits of their product over the "leading competitor," Right Guard spray. Five ads showed Dry Ban spraying on "completely clear and dry," while the other brand left a "white and thick" residue. "Clear Dry Ban helps keep you feeling clean and dry," an announcer's voice promised. Federal Trade Commission (FTC) official Daniel Hanscom charged the company and the ad agency with misrepresentation and, according to the *Wall Street Journal,* recommended a broad order prohibiting further advertising misrepresentation by Bristol-Myers or Ogilvy & Mather. Hanscom recommended the order because, in his words, of "the size and importance of Bristol-Myers's and the nature of the alleged Dry Ban misrepresentations. What is involved in this proceeding isn't simply a question of misrepresentation of the physical characteristics of Dry Ban but an issue of responsibility and integrity in advertising," reported the *Wall Street Journal.*

Not surprisingly, Bristol-Myers challenged the FTC's preliminary ruling, saying, "The attack on our responsibility and integrity in advertising isn't only totally unwarranted, it is inconsistent with the administrative law judge's findings." Bristol-Myers's lawyers contended that the order was too abstract to enforce, that it misinterpreted the terms on which the ad was conducted—clearly, they contended, no one expects a spray to *be* completely dry, only to *feel* dry upon application—and, perhaps most importantly, that it was not in their interests to make unsupportable claims. Lawyers argued, as reported in *Advertising Age,* that "it would be highly harmful commercially when dealing with a product like Dry Ban that depends upon repeat purchases for success, to lead consumers to expect a certain performance if they are likely to find upon using it that the representation has been false."

In the end, after nearly four years of litigation, the FTC dropped its complaint against Ban and, according to *Advertising Age,* "served notice that it isn't interested in looking at ads which don't involve any significant economic or physical harm to con-

sumers." *Advertising Age* saw the ruling as highly favorable to business interests, for it asserted that "petty deception on TV has its own built-in self-destruct, since consumers won't buy the product a second time if they feel cheated." Though Bristol-Myers emerged unscathed from the legal battle, they were unable to find solace in high sales. Patricia Hatry, an attorney with Ogilvy & Mather, remarked "Whatever we think of these commercials, they did not sell the product." Dry Ban never gained more than one percent of the market share.

Ban's next advertising campaign, created by the Daniel & Charles agency, touted the superiority of Ban Roll-On and Ultra Ban 5000. Bristol-Myers had begun claiming that its Ultra Ban 5000 "keeps you drier than any leading antiperspirant spray" in 1972, and by 1973 the ads were, according to *Advertising Age* contributor Nancy Giges, "naming names"—pointing out that Ultra Ban 5000 was superior to competitors Right Guard, Arrid, and Dial. But the ads quickly caught the attention of consumer groups eager to eradicate false claims in advertising. One such group, the Consumers Federation of America, filed complaints against Bristol-Myers with the National Advertising Division of the Council of Better Business Bureaus and the National Advertising Review Board.

Deodorant and antiperspirant manufacturers have always faced a dilemma when they advertise, for they have little recourse to claims of glamour or sex appeal, and their products, relying on very similar chemicals to block perspiration or hide odor, are almost identical. They are marketed primarily on their effectiveness in fighting odor, their comfort on application, and their lack of staining. After all, it is not the kind of deodorant that one wears that helps a person attract a mate; rather, it is the fact that one wears deodorant at all. Under these conditions, allegations about improper claims of superiority could, if proven, be quite damaging. But both review panels, after verifying the data used by Bristol-Myers to make such claims, found those claims "supportable." In this instance, the regulatory process confirmed Bristol-Myers's testing procedures and provided authoritative backing for their product claims. Still, Ban proved unable to capture the leading share of the market.

### Resurgence and Innovation

Shifts in market share within the deodorant and antiperspirant market have often been precipitated by the introduction of a new application method or the decline of an old method. Such was the case when fluorocarbon-based aerosols attracted negative attention in the mid-1970s, and Ban took immediate advantage of the opportunities to boost sales. In 1974, according to the *Wall Street Journal,* researchers reported that "the fluorocarbon gases used in aerosol sprays could impair the atmosphere's ability to screen out excess ultraviolet radiation." As the Food and Drug Administration moved to eliminate fluorocarbon aerosols, consumers looked for alternative deodorant and antiperspirant applications. Right Guard, which had been the market leader for over a decade, quickly lost share to Ban products, which held 16.7 percent of the market share in 1976.

Ban took steps to increase its market dominance in 1977, introducing two versions of a hydrocarbon-propelled antiperspirant spray. Ultra Ban II was introduced in the summer of 1977, behind an advertising campaign geared towards consumers' concern for the environment. The television ads, designed by the Daniel & Charles agency in New York, pictured actor John Gavin pitching the product from a hot air balloon: "Way up here it's hard to believe that fluorocarbon sprays people are using down there may harm the atmosphere above me. But that's why Bristol-Myers is introducing Ultra Ban II, a new kind of aerosol antiperspirant that won't harm the environment . . . because it contains no fluorocarbons." The spot concludes: "New Ultra Ban II, effective for you, good for the world around you." An extensive print campaign and mass distribution of coupons rounded out the advertising push. Bristol-Myers's other hydrocarbon antiperspirant, Ban Basic, quickly attracted competitors from Arrid and Right Guard, whose ads attacked Ban by name. But Ban Basic held three percent of the market share by the summer of 1977, keeping it substantially ahead of its competitors.

## Industry Trends

If the 1970s were the decade of the spray, then the 1980s were the decade of the stick. Solid and stick deodorants and antiperspirants were the most popular applications, and Proctor & Gamble Company's Secret was the most popular of them all. Another significant trend in the 1980s was the diversification of product lines, as manufacturers offered a wide variety of applications and scents to both men and women. In 1990, however, the deodorant and antiperspirant market again ventured into a period of rapid change, driven primarily by the introduction of new "technology." Helene Curtis introduced Degree, a unisex deodorant and antiperspirant that has a unique body-heat activation formula that promises all-day protection. The introduction of Degree and other products had toiletries experts expecting significant shifts in market share in the early 1990s.

Ban also played a part in the innovations with the market, as it launched the first clear deodorant stick in 1992. Ban Clear deodorant was backed by an aggressive advertising campaign by Laurence, Charles, Free & Lawson (LCF&L), part of Bristol-Myers's $17 million 1992 advertising budget that included spending on Ban Clear and the new Ban Fresh & Dry. Bristol-Myers was also the first to introduce a clear antiperspirant when it launched Ban Clear A.P. for women and Ban for Men Clear Anti-Perspirant in the spring of 1993. According to *Brandweek,* manufacturers had been "scrambling to market an antiperspirant stick that leaves no residue." The $17.5 million 1993 campaign, again designed by LCF&L, featured a "Don't mess that dress" tagline for the women's campaign and a *Sports Illustrated* ad for the men's campaign. Analyst Gale Lowy told *Brandweek* that "brand loyalty is very high with antiperspirants [and] marketers won't mind cannibalizing their brands if it's a higher-margin product." Other manufacturers were expected to follow Bristol-Myers's lead.

## Future Prospects

The Ban line of deodorants and antiperspirants appeared very healthy in 1993: Ban's products retained 9.1 percent of 1992

market share, and new product introductions in 1993 promised continued growth. However, according to a 1993 *Advertising Age* report, Bristol-Myers was considering selling its Ban products in order to invest more energy in the health care market, a strategy prompted by its merger with the Squibb Corp. in October 1989. Bristol-Myers Squibb's health care products include Excedrin, Nuprin, and Bufferin pain relievers, and numerous prescription medications. Colgate-Palmolive Co., Unilever, Kao Corp., and Henkel were all mentioned as expressing interest in acquiring the Ban and Clairol brands. Ban's decades-long success has relied upon strong corporate backing to spur the near-constant innovation needed to succeed in the competitive market. Whether Ban continues that success seems entirely dependent on the strength and commitment of whoever markets the brand into its fifth decade.

## Further Reading:

"Ban: It Sold Britons on 'Necessity,' " *Printers' Ink,* July 7, 1961, pp. 41–42.

"Bristol-Myers Claims FTC's Ruling on Dry Ban Ads 'Verges upon Libel,' " *Advertising Age,* February 11, 1974, pp. 3, 66.

"Bristol-Myers Slips Ban into Ogilvy Portfolio," *Advertising Age,* April 27, 1959, pp. 1, 41.

Cohen, Stanley E., "Ban Deodorant Tests Held 'Supportable' by Review Unit," *Advertising Age,* June 12, 1972, pp. 1, 77.

Cohen, Stanley E., "Dry Ban's FTC Win Signals New Policy for Ad Enforcement," *Advertising Age,* May 26, 1975.

"FTC Hits Bristol-Myers, O & M for Dry Ban TV Ads," *Advertising Age,* August 23, 1971, p. 2

"FTC Ponders Appeal to Dry Ban Order; May Be Too Abstract to Enforce," *Advertising Age,* June 3, 1974.

Giges, Nancy, "As Some Bemoan Hexachlorophene Action, Ultra Ban, Stay Dry Get Ads," *Advertising Age,* January 17, 1972, pp. 2, 50; "NARB Upholds Bristol-Myers on Ad Claims for Ultra Ban," *Advertising Age,* February 5, 1973; "Bristol-Myers's Ad Names Names in New TV Drive Ad for Ultra Ban 5000," *Advertising Age,* August 13, 1973.

"How Bristol-Myers Planned Ban's Success," *Printers' Ink,* June 5, 1959, pp. 64–65.

O'Connor, John J., "New Pump Sprays Aim at Ban Basic," *Advertising Age,* July 11, 1977, pp. 2, 173.

Shore, A., "Cosmetics and Household Products Industry Report," *Paine-Webber, Inc.,* April 8, 1993.

Sloan, Pat, "Heat's on Gillette," *Advertising Age,* March 30, 1992, p. 48; "Bristol Mulls Selling Clairol, Ban Lines," *Advertising Age,* March 8, 1993, pp. 2, 8.

Spethmann, Betsy, "Ban First with Clear A.P. Stick," *Brandweek,* March 8, 1993, p. 3.

"Staff's Complaint on Dry Ban Was All Wet, FTC Rules," *Wall Street Journal,* May 27, 1975.

"Wide Order on Bristol-Myers's Ads Is Urged in FTC Aide's Decision on Antiperspirant," *Wall Street Journal,* December 10, 1973.

*—Tom Pendergast*

# BAND-AID®

BAND-AID®

The Band-Aid brand of adhesive bandages was one of the first consumer products manufactured by Johnson & Johnson, the world's largest maker of health-care products. Introduced in 1921, Band-Aid became the company's best-selling product and was so successful that the term was often used generically to describe any adhesive bandage or temporary solution. By 1992, Band-Aid bandages were available in more than 150 countries, including the People's Republic of China, where they were introduced by Johnson & Johnson in a joint venture with Shanghai Hygenic Supply Works.

## Antiseptic Dressings

In 1876, Robert Wood Johnson, then a partner in a flourishing medicinal plasters business in New York, attended a lecture in Philadelphia by Sir Joseph Lister, an English surgeon who had identified airborne germs as a primary cause of infection in the operating room. Although many physicians in the late 19th century were skeptical of Lister's "invisible assassins," Johnson was a believer. He also came away from the lecture with the idea for an entirely new business. At the time, most surgical dressings were made of pressed sawdust gathered from the waste of wood mills. Johnson proposed manufacturing and selling antiseptic surgical dressings made of cloth that would reduce the risk of infection.

Ten years later, Johnson broke with his former partner to join his brothers, James Wood Johnson and Edward Mead Johnson, who had begun their own plasters business in a former wallpaper factory in New Brunswick, New Jersey. The business was incorporated as Johnson & Johnson in 1887. The bulk of the company's first catalog was devoted to an exotic assortment of medicated plasters and ointments. However, the catalog also listed a variety of antiseptic dressings made of cotton and gauze, including some which were sanitized with carbolic acid "according to Lister's formula."

In 1888, Johnson & Johnson published *Modern Methods of Antiseptic Wound Treatment,* edited by Frederick B. Kilmer, the father of poet Joyce Kilmer, who was then proprietor of the Opera House Pharmacy in New Brunswick. The manual was a huge success. More than four million copies eventually were distributed worldwide, and it became the standard text on antiseptic medical practices. The manual also doubled as a sales catalog and made Johnson & Johnson one of the most recognized and respected names in the medical products industry.

Kilmer was enticed to join Johnson & Johnson as director of scientific affairs, and in 1891 the company established a bacteriological laboratory. By 1892, under Kilmer's direction, Johnson & Johnson was using a combination of dry heat and pressurized steam to produce sterile bandages of cotton and gauze. That same year, Johnson & Johnson adopted the slogan, "The Most Trusted Name in Surgical Dressings."

## Band-Aid Adhesive Bandages

Johnson & Johnson had been making bandages for more than 30 years when, in 1920, Earle E. Dickson, a cotton buyer in the purchasing department, suggested a new product for home use. According to company lore, Dickson's inspiration was his new bride, Josephine, who was continually burning or cutting her fingers in the kitchen. Dickson, whose parents and grandparents had been doctors, grew tired of bandaging his wife's fingers with gauze and surgical tape, two products then made by Johnson & Johnson. He later told people, "I was determined to devise some manner of bandage that would stay in place, be easily applied, and still retain its sterility."

Dickson laid a strip of surgical tape on a table, adhesive side up. He then stuck small pads of gauze at intervals along the tape. Finally, he covered the sticky side of the tape with crinoline, a stiff, cotton fabric usually used as a liner in clothing. Whenever his wife needed a bandage, she simply cut a piece from the convenient roll of tape.

Dickson mentioned his invention to a fellow worker at Johnson & Johnson, who encouraged him to pitch his idea to upper management. Dickson later recalled, "The boys in the front office loved the concept." James W. Johnson, then president of the company, was one of those who recognized the potential of adhesive bandages for the care of minor wounds and enthusiastically endorsed the idea. W. Johnson Kenyon, superintendent of the textile mill at Johnson & Johnson, is credited with suggesting the name Band-Aid. Band-Aid brand adhesive bandages eventually became the best-selling product in Johnson & Johnson history. Dickson was rewarded by being named a vice president and member of the board of directors. He retired in 1957 and died in 1962.

## Marketing

The first "J&J Band-Aid Adhesive Bandages" were produced in 1921. They were made by hand, came in a strip 2½ inches wide and 18 inches long, and crinoline was still used to cover the adhesive surface. Salesmen making the rounds of doctor's offices and pharmacies carried scissors to demonstrate how to use the new product. Band-Aid bandages also were promoted heavily in *Red Cross Notes,* a magazine for druggists that was edited by Kilmer. Samples were also given to Boy Scouts across the country, and one industrious salesman gave Band-Aids to every butcher in Cleveland.

Sales, however, were slow until 1924, when mechanization allowed Johnson & Johnson to begin selling Band-Aids in precut strips three inches long and ¾ inches wide. Other improvements soon followed. In 1928, two holes were added to the section of tape over the gauze pads to allow air to reach the wound and promote faster healing. Medicated bandages also were introduced in 1928. Each Band-Aid was wrapped in an individual glassine package, which was opened with a patented tear string. The entire product was made sterile in 1939.

Initially, Band-Aid bandages were promoted as "The New Speed Bandage" and "a protective dressing for minor cuts, burns and abrasions." However, by the 1930s, other companies had introduced competitive brands, and Johnson & Johnson needed to distinguish its original Band-Aid brand from the competition. This prompted a change in advertising, with the focus shifting to the adhesive power. One ad used during the 1930s proclaimed that Band-Aid bandages had "A slicker, quicker sticker," and another promised that Band-Aids would stick "like a day coach window." Sticking power would continue to be a major selling point for adhesive bandages. In the early 1950s, ads touted Band-Aid bandages' "new SUPER-STICK adhesive." By the 1940s, Johnson & Johnson was also attempting to protect its trademark with advertising slogans such as, "All Sparklers Aren't Diamonds/All Adhesive Bandages Aren't Band-Aid."

During World War II, Band-Aid bandages were used extensively by the Armed Forces and in defense plants, where, as the *New York Times* noted in an article about the brand, "unattended cuts and scratches could lead to lost man-hours." Band-Aid "patches" and "spots" were developed for the type of cuts and scrapes encountered in manufacturing. After the war and into the early 1950s, a long-running series of magazine ads urged readers to never neglect even a small injury. The ads also continued to caution that "Not all adhesive bandages are Band-Aid. Only Johnson & Johnson makes Band-Aid. And only Band-Aid brings you Johnson & Johnson dependability." According to the ads, Band-Aid brand was the "6 to 1 choice in doctors' recommendations."

One of the most effective advertising campaigns involving Band-Aid was created in 1948 when Johnson & Johnson commissioned Gladys Rockmore Davis to do a series of 15 paintings that showed children using the company's first aid products. The paintings appeared in full-page color ads in Life Magazine and The Saturday Evening Post with the caption, "Mommy always says you're safe when you use Johnson & Johnson." Pictures and descriptions of Band-Aid bandages and Johnson & Johnson's Red Cross brand adhesive tape, cotton, gauze pads, and gauze bandages appeared at the bottom of the page. The ads ran from 1949 into the early 1950s; the paintings were so popular that later ads offered free reprints from Johnson & Johnson. Reproductions hung in nurseries and doctors' offices for many years.

Johnson & Johnson was an early sponsor of network television. Ironically, the first TV program sponsored by Band-Aid and other Johnson & Johnson consumer products was *The Adventures of Robin Hood.* According to company lore, Robert Wood Johnson II, the founder's oldest son, who was then president of the company, was initially outraged by the sponsorship, calling up his advertising executives and demanding, "What is this business about stealing from the rich and giving to the poor?" Johnson was apparently satisfied that there was nothing immoral about Robin Hood, and the company sponsored the show for three years. Johnson & Johnson went on to sponsor shows such as *Cheyenne, Gunsmoke,* and *The Donna Reed Show.* One well-remembered television commercial from the mid-1950s featured a Band-Aid bandage sticking firmly to an egg even during the "amazing boiling water test."

## Postwar Innovations

In 1951, Johnson & Johnson introduced Band-Aid Elastic Adhesive Bandages. The stretchable Band-Aids were advertised as "Ideal for hard-to-bandage injuries like blisters, boils and scalp wounds! Perfect for hard-to-bandage places like elbows, heels and palms!" However, elastic Band-Aids would soon be replaced by an even more significant improvement. In 1951, Johnson & Johnson announced Band-Aid Plastic Strips, "the new dressing that *doesn't* wash off . . . *does* wash clean!"

Ads for the Band-Aid Plastic Strips said they offered the "Greatest comfort ever!" and the "Neatest appearance ever!" They were thinner and smoother than the version made with adhesive tape. They stretched, didn't fray or curl, could be washed clean, and were waterproof. They were also, according to the ads, "flesh-colored" so "you hardly see them at all." Band-Aid bandages would continue to be "flesh colored" until the 1960s, when corporations became conscious of minority concerns. The color remained the same, but the "flesh-colored" terminology was dropped.

Another appearance-related innovation came on the market in the 1950s: Bauer & Black introduced the "Curad Battle Ribbon," the first colored adhesive bandages for children. Curad, "the ouchless bandage," was then the second-leading brand of adhesive bandages. Johnson & Johnson retaliated with Band-Aid Stars 'n Strips. Eventually, the designs became even more imaginative with animals, cars and trains, and other shapes. In *A Company That Cares: One Hundred Year Illustrated History of Johnson & Johnson,* Lawrence G. Foster, former vice president of public relations, wrote, "the fad raged on until youngsters began using the colored bandages when they didn't have cuts, and parents put their foot down.'' Band-Aid Stars 'n Strips were discontinued in the late 1950s.

However, children's designs made a strong comeback in the late 1980s with a variety of cartoon characters, beginning with the National Patent Medical Company's Mickey and Pals brand adhesive bandages, which featured Mickey Mouse and Donald Duck. Johnson & Johnson introduced Band-Aid brand Sesame Street Adhesive Bandages in 1990.

In 1958, Johnson & Johnson introduced Band-Aid Sheer Strips, which according to *A Company That Cares,* ''propelled the once simple Band-Aid Bandage into the world of high technology.'' Sheer Strips were made of clear plastic with a criss-cross ''flesh-tone'' pattern. Other innovations followed. In 1961, tiny holes were added to the entire Band-Aid. Johnson & Johnson said the air holes prevented ''that whitened, wrinkled look'' when the bandage was removed. Ads touted Band-Aid as ''the breathing bandage.'' Band-Aid brand bandages of tricot mesh and flexible fabric were introduced in 1981. Band-Aid Medicated Adhesive Bandages followed in 1984, and Band-Aid Clear Strips in 1986.

Over the years, Johnson & Johnson extended the brand's product line. In the 1940s and 50s, they marketed a line of foot-care products under the Band-Aid brand name, including Band-Aid Bunion Pads, Band-Aid Corn Pads, and Band-Aid Moleskin Adhesive. The company also sold Band-Aid brand Adhesive Tape into the 1960s, in addition to its better-known Red Cross brand adhesive tape.

## Future Directions

Although Band-Aid bandages were still the overwhelming market leader in the early 1990s, they faced a renewed challenge in the U.S. from Curad, their traditional second-place rival from Kendall-Futuro Company. Curad was introduced in the late 1920s by Bauer & Black, a company cofounded by S. H. Black, a former sales manager for Johnson & Johnson. Ironically, the marketing offensive launched by Curad in 1990 was being directed by Paul Amatangelo, who was senior brand manager for Band-Aid before becoming director of personal care products at Kendall-Futuro in 1988.

In 1990, Kendall-Futuro introduced Curad Kid Size, a smaller version of its regular adhesive bandages that were festooned with pictures of Ronald McDonald, the clown symbol of McDonald's Restaurants. Samples were distributed in 7.5 million McDonald's Happy Meals. Johnson & Johnson responded by introducing Band-Aid brand Sesame Street Adhesive Bandages. The Band Aids had a softer, thicker gauze pad and pictures of Big Bird and Cookie Monster, two characters from the children's television program ''Sesame Street.'' However, *Sales & Marketing Management* reported in 1993 that, ''After years of idling in the No. 2 position, [Curad] currently holds a commanding 36.1 percent of the children's bandage market.'' Band-Aid was in second place at 26.6 percent. Kendall-Futuro was also challenging Johnson & Johnson more aggressively in the adult market with a television advertising campaign stressing that Curad was the adhesive bandage chosen for the American Red Cross first aid kit.

## Further Reading:

*Johnson & Johnson Annual Reports,* New Brunswick, NJ: Johnson & Johnson, 1980–92.

*Brief History of Johnson & Johnson,* New Brunswick, NJ: Johnson & Johnson, 1992.

Foster, Lawrence, *A Company That Cares: One Hundred Year Illustrated History of Johnson & Johnson,* New Brunswick, NJ: Johnson & Johnson, 1986.

Linsenmeyer, Adrienne, ''No Band-Aid Solution,'' *Financial World,* January 21, 1992, pp. 25–27.

Miller, Cyndee, ''Company Slips a Mickey into the Bandage Biz,'' *Marketing News,* June 5, 1989, p. 10.

Nagle, James J., ''News of the Advertising and Marketing Fields,'' *New York Times,* Sept. 13, 1953, p. C8.

*The Story Behind the Band-Aid Brand Adhesive Bandage,* New Brunswick, NJ: Johnson & Johnson.

Swisshelm, George, ''Curad Ads Cover Old Wounds,'' *Television/Radio Age,* June 12, 1989, pp. 44–45.

Wiesendanger, Betsy, ''Profiles in Marketing: Paul Amatangelo,'' *Sales & Marketing Management,* January 1993, p. 12.

*—Dean Boyer*

# BASS®

Bass has been a leading brand in casual footwear for more than a century. The G.H. Bass & Company's most popular shoes, the classic Weejun collection of "penny" and "tassel kiltie" loafers, established a unique market category in casual footwear. Despite the enduring Bass reputation for quality products, G.H. Bass & Company found it difficult to outpace increasing foreign competition in the footwear industry during the 1980s. In 1978 Chesebrough-Pond's Inc. acquired Bass, but failed to revitalize the brand and sold it to Philips-Van Heusen Corporation in 1987. Under aggressive new management, Bass quickly rebounded to the top of the casual footwear market, reclaiming its long history as a reputable and dependable casual shoe brand.

## Brand Origins

In 1876 George Henry Bass founded G.H. Bass & Company in Wilton, Maine. Initially the company produced boots and moccasins for Maine farmers and woodsmen. The founder's guiding principle was clear and sincere, with a hint of backwoods charm: "We will make the best shoe for the purpose for which it's intended." Keeping this goal in mind, G.H. Bass & Company created a number of rugged footwear designs that served their purpose famously: Lindbergh wore Bass boots as he crossed the Atlantic; Bass created Admiral Byrd's footwear for two South Pole expeditions; and the U.S. Army's Tenth Mountain Division in World War II was outfitted in Bass boots. With this kind of exposure, the brand established a solid reputation for quality products.

For years, G.H. Bass & Company maintained its tradition of making "the best shoe for the purpose" by producing a few simple designs of casual and rugged shoes. Several of the Bass brand styles endured for decades. For instance, the original Camp Moc, created in 1910, remained essentially the same for nearly a hundred years. In 1936 G.H. Bass & Company developed its world-famous trademark Weejuns—the name derived from "Norwegian slippers." Through the early 1990s Bass continued to produce the Weejun loafers in the same basic style, as well as a number of variations of the original. During the 1950s and 1960s Weejuns were so popular that the demand for the loafers almost always exceeded supply.

## Changes in the Footwear Market

While the 1970s were a period of continued growth for Bass, during the latter part of the decade, the U.S. footwear industry began losing ground to foreign competition. By the mid-1980s nearly 90 percent of shoes purchased in the United States were produced overseas, and Bass shoe sales began to suffer. In 1978 the Bass family sold G.H. Bass & Company to Chesebrough-Pond's Inc. for $27 million in cash in order to avoid an estate tax, thus bringing to an end a century of family ownership. The footwear industry itself was also undergoing dramatic changes. The public's growing interest in physical fitness greatly influenced footwear fashions. Increased demand for athletic shoes—especially jogging and aerobics footwear—cut into the market for more traditional casual shoes like those made by G.H. Bass & Company.

Bass pursued a number of strategies to adjust to the new fitness-oriented environment, but to no avail. An attempt to enter the athletic shoe market with the Bass Air failed, as did a new line of women's shoes imported from Brazil. G.H. Bass & Company was shifting radically from the founder's original purpose; by the mid-1980s, rather than perfecting a few styles for specific purposes, the Bass brand name encompassed over six hundred models of seventeen different categories.

Concerned primarily with cutting costs, G.H. Bass & Company sacrificed quality and neglected marketing strategies for its core products. Bass lost $72 million between 1983 and 1987; in 1986 alone, Bass lost $46 million on $150 million in sales. Most of the U.S. Bass factories were shut down, with only one remaining in Wilton, Maine, and another in Puerto Rico.

## Changes in Marketing Strategy

Phillips-Van Heusen's purchase of G.H. Bass & Company in 1987 for $79 million was well under its estimated book value of $130 million. Phillips-Van Heusen hired a new chief executive, John Thorbeck, to help revamp the failing Bass division. In the *New York Times* Thorbeck criticized Chesebrough-Pond's management of Bass for focusing too narrowly on "fashion, imports, price"; in other words, imitating European fashion, manufacturing overseas, and selling cheaply in the United States. The new Bass leadership redefined the Bass image by emphasizing the classic design, domestic manufacturing, and the long-standing commitment to quality footwear.

In the late 1980s Bass streamlined its product designs to two hundred patterns in six categories, each of which was intended to reflect a different lifestyle. These included the Weejuns, virtually

## AT A GLANCE

**B**ass brand of footwear founded in 1876 by George Henry Bass, president of G.H. Bass & Company, in Wilton, MN; Bass became a registered trademark, 1911; company sold to Chesebrough-Pond's Inc., 1978; company acquired by Phillips-Van Heusen Corporation, 1987.

**Performance:** *Market share*—(source: Footwear Market Insights) 5.3% of total casual footwear category (top share of 972 million pair market, 1992); 4.4% of women's casual footwear (top share of 147 million pair market); 4.6% of men's casual footwear (fourth place in 46 million pair market). *Sales*—(source: Footwear Market Insights) $333.2 million (total footwear, 1992).

**Major competitor:** (women's casual footwear) Naturalizer, Dexter and SAS; (men's casual footwear) Dexter, Rockport, and Florsheim.

**Advertising:** *Agency*—Cipriani Kremer Design, 1991—. *Major campaign*—"Bass. The look that never wears out."

**Addresses:** *Parent company*—G.H. Bass & Company, 600 Sable Oaks Drive, South Portland, Maine, 04106-9413; phone: (207) 791-4000. *Ultimate parent company*—Phillips-Van Heusen Corporation, 1290 Avenue of the Americas, New York, NY, 10104-0101, phone: (212) 541-5200.

synonymous with the Bass brand name; the Comfort shoes; the more formal Tailor designs; the casual lace-up Saddles and Bucs model; the Outdoor group including loafers, moccasins, sneakers and boots; and finally, the Sunjuns summer footwear.

Bass's strategy was to reestablish the Bass brand's reputation for superior craftsmanship. Thus, several of the new designs were of higher quality and higher price. In 1988 the first advertising campaign in four years appealed to more affluent consumers with a series of multiple-page promotions in high fashion magazines, including twelve-page ads in *Vogue* and *Gentleman's Quarterly*. The Lintas advertising agency developed the slogan: "Bass. The look that never wears out," which continues to be the Bass motto. At that time, Bass spent over $1 million annually on advertising.

In order to create a stronger consumer awareness of the company's style, personality, and values, G.H. Bass & Company emphasized its history in the advertising campaigns. For instance, Bass stressed the founder's dictum, "The best shoe for the purpose," and printed that slogan on all Bass shoe boxes, which were redesigned for each new shoe category. The marketing strategies were highly successful, with sales reaching $240 million in 1989, up from $150 million in 1987.

In the late 1980s and early 1990s, traditional American shoe styles became popular once again, in part because European designers were promoting such styles. According to Engle Saez, senior vice president of product design and development at Bass, who was quoted in *Footwear News,* "Europeans' love affair with genuine American authenticity" redirected shoe fashions toward American styles. He argued that when such a prominent European firm as Gucci made imitations of American loafers, it increased the demand for the original style of the Bass Weejun loafer. In the late 1980s pop star Michael Jackson, who often wore black Bass Weejuns in his performances and music videos, also contributed to boosting the popularity of the Bass brand.

Moreover, during the early 1990s U.S. consumers were increasingly attracted to domestically produced products, in part out of a concern for the sagging economy, according to Mitchell Massey, senior vice president of marketing for G.H. Bass & Company He claimed in *Footwear News* that Americans also benefited from purchasing the domestically made Bass shoes since the company operated in-stock, thus providing customer convenience in distribution.

In the early 1990s Bass once again changed its marketing strategy, targeting middle-American consumers rather than the more wealthy. As Don Sappington, president of Bass, explained in *Footwear News,* "The company was being positioned as a champagne company on a beer budget." Although G.H. Bass & Company continued marketing some of the sleeker versions of its traditional products, the company focused primarily on the core designs of Bass Buc, Compass, and Weejun.

### Product Innovations and Brand Extensions

Increasingly, consumers were expecting more comfortably designed shoes. As Mike Kormos, president of the research firm Footwear Market Insights (FMI), explained in *Footwear News,* "comfort criteria" were established during the fitness craze of the 1980s and subsequently were incorporated into the designs for dress as well as casual shoes. While the dress shoe market deteriorated and athletic shoe sales declined nearly two percent, the unit sales of casual shoes increased ten percent in 1991 alone. As a result, the casual and athletic shoe categories began to converge, creating a greater demand in the active casual category.

The trend toward active casual shoes was also motivated by a progressively less formal dress code at the workplace. Footwear was essentially redefined as more of a comfortable accessory rather than a fashion statement. Consumers were demanding not only more comfortable shoes, but more versatile designs as well. Bass offered a variety of fashionable casuals in canvas and leather in a variety of colors.

In 1988 Bass designed updated versions of the traditional Weejun loafers, aiming at the aging baby-boomer market. Saddle and Buc shoes were especially successful for this age group. In the spring of 1989 Bass also introduced its version of "status sneakers," a canvas, rubber-soled shoe with brass eyelets and leather trim and laces known as the Compass. While projected sales were 30,000 pairs, by the end of 1990 more than one million pairs had been sold.

Early in the 1990s Bass added new comfort technology to some of the classic Oxford and Wingtip designs. Engle Saez explained in *Footwear News* that Bass sought to balance a classic design with more comfort and flexibility, something which he believed the competition was not doing. Previously, shoe technology included a steel shank—which prevented the shoe from curling by separating the rubberized heel and the upper—and a soft heel to provide cushioning. Bass improved this design by shrinking the size of the shank and placing it more strategically as well as adding foam padding at the toe. The comfort technology was later added to a variety of other Bass shoe designs, including the traditional Weejuns as well as a European style of Weejuns. The advertising campaign suggested that Bass footwear was as comfortable and relaxing as standing barefoot on soft grass, featuring the slogan: "Now. Paradise for City Feet."

A new tanning technology called WeatherTuff was also applied to several styles of Bass boots and shoes. The leather uppers of these shoes were tanned in such a way that they created virtually

*The classic Bass Weejun penny loafer was first introduced in 1936.*

impenetrable barriers against water, snow, salt, and stains. Moreover, the WeatherTuff shoe remained comfortable and breathable. Motivated by the expanding market for outdoor and hiking shoes, in 1992 Bass developed the ''World Class'' outdoor shoe collection, which was a combination of Bass Oxfords and Duck boots featuring brass eyelets and speed lacing. The World Class series also featured one hundred percent rubber soles designed to be strong, slip-resistant, and flexible.

In mid-1992 the Bass Retail Division began a pilot program to market a casual apparel line in thirteen locations across the United States. The strategy proved successful in two ways: not only were the clothes popular, but they helped boost the sales of footwear at these locations. Similarly, sales of such Bass accessories as luggage and hosiery also increased. In 1993 the company planned to sell Bass Apparel at most of the company stores by the mid-1990s. For 1994 the G.H. Bass & Company Retail Division planned to extend its name to children's merchandise, calling the new division Bass Kids.

## Performance Appraisal

In 1988, the first year of Phillips-Van Heusen ownership, Bass sales increased by $30 million to $180 million. Sales continued climbing steadily. By 1990, sales reached $270 million, and in 1992 they were $333.2 million, an eight percent increase from the previous year. During the early 1990s, the core products remained the Weejuns, although the growth of Saddle and Buc shoes climbed steadily to one and a half million pairs in 1992, an increase of four hundred thousand from the previous year. Compass shoe sales remained solid after several years of strong growth.

In 1992 total domestic shoe sales were $30 billion, with 60 percent representing casual and dress shoes. Overall, Bass led the casual footwear market with 5.3 percent of the 193-million-pair domestic industry. Pairs of women's casual shoes sold were 147 million, with Bass at the top of that market, with a 4.4 percent share. Men's Bass shoes were ranked fourth, with 4.6 percent market share of the 46-million-pair market.

General market predictions made by FMI president Mike Kormos in the November 23, 1992 issue of *Footwear News* were positive for the casual footwear industry, with an expected growth around five percent between 1992 and 2002. Because the world market was evolving into a technical economy from an industrial one, Jeffery Hallett, chairman of PresentFutures Group Inc., predicted that manufacturers and retailers who could continue to attract new consumers globally would prosper. By the early 1990s, when the Bass brand had been repositioned more favorably in the domestic market, G.H. Bass & Company began concentrating on strengthening its European and Japanese markets. The company established direct sales operations with European agents, and in Japan, arranged for licensing and distribution of the brand. In 1990 Bass started shipping to Italy, France, the Netherlands, and Great Britain. Although Bass's overseas business was only about five percent of total sales in 1992, the company expected to increase that amount to 30 percent by 1995. Overall, G.H. Bass & Company was well-positioned to explore new opportunities in the global market.

## Further Reading:

''Bass Puts Its Best Foot Forward Again,'' *Los Angeles Times,* August 11, 1989, Business sec., p. 2.

Dougherty, Philip H., ''Lintas Print Campaign For G.H. Bass Shoes,'' *The New York Times,* August 4, 1988, sec. D, p. 17.

McAllister, Robert, ''Market Reading,'' *Footwear News,* August 17, 1992, p. S8.

''Phillips Van Heusen Corp.,'' *Disclosure Online Database,* 1993.

Rooney, Ellen, ''Shoe Execs Told To Eye Global Markets For Growth,'' *Footwear News,* November 23, 1992, p. 2.

Tedeschi, Mark, ''Bass is Centering On Dress Shoe Line,'' *Footwear News,* September 17, 1990, p. 2; ''Americana Firms On Safe, High Ground,'' *Footwear News,* September 24, 1990, p. 28; ''Bass Renews Emphasis On Middle America Market,'' *Footwear News,* November 4, 1991, p. 2.

Thorbeck, John, ''The Turnaround Value Of Values,'' *Harvard Business Review,* January-February 1991, p. 52.

Warrock, Anna M., ''Shoemakers Feel The Pinch,'' *New England Business,* October 21, 1985, p. 62.

*—Audra Avizienis*

# BAUSCH & LOMB®

# BAUSCH & LOMB

Soft contact lenses are synonymous with Bausch & Lomb, the company that pioneered the revolutionary lenses and made contact lens wearing more comfortable and acceptable to the masses needing corrected vision. Bausch & Lomb contact lens and eye care products have consistently held formidable market shares because the company backs its products through diversification and heavy investment in research and development. The strong market shares of Bausch & Lomb products support the company's position as one of the top eyecare and health care companies in the world.

## In the Beginning

In 1849, Henry Lomb set out from Burghaun, Germany to Rochester, New York, where he settled down in search of a better life. Several years later, he invested his $60 savings in an eyeglass business run by John Bausch. Because Americans did not seek professional services for eyecare in the late nineteenth century and because Bausch had already launched one optical company that failed, friends initially thought Lomb was headed for financial disaster.

Bausch & Lomb's first success came from making optical instruments and eyeglass frames from vulcanite (hardened rubber) in 1866. More than 10 years later, Bausch & Lomb lenses won free publicity: Dr. Oliver Wendell Holmes publicly endorsed the company's microscopes, and Rochester resident George Eastman used Bausch & Lomb lenses in the Kodak camera he patented in 1888. When Lomb died in 1908, the business in which he invested $60 was producing more than 20 million glass lenses annually, making Bausch & Lomb the largest company of its kind in the world.

The development of non-glare glasses for U.S. Army Air Corps pilots in the 1920s boosted Bausch & Lomb's brand name in the eyeglass industry. The new glasses were named Ray-Ban because they reduced harmful ultra-violet and infrared rays. Ray-Bans continued to sell well into the 1990s. Bausch & Lomb's development of the CinemaScope lens won praise from the Academy of Motion Pictures and Sciences and the company was honored with an Academy Award in 1955. Bausch & Lomb's place on the cutting edge of eyecare technology kept its products ahead of its competition.

## Brand Origins

The soft contact was not invented until the late 1950s when Czechoslovakian polymer chemists Otto Wichterle and Drahoslav Lim at the Institute for Macromolecular Chemistry in Prague created the flexible lenses made out of a porous material. In the early 1960s Wichterle made the soft lenses in his kitchen with a homemade centrifugal spincasting machine that used part of his son's Erector set and part of a bicycle generator. Wichterle told the *Wall Street Journal* that when he got tired of generating, his wife pedaled.

To bring the soft contact to the United States officially, the National Patent Development Corporation (NPDC) had to agree to a patent and national distribution. In 1966, the NPDC granted an exclusive license to Bausch & Lomb to make and sell soft contact lenses in the United States. According to James P. Dodd, retired president of the Bausch & Lomb Soflens Division, company officials "thought we'd be able to market the product in about six months at a cost of about $200,000, but it took almost six years and $4.5 million."

Marketing the lenses was delayed because of disagreement about the soft lenses' safety and effectiveness compared to hard lenses. Bausch & Lomb commissioned Donald N. Zehl, an ophthalmologist at the University of Rochester School of Medicine and Dentistry, to conduct a two and a half-year study that began in 1967. Testing of a new hydrophilic contact lens called Soflens was conducted among private practices in the Rochester area before branching out nationally. The FDA ruled in 1968 that all soft contacts were to be classified as "new drugs," and not as medical devices, prompting Bausch & Lomb to accelerate lab and clinical testing of its Soflens brand of soft contact lenses, which the company was ready to introduce in 1969.

Two years later, on March 18, 1971, the FDA granted Bausch & Lomb approval to market Soflens in the United States, making it the first company to receive such approval. Later that year, the company was granted a sublicense to make and sell Soflens in Japan, the Philippines, Okinawa, Taiwan, South Korea, and Hong Kong. Additional licensing agreements and approvals overseas enabled Bausch & Lomb to expand manufacturing and marketing to Europe by 1973.

The FDA approval was a turning point, transforming Bausch & Lomb into a different company: ". . . Bausch & Lomb ceased to be the quiet and rather dull manufacturer of only dependable eye glasses and scientific instruments, struggling along with earnings fluctuating from year to year," according to *Bausch & Lomb Magazine.* "It had an exciting new product that the public had been eagerly awaiting; it became the stock to watch on Wall Street; it was a growth company."

## Product Changes

Soflens was unveiled and distributed in May 1971, and Bausch & Lomb conducted symposia and workshops in 30 American cities to introduce the new lens care system to eyecare professionals. The first soft lens care kit consisted of a heating unit to disinfect lenses, a bottle of salt tablets and a mixing bottle. Eyecare professionals were charged $25 to attend Bausch & Lomb symposia to learn how to fit the soft contacts on patients, and they also had to pay $2,900 for a lens kit that contained a range and assortment of lenses for nearsighted patients. Some professionals complained about the high charges, causing a rift between physicians and the company. In hindsight, Bausch & Lomb officials were quoted as saying that they would have changed the way Soflens was distributed in the first place. Nevertheless, by the end of 1971, 10,000 American consumers were wearing Soflens.

Soflens soft contact lenses soon became Bausch & Lomb's main and only profit center. Bausch & Lomb announced in an earnings release that Soflens sales netted the company a 57 percent increase in 1971 third quarter profits, thereby resuscitating the company's financial health. Without the Soflens brand, sales would have been "moderately below the results of the third quarter of 1970 due to the continuing weak demand for scientific instrument products," then Chairman of the Board Daniel G.

Schuman and President Jack D. Harby told the *Bausch & Lomb Magazine.* By 1976, more than 1.5 million Americans wore Soflens brand soft contact lenses.

In 1974, Bausch & Lomb introduced a new Low Plus End Series of soft contact lenses to correct far-sightedness and moved its contact lens division to its North Goodman Street location in Rochester, the site of present day headquarters. Bausch & Lomb finally unveiled its first contact lens care line of products in 1979, with Preserved Saline Solution, Daily Lens Cleaner, and Sterile Lens Lubricant that prepared lenses for insertion in the eye and cleaned them as well.

To broaden the customer base for contact lenses, Bausch & Lomb technicians began work on the development and manufacture of a "toric" lens, a combination hard and soft contact lens for correction of astigmatism, in 1979. Toric lenses were introduced in 1981. The following year, another improvement on the lens was revealed with the launch of P.A. 1 Bifocal soft contact lenses, designed to correct presbyopia.

New contact solutions were also developed to meet the increasing demands of contact lens wearers. In 1982, Bausch & Lomb introduced Sensitive Eyes Saline Solution, which eventually became the top selling saline solution in the United States. In Europe, the Fresh Vision system of frequent contact lens replacement was implemented two years before it would be used in the United States.

Other developments throughout the 1980s and 1990s included the introduction of spuncast "70" high water and "0" low water series extended-wear lenses (1983); Naturaltint line of tinted soft contact lenses (1984); Optima Toric soft contacts (1985); Bi-Tech Bifocal soft contacts (1986); SeeQuence disposable contact lenses (1988); the Medalist contact lens to celebrate the company's Olympic sponsorship (1990); and a new concept called Occasions wear (1993).

In addition to the new lenses, new solutions were developed and introduced. In 1987, ReNu Multi-Purpose Solution hit the market and was described as "the first generation of lens care products which combine effectiveness with convenience" for "cleaning, rinsing and disinfecting." Sensitive Eyes Plus, a pH-balanced saline solution, was introduced in 1992.

## Marketing Strategy

Growth in the soft contact lens industry exploded during the 1970s and Bausch & Lomb almost monopolized the industry. Success in the 1970s was followed by loss in the 1980s. In the late 1970s, FDA approval enabled other competitors to enter the contact lens market. Bausch & Lomb began losing market share until it decided to revamp and expand its soft contact lens lines. New manufacturing sites for lenses were built in Ireland, while construction in South Carolina focused on sites for solution production. In addition, the Soflens Division was reorganized, and a Personal Products Division was formed.

Competition was not the only factor that contributed to Bausch & Lomb's difficulties during the early 1980s. Prices of contact lenses dropped dramatically. Bad press about the safety of extended wear contacts also dissuaded consumer purchasing. Other causes for the decline were attributed to the industry focusing on large chain store accounts and private practices, the trend in designer eyewear and a flattening in the percentage of new soft contact lens patients.

*Business Week* described Bausch & Lomb's problem as a "lack of zest for marketing." Bausch & Lomb had the scientific know how—its spincasting process (where a liquid polymer is spun in a mold) was more cost-effective than a competitor's lathe process—but not the business wherewithal to fight competition. Bausch & Lomb's lack of aggression in marketing enabled Warner-Lambert's American Optical Corp. to increase sales through volume discount offers that Bausch & Lomb did not meet. Other companies began flooding the market with thinner lenses, gas permeable hard lenses, extended wear soft lenses, cosmetic tinted lenses, and soft lenses that corrected astigmatism. Bausch & Lomb's market share plummeted from 100 percent in 1974 to less than half that in 1978, at which time Bausch & Lomb had many competitors, including Revlon's Barnes-Hind/Hydrocurve, Cooper-Vision, Syntex, Dow Corning, Johnson & Johnson, Schering, and Ciba-Geigy.

To combat losing more market share, Bausch & Lomb set a new marketing strategy in place. Bausch & Lomb began reducing prices 28 percent (the first soft contacts cost wearers $400), selling lenses to fast-growing high-volume optical chains, and implementing a consignment system making it easier for eyecare practitioners to obtain lenses for same-day trial fitting and dispensing. The company's strategy to sell discounted lenses to optical chains ruffled feathers in the eyecare community, and Bausch & Lomb appeased practitioners by offering them access to toll-free ordering and making experts available to doctors for consultations.

Bausch & Lomb belatedly began making extended wear contacts in 1983. Even with a late start, the Bausch & Lomb brand name helped the lenses win market share. Within four months of the new lenses hitting the market, Bausch & Lomb captured 37 percent of the extended wear market and was the number one seller in 1984, reported *Business Week*. In that year, Bausch & Lomb acquired Polymer Technology Corp. of Wilmington, Massachusetts, a leader in rigid gas permeable lens materials.

The company then set off on a research and development mission by increasing spending and rolled out new lines of contacts and eyecare solutions. By 1986, Bausch & Lomb was at the forefront of rigid gas permeable lenses (with its Boston Lens division), *Barron's Investment News & Views* reported. In revamping the way it marketed contacts, the company established "tiger teams" to brainstorm new products, reported Lois Therrien in a 1987 *Business Week* article. Teams were rewarded with cash or stock options if their ideas went to market. "People aren't afraid to bring forth ideas, and management is saying 'We're behind you,' " research chemist Mark Trokanski told *Business Week*.

### Advertising Innovations

Bausch & Lomb has always tried to make their soft contacts appear to be the most popular brand worn by hyping the fact that their brands are comfortable enough to wear anywhere. The company also has conducted public information forums educating eyecare professionals and potential contact users on proper contact eyecare and wear. Actresses like Connie Sellaca modeled soft contacts in ads about career women in the mid-1970s. Skylab astronauts, who donned soft contacts in 1983, were the first to wear them in space.

Bausch & Lomb also became one of twelve top sponsors of the 1992 Olympic games. Olympic gold medalist and figure skater Dorothy Hamill was signed to endorse the new SeeQuence disposable contact brand in a series of TV and print ads to promote the brand as well as encourage better eyecare. Hamill was chosen by Bausch & Lomb to represent all lenses and solutions because she embodied "quality and trust," company officials told *Advertising Age*. In addition, she appealed to both sexes even though 65 percent of all contact wearers at the time were women.

The 1992 games marked Bausch & Lomb's first Olympic sponsorship, which was launched in tandem with the introduction of the Medalist contact lens. Perhaps in an effort to woo men, the company, through its agency Avrett, Free & Ginsberg of New York, signed a multi-year, multi-million dollar sponsorship agreement with the National Basketball Association in 1992. The sponsorship included network and cable TV ads, NBA publications and a merchandise catalog.

### International

Although Bausch & Lomb has been selling soft contact lenses overseas since the 1970s, it did not establish an international division until 1984. Until that year, overseas businesses were offshoots of the company's U.S. operations. Growth in the international division accounted for 46 percent of total revenues in 1991, compared to 17 percent in its first year, according to Seema Nayyar in *AdWeek's BrandWeek*.

The Far East, including the People's Republic of China, accounts for 15 percent earnings growth and is Bausch & Lomb's fastest growing area, compared to markets established in Latin America, Europe, Canada, and the Middle East. Japan in particular is where Bausch & Lomb reported a more than 40 percent increase in sales in 1991. According to Rahul Jacob in *Fortune*, "turning local managers loose makes all the difference" in the way Bausch & Lomb has succeeded internationally. Jacob cited how the company was able to respond to Japanese consumer demands for a more comfortable gas permeable lens. Next in the strategy is to go after the Chinese and Indian markets.

Bausch & Lomb has followed what it termed an "aggressive policy of geographic expansion and of building markets from the ground up. It is willing to form joint ventures in order to conform to a particular country's regulations," stated *Bausch & Lomb Magazine*. For example, in the early 1990s Bausch & Lomb was building a contact lens plant in India to begin manufacturing contact lenses.

International markets look promising for Bausch & Lomb contact lenses and solutions. Competition has eroded market share in the United States where only about 47 percent of the company's contact lens business was conducted. Fifty-three percent of the company's business was overseas.

### Future Growth

Soft contacts lenses used to be the major driver of company profits, but in the late 1980s Bausch & Lomb began selling off half of its unprofitable businesses and began diversifying into healthcare products such as surgical knives, diagnostic packages for eye surgeons, eye bandages, mouthwash, and other health care pharmaceuticals for what one company official called "above-the-shoulder orifices."

Even though the company has diversified, Bausch & Lomb will continue to strenuously market the brands that made it one of the world's largest eyecare companies. The number of lenses sold is increasing, especially the disposable contact brands, noted *Adweek's Brandweek.* Bausch & Lomb planned to win back market share of disposable contact lenses lost to Johnson & Johnson. Bausch & Lomb began its marketing campaign by raising its prices on its disposable contact lens brand. Harold O. Johnson, senior vice president of the company and president of the Contact Lens Division, said in *Bausch & Lomb Magazine* that the company would use history as its guide to future growth: "... we want to bring back the excitement and the attitude of the 1970s which contributed to our vigorous growth and also learn from any mistakes we had made in the past."

## Further Reading:

"Bausch & Lomb: Hardball Pricing Helps It to Regain Its Grip in Contact Lenses," *Business Week,* July 16, 1984, p. 78.

"Bausch & Lomb: Marketing Vision Bolsters its Role in Contact Lenses," *Business Week,* November 17, 1980, p. 173.

Byrne, Harland S., "Bausch & Lomb, Another Year of Record Earnings," *Barron's Investment News & Views,* November 9, 1992, p. 37.

Fuchini, Joseph J., and Suzy Fuchini, *Entrepreneurs: The Men and Women behind Famous Brand Names and How They Made It,* Boston: G.K. Hall & Co., p. 166.

Jacob, Rahul, "Trust the Locals, Win Worldwide," *Fortune,* May 4, 1992, p. 76.

Nayyar, Seema, "In Your Face," *AdWeek's BrandWeek,* December 7, 1992, pp. 24–31.

"New Contact Lens Due," *New York Times,* March 19, 1993, p. 15D.

Reynes, Roberta, "New Contact Lens Competition Focuses on Bausch & Lomb," *Barron's News & Investment Views,* August 1, 1983, p. 13.

Serve, Cynthia, ed. *Bausch & Lomb Magazine,* Fall 1991.

Sherman, Stratford P., "Bausch & Lomb's Lost Opportunity," *Fortune,* January 24, 1983, p. 104.

Therrien, Lois, "Bausch & Lomb Is Correcting Its Vision of Research," *Business Week,* March 30, 1993, p. 91.

Troxell, Jr., Thomas N., "Broader Focus: Bausch & Lomb Draws on More than Lenses," *Barron's Investment News & Views,* August 18, 1986, p. 35.

Winters, Patricia, "Hamill Lends Her Image to Lenses," *Advertising Age,* May 29, 1989, p. 41.

*—Evelyn S. Dorman*

# BAYER®

Bayer is the world's oldest brand of aspirin. First manufactured by the German firm Farbenfabriken Bayer in 1899, it is used to relieve a variety of ailments, including fever, headache, inflammation, and muscle and joint pain. Because aspirin inhibits blood clotting, it can also be helpful in the prevention of some types of heart attack and stroke.

Ownership of the Bayer brand is divided between two companies. Sterling Winthrop Inc., headquartered in New York City, has exclusive rights to the brand for aspirin and other pharmaceutical products in the United States and Canada. A manufacturer of drugs and consumer health products, Sterling produces not only Bayer aspirin but also a Bayer line of aspirin-free analgesics containing either acetaminophen or ibuprofen.

Bayer AG of Leverkusen, Germany, the successor of Farbenfabriken Bayer, has exclusive rights to the brand outside the United States and Canada. Within the U.S. and Canadian markets, its use is limited to industrial products. A giant chemical firm, Bayer AG is the world's largest producer of aspirin.

## Brand Origins

The long journey toward the development of aspirin—known scientifically as acetylsalicylic acid, or ASA—began thousands of years ago, when the bark of the white willow was discovered to be an effective analgesic. Hippocrates, the famous physician of the 2nd century B.C., prescribed a potion brewed from the willow bark for pain and fever.

Modern science took its first giant step toward an improved pain killer in 1828, when German chemists isolated salicin as the active ingredient in willow bark. Salicylic acid, a simpler form of salican, was synthesized by French researchers ten years later. Although salicylic acid became a popular drug, its harsh side effects—including nausea, ringing in the ears, and burning in the mouth, throat, and stomach—encouraged scientists to continue searching for a safe analgesic.

During the 19th century the dye industry was also benefiting from new research. Especially important was the discovery that dye could be synthesized from coal tar, a gooey residue left over from the production of coal gas. Taking advantage of this new source, Freidrich Bayer and Johann Weskott of Barman (Wuppertal), Germany, established their synthetic dye business in

1863. Called Friedrich Bayer & Company, the firm was initially located in their home kitchens, but when neighbors began to complain about contamination of the water supply, it moved to a piece of land next to the Wupper river. By 1880, the year that Bayer died, the business had again moved, this time to nearby Elberfeld, and took on the unusual name Farbenfabriken vormals Friedrich Bayer & Company (Dye Factory Formerly Known as Friedrich Bayer & Company). It would later build a magnificent plant just south in Leverkusen.

The dye industry was exceptionally competitive, and Farbenfabriken Bayer, with only mixed success in the field, began to look for new areas of production. An answer would soon come from Strasbourg, a city straddling the border between France and Germany, where in 1886 two interns learned by accident that acetanilid, a coal-tar chemical used in the dye industry, reduced fever. Two years later Farbenfabriken Bayer was able to introduce its own coal-tar analgesic, acetophenetidin (Phenacetin), which it made from para-nitrophenol, a by-product of dyemaking.

Because acetanilid and acetophenetidin, like salicylic acid, had unpleasant and potentially dangerous side effects, Farbenfabriken Bayer continued to explore new analgesics. A modified version of salicylic acid known as acetylsalicylic acid, or ASA, was finally discovered in 1897 by Bayer chemist Felix Hoffmann, who had been looking for a milder analgesic to treat his father's rheumatism. Although a crude form of the drug was synthesized as early as 1853, Hoffmann's method of making ASA was superior, and the drug apparently alleviated his father's pain without the corrosive side effects typical of the day's analgesics.

Even so, ASA was initially dismissed by Heinrich Dreser, head of Bayer's pharmacological division. At the time, salicylic acid was wrongly assumed to have a harmful effect on the heart, and Dreser thought that ASA would have a similar problem. Farbenfabriken Bayer, in fact, might never have considered the drug without the determination of Arthur Eichengrün, Hoffmann's boss in the pharmaceutical division, who decided to test the drug on himself. His heart not experiencing the supposed harm, Eichengrün then secretly sent ASA to doctors in Berlin, who tested it on their patients. The results were miraculous. ASA reduced fever, relieved sore joints, and even took care of headaches.

## AT A GLANCE

**B**ayer brand aspirin founded in 1899 by the German firm Farbenfabriken vormals Friedrich Bayer & Company; construction of American plant begun in 1903; American operations, patents, and trademarks confiscated by the U.S. government during World War I and auctioned to Sterling Products, Inc., in 1918; name of parent company changed to Sterling Drug, Inc., in 1942; Sterling Drug acquired by Eastman Kodak Company in 1988 and renamed Sterling Winthrop Inc. in 1991.

**Performance:** *Market share*—17% (top share) of aspirin category; 6% (fourth share) of analgesics category. *Sales*—$120 million.

**Major competitor:** Tylenol (acetaminophen), by Johnson & Johnson; also, Advil (ibuprofen) and Anacin (aspirin and caffeine), by American Home Products Corporation; and Excedrin (acetaminophen, aspirin, and caffeine), by Bristol-Myers Squibb Company.

**Advertising:** *Agency*—N W Ayer, Inc., New York, NY, 1991—. *Major campaign*—"The Wonder Drug that Works Wonders."

**Addresses:** *Parent company*—Sterling Winthrop Inc., 90 Park Avenue, New York, NY 10016; phone: (212) 907-2000; fax: (212) 907-3517. *Ultimate parent company*—Eastman Kodak Company, 343 State Street, Rochester, New York 14650; phone: (716) 724-4000; fax: (716) 724-0663.

After further testing Dreser finally approved the use of ASA, and in January of 1899 the drug was given a new and soon to be famous trademark —aspirin, coined from the Latin name for the genus Spiraea, in which the meadowsweet plant, a source of ASA, was then classified. Because European doctors were strongly against advertising drugs to the public, the first marketing of Bayer aspirin, begun in June of 1899, took the form of free samples to doctors, hospitals, and professors, as well as notices in medical journals. The drug immediately received glowing reports, and by November of 1899 Bayer aspirin was already in wide use across Europe and even extending its reach to Asia and America. A decade later the company would report, "Aspirin has . . . become so popular that it is unsurpassed by any other drug. Surely it is not an exaggeration to say that it is today the most used and beloved medicine we manufacture."

### Introduction to the United States

Soon after its founding Farbenfabriken Bayer began exporting to the United States, and by 1900 its U.S. sales had reached some 7.5 million marks. Bayer products were distributed through both the company's New York office and a contracted sales agent, Schieffelin & Company. Thus, by the turn of the century the company was well prepared to market its new wonder drug, aspirin, which was initially sold only in powder form.

The new Bayer product held a special advantage in the United States. While in many countries Farbenfabriken Bayer easily obtained a trademark for the name aspirin, only in the United States and briefly in Britain was it able to get a patent on the drug itself. For seventeen years, beginning in 1899, the company was the only legal supplier in the United States of ASA, which would represent 21 percent of the company's U.S. sales by 1907 and 31 percent in 1909. Its success came despite an ongoing problem with illegally sold and less expensive aspirin made by other companies.

In the United States, as in Europe, Bayer aspirin was initially advertised just to doctors, usually through flyers, samples, and notices in medical journals. The first attempt at public advertisement began in 1914, when the company switched the form of Bayer aspirin from powder to tablets, which were stamped with the company's logo, the "Bayer Cross" (BAYER spelled both vertically and horizontally, with the two words meeting in the center at the letter Y). Not until 1916, the year the patent ended, did newspaper advertisements appear, and these were quite modest, suggesting only that "The Bayer Cross on every package and every tablet of Genuine Aspirin protects you against all counterfeits and substitutes." Predictably, American doctors were harshly critical of the campaign, especially the company's attempt to distinguish Bayer from other brands of ASA.

Along with increased advertising, sales were also helped by the decision in 1903 to build an American plant, which allowed Farbenfabriken Bayer to reduce shipping costs, avoid the U.S. import tax, and thus sell Bayer aspirin at a lower price. Located in Rensselaer, New York, the new 75-acre facility, dominated by a giant aspirin factory, produced a variety of drugs and dyes.

The one ominous cloud overshadowing the company's early success was its membership in various European cartels, which violated U.S. antitrust laws. As a result, its American branch was replaced in 1913 by two new organizations, Bayer Company and Synthetic Patents Company, which were legally independent of, though still controlled by, Farbenfabriken Bayer. Synthetic Patents Company, as the name suggests, gained ownership over all the German firm's U.S. patents, while Bayer Company took over the U.S. trademarks and property. This reorganization, at the time a sensible move, would soon have disastrous results for Farbenfabriken Bayer.

### Purchase by Sterling Products, Inc.

The history of Sterling Products, Inc., begins with the Neuralgyline Company, founded in 1901 in Wheeling, West Virginia, by two pharmacists, William Weiss and Albert Diebold. Its first product, Neuralgine, was likely an analgesic derived from coal tar, although no record of the ingredients exists. Outstanding salesmen, Weiss and Diebold sold more than $10,000 of Neuralgine in the first year, and by 1912 they were able to acquire various other drug firms, whose products, including laxative and dandruff medicine, helped boost the value of the company to some $4 million. In 1917 the company became Sterling Products, Inc. (changed to Sterling Drug, Inc., in 1942), a name borrowed from Sterling Remedy, one of the firms they purchased.

After the outbreak of World War I Sterling continued to prosper, but it was during this period that Bayer Company began to face serious difficulties. One of its biggest problems was the shortage of phenol, a coal-tar derivative essential to making aspirin but, unfortunately, to making certain explosives as well. The war brought even greater disruption in January of 1918, when the company itself was taken over by the U.S. government's Office of the Alien Property Custodian, charged with holding all German property in trust for the remainder of the war. Congress subsequently ordered the auction of enemy property, and on December 12, one month after the end of the war, Farbenfabriken Bayer's American factory, trademarks, and patents (owned by Bayer Company and Synthetic Patents Company) were sold to the highest bidder, Sterling Products, for $5,310,000. Worse than losing the giant New York facility, the German company could no longer use its own name, Bayer, in the United States.

Sterling was interested only in Bayer Company's drugs, and immediately after the purchase it sold the dye business for $1.5 million to Grasselli Chemical Company of Cleveland. What remained was Bayer aspirin and 63 other drug products. Under a

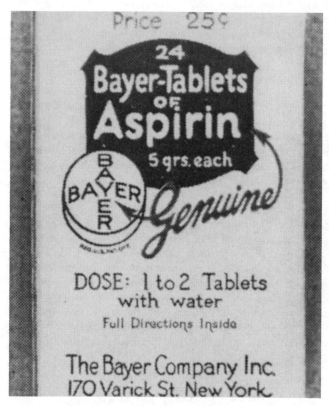

*In 1935 a package of Bayer aspirin cost 25 cents.*

Sterling reorganization, aspirin continued to be made by Bayer Company, and the other drugs were relegated to a newly created Winthrop Chemical Company, named after John Winthrop the Younger (1606–1676), an early chemical manufacturer and governor of the Connecticut colony. One of the primary reasons for Sterling's purchase was, in fact, to acquire the trademark aspirin. Ironically, just 17 months after the purchase, a U.S. judge ruled that "aspirin" had become a generic term for ASA, thus making its use available to any company selling the drug to the public.

One other problem dominated Sterling's early ownership of the Bayer brand. Although Sterling knew how to make aspirin, it was baffled by the technology for producing the company's 63 other drugs. Reluctantly, it decided to approach Farbenfabriken Bayer for help, even though at the time unlicensed trading between American and German companies was against U.S. law. Farbenfabriken Bayer, which continued to sell Bayer aspirin elsewhere in the world, was not pleased to deal with the new owner, and only after torturous negotiations were deals struck in 1920 and 1923. Farbenfabriken Bayer agreed to supply the 63 chemicals, but Sterling gave the German company 50 percent of Winthrop's stock (and thus half of its profit), a percentage of any cost savings from Farbenfabriken Bayer's technical help (especially from the improvement of aspirin production), and 75 percent of all profits

from Bayer aspirin (sold by Sterling but supplied by the Farbenfabriken Bayer) in the then lucrative market of Latin America. Sterling, however, refused to let the German company, which merged into the giant chemical firm IG Farben in 1925, enter the U.S. aspirin market. Beneficial to both companies, the deal would fall apart as World War II approached.

After the war IG Farben was split up by Germany's occupation leaders, and in 1951 the old Bayer company was reinstated as Farbenfabriken Bayer Aktiengesellschaft (renamed Bayer AG in 1972). With little hope of marketing Bayer aspirin in the United States, the German company tried to negotiate with Sterling to buy back the Bayer brand and logo in all other countries. Talks initially led nowhere, and only after 1976—when an Irish judge ruled that both companies could use the brand in Ireland—was a settlement worked out. By 1986 Bayer AG had acquired exclusive rights to the brand and logo everywhere except in the United States and Canada, and even in those countries it obtained limited use of the brand for industrial products.

## U.S. Advertising and Competition

After Sterling acquired Bayer in 1918, the brand's U.S. advertising greatly increased, and for the first time claims were made about the effectiveness of aspirin. An advertisement in 1921, for example, announced that Bayer Aspirin could cure "colds, pain, toothache, neuritis, headache," and "neuralgia."

It was probably name recognition that allowed Bayer to dominate sales in the first decade after World War I, but in the 1930s its competitors began to catch up. Many competing brands, such as Alka-Seltzer, were soluble, while some were a mixture of aspirin and other medicine (for example, Asper-Lax, an aspirin and laxative). To hold back the new competition, Sterling turned to the radio, where Bayer aspirin became one of the most heavily advertised products and was even the sponsor of its own show, the "Bayer Cavalcade of Song." During this period Sterling frequently labeled its competitors as unpure, telling customers, "Thousands of boxes of counterfeit aspirin have been put on the market. Watch out. Take no chances and flatly refuse to accept any box not marked Genuine Bayer Aspirin."

It was after World War II that Bayer began to slip from its dominant position. Its most serious challenge came from three brands: Anacin (founded in 1915), originally a mixture of aspirin, acetanilid, caffeine, and quinine sulfate, though later just aspirin and caffeine; Bufferin (1949), which was aspirin "buffered" with antacids; and Excedrin (1961), initially composed of aspirin, acetophenetidin, caffeine, and salicyclamide. The postwar success of all three brands was largely due to expensive advertising campaigns that focused on the supposed benefit of having extra "pain relieving" ingredients, a tactic that apparently worked, as Bayer's market share dropped to some 25 percent in the early 1950s and almost half of that by 1957, leaving a virtual three-way tie between Bayer, Bufferin, and Anacin for top-share of the analgesics category. In television advertisements in 1957, Sterling tried to defend Bayer by asking, "Why pay more for extra ingredients that can't relieve pain?" The claims of superiority by Bayer's competitors were, in fact, unsubstantiated, but not until the 1970s did the U.S. Federal Trade Commission force drug companies to back up their advertising with clinical studies.

Bayer's market share further tumbled with the rise of two aspirin-free substitutes: Tylenol (acetaminophen), which became popular in the late 1970s, and Advil (ibuprofen), introduced in

1984. Their success can be partially attributed to growing concerns about aspirin, by then thought to be associated with several serious but rare medical problems, such as the childhood illness Reye syndrome. A more common side effect, though still afflicting only about 5 percent of the population, was an upset stomach. Although Tylenol and Advil were not without their own side effects, they quickly rose to the top of the analgesics category, buoyed by savvy advertising and their image as new, state-of-the-art medications. "Doctors recommend Tylenol more than all leading aspirin brands combined" was an effective advertising tag line used during the late 1970s.

Sterling tried several strategies to hold back the new wave of competitors. In 1976, the year Tylenol sales took off, Sterling introduced its own aspirin-free product, Bayer Non-Aspirin, containing acetaminophen. The introduction may have confused customers, who long associated Bayer with "pure aspirin," and despite heavy advertising, the product failed. The following year Sterling tried an aggressive advertising campaign with the slogan, "Makers of Tylenol, Shame on You!" It pointed out that Tylenol was recommended "more than all leading aspirin brands combined" only because doctors rarely specified an aspirin brand. Doctors, in fact, recommended aspirin more frequently than acetaminophen. The Bayer brand, however, continued to slide, with its market share declining to 10 percent in 1977 and 6 percent a decade later. By then Tylenol's share had reached some 30 percent. In 1988 Sterling was acquired by Eastman Kodak Company and three years later renamed Sterling Winthrop Inc.

## Brand Outlook

Although Bayer has lost considerable market share, its future appeared by no means bleak. Most promising have been scientific studies showing new benefits of aspirin. In the 1980s the U.S. Food and Drug Administration approved the daily use of aspirin for the prevention of both recurrent transient ischemic attacks (ministrokes) and second heart attacks. Aspirin's effect on other medical problems, such as first heart attacks, colon cancer, and diabetes, was also being explored. Along with the traditional uses of aspirin, the new indications gave credibility to Bayer's advertising claim as "The Wonder Drug that Works Wonders."

By the early 1990s potential could also be found in the impressive array of new Bayer products, including Extended Release Bayer 8-hour Aspirin, for recurring pain, and Bayer Children's Chewable Aspirin, with only 81 milligrams of aspirin per orange-flavored tablet. Made to be easier on the stomach were Bayer Plus Aspirin, "buffered" with calcium carbonate, magnesium carbonate, and magnesium oxide; and Bayer Enteric Aspirin (designed for people on a physician-prescribed aspirin regimen), which, because of a special coating, allowed the tablet to pass through the stomach and dissolve in the intestines. Especially ambitious was the introduction in September, 1992, of five aspirin-free Bayer "Select" products, containing either acetaminophen or ibuprofen, each designed for a specific pain (head, arthritic, nighttime, menstrual, and sinus). Although with such products Bayer had expanded far beyond its origin as "pure aspirin," the brand's success was likely still tied to its traditional image as a safe, effective, high-quality medicine.

## Further Reading:

Hammonds, Keith H., "Kodak May Wish It Never Went to the Drugstore," *Business Week,* December 4, 1989, pp. 72, 76.

Mann, Charles C. and Mark L. Plummer, *The Aspirin Wars,* New York: Alfred A. Knopf, 1991.

Mellow, Craig, "Winning Hearts and Minds in the Aspirin Market," *Across the Board,* October 1989, pp. 20–27.

Sloan, Pat, "Bayer Buoyed with New Extension," *Advertising Age,* December 2, 1991, pp. 3, 46.

Sloan, "Bayer to Offer Non-Aspirin Pain Reliever," *Advertising Age,* July 13, 1992, p. 12.

Sloan, and Gary Levin, "Lintas Quits Bayer Account," *Advertising Age,* April 22, 1991, pp. 3, 39.

Winters, Patricia, "Bayer Shifts Tactics," *Advertising Age,* January 2, 1989, pp. 3, 30.

Winters, and Steven W. Colford, "Aspirin Marketers Await Guidelines," *Advertising Age,* July 24, 1989, p. 80.

*—Thomas Riggs*

# BIC®

The now-familiar Bic brand name initially graced a line of inexpensive ballpoint pens. Since then the brand has come to include such items as disposable butane cigarette lighters and disposable safety razors. These products are sold in the United States by Bic Corporation, a subsidiary of the French company Société Bic S.A. Bic products were also represented in more than 90 other countries.

## Brand Origins

Marcel Bich, an Italian baron who became a naturalized French citizen, was the production manager for a French ink company in 1945 when he decided to set up his own business outside of Paris making parts for fountain pens and mechanical pencils. That same year, Chicago entrepreneur Milton Reynolds introduced the first ballpoint pen in the United States. The pen created a sensation at Gimbel's in New York even though it sold for a hefty $12.50. Such pens were also becoming popular in Europe, and Bich recognized the potential for a low-cost, reliable ballpoint pen. In 1949 he introduced his own pen, a non-refillable ballpoint with a simple plastic barrel, which he sold for as little as 19 cents. He used a phonetic version of his own name, ''Bic,'' as the brand name.

Many early ballpoint pens were unreliable, often clogging, skipping, leaking or smearing. Bich's pens, however, proved to be of better quality, despite their low price. They were a huge success in the European market, with annual sales exceeding $5 million by 1955. Thus having become the leading maker of ballpoint pens in Europe, Bich turned his attention to the United States.

In 1958 Bich bought the Seymour, Connecticut-based Waterman Pen Company. Waterman Pen had been founded by Lewis E. Waterman, an American insurance salesman and part-time inventor who developed the first practical fountain pen in 1884. At one time, Waterman Pen was the world's leading maker of fountain pens, but in the 1950s, while the company ignored the growing popularity of ballpoint pens and profits began to plummet. Bich initially purchased 60 percent of the company's stock for $1 million. Soon after the purchase, Bich moved the reorganized Waterman-Bic Pen Corporation to Milford, Connecticut, which remained corporate headquarters into the 1990s. The name was changed to Bic Pen Corporation in 1971, then again in 1982 to Bic Corporation.

The inexpensive Bic pens did not catch on as quickly in the United States as they had in Europe, probably because the U.S. market had been flooded with shoddy pens made by other companies. Bich's U.S. managers urged him to make a more expensive ballpoint to compete with the PaperMate brand, which had been purchased by The Gillette Company in 1955. PaperMate pens were then the leading brand in the ''over-a-dollar'' market. Bich, however, was adamant. He reportedly told his advisers, ''Waterman is 100 percent mine. You are going to do what you are told.''

Waterman-Bic then launched an aggressive advertising campaign, claiming that its pens would write ''first time, every time.'' To overcome the skepticism that a 29-cent ballpoint would perform as well as pens costing several times more, the company created a series of television commercials—many of them live—that showed ''Bic Crystal '' pens still working after being drilled through wallboard, shot from guns, fire-blasted, and strapped to the feet of ice skaters and flamenco dancers. Bic pens also were sold through grocery stores and shops near schools where students gathered, rather than in the traditional department stores.

After a rocky start, Waterman-Bic soon established itself as the largest maker of ballpoint pens in the United States. By 1967 the company was turning out nearly 500 million Bic ballpoint pens a year, accounting for nearly 60 percent of the U.S. market. In 1972 a *Time* article opined that ''Baron Bich has done for ballpoints what Henry Ford did for cars: he has produced a cheap but serviceable model.''

In 1974 a *Forbes* correspondent noted that, ''From the start, Bich concentrated on the cheap end of the market—but with a difference. Where his competitors were turning out junk, Bich made a reliable pen that could command a premium, but still cheap price. . . . By the time his competitors figured out how to build an equally good pen for the price, Bich had a lock on the market.'' One of those competitors was Gillette, which introduced its own low-cost line of ballpoint pens under the Write Bros. brand name to compete with Bic and its own PaperMate brand.

For many years, Bic was content to make only non-retractable ballpoint pens, primarily the yellow Bic Stic and the original, clear-plastic Bic Crystal. Then in 1968, the company introduced the retractable Bic Clic. Since then, the company has introduced a variety of Bic pens and mechanical pencils, including the Bic Banana, a fine-line marker marketed in the mid-1970s. In 1992 Bic

## AT A GLANCE

**B**ic brand of ballpoint pens founded in 1949 by Marcel Bich, owner of the French corporation, Société Bic S.A.; Bic pens introduced in United States by Bic-Waterman Corporation, subsidiary of Société Bic, in 1958; U.S. subsidiary name changed to Bic Pen Corporation in 1971, then to Bic Corporation in 1982; brand applied to disposable butane cigarette lighters in 1973 and disposable razors in 1977; Wite-Out brand correction fluid purchased in 1992, renamed Bic Wite-Out.

**Performance:** *Market share*—60% of ballpoint pen market; 56% of disposable lighter market; 45% of disposable razor category. *Sales*—(for pens and other stationery products) $216.2 million; (for disposable lighters) $101 million; (for disposable razors) $74.6 million; (for sporting goods) $5.6 million.

**Major competitor:** The Gillette Company's PaperMate and Write Bros. ballpoint pens; The Gillette Company's Good News! disposable razors; Scripto brand disposable lighters; Liquid Paper correction fluid.

**Advertising:** *Agency*—Slater, Hanft, Martin, New York, NY, 1982—. *Major campaign*—(for lighters) "Flick my Bic"; (for razors) "I'm A Bic Man."

**Addresses:** *Parent company*—Bic Corporation, 500 Bic Drive, Milford, CT 06460; phone: (203) 783-2000. *Ultimate parent company*—Société Bic, S.A.

created a line of multi-colored ballpoint pens called Bic Wavelengths, and in 1993 the company created Bic Body Heat pens, which changed colors when held.

## Bic Enters the Disposable Lighter Market

Bic, whose head-to-head competition with Gillette began with ballpoint pens in the late 1960s, also found itself competing with Gillette in the market for disposable cigarette lighters in the early 1970s. Gillette entered the market first with its 1970 purchase of the S.T. Dupont Company, a French manufacturer whose principal product was a line of luxury cigarette lighters selling for hundreds of dollars, supplemented by the disposable Cricket lighter that the company had developed. Two years later Gillette introduced Cricket in the United States. Bic was not far behind. Late in 1972 a *Time* report stated, "A disposable Bic cigarette lighter that gives 3,000 lights is being test-marketed in Sweden; if it proves out, Bich plans to sell it for less than 90¢."

Bic launched its disposable lighter in the United States in 1973, although it was initially priced at $1.49. To catch up with Gillette, Bic again turned to creative television advertising. A series of commercials, which viewers either found amusing or irritating, showed sensuous women urging cigarette smokers to "Flick My Bic," a catch phrase with off-color connotations that soon became part of the national lexicon.

In 1977 Bic slashed the wholesale price of its lighters by almost one third, allowing them to be sold at retail for less than one dollar and setting off a fierce price war with Gillette's Cricket. By the end of 1978 Bic had pulled ahead of Cricket. In 1984 Gillette acknowledged defeat and pulled the Cricket lighter, leaving Bic with about 65 percent of the market. Gillette later sold Cricket to Swedish Match, which licensed the lighter for distribution in the U.S.

In 1985 Bic introduced the Bic 2000, a fixed-flame, compact version of its original Bic lighter. Early advertising stressed the lighter's advanced technology, but consumers were more fascinated with the lighter's size—it fit inside a pack of cigarettes. Consumers also insisted on referring to it as the "mini Bic," so in 1986 the name was officially changed. A new advertising campaign touted the Mini-Bic as "so advanced it goes where no lighter has gone before." In later years Bic created lighters featuring such decorative motifs as sports, flowers, and western scenes.

## Product Liability

After 15 years on the market, the Bic disposable lighter came under intense scrutiny in 1987 because of safety concerns. Apparently Bic had experienced problems for some time with its lighters flaring up while they were being used or accidentally igniting when not in use. The *New York Times* reported that, "claims began to trickle in soon after Bic introduced its throwaway lighters in 1972, [however] the company has until recently been able to keep the cases quiet by settling them out of court, usually making secrecy one of the terms of the settlement." The newspaper reported that three people had died from incidents involving Bic lighters, and that Bic had settled more than 20 cases out of court for amounts ranging from $5,000 to almost $500,000.

Then in 1986, in the first case to go to trial, a jury found the company liable for extensive burn injuries suffered by a woman who claimed her lighter ignited in a shirt pocket while she was on a camping trip. Design engineers cited evidence that Bic lighters occasionally leaked and that debris could cause the shut-off valve to fail. The woman's lawyers also cited a quality-control audit, conducted by Bic in 1983, that indicated 1.2 percent of the lighters Bic tested failed to extinguish when they were supposed to. Bic eventually paid the woman $3.25 million in damages.

Although more lawsuits followed, Bic maintained that most of the incidents were caused by user negligence. According to the company, it successfully defended itself in more than 50 lawsuits involving lighter liability between 1988 and 1993. It lost three cases, two of which were under appeal in 1993. In its 1992 annual report, Bic said, "The legal expenses of defending product liability claims involving lighters continue to be heavy. However, as a result of our longstanding philosophy to vigorously defend these claims, and our success in doing so, the number of lawsuits continues to decline."

Concerns were also raised in the late 1980s about the number of fires started by children playing with disposable lighters. In 1987 the Consumer Product Safety Commission asked manufacturers to make their lighters "child resistant," and three years later the request became mandatory. The child-safety standards were expected to become effective in 1994.

In the meantime, in 1992 Bic introduced a lighter with a patented "child resistant" latch that, according to the company, was the result of a seven-year, $21 million development program. The Child Guard lighter required that a safety latch be moved to the side and up before it would light. The latch slid back into place automatically after each use.

In one of the lawsuits under appeal in 1993, a jury in Creek County, Oklahoma, found Bic responsible for injuries to three children who were severely burned while playing with a Bic lighter. In 1992 the jury awarded the children $22 million in actual and punitive damages. The lighter allegedly exploded when it was dropped while lit. Attorneys for the children, the oldest of whom was five years old at the time, argued that the lighter should have been more child-resistant. Bic argued that the grandparents should not have allowed the children to play with the lighter.

Bic lighters may also have suffered a legal setback late in 1992 when the U.S. Court of Appeals in Philadelphia ruled that manufacturers of a product that is completely safe when used as it was intended may also have an obligation to make it safe for unforeseeable situations. The ruling involved a case in which a three-year-old child took a Bic lighter from his father's pants pocket and set fire to an infant's bedclothes. The case, Griggs v. Bic Corp., was remanded to the lower court that originally had dismissed the case.

### Bic vs. Gillette, Again

Having confronted Gillette in the market for ballpoint pens and disposable lighters, perhaps it was inevitable that the two companies should also face off over Gillette's best-known product, the razor. Ever since King C. Gillette invented the safety razor in 1903, the company he founded dominated the U.S. market, selling increasingly advanced and profitable "razor systems" that included reusable handles and replacement blades. Then in 1975, Société Bic introduced an inexpensive, disposable razor in the European market. This was followed in 1976 by the American debut of the single-blade Bic Shaver.

Gillette's entry in the U.S. disposable market was the Good News! twin-blade razor, but very little was spent to promote the new product. The company underestimated the disposable market, predicting that disposable razors would account for, at most, only 7 percent of the wet-shave market. Even *Newsweek* reported in 1976 that, "the new razors may prove to be an iffy product." In addition, every Good News! customer meant one less customer for Gillette's more profitable razor systems. As *Esquire* put it in 1980, since disposable razors cost more to make and sold for less that Gillette's replacement blades, "Every time Good News! gains a couple points of market share, Gillette loses millions of dollars in sales and profits."

On the other hand, Bic advertised heavily, again turning to catchy television commercials. In one series of commercials people were blindfolded and then shaved by professional barbers, using either the Bic Shaver or Gillette's non-disposable Trac II razor. In the commercials, 58 percent of the participants said there was no difference between the Bic shave and the Gillette shave. Gillette was so enraged by the ads that the company's vice president of marketing met with representatives of the three television networks and asked them not to run the commercials unless Bic could document its claims.

By the end of 1979 Gillette and Bic each had about 50 percent of the market for disposables, which already accounted for 20 percent of the total market for wet-shave razors. Disposables were especially popular among teenagers and women. Women, in particular, were taken with the Bic Lady Shaver, the first razor specifically designed and marketed with them in mind.

By the late 1980s, disposables accounted for about half the wet-shave market. In the struggle for market share, Bic scored big with the Bic Shaver for Sensitive Skin in 1985 and the Bic Metal Shaver in 1988, but the following year Gillette managed to cut into the market for disposables with its Sensor razor system, which reportedly cost $200 million to develop. At the time, Gillette

stopped advertising its disposable razors to concentrate on its new Sensor system. In 1990 Bic introduced the Bic Pastel, another razor designed especially for women. Two years later Bic launched its first line of twin-blade razors. At the time, Bic and Gillette were nearly even in the disposable market, with about 45 percent each, though Gillette still dominated the total wet-shave market with more than 60 percent, compared to about 20 percent for Bic.

### Brand Name Applied to Other Products

Bic's line of sporting goods included the Bic Sailboard, which was introduced in the early 1980s and quickly became the market leader. However, Bic Sport was forced to stop selling the sailboard in the United States in 1985 when a U.S. District Court ruled that Bic had infringed on a patent owned by Windsurfing International. Bic reintroduced the sailboard to the U.S. market when the patent expired in 1987.

In 1989 Bic launched a line of inexpensive, pocket-sized perfume "spritzers," attempting to do for French perfume what it had done for ballpoint pens and disposable lighters and razors. Marketed under the name Parfum Bic, the fragrances were first introduced by Société Bic in Europe, where they were sold with other Bic products. However, Bic's successes had come from what *Esquire* once called "commoditization," the "devolution . . . of certain expensive durables . . . into inexpensive, nonstatus, more or less disposable items." Analysts were skeptical that U.S. consumers would accept an inexpensive perfume the same way they had accepted other low-cost Bic products, since French perfumes were traditionally marketed with an image of luxury and snob appeal.

The analysts proved right. Despite a print and television advertising campaign touting the fragrances as "Paris in your pocket," at a cost that was estimated by *Advertising Age* to be $22 million, Parfum Bic lasted less than a year on the U.S. market. The fragrances lasted longer in Europe, but were eventually pulled from the overseas market in 1991. Bic also briefly marketed Bic pantyhose in the mid-1970s after Société Bic bought DIM, one of the biggest hosiery companies in France. However, with decreasing demand due to changes in women's fashions and stiff competition from such established brands as L'eggs, the line never succeeded.

### Future Directions

In 1992 Bic purchased Wite-Out Products, Inc., the second largest maker of correction fluid in the United States. The line of correction fluids was reintroduced as Bic Wite-Out. The company also changed the name of its Writing Instruments division to Stationery Products, indicating an intention to market an expanded line of stationery-related items. Although the market for disposable cigarette lighters was beginning to reflect the declining demand for tobacco products, the market for disposable shavers continued to be strong, and Bic was aggressively expanding that product line.

### Further Reading:

"Are the Talents Transferable?" *Forbes,* April 1, 1974, p. 62.

Armstrong, Jeffrey D., "Bic Corp.: 'The stock will strengthen as the issue of lighter safety fades.' " *Barron's,* October 12, 1987, p. 69.

"Ballpoint pens that work," *Changing Times,* April 1973, p. 14.

"Bic abandons the basics," *Packaging Digest,* March 1992, p. 36.

"Bich the Ballpoint King," *Fortune,* August 15, 1969, p. 122.

Cooper, Wendy, "The case of the exploding lighters," *Institutional Investor,* December 1987, p. 209.

"Discovering the potential in Bic," *Business Week,* July 30, 1979, p. 65.

"Extinguished: Gillette puts out its Cricket," *Time,* October 15, 1984, p. 93.

Flax, Steven, "Why Bic got flicked," *Forbes,* September 27, 1982, p. 38.

"Gillette challenges Bic to verify its ad claims," *Business Week,* March 19, 1979, p. 32.

"Going Bananas Over Bic, *Time,* December 18, 1972, p. 93.

Hayes, Linda Snyder, "Gillette Takes the Wraps Off," *Fortune,* February 25, 1980, p. 148.

"An Igniting Controversy," *Time,* April 20, 1987, p. 56.

Ingrassia, Lawrence, "Gillette Holds Its Edge By Endlessly Searching For a Better Shave," *Wall Street Journal,* December 10, 1992, p. A1.

King, Resa W., "Will $4 perfume do the trick for Bic?" *Business Week,* June 20, 1988, p. 89.

Langway, Lynn, "Razor Fighting," *Newsweek,* November 22, 1976, p. 103.

Moskowitz, Daniel, "Courts Tackle Safety Liability in Product Design," *Washington Post,* February 8, 1993, p. WB11.

"Razors & blades," *Consumer Reports,* May 1989, p. 300.

"Scents and Sensibility," *Time,* May 20, 1991, p. 47.

Sloan, Pat, "$22M campaign urges: Spritz your Bic," *Advertising Age,* February 20, 1989, p. 3; "Bic pulls fragrances after flickering sales," *Advertising Age,* March 12, 1990, p. 77.

"Starting To Click; Mainstay Products Help Bic Mark Profit Gains," *Barron's,* June 23, 1986, p. 52

Warner, Liz, "Bic scents a quick killing," *Marketing,* June 30, 1988, p. 1.

"Waterman-Bic Pen Corp.: On the ball with the ballpoint," *Nation's Business,* December 1970, p. 72.

Welles, Chris, "The War of the Razors," *Esquire,* February 1980, p. 29.

Winters, Patricia, "Multi-million-dollar push for Mini-Bic," *Advertising Age,* June 2, 1986, p. 37.

—*Dean Boyer*

# BON AMI®

Like the phoenix rising from the ashes, Bon Ami's trademark little yellow chick is rebounding after a not too recent past of dismal business failures and bad management. Bon Ami, a nonabrasive cleanser with the catchy slogan "Hasn't scratched yet," has been an American brand since the late 1800s. Now owned by the Faultless Starch/Bon Ami Company of Kansas City, Missouri, the brand is expected to stake its claim as the first pure nonabrasive cleanser and polisher.

## Brand Origins

In the late 19th century, it was customary to make cleaning soap out of pulverized quartz, which served as an effective abrasive. Mined from quarries in the northeast, quartz was often embedded with feldspar, a fine, powdery substance that had to be separated from the quartz and was often discarded as useless.

However, Scottish-born John T. Robertson of Manchester, Connecticut, decided to recycle feldspar, which could be used to polish metal to a shiny finish. In 1886, Robertson turned an old grist mill into a soap factory where he mixed discarded feldspar with liquid soap in wooden troughs. He cured and cut the mixture into cakes and called it Bon Ami. Bon Ami was sold in quarter-gross boxes in bar form. During the 1880s the J.T. Robertson Company also manufactured a Sapolio scouring soap made from finely ground quartz and tallow soap.

By 1896, Bon Ami, which means "good friend" in French, had established itself as a brand name. Its distinctive packaging and slogan were widely recognized; the label carried a picture of a yellow chick and the words, "Hasn't scratched yet." The reference was probably more well known at the turn of the century: a newly-hatched chick will not scratch the ground for food for two to three days after it hatches because it can survive off the yolk. Bon Ami used this clever slogan to emphasize its nonabrasive qualities.

## Early Marketing Strategy

Bon Ami became a well-known brand in the northeast and by 1913 was being sold in powder form. A. W. Erickson, the founder of Erickson Advertising and forefather of McCann-Erickson Worldwide is credited with being Bon Ami's first advertising agent. Though the agency did not invent the yellow chick trademark logo or the "Hasn't scratched yet" slogan, it advised the J.T. Robertson Company to never abandon it.

J.T. Robertson Company's early advertising for Bon Ami featured paintings by famous Pennsylvania artist Ben Austrian. Each advertisement was a portrait in oil depicting a "practical, middle-aged housewife" using Bon Ami. Between 1904 and 1913, Erickson switched Bon Ami advertising from newspapers and advertising cards to full-length color ads in leading women's magazines.

Bon Ami as a soft, pure, but powerful cleanser and polisher remained a top seller even through the Depression because it did not scratch porcelain. According to David P. Garino in a 1978 *Wall Street Journal* article, Bon Ami's sales in the 1920s were close to $30 million a year. In the 1930s, he writes, "Bon Ami was one of the 'Golden 16' companies that never failed to pay a dividend."

## Mismanagement

But after 50 years of growth, the brand was undermined by slowing sales and fraud from within the company. According to the *Wall Street Journal*, Alexander Guterma had control of the company in 1958 and "bled its assets and mortgaged its factory." Bon Ami and another held Guterma-held company were suspended from being traded on the New York Stock Exchange, and Guterma was later convicted of fraud and imprisoned.

After the Guterma episode, Bon Ami changed hands several times. Company founders had sold out in the 1950s and by the late 1960s, the Bon Ami cleanser brand almost disappeared from store shelves. Key to the brand's demise was the failure of the company to live up to its promotional promises. For example, grocers had been promised television ad support if Bon Ami was carried, but were left holding the bag.

Bon Ami suffered another public embarassment when the company attempted to advertise the brand during an NBC *Today Show* broadcast. The Bon Ami yellow chick made a guest appearance, but appeared sluggish and drowsy on camera. Irate viewers deluged company headquarters with mail charging company officials with drugging the chick.

Bon Ami cleanser's misfortunes enabled Colgate-Palmolive's Ajax and Procter & Gamble's Comet cleansers to outsell Bon Ami. Both brands gained their substantial shares of the market

## AT A GLANCE

**B**on Ami brand of cleanser invented in 1886 by John T. Robertson, who combined soft, powdery mineral feldspar and liquid soap into a non-abrasive cleanser in cake bar form; Bon Ami first marketed in 1892; Bon Ami offered in powder form in 1913; trademark registered in 1916; J.T. Robertson Company sold to the Faultless Starch Company, manufacturer of consumer laundry and household cleaning products, 1971; company renamed Faultless Starch/Bon Ami Company, 1974.

**Performance:** *Market share*—5% (third-largest share) of cleanser category.

**Major competitor:** Clorox's Soft Scrub; also Procter & Gamble Company's Comet and Colgate-Palmolive Company's Ajax.

**Advertising:** *Major campaign*—Print campaign led by an in-house advertising department depicting a little yellow chick emblem with tagline, "I Hasn't Scratched Yet."

**Addresses:** *Parent company*—Faultless Starch/Bon Ami Company, 1025 W. 8th St., Kansas City, MO 64101; phone: (816) 842-1230; fax: (815) 842-3417.

with the help of million dollar advertising budgets. The ad budget for Bon Ami did not exceed $250,000 annually until the 1970s, and this meager investment was clearly insufficient to compete with the marketing giants Colgate-Polmolive and Procter & Gamble. In 1971, Bon Ami held only 1 percent of the market.

It wasn't until 1971 when the family-owned Kansas City-based Faultless Starch Company purchased Bon Ami that the cleanser's luck began to change. The Faultless Starch Company manufactured and marketed laundry and household cleaning products, and, like Bon Ami, began in 1886. Major Gordon T. Beaham and his descendants have led the company from a single-brand focus—laundry starch—to its biggest acquisition, Bon Ami Cleanser.

### Brand Development

Gordon T. Beaham III (Major Beaham's great grandson) saw his company's biggest purchase as a gamble. When Faultless Starch had purchased the brand it included the soap bar form (still made on a 1905 soap cutting machine that used piano wires), the powder version, and Bon Ami Deluxe Polishing Cleanser, an updated formula of the powder with detergent and bleach. To highlight its purchase of Bon Ami, the company changed its name to Faultless Starch/Bon Ami Company in 1974. Company documents state that sales management had "become weary of so many customers saying: 'Oh, I didn't know you had Bon Ami, too!'"

Beaham III began his efforts to revive the brand by rectifying previous marketing mistakes and by increasing advertising spending. The brand began to turn a profit for the first time in 1977, and by 1978 it was reported in the *Wall Street Journal* that Bon Ami sales had "quadrupled to about $4 million annually" and that the brand had regained 3 percent of the U.S. cleanser market.

Beaham III launched 30-second television spots, but the mainstay of the advertising for Bon Ami, with its $750,000 annual ad budget, remained in women's magazine print ads. He then appealed to supermarkets and grocery stores for shelf space by visiting stores and handing out samples to shoppers. A team of 68 brokers distributed Bon Ami to the major supermarket chains,

including Kroger, Safeway, and A&P. However, it wasn't easy wooing some supermarkets. Kroger Supermarkets in the Nashville, Tennessee, area had refused to stock the brand because of its limited sales potential. Beaham III told the *Wall Street Journal* in 1978 that he had even been thrown out of some stores.

Other attempts at reviving the brand consisted of obtaining endorsements from cookware manufacturers, relying on loyal users, pitching the benefits of Bon Ami to newlyweds, and hyping the product's many uses. The University of Maryland's Natural Resources Institute was known to use Bon Ami to clean laboratory bowls used in raising crab larvae. Martin Marietta Corp. in the early 1970s used Bon Ami to clean scuff marks off the interior of Skylab. General Motors' Delco Division was even using Bon Ami to test windshield wipers. A customer wrote Faultless Starch/Bon Ami saying she wanted to try using Bon Ami as a shampoo to get rust out of her hair.

### Advertising Innovations

In 1980, Faultless Starch/Bon Ami Company launched a major advertising campaign to boost sales of Bon Ami Cleanser. The campaign focused on magazine spreads that featured the original Bon Ami trademark and by the headline: "Never Underestimate the Cleaning Power of a 94-Year-Old Chick With a French Name." Company documents indicate that during the first six

*An early cake of Bon Ami soap, complete with chick and slogan.*

months of the campaign, sales increased 12 percent. Heavy promotion had paid off. Bon Ami print advertising won the 1980 *Sales & Marketing Management Magazine Excellence* Award as the best print advertising campaign for that year. The same campaign also won the Golden Effic Award for consumer product print advertising, presented annually by the New York Chapter of the American Marketing Association.

In 1986, *Consumer Reports* described Bon Ami as "one of the most effective, yet one of the gentlest products" and rated it higher than Comet, Ajax, Soft Scrub, and Old Dutch. Bon Ami soon began finding new users among environmentalists who praised the brand for its purity and non-abrasiveness. Bon Ami Cleanser is a biodegradable, grease-cutting detergent that contains no perfume, dyes, or chlorine. Doctors recommend it to patients who are sensitive to the perfumes and chemicals found in other household cleaners.

In part because it doesn't scratch or leave a gritty residue like cleansers that contain silica, such top brands as Corning Ware, Farberware, Anchor Hocking, Pyrex, Rival, U.S. Ceramic Tile, West Bend, and Kohler started recommending Bon Ami for their products. Bon Ami can be used in a wide variety of ways: In addition to using it on everything from bathroom surfaces to cookware, Bon Ami, mixed with other materials, can help remove blood and wine stains from fabrics. It can clean vinyl and polish chrome, as well as clean windows and mirrors.

## Future Growth

According to Faultless Starch/Bon Ami Company records, the Bon Ami line is distributed nationally and has approximately 5 percent of the cleanser market, ranking as the third best selling powdered cleanser in the United States. When Faultless Starch/Bon Ami purchased the company and brand name in 1971, it also purchased the brand name in 47 countries. Bon Ami had been sold worldwide from 1910 through the 1940s, and company officials stated recently that they hoped to reintroduce the brand worldwide at some future date. The challenge for the Faultless Starch/Bon Ami Company will be to sell younger consumers on Bon Ami's reliability as an old brand name. Bill Saporito in *Fortune* underscored part of the problem when he asked, "How many consumers under age 70 even understand Bon Ami's famous 'Hasn't Scratched Yet' slogan?" He added, "Another problem: the company can't afford much for advertising."

The current trend toward natural products that don't pollute may help relaunch Bon Ami Cleanser; if so, it's likely to happen with little fanfare. Company officials in the fall of 1993 planned full-size advertisements in environmental newsletters and periodicals. However, as a small company on a small budget, Faultless Starch/Bon Ami is unlikely to launch a major advertising campaign on the scale of its glitzy competitors in the near future. For the moment, Bon Ami continues to hold its own.

## Further Reading:

"Cleansers: One Stood Out," *Consumer Reports,* January 1990, p. 61–63.

Garino, David P., "A Cute Little Chick, A Catchy Slogan—And An Uphill Battle," *Wall Street Journal,* May 18, 1978, p. 1.

Saporito, Bill, "Has-Been Brands Go Back to Work," *Fortune,* April 28, 1986, p. 123.

"Scouring Cleansers," *Consumer Reports,* December 1986, p. 224.

*—Evelyn S. Dorman*

# BORAXO®/20 MULE TEAM® BORAX

Boraxo and 20 Mule Team Borax, a natural detergent booster, are among the oldest brands in the United States. Borax's familiar trademark, a 20 mule team and wagons, has graced the product's packaging for over 100 years. The story of 20 Mule Team Borax is directly tied to the lore and mystique of Death Valley, where a deposit of borax—a white crystalline, mildly alkaline salt—was discovered in the 1880s. Borax miners used huge wagons hitched to 20 mule teams to haul borax out of the rocky, desolate valley to Mohave. The product may have reached the apex of its popularity when 20 Mule Team Borax sponsored "Death Valley Days," first a radio show and later a television show hosted by actor and future U.S. President Ronald Reagan.

20 Mule Team Borax eventually came to be a big seller for The Dial Corp, which owns the 20 Mule Team product line. In addition to its laundry booster, the line includes such products as Boraxo Tile, Porcelain and Fiberglass Cleaner, Boraxo Waterless Hand Cleaner, and Borateem bleach. The major ingredient in most of the 20 Mule Team products is borax, a naturally occurring mineral composed of sodium, boron, oxygen, and water.

## Brand Origins

The 20 Mule Team brand name was adopted around 1891 at the urging of a young advertising manager for Pacific Coast Borax Company. Francis Marion Smith, the president of the company and a major producer of borax since 1873, had been decorating his borax packages for years with a distinctive cartoon of a mule team and wagons, first placed there by his brother and former partner, Julius. Although Smith had originally favored using his own name as the brand name, he eventually recognized that 20 Mule Team Borax was the logical choice, according to Richard Lingenfelter in *Death Valley and the Amargosa.*

Smith, a prospector and woodcutter, had "struck it rich" by discovering borax in Teel's Marsh, Nevada, in 1872. He and his brother formed a borax refinery, Smith Brothers, the following year. In 1880, acting alone, Smith purchased the Pacific Borax Company. Soon after, he learned of borax deposits in Death Valley, promptly acquired the rights to them, and established the Harmony Borax Works to refine the borax. It was there, in 1883, that the famous 20 mule teams began hauling borax in specially designed wagons to the railroad at Mojave, 165 miles to the southwest. Several of Smith's borax interests were consolidated

into Pacific Coast Borax Company in 1890, with Smith named president and majority stockholder.

## Early Marketing Strategy

When Smith first began mining borax, he was faced with a dilemma: how to market a relatively unknown product in a depressed American economy. He decided to open a small office in New York City and launch a marketing campaign to sell borax to the public. In keeping with the exaggerated advertising claims of the era, Smith produced literature proclaiming that borax was not only ideal for use in the laundry, but would clean black cashmere, cameos, and coral; keep milk and cream sweet; cure "nervous headache"; and act as a preventative against diphtheria, "lung fever," and kidney trouble.

In the mid-1870s, Smith joined forces with William T. Coleman and Company, a marketing firm that had been a selling agent in the borax industry for many years. U.S. Borax and Chemical Company, the lineal corporate descendent of Smith Brothers, still retains hand-out cards dating from the mid-1870s, which advertise the many uses of Smith's product—washing, starching, preventing the appearance of moths and cockroaches, dressing wounds, softening chapped skin, bathing, cleaning clothes, and preserving milk and cream. "Very likely F. M. Smith himself used these very cards in his opening sales campaign in New York City in 1885," wrote George Hildebrand in *Borax Pioneer: Francis Marion Smith.*

## Advertising Innovations

As head of the Pacific Coast Borax Company, Smith became involved in several innovative schemes to promote borax. Stephen Tyng Mather, the young man who urged him to adopt the "20 Mule Team" brand name, approached Smith about 1891 with the idea of drawing on the lore and mystique of Death Valley to sell borax. A former cub reporter for the *New York Sun,* Mather arranged to have one of the *Sun*'s feature writers go to Death Valley and write the story of borax and its Death Valley connections. The result was the first popular book on the valley, *Illustrated Sketches of Death Valley and Other Borax Deserts of the Pacific Coast,* published in 1892.

Smith was so impressed with the result that he hired Mather to launch a campaign to develop a home market for borax. Since

## AT A GLANCE

**2**0 Mule Team Borax brand of detergent booster developed by Pacific Coast Borax Company president Francis Marion Smith around 1892; sold by a succession of companies over the years; product line owned by The Dial Corp beginning in 1988.

**Addresses:** *Parent company*—The Dial Corp, Dial Tower, Phoenix, AZ 85077; phone: (602) 207-4000; fax: (602) 207-5900.

Smith was unwilling to spend much money on advertising, Mather had to come up with innovative marketing strategies. Using press releases and letters to the editor, he offered a dollar to anyone who sent in a published testimonial letter extolling the virtues of borax. He compiled the testimonials—along with some of his own planting—into a booklet entitled "Borax: From the Desert, Through the Press, Into the Home: 200 Best Borax Recipes from More than 800 Issues of 250 Different Publications in 33 States of the Union." Mather set up a distribution office in Chicago and launched several other successful promotions that helped make borax a household word across the country. He stayed with the firm until 1903.

Despite Mather's departure, Smith continued to come up with innovative approaches to marketing his product. In 1904, he resurrected two of the old Death Valley wagons, trained a new team and sent them to the St. Louis Exposition. He even created the character of "Borax Bill," the driver of the team, to add to the excitement. The St. Louis appearance was so successful that Smith sent the team on a tour of the East to hand out free samples of the product.

At the same time, Smith published another booklet, entitled "The 20 Mule Team and a Sketch of its Famous Driver: Borax Bill." William Parkinson, who played the character, had never actually driven the Death Valley teams but looked the part. "A short, stout, feisty man with a walrus moustache, he put the big team through its paces with a black snake whip and a string of curses that made the crowds gasp," wrote Richard Lingenfelter in *Death Valley and the Amargosa*. In 1916, the Pacific Coast Borax Company once again resurrected the old 20 mule team wagons, recruiting a new Borax Bill, Frank Wilson, to drive them from the Pasadena Rose Parade through the Eastern states for a five-year tour. Even the company that made the machines that boxed the borax for market, the Pneumatic Scale Corporation, got into the act. They published a booklet entitled "The Romance of the Desert," which repeated the tales of the borax teams and told of their role in ensuring full measure in every box, so that old "Borax Bill did not work in vain," according to Lingenfelter.

The 20 Mule Team products continued to maintain a high profile through the 1950s, thanks to a popular show first made popular on the radio and later broadcast on television. Many people still remember with fondness the show, "Death Valley Days," sponsored by 20 Mule Team products. The first half-hour radio show was broadcast in 1930. The show made its TV debut in 1952, with Ronald Reagan as host. Over the years, many Hollywood celebrities promoted the products, including Robert Taylor, Rosemary DeCamp, and Dale Roberts. The product line garnered some free publicity in 1940 when a short film, *Twenty Mule Team,* toured the country's movie houses. The film starred Wallace Beery and told the tale of the famous 20 mule teams.

Today, The Dial Corp, which owns the 20 Mule Team product line, does virtually no advertising for the products. Instead, Dial counts on loyal users to spread the word, according to a newsletter published by U.S. Borax, which sold the 20 Mule Team product line to Dial in 1988 and continues to sell the company borax. "In the past, parents have shared their laundry secrets with their children, and, in turn, their children have passed the secrets on to the next generation," the newsletter stated. Dial did, however, redesign a former U.S. Borax booklet entitled "The Magic Crystal," that describes how borax can be used around the house. More than a quarter of a million people requested the brochure in 1992.

### Brand Development

20 Mule Team Borax, which celebrated its 100th anniversary in 1991, remains the same after all these years—99.5 percent pure borax. Trace minerals comprise the remaining .5 percent. Although borax is primarily used as a laundry water conditioner to help boost cleaning power, it has many other uses: all-purpose household cleaner, deodorizing the refrigerator, washing fine china, cleaning windows and floors—even preserving fresh cut flowers. In earlier times, 20 Mule Team Borax was proclaimed to be a "magic crystal" and was thought to aid digestion, keep milk sweet, and even cure epilepsy. Homemakers found dozens of other uses for borax over the years—from killing cockroaches and spiders to fertilizing soil. The company now makes no claims that it is either safe or useful for those special purposes.

Although 20 Mule Team Borax hasn't changed over the years, the package has. In 1992, legendary Borax Bill disappeared from the box. Borax Bill, often mistaken as a girl with wavy locks, first appeared on the box in 1986. Neon orange type on a bold green box has replaced the little "mule skinner." The change was designed to help new buyers identify with the product's uses more quickly. The words "Natural Laundry Booster" took the place of "Nature's Freshener," and the box features a small collage of freshly washed clothes and the familiar 20 mule team and wagons.

Since 20 Mule Team Borax was first introduced, many other products have sported the 20 Mule Team trademark. The major ingredient in most of the products has been borax. In 1905, Boraxo, a polishing cleanser of borax and soap powders, was introduced under the 20 Mule Team trademark. Many people still remember the product's familiar tin package, designed in 1935 and decorated with a 20 mule team. Today, the 20 Mule Team product line includes such products as Borateem, a laundry bleach containing borax, enzymes for stain removal, whitening agents, and perfume; Boraxo Powdered Hand Soap; and Boraxo Tile, Porcelain, and Fiberglass Cleaner.

### International Market

20 Mule Team Borax has been marketed internationally since 1896, when Francis Marion Smith, president of Pacific Coast Borax Company, took a trip to Europe in search of international markets. As the result of that trip, Pacific Coast Borax Company merged with Redwoods Chemical Works in England to form the Pacific Borax and Redwood Chemical Works Limited. The company became multinational in scope in 1899 with the acquisition of other borax producers and the formation of Borax Consolidated Limited.

Today, Dial continues to market its 20 Mule Team products internationally, as part of its Personal Care and Laundry/Household Divisions. Major growth in this area has come from operations in Korea, Taiwan, Thailand, Mexico, and Canada.

## Performance Appraisal

Although borax production made F. M. Smith a very wealthy man, early sales figures for 20 Mule Team Borax are unavailable. Today, the 20 Mule Team product line is part of Dial's Laundry/Household and Personal Care Divisions. Sales and market share figures for the product line are not broken out in the company's annual report. However, Neri reported in a U.S. Borax newsletter that the entire 20 Mule Team product line contributed to strong profits to Dial in 1991 and 1992. "We think it was a good buy," he said. "It helps to complete the Dial product line in the laundry and household division."

For over 100 years, 20 Mule Team Borax has given homemakers a vast range of cleaning help. As always, it is 100 percent natural, produced from naturally occurring minerals that can be used safely with no adverse effect on the environment. Borax contains no phosphates or chlorides and is harmless to washing machines, plumbing, and septic tanks. 20 Mule Team brand is packaged in recycled paperboard. Market research has shown that borax users have an above-average concern with environmental safety and that many consider the impact on the environment when choosing household and laundry products. With the public's increasing interest in natural products that won't harm the environment, it seems that 20 Mule Team Borax is likely to appeal to today's consumer.

## Further Reading:

*The Dial Corp 1992 Annual Report,* Phoenix, AZ: The Dial Corp.

Hildebrand, George H., *Borax Pioneer: Francis Marion Smith,* LaJolla: Howell-North Books, 1982.

Lingenfelter, Richard E., *Death Valley & the Amargosa,* Los Angeles: University of California Press, 1986.

Additional information for this essay was obtained from literature published by U.S. Borax and The Dial Corp.

*—Pam Berry*

# BOUNTY®

# Bounty

Bounty is the nation's top-selling brand of paper towels. Introduced by Procter & Gamble Company in 1965, Bounty paper towels were two-ply sheets promoted as being quickly absorbent. Consumers have found that the brand offered all of the qualities necessary in a paper towel. A paper towel must have durability and should not shred or tear while being used. It must be able to stand up to wet scrubbing when it is being used for such heavy duties as cleaning tiles or oven walls or lighter duties such as cleaning a mirror. A paper towel must also have absorbency and wet strength. It must be able to soak up spills quickly and completely while remaining intact. Since their introduction, Bounty paper towels have met these expectations.

Throughout the years the company has developed new types of Bounty paper towels in order to satisfy various consumer tastes, preferences, and needs. Some changes improved on the properties of the paper towels, while others were enhancements in product design and packaging. By offering products to fit any consumer interest, Procter & Gamble has been able to gain a competitive edge for Bounty and retain consumer loyalty to the brand. Despite the many brands crowding store shelves, the company has successfully maintained the brand's leadership position.

## Brand Development

Throughout the 1970s, Bounty was improved in absorbency as well as marketed in different styles. Bounty towels appeared in prints to make them more attractive to consumers including Fun Prints, Designer Prints and Medley Prints. Subsequent introductions included specialized types of Bounty and further improvements in absorbency.

Specially formulated for use in microwave ovens, Bounty Microwave was introduced in 1984. Microwave ovens were just becoming popular with consumers in the early 1980s, but only certain cookware could be used in them. Specifically, paper and plastic products were considered to be microwave-safe. Bounty Microwave was recommended for microwave cooking because it provided certain advantages. For example, food wrapped in a paper towel wouldn't splatter in the oven while cooking. Additionally, the paper towels absorbed excess moisture produced while cooking; consequently, foods wouldn't dry out or become soggy.

In 1991 an improved Bounty was promoted as "more absorbent than ever." The new towels were reportedly 10 percent more

absorbent than the old product. Because fewer towels would be necessary for a given task, consumers would save money. Bounty Select-a-Size was introduced in 1992. The objective of this product was to give consumers choices in selecting the size needed for a given task. A Bounty brand spokesperson explained that with standard paper towel sheets you sometimes get too much or too little to tackle a task. Bounty Select-a-Size is versatile, allowing you to choose the right size. The roll is 50 percent longer than regular Bounty and consists of special small-sized sheets. This product is available in white or color design and is reportedly more convenient and easy to use yet just as strong and absorbent as other Bounty products.

Most paper towel sheets are 11 inches by 11 inches. Bounty Select-a-Size is perforated every 6 inches in order to provide small-sized sheets. The consumer chooses the length desired for different tasks by using a certain number of sheets. A 6 inch sheet is recommended for such jobs as cleaning small spills and drying hands and can also be used as a napkin. A consumer could tear the sheet at the 12 inch perforation for regular jobs such as draining, scrubbing, cleaning and cleaning regular size spills. Three 6 sheets will provide an 18 sheet needed for large jobs such as washing windows and cleaning big spills. This long sheet can also be used as a placemat.

## Packaging

Bounty paper towels are packaged in different-sized rolls in single or multiple roll packages. All Bounty paper towels are 2-ply in contrast to some competing brands that are 1-ply.

Bounty regular contains 80 2-ply sheets and measures 67 square feet. Bounty Microwave rolls also contain 80 2-ply sheets. Both products are available in white or in designer prints. The improved Bounty, first marketed in 1991, contains 72 2-ply sheets and measures 60 square feet per roll. The Bounty Select-A-Size roll contains 198 two-ply sheets, and measures 90.7 square feet.

## Advertising Innovations

Bounty paper towels were originally promoted with the tagline, ''Absorbs like Magic.'' The brand's most popular television advertising campaign, however, featured actress Nancy Walker portraying a diner waitress. In these ads Walker used Bounty to quickly clean up after a customer and commented, ''Bounty, it's the quicker picker upper.'' This tagline also appeared on the package. Other product in the Bounty line of paper towels were advertised with demonstrations of how they could be used for different purposes. For example, Bounty Microwave was shown wrapped around a food that was being placed in a microwave oven.

## Price-Cutting Strategy

The paper towels market is smaller than that of other paper products, such as facial or bathroom tissues. Consumers perceive paper towels more as luxuries than necessities, particularly during poor economic times. Consequently, price is a particularly important factor in attracting consumers to purchase specific paper towel brands. With so many major brands in the marketplace, including regional, private label, and store brands, pricing was becoming extremely competitive. In 1992 Procter & Gamble decided to embark on a new marketing strategy, cutting list prices and reducing promotions to supermarkets. The aim was to lower prices for all their products so that consumers would not choose lower-priced brands.

## Performance Appraisal

The paper towel industry generated an estimated $1.7 billion in annual sales in the early 1990s. Bounty controlled an estimated 22 percent of the market, earning approximately $374 million. Bounty has maintained its leadership position throughout the years because it has offered consumers choices and variety, as well as high quality.

## Further Reading:

''Bounty Adds New Dimension to Old Kitchen Stand-By,'' Bounty Press Release, 1993.

Bounty Select-A-Size Fact Sheet, Cincinnati, OH: Procter & Gamble Company, 1993.

Freeman, Laurie, '' 'Green' Rolls On,'' *Advertising Age,* March 12, 1990, p. 66.

''Less Bountiful,'' *Consumer Reports,* August 1991, p. 567.

''Paper Towels,'' *Consumer Reports,* January 1992, pp. 27–31.

Weinstein, Steve, ''Will Procter's Gamble Work?,'' *Progressive Grocer,* July 1992, pp. 36–40.

*—Dorothy Kroll*

# BRECK®

A family-owned brand for its first 55 years, Breck hair care products were named for the chemist who created them, John H. Breck. Once limited to sales in professional beauty salons, Breck was mass marketed in 1946 and soon became the country's highest-selling brand of shampoo. Breck lost market share in the highly competitive hair care market of the 1970s, however, and its share of shampoo sales dwindled to 1.3 percent by the end of the 1980s when Breck was under the custody of American Cyanamid. The brand was purchased in 1990 by The Dial Corp and joined this company's line of personal care products that included: Dial, Tone and Liquid Dial soaps, Purex detergents, Brillo soap pads, Lunch Bucket microwave meals, and Armour Star canned meats. Dial worked hard to reposition Breck shampoo as a premium brand in the early 1990s, and ambitious undertaking in the saturated, still competitive, and slow-growth hair care market at that time.

## Brand Origins

Dr. John H. Breck, the man who introduced modern shampoo to America, was born in Holyoke, Massachusetts, in 1877 and started working at the age of 14. At 19 Breck moved to Chicopee, Massachusetts, and joined the Chicopee Fire Department, becoming the country's youngest fire captain at 21 years old. Breck became interested in hair care around that time because he was balding prematurely. Breck began studying chemistry during his time off from firefighting, attending classes at Amherst College.

Shampoos had been used in Europe since before the turn of the twentieth century, but Americans still used multi-purpose bar soap to infrequently wash their hair. Although Breck wasn't able to keep his hair from falling out, he did succeed in developing one of the first liquid shampoos in the United States. Breck's hair cleaning preparation was promoted among friends and customers by word of mouth until 1908, when Breck quit firefighting and opened an office in Springfield, Massachusetts. He started with three employees, and his Breck Preparations were sold to local hairdressers. Breck shampoos were sold exclusively to beauty salons until 1946.

In 1928 a representative of the Edward E. Tower Company, a Boston-based beauty supply dealer, approached Dr. Breck with an offer to distribute his well-liked Breck Preparations. The Tower Company helped Breck expand his distribution sphere to other New England states, and the business was incorporated as the John

H. Breck Corporation in 1929. Sales that year totaled about $10,000.

After twelve years of research into hair and scalp treatments, Breck introduced the first pH-balanced shampoo in 1930. Three years later Breck developed shampoos for oily and dry hair, becoming the first line of shampoo to segment products by hair type. The gold-foil-covered box and label gave the Breck brand a look of premium quality and elegance.

## Advertising—the "Breck Girls"

In line with Breck's professional hair salon distribution, the brand's first advertising was placed in trade magazines. The first ad appeared in the January 1932 issue of *Modern Beauty Shop* magazine. By 1936 Edward Breck, a son of the founder, had risen to the position of president and general manager of the company. That year, he met Charles Sheldon, a portrait and poster artist who had trained under Alphonse Mucha, a celebrated French proponent of the Art Nouveau style. Sheldon had painted motion picture actresses for covers of *Photoplay* magazine since the 1920s, but as the film industry faltered during the Great Depression, Sheldon sought other work. He painted several pastel portraits for "Beautiful Hair Breck" that formed the basis of the shampoo's print campaign and launched one of America's longest-running ad themes, the "Breck Girl."

The Breck account provided Sheldon with enough income to form his own advertising agency around 1940. The first Breck Girl was Olga Nelson, a Springfield woman. But it was 17-year-old Roma Whitney who would become one of the most famous Breck Girls after her portrait was completed in 1937. The blonde was posed with her chin thrust out proudly against a deep sapphire background. The portrait was used in Breck's first national advertising effort, which appeared in *Ladies Home Journal* in 1946. The ad campaign, which cost $112,000, marked the beginning of mass distribution of Breck shampoos. Ms. Whitney's likeness was registered as Breck's trademark in 1951.

Sheldon had a policy of eschewing professional models for "ordinary women." He painted women from his own ad agency, as well as members of the Breck family. Three daughters of Edward J. Breck and two daughters-in-law of founder John Breck, sat for portraits. Sheldon would go on to produce 34 portraits of members of the Breck family, 45 different portraits of 19 Sheldon ad agency employees, and other portraits of friends, neighbors, and family. Most of the works featured a beige background and subjects wearing a V-neck and little or no jewelry. Sheldon completed over 100 portraits between 1936 and 1959. They were the focal point of ads that appeared in hundreds of millions of issues of *Ladies Home Journal, Harpers Bazaar, Vogue, Woman's Home Companion, Seventeen, Glamour,* and *True Story* magazines. The ads documented the ideal "girl next door" for decades.

Breck was first promoted on television in 1955. Early ads appeared on ABC-TV's "Afternoon Film Festival." After placing ads in several slots, the company settled on a TV formula that projected an air of quality. The television budget was maximized with the purchase of sole sponsorships of prime time drama and musical specials. Television helped the John H. Breck Corporation double its sales volume from 1956 to 1961.

Ralph William Williams was hired to create the trademark pastel portraits upon Sheldon's retirement in 1957. Williams had earned an international reputation for the design of stained glass windows in the Washington National Cathedral and the Christian Science Mother Church. Williams changed the style slightly by employing brighter colors, and his portraits helped launch the careers of several well-known model/actresses. Brooke Shields was 11 when she appeared in a 1974 Christmas ad. Breck's sponsorship of America's Junior Miss contests brought Junior Miss Tennessee Cybill Shepherd into the spotlight. Kim Basinger appeared as a strawberry-blonde bride. Jaclyn Smith told television audiences that her Breck hair was "second nature." Other stars launched by Breck ads were Cheryl Tiegs, Erin Gray, Christie Brinkley, and Connie Sellecca. Williams created almost 300 pastel portraits before his death at the easel drawing the winner of the 1976 Junior Miss Pageant.

## New Products

In 1957 the brand brought out Breck Hair Set Mist and professional shampoos with protein and shampoo for color-treated hair. By 1961 more than 40 Breck products were being marketed, most of which were sold only for professional use. Five products were mass marketed in drugstores and supermarkets: Breck Hair Set Mist, Breck Children's Shampoo, Breck Banish Dandruff Treatment Shampoo, Breck Creme Rinse, and the three basic Breck shampoos, which brought in 75 percent of retail sales volume. Although Breck was notoriously reticent about its sales and mar-

ket share figures, retail sales in the early 1960s were estimated at over $50 million, and the brand held approximately 20 percent of the liquid shampoo market. In 1962 Reach, McClinton & Humphrey purchased the Sheldon agency and operated it as a branch.

The John H. Breck Corporation was acquired by American Cyanamid of Wayne, New Jersey, in 1963. That same year, the brand's advertising contracts were awarded to Young & Rubicam. Cyanamid launched Breck in Great Britain in 1964. The British market was fraught with competition: over 400 brands scrambled for market share in a country where shampoo brand loyalty was virtually unknown.

During the 1960s Breck concentrated strongly on the teen market. It introduced Miss Breck hair spray with "Doodle-Do Parties"—seminars on grooming habits—at department stores around the country. However, this imaginative effort wasn't supported with the kind of concerted, national campaigns that had carried the brand to the top of the market it created. In fact, American Cyanamid expected local department stores to pay for all advertising surrounding the "Doodle-Do" events. No national advertising supported the introduction of Miss Breck. It was the beginning of an unfortunate trend that allowed Breck to plummet from the number one shampoo to an obscure, outdated, bargain brand.

## Decline

Several factors contributed to the decline of the Breck brand in the 1970s and 1980s. The Breck Girl image was not in keeping with the growing feminist movement. While she evolved into the Breck woman in the late 1960s and early 1970s, the Breck Girl ended up with an identity crisis. Marketers tried to update her with "flower-power" portraits of long-haired hip blondes and African-American women with Afro hairstyles, but the campaign had lost its effectiveness, and the Breck Girls were pulled in 1978. After a ten-year hiatus, the Breck Girl was briefly revived, but the new "80s Woman" did not have the impact of the original theme.

At the same time, the hair care market exploded with increased use of shampoo and intense competition. One survey showed that, while only 12 percent of young women washed their hair daily in 1966, 39 percent did so in 1977. More washings meant more shampoo sales, and the growing market lured some of the country's largest personal products companies into the fray. Shampoos for cosmetic, medicinal, and other purposes were introduced. There were shampoos "fortified" with milk, beer, henna and jojoba from such giant corporations as Procter & Gamble, S.C. Johnson & Son, Bristol-Myers and Gillette Company. Consumers felt no brand loyalty, and were highly price sensitive, so new product introductions and heavy promotions were vital to maintain market share.

At this point American Cyanamid lost interest in its consumer products group and stopped spending money on advertising and promotion. To make matters worse, former Breck Girl Jaclyn Smith appeared in television commercials for Wella Balsam conditioning shampoo saying, "I switched." American Cyanamid failed to meet the challenge of competition, and by the end of the 1970s Breck's share of the market had dropped to 4.2 percent. At the end of the next decade, Breck's share had plummeted still further to 1.3 percent, prompting American Cyanamid to divest all of its consumer products businesses. In 1990 Greyhound Dial Corp. (now The Dial Corp) purchased the Breck trademark and operations for less than $50 million, and set out immediately to revitalize the brand.

## Restaging under The Dial Corp

Dial worked to improve all aspects of Breck, including packaging, formulation and fragrance. The new parent employed a scientific approach to re-establish Breck, in many respects returning to the brand's origins in the chemistry lab. Breck was reformulated with "Vitasomes," a delivery system that permeated the hair with vitamins E and C, Panthenol (provitamin B-5), and wheat protein.

*The 1937 portrait of Breck Girl Roma Whitney became the brand's registered trademark in 1951.*

The new formulations were based, in part, on consumer research that showed consumers preferred shampoos and conditioners that rinsed well and imbued the hair with shine. Dial's studies also showed that fragrance was a pivotal factor in the consumer decision-making process. The Breck research and development team chose a signature fragrance for the entire line of 23 hair care products. The scent was a blend of citrus, peach, and floral bouquets that augmented the sensation of clean, healthy hair.

Breck hair sprays had been the brand's best-performing products in the 1980s, and retained a 4 percent share of the hair spray market. Dial expanded the line of styling fixatives, bringing it more up-to-date with mousse, gel, and styling spritz. The basic hair sprays provided various levels of control and delivery.

The new packaging featured a rich, yet feminine peach color and gold logo that harkened back to Breck's original gold-foiled box and reflected the brand's premium positioning. Dial supported "new Breck" with a romantic television ad filmed in sepia tones that featured a man shampooing a woman's hair. As Blair Sabol observed in the *New York Times*, Breck seemed to have "shifted its focus from the ideal woman to the ideal relationship." The new parent had no plans to resurrect the Breck Girl in its advertising, but the company did not ignore her. Many of the original portraits depicting Breck Girls had been lost or given away, while the

remainder were stashed away in warehouses and storerooms. After years of neglect, however, the 150 surviving portraits were restored for public display in the "Breck Girl Hall of Fame" at The Dial Corp headquarters in Phoenix, Arizona.

Unfortunately, the restaging and 1992 reintroduction of Breck didn't even merit a mention in *Drug & Cosmetic Industry's* review of the 1992 hair care market. Citing more than 20 brands with shares ranging from 12 percent to 1 percent, Breck was ranked among the "others." In addition, while hair care is considered a "recession-proof" market, industry observers noted the snail's-paced two to three percent growth during the recessionary years of the early 1990s. The stagnant market translated into an even smaller pie for the individual hair care brands, further heightening competition and fragmentation. Breck and The Dial Corp clearly have their work cut out for them.

## Further Reading:

Baltera, Lorraine, "Wella's new star of TV ad campaign is ex-Breck Girl saying, 'I switched,' " *Advertising Age,* February 9, 1976, pp. 1, 57.

"Breck, Alberto invading British shampoo market," *Advertising Age,* September 28, 1964, pp. 80–81.

"Breck arranges doodle-do parties to attract teens," *Advertising Age,* May 17, 1965, pp. 2, 113.

"Breck buys into 'Garry Moore,' sets print fall ads," *Advertising Age,* June 27, 1966, p. 25.

"Breck Girl goes into TV ads a real live doll," v.37, *Advertising Age,* March 21, 1966, p. 16.

"Breck Girl marks ad birthday—even tells age (it's 30)," *Advertising Age,* June 6, 1966, p. 25.

"A brief history of Breck, America's first shampoo," Phoenix: The Dial Corp, [1992].

Davis, Donald A., "The hair care market," *Drug & Cosmetic Industry,* April 1992, pp. 19–22.

"The Dial Corp establishes Breck Girl Hall of Fame," Phoenix: The Dial Corp, [1992].

"Dial Corp unveils healthy, new Breck," Phoenix: The Dial Corp, [1992].

Giges, Nancy, "Shampoo competition heats up, *Advertising Age,* February 26, 1979, p. S-30.

"Golden moments in Breck history: a chronology," Phoenix: The Dial Corp, [1992].

"How Breck found its own TV formula," *Broadcasting,* October 23, 1961, pp. 26, 28.

Lynch, Jacqueline, "A little dream goes a long way," *In Chicopee* (Massachusetts), February 19, 1992.

"Reach, McClinton absorbs Charles Sheldon agency," *Advertising Age,* July 23, 1962, pp. 1, 87.

Sabol, Blair, "Forever Breck," *New York Times,* June 14, 1992, sec. 9, p. 3.

Schneidman, Diane, "Breck Girl is back as 'Woman of the '80s,' " *Marketing News,* August 14, 1987, p. 1, 19.

Sloan, Pat, "Shampoo market is in a lather," *Advertising Age,* October 6, 19–, p. 52.

"Today's marketing: American Cyanamid Co.," *Sales Management,* November 10, 1969, p. 94.

Turner, Richard, "Greyhound Dial purchases Breck hair-care lines," *Wall Street Journal,* September 11, 1990.

Wurdinger, Victoria, "Hair care report," *Drug & Cosmetic Industry,* April 1993, pp. 26–28, 111.

*—April S. Dougal*

# BRILLO®

Brillo, the steel wool pad filled with pink soap, was the second leading soap-filled scouring pad on the market in 1992, with sales of nearly $20 million. The brand, owned by The Dial Corp, accounted for about 25 percent of the market, compared to nearly 60 percent for S.O.S pads from Miles, Inc. More than 3.5 million Brillo soap pads were produced every day at a plant in London, Ohio. Other products to carry the Brillo name included Flip Pads, Brass Cleaning Pads, Stainless Metal Pads, Plastic Knit Pads, Copper Knit Pads, Dobie Cleaning Pad, Nylon Scrubbers, and Scouring Cloths.

## Brand Origins

According to corporate lore, Brillo was the ingenious invention of an itinerant peddler of pots and pans and his brother-in-law, a jeweler in New York City. The peddler, known only as Mr. Brady, traveled around New England in the early 1900s selling shiny aluminum cookware to women who were happy to be rid of their heavy, black cast-iron pots. Unfortunately, his customers were not so pleased to see him on his return trips. Cooking over a coal stove quickly covered the aluminum pots and pans with grime, and even gas stoves left the cookware blackened. The women wanted a way to keep their aluminum pots and pans as shiny as when they were new.

Brady took his problem to his brother-in-law, Mr. Ludwig, who suggested using soap, jeweler's rouge, and fine German steel wool to scour the grease and grime from the aluminum pans. Rouge is a reddish powder made of ferric oxide that is used to polish metals and glass. At a time when there were few commercial cleaning products on the market, Brady's concoction worked so well that it was soon out-selling his pots and pans.

Milton B. Loeb, an attorney hired by Brady and Ludwig to help them set up a company to market their discovery, is credited with creating the name Brillo from the Latin word "beryllus," which means "to shine." Brillo was patented in 1913, and the name was registered as a trademark. The Brillo Manufacturing Company of Brooklyn, New York, was incorporated soon afterwards. Loeb, who was offered a share of the company in lieu of payment for his services, went on to become known as "Mr. Brillo." He later bought out his partners, sold stock in the company, and served as president from 1925 until it was purchased by the Purex Corporation in 1963. He stayed on as a member of the Purex board of

directors and continued to oversee the company's British operations until his death in 1972.

Coincidentally, the S.O.S soap pad, which would become Brillo's chief competition, was created about the same time as Brillo on the other side of the country. Erwin W. Cox, a door-to-door aluminum cookware salesman in San Francisco, filed a patent application for a soap-impregnated steel-wool pad in 1917. The story is that Cox's wife gave the pads the name S.O.S because the letters were the universal call for help and because they stood for "Save Our Saucepans." The General Foods Corporation purchased the S.O.S Company in 1958, then sold the brand to Miles Inc. in 1968.

## Early Marketing

For the first few years, Brillo pads were sold almost exclusively by salesmen like their creator Brady, who went house to house with their aluminum cookware. Eventually, hardware retailers, who stocked most of the cleaning products of the day, also began selling Brillo. But the big break for the young company came in 1918, when the New York-based F. W. Woolworth Company agreed to carry Brillo. At the time, Woolworth, a chain of five-and-ten-cent stores that had been founded in 1912, had nearly a thousand stores throughout the eastern half of the country. In the 1920s, grocers also began carrying cleaning products, and grocery stores soon began to account for most of Brillo's sales.

Until 1930, a box of Brillo pads consisted of several wads of steel-wool and a cake of reddish polishing soap. Then in 1930, the company perfected a process to infuse soap into the steel-wool pads, following the lead of S.O.S, and making Brillo even more useful and convenient. About this time, the company also introduced several other products that carried the Brillo name, including Brillo kosher soap, Brillo cleanser, and a line of Brillo pads for floor scrubbing machines. Most of those products have since disappeared from the marketplace. During World War II, both S.O.S and Brillo all but disappeared from grocer's shelves. The large rolls of steel wool, originally destined to become soap pads, were painted brown and green to create camouflage canopies for Allied guns and tanks.

After the war, demand for consumer products soared, and in 1955 the Brillo Manufacturing Company purchased the Williams Company of London, Ohio, a maker of steel wool since 1920, thus

## AT A GLANCE

**B**rillo brand of scouring pads registered as a trademark in 1913 by Brillo Manufacturing Company of Brooklyn, NY; company purchased by Purex Corporation, 1963; Purex Consumer Products, including Brillo, acquired by the Greyhound Corporation, 1985; corporate name changed to Greyhound Dial Corporation, 1990; corporate name changed to The Dial Corp, 1991.

*Performance:* *Market share*—24.5% of scouring pads. *Sales*—$19.7 million.

*Major competitor:* S.O.S soap pads, by Miles, Inc.

*Addresses:* *Parent company*—The Dial Corp, 1850 North Central Ave., Phoenix, AZ 85077; phone: (602) 207-4000.

ensuring the company of a consistent supply of steel wool for its products. Brillo would become for a time the world's leading producer of steel wool and steel wool products. Brillo soap pads have been made at the London, Ohio, facility since 1969. Ironically, the only other facility making Brillo soap pads was in London, England; it was owned by the Brillo Manufacturing Company of Great Britain, Ltd.

### Brillo and Andy Warhol

In 1963, the Brillo Manufacturing Company and its Brillo, Paddy, and Dobie brands of cleaning products were purchased by the Purex Corporation, Ltd., a major producer of household products. Although Brillo had been advertised on television before, Purex immediately expanded that advertising to include all three major networks. In 1964, for example, Brillo sponsored "I Love Lucy," "Pete and Gladys," "Concentration," and "The Loretta Young Show," all daytime television shows popular with women. Brillo was also one of several products advertised regularly on the nighttime show "Hollywood and the Stars," which was sponsored solely by Purex. The commercials used the theme, "You'll find the women's touch in every Purex product." In 1965, Purex announced the first celebrity spokesman in Brillo's history when it signed comedian Allan Sherman to do several television commercials with the themes, "Brillo Soap Pads, the soap pads with muscle" and "Made better, to work harder."

It was during this time of intensive television advertising that Brillo received free publicity from a most unlikely source. Andy Warhol was a pioneer in the controversial art form known as Pop Art that developed in the 1960s, which often took commercial illustrations as its subject matter. Warhol is perhaps best known for his oversized paintings of Campbell Soup cans. However, in 1964, a Pop Art show opened at the Stable Gallery in New York, which featured a room filled with oversized replicas of cardboard packing crates, including cartons of Del Monte peaches, Campbell's tomato juice, Heinz ketchup, and Brillo soap pads. It is not known why Warhol had chosen Brillo soap pad boxes to be his first sculptures. But the Brillo boxes were a smash artistic success for a short time, selling for as much as $300 apiece. Famed artist

Robert Indiana once said, "The most striking opening of that period was definitely Andy's 'Brillo Box' show. You could barely get in, and it was like going through a maze. The rows of boxes were just wide enough to squeeze your way through."

The Brillo boxes did not last long as an art form, however. The Canadian National Gallery of Art in Toronto had scheduled a showing of the Brillo boxes and other Warhol art, but the show was canceled when the museum director decided the grocery boxes were not art, and therefore subject to a 20 percent import duty. By that time, Warhol had lost interest in Brillo. He told *The New York Times*, "I really don't care. I think with some of the important things happening they must have more to worry about than some dumb little boxes." Brillo made a brief return to the art world in 1988 when boxes of soap pads were given away during an auction of Warhol memorabilia.

### Future Directions

In 1985 Purex was purchased by the Greyhound Corporation, then best known as a motorcoach company, but which had been diversifying into non-transportation businesses since the 1960s. Greyhound had purchased Armour Foods (including Dial soap) in the 1970s. The corporate name was changed to Greyhound Dial Corporation in 1990 and then changed to The Dial Corp in 1991.

In 1992, Dial announced "an advancement that will eclipse all others in the hearts of every pot and pan owner in America: new rust-resistant, longer-lasting soap pads." The company said the new Brillo soap pads would resist for several scrubbings the natural tendency for steel wool to rust. The improved product would not receive much advertising, however. Considered to be established brands in a mature, $80 million-a-year market, neither Brillo nor its chief competitor, S.O.S soap pads, were heavily advertised during the late 1980s or early 1990s. Although there was speculation in 1993 that a new product from the Minnesota Mining & Manufacturing Company (3M), Scotch Brite Never Rust, could spur an increase in advertising, The Dial Corp denied plans to resume advertising Brillo.

### Further Reading:

Bockris, Victor, *The Life and Death of Andy Warhol*, New York: Bantam Bks., Inc., 1989, pp. 142–163.

*Brief History of S.O.S*, Miles, Inc.

*A Brilliant Idea Continues to Shine*, The Greyhound Corporation, 1988.

"Brillo Joins Purex," *Purex News & Views*, November 1963, pp. 4–5.

"Brillo Technology Leaps Forward, Now Resists Rust," The Dial Corp, April 1992.

Goldman, Kevin, "Scouring-Pad Rivals Face 3M Challenge," *Wall Street Journal*, January 11, 1993, p. B8.

"The Idea Was Brilliant," *Go Greyhound*, The Greyhound Corporation, Fall 1985.

Kynaston, McShine, *Andy Warhol: A Retrospective*, New York: The Museum of Modern Art, 1989.

"Milton Loeb, Mr. Brillo, Dies at 84," *Purex News & Views*, March 1972, pp. 3–4.

—*Dean Boyer*

# BRITISH KNIGHTS®

British Knights athletic shoes burst onto the scene in the mid-1980s with radical, youth-oriented designs and quickly captured almost three percent of the U.S. market. However, after peaking as the seventh most popular brand of athletic shoes in 1988 with U.S. sales of $120 million, British Knights slumped in the early 1990s. By 1992 British Knights had fallen to the 13th best-selling brand with about 1.5 percent of the U.S. market and domestic revenues of $89 million and worldwide sales of $121 million. British Knights brand shoes, also referred to as BKs, are manufactured by Jack Schwartz Shoes Inc., the largest privately owned shoe company in the United States.

## Brand Origins

Jack Schwartz Shoes Company was founded in 1936 and manufactured men's dress shoes, including the Charles Walker and Kent & Howard brands, until 1976. The company then moved into athletic footwear and achieved some early success with its Pro Players brand, which was popular in the Midwest and on the East Coast. Then in 1983, the company introduced a canvas boat shoe bearing the name British Knights. According to Larry Schwartz, grandson of the company's founder and executive vice-president in the early 1990s, the name was chosen because "British" symbolized quality in shoes and "Knights" "just sounded good." The shoes were only mildly successful, but the brand name was a hit. In 1985 the company began phasing out Pro Players and expanded the British Knights brand to encompass all its athletic shoes.

## Marketing

From the beginning, British Knights brand shoes stressed style while most other athletic shoe companies touted superior technology. Schwartz commented in the *New York Times* in 1991, "From a technical standpoint, all shoes are basically the same. We think we can stand out by being more fashion oriented." British Knights shoes were among the flashiest and most colorful on the market.

British Knights also targeted inner city youth with its marketing. In a press release, Schwartz said, "The inner city is the key to many industries, but it is the lifeblood of the sneaker industry. What people in the [neighborhood] wear defines what's cool for the entire country. . . . The most difficult thing about marketing to the 'hood is that if you appear to be trying to sell them, you have no choice. You can't tell them what's cool. You must be in tune to what they are thinking and develop products they'll be attracted to on their own. Literally, these days the only way to get a middle-class suburban high school kid to buy your product is to have an inner city kid wear it."

British Knights were also advertised heavily on MTV, the youth-oriented cable network, and the Fox Broadcasting Company network. British Knight commercials were fast-paced and featured both the images and the language of the inner city. The rebellious image caught on quickly with image-conscious young buyers, who also began referring to the brand as "BKs." British Knights

later copyrighted the BK brand and began attaching a BK button to its shoes.

## Sneakers with an Attitude

British Knights' spectacular growth stalled in the early 1990s, and in an effort to revitalize its image, British Knights adopted an irreverent attitude in its advertising that it hoped would set the brand apart from the leading sneaker companies and catch the attention of independent-thinking young buyers. "Our success in the late 1980s was clearly a fad," Schwartz admitted. "Our challenge is to turn a fad into a brand."

Television commercials launched in 1991 updated the classic children's insult "your mother wears combat boots" to "your mother wears Nikes." One commercial featured a group of gray-haired women wearing Nike brand athletic shoes while they lounged around a tennis court gossiping, then cut away to a close-up of British Knights shoes. Another commercial featured rapper M.C. Hammer delivering the same message. Donny Deutsch, then executive vice-president of Deutsch, Inc., the advertising agency that created the commercials, told the *New York Times*, "We want to be seen as the sneaker company for rebellious young people. Reebok and Nike have become so mainstream they're the sneaker of choice for little old ladies."

Even the press releases for British Knights were irreverent. Early in 1993, the company sent out an announcement entitled: "Enough . . . Enough John Stockton . . . Enough Godzilla . . . Much too much Deion Sanders . . . Oh my God, Larry Johnson is wearing a dress . . . Move over stooges, my sides are achin' . . . And as far as we're concerned 'Hey buddy, pump this' . . . Good bye nonsense . . . Hello face." The press release declared 1993 "The Year of the Attitude" and promised, "We've got the athletes. We've got the look. We've got the technology. But most of all, we got this attitude thing. It's like a mood with a little nasty thrown in . . . and a dash of cocky." The press release ended by telling parents, "So, if you don't want your kid to be a hall monitor with a pocket guard and his pants pulled up to his chest, get him a pair of BKs."

## "Sweet Pea" Daniels

British Knights also signed Lloyd "Sweet Pea" Daniels, a professional basketball player, in 1991 to endorse its shoes. Daniels, then playing for the San Antonio Spurs of the National Basketball Association (NBA), was a controversial choice because of a past that included drug abuse and violence. While growing up in New York City, he was once shot while buying drugs and still carried a bullet in his shoulder. But British Knights saw Daniels as a way to reach inner city youths who could relate to the problems that the basketball player had managed to overcome. The company acknowledged the risk it took in signing Daniels but added in a press release, "There are a lot of kids in trouble out there and it is important to show that it's never too late to turn things around. That is why we signed [Daniels], because he's

## AT A GLANCE

**B**ritish Knights brand of athletic shoes founded in 1983 by Jack Schwartz, owner of Jack Schwartz Shoes Inc., which began in 1936; brand originally a line of canvas boat shoes; brand extended in 1985 to encompass all Jack Schwartz athletic shoes.

**Performance:** *Market share*—1.5% of U.S. athletic shoe category; 1% of international market. *Sales*—(U.S.) $89 million; (worldwide) $121 million.

**Major competitor:** Nike; also, Reebok.

**Advertising:** *Agency*—Deutsch, Inc., New York, NY, 1990—. *Major campaign*—Television commercials featuring professional basketball star Lloyd "Sweet Pea" Daniels as spokesperson.

**Addresses:** *Parent company*—Jack Schwartz Shoes Inc., 155 Avenue of the Americas, New York, NY 10013; phone (212) 691-4700; fax: (212) 260-4168.

proven that he is worth taking a risk and he represents the dreams of many of the kids who lace up our sneakers.''

In addition to television commercials featuring Daniels, British Knights also sponsored a series of seminars around the country at which Daniels talked candidly to inner city youths about drug abuse. Patterned after the well-known ''Scared Straight'' programs about life in prison, the British Knights ''Scared Clean'' clinics presented a graphic look at the dangers of using drugs. ''Frankly, we hope to literally scare the living daylights out of the kids,'' Schwartz said in announcing the program. ''If drugs are reality to them, we're going to show them how destructive that reality can be.''

British Knights offered a free pair of shoes to anyone who attended a ''Scared Clean'' clinic and signed an agreement not to use drugs. To get the shoes, the youths had to send in an anti-drug poster of their own design. Schwartz explained, ''We wanted to give away the sneakers to make sure the kids come, but then we thought we should get some type of commitment to stay clean. I don't know if it will last, but I want these kids to go home having done something that will remind them of Sweet Pea's life and what was said at the seminar.''

### Trends

In 1993 British Knights brought back the canvas basketball shoe, long abandoned by athletic shoes companies in the move to

leather. The canvas shoes, named the Predator, reinforced British Knights' claim as the brand designed for the rugged basketball of the inner city playgrounds. In a press release, British Knights declared, ''This sneaker wasn't made for the slow paced, zone defense, gym game. The Predator was designed to give an edge to the street ball player.'' British Knights said the soles of the Predator basketball shoes were designed to withstand rugged use on concrete or asphalt outdoor courts and, because the uppers were made of canvas, kept feet cooler in hot summer weather.

To promote its canvas shoes, British Knights sponsored a smelly sock contest. The company invited sneaker wearers to send their smelliest socks to British Knights—in a sealed plastic bag. The winners would receive a free pair of British Knights Predators every year for three years. Combining its playground heritage with some fun at the expense of ''pump'' shoes from Nike and Reebok, Predators also came with an attached air-pump needle ''for those days when everyone has a ball, but no one has a pin to pump it up with. Thus, the Predator [brought] new meaning to getting pumped and getting air on the playground.''

The British Knights brand, which would grace a line of clothing and accessories in 1994, also explored new territory in 1993 by letting Derrick Coleman of the New Jersey Nets direct his own television commercial for BK shoes. The commercial showed Coleman at home, at his local gym, and hanging out with friends. British Knights said the commercial showed ''how, where, and why'' Coleman wore British Knights shoes. In what had become typical British Knights fashion, a press release about the commercial asked, ''So, what's it going to be? Another commercial where the athlete has neat little lines written for him, some clever tidbits that an adman thought up? How about some million dollar budget or an over used slogan? This time the player calls the shots . . . this time it's his words.'' Coleman, former bad-boy rookie of the year in the NBA, was also seen in a commercial for British Knights as a street monster created by a mad scientist and powered by British Knights Dymacel basketball shoes and as an animated stick figure with an oversized head.

### Further Reading:

British Knights press releases, New York: Jack Schwartz Shoes Inc.

Foltz, Kim, ''Campaign for British Knights to Escalate Sneaker Wars,'' *New York Times,* February 20, 1991, p. D17.

Magiera, Marcy, and Pat Sloan, ''Rival's Ads Hammer Nike,'' *Advertising Age,* February 28, 1991, p. 1.

*—Dean Boyer*

# BROOKS BROTHERS®

Brooks Brothers, Inc. is the oldest retail clothing store in the United States and has sustained a reputation for prestigious, tasteful, and conservative business attire for much of its history. A Brooks Brothers suit was considered de rigueur for generations of corporate executives and ambitious managers. When Brooks Brothers discontinued custom tailoring in 1976, the news made the front page of the *New York Times*.

Brooks Brothers offered a complete line of men's wear, including socks, underwear, shirts, ties, and hats. The company also began marketing women's clothing in the 1950s, although men's clothing accounted for more than 80 percent of the company's sales as late as 1992. By the early 1990s Brooks Brothers, Inc. operated more than 50 retail stores, a dozen factory outlets, and a direct-marketing catalog facility in the United States. International operations included stores in Japan and a wholesale operation in Italy.

## Brand Origins

Henry Sands Brooks, the son of a Connecticut doctor, was a successful New York grocer in the early 19th century who enjoyed shopping for fashionable clothes in Europe. When his friends requested that he bring back clothing for them as well, he decided to enter the clothing business himself. In 1818 he opened the H. & D.H. Brooks & Co. clothing store at the corner of Catharine and Cherry Streets in the heart of New York City's financial district. With the guiding principle, "To make and deal only in merchandise of the best quality and to sell it at a fair profit only, and to deal with people who seek and are capable of appreciating such merchandise," Brooks began an operation that would continue to exemplify his high standards for generations.

After Brooks' death in 1833 the business went to his eldest son, Henry Jr. It was Henry Jr. who reportedly introduced the first ready-made suits in the United States in 1845, thus making professionally-tailored business attire more affordable. Henry Jr. died in 1850 and his sons, Daniel, John, Elisha, and Edward renamed the business Brooks Brothers in 1855. The Catharine Street store closed in 1874 and a larger, grander store on Madison Avenue opened in 1915.

## Famous Customers

Brooks Brothers clothed many of the richest and most powerful men of the 19th century, including members of the Vanderbilt and Rockefeller families and business tycoon J.P. Morgan. Brooks Brothers also created a silk-lined coat, patterned with American eagles and containing the embroidered inscription "One Country, One Destiny" that Abraham Lincoln wore to his second inaugural. The coat that Lincoln was wearing when he was assassinated five weeks later was also a Brooks Brothers design.

Presidents Ulysses S. Grant, Theodore Roosevelt, and Woodrow Wilson also wore Brooks Brothers suits to their inaugurations. When Franklin D. Roosevelt met with Winston Churchill and Joseph Stalin at the historic Yalta summit in 1945, he wore a cape from Brooks Brothers intended to disguise his illness from the Russian leader. In 1992 Hillary Rodham Clinton gave President Bill Clinton a suede bomber jacket from Brooks Brothers for their 17th wedding anniversary.

When Charles Lindberg landed in Paris after the first solo transatlantic flight in 1927, Ambassador Myron T. Herrick lent him a Brooks Brothers suit to wear. Shortly thereafter, Brooks Brothers custom-tailored a suit overnight for Lindberg to wear during his ticker-tape parade in New York City. Other celebrity Brooks Brothers patrons included actors Douglas Fairbanks, Sr., John Barrymore, Cary Grant, Rudolph Valentino, Clark Gable, and Errol Flynn.

## The Golden Fleece

Brooks Brothers adopted its famous Golden Fleece logo in the 1850s. The trademark consisted of a golden sheep suspended from a sling made of ribbon and was adopted from the Order of the Golden Fleece, an Order of Knighthood founded in 1429 by Philip the Good, Duke of Burgundy. The symbol was later used by tradesmen in Great Britain who sold wool.

The original symbol may have been symbolic of the Lamb of God or in reference to the mythological Golden Fleece sought by Jason and the Argonauts. *The Haberdasher,* a clothing business trade journal, said of the symbol in 1892 that "The lamb that figures on [Brooks Brothers] billheads is probably symbolical and signifies that the principles of the firm are 'all wool and a yard wide.' It is a faithful, patient, productive beast, and has certainly proven to the firm of Brooks Brothers to be the 'Lamb with the Golden Fleece'." The logo appeared on Brooks Brothers stationary, packages, advertising, as well as on its luggage, suits, knit shirts, and other clothing. Some customers were known to pur-

## AT A GLANCE

**H**. & D.H. Brooks & Co. clothing store established in New York City by Henry Sands Brooks in 1818; business renamed Brooks Brothers in 1855; company purchased by Julius Garfinckel & Co. in 1946; Garfinckel department store chain acquired by Allied Stores, Inc. in 1981; Allied acquired by Campeau Corporation in 1986; Brooks Brothers sold to Marks & Spencer PLC in 1988.

**Performance:** *Sales*—$338 million (1992).

**Advertising:** *Agency*—Ogilvy & Mather, New York, NY, 1993—. *Major campaign*—175th anniversary celebration (1993).

**Addresses:** *Parent company*—Brooks Brothers, Inc., 346 Madison Avenue, New York, NY 10017; phone: (212) 682-8800; fax: (212) 986-1854. *Ultimate parent company*—Marks & Spencer PLC, London.

chase the least expensive Brooks Brothers item containing the logo and then transfer it to suits of another maker.

### Style Setting

After pioneering off-the-rack suits in the mid 1840s, Brooks Brothers further influenced U.S. fashion with the introduction of the "sack suit" in 1895. The sack suit featured a single-breasted jacket with a center vent, flap pockets and natural, unpadded shoulders which soon became the American standard. The trousers had a plain full front with straight legs. The comfortable, boxy-looking suit was a departure from the padded-shoulder, tight-fitting jackets and pleated trousers that had been popular in Europe. The sack suit was particularly well-styled for the older businessman who might be trying to hide a few extra pounds.

The sack suit was considered the first genuinely American business suit. Fashion critics panned it, but the suit soon became the appropriate outfit for nearly all occasions. A Brooks Brothers golf catalog in 1920 offered merchandise ranging from a cape and chamois gloves to wing tip shoes with crepe rubber soles. It also listed "Sack Suits with Knickerbockers to match, in various patterns and materials, suitable for golf and general country wear." The sack suit evolved into the Ivy-League look of the 1950s and the celebrated gray flannel suit of the 1960s. Virtually unchanged after nearly 100 years, the suit accounted for more than a third of Brooks Brothers' sales in 1992.

Brooks Brothers also introduced the button-down collar on men's business shirts. In 1896 John Brooks, grandson of founder Henry Sands Brooks, was watching a polo match in England when he noticed that the players buttoned the points of their collars to keep them from flapping in the wind. A third button secured the collars in the back. Brooks brought the idea back to New York City, and in 1900 Brooks Brothers marketed the first button-down oxford shirts. Although the third button was seldom used, it remained part of the shirt's design until 1946. After that Brooks Brothers would sew a button behind the collar and add a button hole on request. The button-down oxford was still Brooks Brothers best selling shirt in the early 1990s.

Other European fashions brought to the United States by Brooks Brothers in the first years of the 20th century included the Shetland wool sweater from Great Britain and a loose-fitting

overcoat known as the polo coat. Originally white with pearl buttons, the polo coat was later offered in gray and camel's hair. In 1920 Brooks Brothers introduced Indian madras fabric to the United States with colorful jackets, trousers, and shorts for men. The company also manufactured the first summer suits made of seersucker and lightweight corduroy in 1930.

Another enduring Brooks Brothers creation was the diamond-pattern argyle sock. John Wood, president of Brooks Brothers in the late 1940s, noticed a striking pair of socks on a fellow golfer at the Creek Club in Locust Valley, New York. The golfer told Wood that the socks had been knitted by his wife from a pattern in a book handed down from her great grandmother. Wood borrowed the pattern book, and in 1954 Brooks Brothers introduced the first argyle socks.

### Overseas Expansion

The conservative Brooks Brothers look became popular with Japanese businessmen in the 1970s, and Brooks Brothers stores on the West Coast began catering to the needs of their growing Japanese clientele. Frank T. Reilly, then president of Brooks Brothers, told *Newsweek*, "Most Japanese men are conservative dressers. They are also very conscious of high quality and prestigious names." This reasoning led to the first Brooks Brothers overseas venture in Tokyo. At the store's opening in 1979, a *Newsweek* reporter commented: "From its dignified, gray granite facade to the racks of gray and blue flannels within, the newest branch of Brooks Brothers seems reassuringly familiar. And last week's opening day attracted the same kind of customers—conservatively dressed businessmen—who flock to the flagship Brooks on New York's Madison Avenue."

Brooks Brothers Japan Ltd., which had expanded to more than 40 stores by the early 1990s, was a partnership with Daido Worsted Mills Ltd. of Japan in which Brooks Brothers controlled 51 percent of the stock. Brooks Brothers supplied most of the Japanese stores' merchandise from the United States with only about ten percent manufactured in Japan to Brooks Brothers' specifications. Brooks Brothers clothing was also available in Italy through a wholesale arrangement with S.R. Imports Inc., which had more than 100 outlets in the early 1990s.

### Corporate Ownership

Brooks Brothers remained family-owned and operated for over 100 years until 1928 when president Winthrop H. Brooks sold controlling interest in the company to Julius Garfinckel & Co., a Washington, D.C.-based department store chain. The Brooks family remained active in the company until 1975 when Ashbel Tingley Wall, the great-great-great-grandson of Henry Sands Brooks, retired as a vice president.

Brooks Brothers was sold three times during the 1980s. Garfinckel, Brooks Brothers, Miller & Rhoads, the 18th largest department store retailer in the United States began looking for someone to buy its Miller & Rhoads stores early in 1981. However, Garfinckel attracted the attention of Allied Stores Inc., then the eighth largest chain of department stores, who launched a hostile takeover of Garfinckel. Allied Stores was purchased by the Campeau Corporation in 1986 and the Campeau Corp. sold Brooks Brothers to Marks & Spencer two years later.

Marks & Spencer paid $750 million for Brooks Brothers, which was 30 times the company's net annual profit and more than twice what many analysts believed the company was worth. However, Marks & Spencer, Great Britain's largest retailer, was seeking an entry into the U.S. market and recognized the value of the Brooks Brothers name. William Roberti, then president of Brooks Brothers, told *M Inc.*, "One of the big things that came out of our discussion with Marks & Spencer is that Brooks is really a brand name, and we should recognize it as one."

Brooks Brothers began to wholesale its clothing to specialty stores in an attempt to establish the label as a brand name. This development marked the first time that Brooks Brothers merchandise was available in the United States outside of a Brooks Brothers store or catalog. Alan Millstein, publisher of *Fashion Network*

*Established in 1818, Brooks Brothers began using the famous Golden Fleece logo in the 1850s. The image was adapted from the crest of a medieval Order of Knighthood.*

*Report*, called the decision "a bright idea bordering on brilliant. All over America there are small-town businessmen who've wished they could buy Brooks but haven't wanted to get on a plane to Chicago or St. Louis or Atlanta."

## Updating Brooks Brothers

Brooks Brothers' subdued, richly furnished stores reflected a club-like atmosphere that began in 1889 when Frederick Brooks closed the New York store on Saturdays because of "outsiders" who wandered in to shop. Brooks supposedly asked, "Who are all these people? We must save the merchandise for all our regular customers." This attitude endured until Marks & Spencer acquired Brooks Brothers and began updating its image. Marks & Spencer allowed merchandise to be displayed outside their glass cases so customers could browse and installed bright lights and escalators as part of the mahogany-paneled flagship store's $7 million facelift.

The changes commended attention. Novelist Tom Wolfe quipped, "Escalators remind me of the '30s. That brings them up to within 50 years of the present day." Brooks Brothers president Roberti told the *New York Times*, "The notion for years was that Brooks Brothers was a private club, and that doesn't make good

business sense. The fact is that the only denominator is good taste, good quality, and good value."

Brooks Brothers also began updating its line of merchandise to attract a younger clientele. In addition to its traditional business attire, Brooks Brothers began offering pleated trousers and two-button suits. It also began offering denim jeans, a Brooks Brothers-labeled varsity jacket with snaps, multi-colored cummerbunds, and even lingerie and suede skirts for women; all of which prompted *Business Week* to ask in a 1993 headline, "What's Next, Grunge Bathrobes?" *Business Week* noted that "some of the changes annoy traditional Brooks Brothers customers—and bear out the dire predictions of critics who thought the pairing of a Wal-Mart-style parent with an old-guard haberdasher was a bad idea to begin with."

In 1989, the Brooks Brothers launched its first nationwide print advertising campaign which placed full-color ads in magazines. Previously, Brooks Brothers had relied on black and white advertising in local newspapers. Most upsetting of all the changes, according to *Business Week,* was that Brooks Brothers stopped manufacturing much of its clothing except for suits, ties, and some shirts. But the company maintains that its clothing was still made to its exact specifications by U.S. manufacturers. In 1990 Roberti sent a letter to the more than one million Brooks Brothers customers with charge accounts that said, "We remain firmly focused on the values that have made us the authority for classic American style for 172 years."

## 175th Anniversary

Brooks Brothers launched a major advertising and promotional campaign in the fall of 1993 to celebrate its 175th anniversary. The campaign included national advertising in major business-oriented publications and a six-page insert in *American Heritage* written by George Plimpton. The print ads capitalized on the reputation of Brooks Brothers clothing as the "uniform" of successful businessmen and the expanded line of more casual clothes. "These days you never know . . . Success today is often out of uniform, but wears the same label it has for 175 years."

Promotional efforts included a 45-minute documentary video to be shown in Brooks Brothers stores, a commemorative publication for customers, and a special catalog of classic merchandise filled with historical anecdotes called "The Best of Brooks Brothers." The company also planned a series of special events around the theme "175 Years of American Style." A traveling exhibit of Brooks Brothers history was scheduled to appear at its stores in New York, Boston, San Francisco, Chicago, and Washington, DC.

## Further Reading:

Barron, James, "Pleats? Cardigan Cuddling? Brooks Brothers Unbuttons," *New York Times,* Nov. 11, 1989, p. B1.

Barmash, Isadore, "Brooks Brothers Stays the Course," *New York Times,* Nov. 23, 1990, p. D1.

Better, Nancy Marx, "Unbuttoning Brooks Brothers," *M Inc.,* March 1991, p. 18.

Bhargava, Sunita Wadekar, "What's Next, Grunge Bathrobes?," *Business Week,* June 21, 1993, p. 64.

*Brooks Brothers Celebrates 175 Years of Clothing Originals; A Look At Fashion Firsts,* DeVries Public Relations, New York, 1993.

*Brooks Brothers Celebrates An Illustrious 175 Years,* DeVries Public Relations, New York, 1993.

*Brooks Brothers Milestones,* DeVries Public Relations, New York 1993.

"Garfinckel Sheds a Profit Problem," *Business Week,* Aug. 17, 1981, p. 32.

"Garfinckel Struggles to Foil Allied's Bid," *Business Week,* Aug. 31, 1981, p. 52.

Graham, Judith, "Brooks Bros. Spiffs up Its Image," *Advertising Age,* Oct. 30, 1989, p. 68.

Maremont, Mark, "Marks & Spencer Pays a Premium for Pinstripes," *Business Week,* April 18, 1988, p. 67.

Millstein, Gilbert, "The Suits on the Brooks Brothers Men," *New York Times Magazine,* Aug. 15, 1976, p. 28.

Palmieri, Jean E., "An American Icon Celebrates a Milestone; Brooks Brothers still Spry at 175," *DNR,* May 31, 1993, p. 4.

Plimpton, George, "Under The Golden Fleece," *American Heritage,* November 1993, p. 40.

Sheils, Merrill, "The Brooks Look Moves to Japan," *Newsweek,* Sept. 10, 1979, p. 65.

Van Gelder, Lawrence, "Brooks Bros. Will End Customer Tailoring," *New York Times,* May 8, 1976, p. 1.

"Why Garfinckel Had to Give in to Allied," *Business Week,* Sept. 14, 1981, p. 33.

*—Dean Boyer*

# BUFFERIN®

Bufferin aspirin has been a leading brand of aspirin since the 1950s and in the early 1990s was the fourth-best-selling brand, behind Anacin, Bayer, and Excedrin. Its unique formula combines two antacids with aspirin, to protect the stomach from the upset some aspirin users experience. The antacids also cause the aspirin to dissolve faster in the stomach. This has long been the basis of Bufferin's advertising campaigns, which promise faster relief than with ordinary aspirin.

## Early Marketing

The effects of aspirin (acetylsalicylic acid) had been documented as early as the mid-19th century, and aspirin became a popular drug worldwide in the early years of the 20th century. Anyone could make and sell aspirin, but one brand, Bayer, dominated the American market. Bufferin was invented by the Bristol-Myers company in 1949 and promoted as something better than existing aspirins. Bristol-Myers' researchers had added antacids to their aspirin formula, with the original intention of aiding the multiple complaints of hangover sufferers. This in itself set Bufferin apart from its competitors, but Bufferin had another advantage. Chemists at Bristol-Myers noted that the combination of aspirin and antacids worked to speed up the rate at which the aspirin was absorbed into the bloodstream. Bufferin debuted with the marketing pitch, "Bufferin acts twice as fast as aspirin!"

Early advertising for Bufferin called it a "new, remarkable product for the relief of pain." It was the "modern, faster-acting headache remedy" and the "modern antacid pain-reliever." These phrases did not spell out that Bufferin was actually aspirin, and the "twice as fast as aspirin" slogan also made it seem that Bufferin must be something other than that familiar drug. Print ads showed the miseries of a variety of ailments, all cured best with Bufferin. A housewife in an apron holds her head in anguish as two little boys brandish toy guns and clubs at each other. She has a tension headache. A young man in rumpled pajamas sits staring woozily, showing the headache of over-indulgence. A business man is shown in the act of sneezing, his face wrinkled up, eyes screwed shut, handkerchief inches from his face. He needs Bufferin for his "cold miseries." A fourth drawing crowded into the advertisement demonstrates Bufferin's fast action with a cut away view of a throat and stomach, drawn to look like plumbing parts. Bubbles of text explain how "medical science knows" that a pain reliever must get through the stomach to the blood stream, and that

Bufferin performs this task twice as fast as aspirin. Another line claims that Bufferin "won't upset your stomach the way aspirin often does."

The drawing of the body filled with pipes became an animated cartoon television commercial. This commercial contrasted one set of human piping taking aspirin, and a second one taking Bufferin. Little "A"s of aspirin drop into the first stomach and sit there. Little "B"s of Bufferin drop into the second stomach and are immediately changed into bubbles that flow on through to the rest of the plumbing. This represented Bufferin hitting the blood stream twice as fast. An accompanying song ran, "Don't let it last and last! Get quick relief with Bufferin, it's fast . . . fast . . . fast!" The "fast . . . fast . . . fast" echoed the claim of another aspirin competitor, Anacin, which gave "fast, fast, fast relief."

Bufferin's advertisements were effective. When Bufferin debuted in 1949, Bristol-Myers spent less than $350,000 on promotion. Seven years later, Bristol-Myers was lavishing more than $13 million annually on Bufferin. Market share began at only 2 percent but climbed rapidly, to stand at 15 percent by 1957. Bayer, which had long been the top-selling brand, lost market share to Bufferin and the other major aspirin brand, Anacin; the three-way competition was intense.

## Contested Claims

Each of these three brands strived to differentiate themselves from one another, though the main pain-reliever in each was chemically identical. Bufferin described itself in one campaign as the best painkiller for "sensitive people." In one television ad, a housing official faced with the unpleasant task of evicting two elderly people from their home takes Bufferin. This relieves his headache and upset, and he is able calmly to deliver his unwelcome message. An announcer wraps up the ad with the line, "Bufferin. For sensitive people. It's much better than plain aspirin."

Claims like this that compared Bufferin to plain aspirin angered Sterling, makers of Bayer. Of the top three pain relievers, Bayer was the only one that was all aspirin, and its ads had stressed Bayer's purity. A 1957 Bayer ad struck back at Bufferin, and Anacin as well, warning consumers not to pay more for "aspirin in disguise" and for "extra ingredients that can't relieve pain." Besides taking its grievance to the public through advertising,

## AT A GLANCE

**B**ufferin brand aspirin first marketed by the Bristol-Myers Company, New York, NY, 1949; company changed its name to Bristol-Myers Squibb Co., 1989.

**Performance:** *Market share*—9.3% of aspirin category. *Sales*—$64 million.

**Major competitor:** American Home Products Company's Anacin; also, Sterling Winthrop Inc.'s Bayer.

**Advertising:** *Agency*—Laurence, Charles, Free & Lawson,, New York, NY. *Major campaign*—None in 1993.

**Addresses:** *Parent company*—Bristol-Myers Squibb Co., 345 Park Ave., New York, NY 10154; phone: (212) 546-4000.

Sterling asked the Federal Trade Commission (FTC) to stop Bufferin from making its "twice as fast as aspirin" claim. The FTC was in charge of regulating over-the-counter drugs, but at first it was reluctant to take up the charges against Bufferin. Sterling complained that Bufferin could not be twice as fast as aspirin since it *was* aspirin, and therefore its ads were false. But the FTC ruled that there was no way to tell whether Bufferin was twice as fast or not. No scientific studies had been done to compare the effectiveness of different aspirin brands, and without this, there was no case.

But eventually the FTC did act. Researchers completed a study comparing the top aspirin brands in 1960, and found no difference in effectiveness. In 1961 the FTC decided it had grounds to charge false advertising against four drug companies, including Bristol-Myers for its Bufferin ads. The makers of Anacin, St. Joseph's Aspirin, and Bayer were also charged, since all had claimed that their products were in some way better than the others. Bristol-Myers issued a strong statement claiming that more than ten years of clinical research had proven the truth of Bufferin's advertising claims. But this case dragged through FTC hearings for more than ten years. In the meantime, Bufferin did not substantially alter its marketing approach. A 1968 advertisement told television viewers that Bufferin worked in half the time of regular aspirin. A wristwatch cut in half ticked away on a man's wrist, accompanying the words: "You've a headache. You've taken aspirin. How long before it goes to work? You should have taken Bufferin. . . . Bufferin can cut the time in half. Half the time. That's Bufferin time." Half the time or twice as fast, the message was the same.

Though the 1960 study had shown the major aspirin brands to be virtually identical in effect, a later study seemed to show promise for Bufferin's role in easing arthritic pain. This study appeared in the *Journal of the American Medical Association* in June of 1965, and Bufferin was quick to incorporate the study's findings into new advertising. The ads used a before and after drawing to demonstrate the results achieved by patients who took Bufferin for their pain. It also quoted the study to imply that 87 percent of the patients involved had benefitted from taking Bufferin. The FTC brought a new suit against Bristol-Myers regarding this ad campaign, which had appeared in newspapers and magazines in mid-1966. The FTC claimed that Bristol-Myers had distorted the study's findings to make it seem that a regular dose of Bufferin would ease arthritis pain. The patients in the study had actually taken massive doses of Bufferin under close medical supervision, and the 87 percent who had experienced remission may not have had long-lasting or permanent relief from their

condition. The FTC also took issue with Bristol-Myers' contention that it was "a leader in arthritis research," as the ad had stated.

Bristol-Myers called the FTC charges in themselves false and misleading. Having spent nearly $1 million over the past ten years sponsoring arthritis research, the company felt no embarrassment in calling itself a leader in that field. The company declared that its advertising had been a simple and forthright attempt to report the favorable results of the study. While one FTC examiner called for his agency to drop the complaint, the case was eventually settled in 1968, when the FTC found Bristol-Myers guilty of using misleading advertising. However, the agency did not require the company to issue a retraction, and Bristol-Myers went on to promote a new product called Arthritis Strength Bufferin.

The original FTC complaint against Bufferin finally came to a conclusion in 1973. An FTC judge found that Bristol-Myers was guilty of false advertising because it was unable to substantiate its claims that Bufferin offered pain relief twice as fast as aspirin. At the same time, there was no evidence that it didn't. The judge also ordered that Bufferin disclose its ingredients, and cease to claim that Bufferin could relieve stress or tension, but Bristol-Myers was not required to run any corrective advertising. The legal process had been exhausting for Bristol-Myers, yet the company did not come off too badly. A company statement reasoned that the "most important consideration is that millions of . . . people have used Bufferin . . . for years. These people are familiar with our ad claims, have used the products over and over again, and must be satisfied that these products live up to our claims." Bufferin continued in its number three status behind Bayer and Anacin. Doctors continued to recommend Bufferin, with a 1975 survey showing Bufferin the second most recommended pain reliever. Clearly Bufferin had to be careful of the wording of future advertising. But its biggest threat came not from government regulation but from new competitors in the painkiller market.

### Changing Market Conditions

During the 1970s Bufferin's market share fell, reaching 9.5 percent in 1977. The decline hit the other established aspirin brands as well, when one of the most successful product introductions ever transformed the analgesic market. Tylenol, an aspirin-free painkiller that had for years received little advertising, suddenly swept to the number one spot in 1977. Soon Tylenol had almost a third of the total analgesic market share. Bufferin shopped for a new ad agency, and aired a television commercial claiming that it had anti-inflammatory powers that Tylenol lacked. But Bufferin's market share continued to slip, falling to 7.3 percent in 1981. Instead of attacking the powerful Tylenol, Bufferin decided to return to its old foes, plain aspirin brands.

But the aspirin market shrank even more. Market leader Tylenol was made of acetaminophen, and several other acetaminophen products vied with it. When a third type of painkiller, ibuprofen, came on the market in 1985, its leading brands Advil and Nuprin combined took almost 15 percent of the pain relief market in 1986, leaving even less room for aspirin. By 1987, Bufferin was taking only 4.5 percent of the total analgesic market, and its advertising budget had shrunk to $9.6 million.

A big boost for Bufferin came the next year. A study conducted by Harvard University found that healthy men who took an aspirin every other day could lower their risk of heart attack by 47 percent. Bristol-Myers had donated Bufferin for use in the study, and the company was quick to capitalize on the report's good news. The company came out with Tri-Buffered Bufferin, which promised fewer stomach upsets for people who took aspirin regularly. A new advertisement used a celebrity testimonial, stating: "Under the supervision of his doctor, Arthur Ashe uses the Bufferin brand of buffered aspirin." This advertisement did not explain what condition the tennis star used Bufferin for, but the "supervision of his doctor" phrase hinted that he was not casually taking aspirin for headaches. The Food and Drug Administration was wary of allowing Bufferin and the other aspirin brands to use the new heart study specifically in advertising, pending further research. Nevertheless, as aspirin was called a "miracle drug" in a *Business Week* cover story, media hype was enough to send aspirin sales way up in the weeks following the announcement of the Harvard study results. Bufferin was allowed to run ads that affirmed the results of an earlier study showing aspirin could be used to prevent second heart attacks, and its new slogan was, "When you take aspirin more than once a week."

## Performance Appraisal

Despite the impact of the 1988 heart health study, the surge in aspirin sales was short-lived. Even though Bufferin was the brand that had been used in the Harvard study, this did not significantly advance Bufferin's status with consumers. By the next year, Bufferin had already changed its advertising. The new ads shied away from the "doctor's supervision" and "more than once a week" themes that had been meant to promote Bufferin's preventive heart care faculties. The new message was aimed at consumers 50 years old and up, who would take Bufferin to deal with the ordinary aches and pains of aging. Print and television ads featured actress Angela Lansbury declaring that a cup of tea and Bufferin were what helped her enjoy her golden years. This new campaign was targeted at a growing demographic group, and at the same time harkened back to Bufferin's advertising of the 1950s. A marketing director at Bristol-Myers had looked back over Bufferin's advertising history and found the most convincing ads to be simple testimonials made by television personality Arthur Godfrey. The Lansbury spots intended to recapture the directness of those earlier ads, and speak to older people who still preferred aspirin to the newer pain relievers.

By the late 1980s, Bufferin was the fourth-place aspirin brand, with about 10 percent of the aspirin market. But the aspirin market was shrinking, to less than 40 percent of the total analgesic market. The aspirin market remained flat in the 1990s, as aspirin's appeal paled next to acetaminophen and ibuprofen. Hope for change still lay in medical research that showed aspirin's benefits in fighting a variety of diseases. But even the overwhelming good news of the 1988 Harvard study had done little to help Bufferin's sales. Bufferin's early marketing had cleverly advertised Bufferin as better than aspirin, though it was in fact aspirin. It was very difficult to fight the new pain relievers, which promoted themselves as better than aspirin, and in fact were not aspirin.

Bufferin's stagnation was only a piece of the sluggishness of all the major aspirin brands. A 1992 report showed that aspirin manufacturing was only operating at 65 percent capacity. Sterling Winthrop Inc., maker of Bayer, stopped producing its own aspirin powder and shut down its plant in 1991. This same report suggested that the major aspirin marketers would have to work together to bring back their brands' lost prestige. And the aspirin makers would have to get cooperation from the Food and Drug Administration to be allowed to properly advertise the results of new medical research. This would be a departure from the rugged competition that drove Bufferin in its early years. Without a major change in overall market conditions, it does not seem likely that Bufferin will do more than maintain its current position.

## Further Reading:

"Aspirin Makers Look to Offset Inroads by Other Analgesics," *Chemical Marketing Reporter*, February 24, 1992, p. 14.

"Bates Ads Boost Anacin, Bufferin!," *Advertising Age*, March 4, 1968, p. 2.

"Bristol-Myers Charges CBS with Libel over Statements on Company Studies, Ads," *Chemical Marketing Reporter*, October 22, 1979, p. 1.

"Bristol-Myers Draws FTC Blast for Bufferin Ad," *Advertising Age*, October 7, 1968, p. 1.

"Bristol-Myers, Sterling, Plough Defend Ad Claims," *Advertising Age*, March 22, 1961, p. 2.

"Bufferin Answers FTC Ad Complaints," *Broadcasting*, March 6, 1967, pp. D38–39.

"Drop Plaint on Bufferin Ad, FTC Examiner Urges," *Advertising Age*, November 27, 1967, p. 1.

Freeman, Laurie, "Sales of Aspirin Soar after Study," *Advertising Age*, March 28, 1988, p. 3.

"FTC Issues Plaint against Three in Analgesic Ad Case," *Advertising Age*, March 19, 1973, p. 2.

"FTC Plaint Hits Bufferin Ad; B-M Calls Charge False," *Advertising Age*, January 30, 1967, p. 3.

Giges, Nancy, *Advertising Age*, "B-M Sets Big Ad Drive for New Bufferin," December 6, 1971, p. 1; "Bufferin Seeks Creative to Break Analgesic Mold," August 22, 1977, p. 2.

Gordon, Richard L., "FDA's Panel Urges Tougher Restrictions on Analgesic Ads," *Advertising Age*, October 25, 1976, p. 1.

Hamilton, Joan O'C, and others, "Miracle Drug," *Business Week*, August 29, 1988, pp. 56–61.

Hiestand, Michael, "New Health Study on Heart Attacks Sends Aspirin Makers Racing to Ads," *Adweek's Marketing Week*, February 1, 1988, p. 1.

Mann, Charles C. and Mark L. Plummer, *The Aspirin Wars: Money, Medicine, and 100 Years of Rampant Competition*, New York: Alfred A. Knopf, 1991.

"New Headaches in the Painkiller Market," *Fortune*, September 15, 1986, p. 10.

O'Gara, James V., "Bates Trades Anacin for Bufferin Business," *Advertising Age*, November 20, 1967, p. 1.

Sloan, Pat, "Aspirins Ready New Strategies," *Advertising Age*, February 2, 1981, p. 1.

Winters, Patricia, "Bufferin Aims at 50-Plus," *Advertising Age*, October 23, 1989, p. 4.

*—A. Woodward*

# BURMA-SHAVE®

"Our fortune/Is your/Shaven face/It's our best/Advertising space/Burma-Shave." Ask anyone over 40 years old if they have ever heard of Burma-Shave shaving cream and they are likely to wax nostalgic about those signs they remember reading along the highway that always had some humorous jingle about getting rid of facial hair. The famous Burma-Shave signs, sets of six spaced at 100 feet apart, graced the United States' most traveled routes from 1926 until the mid-1960s, becoming American icons. Perhaps no other company has experienced the phenomenal advertising success of the Minnesota-based Burma-Vita Company, which was founded by the Odell family.

## Brand Origins

Burma-Shave, which later came under the ownership of American Safety Razor, was developed from a liniment that the Odell family had mixed and tried to market to local druggists. As Leonard Odell recalled in Frank Rowsome's *The Verse by the Side of the Road,* Odell's grandfather got the liniment recipe from an old sea captain. "Grandfather made it in his office up in the old Globe Building. It was a potent liniment both in action and smell. You could smell it on the ground floor when he was mixing it on the fifth floor, which probably didn't endear him to his fellow tenants."

The liniment's curative powers were discovered when a relative was severely burned with hot fat. "In desperation she stuck her hand into this liniment and in spite of what you might think, the pain stopped immediately. She had no blisters and no scars. It was a marvelous thing," Leonard was quoted as saying.

That was when Clinton Odell, Leonard's father, decided to market the concoction. Clinton made out a royalty arrangement with his father, who had been disabled by a stroke by then, and set out to sell it. He chose the word "Burma" because most of the essential oils—camphor, cassia and cajeput—in the product came from the Malay peninsula; and he added "Vita," which means life and vigor in Latin. Hence, the name Burma-Vita denoted "life from Burma."

Early sales of Burma-Vita were not impressive. As Leonard later recalled to Rowsome: "We nearly starved to death on that product for a couple of years." The Odells—Clinton and sons Leonard and Allan—were advised by druggists to find something they could market universally instead of only to the sick. One person gave Clinton a sample of Lloyd's Euxesis to see if he wanted to sell it. Lloyd's Euxesis, the original brushless shaving cream on the market, was produced England. Soon Clinton had an idea.

A couple of years before, Clinton had befriended a chemist who had succumbed to illness and moved to Arizona in an effort to save his life. Touched by the story, Clinton sent his friend a $25 check for Christmas. In 1925, just when the Odells were about to throw in the towel, the chemist, Carl Noren appeared announcing, "I'm well and what can I do for you?"

Clinton asked Noren if he had ever thought about inventing a brushless shaving cream. Noren, who used to be the chief cosmetic chemist for the Old Minneapolis Drug Company, said he had never heard of such a thing but thought he would give it a try. (Noren would eventually serve as director of the Burma-Vita Company.) Noren's first batch was "frankly, terrible stuff," according to Rowsome in his book *The Verse by the Side of the Road.* About 300 formulations were made until the Odells went back to Formula 143 (some historians claim it was number 153); they apparently discovered that an aged jar "gave a person a real fine shave." With that, Burma-Shave was invented.

## Early Marketing Strategy

Early marketing of the shaving cream formulation centered around a "Jars on Approval" program. Jars of Burma-Shave were given to men off the street. The Odells would explain how to use this new brushless shaving cream. If the customer was satisfied after using it, he agreed to give them 50 cents; if not, he was asked to return the used jar.

Sales during the Jars on Approval campaign lagged, and a new strategy was desperately needed. Then one day, Allan Odell noticed on his way from Aurora to Joliet, Illinois, a set of small serial signs advertising such things as gas, oil, and restrooms, with the last sign pointing to the gas station. He thought it might be effective to market a product that way. But advertising agents at the time told the Odells it wouldn't work. Luckily Allan refused to listen. With $200 loan from Clinton, Allan and younger brother Leonard bought secondhand wooden boards from Rose Brothers Wrecking Company, then recut, painted and stenciled them. The first Burma-Shave signs, placed along farmers' fields, did not have the rhymed jingles that eventually made them famous, but had something like this: "Shave the modern way/Fine for the skin/Druggists have it/Burma Shave."

The first "trial" of 10 to 12 sets of crudely stenciled signs was conducted along two roads—Route 65 to Albert Lea and to Red Wing out of Minneapolis. By the beginning of 1926, the Odells were receiving repeat orders from druggists for the first time since marketing Burma-Shave. Father Clinton was finally convinced that Allan had a good idea except that Burma-Vita was now bankrupt. To stay afloat, he incorporated Burma-Vita and sold 49 percent of his stock. Burma-Shave was well on its way to becoming a definite sign of the times.

## First Commercial Success

The Odells established their first sign shop, where they made silk screen signs, in 1926. Locations were purchased, and Allan Odell and his father wrote most of the early verses, which were targeted at hairy men: "He played/A sax/Had no b.o./But his whiskers scratched/So she let him go." Rowsome noted, "There was also an impious absurdity that was captivating, for no advertisers had ever spoken to consumers this way before: 'Does your husband/Misbehave/Grunt and Grumble/Rant and rave/Shoot the

## AT A GLANCE

**B**urma-Shave brand of shaving cream developed in 1925 by Clinton Odell from his father's liniment made of camphor, cassia, and cajeput oils; Odell purchased his father's Burma-Vita Company in the mid-1920s; Burma-Shave advertised by a series of roadside signs, beginning in 1926. Burma-Vita purchased in 1963 by Philip Morris, Inc., which discontinued roadside advertising in 1965; Philip Morris dropped all Burma trademarks and Burma-Shave division purchased by American Safety Razor of Staunton, VA, 1978; Burma-Shave trademark registered in 1979 by American Safety Razor, 1979 and brand no longer actively marketed, produced, or advertised.

**Performance:** *Sales*—$3 million in the brand's heyday.

**Major competitor:** Pfizer's Barbasol; also Molle, Krank's Shaving Cream, Colgate-Palmolive's Colgate, and S.C. Johnson's Edge.

**Advertising:** *Major campaign*—The campaign from 1926 to 1965 was the placement along U.S. highways of sets of six roadside signs, each sign containing a line of a humorous jingle.

**Addresses:** *Parent company*—American Safety Razor, P.O. Box 500, Staunton, VA 22401; phone: (703) 248-8000, or (800) 445-9284; fax: (708) 248-0522.

brute/Some Burma-Shave.' '' It took three seconds to read each sign if the car was traveling at 35 miles per hour. The signs became so popular that Alexander Woollcott remarked it was as difficult to read one Burma-Shave sign as it was to eat one salted peanut.

Selling a new shaving cream—one that was brushless—required the changing of ingrained habits, so the Odells sold Burma-Shave on its convenience, speed, and modernity. The competition, however, was not far behind. Molle, Krank's Shaving Cream and Barbasol soon launched brushless shaving creams, followed by the Colgate-Palmolive and Williams companies. Private brands appeared during the Great Depression through drugstore chains and discount stores. Barbasol even legally challenged the Burma-Shave jingle ''No brush/No lather/No rub-in,'' alleging that it was Barbasol's exclusive property. A similar line was sung on the radio as the theme song of Barbasol: ''Barbasol, Barbasol, no brush, no lather, no rub-in—wet your razor and begin.''

By the end of the 1920s, Allan and Clinton ran out of fresh jingles. To revitalize advertising, Allan held an annual contest and paid $100 for each verse accepted. Entries poured in by the thousands. Some of the ideas were censored in an effort to ''protect the American highway against anything scatological or off-color.''

The first public service jingle appeared in 1935 and was written by Allan: ''Keep well/To the right/Of the oncoming car/Get your close shaves/From the half-pound jar.'' In addition to protecting the highways from immoral advertising, the Odells felt they needed to be helpful in terms of not contributing to highway accidents with distracting signs. They tried to instill some sort of goodwill even though billboard backlash in the 1960s would spell the signs'—and the company's— demise. Jingles in the 1950s encouraged the prevention of forest fires. During the war years, the signs exhorted drivers to buy war bonds: ''Let's make Hitler/And Hirohito/Look as sick as/Old Benito/Buy defense bonds.''

Signs appeared from Maine to Texas with 20 to 25 new jingles installed regularly. Annual advertising costs started with as little as $25,000 in 1926, when signs were placed in Minnesota, Wisconsin, and Iowa, netting sales of $68,000. The following year, sales doubled, with $45,000 spent on signs, which popped up throughout the Midwest. By 1929, Burma-Vita was spending approximately $65,000 in ads, with sales averaging around a quarter of a million. The company eventually began grossing more than $3 million a year as signs could be found from coast to coast.

The only states where jingles did not appear were Arizona, Nevada, and New Mexico, due to low traffic density, and Massachusetts, because of its many winding roads. Burma-Shave signs required highway locations that were fairly level and straight, with no other interfering big billboards. Farmers were offered jars of Burma-Shave to break the ice, and negotiations would begin. With extended leases that could last for decades, some farmers would reap slight profits from allowing Burma-Vita to lease their land. Road crews of advance men, post hole diggers, and samplers would descend on U.S. roadways installing and maintaining signs nearly year round. Signs located near college towns were often stolen, but company officials fixed that by reinforcing post holes. Wood-eating rodents as well as horses using the signs as back scratchers posed other challenges.

The signs, originally in red and white lettering, were eventually placed practically everywhere—even in the South Pole upon request by the U.S. Navy to help boost the morale of officers stationed in Antarctica. The same idea was used during World War II on the roads leading to the front in Italy: ''A G.I. Joe/From Venafro/Passed on a curve/Now he's/Six feet below,'' as quoted by William K. Zinsser in the *Saturday Evening Post*.

Other colors besides red and white, such as orange and black, were used but were eventually discontinued. Burma-Vita had to adhere to some state regulations requiring various colors for safety reasons, thus blue and white Burma-Shave signs appeared along South Dakota roadways.

Rowsome observed that the signs were comforting to viewers in part because of the friendly, folksy language: ''The impression was given that the company sure must be made up of friendly plain folks, very different from those other advertisers of drugstore products, who noisily threatened malodorousness, disease and decay.''

### The Party Ended

All good things come to an end, and the end for Burma-Vita Company was evident in 1948, when sales declined and costs increased, prompting salary cuts. Eventually the jingles just wore out and were temporarily abandoned in favor of television and radio advertising. People were also beginning to drive too fast to read the signs. The old time highways of yore were turning into high-speed expressways. Signs were becoming costlier and less effective, and complaints about billboard pollution mounted.

Clinton Odell, who had served as chairman of the board, died at age 80 in 1958. His son Allan succeeded him as president until the early 1960s, when younger son Leonard took the helm. On February 7, 1963, it was announced publicly that the Burma-Vita Company had been sold to Philip Morris, Inc. Immediately, Philip Morris decided to retire the road signs, which were costing an average of $200,000 in advertising, and switch to more profitable media such as radio and television. The signs were gone by 1965.

Attempts were made to translate the jingles to television in 1965 and 1967, but advertising was virtually discontinued.

By 1978, Philip Morris discontinued all rights to such Burma-Vita trademarks as Burma-Shave, Burma Bey, Burma Blockade, and Burma Face-Guard, reported John J. O'Connor in *Advertising Age*. By this time, Burma products had not been marketed for nearly a year. Philip Morris sold the Burma trademarks to American Safety Razor Products, then a division of Philip Morris. Allan Odell, the mastermind behind the signs, would enter into semi-retirement serving only as a consultant, making Leonard president of the new division under American Safety Razor.

The discontinuation of Burma-Shave jingles met with public farewells conducted in the mainstream press. The Advertising Club of New York held a luncheon to bid adieu and introduce a Eurasian actress who would become the Burma-Shave TV spokesperson. Some of the signs were given to the Smithsonian Institution for posterity. In all, some 35,000 individual Burma-Shave signs had dotted the United States' highways and byways.

The Burma-Shave signs were a stroke of advertising genius—an idea that happened at the right place at the right time. "We've had fun with this business," Leonard Odell commented to Zinsser in the *Saturday Evening Post*. "We were the last of the four independent brushless shaving-cream companies to sell out to a big corporation. But it's increasingly important to compete in the modern market." Allan agreed and told Zinsser, "I don't know if I'd get the same response if I started putting up those signs today [the 1960s]. Some of the fire and vigor have gone out."

## The Future Is Past

American Safety Razor of Staunton, Virginia, no longer makes Burma-Shave in quantities and does not actively market the brand. On special request, the company has provided samples but does not include any Burma brand in its price list of products that focus primarily on private label razors and bar soaps. In 1993 American Safety Razor filed for an initial public offering to raise a needed $80 million to get out of debt. The company came under the ownership of an investing group led by Jordan Co. of New York, which purchased American Safety Razor in 1989 for $140 million.

## Further Reading:

Barach, Arnold B., *Famous American Trademarks,* Washington, DC: Public Affairs Press, 1971, pp. 25–26.

Kansas, Dave, "Razor Concern Plans to Make Initial Offering," *Wall Street Journal,* April 5, 1993, p. B70(E).

O'Connor, John J., "Burma-Shave, Once a Star, May Now Be Mark of ASR," *Advertising Age,* March 6, 1978, p. 45.

"The Unsung Bards of Burma-Shave," *Changing Times,* February 1965, p. 47.

Rowsome, Frank, Jr., *The Verse by the Side of the Road,* Vermont: Stephen Greene Press, 1965.

Zinsser, William K., "Good-Bye Burma-Shave," *Saturday Evening Post,* September 5, 1964, pp. 65–66; "Good-bye Burma-Shave," *Reader's Digest,* February 1965, pp. 103–06.

—*Evelyn S. Dorman*

# BUSTER BROWN®

Since 1904 the name Buster Brown has been synonymous with children's shoes. The venerable trademark is one of the oldest in the nation and is owned by Brown Group, Inc., a footwear and specialty retailing company. The Brown Group's other brands include Connie, Naturalizer, and Life Stride; the company also owns the Famous Footwear shoe store chain. Although children's shoes account for only a small portion of Brown Group's sales, Buster Brown shoes remain popular with children and parents alike because of their durability and kid-pleasing styles.

## A Brand for Everyone

Buster Brown originated as a character in the nation's first four-color, full-page comic strip. In 1902 cartoonist Richard Fenton Outcault created the youthful prankster Buster, as well as his dog Tige and his sister Mary Jane for the *New York Herald*. According to "The Life and Times of Buster Brown," "Buster's Lord Fauntleroy clothes and antic behavior were as familiar to those who read the 'funnies' at the turn-of-the-century as [Little Orphan] Annie's blank eyes or [Charlie Brown's] inability to coach a winning baseball team were later." John Bush, a young sales executive at the Brown Shoe Company, quickly perceived the promotional value of the Buster Brown character and convinced the company to negotiate trademark rights with Outcault. Bush's foresight paid off when he became president of the company in 1915. The Buster Brown brand debuted at the St. Louis World's Fair in 1904, where the Brown Company's model shoe factory featuring the character won the shoe exhibit's Double Grand Prize. The brand was off to an auspicious start; but there was one problem—the contract with the cartoonist did not give the Brown Company exclusive rights to the mischievous boy character. At the same time the Brown Shoe Company was touting its new brand of shoes, Outcault was selling the Buster Brown name left and right at his own booth at prices ranging from $5.00 to $1,000. Within a very short time, there were as many as 50 products on the market carrying the Buster Brown name, from wheat flour, apples, coffee, cigars, candy, raisins, bread, and bourbon to harmonicas, horseshoes, pocketbooks, waffle irons, egg-dye, pocketbooks, and textiles. The popular Buster Brown apparel line formed at this time and was owned by the Gerber Company of Chattanooga, Tennessee, until it was sold in 1993 to a group of investors.

## Buster Comes to Life

The Buster Brown cartoon characters were inspired by Outcault's own son, daughter, and family dog. The cartoon strip was published until 1926 and its light-hearted, entertaining combination of mischief and morality made it a favorite of all ages. From 1904 to 1915 and again from 1921 to 1930, the Brown Shoe Company capitalized on Buster Brown's popularity by producing an enormously successful live act that traveled to theaters, shoe stores, and department stores around the country. The act employed 20 different people to play the character of Buster; the most famous of these was Ed Ansley, who visited every county in the United States drawing upwards of 25,000 spectators for his performances as Buster Brown. The act also featured a real dog in the role of Buster Brown's pal, Tige.

With the words, "I'm Buster Brown; I live in a shoe. (WOOF! WOOF!) That's my dog Tige: he lives there too," the performance began which included an improvised discussion with the audience and concluded with prizes for the kids. According to William Harris in *Forbes*, it was a "fabulous promotion" that "helped the company sell thousands of pairs of shoes." The credit for the success of these shows goes to John Bush, claimed David Powers Cleary in *Great American Brands: The Success Formulas That Made Them Famous*. Because of his clever use of a living trademark, "Bush was an important pioneer in the art of advertising to children," wrote Cleary. Most shoe companies at the time assumed that parents chose their children's shoes and that advertising for children was a useless tactic, but "Decades later," Cleary continued, "Brown Shoe Company's marketing research would find that children are the predominant influence in the shoe brand selection—beginning at the age of five."

## Print, Radio, and TV

In addition to the live act, other early marketing campaigns included national magazine advertisements. A 1920 ad in *Vogue* read as follows: "Charming Children, Like Fragrant Flowers, Deserve Constant Care. . . . Their shoes are even more important than their frocks. Dainty frocks enhance the child's beauty—but Buster Brown Shoes develop the feet upon Nature's graceful lines, and thus preserve their natural beauty, with the aid of the Brown Shaping Last." Other promotions further illustrated the company's penchant for performance, such as the 1926 opening of a new plant in Vincennes, Indiana, in which Brown Shoe President

## AT A GLANCE

Cartoonist Richard Fenton Outcault sold the rights to the Buster Brown name to Brown Shoe Company executive John Bush at the 1904 World's Fair in St. Louis; Brown Shoe Company renamed Brown Group, Inc., 1972; the Buster Brown brand was transferred to the Brown Group's Pagoda business in 1991.

*Performance:* *Sales*—1.8 billion (1989; company wide, including Nautralizer and Connie brands).

*Major competitor:* Stride Rite; also Keds.

*Advertising:* *Agency*—The Puckett Group, 1992—. *Major campaign*—"My First Buster. There's a little kid in every shoe."

*Addresses:* *Parent company*—Brown Group, Inc., Buster Brown Division, 8300 Maryland Avenue, St. Louis, MO 63166; phone: (314) 854-4000; fax: (314) 854-4274.

John Bush and other executives arrived by railroad car, accompanied by Buster Brown and Tige.

In 1943 the characters were granted their own variety show on the West Coast NBC radio network called *The Buster Brown Gang.* Within two years the gang and their host, "Smilin' " Ed McConnell, could be heard on 165 stations throughout the United States. In 1951 the show made the transition to television where it aired until 1955, a year after McConnell's death.

Other forms of advertising over the years included distribution of decals and advertising cards to storekeepers and novelty giveaways for the consumer, many of which have become collectible items. From the late 1950s through the early 1990s, the Brown Company has regularly promoted its brands both on television and in print. A 1957 campaign in *Life Magazine* featured a different Brown brand each week and also introduced a new logo designed to strengthen corporate identity.

### Brown Shoe Becomes Brown Group

In the years following World War II, the company embarked on a large-scale program of plant modernization and company expansion. In 1951 the Brown Shoe Company merged with the Wohl Shoe Company, a wholesale and retail business headquartered in St. Louis. The Wohl Shoe Company posted annual sales of $33 million, 90 percent of which came from women's shoes. The merger provided a large new market for the Brown Company because Wohl wholesaled shoes through 2,500 stores throughout the United States, Canada, Mexico, and Cuba, and operated several hundred retail stores and department store shoe salons. It was the Brown Company's first major acquisition and represented a giant step toward diversifying its operations into both manufacturing and retailing. Several other mergers and acquisitions followed, but by far the most significant was the 1956 acquisition of G.R. Kinney Corporation, then the largest operator of family shoe stores in the country. The Brown Company was the fourth-largest U.S. shoe manufacturer at the time and the deal was ultimately challenged as a violation of antitrust laws and struck down, but not before the Brown Company became the number one in shoe manufacturer in the United States. Following a 1962 Supreme Court ruling, the Brown Company sold Kinney to F.W. Woolworth.

The Brown Shoe Company changed its name in the 1970s to the Brown Group, a move that reflected its diversification into non-footwear subsidiaries. The Buster Brown brand still commanded enough interest among youngsters to have its own Saturday morning cartoon show, but the brand no longer occupied center stage within the burgeoning Brown Group. Women's shoes, at 75 percent of corporate sales, were the company's focus and thus received the bulk of the company's advertising dollars. The Buster Brown brand further suffered along with the rest of the shoe industry from the rise of imported shoes. The Brown Group's situation was additionally affected by the surging popularity of athletic shoes and its own unproductive non-shoe subsidiaries. So severe was the situation that the company's profits fell more than 50 percent over a six-year period in the 1980s.

In response to the changing consumer market, the Brown Group aimed to revive its sales by divesting into shoe importing. The company acquired Arnold Dunn, Inc., a women's shoe importer, in 1984, the same year that they established an importing division, Brown Group International. Two years later the company acquired the Pagoda Trading Company, a Far-East importing firm that has fueled new growth for the company. This strategic realignment also included a renewed emphasis on marketing the company's best-known brands, including Buster Brown, Naturalizer, and Connie. Lesser known and unprofitable brands were

*In 1904 cartoon character Buster Brown and his dog Tige began representing a line of shoes for the Brown Shoe Company.*

discontinued. In 1991 the Brown Group transferred the Buster Brown brand to Pagoda, and it is now being marketed not only in the United States, but also in Europe, Latin America, and the Far East.

### A Buster for the 1990s

For decades the Buster Brown logo remained unchanged. In *Famous American Trademarks,* Arnold B. Barach wrote that "Not an eyelash of boy or pup has been altered over the years," from the smiling, bug-eyed dog to the winking Buster with his page-boy haircut. However, in an effort to update the brand's image, the Brown Group created a new logo featuring a baseball-capped all-American boy and his kerchief-wearing dog. In addition, a revised take on the original logo accompanied the "My First Buster" promotion in 1992 which featured the former logo in a side profile with Buster's familiar pie hat. The new catch-phrase was "Buster Brown. There's a little kid in every shoe." In a related promotional pamphlet, the company boasts that "After nearly 90 years of making children's shoes, we've learned a lot about the feet that go in them."

## Further Reading:

Barach, Arnold B., "Buster Brown," *Famous American Trademarks,* Washington, D.C.: Public Affairs Press, 1971, pp. 27–8.

*Brown Group: The First Hundred Years,* St. Louis, MO: Brown Group, Inc., 1978.

Byrne, Harlan S., "Brown Group: Prosperity Following a Shakeout," *Barron's,* March 15, 1993, pp. 46–7.

Cleary, David Powers, "Buster Brown Shoes," *Great American Brands: The Success Formulas That Made Them Famous,* New York: Fairchild Publications, 1981, pp. 36–9.

Harris, William, "Buster Brown Lives," *Forbes,* July 19, 1982, p. 50.

"The Life and Times of Buster Brown," St. Louis, MO: Brown Group, Inc., 1992.

"Midget Who Did Tours as Buster Brown Dies," *New York Times,* September 28, 1972, p. 50.

Morgan, Hal, *Symbols of America,* New York: Penguin, 1986.

Moskowitz, Milton, et al, editors, "Brown Group, Inc.," *Everybody's Business: A Field Guide to the 400 Leading Companies in America,* New York: Doubleday, 1990, pp. 97–8.

Wax, Roberta, " 'Hi, I'm Buster Brown . . . ,' " *Los Angeles Magazine,* October 1986, pp. 208–10.

*—Jay P. Pederson*

# BVD®

Since its 1876 origins as a manufacturer of undergarments for men and women, BVD has distinguished itself as a leader in quality, comfort, and marketing prowess. Though much of its early success stemmed from innovation in bustles for women, the brand became primarily known for its men's underwear after the tremendous success of its one-piece "union suit," made in lightweight, perforated fabric called Nainsook Cloth. After several changes in ownership, BVD was acquired by Union Underwear Company in 1976, thereby joining the world's largest manufacturer of underwear, including the rapidly growing Fruit of the Loom brand. After acquiring Union in 1985, Farley, Inc., effected a major restructuring effort in which Fruit of the Loom, Inc., spun off as an independent, publicly owned company controlling BVD and other major brands and claiming a leading 40 percent of the men's and boys' underwear market by the early 1990s. Although BVD retained much of its singular identity as a leader in men's underwear, its association with Fruit of the Loom, Inc., provided it with unprecedented support in marketing, distribution, and line expansion.

## Brand Origins

In 1876 Messrs. Bradley, Voorhees, and Day started manufacturing women's and men's undergarments in New York City, naming their new enterprise after the first initials of their names. B.V.D. quickly earned its reputation from a spiral bustle for women, marketed as "The Only Bustle Not To Break Down." The men's line consisted of long-sleeve and long-legged garments made of heavy knitted, cotton and wool blend fabrics. Though uncomfortable by later standards, B.V.D.'s early products appealed to consumers as durable, relatively comfortable, and affordable apparel.

From its vantage point in the 1870s, B.V.D. benefited from centuries of underwear traditions, borrowing and altering them to accommodate new markets. Precursors of underwear dated back to ancient times, where loincloths, described in the Bible and other ancient texts, were commonly worn in hot climates. In colder, more northern climates, variations on long johns, often called drawers or braies, prevailed after the 12th century. Serving as protection from coarse outer garments and as warming insulation, drawers varied in fabric and style, according to region and social status. Whereas the lower classes generally resorted to wool articles, higher strata could afford linen or hemp, with silk for the

extremely wealthy. Styles ranged from briefs to ankle-lengths, to stockings that peasants stretched over braies and tied to primitive waist girdles for support.

With the 17th and 18th centuries, underwear followed the class-conscious fashions of upper society, defining status by volume of ruffles or by *finesse* of material. As bathing was a rare luxury, even among the upper classes, underwear functioned as a hygienic barrier between less-than-clean skin and often costly outer garments. It also served more aesthetic ends, including waist retention, back support, and calve-enhancement by padding worn under stockings. A new age of prudishness and austerity effected underwear fashions in the late 18th century. Beau Brummel, the influential dandy who emphasized cleanliness as a social virtue, contributed greatly to elitist requisites of regular changes of underwear. Prodigiously stiff collars and corsets were the mode for dandies well into the 1850s. Underwear fashions appealed primarily to the upper classes.

In the late Victorian era, however, much of the status-driven appeal of underwear lost ground to the mass marketing of less expensive, more practical fashions accessible to a wider consumer base. Starting operations in 1876, B.V.D. tapped into this trend, becoming an innovator in underwear marketing, design, and manufacture for decades.

## First Commercial Success

The brand began to outstrip underwear competitors in 1908, when the textile company Erlanger Brothers, Inc. bought the B.V.D. Company and its trademark and increased both marketing efforts and line extensions. An early print advertisement, for example, promoted the benefits of loose-fitting garments as opposed to conventional, bulky and tight fitting underwear. A generic man clad in drawers and a sleeveless shirt, opening one side to expose his chest and the supportive waistline of the shorts, is accompanied by the copy, "In Hot Weather, All Tight Fitting Underwear Is Sticky and Disagreeable. Loose Fitting B.V.D. Coat Cut Undershirts and Knee Length Drawers Are Cool and Comfortable." Before long, a new, athletic design combined drawers and shirt into a one-piece suit, the "Union Suit," that became the company's biggest seller.

After World War I, exposed shirtsleeves became more widely accepted, and underwear materials expanded to include cotton, marino, llama, flannel, viyella, and china spun silk. For B.V.D. brand, the greatest breakthrough was the use of a new lightweight waffle-like fabric called Nainsook Cloth. Though used in other styles, the new material clung tightest in the Union Suit, pushing its sales to over seven million pair by the mid-1920s.

### Early Marketing Strategy

In addition to product innovation, B.V.D. depended on new marketing strategies to increase underwear sales. In addition to the catchy slogan, "Next To Myself I Like B.V.D. Best," a growing series of print advertisements extolled the brand's comfort, stylishness, and its expanding product line, which ranged from swimsuits to socks. A 1914 ad from *Cosmopolitan* magazine capitalized on the insulating properties of the underwear by suggesting its use on ocean cruises. "There's 'An Ocean of Comfort' in B.V.D." claimed the copy. "You wear a coat and a smile with B.V.D. On land or sea, in city or country, outdoors or in the office." It was accompanied by a picture of well-dressed socialites comfortably competing at shuffle-board on a ship deck. In fine print, the ad continued, "For your own welfare, fix the B.V.D. Red Woven label in your mind and make the salesman *show* it to you. If he can't or won't, *walk out!*" The ad concluded with one last appeal: "If you dance, B.V.D. leaves you arm, leg and body-free."

A 1929 ad from *Liberty* magazine focused on comfort and price. It depicted a classically handsome man lounging in a bathrobe, open to display his white Union Suit. The copy described the virtues of B.V.D. quality, the comfortable design of the Union Suit and Nainsook material, and the growing number of additional products made by the same company—knit pull-over shirts and

knee drawers, in different colors and patterns. By the 1930s, B.V.D. had also moved into swimwear, using publicity stills of Olympic swimmer Johnny Weismuller to promote the trend toward topless trunks for men, and featuring movie star Jean Harlow to model skirtless, one-piece suits for women. Later, after the Navy introduced the widespread use of T-shirts in World War II, B.V.D. also moved into that market.

### Merchandising Innovation

In August of 1951, the B.V.D. trademark was sold to Superior Mills, in Piqua, Ohio, which subsequently changed its name to the B.V.D. Company. The company initiated a series of new merchandising techniques and marketing schemes that not only influenced the rest of the industry, but also secured a leading position for B.V.D. The company introduced the first 3-pair package in bright, attractive store fixtures. In addition, unprecedented emphasis was placed on consumer and dealer promotions, point of sales materials, and appealing displays. B.V.D. was also the first major national brand to expand distribution to mass merchandisers on a fair-trade basis; this move would pay off in the 1980s and 1990s, when medium-priced apparel sales exploded at mass merchandisers such as Wal-Mart and Kmart. To facilitate these moves, B.V.D. virtually pioneered basic stock controls for the underwear industry. In order to maintain lean and efficient inventories, the company used electronic data interchange (EDI) along every point of the manufacturing and sales process, ushering in an age of quick response bookkeeping.

In addition to improving marketing operations, Superior Mills also instigated superior manufacturing efficiency. The company purchased four new underwear manufacturing plants and Craftspun Mills, a plant designed to spin yarn from raw cotton. Craftspun was quickly supplemented by another plant to knit, dye, and finish yarn. B.V.D. had become a vertically integrated company, controlling operations from the purchase of raw cotton to the sale of finished products.

### Brand Development

In the 1960s and 1970s, B.V.D. continued to improve and expand its product line. Responding to a tremendous surge of style in the apparel industry, in the mid-1960s the brand developed a line of fashion underwear, ranging from silk bikini briefs to paisley-patterned boxer shorts. B.V.D. was also among the first branded underwear lines to introduce nylon tricot and mesh underwear to the retail trade. In addition, it developed the B.V.D. Sportop, a successful tee-shirt line featuring a pocket, which appealed to consumers as both a casual outer shirt or a convenient utility shirt.

To accommodate the fashion trends of the 1970s, B.V.D. further diversified its products. A full line of "Skins" underwear, made of Antron II stretch nylon, was introduced and marketed to meet a growing demand for sports apparel. The company also adjusted to the soaring popularity of blue jeans by developing a line of briefs, tank tops, and tee shirts in denim rib material, with a wide selection of colors. In a campaign to appeal to the so-called "Jean Set," B.V.D. developed an entire, coordinated underwear line to match contemporary trends. Items included a lower V-neck tee shirt to compliment the mode of open neck sport shirts; lower-rise briefs; all-cotton tee-shirts and athletic shirts in medium and pastel shades; and specially tapered boxer shorts.

In 1976 B.V.D. was acquired by Union Underwear Company, a subsidiary of Northwest Industries, Inc., and the largest manufacturer of underwear in the world. The periods were taken out of the brand name to yield BVD, and the new owners assured investors that BVD's tradition of quality would be maintained and supported by greater levels of trade and consumer marketing support. By the early 1980s, the company had launched an aggressive campaign to uphold its promise. Among other marketing strategies, one advertising campaign featured a photograph of actor Larry Hagman tipping his cowboy hat under the headline, "What does this man love as much as great quality?" Transcribed alongside his face was the answer, "A great deal . . . darlin'!," referring to the money-back coupon appended at the bottom of the page: a $3 refund on two packages of BVDs or $1 back on one package. Despite such efforts, Union Underwear moved into the 1980s with diminished profits and increasing debt burdens, making it susceptible to a takeover.

## Farley Reorganization

For the first nine months of 1985, Northwest racked up a net loss of $82.3 million and a negative cash flow of $45.5 million, according to a January 13, 1986, article in *Crain's Chicago Business.* On July 31 of that year, William Farley, the financier and head of Farley, Inc., acquired Northwest in a leveraged buyout, creating Farley/Northwest Industries, Inc., the largest manufacturer of men's and boys' underwear in the United States. As part of a major financing scheme, in 1986 Mr. Farley created a holding company called Farley Apparel, Inc., stressing consumer soft goods. That same year, Farley spun off Fruit of the Loom as a separate company, marketing a growing variety of products under such popular brands as BVD, Fruit of the Loom, Screen Stars, and Munsingwear. His strategy was to use the Fruit of the Loom brand identity to secure existing business and to enter the growing market for active wear and casual clothing. In 1987 Farley took Fruit of the Loom public, using proceeds to expand capacity, bolster advertising and marketing budgets, and whittle down some of the takeover-related debt. By the late 1980s, BVD helped bolster the Fruit of the Loom company, named after the brand that had been a major competitor less than two decades earlier.

## New Ad Efforts

In addition to financial reorganization of Fruit of the Loom, Farley transformed the company from primarily a manufacturer of men's and boys' underwear into a diverse, vertically integrated maker of men's, women's, and children's apparel. Rigorous marketing efforts bolstered these new markets and increasingly supported products in mass-merchandise and discount stores, which accounted for 75 percent of all underwear sales by 1987. BVD brand benefited from a new generation of advertisements to better define it as the higher quality, pricier end of Fruit of the Loom underwear.

In June of 1987, BVD changed its account from Saatchi & Saatchi in Compton, New York, to Warwick Baker & Fiore, Inc., New York, ushering in a wave of highly effective advertisements. Billings were around $4 million to $5 million, according to the *New York Times* on June 17, 1987. The company began a push to increase sales and brand awareness through celebrity endorsers. Combining humor with nastiness, a 1987 televsion spot featured Larry Hagman. He bests BVD competitors in a nefarious business deal and then sneers, with assistance from the ad's voice-over, "Isn't it time you changed your underwear?" Other celebrities

were featured in a 3-year campaign themed, "America, do it better. Do it in your BVDs." In a full-color, one-third-page *People* magazine spread, for example, Milton Berle was shown smiling alongside the quote, "I've done almost everything in my BVDs." The copy continued, "Whatever you do BVD brand underwear will help you do it better. That's because BVD is the name to turn to for extra comfort and fit."

By 1990, Warwick had moved to another campaign, which used humor infused with sex appeal and displayed the product in use. The fit young actor Bill Bumiller is locked out of his hotel room. As an announcer touts the benefits of BVDs ("strong waistband, 100 percent combed cotton, etc.), the semi-nude model slinks past an attractive young woman, an elevator of conventioneers, and finally a desk clerk who hands him the key. The slogan summarizes, "BVDs. You're better off with them on." David Frescher, executive VP-marketing of Fruit of the Loom, Inc., told *USA TODAY* that we're delighted we're able to show the product in use, as opposed to just sitting on a countertop." New policies in television network advertising were passed in 1988, allowing ads to show actors clad only in underwear.

In 1992 Warwick started a campaign emphasizing the durability of BVDs with "The Not-So-Brief Brief" slogan. The campaign depicted worn-out men's underwear serving different rag functions—a buffing rag for polishing silverware, a shoe-shine rag, a car waxing cloth, and a paintbrush cleaner—in crisp, high-contrast color photographs appealing to the eye. The ads' headlines asked, "What will your underwear be doing a year from now?" The right column provides the answer, "Chances are, if they're BVD Underwear, you could still wear them," along with copy outlining the quality features of the brand, including long cotton fibers, Lycra-spandex legbands, wash-resistant rubber, and so on. The success of these campaigns prompted further investment in advertising. In 1992 alone, Fruit of the Loom spent $75 million to build brand awareness and projected a budget increase of 25 percent to $93.8 million in 1993, Mark Steinkrauss, a spokesman for the company, told *Investor's Business Daily* in 1993. Warwick's performance with BVD was so successful that Fruit of the Loom brand was prompted, in 1992, to transfer its 42-year-old account with Grey Advertising, New York.

## International Market

In addition to increased brand awareness through marketing, another top priority for BVD brand was expansion outside the United States. In a 1987 strategic move to increase its penetration of the vast European market, the company (then Union Underwear Co., Inc.) made a joint venture with W. P. McCarter & Co., Ltd., an Irish company with an apparel manufacturing facility in County Donegal. The arrangement tripled the capacity of the McCarter plant for the production of products to be sold in Europe under the BVD, Fruit of the Loom, and Screen Stars brand names.

By 1993, BVD had become a world traveler. Several new sales offices were established in Europe, including Brussels, to focus on the Belgian and Dutch markets. In addition to exploiting new opportunities in Eastern Europe, the company increased shipments to retail accounts in the Czech and Slovak Republics. Planning for expansion into Central and South American countries was expedited by the arrival of Tony Lyra, formerly president and general manager for a large consumer products company in Mexico, as Fruit of the Loom president of international operations in the Southern Hemisphere. In 1992 13 percent of the company's sales came from overseas, with estimated growth of about 20 percent by 1994, according to Mr. Steinkrauss. In 1992 European sales rose 42 percent.

## Performance Appraisal

*Standard & Poor's* 1992 survey for the apparel industry cited two key determinants for growth in 1990s: development of basic apparel (T-shirts, denims, and fleece wear) stressing casualness and comfort for the value-oriented consumer; and penetration into the mass merchandise market (Kmart, Wal-Mart, etc.). Under Fruit of the Loom, BVD has closely followed those determinants. From 1988 to 1993 Fruit of the Loom earnings increased at an annual rate of 24 percent. Profit growth was forecast at a rapid pace, with an estimated rise in earnings of 27 percent to about $3.15 a share for the remainder of 1993, and another 21 percent to $3.80 in 1994, according to *Investor's Business Daily.*

A 1988 article in the *New York Times* maintained that "Mr. Farley likes Fruit of the Loom 'because everybody wears underwear,' " making it a stable market. If that is the case, and if Fruit of the Loom continues to benefit from the aggressive growth strategies initiated by Farley Inc. in 1985, then BVD may, in fact, turn out to be the "not-so-brief brief." It may, in fact, continue to lead the market, over a hundred years after Bradley, Voorhees, and Day risked loosing their shirts to get it started.

## Further Reading:

Benedict, Helen, "A History of Men's Underwear," *American Fabrics and Fashions,* winter 1982, pp. 89–94.

Boland, John, "A Well-Dressed I.P.O.," *New York Times,* October 19, 1986, sect. 3, p. 12.

Bremner, Brian, "Stripped to its Kivvies, Farley Seeks Equity Heat," *Crain's Chicago Business,* September 1, 1986, p. 1.

"B.V.D. History," Bowling Green: Fruit of the Loom, Inc., 1993.

Cole, Robert J., "Farley Bids $1.3 Billion for Pepperell," *New York Times,* October 24, 1988, p. D6; "Pepperell Offer Raised By Farley to $52 a Share," *New York Times,* February 2, 1989, p. D2.

Dagnoli, Judann, "BVD Dresses Up Spot With Athletes and Stars," *Advertising Age,* November 30, 1987, p. 88.

Dougherty, Philip H., "Warwick Gets Account For BVD Underwear," *New York Times,* June 17, 1987, p. D19.

Elliott, Stuart, "News Involving 2 Accounts Puts Some Pep Into August," *New York Times,* August 24, 1992, p. D7; "Dr. Pepper Loses the Loner Image," *USA TODAY,* November 14, 1990, p. 10B.

"Farley Apparel Files Registration Statement," *PR Newswire,* August 26, 1986.

"Farley Inc. Goes Public to Pay Debt," *Chicago Tribune,* August 27, 1986, p. C3.

"Fruit of the Loom Concludes Record Breaking Year" *Business Wire,* February 3, 1993.

"Fruit of the Loom Reports Solid Operating Results for its First Quarter," *PR Newswire,* April 21, 1993.

Greenfield, Jeff, "Beware the Schizoid Tube," *Los Angeles Times,* June 21, 1987, p. 6.

Hass, Nancy, "Fruit's Salad Days," *Financial World,* June 22, 1993, p. 46.

Labich, Kenneth, "Bill Farley Has A Dream Machine," *Fortune,* May 27, 1985, p. 114.

Merrion, Paul, "William Farley Winning Fight to Tame Northwest Ind. Debt," *Crain's Chicago Business,* January 13, 1986, p. 3.

Much, Marilyn, "Executive Update, Strategy," *Investor's Business Daily,* April 14, 1993, p. 3.

"Union Underwear Increases Aim at European Market," *Business Wire,* March 4, 1987.

*—Kerstan Cohen*

# CALVIN KLEIN®

# Calvin Klein

American fashion designer Calvin Klein helped popularize designer clothing as his name appeared on the back pocket of the designer's jeans in the late 1970s, initiating the designer jean fad of the 1980s. The jeans trend made the Calvin Klein brand name accessible to the general public, which opened new markets for ready-to-wear versions of Calvin Klein's collection of designer clothing. Through licensing agreements, Calvin Klein jeans and sportswear filled department and specialty stores and soon became the most profitable portion of Calvin Klein Industries—even though the designer focused mainly on the image of his high-cost collection. The Calvin Klein brand name further infiltrated the market and increased profits with the introduction of Calvin Klein's fragrances. In 1985 the controversial advertising for Obsession perfume for women reaped both profits and publicity for the Calvin Klein name. By 1993 the Calvin Klein name graced six fragrances, jeans, various accessories, menswear, sportswear, bridge fashions (reflections of the exclusive collection at more modest prices), and the designer collection.

## From Coats to Couture

The Calvin Klein brand name has become one of the most recognized symbols of American fashion since its debut in 1968. In that year, Calvin Klein, after graduating from the Fashion Institute of Technology in New York and spending five years designing at three different companies, decided to open his own shop. Klein and his childhood friend Barry Schwartz formed Calvin Klein Ltd., continuing the entrepreneurial spirit of their fathers who both had their own Harlem grocery stores. Schwartz, who invested $10,000 in the venture, directed the business end of the company while Klein focused on designing. Klein told *Fortune* contributor Walter McQuade, "Barry runs the company in a tough, tight way, and I support him," adding "I give Barry my collection, and he turns it into money."

Klein's first sale was famous and revealed his dedication to his product. After a Bonwit Teller executive mistakenly entered Klein's shop, he noticed the quality of Klein's coats and made Klein an appointment with Bonwit Teller's president. Klein pushed his coats on a rack with a broken wheel 23 blocks through the streets of New York City to the appointment because he did not want them to be wrinkled when they were shown. Upon seeing his wares, the president told him to raise his prices by ten dollars, and she then placed an order for $50,000.

Klein expanded his repertoire from coats to general sportswear in 1970, a risky venture according to Schwartz, who commented in *Fortune* that "buyers are funny: they won't buy sportswear from a coat house, or vice versa." Schwartz, however, used his determination to persuade buyers. "I am a very stubborn man. I decided that even with our best accounts, if they wouldn't buy our sportswear we wouldn't sell them our coats."

Klein's designs and Schwartz's stubbornness enhanced the status of the Calvin Klein brand name. Schwartz explained to *Fortune* in 1980 that "the Calvin Klein image is the most important thing we have." Klein, however, credited Schwartz with their success, telling *People* that "there are many good designers, but the difference is that I have Barry." In 1973 Klein won his first of three consecutive Coty awards, the fashion industry's equivalent of an Oscar. The first award commented on Klein's "nonconformist" but "classic" designs. *Vogue* magazine remarked upon on the quintessentially American qualities of Klein's clothes, claiming "if you were around 100 years from now and wanted a definitive picture of the American look of 1975, you'd study Calvin Klein." Calvin Klein's clothes came to represent simple, understated design in the form of sportswear, jeans, and haute couture.

The Calvin Klein image is of utmost importance to the company. Even though sales of the ready-to-wear collection rose from $500,000 in 1968 to $30 million by 1977, the partners held back expansion, cutting over 1,000 retail outlets to 250. They did not "wish to dilute the exclusive aura of the Calvin Klein label," Walter McQuade wrote in *Fortune*. To bolster the label's image after winning his first Coty award, Klein pronounced the polyester he had used to make Trevira blouses and printed dresses "slimy" and upgraded his fabrics to include sheer wool, silk, and cashmere. The upgrade helped the brand image, but sales of Calvin Klein's top-of-the-line collection were held to a level conducive to exclusivity. According to a 1992 *Los Angeles Times* article, the "successful top-of-the-line clothes have accounted for only ten percent of sales at Calvin Klein Ltd."

## Calvins Replace the All-American Jean

The prestige of Calvin Klein's more expensive clothes created the Calvin Klein brand image, but Calvin Klein jeans broadened appeal for the brand name and garnered more profits for the company. In 1976 the first of Klein's designer jeans debuted in his spring collection and sold well at the high price of $50 per pair. The shapely jeans with the Calvin Klein name sewn on the rear pocket resulted from Klein's discussion with Bloomingdale buyer Connie Dowling, who, a year earlier, had suggested that Klein redesign jeans as a fashion garment. The jeans were the first to display the name of a Seventh Avenue designer. The redesigned jean became a huge success, selling "200,000 pairs the first week they hit the market," reported Linda Grant of the *Los Angeles Times.*

By 1978 Schwartz, wishing to further the success of the jeans, had arranged a very unusual and profitable licensing agreement with Puritan Fashions. The agreement stipulated that Puritan would market the jeans and pay Klein a one dollar royalty on every pair, with a minimum of one million dollars in royalties over five years. Even though Puritan had not made jeans before the Calvin Klein license, by 1979 it made 125,000 pairs each week, according to *Business Week. Forbes* contributor Pamela Sherrid noted that the jeans sales had risen to $60 million by 1979.

Advertising strategies were essential to the rate of sales for Calvin Klein jeans. Calvin Klein would not let Puritan advertise his jeans on television because, McQuade noted, he called the approach "tacky." After losing millions of dollars in sales because of inferior advertising methods, Klein changed his mind and bought $5 million worth of television time for commercials he had directed himself. He paid 15-year-old model Brooke Shields $500,000 to recline in his skin-tight jeans and say "You know what comes between me and my Calvins? Nothing." The ad was decidedly controversial, and many stations banned it. Dismayed, Klein had Jimmy Carter's pollster Pat Caddell figure out what market segment was raising issue with his ad. Klein reported in *People* that "It was mostly an older group who objected. It was someone who couldn't relate to why anyone wears jeans, which is a very sensual thing to begin with." The ad did accomplish Klein's objective, however, for it propelled his jeans into the top-selling position, above Murjani jeans.

Designer jeans remained a growing business until 1982. At that time, Puritan's president Carl Rosen had been succeeded by his 27-year-old son, whose plans to discount the jeans did not impress Calvin Klein Ltd. "You can't sell $140 perfume and have your jeans at K-Mart," a Calvin Klein Industries executive explained to *New York* magazine. Calvin Klein Ltd. made a leveraged buy-out of Puritan for an estimated $61 million, consolidating the companies as Calvin Klein Industries.

Operating Puritan proved difficult, however, for profits from the sale of designer jeans declined due to the recession, competition, and the aging of the baby boom generation. The jeans division sales peaked at $400 million in worldwide sales in 1983, but began to drop as "aging consumers switched to looser-fitting sportswear such as sweats and tennis warmups," according to the *Los Angeles Times.* By 1988 the slowed Calvin Klein Sport division accounted for 84.2 percent of the company's revenues. The company remained buoyant, however, as Klein concentrated on other aspects of his empire, such as his top-of-the-line clothes and his myriad licensed products, including perfume and underwear.

### Reviving Faded Jeans

In 1990, in an effort to revive the designer jeans, Calvin Klein ran five different 30-second television ads. *Advertising Age* contributor Bob Garfield said the ads' imagery went "beyond suggestiveness and way past aphrodisia." He noted that "this time [the jeans] are positioned as a sort of sex organ in their own right." In one spot a man complains to his girlfriend about her lack of commitment even though they have been "exchanging bodies for months." She responds, saying "I've tried to forget you, but my Calvins won't let me." In another ad, a man says of a woman, "all she has to do is wiggle her Calvins to make my Calvins crazy." Yet another ad describes a man in love: "I'd do a low crawl over two miles of broken glass just to smell the tracks of the truck that hauled her Calvins to the laundry." Garfield rated the ads mediocre, concluding that "it is just a reprise of Brooke Shields, with all of the lasciviousness but none of the surprise. Once you've done pantiless jailbait half on her back, there's no more shock value to exploit and no more dignity to lose." The ads were ineffective; *Women's Wear Daily* reported that the Calvin Klein Sport division lost $14.2 million in 1990.

Klein redoubled his efforts to grab attention and sales for his jeans in 1991. *Women's Wear Daily* contributor David Moin reported that "Calvin Klein officials say the designer has put new emphasis on jeans this year. He reportedly has increased his advertising budget dramatically, to $10 million on jeans this year, and for the first time staged a Calvin Klein Sport show." He introduced two new styles: "The Radically Relaxed" jean with a zip-front, cut fuller through the thighs and knees, and "The Stovepipe" jean with a button-front, straight legs, and a wide waist meant to be tightened with a belt. The jeans were introduced in colors of red, navy, olive, and wheat.

To garner more attention than the 1990 television commercials on a lower budget, Klein brainstormed a special advertising project, the culmination of which was a $1 million, 116-page advertising supplement to the October issue of *Vanity Fair.* According to *Vanity Fair* publisher Ron Galotti, the supplement was the "largest to run in the United States" at that time, and it was "the equivalent of 29 ad pages." The supplement was a picture story of the "fast-lane rock 'n' roll world," featuring model Carre Otis and several muscle-bound men in various states of undress. Though the supplement became a collector's item and generated controversy, it did not translate into a surge in new jeans sales.

Calvin Klein, however, continued to lead the denim market, according to the *Daily News Record.*

In the face of stagnant sales, Calvin Klein refocused his jeans division. Marketing to baby-boomers in the 1980s spelled success, but as that generation aged, Calvin Klein tried to win a younger generation—his daughter's peers. To revamp his image in 1992, Calvin Klein renamed the Calvin Klein Sport line CK Calvin Klein and retargeted his advertising to a younger audience. Sarah Mower of *Harper's Bazaar* said his plan was "the hottest marketing of jeans the industry has seen since . . . Brooke Shields." The new ads appealed to a new generation, featuring sometimes-topless 18-year-old fashion model Kate Moss and muscled rapper Marky Mark. The new line was positioned in the higher priced bridge-market floors of Bloomingdale's and Saks Fifth Avenue, in addition to about 75 CK shops opened in Dillard's stores throughout the United States. The bridge market is priced below the top-of-the-line haute couture but above the middle-priced clothing collections. Klein's new approach seemed on target to increase sales; jeans sales were predicted to rise from 1991 sales of $41 million to $57 million, according to *Women's Wear Daily.*

### Licensing for Profit

To increase profits while keeping capital requirements and operating expenditures low, the company began a licensing program in 1974. Under licensing agreements, the Calvin Klein trademark is attached to products that are either designed or approved by Calvin Klein Industries but made, marketed, and sold by the licensee. The company's licensees pay the company from five to ten percent of sales, and if the licensees meet specific sales levels, the agreements are renewable for three to five years. Calvin Klein Industries' revenues from licensing rose from $7.3 million in 1984 to $14.8 million in 1988, accounting for 6.4 percent of the company's 1988 revenues. Products licensed included fragrances, sewing patterns, women's footwear, sleepwear, hosiery, underwear, handbags, small leather goods, scarves, and luggage.

Calvin Klein kept close control over his licensed products. In 1977, for example, Bidermann Industries held a license to produce all Klein's menswear. When Puritan won the license for jeans in 1978, however, Klein allowed Puritan to manufacture some men's jeans and Western shirts. Arguments between Bidermann and Klein festered as his menswear sales declined, top Bidermann executives left the company, and Klein stopped approving designs and then "refused to work," said a former Bidermann executive. The license for menswear with Bidermann ended in 1984 and Klein discontinued his men's collection.

In 1992 Klein re-entered the higher-priced men's clothing industry through a license with GFT USA Corp. "Our strategy was to step out of clothing, dress shirts, and sportswear for four years, and just have a jeans product," Klein commented in *Women's Wear Daily.* "Now its time. I'm ready and the stores are ready." The new collection benefitted from the established image of the other Calvin Klein products. Even though the designer had not produced a men's collection for four years, he told *Daily News Record* that "the general consumer is not aware the product hasn't been out there." The high-end of the collection was scheduled to debut in 12 to 15 stores while the mid-priced clothing entered 190 stores. The collection was sold in stores that afforded it 1,000 to 1,500 square-feet of space, including Klein's company-owned stores in Dallas, Texas; Cleveland, Ohio; Palm Beach, Florida; Costa Mesa, California; and Chestnut Hill, Massachusetts, and

prestigious stores such as Barneys New York, Neiman Marcus, Wilkes Bashford, and Saks Fifth Avenue.

Calvin Klein selected the stores that would carry his line carefully, insuring that the men's collection and second-tier classification assortment had been arranged carefully to protect the integrity of the line. The *Daily News Record* noted that the company felt " 'very strongly' that each [shop] buys the entire collection. Stores that are buying the upper-end collection can also buy the classification as well, but the two collections can not be mixed together." GFT produced the higher priced collection in Italy and the United Kingdom and the mid-priced clothes in its Riverside, New Jersey plant. Klein's personal involvement in the designing and marketing of the line spurred its sales.

### Unusual Underwear

When women were borrowing from men's wardrobes in the early 1980s, Calvin Klein underwear capitalized on the trend. His women's underwear was patterned after men's underwear, featuring 100 percent cotton knit and wide white elastic waistbands. The boxer shorts even sported a fly. Though he considered leaving off the fly, Klein told *Time* that "It's sexier with the fly. These things are seriously thought out." "In the box it's masculine. On the body it's feminine," Pam Gau, president of Calvin Klein Underwear division, told *Forbes.* "It's part of the popular androgynous look." The look did appeal to the consumer; women bought 400,000 pairs and the company reaped $50 million in profits in 1984. The Calvin Klein image was the impetus behind the success of the underwear. *Forbes* contributor Jeffrey A. Trachtenberg wrote that "The woman buying $7.50 panties doesn't get much that she can't find at $3. The difference is that insecure people feel better wearing designer labels—and there are plenty of insecure people around." Pam Gau, commenting on the designer price of the underwear in *Marketing and Media Decisions* said, "We still have the one thing that women desire most: Calvin Klein."

The advertising campaign for the underwear was based on Klein's notion that underwear is white. Shot in black and white, the print ads highlighted a white tank top and white briefs on a deeply-tanned, reclining model. The ads ran in *Vogue, Mademoiselle, Women's Wear Daily, Harper's Bazaar, Seventeen, Glamour, and Interview. Interview* carried some ads with a bare-breasted model. The ad campaign continued into the 1990s but featured model Kate Moss topless and rapper Marky Mark, who had popularized Calvin Klein men's underwear by wearing his jeans below his white Calvin Klein waistband.

### Fragrances of Fortune

The Calvin Klein image became synonymous with Calvin Klein himself during the marketing of fragrances. In his early years as a designer, Klein shunned the press, stating in 1969, according to *New York* magazine, "What can be great about designing fashion? Being a doctor, now, that's great." *Financial World* reported ten years later that "other designers court fame by mingling with socialites and selling to the jet set. But Klein has carefully avoided the gossip column route." In similar fashion, he kept his popular jeans from being advertised on television until 1980 because it was "tacky."

But Klein's personal style changed in the 1980s, along with his advertising techniques. He divorced his wife and began frequenting New York's most popular nightclubs, dating several women, and dancing in gay discos. Klein described this "very wild period'' in a *Playboy* interview: ''I've fooled around a lot. I stopped at nothing. I would do anything.'' A former Calvin Klein executive told *New York* magazine that ''It's harder to create an image than a fall look. He created an image. He was everyone's fantasy of style, sophistication, and creativity. It was the life-style of the times. You could be any sex you wanted. The more outrageous you were the better. He pushed the edge of the envelope.''

As Klein increased his personal media exposure, his products benefitted. The 1985 introduction of Obsession for women was the first to benefit from the gossip column reports of Klein's personal life and was a stellar success. Obsession rose to be a prestige fragrance ''almost overnight, with wholesale sales of more than $40 million a year in the United States, $100 million worldwide,'' according to *Cosmopolitan* in 1991. The perfume sales had doubled since 1985.

The quick growth of Obsession was spurred by Calvin Klein's personal image. ''Luckily, Calvin's somewhat controversial sexy side had already been revealed to the public,'' a Calvin Klein executive told *Harper's Bazaar.* Calvin Klein had married his personal image to his marketing approach. ''Obsession was about insanity, not just my own personal insanity,'' Klein told *Vogue.* ''It was society's obsession with work and love, insanity as a reflection of the times.''

The initial print campaign showed naked bodies intertwined in complex, provocative ways. *Cosmopolitan* noted that ''you couldn't tell what was going on, but it wasn't hard to imagine anything from group sex to incest.'' The ads were memorable, however. They ads were ranked number one in the 1989 survey by a New York based firm named Video Storyboard Tests. *Los Angeles Times* writer Bruce Horovitz declared that ''the campaign has helped to make Calvin Klein one of the most familiar names in fashion.''

Television commercials for Obsession did not attract as much attention as the print campaign. Directed by David Lynch, producer of the *Twin Peaks* television program, the television commercials featured men and women absent-mindedly walking around quoting famous authors like Ernest Hemingway, F. Scott Fitzgerald, D. H. Lawrence, and Gustave Flaubert. About the commercials, a Calvin Klein executive told *Cosmopolitan* that ''our objective was to maintain some of the mystery but to concentrate more on romance than on promiscuity.''

The dialogue resulting from the odd quotes did not please critics. Robert Stricklin, writing in the *New York Tribune,* summarized the first commercial:

FACE (maniacally wide-eye): ''Members of the jury, the accused stands before you on trial for his sins!''
ACCUSED (A young man with a bad haircut): ''Forgive me I loved you all.''
GIRL: ''Liar! You only loved your dreams!''
ACCUSED: ''But dreams are where a man invents himself! Is that a sin?''
MOTHER (to ACCUSED as a young boy snipping off a lock of his own hair with a pair of scissors): ''Yours will be a great and lonely life.''
ACCUSED (consumed in flames): ''If living with obsession is a crime—then let me be guilty!''
VOICEOVER: ''Ah-h-h . . . the smell of it.''

Stricklin called the commercials ''esoteric, portentous drivel.'' Consumers may have agreed with Stricklin; the president of Video Storyboard commented in the *Los Angeles Times* that ''Calvin

Klein is one of the few companies whose print advertising is actually more memorable than its television advertising.''

In 1988, a new fragrance, Eternity, was launched. The campaign for Eternity reflected the return to traditional, monogamous relationships, mirroring Klein's marriage to Kelly Rector and his retreat to a more sedate, private life. The ad campaign featured a family spending a day at the beach. The perfume was introduced nationally in September with a ten-page print ad after a summer of sales at Saks Fifth Avenue in New York City and Southampton, New York. Television spots focused on the couple's romantic relationship. One commercial has a man ask a woman ''Would you still love me if I were a woman?'' The women answers, saying ''Of course. If I could be your man.'' *Advertising Age* reported that the print campaign cost $1.3 million and the television spots $4 million. In line with the changing trends of the 1990s, the Obsession ads were updated. ''The new Obsession ads will continue to stand for sex, but sex between two people instead of a menage a trois or quatre,'' Calvin Klein Cosmetics Corp. executive Robin Burns told *Advertising Age.*

Obsession and Eternity depicted ''two facets of a couple's relationship,'' according to Burns in *Harper's Bazaar.* A third facet was introduced in 1991 with the debut of Escape perfume. Klein told *Vogue* that ''Everyone I know is talking about wanting to escape the rat race.'' The inspiration behind the new fragrance was Klein's life with his wife Kelly. He added in *Vogue* that Escape is ''about Kelly and myself, what we do and how we live.'' The print campaign continued to feature black and white photographs by famous photographers Bruce Weber and Irving Penn, and highlighted people involved in sensual but sporty activities like swimming. Escape for men was introduced in 1993 with a similar campaign but with an unprecedented advertising budget of $30 million.

The Calvin Klein image is not the only key to the perfumes' success. Calvin Klein employed the best professionals in the fragrance industry. Industry consultant Allan Mottus told *Advertising Age* that Calvin Klein Cosmetics president Kim Delsing ''has proven better than anyone at both maintenance of existing brands and launch of new brands.'' Calvin Klein has also had the help of one of the most sought after noses in the perfume business. Ann Gottlieb, a fragrance consultant, was essential in the creation of Klein's three fragrances for men and women. Gottlieb told the *Wall Street Journal* that ''I see myself as translating an image into a fragrance.'' She concentrates on making each fragrance different from all others and yet marketable to the large numbers of people her clients want to reach. President of Calvin Klein Cosmetics Kim Delsing commented on Ms. Gottlieb's essential role in the fragrances' success in the *Wall Street Journal,* saying ''because Ann is a consultant and works for our competitors, she more than anyone else has her finger on the pulse of the industry. The service she provides is invaluable.'' The wholesale volume of Klein's fragrances worldwide in 1991 was $300 million, according to *Women's Wear Daily.*

## International Moves

Klein wants his name to be a household word in Europe by the year 2000, according to *Women's Wear Daily.* By 1990 the company sold products in Canada, Asia, and Central and South America, although it did not sell its wares in South Africa. The company continued to look for new markets in which to increase profits, but some aspects of international licensing—such as changing currency exchange rates and governmental control of royalty rates—were out of the company's control. Expansion overseas is patterned after Klein's fragrance distribution. The fragrances are first introduced in an area and are followed by the collection business and then the general sportswear.

## Future Expectations

Calvin Klein's image continues to represent American style, but it has become more understated each year. By the 1990s, he seemed to be recapturing the spirit of his minimalist top-of-the-line designs. Klein told *San Jose Mercury News* writer Mary Gottschalk that "being a minimalist and trying to understand the way women really live, I think simplicity of design becomes far more important than how many accessories can I put on the clothes. . . . I'm trying to make [women] feel as comfortable and look as beautiful and as feminine as possible and still fit into a modern way of living. That's my goal." With that goal and the popularity of the Calvin Klein brand name, Calvin Klein is poised to continue influencing the way Americans and other nationalities dress, scent themselves, and view advertising.

## Further Reading:

Alter, Jonathan, and Ann Hughey, "Calvin and the Family Firm," *Newsweek*, December 12, 1983, p. 91.

Behbehani, Mandy, "Nothing Between Success and Calvin," *San Francisco Examiner*, January 30, 1992.

"The Big Three in Bridge: Two Kleins and an Ellis," *Stores*, October, 1987, pp. 24–25.

"Calvin Klein's Bold Strategy in U.S., Europe," *Women's Wear Daily*, June 19, 1991, p. 1.

"Calvin's New Gender Benders," *Time*, September 5, 1983, p. 56.

"Calvin Klein's Obsession," *Cosmopolitan*, May, 1991, p. 236.

"Calvin Klein's Obsession," *Harper's*, August, 1984, pp. 24–25.

"Calvin Klein Sport," *Daily News Record*, May 10, 1991, p. 5

"Calvin Klein—Sports Division," *S1 SEC Registration*, June 1, 1989.

Choney, Suzanne, "Ads Get Sexier than Ever," *San Diego Union*, March 26, 1987.

Clurman, Shirley, "Nothing but $750 Million a Year Comes between American Women and Their Handsome King of Clothes: Calvin Klein," *People*, January 18, 1982, pp. 94–96.

Dodero, Tony, "Calvin Klein Follows Trend, Opens His Own Retail Store," *Orange Coast Daily Pilot* (Costa Mesa, California), November 21, 1990.

Garfield, Bob, "Nothing Comes Between Jeans and Sex in Calvin Klein Spots," *Advertising Age*, September 24, 1990, p. 60.

Gottschalk, Mary, "Images of Calvin," *San Jose Mercury News* (California), October 5, 1991.

Grant, Linda, "Can Calvin Klein Escape," *Los Angeles Times*, February 23, 1992.

Gross, Michael, "The Latest Calvin: From the Bronx to Eternity," *New York*, August 8, 1988, pp. 20–29.

Horovitz, Bruce, "Lingering Scent," *Los Angeles Times*, May 24, 1989.

Jereski, Laura Konrad, "Hold Your Undershirts! Calvin Sews Up $50 Million in Men's Undies for Women," *Marketing & Media Decisions*, spring, 1984.

Kanner, Bruce, "The New Calvinism," *New York*, September 17, 1984, pp. 31–36.

Kaufman, Joanne, " 'The Nose' Knows Winning Scents," *Wall Street Journal*, June 9, 1992, sec. A, p. 14.

Kay, Andrew, "The Mood of Calvin Klein," *Harper's Bazaar*, November, 1982, pp. 215–16, 258.

Loar, Russ, "South Coast Plaza to Get First West Coast Calvin Klein Store," *Orange Coast Daily Pilot* (Costa Mesa, California), May 18, 1990.

Lockwood, Lisa, *Women's Wear Daily*, June 20, 1991 p. 2.

McLaughlin, John, "A Nose for Business," *Harper's Bazaar*, January, 1990, p. 32.

McQuade, Walter, "The Bruising Businessman Behind Calvin Klein," *Fortune*, November 17, 1980, pp. 106–118.

Moin, David, "Calvin Klein Jeans Sales Surging, Says Bloomingdale's," *Women's Wear Daily*, September 30, 1991, p. 2.

Mower, Sarah, "Calvin in Control," *Harper's Bazaar*, November 11, 1992, pp. 121–122.

Orth, Maureen, "A Star Is Reborn," *Vogue*, September, 1988, pp. 692, 695, 754.

Parola, Robert, "Calvin Klein Co. Sets Store Lineup," *Daily News Record*, April 3, 1992, p. 2.

Peer, Elizabeth, "Stylish Calvinism," *Newsweek*, November 3, 1975, p. 48.

"Perfume Makers File Suit," *Waterbury Republican* (Connecticut), November 7, 1986.

"Puritan Fashions: A Little Chic Goes a Long Way," *Financial World*, July 1, 1979, pp. 18–19.

"Puritan Fashions: Trying to Protect a Bonanza Built on Designer Jeans," *Business Week*, August 13, 1979, pp. 68–69.

Rich, Andrew, "Calvin Klein of Minnetonka Obsessed with Sex," *City Business/Twin Cities* (Minneapolis, Minnesota), March 19, 1986.

Sherrid, Pamela, "Ragman," *Forbes*, February 15, 1982, pp. 33–34.

Sloan, Pat, "Calvin Aiming Designer Briefs Ads at Females," *Advertising Age*, September 27, 1982, p. 74.

Sloan, Pat, "Calvin Klein Bets $30M on Escape," *Advertising Age*, March 29, 1993, p. 4.

Sloan, Pat, "Calvin Klein Seeks Shop," *Advertising Age*, November 20, 1989, p. 40.

Sloan, Pat, " 'I Don't Have Long-Term Plans. I Just Act Instinctively,' " *Advertising Age*, May 18, 1992, p. 3.

Sloan, Pat, "New Fragrances Continue to Be In Fashion," *Advertising Age*, June 9, 1986, p. 28.

Sloan, Pat, and Scott Donaton, "Klein 'Outsert': New Trend?" *Advertising Age*, September 9, 1991, p. 12.

Stanley, Alessandra, "Riding High," *Vogue*, August, 1991, pp. 230–38.

Stricklin, Robert, "Today's Advertisements: 'Oh-h-h, The Smell of It,' " *New York Tribune*, December 8, 1988.

Trachtenberg, Jeffrey A., "Between Me and My Calvins," *Forbes*, April 9, 1984, p. 139.

Wentz, Laurel, "Calvin Klein Designs Brazilian Launch," *Advertising Age*, August 23, 1982, p. 29.

White, C. R., "CK: Calvin's Big Turnaround," *Women's Wear Daily*, December 23, 1992, p. 4.

Youngblood, Dick, "Calvin Klein's Costly Obsession Elixir of Profit for Chaska Firm," *Minneapolis Star and Tribune*, July 8, 1985.

*—Sara Pendergast*

# CARTER'S®

![Carter's logo]

Known primarily for its children's wear, the Carter's brand was connected with adult undergarments throughout the last half of the nineteenth century. By the early 1990s, the William Carter Company had become one of the oldest and largest manufacturers of premium infants and children's apparel in the world, having clothed over 300 million children since its founding. One of the most widely recognized children's wear labels, Carter's brand has earned a reputation for marketing long-lasting products that are passed on from generation to generation. The branded products are manufactured at eleven plants in Georgia, Texas, Mississippi, and Pennsylvania and are distributed primarily through department and specialty stores.

## Brand Origins

Founder William Carter was born in 1830 in England's northern textile district and learned the trade from his grandfather, a knitting machine manufacturer. When industrial turmoil shook England's mid-nineteenth century world of work, Carter joined the flood of immigrants to America. After arriving in New York in 1856, he worked his way to the textile towns of Massachusetts, finally settling in Highlandville (now Needham Heights). The first garments bearing the Carter name were produced in William's home on a second-hand knitting machine set up in the kitchen.

Carter started out making cardigan sweaters, and by 1870 had built up his business to the point that he had to construct a workshop to house more knitting machines. With more manufacturing capacity came a more diverse product line, including men's and women's undergarments. Carter's one- and two-piece underwear were made from oatmeal-hued cotton fabric that was far softer and more comfortable than the wool and flannel fabrics that enjoyed wide use at that time. By the 1880s, when Carter expanded his manufacturing capacity again, he had added worsted mittens to the line of apparel bearing his name. Carter entered the field of children's wear almost by accident when a retail customer offered him some salvage yarn that Carter made into his first child-size product: mittens.

## First Commercial Success

Carter's sons helped to transform apparel marketing in general when they suggested to their father that they utilize direct sales and brand each Carter's garment. In the past, manufacturers had sold their unmarked goods to jobbers, who then sold the garments to retail stores. Branding was in its infancy, and had not often been used to differentiate products' varied quality. Carter's three-man sales force began to sell directly to retailers. The brand's first slogan urged consumers to "Distinguish the Best from the Rest," and often appeared right on Carter's boxes. Since then, packaging has remained an important point-of-purchase advertising medium for the brand.

At first the direct sales method appeared to fail. After the first year of using the technique the company lost money, leaving Carter and his two sons chagrined. But the following year Carter's earned more than all previous years combined by eliminating the middleman.

## Early Advertising

One of the earliest ads for Carter's depicted a woman holding up a union suit. Copy extolled the garment's wide rear flap as the key to "the fit and comfort of Carter union suits." Another turn-of-the-century promotion featured three underwear-clad women with copy that spoke of undergarments as more intimate than any friend and urged customers to choose well. These first print campaigns appeared primarily in women's magazines, and a typical year's advertising budget ran around $6,000.

The brand's first efforts were probably prepared in-house, but as advertising became more professionalized, Carter's brought on the J. Walter Thompson agency. The brand switched to its longest-running agency, Batten, Barton, Durstine & Osborn (BBDO), in 1932. BBDO launched Carter's popular illustrated ads shortly after World War II, when the postwar baby boom was just getting underway. These campaigns featured color illustrations of children wearing Carter's apparel and ran for over fifteen years; the ads were so well liked that some consumers saved the drawings for framing.

However, by the early 1960s BBDO and Carter's agreed that the campaign was outdated. Sales of private-label clothing had eroded Carter's market share, making the demand to modernize the ads more urgent. A focus group revealed that although women liked ads with illustrations of children as well as those with live models, they identified more closely with photographed children. Accordingly, a new campaign was released in 1961. Readership of the new ads surpassed the old, sales of the advertised products

## AT A GLANCE

Carter's brand of children's apparel founded in 1865 by William Carter in Needham, Massachusetts; under joint ownership of Mutual Benefit Life Insurance Company, the William Carter Company's management, and Wesray Capital Corporation since 1987.

**Performance:** *Market share*—No. 1 in infant sleepwear and layettes. *Sales*—$200 million.

**Major competitor:** Oshkosh B'Gosh; also VF Corp.'s Healthtex.

**Advertising:** *Agency*—Murrie White Drummond Lienhart and Associates, Chicago, IL. *Major campaign*—Print advertisments with a nursery rhyme theme featuring the tagline, "The tradition that never wears out."

**Addresses:** *Parent company*—William Carter Company, 1590 Adamson Parkway Suite 400, Morrow, Georgia 30260; phone: (404) 961-8722.

increased by 50 percent, and the Carter brand name achieved even higher recognition than it had in the past.

### Product Development

The William Carter Company developed innovative apparel designs that made children's clothing more comfortable and functional, and thus contributed to the brand's success. "NevaBind" seams ended chafing, and "Handi-Cuff" mitten sleeves kept tiny infants from scratching their own faces. Horace Carter, second son of the founder, invented the "Jiffon" neck, a collar that expanded to stretch comfortably over a child's head.

Despite the move into children's garments, adult underwear remained a significant segment of Carter's merchandise until the 1960s, when Carter's decided to drop the adult line of clothing and focus on children's wear. The new emphasis on children's apparel also brought a focus on fashion. Corporate folklore relates that when expectant mother Shirley Temple asked Carter's to produce garments in new colors, the company indulged her with a whole new array of colors, including yellow, green, and purple for its layette and toddler lines.

Another era of changing styles occured in the mid-1970s, when the "Euro-look" burst on the scene. Suddenly color and a new variety of styles were important. Children's wear designers became even more aware of fashion and adapted adult clothing trends to fit children's specific needs. The fashion trend was driven in part by the declining birth rate in the 1960s and 1970s that forced competition among apparel makers. The trend gained momentum in the 1980s and 1990s, as more couples postponed their first child. Later births generally meant wealthier parents, grandparents, and friends, which led even further from a competitive pricing strategy to a focus on fashion.

### Licensing

The William Carter Company capitalized on the value of its brand name when it agreed to several licensing ventures in the late 1980s and early 1990s. StoneMark, a manufacturer of children's shoes, used the brand name on shoes sized for infants to school-age children. Diaper bags by Mitzi International carried the name

as well. In 1991 Carter's agreed to name a line of baby toiletries manufactured by skin care company Gerwin Inc. after the venerable brand. Carter's Naturals included baby oil, baby lotion, baby bath, shampoo, and a vegetable-based jelly. The hypoallergenic and noncomedogenic line differed from conventional baby toiletries in that it was not baby-scented or colored. The products took advantage of two early 1990s marketing trends: clear formulations and environmentalism. No mineral oils or petroleum products were used in the line, and formulas were based primarily on vegetable and fruit derivatives. To appeal to Carter's slightly upscale target customer, the products were not tested on animals, and were priced somewhat higher than market leaders Johnson & Johnson and Mennen's Baby Magic.

A licensing agreement for the production and marketing in Canada of all Carter's children's wear lines was inked in 1990, and licensing in Europe and Asia was under consideration.

### Marketing and Distribution

Increased competition from mass merchandisers in the late 1980s and early 1990s forced the William Carter Company to adjust its marketing and distribution strategy. Recognizing that its marketing standards had slipped in the 1980s, the company reduced the number of company-owned retail outlet stores to diminish competition among retailers and planned to further upgrade its reputation by eliminating over 2,000 accounts in the early 1990s. The company also cancelled contracts with some private label and secondary brands that were determined to be outside the brand's upscale purview.

Carter's Classic Collection, a line that replaced the Today's Baby merchandise, was offered through upscale retailers and featured 100 percent cotton designs. The line's higher pricing made it a good candidate for gift purchases.

A new print advertising campaign depicted children wearing Carter's clothing in nursery rhyme settings and incorporated the tagline, "The tradition that never wears out." A "design your own pj's contest" was also promoted in 1990. Packaging changes included an updating of the Carter's logo, a clearer delineation between boys' and girls' garments, and new labels. The modifications were complimented by a national "buy two get one free" underwear promotion. To reinforce brand loyalty among new mothers, Carter's also offered over 1.8 million postpartum women a free Carter's bodysuit for the newborn.

Carter's planned to move into clothing for older children in the 1990s. The decision entailed a shift in target audience from mothers to children, since research showed that older children were closely involved in the purchase decision.

Despite moves into more upscale markets, the Carter's brand did not desert its primary, middle-American customer. The basic Carter's line maintained its quality, good fit, and updated styling at upper moderate prices. The clothing was distributed in large specialty stores, department stores, and major children's wear stores, and continued to include all infant apparel needs from layette to toddler playwear. Carter's playwear appealed to fashion-conscious children by incorporating screenprints, embroidery, and bold graphics in keeping with ever-changing trends, yet did not stray too far from the enduring, but sometimes conservative, "Carter's Look."

## New Brand Management

In mid-1992 four executives from Lee Apparel Co., including president Fred Rowan and marketing vice president Joe Pacifico, took comparable positions at Carter. Although the Carter's brand continuted to hold the leading position in infant sleepwear and layettes, rival Healthtex (a division of VF Corp.) overtook Carter's in baby playwear. Competition from discounters and mass merchandisers precipitated the change in management. Carter hoped that Rowan, who had effected a turnaround for Lee's brand blue jeans, would apply his experience with in-depth consumer research to the children's wear brand.

## Further Reading:

Black, Susan S., "A Market to Count On," *Bobbin,* April 1990, 38–48.

"Carter's: The Tradition that Never Wears Out," Morrow, Georgia: William Carter Company, August 1990.

"Centennial Is Motif of $1,500,000 Carter Push," *Advertising Age,* November 23, 1964, p. 4.

"Children's Wear: Fashion Looks Too," *Stores,* February 1977, pp. 42, 45.

Corwin, Pat, "Vigorous, Healthy Sales in Infants' Wear," *Discount Merchandiser,* August 1989, 84-88; "Today's Tots Are Trendier," *Discount Merchandiser,* June 1991, pp. 32–34, 63.

Dagnoli, Judann, "Carter Line Cooks with Campbell," *Advertising Age,* June 13, 1988, p. 10.

"Improving a Successful Ad Formula," *Printers' Ink,* December 14, 1962, pp. 46–48.

"Rejuvenating Children's Wear," *Stores,* May 1975, pp. 14, 26.

Rudie, Raye, and Ellen S. Gang, "Novelty Knits Promise Newness; Trim's No Kid Stuff," *Bobbin,* January 1989, pp. 100–7.

Underwood, Elaine, "Carter's Taps Rowan for Lee-Like Results," *Adweek's Marketing Week,* June 29, 1992, p. 4.

*—April S. Dougal*

# CHAMPION®

Champion is the most widely recognized brand of athletic fleece-wear in the United States. The story of Champion's success, far more so than that of most superbrands, is one that is still only beginning to unfold. As recently as 1990, fully half of Champion's sales were to institutional markets—high school, college, and professional sports teams, as well as campus bookstores. It was upon such markets that Champion quietly built a name for itself, a name associated with durability, classic styling, and innovation. Uniform sales and special imprint sales will no doubt always be a mainstay with Champion. However, its focus since 1985 has been on sporting goods and department store sales, a long-neglected retail market. At that time Roger Holland was brought in to provide new direction for the family-owned company. According to Kathy Murray of *Forbes,* "Holland remembers the advice he received from a departing executive: 'Don't mess with retail, it's a loser and it's not something we should do.' " Holland chose not to listen.

Champion products, through a number of licensing arrangements, were then among the hottest on the European market. Holland and retailing vice-president Frederick Lulof reasoned that the same success could be had in the United States, with a large infusion of marketing capital. They were right. Unfortunately, the company quickly became a takeover target by New York brokerage firm Walsh Greenwood. By early 1989 the threat had become so serious that Champion Products decided to seek non-hostile bids from other companies. Sara Lee Corp. and Champion came out winners. Although traditionally associated with food, Sara Lee ranked as the largest apparel company in the United States in the early 1990s. In addition to Champion, the parent company owns such respected clothing brands as Hanes, L'Eggs, Isotoner, Playtex, and Bali. Robert Sharoff reported: "With Hanes and Champion leading the way, Sara Lee Corp. plans to aggressively expand its apparel operations over the next few years." A megabrand in the making, Champion is expected to more than triple its sales in the 1990s while going head-to-head with market leader Russell Athletic. Name recognition and Sara Lee's experience with big-brand marketing are on its side.

## Brand Origins

Champion began humbly in 1919 as the nascent brainchild of brothers Abe and Bill Feinbloom of Rochester, New York. "Working on opposite sides of a single desk," according to the

official history, "they hired a few employees and began what was to be a revolution in the apparel industry." The Feinblooms observed that students were appropriating the sweatshirt "fashion" of outdoor laborers. This potential market could be expanded if students were given an added incentive to sport the new style. Raised-letter logos were the answer, and their sweater mill company, Knickerbocker Knitting, became the first clothes manufacturer to sell imprinted sweatshirts. The tie-in to athletics arose in the same manner: because students were wearing their Champion sweats to team practices, the Feinblooms decided they could again carve out a new market, this time by modifying their Army surplus union suit into a team athletic jersey.

In 1938 Champion salesperson Sam Friedland patented a "reverse weave" process that helped maintain the original form of Champion sweats over time. The advancement came in response to complaints from athletes that their sweatshirts tended to stretch through the middle and shrink in length. Friedland's reverse weave process was still employed in the early 1990s throughout the Champion collection. The Champion brand and the Big-C logo soon defined the Rochester company, even to the point of renaming it. Champion's clear niche became that of high school, college, and professional team supplier. "By the time college bookstores were supplying the rest of the student body," wrote Hilary Sterne, "[Champion] shirts were as legendary as tousle-haired touch-football games on the Kennedy lawn."

The 1960s may well have been an era when the Champion brand attained classic status, but for the Champion company it was a time of woeful mismanagement. It was then, wrote Murray, that the Feinbloom family brought in leadership from the outside. "Outside, and not very bright. They continued to sell Champion's uniforms directly to coaches and school athletic departments, thereby alienating the sporting goods stores. That proved costly when the fitness boom took off, and gave competitors like Russell Corp. [which by 1988 had sales of $480 million] a big toe in the athletic apparel retailing door." In campus bookstores Champion continued to excel; unfortunately, it did so while ignoring the larger retail market.

Then, in 1976, came a tantalizing possibility. Minneapolis-based Jostens Inc., a leader in the manufacture of school rings and other school-related products, posed a merger with dominant school sweats maker Champion. In April both boards of directors

## AT A GLANCE

**C**hampion brand of athletic fleecewear founded in mid-1930s in Rochester, NY, by Abe and Bill Feinbloom, owners of Knickerbocker Knitting Company; company renamed Champion Products, Inc.; Champion Products acquired by Sara Lee Corp., 1989.

**Performance:** *Market share*—Top share of imprinted sportswear to college bookstores; 17% (top share, with Hanes and Pannill) of sweatshirt category; 25% (middle share, with Hanes) of overall T-shirt category. *Sales*—$300 million (estimated).

**Major competitor:** Russell Corp.'s Russel.

**Advertising:** *Agency*—Rumrill-Hoyt, Rochester, NY. *Major campaign*—Print ads featuring amateur athletes sporting bright-colored Champion outerwear.

**Addresses:** *Parent company*—Champion Products, Inc., 3141 Monroe Ave., Rochester, NY 14618; phone: (716) 385-3200; fax (716) 385-2452. *Ultimate parent company*—Sara Lee Knit Products Inc., P.O. Box 3019, Winston-Salem, NC 27102; phone: (919) 744-2400.

agreed to the deal, but by August they mutually terminated negotiations. Most likely the merger was thwarted by lower than expected earnings by Champion. Whatever the case, Champion proceeded in the late 1970s to boost sales by confidently entering the retail market, buoyed by newly acquired license rights to major league baseball, the National Football League (NFL), the National Basketball Association (NBA), the National Collegiate Athletic Association (NCAA), and the North American Soccer League. But by the mid-1980s Champion had not only largely retreated from retail, it had also embroiled itself in royalties disputes with such collegiate customers as the University of Southern California, the University of California, Los Angeles, and the University of Pittsburgh.

When Holland came on board in 1986 sales were sluggish and the competition was fierce. Taking drastic measures, he transferred knitting operations to a new plant, excised most of Champion's upper management, and then successfully lobbied the board for approval of a $9 million, three-year advertising campaign—an enormous commitment for the conservative financially squeezed company. Within two years Holland tripled Champion's profits and boosted sales by 50 percent. The return to high-margin retail markets, of course, was key to the Holland turnaround. The reason it worked this time, other than a heightened emphasis on advertising, was Holland's decision to revamp Champion's sales force. In effect he created two organizations, one comprised primarily of ex-athletes and ex-coaches and devoted to campus bookstores and sports teams, and the other, of an expert force for the retail arena.

Although Champion's 1988 figures ($219 million in sales and $14.9 million in net income) were dwarfed by Russell's, Champion Products was now firmly in the fight for sales share. As Champion entered the 1990s under new ownership and new leadership, it was, in Warren Berger's words, "by no means the largest brand of fleece-based athletic apparel in the U.S." Rather, it was in fourth place, behind Russell, Tultex, and Bassett-Walker (VF). "Unlike the others, however, Champion is the most widely known among consumers because the company sells its merchandise through large retailers." Champion's brand management during

the early 1990s was taken on by president Terry Owen, marketing vice-president Paul Wold, and the Rumrill-Hoyt agency. In contrast to hard-hitting, jock-oriented "perspiration-heavy" marketing of the brand during the mid-1980s, this new team emphasized mass lifestyle appeal: print ads featuring Frisbee players and other amateur athletes sporting a variety of Champion outerwear in neon and other bold colors. The ads were accompanied by clever observations of action-filled lifestyles. For example, a Champion-clad couple hauling their bicycles over rugged train was captioned: "The mountains supply altitude. We supply attitude."

The teenage and over-30 markets were chief targets of the campaign. Despite what Wold said to Berger—"We're not making any attempt to be trendy. The strength of the Champion name is that it's a classic"—a hot new trend was launched. "Kids are going nuts for the stuff," said a New York sporting goods store owner. "The gray sweats still sell best, but the teen business is exploding." Since the campaign began, sales of Champion's non-fleece items, such as tank tops, Jam shorts, and jackets, have grown markedly. Meanwhile, Champion has been careful not to neglect its collegiate and professional sports ties and, in fact, has parlayed these long-term relationships into greater retailing power. Champion now supplies seven NFL teams and is the official supplier to the NBA. In addition, Champion was positioned as a major sponsor and supplier of activewear for the 1994 and 1996 U.S. Olympic teams.

In fiscal 1992 Champion launched Sara Lee Champion Europe in an effort to "coordinate sourcing for Champion's independent international licensees." Both European and Pacific Rim countries remain important to Champion's future growth as a megabrand. With one long and relatively obscure chapter of its story concluded, Champion now faces a high-stakes, high-profile future under Sara Lee. Concept shops, windwear, outerwear, further licensing agreements, and sourcing arrangements with its sister companies are all means by which the brand will likely advance. However, as Champion Chief Executive Officer Susan Engel summarized for *Sporting Goods Business:* "One of the advantages of Champion is its superb name recognition. Wherever you go, and regardless of whom you talk to, from retailers to reps, everyone knows the name."

### Further Reading:

Arlen, Jeffrey, "Champion Brands Overseas Markets," *Daily News Record,* April 18, 1985, p. 4.

Berger, Warren, "Champion Starts to Show Its True Colors Off the Field," *Adweek's Marketing Week,* April 23, 1990, pp. 20–21.

"Champion Products Agrees to Buy Sweatshirt Maker," *Wall Street Journal,* December 16, 1968, p. 8.

"Champion Products, Jostens, Inc. Dropping Plans for a Merger," *Wall Street Journal,* August 12, 1976, p. 4.

"Designs on Europe's Knickers: 'Can Sara Lee Do in Europe What It Has Done in America?'" *Economist,* November 14, 1992, p. 86.

"Directors of Jostens, Champion Products Approve Merger Pact," *Wall Street Journal,* April 21, 1976, p. 8.

Heuslein, William, "The Price Was Right," *Forbes,* May 15, 1989, p. 10.

Kentouris, Chris, "Boosted by WestPoint, Champion, Fashion Shares Outdo Market," *Daily News Record,* October 26, 1988, p. 9.

Leibowitz, David S., "Two Cases Where Quality Will Out," *Financial World,* June 23, 1992, p. 103.

Murray, Kathy, "Thanks for the Advice," *Forbes,* May 2, 1988, pp. 62, 64.

"New Champion CEO Focuses on Future," *Sporting Goods Business,* January 1992, p. 14.

Phalon, Richard, "Walking Billboards," *Forbes,* December 7, 1992, pp. 84–85.

Robb, Gregory A., "Champion Products Accepts Bid," *New York Times,* February 14, 1989, p. D5.

*Sara Lee Corp. Annual Report,* Chicago: Sara Lee Corp., 1992.

"Sara Lee Net Rose 12% in Its 4th Period Despite Weakness in Foreign Markets," *Wall Street Journal,* August 10, 1993, p. B4.

Sharoff, Robert, "Sara Lee Predicts Huge Growth for Hanes, Champion Divisions," *Daily News Record,* October 30, 1992, p. 2.

Sterne, Hilary, "Honest Sweats: Champion's Cotton Shirts Are the Real McCoy," *Gentlemen's Quarterly,* May 1992, p. 43.

Troxell, Thomas N., Jr., "One Strike's Not Out: Champion Products Is Recovering from the NFL Walkout," *Barron's,* April 18, 1983, pp. 62–63, 65.

*—Jay P. Pederson*

# CHANEL®

# CHANEL

It can be said that no other fashion designer has impacted the way women dress as greatly as Gabrielle (Coco) Chanel. Originally intended as a bold challenge to the restrictive clothing of the early 20th century, Chanel designs have grown to become worldwide classics. Over the years Coco Chanel's legendary line of hats, couture, and perfume has expanded to include seven fragrances, a ready-to-wear line of clothing, and the Beaute line of cosmetics and skin care. The Chanel name achieves a 97–98 percent customer awareness rating in company-directed polls, and fragrances such as Chanel No. 5 consistently rank among the top five in fragrance sales worldwide. The Chanel brands are managed by Chanel Inc., a privately held company 100 percent owned by Pameco, the Swiss holding company for the Wertheimer family. The family has owned rights to the brand since 1924. The family releases no financial information concerning the Chanel brand. A 1989 *Forbes* article, however, estimated the brand to be worth over $1 billion.

## Origins

Inextricably intertwined with the Chanel brand is Gabrielle ''Coco'' Chanel, a Frenchwoman born of peasant parents in 1883 who grew to become perhaps the most legendary woman in modern France. No knowledge of 20th century fashion is possible without studying Chanel, the first designer to create elegant clothing free of corsets, heavy hats, and extraneous ornaments.

Chanel's origins were humble: abandoned after the death of her mother when she was 12, Gabrielle lived in an orphanage and later in a convent in Moulins. At the convent she was reunited with a young aunt, Adrienne Chanel, who grew to become one of her closest friends.

The women left the convent when Gabrielle was 20, and found employment selling linens in the town of Moulins. The simple life of a shop girl was not to last long for Gabrielle. Young, attractive, and fiercely unconventional, she soon left for the resort town of Vichy where she pursued a dream of becoming a star vocalist in France's popular music halls and garnered the nickname ''Coco'' along the way. In Vichy Chanel met her first love, a young infantry officer and member of the ''grande bourgeoise'' named Etienne Balsan. She agreed to become his mistress (marriage was out of the question) and moved with him to his country estate where she entered the world of high society, famous actresses, and courtesans.

Fashion at the turn of the century consisted of an elaborate combination of tight corsets, heavily beaded dresses, and large hats piled high with ornaments. Chanel deliberately stripped her clothing of all bric-a-brac in an effort to set herself apart from the women of the ''demi-monde,'' a term referring to women of humble origin who entered the aristocracy by becoming mistresses of wealthy men. Her approach to dressing was unconventional, yet very pragmatic. To the races, for example, she wore clothing she considered suitable for the event: small, simple hats and her lover's overcoat. With her unconventional flair and elegance, Chanel attracted the attention of high society. Before she had even gone into the fashion business, Chanel was making a name for herself.

### Modes Chanel

Around 1910 Chanel decided to go to Paris and establish herself as a milliner. Balsan thought it a charming idea but did not feel that it was socially proper for the mistress of a wealthy man to work as a milliner. Chanel found a friend, however, in Boy Capel, a young British friend of Balsan with a keen sense of business. He offered to set Chanel up in Paris, and by the end of that year, she began selling her first hats out of a small apartment on Boulevard Maleshergbes.

Chanel bought small straw hats at the Paris department store Galeries Lafayette and decorated them with simple elegance. She initially sold her hats to the fashionably dressed women in her circle of friends, some of which were very high profile actresses. Her best marketing strategy was instituted in 1912, when she convinced actress Gabrielle Dorziat to wear an elegant and simple Chanel hat in the play *Bel Ami*. Soon many stars were wearing Chanel hats, and women in the audience were flocking to Chanel's door.

In 1913 Chanel created her first dress: black velvet with long, simple lines and embellished only by a collection of white lawn petals sewn together to form a collar. With financial backing from Boy Capel, she opened her first dress shop that year in the seaside town of Deauville. Her marketing technique was similar to the one used to promote her hats. Each morning she sent her aunt Adrienne (who was by then a well-known actress) on a promenade by the seashore wearing the latest Chanel dress and hat. Bit by bit, the curious customers came to her door.

## AT A GLANCE

Gabrielle (Coco) Chanel opened her first milliner shop in Paris in 1910; first clothing boutique opened in 1913 in the French costal town of Deauville; Chanel No. 5 perfume created in 1921; Chanel entered into agreement with Pierre Wertheimer of the Bourgeois fragrance and cosmetic company to manufacture and distribute Chanel perfumes in 1924; all rights to Chanel name reverted to Wertheimer family upon death of Chanel in 1971; Chanel is managed by Chanel Inc., a privately held company wholly owned by Pameco, a Swiss holding company controlled by the Wertheimer family.

**Performance:** *Market share*—Chanel No. 5 consistently ranks in top 5% of prestige perfume category. *Sales*—Perfume: $95 million; cosmetics: $95 million.

**Major competitor:** Calvin Klein.

**Advertising:** *Agency*—DDB Needham, New York, NY. *Major campaign*—Long-running print ads for cosmetics and perfumes featuring models Ines de la Fressange and Carole Boquet.

**Addresses:** *Parent company*—Chanel Inc., 9 West 57th Street, New York, NY 10019; phone: (212) 688-5055; fax: (212) 752-1851. *Ultimate parent company*—Pameco, Switzerland.

When the Germans invaded France during World War I, French aristocrats fled Paris and took up residence in Deauville. Through creativity and innovation, Chanel managed to keep her shop open, despite massive shortages. She purchased a quantity of Rodier jersey (a soft fabric that had been used to make men's undergarments), cut them into loose-fitting, fluid dresses, and created the first "sportswear." The dresses allowed women greater ease of movement and were designed for forays to the beach or race track. That year, Chanel also introduced her first bathing suit, cut from the fabric of Boy Capel's sweater.

World War I created a climate that greatly benefitted Chanel's innovative style. The cumbersome trappings and the elaborate couture of France's aristocracy were wiped out. As the men went off to fight, women began assuming their tasks at home and became more active. Chanel's practical yet stylish clothing hats suited their needs well. By 1916, Chanel was employing over 300 seamstresses and milliners in Paris and had opened a shop in Biarritz. Also that year, the American fashion magazine *Harpar's Bazaar* featured one of Chanel's creations, planting the seeds of her popularity in the United States.

### The Golden Age of Chanel

Chanel's reputation reach unparalleled heights during the era between World War I and World War II. During this time, she made liaisons with some of the most famous artists of her time: Igor Stravinski, Vaslav Nijinsky, and Pablo Picasso. She designed costumes for *Le Train Bleu*, a hugely successful ballet by Les Ballets Russes, and for the famous play *Antigone*, adapted by Jean Cocteau with sets by Picasso.

Working out of her mirrored salon on rue Cambon, Chanel produced fashion that both influenced and was influenced by members of the European aristocracy. From her brief affair with Grand Duke Dimitri Pavlovich, nephew of the last tsar of Russia, she developed a taste for the old Russian style of tunics, embroidery, baroque jewelry, and perfumes, all of which she incorpo-

rated into the Chanel style of the early 1920s. During the years 1926 to 1931, Chanel created a decidedly British style inspired by her association with the Duke of Westminster. It became the hallmark of the Chanel look: tweed jackets, sporty coats, and a series of simple, elegant, and comfortable suits.

This was the decade of Chanel introductions that were to completely alter women's fashion in the 20th century. She reportedly was the first to make a suntan fashionable and the first to bob her hair. In 1925 Chanel introduced a line of pants for women. One year later, she created the "little black dress," which soon became a fixture in women's wardrobes on both sides of the Atlantic. The style was so popular that the American *Vogue* dubbed it the "Chanel Ford" and crowned her "the greatest mind in fashion." By the end of the 1930s her personal fortune was rumored to be $15 million.

### Parfums Chanel

Although Chanel earned international acclaim for revolutionizing the way women dress, her most lucrative creation was the fragrance Chanel No. 5. In the early 1920s Chanel had hired chemist Ernest Beaux to create five different blends for Chanel to sample. She chose the fifth vial, labeled No. 5, and (in keeping with her penchant for simplicity) did not change its name. Chanel No. 5 debuted on May 5, 1921, in a bold, square cut crystal vial inspired by toiletry bottles designed for travel. Its rectangular white label with, "No. 5, Chanel, Paris" printed in black letters stood in stark contrast to the elaborate and flowery fragrance bottles of that time. In 1922 Chanel launched her second perfume, packaged in the same clean cut crystal bottle, with the same simple black and white label. She named it No. 22, for the year in which it was launched.

In 1924 Chanel founded Parfums Chanel with Pierre Wertheimer, owner of the Bourgeois cosmetic company, then the largest fragrance and cosmetics company in France. In the agreement, Bourgeois would manufacture and distribute the perfume, Wertheimer would receive 70 percent of the rights to Chanel fragrances, Chanel 10 percent, and Theophile Bader (founder of the Galeries Lafayette department store) received a 20 percent share for brokering the agreement. That year, Chanel No. 5 was launched in the United States, setting it off on the route to becoming the most widely recognized and best-selling perfume in the world. Chanel and Wertheimer immediately began launching new perfumes: Gardenia in 1925, Bois des Iles in 1926, and Cuir de Russie in 1927. Yet none would achieve the phenomenal success of No. 5 and No. 22.

For almost 20 years, Chanel reigned as queen of world fashion. In 1938 she was toppled from her throne when Italian designer Elsa Schiaparelli stole the hearts and minds of the fashion world. Almost overnight, Chanel's decades-old sway over the way women dressed faded. She showed a final collection in fall of 1939, then closed her couture operations on rue Cambon, leaving only her boutique open to sell costume jewelry, cosmetics, and perfume.

World War II broke out and Chanel cloistered herself in the Ritz hotel, then took refuge in Switzerland while the war raged through Europe. During the war, the only successful product bearing the Chanel name was No. 5. Early in the war, German soldiers lined the walk, waiting to buy a bottle for their mothers or sweethearts back home. After the war, the German soldiers were replaced by American soldiers seeking the same perfume.

Chanel realized she had signed away her rights to the most profitable portion of her business. Throughout her life, she remained angry over her perfume deal with Wertheimer and sought numerous ways to renegotiate the agreement. During the war, she allied herself with a young German officer, attempting to use German occupation regulations to seize the assets of the Wertheimer family, who were Jewish and had fled to the United States. After France was liberated, Chanel was arrested by the French resistance for her dealings with the Germans. However, according to several biographers, her former lover, the Duke of Westminster, intervened on Chanel's behalf. Within 24 hours, she was set free.

Chanel continued her battle with Wertheimer for a large share of fragrance profits, concocting a perfume called Mademoiselle Chanel No. 5, which had a scent similar to the original. Aware that Chanel's personal image was integral to the success of any product bearing her name, Wertheimer sought to avoid any public scandal that might dig up her wartime activities. He paid her $40,000 in cash plus two percent royalties on all products bearing her name. Later Chanel entered into a no-competition agreement in exchange for a monthly fee paid by Wertheimer.

The popularity of Chanel No. 5 grew unabated, even as Chanel herself no longer created the couture that had initially given the fragrance its allure. By 1954, however, even perfume sales were down. With financial assistance from Wertheimer, Chanel returned to reopen her Paris salon in hopes of rekindling profits for her fragrance.

## Chanel Comeback

According to the French press in 1954, Chanel's first new collection in 15 years was a disaster. Her jersey-and-tweed suits were found "tacky" by some, and touchingly sad by others. But buyers were buying. In the United States, designers began incorporating elements of Chanel's design into their new collections. Christian Dior, the reigning Parisian designer, borrowed heavily from Chanel's boyish 1920s look. Chanel had staged her comeback, and followed it up with a small, private showing in October and an much larger one in February of 1955.

In the ten years that followed, Chanel's suits, loose-fitting dresses, and elegant accessories were the fashion of choice among many women in the United States and Europe. When asked, "Who do you dress?," Chanel's response was, "Ask me who I don't dress." Celebrities and elegant women from Jacqueline Kennedy to Marilyn Monroe wore Chanel. Knock-off styles abounded, some going at fractions of the cost of the original, while others sold for twice the price.

In her early years, Chanel was an innovator. As she grew older, however, her image grew more conservative. The social upheavals that began in France and the United States in 1968 also generated a revolution in women's clothing that was the antithesis of Chanel's simple and seemingly austere style. In 1971, one year after introducing her highly successful Chanel No. 19 perfume in Europe, Coco Chanel died quietly in her quarters at the Ritz. At the time of her death, the House of Chanel was earning over $160 million a year.

## Chanel after Chanel

When Chanel died, all rights to the Chanel name and products were transferred to the Wertheimer family. Quite predictably,

Chanel's death left a void in the House of Chanel. Couture designs floundered aimlessly during the early 1970s, and its sales slumped. Perfume sales, however, remained strong, with Chanel No. 5 ranking consistently among the international best-sellers.

The Wertheimers were in the perfume and cosmetic business, and began concentrating their efforts on what they knew best. In the years immediately following the death of Chanel, Parfums

*Designer Coco Chanel's now-famous simple elegance is reflected in the brand's logo.*

Chanel focused almost exclusively on the launch of new perfumes and Chanel Beaute, an exclusive line of color cosmetics and skin care products inspired by Coco Chanel's small cosmetic line during the 1930s. Chanel No. 19 was successfully introduced in the United States in 1972.

By 1974, however, as Chanel was gearing up to introduce Chanel Beaute, its image was tarnished by the fading memory of Coco Chanel and wide-spread distribution that allowed an aging clientele to easily purchase Chanel No. 5 at the corner drugstore. Alain Wertheimer, grandson of Pierre, stepped in to spruce up Chanel's image. He skillfully maneuvered around U.S. laws to reduce the number of Chanel outlets from 18,000 to 12,000. He also put millions of dollars behind the European launch of Chanel Beaute, supported by simple yet elegant advertising. First year sales topped $5 million.

Chanel Parfums was on a roll, introducing Cristalle, another successful fragrance, in 1975. Chanel then poured millions of dollars into advertising to support the U.S. launch of Chanel Beaute and Cristalle in less than 500 high-end outlets. In 1978 Wertheimer moved his attention to Chanel's lagging couture division and created Chanel's first ready-to-wear line. This was soon followed by a relaunch of higher priced Chanel accessories: quilted handbags selling for $960, slippers for $225, and long strands of faux pearls for $360. Wertheimer had successfully recreated an exclusive image around a slew of new Chanel products. However, the excitement that had surrounded the Chanel name when Coco was creating her own couture was slow coming.

In 1983 the House of Chanel wooed designer Karl Lagerfeld from his position at Chloe. Within a year, Lagerfeld's $150,000 gold-buttoned variations of the traditional Chanel suit were worn by Princess Caroline of Monaco, Ivana Trump, and the Queen of Jordan. A new excitement surrounded Chanel products, which soon rubbed off on Chanel perfumes, cosmetics, and accessory sales.

The 1980s marked a decade of expansion for Chanel. One year after hiring Lagerfeld, Chanel introduced Coco, a fragrance dedicated to its founder, and opened the first free-standing Chanel boutique in the United States. In the five years following, five more free-standing Chanel boutiques were opened in U.S. cities. Chanel also expanded into the men's fragrance industry introducing Chanel Antaeus in 1981 and Pour Monsieur in 1988.

Chanel Beaute also expanded during the 1980s and made a name for itself in the 1980s as an innovator in skin-care treatment, introducing a number of cosmetic industry firsts: Teint Naturel, the first totally non-occlusive foundation (1981); Creme Extreme Protection, the first day-time moisturizer with a built-in sunscreen (1982); Lift Serum, the first corrective skin care product to address primary, secondary, and tertiary wrinkles (1986); Soleil Chanel, the first totally waterproof line of sun care products (1987); and others. In 1990 Chanel redesigned its color cosmetics line to suit not only a woman's complexion but also the colors in her wardrobe; the line was introduced under the name Colour Confidence with hopes of capturing 25 percent of the prestige color cosmetics market.

## Performance Appraisal

Until 1971 the success of the Chanel name was directly tied to the success of Coco Chanel as a designer. After the death of Chanel, the Chanel name risked loosing its identity. Although the brand floundered for several years after Chanel's death, the Wertheimer family succeeded in firmly re-establishing the Chanel name in the prestige market. Company-generated surveys found that consumer recognition of the Chanel name never dropped below 97 to 98 percent during the 1980s, fueled primarily by the continuous introduction of new perfumes, cosmetics, and boutiques.

The Wertheimer family successfully built upon the unique image established by Coco Chanel. By 1990, wholesale volume for Chanel fragrances and cosmetics were estimated at $95 million each, supported by strong sales in North America and the Pacific Rim. Chanel is now firmly established as a leader in the prestige cosmetics and fragrances markets. The brand's continued success depends on a marketing plan that successfully balances the tradition of Coco Chanel with innovation and changing consumer desires.

## Further Reading:

Berman, Phyllis and Zina Sawaya, "The Billionaires behind Chanel," *Forbes,* April 3, 1989, p. 104.

"Chanel No. 1," *Time,* January 25, 1971, p. 54.

"Chanel Widens U.S. Spotlight for No. 19," *Women's Wear Daily,* December 16, 1988, p. 10.

"Cristalle Is Chanel's First Named Scent," *Advertising Age,* March 14, 1977.

Deeny, Godfrey, "Chanel No. 5 Tops List of Bestsellers in Paris," *Women's Wear Daily,* September 7, 1990, p. 32.

Edelson, Sharon, "Zimmerman: Chanel's Ace Juggler," *Women's Wear Daily,* August 3, 1990, p. 8.

"Feeneesh?," *Time,* February 15, 1954, p. 28.

Furukawa, Tsukasa, "Dior, Chanel Tops in Japan," *Women's Wear Daily,* June 10, 1988, p. 88.

"H Hour, H Line," *Newsweek,* August 9, 1954, pp. 51–52.

Ludington, Callaway, "Coco Blossoms in Many Versions," *Women's Wear Daily,* June 9, 1989, p. 74.

*Mademoiselle Chanel,* New York: Chanel Inc., 1992.

Oliver, Joyce Anne, "She Innovates without Destroying a Legend," *Marketing News,* December 10, 1990, p. 10.

*The Story of Chanel,* New York: Chanel, Inc.

Wood, Dana, "Chanel's Confidence Game," *Women's Wear Daily,* April 13, 1990, p. 11.

*—Maura Troester*

# CHAP STICK®

More than just a brand name, Chap Stick is a household product synonymous with lip care. Millions of people rely on the soothing and smoothing effect of this petroleum product. The *Physician's Desk Reference for Nonprescription Drugs* described Chap Stick as a balm "which forms a barrier to prevent moisture loss and protect lips from the drying effects of cold weather, wind and sun which cause chapping," and cited its "special emollients" as the key to its effectiveness at "restoring suppleness to the lips, and preventing drying." While many lip balms have been introduced into the consumer market in the 1970s and 1980s, none have shaken Chap Stick's reign.

## Brand Origin and History

Chap Stick was invented in the 1880s by Dr. C. D. Fleet, a Lynchburg, Virginia, doctor who combined petroleum and wax into a molded stick. For a number of years, Dr. Fleet made the product himself, wrapped it in foil, and sold it locally. In 1912 he sold the rights to the product to Lynchburg resident John Morton for five dollars. After securing a small business loan, Morton and his wife began to make Chap Stick in bulk quantities. Mrs. Morton mixed and melted the formula on her kitchen stove, poured it into molds of brass tubes, and set it out on the porch to cool. After the sticks hardened, Morton pushed them out of the tubes with a metal rod, chopped them into the appropriate size with a self-designed gadget, covered them in silver foil, and shipped them in paste-board boxes to wholesale druggists near and far. The business thrived, and Morton incorporated his business into the Morton Manufacturing Corporation in 1919.

The United States' economy typically flourishes during war, and World War II proved especially beneficial to the growth of Chap Stick. The government bought quantities of the product and issued it in olive-drab tubes to the troops; soldiers going to the tropics received one kind, those fighting in colder climates another. Chap Stick so impressed the servicemen that they continued to buy the product after they returned home, and sales boomed.

Encouraged by the commercial success of Chap Stick, Morton Manufacturing began to branch out into other health and beauty products as well as cleaning and food products. Morton's Snow White brand of beauty products included shampoo, face powder, deodorant, perfume, and bleaching cream; the same type of products were also sold under the name Lady Wayne. Their Blair trademark included air freshener, household disinfectant, silver polish, stove polish, furniture polish, and floor wax. Morton manufactured food products such as flavoring extracts and puddings under the name Ann Elizabeth Wade. Talcum powder and hair tonic was marketed under the trademark Coat of Arms. The major line extension was a new line of hand cream, Chap Ans, introduced in 1948. Their major development, was the "Lipotropic Substance," the ingredient Moistutane, whose name they registered in 1961.

## Product Development

Since buying Chap Stick in 1963, A.H. Robins Co. has improved and extended the product line. One of the first innovations was adding flavors to the original formula. In 1971 A.H. Robins introduced cherry, mint, and grape flavored Chap Stick; they added orange in 1978, strawberry in 1981. In addition, A.H. Robins continued to improve the basic formula in response to the continuing growth of the competition. In their 1985 Annual Report, A.H. Robins announced that "a new softer, smoother feeling formula now being introduced is expected to strengthen Chap Stick's franchise in the lip balm market."

Recognizing the growing market for sunscreens, they unveiled Chap Stick Sunblock 15 in 1980. Designed for year-round use, Chap Stick Sunblock 15 contained the same dry-lip protection as regular Chap Stick with the added benefit of two FDA-approved sunscreen agents whose overlapping ultraviolet absorption rates provide maximum protection. In 1986, A.H. Robins introduced Chap Stick Petroleum Jelly Plus, and Chap Stick Petroleum Jelly Plus with Sunblock 15 in squeeze tubes. The "Plus" referred to the addition of aloe and lanolin to 99 percent white petrolatum (petroleum jelly), or to 89 percent petrolatum in the sunscreen formula. Regular Chap Stick contains 44 percent petrolatum.

The concept and the ingredients of Chap Stick have spawned several new product lines for A.H. Robins. In 1975 they created Lip Quenchers, a lipstick that incorporated the conditioning and protective properties of Chap Stick. The following year the company introduced Face Quenchers, a foundation makeup with the similar qualities. Several years later they launched a new line of flavored lipsticks, Lip Treat, geared towards teenage consumers.

American Home Products Corporation acquired A.H. Robins in 1989 and continued research and product development for the Chap Stick line. In the early 1990s, the company pioneered a

## AT A GLANCE

**C**hap Stick brand of lip balm founded in the 1880s by Dr. C. D. Fleet; became a registered trademark in 1912 owned by John Morton, president of the Morton Manufacturing Corporation; brand and company sold to A.H. Robins, 1963; was aquired by American Home Products in 1989.

**Major competitor:** Blistex; also Sterling Drug's Campho-Phenique.

**Advertising:** *Agency*—Scali, McCabe, Sloves, New York, NY, 1991—.

**Addresses:** *Parent company*—A.H. Robins, Co., Consumer Products Division, 1407 Cummings Drive, Richmond, VA 23220; phone: (804) 257-2000; fax: (804) 257-2726. *Ultimate parent company*—American Home Products Corporation, Five Giralda Farms, Madison, NJ 07940.

medicated form of the product available in stick, tube, and jar forms. The new ingredients included camphor, menthol, and phenol which aided not only dry and chapped lips, but also fever blisters and cold sores; camphor relieved the itching and burning, menthol reduced pain, and phenol numbed the area.

### Rising Competition

Even though Chap Stick was invented before the turn of the century, competing products have been developed only recently. Prior to World War II, the Trademark Registration File shows only one other registered lip balm, Physician's Formula, which was introduced in 1937. In the 1950s two new products were introduced, the antibiotic Blistex and the medicated Lip-Guard, which was manufactured by American Home Products. However, competition increased in the 1970s when Sea & Ski, first produced in 1965 by Wild Surf; Lip Saver; and Zone Defense by the Givaudan Corporation became popular. Other new products introduced in the 1970s included Questor's Spalding Lip Balm, Chesebrough-Pond's Constant Care, Village Bath Products' Lip Lickers, Chattem Drug and Chemical Company's Tip-a-Lip, Plough's Winecooler, Browne Drug Company's Palmer's Lip Balm, and lip balms by Shaklee and Key West. Further competition arose in the 1980s with Campho-Phenique, a medicated lip balm introduced by Sterling Drug Inc., Aloe Up, by J. Benson Corporation, the Merchandising Company's Lip Rx, Chesebrough-Pond's Lip Therapy, and Balassa Laboratories' Solar Stick, as well as lip balms by Nature's Aloe and Aloe Advantage.

Despite the number of new entries onto the market, Chap Stick sales continued to climb yearly under A.H. Robins management. However, their market share slipped from 60 percent in the mid 1970s to 55 percent by 1982. A.H. Robins counteracted with aggressive advertising and promotional campaigns, and by 1984 Chap Stick market share was up to 56 percent. Sales have continued to be strong.

### Advertising and Marketing

When A.H. Robins bought Chap Stick, an aggressive national advertising campaign was initiated. Not only did they advertise extensively in print in national newspapers and large-circulation magazines, but they also aired television commercials. Both Chap Ans and Chap Stick were promoted seasonally on NBC's *Today* show, and several of the United States' top sports figures were

hired to endorse the product in magazines, college newspapers, and on television. In 1975, the company experimented in select markets with year-round advertising to stress the effectiveness of the product in both summer and winter; this proved so successful that all-season advertising continued in the following years on a national level.

In addition to its national advertisements, in-store displays continued to play a part in Chap Stick's promotion. In 1979 the company changed the color of its label to include yellow, white, and blue in order "to symbolize the product's year-round use," states the 1979 *Annual Report*. Chap Stick Sunblock 15 was initially promoted directly to dermatologists and other physicians as well as to the consumer. The sunblock version was also placed in special displays in the suntan lotion department of stores to create additional activity during the summer months. Three years after its introduction, Sunblock 15 was repackaged using colors that were more compatible with those used for other sunscreen products, and a new promotional theme built on the growing consumer awareness of the sun's damaging effects identified it specifically as a product to prevent sunburned lips.

In 1982, the company expanded their distribution with checkout stand displays. They also hoped to increase sales by becoming a sponsor of the U.S. Olympic team. The following year they

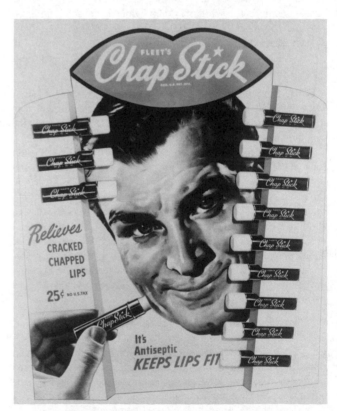

*A Chap Stick promotional display as it appeared in 1948.*

changed wrapping again, and Chap Stick was given a new, more attractive package. Again in 1991, this time under American Home Products, "major revisions in packaging design were made by Robins for Chap Stick lip balm," according to the 1991 *American Home Products Corporation Annual Report*.

By 1975 when A.H. Robins introduced Chap Stick onto the international market, the company was already marketing many of their other products through their International Division in more than one hundred countries worldwide through distributors, licensees, and their fifteen subsidiary companies. Initial foreign sales of Chap Stick were so successful that the company has continued to introduce the product into other countries. In 1977 Chap Stick reached Japan through A.H. Robins's Tokyo-based subsidiary, the American Drug Corporation. By 1983 Chap Stick was available in Spain.

## Product Health and Future

The purchase of Morton Manufacturing by A.H. Robins in 1963 has proved beneficial for Chap Stick, providing the brand with more advertising dollars and a wider reach into foreign markets which resulted in increased sales almost every year. However, Chap Stick has proved profitable for the company as well. The strength of the A.H. Robins Consumer Products Division carried the company through difficult years when problems with the Dalkon Shield in-utero birth control device, for which A.H. Robins acquired the rights in 1970, drove the company into Chapter 11 proceedings in 1985. By the end of the decade, however, the conglomerate American Home Products stepped in to buy A.H. Robins for $3.2 billion and effectively resolved A.H. Robins's debt.

It was partly Chap Stick's profitability that made it worthwhile for American Home Products to pull A.H. Robins out of debt.

American Home Products, owners of Jiffy Pop, Black Flag, and Woolite, among other products, was ready to expand their consumer products business. A.H. Robins's Consumer Products Division, with Chap Stick as one of the best and most secure sellers, offered AHP some $300 million in annual revenues. Even during the bankruptcy proceedings, Chap Stick was breaking sales records with annual increases of more than ten percent in 1985 and 18 percent in 1986. By acquiring A.H. Robins, American Home Products enabled Chap Stick to retain its market share. In return, the company recognized the product in its 1989 *American Home Products Corporation Annual Report* as a "long standing leader in its category."

## Further Reading:

A.H. Robins Co., Inc. Annual Report, Richmond, VA: A.H. Robins, Co. Inc., 1964–1988.

American Home Products Corporation Annual Report, New York: American Home Products, 1989–1992.

Baldo, Anthony, "Syrupy Smooth: In Swallowing A.H. Robins, American Home Products Can Only Get Healthier," *Financial World,* January 23, 1990, p. 35.

"Chap Stick Bought for $5!" *Counterpoint,* January/February, 1991.

*Physician's Desk Reference for Nonprescription Drugs,* Montbale: Medical Economics Data Production Company, 1993.

Robinson, Richard, *United States Business History 1602-1988: A Chronology,* New York: Greenwood Press, 1990.

*—Robin Armstrong*

# CHARMIN®

Charmin, the nation's leading brand of bathroom tissue, is a premium brand valued for its softness, strength, and absorbency. In a highly competitive field, Charmin has maintained its leadership by focusing chiefly on these qualities. The development of a special technology enabled the Procter & Gamble Company to make a one-ply tissue that was comparable in strength and softness to brands using two sheets. In addition, for 21 years an advertising campaign featuring a fictional grocery clerk named Mr. Whipple reminded consumers about the product's qualities. Years after the campaign ended, consumers still remembered Mr. Whipple, associated the product with him, and even suggested that the company bring him back.

## Brand Origins

Charmin was originally manufactured by John Hoberg, a German immigrant who founded the Charmin Paper Company in 1892. The company name was changed to Charmin Paper Mills in 1953. Four years later Charmin Paper Mills was acquired by Procter & Gamble.

While most manufacturers of bathroom tissue used two plies of paper to make their brands soft and strong, this method was expensive. In the early 1960s, however, Procter & Gamble succeeded in developing a technique that would give Charmin such qualities with a single sheet of tissue. By air-drying the fibers in one-ply paper, the tissue was made softer, without lessening its strength.

## Product Changes

During the 1980s, the company introduced new variations of Charmin that provided consumers with several purchase options. Charmin Plus had a touch of lotion added to the tissue; Charmin Free did not contain inks, dyes, or perfumes; and Charmin Potpourri had potpourri scent on the core, not the paper. In addition, Charmin Big Squeeze containing 60 percent more sheets per roll was launched.

In 1993 Procter & Gamble began marketing Charmin Spacemaker. The new design allowed eight full-size rolls to be stored in the amount of space taken up by a regular four-roll pack. The aim was to bring greater convenience to consumers living with the "shrinking space syndrome," in households where space was at a

premium. Charmin Spacemaker also reduced package volume by 35 percent, making the product more environmentally friendly.

## Advertising Innovations

Advertising bathroom tissue was at times difficult because many manufacturers were reluctant to use the phrase "toilet paper" in TV commercials. Procter & Gamble, however, experienced great success in marketing Charmin. From 1964 to 1985 advertising for the brand revolved around Mr. Whipple, the worried grocery store clerk who admonished people about squeezing the tissue yet couldn't resist squeezing it himself. The tagline, "Please don't squeeze the Charmin" became part of advertising folklore. Years after the campaign ended, consumers still associated Charmin with Mr. Whipple.

Procter & Gamble tested a Charmin TV commercial in which a clown enters the men's room and closes the door of a stall. His head appears over the door, and his expression is one of obvious distress. His face is red and steam is pouring out of his ears, presumably because the toilet paper he used made him so uncomfortable. He remarks, "Life Without Charmin Can Really Be a Pain." While market research showed that people didn't find the commercial offensive, it did not always create brand identity because some people found it difficult to remember the name of

---

### AT A GLANCE

**C**harmin brand of bathroom tissue founded in 1892 by John Hoberg, owner of Charmin Paper Company; company name changed to Charmin Paper Mills, 1953; in 1957 Charmin Paper Mills was acquired by the Procter & Gamble Company.

**Performance:** *Market share*—31% (top share). *Sales*—$806 million (1991).

**Major competitor:** Scott Paper Co.

**Advertising:** *Agency*—D'Arcy Masius Benton & Bowles, New York, NY. *Major campaign*—"Please don't squeeze the Charmin"; also "CharminLand."

**Addresses:** *Parent company*—Procter & Gamble Company, One Procter & Gamble Plaza, Cincinnati, OH 45202-3315; phone: (513) 983-1100; fax: (513) 562-4500.

the product. In 1992 a new TV campaign using animation introduced viewers to CharminLand. This was the factory where cartoon babies made Charmin squeezably soft.

### Price-Cutting Strategy

In 1992 Procter & Gamble initiated an overall strategy of lowering list prices and reducing promotions to supermarkets for all its products. In the bathroom tissue market, a crowded field of lower priced brands tempts consumers to shop solely on the basis of cost, causing higher priced brands to lose market share. By making Charmin more price-competitive, the company hoped to retain consumer brand loyalty. The company's new system changed a pricing and promotional program that had been in place for 20 years.

In the early 1990s, estimates for total sales of bathroom tissue ranged from $2.2 to $2.9 billion. Charmin was estimated to have sales of $750 million in 1990 and $806 million the following year, representing the top share with 30-31 percent of the market. While the manufacture and marketing of bathroom tissue remains highly competitive—the field is crowded with major brands as well as private label and store brands—a company spokesman stated,

"We are very committed to this category as an important business for us, and P&G will continue to lead in the market and grow in the category."

### Further Reading:

"Bathroom Tissues," *Consumer Reports,* September 1991, pp. 606–09.

Charlier, Marj, "Kimberly-Clark Enlivens Market for Toilet Paper," *Wall Street Journal,* July 23, 1990, pp. B1, 6.

Klepacki, Laura, "Bathroom Tissue Battle Flushes Out Shoppers," *Supermarket News,* September 2, 1991, pp. 13, 15.

Lawrence, Jennifer, "Say Goodbye to Mr. Whipple: Say Hello to Charmin-Land," *Advertising Age,* August 10, 1992, p. 2.

Lipman, Joanne, "Bathroom Talk No Longer Taboo in Ads," *Wall Street Journal,* January 19, 1990, p. B4.

The Procter & Gamble Company Annual Report, Cincinnati, OH: The Procter & Gamble Company, 1992.

"Toilet Paper," *Consumer Reports,* August 1986, pp. 440–42.

"Spacemaker Charmin," Cincinnati, OH: The Procter & Gamble Company.

Warner, Fara, "Kleenex Goes National With High-Tech Bathroom Roll," *Adweek's Marketing Week,* November 25, 1991, p. 7.

*—Dorothy Kroll*

# CHEER®

# cheer

Cheer detergent, launched in 1950 by the Procter & Gamble Company, has been one of the most popular laundry products in the United States, second only to Tide among powdered detergents for most of four decades. Early advertising positioned "New Blue Cheer" as the detergent with built-in whiteners. Later, when consumers began washing clothes in cold water or warm water because of the energy crisis and the proliferation of new, colorful fabrics, Cheer became best known as an all-temperature laundry product.

## Brand Origins

In 1946, when Procter & Gamble introduced Tide, the first heavy-duty synthetic laundry detergent for household use, other soap companies were already developing formulas to compete with Tide in the marketplace. Procter & Gamble, meanwhile, adopted an unusual but calculated strategy: If someone was going to develop a detergent that would challenge Tide's supremacy, that someone would be Procter & Gamble itself. By 1950, Procter & Gamble had created a new formula—known during top-secret development as "Project J"—which it introduced to the market as Cheer.

The decision to introduce a second brand of detergent to compete directly with Tide reflected a system of brand management that had begun to develop at Procter & Gamble in the 1920s, when Neil McElroy, who would become president of Procter & Gamble in 1948, was responsible for promoting another new product, Camay soap. Initially, Camay did not do well, and Procter & Gamble decided that its advertising agency was putting too much emphasis on the company's flagship product, Ivory soap. The Camay account was turned over to a competing advertising agency, which could devote its full attention to Camay without worrying about the effect on Ivory. Freed of any possible conflict of interest, Camay became a very successful brand.

In 1931 the Harvard-educated McElroy drafted a three-page memo outlining a complete system of brand management that would, in effect, set up each Procter & Gamble brand as a separate business, with a brand manager responsible for each product's performance. *Time* magazine described the proposal as a "free-for-all among P&G brands, with no holds barred." The magazine also quoted McElroy, who admitted, "At first some of the more conservative members of the company cringed at the idea of having a punch taken at ourselves by ourselves." But the magazine concluded, "Eventually McElroy won his point. He persuaded his elders that the way to keep fast-growing Procter & Gamble (P&G) from becoming too clumsy was indeed to have it compete with itself." P&G became one of the first companies to operate on a brand-by-brand basis.

## New Blue Cheer

Despite Procter & Gamble's spectacular success with Tide, Cheer was initially a disappointment in the marketplace. For almost two years, the company struggled to establish an identity for Cheer, something that would set it apart from all the other detergents that were being introduced. Then, in 1952, Procter & Gamble decided to add a bluing compound to the Cheer formula. Bluing was a coloring agent that many homemakers added to their laundry to counteract the yellowing that occurred in white fabrics by giving them gave a slightly bluish tint. The product was renamed Blue Cheer, and commercials proclaimed, "It's new! It's blue."

With that simple change, Cheer became a success and a major brand of laundry detergent. As Oscar Schisgall wrote in *Eyes on Tomorrow: The Evolution of Procter & Gamble,* "Cheer's addition of blueing represented still another stride in the whiteness race." Procter & Gamble named its new ingredient "Blue*Magic Whitener," and Cheer was advertised as the "first and only washday detergent of its kind!" Despite the fact that bluing had been used for decades, the company claimed its Blue*Magic Whitener was a "scientific discovery that works in the newest, most modern way." In addition to laundry, Cheer was promoted for washing dishes.

As Procter & Gamble had intended when it created Cheer, the detergent soon became the No. 2 brand in the United States, behind Tide, a position it held until Procter & Gamble introduced Bold in 1965. Bold was a low-suds detergent that contained a high-level of fluorescents and a color-safe bleach in addition to bluing agents. Cheer would eventually reclaim second place in the 1970s and hold that spot until the mid-1980s, when the growing popularity of liquid detergents would vault Lever Brothers' Wisk into the No. 2 slot.

## All Temperature Cheer

In 1973 the Organization of Petroleum Exporting Countries (OPEC) imposed an oil embargo on the United States and other countries dependent on Mideast oil. It also raised the price of crude oil by as much as 130 percent. The result of the cartel's actions was an energy crisis throughout much of the industrialized world, symbolized by shortages and long lines at gasoline stations. The embargo also affected the way people washed their clothes because it affected the cost of heating water.

Procter & Gamble responded by changing the formula for Cheer to be more effective in cold water, and began advertising the reformulated detergent as All-Temperature Cheer. The strategy was especially effective in Japan, a country that must import all its oil and was hit especially hard by the oil embargo. Soon after being introduced in Japan in 1973, Cheer was the leading brand of detergent in the island nation with more than ten percent of the market. In the late 1970s Cheer lost market share because of worries about phosphates and, according to *Forbes* magazine, hard-sell commercials that offended Japanese sensibilities.

## Environmental Concerns

In the early 1960s, environmentalists began campaigning against laundry detergents, which were seeping into rivers and foaming up for all to see. After considerable public debate, manufacturers switched to surfactants that were biodegradable, which all but eliminated the sudsing problem in the nations waterways. However, environmental concerns about detergents and water pollution were far from over.

In 1967 Stewart L. Udall, then Secretary of the Interior, called upon U.S. detergent makers to eliminate the use of phosphates, which studies showed greatly accelerated eutrophication, the process in which freshwater lakes eventually become clogged with organic material, especially algae, causing fish and other marine life to die. Many companies complied and began selling phosphate-free or reduced-phosphate detergents. Procter & Gamble refused, saying that it would not market inferior or dangerous products. Phosphate-free detergents clearly were less effective than detergents with phosphates, and many of the phosphate replacements were caustic and considered potentially harmful. (Initially, Procter & Gamble did reduce the amount of phosphates in Cheer, replacing it with sodium nitrilotriacetate [NTA]. But when the government called for more testing of NTA, raising doubts about its safety, Procter & Gamble quit using NTA and went back to phosphates.)

When several communities and, eventually, entire states banned phosphates outright, Procter & Gamble pulled Cheer and its other detergents from supermarket shelves in a few areas. The outrage over Procter & Gamble's action was so great that the company was forced to address the issue in its annual report for 1971. Howard J. Morgens, then chairman of the company, wrote, "We did not introduce nonphosphate detergents because we felt strongly that it would be irresponsible for us to do so. The present nonphosphate detergents, as we view them, fall into two general classes. There are those that just won't get dirty clothes clean, and we feel housewives will quickly recognize their ineffectiveness. Then there are those that are dangerous to use in the home."

The uproar over phosphates eventually died down as the detergent industry developed safe and effective substitutes, and environmental scientists came to agree that sewage and other chemicals were probably more to blame for eutrophication than phosphates anyway. In 1993 about a third of the United States still banned phosphates, whereas other states set limits on the amount of phosphates they allowed in detergent formulas.

## Cheer with Advanced Color Guard

In January of 1993 *The Wall Street Journal* reported, "In the past two years, U.S. consumers have fundamentally changed the way they go about performing one of life's perpetual chores: washing their clothes. For four decades, people spilled powdery soap out of giant-sized boxes into their washing machines. In recent years, many consumers switched to liquid detergents. But now, most are flipping up the top of a small cardboard cube and measuring out a prudent dose of concentrated granules with a recyclable scoop." The superconcentrates, originally developed for the Japanese market, had arrived.

Colgate-Palmolive introduced the first concentrated powder, Fresh Start, in 1980, but it was never well received. However, by the 1990s, laundry habits were changing. Consumers were washing bigger loads and less often. In addition, environmental concerns had shifted from phosphates to wasted packaging. In 1990 Lever Brothers introduced a superconcentrated powdered detergent under the Wisk brand name, Wisk Power Scoop, in response to P&Gs launch of Ultra Tide the same year, which rapidly became the best-selling detergent in the country.

In 1992 Procter & Gamble also launched Cheer with Advanced Color Guard, a superconcentrated granular detergent that the company said was reformulated to prevent fading and extend the wearability of cotton clothes. Television and coupon advertising carried the theme, "Cheer helps keep clothes looking newer, longer." According to Information Resources, Inc., the new Cheer accounted for about 6.7 percent of detergent sales in the last quarter of 1993.

## Further Reading:

"Back to Enzymes," *Newsweek*, November 29, 1971, p. 62.

"Back to Phosphates," *Newsweek*, September 27, 1971, p. 123.

Bird, Laura, "Detergent Industry Spins into New Cycle," *Wall Street Journal*, January 5, 1993, p. B1.

Donohue, Janet, "Laundry Detergents Continue to Grab Industry and Consumer Attention with Strong New Product Activity and Heavy Marketing Support," *Soap/Cosmetics/Chemical Specialties*, January 1987, pp. 30–32.

Freeman, Laurie, "The House that Ivory Built," *Advertising Age*, August 20, 1987.

Rice, Faye, "The King of Suds Reigns Again," *Fortune,* August 4, 1986, pp. 130–34.

Rukeyser, William Simon, "Fact and Foam in the Row over Phosphates," *Fortune,* January 1972, pp. 71–75.

Schisgall, Oscar, *Eyes On Tomorrow: The Evolution of Procter & Gamble,* Chicago: J.G. Ferguson Publishing Co., 1981.

Shapiro, Bill, "Procter & Gamble's Comeback Plan," *Fortune,* February 4, 1985, pp. 30–34.

"Soap Opera," *Consumer Reports,* July 1987, pp. 413–14.

"Sudsy Dilemma," *Newsweek,* January 17, 1972, pp. 62–63.

Trachtenberg, Jeffrey, " 'They Didn't Listen to Anybody,' " *Forbes,* December 15, 1986, pp. 168–69.

Walley, Wayne, "Genesis of the 'Soaps'," *Advertising Age,* August 20, 1987.

"Why Detergent Makers Are Turning Gray," *Business Week,* February 20, 1971, pp. 64–65.

—*Dean Boyer*

# CHINET®

The Chinet brand of disposable dinnerware is one of more than 400 products produced by Keyes Fibre Company. The company's output is dominated by items that, like Chinet, are made from paper pulp. They include egg packaging, flourescent tube packs, cup carriers, berry baskets, and apple trays. The Chinet line consists of disposable plates of varying sizes and shapes made from paper pulp; paper napkins; dinner and luncheon size plastic flatware; and disposable dinnerware in various holiday themes.

## Product Origins

The molded pulp pie plates that predated Chinet by about two decades were invented by Martin Keyes (surname rhymes with "eyes"), a man whose lifelong experiences in the paper industry were combined with his innate creativity. Born in Lempster, New Hampshire, in 1850, Keyes started work at his father's saw and grist mill at a young age. His inventive capacity also became evident in his youth and impelled him to keep pencil and paper on hand in order to write or draw ideas at any time. Keyes's entire career would involve the paper business, especially *papier-mâché*.

There are two corporate fables regarding the origins of the sturdy, yet disposable, paper dishes that led to the development of Chinet. One story recounts that inventor Martin Keyes saw workers at a veneer plant in New York eating their lunches on pieces of maple veneer and that their impromptu plates got him thinking about disposables. The other tale states that Keyes's mother urged her enterprising son to improve upon the pressed wood pie plates that were available at the turn of the century. Before Keyes's invention, there were inexpensive plates stamped from a heavy paper stock, but these weak, absorbent disposables were unreliable.

At first, Keyes steamed veneer into plates, but he later arrived at a plan to form pulp with a mold. Carrying out that plan took at least two years: the inventor had to develop a machine that would mash the wood pulp and then mold, dry, and package the plates. Once he had done so, he ran into another problem.

When Keyes filed for a patent for his machine, he was notified that the process was already registered. Realizing that someone had stolen his idea, Keyes sued to prove that the paper plate machine originated with him. Although the original patent seemed inarguable at first, Keyes was able to produce a daily diary that unquestionably recounted the progression of the machine from concept to reality. Martin Keyes won the case on the strength of the diary and acquired the patent that provided the basis for the development of Chinet brand plates.

In 1903 Keyes, with the help of a business associate and two brothers-in-law, was able to incorporate the Keyes Fibre Company in Shawmut, Maine, to produce paper pie plates. The company's first shipment went out in the summer of 1904, but Keyes's mill was forced to close the following spring as a result of cost competition. The plates were indeed better, but they also cost twice as much as alternatives.

After cutting prices drastically and applying all his personal finances to the business, Keyes was able to resume production of his unique product in the fall of 1905. The product benefitted from a well-known tragedy, in which an entire shipment was sold in San Francisco after the earthquake and fire of 1906 had created high demand for disposable dishes.

## Refinement of Chinet

Keyes's first consumer product, a "picnic package" with different sized plates, was introduced shortly after the Keyes Fibre Company relocated to Waterville, Maine, in 1908. Another corporate shake-up precipitated the establishment of the Chinet brand. In 1926 a serious threat to the company's future brought a change in ownership. A former employee had come up with significant, patentable improvements on the original Keyes process. The competitive threat came at the same time Keyes's original patents were about to expire. Within a year, the company was sold for $4.5 million to the Rex Pulp Products Company, which maintained the valuable Keyes name with a slight change, to Keyes Fibre Company, Inc.

The new management pushed for a more diversified product line and by the end of the decade had added ice cream dishes, drinking cups, and the smooth-finished line of paper dinnerware called Chinet. The even, moisture-resistant finish of the new product was devised by Walter Randall, who developed a distinctive drying and sizing process for the molded plates. Keyes was also the first company to manufacture a popular molded sectional plate. The block-lettered Chinet trademark and product were registered in 1933.

## AT A GLANCE

**C**hinet brand of disposable dinnerware founded in 1903 by Martin Keyes, president of the Keyes Fibre Company; product refined in late 1920s by Walter Randall; brand trademarked in 1933 and used in food service industry; Chinet brand introduced to consumer market, 1965. Keyes Fibre Company incorporated in Shawmut, Maine, 1903; closed briefly, 1905; moved to Waterville, Maine, 1908; sold to Rex Pulp Products Company and name changed to Keyes Fibre Company, Incorporated, 1927; reorganized and name changed back to Keyes Fibre Company, 1935; Keyes purchased by Van Leer Holding Inc., 1982.

**Performance:** *Market share*—8% (total dollar volume) of disposable dinnerware. *Sales*—$75 million.

**Major competitor:** Hefty's line of plastic foam plates; also Dixie Livingware.

**Advertising:** *Agency*—Gregory & Clyburne, Stamford, CT, beginning in 1989. *Major campaign*—"Nothing stacks up to Chinet."

**Addresses:** *Parent company*—Keyes Fibre Company, 301 Merritt 7, P.O. Box 5317, Norwalk, CT 06856; phone: (203) 846-1499; fax: (203) 849-4157. *Ultimate parent company*—Van Leer Holding Inc., 301 Merritt 7, P.O. Box 5317, Norwalk, CT 06856.

Because it promoted labor and equipment cost savings and eliminated breakage and pilferage losses, Chinet grew very popular with such institutional food service markets as hospitals, colleges, and industrial cafeterias. Rising labor costs in the 1960s and 1970s made disposables even more attractive.

In 1965, when the product was moved into the consumer market, Keyes changed the Chinet trademark to script lettering. The company was able to claim that there was "virtually no comparable product on the market," even as late as 1968. Brand management reasoned that it had a ten-year lead on any competitor who might come up with a comparable product with as high a quality as Chinet. Sales of the branded plates outran production capacity in the late 1960s, yet management acknowledged that it had not fully exploited the home consumer market.

### International Market

Keyes Fibre Company first licensed Martin Keyes's patents for molded paper pulp items to companies in Canada, Norway, and Australia in the 1930s. But Chinet's parent company became more directly involved in the international promotion and distribution of its products in the 1960s, when it entered the Japanese and Mexican markets. By the 1990s, Chinet was Canada's top brand of disposable dinnerware, and Keyes management focused more intently on strengthening its position in the Australian, European, and Japanese regions.

### Further Reading:

"Keyes Fibre Company," *Wall Street Transcript,* September 23, 1968, p. 14432; February 21, 1977, p. 46275.

Marriner, Ernest C., "Dishes from Molded Pulp: a History of the Keyes Fibre Company," 1963; "Pulpwood to Pie Plates—The Keyes Fibre Story," *Down East: The Magazine of Maine,* March 1964, pp. 6–15.

Miller, Cyndee, "Chinet Maker Launches PR Drive to Promote Composting," *Marketing News,* July 5, 1993, pp. 14 and 18.

*—April S. Dougal*

# CITIZEN®

**⬤CITIZEN.**

Since their 1930 introduction in Japan, Citizen watches have ticked along with changing timepiece markets to attain the leading position in world watch production by 1986. After operations were firmly established in the United States in 1975, nearly a decade passed with little growth and weak brand recognition. Starting in the mid-1980s, however, Citizen experienced a veritable explosion in growth, sparked by an aggressive strategy of product development, marketing, and distribution. Under the guidance of executives Laurence Grunstein and Masao Itoh (followed by Katsuaki Noji in September of 1991), Citizen realized a U.S. market share increase of over 300 percent from 1986 to 1992, moving it to second place behind Seiko in the mid-price category. Innovative advertising campaigns helped distinguish the rising star. The Hannimals campaign, which introduced the new Noblia Timepiece line, featured watchbearing forearms made up to resemble exotic animals in various settings. In addition, the company capitalized on the high visibility of the America's Cup sailing regatta, as Citizen was named the Official Timer and the Official Watch of the event in 1992 and 1995. Sailing into the 1990s with these and other efforts, Citizen continued its push toward the number one position in mid-priced U.S. watches, despite the pressures of a weak global economy and an appreciating yen.

## Brand Origins

The roots of Citizen date back to 1918, when Shoki Watch Research Institute began marketing timepieces. Mr. Shinpei Gotoh, the mayor of Tokyo at that time (the Taisho Period), bestowed the name "Citizen" on the young company's products, connoting their "closeness to the hearts of people everywhere." When Citizen Watch Co., Ltd., came into being in 1930, the mayor's pet name for the watches became the official name of the company and the brand.

Although the brand entered the international market in 1936, exports were abruptly cut off by World War II and did not resume until the late 1950s—and then only in Europe and Southeast Asia. Business in the United States did not resume until the 1975 establishment of Citizen Watch Co. of America, Inc. Though the U.S. office was staffed with Japanese business people who were very well versed in the watch industry, their lack of familiarity with American retailing and marketing culture resulted in slow initial growth. During its first ten years in the United States,

Citizen managed to use the time as a learning period for its personnel and an adapting period for the company; it did not make great strides in selling its product line.

The brand's entry into the U.S. market coincided with advances in digital technology that changed both the face of watchmaking and Citizen's role in that industry. Conventional clock faces were increasingly replaced by numerical readouts that could be mass produced at extremely low costs. With the leading edge in new technology, U.S. electronics and semiconductor companies such as Texas Instruments Inc. and National Semiconductor Corp., saw the advent of digital watches as a perfect opportunity to carve out their own chunks of a new consumer market. Many large companies hired whole staffs of watch designers and watch marketing specialists and integrated their manufacturing to penetrate the mass market. Japanese watch leaders, such as the top-ranked Hattori & Co. and Citizen, watched the U.S. digital market closely. In an October 27, 1975, *Business Week* article, Yukio Asano, general manager of Hattori's merchandising department, described digital watches as a passing fad that "lacked reliability." Hattori, Citizen, and other key players were heavily committed, instead, to analog quartz watches, which combined an integrated circuit and quartz time base with a miniature motor and gears that drove conventional hands. Citizen Trading Co.'s Yasuo Okamoto, manager of overseas trade, recognized the potential of digitals, noting that U.S. companies commanded the technological lead in electronics and would assume the leading role in a potentially successful digital watch blitz. If the watches declined in price to between $25 and $30, "then the whole market in the developed world will change," he told *Business Week*.

Digital prices did drop, and the world watch market shifted dramatically, thought not in favor of U.S. producers. By the early 1980s, virtually all U.S. watchmaking had disappeared, Swiss leaders had been forced to consolidate, and the bulk of production had shifted to Hong Kong and Japan, where industry survivors became enmeshed in a vicious battle for market share. The preferred weapon became volume production, which oversupplied the market and triggered price cuts that slashed profits across the board. In 1983 alone, Hong Kong churned out 250 million watches, with 102 million coming from Japan and 47 million from Switzerland. That year, Hattori shipped 46 million watches, followed closely by Citizen, which shipped 45 million. But even though Citizen outsold its Japanese competitor in world sales,

## AT A GLANCE

**C**itizen brand name coined by Mr. Shinpei Gotoh, Mayor of Tokyo in the Taisho Period, with the establishment of Citizen Watch Co., Ltd., successor to the Shoko Watch Research Institute, in 1930; U.S. office, Citizen Watch Company of America, Inc., established in 1975; in 1985 two executives, Masao Itoh and Laurence Grunstein, launched sales, marketing, and distribution campaign that dramatically increased Citizen's market share by the early 1990s.

**Performance:** *Market share*—17% of U.S. midprice wristwatch category in 1990 (second to No. 1 Seiko); market leader in the $50 to $125 retail price range (1992). *Sales*—$1.204 billion (122,533 million yen) for wristwatches and parts by Citizen Watch Co., Ltd. in 1991.

**Major competitor:** Hattori Seiko Co.'s Seiko watches.

**Advertising:** *Agency*—D'Arcy Masius Benton & Bowles, New York, 1992—. *Major campaign*—Approximately $12 million to support general advertising and sports sponsorships (such as America's Cup '95 and U.S. Open Tennis Championship).

**Addresses:** *Parent company*—Citizen Watch Company of America, Inc., 1200 Wall Street West, Lyndhurst, New Jersey, 07071; phone: (201) 438-8150; fax: (201) 438-4161. *Ultimate parent company*—Citizen Watch Co., Ltd., P.O. Box 235, 20F, Shinjuku Mitsui Building, 1-1,2-Chome, Nishi-Shinjuku, Shinjuku-Ku, Tokyo 163-04, Japan; phone: (03) 3342-1231; fax: (03) 3342-1280.

Hattori still dominated the U.S. market by a wide margin. Nine years after entering the United States, Citizen ranked sixth in the mid-priced watch segment, with unit sales at a half-million pieces and a brand identity that had gained respect but relatively little popular recognition.

### Brand Development

From its 1956 entry into the international marketplace until its ascent as the world's largest watch producer in 1986, Citizen distinguished itself as a timepiece innovator. The brand laid claim to Japan's first shockproof watches, as well as the first waterproof and electronic models, and produced the first analog quartz watch accurate to within three seconds a year. Citizen also pioneered analog solar battery watches and introduced, in 1992, a multi-zone radio controlled watch that received VLF radio signals to automatically set itself.

Even with such a profile, Citizen moved into the competitive U.S. market of the mid-1980s with a far smaller share of the market than it aimed for. In 1985 it sold approximately a half million watches annually and held six percent of the mid-priced watch segment ($50 to $350). To tighten its hold on the American wrist and wallet, the company would have to expend tremendous efforts. That is precisely what it did.

In the mid-1980s, Masao Itoh became chairman of the board in the United States and launched an intensive campaign to increase market share and penetration. Itoh teamed up with another new executive, Laurence Grunstein, who had formerly served as chief operating officer of the North American Watch Co. Together, Itoh and Grunstein restructured Citizen's sales, marketing, and distribution systems, accelerated the introduction of new collections, and boosted ad spending to over $20 million annually. In an effort to "image up" the brand, the team of executives placed greater emphasis on higher-priced fashion and sports watches in the $125+ segment, expected to be the fastest growing area of the mid-price watch market through the 1990s. The ultimate goal of these initiatives was to replace longtime rival Seiko as No. 1 in the mid-price category.

Despite financially tight times, Citizen's efforts paid off with a burst of growth in the late 1980s. Between 1985 and 1988, the yen rose nearly 100 percent against the U.S. dollar, severely eroding its price advantage and prompting many watchmakers to curtail production and cut costs in anticipation of an onslaught by Hong Kong watchmakers. According to the *Japan Economic Journal* of September 1989, Citizen did exactly the opposite, using other manufacturer's cutbacks to its competitive advantage and upping capacity to out-produce Seiko by 17 million watches in 1988. The brand saw staggering success: by 1989 Citizen had reached its goal—one year ahead of schedule—of 2.5 million watches sold in the United States. From 1986 to 1992, Citizen's market share more than tripled, making it the leading brand in market share for watches priced between $50 and $125.

### Fashion Watches

Much of Citizen's growth stemmed from its attention in the early 1980s to the increasing popularity of so-called fashion watches—timepieces with a primary focus on design, even (sometimes) at the expense of durability and craftsmanship. The fashion watch craze was ushered in by the landslide success of Swatch watches, all battery-operated analog models that were introduced in 1983 at $19.95. Their low cost and availability in multiple colors (and 246 different styles by 1988) encouraged multi-ownership and even the wearing of several Swatches simultaneously. The design craze in watches also helped settle the ongoing battle between analog watches (with hands) and digitals (with displays) in favor of analogs. The dominance of digitals in the late 1970s and early 1980s made way for a resurgence in the popularity of more conventional watch faces by 1985, when 173 million analogs were sold versus 149 million digitals. By 1990 analogs had outpaced their display-faced brethren by 405 million to 242 million and were in the lead to stay, according to industry analysts. Citizen responded to these changes with strategic plans aimed at gaining mid-price market share.

Following the success of Swatch, other watch manufacturers, including Citizen, moved quickly to tap the new design-driven market, especially in low-end models. In 1985 Timex introduced Watercolors, colorful plastic watches targeted at teens, and later expanded to women's fashions with the Big Bold Beautiful line and the men's market with the Carriage Collection. Bulova Watch Co. introduced Benetton watch line, and other major players, including Casio and Seiko, joined the bandwagon. Looking back at the rise of the inexpensive fashion watches in *Crain's New York Business* issue of October 29, 1990, Citizen's Laurence Grunstein said, "I knew then design had to be central to our strategy. Watches aren't just timekeepers to most people, they're expressions of style. And to grow we need to be leaders in style."

### Upgraded Styling

Combining its drive to become a leader in style with strategic plans to corner the mid-price watch market, Citizen helped broaden the meaning of "fashion watch." Joe Thompson, editor-in-chief of *Modern Jeweler,* noted in a July 18, 1988, *Advertising Age* article that "Whereas once fashion watches referred to those that were colorful and plastic, now any watch whose emphasis is on design is a fashion watch.'' By the late 1980s, Citizen had developed three mid-priced product lines: The basic $59-to $195 Citizen targeted middle America; the $100-to-$195 Elegance line had the look and feel of luxury pieces; and the Noblia Timepieces line was designed for those Americans capable of handling luxury price tags.

These three fundamental lines continued to change into the 1990s. Conveying a ''watches and lifestyles'' message, the brand offered several new series: Citizen Pro Master for sports enthusiasts; Citizen of the World analog multihand watches for business executives; the Clariti series for women interested in high fashion; and the super-lightweight Titanium Collection. In December 1992 Citizen Trading Co., the watchmaker's export/import arm, began selling four varieties of watches, priced at $390, in the Japanese domestic market under the designer name Yves Saint Laurent.

## Advertising Innovation

Citizen's tremendous growth was spurred by aggressive advertising support that consistently drew on a $20 million-plus annual budget in print, radio, and television by the early 1990s. The brand made its network TV debut in a 1986 ad based on the Al Jolson hit, ''About a Quarter to Nine.'' Designed by Levine, Huntley, Schmidt & Beaver, a subsidiary of Grey Advertising, the ad featured roughly 25 quick cuts and five close-up shots of the products, projected to the accompanying music. Success of the Al Jolson spot led, two years later, to another TV ad for the brand's higher-priced Elegance line that was set to the 1940s Louis Armstrong hit, ''It Takes Time.'' Written by Arthur Korb in 1947, the song's lyrics helped to project a feeling of romance.

In 1988 the brand also introduced an innovative print campaign, run in high-fashion magazines, for its higher-priced Noblia line. The distinctive ''Hannimal'' ads featured the wristwatches as animal collars on hands and forearms painted to resemble alligators, race horses, and panthers. The campaign also included one giant billboard of an 80-foot zebra and a 30-second TV spot and print campaign for the related Noblia-Spirit line of watches. In December of 1992 Citizen shifted its $10 to $12 million account from Young & Rubicam to D'Arcy Masius Benton & Bowles.

## Model Citizen: Public Relations

In conjunction with advertising efforts, Citizen focused increasingly on public relations and high-visibility promotions to boost brand awareness and image. In 1991 the company established its ''Citizen of the Year'' award to honor remarkable contributions to society by ordinary people. A selection committee of ten employees combed through newspapers seeking finalists to be recognized for a wide variety of deeds: honorees included a bus driver who deviated from his route to take a fainted bystander to the hospital and a boy who distributed Braille calendars to the blind. Citizen also established a scholarship fund encouraging German high school students to study in Japan. Over the years, the brand installed various eye-stopping billboards and clocks to increase its visibility: in 1975 a Citizen neon sign was installed at Place de l'Opera in Paris, France; a precision sundial was built in Hamburg, Germany, in 1976; the Citizen Digital clock tower was installed at Shinjuku Prince Hotel in 1978; a clock tower was donated to Masan City, Korea, in 1979; and the world's largest neon sign was installed in the Wanchai district of Hong Kong in 1982. Other notable PR activities included the publication of

*Salesways,* a house magazine used by distributors and key dealers after 1981; and the 1986 ''Citizen study tours,'' designed for European journalists.

After the 1990 appointment of Katsuaki Noji as chairman of the board for U.S. operations, Citizen placed unprecedented emphasis on sports sponsorship. In 1991 the brand began implementing its sponsorship of the 1992 America's Cup, based on its appointment as the Official Timer and Official Watch of America's Cup '92, the Louis Vuitton Cup Challenger Races, and the Defender Selection Series of the regatta. Such an honor cost more than $7.5 million in marketing and promotional expenses. Citizen's president, Laurence R. Grunstein, participated directly in the Defender Trials of January 14, 1992, serving on board Stars & Stripes as the ''17th man'' of Team Dennis Conner. Citizen has sponsored the event for a second consecutive time and has been designated the first title sponsor of the Defender Race Series for the America's Cup, thereafter called the Citizen Cup. (The winner of the Citizen Cup meets the winner of the Louis Vuitton Challenger's Cup in the final series of races for the America's Cup.) Once again, Citizen is utilizing its specially designed cellular timing system throughout the races.

Other sporting events sponsored by Citizen include the Federation Cup tennis series, the World Figure Skating Championships, the Fukuoka International Marathon, the Paris-Cape Town Cross Country Marathon Raid, and car sponsorship for the Paris-Dakar Rally of 1985. In 1993 the brand was also selected as the official timer of the U.S. Open Tennis Championships.

## International Growth

After Citizen began to export watches in 1936, activity was temporarily suspended by World War II. Exports resumed in the late 1950s to Southeast Asia, the United States, and Europe, with the first overseas subsidiary, Citizen Watch Europe GmbH, established in 1969. Just as Citizen jump-started its U.S. watch business in the mid-1980s, its parent company expanded overall European operations in preparation for a single European market. In 1986 Citizen Machinery Europe GmbH was established to manufacture and market precision industrial machinery, a segment that was then expanded in 1992 by the acquisition of Boley GmbH, a German machine tool firm. Office Automation (OA) equipment manufacturing was also anchored in Europe by the establishment of Citizen Manufacturing (UK) Ltd. and a network of supporting sales subsidiaries set up in the United States, the United Kingdom, and Germany. Watch production also expanded in the same period: Citizen set up a factory in South Korea to start production in September 1988 because Citizen of Korea Co., an affiliate that produced watches and small printers, lacked space to increase its production capacity. In July 1988 Citizen announced that it would start assembling low-priced mechanical watches in Jiangmen, China; and in September 1993 Citizen worked with Asia Commercial Holding Co. Ltd., and Sun International Ltd., to set up a watch production and sales base in Dongguan, China, for an expanding Chinese market. By 1992 Citizen operated 23 production facilities in nine countries and 20 sales offices in 11 countries worldwide.

## Performance Appraisal

As Citizen continued its vigorous campaign to surpass Seiko in the mid-price watch segment of the 1990s, economic recession constrained the kind of business growth enjoyed in the 1980s. In 1993 financial malaise in Japan was compounded by the yen's appreciation in foreign currency trading, placing additional pressure on Citizen's earnings. To offset the pressure, Citizen announced several compensating measures, including discontinuation of programs and shifts to overseas production. Nevertheless, the growth momentum of the mid-1980s continued to carry along the elements of advertising innovation, product development, and strategic management necessary for continued growth. Whether the brand is able to match the 300 percent growth rate it achieved between 1986 and 1992, only time will tell.

## Further Reading:

Barmarsh, Isadore, "Watchmakers Stress Fashion, Sports Lines in Tight Market Race," *The Houston Chronicle,* November 17, 1991, p. 5.

"Citizen's Soar to Success," *Watch & Clock Review,* May, 1993, p. 26–9.

*Citizen Annual Report,* Lyndhurst, NJ: Citizen Watch Company of America, 1993.

"Citizen Watch Sees Earnings to 1994 Under Pressure From Tight Yen," *AFX News,* May 13, 1993.

"Digital Watches: Bringing Watchmaking Back To the U.S.," *Business Week,* October 27, 1975, p. 78.

Dougherty, Philip H., "Citizen Watch in U.S. Push," *The New York Times,* April 25, 1984, p. D19.

Edwards, Larry M., "America's Cup Organizer Gets First Corporate Sponsor for '95," *San Diego Business Journal,* June 14, 1993, Vol. 14, No. 24, Sec. 1, p. 4.

Fahey, Allison, "Timex, Swatch Push Fashion; New Fancy Watches Will Get Even Fancier," *Advertising Age,* July 18, 1988, p. 4.

Gault, Ylonda, "A Better-Designed Citizen Thinks its Time Has Come," *Crain's New York Business,* October 29, 1990, p. 43.

"Price Wars and a Glut Have the World's Watchmakers in Chaos," *Business Week,* February 20, 1984, p. 102D.

Schnorbus, Paula, "Tick Tock; Brand Report," *Marketing & Media Decisions,* 23, No. 10, October 1988, p. 117.

Shuster, William George, "Citizen Aims to be Top Midprice Brand," *Jewelers' Circular-Keystone,* March, 1991, p. 121.

Tanaka, Kirofumi, "The Battle for Market Share; Watches: Seiko Finds Itself Playing Catch-Up with Citizen," *Japan Economic Journal,* September 16, 1989, p. 4.

*—Kerstan Cohen*

# CLAIROL®

# C L A I R O L

Clairol is the United States' leading hair color brand, with a market share of more than 50 percent. Clairol markets several popular hair color lines, including Ultress, Nice 'n Easy, Miss Clairol, Loving Care, and Option for Men; lighteners and highlighters such as Summer Blonde and Frost & Tip; Final Net, a non-acrosol hair spray; and a variety of shampoos and conditioners. Clairol has also marketed cosmetics and hair setting appliances, but hair color has always been the core of the brand. Clairol's innovations both in the chemistry of hair dye and in its marketing led to explosive growth in the category, so that in the 1990s an estimated 40 million American women were coloring their hair.

Clairol, produced by Clairol Inc., was introduced in the 1930s at a time when hair coloring was an expensive, time-consuming process that could only be done in a salon. Moreover, hair coloring bore a social stigma, and only a small percentage of women tinted their hair. Clairol transformed the American perception of hair coloring, making it a socially acceptable and widely popular beauty treatment. But it took many years of marketing perseverance before this transformation came about.

## Brand Origins

Clairol was invented in Germany and used in France, but it took an enterprising American to make a true success of the formula. New Yorker Lawrence Gelb had worked in the chemistry field as both a manufacturer of specialty chemical products and as a chemical broker. In the midst of the Depression, he set sail for Europe with his wife, Joan, and two young sons in search of some new and exciting chemistry venture. He studied a variety of European cosmetics and perfumes, but it was a unique Parisian hair dye that caught his attention.

This product, already called Clairol and marketed by the French company Mury, had several major advantages over existing dyes. Instead of merely coating the hair, Clairol penetrated the hair shaft, leaving a much more natural-looking color than anything else then on the market. Clairol had a pleasant consistency as well, like a rich, foaming shampoo. Other colorants at the time tended to be thin and watery and would run down a person's face and neck during application. It was Joan Gelb who was truly entranced with Clairol. She was struck by the seemingly ageless beauty of Parisian women and wondered if Clairol might be part of their secret. She and her husband returned to America with U.S. marketing rights to Clairol and $200 worth of the formula.

## Early Marketing

Joan Gelb herself became president of the new Clairol Corporation, and she was instrumental in the early promotion of the product, which the Gelbs called Instant Clairol Oil Shampoo Tint. Using the name Joan Clair, she and Lawrence Gelb demonstrated their product at salons throughout the country. Newspaper photos from the 1930s depict Joan as a woman of great elegance and beauty with a serious air, which was just what Clairol needed to cut through the public's disdain for hair coloring. The Gelbs' biggest task was to overcome this social stigma. Earlier hair dyes did not give the natural colors of Clairol, and their use was considered rather vulgar. Actresses may have colored their hair, but not respectable housewives. The Gelbs wanted women to view Clairol as they would any other cosmetic, that is, as a beauty aid and not as something that was cause for scandal.

The husband and wife team lectured and demonstrated at beauty trade shows and at hair salons, teaching people how to use Clairol. They published and distributed free instruction materials to help hairdressers apply Clairol and, in order to develop and improve the product, began a research laboratory headed by an Austrian biochemist. Joan Gelb convinced hairdressers at the best salon chains, including Antoine's, Seligman & Latz, and Glemby, to use Clairol, and chemist Lawrence Gelb was hailed in advertisements as a "noted hair expert." Sales began to grow as more and more beauty salons learned the virtues of the new coloring agent. While old-style dyes had sometimes taken a hairdresser all day to apply, Clairol was comparatively quick and easy to use. Clairol was clearly a superior product, yet it took the Gelbs' intensive education program to begin to dispel the public's dim view of hair coloring.

In 1938 Lawrence Gelb secured the complete North, South, and Central American marketing rights to Clairol from Mury in France, and he paid the German inventor $25,000 for rights to the original Clairol formula. Sales had reached $900,000, and Clairol moved to larger production headquarters, then to an even larger factory. Nevertheless, banks still refused to finance Clairol, regarding hair tint as a "questionable" product.

## Bigger Success

The real breakthrough for Clairol did not come until the 1950s. Clairol's chemists had been working on improvements to the

## AT A GLANCE

**C**lairol brand of hair color originally marketed in France by the Mury company; introduced as Instant Clairol Oil Shampoo Tint in the United States in 1931 by Lawrence and Joan Gelb. Clairol Inc. acquired by Bristol-Myers Squibb Co., 1959.

**Performance:** *Market share*—More than 50% (top share) of retail hair color category. *Sales*—$350 million (estimated for all Clairol brands).

**Major competitor:** L'Oréal's line of hair color products.

**Addresses:** *Parent company*—Clairol Inc., 345 Park Ave., New York, NY 10154; phone: (212) 546-5000; fax: (212) 546-2993. *Ultimate parent company*—Bristol-Myers Squibb Co., 345 Park Ave., New York, NY 10154; phone: (212) 546-4000; fax: (212) 546-4020.

formula for more than ten years. One assignment took the lab from 1942 to 1950 to complete, but they came up with exactly what they were looking for—a one-step hair coloring product. Though Instant Clairol Oil Shampoo Tint had been a vast improvement over any other dye on the market, it still required a considerable amount of time and attention to apply. The hair had to be pre-lightened, shampooed, and dried before the color could be applied. The new product, called Miss Clairol Hair Color Bath, did away with the pre-lightening step. Using Miss Clairol was almost as easy as shampooing, and the color looked more natural than ever.

Miss Clairol was a huge success at trade shows. So amazing was the one-step process, Clairol demonstrators tinted models' hair on stage, using buckets to rinse, so the audience would believe there was no trickery involved. The Clairol sales team set off across the country to demonstrate the new product. Some of the hair salons located in fashionable department stores such as Saks and Bullocks agreed to run Clairol ads under their store banners, lending their prestige to Miss Clairol. As more hairdressers wanted to learn about the new one-step process, Clairol set up a teaching institute in 1952 and even published a textbook, *How to Do Better Haircoloring.*

Clairol grossed its first $1 million in 1950 and continued to grow, yet the company was aware that a large market was still untapped. The department store ads helped Clairol but running magazine ads proved difficult. The Hearst publications had a blanket order not to write about or advertise hair colorants, for example, and other publications were just as leery of this "racy" topic. And by 1955 only an estimated eight percent of American women tinted their hair. So Clairol hired the New York advertising firm of Foote, Cone & Belding to break through to a general audience and get "the girl next door" to try coloring.

Young copywriter Shirley Polykoff was the mastermind behind Clairol's successful campaign. Her theme was "Does she . . . or doesn't she? Hair color so natural only her hairdresser knows for sure!" When Polykoff gave the ad to *Life* magazine, then the leading general consumer magazine, the editors refused to run it, finding it too suggestive. Polykoff insisted that *Life* poll its female employees and see what they thought of the ad. Not one of these employees would admit finding sexual innuendo in the phrase "Does she . . . or doesn't she?" and the editors gave in. The ad then ran for 18 years in both print and broadcast, while sales of Clairol more than quadrupled. The percentage of women using hair color jumped from eight percent to almost 50 percent.

Shirley Polykoff's catchy slogan was not the only winning factor in Clairol advertising. To emphasize the naturalness of Clairol color, its advertising models were good-looking but not glamorous; models auditioned in their own clothes, without make-up, and ads showed such ordinary scenes as mothers with their children. The message was that Miss Clairol was a wholesome product for every woman.

### Brand Development

The hair color market took off in the 1950s, and Clairol soon found itself with a lot of competitors. Though Clairol held at least a 50 percent market share by 1960, the Gelbs did not sit still; instead, they investigated new products. Realizing that many women preferred their natural hair color and didn't want to go gray, Clairol introduced Loving Care in 1960. Loving Care, a mild dye that covered gray and washed out after several shampoos, did not change a woman's original color. The product was a big success, thanks in part to the advertising savvy of Shirley Polykoff, who invented the slogan, "Hate that gray? Wash it away."

For women who were a little bolder about coloring, Clairol introduced a series of lighteners that would bleach any color hair to blonde. Lady Clairol Whipped Creme Toner debuted in 1951 and reappeared in even lighter shades in 1962. Lady Clairol projected a more elegant, less down-home image than Miss Clairol. Copywriter Polykoff came up with an adventurous slogan for this new product, "If I've only one life . . . let me live it as a blonde!" Another slogan asked, "Is it true . . . blondes have more fun?"

Clairol's most successful new product was a shampoo-in colorant called Nice 'n Easy. Several other hair color manufacturers had put out quick, shampoo-in colors in the early 1960s, and when these proved successful, Clairol followed suit. Nice 'n Easy came out in 1965 and became the largest-selling hair coloring ever. By 1974 Nice 'n Easy had a 21 percent share of the retail hair color market, while Miss Clairol had 15 percent, and Loving Care followed with 9.9 percent. The total Clairol market share added up to more than 67 percent, with its closest competitor, L'Oréal, holding a little less than 10 percent.

Clairol also produced some new shampoos, including Herbal Essence, and such conditioners as Long & Silky and Kindness. New hair color products included Picture Perfect, a color rinse to tone down bright or brassy colors between dye jobs, and Frost & Tip, which added blonde highlights. Some of these products did better than others, but none reached the status of the "big three": Miss Clairol, Nice 'n Easy, and Loving Care. Sales for these products continued on an upward trend throughout the 1970s, until changing market conditions began to slow Clairol down some.

### Later Market Conditions

Clairol Inc. had practically invented the American hair color market with its breakthrough advertising in the 1950s, and the company ran away with a huge market share. But growth in the hair care market slowed by the mid-1970s, and Clairol sales began to level off. More women were opting to keep their natural color and thus visited salons less often. Most importantly, there were fewer women moving into the 30-and-over category, traditionally the largest segment of the hair color market. A cancer scare directed at one hair color ingredient sent a brief shock to the industry in 1978. Clairol came out with a new line, Clairesse, that was free of the offending chemical, then switched the formula for its entire line.

Another change came when Clairol began to market its products in supermarkets. With the introduction of the one-step coloring process, women had been able to color their hair at home, and they were used to buying their Clairol products at drugstores. Eventually, however, one-stop shopping became popular, and consumers liked the convenience of picking up their hair colorant with their groceries. By 1981 Clairol did more than a quarter of its volume in food stores.

Meanwhile, Clairol's longtime competitor, L'Oréal, began to grab a bigger share of the U.S. market, though it remained in a distant second place. Aggressive L'Oréal ads in the 1970s took on Clairol by offering a free box of L'Oréal's Preference brand hair color to consumers who sent in a box top of any other brand of color. L'Oréal's Preference cost more than Miss Clairol and had an image of better quality that seemed to be the basis of its success over other lesser known brands. Its advertising urged consumers to "Spend more for L'Oréal. You're worth it." By 1976 market share for Preference stood at 12 percent, with Miss Clairol at 15 percent. One Clairol response was to take out advertising for Miss Clairol that encouraged consumers to shun the idea of spending more, with ads that gave a well-known actress the line, "Some people have to pay more to feel secure. I don't." Nevertheless, Clairol brought out more glamorous, high-end products in the 1980s.

One of these was the Clairol Color Renewal System, which premiered in 1982. Color Renewal, a semi-permanent colorant, projected a more stylish image than Clairol's earlier products. It was aimed at women aged 15 to 34, an important market to capture, as these women could be induced to try more permanent colorants as they grew older. Ads for Color Renewal likened hair care to skin care, and emphasized that Color Renewal conditioned and moisturized hair, offering color and shine without a drastic change of shade.

Color Renewal System was not a huge success, and a few years later Clairol came out with another new product, called Ultress. Ultress was a permanent hair coloring like Miss Clairol, but it sold at a higher price. Its advertising spokesperson was actress Linda Evans, star of the popular television show *Dynasty*. She was a glamorous figure who told consumers, "Let's face it: 40 isn't fatal." Ultress came in a new gel form, but its main attraction seemed to be its pricier image, designed to match L'Oréal's brands.

Ultress came out in 1985, and its ads were handled by Grey Advertising. In 1986 Clairol moved the rest of its brands out of the Foote, Cone & Belding agency, whose Shirley Polykoff had written so many early successful campaigns. Clairol cited changing conditions as its reason for parting with the agency it had worked with for 30 years. Increased competition from L'Oréal, whose market share increased in the 1980s to almost 25 percent (Clairol's dropped to around 60 percent), had led Clairol to extend its advertising budget significantly. But increases in sales remained slight.

In the 1990s Clairol found itself defending its market share with yet more innovations. Clairol tried to reach out to a new, unexplored market category—men's hair coloring—in 1989. Option for Men, in both Instant and Gradual formulas, was an easy-to-use, one-step tint that covered gray hair. A 1989 survey found that only 8 percent of men colored their hair, so Clairol hoped there might be significant growth in this market niche. Clairol also spotted a salon trend in 1991: a 25 percent increase in the number of salon customers who had themselves made over as blondes. Noting that several dark-haired celebrity models and actresses had recently converted to blonde, Clairol promoted a one-step lightener called Ultimate Blonde. L'Oréal, too, promoted a special blonde line, Preference Les Blondissimes.

## Performance Appraisal

Clairol's huge successes in the 1950s, 1960s, and 1970s were behind it by the 1980s, and the hair color market as a whole was no longer rapidly expanding. The brand finally had to take its competition seriously as well, after many years of standing almost alone as the household name in hair coloring. By the early 1990s Clairol's market share was estimated by industry analysts to be between 50 and 60 percent, and L'Oréal had taken about 25 percent of the retail hair coloring market. But even though L'Oréal had managed to double its market share since the 1970s and Clairol's had fallen off, Clairol remained far ahead. In addition, because the hair coloring industry as a whole experienced a slowdown in growth in the 1980s and 1990s, no major shake-up appeared likely. In this less explosive market, brand innovations as well as careful monitoring of new trends seemed important to Clairol's continued viability. Though Clairol's sales growth in the early 1990s could not match the glory of earlier decades, the brand remained an impressive leader in market share—a position many companies would envy.

## Further Reading:

"A Bad Case of Jitters for Hair Dye Makers," *Business Week,* January 30, 1978, pp. 23–24.

Balter, Lorraine, "Spend More for L'Oréal ? Not Me, Says Clairol Girl," *Advertising Age,* November 8, 1976, p. 2.

"Clairol Ads Stress Results, Not Use, FC&B's Polykoff Tells AA Workshop," *Advertising Age,* July 25, 1966, p. 2.

"Clairol Launches Picture Perfect Color 'Refresher,' " *Advertising Age,* July 11, 1966, p. 1.

"Clairol's 'Does She' Theme is Fading," *Advertising Age,* March 13, 1972, p. 8.

"Clairol's Fast Formula Switch," *Business Week,* September 4, 1978, p. 29.

Jones, Abbott C., "Clairol: Quiet Revolution," *Advertising Age,* January 25, 1981, pp. 47–48.

"L'Oréal Aims at Clairol in $3,200,000 Print, TV Push," *Advertising Age,* April 16, 1973, p. 90.

Sloan, Pat, "Clairol's Color System Signals New Directions," *Advertising Age,* December 27, 1982, p. 3; "New Luster Seen for Hair Color Market," *Advertising Age,* May 2, 1983, p. 10; "Clairol Ultress Adds Color to Dull Market," *Advertising Age,* April 1, 1985, p. 66; "Clairol, Sassoon Add Hair Coloring," *Advertising Age,* September 16, 1985, p. 2; "Clairol Moves out of FCB," *Advertising Age,* February 17, 1986, p. 6; "Clairol Expanding Its Options," *Advertising Age,* May 1, 1989, p. 12; "Blond Faith in '90s," *Advertising Age,* January 6, 1992, p. 3.

Stein, Mimi, *Fifty Colorful Years: The Clairol Story,* Clairol, Inc., 1982.

"Top Shampoo Brands Weaker During First Half, Maxwell Says," *Advertising Age,* January 12, 1976, p. 34.

"What Clairol Learned While Developing 'Option' for Men," *Adweek's Marketing Week,* October 9, 1989, pp. 52–53.

*—Angela Woodward*

# CLOROX®

Clorox—manufactured by its namesake, The Clorox Company—is the leading American brand of household bleach. A staple of home cleaning, Clorox is used to disinfect kitchens, brighten or whiten laundry, and destroy bathroom mold and mildew. A simple but highly effective product, Clorox bleach is one of the nation's most widely used brands.

## Brand Origins

In 1913, five entrepreneurs in Oakland, California, contributed $100 each to set up a small factory to manufacture liquid chlorine bleach. Of the five principals, Edward Hughes, Charles Husband, Archibald Taft, Rufus Myers, and William Hussey, only Hussey had practical knowledge of chemistry. But the five knew that brine, a prime ingredient in chlorine bleach, was freely available in the salt ponds of San Francisco Bay. All they had to do was retrieve it. Using a complex electrolytic process, they converted brine into sodium hypochlorite bleach. The business was incorporated May 3, 1913 as The Electro-Alkaline Company, with headquarters at Oakland's Bacon Building. Three months later it purchased its first manufacturing facility, at 809 High Street, a property the company still owns.

## Early Marketing Strategy

The Electro-Alkaline Co. manufactured its chlorine bleach in a 21 percent industrial strength solution. At this degree of concentration, the partners hoped to win business from San Francisco's commercial laundries, walnut bleachers, municipal water companies and brewers, as well as janitors throughout the San Francisco Bay area. The company's bleach was shipped in jugs carried by horse-drawn wagons.

When the product hit the market, an engineer for one of the company's suppliers, Abel M. Hamblet, recommended that Electro-Alkaline give its bleach a catchier name. Hamblet offered his own suggestion, combining the words "chlorine" and "sodium hydroxide"—the two primary ingredients in sodium hypochlorite bleach—to produce "Clorox." Simple and distinctive, the Clorox name was considerably less industrial sounding than "Electro-Alkaline," which may have sounded harsh or dangerous.

Hamblet also suggested a simple logo for the product, an oblong diamond with "Clorox" written across the center axis. Outside of the diamond, along each line, he thought there should

be some appropriate wording to describe the product. The founders eventually settled on "Liquid Bleach Cleanser Germicide." The design was immediately registered as a company trademark. It is not known whether Hamblet was compensated for his good-spirited volunteerism; he did, after all, create one of the most widely recognized corporate emblems in America.

## Brand Development

As is common with new products, the founders of Electro-Alkaline misjudged their market. Sales of Clorox bleach were nowhere near their projections. By 1915, cash flow was so low that Electro-Alkaline was unable to make mortgage payments on the High Street plant. Foreclosure was imminent.

William C.R. Murray, an Oakland grocer and early investor in Electro-Alkaline, believed strongly in the superior qualities of Clorox bleach. He agreed to cover the company's obligations, and was named general manager of the operation. Murray suggested offering a diluted version of Clorox bleach for household use. He felt that housewives would welcome a safe bleach for laundry and cleaning, particularly with the number of wooden drains in use at the time. The sodium hypochlorite concentration was reduced to 5.25 percent, a quarter of the industrial product.

While running The Electro-Alkaline Company, Murray left the operation of his grocery store to his wife Annie. She liked the idea of household bleach and arranged to give away free samples of the product in 15-ounce amber "pint" bottles. Unknown to her, word began to spread among her customers. Before long she was receiving inquiries about Clorox bleach from across the United States and Canada. Meanwhile, William Murray appointed Kelley-Clarke, a food broker, to manage wider distribution of Clorox bleach. Sales slowly picked up, and company profitability was restored.

With its growth in popularity, Clorox inspired a number of imitators, many of whom unabashedly attempted to win customers through a campaign of confusion. A product called "Cloro" was reportedly on the market in Los Angeles. Another company introduced a brand of toothpaste called "Chlorox." Electro-Alkaline was unable to register the Clorox name in Canada because someone had already claimed it for a toothpaste with the Canadian Patent Office. Eventually, these and many other cases were settled.

## AT A GLANCE

**C**lorox brand bleach introduced as an industrial product in 1913 by The Electro-Alkaline Company; named Clorox Bleach, 1914; diluted for household use, 1915; production maintained during World War II for possible application of neutralizing poison gas; Clorox 2 perborate enzyme bleach introduced, 1969; Clorox Detergent introduced, 1986, phased out, 1991.

**Performance:** *Market share*—50% plus of bleach category.

**Major competitor:** Purex; Bo-Peep; various store brands.

**Advertising:** *Agency*—Foote, Cone & Belding, 1925—(at first under the name Erwin Wasey Company). *Major campaign*—"Germicide, Disinfectant"; also, "The White Line is the Clorox Line."

**Addresses:** *Parent company*—The Clorox Company, 1221 Broadway, Oakland, CA 94612.

Electro-Alkaline soon lost its identity in Clorox, which by 1922 had become a household name. The company was reorganized that year as the Clorox Chemical Corporation. In 1928 the partnership gave way to public incorporation and the corporation was reorganized as the Clorox Chemical Company. As demand for Clorox bleach grew across the nation, the company established additional plants. The first of these was established in Jersey City, New Jersey in 1938. Others were added in Chicago in 1939, Cleveland in 1948, Los Angeles in 1949, Tampa in 1950, Camden (New Jersey) and Kansas City in 1951, Charlotte in 1952, and Seattle in 1954.

The success of Clorox in the United States translated well to foreign countries, where postwar concerns with sanitation mirrored those in America two decades earlier. This concern created a demand for chlorine bleach products and provided the Clorox Company with an easy opening into many foreign markets.

Clorox bleach and other products were manufactured at 35 plants in the United States, Puerto Rico, Argentina, Barbados, Canada, Colombia, Egypt, Mexico, Panama, the Republic of Korea, Saudi Arabia, and Yemen in the 1990s.

## Health Claims

Bleach possesses well-known germicidal qualities. As the first major household brand, Clorox had little difficulty gaining a reputation as an effective cleanser, stain remover, deodorant, and disinfectant. Clorox was so effective in killing germs and preserving the public health that, when war broke out in Europe in 1940, the Surgeon General insisted that bleach production not be curtailed. The government had authorized reduction of the sodium hypochlorite level in household bleach by as much as 40 percent. The Surgeon General, however, was outspoken in his insistance that manufacturers be allotted at least minimal production materials as a public health measure. In addition to fighting germs, chlorine bleach was an effective decontaminant to poison gas. The company even ran ads with detailed instructions on how to use Clorox bleach in the unlikely event of a poison gas attack. In fact, when the United States became involved in the war a year later, chlorine supplies were put under government control, and a small amount was set aside for chemical manufacturers.

Clorox had long term supply contracts with numerous suppliers that locked in low prices for chlorine. But during the war, with

the price of chlorine so high, Clorox released its suppliers from these contracts and negotiated new ones at market prices. "If the shoe were on the other foot," said company president William J. Roth, "I'd resent being held to a contract under those circumstances." As it was, Clorox was limited in the amount of bleach it could produce during the war. But production was sufficient enough that, with careful use, there was enough Clorox available for basic germicidal uses.

During the war, a competitor cut the strength of its bleach to meet demand. Clorox, however, had an electrolytic process for producing chlorine. Combined with the limited amount of chlorine available on the market, this enabled Clorox to maintain the strength of its bleach while meeting consumer demand. By the end of the war, the competing brand had gained a reputation for being a weak bleach and lost its lead in the market to Clorox.

## Advertising

When it was first introduced, Clorox bleach carried a strong reference to the difficult electrical process used to manufacture the product. As if the name "Electro-Alkaline" were not enough, labels of the company's bleach carried the high-tech boast, "Made with Electricity." At first, this was a highly unusual and distinctive claim. Later, as the use of electricity became more common, the reference was dropped.

The first print ads for Clorox appeared in 1925. These were placed by the Erwin Wasey Company, a West Coast agency that later became part of Foote, Cone & Belding. One of the first printed ads for Clorox proclaimed, "Women who know use Clorox for washing and cleansing." A common Clorox tagline around 1920 was, "The white line is the Clorox line," referring to laundry clotheslines. The company also constructed a 100-foot by 20-foot billboard on a ferry approach in San Francisco Bay.

To reach more consumers in more places, the company paid men to drive cars emblazoned with promotional slogans through numerous cities. These promotion men also laid portable signs along roadways and sold Clorox to motorists out of their trunks. Clorox was advertised on radio during the 1930s and throughout the war. By 1950, however, a new, potentially more powerful advertising medium emerged: television. Clorox made its first television ads in 1953, sticking to the same themes it carried in radio and print.

Wartime applications of bleach for public health purposes prodded the company into changing the wording of its diamond logo. The words "disinfectant" and "deodorant" were added to the emblem. In 1947, all wording was removed from the perimeter of the logo, and a mascot character was introduced. Because the personification of packages was in vogue, Clorox introduced a representation of its bottle with an animated face. The character, called "Butch," was featured in advertising—speaking the brand's claims directly to the reader—and along both sides of the diamond logo. The complex logo was simplified in 1957 when Procter & Gamble, which briefly acquired Clorox, requested a simpler design for stationery and other purposes. Accordingly, Butch was phased out in favor of a more conservative approach to advertising.

The logo was simplified further in 1972. The diamond shape was streamlined slightly and white lines were added at each corner. In 1987 the Clorox name took bolder type, and the open corners at the top and bottom of the diamond were closed. Previously, the diamond looked like a stencil, suggesting an industrial identity.

## Packaging

The first supplies of industrial strength Clorox bleach were shipped in returnable five-gallon crockery jugs. With the introduction of a household concentration, the company began using 15-ounce bottles. Hand-filled on a production line with overhead hoses, the bottles were sealed with a simple rubber stopper. Huge freight trains were assembled, using as many as 66 boxcars to transport Clorox bleach to the East Coast in a single shipment.

The 15-ounce amber bottle was common stock, used by several manufacturers for a variety of products. If the glued-on Clorox label came off, it was impossible to distinguish a bottle of Clorox bleach from any other product. This remained a problem until 1929, when the company introduced a more unique full quart-size

*Clorox Company retiree Virginia McElligott poses with bleach containers as they have appeared through the years.*

bottle with the diamond trademark on the bottom. The quart-size bottle was followed in 1938 by a half-gallon bottle with a finger ring that was developed specifically to reduce shipping weight and packaging and warehousing costs. A metal screw cap replaced the rubber stopper in 1940.

The amber glass bottle was retired in 1960. In its place, Clorox used a lightweight white polyethylene bottle with a plastic screw cap and four-finger carrying ring. This further reduced shipping costs and enabled Clorox to offer its bleach in even larger bottles. In 1964, this king-size bottle was replaced by a one-and-a-half gallon plastic jug. More recent designs used the channel of the finger ring to pass air into the bottle as it was being emptied. This

enabled consumers to pour Clorox bleach without troublesome gurgling and splashing.

## Market Relationships

Clorox emerged from the war as a major brand and an essential ingredient in household cleaning. Detergent was no longer enough; a thorough job needed bleach. Procter & Gamble saw a natural fit between Clorox and its own lines of detergents and cleansers, and in 1957 it acquired the Clorox Chemical Company. Within three months of the deal, however, the Federal Trade Commission intervened, charging that Procter & Gamble's acquisition of Clorox could cause it to exercise a degree of monopoly power in the bleach industry. Purex, in particular, charged that Procter & Gamble wielded enough promotional muscle to drive other bleach manufacturers out of business.

The Clorox Company (the word ''Chemical'' was dropped from the name) continued to operate as a virtually autonomous division of Procter & Gamble, receiving no promotional subsidies from its parent company. Finally, in 1963, the Federal Trade Commission ruled that Procter & Gamble must divest itself of Clorox. The company became fully independent of Procter & Gamble on January 2, 1969. As a result of its experience as a division of Procter & Gamble, Clorox's directors realized they could not maintain growth as a one-product company. The first move came with the acquisition of Liquid-Plumr later in 1969.

## Extensions

In September of 1969, shortly after acquiring Liquid-Plumr, the Clorox Company introduced a dry non-chlorine bleach called Clorox 2. This perborate enzyme brand was developed specifically in response to the rise of competing enzyme laundry detergents, which boasted colorfast cleaning. But these brands soon lost their novelty when it was discovered that enzymes alone could not whiten clothes as well as Clorox, or brighten colors as well as Clorox 2.

The Clorox Company continued to diversify its product line through the 1970s, adding such products as Formula 409, Tilex, Soft Scrub, Fresh Step cat litter, Hidden Valley Ranch salad dressing, and Kingsford charcoal briquets. The Clorox name, however, was not extended to another brand until 1986, when the company went head-to-head with its former parent Procter & Gamble. The company introduced Wave, later called Clorox Detergent, as part of an effort to further reduce its dependence on profits from bleach. The effort was a none-too-subtle attack on Procter & Gamble's Tide.

Clorox test marketed Wave for years, allowing Procter & Gamble to speed up development of Tide with Bleach. The Clorox detergent never went national and was never afforded the tremendous promotion that is common with Procter & Gamble products. In response, Procter & Gamble rolled out its own extension, Tide with Bleach, and test marketed a liquid chlorine bleach under its Comet brand.

To complicate matters, several detergent manufacturers had developed concentrated washing powders. Clorox, playing catch-up, rushed into that market with Ultra Clorox detergent. The company was ill-prepared for challenges outside of its flagship bleach product, however. As a result, Clorox was plunged into an identity crisis: was Clorox a bleach, a detergent or both? In the end, Tide and Tide with Bleach succeeded in stopping the sale of

Clorox detergent and did significant damage to Clorox 2 sales. In fact, many consumers wondered, if Tide already has bleach, why add Clorox bleach at all?

As a result of its costly and disastrous battle with Procter & Gamble, Clorox struggled to regain its balance. Clorox returned to being promoted only as a bleach. Despite its ill-conceived invasion of the detergent market, Clorox emerged with its most important possession intact: Clorox remained the most respected name in bleach. This has allowed the company to sustain challenges to its market and retain its leading market share. It is unlikely that the Clorox name will be freely extended to any other product in the future. As Clorox detergent demonstrated, brand extension can help launch a new product, but it also can dilute the good name of the original product.

## Further Reading:

"A Bright Idea Clorox Wishes It Never Had," *Business Week,* June 24, 1991, p. 118.

"Clorox Dumps Its Detergents and Sticks to Its Core Brands," *Adweek's Marketing Week,* May 27, 1991, p. 6.

"Clorox Ups Ante in War with P&G," *Advertising Age,* August 1, 1988, p. 1.

"Clorox's Identity Crisis," *Advertising Age,* May 6, 1981, p. 1.

"Collectors Guide to Clorox Bottles," The Clorox Company.

"Evolution of a Corporate Symbol," *Company Backgrounder,* April 1988.

"History of the Clorox Company," *The Diamond* (The Clorox Company Magazine), Spring 1988.

"Oakland's Clorox Company Celebrates 75 Years," The Clorox Company News Release, April 15, 1988.

"Still Number One," *Barron's,* August 2, 1982, p. 38.

"Still the Leader," *Barron's,* March 25, 1985, p. 57.

"Wash-day Washout," *Advertising Age,* June 3, 1991, p. 54.

*—John Simley*

# CLOSE-UP®

Close-Up, marketed by Chesebrough-Pond's USA Company, was in the early 1990s the best-selling "cosmetic" toothpaste in the United States. Among all toothpaste brands it ranked fourth. Unlike the white pastes of many of its competitors, Close-Up was a translucent red gel flavored with mouthwash.

The brand was introduced in 1967 by Lever Brothers, the U.S. subsidiary of Unilever N.V., a giant holding company based in Rotterdam and London. Marketing and distribution of Close-Up was switched to Chesebrough-Pond's shortly after Unilever acquired that company in 1986. Despite the entry of a dozen or so imitators, Close-Up, the leading toothpaste brand of Chesebrough-Pond's, has been able to maintain its leading market position through a combination of product promotion and advertising based on the brand's established, traditional equities.

## Brand Origins

In December of 1967, when the brand was first introduced in Denver, Close-Up represented something of a revolution in the traditionally staid dentifrice market. Until that time virtually all toothpastes were opaque, foaming abrasives made palatable only by the inclusion of minty extracts. In addition to covering up the chalky detergents in toothpaste, the flavorings afforded various brands a degree of taste differentiation and left the consumer with a mouth that felt fresh and cool.

During the late 1950s the Procter & Gamble Company bounded into the mouthwash market with a new brand called Scope. This minty, clear-green liquid stole away much of the market from the best-selling brand, Listerine. Procter & Gamble also battled Colgate-Palmolive Company for supremacy in the toothpaste market, hoping to piggyback sales of cosmetic applications, such as mouthwash, which were marketed to "vain" or "self-conscious" consumers. The advertising war that ensued raised the public consciousness for mouthwashes, which perfumed the mouth with a flavored detergent and temporarily retarded the growth of germs with a heavy shot of alcohol.

Lever Brothers—after properly identifying this preoccupation with mouthwash as an important new equity with great sales potential—designed a new toothpaste radically different from the leading brands (Crest, Colgate, and Pepsodent). The new toothpaste incorporated the characteristics of mouthwash, and as such it was seen as two products in one. Rather than mint, the flavor of every leading brand, Lever Brothers used flavorings similar to those in a mouthwash. The result was a mild spicy cinnamon taste similar to Lavoris.

To provide greater visual differentiation and cement the brand's association with mouthwash, the company made the toothpaste a clear red. This was a novel characteristic for a toothpaste, but it necessitated the use of less opaque abrasives in the formula. The resulting brand was a detergent- and flavor-intensive dentifrice.

Concerned that such a radical departure from conventional toothpastes (which were now loaded with fluoride compounds) might not be taken seriously, Lever Brothers mapped out an equally radical identity for the new brand. Because the brand was aimed at a self-conscious consumer who was likely to use mouthwash, breath sprays, and mints, Lever Brothers decided that its new brand should be positioned as *the* toothpaste for modern, attractive people who exuded independence and sex appeal. The target market was liberated young people who were socially active, paid close attention to their appearance, and were taken to public displays of affection.

## Early Marketing Strategy

Lever Brothers' new brand required a name that supported this identity. Rather than featuring average consumers or dentists making testimonials to the effectiveness of the brand, the company decided to depict youthful adults having fun by blowing innocent kisses at each other. This was art, not science, and because the product was, after all, a toothpaste, it required a name that supported its subtle social nature. "Close-Up" communicated intimacy and self-assurance without hopelessly overselling the brand. Several other products capitalized on this approach but were so unabashed in their claims that they became self-parodies. In a fine example of overselling, Hai Karate after-shave depicted men who had to fight off women with karate—an idea whose novelty was quickly exhausted, particularly among women.

Close-Up would be introduced in the same familiar collapsible tube that was common among all leading brands. The Close-Up tube featured a red and white color scheme, similar to Colgate, and was packaged in a red cardboard box. Its white lettering, bold and modern-looking, was printed in sans serif italic. In fact, the brand looked just like any other until the dramatic moment when

## AT A GLANCE

Close-Up brand of toothpaste introduced by Lever Brothers in 1967; marketing and distribution switched to Chesebrough-Pond's USA Company in 1986; high-fluoride extension introduced in 1987; Crystal Close-Up introduced in 1993.

**Performance:** *Market share*—5% (fourth-largest share) of toothpaste category.

**Major competitor:** Colgate-Palmolive Company's Colgate; also Procter & Gamble Company's Crest and Ultra-Brite and SmithKline Beecham's Aquafresh.

**Advertising:** *Agency*—J. Walter Thompson, New York, NY. *Major campaign*—"Brushes Out Bad Breath"; "Put Your Money Where Your Mouth Is."

**Addresses:** *Parent company*—Chesebrough-Pond's USA Company, 33 Benedict Place, Greenwich, CT 06836-6000; phone: (203) 661-2000; fax: (203) 625-1602. *Ultimate parent company*—Unilever N.V., P.O. Box 760, 3000 DK, Rotterdam, Netherlands; phone: 011-31-10-46-45-911.

the clear red gel emerged onto the consumer's toothbrush. Pictures of models would frequently accompany the package in display ads, providing a visual association between the brand and the typical user.

## Advertising

After being test-marketed in 1968 with the slogan "Brushes out bad breath," Close-Up went into national distribution. The brand hit the market shortly after the introduction of Ultra-Brite, another cosmetic toothpaste from Colgate-Palmolive. Ultra-Brite contained highly abrasive cleaning agents, and advertisements boasted that using the brand would result in whiter, brighter teeth—although possibly at the expense of damaging tooth enamel.

Ultra-Brite targeted the same market as Close-Up, but its advertising bordered on the ridiculous. After brushing with the brand, models produced smiles with bright pinpoint reflections that made a "ting" sound. To top it off, Ultra-Brite claimed to give its users sex appeal, probably the first reference to sex in public commercials.

Given the competition, Lever Brothers' ads for Close-Up were only slightly less outrageous. Female models in Close-Up ads literally blew kisses at unsuspecting male models. As if gently slapped in the face, the surprised men looked over their shoulders to reveal perfectly drawn pairs of lips on their cheeks. Later ads portrayed the playful moments before a first kiss. These subtle sexual references appealed strongly to a broad range of consumers, almost all of whom could identify personally with the exciting moment of discovery and intimacy associated with a first kiss.

## Brand Development

While only a small threat to the commanding market share of Crest and Colgate, cosmetic brands had clearly found a place in the market. On the strength of its cute, kitschy advertising, Close-Up bolted past Ultra-Brite to garner 15 percent of the toothpaste market and to become the third-best-selling dentifrice behind Crest and Colgate. As a host of imitators crowded into the market,

Colgate-Palmolive struck back quickly against Close-Up. The company began a heavy promotion for an Ultra-Bright cool-mint extension, which by 1973 had caused Close-Up's market share to fall to just 10 percent.

That year Lever Brothers switched its Close-Up advertising account to J. Walter Thompson, which developed for the red gel a bold new campaign containing an interesting double entendre. The brand's new tag line, "Put your money where your mouth is," implored consumers who really cared about their appearance to invest in a tube of Close-Up. Meanwhile, in a roundabout way it dared Colgate-Palmolive to substantiate its tongue-in-cheek claims for Ultra-Brite. Few outside the industry caught on to the latter meaning, but, as with kiss-blowing, it was an immediate hit with the public. Simply by relentless repetition, the old expression once again came into popular use, and the barrage of advertisements established an enduring association between the expression and the brand. Even 20 years after the campaign ceased, many people continued to think of Close-Up (or at least toothpaste) when they heard it.

Close-Up was relaunched in 1979 in a new campaign intended to avoid market losses to SmithKline Beecham's red-, white-, and green-striped fluoride brand called Aquafresh. Lever Brothers promoted Close-Up in a new formulation that had "an even fresher-tasting mouthwash for irresistibly fresh breath, and it still keeps your teeth their whitest." In 1980, however, sales of Close-Up were hurt badly by the introduction of numerous line extensions, including gel toothpastes, from Colgate-Palmolive and Procter & Gamble.

## Brand Extensions

As early as 1971, when Colgate-Palmolive rolled out its cool-mint Ultra-Brite and a green gel called Appeal, Lever Brothers briefly test-marketed a green mint-flavored version of Close-Up. Lever Brothers' brand extension later evolved into a second brand, Aim, a blue fluoride-containing gel. This new brand was created specifically to raid market share from Colgate and Crest and defend against competitors in the cosmetic category. But initially Aim merely cannibalized market share and advertising dollars from Close-Up, further weakening the red brand's position in the market. By 1975, however, both brands had stabilized, with Close-Up holding some 10 percent of the market and Aim about 15 percent. A second, more serious threat to Close-Up came from Aquafresh. While the colorful new brand grew mostly at the expense of Colgate and Crest, it dropped Close-Up's share by yet another point.

A new version of Close-Up, an opaque white brand like traditional toothpastes, was introduced in 1987. Containing twice the fluoride as its red counterpart, the new Close-Up hit the market just as Colgate-Palmolive and Procter & Gamble began battling over the new tartar-control toothpaste segment. Neither Colgate nor Procter & Gamble, however, left a large enough opening in the fluoride toothpaste market to accommodate the new Close-Up, which was subsequently phased out.

Chesebrough-Pond's, purchased by Unilever in 1986, assumed control over Close-Up the following year, and in 1990 it brought the flagging brand back to its roots with a new campaign. The company also introduced a revised formulation of Close-Up, which had more whitening agents and mouthwash and was available in a variety of extensions, including regular fluoride, mint fluoride, tartar control, and pink-colored gel.

The new brand extensions were promoted with some familiar-sounding copy: "Close-Up is as good as other toothpastes, plus it has something extra, the added benefit of mouthwash protection." The tag lines emphasized Close-Up's established cosmetic qualities and distinguished it from the therapeutic messages to which Colgate and Crest had returned. In 1993 Chesebrough-Pond's introduced another extension of Close-Up, a trendy clear gel called Crystal Close-Up. Taking its lead from Crystal Pepsi and a plethora of clear dishwashing liquids and shampoos, Crystal Close-Up represented a bold attempt to win back that fluid segment of customers who were attracted by such novelties.

## Health Claims

The strongest health equity among toothpaste brands has been the claim of fighting cavities. The American Dental Association (ADA) has maintained that the best protection against tooth decay is regular, thorough brushing, but this advice has left no room for product differentiation.

In 1955, in an effort to win a leading place among toothpastes, Procter & Gamble developed Crest, a brand that contained tooth-hardening fluoride. The formula won Crest a valuable seal of acceptance from the ADA. While fluoride was later added to Colgate, Cue, Fact, and Lever Brothers' own Super Stripe, cosmetic brands including Close-Up ignored the fluoride issue for some years. From a scientific standpoint the proliferation of fluoridated water—and the fact that too much fluoride can turn teeth brown—rendered the fluoride issue virtually moot. But from a marketing standpoint fluoride and the coveted seal of acceptance from the ADA became powerful selling devices. Close-Up contained only a small amount of fluoride until 1987, when its high-fluoride brand was introduced.

## Brand Outlook

For all the efforts made to repair the Close-Up franchise, the brand has continued to operate with only a fraction of the market enjoyed by Crest, Colgate, and Aquafresh. Even so, it has been able to occupy a valuable niche, one defined by a customer segment given to cosmetic applications. It has defended this position against a flurry of competing gels from Colgate and Crest, others in the form of Aquafresh and Check-Up, and enduring cosmetic brands like Ultra-Brite, Pearl Drops, and Gleem.

Despite the worldwide presence of Unilever, Close-Up seemed likely to remain a major brand only within the United States. Its strong cosmetic appeal, designed specifically for the unique mores of American society, did not translate well in countries outside North America, where different marketing approaches would be more effective. In the United States, where it was an established, well-recognized brand, Close-Up was seen as having a promising sales potential.

## Further Reading:

"Aqua-fresh Test Shakes Market," *Advertising Age,* July 30, 1979, p. 3.

"Close-Up Goes Back to Its Roots," *Advertising Age,* January 22, 1990, p. 40.

"Close-Up in New Premium Drive to Spur Share Growth," *Advertising Age,* September 24, 1973, p. 10.

"Close-Up Sales Big Factor in Lever '70 Profit Hike," *Advertising Age,* March 15, 1971, p. 3.

"Crest, Aim Jump on Pump Segment," *Advertising Age,* September 24, 1984, p. 1.

"Lever's Battle to Rise Again," *New York Times,* March 12, 1983, p. 21.

"Lever Brothers Tests Close-Up," *Sales Management,* December 1, 1967, p. 51.

"Lever Moving Out Aim at Risk of Close-Up Loss as Share Fight Heightens," *Advertising Age,* March 25, 1974, p. 1.

"New Items Greet '87; Lever to Take Fluoride Route for Aim, Close-Up Additions," *Advertising Age,* December 1, 1986, p. 3.

"P&G's Crest Efforts Taking Aim Against Growing Lever Share," *Advertising Age,* January 26, 1976, p. 2.

"Put Your Money Where Your Mouth Is," *Consumer Reports,* March 1984, p. 129.

*—John Simley*

# COACH®

The distinctive Coach leather tag attached to handbags and brief-cases is more than just a status symbol. For more than 50 years, the tag and the name Coach have been synonymous with quality leatherware and have been thought to identify those who appreciate understated quality and elegance. Today, in addition to the original handbags and briefcases, the Coach line includes leather accessories, outerwear, scarves, ties, and socks. Since 1985 the company has been part of Sara Lee Corporation's Sara Lee Direct division, which also owns such well-known brands as Hanes hosiery, Aris Isotoner, and L'eggs pantyhose, and directly markets these products through company-owned stores and catalogues. From its humble beginnings with a handful of employees to its current world-wide presence, Coach has maintained its reputation for remaining on the forefront of fashion.

## Brand Origins

Coach was founded in 1942 in what was then the bustling garment district of New York City. A handful of highly-skilled leather crafters, mostly recent immigrants from eastern Europe, worked in a small factory making wallets. Coach's founder wanted to bring the softness and comfort of a well-worn leather baseball glove to small personal leather goods. In order to achieve a high level of quality, the finest in leather was essential, but the structure and craftsmanship of the products were also important.

In 1946 shortly after the company's founding, a young man named Miles Cahn came to work for Coach. In 1961 Cahn and his wife Lillian bought the company and decided that the profits to be made from billfold production would not carry the company into the future. The Cahns designed their own simple handbags but maintained the same high quality standards established by the brand's founder. Miles and Lillian Cahn's simple but elegant bag designs proved timeless and rarely changed in the 25 years the couple ran Coach. The bags were stylish, but they were also roomy, practical, and extremely durable. Their excellence was reliable due to the "quality control" the Cahns practiced long before it became a corporate buzzword.

Although demand rose sharply over the years, the Cahns were determined to remain headquartered in the heart of New York, partly out of allegiance to the city and partly because of the large pool of skilled workers available there. They paid their workers a substantially higher hourly wage than the rest of the industry, provided excellent retirement benefits, awarded $2,000 Christmas bonuses, and made a habit of consulting the union before enacting changes that affected the workers. It was perhaps because they treated their workers better than most in the garment district that they produced such high quality merchandise and won a fiercely loyal and fast-growing customer base. Demand for their products became so high in the early 1980s that the Cahns were forced to ration bags to department stores.

## Changes in Ownership

By 1986 the Cahns were becoming increasingly more interested in their farm in the Hudson River Valley and feeling more alienated from the "hands-on" aspects of their business. None of their three children were interested in taking over Coach, so Miles and Lillian Cahn went shopping for a buyer. Sara Lee Corporation soon approached them and a deal was completed, leaving the Cahns with an estimated $30 million, $1 million of which they divided between company employees. The Cahns took up full-time residence at their aptly named Coach Farms and began producing goat cheese.

Sara Lee appointed Lew Frankfort as Coach's president, and he remained in that post through the early 1990s. When Coach's new corporate parent began to apply its marketing savvy, the brand grew from a small, highly-respected company with impressive brand loyalty to a $200 million per year brand with a significant international presence.

## Product Line Expansion

Although the classic designs of the Cahns' handbags and billfolds had proven tremendously successful for Coach, new owner Sara Lee felt that the brand could be expanded without compromising its quality or mystique. Shortly after the acquisition, Coach developed a new line called "Lightweights," made from a lighter weight of leather and featuring softer silhouettes. The "Lightweights" line, manufactured at the company's Miami, Florida, plant and intended to appeal to customers in warmer climates, helped Coach broaden its customer base. During this same period, Coach expanded its line of business accessories, adding briefcases, wallets, and business diaries to the line. In October of 1988 Coach announced the introduction of a line of scarves, the company's first nonleather product. Four styles were featured, retailing for approximately $60, and were intended to compliment Coach leather handbags.

## AT A GLANCE

**C**oach brand of leatherware founded in 1941; brand sold to Sara Lee Corporation, 1985.

**Performance:** *Sales*—$200 million.

**Major competitor:** Hermès; also Dunhill.

**Advertising:** *Agency*—Kirshenbaum & Bond, 1991—. *Major campaign*—descendants of famous Americans pictured with Coach products.

**Addresses:** *Parent company*—Coach Leatherware Company, Inc., 516 W. 34th St., New York, NY 10001; phone: (212) 594-1850; fax: (212) 594-1682. *Ultimate parent company*—Sara Lee Corporation, Chicago, IL.

---

A July, 1991 article in the *New York Times* reported that "Coach is moving to conquer the market for expensive accessories and extend the Coach appeal to younger customers," and aggressive line expansions were a means to that end. In addition to appealing to a broader, younger audience, brand expansion served other purposes. According to Jon Bernstein, vice president of marketing, "To extend a proven brand name into other categories is cost-efficient versus starting a new brand from scratch." At the end of 1992 Coach announced its intention to introduce a line of small fabric luggage and offer new styles and colors of handbags. The "Manhattan Collection" would feature the brand's first line of brightly colored bags. A new line of leather outerwear initially included five unisex items using textured lamb, burnished lamb napa, lightweight cow napa, and nubuc in black, dark brown, and olive. Coat styles included a car coat, bomber jacket, parka, and anorak and were all water-resistant.

For fall of 1992 Coach brought out "Sheridan," a group of textured, treated leather bags designed to be more scratch-resistant than traditional Coach styles. The company also offered "Camden," a line with distinctive brass hardware. In 1992 the company saw potential for new line expansion in gift items, such as frames, and an updated, expanded belt line. According to Sara Lee's 1992 annual report, new categories for Coach included an all-leather travel collection and a casual dress sock line.

### Domestic Retail Outlets and Catalogues

During the stewardship of Miles and Lillian Cahn, Coach opened six free-standing stores in addition to the original on Madison Avenue in New York. Within the first two years that Sara Lee owned the company, the number of stores jumped to 40 and store expansion grew steadily during the early years of their ownership. The total number of stores rose to 69 by 1992.

In 1987 Coach opened a new 2,050 square foot flagship store, and New York Mayor Ed Koch presided at the ribbon-cutting. In 1991 the flagship Coach for Business store opened, also on Madison Avenue, intended to appeal primarily to men. A west coast flagship store was opened in San Francisco in May of 1992 and with 18,000 square-feet of space, was one of the company's largest. The company felt that demand necessitated a large San Francisco store—the previous, much smaller San Francisco outlet had generated excellent sales. The large volume of sales in San Francisco was attributed to the influx of Japanese customers in certain seasons, sometimes accounting for 40 percent of the store's sales.

The company began producing catalogues in 1985, and by 1992 the mail order division had become its most profitable segment. In light of that success, Coach began mailing 10 million catalogues annually to store customers and prospective customers. In addition to providing a cost-effective revenue stream, the direct mail segment provided a list of names that was valuable to other divisions of Coach and Sara Lee. A large percentage of those receiving catalogues actually purchased items at Coach stores. In addition to annual mailings of the catalogue, the company also used the list to send announcements of store openings and new product introductions, and to remind customers of gift-giving holidays, such as Mother's Day.

In late 1992 Coach participated in "High Street," a catalogue offered by five major U.S. domestic airline carriers and featuring the merchandise of major retailers. The service allowed customers to select items from the catalogue while in flight, order with a 24-hour toll-free phone call, and either pick their orders up at one of five major airports or have them delivered within one of the airport's metropolitan areas. Other retailers included in the program were Bloomingdale's, Hammacher Schlemmer, and Chef's Catalog. Prices of items in the High Street catalogue were the same as those offered in other direct mail catalogues.

### International Growth

In 1988 Coach hired a new vice president of international sales, Peter Emmerson, specifically to launch the brand in key foreign markets. Encouraged by heavy traffic from foreign tourists in U.S. stores, Coach announced the opening of the first in-store shops in 1988. Boutiques in Harrod's in London and in four Mitsukoshi department stores in Japan featured the full Coach line. The decor imitated the free-standing stores in the United States with natural wood fixtures and marble, and Coach staffed the store with company-trained employees. The location of the boutiques within popular upscale foreign department stores provided immediate credibility and prestige and allowed Coach to gain a foothold in these countries without paying the high rents of free-standing stores.

Quickly following the opening of the first in-store boutiques, Coach opened its first free-standing overseas store on London's chic Sloane Street and added 3 in-store shops in Mitsukoshi stores in 1989. By 1990 the international expansion was well underway with 17 in-store Mitsukoshi shops, and the company was projecting between six and seven percent of total volume to come from overseas sales. In 1990 in-store shops opened in Singapore and in the Regent Hotel in Taiwan, and a free-standing store opened in Stuttgart, West Germany. Also in 1990, Coach announced that it would award sole Japanese distributorship of its products to Mitsukoshi. By 1991 Coach boasted 21 shops in Mitsukoshi stores and was receiving ten percent of its revenues from overseas sales.

### Advertising

Advertising had never been a concern for Coach Leatherware prior to its acquisition by Sara Lee. In fact, under the Cahn's ownership, difficulties in keeping up with demand overshadowed any need or desire to advertise. Coach enjoyed an almost unprecedented word-of-mouth publicity. Nevertheless, under the Sara Lee Corporation, advertising was an integral part of the brand's expansion in foreign and domestic markets.

Initial advertising under the Sara Lee Corporation was created by Lord Einstein O'Neill and Partners and played on the company's strong point—its products. Print ads featured large color photographs of bags, briefcases, and accessories, accompanied by the style numbers. Lord Einstein handled the campaign until they were dismissed in December 1990. Advertising was handled in-house for several months before the final choice of a new agency was made.

In 1991 Coach hired Kirshenbaum & Bond, an aggressive, cutting-edge advertising agency. Although the pairing seemed unorthodox to industry observers, it produced a campaign in keeping with the company's reputation of timeless quality. The print ads featured descendants of famous Americans and their favorite Coach products, with the tag line "An American Legacy." The offspring of Mark Twain, Davy Crockett, J.P. Morgan, Paul Revere, Sitting Bull, and George Washington were photographed in sepia tones, the Coach products in color. The campaign effectively communicated both the brand's timeless quality and its awareness of current fashions. In addition, by featuring famous Americans, Coach was able to capitalize on the fact that it was a quality American product.

In 1990 Coach filed suit against several retailers and manufacturers, including Ann Taylor and Laura Leather Goods, for too closely copying their distinctive style. Laura Leather Goods had imitated the Coach leather tag and used identical dimensions and designs for its bags. In November of that year, a New York federal court ruled in favor of Coach, finding the defendant companies liable for trade dress infringement and common law unfair competition. The suit demonstrated the Sara Lee Corp.'s aggressive protection of its Coach brand, and was intended to send a message to any other would-be copycats.

## Performance Appraisal

Coach Leatherware has enjoyed steady growth since its founding. Unlike most businesses, its problems have always been those of keeping up with demand and limiting distribution of their products. The "Coach mystique" has depended on a certain amount of short supply, and Coach has always been very particular about which retailers could sell its products. There is no indication that at any point in the company's history it has experienced declines in sales, cut its staff, or reduced production. In fact, Coach is one of the few consumer products that is virtually never on sale. According to the company, "Coach never needs to go on sale because demand is always greater than supply."

The brand's history can really be divided into two eras: the Miles and Lillian Cahn ownership years and the Sara Lee Corporation ownership years, beginning in 1986. During the first era, Coach was a highly-successful company with enviable customer loyalty. It was a small, family-like company and intended to remain so even to the point of resisting growth. Under the ownership of corporate giant Sara Lee, Coach had the support, the expertise, and the mission to gain worldwide recognition for its brand.

During one of the first years of Sara Lee's ownership of the company (1987), sales increased by 94 percent. Impressive growth continued, and, within the first four years of owning the brand, sales quintupled to $100 million in 1989. By 1991 sales had increased again by 50 percent to $150 million and in 1993 were $200 million.

The rapid expansion of the Coach line into accessories, outerwear, and international markets has apparently made the brand stronger than ever. The Coach brand name has been well-protected and used only in ways that enhance the brand's image. Other competitors have not been as prudent. According to marketing consultant Stewart Owen: "When YSL [Yves Saint Laurent] was on $2,000 and $3,000 dresses at the same time it was on a $19.95 men's polyester dress shirt, it destroyed the exclusivity of the brand." The fact that Coach has no easily discernable direct competitor also helps maintain the brand's position. Although companies like Hermès and Dunhill are closest to being considered competition, they do not enjoy the same immediate name recognition as Coach, nor are they as directly related to leather goods.

In many ways, Coach provides a textbook example of how to build a successful company: produce a superior product; build consumer loyalty from a solid reputation for quality, style, and durability; increase sales while carefully controlling supply; and, finally, leverage the brand into foreign markets, additional product lines, and new domestic markets.

According to the company, "Coach remains steadfastly committed to creating the highest quality products made of the finest materials, sold at a fair price." The *New York Times* indicated in 1991 that the "parent company is grooming Coach's name in much the same way it cultivated Hanes, once a small hosiery company that analysts say is now probably Sara Lee's single biggest source of income." With the support of such a large, successful corporate parent, the Coach brand should continue to be equated with practical elegance well into the future.

## Further Reading:

Berman, Phyllis, "Goat Cheese, Anyone?," *Forbes,* September 18, 1989, p. 220.

Gault, Yolanda, "Buyers Riding Coach; Leather Maker Growing," *Crain's New York Business,* May 6, 1991, p. 3.

Newman, Jill, "Getting Serious About Sell-Through; Accessories Industry 2nd-Half Forecast," *WWD,* July 17, 1992, p. 11; "Plotting New Horizons; Accessories Manufacturers Prepare for 1993," *WWD,* December 4, 1992, p. 15.

Sara Lee Corporation Annual Reports, Chicago: Sara Lee Corporation, 1986–1992.

Serrin, William, "Skilled Workers Help Some Plants Buck a Trend and Stay in Northeast," *New York Times,* June 2, 1985, p. 51.

Strom, Stephanie, "A Women's Chain Beckons to Men," *New York Times,* July 24, 1991, p. D1.

Wilson, Melinda, "Some Merchants Still Say 'No Sale!'" *Detroit News,* November 28, 1999, p. 9.

*—Kate Sheehan*

# COLGATE®

Contrary to what advertisements for toothpaste may lead consumers to believe, the most important factor in brushing teeth is the physical action of brushing. Plaque, the material that builds up on teeth, produces acids that cause tooth decay and can be removed only by brushing. Colgate, produced by the Colgate-Palmolive Company, is a leading presence in the competitive market to provide consumers with the means to sweep that plaque away. Colgate has been developed over the years to make teeth more resistant to decay, provide fresher breath, and even combat gum disease.

## Brand Origins

The origin of toothpaste dates back several hundred years, when early scientists noted the formation of white substances on their teeth hours after eating. Anton van Leeuwenhoek, inventor of the microscope, analyzed this matter under a microscope and was amazed to find it populated with millions of living organisms. But even less learned people knew that the substance caused bad breath and dental problems, and that these could be controlled by brushing the teeth.

The first dentifrices were introduced in Europe during the eighteenth century. These were mostly salty powders not terribly far removed from common baking soda. By the middle 1800s, several brands of dentifrice were available in liquid, powder, and paste form. Until the Civil War, most brands had to be imported from Europe and all were expensive.

Colgate, primarily a manufacturer of soaps at the time, introduced its own brand of aromatic toothpaste in 1873. Formulated with a mild abrasive (slightly heavier than chalk), a detergent, and mint extracts, Colgate entered the market as an entirely new concept in dental care: a palatable dentifrice.

## Early Marketing Strategy

From its earliest concept stages, Colgate toothpaste was intended for parallel distribution with the company's soap products. As the company had a well-established reputation with grocers and other retailers, Colgate toothpaste could easily be shipped and displayed with Colgate soap. In addition, retailers had grown to trust Colgate, which by 1873 had already been in business for 67 years.

A better tasting alternative to chalky, soapy-tasting competitors, Colgate was introduced as a major brand. During the late 1800s, however, dental care was extremely primitive. Few people used toothpaste, which at the time was a costly luxury.

The promotional men at Colgate knew that the toothpaste's pleasant minty flavor made it a favorite of children who, considering the alternative, would sooner not brush. But understanding that habits, once formed, are difficult to break, Colgate launched a campaign aimed directly at children. In 1911 and 1912, when toothbrushing was still sporadically practiced, Colgate distributed two million free tubes of toothpaste—and several thousand toothbrushes—to schools. The schools, eager to instill good grooming habits in students, happily passed out the free samples to children. Colgate also included literature aimed at parents, stressing that the toothpaste was so appreciated that "children use it without urging."

This single effort did more to instill habitual brushing in American society than perhaps any other marketing stunt, and while all brands of toothpaste benefitted from the campaign, none came out further ahead than Colgate, whose name and reputation had become firmly established. The school care program is still practiced by Colgate-Palmolive.

## Health Claims

As was common with most products in the late 1800s, toothpaste brands made wild claims about the medicinal qualities of their products. Some claimed to cure pyorrhea, a chronic inflammation of the gums that often led to abscesses and tooth loss. Others purported to correct "acid mouth," firm the gums, and even fill cavities.

Colgate, however, never made such ridiculous claims. In fact, the company went to great lengths in its advertising to say that no brand of toothpaste could perform such fantastic feats. By being honest with the public, Colgate built a strong trust equity with consumers. The greatest health claim made by Colgate in the early days was that its toothpaste was merely a safe cleansing agent that was refreshing, pleasant tasting, and economical.

By the 1950s, the formulation in Colgate toothpaste had been given a special proprietary name: Gardol. Packages of the product carried "with Gardol" on the label. In 1955, after the introduction of Procter & Gamble's Crest, which contained decay-fighting stannous fluoride, Colgate's leading market share began to fall. In 1960 Crest won recognition from the American Dental Association for its ability to help reduce the incidence of tooth decay. Colgate's response was to introduce its own fluoride toothpaste, Cue. In 1968, after Colgate had lost its lead to Crest, the company introduced a reformulated toothpaste, Colgate with monofluorophosphate (MFP). More stable than stannous fluoride, Colgate's fluoride compound helped the brand to gain ADA recognition in 1969 that was identical to that enjoyed by Crest.

### Packaging

The first toothpastes were packaged in porcelain jars, which obliged people to dip their toothbrushes into the paste. In households where the jar was shared, this was highly unsanitary. In the late 1800s, Dr. Tracy L. Sheffield, son of a Connecticut dentist and toothpaste manufacturer, returned from Europe with samples of food packed in collapsible tin tubes. This inspired the elder Washington Wentworth Sheffield to package his toothpaste in tubes imported from Europe. Later he purchased his own tube making machine. The tube business later became so popular that Sheffield quit making toothpaste to concentrate on tubes.

In 1896, four years after Sheffield began packing toothpaste in tubes, Colgate introduced its own toothpaste in tubes. It was labelled as an "aromatic tooth paste (for cleaning and preserving the teeth and refreshing the breath)." The all-tin tubes were pasted with a pinkish-tan paper label and maroon lettering. The base of the nozzle was clipped to the head of the tube and molded with the words "Colgate & Co., New York." The tube was packaged in a bronze-colored cardboard box that featured a signed guarantee from Samuel Colgate and a testimonial from Professor Henry Leffman of the Pennsylvania College of Dental Surgery. One of the first "scientific" endorsements, Professor Leffman's claim read, "I have analyzed the tooth paste and recommend it as a pleasant and agreeable stimulation to the teeth and gums, imparting an agreeable fragrance to the breath."

Colgate's color scheme was changed radically in 1933. At the time, S. Bayard Colgate, a fourth generation descendant of the company's founder, William Colgate, had just become president of the newly formed Colgate-Palmolive-Peet Company. Bayard Colgate oversaw the creation of an all white tube with a thick scarlet band printed across it. The carton was changed over to this new design in stages. Within that band, the name Colgate was printed in streamlined white letters. This enduring modern design has remained basically unchanged ever since.

### Metamorphosis of the Tube

Many toothpastes in existence at the turn of the century were hard pastes, with roughly the same consistency as spackle. As a growing number of these dentifrices were packaged in tubes, an interesting dilemma developed.

The circular nozzle of toothpaste tubes produced a perfectly round section of toothpaste. Because the paste was hard, it did not attach firmly to toothbrushes. As a result, the slightest lateral movement of the toothbrush caused the toothpaste to roll off the brush and into the sink (or onto the floor).

Rather than develop softer toothpaste (a solution that was not utilized by toothpaste manufacturers until decades later) Colgate altered the shape of the opening on its nozzle. Rather than a simple round hole, Colgate developed a flat rectangular opening. When extruded from the tube, Colgate toothpaste came out in a flat bar. Impervious to all but the most severe angles, Colgate toothpaste thus remained on the toothbrush. Colgate marketed the novel shape of its toothpaste, and Colgate Dental Cream, as it was then called, became Colgate Ribbon Dental Cream.

The first Colgate tubes were imported from G. Richter Metallindustrie in Germany and an associate firm located in France. Shortly before World War I, Richter's firms moved to the United States, where they continued to supply Colgate. Richter introduced a printing mechanism in 1900 that eliminated the need for paper labels and allowed Colgate tubes to be directly decorated.

In 1910 Colgate purchased a chocolate drop candy machine, adjusted the calibration, and used it to squirt toothpaste into a line of several tubes all at once, speeding up production. Sealing the tube, however, still had to be done by hand. The following year Colgate installed a machine from the Arthur Colton Company that folded the end of the tube. Two Colgate engineers, C.C. Schwarz and K.T. Katz, then added an automatic clipping device to fasten the fold. In 1912 the company purchased a carton-making machine and later devised a method to insert the tube into the box. Caps to the nozzles, which had been screwed on by hand for years, were attached automatically after 1928. Two years later, Colgate eliminated tube clips in favor of a method in which the tube was folded three times and crimped into place.

Engineering the rectangular opening proved a substantial feat. The distinctive rectangular opening was possible only with tin tubes. During World War II, when supplies of tin were diverted to military use, Colgate was forced to switch to the only available metal, aluminum. Colgate, however, found it impossible to fashion a reliable rectangular opening using aluminum. Instead, the company reverted to a circular opening and, like competing brands, softened its toothpaste. The new formulation caused Colgate toothpaste to stick vigorously to toothbrush bristles. Even when completely inverted, the toothpaste would remain on the brush.

### Advertising

Colgate was one of the first companies to make use of transit advertising, purchasing space for printed cards on urban streetcars and other rail systems. Beginning in 1910, the company distributed tens of thousands of cards with the slogan "Take home a tube."

The introduction of the rectangular nozzle opening in 1908 led to an entire advertising campaign based on the shape of Colgate toothpaste. For years, Colgate ads carried the slogan, "Comes out a ribbon; lies flat on the brush." In order to dispel fears that the ribbon was just a cute gimmick, ads included the claim, "We couldn't improve the product, so we improved the tube."

Ted Bates, the advertising firm that conducted advertising for Colgate, continued to emphasize Colgate's qualities until the late 1950s, when Crest hit the market. But it wasn't until the mid-1960s that competition from this new brand became serious. A reformulation of Colgate in 1968 enabled several new angles to be introduced, including the claim that Colgate was "unsurpassed" in cavity protection. This carefully stated proclamation did not say that Colgate was superior to Crest, merely that it was at least equal. The distinction was necessary, as the American Dental Association had endorsed both brands as effective dentifrices and refused to be misrepresented as favoring one over another.

The Colgate advertising account was later switched to Young & Rubicam Inc., which continued many of the traditional themes. The arrival of extensions, however, allowed many more angles to be used. Each was like an entirely new brand with another opportunity to pry market share from Crest. But, like Crest's advertising, spots for Colgate during that period are not particularly memorable. The prevailing focus has been on conservative, fairly understated explanations of the brand's superior qualities and ADA approval.

## Extensions

The emergence of Crest in 1955 so threatened Colgate Palmolive's leading toothpaste that it was forced to rush out an extension called Cue. Like Crest, Cue contained cavity-fighting stannous fluoride. The brand faltered in the market and after several years was withdrawn.

Colgate began the revolution in so-called cosmetic toothpastes in 1968. That year the company introduced a brand with a strong abrasive called Ultra Brite. While this toothpaste did whiten teeth, it also caused serious abrasion of dental enamel. But with clever advertising (promoting "sex appeal"), Ultra Brite became a major brand.

The first extension to use the Colgate name came in the early 1960s, when the company introduced a mouthwash called Colgate 100. A second extension of the name came in 1981 when Colgate became available in a blue gel. The extension was created to stem losses in market share to other gel toothpastes, such as Aim, Close-Up, and striped Aquafresh.

In 1984 a new competitor called Check Up hit the market with a novel gimmick. It was packaged in an upright tube that contained a pump. Colgate-Palmolive responded quickly with its own pump package. When Crest attempted to follow, it was held back by manufacturing and distribution difficulties. With heavy promotional muscle, Colgate succeeded in tying up about half the pump market, achieving a position that Crest's pump could not overcome.

The next shot fired came with development of a tartar control extension in 1986. Colgate-Palmolive and Procter & Gamble developed tartar control brands at virtually the same time, and neither gained a special advantage. Tartar, a hard substance that builds up along the gum line, does not cause tooth decay like plaque, but can lead to gum disease. Colgate Tartar Control proved effective in controlling tartar buildup and helped the brand to gain another small, but important share of the market.

Colgate and Crest introduced extensions specially formulated for children shortly after the introduction of a rival's Muppets toothpaste. Colgate for kids is slightly less abrasive and more palatable to children. The major selling point is identical to that used 70 years previously: "children use it without urging."

Colgate also introduced a baking soda toothpaste in 1992, in regular and gel formulations. Baking soda, with its high pH, is effective in neutralizing the acids produced by plaque that damage tooth surfaces.

## Performance Evaluation

Colgate, which is manufactured mostly at facilities in Jeffersonville, Indiana, is available in many markets internationally. Because good dental care is considered a priority only in advanced economies, Colgate—like other quality toothpastes—is not commonly available in developing countries. Colgate may be purchased in Canada, Europe, Hong Kong, Latin America, and other areas.

Colgate toothpaste, which had been a virtually unchallenged market leader since 1900, saw its most serious threat from Crest. Procter & Gamble promoted its brand vigorously after its introduction, but was unable to collect more than a 10 percent market share over the years. But after Procter & Gamble began promoting Crest's ADA approval in 1964, Colgate gradually gave up share to the new brand. Before the end of the 1960s, Crest had overtaken Colgate as the number one selling toothpaste in America.

Colgate won its own ADA approval in 1969, and the company wasted no time trumpeting this on its product packaging and in advertisements. The approval helped to stem continued losses to Crest and stabilize Colgate's market share in a range between 20 and 28 percent. Colgate has proven quicker to the market than Crest with trendy extensions, such as with the clear gel extension and the pump package. Such sound reflexes have helped Colgate gain momentary leads over Crest and, occasionally, bring sales of the two brands almost neck and neck. The competition between the two leading brands remains fierce, and it is likely that the two will continue to battle for the top market share for some time to come.

## Further Reading:

"Bates Gives Brush Up to Colgate Spots," *Advertising Age*, March 3, 1986, p. 64.

"Colgate Closes Gap with Crest," *Advertising Age*, February 13, 1989, p. 12.

"Colgate Dental Cream, *Modern Packaging*, May, 1949, p. 100.

"Colgate Joins Shift to Pump for Dentifrice," *Advertising Age*, May 28, 1984, p. 1.

"Colgate Puts the Squeeze on Crest," *Business Week*, August 19, 1985, p. 40.

"Colgate Sees Itself Ousting Crest as No. 1," *Advertising Age*, January 13, 1969, p. 8.

"Colgate-Palmolive Company, Memorable Dates," Colgate-Palmolive, n.d.

"Colgate's Product Battle Plan," *Advertising Age*, August 4, 1980, p. 3.

"FDA Report Gives Nod to Therapeutic Claims for Crest, Colgate with MFP," *Advertising Age*, July 27, 1970, p. 6.

"FDA Snaps at Oral Care Ads," *Advertising Age*, October 10, 1988, p. 3.

"Put Your Money Where Your Mouth Is," *Consumer Reports*, March, 1984, p. 129.

"Timeline: Oral Care," Colgate-Palmolive, n.d.

*—John Simley*

# COMET®

Since Procter & Gamble Company (P&G) introduced Comet cleanser to national markets in 1957, the scouring powder cleanser has remained a market leader, gently eliminating dirt on surfaces where it has less gently beat out competitors. Over the years, P&G supported Comet with aggressive marketing strategies to maintain its leading position. Early brand identity was forged in the 1960s by a series of commercials featuring actress Jane Withers as "Josephine the Plumber." Since its introduction, Comet, like the product's advertising campaigns, has undergone changes: new plastic packaging was introduced in 1965; a liquid form of Comet cleanser was introduced in the late 1970s; and lemon-scented Comet cleanser entered the market in the 1980s. In 1987, P&G began a comprehensive restructuring plan that provided greater support for successful brands like Comet in order to increase international sales. By 1989, P&G was supporting its cleaning products with $31.5 million worth of measured media to increase product visibility and maintain Comet's leading market share.

## Brand Origins

Comet was among the products that emerged from the post-World War II development of detergents, cleaning agents made from chemicals. Originally used as special wetting agents by the textile industry, detergents were modified after the war for broader use in commercial laundries, household washing machines, dishwashers, and increasingly in all-purpose cleaners. By 1948, synthetic items accounted for approximately 14 percent of the total soap and detergent tonnage produced in the United States, according to a July 5, 1958, article by Marius Jalet in the *Magazine of Wall Street.* By 1953, that figure had risen to nearly 50 percent, and by 1958 detergents accounted for 72.2 percent of the total soap and detergent volume. Inventories of soap-making animal fats (tallow) and oils (coconut, palm) were replaced by growing varieties of chemical-based replacements. An increasingly competitive market was dominated in the United States by three companies: Procter & Gamble Company, Colgate-Palmolive Company, and the Lever Brothers division of the internationally-owned Dutch concern, Unilever, N.V. Friction among these competitors resulted in the introduction of new cleaners, including Comet, which owed its genesis, in large part, to competition between P&G and Colgate.

In 1947, Colgate introduced an innovative new scouring cleanser, Ajax, designed specifically for contemporary sinks which were commonly made of glazed, porcelain-like materials. Traditional, abrasive cleansers tended to leave small pits on such surfaces, making them dull, prone to stains, and hard to clean. Ajax, too, relied on pumice-like abrasives that could scratch surfaces over time. With an eye on the shortfalls of Colgate's successful "foaming cleanser" (Ajax won nearly half the scouring cleanser market in its early years), P&G researchers introduced Comet for market tests in 1956. Their new scouring powder featured a chlorine bleach ingredient, chlorinol, that served as an extremely effective stain remover. Comet was also less abrasive than its competitor. As late as January 1990, *Consumer Reports* paid tribute to Comet's gentle cleaning qualities by ranking it among the six gentlest powder cleansers, along with White Magic Softer Formula. Two other features of P&G's new product—a slight chorine odor and a blue-green color—proved positive distinctions in market tests. By 1957, Comet was sold nationally and quickly caught up with Ajax in popularity. The two brands, and later additions, have been in a continuous rub ever since.

## Marketing Innovations

To compete against Ajax and other strong cleanser brands, Comet depended on well-funded and innovative marketing efforts. Beginning in 1962, Compton Advertising, Inc. developed a series of television advertisements for Comet, featuring the actress Jane Withers, as "Josephine the Plumber." The ads were successful, and "Josephine's" fame helped forge a strong brand identity for Comet. Also in the early 1960s, P&G shifted its advertising tone, employing what *Advertising Age* called the "new look" in a December 23, 1963, feature. That "look" involved television ads that featured ordinary people giving testimonials of their satisfaction with Comet. In print, the approach favored a quiet, editorial tone. One magazine ad from that year, for example, depicted a sink drain encircled by six different stains occupying the top two-thirds of the page. In the bottom third a centered subheading read, "6 tough sink stains—and the most effective way to remove them all." Four concise paragraphs outlined the cleaning virtues of Comet, concluding that "Every product you use should do its job as well as this one does!"

By the late 1970s these advertising efforts had paid off; Comet was the top-selling cleanser, with approximately 50 percent of the $125-million-plus scouring powder market for the United States in 1978. Ajax controlled roughly 39 percent of the U.S. market,

## AT A GLANCE

Comet brand of cleanser introduced to national markets in 1957 by the Proctor & Gamble Company (P&G); Comet liquid introduced in 1976; other line additions included lemon-scented Comet cleanser in the 1980s and Comet Non-abrasive Bathroom Cleaner in 1992.

**Performance:** *Market share*—28.1% (top share) of household-cleaner category (all P&G cleaner brands). *Sales*—$63.8 million (1991 estimate).

**Major competitor:** (for cleanser) Colgate-Palmolive Company's Ajax; (for bathroom cleaner) Dow.

**Advertising:** *Agency*—Saatchi & Saatchi, New York, NY, 1957—. *Major campaign*—Comet Non-abrasive Bathroom Cleaner ads stressing product's superior ability to clean soap scum and hard water stains.

**Addresses:** *Parent company*—Procter & Gamble Company, 1 Procter & Gamble Plaza, Cincinnati, OH 45202; phone: (513) 983-1100; fax: (513) 562-4500.

while remaining the worldwide market leader. In ads created by Compton Advertising, Comet was described as "the cleaning muscle that saves your own," while Norman, Craig & Kummel advertising sold Ajax as "the one tough cleanser." With such close competition, as well as market shares lost to other powdered cleansers, Comet relied on a wide variety of marketing strategies to distinguish itself. The 1986 appearance of Halley's Comet marked a perfect promotional opportunity. Capitalizing on public interest in the comet, P&G commissioned Benjamin Company, a publishing and marketing organization in Elmsford, New York, to produce one million "Halley's Comet" booklets written by an eminent scientist. These booklets were given away free with the purchase of Comet cleanser.

In 1988 P&G returned to earth to sponsor the Clasico Internacional Series, a series of international soccer matches between The American National Team and top Latin American opponents under the auspices of key P&G brands including Comet, Tide detergent, Biz bleach, and Ivory soap. "We believe this program will be of great assistance to the Federation in one day winning both an Olympic Gold Medal and a World Cup championship," said Bob Jordan, Hispanic Marketing Manager at P&G in a February 11, 1988 *Business Wire* article.

### Feminist Friction

The success of Comet cleanser was largely attributable to a female consumer base, which was targeted in the product's early marketing campaigns. Starting in the 1960s, however, growing feminist sensibilities, paired with rising numbers of working women, forced the brand to adapt new strategies. By the 1970s the sink-scrubbing housewife portrayed in mid-day television ads had become an outdated stereotype. By 1973, 45 percent of all U.S. women worked part or full-time outside the home, and 41 percent of the married working females continued to bear responsibility for managing households. In the early 1970s, P&G ad bosses moved their television spots into hours when working women would more likely be in the viewing audience, according to a March 26, 1973, *Advertising Age* article. Under a new plan, network spots catered primarily to housewives and other day-

time viewers, while additional network ads were developed for evening air time to reach professional women and their male counterparts.

In addition to changes in media planning, actual advertisements also began to shift emphasis. After losing some of its appeal with Comet consumers, the "Josephine the Plumber" campaign was retired in 1974. New commercials featuring different women in hidden camera situations were designed to be more direct and harder hitting than the earlier campaign.

One 1974 commercial for Comet opened with a woman cleaning her sink, while an accompanying male voice-over explained that Mrs. Pavlovsky was "testing her leading cleanser and Comet on tough food stains, pot marks, and cooking grease." Using a combination of Socratic and sales techniques, the commercial tested the product's effectiveness—Man: "How is the Comet working?" Mrs. P.: "Very well." Man: "Okay, now we'd like you to clean the other side with the same amount of your cleanser. How is your cleanser working?" Mrs. P.: "I have to work harder." Man: "Why?" Mrs. P.: "It's not coming out as easily as Comet." After demonstrating Comet's superiority to the competition, the man concludes that "it can change your mind about cleanser." To support similar Comet campaigns, P&G spent $5.2 million in 1973, according to *Advertising Age*.

While women were the main focus of Comet marketing from the 1960s onward, numerous groups criticized the brand's characterization of somewhat naive women instructed by authoritative male voices. In a May 18, 1993, article for the *Plain Dealer*, "Battling Gender Bias in Ads," Kathleen Brunkala noted that "The makers of Comet cleanser show grown women not quite smart enough to know the correct names for soap scum and hard water stains lurking in their bathrooms." In the commercial at issue, women begrudged "That slippery slime on my tub; that grimy gunk on my shower walls; on my shower door, that, THAT STUFF; it even cleaned that nasty drip mark thing." A male voice rattled off the proper names while the woman cleaned. While the industry at large began to address complaints like Brunkala's, advertising, and P&G in particular, continued to base its decisions not as much on politically fashionable ideologies as on tested market success. The strongest feminist objections to Comet marketing would have to come directly from consumers' loudest mouths, their wallets.

### Competition

Even as a market leader with an unparalleled marketing budget, Comet has had to fend off growing numbers of imitation and generic brands. In 1978 American Home Products Corp. (AHP) revived its old brand, Zud heavy-duty scouring powder, with a new ad campaign focusing on the cleanser's heavy-duty and rust-removing capabilities. Though Zud was more expensive than Comet and Ajax, AHP promoted it as the product to use "when ordinary cleanser fails." In addition to Zud, the market was inundated with new powder cleansers, ranging from name brand products to generic brands introduced by many mass-merchandisers.

Market competition intensified with the emergence of new types of scouring cleansers designed to compete with powder cleansers. In 1986 sales of liquid cleansers rose about 5 percent, while sales of powder cleansers remained steady, according to a January, 1987, article in *Chemical Marketing Reporter*. Clorox held a leading 12 percent of the 1986 liquid scouring market with its Soft Scrub, and was also test marketing a heavy-duty liquid abrasive called Strike, which contained silica, the abrasive commonly found in powders. P&G held its ground by introducing Mr. Clean cleanser with soft abrasive that same year, supplementing its already-established Comet liquid, which had been introduced for limited distribution in 1976.

## Brand Development

Since its introduction, Comet has continually adapted to the competitive and ever-changing market. In 1965, P&G used new packaging to distinguish Comet from its competitors, introducing all-plastic, rust-proof containers with closeable lids (touted as a safety device for households with children). As supplements, not replacements, for the conventional paperboard containers, the new packages were introduced in two forms: six-ounce plastic cans shrink-wrapped in bundles of four, called the Bathroom Bundle; and a 17-ounce decorator container advertised in 60-second television commercials by Compton Advertising, Inc.

The brand was also enhanced with new formulas and ingredients. In 1976, responding to consumers' increasing preference for liquid cleansers, P&G introduced Comet liquid for limited distribution. Similarly, responding to the popularity of lemon-scented cleaners in the 1980s, P&G offered lemon-scented Comet cleanser. "Lemon is by far the most popular scent in household cleaning products," said Phylomena M. Augurusa, manager of soap and household products at New York-based International Flavors & Fragrances, the United States's largest producer of smells and flavors, in an August 25, 1987, article in the *Los Angeles Times*.

In 1992, Comet liquid was phased out in favor of Comet Non-abrasive Bathroom Cleaner, which was promoted as a superior cleaner of bathroom soap scum and hard water stains. P&G also began advertising its other cleaning products with innovative package advertising. Adhesive stickers covering the sifting dispensers of standard Comet powder cleanser containers challenged consumers to "Try New Comet Bath Spray."

In the 1980s, manufacturers began addressing consumers' ecological concerns on Comet packaging. Both plastic and paperboard containers, noted that "Comet contains no phosphorous. The surfactants in Comet are biodegradable." Comet Bathroom Cleaner listed the same features, replacing "surfactants" with a less technical "cleaning agents."

## International Growth

Due to the international growth of its parent company, Comet was available worldwide by the late 1980s. P&G was active in 27 countries in 1985, and by 1989 it had operations in 48. Increased growth in international markets was likely in the early 1990s as P&G followed global growth of other international competitors like Japan's Kao Corp. and Anglo-Dutch Unilever. In an October, 1989 *Business Week* article, "P&G's Worldly New Boss Wants a More Worldly Company," CEO John G. Smale predicted that more than half of P&G's sales would come from outside the U.S. by the early 1990s. In the early 1980s, the company had already started aggressive marketing initiatives to capture the

European market from its key competitors there, Henkel KGAA, Unilever, and Colgate-Palmolive.

## Future Outlook

In 1985, P&G profits dropped for the first time in three decades. After rebounding in 1986, sales fell again in 1987—just in time for the company's sesquicentennial celebration. That year Smale launched a major restructuring plan. Among the plan's new strategies, P&G shifted emphasis from soap and food to health care and nutrition and became the United States's biggest manufacturer of over-the-counter drugs by the end of the 1980s. Notorious for bureaucratic sluggishness, the company also took measures to revamp its management style. Not least of all, P&G also moved to support its most successful brands, like Comet, with renewed marketing strategies backed up by substantial budgets. From the early 1980s onward, P&G remained the biggest advertiser in the United States, with dollar appropriations of $2.2 billion. In 1986 alone, its cleaners, including Mr. Clean soft-abrasive and Comet cleanser, were supported with $31.5 million in measured media.

The 1992 introduction of Comet Non-abrasive Bathroom Cleaner showed continued support for one of the company's most successful brands. With P&G's massive support, the brand had managed to hold ground as a leader in a fiercely competitive market. In July of 1993, P&G announced further declines in profits, which forced the company to reduce its work force by 12 percent. Company sources insisted that the move reflected positive steps toward greater efficiency and continued growth into the twenty-first century. Prospects for a strong future at P&G ensured continued success of Comet.

## Further Reading:

Alter, Stewart, and Nancy Giges, "P&G, Colgate Strike Back," *Advertising Age*, June 2, 1986, p. 1.

Brunkala, Kathleen, "Battling Gender Bias in Ads," *Plain Dealer*, May 18, 1993, p. 2C.

Carahan, Bill, "Procter & Gamble Strategy: Stay With What Works," *Advertising Age*, November 13, 1979, p. S-38.

"Cleansers: One Stood Out," *Consumer Reports*, January 1990, p. 61.

Colt, George Howe, "Here Comes Halley's," *Life*, October 1985, p. 30.

Christopher, Maurine, "P&G in Major Spot TV Shift to Reach More Working Women," *Advertising Age*, March 26, 1973, p. 1.

Elliott, Stuart, "The Media Business: Advertising—Saatchi Is Picking up Spic & Span Account," *New York Times*, June 19, 1991, p. D19.

Giges, Nancy, "P&G's Josephine is Down the Drain," *Advertising Age*, September 9, 1974, p. 1.

——, "Two Scouring Marketers Become More Abrasive," *Advertising Age*, March 27, 1978, p. 3.

Jalet, Marius, "Procter and Gamble, Colgate-Palmolive; Leader and Runner-up in Soap, Detergents and Toiletries," *Magazine of Wall Street*, July 5, 1958, p. 421–3, 442.

McGraw, Carol, "The Perils of Jane—They Finally Wither Away," *Los Angeles Times*, February 10, 1985, sec. 1, p. 32.

McCoy, Michael, "Cleanser Market Set for 'Lively' Year in '87," *Chemical Marketing Reporter*, January 26, 1987, p. 35.

"Procter & Gamble; Joint U.S. Soccer Federation," *Business Wire*, February 11, 1988.

"P&G Puts Comet in Plastic Cans," *Printer's Ink*, October 22, 1965, p. 79.

Potts, Mark, ''P&G Hones A Strategy For Its Future,'' *Washington Post,* July 26, 1987, p. H1.

Schiller, Zachary, ''P&G's Worldly New Boss Wants a More Worldly Company,'' *Business Week,* October 30, 1989, p. 40.

Schisgall, Oscar, *Eyes on Tomorrow,* New York: J. G. Ferguson Publishing, 1981, pp. 3–4.

Sharman, Howard, ''P&G on the Warpath Throughout Europe,'' *Advertising Age,* May 23, 1983, p. 5.

Shiver, Jube, Jr., ''Pervasive in Products; These Days, Lemons Are Cleaning Up,'' *Los Angeles Times,* August 25, 1987, sec. 1, p. 1.

Singer, Penny, '' 'Instant Publishing' Making its Mark,'' *New York Times,* February 15, 1987, sec. 11WC, p. 14.

Tyler, William D., ''Procter & Gamble's New Look,'' *Advertising Age,* December 23, 1963, p. 32.

—*Kerstan Cohen*

# CONTAC®

Contac cold medicine revolutionized the cold medicine market by providing up to 12 hours of extended relief from upper respiratory symptoms of the flu and colds. The capsules provide medication that is released into the body over a 12-hour period. Contac is marketed in several formulas, all of which are multi-symptom remedies for a specific group of symptoms. Contac, manufactured by SmithKline Beecham Consumer Brands, is sold in capsule, caplet, tablet, and liquid forms.

Each Contac formula combines two or more classes of active ingredients. The classes of ingredients found in Contac products include decongestants to relieve nasal or sinus congestion; antihistamines to relieve runny nose and sneezing; analgesics to relieve fever, aches, and sore throat; cough suppressants to relieve coughing; and expectorants to clear chest congestion. Contac's non-drowsy formulas are for those sensitive to antihistamines.

There are four categories of upper respiratory tract disorders that Contac products treat. These are influenza, or flu; allergies; the common cold; and sinusitis. Flu is highly contagious and often manifests itself through fever, aches, and inflamed mucous membranes. Allergies are reactions to allergens, or foreign substances. Mucous membranes are usually inflamed during allergic reactions. In the common cold, upper respiratory tract membranes are usually inflamed, and aches, coughing, and fever may prove uncomfortable to sufferers. Sinusitis is also characterized by inflamed mucous membranes. These membranes line the sinus passages and create pressure when inflamed. The Contac medications treat all of these symptoms, providing unique timed-release relief.

Contac Cold Capsules were introduced in 1961 by Smith Kline & French Laboratories under the Menley & James Laboratories name. Smith Kline & French used the Menley & James appellation to distinguish the over-the-counter medications manufactured by the company from its prescription drugs. In 1985 the Menley & James division was renamed SmithKline Consumer Products. By 1989, when Beecham P.L.C., a large British pharmaceutical company, merged with SmithKline Beckman to become SmithKline Beecham, Contac was a comprehensive line of adult cold remedies. The resulting company had a large market share of the United Kingdom's cough-cold-allergy market, and was aiming to increase its market share in the United States.

## Contac Brand Extensions

The flagship Contac product is cold capsules, which were introduced in 1961. Other Contac products include Contac Jr. Liquid, introduced in 1976; Contac Severe Cold Formula Caplets, introduced in 1981 as a capsule, in 1986 as caplet, and in 1987 (renamed Contac Severe Cold and Flu at this time) with an improved formula with antitussive; Contac Cough Formula Liquid, introduced in 1987; Contac Maximum Strength Cold Caplets, introduced in 1986; Contac Nighttime Cold Medicine, introduced in 1987; Contac Cough and Sore Throat Formula Liquid, introduced in 1987; Contact Sinus, introduced in 1989; Contac Cough & Chest Cold and Contac Severe Cold & Flu Hot Medicine, introduced in 1991; and Contac Day & Night, introduced in 1991 in both Cold/Flu and Allergy/Sinus varieties.

## Advertising and Product Innovation

The manufacturers of Contac know that everyone is afflicted by illnesses on occasion. SmithKline Beecham aimed to reach these sufferers and introduce them to the relief provided by Contac products. The first advertising agency to promote Contac cold medicines was BBDO, which handled the account for its first decade. Foote, Cone & Belding took over from 1970 until 1990. Grey Advertising has been given the job of taking Contac into the 21st century. Media expenditures in 1990 were between $10 and $15 million.

According to SmithKline Beecham, Contac holds a 44 percent rating in brand awareness in the cold medication category. This is the highest brand awareness in the category, and is ahead of competitor NyQuil, made by Richardson-Vicks Co., by several percentage points. However, the manufacturers of Contac struggled against the dominating sales of NyQuil in the nighttime relief market.

In 1991, SmithKline Beecham came out with its Contac Day & Night formulas, which were specifically designed to challenge NyQuil by providing both daytime and nighttime ingredients with different formulas sold in one package. Similarly, Bristol Myers had been eyeing NyQuil, and introduced their Comtrex Day & Night only one month before SmithKline Beecham brought out Contac Day & Night. The Contac product was introduced with more than five million dollars in media support. Two years later, Contac Day & Night Allergy/Sinus was supported by three million

## AT A GLANCE

Contac cold medicine introduced in 1961 by Smith Kline & French under the Menley & James Laboratories name; Menley & James Laboratories renamed SmithKline Consumer Products, 1985; parent company renamed SmithKline Beecham PLC after 1989 merger of British pharmaceutical company Beecham P.L.C. and SmithKline; brand extensions include Contac Severe Cold & Flu Hot Medicine and Contac Day & Night.

**Performance:** *Market share*—5% of cold medications market. *Sales*—$80 million.

**Major competitor:** Richardson-Vicks' NyQuil; also, Burroughs Wellcome & Co.'s Sudafed; Sandoz Pharmaceuticals Corporation's TheraFlu; Bristol-Myers' Comtrex; and Schering Plough's Drixoral.

**Advertising:** *Agency*—Grey Advertising, New York, NY, 1990—. *Major campaign*—Contac Day & Night: "The right medicine at the right time!"; Contac 12-hour caplets: "Contac turns sick days into work days."

**Addresses:** *Parent company*—SmithKline Beecham Consumer Brands, 100 Beecham Drive, Pittsburgh, PA 15205; phone: (412) 928-1000; fax: (412) 928-5864. *Ultimate parent company*—SmithKline Beecham PLC

dollars in media spending. The brand as a whole spent close to $20 million in media in 1993.

The advertising campaign for Contac Day & Night emphasized the ability of Contac to take care of sufferers with time-appropriate medicines. The slogan carried in print advertisements as well as in television and radio spots was "The right medicine at the right time." The medicine for daytime was non-sedating, relieving headache, cough, congestion, and sinus pain during working hours without drowsiness. The medicine for night relieved the same aches and pains with an added antihistamine to let the consumer rest. The active ingredients in the daytime formula were the analgesic acetaminophen and the decongestant pseudoephedrine. The nighttime ingredients included both of those, and added the antihistamine diphenhydramine. The market was segmented by Contac's creation of two versions of Contac Day & Night. One was aimed at allergy and sinus sufferers, and the other was specifically designed for colds and the flu.

One television advertisement for Contac Day & Night Cold/ Flu began by stating: "Contac wrote the book on cold medicine." It described the medicine's patented packaging as the pages in a book. The yellow caplets on one page were the daytime formula designed to work without drowsiness, and the blue caplets on the next page were the nighttime formula allowing rest and relief. The commercial concluded, "Both formulas control your cold with the right medicine at the right time."

As SmithKline Beecham responded to the success of the nighttime dominance of NyQuil with Contac Day & Night, another competitor, Sandoz Pharmaceuticals Corporation's TheraFlu, had found success marketing hot liquid medicine for relief of flu symptoms. In 1991, SmithKline Beecham brought out Contac Severe Cold & Flu Hot Medicine with about four million dollars in television spending to support it.

Grey also did the advertising for the British versions of Smith-Kline Beecham's cold remedies. In 1992, Grey's campaign added a character in the television advertisements for broadcast in the United Kingdom. The commercials featured a coffee mug with symptoms of a cold, and ran with the slogan "Put a smile on your mug." But the new campaign, with Mr. Beecham offering help to cold sufferers, was created to personalize cold treatment by adding human warmth. In the United Kingdom, Beecham's cough and cold remedies claim a 45 percent share of the market.

In the United States, the company targeted users of short-acting medications, such as Actifed, Sudafed, and Dimetapp. Because the consumer of Contac was a young adult, aged 25 to 49, emphasis was placed on the brand's long-lasting effects in contrast with the four-hour wearing-off period of other medications. A television commercial for Contac 12-hour caplets took aim at this generation's concern about missing work due to illness. A working man in the advertisement says, "You better take something that's going to get you down there working." It concludes with the slogan "Contac turns sick days into work days."

With the emphasis on workplace wellness getting tremendous media attention in the 1990s, SmithKline Beecham seized an opportunity to gain some good publicity. The company created an awards program entitled "We Never Miss a Day." Flyers went to large and small companies across the United States describing the program. The program encouraged employee attendance during winter months and promoted good health in the workplace. The program was sponsored by Contac cold and flu medications, and participating companies received coupons for product discounts as well as gift items and posters. They also were given such educational materials as booklets about the common cold, slide presentations about workplace health, and a desktop "winter wellness" kit for all employees. Winning companies were judged on employee absenteeism due to illness as well as the way the program was implemented. The grand prize options were health-related awards such as exercise equipment, prescription reimbursements, and health insurance deferments to offset employees' deductibles.

### Product Tampering

A product tampering incident in 1986 was far less traumatic to Contac than a similar incident had been to Tylenol several years earlier. In the 1982 Tylenol incident, several people died. In March 1986, only six weeks after another Tylenol poisoning had left a woman dead, Contac cold medicine capsules were recalled. The company acted quickly and efficiently to recall the capsules even before the Federal Bureau of Investigations (F.B.I.) deemed a recall necessary. In all, eight capsules were found with trace amounts of warfarin, an ingredient used in rat poison. The tampering did not harm the brand image or its parent company since Contac and the other two affected products produced less than three percent of the company's annual sales, and the tampering came at the end of the cold and flu season, when retail inventories were relatively low.

Two months later, in May 1986, Contac returned to the market in tamper-resistant caplets and capsules. Surveys showed half of all consumers preferred capsules, so the company redesigned Contac capsules. The new capsules were completely clear, and had what the company called "Perma-seal." This was a double seal of gelatin topped by a red seal. This enabled consumers to detect any tampering immediately. They kept the plastic blister packs with foil backing and added a clear plastic overwrap to each package, emphasizing the tamper-resistance of the packaging.

Besides the tampering incident, ecological concerns played a role in designs for packaging of Contac products. SmithKline Beecham reduced the size and weight of packaging for 10-, 20-, and 30-count sizes of Contac, the carton's blister strip, and its film wrap. The company's packaging machinery had to be retrofitted, but the investment was found to be worthwhile for the company.

Packages of Contac contain varying amounts of medicine. Contac 12-hour caplets and capsules both come in packages of 10, 20, or 40, while Contac Sinus tablets and caplets come in packages of 24. Liquid Contac medicines, such as Contac Cough and Sore Throat and Contac Nighttime Cold Medicine come in four- or six-fluid ounce jars. All of the packaging is now tamper resistant, and a number of the packages are designed to be child resistant.

### Restructuring

SmithKline Beecham showed its insistence on marketing expertise when they hired John B. Ziegler to be president of U.S. Consumer Brands in 1991. His background was in health-care marketing, and he had worked for Johnson & Johnson on Tylenol, and for Procter & Gamble before that. In 1992, SmithKline Beecham announced it was combining U.S. over-the-counter pharmaceutical brands into a partnership with Dow Chemical Co.'s Marion Merrell Dow. The venture was 90-percent owned by SmithKline Beecham, and planned to market Contac as well as Aqua-Fresh, Tums, and other over-the-counter products manufactured by SmithKline Beecham. Led by SmithKline U.S. Consumer Brands president Ziegler, SmithKline Beecham Consumer Brands capitalized on a national trend toward self-medication. The hope was that as Marion Merrell Dow contributed more products to be marketed by the group, ownership of the venture would be more evenly split, and the company would be called SmithKline Beecham Marion. They planned to bring some prescription drugs over the counter, including the Nicoderm nicotine patch and Seldane antihistamine, both of which were Marion Merrell Dow products.

In 1993, SmithKline Beecham Consumer Brands put a new worldwide management structure in place to expand their health-care brands into global over-the-counter products. Contac fell into the Over-The-Counter Upper Respiratory division, which represented cough and cold brands. The new structure was to allow advertising, packaging, and positioning plans that could be adapted for use in foreign markets. Six units were created, and the Over-The-Counter Upper Respiratory unit was one of the first to show success as more consumers purchased over-the-counter drugs.

### Further Reading:

Armstrong, Michael W., "Former SmithKline Brands Help Start Drug Company," *Philadelphia Business Journal,* July 23–29, 1990, p. 4.

Cuff, Daniel F., "SmithKline U.S. Brands Has a New President," *New York Times,* February 15, 1991.

Freudenheim, Milt, "2 Companies Join in Selling Medications," *New York Times,* August 19, 1992, p. D4.

Latham, Valerie, "Beecham Warms Up Its Cold Remedies," *Marketing,* October 1, 1992, p. 5.

"Machine Makeover Relieves Contac," *Packaging Digest,* June, 1992, p. 86.

McCarthy, Michael, "Cure for Cold Season: An Ad Flurry," *Adweek,* October 7, 1991, p. 4.

"100 Leading National Advertisers," *Advertising Age,* September 25, 1991, pp. 63–64.

"100 Leading National Advertisers," *Advertising Age,* September 23, 1992, pp. 59–60.

Prokesch, Steven, "SmithKline's Expiring Patents," *New York Times,* April 10, 1991, p. D10.

"Reintroduction Set for Contac," *New York Times,* May 22, 1986, p. D8.

Shenon, Philip, "Capsules of Three Drugs Are Tainted," *New York Times,* March 21, 1986, p. A1.

——, "Traces of Poison Lead to Recall of Three Drugs," *New York Times,* March 22, 1986, p. A1.

Sloan, Pat, "Shops Watch SmithKline-Marion Linkup," *Advertising Age,* August 24, 1992, p. 27.

"SmithKline Considers Sales," *New York Times,* July 10, 1992, p. D2.

Winters, Patricia, "SmithKline Realigns by Category," *Advertising Age,* March 8, 1993, p. 17.

*—Fran Shonfeld Sherman*

# CONVERSE®

**CONVERSE®**

Converse Inc., the largest U.S. manufacturer of athletic footwear, became an industry leader with the 1917 introduction of its canvas Converse All Star basketball shoe. Under the endorsement of player Charles "Chuck" H. Taylor, the Converse Chuck Taylor All Star—known as "Chucks"—became the first basketball shoe worn throughout the United States. By 1992 more than 500 million pairs, in over 56 colors and styles, had been sold in over 90 countries worldwide. In addition, the brand diversified into athletic shoes for most major sports. Starting in the 1970s, however, Converse lost market share to a new wave of competitive, high-performance athletic shoe brands such as Nike and Reebok. In the 1980s, Converse launched aggressive new marketing and design initiatives aimed at reclaiming center court.

## Brand Origins

The origins of Converse athletic footwear date back to 1908, when Marquis M. Converse founded the Converse Rubber Company in Malden, Massachusetts. Having attained the position of general superintendent of Houghton & Dutton, Inc., one of Boston's biggest department stores, Converse shifted to the rubber footwear business, joining Beacon Falls Rubber Shoe Company. When the company was absorbed by U.S. Rubber, Converse started his own firm. Within one year, 350 employees were integrated into a full production team. By 1910 the company had expanded its plant to produce 4,000 pairs of boots and rubber footwear daily. The Converse brand of footwear had taken its first steps toward the market dominance that it would enjoy after World War I.

## The All Star Shoe

The brand experienced a dramatic jump in success after its 1917 introduction of the Converse canvas All Star, one of the world's first basketball shoes. The game of basketball was still in its infancy, having been invented by James Naismith in 1891. As basketball gained international popularity, so did All Stars, eventually extending beyond the court and into the world of fashion. By the early 1990s, customers ranging from fashionable urbanites to rock n' roll fans could choose from over 20 colors, various styles, and sizes from infant to adult.

The All Star's rapid ascent in the footwear market was spurred by the reputation and marketing savvy of basketball star Charles "Chuck" H. Taylor, who joined the Converse sales force in 1921 to become the brand's first player endorser. Chuck Taylor grew up in a town outside of Columbus, Indiana, and progressed from high school directly to a career in basketball. Professional teams were still not established, so Taylor joined such barnstorming basketball teams as the Buffalo Germans and the Akron Firestones. In 1921, he joined Converse's Chicago sales office and began travelling around the country to sell the shoe and promote the sport in basketball clinics.

This innovative approach to sports marketing both increased sales and contributed to product development. Increased traction and ankle support and a sturdier sole were among the ideas Taylor brought in from the sales field. His input was so effective that his signature was added to the All Star ankle patch in 1923. With Taylor serving as the official "Ambassador to Basketball," Converse garnered between 70 and 80 percent of the basketball shoe market by the mid-1960s. In 1968, a year before his death, he was inducted into the Naismith Memorial Hall of Fame, a tribute to the sport in which he starred and in which he planted the All Star shoe.

Sustained success of the All Star spurred growth in a diverse line of athletic footwear. The Converse brand expanded into shoes for tennis, cross-training, team sports, children's activities, running and walking, as well as a full line of basketball footwear beyond the All Star classic. Underlying such brand changes were fundamental shifts in company ownership: after changing ownership twice in its early years, Converse Rubber Co. was purchased by the influential Stone Family of Boston, Massachusetts; in 1972 Eltra Corporation of New York became the new owner until 1979, when Allied Corporation acquired Converse; Allied decided to eliminate consumer goods from its operations, and Converse was spun off as an independent private company; in 1986 it was acquired by INTERCO Incorporated, which remained the parent company into the 1990s.

## Jump in Competition

Beginning in the late 1970s, Converse faced increasing pressure from new competition in the footwear industry. The company worked to fend off imported brands while resisting transplanting its United States-based facilities in countries with lower production costs. "We are committed to remaining predominantly a domestic athletic shoe manufacturer," explained John O'Neil, president of Converse, in a February 13, 1984, *Footwear News* article. Converse's Lumberton plant in North Carolina developed

## AT A GLANCE

**F**irst Converse basketball shoe, the All Star, introduced in 1917 by Converse Rubber Company, which was founded by Marquis M. Converse in 1908; Charles "Chuck" H. Taylor's signature added to All Star logo, 1923; Converse diversified into tennis, cross-training, team sports, children's, running and walking shoe lines; All Star line expanded in 1970s; company launched state-of-the art designs in 1980s; Converse is official shoe of the National Basketball Association (NBA), USA Basketball, the Women's Basketball Coaches Association (WBCA) and the Federation Internationale de Basketball (FIBA).

**Performance:** *Market share*—3.9% of athletic footwear category (1991 worldwide figure); 3.09% of U.S. athletic footwear category. *Sales*—$200 million.

**Major competitor:** Nike; also Reebok.

**Advertising:** *Agency*—Houston, Effler & Partners, Inc., New York, NY, 1992—. *Major campaign*—Humorous caricatures featuring Larry "Grandmama" Johnson.

**Addresses:** *Parent company*—Converse Inc., One Fordham Road, North Reading, MA 01864-2680; phone: (508) 664-1100; fax: (508) 664-7268. *Ultimate parent company*—INTERCO Incorporated, 101 S. Hanley Rd., Saint Louis, MO 63105-3493; phone: (314) 863-1100.

new manufacturing methods that were then adopted at smaller plants in Puerto Rico and Presque Isle, Maine. In addition to organizing highly integrated new machines ranging from high-speed waterjet cutters to multi-color sewing machines, the plant improved employee management. By frequently convening in "quality circles" to discuss quality, productivity and other work-related topics, workers also contributed to the overhauling efforts of the brand.

Converse also faced competition from other domestic shoe companies that were streamlining operations and aggressively seeking market share. In the early 1970s, the introduction of high-performance, leather athletic shoes strained Converse's leading position with its simple, canvas classic. By January of 1986 the *New York Times* reported that "Nike of Beaverton, Oregon, maker of Air Jordan basketball shoes, appears to be outrunning such competitors as Reebok International Ltd., Converse Inc. and Hyde Athletic Industries."

Realizing that the canvas shoe could not hold out on the court alone, Converse repositioned it as a fashion and street-wear item, developing a new fashion line including such colors as pink, camouflage, Aztec, Montezuma, and Prince of Wales.

To ensure continued development of innovative and well-designed footwear, Converse invested in an advanced-technologies lab staffed by a 70-member research and development team. When it was established in the early 1980s, it was one of only two in-house, biomechanical footwear labs in the country. The facility included work stations equipped with powerful computers and robots. A "foot morphology platform" enabled designers to observe podiatric subtleties among test subjects; prototype shoes were subject to extensive stomp tests on a biolab force plate and were twisted and bent by a whole shoe flex tester. These and other standards contributed to quality and design improvements throughout Converse's growing lines.

## Converse Sponsorship

In addition to its attempts to design the most durable and stylish shoes possible, Converse enhanced its reputation by sponsoring major basketball organizations and events worldwide. By the early 1990s, the brand had positioned itself as the official shoe of the National Basketball Association (NBA), USA Basketball, the World Association of Basketball Coaches (WABC) and the Federation Internationale de Basketball (FIBA).

Converse was the first company ever named the official shoe of the NBA. Valid from 1985 to 1995, the contract granted the company permission to use the NBA name in all advertising and promotions, and to manufacture shoes with logos of NBA teams or other affiliations. Converse also supplied merchandise to cheerleaders and ball retrievers throughout the league.

Converse was also a sponsor of USA Basketball since its inception in 1975. The Colorado Springs-based group was responsible for selecting national teams to represent the USA in various international competitions and served as a Class A member of the United States Olympic Committee. After 1977, Converse was contracted as the official shoe of USA Basketball, which agreed to "use [its] best efforts to outfit players in Converse shoes," according to Jeffrey Orridge, assistant executive director for corporate and legal affairs for the sports group, in a September, 1992 article in *American Lawyer*. That agreement later caused legal conflicts, as some USA Basketball team members held contracts with competing shoe companies. Requiring players to wear Converse introduced ethical and legal problems that had to be resolved with special care.

With the globalization of basketball, Converse increased its overseas presence. In 1988 Converse signed a sponsorship for the World Association of Basketball Coaches (WABC). Located in Rome, Italy, the WABC was responsible for training coaches at over 50 clinics worldwide, each involving 300 coaches on average. In February of 1990, Converse began a five-year, seven-figure contract as the sponsor of the Federation Internationale de Basketball (FIBA). Founded in 1932 and based in Munich, Germany, FIBA included 176 member countries and approximately 119 million registered players. Its competitions included the European Championship Club Cup Final and the European Championship for both men and women.

Converse also competed in the sponsorship of the Olympic Games. Though Converse provided footwear to the Olympic Games since 1936, in 1984 it became the first footwear supplier ever chosen to officially represent the games. The honor was not cheap: Converse paid the Los Angeles Olympic Organizing Committee (LAOCC) $4 million for the right and spent an additional $3.5 million for national television advertising. Total promotional costs approached the $10 million mark.

Olympic sponsorship was not without conflicts of interest and legal confusion. Though the 1992 Olympic Games were officially sponsored by Reebok, many other companies managed to claim credit by touting key athletes with whom they held endorsement contracts. The U.S. Olympic Committee's top executive, John Krimsky, Jr., identified Converse as one such "ambush marketer." Though Converse was neither a U.S. nor a worldwide Olympic sponsor that year, it ran an ad campaign showing two of its key endorsers defeating the Olympic opposition. Though Mr. Krimsky directed a "cease and desist letter" to Converse, the company denied any wrongdoing.

## Pro Support

Converse has consistently relied on high-profile sports celebrities and athletes to promote its footwear since Chuck Taylor served as the first player endorser. By 1990 Converse had contracted endorsements with over 14 professional players representing 11 different teams across the United States. In addition, company statistics showed that roughly 21 percent of all professional basketball players wore Converse shoes. The list has included Earvin "Magic" Johnson from the Los Angeles Lakers; 1992 Rookie of the Year Larry "Grandmama" Johnson of the Charlotte Hornets; Kevin Johnson of the Phoenix Suns; Larry Bird from the Boston Celtics; and, beyond basketball, all-pro quarterback Bernie Kosar of the Cleveland Browns; and women's tennis champion Chris Evert.

In the case of basketball endorser Earvin "Magic" Johnson, Converse received more publicity than it may have anticipated. In 1979 Johnson was enlisted as an official company endorser until 1994. By the late 1980s, Johnson showed dissatisfaction with the deal. Though Johnson was paid about $2 million for endorsing Converse shoes, Michael Jordan earned nearly three times that for endorsing Nike, according to a July 23, 1992, article in the *Boston Globe*. After Converse filed suit against the player for failing to comply with his long-term endorsement contract in 1987, matters were temporarily resolved.

When Magic Johnson won the National Basketball Association's most valuable player award, Converse created a 30-second highlight piece of his best moves in the NBA tournament filmed in slow motion to the accompaniment of "Amazing Grace." And in 1990, the company allotted a quarter of its $40-million advertising campaign to launch its Magic Johnson footwear and apparel line. After the player announced in the winter of 1991 that he had tested positive for the HIV virus that can cause AIDS, Converse aired a $1-million public service campaign called "Magic's Athletes Against AIDS." Yet in 1992, old friction resumed with Johnson's public statements that Converse marketing was outdated and that he was terminating his contract before the official date. "Converse as a company is stuck in the '60s and '70s. They think the Chuck Taylor sneaker days are still here," Johnson told reporters in Monte Carlo after the U.S. basketball team practiced for the Olympics. "I've been trying to get out for years," he added.

## Creative Marketing Strategies

Despite Johnson's criticism, Converse moved into the late 1980s and early 1990s with new and innovative marketing strategies aimed at regaining lost market share. In 1985, the company joined two rival coaches—Denny Crum from the University of Louisville Cardinals and Joe B. Hall of the University of Kentucky Wildcats—on one poster to promote the Converse brand. A lead story in the *Louisville Courier-Journal* showed a reproduction of the spread with the heading, "Joe, Denny friendly rivals? Oh, well, anything for shoe biz."

Other promotional strategies vary widely. To introduce a new line of running shoes at the 1985 Sports & Runners Expo in Boston, Converse maintained a test van stocked with shoes available for free trial runs. In 1991, Converse announced a program coordinated with the Windstar Foundation, a Snowmass, Colorado organization devoted to solving environmental problems, to develop hiking and walking shoes from which substantial proceeds would be donated to environmental programs. Converse also sponsored the Hoop-It-Up three-on-three basketball tour, bringing the game of American streetball to 13 European cities and to youth groups across America.

## Jumpy Advertising

In the late 1980s, Converse initiated advertising and promotional campaigns to compete with such brands as Nike, Reebok, L.A. Gear, and Keds that had surpassed it in key categories. Even under the financial strain of its bankrupt parent, INTERCO, Converse garnered an effective creative team at the New York advertising agency Ingalls Quinn and Johnson. Headed by Peter Favat, Richard Herstek and Harry McCoy, the team developed a hit campaign featuring NBA Rookie of the Year Larry Johnson dressed up as his basketball-playing Grandmama, who in her new, light Converse shoes, could blow by you "faster than a passing thought. She'll eat point guards for lunch and pick her teeth with a power forward."

In June of 1992 the same team startled Madison Avenue by pulling up stakes at Ingalls and moving across town to Houston, Effler & Partners Inc., with the $25 million Converse account following along one day later. INTERCO's subsequent emergence from bankruptcy freed up new funds for Converse investments and marketing plans, and Houston was able to take off with a new generation of slick ads to sell hip new shoes. In 1993 Converse introduced its Run 'N' Gun, featuring a patented React cushioning device with a combination of gas and gel built into the heel to absorb shock and provide additional maneuvering control. The shoe incorporated cushioning features of a performance basketball shoe with the streamlined profile and light weight of a running shoe. After religious leaders objected to the shoe's name, Converse changed it to Run 'N' Slam. Houston designed a 30-second TV spot featuring Kevin Johnson of the Phoenix Suns, with music by En Vogue, a group also known as the "funky divas of soul." "It's a hip, upbeat, funky commercial," said Converse spokeswoman Jennifer Murray in a March 7, 1993, article for the *Chicago Tribune*. The spots primarily targeted cable channels such as the Black Entertainment Network and MTV.

With a continued series of vivacious and entertaining ads for Converse, Houston itself bordered on becoming a "funky diva" in its own right. In a 1993 campaign for the new AeroJam shoe, the agency again played off Larry Johnson's "Grandmama" theme. The AeroJam featured REACT juice for added support in both the heel and ankle areas, as well as a unique Visiheel displaying the bright yellow fluid. While Grandmama performed staggering jumps and dunks in her AeroJams, Johnson narrated: "There was an old lady who lived in a shoe. A fresh little crib, you know, and brand spankin' new. And that shoe let her do things that no man could do."

In March of 1992, another campaign with 30-second spots featured both KJ and Grandmama in a "Hairdryer" episode. Sitting under a hairdryer, Grandmama bragged to her manicurist about how she "dissed Kevin Johnson" and "practically knocked him into the past tense." After quick shots of Johnson practicing in his new Accelerator III shoes with REACT Juice, he barged into the beauty salon to challenge his foe. The ad built off the original Grandmama commercial, which won several advertising awards, including the New England Broadcasters Association (NEBA) 1992 Best Produced Television Commercial, and was selected as one of "Adweek's Best Spots of 1992."

Another commercial introduced a new line of Converse high performance basketball shoes designed for tough outdoor playing.

Converse Tar Max were created with exceptionally durable Tar Max outsoles and water resistant leather uppers. The commercial was shot at night, on site at the Dallas outdoor court where Larry Johnson first learned to play the game. The entire take is filmed in black and white except for the flashing of black, red, and yellow outsoles of the shoes. After slam dunking the ball Johnson says, "Still the same. Nothing changes, man, nothing except maybe the game gets meaner and shoes get tougher."

## Brand Appraisal

From its early days as a basketball shoe innovator, Converse grew into one of the world's largest manufacturers of athletic footwear. Over the years, the brand adapted to changing market trends, as evidenced in its repositioning of the classic Chuck Taylor All Star from a basketball shoe to a fashion-oriented shoe. After the 1980s, however, the brand faced unprecedented competition and experienced drastic losses in market share. Yet Converse entered the 1990s with financial hope, as its parent company emerged from bankruptcy and its new line of high-performance shoes attracted both consumers and advertising professionals. From canvas and rubber sneakers for barnstorming teams to computer-designed footwear promoted by multi-million dollar endorsements and marketing budgets, Converse had adapted to the changing needs of athletes and consumers alike. Though the brand had slipped to roughly 3.9 percent of the athletic footwear category by 1991, it had the experience, design expertise, and growing marketing skills to become an offensive player in the increasingly competitive leagues of athletic shoe manufacturers.

## Further Reading:

Converse Inc. Press Kit, North Reading: Converse Inc., 1993.

Bidlake, Suzanne, "Converse Steps Away From Plan to Launch Across Europe; Athletic Footwear Manufacturer," *Marketing Publications Ltd.* (England), April 19, 1990, p. 2.

Carter, Leon H., "Timeout; Bird Won't Fly From Converse," *Newsday,* July 26, 1992, p. 19.

"Converse and 'Grandmama' Hoop-It-Up For the First Time in Boston," *PR Newswire,* July 16, 1993.

"Converse Basketball Goes Global With NBA Stars," *PR Newswire,* July 7, 1993.

"Converse Launches Environmental Program With the Windstar Foundation," *PR Newswire,* June 27, 1991.

"Converse Seizes 100 Pairs on N.C. Fakes, Goes to Court," *Footwear News,* August 13, 1984, p. 20.

Farley, Maggie, and Bob Ryan, "Magic Kicking Converse," *Boston Globe,* July 23, 1992, p. 45; "The $25 Million Heist; Ingalls' Biggest Ad Account Gets Away," *Boston Globe,* July 12, 1992, p. 45.

Jankowski, Dianna, "Boston Expo Crowd Belies Running's Decline," *Footwear News,* April 22, 1985; "Converse Lab Tackles Many Problems," *Footwear News,* November 12, 1984, p. 28.

"Kevin Johnson Demands Grudge Match With Grandmama and Larry Johnson Puts the Rock in the Hole in Converse TV Ads," *PR Newswire,* March 8, 1993.

Lee, Sharon, "Converse Shoots for Fashion," *Footwear News,* March 5, 1990, p. 34.

Palmer, Thomas, "If Converse Can't Pay, Will Its Stars Leave?" *Boston Globe,* March 9, 1991, p. 15.

Rattray, Jim, "Converse Sues Magic Johnson," *United Press International, BC Cycle,* December 4, 1987.

Rifkin, Glenn, "The Machines of a New Sole," *New York Times,* February 10, 1993, p. D7.

"Spreading the Action; Converse Betting on Magic Ads—$10 million Worth," *Footwear News,* February 12, 1990, p. 106.

Vartan, Vartanig G., "A Brisk Pace Is Set by Nike," *New York Times,* January 21, 1986, p. D12.

Wessling, Jack, "Converse Improves Productivity," *Footwear News,* February 13, 1984, p. 126; "Converse Inks Big Name in College Basketball," *Footwear News,* January 21, 1985, p. 33.

Yerton, Stewart, "Dream Job With the Dream Team," *American Lawyer,* September 1992, p. 40.

*—Kerstan Cohen*

# COPPERTONE®

# Coppertone®

Coppertone, the leading brand of suntan lotion, has been a major presence in the American sun care market since the 1950s. Now a part of the Schering-Plough Healthcare Products line, it began as a product to help sun bathers achieve a fashionable, dark tan. Over the years, due to recent discoveries about the role of sun exposure in skin cancer, it has evolved into a necessary health care item. Coppertone has been an innovative brand, pioneering many off-shoots of the original product, including a sunless tanning cream in the 1960s, special children's products in the 1980s, and sun blocks for athletes in the 1990s. Moreover, Coppertone researchers worked with the Food and Drug Administration in the 1970s to determine industry-wide standards for Sun Protection Factor (SPF) numbers that inform consumers of the sunscreen strength of various tanning products. Sun care products marketed under the Coppertone name range from highly protective sun blocks to instant indoor tan lotions to classic tan promotion lotions.

## Brand Origins

Coppertone was developed by Benjamin Green, a Miami Beach pharmacist. Located in a prime sunbather's haven, Green noticed the variety of homemade substances that tourists used on their skin. He decided to make a packaged suntan lotion for this market. He experimented with cocoa butter cooked in his wife's granite coffee pot, and used his own bald head as his testing ground. In 1944 he came out with what he called Coppertone Suntan Cream. The bottles bore an Indian chief logo and the slogan "Don't be a paleface." The next year, Green produced Coppertone Suntan Oil as well. In 1950 he sold his business to three partners, C.E. Clowe, George U. Robinson, and R. Ernest Nitzche. They formed Douglas Laboratories, then incorporated as the Coppertone Sales Corporation.

## Early Advertising

One of the most notable achievements of the Coppertone Sales Corp., was the creation of the "Little Miss Coppertone" logo. This image was created in 1953 by a Manhattan commercial artist, Joyce Ballantyne, in collaboration with the Miami advertising agency Tally Embry. Ballantyne created a drawing of a little girl in pigtails turning in surprise as a black cocker spaniel tugs at her shorts. Her half-bared bottom is white, showing by contrast how deep and dark her suntan is. Next to her was the slogan "Don't be a paleface!" This drawing soon appeared on a 50-foot wide billboard on the side of Miami's downtown Parkleigh Hotel. Other signs followed and eventually became Miami landmarks.

In 1962 Miami Commissioner Alice Wainwright compiled a list of "distasteful" billboards that should be torn down and included the downtown Coppertone sign on her tally. Though the sign survived the Commissioner's wrath, Coppertone's little girl had become a local joke—the "moon over Miami." Bad weather had at times managed to ruin Little Miss Coppertone's scanty clothes, when storms ripped her towel off the billboard. This left her bare bottom shining over Interstate 95. The little girl logo was used in television advertising as well. An animated version of her appeared at the end of a 1965 commercial. This ad also featured actress Jodie Foster, then three years old.

The little girl logo disappeared from Coppertone consumer advertising between the years 1979 to 1987. Researchers had uncovered some of the ill effects of tanning, especially for children, and Coppertone's parent company felt that the Little Miss Coppertone image was inconsistent with the brand's new, more health-conscious approach. In 1991 executives at Schering-Plough, Coppertone's parent, decided to tear down the Miami billboards. They were surprised to find that the "distasteful" signs had completely endeared themselves to the Miami community. The local preservation society rallied to protest the company's decision. The little girl had become a piece of Americana, and Miami did not want to let her go. Schering-Plough acquiesced, and the billboards remained. The Little Miss Coppertone logo was revived for the 1987 launch of Coppertone's Water Babies children's line, and a 1991 television commercial used a four-year-old actress to portray her. A scene with the live actress accompanied by a black spaniel dissolved into the illustration. Remarkably, in 40 years the illustration has not been altered or updated.

The other notable advertising used by the Coppertone Sales Corp., was the slogan "Tan, don't burn . . . use Coppertone." This line was first used in 1955, and, along with "Don't be a paleface," became a classic Coppertone motto.

## Brand Development

In 1957 Plough, Inc., a Memphis, Tennessee-based health care products company, acquired the Coppertone Sales Corp. Under the new company, the Coppertone brand received a boost in advertising expenditure. Bikinis were in fashion at the time, and a

## AT A GLANCE

**C**oppertone brand first appeared as Coppertone Suntan Cream, invented by Benjamin Green, a Miami Beach pharmacist, in 1944; a company to market his product was incorporated circa 1950 as the Coppertone Sales Corp.; company and brand acquired in 1957 by Plough, Inc., (now Schering-Plough Corp.).

**Performance:** *Market share*—33.5% (top share) of the sun care category.

**Major competitor:** Tanning Research Laboratories' Hawaiian Tropic; Procter & Gamble's Bain de Soleil.

**Advertising:** *Agency*—Messner, Vetere, Berger, McNamee, Schmetterer Agency, New York, 1985—. *Major campaign*—New product introduction for Coppertone Sport, with the slogan "For those who don't take the sun lying down."

**Addresses:** *Parent company*—Schering-Plough HealthCare Products, 110 Allen Road, Liberty Corner, NJ 07938; phone: (908) 320-2011. *Ultimate parent company*—Schering-Plough Corp., One Giralda Farms, Madison, NJ 07940; phone: (201) 822-7000.

deep, dark tan was regarded as a sign of a healthy and fun-filled life. The market for tanning products grew, and Coppertone soon held more than half the market share. By 1963 Coppertone's parent company was spending more than $2.5 million in television, print, and outdoor advertising for the brand, and Coppertone had 56 percent of the total suntan lotion market. Its net sales were reported to be 150 percent higher than those of its nearest competitor, Sea & Ski. By the next year, Coppertone had increased ad spending to over $3 million, and by 1967, the figure was up to $4 million. Various advertisements featured bikini-clad actresses such as Mitzi Gaynor, while others cited a Miami test that indicated that Coppertone gave a faster, deeper tan than its competitors.

The brand began to proliferate as well, with new products such as Coppertone Lipkote and Noskote for face protection, and Royal Blend, a beauty tanning lotion. The first sunless tanner, Coppertone's QT, was introduced in 1960. In children's products, Coppertone marketed Shades, for children with sensitive skin, and Coppertone Baby Tan. This last was to counter the popularity of Johnson & Johnson's baby oil as a suntan preparation. Most of these products were geared towards consumers who wanted to maximize their suntan.

### Changing Market Conditions

Coppertone had taken an early lead in the growing suntan lotion market, and for many years the brand's only major competitor was Sea & Ski. But by the mid-1970s, a number of other companies were marketing sun care products. Coppertone's market share remained far larger than any other brand's, but still fell from over 50 percent to an estimated 35 percent by 1978. The public's attitude toward tanning was changing as well, as links between over-exposure to the sun and skin cancer were widely reported. By 1978, though 35 percent of the American sun care market was devoted to conventional tanning lotions like the original Coppertone, and 25 percent went to high tanners like Royal Blend, another 25 percent of the market was made up of sunscreens. Rather than promote tanning, a sunscreen works to shield the skin from harmful sun rays. Coppertone introduced a new high

tanner, Tropical Blend, in 1975, but clearly sunscreen products were increasing in popularity at a rapid pace.

Coppertone established a Solar Research Center in 1974 to work with the Food & Drug Administration on classifying the strength of sunscreen products. The FDA soon adopted the Sun Protection Factor (SPF) numbers. The SPF number indicated how much longer a person could remain in the sun using a particular sunscreen than when using no protection—an SPF of 4 meant four times longer, and SPF 15 meant a person could stay out in the sun fifteen times longer. Coppertone began labelling its products with SPF numbers in 1977. Two years later, sunscreens made up almost 30 percent of the American suncare market. Though most of Coppertone's sales came from its original lotion, the introduction of its own competitive sunscreen products helped the brand boost its market share from an estimated high 30th percentile in 1978 to over 50 percent by 1979. Coppertone's new Super Shade went up against established sunscreens such as Westwood Pharmaceuticals' PreSun brand and Johnson & Johnson's Sundown, but backed by the Coppertone name and Coppertone's $4 million ad budget, it sold well.

Coppertone continued to develop its sunscreen line, though it came out with other kinds of tanning products as well. Several years of consumer research led Coppertone to develop a nongreasy tanning formula for the face, called For Faces Only. This came out in 1980, in SPFs ranging from 2 up to 15, the highest then allowed. Coppertone also reformulated two of its traditional products, Dark Tanning Oil and Tropical Blend, into lighter, less greasy forms. In spite of the market's overall move toward higher protection formulas, Coppertone's basic advertising still stressed the beauty of a dark tan. "Flash 'em a Coppertone tan" was the theme used in Coppertone's print and television ads beginning in 1979. These advertisements featured young, athletic-looking people showing off their bronzed skins. But by 1982, Coppertone had secured 16 percent of the sunscreen market, due mostly to the success of its Shade products. For its product line overall, Coppertone was far and away the market leader, with approximately 40 percent of the total market. Its next closest competitor was Tanning Research Laboratories' Hawaiian Tropic, with an estimated 23 percent.

### Product Changes

By the mid-1980s, the skincare market's tilt toward sunscreens and sunblocks was even more pronounced. Some other products also sold well compared to traditional tanning lotions. Upscale brands with sophisticated packaging gained in appeal, and one of these, Charles of the Ritz Group's Bain de Soleil, claimed to be the number two seller after Coppertone in 1985. (Tanning Research Laboratories' Hawaiian Tropic also claimed to hold the number two spot.) Other upscale tanning lotions with French names, such as Lancome Conquette du Soleil, and tan lotions put out by Estee Lauder and Clinique, gained footholds in the high end of the suncare market. As a result, the market grew increasingly segmented, as traditional tanning lotions, sunscreens, and "fashion" tanners became more discrete categories.

Sunscreens became even more potent. Though the FDA only claimed effectiveness for SPFs up to 15, more brands came out with ever higher numbers. One new brand in 1987 came out under the name Skin Cancer Garde, with the ominous slogan "The sun. A matter of life and death." But even Skin Cancer Garde's SPF of

33 was not the highest on the market. Two brands had SPFs as high as 34 and 36, and Coppertone added an SPF of 25 to its line.

With the market increasingly segmented and competitive, Coppertone changed its product line. What had been called Coppertone Super Shade up until 1985 was reformulated and repackaged as a complete line of waterproof sunscreen called Shade. Marketers at Plough, Coppertone's parent, seemed to think this gave them a better guarantee of growth in the sunscreen end of the market, which was posting double-digit sales gains averaging 15 percent a year in the mid-1980s. At the same time, traditional Coppertone lotion kept pace with the trend toward higher SPFs, and when Shade went up to SPF 30, regular Coppertone could be found with SPF 30+.

To keep up with the fashion end of the tanning market, Coppertone added several new products. 1986 saw the debut of Coppertone Dark Tanning Mousse, Coppertone Gel, and Coppertone After Sun Moisturizer. When Estee Lauder and Clinique began marketing tan accelerators, Coppertone too came out with its Coppertone Natural Tan Accelerator. Also in 1986 the original Coppertone formula was updated. Aloe and vitamin E, popular moisturizer ingredients, were added, the lotion became more waterproof, and its packaging was given new graphics.

Coppertone created a new suncare market category in 1987 with the introduction of its Water Babies line. Water Babies was formulated specifically for children's sensitive skin, was waterproof, and designed not to wash off during swimming or play. Originally offered with an SPF of 15, by 1993 the line went all the way up to SPF 45. Water Babies carried the Coppertone name and the famous Little Miss Coppertone logo on its packaging. But to further expand the children's category, Coppertone came out with another waterproof pre-teen formula in 1993, called Coppertone Kids Sunblock Lotion. Other brands followed with children's sunblocks such as Bain de Soleil Kids Sport, but by 1992, Water Babies was the number one children's suncare product.

As some consumers wished to get their tans with no exposure to the sun whatsoever, Coppertone had sold QT, a sunless tanner, since 1960. In 1991 sunless tanners suddenly became the hottest sales item in the entire suncare market. Besides QT, Coppertone sold a line of Coppertone Sunless Tanning Lotion, and this line received a large proportion of the brand's early 1990s advertising. Coppertone Sport premiered in 1991, spurring imitation by other brands. Targeted for athletes, Coppertone Sport got the bulk of Coppertone's advertising for 1993 under the theme "For those who don't take the sun lying down." Coppertone Sport was meant to reach young men aged 18–30, who wouldn't usually bother with toiletries. Coppertone Sport was one indication of how much the brand had changed its image. Originally a product that enhanced the acquisition of a beautiful tan, its latest message was

clearly that every one needed protection from the sun's harmful rays.

## Performance Appraisal

Though Coppertone has been a major brand for a relatively brief 40 years, it has seen extreme changes in the use and appeal of suntan lotions. Where the brand was originally the best seller among only two major brands, by the 1990s it had a host of competitors, each vying to come out with some new twist on the skincare scene. Its early major competitor, Sea & Ski, saw its market share drop until it lagged far behind newer brands. Though Coppertone held roughly a third of the tanning skincare market in the 1990s, as opposed to over half in its heyday, it has always remained in the top spot. Coppertone's makers have proven to be a flexible force in the marketplace, always ready with innovative products that either start trends or successfully follow the advances of other brands. Coppertone's variety of products, which include special face formulas, children's formulas, an entire range of SPFs, sports products, fashion products, accelerators, super sunblocks, and more, let the company cover every niche of the highly segmented suncare market. Schering-Plough has long shown an eagerness to explore growth areas with its Coppertone line while simultaneously pleasing a loyal core of consumers. In this way the brand has successfully met the challenges of a rapidly shifting and highly competitive market. Coppertone has proven its adaptability, and will likely continue to be a major force in the future of suncare products.

## Further Reading:

Appelbaum, Cara, "Coppertone Says Good-Bye to Summer," *Adweek's Marketing Week*, September 16, 1991, p. 6; "Coppertone Targets Jocks," *Adweek's Marketing Week*, December 10, 1990, p. 10.

"Coppertone Plans $3,000,000 Drive to Reach Tanners," *Advertising Age*, June 15, 1964, p. 42.

"Miami's Icon of Kitsch Faces Toppling Over Bottom Line," *New York Times*, August 25, 1991, p. 28 (L).

Miller, Cyndee, "Tan Fans Shun Sun for that Bottled Bronze Look," *Marketing News*, August 3, 1992, p. 2.

"Plough Summer Push for Suntan Products is Largest to Date," *Advertising Age*, June 17, 1968, p. 2.

Sloan, Pat, "Plough Aims to Shade Rivals," *Advertising Age*, January 1, 1985, p. 56; "Spotlight Falls on Sunscreen," *Advertising Age*, June 11, 1979, p. 3; "Suncare '82 Outlook Partly Cloudy," *Advertising Age*, February 15, 1982, p. 45; "Suncare Arena Heats Up," *Advertising Age*, March 3, 1980, p. 2; "Suncare Marketers Raise Their Screens," *Advertising Age*, May 25, 1987, p. 1; " 'Sunless' Tans Shine," *Advertising Age*, March 16, 1992, p. 16; "This Year It's Tan, Not Toasted," *Advertising Age*, April 18, 1988, p. 4.

*Sun Care Information Guide 1993*, Schering-Plough HealthCare Products, 1993.

—*A. Woodward*

# COVER GIRL®

# COVERGIRL

Ask any woman born in the last 30 years what the name Cover Girl means and she's likely to hum the brand's memorable theme song: "Clean makeup, Cover Girl's the one for clean makeup. . . . " Equally memorable have been the brand's advertisements featuring such famous, fresh-faced, squeaky clean spokesmodels as Cybil Shepherd, Cheryl Tiegs, and Christie Brinkley, who were used specifically to exemplify "natural beauty." The makers of Cover Girl cosmetics have spent a fortune to ensure that their brand is considered the cleanest, purest, and most natural. Their efforts have succeeded, making Cover Girl the top-selling makeup brand, and the company hopes the new "cover girls" for the 1990s will keep the brand going strong.

## Brand Origins

Cover Girl makeup uses as a base the Noxzema cold cream formula developed by Baltimore pharmacist George Bunting in 1914. Bunting's cold cream was a mixture of clove, eucalyptus, menthol, and camphor. After a customer told him it cured his eczema, Bunting named the product Noxzema from the phrase "No-eczema." In 1917 Bunting formed the Noxzema Chemical Company to sell Noxzema, and marketed it first as a cure for sunburn. Soon, the problems it was thought to help multiplied: acne, chapped skin, tired feet, and facial blemishes were all to be relieved by the application of some Noxzema. At one time, Noxzema was even touted as a shaving cream. By 1920, demand for Noxzema prompted Bunting to establish his first factory in Baltimore. Three years later, his company turned a profit. By 1925 Noxzema sales reached $100,000, and the brand was sold nationally.

Noxzema print ads featured testimonials from housewives and nurses who praised the brand's medicinal properties. Noxzema salesmen emphasized the brand's purity by actually tasting the cream in front of customers and rubbing it into their suits to prove Noxzema was safe and greaseless. The brand gained the national spotlight when explorer Richard E. Byrd took a case of Noxzema to the South Pole in 1929 and tested it under severe weather conditions. Bunting's company supplied soldiers with little blue jars of Noxzema during World War II. Brand recognition through radio advertising spots also helped boost sales to $3 million by 1944.

In 1950 a company employee mentioned to a Noxzema executive that she washed her face regularly with the brand because it didn't irritate or dry her face like soap did. An idea was born, and advertising touted Noxzema as a replacement for soap. The company capitalized on consumer's loyalty to the brand by adding new products that used Noxzema as a base: Noxzema Complexion Lotion, shave cream and mentholated shave cream, brushless lather, and cold cream.

In 1961 the company continued this trend when it introduced a line of makeup that contained Noxzema as a key ingredient. Bunting did not live to see this major expansion of the Noxzema brand name, having died in 1959 at the age of 89. His son and grandson would head the company through the next two decades and see this new product to fruition. Noxzema named its new makeup line Cover Girl and backed it with an advertising blitz that featured famous American models.

## "Who's That Girl?"

Cover Girl was initially advertised as "good for the skin." Beautiful models like Cheryl Tiegs were used to represent the brand, and their clean, fresh appearance underscored the company's claim that by wearing Cover Girl liquid and powder makeup, women looked "natural." Sales by the end of 1961 exceeded company projections by 74 percent. In 1964 Cover Girl lipstick was introduced and started the brand expansion that resulted in more than 500 items being offered by the 1990s. The Noxzema Chemical Company in 1966 changed its name to the Noxell Company and moved its headquarters to the Baltimore suburbs.

Choosing the right models to represent Cover Girl has always been of the utmost importance to the brand's advertising experts. In fact, using a model as a spokesperson to sell a product line was deemed revolutionary in the 1960s. Cover Girl used professional models as beauty experts and photographed them on fake magazine covers taking breaks between television commercials. According to Robert E. Sullivan, Jr., in *Vogue,* one of the first commercials featured a 1961 television announcer saying, "It's lovely Cover Girl Jane Rylander using Cover Girl Clean Make-Up, medicated so it keeps your puffs germ free." Rylander would then say "Noxzema makes it, so I trust it."

Noxell began using New York-based Lintas to choose models for its advertising campaigns. The agency usually chose from a bevy of so-called supermodels who were predominantly fair-

## AT A GLANCE

**C**over Girl brand of cosmetics created in 1961 by the Noxzema Chemical Company of Baltimore, using Noxzema as its key ingredient; company became Noxell Corporation in 1966; Procter & Gamble acquired Noxell Corp. in 1989.

**Performance:** *Market share*—21.5% of the overall cosmetics market, ranking first in terms of second quarter 1992 sales at all outlets; 55% of the face makeup market; 31% of the lipstick market; 15% of the color cosmetics category, second after Maybelline; 0.4% of the nonwhite or ethnic cosmetic market. *Sales*—$370 million (1991).

**Major competitor:** Maybelline; also Revlon (Revlon's Almay brand), Max Factor, L'Oreal, and Avon.

**Advertising:** *Agency*—Grey Advertising, New York, NY, 1989. *Major campaign*—Niki Taylor, as the new cover girl promoting the brand's "Clean Makeup"; also, African-American models Lana Ogilvie and Tyra as the Cover Girls promoting the new foundation shades for women of color. Other campaign slogans: "Where naturally beautiful skin begins"; "Cover Girl: Redefining Beautiful."

**Addresses:** *Parent company*—Procter & Gamble Cosmetic & Fragrance Products, 11050 York Rd., Hunt Valley, MD 21030; phone: (410) 785-7300. *Ultimate parent company*—Procter & Gamble Company, One Procter & Gamble Plaza, Cincinnati, OH 45202; phone: (513) 983-1100; fax: (513) 562-2062.

haired and blue-eyed. Recalled Dick Huebner, "keeper of the flame in terms of image" at Lintas, in an *AdWeek* interview, "We could call Ford [Models] and say, 'Send us all your pretty blondes.' "

Although models helped place Cover Girl make-up in the forefront of the cosmetics market, many a model's career took off after she was proclaimed a true Cover Girl. The brand's spokesmodels have included Jennifer O'Neill, Carol Alt, Christie Brinkley, Cybil Shepherd, and Rachel Hunter. Cheryl Tiegs reigned as the Cover Girl for an unprecedented 19 years.

Lintas held the Cover Girl account for 25 years until 1989 when Procter & Gamble took over Noxell and switched to Grey Advertising of New York. Huebner also switched to Grey and has been in charge of finding "the right face" ever since. He has also tried to steer Cover Girl through the tides of change. In the 1980s, in an attempt to find cover girls who represented a wider spectrum of American women, Huebner began looking beyond the traditional blue-eyed blond Cover Girl, and chose in 1992 models Niki Taylor, who at 17 is the youngest Cover Girl ever, and Lana Ogilvie, the first African-American Cover Girl under contract; 1993 additions include African-American model Tyra, and Patricia Velasquez, the first Hispanic Cover Girl under contract. Women who represent Cover Girl are "considered accessible, both literally and figuratively, to American women," Cathy Taylor reported in *AdWeek.* Yet they must still "fit the brand's squeaky clean, mass merchandise image."

### Commercial Successes

Cover Girl continued to enjoy wide success, especially as a relatively inexpensive makeup for teens and young adult women. The brand became the foundation of Noxell's business. Throughout the 1970s, Noxell built upon the brand's success by steadily

introducing new Cover Girl products, including Cover Girl Eyes eye-shadows in 1971; Super Sheer Liquid Powder Blush in 1972; MoistureWear Make-up and Moisture Cover Stick in 1973; Long'n Lush Mascara and Soft Line Eyeliner in 1974; 9-Hour Eye Polish (liquid eye shadow) and Shiny LipSlicks in 1975; Oil-Control Liquid Make-up and MoistureWear Make-up in 1976; Cover Girl Nailslicks in 1977; and in 1979, Professional Mascara.

Cover Girl continued to experience 11 percent growth in sales annually until the late 1980s, placing it ahead of Revlon and Maybelline as the leader of the $2.6 million mass-market segment in 1986. However, increasing competition slowed the brand's growth to about 7 percent in 1988, *Business Week* reported. Noxell's 1986 introduction of Clarion, a hypoallergenic makeup was intended to pick up the slack from slowed Cover Girl sales, but that brand had to be revamped. Demographic changes also forced a revision of the Cover Girl lines. The declining population of teens hurt the brand, yet the company hoped to reach the burgeoning market of older and working women. In an attempt to keep earnings strong, the company began marketing to these groups by introducing Cover Girl's Extremely Gentle line of fragrance-free cosmetics for sensitive skin, MoistureWear, and Replenishing makeup, and by allowing its young cover girls to "age gracefully." The strategy didn't work with Cover Girl, which continued to be seen as a brand for teens and young adults.

### New Name, New Face

Procter & Gamble, the Cincinnati-based packaged-goods company, purchased Cover Girl in 1989 and continued Noxell's plan to change its image from a budget makeup for teens to a makeup used by all kinds of women. Procter & Gamble increased its Cover Girl budget to $38 million in 1990 and continued Noxell's plan to repackage many products in sleek compacts and eye shadow containers stamped with a textured imprint. At the time of the acquisition, Cover Girl was introducing its first fragrance, NaVy, which Procter & Gamble backed with a $14 million rollout. The fragrance line was later expanded to include a new perfume called Incognito.

In 1992 Cover Girl, joining the trend of mass-marketed makeup firms trying to reach the ethnic or nonwhite market, unveiled its shade extensions for Women of Color. Cover Girl hired African-American model Lana Ogilvie to represent the line extension, which included pressed powders and foundations in ten shades complimenting African-American skin; three shades of finishing powders; and various shades of blush, eye shadows, lipsticks, and nail enamels.

The new shades for Women of Color were packaged in the same Cover Girl packaging and consisted of 72 new units for face, eyes, lips, and nails. *Women's Wear Daily* quoted industry experts as estimating that the new African-American makeup line would account for ten percent of total Cover Girl sales in the first year after introduction. "It's hard to say when you get into the color cosmetics area which shade is exclusively for a black, Hispanic, or Caucasian woman. We have always had a lot of crossover. Dark skinned women have always used Cover Girl products, like our mascara, and lighter skinned woman might like the darker shades for the evening." said A. Randy Floss, advertising manager for Cover Girl, to *Women's Wear Daily.*

In the next year, Procter & Gamble launched Cover Girl Clean SkinCare, hoping younger makeup users would be attracted to the brand early on and then stick with it throughout their lives. This new ten-product line of astringents, toners, moisturizers, anti-acne pads, and hydro-gels marked the brand's single largest new product introduction in 16 years. Procter & Gamble backed it with an $11 million advertising campaign. Each item was color-coded (green for oily skin, blue for dry skin, etc.) to help consumers determine which product fit their facial needs. Ad manager Floss stated in company press materials that "with imagery and advertising that have consistently focused on the 'clean and natural' look, it's logical for Cover Girl to develop a line of products that addresses the state of a woman's skin before she applies her make-up."

In early 1993 Cover Girl also revamped its line of mascaras, which included a nine-product line of waterproof, thick lash, non-smudging, clear mascara and a formula for women with sensitive eyes.

## Future Growth

Cover Girl has always been perceived as an All-American makeup and, in fact, only experienced 15 percent of its sales outside the United States, most of them in Canada. However, Procter & Gamble's 1991 acquisition of Revlon's Max Factor makeup lines and the German Betrix cosmetics for $1.1 billion, gave the company an entry into foreign markets and a way to push the Cover Girl brand overseas. Seventy-five percent of Max Factor's sales were in Europe and Japan. Betrix, with $200 million in sales, was the leading makeup brand in Germany, reported *AdWeek's Marketing Week*. The purchases of these companies were said to have given Procter & Gamble more than 30 percent of the $1.9 billion cosmetics market.

Cover Girl cosmetics ranks as the number one cosmetics brand over such competitors as Revlon and Maybelline. Procter & Gamble also outspends its competitors in terms of advertising and has thus helped Cover Girl keep its lead despite a worldwide recession. Cover Girl has stayed ahead of the game by diversifying its brand line to offer something for almost every woman.

Ethnic and teen beauty products are projected as the fastest growing areas in the cosmetics industry, and Cover Girl is planning to capitalize on it. In fact, Cover Girl has made a habit of purchasing particular magazine issues—such as *YM*'s "Love Special" issue—hoping to position itself as a young woman's confi-

dant and friend. Cover Girl has a strong presence in the supermarket and drugstore chains, which have traditionally sold less expensive cosmetics, making Cover Girl much more accessible than high-end brands like L'Oreal and Clinique.

According to Cover Girl press materials, in 1991, women spent a total of $2.3 billion on skin care products, $1 billion of which came from supermarket and mass merchandiser purchases. The skin care market is likely to grow an estimated six percent annually by 1995, and Procter & Gamble anticipates Cover Girl growing along with it.

## Further Reading:

Appelbaum, Cara, "Cover Girl, Maybelline: On the Ethnic Edge," *WWD,* October 9, 1992, p. 8; "A New World of Beauty for P&G," *AdWeek's Marketing Week,* April 15, 1991, p. 4; " 'Mr. Maybelline' Gives Cover Girl the Edge," *AdWeek's Marketing Week,* October 22, 1990, p. 6.

"Cover Girl to Market New Line," *Supermarket News,* November 23, 1992, p. 35.

Dunkin, Amy, and Christine Dugas, "How Cosmetics Makers Are Touching Up Their Strategies," *Business Week,* September 23, 1985, p. 66.

Huhn, Mary, "Cover Girl to Sponsor a Special June Issue of *YM* on Topic of Relationships," *MediaWeek,* April 26, 1993, p. 4.

Kagan, Cara A., "Cover Girl Turns a Page," *WWD,* November 6, 1992, p. 6.

Moskowitz, Milton, Robert Levering, and Michael Katz, *Everybody's Business,* New York: Doubleday, 1990, p. 161.

Muirhead, Greg, "Revlon, P&G Plan Ethnic Cosmetics," *Supermarket News,* April 6, 1992, p. 32.

Nayyar, Seema, "Beauty's Marketing Makeover," *AdWeek's Superbrands* supplement, October 1992, p. 64; "The Cash Flows in Cosmetics," *AdWeek's Marketing Week,* March 23, 1992, p. 22; "Cover Girl Aims to Capture Teen Set," *BrandWeek,* September 28, 1992, p. 2.

Nayyar, Seema, and Cathy Taylor, "P&G Unveils Cover Girl Ethnic Line," *AdWeek's Marketing Week,* June 22, 1992, p. 1.

Rice, Faye, "Making Millions on Women Over 30," *Fortune,* May 25, 1987, p. 75.

Riddle, Judith Springer, "Ethnic Marketing: Mining the Non-white Markets," *BrandWeek,* April 12, 1993, p. 29.

Taylor, Cathy, "The Beholder's Eye," *AdWeek,* November 9, 1992, p. 24.

Weber, Joseph, "Why Noxell Is Touching Up its Latest Creation," *Business Week,* July 11, 1988, p. 92.

"Winnowing the Winners in Personal Care," *Fortune,* March 18, 1985, p. 177.

*—Evelyn Dorman*

# CRAYOLA®

**Crayola**®

"Fun, creative, colorful." These are the words that Binney & Smith Inc. used to describe both its historic, top-selling brand, the Crayola crayon, and the company's product line of the early 1990s. Children have been drawing with Crayola's eight original colors since 1903. In 1993 Binney & Smith produced more than two billion crayons in 112 colors for customers in 80 countries worldwide.

Binney & Smith ensured the success of Crayola crayons by listening to consumers, continually updating the product, refining production processes for maximum efficiency, and aggressively marketing the crayons. Recognized by 99 percent of Americans, according to the brochure *Binney & Smith,* the Crayola brand name has accumulated enough marketing power to support an entire line of Crayola products, including markers, colored pencils, chalk, paints, clay, and assorted "creative development products." Such brand expansion and development became crucial for Binney & Smith's continued growth during the 1970s and 1980s as they found themselves dominating the U.S. crayon market and entangled in two art-supply price fixing lawsuits. Fun is serious business at Binney & Smith, now owned by Hallmark Cards, Inc. the company's continued growth depends on its creative use of the Crayola brand name and its ability to keep re-inventing the primary Crayola product, the Crayola crayon, to make it perennially colorful for both new and old users.

## Nineteenth-Century Origins

While the Crayola crayon was born in 1903, the roots of the Crayola lie in a firm created in the mid-nineteenth century. In 1864 Joseph Binney founded the Peekskill Chemical Company in Peekskill, New York, to produce hardwood charcoal and lampblack, a black pigment. After some success, Binney opened an office in New York City in 1880 and invited his son, Edwin Binney, and his nephew, C. Harold Smith, to join the business. Five years later, Joseph Binney retired and left the operations to the younger generation. At that time, Edwin Binney and C. Harold Smith formed a partnership named Binney & Smith and immediately expanded their organization and product line. They introduced shoe polish and printing ink in 1885 and, in 1900, bought a water-powered stone mill along the Bushkill Creek, near Easton, Pennsylvania, and the region's slate quarries, to produce slate pencils for schools.

Once in the educational market, Binney & Smith discovered the children's art niche by listening to teachers. Teachers wanted chalk with less dust and affordable, quality crayons. Binney & Smith responded; chemists at the company soon developed An-Du-Septic Dustless Chalk, which won a gold medal for excellence at the 1902 St. Louis Exposition. Chemists had also created a new, carbon black wax crayon to mark crates and barrels. The new technology, they reasoned, could be applied to crayons for children.

Realizing that the crayons might be chewed—or even swallowed—researchers developed synthetic, nontoxic pigments to replace toxic organic colorings. To match the color uniformity and consistency of fine imported crayons, small batches of liquid crayons—a blend of certain amounts of wax and pigment—were hand mixed after precise measurements were taken. The production process was complete after the crayons were pulled from their molds and labelled. In 1903 the new crayons were ready for the market, yet they were without a name.

This final step was taken care of by Mrs. Alice Stead Binney, Edwin Binney's wife. A former schoolteacher, Alice Binney was excited by the affordable, high-quality color crayons. She invented the name "Crayola" for them by combining the French word *craie* (chalk or stick of color) and "ola," from "oleaginous" or oily. Crayola crayons were available in 1903 for five cents per box. They came in eight basic colors: black, blue, brown, green, orange, red, violet, and yellow. This blend of pigment and oil-derived paraffin wax gave countless schoolchildren the opportunity to draw colorful pictures.

## Robust Expansion at Mid-Century

By the end of World War II, Crayola crayons were so popular that Binney & Smith saw an opportunity to diversify into related products under the Crayola brand name. Crayola poster, finger, and watercolor paints, and Crayola modelling clay, paste, glue, and new assortments of chalk were all introduced in 1948. Crayola crayons themselves also received a high-octane boost; 40 more colors were added. Now color offerings included Apricot, Bittersweet, Magenta, Mahogany, Maize, Pine Green, Sea Green, and Turquoise Blue. Binney & Smith was thus prepared for the post-World War II baby boom. Beginning in the 1950s, Crayola crayons and Crayola products began a sharp rise in sales that

## AT A GLANCE

**C**rayola brand of crayons developed in 1903 in Easton, Pennsylvania, by Edwin Binney and C. Harold Smith, owners of Binney & Smith Inc.; Binney & Smith became a division of Hallmark Cards, Inc., 1984.

**Performance:** *Market share*—80% (top share) of U.S. crayon market (1981). *Sales*—$44.0 million (1981)

**Major competitor:** None.

**Advertising:** *Agency*—Avrett, Free & Ginsberg, New York, NY. *Major campaign*—A grandmother, mother, and daughter draw together to the theme, "Crayola: Drawing families together for generations."

**Addresses:** *Parent company*—Binney & Smith Inc., 1100 Church Lane, Easton, PA 18042; phone: (215) 253-6271. *Ultimate parent company*—Hallmark Cards, Inc., 2501 McGee Trafficway, Box 419580, Kansas City, MO 64141; phone: (816) 274-5111.

would fuel further Crayola development and marketing in the United States and overseas.

To support sales, Binney & Smith needed a center for its broadening operations. In 1952 the company opened a manufacturing and distribution center in Winfield, Kansas. In 1958 manufacturing plants sprang up in Ontario, Canada, and Bedford, England. By 1975 facilities in Mexico, which sold crayons, chalk, and tempera paint, and the Netherlands, mainly producing chalk, were added. Crayola became an internationally recognized brand name, yet the Crayola crayon, accounting for 87 percent of the $13.8 million in 1963's sales, still was the heart of the enterprise.

In 1958 the yellow and green 64-box of Crayola crayons with the built-in sharpener—now a recognized classic—was introduced. Colors such as Copper, Lavender, Mulberry, Raw Umber, and Sky Blue joined the previous 48. Several old colors were also renamed: in 1958 Prussian Blue was renamed "Midnight Blue" in response to teachers' requests, while in 1962 Flesh was renamed Peach. (In *Crayola Crayon Color History,* Binney & Smith explained that the latter change arose voluntarily and "partially as a result of the U.S. Civil Rights Movement.")

### Tough 1970s Market

"Almost two decades ago, Binney & Smith was profiting handsomely from a post-World War II baby boom that provided built-in growth for its mainstay Crayola crayons," *Business Week* wrote in 1981. In the 1970s, however, Crayola's market declined along with the birth rate, the profit margin shrank as raw material prices rose, and larger corporations eyed Binney & Smith as a potential takeover target. The glory days of the early- and mid-century were gone.

The company responded by pressing for further international growth, updating its distribution system, modifying Crayola color names, and diversifying into related industries. The 1975 expansion into Mexico and the Netherlands proved crucial for Crayola's continued sales growth given a declining U.S. market. In the United States, Crayola prices were raised, warehouses were sold off, production and purchasing were computerized and made more efficient, and the hiring of summer production help leveled off.

These changes adapted Crayola production and sales for both a tougher U.S. market and a shifting world market.

In 1972 Crayola gained eight new colors including Atomic Tangerine, Outrageous Orange, Screamin' Green, Shocking Pink, and Wild Watermelon. With new colors and an adapted Crayola production and distribution system, Binney & Smith was able to slow the tide of profit declines and even demonstrate periodic profit increases. Still, the company wished to reduce its reliance on Crayola as a sole supplier of revenue. Binney & Smith had begun this process in 1964 by diversifying into artists' paints when it acquired Permanent Pigments Inc., a Cincinnati company, and its Liquitex acrylic paints. In 1975 the company bought the manufacturing rights to Silly Putty, a popular art toy for children.

### Ambitious 1980s and 1990s

Chief Executive Officer Jack F. Kofoed sought to bolster Crayola recognition while taking advantage of its popularity. Five products were introduced in 1981, followed by additional ones in succeeding years. In 1981 a Crayola Fun Center in-store display—holding 37 Crayola-brand items—was introduced for large retailers such as K-Mart, Woolworth, and Toys 'R' Us. The same year Crayola crayon sales accounted for less than 45 percent of sales, down from 87 percent in 1963. Yet earnings were up 50 percent over 1980, to a record $8.8 million. In 1982 Binney & Smith needed a $15 million capacity expansion project at its home plant in Easton, Pennsylvania, just to keep up with orders for Crayola Fun Center products.

Not everything was upbeat in the early 1980s. In 1980 Binney & Smith and two other companies, the Joseph Dixon Crucible Co. and the Milton Bradley Co., were named in a lawsuit accusing them of fixing the prices of educational art materials. Although Binney & Smith did not admit guilt, the company paid a $1 million settlement and was barred, along with the other companies, from any future price fixing. Between 1979 and 1980, art supply dealers filed a class-action lawsuit against the three companies and the American Art Clay Co. In 1983 Binney & Smith paid $5 million to the dealers to settle that suit.

Diversity was a chief goal at Binney & Smith, and in 1984 Binney & Smith accepted an offer to become a subsidiary of Hallmark Cards, Inc., the world's largest greeting card manufacturer. In addition to diversification and intensive domestic marketing, international marketing of Crayola also took high priority at Binney & Smith. By 1987 the company added a manufacturing facility in Australia to its existing plants in the United States, Canada, Mexico, and England. Licensee arrangements enabled Crayola crayons to be produced in the Philippines and Japan. By 1993, Binney & Smith could boast that its products were sold in over 80 countries worldwide, with sales and distribution centers in Australia, Belgium, Canada, France, Germany, Mexico, Spain, and the United Kingdom.

Entering the 1990s, the Crayola crayon was still being reinvented and intensively marketed in the United States. In 1990 Binney & Smith retired eight Crayola colors and replaced them with more vivid hues such as Fuchsia and Wild Strawberry. Out of nostalgia, a group called RUMPS (Raw Umber and Maize Preservation Society) protested the replacement. Binney & Smith leaked word of the group to the press, which covered the story and brought significant free advertising to the Crayola brand. One year later, Binney & Smith re-issued the colors in a special commemorative tin case as "classics"; the eight-crayon package, including notes on the crayons and their retirement, was available during the Christmas season of 1991 at $6.99 each.

In 1992 Crayola crayons became available in yet another eight-pack, the "Global Pack" of multicultural colors, according to the *New York Times*. This new offering was in response to teacher requests for a full range of skin-toned colors available for children to draw pictures of themselves. In 1993 the Crayola "Big Box" was launched in celebration of the Crayola brand's 90th birthday. The new box contained 96 colors, including 16 new ones.

Central to the aggressive marketing of Crayola in the early 1990s has been a series of advertising and promotional campaigns. Binney & Smith launched an MTV-style campaign featuring the pop group Milli Vanilli. (The campaign backfired when Milli Vanilli was caught up in scandal, but the ad nonetheless represented an attempt to re-associate Crayolas with contemporary youth.) In 1992 Crayola ran a television advertisement featuring a grandmother, mother, and daughter drawing faces together with Crayolas. A Crayola coupon and coloring book distributed to 54 million households also provided a significant boost to 20 Crayola brands, including the Crayola crayon.

Passing 90 years of age in 1993, Crayola crayons have become a worldwide brand with significant nostalgic value in the United States. Since Binney & Smith has continually updated the brand and found new ways to make the Crayola brand name profitable, the Crayola crayon should continue to thrive well into its second century.

## Further Reading:

*Adweek's Marketing Week,* June 24, 1991, p. 9; November 26, 1990, p. 5; September 3, 1990, p. 8.

*Binney & Smith,* Easton, PA: Binney & Smith Inc., 1992.

*Brandweek,* March 22, 1993, p. 25.

"Crayolas Color the World," *Global Trade Executive* February 1987, pp. 10, 16.

*Crayola Crayon Color History,* Easton, PA: Binney & Smith Inc., 1993.

Flax, Steven, "The Greening of Crayola," *Forbes,* April 12, 1982, pp. 190, 192.

"Higher Tabs Help Binney & Smith Earnings Enjoy a Brighter Hue," *Barron's,* November 10, 1975, p. 62.

*History and Development of Crayons,* Easton, PA: Binney & Smith Inc., 1993.

Morgan, Hal, *Symbols of America,* New York: Penguin Books, 1986.

*New York Times,* January 16, 1992, p. C3; October 3, 1991, p. C9.

"Redrawing the Crayola Image," *Business Week,* August 31, 1981, p. 83.

Roberts, Jeff, "Irv Hockaday Is Leaving His Mark on Hallmark: Diversity," *Business Week,* November 12, 1984, pp. 73, 76.

*Wall Street Journal,* June 27, 1983, p. 15; July 11, 1980, p. 21.

*—Nicholas Patti*

# CREST®

Procter & Gamble Company's Crest is the best selling brand of toothpaste in the United States. Formulated with a unique blend of abrasives, detergents, and other ingredients, Crest has a distinctive flavor and special chemical qualities that inhibit tooth decay. This has earned the brand recognition from the American Dental Association, which allows Procter & Gamble to feature the organization's seal of acceptance on Crest's labels.

The quality of the toothpaste is less a factor in removing decay-causing plaque than the physical action of brushing. Toothpaste provides a detergent medium for suspending the dislodged plaque so that it may be flushed out of the mouth. Crest was created not to destroy plaque or make brushing any easier, but to provide longer term protection of teeth by making the enamel, or outer layer, of teeth more resistant to decay. During the 1930s, scientists discovered that fluoride compounds appeared to harden the enamel of teeth. This made it more difficult for the acids produced by plaque to eat away at teeth and cause cavities. The commercial application of fluoride to toothpaste, however, did not occur until 1955.

## Brand Origins

Early toothpastes were palatable powdered cleansers containing mint extracts that left the mouth feeling fresh. Baking soda was often used for brushing teeth and proved useful in neutralizing acids from plaque. Baking soda, however, was only helpful as long as it remained in the mouth.

Procter & Gamble first entered the dentifrice market in 1938, when it introduced a brushing liquid called Teel, which proved unsuccessful. Consumers preferred Colgate toothpaste because it was soft, foamy, and minty. In 1952 Procter & Gamble marketed its own dental cream called Gleem. Like other toothpaste, Gleem was little more than a medium for brushing, but it had all the qualities of Colgate and captured second place in the market. Procter & Gamble, however, wanted a market leader.

With the discovery of its medicinal qualities, Procter & Gamble decided to develop a new brand of toothpaste containing fluoride. Rather than merely promote the unique fluoride quality, Procter & Gamble sought scientific affirmation that the brand was superior to others. In developing the new brand, the company faced a dilemma over which type of fluoride compound to use, sodium fluoride or stannous fluoride. Eventually, Procter & Gamble settled upon the latter after lab tests indicated that it would provide some measurable benefits. The company then sponsored several months of independent laboratory research at the University of Indiana under Dr. Joseph Muhler.

This testing was very costly and required a tremendous investment in time. Procter & Gamble supported nine years of research, paying for 11,000 dental examinations and 64,000 x-rays. When it was finally completed, the research proved that the stannous fluoride toothpaste, which Procter & Gamble named Crest, did reduce tooth decay with regular brushing and dental check-ups. The findings also confirmed that the benefits were as strong in adults as in children.

## Early Marketing Strategy

The evidence garnered from the laboratory experiments formed the crux of Procter & Gamble's marketing strategy for Crest. More than just another toothpaste, Crest was positioned as a scientific breakthrough, a technological achievement that rendered all other toothpastes obsolete. Crest was also promoted as a supplement, rather than a substitute for fluoridated water. The unique formula for Crest, which contained 0.4 percent stannous fluoride, was patented under the name trademarked Fluoristan.

The very first advertisements for Crest appeared in a series called *Milestones in Modern Medicine*. One proclaimed "Triumph over Tooth Decay," stating that Crest "actually strengthens tooth enamel to lock out tooth decay." Accompanying copy explained the chemical qualities of fluoride in great detail. The ads emphasized the scientific origin of Crest and the conclusive results of tests on the brand. Further copy invoked the endorsement of dentists who had professional experience with the amazing qualities of Crest.

## Health Claims

The claims made by Procter & Gamble in relation to the superiority of Crest were substantiated by tests that were paid for by the company. While few could challenge the results (the tests were scientifically valid), Crest still held only about ten percent of the toothpaste market in 1960, and was in third place behind Colgate and its sister brand Gleem. Meanwhile, Colgate-Palmolive introduced its own stannous fluoride brand, Cue. Similar to Crest, Cue grew steadily in market share and began to chip away at Crest's position in the market.

## AT A GLANCE

Crest brand of toothpaste with stannous fluoride introduced by Procter & Gamble Company, 1955; gained recognition for prevention of tooth decay by American Dental Association, 1960; began advertising ADA acceptance, 1964; in 1981 a gel formula was launched, while original was reformulated using sodium fluoride; Tartar Control Crest and pump dispenser marketed in 1985.

*Performance:* *Market share*—36% (top share) of the toothpaste market. *Sales*—$340 million.

*Major competitor:* Colgate; also Close-Up and Aquafresh.

*Advertising:* *Agency*—D'Arcy Masius Benton & Bowles/New York. *Major campaign*—"Fighting cavities is the whole idea behind Crest."

*Addresses:* *Parent company*—Procter & Gamble Company, 1 Procter & Gamble Plaza, Cincinnati, OH 45202; phone: (513) 983-1100; fax: (513) 983-7847.

Procter & Gamble fought back by leading a quiet campaign of negotiation with the highest authority on dentistry in the United States, the American Dental Association (ADA). A group of experts and lawyers from Procter & Gamble lobbied the ADA for months, providing scientific data on Crest and hoping to win an official endorsement of the brand. In 1960 the ADA formally proclaimed Crest effective in reducing tooth decay, when used in conjunction with regular brushing and dental examinations. While the ADA took no compensation for its endorsement, it did not come without costs for Procter & Gamble, which spent tremendous sums on its studies and lobbying efforts. Nevertheless, the investment paid off handsomely. The ADA's public endorsement was worth millions of dollars in added sales of Crest.

In 1988 the United States Food & Drug Administration charged several dentifrice manufacturers with making unfounded medical claims. Several brands claimed to combat gingivitis, a form of gum disease. While Procter & Gamble was not cited, it had claimed that Crest could help prevent gingivitis. In light of the FDA action, Procter & Gamble voluntarily removed the reference to gingivitis control from packages of Crest.

## Brand Development

Crest is typical of Procter & Gamble brands in that it was meticulously researched before its introduction, had a highly specific quality in fluoride, and was vigorously promoted when it hit the market. Still, it could muster no better than a ten percent share of the market. After the ADA endorsement in 1960, however, sales of Crest increased dramatically. By 1962 it led all brands—including Colgate, Pepsodent, and Ipana—with 33 percent of the market. Now competitors such as Colgate-Palmolive and Lever Brothers were knocking on the ADA's door with bundles of test results.

In time, Cue, Bristol-Myers's Fact, and Lever Brothers's Super Stripe won ADA acceptance, but supporting clinical evidence was inconclusive and none were allowed to advertise the endorsement. As a result these brands were unable to overcome Crest's commanding lead in the marketplace, and all were eventually phased out. The company completely missed the emergence of flashy cosmetic toothpastes. While highly abrasive to the enamel, brands such as Ultra-Brite captured a small but significant share of the market during the late 1960s.

In 1969, after years of preparation, arch-rival Colgate-Palmolive received identical approval from the American Dental Association. Nevertheless, Crest remained the market leader throughout the remainder of the 1960s and 1970s. In 1974, Lever Brothers introduced Close-Up, a breath freshening red gel toothpaste that quickly gained popularity. In 1979 another new toothpaste entered the market, robbing Crest and Colgate of a significant amount of market share. The new brand, Aquafresh, was a striped opaque white and blue gel. Its selling point was that it was two toothpastes in one, a breath freshener like Aim and Close-Up, and a fluoride toothpaste like Crest and Colgate.

The Crest formula was changed in 1981, when the company dropped the stannous fluoride compound in favor of sodium fluoride. Stannous fluoride was found to be partially unstable due to the abrasives in use at the time. Because it was likely to break down after only months, older tubes of Crest were much less effective. Sodium fluoride, however, was highly stable and would provide a longer shelf life for the brand. Procter & Gamble also changed the abrasive component of Crest to silica. In tests, this indicated that sodium fluoride was better able to react with tooth surfaces to resist decay. The new sodium fluoride brand was called Advanced Formula Crest. Clinical studies showed that the new formula was almost twice as effective against cavities as original Crest.

## Marketing Strategy

The ADA endorsement became the centerpiece of Crest's advertising campaign. As the only toothpaste officially accepted by the ADA, Crest could be called the best toothpaste on the market. The entire series of ads developed by Benson & Bowles, the advertising agency responsible for Crest since its inception, drew heavily on the ADA endorsement. Procter & Gamble began featuring the ADA's seal of approval on packages of Crest in 1964 when the toothpaste received this distinction.

Crest advertising was carried mostly on television until 1968, when the company made a major move back into magazine buys. The decision was made in part to appeal more strongly to magazine-reading mothers who made purchasing decisions for the family, and partly to cross promote ads in other media, such as television. A similar mix has been used since that time. The ads themselves are strictly message-oriented, repeating the brand's strong qualities and the ADA endorsement.

When Procter & Gamble introduced its revolutionary new toothpaste, it had two packaging objectives. The first was to use a tube whose neck would not discolor toothpaste that spilled over onto the nozzle after use. The second goal was to develop a unique color scheme.

In solving the first problem, Procter & Gamble used a wax lined collapsible lead tube coupled with a white plastic nozzle (which had been featured on tubes of Macleans toothpaste for some years). The nozzle was fitted to the tube with a small flange. Wax from the tube lining closed the remaining gap, preventing the contents from spilling out around the nozzle. After filling, the tube was rolled up at the opposite end and pressed, fusing the lead and keeping the tube from unravelling.

The tube was painted all white and used alternating red and blue letters to spell Crest. The rolled end of the tube had a triangle in which "with fluoristan" was printed. The design was repeated on the cardboard box that held the tube. This basic design has remained virtually unchanged since Crest was introduced.

Crest was exclusively a tube toothpaste until 1985. The previous year, Colgate introduced a pump package that stood upright and extruded toothpaste with a small finger pump. Procter & Gamble had difficulty getting the Crest pump to market, enabling Colgate and other trendy pump brands to snap up much of the $150 million pump toothpaste segment. In addition, Crest's pump had the same problem as all other pump brands: it wasted a significant amount of product. Finally responding to consumer complaints about the wasteful pump, Procter & Gamble rolled out a Neat Squeeze tube. The upright container had fewer parts and allowed nearly all of the contents to be used. Furthermore, it required 40 percent less packaging than the pump. Reduction of costly packaging overhead was a major goal of Procter & Gamble.

## Brand Growth

The first extension of Crest came in 1966 when Procter & Gamble test marketed a mint flavored Crest in Columbus, Houston, and Seattle. The mint flavor appealed to a wider variety of people who were attracted by the refreshing qualities of other minty brands. National roll-out of mint Crest occurred in 1967. Later, the rise of gel toothpastes led Procter & Gamble to introduce Crest Gel in October of 1981. This new version forestalled a slow loss of Crest's market share to Close-Up, Aim, and Aqua-fresh.

A month after the introduction of a cool mint gel variation in February of 1985, Procter & Gamble rolled out Tartar Control Crest. Tartar, a hard naturally occurring substance that builds up along the gumline, does not cause cavities like plaque, but can lead to gum disease. Crest's Tartar Control, which also received ADA acceptance, was developed to combat the buildup of tartar. The brand was introduced nationally in 1985. Tartar Control Crest helped boost the market share of the entire Crest line from a sagging 29 percent to nearly 40 percent within a year, despite cannibalization of the flagship brand. Claiming superior qualities, a rival tartar fighter from Colgate-Palmolive entered the market in 1987, but was unable to stem Crest's lead.

In August of 1987 the company introduced Crest for Kids, with a flavor that appealed to children. The selling point to mothers was that, because it tastes better, kids will brush more. Procter & Gamble also extended the Crest name to a mouthwash product called Crest Tartar Control Mouth Rinse. While effective, the product failed to catch on in test markets. Such product extensions held off Colgate for several years, but by 1989 Crest had fallen to a 36 percent market share, while its competitor had climbed from 20 to 28.

Crest is available in many countries in Europe and Asia, but it is not as dominant a brand as it is in the United States. Still, Procter & Gamble pursues growth markets wherever they emerge. The collapse of communist governments in Eastern Europe provided just such an opportunity in 1991. The company purchased a few local producers serving Poland, Czechoslovakia, and Hungary and began production of a variety of products. In whatever direction the brand evolves, however, Procter & Gamble may be expected to maintain vigorous promotion and placement of Crest. Therefore Crest is likely to remain the market leader for many years.

## Further Reading:

"Adult Approach," *Chemical Week,* April 2, 1955, p. 80.

"Colgate Closes Gap with Crest," *Advertising Age,* February 13, 1989, p. 12.

"Colgate Puts the Squeeze on Crest," *Business Week,* August 19, 1985, p. 40.

"Colgate Sees Itself Ousting Crest as No. 1," *Advertising Age,* January 13, 1969, p. 8.

"Crest, Aim jump on pump segment," *Advertising Age,* September 24, 1984, p. 1.

"Crest Gets an Aqua-Fresh Cavity," *Advertising Age,* December 17, 1979, p. 1.

"Crest History," Cincinnati, OH: Procter & Gamble Company.

"Dentifrice Marketers Bare Teeth," *Advertising Age,* March 16, 1981, p. 1.

"Dentists Endorse Colgate Formula," *Business Week,* October 11, 1969, p. 46.

"FDA Report Gives Nod to Therapeutic Claims for Crest, Colgate with MFP," *Advertising Age,* July 27, 1970, p. 6.

"FDA Snaps at Oral-Care Ads," *Advertising Age,* October 10, 1988, p. 3.

"New Toothpaste Hits Copy-Crest," *Advertising Age,* August 26, 1955, p. 45.

"P&G Gives Crest a 'Neat Squeeze,' " *Adweek's Marketing Week,* April 22, 1991, p. 7.

"P&G Marches into Eastern Europe," *Advertising Age,* September 28, 1991.

"P&G pumps Crest with new promotion," *Advertising Age,* p. 8.

"P&G Rides Crest With Leverage," *Adweek's Marketing Week,* October 5, 1987, p. 58.

"P&G's Crest Gets Modernity, Dimension in Magazines," *Advertising Age,* October 20, 1969, p. 156.

"Procter & Gamble," *Forbes,* April 15, 1969, p. 36.

19.

"Pure White Crest," *Modern Packaging,* October 1956, p. 126.

"Toothpaste Ads Vie for Favor on Flavor," *Advertising Age,* August 1, 1966, p. 2.

"Toothpaste Tempest," *Chemical Week,* August 22, 1964, p. 53.

*—John Simley*

# DANSKIN®

DANSKIN

The logo for Danskin—a silhouette of a woman in a balletic mid-leap—ably personifies the line of fashionable athletic wear that has been the choice of active women for decades. Danskin, in fact, "is to leotards and tights what Coke is to soft drinks and Kleenex is to paper tissues—a brand name with an impressive consumer recognition rating," according to *Forbes* reporter Robert T. Grieves. As a leading brand name in its field, Danskin has become popular enough to eclipse its original market and move into mainstream "streetwear." The line's versatility is reflected in its best-known slogan, "Danskin—Not Just for Dancing."

## Brand Origins

Despite its successful crossover into streetwear, the brand, held by Danskin, Inc., was originally created for dancing. In 1882, brothers Joel and Benson Goodman founded a dry goods business on Walker Street in New York City. Goodman Brothers dealt in retail hosiery, leatherwear and apparel, but always bought their merchandise from other manufacturers. In 1923, when the Goodmans' sons took over the business, mass-produced knit hosiery was more popular than ever and the sons bought into the Triumph Hosiery textile mill in Philadelphia.

This acquisition enabled Goodman Brothers to produce their own line—called Triumph Hosiery—which proved so profitable that the original textile mill was expanded into a new facility in York, Pennsylvania, in 1927. The fine cotton and silk brands continued to flourish throughout the 1930s and 1940s, and Triumph Hosiery was especially valued among actors and dancers for its ability to hold its shape through the rigors of dancing. The brand was also notable for producing hard-to-fit sizes.

When nylon was introduced to the hosiery field in the early 1950s, better-fitting, long-lasting stretch tights could be produced in mass numbers for an appreciative public that was tired of tights with baggy knees and saggy ankles. Triumph's version of this close-fitting hosiery was given a new name—Danskin—during that time. The name, an amalgam of "dance" and "skin," caught the attention of dancers and other athletes. Throughout the first half of the century, professional dance outfits were made of cottons that tended to hinder free movement, but that changed when Danskin produced its first line of stretch nylon leotards in the 1950s. In addition to tights, Danskin garments provided just the right support for a dancer's kicks, spins and stretches.

In its early years Danskin built a reputation for innovation, introducing such new looks as the fish-net stocking, and the now-classic "Ballet Pink" and "Theatrical Pink" stagewear colors. On the heels of its success with leotards, Danskin expanded its product line in the 1960s with knitwear and sweaters, and by the mid-1960s Danskin was a leading brand in children's clothing. In a 1988 interview with *Forbes* magazine, Danskin president, Podie Lynch, commented that the popularity of the brand's children's wear has grown because "every little girl wants to be a ballerina."

In the early 1970s, Danskin introduced a landmark product—the bodysuit. The unitard came in a range of colors and styles and allowed dancers and athletes unprecedented freedom of movement. The sudden burst of popularity in women's gymnastics in the early 1970s was largely responsible for the dramatic success of the Danskin bodysuit. Sales of Danskin brand products rose dramatically in response to the growing demand for increasingly sophisticated athletic wear. The company has kept a continuous interest in the lucrative business of producing athletic wear for gymnasts, sponsoring the Gymnastrada Skills Test program in 1978. The program, designed to help young gymnasts chart their progress, had an enrollment of more than 250,000. In 1978, Danskin's continuing leadership in its field was recognized when the company won a special Coty Award, the fashion industry's highest honor. The award acknowledged Danskin's efforts in total body dressing.

In the 1980s, Danskin found itself facing increasing competition as more brands began producing leotards, bodysuits and tights for the burgeoning market of aerobics exercise wear. Profit slowed as consumers tested each new entry in the field; but Danskin's well-regarded reputation proved a saving grace. As the dancewear market "topped out" in the mid-1980s, Danskin retained its position as a brand leader, while lesser-known brands languished. During this period, Danskin introduced its first line of combination swimsuits/leotards. Constructed of a strong and flexible nylon/spandex blend, the one-piece "Maillot" suits provided both style and support for virtually any athletic need—gymnastics, dance, diving, aerobics, or running.

Since then, Danskin has remained a vital name in the fitness industry, providing a full line of activewear in cotton, nylon, and Supplex blends, often in eye-catching colors and patterns. Such

## AT A GLANCE

**D**anskin brand of hosiery and leotards introduced as Triumph Hosiery in New York City by Goodman Brothers in 1923; company incorporated as Triumph Hosiery, 1923; changed name to Danskin, Inc., early 1950s; acquired by International Playtex, Inc., 1980; bought by investor Esmark Group, 1986, and Danskin, Inc., became a wholly owned subsidiary of Esmark Inc.

**Performance:** *Market share*—50% of women's activewear category (1988). *Sales*—$134.5 million (company-wide).

**Major competitor:** Weekend Exercise Company brands; also Gilda Marx, Nike, and Reebok.

**Advertising:** *Agency*—Pagano Schenck & Kay, Rhode Island, since 1993. *Major campaign*—"Danskin—Not Just for Dancing"; "All the World's a Stage."

**Addresses:** *Parent company*—Danskin, Inc., 305 State St., York, PA 17403; phone: (717) 846-4874. *Ultimate parent company*—Esmark Inc., 111 West 40th St., New York, NY 10018; phone: (212) 764-4630; fax: (212) 764-7265.

diversity made possible the company's successful foray into streetwear—a Danskin leotard, for instance, could easily double as a tank top to layer under a sweater, and bring truth to the brand's "Not Just for Dancing" theme.

### Advertising and Promotion

The slogans "Not Just for Dancing" and "All the World's a Stage" boosted Danskin brand recognition in the 1990s. Simple print ads displaying Danskin products have proven most successful in athletic and mainstream women's magazines. In fact, a marketing survey quoted by *Forbes* revealed that almost half of the women who purchase Danskin products are more interested in fashionable apparel than athletic wear. Of the wide range of Danskin styles and colors available, the most popular color has been black and the highest-selling products have been basic leotard/tights combinations, comprising approximately 70 percent of the brand's net sales.

Sales promotion efforts for Danskin have included the company's sponsorship of "Team Danskin," a consortium of notable female athletes from various sports (including volleyball, body-building, climbing and fencing). Members of Team Danskin appeared in ads and mailers wearing the company's athletic wear in public meets and served as consultants and spokeswomen. Such well-known names as Olympic gymnast Kim Zmeskal, ballet dancer Darci Kistler, and two-time Olympic gold medal figure skater Katarina Witt have all been a part of Team Danskin. Witt, in fact, went on to design and endorse her own line of Danskin wearables. A photograph of Team Danskin was produced as a poster and made available to the company's 3,000 authorized retailers for in-store display.

In another cross-promotional effort, the company introduced "Danskin Women's Triathlon Series" in 1990. The first event of its kind, the Series invited women to compete in traditional triathlon sports—marathon running, long-distance swimming and biking. In three years the Series expanded from three to seven U.S. cities, and an international meet in Germany.

### The Business End

Since the brand's inception, Danskin had provided a wide variety of workout and fashion apparel to meet particular needs. By the 1990s, the company had solidified its product line into three distinct categories: the overall "Danskin" label for mainstream dance and streetwear, fashion tights, and sportswear ensembles; "Danskin Pro," the Team Danskin-endorsed line of high-performance wear for such sports as gymnastics, skating, track, volleyball, water sports and sport climbing; and "Danskin Plus," for larger-sized women. In addition, Danskin selectively licensed out its name for products like outerwear, underwear and socks.

While Danskin got its start as a family-run business, in 1980 the company joined International Playtex, Inc., then a subsidiary of the Beatrice Corporation. By 1986 Playtex divided its stock into Esmark Inc.; and in June of that year a group of investors purchased Esmark. The Esmark group, operates three divisions: Danskin, Dance France, and Pennaco hosiery. In addition to Danskin garments, other products in the corporate lineup include Shape, Round-the-Clock, Anne Klein, and Givenchy hosiery.

With its estimated 85 percent awareness rating, Danskin was one of the best-recognized names in its field in the early 1990s. The company finished fiscal 1993 with $134.5 million in sales, up almost four percent from the previous year. This rise in sales was partially attributed to the introduction of a new latex fabric called Supplex (a trademark of Du Pont) in several Danskin garments.

In the early 1990s, Danskin was the only major bodywear/ exercise apparel vendor that manufactured a majority of its merchandise in the United States. Approximately 800 employees designed, produced and distributed more than 90 percent of the Danskin line from the company's facility in York, Pennsylvania.

Danskin brand products are represented in some 13,000 stores altogether, with the biggest market continuing to be in sporting-goods and dance specialty stores, and company-owned outlet venues. In fiscal 1993 department store sales accounted for a full 28 percent of Danskin's wholesale revenue; international sales, while accounting for only 10 percent of total sales, also enjoyed significant increases in the early 1990s.

### Plans for Future Growth

Danskin's long-range plans, as outlined by CEO Byron Hero in January of 1993 in *Apparel Industry Magazine,* were to "take advantage of the tremendous growth opportunities in licensing, by developing the existing brands, and by continuing to build its international business." The company also intended to improve its distribution by expanding wholesale distribution networks and increasing the number of retail outlets and full-price stores. Since the public offering in August of 1992, Danskin has been encouraged by the performance of its Shape line of value-priced activewear, expected to have 32 retail outlet stores and one full-price flagship store opened by the end of fiscal 1994.

### Further Reading:

Danskin Inc. company prospectus, New York: Danskin, Inc., August 19, 1992.

Danskin press releases, New York: Danskin, Inc.

Grieves, Robert T., ''Stretching the Image,'' *Forbes,* April 18, 1988, p. 99.

Moore, Lila, ''Danskin Leaps Back From the Bunk,'' *Apparel Industry Magazine,* January 1993, p. 24.

*—Susan Salter*

# DIAL®

Soapmaking has changed little since the Phoenicians boiled goat fat and caustic wood ashes to make the first batch over 2,500 years ago. Cleaning effectiveness in modern soap still relies on a fat and an alkaline substance, a recipe that usually consists of beef tallow or vegetable oil and lye. The key ingredient of fat made soapmaking a natural business line extension for meatpacker Armour & Company. The company achieved diversification by using almost every part of their stock of hogs and cows, including the animals' fat for soap. Armour tapped the emerging public awareness and concern for hygiene with the introduction of Dial soap in 1948. Dial, later a product of The Dial Corp, was the first soap to have a germicide in its formula; thus, giving it effective deodorant properties. By the 1990s, consumers bought more than a million bars of Dial soap every day of the year.

Two key events simplified the soap manufacturing process. The first was the invention of the Le Blanc process for making caustic soda, and the other was the destruction during World War II of European plants that used the traditional, slow and cumbersome kettle soap process. The latter event was an impetus for Armour & Company to develop a unique new product to gain a larger share of the growing post-war soap market. An employee suggested a revolutionary but timely idea—a soap that contained deodorant. Personal hygiene was just beginning to be an important social concern; while soaps of the time promised to clean, deodorant protection was still a novel idea.

"The Story of Dial Soap; Forty-Five Years of Success" recounts how an Armour laboratory chemist added to the soap a germicidal ingredient similar to one that a German chemist had tried to promote in the United States. When the product was tested, company researchers found that soap containing the germicide reduced bacteria on skin by approximately 95 percent, while soaps without the germicide reduced bacteria by only 15 percent. Since it was known that bacteria caused body odor, researchers determined that the germicide was the ingredient they needed for deodorant soap. Armour chemists used the germicide and created a soap that was nonirritating to even the most sensitive skin. With the addition of a distinctive fragrance, the very first effective deodorant soap was ready to hit the market. Armour reviewed more than 700 potential names for their product. The search ended with the selection of a name denoting the soap's ability to provide 24-hour protection from body-odor causing bacteria—Dial. The

brand's first slogan, "Round the Clock Protection," reflected the soap's name and its claims.

## Fragrant Launch

Dial soap had a fragrant send-off in a full-page advertisement in a 1948 edition of the *Chicago Tribune*. The ad invited readers to smell the newspaper because, "this very page carries Dial's refreshing fragrance! Hold it close to your face—you'll find pleasant proof that Dial smells good!" Chicagoans that morning could indeed smell the distinctive scent of brand-new Dial soap. By nightfall one of Chicago's leading department stores sold 4,000 bars. It is unknown whether newspaper employees added the perfume to the ink supply for the presses or, as one anecdote says, four mischievous Armour employees dumped the fragrance into the supply. Either way, the Dial ad was probably the first instance of a perfumed advertisement.

Because the soap's manufacturer desired consistency in its advertising, it used the same basic theme for Dial over the years. The famous Dial slogan, "Aren't you glad you use Dial? Don't you wish everybody did?" originated in 1953. It is one of the best-known company slogans in the history of advertising and remained in use by The Dial Corp 40 years later.

## Brand Progress

In the 1950s, scientists discovered a new class of chemicals called bacteriostats that controlled bacteria that caused sweat to break down into malodorous components; the chemicals stayed on skin to provide long-lasting protection. Of these antimicrobial agents, hexachlorophene was the most important one used in soaps, including Dial. However, in the early 1970s, the U.S. Food and Drug Administration (FDA) raised questions about the safety and efficacy of antimicrobial agents. The inquiry led to the banning of hexachlorophene and the chemical TBS, although other antimicrobial agents remained in use. The soap industry defeated a proposal by the FDA requiring that labels of soaps containing antimicrobial agents include a warning against their use on infants.

In spite of the FDA action, Armour still produced a Dial soap with a distinctive fragrance and germ-killing properties. These qualities led the brand to become the top selling deodorant soap in the United States in terms of both dollars and ounces in 1963. Dial continued to hold that position into the 1990s. Initially, Lever

## AT A GLANCE

**D**ial brand of soap created in 1948 by Armour & Company; brand sold to Greyhound Corp., 1970; Greyhound renamed Greyhound Dial, 1990, then The Dial Corp, 1991.

**Performance:** *Market share*—12% (top share of deodorant soaps; number two of bar soaps) of toilet soap category. *Sales*—$160 million.

**Major competitor:** Lever 2000; also Lifebuoy, Ivory, Safeguard, Coast, Shield, Zest, and Irish Spring.

**Advertising:** *Agency*—DDB Needham, Chicago, IL. *Major campaign*—"Aren't you glad you use Dial? Don't you wish everyone did?"

**Addresses:** *Parent company*—The Dial Corp, Consumer Products Group, Dial Tower, 1850 N. Central Ave., Phoenix, AZ 85077; phone: (602) 207-5338; fax: (602) 207-5900.

Brothers' Lifebuoy deodorant soap was perceived as Dial's only competition in the soap market. However, Dial did not build sales by going head-to-head with Lifebuoy; instead, it built sales in the segment of the soap market that was dominated by complexion bars like Lux and Camay. The brand capitalized on consumer interest in the new underarm deodorant and antiperspirant products being heavily advertised. In fact, the company eventually extended the Dial brand to underarm deodorant products.

Greyhound Corp. bought Armour & Company and its Dial brand in 1970. The brand was the foundation on which the company began a transformation in the mid-1980s from a corporation providing transportation services to one selling exclusively consumer goods and services in the 1990s. Corporate name changes paralleled the transformation and built on the company's only well-known consumer product, Dial soap. The company became Greyhound Dial in 1990 and was renamed The Dial Corp in 1991.

The new owner of Dial carefully monitored consumers, educated sales staff and retailers, and observed and tested the brand against other brands. By 1977, Dial had more than 20 percent of the bar soap market, and in 1979 cut into the market share of the Coast brand and the perennial leader, Ivory.

The company made product improvements and developed brand extensions to further increase market share. It relaunched its gold Dial soap in 1984 with a new formula, which purportedly killed twice as many odor-causing bacteria than the previous version, and introduced Dial Deodorant White bar soap. In 1990, Mountain Fresh Dial came out, targeting those consumers who liked a high fragrance level in soap in addition to deodorant protection. The soap bars were packaged in foil wrappers and marketed at young adult men between the ages of 18 and 39.

Liquid Dial was yet another brand extension. Liquid soap first appeared in the 1940s, but because of its harsh chemistry it was positioned for the industrial and institutional markets. Detergent improvements in the 1950s and 1960s eventually led to the introduction in the late 1970s of a liquid soap brand positioned for general in-home use. Liqua 4 was Dial's first liquid soap product for the consumer market. The product was packaged in a plastic container shaped like a bar of soap; however, the product was unpopular because consumers found it difficult to squeeze the package to dispense the soap.

However, decorator pump dispensers and milder formulas improved sales of liquid soap during the next decade. The increasing popularity of the products attracted Greyhound's attention and the company reentered the liquid soap market in 1987 with Liquid Dial. In the March 1992 issue of *Soap—Cosmetics—Chemical Specialties* Nancy Dedera, director of public relations, commented, "Since we are soap experts, we wanted to pursue the idea of liquid soap, and since we are germ killing antibacterial experts, we decided to come up with a liquid soap of a kind never available to consumers." A team of scientists and soap manufacturing specialists experimented with dozens of formulas over two years before deciding on a chemical makeup that included special moisturizers and the antibacterial ingredient Triclosan. The liquid killed germs on contact and had a residual effect that prevented the growth of germs after being rinsed off.

Several antibacterial liquid soaps had been developed for doctors, nurses, and other health care professionals, but they were too harsh for the general population. Consequently, Liquid Dial fulfilled an unrecognized need in the consumer market. Liquid Dial's container, amber gold color, perfume, good feel, and antibacterial ingredients were all popular with consumers and the product was an instant success. People used the product to fight germs and infection and to get rid of ordinary dirt, too. Many consumers wrote unsolicited letters to the company applauding Liquid Dial and suggesting additional uses for the soap, including application as a shampoo.

The product immediately became the number one antibacterial liquid hand soap on the market and took the lead in the overall liquid soap market in 1988, representing 27 percent of the more than $100 million market. *Consumer Reports* gave Liquid Dial its best rating for liquid soaps in 1990. However, the original liquid soap brand leader, Softsoap, achieved the top share again in 1991.

### Brand Outlook

In 1985, Greyhound's research and development department was revamped to permit more input from all areas of the company. To better meet consumer demands and to avoid wasting time developing products that would not sell, sales and marketing were involved in the first phase of product development. This emphasis on consumer demands is maintained by The Dial Corp as a means to compete successfully in a mature soap market that increasingly looks to segmentation to gain share.

Dial bar soap and its liquid counterpart were positioned to sustain and even increase share, particularly as the antibacterial liquid soap market expanded rapidly in the early 1990s. The brand's sales were expected to continue growing as The Dial Corp expanded distribution in foreign countries. In 1993, Europe remained an untapped market, although the company had new distribution channels in Korea and Singapore, overseas licensing agreements, and a plant in Mexico. Meanwhile, in the United States the Dial brand retained a leadership position.

### Further Reading:

Coleman, Lynn, "Promotions Hail Longevity of Camel, Dial, Chips Ahoy!" *Marketing News*, May 23, 1988, pp. 1–2.

Darconte, Lorraine, "Soap Wars: Liquids Bubble Over as Bars Begin to Slip," *Soap—Cosmetics—Chemical Specialties*, December 1990, p. 24.

Hardman, Adrienne, "Tortoise Triumphant," *Financial World*, April 13, 1993, pp. 32–34.

Hoover, Gary, editor, *Hoover's Handbook of American Business 1993,* Austin, TX: The Reference Press, Inc., 1992, p. 239.

Johnson, Bradley, "Teets Focuses Dial on Personal Care," *Advertising Age,* September 16, 1991, p. 42.

Jungerman, Eric, "Toilet Soaps: New Trends and Technologies," *Soap—Cosmetics—Chemical Specialties,* March 1985, p. 30.

Kintish, Lisa, "In a Lather: The Grab for Market Share Is Intense in the Bar and Liquid Soap Market," *Soap—Cosmetics—Chemical Specialties,* December 1992, p. 34.

Lazarus, George, "Dial Lathering Up Liquid Soap World," *Chicago Tribune,* October 7, 1988, sec. 3, p. 4.

Lundmark, Larry, "The Evolution of Liquid Soap; Bath & Spa Beauty Products," *Cosmetics and Toiletries,* December 1992, p. 49.

Morris, Gregory D. L., Peter Savage, Sophie Wilkinson, and Catherine Brady, "Soaps & Detergents," *Chemical Week,* January 18, 1989.

Rosendahl, Iris, "Soaps Are Steady Sellers in Drugstore," *Drug Topics,* September 23, 1991, p. 83.

Schisgall, Oscar, *Eyes on Tomorrow: The Evolution of Procter & Gamble,* Chicago: J. G. Ferguson Publishing Co., 1981, pp. 236–37.

Shapiro, Eben, "Dial to Concentrate on Consumer Goods," *New York Times,* October 30, 1991, sec. D, p. 4.

"Soaping Up," *Consumer Reports,* October 1990, p. 644.

*The Story of Dial Soap; Forty-Five Years of Success,* Phoenix, AZ: The Dial Corp.

Stradberg, Keith W., and Suzanne Christiansen, "Research and Development: The Roots of A Product," *Soap—Cosmetics—Chemical Specialties,* March 1992, p. 28.

"Tracing Household Product Sales," *Chemical Week,* January 24, 1979, p. 44.

Ward, Leah Beth, "Dial's Big Consumer Play: Safety in the Second Tier?" *New York Times,* July 18, 1993, p. F16.

Wilkinson, Sophie, Catherine Brady, Lisa Tantillo, Natasha Alperowicz, Emma Chynoweth, Debbie Jackson, and Lyn Tattum, "Soaps and Detergents; New Opportunities in a Mature Business," *Chemical Week,* January 31, 1990.

*—Doris Morris Maxfield*

# DIXIE® CUPS

Owned by the James River Corporation of Virginia since 1982, Dixie Cups and other Dixie brand products are among the leaders in both the consumer and commercial markets for disposable cups, plates, tableware, and other food-service products. In 1993 the James River Corporation operated ten cup and plate plants in the United States and four in Canada. A joint venture, Dixie-Benders Ltd., operates in London.

## Brand Origins

Dixie Cup, the namesake for all other Dixie brand products, traces its origins back to the early years of the 20th century and the marketing ingenuity of a Harvard University dropout by the name of Hugh Moore. In the early 1900s most commercial transportation facilities and public buildings still offered patrons free water that was drunk from tin dippers—an effective way to spread communicable diseases. Moore, a Kansas native, was horrified by the lack of public sanitation and decided that people would be willing to pay for safer drinking water once they knew as much about germs as he did.

In 1908 Moore dropped out of Harvard, and along with a fellow Kansan, Lawrence Luellen, he established the American Water Supply Company of New England. They took their idea for a water cooler that dispensed individual paper cups to New York where they met an investment banker, Edgar Marston. Marston, who had reacted the way Moore predicted when he was told about the hazards of drinking from public dippers, put the two entrepreneurs in touch with William T. Graham, president of the American Can Company. Graham agreed to invest $200,000 in their venture, which they incorporated in 1909 as the Public Cup Vendor Company. Nearly 50 years later, the American Can Company would purchase the Dixie Cup Company.

## Early Marketing

Moore and Luellen began making expensive porcelain vending machines, with separate compartments for ice, a five-gallon bottle of spring water, a stack of clean paper cups, a drain for waste water, and a receptacle for trash. Customers received five ounces of water for a penny. The cup was a clumsy flat-bottomed container with a rough brim.

Moore and Luellen set up their water coolers in public locations, such as trolley-line transfer points, and they later received the endorsement of the Anti-Saloon League, which believed that many men would settle for a cool drink of water over a tavern. Sales, however, were disappointing. Advertising urged customers to "quaff Nature's Nectar from this chalice," but the community was unwilling to pay for something they could get for free, despite its health claims.

The medical community was far more receptive, and it was a meeting between Luellen and a hospital-supply representative that suddenly changed the company's focus from selling drinking water to selling cups. Luellen learned that hospitals were looking for small paper cups to collect sputum samples. That led Moore and Luellen to consider abandoning their cumbersome water coolers and to concentrate on selling paper cups from simpler machines. Moore later said that "We had to sell the idea that drinking out of dirty glasses was dangerous."

Ironically, Moore and Luellen received their first significant support from their home state of Kansas. For years Dr. Samuel Crumbine had tried to convince the public that tuberculosis was spread by the use of communal drinking cups on passenger trains. Then in 1909 he became the Kansas state Health Officer and immediately ordered that shared drinking cups be eliminated in public places, including on all trains passing through Kansas.

Although the railroad companies resisted, Moore and Luellen had the opening they needed. As a vice president for the Pullman Company, whose sleeper and dining cars were used on practically every railway in the United States, said, "This damn little Health Officer in Kansas has ordered us to take out the glasses we have always used. We have nothing to take their place."

The Lackawanna Railroad, which had made a point of appealing to women customers with a fictional spokesperson named Phoebe Snow, was the first to carry Moore's paper cups. In campaigning for the railroad's business, Moore had imitated Lackawanna's advertising with the ditty, "Phoebe dear . . . you need not fear . . . to drink from cups . . . that you find here. With cups of white . . . no bugs will bite . . . upon the road of anthracite."

About the same time, Dr. Alvin Davison of Lafayette College in Pennsylvania published a report of the disease-causing germs he had found on public drinking cups. Soon afterward, more states began passing laws against communal drinking cups.

## AT A GLANCE

**D**ixie brand of paper cups introduced in 1909 by the Public Cup Vendor Company; company renamed the Individual Drinking Cup Company in 1910; first brand name, Health Kup, adopted in 1912, when company changed its name to the Health Cups Company; brand and company names changed to Dixie Cup in 1919; company purchased by American Can Company in 1957; brand sold to James River Corporation of Virginia in 1982.

*Advertising:* *Agency*—DDB Needham, NY.

*Addresses:* *Parent company*—James River Corporation of Virginia, 120 Tredegar Street, Richmond, VA 23219; phone: (804) 644-5411; fax: (804) 649-4428.

Moore and Luellen soon abandoned the penny cup-vending machines, and instead began selling paper cups and free dispensers for use on railroads, in schools, and at office and government buildings. In 1910 they again changed the name of their company to capitalize on the growing awareness of the hazards of shared drinking cups, calling it the Individual Drinking Cup Company. In 1912 the company and its sole product became known as Health Kups.

### Dixie Cups

The name Health Kups lasted until 1919, when Moore began looking for a catchy name that would sound less clinical. He did not have far to look. In the very same New York building where Health Kups were being produced was the Dixie Doll Company.

The term ''Dixie'' apparently referred to $10 notes issued by a New Orleans bank in the early 1800s, when there was no national paper currency. The French word for ten, ''dix,'' was printed on the face of the bank notes, which were circulated widely along the Mississippi River trade route. Rivermen referred to the notes as ''Dixies,'' and Dixieland came to refer to the South. Moore was taken with the name Dixie and asked the owner of the Dixie Doll Company if he could borrow it for his paper cups. The first Dixie Cups were sold in 1919.

### Ice Cream Containers

Moore now had the name he wanted, but it would be four more years and a move from New York City to Easton, Pennsylvania, in 1921 before the Dixie Cup Company really began to grow. This eventual growth was due mainly to the fact that drinking cups became the ideal container for single servings of ice cream.

Until 1923 ice cream was sold only in large containers. But the industry needed a way to compete with the growing popularity of candy bars among children. The solution seemed to be to pack ice cream in small, convenient containers. The first attempts at using Dixie Cups failed. The paper containers either came apart when they were capped or they were crushed in the packing process. Finally, however, Moore and Luellen created a 2.5-ounce Dixie Cup container that met ice cream manufactures' requirements. Eventually, asking for a Dixie Cup became an integral part of ordering single servings of ice cream.

### The Consumer Market

If any doubts remained about the public-health value and convenience of paper cups, they disappeared during World War II, when the Armed Forces, hospitals, the American Red Cross, and factory cafeterias made extensive use of disposable products. When paper rationing ended after the war, the Dixie Cup Company entered the consumer market for the first time with a kitchen dispenser for five-ounce cups. In the 1950s the company began selling a line of printed paper plates with the Dixie brand name.

In 1957 the American Can Company, whose former president had invested $200,000 to back the Public Cup Vendor Company in 1909, purchased the Dixie Cup Company. The most popular Dixie Cup product, the bathroom dispenser with three-ounce cups, were introduced in 1962.

### James River Corporation

The brand changed hands again in 1982 when the James River Corporation of Virginia purchased the Dixie/Northern paper products division from the American Can Company for $450 million. The James River Corporation was founded in 1969 when the Ethyl Corporation, a paper products company in Richmond, Virginia, sold its original paper making facilities on the north bank of the James River to two former company executives, Brenton S. Halsey and Robert C. Williams. James River more than doubled in size during its first ten years through a series of acquisitions, but it was still primarily a company making specialty papers for industrial uses. Then in 1982, after a year of negotiations, the company again doubled in size by acquiring the Dixie and Northern brands.

At the time Dixie was the top-selling paper cup in the United States, but other Dixie-brand products were on a downslide, losing market share in the critical food-service industry to the Maryland Cup Corporation. Part of the problem was that the American Can Company reportedly had ''lightened up'' on Dixie products by using less paper and wax in an effort to cut costs. In addition, the growth of molded plastic and plastic foam products cut into the demand for paper products. James River moved quickly to stop the slide by introducing Superware and Livingware, two new lines of coated paper plates with the Dixie name.

The company also tripled the amount of money spent to advertise Dixie products. James River has since expanded the Dixie brand to include plastic eating utensils, brightly colored plastic party cups, and a line of foam cups, plates and bowls. In 1984 *Forbes* called the James River Corporation ''The best little paper company in America.''

Since buying the Dixie brand, James River has continued to promote the use of Dixie Cups as a way to prevent the spread of germs, just as entrepreneur Hugh Moore did in 1908. An advertising campaign for the winter of 1992 urged consumers to ''Stop those Germs with Dixie Bathroom Cups.'' The ''Dixie Cold & Flu Prevention Quiz,'' a brochure distributed with a coupon for Dixie bathroom cups, included the same advice that Dr. Crumbine, the Kansas Health Officer, might have given: ''Drinking from the same cup or glass . . . enable[s] the virus to be easily transferred to others. Disposable bathroom and kitchen paper cups are hygienic and reduce the possibility of infecting others.''

### Looking Ahead

Emphasizing its commitment to the Dixie brand, in 1992 the James River Corporation opened a new plant in Bowling Green,

Kentucky, to manufacture paper plates. The company also introduced a stronger version of Dixie Superware, which it considered to be a flagship product. In its 1992 annual report, the James River Corporation said that "leveraging the Dixie brand is a major ongoing business initiative," and announced that Dixie packaging would be redesigned for 1993.

## Further Reading:

*1992 Annual Report,* Richmond, VA: James River Corporation, 1992.

Campbell, Hannah, *Why Did They Name It . . . ?,* New York: Fleet Publishing Corporation, 1964, pp. 195–200.

"The Best Little Paper Company in America," *Forbes,* January 2, 1984, p. 172.

Carpenter, Kimberly, "A Southern Papermaker's Yankee Campaign," *Business Week,* October 14, 1985, p. 82.

Gershman, Michael, *Getting It Right the Second Time,* Reading, MA: Addison-Wesley, 1990, pp. 24–30.

*James River Corporation 1969-1989: Twenty Years of Growth,* Richmond: James River Corp., 1989.

"James River: The Biggest Test Yet in Upgrading Paper Acquisitions," *Business Week,* August 23, 1982, p. 112.

Sherman, Stratford P., "James River Just Keeps Rollin'," *Fortune,* May 2, 1983, p. 91.

Smith, Geoffrey, " 'Look Right in Your Own Backyard'," *Forbes,* March 3, 1980, p. 69.

*—Dean Boyer*

# DIXON TICONDEROGA®

Dixon Ticonderoga pencils have helped write the American chapter on the modern-day pencil. The namesake brand of the Dixon Ticonderoga Co. is one of the nation's premium graphite lead pencils, easily recognizable by its yellow exterior and yellow and green metal band eraser tip.

## The First Pencils

Historians consider the Romans, who used tiny reed brushes dipped in ink, to be the earliest users of the pencil. The Romans called their creation "penicillum" from "peniculus," which means little tail. According to Henry Petroski in his book *The Pencil,* the Greeks and Romans also used metallic lead to mark papyrus.

The modern pencil no longer uses lead, but graphite, whose use dates to 1564 when, according to legend, a violent storm blew down a large tree near Borrowdale in Cumberland, England, exposing a black mineral deposit at the tree's roots. The deposit was called "plumbargo," or "black lead," and was noted to be the purest graphite ever uncovered in the British Isles. This spot became the site of a famous graphite mine during the reign of Queen Elizabeth. Pieces of the mother lode were used to brand sheep, and street vendors cut it into sticks, wrapped them with string, and sold them on London streets as "marking stones," according Jerome Bromfield in *Kiwanis Magazine.*

These early marking sticks were inefficient because they stained the user's hand and crumbled easily, and pencils encased in wood became available by the end of the 17th century. In 1761 Kaspar Faber, a German craftsman and part-time chemist, mixed powdered graphite, sulphur, antimony, and resins to help solidify the graphite. Napoleon Bonaparte was said to have inspired yet another improvement in 1790 by prompting French chemist and inventor Nicolas Jacques Conte to mix clay with sparse supplies of graphite. The clay adhered to the graphite and the firing process made it a durable writing stick. By controlling the amount of clay, Conte could make the graphite in varying shades and strengths (from light to dark and soft to hard). Conte, too, encased his new graphite blended pencil in wooden slats.

## Brand Origins

Joseph Dixon, born in 1799 in Marblehead, Massachusetts, eventually became one of the most successful marketers of pencils in the United States. His father, a ship owner, used Ceylonese graphite as ballast on homeward runs from the Orient. The graphite ballasts were discarded into the bay at Marblehead, and Dixon soon learned how to reuse them. His friend Francis Peabody, a local cabinetmaker and chemist, showed the young Dixon how to groove wooden slats and make a mixture of graphite and clay.

At the age of 23, Dixon married Hannah Martin, the daughter of well-known cabinetmaker Ebenezer Martin. At their home in Salem, Massachusetts, Dixon made the first of his Dixon graphite lead pencils in 1827. While Dixon eventually pursued careers in printing, chemistry, and medicine, it was the pencil that he kept coming back to. The first Dixon pencils were not acceptable to local merchants; according to *The Pencil,* "a dozen Dixon pencils dating from about 1830 were found to have gritty leads that were not laid evenly in the wood case, which itself was only roughly finished. Even the label, lithographed by Dixon himself, was flawed, for it contained a typographical error, the "a" being omitted from Salem. . . . "

The Dixons experimented with graphite and clay formulas and accidentally discovered that graphite was an excellent stove polish. The Dixons patented and sold Dixon's Stove Polish and used the profits to enable Joseph to sell pencils at 10 cents apiece.

But demand was low and the Dixons had to turn to other inventions to fund their fledgling company. Dixon invented a heat-resistant graphite crucible widely used in the production of iron and steel during the Mexican-American War of 1846. The success of this hardy crucible spurred the formation of the Dixon Crucible Company factory in Jersey City, New Jersey, in 1847, which manufactured his stove polish, crucibles, and Dixon pencils. In his first year of business it was obvious which product was underwriting the other: Dixon had a net profit of $60,000 on crucibles and a $5,000 loss on pencils.

The demand for pencils did not increase until the Civil War. Dixon pencils were made of "solid black lead, one-half inch square, four-inches long," *The Pencil* states. Dixon began to make quality cedar wood pencils once faced with competition from German pencil manufacturers setting up shop in America. He invented a wood planing machine in 1866 that could produce 132 pencils a minute, and by 1872, the factory was producing 86,000 pencils a day, or about one-third of American consumption. The cheapest pencils were made of pine, the common grades were

## AT A GLANCE

**D**ixon brand of pencils founded in 1827 in Salem, MA, by Joseph Dixon; brand name changed to Dixon Ticonderoga in 1873 when Dixon purchased the American Graphite Company of Ticonderoga, NY.

*Performance:* *Market share*—70% of the high-end pencil category; *Sales*—$60 million in pencils, pens, crayons, art supplies.

*Major competitor:* Faber-Castell; also Empire Berol.

*Advertising:* In house.

*Addresses:* *Parent company*—Dixon Ticonderoga Co., 2600 Maitland Center Parkway, #200, Maitland, FL 32751; phone: (407) 875-9000; fax: (407) 875-1475.

made of red cedar, and the standard grades were made of Florida Keys cedar, which is soft, close-grained, and of superior quality.

Soon Dixon's Jersey City company was being described as "the birthplace of the world's first mass-produced pencils." Dixon Pencils became a registered trademark in 1873. Dixon himself was later able to capitalize on patriotic sentiment by emphasizing that his success was due to "purely American principles." To protect his new and improved pencils from imitators, Dixon identified each one with a "skeleton crucible," and used a new system of grading that became the registered trademark "American Graphite."

By the time of his death in 1869 at the age of 70, Dixon had designed the forerunner of the camera viewfinder, patented a double-crank steam engine, developed a photolithography process for foiling counterfeiters, and invented a new way of tunneling under water; still, according to company documents, Dixon "considered the wood-cased pencil his most important achievement."

The company was headed by Dixon's son-in-law after Dixon's death. In 1873 Dixon purchased the American Graphite Company of Ticonderoga, New York, inspiring a name change for the brand from Dixon to Dixon Ticonderoga (the Dixon Crucible Company did not change its name to the Dixon Ticonderoga Co. until 1983). The company fell into the receivership of Edward F. C. Young, a bank president, in 1880. Young revived the company, which continued to do well under the direction of his own son-in-law, George T. Smith.

## World War I

By World War I, European pencil manufacturers had entered the world market. The Dixon Crucible Company distinguished its brand pencils as made of American Graphite Polygrade. In 1919 the Dixon company introduced its Eldorado brand of drawing pencils for artists and engineers. Eldorado was distinguished by a blue finish and gold lettering and graded according to a European system. A 1919 advertisement declared that "during the war, when most needed in the tasks of victory—Dixon's Eldorado, 'the master drawing pencil,' rendered a real National Service."

Although 90 percent of the American market was dominated by the "Big Four"—Dixon, Eberhard Faber, American, and Eagle pencil companies—by 1921 these companies were demanding increased tariffs to thwart cheaper imported pencils from Germany and Japan. By 1934 the Big Four accounted for only 75

percent of domestic pencil production and faced an uphill battle against increased foreign competition and lack of demand during the Great Depression.

More than 1.5 billion pencils were being produced annually in 1942—enough for more than 10 pencils for every man, woman, and child in the nation. During World War II, American companies were cut off from key supplies of graphite and clay, and shortages led to a ban on the use of rubber or any kind of metal on pencils. Plastic and rubber substitutes were used instead for ferrules and erasers. The war's end did not resolve a worldwide shortage of pencils. Pencil manufacturers used more plastic and other new techniques to make even more pencils to fill a seemingly unquenchable demand.

By 1953 American demand had tapered slightly to 1.3 billion pencils a year. There were 23 pencil manufacturers, but the Big Four (which included Dixon) controlled all aspects of pencil making—from the leads and wood slats to the eraser tips. Control was so tight that in 1954 the Big Four were charged with violating the Sherman Antitrust Law. The U.S. government alleged that as early as 1949 these companies had conspired to fix prices, rig bids, and allocate sales of pencils to local government agencies and industries. Annual sales combined for the Big Four were more than $15 million, accounting for 50 percent of domestic and 75 percent of export sales. The companies all entered pleas of no defense and paid fines of $5,000 apiece. All agreed in a consent decree to abstain from further illegal practices.

In the wake of the suit and increasing competition by Empire, the fifth-largest pencil maker, Dixon redesigned its packaging in an effort to distinguish its brand. In 1957, in an effort to supplement its line of graphite lead pencils, Dixon merged with the American Crayon Co. of Sandusky, Ohio, and expanded its pencil line to include "Old Faithful" pencils, Prang school and marking crayons, and Tempera colors and art materials.

## Mergers and Acquisitions

Twenty-five years later, Dixon purchased the Wallace Pencil Co., which had facilities in Versailles, Missouri, and Vandalia, Illinois, as part of an overall plan to phase out Dixon's pencil-making operations in Jersey City and move them to the new subsidiary's headquarters in Missouri. Dixon Crucible Company buildings in New Jersey were purchased by a developer who converted the factory into apartments in a self-contained neighborhood setting, called "Dixon Mills."

The Dixon Crucible Company became Dixon Ticonderoga Co. in September 1983, named after its oldest and most famous yellow and green Ticonderoga pencil, after merging with the Bryn Mawr Corp. of Vero Beach, Florida. Bryn Mawr's history goes back further than Dixon's, tracing its origins to 1785. Dixon Ticonderoga Co. headquarters were moved to Vero Beach.

The Bryn Mawr merger was part of a Dixon strategic plan that stated: "The overall goal of Dixon Ticonderoga is to be a marketer and producer of high quality products which will command higher margins through proprietary characteristics, either in and of themselves, by packaging, or by brand name development and marketing (rather than commodity products).

"Concentrating on writing and art products, graphite and graphite products, real estate development, restaurants and transit, the company's current goal is to be well-planned and market driven with tight central management control.''

The merger "looked like a real winner," according to *Barron's Investment News & Views,* but Dixon Ticonderoga had a rocky start financially. The company suffered losses and was set back by the 1985 earthquake in Mexico City, which affected a major contract Dixon Ticonderoga had for supplying Mexican schools with pencils.

In 1986 Dixon Ticonderoga, under the leadership of CEO Gino N. Pala, increased the prices of its pencil and crayon line, tightened inventories, and implemented other cost-saving measures, including moving its graphite production for lower-priced pencils from Illinois to Mexico. Pala also consolidated operations, upgraded Dixon's aging factories, and reduced manufacturing costs.

The company also entered mass markets for the first time in its history by offering a specially packaged, lower-priced pencil. In 1987 Dixon Ticonderoga purchased privately owned David Kahn, Inc., and its Wearever writing instruments line, which was expected to be the "biggest single boost to profits," *Barron's* reported. The Wearever pen line, which also included desk accessories, was expected to generate about $250,000 in profits on about $45 million of volume in 1987, and perhaps double that amount in 1988.

Dixon Ticonderoga pencils and crayons were expected to provide more than $8 million in operating profits on about $50 million in revenues in 1987, compared to $6.4 million in 1986. In 1981 the Dixon company (pencils and graphite business together) earned only $1 million on revenues of $64 million; in 1982, it lost $1 million on $57 million. Industry analysts estimated that for 1988, profits would be around $9.5 million on sales of about $55 million, *Barron's* reported.

## Corporate Performance

Pala is credited for reshaping Dixon Ticonderoga after the merger and helping to boost overall sales 40 percent to $80 million, in part due to his aggressive marketing of the company's writing instruments to stores like Kmart and Wal-Mart. In 1988 new product introductions included a self-advancing mechanical pencil (SenseMatic), a designer pen, and a dust-free white marker for blackboards, making Dixon a major player in the market again. As a result, Dixon Ticonderoga became a hot stock choice. The company's other products are graphite, real estate, industrial lubricants, and heat resistant materials used in cookware, tiles, and ceramics.

In 1988 Dixon Ticonderoga also purchased and consolidated the Ruwe Pencil and National Pen & Pencil companies, helping reduce the fixed cost of the company's annual American pencil production of 2.5 million gross by 30 cents a gross, reported Fleming Meeks in a 1989 *Forbes* article. By 1990, however, Dixon Ticonderoga reported losses in every quarter, attributed to slow sales and overstocked pencil and crayon inventories. The company's shares shrank from a high of 18⅝ to 4¼.

## Advertising

Since the turn of the century, Dixon Ticonderoga pencils have always been promoted as being born of American know-how and ingenuity. Promotional literature at the time linked Dixon pencils to: "American industry, American materials, American capital, American brains, American labor and American machinery." The

Ticonderoga brand name evoked memories of the American Revolution and Ethan Allen at Fort Ticonderoga (and, one could suppose, America's liberation from dependence on Britain's Borrowdale graphite mine and British pencils).

The Dixon Crucible Company commissioned Norman Rockwell to paint several portraits depicting the many uses of the Dixon Ticonderoga pencil in American settings. One shows an older man demonstrating to a boy how to use a knife to sharpen pencils; another features a boy buying pencils for school. Another artist, Frances Tipton Hunter, also painted portraits of people using Dixon Ticonderoga pencils that were used for advertisements during World War II.

Dixon's advertising has also attempted to link the brand name with key events in American history. For example, one of Dixon's advertisements featured the ghost of a Revolutionary War hero riding above the launch of the U.S.S. Ticonderoga aircraft carrier, and a Ticonderoga pencil superimposed over the photo with the tag line: "To the American People: This fine pencil with its fine American name points out that the War Bonds we buy today underwrite our prosperity tomorrow! Signed Dixon Ticonderoga."

In recent years Dixon Ticonderoga has not actively promoted its brand of pencils. Even so, the brand's recognition appears to be durable: company sources say that Ticonderogas were used on the television show *Leave It to Beaver,* the shipwrecked crew of *Gilligan's Island* held on to their Dixon Ticonderoga pencils, and cartoon character Bart Simpson has been spotted using one.

## Future Growth

Dixon Ticonderoga began getting back on track in 1992 when it began reporting a profit for the first time since 1988, thanks to corporate restructuring, the closing of two factories, and other cost cutting measures. From the start, the company has never really relied on just the pencil. By developing its products from one main material—graphite—Dixon Ticonderoga has been able to successfully manufacture pencils, crucibles, stove polish, graphite oils, and lubricants. The company's strategy to acquire and merge with other pencil and writing instrument companies has expanded its writing instrument and desk accessory lines to include crayons, art supplies, rubber bands, erasers, felt tip markers, lumber crayons, and industrial markers.

Under Pala's leadership, the company has tried to erase its heavy debt with cost-containment strategies and is attempting to use technology to "drag us out of the 19th century into the 21st century," Pala told the *Orlando Business Journal.* In terms of the pencil market, Dixon Ticonderoga is continuing its aggressive marketing by seeking exposure of its writing instruments line in stores such as Office Depot, Bizmart, and other national office wholesalers. Future growth may depend on the company's push into the colored pencil market, which has shown an annual growth rate of 12 to 14 percent.

The demand for pencils is not likely to abate soon. As Petroski wrote in *The Pencil,* "reports of the pencil's impending passing have been so greatly exaggerated that its staying power has come to be the subject of amusement." Despite the widespread adoption of the typewriter and the computer, pencils are currently being manufactured worldwide at the rate of about 14 billion a year.

**Further Reading:**

Bromfield, Jerome, "Everything Begins with a Pencil," *Kiwanis Magazine,* 1976, p. 25–33.

Frankenstein, Diane, *Brandnames: Who Owns What,* Facts on File, 1986, p. 174.

"Growing Sharper, Dixon Ticonderoga Points to Earnings of $2 a Share This Year," *Barron's,* April 16, 1987, p. 64.

"Companies Involved in Largest Insider Purchases," *Insider's Chronicle,* March 4, 1991, p. 3.

Marcial, Gene G., "This Penmaker Has Written Itself A Hot New Script," *Business Week,* May 9, 1988, p. 134.

Meeks, Fleming, "Better than an M.B.A.," *Forbes,* June 26, 1989, p. 88–94.

Meeks, "Easier Does It," *Forbes,* October 29, 1990, p. 10.

Perrault, Mike, "Pencil in Profits, Dixon Ticonderoga to Erase Losses," *Orlando Business Journal,* June 26, 1992, p. 1.

Petroski, Henry, *The Pencil: A History of Design and Circumstance,* New York: Alfred Knopf.

"Lowly Pencil Involved in Global Controversy," *Wall Street Journal,* October 19, 1990, p. B1(E).

—*Evelyn S. Dorman*

# DOCKERS®

In 1986 Levi Strauss & Co. introduced the Dockers brand of casual wear in the United States as a comfortable alternative to jeans for aging baby boomers. Dockers all-cotton, pleated slacks offer a roomier fit and a slightly more upscale style. Recognizing the potential for growth in the baby-boomer market segment, Levi Strauss & Co. promoted its Dockers brand aggressively, and Dockers soon reached the top of the casual wear market with sales of $1.8 billion in 1992. By the early 1990s, Dockers was the fastest-growing apparel brand in U.S. history and had the highest level of brand awareness in the men's casual pants category. "If the brand were a separate company," boasted Levi Strauss & Co., "it would be the world's sixth largest apparel concern."

## Brand Origins

Levi Strauss, the founder of Levi Strauss & Co., came from a rather humble background. He emigrated from Bavaria to the United States in 1853 to join his brother-in-law, David Stern, who owned a dry goods business in San Francisco. Strauss brought a selection of fabrics from New York, but on the clipper-ship journey to California, he sold all of the higher quality materials. All that remained was some brown canvas-like material that Strauss hoped would be needed for tent material and Conestoga wagon covers.

However, as the company legend goes, an old weathered miner complained to Strauss, "You should've brought pants. Pants don't wear worth a hoot up in the diggin's." The savvy Strauss brought his canvas fabric to a tailor and asked him to sew a pair of pants out of the sturdy material. The word quickly spread around town, especially among miners, about the superior durability of "those pants of Levi's." Within a short time, Strauss created the prototype "denims" using a heavy, cotton fabric from Nimes, France, and an indigo dye.

Strauss made only a few alterations, adding snaps and applying patented copper riveting for strength at the seams. He also added a two-horse brand patch on the back pocket. (The famous red tab at the right hip pocket first appeared in 1936.) By 1890, Levi Strauss & Co. was formally incorporated and a few decades later was selling products overseas. Levi Strauss & Co.'s enduring success throughout the twentieth century was attributed to its commitment to producing quality products. A "Levi's Promise" card was attached to the two and a half billion pairs of jeans sold worldwide to date.

Levi Strauss & Co. continued to successfully expand its jeans market until the early 1980s, when it began losing the core jeans consumers, the 77 million baby boomers whose tastes were changing and waistlines expanding. In response to these changing demographics, Levi Strauss & Co. introduced Dockers in 1986.

## Early Marketing Strategy

In the late 1980s, Dockers casual wear appeared to be somewhat of a radical idea. Levi Strauss & Co. placed Dockers in the "new casual" segment, a market niche of sportswear, somewhere between jeans and dressier pants, which the company felt had been virtually untapped. According to apparel industry analyst John Tugman in *Fortune,* "Dockers is a major category that didn't even exist before. The beauty is that it's a natural extension of the jeans business, and Levi had either the wisdom or the luck to be the first to develop a brand position."

Appealing to customers between 25 and 49 years old, the Dockers brand featured a roomy "reverse silhouette" design, that was wider at the waist, narrower at the ankles, and boasted deep side pockets. The all-cotton, pleated slacks were made of soft and pre-washed fabrics, such as twill and chambray, and came in a variety of colors.

*Fortune* contributor Brenton R. Schlender noted that Levi Strauss & Co. had even used the Dockers brand name previously on twill work pants sold in Japan and Argentina. The new Dockers brand was improved in several ways: a greater selection of colors and fabrics existed, and later an assortment of shirt coordinates of knit and woven fabrics were available. Convinced of the brand's potential, Levi Strauss & Co. invested millions of dollars promoting Dockers.

## Brand Extensions

Initially a menswear brand, Dockers soon expanded to include women's apparel. Women's Dockers were also made of all-natural fabrics and had a looser fit, but were targeted at 22 to 39 year olds—a slightly smaller focus group than the men's. Women's double-pleated Dockers slacks featured a contoured waist and were casual, comfortable, and fashionable. Vince Tavani noted in *Women's Wear Daily* that sales of women's Dockers were primarily driven by the clothing's superior fit.

## AT A GLANCE

**D**ockers brand of casual wear introduced by Levi Strauss & Co. in 1986; originally a line of just men's clothing, brand was expanded to include women's and boys' apparel; brand also includes a line of shoes and leather accessories.

**Performance:** *Market share*—11.2% share of men's casual pants category (of 91 million pair market). *Sales*—$1.8 billion total Dockers brand, including menswear, womenswear, youthwear, and related merchandise.

**Major competitor:** Haggar Apparel Company's Renegade brand; also Bugle Boy Industries' "M" brand; also Farah Manufacturing Company's Savanne brand.

**Advertising:** *Agency*—Foote, Cone & Belding, San Francisco, CA, 1930—. *Major campaign*—"Nobody does colors like Dockers"; for Dockers Authentics: "Something new that has been there all along."

**Addresses:** *Parent company*—Levi Strauss & Co. Dockers Division, 1155 Battery Street, San Francisco, CA 94111; phone: (415) 544-6000. *Ultimate parent company*—Levi Strauss & Co. Associates Inc., 1155 Battery Street, San Francisco, CA 94111; phone: (415) 544-6000; fax: (415) 544-1693.

By the early 1990s, the Dockers brand included a variety of casual clothing for women, men, and boys, including shorts, skirts, shirts, jackets, and sweaters. The Dockers brand also included a Sport line of activewear separates, Dress Dockers, a line of shoes, socks, and small leather accessories.

In the summer of 1993, Levi Strauss & Co. introduced a new, more upscale version of Dockers, called Dockers Authentics, for the younger half of male baby boomers—those between 21 to 35. The more fashionable cuts and fabrics were designed to capture a casual wear market niche somewhere between original Dockers and designer collectibles. In part, Dockers Authentics were designed to take advantage of a general fashion trend during the early 1990s toward a more casual dress code at the workplace. The classic Authentics sportswear cost approximately ten percent more than Dockers. Levi Strauss & Co. officials predicted that by the mid 1990s, Dockers Authentics would account for roughly ten percent of men's Dockers sales.

Levi Strauss & Co. added wrinkle-free fabrics to Dockers menswear in the fall of 1993, citing consumer demand for casual attire that looked crisp and neat and was appropriate for work. Levi Strauss & Co. was also interested in adding wrinkle-free fabrics to women's and children's Dockers and eventually to shirts once the company had developed a wrinkle-free chemical treatment appropriate for lighter-weight materials.

## Advertising

From the outset, Levi Strauss & Co. invested millions of dollars in advertising the Dockers brand. Within two years of its inception, the Dockers advertising budget reached $10 million. The dynamic advertising campaigns, created by Foote, Cone & Belding—representatives for Levi Strauss & Co. since 1930—contributed greatly to establishing brand recognition with the U.S. public. Foote, Cone & Belding helped develop what Steve Goldstein, the director of consumer marketing for menswear, called: "Dockers World, the mythical place where our Dockers consumer feels comfortable."

One of the first Dockers television campaigns featured the slogan: "If you're not wearing Dockers, you're just wearing pants." Directed by Leslie Dektor in his cinema *verite* style, the mood of the advertisements was casual, as suggested by the shaky camera movements and the improvised dialogue rambling in a stream-of-consciousness manner.

In 1991 a new Dockers television campaign was introduced during Levi Strauss & Co.'s first Super Bowl Sunday appearance. Levi Strauss & Co. spent approximately $2 million on four of these football spots. Directed by Joe Pytka, the overall theme was "Relax—you're among friends." The commercials depicted men in their 20s through 40s, pleasantly spending time together in various settings, such as in a park, at a pool hall, or at a wedding. A voice-over added endearing and humorous dialogue. The company invested between $15 and $20 million on this advertising campaign.

The following year, the media budget increased once again, to an estimated $20 to $25 million. The campaign focused less on product information and appropriate occasions for wearing Dockers, instead placing emphasis on fashion and the wide selection of Dockers colors. According to the *New York Times,* these ads tried to establish "that Dockers come in many different flavors." During each of the segments, a voice-over narrated various scenarios about colors, such as: "Gray. It's what black would look like if it could just lighten up a little. Flint and steel, stone and mist. Gray. A color for any age, any time." Meanwhile various gray-clad men moved about in slow motion through a predominantly gray setting. The spot ended with the line, "Nobody does gray like Dockers."

This highly acclaimed campaign won the praises of many in the advertising industry. *Advertising Age* chose the "Gray" commercial as one of the best in 1992 and also honored its cinematography. Bob Garfield of *Advertising Age* commented that this spot was "one of the most pleasing, most seamlessly integrated syntheses of market, selling strategy, creative solution and audiovisual style." The brand was so successful that Dockers became the generic name for imitations. According to Robert Hanson, Levi's director of consumer marketing for menswear, one of Levi's goals for the 1992 and subsequent campaigns was to distinguish Dockers from the imitations.

The 1993 advertisements for Dockers Authentics, also created by Foote, Cone & Belding, portrayed the brand extension as "something new that has been there all along." The ads were more understated than those for Dockers of the early 1990s, and the media budget for the Authentics line accounted for about 20 percent of total men's Dockers, or approximately $4 to $5 million annually.

An early print advertisement for women's Dockers appealed specifically to a young professional woman. It read: "If you took some Levi's jeans, added a BMW convertible and a well-worn Cartier Tank watch and a Bass Weejun loafer, plus the way it feels to really trounce your tennis instructor, and then whipped it all together in a Cuisinart, what you'd get is Levi's Dockers." While previously allocating a total of about $8 million for advertising on women's Dockers and jeans in the early 1990s, in 1993 Levi's planned to spend between $30 million and $40 million on total womenswear, about half of the menswear media budget.

## Performance Evaluation

The Dockers brand was virtually an overnight success. It was one of the most dramatic product introductions in the apparel industry in U.S. history. In its first year Dockers sold $40 million in slacks. By 1990, sales reached $500 million. The $800 million in sales in 1991 represented 21 percent of total sales of Levi Strauss & Co. In 1991 Dockers captured 11 percent market share (of total sales of 91 million pairs of casual men's pants), up from nine percent the previous year.

Sales of women's Dockers also exploded in the first year, reaching close to $40 million. In *Women's Wear Daily* Thomas Kasten, president of Levi's Womenswear, noted that women's Dockers were "actually higher on the power [growth] curve than men's was at the same time in their history." The popularity of all Dockers products continued to increase dramatically throughout the early 1990s. By 1992, total sales of the Dockers brand exceeded $1.6 billion, representing 28 percent of total Levi's sales of $5.6 billion.

## Future Growth

Levi Strauss & Co. predicted that the Dockers brand would continue to expand in all categories, including menswear, womenswear, youthwear, and Dockers accessories. The exceptionally strong position of Dockers in the U.S. market during the early 1990s suggested that the brand would maintain its lead in the casual wear market throughout the mid-1990s. Dockers were successfully introduced into a number of foreign markets, including Canada, Central and South America, Asia, and New Zealand. Because the labor content of Dockers products was twice that of Levi's jeans, most of the Dockers products were manufactured in the Caribbean basin, where labor was comparatively cheaper than in the United States. Levi Strauss & Co. plans to continue developing Dockers markets abroad as well as in the United States.

## Further Reading:

"Apparel & Accessories," *Advertising Age,* May 3, 1993, p. S-10.

Beckett, Jamie, "Price Comparisons Dominate New Spots," *San Francisco Chronicle,* January 14, 1991, p. C3.

Bloomfield, Judy, "Casual Pants: Hot Ticket For Holiday," *Women's Wear Daily,* August 3, 1988.

Elliott, Stuart, "Can Levi Strauss & Co. Extend Its Success With Dockers?" *New York Times,* February 24, 1992, sec. D, p. 10.

"Fashion Statement," *San Francisco Business Magazine,* October, 1992, p. 30.

Garfield, Bob, "Levi's Dockers Show Their Colors Perfectly," *Advertising Age,* March 2, 1992, p. 34.

Magiera, Marcy, "Dockers Tackles New Ads," *Advertising Age,* January 14, 1991, p. 41; "Levi Gives Women A Taste Of The Blues," *Advertising Age,* July 18, 1988, p. 23.

Simpson, Blaise, "Levi's Makes Push In Women's Wear," *Women's Wear Daily,* March 2, 1988, p. 1.

Sloan, Pat, "Levi Redraws Women's Jeans Campaign For TV," *Advertising Age,* August 9, 1993, p. 3.

Schlender, Brenton R., "How Levi Strauss & Co. Did An LBO Right," *Fortune,* May 7, 1990, p. 105.

*—Audra Avizienis*

# DOVE®

*Dove*®

The leading toilet bar soap is not a soap at all. Dove Beauty Bar is composed primarily of synthetic detergents and fillers. The active ingredient is a relatively mild surfactant combined with a high level of stearic acid, presumably the one-quarter moisturizing cream in the formula. In a mature market that has had to rely on segmentation for growth, Dove first emerged as a hard water soap that fixed the "bathtub ring" problem and later was marketed as a cleansing and beauty bar for the face.

A company with a long history in the soap industry, Lever Brothers Company commercialized the Dove Beauty Bar in 1957. William Hesketh Lever, who had worked in his family's grocery business, formed Lever Brothers in England in 1855 with his brother James. At the time, most soaps were coarse and sold in nameless blocks cut to the customer's order. From its first product—Sunlight, the world's first packaged, branded laundry soap—the company extended its business into a variety of fields and into several countries. Lever Brothers became the world's largest soap seller and its eventual parent company, Unilever, became known as the world's largest consumer goods company.

Soapmaking originated with the Phoenicians in 600 B.C., survived the Middle Ages in Europe, and came to the North American continent around 1600. Although soap had a long history, the basic method and recipe for making it changed little until the twentieth century. Well into the nineteenth century most households made their own soap combining fat and wood ashes and boiling the mixture in a kettle. These homemade soaps cleaned, but were harsh on the skin.

Soapmaking expanded as a commercial enterprise in the twentieth century, especially around World War II. The market opened to more technologically advanced production methods after battles in Europe destroyed numerous soap plants and left capacity limited there. Manufacturers leaped at the opportunity to improve production and concurrently responded to consumer demands for soaps that were more gentle to the skin and which addressed health and hygiene concerns.

A formula similar to the basic Dove bar formula was used in World War II as a non-irritating skin cleanser for the treatment of burns and wounds. Later, scientists at the Lever Research Center in Edgewater, New Jersey, refined the formula and commercialized the Original Dove Beauty Bar. Dove was a "first of a kind" product as the first cleansing beauty bar containing moisturizing cream. The Dove formulation comprises two principal ingredients: an ester of vegetable oil fatty acids to provide cleansing and lathering properties in hard or soft water and a substance commonly found in cleansing creams to provide mildness and moisturizing benefits. Lever developed a special production process that made it cost effective to mass produce the mild direct esterified fatty isethionate (DEFI) cleansing agent in Dove. Original Dove became available nationwide in the 1960s.

## Advertising Claims

The non-drying properties of Dove was its biggest selling point. An independent clinical dermatological study in the 1970s proved Dove Beauty Bar was milder than 17 leading bar soaps. That mildness led Dove to become the number one physician-recommended cleansing bar in the 1980s.

In the 1990s, Lever advertised Dove as the number one dermatologist recommended cleanser. Dermatologists found the cleansing agent in Dove suitable for all skin types, including that of children and the elderly. The endorsement followed advertising targeted to the specialists that stated patients found Dove complemented Retin-A therapy since, unlike mild soaps which tended to intensify the drying effect of the drug, it lessened the exacerbation of dryness, itching, and redness.

Nondrying properties in cleansers were of increasing importance to an aging population. Early themes were "Dove creams your skin while you wash" and "For softer, smooth skin switch to Dove." Further, the emphasis on moisturizing led Lever to modify its slogan from "Dove is ¼ cleansing cream" to "Dove contains ¼ moisturizing cream. It won't dry your face like soap." The new claim reflected skin care beyond simple cleaning.

The Dove "Real Women" campaign showed real women who looked great but not like professional models, and included each woman's name, hometown, and number of years they had used Dove. Another campaign was centered around the theme that Dove users could feel the difference in their skin after using it for seven days.

## Brand Extensions

Besides the moisturizing trend, Lever Brothers pursued other consumer demands. The company introduced White Unscented

## AT A GLANCE

**D**ove Beauty Bar brand introduced in 1957 by Lever Brothers Company, which was founded in 1855 by William and James Lever; market extensions include White Unscented Dove Beauty Bar (introduced in the 1980s) and Regular and Unscented Liquid Dove Beauty Wash (introduced in 1990).

**Performance:** *Market share*—16.5% (number one share) of toilet soap category. *Sales*—$235 million.

**Major competitor:** Oil of Olay Conditioning Bath Bar.

**Advertising:** *Agency*—Ogilvy & Mather, New York, NY, 1957—present. *Major campaign*—"Contains ¼ moisturizing cream. It won't dry your face like soap."

**Addresses:** *Parent company*—Lever Brothers Company, 390 Park Ave., New York, NY 10022-4698. *Ultimate parent company*—(In the United Kingdom) Unilever PLC, P.O. Box 68, Unilever House, Blackfriars, London EC4P 4BQ United Kingdom. (In the Netherlands) Unilever NV, P.O. Box 760, 3000 DK Rotterdam, Netherlands.

Dove Beauty Bar in the 1980s and Original and Unscented Liquid Dove Beauty Wash in 1990. In a 1990 *Consumer Reports* article, White Unscented Dove Beauty Bar was the top rated brand of all the soap products tested. Lever also sells Dove Dishwashing Liquid.

Liquid Dove Beauty Wash was aimed to capture the popularity of non-soap and wash-off cleansers for facial use. Although liquid soap first appeared in the 1940s, several decades elapsed before detergent innovations and pump dispensers positioned liquid soaps for general in-home use. By the mid-1980s, the market was ready for segmentation. Appealing to aging female baby boomers, Liquid Dove Beauty Wash was mild and cleaned without stripping the natural oils that keep skin moist. Lever backed the introduction of Dove Beauty Wash with strong print and television ads and coupon drops.

## Market History and Outlook

Although synthetic detergent bars gained a 15 to 20 percent share of the market within a few years of introduction, it was not until 1983 that Dove unseated long-time soap market leader Ivory. Dove gained nearly a 12 percent dollar share in 1984, then lost the top spot to Dial. In 1989 Dove retook the top spot on the strength of a consumer movement toward upscale moisturizing products. By 1991, the beauty segment accounted for 32 percent of total bar soap dollar sales and Dove passed Procter & Gamble in toilet soap revenue, attaining the number one brand in the $1.5 billion bar soap category.

Lever Brothers cultivated the growth of the Dove brand by repositioning the product intelligently and capitalizing on the brand's image as a non-drying beauty bar. In 1992 the company restaged Liquid Dove Beauty Wash in a new proprietary bottle and packaged Dove bars in preprinted cartons with an easy-open tab. Bar and liquid versions of Dove are packaged in plain white boxes, with the logo in blue letters for the Original scent and green letters for Unscented; a tan dove graces the package above the word "Dove." Concurrently, Lever boosted the presence of Dove bar and liquid cleanser in the United States in chain department stores.

Also in 1992, Dove bar was launched as a new brand in Europe, supported by a brand strategy created to communicate a high quality, functional identity via major advertising and promotions. The introduction spread brand distribution worldwide.

Sustained by marketing efforts, the Dove brand is positioned to enjoy continued market share. The beauty bar and liquid wash each fill a niche as the market grows more segmented, and as it becomes more popular for people to have their own soap or cleanser instead of sharing one with everyone in the household. Additionally, Dove was a high value, premium product that had an easily understood and motivating consumer proposition with its claim of moisturizing agents. It was one of the few grocery goods that contained sodium cocoyl isethionate, an ingredient usually in products found only in the specialty skin care section of pharmacies. The brand had the added benefit of the trademark Lever unconditional guarantee of quality and dependable performance.

## Further Reading:

Adkins, Lynn, "Tough Times for P&G," *Dun's Business Month*, August 1984, pp. 53, 56.

Bassin, Amelia, "Why Is Our Advertising So Wasted; Cosmetic Marketing Interview," *Drug & Cosmetic Industry*, March 1992, p. 51.

Darconte, Lorraine, "Soap Wars: Liquids Bubble Over as Bars Begin to Slip," *Soap—Cosmetics—Chemical Specialties*, December 1990, p. 24.

"Dove Bar History," Lever Brothers Company, n.d.

Freeman, Laurie, "Franchise Players: Brand Expansion Preferred Route," *Advertising Age*, August 18, 1986, pp. 3, 61.

Goldemberg, Robert L., "Serendipity; Interesting Results of Dermatologic Research," *Drug & Cosmetic Industry*, May 1990, p. 46.

Henderson, Clare, "Clean Living; UK Toiletries Market," *Soap, Perfumery & Cosmetics*, July 1992, p. 28.

Hoover, Gary, ed., *Hoover's Handbook of American Business 1993*, The Reference Press, Inc., 1992, p. 549

Jungerman, Eric, "Toilet Soaps: New Trends and Technologies," *Soap—Cosmetics—Chemical Specialties*, March 1985, p. 30.

Kintish, Lisa, "In a Lather: The Grab for Market Share Is Intense in the Bar and Liquid Soap Market," *Soap—Cosmetics—Chemical Specialties*, December 1992, p. 34.

"Lever Brand Extensions Boost Flagging Soap Market; Lever Brothers Co.'s Line Extensions and Innovations on Lux and Dove," *Cosmetics International*, April 25, 1992, p. 3.

Lundmark, Larry, "The Evolution of Liquid Soap; Bath & Spa Beauty Products," *Cosmetics and Toiletries*, December 1992, p. 49.

Moskowitz, Milton, Robert Levering and Michael Katz, eds., *Everybody's Business: A Field Guide to the 400 Leading Companies in America*, Doubleday, 1990, pp. 137–39.

Morris, Gregory D. L., Peter Savage, Sophie Wilkinson, and Catherine Brady, "Soaps & Detergents," special report in *Chemical Week*, January 18, 1989.

"1992: A Year in Review; Cosmetics and Perfumes Industry, Part 1 Industry Overview," *Cosmetics International*, November 25, 1992, p. 5.

"Procter & Gamble Restage Camay," *Cosmetics International*, April 25, 1991, p. 6.

Rice, Faye, "Trouble at Procter & Gamble," *Fortune*, March 5, 1984, p. 70.

Rosendahl, Iris, "Soaps Are Steady Sellers in Drugstore," *Drug Topics*, September 23, 1991, p. 83.

Sharp, Harold S., *Advertising Slogans of America*, Metuchen, NJ: Scarecrow Press, Inc., 1984, p. 323.

Singletary, Lynda, "Bar Soaps: No-Soap Soaps Up," *Chemical Marketing Reporter*, January 27, 1992, pp. SR23–24.

Sloan, Pat, "Olay Bath Bar Takes Aim at Dove," *Advertising Age,* February 4, 1991, p. 9.

"Soaping Up," *Consumer Reports,* October 1990, p. 644.

"Soaps and Detergents; New Opportunities in a Mature Business," special report in *Chemical Week,* January 31, 1990.

"Tin Horse; Tin Horse Design," *Cosmetics International,* November 10, 1992, p. 12.

Wells, Ken, "Selling to the World: Global Ad Campaigns, After Many Missteps, Finally Pay Dividends," *Wall Street Journal,* August 27, 1992, Sec. A1.

*—Doris Morris Maxfield*

# DOWNY®

Downy brand fabric softener, in its original formula, is the top-selling fabric softener in the United States. Packaged in the trade-marked plastic bottle or the cardboard box featuring a picture of a blanket-bundled baby's face, Downy has been softening consumers' laundry and preventing static-cling for more than 30 years. Fabric softeners have evolved from the "basic blue" laundry additives of the 1960s to the trendy concentrates of the 1990s that have been influenced by technology and consumers' environmental concerns. As competing brands proliferated in the 1960s and 1970s, the Downy brand consistently outsold such heavyweight competitors as Bounce and Snuggle fabric softeners. Just one of Procter & Gamble's (P&G's) multitude of consumer products, the Downy brand has remained a market share leader due to years of pleasing consumers and responding to their concerns.

## Brand Origins

During the years following World War II, technological advances led to the production of synthetic fabrics—low-maintenance materials that required little care and proved popular with the busy American woman trying to juggle family and job. Two consistent problems with these wonder fabrics, however, were stiffness of fiber (necessary to maintain shape) and static cling. The Procter & Gamble Company saw the opportunity to use its laboratory resources to address these concerns by developing a no-mess fabric softener which could be used in washing machines. The result of P&G's efforts was Liquid Downy, introduced in 1960. Twice as concentrated as the existing brands available at the time and sold in convenient, lightweight, unbreakable plastic bottles, Downy softener claimed superiority to other brands which were marketed in glass bottles.

## Early Marketing Strategy

P&G's marketing strategy for Downy fabric softener utilized techniques originated by Harley Procter in 1882 for P&G's Ivory soap campaign; product image, brand promotion, and consumer orientation were the integral components of this strategy. P&G allocated large amounts of time and money to its "marketing mix" for the Liquid Downy brand which included media and direct-mail advertising, point-of-purchase materials, samples, coupons, demonstrations, package offers, and refunds. With these extensive techniques, P&G hoped to make Downy a household product.

To soften laundry, a small amount of Downy liquid is poured into the rinse cycle of a washing machine to lubricate fabric—a process similar to hair conditioning. The lubricating action fluffs garments' fibers and prevents them from congealing into harsh clumps in the dryer. Downy softener eliminates the build-up of static charges in the dryer through its action in the washer. Static electricity occurs in the dryer when fabrics composed of fibers such as nylon, rayon, cotton, and polyester brush against one another and exchange electrons. Low humidity in the drying cycle forms the perfect environment for the unequal build-up of charges in fabrics which causes them to cling together. To counteract this, softener molecules transfer to the fabrics, making the dissimilar fibers more alike. When these softened fibers rub together in the dryer, they do not generate a charge. Liquid Downy softener provided maximum benefits to machine-dried clothing because the tumbling action of the dryer continually fluffed fabric fibers, but the product also aided line-dried clothes, even though the weight of the water matted the fibers. Though line-dried clothing would not be as soft as machine-dried clothing, Downy was promoted as better than nothing in such situations.

P&G also suggested Downy fabric softener for delicate clothes that required hand-washing. As with machine-washing, Liquid Downy could be added to the final rinse to eliminate static. Temporary spotting, which occurred if any undiluted fabric conditioner came into contact with clothing, was easily eliminated by moistening the spot with warm water, rubbing with mild bar soap (P&G suggested Ivory), rinsing, and rewashing the item with detergent. This versatility increased Downy's chances of becoming a consumer mainstay.

One attribute that contributed to Downy's popularity was that the fabric softener worked effectively in both hard and soft water; thus people could use it regardless of their water source. Though Liquid Downy was safe to use on all washable fabrics, the product was not recommended for use on children's cotton sleepwear because it might reduce the efficacy of the garments' flame-resistant finishes.

## Advertising Innovations

In addition to sponsoring wholesome television shows that fostered family values, P&G utilized the print media to promote its Downy brand. Other campaigns included grocery store point-of-purchase displays featuring refund tear-off forms, coupons included with the Sunday paper, and direct-mail efforts that distributed trial size Downy bottles to prospective consumers. P&G's intense market research and mail surveys also served to elicit consumers' needs. To further expand their knowledge of consumer trends, in the late 1970s P&G became one of the first companies to include toll-free telephone numbers on its packages.

In October of 1991 P&G inaugurated its new EDLP (Every Day Low Price) policy, a new marketing strategy that lowered a retailer's cost for P&G products but eliminated the retailers' generous trade allowances. The Everyday Low Price policy was part of CEO Edwin L. Artzt's vision of a new P&G—a more profitable company driven by lower costs and higher brand loyalty derived from streamlined manufacturing operations, increased control over trade promotions, and consumer-oriented advertising. However, this "value pricing" program was not welcomed by retailers. As a trade-off, one of P&G's agencies, J. Brown and Associates in New York City, developed the Bonus Media Program in which specially "tagged" TV spots mentioned a local retailer's name at the end of a P&G-sponsored TV commercial. These spots promoted the local retailer as well as the P&G product—a win-win situation.

## AT A GLANCE

**D**owny brand fabric softener founded in 1960 at the laboratories of the Procter & Gamble Company in Cincinnati, Ohio.

**Performance:** *Market share*—35.5% of the fabric softener market (1991).

**Major competitor:** Procter & Gamble's Bounce; also Lever Brothers's Snuggle.

**Advertising:** *Agency*—Grey Advertising, New York, NY. *Major campaign*—"Deep down fluffy softness!"

**Addresses:** *Parent company*—Procter & Gamble Company, One Procter & Gamble Plaza, Cincinnati, OH 45202; phone: (513) 983-1100; fax: (513) 983-7847.

### Brand Development and Product Changes

As trends changed, so did Downy. Few alterations occurred in the years following the introduction of the Downy brand until 1981's test-marketing of "new" Downy fabric softener in the Boston area. The "new" Downy claimed to be a bluer, thicker, more perfumed formula developed to leave cloth even softer and more static-free. The formula was well-received by consumers and in 1983 "new" Downy fabric softener was rolled out nationally. Minor adjustments were incorporated later; perfumes were modified in 1985, caps were redesigned, and graphics were updated. The 1987 advertising slogan became "deep down fluffier softness."

By 1993 several variations of the Downy brand were on the market. Downy Regular Concentrate in the April Fresh Scent was the leading liquid conditioner in the U.S. marketplace despite the rising popularity of dryer-added sheets. Ultra Downy brand, a concentrated form of Liquid Downy, which required only one capful per load, also sold well. Downy refill cartons, the contents of which could be poured into an existing Ultra Downy bottle, appealed to consumers concerned with solid waste problems. Downy's line included various sizes and scents, including April Fresh, Sun Rinse Fresh, Mountain Spring and the unscented Downy Free. Environmentally-friendly, all Downy bottles were composed of 100 percent post-consumer HDPE (high-density polyethylene) recyclable plastic. Furthermore, the Ultra Downy refill carton was constructed of paperboard which was laminated with thin layers of plastic that P&G claimed was designed to be safely landfilled, incinerated, or composted. The refill carton, which resembled a cardboard milk container, utilized 75 percent less packaging than did the 64-ounce container of regular Downy.

Regular Concentrate Downy and Ultra Downy were intended to be added at the beginning of the rinse cycle and designed to be the last water solution to touch one's clothes. However, the presence of the fabric conditioner and detergent in the same cycle contributed to fabric staining, and both types of Downy had to be used in top-loading washers with Downy dispensers that could be ordered from Procter & Gamble. These dispensers enabled the user to "catch" the rinse cycle if the user placed a dispenser in the machine during the wash cycle, thus eliminating the need to be present for the rinse cycle. The next development at P&G was to create a cellulose-based sheet for dryer use that would soften fabric as well as Downy liquid. Available in 1993 in April Fresh and Sun Rinse Fresh scents, Downy dryer sheets were single-use sheets designed to be added to the start of each dryer load. As the

Downy sheet tumbled with the laundry, the heat of the dryer released of the softening ingredients and static control agents. The sheets could be used for all dryer-safe fabrics including synthetics, natural fibers, permanent press, colors, and whites. Small translucent spots or streaking which might appear on some synthetics or blends could be avoided by using a low heat setting and drying full loads instead of a few small items. P&G scientists discovered, however, that some polyesters would spot consistently when dryer softeners were used, and for those P&G recommended the traditional Liquid Downy.

### Environmental Controversy

By 1993 P&G maintained that ingredients in Liquid Downy and Downy dryer sheets were biodegradable and/or satisfactorily removed during sewage treatment and would not contribute to landfill contamination or injure aquatic life. Originally, however, P&G had used alkyl benzene sulfate as a cleaning agent in Downy softener. Although the compound was effective and affordable, it had serious flaws—it did not break down during sewage treatment, and it left white foam along the banks of rivers and streams. Even though P&G proved in congressional investigations that Downy's alkyl benzene sulfates did not pose a public health hazard, the company voluntarily switched to linear alkyl sulfate. However, the suds along waterways persisted, and environmentalists pushed for further governmental intervention.

P&G's next ecological snag occurred when an international commission composed of representatives of Canada and the United States was appointed to study the effects of phosphates in the Great Lakes. The commission concluded that phosphates from consumer products resulted in "accelerated eutrophication"— over-fertilization and decay of algae that consumed oxygen needed by fish and other marine life to survive. The commission's report stated that although eutrophication was a natural process, manufacturers' detergent phosphates had accelerated the process to the point that fish and other aquatic life were suffocating and the lakes' fragile ecosystem had become unbalanced. As a result of this report, more stringent governmental rules were enacted to prevent a product's national introduction until it was determined to be environmentally safe. The new policy prompted P&G to funnel generous funds into research and development to ensure compliance with environmental regulations.

### Future Predictions

Since its debut in 1960 as Procter & Gamble's first fabric softener, the Downy brand has remained a market share leader in the United States. Although the product's perfume was imported from France, as of 1993 P&G did not market Downy internationally. P&G strives to keep pace with progress by querying consumers, providing samples and generating advertising in an effort to address consumers' changing needs. As a P&G researcher once remarked: "It isn't enough to invent a new product. Through constant improvement, we must manage every existing brand so that it can flourish year after year in an ever-changing, intensely competitive marketplace. . . . At P&G, we create the future."

### Further Reading:

*Answers About Marketing,* Cincinnati, OH: Procter & Gamble Company, 1993.

Cleary, David Powers, *Great American Brands,* New York: Fairchild Publications, 1981.

"Fabric Softeners," *Consumer Reports,* February 1991, p. 109.

"Fabric Softeners," *Consumer Reports 1988 Buying Guide,* December 1987, p. 79.

"Fabric Softeners," *Consumer Reports 1989 Buying Guide,* December 1988, p. 81.

*Facts About Procter & Gamble,* Cincinnati, OH: Procter & Gamble Company, 1993.

Freeman, Laurie, "Downy to Get Refill: P&G Container Resembles Milk Carton," *Advertising Age,* November 13, 1989, p. 92.

"Ivorydale—A Procter & Gamble Landmark," Cincinnati, OH: Procter & Gamble Company, 1993.

Koeppel, Dan, "P&G Launches 'Environment-Friendly' Downy," *Adweek's Marketing Week,* November 20, 1989, p. 6.

Lawrence, Jennifer, "P&G's Downy Goes Ultra: Concentrate Features Smaller Bottle, Recycled Plastic," *Advertising Age,* June 15, 1992, p. 2; "P&G Hooks up Interactive Product-Sampling Hot Line," *Advertising Age,* October 5, 1992, p. 3; "P&G Customizes Ads to Plug Retailers, *Advertising Age,* February 8, 1993, p. 28; "Will P&G's Pricing Policy Pull Retailers Over to Its Side?" *Advertising Age,* April 19, 1993, pp. 1, 42–43.

Lief, Alfred, *"It Floats"; The Story of Procter & Gamble,* New York: Rinehart, 1958.

*The Procter & Gamble Company,* Cincinnati, OH: Procter & Gamble Company, 1993.

The Procter & Gamble Company Annual Report, Cincinnati, OH: Procter & Gamble Company, 1992.

*Procter & Gamble: The House That Ivory Built,* Lincolnwood, IL: NTC Business Books, 1988.

Schisgall, Oscar, *Eyes on Tomorrow: The Evolution of Procter & Gamble,* Chicago: J.G. Ferguson Publishing Company, 1981.

"The True Performance of Fabric Softeners," *Consumer Reports,* July 1987, pp. 420–22.

*—Virginia Barnstorff*

# DR. SCHOLL'S®

The Dr. Scholl's brand comprises the best-known and best-selling line of foot care products in the United States. Dr. Scholl's has almost two-thirds of the total foot care market share, close to 90 percent of the market share for shoe insoles and inserts, and more than 50 percent of the market share for athlete's foot remedies; foot deodorants and anti-perspirants; and corn, bunion, and wart treatments. The brand originated with a Chicago doctor's invention in 1904. The resourceful and enterprising Dr. William Scholl patented products for every aspect of foot health, and his arch supports, corn pads, insoles, and foot powders were soon sold around the world. The Dr. Scholl brand could be found at specialty Dr. Scholl Foot Comfort Shops in the United States and Europe, as well as in shoe stores and drug stores. The brand also included a line of therapeutic shoes for men and women. The Dr. Scholl's Exercise Sandal became a fashion must in the 1970s, and was one of the brand's most well-known items. Currently, the Dr. Scholl brand is marketed by the Schering-Plough HealthCare Corporation. Schering-Plough revamped the line in the 1990s using the latest technology, anticipating continued double-digit growth in the foot care market. But the brand is still sold in the familiar yellow and blue packaging designed early in its history, maintaining a strong tie with tradition.

## Brand Origins

The Dr. Scholl brand was the inspiration of William Mathias Scholl, a medical doctor who devoted his life to inventing and promoting a huge array of products to ease foot discomfort. He was born in 1882 on a dairy farm in La Porte, Indiana, and he learned to make shoes from his grandfather. At this time, there was no such thing as standard shoe sizes, and shoes were made in only two widths—wide and narrow. Even the practice of making differently shaped shoes for the left and right foot was new when Scholl was young, the custom having come into vogue only after the Civil War. Scholl moved to Chicago in 1899 to attend medical school, and he supported himself by working in a shoe store. There he saw the ill-effects of city living on his customers' feet. Poorly fitted shoes, walking on concrete, and standing up all day all led to a variety of foot stresses. Scholl concentrated his medical studies on the anatomy and care of the foot, and though he received his medical license in 1904, he never practiced general medicine. Even before he graduated from medical school he had patented his Foot-Eazer arch supports, and as soon as he was out of school he began making them by hand and peddling them to Chicago shoe

shops. The Foot-Eazer was made from leather, with a self-adjusting double spring below, and fit inside a shoe to help hold up a weak arch. The young doctor's flair for salesmanship equalled his designing talent. He carried a skeleton of the human foot in a special pocket of his coat, and he would take this out to demonstrate scientifically how his Foot-Eazer worked.

Scholl's business grew rapidly. He incorporated the Scholl Manufacturing Company in 1907, and two years later he opened his own factory in Chicago. The factory was soon making a variety of products with the Dr. Scholl name, including his Zino Pads for corns, foot plaster, foot soap, foot powder, and more. These were packaged in the bright yellow and blue colors that are still used for Dr. Scholl products today. Dr. Scholl worked tirelessly to educate the public and the shoe business in the proper care of the foot. He campaigned to get shoe manufacturers to standardize shoe sizes and to offer more widths. And in 1912 he founded the Illinois College of Chiropody and Orthopedics, later re-named the Scholl College of Podiatric Medicine.

Meanwhile, searching for new markets for his products, Scholl traveled to Europe. On one trip he fitted arch supports for Kaiser Wilhelm II. Another star customer was Olympic champion Paavo Nurmi, "the flying Finn"; Scholl hand-built special arch supports for the athlete's running shoes. Dr. Scholl found Europe promising and decided to send his brother, Frank, to London to work the business from there.

## Early Marketing

Frank Scholl, William's younger brother, had joined the Scholl company in 1908 and brought to the business a unique eye for retailing. It was Frank's idea to open the first Dr. Scholl Foot Comfort Shop to sell the Scholl line. William Scholl was skeptical, because he did not want to compete with the drugstores and shoe stores that sold Scholl products, but Frank won out and opened his London shop in 1913. There were eventually hundreds of company-owned and franchised shops throughout Europe and America.

Frank's motto was "a well dressed window pays your rent," and the Comfort Shop windows were quite spectacular. An imposing front window display was crammed with Dr. Scholl's products from floor to ceiling-level, all in the same eye-catching yellow and blue packaging. Model legs and feet demonstrated

## AT A GLANCE

The first Dr. Scholl's product was patented in 1904 by Chicago doctor William Mathias Scholl, and his Scholl Manufacturing Company was incorporated in 1907; company was acquired by the Schering-Plough Corp. in 1979.

**Performance:** *Market share*—67% (top share) of the foot care market.

**Major competitor:** No major competitor in insoles and inserts category; Combes' Odor Eaters in odor and wetness category.

**Advertising:** *Agency*—Messner, Vetere, Berger, McNameee, Schmetterer, New York, NY. *Major campaign*—Television spots for insoles and inserts featuring an elephant perched on a woman's shoulders, a sumo wrestler on a man's shoulders, to demonstrate the enormous weight the average person puts on his or her feet daily.

**Addresses:** *Parent company*—Schering-Plough HealthCare Products, Inc., 110 Allen Road, Liberty Corners, NJ 07938; phone: (908) 320-2011. *Ultimate parent company*—Schering-Plough Corp., One Giralda Farms, Madison, NJ 07940; phone: (201) 822-7000.

products, and large advertisements and posters explained them. One moving display graphically illustrated the burden the human foot carries: an oversized sledgehammer, emblazoned "140 pounds, the weight of the average man," smashed down on the knee of a model skeleton leg, causing the foot beneath to flatten. This hammer pounding away in the shop window showed walking to be quite a painful process.

The elaborate Comfort Shop windows were designed to draw in anyone who might walk by. At the same time, the Scholl company worked hard to educate a more specific clientele, shoe salesmen, so that they could confidently recommend Scholl products to their customers. Dr. Scholl launched a series of correspondence and classroom study courses in 1915 that taught salesmanship as well as foot anatomy. The graduate of a Scholl course in "practipedics" might offer to take a "pedograph" of his customer's foot and scientifically analyze this impression. A "master shoe fitter" also learned to "read" his customers' shoes, and note from the way the shoes wore down the signs of a turned ankle, cramped toe, weak arch, or other problem. A full-page advertisement for Dr. Scholl's products from the 1930s illustrated shoe reading with the slogan, "If shoes could talk, read what these shoes would say." The shoes depicted explained such things as, "I wear holes in my owner's hosiery because I slip out at the heel," and, "My shank is broken down, the front of my heel is worn off, and my uppers bulge around the ankle owing to a flat foot condition." These shoes explained problem after problem, and the remedies were to be found in Dr. Scholl's products. The extent of the Scholl line was quite ample—more than 500 foot and leg care products had been introduced by the 1970s.

## Shoes

The Dr. Scholl brand eventually included shoes as well as shoe appliances. A national chain of Scholl shoe stores opened in 1933. The Scholl brand shoes were well built, designed for maximum wearer comfort. The basic men's shoe was a sturdy black oxford with extra padding in the uppers and thick, soft soles. Women's shoes, too, were made for comfort and durability, not style, and

they were preferred by people who worked on their feet. In the late 1940s the Scholl company bought a custom shoe manufacturing plant in Wisconsin and added their hand-made "Co-Peg" shoes to the Scholl line.

Dr. Scholl's shoes were not designed to be fashionable, so it was something of a shock to the company when Dr. Scholl's Exercise Sandals became a youth fashion statement in the 1970s. The exercise sandal had a contoured beechwood sole, which secured itself to the foot with a simple leather strap. The action of the big toe gripping the wooden sole was supposed to tone the leg muscles. Scholl began marketing them in 1965, and they soon became a hit with young British women. The craze for Dr. Scholl's sandals spread to the United States, and the Scholl company backed the product with radio, television, and print ads. The exercise sandals were endorsed by the U.S. ski team and the British Royal Ballet. Scholl's marketers placed the sandals in self-service display racks in drug stores, instead of limiting them to Scholl shoe shops. This strategy was meant to have several effects. It brought awareness of Dr. Scholl's foot care line to much younger customers and so helped to banish the image of Scholl products for only the old and tired. It brought profits to the company as well. The sandals were an impulse buy that cost close to $13.00, and so the Scholl company made them as broadly available as possible.

## Corporate Changes

Dr. William Scholl died in 1968. A life-long bachelor, he left the company to two nephews. Jack Scholl ran the U.S. side of Scholl, Inc., from Chicago as vice president and general manager. His cousin William Scholl became president of the company and was in charge of international markets. He lived in England and managed markets in Japan, Canada, Latin America, Europe, and New Zealand. The cousins reorganized and modernized the Dr. Scholl brand, updating the packaging, dropping less successful products, and collecting marketing talent from other companies. The Scholl fortune climbed steadily: in the first six years after Dr. William Scholl's death, sales and profits had risen by 100 percent. The company, which had been 99 percent family owned until Dr. William Scholl's death, made a public stock offering in 1971 in order to settle the Scholl estate. 650,000 shares sold for $14.3 million. Sales in 1972 were $127 million and by 1978 were up to $245 million. The brand proved "recession proof" as well, as people tended to spend more on shoe upkeep during business downturns.

## Later Market Conditions

Because people were wearing more comfortable shoes than in the days when Dr. Scholl had visited shoe shops with a foot skeleton in his coat pocket, the market for such items as corn and callous cures had actually decreased. Yet sales had increased in other areas to make up for it. Foot sprays and powders were a hot growth area in the 1970s, and several companies launched products in competition with Dr. Scholl's. Beside the other established brands Desenex and Quinsana, Gillette came out with Foot Guard and the Carter-Wallace Company introduced Arrid Extra foot spray and a foot powder called Dri-Power. This segment of the market was estimated as having sales of $15 million in 1971, which was only half the sales figure for feminine hygiene deodorants and five percent of underarm deodorant sales, leaving plenty of room for expansion.

Dr. Scholl's ads of this era tried to steer away from an image of sick, old feet. Humorous television commercials for the brand depicted the trauma of foot odor and the agony of hot, overworked feet in far-fetched scenes that did not target any specific market segment. A commercial for Gillette's competing foot spray, for example, showed a mother spraying deodorant into her daughter's boots, as women who wore plastic boots had been found to have foot odor problems. In contrast, the Dr. Scholl's commercial showed a medieval street scene with a man locked in stocks. The smell of his protruding feet cause even a dog to faint. In the same vein, a commercial for a cooling aerosol foot spray showed an Indian man walking barefoot across a bed of coals, then rushing out of sight of his audience to spray on some Dr. Scholl's. These light-hearted ads were in keeping with the Scholl company's aim to appeal to younger customers.

The Dr. Scholl's brand had enjoyed a large market share and steady sales for most of its first 75 years. After the death of Dr. William Scholl, when the company went public for the first time, Scholl, Inc., found itself pursued by larger companies looking for an acquisition. Jack Scholl claimed that "just about everybody in the Fortune 500" had made offers. To pre-empt a possible hostile take-over, Scholl, Inc., arranged a merger with the Schering-Plough Corp., which paid $130 million for the foot care company in 1979. Schering-Plough was a large health care and consumer products firm that marketed well-known brands such as Coppertone suntan lotion and Di-Gel antacid. Schering-Plough also sold the athlete's foot drugs Lotrimin AF and Tinactin as well as DuoFilm wart medication; these combined with Dr. Scholl's products made an even more comprehensive foot care line. Schering-Plough continued to promote and develop the Dr. Scholl brand during the 1980s, and in the 1990s significantly updated the line using new technology. Using advanced computer assisted designs and new shock absorbing materials called Poron and IMPLUS, Schering-Plough developed more efficient shoe insoles. These were marketed in a men's and women's line that included insoles tailored for special needs: Toe Squish Preventer Cushions and Ultra-Thin Insoles were meant to be worn in high heels, and the men's line included inserts for sports shoes as well as dress and casual shoes. Other new product developments included a Bunion Guard made of a new malleable material, Odor Destroying Sports Insoles, Super Absorbent Foot Powder, and BackGuard, a shoe insert made to reduce lower back pain.

## Performance Appraisal

Dr. William Scholl's lifelong dedication to easing foot discomfort led him practically to invent the modern foot care market. His scientific designs coupled with creative and persistent promotion of his products led to the early success of his brand. No other brand offered as complete an array of foot care products. Yet when Schering-Plough acquired Scholl, Inc., in 1979, a financial writer for *Forbes* magazine characterized Scholl as a mature business, and doubted that there was any growth left in such a company. Though sales had been increasing, so had inflation, and overall profits were not growing. However, Dr. Scholl's new parent company researched the foot care market carefully and found great opportunity for reaching new consumers. The demographics of the post-war baby boom meant that by 1996, more than half of the U.S. population would be 35 years old or older, and this aging population would presumably experience common shoe and foot-related problems. And though the foot care category was only the ninth-largest consumer health care area in terms of sales, it was the fourth-fastest-growing category in the late 1980s. Growth of the total foot care market between 1986 and 1991 equaled 47 percent, and sales across the board in 1991 were $520 million. Schering-Plough expected this figure to double by 1996. The company also expected younger and more affluent consumers to be attracted to Dr. Scholl's products, as baby boomers looked for ways to increase their shoes' performance. Schering-Plough resolved to do its best to attract this expanding market by relaunching the Dr. Scholl's line, using more technologically advanced materials. The company also updated the packaging and retail display of the Dr. Scholl's line and outspent its competitors in advertising and promoting the brand. Schering-Plough's market research and dedication to new design and materials seemed a continuation of the original mission of Dr. Scholl, thus the brand should continue its vitality in coming years.

## Further Reading:

Ackland, Len, *Chicago Tribune*, "Scholl Is Heading for Tennessee," August 7, 1979, sec. 4, p. 7; "Those Footsteps Are Scholl's—Out of Town," August 12, 1979, sec. 5, p. 1.

"Feet First—The Scholl Story," Exhibition at Dr. William M. Scholl College of Podiatric Medicine, 1993.

Nagelberg, Alvin, "Scholl's Emphasis Shifts to Comfort," *Chicago Tribune*, September 3, 1973, sec. 3, p. 7.

O'Connor, John J., "Foot Spray Market about to Take Giant Strides," *Advertising Age*, June 28, 1971, p. 8.

"Price Increases Step Up Pace of Earnings Recovery at Scholl," *Barron's*, September 2, 1974, p. 23.

Schering-Plough HealthCare Corp. press releases, 1993.

Seneker, Harold, "Is There Growth in Corn Plasters?," *Forbes*, January 21, 1980, p. 78.

"Those Aching Feet," *Time*, August 24, 1962, pp. 60–61.

"Young Dr. Scholl," *Sales Management*, June 12, 1972, p. 3.

*—A. Woodward*

# DRĀNO®

Drāno has been the leading drain opening product since its introduction in 1923. Through much of its history it defined the sector, controlling up to 90 percent of the market share. Drāno was also the first major commercial success of its founder, the Drackett Co., which went on to become a major player in the homecare products field. Drackett, a subsidiary of Bristol-Myers Squibb since 1965, was bought by S.C. Johnson & Son, Inc. in 1992; Drāno and a number of other successful Drackett brands switched to the S.C. Johnson Wax label as a result.

Drāno's tremendous commercial success was in large part due to its early arrival on the scene of the booming indoor plumbing industry. As the first product of its type marketed specifically for home use, Drāno captured a huge market in its infancy and managed to retain that market on an almost exclusive basis for almost half a century. It was only in the 1970s that competitors, most notably Clorox's Liquid Plumr, began to pose a serious threat to Drāno's dominance of the market.

## Brand Origins

The successful introduction of Drāno can be attributed to a single phenomenon; the huge expansion in the availability of indoor plumbing in the early twentieth century. As discussed in *Never Done*, Susan Strasser's definitive book on American housework, it was not until the early twentieth century that both public policy and the industrialization of the plumbing fixture industry made plumbing available to the majority of homes. After World War I the manufacture of plumbing fixtures boomed, more than doubling between 1921 and 1925. Drāno's launch in 1923 was a direct response to this new trend. Although the introduction of indoor plumbing was a welcome relief to the unpleasant chores of carrying water and disposing of sewage, a number of concerns surrounded the new technology. American householders, always reluctant to attach their homes to public facilities, felt uneasy with the notion that sewage would leave their home through pipes leading to an unseen sewage system. Stories abounded about porous sewers and faulty fixtures leaking invisible, contaminated "sewer gas" into unsuspecting homes. While there was little foundation for these concerns, keeping drainage pipes clean and free-running was perceived as necessary not only for effective plumbing, but also for the very health of American families. Drackett's Drāno was marketed to take advantage of this concern.

The Drackett Company was a small manufacturer of chemicals for industrial use when it was incorporated in 1915. Among its products was sodium hydroxide, commonly known as lye, a caustic cleansing agent used in a variety of industrial applications. When dissolved in water, lye releases a great deal of heat, literally melting many types of dirt and grease. It also chemically alters the structure of fat, gradually turning it into a water-soluble soap. Lye was clearly the ideal substance for chemically cleaning drains since, when flushed with water, it was effective at dissolving just those sorts of protein and fat based substances, such as grease and hair, which are likely to lodge in a pipe. Lye also reacts with certain metals, forming a fizz of hydrogen gas. Drackett realized that the inclusion of tiny metal nuggets with the pellets of lye would cause the fizzing hydrogen to actually physically loosen up debris, creating what would be called in advertisements the "churning action" of Drāno crystals. Sold in quantities ranging from a 50-pound drum to a 12-ounce tin, Crystal Drāno's simple combination of solid lye and metal pellets would become virtually the only chemical drain cleaner to be used in American households for some 50 years after its launch.

## Product Development

The dry crystal version of Drāno has undergone relatively little change since its introduction in 1923. The cleaning and sanitizing aspect of the product has been emphasized with the introduction of a variety of scents, including a pine-odor fragrance launched in 1968 with the distribution of live pine trees to buyers. The major product innovation occurred in 1966 with the introduction of Liquid Drāno. Although relatively effective at clearing blocked drains, Crystal Drāno had two major drawbacks. Because of the risk of corrosion from the chemical action and heat it generated, Crystal Drāno could not be used in more complex mechanisms such as garbage disposals. In addition, Crystal Drāno dissolved quickly in water so that all standing water had to be removed from a blocked drain if Drāno were to effectively reach the clog. Liquid Drāno was designed to solve these two problems. Composed of a liquid solution of 2.4 percent sodium hydroxide (lye), six percent sodium hypochlorite (bleach), and a corrosion inhibitor, Liquid Drāno was far less corrosive than the crystal formula, which was composed of up to 54 percent lye. The liquid product could therefore be used to clean drains connected to garbage disposals, an appliance that became increasingly popular in the 1960s. Liquid Drāno also did not dissolve in water; it could thus be poured

## AT A GLANCE

**D**rāno brand of drain cleaner founded in 1935 in Cincinnati, Ohio, by Drackett Co.; Drackett bought as subsidiary by Bristol-Myers Squibb, 1965; Drackett bought by S.C. Johnson & Son Inc., 1992.

**Performance:** *Market share*—41% (top share) of drain cleaner category. *Sales*—$58,000,000.

**Major competitor:** Clorox's Liquid Plumr.

**Advertising:** *Agency*—DDB Needham Chicago, IL, 1993.

**Addresses:** *Parent company*—S.C. Johnson & Son, Inc., 1525 Howe St., Racine, WI 53403; phone: (414) 631-2000; fax: (414) 631-2000.

directly into blocked drains where standing water had accumulated. At the same time, however, Liquid Drāno was not as effective at clearing completely blocked drains as was the caustic crystal product. It was therefore marketed primarily as a drain "cleaner." Following the introduction of a professional strength product by Drāno's major competitor, Clorox's Liquid Plumr, in 1991, Drackett also came out with a stronger formula of Liquid Drāno, Drāno Plus, which contained 2.5 percent lye and ten percent sodium hypochlorite.

Traditionally all Drāno products and their major competitors had used lye as their principle active ingredient. In the mid-1980s, however, a new type of drain cleaner was introduced as the result of research in biotechnology. Launched by a variety of smaller brands, these products made use of genetically engineered enzymes specifically designed to eat the hair and grease of clogged drains. The enzymes used in these drain cleaners did not present the chemical hazards of caustic drain cleaners, hazards which had prompted increasing concern in the environmentally conscious 1980s. Unfortunately, although the enzymes could be designed to soften either hair or grease, they couldn't seem to successfully eat through the diverse materials which made up a typical blocked drain. In 1993 both Drāno and the chief competitor, Liquid Plumr, launched enzyme-based build-up removers in an attempt to exploit the potential of this new technology. These products were described only as drain cleaners with no claim to open completely blocked drains. It was argued that with regular use the liquid build-up remover would clear the greasy sludge that builds up in drains and thus prevent future blockages. This was precisely the argument that had been used all along by the marketers of Drāno, even though consumers had continued to perceive Drāno products as primarily useful for unclogging slow-running or blocked drains.

### International Presence

The highly successful Drackett Co. began to expand its international operations in the late 1950s and early 1960s. The company's first move outside the United States involved the founding of a wholly-owned subsidiary, Drackett Canada. By 1964 Drackett was distributing Drāno in Germany, Australia, and England and test marketing the product in other common market countries. A spokesman for the company at that time commented in the *Investment Dealers' Digest* that the potential distribution of Drāno was limited only by that of indoor plumbing. The acquisition of Drackett by Bristol Myers Squibb in 1965 further expanded the distribution of Drāno as Bristol Myers established distribution networks in the Middle East and Far East regions. S.C. Johnson & Son, who

purchased Drackett in 1992, also maintained a very strong overseas presence, meshing conveniently with the already established distribution system for Drāno.

### Government Regulation

Drāno has faced an ongoing battle with image, both because of its association with drains and waste products, and because of its extremely corrosive formula. Lye-based drain cleaners like Crystal Drāno are among the most dangerous household products when used improperly and have consequently faced a variety of federal regulations. The very properties that make Crystal Drāno so effective at cleaning drains also make it extremely dangerous when touched or ingested by humans. Just as it dissolves the grease and hair of drain clogs, Drāno dissolves the fats and proteins on the surfaces of human cells and can cause severe damage to the eyes, skin, and mucous membranes. If ingested even in relatively small quantities, Crystal Drāno can be fatal. When Drāno was introduced in 1923 there were no federal regulations regarding the labelling or packaging of household products but by 1929 the federal government passed the Federal Caustic Poison Act, which required a limited warning label on lye-based products. By 1959 the large number of new chemicals on the market and an alarming rise in the number of household poisonings prompted the federal government to take stronger measures and a new Hazardous Substances Act was enacted. Under this act and subsequent amendments, sodium hydroxide, the major active ingredient in Crystal Drāno, became a heavily regulated chemical requiring the designation "Poison" and the skull and crossbones symbol on the front of all product packages containing more than a ten percent concentration. In 1970 liquid drain cleaners containing more than a ten percent solution of sodium hydroxide were banned outright, presumably because of the greater danger of ingestion and spillage of the liquid product.

### Marketing and Advertising

From its inception, Drackett Co. had promoted Drāno for its ability to maintain clear drains through regular use rather than exclusively as a drain opener. This marketing strategy had the double advantage of promoting the benefits of the product while encouraging its frequent use. When Liquid Drāno was introduced in the mid-1960s this aspect of product promotion was emphasized even more strongly since the liquid version of the product did not perform well on completely blocked drains. Advertisements and packaging stressed the convenience of the new Liquid Drāno, suggesting that it be used regularly in order to prevent the buildup of greasy clogs. While the earliest Drāno advertisements stressed the potential health hazards of dirty drains, as people became more and more comfortable with the notion of public drainage systems this argument for the use of drain cleaners began to lose its force. The idea that sanitary drains were important for health reasons was in part replaced by an appeal that reminded consumers of the odor of unclean drains, and scented versions of Drāno were introduced.

Drāno's inherently unglamorous image has posed a challenge to its marketers over the years. While Windex, Drackett's other very successful brand, could be promoted through imagery of sunlight shining through gleaming windows to the accompaniment of inspirational music, the notion of gleaming drains was not likely to excite the same emotional response. Drāno's marketers sought to overcome this difficulty through the use of simple demonstration advertisements and, even more importantly, humor.

By the 1950s television had become a major advertising vehicle for the Drackett Company, who became the sponsors of the hugely popular Jackie Gleason show. Gleason delivered comical lead-ins to the Drackett commercials, posing with a shopping cart full of oversized Drackett products, including a two-foot-high can of Drāno. Humor remained an important marketing technique for Drāno through the 1980s. A 1987 campaign by Grey Advertising even featured a naked man after his bath joyfully unclogging the drain with Drāno to the tune of the Bobby Darin hit "Splish Splash, I was taking a bath."

## Major Competitors and Performance

Drāno held a virtual monopoly in the chemical drain cleaner market for almost fifty years after its introduction in 1923. In 1959 Drāno could claim over 90 percent of the drain cleaner segment. The first and only significant threat to Drāno's dominance of the market has been Clorox's Liquid Plumr. Liquid Plumr was developed by the Jiffee Chemical Company in the early 1960s but in 1969 the brand was bought by Clorox, which hoped to gain a share of the then $40 million drain cleaner sector. Liquid Plumr was chemically very similar to Liquid Drāno, essentially relying on a liquid solution of sodium hydroxide (lye). Clorox began heavy promotion of its newly acquired brand, pitting it directly against Liquid Drāno in advertising campaigns. Perhaps because of its descriptive name and Drāno's association with the well-established crystal format, Liquid Plumr quickly picked up a sizable share of the drain cleaner market, surpassing Liquid Drāno in sales of liquid drain cleaners. Drāno responded with comparison ads of its own but its stranglehold on the drain cleaner market had been lost for good. The two liquid products were running virtually neck and neck, struggling to gain each market point, when Liquid Plumr brought out a stronger Professional Strength formula in 1990. Drāno quickly followed with Drāno Plus, a product that claimed to contain 35 percent more active ingredients. The advertising campaign for Drāno Plus started an advertising war between the two brands that eventually led both companies to bring complaints to the National Advertising Division of the Council of Better Business Bureaus. As reported in *Advertising Age* in 1992, the NAD found in favor of both complainants. The NAD argued that Drāno Plus should modify its ad to clearly identify the target product of the "35 percent more active ingredients" comparison claim as being regular strength Liquid Plumr (rather than the more potent Professional Strength formula) and that Professional Strength Liquid Plumr drop its claim that "all other liquid drain openers dilute . . . and wimp out." The NAD did, however, support Liquid Plumr's claim to superior performance on completely clogged drains despite Drāno Plus's contention that the clogs illustrated were not common in real-life situations.

While Drāno and Liquid Plumr were essentially very similar sodium hypochloride-based products, a number of other chemical drain cleaners on the market used acid-based formulations instead. These ranged from Lime-O-Sol's The Works, which uses primarily hydrochloric acid, to Rooto Professional, made from sulfuric acid. None of these products made any great impact on the drain cleaner market, as they were either no more effective than lye at clearing blockages or sufficiently dangerous to seriously inhibit household use. New developments in biotechnology created an entirely different type of drain cleaner in the 1980s. Launched by a variety of smaller companies, these brands, including Dispoz-all and Microbe Lift II, are safer than lye- or acid-based formulas. These products, however, proved to be less effective at clearing blocked drains and failed to capture a significant share of the drain cleaner market. In 1993 Drāno and Liquid Plumr officially launched their own versions of enzyme-based drain build-up removers.

S.C. Johnson & Son, Inc. continues its efforts to improve Drāno, in part because of environmental issues. It is possible that increasingly environmentally conscious consumers may become reluctant to buy products with the harsh chemicals of traditional drain cleaners. Drāno continues in 1993 as a market force, with a 41 percent share of the $141 million drain cleaner market, second only to Liquid Plumr's 50-percent share.

## Further Reading:

"Drain Cleaners," *Consumer Reports,* January, 1988, p. 60–63.

"Drackett Brands," *Advertising Age,* April 12, 1993, p. 41.

"Drackett Earnings Gleam on Research, Promotion," *Barron's,* February 9, 1959, pp. 34–6.

"Drackett Heads for National Distribution of Pine-Odor Drāno," *Advertising Age,* April 22, 1968, p. 4.

"Drackett Pushes Its New Drāno as Safe, Easy to Use," *Advertising Age,* April 18, 1966, p. 54.

Freeman, Laurie, "Drackett fights to keep household edge," *Advertising Age,* February 27, 1989, p. 35.

Gibson, Richard, "Bristol-Myers To Sell Drackett to S.C. Johnson," *The Wall Street Journal,* October 28, 1992, p. B1.

Harte, John, "Sodium Hydroxide," *Toxics A to Z,* Berkeley: University of California Press, 1991, pp. 398–400.

Jensen, Jeff, "NAD clears drain opener dispute," *Advertising Age,* December 14, 1992, p. 39.

Kelly, Janice, "NARB to review Drāno Plus case," *Advertising Age,* May 4, 1992, p. 46.

Lippert, Barbara, "Drāno Breaks Through With Some Bubbly Sex Appeal," *Adweek's Marketing Week,* September 21, 1987, p. 30.

Marchand, Roland, *Advertising the American Dream,* Berkeley: University of California.

Mathews, Carol, "Stick-To-It-iveness Pays Off For Drackett Co.," *Investment Dealers' Digest,* February 24, 1964, pp. 30–31.

Mitchell, Thomas, "J-Wax completes $1.1 billion cash buyout of Drackett Co.," *The Journal Times,* January 1, 1993, p. 6.

Strasser, Susan, *Never Done,* New York: Pantheon Books, 1982.

*—Hilary Gopnik*

# DRISTAN®

# Dristan®

When people reach into their medicine cabinets, they are often looking for quick relief, easily administered. With a wide array of products and a highly recognizable name, Dristan has been providing such relief for more than 35 years. To understand the appeal of Dristan products is to acknowledge what life was like before them. Cold, flu, and allergy sufferers once had little in the way of accessible treatment for their ills; aspirin did not always do the job, doctors' prescriptions could be costly, and the combination of ingredients needed to produce results could be confusing.

In 1957, Whitehall Laboratories, now a division of American Home Products Corporation, introduced its first multi-symptom relief formula called Dristan. Dristan tablets' combination of active formulas set them apart from other over-the-counter products. One dose of Dristan provided a *decongestant* to clear nasal passageways, an *antihistamine* to dry out runny noses and eyes and relieve sneezing, and an *analgesic* pain reliever for the headaches that often accompanied colds and flu. Future Dristan products would also contain a cough suppressant.

## Fast Relief

Dristan became popular quickly because it provided fast relief in one convenient dose. Naturally, the widespread availability of decongestants and antihistamines sparked competition from other laboratories, but Dristan prevailed by virtue of its innovation in the marketplace. The product went on to become one of the top-selling over-the-counter brands, and remained a formidable market presence into the 1990s.

As well as Dristan tablets worked, however, there was still room for faster relief. And so in 1958 a new kind of Dristan product emerged. Dristan Nasal Spray combined the same decongestant and antihistamine as the tablets but was based on a unique concept: topical (inhaled) application. The idea of something that worked even faster than a tablet appealed to scores of Americans immediately. Dristan Nasal Spray, like the pills, beat out the competitors to become America's leading nasal spray. More recently Dristan Nasal Spray has captured 8.8% of the $195 million-per-year nasal spray market, behind competitors like Afrin and Sinex.

## New Formulas for Relief

The cold-relief business relies in part on a distinction between over-the-counter and prescription medicines. The regulations that govern drugs vary; a prescription-only medicine in the United States may be available over-the-counter in other countries. But when a drug is deemed safe enough for U.S. public consumption, manufacturers hurry to incorporate it into their formulas. Such was the case with Dristan Nasal Spray. For almost two decades it provided temporary relief of sinus congestion, any stronger medication would have to be prescribed. Then, in 1976, after several years as a prescription medication, the stronger drug Xylometazoline was made available over-the-counter. Dristan quickly adopted this higher-strength decongestant into its sprays. The result was the creation of Dristan Long-Lasting Nasal Spray and Dristan Long-Lasting Menthol Nasal Spray, each providing up to eight hours of relief.

The long-lasting nasal spray formulas were reformulated in 1981 to improve their efficiency. A few years later, another drug was made available to manufacturers. The new drug, Oxymetazoline, replaced the old Xylometazoline as Dristan Nasal Spray's "active ingredient." With the new formulation, up to 12 hours of relief from sinus congestion could be expected. By 1987, both regular and long-lasting nasal sprays were reformulated once again with the addition of an agent called Methylcellulose. This ingredient complemented the decongestant by providing a layer of soothing cellulose, a glucose-like organic substance.

Not all improvements to Dristan were chemical. In 1987, the Dristan sprays received a lengthened applicator nozzle, making the sprays easier to use. In 1988, Dristan addressed this issue with a metered dose extension line of its regular and long-lasting nasal treatments. One traditional drawback to nasal sprays is the tendency some people have to inhale too much, or not enough. With the metered system, each spray ejects the precise pre-measured dose with every application.

Seasonal "dry nose," a problem for many allergy sufferers, was addressed by the creation of a new Dristan product. For these needs, Dristan introduced the non-medicated Dristan Saline Spray in 1992. As many times a day as needed, an adult or child can use this spray to moisten nasal passages and improve breathing.

While all the nasal sprays were being formulated and reformulated, traditional Dristan tablets, caplets, and easy-to-swallow "gelcaps" were expanding the company's product line further. In 1988, for instance, Maximum Strength No-Drowsiness Dristan was introduced with great success. Two years later, Dristan Sinus

## AT A GLANCE

**F**irst Dristan product, a multi-symptom cold-relief formula, introduced in 1957 by Whitehall Laboratories, now a division of American Home Products; Dristan Nasal Spray introduced in 1958.

**Performance:** *Market share*—Dristan Nasal Sprays: 8.8% of nonprescription nasal sprays market segment. *Sales*—$17 million; Dristan annual combined consumer sales: $35 million.

**Major competitor:** Sinex; also, Afrin and Neo-Synephrine.

**Advertising:** *Agency*—McCann-Erickson, New York, NY, 1986—. *Major campaign*—"When you can't call in sick, call on Dristan" (1988); "Smell the Orange" (1991).

**Addresses:** *Parent company*—Whitehall Laboratories, 685 Third Avenue, New York, NY 10017-4076; phone: (212) 878-5500. *Ultimate parent company*—American Home Products Corporation, 685 Third Avenue, New York, NY 10017-4085.

formula hit the market to join the ever-growing legion of sinus-only medications. Dristan Sinus has the active ingredient of ibuprofen, a drug often associated with the pain reliever Motrin. The addition of ibuprofen made Dristan Sinus one of the strongest pain-relieving sinus medicines available over the counter.

## An Industry First

For years, one of the main pieces of advice for the cold or flu sufferer was to "drink plenty of liquids." In 1991, Dristan unveiled a formula that played off that very idea. Dristan Cold and Flu medication is a powder that mixes into hot water to provide sipping relief. During the same time, Dristan Allergy was introduced; it contains one of the strongest non-drowsy antihistamines available without prescription and acts with a decongestant to clear breathing passages.

In 1992, another two products expanded the Dristan family. Dristan Juice Mix-In, a non-drowsy, portable powder that mixes into any kind of juice. This product was a unique addition to the "powdered segment" of nonprescription medications; all previous powders had to be combined with hot water. "The idea is that most doctors recommend juice for colds, and this way you get your juice with your medicine," an American Home Products spokeswoman told *Advertising Age*. *Advertising Age* contributor Patricia Winters added that the new powdered segment "is getting attention because it offers a new delivery system, has received considerable ad support, and has 'something of a home remedy image,'" according to a management expert. Dristan Juice Mix-In's active ingredients, cough suppressant, decongestant, and analgesic, do not alter the taste of the juice.

The introduction of Dristan Juice Mix-In brought publicity to the company. *Advertising Age* acknowledged the innovation by noting that "the product's portability, plus American Home's effort to sell Dristan Juice Mix-In in the juice and health aisles of stores, are interesting angles in a very tough market." Innovative in-store displays for Dristan Juice Mix-In featured floor stands in the shape of a juice carton.

The other brand extension in 1992 was a gel caplet. Gel caplets came on the market to help those who have difficulty swallowing larger tablets and pills. Dristan Gel formulas include Multi-Symptom Gel Caplets (maximum strength), and Dristan Cold No Drowsiness Gel caplets. Between various cold, flu, sinus, and allergy treatments, Dristan numbered ten different nonprescription medicines to offer consumers by the end of 1992.

## Advertising Themes

With so many brand-name and generic cold-relief formulas dotting drugstore shelves, several advertising themes have been employed to position Dristan as an innovative brand. A television campaign from 1988 featured football coach Mike Ditka, who advised, "When you can't call in sick, call on Dristan." A hidden-camera campaign in 1990 introduced the theme "The Face of Relief Today," which continued into the 1992 ads. For Dristan Nasal Spray, the theme "Smell the Orange" was rolled out in 1991. Dristan Juice Mix-In commercials were targeted toward upscale and wide-reach audiences simultaneously by sponsoring narrowly targeted television shows like "Northern Exposure" and "Mad About You" as well as mass-market shows like "Family Matters."

The most current design of Dristan products is meant to catch consumers' eyes on a shelf crowded with competitors. The graphics are kept simple—even those who don't read English can look at the photo of a man's face with arrows pointing up his nasal passages and understand that this product is a decongestant. The bright background colors suggest what each product is about—green, the color of grasses and weeds, for Dristan Allergy, or orange, the color of juice, for Dristan Juice Mix-In. Even though the products are not market leaders, Dristan enjoys long-term loyalty in the market and has an awareness rating of 98 percent. Sales of Dristan Nasal Spray reached $17 million in the early 1990s, according to company figures; Dristan combined sales earned $35 million.

## Further Reading:

Gannon, Kathi, "The Name of the Game in OTCs Is Brand Names," *Drug Topics*, October 12, 1992, p. 40.

Winters, Patricia, "Dristan Juices Up Cold Remedy," *Advertising Age*, October 19, 1992.

*—Susan Salter*

# DURACELL®

The only household battery sold worldwide under a single brand in the early 1990s, Duracell maintained clear leadership in the overall U.S. battery market and in the international long-life battery segment. Based on aggressive marketing and advertising, to which other established marketers were slow to respond, Duracell batteries rose from relative obscurity in the early 1970s to world prominence by the early 1990s. Introduced in the early 1970s by the Mallory Battery Company division of P.R. Mallory & Co. Inc., Duracell's marketing strategy has remained essentially the same despite a number of ownership changes. Known as the "Copper Top" battery, the Duracell brand's alkaline battery lasts up to six times longer than traditional zinc carbon batteries.

Duracell International Inc. was the largest manufacturer and marketer of alkaline batteries in the world in 1992. Although alkaline batteries contributed over 80 percent of the revenue for Duracell International in 1992, the company also produced other kinds of batteries, including high power lithium batteries and zinc batteries principally used in hearing aids. Duracell International entered the mid-1990s with plans to become a major factor in the growing rechargeable battery business, as related to high power devices like cellular phones and portable computers, and with yet more grand marketing plans and worldwide ambitions.

## Origins: Quick Moves

During the early 1970s, battery markets were dominated by the traditional zinc carbon battery. Each major market had its dominant brand: Union Carbide's Eveready brand dominated the U.S.; Ever Ready of Britain (unrelated to the U.S. Eveready) controlled British markets; Varta led in Germany; Mazda in France; and so on. Then in the United States a company threw itself into the global marketing fray by aggressively marketing longer life Duracell alkaline batteries. This relatively small company, P.R. Mallory & Co. Inc., would alter world battery markets irreversibly in ten short years with its Duracell brand long-life alkaline battery.

P.R. Mallory may have been small upon entering the field of battery manufacturers, but it moved quickly on new opportunities. Founded in 1916 by Philip Rogers, P.R. Mallory was hungry for expansion by the early 1940s. The company focused on the newly emerged alkaline technology and expanded it with success. Even in 1971, observers noted that the upstart alkaline battery might shake things up in the industry. "The familiar carbon-zinc unit used in flashlights, transistor radios, toys and novelties is being challenged in some areas by the more expensive but longer-lasting alkaline manganese variety," *Barron's* reported in 1971. A study by Arthur D. Little & Co. predicted a 7 percent annual growth rate for alkaline batteries and only 3 percent for carbon-zinc.

P.R. Mallory would in fact drive Duracell brand sales much higher in the generally favorable market. In 1973, *Financial World* reported that P.R. Mallory had doubled its sales—as had a number of battery manufacturers—over the previous decade. In 1973, P.R. Mallory revamped its battery sales strategy by attacking the consumer market. P.R. Mallory then formed a consumer battery division, Duracell Products Company, to be dedicated to marketing the Duracell brand. Meanwhile, Mallory Battery Company, now a second division, would continue to hold responsibility for all U.S. battery engineering, manufacturing, and sales to industrial and government accounts. These moves, *American Metal Market* reported, would bolster P.R. Mallory's position as a leading supplier of batteries and battery systems.

Duracell was a hot item in the mid-1970s. In 1977, Mallory built a third U.S. plant in Lancaster, South Carolina, to produce more Duracell batteries for the consumer battery market. P.R. Mallory's chief executive officer Charles A. Barnes, was quoted as saying in *American Metal Market* that he expected worldwide high-performance battery sales to total over $170 million in 1975 and to double by 1980.

## Rapid Growth Yields Frequent Reorganization

Despite its attention to Duracell and battery systems, P.R. Mallory still manufactured other goods. Sales from batteries accounted for 79.7 percent of pretax earnings and 55.7 percent of total sales volume in 1977. In 1978, following Dart Industries acquisition of P.R. Mallory, the company would cease its other activities and focus exclusively on batteries. In 1979, Dart Industries Inc. acquired P.R. Mallory and disposed of all remaining P.R. Mallory nonbattery businesses.

This acquisition represented only the beginning of several parent company reorganizations which culminated in one of the largest leveraged buyouts in history. One year after Dart Industries bought P.R. Mallory, Dart merged with Kraft, Inc., to form Dart & Kraft, Inc. In 1980, Dart & Kraft changed P.R. Mallory's name to Duracell International, more accurately reflecting the company's mission and support of its primary product.

## AT A GLANCE

**D**uracell brand of batteries first sold in the mid-1960s by the Mallory Battery Company, a division of P.R. Mallory & Co., Inc.; launched as a multi-purpose household battery brand by the Duracell Products Company in 1973; P.R. Mallory acquired by Dart Industries Inc. in 1978; Dart Industries Inc. merged with Kraft, Inc. to form Dart & Kraft, Inc., a new Duracell battery sales and marketing arm of P.R. Mallory, which was renamed Duracell, in 1980; Duracell remained a subsidiary of Kraft Inc. during a split of Dart & Kraft in 1986; Duracell bought from Kraft by Duracell management and Kohlberg Kravis Roberts & Co. in 1988; renamed Duracell International Inc. in 1991.

**Performance:** *Market share*—48% (top share) of consumer alkaline battery category (estimate). *Sales*—$1.62 billion (company-wide).

**Major competitor:** Ralston Purina's Energizer.

**Advertising:** *Agency*—Ogilvy & Mather, New York, NY. *Major campaign*—Known as the "Copper Top" battery, Duracell alkalines have been continually featured with toys in ads proclaiming, "You Can't Top the Copper Top."

**Addresses:** *Parent company*—Duracell Inc., Berkshire Corporate Pk., Bethel, CT 06801; phone: (203) 796-4000; fax: (203) 796-4096. *Ultimate parent company*—Duracell International Inc., Berkshire Corporate Park, Bethel, CT 06801; phone: (203) 796-4000; fax: (203) 796-4096.

Dart & Kraft provided Duracell with the flexibility to expand commensurate with its strong growth. In 1982, Duracell bought the continental European operations of British Ever Ready for $60 million. Interbrand wrote in its survey, *World's Greatest Brands,* that Duracell had entered the British market in 1979, when alkaline batteries were but "a tiny specialist sector." As in the United States, however, after two short years in the British market, "Duracell had again caught the market leader napping and profited mightily from this." By 1982, Duracell controlled all of what had been British Ever Ready's operations in West Germany, Italy, Belgium, Holland, Denmark, Norway, Sweden, Greece, and Portugal. The acquisition represented a yearly sales volume in 1981 of $100 million—almost one-fifth of Duracell's total 1981 world sales of $535 million, according to the *Wall Street Journal.*

By 1986, several of Dart & Kraft's businesses formed a drag on Kraft's value on the stock market. In 1986, all of the remaining Dart-related operations except Duracell were to be spun off into a separate corporation. In 1986, Duracell was expected to continue its spectacular 15 percent annual growth, *Business Week* reported.

Kraft sold Duracell to Kohlberg Kravis Roberts & Co. in 1988, a move that was not a complete surprise. Although Duracell's management had proposed taking Duracell private, the final sale price of $1.8 billion—15 times their yearly earnings—coupled with more than $1.45 billion in debt somewhat worried Duracell's chief executive officer, C. Robert Kidder. "We were concerned the price might go over the top—that the financing would not allow us to carry forward the strategic priorities of the business," Kidder was quoted as saying in *Fortune.* After a heated bidding war between Kohlberg Kravis Roberts & Co. (KKR) and Forstmann Little though, KKR won by putting up $350 million in equity to make the buyout possible. In one of the most famous leveraged buyouts of the 1980s, Duracell became a privately owned enterprise. At the time of the KKR buyout, about 35 senior Duracell managers invested nearly $6 million in equity in the company.

### Aggressive Expansion

During the few years before the buyout, Duracell had gained still more market share from Eveready—Eveready fell from 60 percent to 42 percent from 1986 to 1989 while Duracell gained significantly to a 36 percent share in 1989. One year after Duracell International became an independent company, Julie Liesse Erickson interviewed the president of Duracell North America, Charles Perrin, for *Advertising Age.* Perrin said that Duracell's goals had not changed since the buyout, but Duracell's drive had. "We're a very focused company—we want to be the worldwide leader in consumer batteries," he asserted. To achieve that goal meant transforming the market at home and abroad, especially shifting perceptions of the consumer battery category from a commodity market to a more highly differentiated consumer market. To that end, Duracell increased its spending in corresponding areas: "We are spending record levels on advertising, promotion, [research and development]," Perrin said.

Duracell's advertising and promotion, its Copper Top brand image, and its relationship with trade customers are the top three strategies contributing to Duracell's strength in the marketplace, Perrin told Erickson. Duracell began with an advertising campaign focusing on toys and the Copper Top image and has never departed from the approach.

Duracell's promotional energy continued to pay off. In 1990 Duracell held 44 percent of the consumer battery market against Eveready's 38 percent, although Eveready claimed market leadership in the estimated 30 percent of sales not tracked by A.C. Nielsen. In December of 1992, Julie Tilsner of *Business Week* reported Duracell International's quick recovery from the heavy debt burden of the buyout. With a higher than expected cash flow and continually rising profits, and by taking the company public, Duracell was able to pay down its debt from $1.45 billion in 1988 to $724 million—a manageable level—by 1992. Tilsner questioned, however, how much more of the market Duracell could claim when it already held nearly 48 percent of the $3.2 billion U.S. retail market for consumer alkaline batteries. "Given the maturity of the battery market and Duracell's huge market share . . . U.S. sales growth is expected to slow to 5 percent in the current year [1993]," Erickson wrote.

What is Duracell to do from the top? Erickson reported company officials looking to new overseas markets and to new products. Duracell chief executive officer C. Robert Kidder has targeted Asia in particular for future growth. The *Duracell 1992 Annual Report* highlighted Spain, Brazil, and selected Asian markets for immediate expansion. The report cited these as the most fertile of its established yet growing markets in "most of the developed countries in North America, Europe, Latin America, the Pacific Rim, the Caribbean and the Middle East." In addition to established markets, Duracell looked as well to markets "practically untapped by Duracell or any other global competitor." These markets included Russia, India, China, most of Africa, Indonesia, and Eastern Europe. As the world alkaline battery category leader, Duracell hoped to benefit significantly from further conversion of the world market from zinc carbon to alkaline. The overall world battery market had reached only 25 percent alkaline in 1992, according to the annual report.

Meanwhile, Duracell prepared for the mid-1990s with brand innovation. Duracell reached an agreement in 1992 with world competitors Toshiba Battery Co. of Japan and Varta Batterie of Germany to develop together a new, longer-lasting rechargeable battery. The new nickel metal hydride battery would be used in camcorders, cellular phones, and laptop computers and would last up to 40 percent longer. Duracell introduced the new battery in 1993. In 1992, Duracell boosted sales with its new Copper Top Tester, an on-pack battery tester that allowed customers to know when to replace used Duracell batteries. Finally, Duracell eliminated added mercury from its alkaline batteries without affecting their performance. Also in service of the new environmental strategy, Duracell planned to discontinue sales of mercury and nickel cadmium batteries and to use recycled and recyclable packaging.

In its 1992 annual report, Duracell described all of its efforts to prepare its brand for the mid-1990s with the phrase ''adding value.'' Duracell wrote that, ''Adding value means doing these things well, doing them consistently, and doing them around the world. It all adds up to a global brand that consumers know and trust.''

## Further Reading:

*American Metal Market,* August 23, 1978, p. 21; October 29, 1975, p. 17; November 11, 1974, p. 25; June 15, 1973, p. 7.

Donnelly, Richard A., ''Power in Batteries,'' *Barron's,* August 2, 1971, p. 5.

*Duracell 1992 Annual Report,* Bethel, CT: Duracell International Inc., 1992.

*Duracell Primary Battery Systems,* Bethel, CT: Duracell Inc., 1991.

Ellis, James E., ''Dart & Kraft: Why It'll Be Dart and Kraft,'' *Business Week,* July 7, 1986, p. 33.

Erickson, Julie Liesse, ''Perrin Leads Duracell's Charge,'' *Advertising Age,* June 26, 1989, p. 60.

Farnham, Alan, ''What's Sparking Duracell,'' *Fortune,* July 16, 1990, p. 74.

*Industry Week,* July 21, 1980, p. 11.

*Moody's Industrial Manual,* Moody's Investors Service, 1992, 1988, 1978.

Stern, Richard L., and Tatiana Pouschine, ''Junk Equity,'' *Forbes,* March 2, 1992, pp. 40–42.

Tilsner, Julie, ''Duracell Looks Abroad for More Juice,'' *Business Week,* December 21, 1992, pp. 52, 56.

*Wall Street Journal,* December 20, 1982, p. 9.

*World's Greatest Brands: An International Review by Interbrand,* John Wiley & Sons, p. 84.

*—Nicholas Patti*

# ELMER'S® GLUE

Elmer's Glue-All, one of an extensive line of Elmer's products, is the most popular glue on the market. Packaged in a convenient squeeze bottle with a handy applicator top—and with Elmer the Bull as "spokesbull"—Elmer's has been one of Borden, Inc.'s top selling products since the 1950s. Over the years, Elmer's has introduced nearly 150 types of glues, adhesives and caulks. These include specialty white glues, such as Craft Bond I, formulated for craft applications; Stix-All, for special applications; and Carpenter's Wood Glue for woodworking.

## Brand Origins

The product known today as Elmer's Glue-All was first introduced in 1947. It was named "Cascorez" and came in a small glass bottle with a wooden applicator. Initially, sales of the product were unimpressive. However, product sales quickly improved when the product was renamed Elmer's Glue-All in 1951 and repackaged in a more convenient plastic squeeze bottle in 1952.

## Early Marketing Strategy

In the late 1940s, Borden's new Chemical Division wanted to use Elsie the Cow, the "spokescow" for Borden dairy products since the 1930s, as a marketing symbol for its white glue product. Company advertising officials recoiled at the thought of their beloved Elsie representing a non-food product. As a compromise, Elmer the Bull was loaned to the division as its "spokesbull." Elmer, Elsie's husband, had been created for a 1939-40 New York World's Fair exhibit and was a popular character with the public. In 1951, Elmer was selected as the marketing symbol for Elmer's Glue-All. Just over a year later, the glue was repackaged into the familiar plastic squeeze bottles with the applicator top.

## Brand Development

Since Elmer's Glue-All was introduced, Elmer's has added nearly 150 other glues, adhesives and caulks to its product line. These products fall into five basic categories: household and school glues, caulks, building adhesives, instant adhesives, and special adhesives. The household and school glues category includes Elmer's School Glue, which washes out easily, even after drying; and Elmer's Glue Stick, which has a handy twist-up applicator. In the home repair products category, there are such handyman helpers as Elmer's Professional Carpenter's Wood Glue, specially formulated for wood; and Elmer's Redi-Spack

Spackling Compound, with its fast-drying, sandable acrylic formula. There are 15 products in the caulks category, including Elmer's Silicone Rubber Sealer, which provides a permanent, flexible, waterproof seal.

Of the six products in the building adhesives category, the newest is Elmer's Neoprene Contact Cement, which offers instant adhesion and excellent bonding strength and water resistance. The specialty adhesives category includes Elmer's Stix-All, an adhesive that bonds almost everything—except skin. *Consumer Reports* found that, while somewhat weak on wood and steel, its elasticity, water resistance and gap-filling abilities let it serve as a sealant and caulk as well as an adhesive. Another product in that category is Elmer's Wonder Bond Plus, a cyanoacrylate or "instant" glue, that bonds most non-porous materials in seconds with a tensile strength of up to 5,000 pounds per square inch. *Consumer Reports* indicated that while the glue is not intended for use on wood or porous materials, it grips well on wood as well as metal. In the specialty adhesives category, there are such products as Elmer's White Silicone Rubber Tub & Tile Caulk and Krazy Lock, an anaerobic multi-purpose thread locker that keeps nuts, bolts and screws tight.

In the early 1990s new brand developments included Elmer's GluColors Decorative Color Glue, uniquely formulated in an array of mostly neon colors, and Elmer's Fun Kits, children's activities kits designed for use with the GluColors line and introduced in 1993. Borden expanded its GluColors line in 1992 by adding black and opaque white glues and larger sizes. Also that year, Borden introduced a new glue in gel form that it described as the first advance in the school glue category in 25 years. Elmer's School Glue Gel, designed to be faster grabbing than traditional white school glues, has a thicker gel formula that does not run, drip or spill.

---

### AT A GLANCE

Elmer's Glue-All brand of glue established in 1952 by Borden, Inc.

**Advertising:** *Agency*—Grey Advertising, New York, NY.

**Addresses:** *Parent company*—Borden, Inc., 180 East Broad Street, Columbus, OH 43215; phone: (614) 225-4000; fax (614) 225-3410.

## Advertising Strategies

Borden is the strongest advertiser in the consumer adhesives category, according to company-published literature. In 1992, the Elmer's and Krazy Glue line, both distributed by Borden, represented an estimated 81 percent of total advertising in the adhesives category. Borden uses a combination of television and print advertising and point of purchase displays to promote its Elmer's brand products. In 1993, Elmer's advertising campaigns targeted the American family with messages on television and in magazines that showed how Elmer's can be used to create, build and repair. Elmer's also demonstrated many new and creative uses for its products through special ads directed at teachers. Commercials and print ads for Elmer's GluColors were shown during popular children's programs and in leading magazines for moms and kids. A 1993 ad for Fun Kits promised, "With nine Fun Kits to choose from, you'll never be bored." Elmer's also told millions of consumers about School Glue Gel in seven leading national publications directed at both kids and moms.

Another product that was widely advertised in 1992 and 1993 was Squeeze-N-Caulk, an improvement on the caulking gun. Consumers doing home repairs learned of the convenience and benefits of the product through television commercials and advertisements in do-it-yourself magazines.

## Performance Appraisal

Sales within Borden's Non-Food Consumer group, which includes the Elmer's line, totaled $613 million in 1992. More than half of the sales within that group resulted from international business. Elmer's is currently being sold in Canada, Ecuador and the Philippines. The Non-Food Consumer group is part of Borden's Packaging and Industrial Products division, which had sales totaling $1.95 billion in 1992. The division's sales benefited in part from sales and income gains in consumer adhesives, including Elmer's, according to the 1992 annual report. Elmer's is a favorite among consumers in the area of household adhesives, home improvement products and instant glues, the report noted. Considering Elmer's sales performance and popularity and Borden's commitment to advertising, unifying its sales and marketing efforts and introducing new products, further growth of the brand's sales seems assured.

## Further Reading:

*Borden 1992 Annual Report,* New York: Borden.

"Borden Expands Elmer's Glue Line," *Supermarket News,* June 8, 1992, p. 298.

"Household Glues," *Consumer Reports,* December 1988, p. 354.

Morgan, Hal, *Symbols of America,* New York: Penguin, 1986.

"Pipher Shoots the Caulking Gun," *Back Stage-SHOOT,* July 3, 1992, p. 16.

"Which Glue Is for Which Job," *Consumer Reports,* January 1988, p. 46.

Additional information for this essay was obtained from Borden and Adbank, an advertising service based in New York, New York.

*—Pam Berry*

# ENERGIZER®

Energizer brand alkaline batteries have enjoyed much success since their introduction. Introduced in 1980 by the Battery Products Division of the Union Carbide Corporation to expand the Eveready franchise into the fast-growing alkaline segment, the Energizer became a serious competitor with Duracell only after the Ralston Purina Company mastered battery marketing techniques and initiated one of the most innovative advertising campaigns of the early 1990s, the Energizer Bunny campaign. The award-winning Energizer Bunny advertising campaign transformed the Energizer from a trailing second-place brand into an industry leader. In 1991, Energizer sold over one billion alkaline batteries to overtake Duracell as the leader of the high-performance alkaline battery market in North America. In 1992, Energizer broadened its lead. Building on this success, Energizer's producer, the Eveready Battery Company, the world's largest manufacturer of batteries and flashlights and a subsidiary of the Ralston Purina Company, continued to expand the brand and to market it aggressively worldwide in 1993.

## Brand Origins

Union Carbide was a relative late-comer to the high-performance alkaline battery market with its Energizer brand. Union Carbide's Eveready battery made of carbon zinc dominated the overall battery market through the mid-1970s. Not until the P.R. Mallory & Co., Inc.'s Duracell alkaline battery had gained significant market share in the late 1970s did Union Carbide enter the alkaline market. It was not that Union Carbide lacked access to alkaline battery technology—they had created the first standard alkaline battery in 1957. Interbrand described Union Carbide's initial reluctance to enter the alkaline battery market in its survey, *World's Greatest Brands:* "Union Carbide complained that 'Duracell sneaked in on us' but the truth is that the market leader saw little to gain from obsoleting its production capacity and introducing a new product which lasted several times as long as existing products. It was a sitting duck."

Recognizing that the alkaline segment was growing to over 70 percent of total sales value for batteries by the mid-1980s, Union Carbide could not afford to delay its entry into the market any longer. Union Carbide augmented its historic Eveready brand with a high-performance alkaline battery to compete with Duracell. In 1980, Union Carbide introduced the Energizer.

## A "Supercharged" Energizer

With its sister brand Eveready, the new Energizer quickly became a major brand and received substantial advertising and development support. In 1985, Laurie Freeman reported in *Advertising Age* that Eveready of Union Carbide had recently introduced a new "Supercharged" Energizer battery. Primetime network and cable television advertisements featured the Olympic gold-medalist Mary Lou Retton as the spokeswoman. Freeman quoted an Eveready representative who said that the advertisements would "focus on the long-lasting energy of Mary Lou Retton and America's newest bundle of energy—the Energizer new supercharged 'AA' battery." The new Energizer claimed 42 percent of the battery market, following Duracell with 48 percent.

## A Valuable Acquisition

By 1986, Energizer and Eveready brands were a formidable business unit, holding 60 percent of the U.S. battery market and 30 percent of the world market. When in the mid-1980s corporate raids were prevalent, Eveready and Energizer would have to shift hands to prevent a buy-out of Union Carbide. Fending off a hostile takeover, Union Carbide was forced to restructure and to sell what its purchaser, Ralston Purina, would later call "its crown jewel." Meanwhile, Ralston Purina had too much excess cash on its ledger and not enough debt—it too was a prime target for a corporate raider.

In a gesture of defense for both companies, Union Carbide sold Eveready and Energizer to Ralston Purina for $1.4 billion, according to Kenneth Dreyfack of *Business Week.* After the purchase, Ralston Purina could boast a sufficiently burdensome debt load of $1.8 billion, an amount which rendered the company safe from potential buyouts. Ralston hoped to make the purchase worth the debt by increasing Energizer and Eveready advertising and sales. Based on Ralston's expertise in developing and marketing branded consumer goods, Ralston expected to significantly boost sales of these already-established brands. Ralston named its new operation the Eveready Battery Company and began its intensive efforts.

## A Rough New Start

Ralston Purina had no prior experience in the battery business, however; over the next two years they would discover that their

## AT A GLANCE

Energizer brand alkaline batteries introduced in 1980 by the Battery Products Division of the Union Carbide Corporation to expand the Eveready franchise into the high-performance alkaline battery market; sold with Eveready in 1986 to the Ralston Purina Company, who organized the Eveready Battery Company as an immediate parent.

**Performance:** *Market share*—36% of alkaline battery segment (1991). *Sales*—$684.0 million.

**Major competitor:** Duracell of Duracell International Inc.

**Advertising:** *Agency*—Chiat/Day/Mojo, Venice, CA, 1989—. *Major campaign*—The Energizer Bunny interrupts a variety of phony commercials to a voice-over saying that the Energizer keeps "going and going."

**Addresses:** *Parent company*—Eveready Battery Company, Checkerboard Square, St. Louis, MO 63164; phone: (314) 982-1000; fax: (314) 982-2752. *Ultimate parent company*—Ralston Purina Company, Checkerboard Square, St. Louis, MO 63164; phone: (314) 982-1000.

strategies for other consumer markets such as groceries did not apply to batteries. As quoted in *Advertising Age* in 1989, one securities analyst warned Ralston Purina's Chairman-CEO William Stiritz at the time of the acquisition in 1986 that "You can't sell batteries like you sell dog food." But Ralston Purina tried. In accordance with what one industry executive called in *Advertising Age* the "grocery product marketing model," the Eveready Battery Company of Ralston Purina immediately introduced new products and line extensions. Eveready split its battery line into a number of brands. The old zinc carbon Eveready was itself split into two brands, the Eveready Classic and the Eveready Super Heavy-Duty. The Energizer brand then received new brightly-colored packaging to coordinate with Christmas wrapping paper—hence the new "GiftMate" Energizer. In addition, Eveready changed the chemistry of the Energizer slightly to specialize a new brand, the "Conductor," for audio equipment. By its third season in 1989, the GiftMate brand was dropped. Similarly, one year after spending $10 million to back the Conductor in 1988, all ad support was pulled for the stagnant brand. *Advertising Age* reported that Eveready's brands—including Energizer and Eveready—had slipped from 52 percent of the total battery market in 1986 to 47 percent in 1988.

Ralston Purina realized a different strategy would be necessary. Consumers in the battery industry historically have been uninterested in brand proliferation and Eveready offered consumers no significant technological advances behind their Eveready and Energizer line extensions, *Advertising Age* reported.

In 1989, Ralston Purina realized it would have to square off with Duracell directly if it wished to gain back lost market share for Eveready and Energizer. Julie Liesse Erickson of *Advertising Age* quoted an anonymous source who described Ralston's change of strategy: "Originally, Ralston came in and didn't want to go head-to-head with Duracell in alkaline batteries, but now they've come to the realization that they need a bigger alkaline brand, and Energizer is the only one that can do it for them. To rebuild it, they will match if not outspend Duracell." Duracell was the leading brand in the alkaline category.

## The Bunny to the Rescue

The Energizer Bunny campaign of October 1988 grew directly out of Ralston's strategy to challenge Duracell directly. The Energizer Bunny television commercial represented a direct attack on Duracell's advertising theme. In their advertising, Duracell had raced toys charged with Duracell against those with "ordinary" batteries—those of carbon-zinc and not alkaline. Duracell's toys kept going longer than the "ordinary" toys. In Energizer's new commercial, a crowd of toy bunnies similar to those made famous in Duracell commercials went about their drumming across the screen. They were soon interrupted, however, by the larger Energizer bunny who drummed its way onto the scene to the sound of a voice-over explaining that Duracell had never "invited us to your party," *Advertising Age* reported.

That frontal attack on Duracell's advertising marked the first stage of the Energizer Bunny campaign. The ad agency behind the idea, DDB Needham, saw the ad as a temporary move and not the basis for a long-term Energizer advertising theme. "We don't think we can campaign this out," Eveready Chairman-CEO J. Patrick Mulcahy told *Advertising Age*. "We think it's a one-shot deal, a limited tactical vehicle. We should put it on air for a while and then go back to something else."

After less than two years with DDB Needham, then, the Energizer advertising account went back into review. Out of that review process emerged the novel and award-winning second version of the Energizer Bunny campaign, designed by Chiat/Day/Mojo of Venice, CA. In that campaign, debuted in October of 1989, the Energizer Bunny began to parody a number of advertising styles by interrupting phony commercials for imaginary products. After a year and a half, the Bunny broke in on about 20 different fake commercials, according to *Advertising Age*.

In early 1991, *Adweek's Marketing Week* had nothing but praise to write about the Energizer Bunny campaign: "What the campaign does so well is let the viewer in on an advertising joke, poking fun at the sanctity of commercial styles. The campaign has actually gotten better since it began, which is as unusual for ad series as it is for movie sequels." Examples of the parodies include a promotion for "J.P.'s Pigskin Porkrinds" by spokesman Lyle Alzado and a Dr. Pepper spoof featuring a dancer who nimbly climbs the walls with a can of soda before being interrupted by the gong of the Energizer Bunny's drum. Eveready Chairman-CEO J. Patrick Mulcahy could boast in his "First Quarter Report to Shareholders" in 1992 that an *Ad Week* poll had just ranked the Energizer Bunny campaign number two in American advertising, second only to Pepsi.

The development of the advertising campaign has not been without its problems, however. While the campaign was predicated on the parody of other advertising styles, Eveready had difficulty accepting similar criticism directed at the Energizer. For instance, the Coors Brewing Co. ran an advertisement by Foote, Cone & Belding of Chicago in May of 1991 that featured the actor Leslie Nielsen, star of "The Naked Gun" and "Airplane," dressed up as a kind of Coors Light Bunny. In this ad, a typical macho beer commercial, complete with a deep, resonant voice-over and a close-up of beer pouring into a glass, is interrupted by Leslie Nielsen "clanging" a big Coors Light drum in true Energizer Bunny style, according to Ira Teinowitz of *Advertising Age*. In place of the Energizer commercial voice-over that the battery keeps "going and going," Coors Light's spot states that its beer sales keep "growing and growing." Infuriated, Eveready took

Coors to court. There a judge denied Eveready's request for a preliminary injunction to block the airing of Coors's commercial. Coors premiered its spot on NBC during Saturday night coverage of the National Basketball Association playoffs in May of 1991. "We did it for awareness," said Bob Simon, senior vice-president

*The Energizer Bunny began drumming his way through ads in 1988.*

and group creative director at Foote, Cone & Belding, in *Advertising Age.* "I think people drink beer in part for the likability factor."

While Eveready reacted strongly to Coor's parody on the Energizer Bunny, Coors's parody was not the first. Numerous television shows such as "Late Night with David Letterman," as well as comic strips and editorial cartoons had already played on the Energizer Bunny motif. Finally, a Ford Bronco ran over the Energizer Bunny a year earlier in a commercial designed by W.B. Doner & Co. of Baltimore for the Washington, D.C.-area Ford Dealers Association. All this exposure undoubtedly contributed to the Energizer Bunny's fame and to its effectiveness.

While the campaign worked through some early customer confusion as to which product was being advertised, Duracell or Energizer, and more confusion later when the Bunny appeared for a brief spell in supposedly fake commercials featuring other Ralston products, the Energizer Bunny campaign eventually brought significant results in the market. In 1991, Julie Liesse of *Advertising Age* reported that Energizer's market share declines had finally reversed course. During 1990, both Energizer and Duracell gained market share in a growing alkaline market. In its 1992 Annual Report, Ralston Purina attributed much of the seven percent of 1992 dollar value Energizer sales growth to the "continued success of the Energizer Bunny Campaign."

## Ongoing Innovation and International Marketing

While the Energizer Bunny advertising campaign was certainly effective, it was not the only factor behind the success enjoyed by the brand. Energizer has also been a central focus of Eveready's brand research and development efforts as well as Eveready's aggressive international marketing strategy. During 1992, a new Energizer had been brought from development to market. The AA Energizer Lithium battery, heralded by Eveready as a "technically superior and unique new product," was introduced in Japan in June of 1992 and in the United States in January of 1993. Eveready extended its brand family in 1992, as well, adding a new "zero-mercury added" alkaline battery called "Green Power" to its Energizer and Eveready franchises.

Eveready has also actively marketed Energizer internationally. In February of 1992, Eveready acquired the leading battery manufacturer in Spain and Portugal from Sociedad Española Del Acumulador Tudor. Tudor manufactured alkaline batteries in Spain and carbon zinc batteries in Portugal. In July of 1992, Eveready finished the purchase of Ever Ready Limited from Hanson PLC in the United Kingdom. Ever Ready was the leading battery company in the United Kingdom, producing alkaline, carbon zinc, and rechargeable batteries as well as flashlights and related lighting devices. These two acquisitions provide Eveready and its Energizer brand with greater access to the European market.

In addition to expansion in Western Europe, Eveready continued to expand into other regions of the world as well. In 1992, Eveready established the Beijing Eveready Battery Company in China and embarked on a new joint venture in Turkey called Eveready Pil Sanayii. Eveready also began a joint venture in Czechoslovakia, which will also serve markets in Hungary and Poland. Already the world's largest manufacturer of batteries and flashlights, producing from 43 plants for over 162 countries around the world, Eveready continued in the early 1990s to expand its marketing internationally.

With alkaline as the fastest-growing segment of the battery market worldwide, Eveready continued to expand their flagship alkaline brand, the Energizer. In the Eveready 1993 "First Quarter Report to Shareholders," Mulcahy stressed the importance of alkaline batteries to Eveready's overall strategy for the 1993 fiscal year: "Our key international objectives for fiscal year 1993 will be to continue to drive for alkaline volume growth, integrate and consolidate the new acquisitions in Europe to reduce costs and improve our alkaline share and continue geographic expansion, particularly in China and the Far East." When Mulcahy strives for alkaline sales growth worldwide, he pushes for the growth of the Energizer.

## Further Reading:

"America's Favorite Advertising," *Adweek's Marketing Week,* March 11, 1991, p. 36.

Dreyfack, Kenneth, "What Purina Really Wanted from Carbide," *Business Week,* April 21, 1986, p. 33.

Eveready Battery Company, Inc., *Eveready Battery Company History,* St. Louis, MO: Eveready Battery Company, Inc., 1993.

Freeman, Laurie, "Rayovac Back on Beam in Battery Market," *Advertising Age,* September 16, 1985, p. 47.

Liesse Erickson, Julie, "Ralston Lesson: Batteries Aren't Groceries," *Advertising Age,* November 27, 1989, p. 114.

Liesse, Julie, "Batteries Getting Greener," *Advertising Age,* February 17, 1992.

Liesse, Julie, ''How the Bunny Charged Eveready,'' *Advertising Age,* April 8, 1991.

Ralston Purina Company, *Ralston Purina Company Annual Report,* St. Louis, MO: Ralston Purina Company, 1992.

Ralston Purina Company, *First Quarter Report to Shareholders,* St. Louis, MO, 1992–1993.

Rouland, Renee Covino, ''Batteries Have Staying Power!,'' *Discount Merchandiser,* August 1992, pp. 72–4.

Teinowitz, Ira, ''Coors in a (Rabbit) Stew Over Parody,'' *Advertising Age,* April 29, 1991.

Teinowitz, Ira, and Julie Liesse, ''Coors 'Bunny' Ad Gets Going,'' *Advertising Age,* May 20, 1991.

''Union Carbide Corporation,'' *International Directory of Company Histories,* Chicago: St. James Press, vol. 1, 1988, pp. 399–401.

*World's Greatest Brands: An International Review by Interbrand,* New York: John Wiley & Sons, 1992, p. 84.

*—Nicholas Patti*

# ESPRIT®

ESPRIT

With a sweep of natural fabric and a dollop of common-sense good looks, the Esprit image has come to be known in fashion circles as a formidable presence. Produced by the company Esprit de Corp., the Esprit brand name graces clothing, shoes, accessories—anything a woman can wear with comfort both at work and at play. As *W* magazine put it, Esprit fashions are "part of that huge, growing category of well-priced clothes that range from the street-smart style of DKNY [Donna Karan New York] and CK Calvin Klein to the career-oriented mood of Ellen Tracy and Anne Klein II."

Many report that the most distinguishing features of Esprit fashions are what the clothing *isn't*. Items never associated with Esprit are the clingy cocktail dress, the stifling "power suit," or the crippling high-heeled pump. Instead, a typical Esprit outfit shows, for example, a looser-fitting rayon vest or tunic over wide-legged pants or perhaps a flowing, calf-length skirt made of soft cotton. An Esprit shoe is low-heeled for comfort, and durable for the woman who spends much of her day on her feet.

According to the journal *View on Colour,* Esprit "has come to epitomize the Northern California lifestyle, an informative mix of a sunny climate, bold colors, outdoor sports, eternal youth, and social values. Esprit's saucy sportswear, sometimes emblazoned with messages such as 'save the whales,' rocketed the company into international prominence in the early '80s and encouraged (if not triggered) the worldwide sportswear boom."

This success was no accident. Rather, it was the result of the personal vision of Esprit de Corp.'s co-founder, Susie Tompkins. Born into affluence but a product of the countercultural 1960s, Tompkins has been the guiding force behind the company, and has been its main arbiter of fashion. "Esprit's style is like Tompkins herself: comfortable, appropriate and stylish, but with an individualistic twist," said Gayle Sato Stodder in *Entrepreneurial Woman.*

## From Plain Jane to Esprit

A designer from early on, Tompkins got her start, along with partner Jane Tise, in her native San Francisco in 1968, selling homemade frocks under the name Plain Jane. "Neither of them knew how to sew or run a company," noted Stodder. "All they had was a hot idea." That idea was to market whimsical, affordable fashion for the workaday woman. And with Tompkins' husband, Doug, joining the company in the early 1970s, the newly

named Esprit de Corp. began to make its mark in better boutiques. As the 1970s gave way to the 1980s, Esprit had expanded its client base into more than 30 countries.

For its first several years, the line was especially popular with teenagers; fashions reflected their tastes with easy-to-wear casual clothes in durable fabrics and engaging colors. Eventually, Esprit clothing would represent both youthful style and career-minded fashion—that is, playful looks that can be worn in more grown-up settings, such as the casual office. Tompkins and company refer to it as "creative career" dressing, noted Constance C. R. White in a *Woman's Wear Daily* article. White went on to quote Tompkins, saying that the line is "for a woman who is very confident but who is still playful. Women today have a lot of work to do. They love fashion and they want to look appropriate, but they don't have time for hysterical mornings any more. They also don't want to look like they've been shopping." This "bridge" line of clothing, named after its founder Susie Tompkins, was hailed for bringing the carefree feeling of Esprit into a more classic, career-oriented style.

## Near Misses for Esprit

Shopping, of course, is the prime way to gain access to Esprit fashions; ironically, retailing nearly was the downfall of the Esprit de Corp. organization. It all began in the early 1980s. Esprit was a leading sportswear manufacturer, selling in all the major department stores and boutiques. But, as *Working Woman* writer Ellie McGrath described it, "the company's decision [in 1981] to create boutiques within major department stores—there are 102 nationwide—was akin to booking passage on the *Titanic*. Retail giants like Macy's and Bloomingdale's are struggling under the weight of heavy debt and poor sales. Meanwhile, Esprit faces big-time competition from the Gap and the Limited, which invested in freestanding stores and now dominate the very niche that Esprit pioneered." Fashion expert Alan Millstein gave McGrath a different slant on that era: "Esprit missed the market for five years," he says in the article. "They missed 20 seasons. That means they lost half a generation of kids."

The rejuvenation of Esprit came about in spite of—or perhaps because of—the turmoil occurring in Tompkins' personal life. Esprit had enjoyed fruitful years between 1975 and 1987, with worldwide sales reportedly approaching $1 billion. But by 1987 "Susie and Doug disagreed about Esprit's future direction, and

## AT A GLANCE

**B**rand originated in 1968 as Plain Jane in San Francisco, CA, by Susie Tompkins and Jane Tise; company incorporated as Esprit de Corp., c. 1976; formerly owned by both Doug and Susie Tompkins; bought by Susie Tompkins and investor group, June, 1990.

*Performance:* *Sales*—$900 million (worldwide).

*Major competitor:* For Esprit line: Gap brand clothing; also, Limited brand clothing. For Susie Tompkins line: DKNY; also, Ellen Tracy, Calvin Klein, and Anne Klein II.

*Advertising:* *Agency*—In-house. *Major campaign*—"Real People," 1980s; "What Would You Do?," 1991.

*Addresses:* *Parent company*—Esprit de Corp., 900 Minnesota St., San Francisco, CA 94107; phone: (415) 648-6900.

sales dropped," wrote Stodder in *Entrepreneurial Woman*. In fact, as *Business Week* elaborated, in June of 1987 "Esprit's sales had reached $412 million in the U.S., but operating profit had fallen 92%, to $5 million."

The drop in business came as a direct result of Susie and Doug's growing estrangement. And by 1990, Susie Tompkins, the founding spirit of Esprit, was "down and almost out," as McGrath put it. "Her rocky, 25-year marriage to Doug Tompkins had finally ended," and Susie was no longer running the business end of Esprit, having seriously considered Doug's offer to buy her out.

A meeting with another fashion entrepreneur provided epiphany. Tompkins got together with Bruce Katz, who had founded Rockport Shoe Co. and made a fortune as a "key promoter of the 1980s walking-as-exercise trend," as the *Working Woman* article noted. Katz, who had sold Rockport in 1986 for $118 million, told Tompkins that selling out a company he'd founded was a decision he had come to regret.

### On the Rebound

"Awakened" (as Tompkins described it) by Katz's advice, the designer elected to buy out Doug instead. She enlisted the financial support of Katz, as well as several other investors. But time was of the essence: according to the Tompkins' agreement, "if one of them didn't buy out the other by June of 1990, Esprit, which was [then] reportedly worth at least $380 million, would be sold on the open market to the highest bidder," wrote McGrath.

With days counting down before the final deadline, the estranged Doug and Susie met to work out the future of Esprit. They came to the decision that Susie would buy back the company, and Doug would bow out to the tune of $125 million—"considerably less," pointed out McGrath, "than the amount he probably would have made had the company gone on the block." And so Susie Tompkins was back at the helm of Esprit, but this time with a difference: "For one thing, she isn't running the company," Stodder explained. "Instead, she provides input, she voices opinions."

Chief among those opinions are Tompkins' concerns over environmental issues and how Esprit can make a positive difference. Under Tompkins' direction, the company initiated the Ecollection line of clothing in the spring of 1992—"a big step, even for trend-setting Esprit," according to *View on Colour*. The Ecollection fashions are notable for being produced in the most envi-

ronmentally friendly way possible. From organically grown cotton (raised on land free of chemical treatment), to recycled wool, to biodegradable enzyme washes and metal-free dyes, this line of casual sportswear supports the more environmentally conscious lifestyle of the 1990s. Even the accessories are earth-friendly and socially conscious: reconstituted glass for necklaces and bracelets, handpainted buttons (providing gainful employment for a rural North Carolina area), and recycled sea shells are part of Esprit's Ecollection.

Ecollection isn't the only Esprit subsection. Since the 1970s the company has initiated several product lines. Besides the regular Esprit-branded products, there are Esprit Footwear and Accessories, Esprit Kids (which incorporates Baby, Girl Toddlers, Boy Infant and Toddler, Mini, Kids, and Teens), and, of course, the separate Susie Tompkins signature line. Considered more sophisticated, the latter bridge line is "aimed at the grown-up Esprit customer, a working woman over the age of 25," an article stated in *View on Colour*. In the same article, Tompkins described the line as everything from responsible, to sympathetic, to sensible, gentle, and socially conscious, "adjectives [that] have prompted her critics to charge her with being 'anti-fashion,' " noted the profile.

### Real People, Real Messages

Esprit advertising and marketing efforts are as low-key as the fashions they represent. The most famous campaign, developed in-house in the early 1980s, was a line of print ads showcasing real Esprit customers. The copy described the customer's lifestyle, habits, and general worldview, while the Esprit fashions themselves played almost a secondary role. The campaign effectively positioned Esprit as a youthful-oriented clothing line. Iron-

*The signature of Esprit co-founder Susie Tompkins is also the logo for a line of clothing.*

ically, though, a look-alike series of Gap ads, this time featuring celebrities modeling Gap fashions, all but eclipsed Esprit's original idea.

True to form, Esprit advertising also has a history of a social consciousness. The "Real People" ads were followed by a powerful, full-page installment in Esprit's 1987 catalogue; titled "AIDS: A Global Epidemic," the text advised consumers to practice safe sex in order to avoid contracting the disease, contained up-to-date facts that served to dispel rumors about AIDS, and provided a national hot-line. The article positioned Esprit as the first major fashion manufacturer to address the AIDS crisis. In 1991 another campaign, called "What Would You Do?," also addressed the social concerns of Esprit's typical customers. These print and TV spots, according to *Business Week,* "feature sober black-and-white photographs of urban teenagers expressing abbreviated, liberal political views. Some aren't wearing Esprit clothes." As reporter Laura Zinn went on to say, this campaign caused no small consternation between Tompkins, who "loves the ads," and partner Katz, who "sparred with her about their appeal." Meetings on this subject "blew up," said Zinn, and the campaign eventually evolved "into color ads with teenagers wearing Esprit apparel."

In the field of marketing, Esprit works hard to keep its brand name outstanding. In chain department stores, Esprit clothing is clustered in one area, and even in discount stores like T. J. Maxx, Esprit fashions are often grouped together for convenience. Esprit also distributes its fashions as widely as possible: company-owned stores are located in California and Colorado; franchises range in location from Hawaii to Puerto Rico; and Esprit maintains outlet stores throughout the United States. Company catalogs also help the cause. And Susie Tompkins' energetic attention to environmental issues provides a fair amount of free publicity.

### Esprit Looks Ahead

But no amount of publicity can take the place of hard work and dedication to success. In March of 1993 Tompkins outlined Esprit's future for *Women's Wear Daily*'s Constance C. R. White.

The aim, according to the article, "is to develop business with existing customers as well as with existing stores." As Tompkins told White: "Esprit, like the entire junior market, is in the process of reevaluating the customer today, and I'm continuing to pursue this marketplace with consideration of the roots and culture of this company." And, just as important, Tompkins wants to make sure that Esprit "isn't trendy," as she stated in a *San Francisco Focus* article. "We don't have to be doing what everybody else is doing. We just have to do *our* style, which is a kind of eclecticness and an integrity of design. Mixing old things with new things. Having a really nice way of presenting color. We try not to use the cliche teen colors. We wouldn't use a powder-pink, we'd use a dusty-pink, colors that are more sophisticated. Being young but still appropriate for an older customer."

### Further Reading:

Benson, Heidi, "Reinventing Esprit," *San Francisco Focus,* February 1991.

McGrath, Ellie, "Esprit, the Sequel," *Working Woman,* September 1991.

Stodder, Gayle Sato, "A Perfect Fit," *Entrepreneurial Woman,* summer 1993.

"Susie's New Spirit," *W,* May 10, 1993.

*View on Colour,* January 1992.

White, Constance C. R., "Susie Tompkins: Crossing a New Bridge," *Women's Wear Daily,* March 10, 1993.

Zinn, Laura, "Will Politically Correct Sell Sweaters?," *Business Week,* March 16, 1992.

*—Susan Salter*

# ESTÉE LAUDER®

# ESTĒE LAUDER

Estée Lauder is one of the best known brands in the U.S. cosmetics and perfume industry. Over 90 percent of Estée Lauder products are sold in department stores, consistently out-selling other brands by a wide margin. Nearly half of all cosmetics and perfumes carried by department stores are Estée Lauder products—an impressive percentage considering that Estée Lauder arrived on the cosmetics market well after established brands like Elizabeth Arden and Helena Rubenstein. The Clinique cosmetics line introduced by Estée Lauder in 1968 has become the most profitable of Estée Lauder's five divisions, and Aramis, the company's men's toiletry line, offers one of the best-selling men's colognes in the country. Estée Lauder, Incorporated is the largest privately owned cosmetics company in the world.

## Brand Origins

Estée Lauder was founded by Queens, New York, native Josephine Esther Mentzer, whose business sense made her one of the rare self-made billionaires in the United States. Her childhood as one of nine children of Hungarian parents was lean and devoid of the glamour she later came to symbolize. Yet as early as age twelve she was fascinated by her uncle's chemistry laboratory and desired to be a skin doctor. John Schotz invented many of the creams and lotions that his niece later made and marketed on her own. With the knowledge she gained from her uncle, she launched her own line of cosmetics in 1937 with support from her husband, Joseph Lauter.

The new skin creams and lotions debuted under the name Estée Lauder—a frenchification of Mentzer's first and married names. Lauder sold the products herself from behind the counters of such New York department stores as Bonwit Teller; it was a bold move for an unknown cosmetologist with little financial backing. But Lauder was an imaginative and persistent businesswoman—she was known to stop strangers on the street to offer them makeup advice and sell them her products. Lauder aspired to sell her cosmetics to the most fashionable store of the day, Saks Fifth Avenue, a move which she felt would ensure her products' success and profit. She finally achieved this in 1946 after a particularly successful lecture and demonstration at the Waldorf Astoria hotel that encouraged scores of well-to-do women to try the products. Feeling secure in her business acumen, Lauder and her husband founded Estée Lauder, Inc. in New York City later that year.

## Early Marketing Strategy

Estée Lauder steadily built a clientele in New York and other large cities by offering leading department stores creative ways to market her products. Shocked that $50,000 was not enough to attract even a small advertising agency, Lauder decided instead to expend that sum on gift items to be included with purchases of her products. Though now a common practice, this strategy was unheard of in the early 1950s and puzzled many traditional retailers and customers. However, it proved so successful that other cosmetics companies soon followed suit when they discovered that sample products whetted the consumer's appetite for more.

When Estée Lauder's first perfumed bath oil, Youth Dew, was developed in 1953, it met with immediate success. Within several years almost 80 percent of Estée Lauder's sales were derived from Youth Dew, which had been transformed into a bottled perfume. Originally distributed as gift packets included with a customer's purchase, Youth Dew boosted sales of the other skin care items, and by 1960 Estée Lauder sales totalled one million dollars. With the opening of the first overseas Estée Lauder branch in Harrods department store at this time, the company commenced its international expansion. In an attempt to remain competitive, Estée Lauder introduced the European-styled skin care lotion Re-Nutriv at a pricey $115 a pound in 1960. Re-Nutriv was the first in a long line of Estée Lauder products marketed with its scientific formulation in mind. In order to advertise Re-Nutriv face cream, Estée Lauder created its first full page advertisements for *Harper's Bazaar* entitled: "What Makes a Cream Worth $115.00?" The eye-catching campaign generated good publicity that helped propel the company to the forefront of the cosmetics industry. The resulting success of Re-Nutriv inspired the development of a new product line for men called Aramis.

## Product Innovation

By the early 1960s Estée Lauder's son Leonard was a rising star in the company. In his efforts to dissociate men's fragrances with effeminacy, he developed the Aramis line that included cologne and other skin care products. Though it started slowly, Aramis eventually became the most successful men's fragrance on the market—a position it retained until competitors caught up with it in the 1980s. By the 1990s the Aramis division contained over forty products.

## AT A GLANCE

**E**stée Lauder skin care products founded in 1937 in New York City by Estée Lauder; the Estée Lauder Company was incorporated in 1946; company added Aramis division in 1964, Clinique in 1968, Prescriptives in 1979, and Origins Natural Resources in 1990.

**Performance:** *Market share*—40% of department store cosmetics market (1991).

**Major competitor:** Elizabeth Arden; also Calvin Klein.

**Advertising:** *Agency*—AC&R, New York, NY, 1965—.

**Addresses:** *Parent company*—Estée Lauder, Incorporated; 767 5th Ave., New York, NY 10153; phone: (212) 572-4200; fax: (212) 572-6745.

Another of Leonard Lauder's efforts, Clinique was developed to appeal to a younger sector of the market than Estée Lauder's original products. Established as a separate division in 1968, many Clinique products at first glance appear to be similar to the parent company's products. However, the ingredients, appearance, and the consumers differ. The Clinique brand put less emphasis on color and glamour and was within the price range of most working women. Clinique by its very name was meant to emphasize healthy skin care; products were fragrance-free and hypoallergenic. Non-skin care products such as lipsticks, mascara, and eye shadow were offered in less elaborate containers than the Estée Lauder products. The Clinique brand was presented as a complete system that would create and maintain healthy looking skin—a strategy that coincided nicely with consumers' growing concern with fitness.

In 1979 a fourth Estée Lauder division, Prescriptives, debuted with products that catered to different skin types. Based on the philosophy that every skin tone requires a matching makeup, the division hired in-store "skin analysts" who would customize skin treatment programs for consumers. Due in part to its highly specialized nature, Prescriptives became the most expensive Estée Lauder product line.

The newest division of Estée Lauder, launched in 1990, was Origins Natural Resources. Extending a concept that began with Clinique, the new products further stressed healthy-looking skin over mere color. According to market analysts, the Origins Natural Resources line was developed in response to the rapid U.S. expansion of the England-based Body Shop, a company whose products exhibited an environmental-friendliness that proved quite profitable. With Origins Natural Resources, Estée Lauder became the first major cosmetics company in the United States to develop its own makeup and skin care products utilizing recyclable packaging and natural ingredients that have not undergone animal testing. Origins' ventured one step further than the competition, however, by developing "sensory therapy" products designed to ease tension. Advertised as the "no makeup makeup," Origins' sales in its first year exceeded company expectations by 70 percent.

## Advertising

Since Estée Lauder's original marketing innovation of including free samples with purchases, the company's advertising campaigns have expanded in scope and medium. Most of their early magazine ads featured stylish black and white photographs because they were less expensive than color ads. In 1971 model Karen Graham became the focus of many Estée Lauder ads and represented the company's image for years. Other Estée Lauder divisions customized advertising strategies to emphasize their products' uniqueness. For example, Prescriptives' newest product line, All Skins, included Asian, Hispanic, and Afro-American women in all of its print advertising. As a result of Estée Lauder's efforts to diversify its clientele, sales of All Skins rose 45 percent a year after being launched. The uniqueness of Origins Natural Resources, with its combination of environmental and "new age" characteristics, similarly called for distinctive advertising. Instead of heavy television advertising, Estée Lauder advanced awareness of Origins through tree planting ceremonies, in-house promos, and a barrage of press releases.

## International Growth

Soon after reaching the million dollar sales mark in 1960, Estée Lauder products were introduced in London. With the subsequent establishment of Estée Lauder International, exports reached more than 80 countries by the early 1990s, and overseas sales constituted nearly half the company's annual revenue. Even before the fall of communism in the former Soviet Union, Estée Lauder opened a boutique a few blocks from the Kremlin. The boutique's immediate success was due in part to the unheard of concept of gift packets and the store's acceptance of rubles for payment. Estée Lauder planned to further expand in Russia and enter the untapped market of China as well.

After his first visit to China in 1982, Leonard Lauder sought to make the same high-quality skin care products available to Chinese women that U.S. women had enjoyed for years. By the early 1990s Clinique and Estée Lauder products could be found in a Shanghai department store. Because of the saturation of the U.S. and western European cosmetics markets and the rise of mass market outlet store like Kmart and Wal Mart, international expansion seems to be the best way for Estée Lauder to secure market share and profits in the wake of declining U.S. sales.

The continuing success of Estée Lauder depends on the company's ability to maintain competitiveness in a stagnant market. From a modest six-product line during World War II to five divisions that offer thousands of products for all consumers, Estée Lauder continues to offer some of the most widely recognized products in the industry. Recently developed perfumes such as Cinnabar and Spellbound along with Prescriptives' All Skins makeup have widened the market by appealing to diverse ethnic groups. Responding to consumers' environmental concerns, Estée Lauder has also produced a successful line of sunscreens.

## Further Reading:

Born, Peter, "Russian Front," *Women's Wear Daily,* Feb.19, 1993, p. 6; " 'Origins' TV Debut," *Women's Wear Daily,* May 14, 1993, p. 4.

"Estée Lauder to Enter Chinese Market Today," *New York Times,* June 9, 1993, p. C3(N), p. D3(L).

Fearnley-Whittingstall, Sophy, "Lauder Stands Out in Sluggish Midwest," *Women's Wear Daily,* August 6, 1993, p. FC16.

Israel, Lee, *Estée Lauder: Beyond the Magic; an Unauthorized Biography,* New York: Macmillan, 1985, 186p.

Lauder, Estée, *Estée: A Success Story,* New York: Random House, 1985, 222p.

''New Life for Youth Dew at 40 (Estée Lauder's Oldest Scent),'' *Women's Wear Daily,* May 28, 1993, p. 4.

Omelia, Johanna, ''Dipping a Cosmetic Toe into Eastern Europe,'' *Drug & Cosmetic Industry,* February 1993, pp. 30–32.

Pottker, Jan, *Born to Power: Heirs to America's Leading Businesses,* New York, Writer's Cramp, Inc., 1992, 460p.

Zinn, Laura, ''At Estée Lauder, the Sweet Smell of Survival,'' *Business Week,* September 14, 1992, pp. 52, 56.

—*Sina Dubovoj*

# EX-LAX®

**ex-lax**®

Ex-Lax, introduced by the Ex-Lax Co. in 1906, was the best-selling brand of laxative in the United States for more than 70 years. It is available in its original chocolate-flavored formula and in unflavored pill form. The Ex-Lax Company was acquired by General Cigar and Tobacco in 1969. The brand has been owned by the Sandoz Corporation, the U.S. subsidiary of Swiss-based international pharmaceutical and chemicals giant Sandoz Ltd., since 1981.

## Brand Origins

Ex-Lax was created in the early 1900s by Max Kiss, a Hungarian-born pharmacist who set out to develop a laxative that would be more palatable to children than the foul-tasting castor oil that was then the most common cathartic. Kiss, born in 1882, immigrated to the United States in 1898, arriving in New York without any money and without a job. The first work he found was as a skin nailer for a New York furrier. Kiss then decided to become a pharmacist and served as an apprentice for several New York druggists. He later attended the Columbia University College of Pharmacy, graduating with a Ph.G. degree in 1904. After graduation he returned to Hungary to visit his family. On the voyage he apparently met several physicians aboard ship from whom he learned of phenolphthalein, a tasteless powder discovered by Farbenfabriken vormals Friedrich Bayer & Co., the German chemical manufacturer that also developed aspirin.

Phenolphthalein was used in winemaking to gauge acidity. But when drinkers noticed that wines with the additive also had a cathartic effect, physicians in Europe began prescribing phenolphthalein as a laxative. Kiss tested a small dose on himself and found that it worked. He then realized that if he combined the right amount of phenolphthalein with a chocolate base, he could produce a laxative that even children would like.

Kiss experimented with various formulas for a year before hitting on the right combination. According to one account, Kiss initially planned to call his laxative Bo-Bo, but changed his mind after reading a Hungarian-language newspaper that used the term "ex-lax," which was slang for parliamentary deadlock. Kiss saw the term as a contraction of "excellent laxative," and took it as the name for his chocolate-flavored laxative. Kiss convinced Israel Matz, a Lithuanian immigrant and successful drug wholesaler in Manhattan, to back his venture and together they founded the Ex-Lax Company in 1906.

Matz, a noted Hebrew scholar and pioneer Zionist, served as president of Ex-Lax, Inc., for 42 years until his death in 1950 at the age of 81. Kiss's tenure with the company was of even longer duration. Until he died in 1967, at the age of 84, Kiss was active as the company's chairman and treasurer.

## Marketing

Ex-Lax quickly became a popular item in medicine cabinets of early 20th century America, where laxatives were often administered for many ailments in addition to constipation. Moreover, judging from early advertisements, "staying regular" was a national obsession. An Ex-Lax advertisement in *Hearst's International-Cosmopolitan* in 1931 carried the headline, "Your very health depends on this!" It went on to warn American consumers, "The poisons of constipation are as real as any poisons put up in bottles! So when Nature fails, the prompt aid of a good laxative is essential to the maintenance of good health." "When Nature forgets, remember Ex-Lax" was the product's slogan.

Early Ex-Lax advertising also was true to Kiss's training as a pharmacist as it emphasized that phenolphthalein was the laxative "that most closely approximates Nature's own way of moving the bowels." The advertisements also displayed little inclination to dance around the subject. Many of the early advertisements were graphic (and scientifically careless) in tone. One magazine advertisement purported to show x-rays of intestines convulsed with harsh laxatives instead of mild Ex-Lax. The text cautioned, "There are two kinds of laxatives. The wrong kind and the right kind. If you only knew what happens inside of you when you take the wrong laxative, you would never gamble with your health again." The ad then went on to describe how the peristaltic muscles of the bowels work "to eliminate the food wastes from your body." "They should churn and knead steadily to perform this vital task . . . The right kind of laxative—such as Ex-Lax—gently reminds and stimulates your bowel muscles to do their work calmly and easily."

Although Ex-Lax was created with children in mind, it was also marketed to adults and the elderly. Advertisements generally targeted the mother of the family, who purchased most of the over-the-counter medicines and almost always administered the laxatives. "Ask mother. She knows!" said one ad in the early 1930s. "For 28 years mothers have known Ex-Lax. And today more mothers select Ex-Lax as the family laxative than any other laxa-

## AT A GLANCE

Ex-Lax brand created by Max Kiss and introduced in 1906 with Israel Matz, who co-founded the Ex-Lax Company with Kiss; owned by General Cigar and Tobacco from 1969 to 1981; company sold to Sandoz Corporation in 1981.

*Advertising:* Agency—Bloom FCA, Dallas, TX, 1986—. *Major campaign*—"For regular people who sometimes aren't."

*Addresses:* Parent company—Sandoz Pharmaceuticals Corporation, 59 Route 10, East Hanover, NJ 07936; phone: (201) 503-7500. *Ultimate parent company*—Sandoz Corporation, 608 5th Ave., New York, NY 10020; phone: (212) 307-1122; fax: (212) 246-0185.

tive in the world." For many years, free samples of Ex-Lax were offered to anyone who wrote to the company.

The Ex-Lax Co. also developed commercials for Ex-Lax that were shown in theaters. One commercial depicted youngsters climbing a tree to pick apples, only to get stomachaches after overeating. Running home to mom, they took Ex-Lax and the stomachaches went away. Kiss later recalled that "there were no apples on the tree, so I bought some and tied them on." It was only after the filming of the commercial was complete that he was told the tree was an oak. Kiss's sons and their friends appeared in the commercial.

Soon after forming the Ex-Lax Co., Matz and Kiss also introduced a fig-flavored version of their laxative, but it never achieved the popularity of the chocolate-flavored Ex-Lax product and was discontinued. Ex-Lax then remained virtually unchanged until 1965, when the company introduced Ex-Lax Unflavored Pills. Later brand extensions included "Extra Gentle Ex-Lax," unflavored pills with a stool softener, and "Ex-Lax Gentle Nature," unflavored pills with a natural vegetable formula instead of phenolphthalein. "Maximun Relief Formula Ex-lax Pills"—50% more medicine.

A series of television commercials for Ex-Lax were introduced in 1991 that presented a softer approach to selling Ex-Lax than early advertisements. The commercials showed everyday people politely mentioning that they occasionally became constipated and used Ex-Lax for relief. The commercials used the tag line, "For regular people who sometimes aren't." The commercials avoided the pseudo-medical and descriptive language of early advertisements and never mentioned the active ingredient phenolphthalein.

### Further Reading:

"Israel Matz Dies; Hebrew Scholar," *The New York Times*, February 11, 1950, p. 15.

"Max Kiss is Dead; Created Ex-Lax," *The New York Times*, June 23, 1967, p. 39.

*—Dean Boyer*

# EXCEDRIN®

Extra Strength Excedrin is a leading brand of nonprescription headache and pain-relief medication marketed by the Bristol-Myers Squibb Company, a major manufacturer of pharmaceuticals and personal-care products. Brand extensions include Aspirin Free Excedrin, Excedrin PM, Sinus Excedrin, Excedrin IB, and Excedrin Dual. Collectively, Excedrin products are the number three pain-relief medication behind Tylenol brand products, made by Johnson & Johnson, and Advil brand products, produced by American Home Products Company. Bristol-Myers Squibb also produces Bufferin and Datril. ''The Headache Medicine'' is a trademark of Excedrin.

## Brand Origins

Extra Strength Excedrin was introduced by the Bristol-Myers Company in 1960. Initially, Excedrin was a combination of aspirin, acetophenetidin, and salicylamide, a drug related to aspirin. The acetophenetidin was replaced with acetaminophen in 1963 because of growing concerns about the safety of the former drug. Original Excedrin also contained caffeine, which some studies indicated enhanced the effectiveness of pain-relieving drugs.

Aspirin is probably the most widely used drug in the world. It was originally a brand name created in 1899 by a German chemical company, Farbenfabriken vormals Friedrich Bayer & Co., for acetylsalicylic acid, which had been discovered in the mid-1800s. Bayer was still the best-selling brand of aspirin in 1993. Over the years aspirin, often called the ''wonder drug,'' has been shown to be effective in relieving the pain from headaches and arthritis, and reducing fever and inflammations caused by illness or injury. In recent years, research indicated that aspirin may also reduce the danger of strokes, heart attacks, and colon cancer.

Acetaminophen, the other principal ingredient in Excedrin, was discovered in 1878, also in Germany. It was first used as a medicine in the late 1800s. It was not widely available in the United States, however, until after 1951, when the Institute for the Study of Analgesic and Sedative Drugs sponsored a symposium on its use.

The best-known acetaminophen product was Tylenol, introduced in 1955 by McNeil Laboratories as a flavored medicine in liquid form for children. Johnson & Johnson purchased McNeil in 1959, and Tylenol eventually became the leading headache medicine in the United States. Ironically, the Squibb Pharmaceutical

Company, which merged with Bristol-Myers in 1989, introduced a prescription drug in 1950 that combined aspirin, acetaminophen, and caffeine. However, the drug, known as Trigesic, was pulled off the market when two users developed a rare blood disease, later proven to be unconnected to the drug.

## ''The Excedrin Headache''

In 1967 Bristol-Myers created ''The Excedrin Headache,'' an advertising campaign that featured a series of vignettes of tension-filled situations that led to excruciating headaches. Each of the situations was assigned an Excedrin headache number. Excedrin Headache No. 9 was a visit from the mother-in-law. Excedrin Headache No. 1040 was a tax audit. Although they aired for only 18 months, the spots were among the most remembered television commercials more than two decades later.

The Excedrin headache was revived briefly to promote Aspirin Free Excedrin in 1991. Also in 1991 Bristol-Myers commissioned a survey about headaches among men and women from ages 20 to 49, and issued a series of media releases under the heading, ''The Excedrin Headache Report.''

## Charges of False Advertising

Aspirin and other headache medications were among the most heavily advertised consumer products on the market, with brands often claiming faster, gentler, or more effective pain relief. In the early 1960s, just when Bristol-Myers was introducing Excedrin, the Federal Trade Commission (FTC) launched an investigation into these advertising claims. It was another ten years, however, before the FTC actually began to bring charges of false advertising against the drug companies. The FTC ordered the companies to back up their advertising claims with documented medical studies and to reveal any studies that had not supported the claims.

Bristol-Myers had capitalized in its advertising on the fact that Excedrin contained four ingredients, while other products contained only one or two. Bayer aspirin, for example, was pure aspirin. Anacin, on the other hand, had started out in 1915 as a mixture of acetanilid, caffeine, and quinine sulfate, but was later reformulated to contain aspirin and caffeine. The FTC challenged Excedrin's claim that more ingredients meant faster or more effective pain relief.

After years of legal wrangling, the FTC's complaint against Excedrin finally went to trial in 1978. In its defense, Bristol-Myers relied on a study conducted at Philadelphia General Hospital that showed Excedrin to be more effective in relieving pain suffered by women following childbirth. Results of the study had been featured in an advertising campaign in 1968 and 1969 that starred David Janssen, an actor who had played a doctor wrongly convicted of murdering his wife on the popular 1960s television series *The Fugitive*. Janssen, shown at a medical convention in Atlantic City, told viewers of "an amazing new experiment." "In this study," Janssen said, "it took more than twice as many aspirin tablets to give the same pain relief as two Excedrin. Not three aspirin, not even four aspirin."

The FTC argued that the study was flawed because the women given Excedrin had higher levels of pain to begin with and, therefore, were more likely to experience relief. In addition, Bristol-Myers was forced to release the results of another study, done at Massachusetts General Hospital, in which researchers could not document more effective relief from either Excedrin or plain aspirin.

Bristol-Myers eventually was ordered to acknowledge the existence of the other study in its advertising. Other big drug companies were also censured. However, although the companies were more careful about their claims after the FTC investigations, the advent of Tylenol as the dominant competitor served to intensify the advertising.

## Excedrin PM

In 1969 Bristol-Myers introduced Excedrin PM, a combination of acetaminophen and diphenhydramine, an antihistamine that induced drowsiness. For more than two decades, Excedrin PM was the only major nonprescription product sold exclusively for nighttime pain relief. Then, in 1991, Johnson & Johnson introduced Tylenol PM. American Home Products followed with Anacin Aspirin-Free PM Caplets. Bristol-Myers Squibb also introduced Bufferin Nite Time, although Excedrin PM and Tylenol PM, which contained identical ingredients, were the overwhelming market leaders.

The *Wall Street Journal* suggested in 1992 that the sudden interest in nighttime pain relief was related to stress caused by a worsening economy, although the newspaper also attributed the interest to aggressive advertising and the need of drug companies to increase sales by creating demand. Television commercials for Excedrin PM focused primarily on headaches caused by everyday stress that could result in sleepless nights. Commercials for Tylenol PM focused on pain relief and how pleasant one's life could be after a good night's sleep.

Tylenol PM quickly replaced Excedrin PM as the sales leader, despite a court battle that threatened for a time to force Tylenol PM off the market. Soon after Tylenol PM was introduced, Bristol-Myers Squibb filed suit against Johnson & Johnson over the use of "PM" in the brand name. The suit also contended that Tylenol PM's blue box with a green stripe was deliberately calculated to confuse consumers, since Excedrin PM came in a blue-green box. Both products were sold as blue-colored pills. In 1992 a U.S. district court initially issued a preliminary injunction against Tylenol PM, but a federal court of appeals ruled that Johnson & Johnson could use "PM" as part of its brand name and that the similar boxes were unlikely to confuse consumers.

## Product Tampering

In the fall of 1982 seven people in the Chicago area died after taking Tylenol capsules that had been intentionally contaminated with cyanide. Tylenol was then the leading headache medicine on the market, but in the weeks to come that share would fall from nearly 30 percent to 8 percent. Almost lost in the publicity over the Tylenol tamperings was a similar scare in Colorado in which Excedrin capsules were found to contain traces of mercuric chloride. Tylenol would eventually regain its lost market share, but the deliberate tampering would forever change the over-the-counter drug industry. Nearly every drug manufacturer rushed to introduce tamper-resistant packages, including Bristol-Myers.

Unfortunately, tamper resistant did not mean tamper proof. In January of 1986 a woman in New York died after taking Tylenol capsules laced with cyanide. That summer, two people died in the Seattle area after taking Excedrin. The Excedrin capsules had also been laced with cyanide. Bristol-Myers immediately recalled all of its nonprescription drugs then sold in capsule form, including Excedrin, Bufferin, Datril, and Comtrex. Following the lead of Johnson & Johnson, within days the company also announced that it would no longer sell any nonprescription drugs in capsule form, although the company held out the possibility of reintroducing capsules if tamper-resistant technology were developed.

## Aspirin Free Excedrin

After 30 years of selling Excedrin, which contained a combination of aspirin and acetaminophen, Bristol-Myers introduced Aspirin Free Excedrin in 1990. Aspirin Free Excedrin was immediately challenged on television and in court.

Aspirin Free Excedrin was made from a combination of acetaminophen and caffeine, and the initial advertisements claimed that the combination of ingredients was more effective than acetaminophen alone. By inference, that meant that Aspirin Free Excedrin was better than Tylenol. Although caffeine had been used in aspirin products, including regular Excedrin, Aspirin Free Excedrin was the first non-aspirin headache remedy to include caffeine. Johnson & Johnson filed suit, arguing that there was no basis for the claim that caffeine enhanced the effectiveness of acetaminophen, and won an injunction against the ads. Less than a month later, Johnson & Johnson also launched a new advertising campaign for Tylenol that urged consumers to check the label of their pain relievers for the presence of caffeine because "you certainly don't want to find it in unexpected places."

Forced to rethink its advertising for Aspirin Free Excedrin, Bristol-Myers revived the famous "Excedrin Headache" concept of the 1960s. A commercial that debuted in January of 1991 showed a segment of a 1968 "Excedrin Headache" commercial involving a housewife and an out-of-control washing machine. An announcer explained that Aspirin Free Excedrin was a new product to cope with old problems.

Then, perhaps because the 1960s' "Excedrin Headache" commercial could have been considered sexist in the 1990s, Bristol-Myers followed up the next month with another commercial for Aspirin Free Excedrin and a new advertising tag line. This time, the commercial showed a woman working at a computer in a cluttered home office. As the woman rubbed the temples of her head, her husband recommended Aspirin Free Excedrin. An unseen announcer added, "Aspirin-free relief, for a headache so bad it shows." Bristol-Myers also teamed up with H&R Block, the tax-return preparation company, to advertise Aspirin Free Excedrin in early 1991. As a tax interview ended, the tax preparer pulled out a box of Excedrin and told his client, "This, for your headache." In 1993 advertisements claimed that Aspirin Free Excedrin "contains more medicine than regular strength pain relievers."

## Excedrin IB

In 1991 Bristol-Myers Squibb introduced Excedrin IB, a pain-relief medicine containing ibuprofen, an extremely effective drug developed in England in the late 1960s. In clinical tests, ibuprofen was shown to be 16 times more powerful than aspirin as an analgesic, and 20 times more powerful as an anti-inflammatory medication.

Initially, ibuprofen was a prescription drug and was marketed in the United States by the Upjohn Company under the name Motrin. By 1983, Motrin was the fourth most popular prescription drug in the United States. Then, in 1984, the Food and Drug Administration authorized ibuprofen as an over-the-counter (OTC) drug. Both American Home Products and Bristol-Myers acquired the right to market OTC products with ibuprofen. American Home introduced Advil, while Bristol-Myers introduced Nuprin. By 1992, sales of ibuprofen-based pain relievers had surpassed aspirin. As a late entry, Excedrin IB was the fourth-best-selling brand containing ibuprofen.

In 1992 Bristol-Myers continued the move to dual-purpose medications begun with Excedrin PM with the introduction of Aspirin Free Excedrin Dual, a combination of acetaminophen and antacid for upset stomachs.

## Further Reading:

Agovino, Theresa, "Expectations Give Firm an Excedrin Headache," *Crain's New York Business,* May 14, 1990, p. 2.

Deveny, Kathleen, *Wall Street Journal,* "Ibuprofen's Success Pains Aspirin Makers," January 12, 1993, p. B1; "Stresses, Strain and Shrewd Marketing Ignite Sales of Nighttime Pain Remedies," September 24, 1992, p. B1.

DiBacco, Thomas V., "Aspirin's Long Record Began with Germany, World War I," *Washington Post,* January 12, 1993, p. 18.

Dwyer, Augusta, "The Pain-Killer Market; The Competition Reflects the High Stakes," *Maclean's,* July 16, 1990, p. 42.

Freudenheim, Milt, "Judge Bars Tylenol PM as Lookalike," *The New York Times,* February 22, 1992, p. 17.

Garfield, Bob, "Excedrin Pounds Home Message for Its Asprin Free Medication," *Advertising Age,* February 25, 1991, p. 54.

Kipman, Joanne, "H&R Block, Excedrin Discover Joint Promotions Can Be Painless," *Wall Street Journal,* February 28, 1991, p. B7.

Mann, Charles C. and Mark L. Plummer, *The Aspirin Wars: Money, Medicine, and 100 Years of Competition,* New York: Alfred A. Knopf, 1991.

Todd, David, "The Wonder Drug," *Maclean's,* July 16, 1990, p. 38.

Winters, Patricia, *Advertising Age,* " 'Excedrin Headache' Comes Back," January 28, 1991, p. 9; "Excedrin Bangs Tylenol: New Aspirin-Free Product Claims It's Better," August 13, 1990, pp. 3–4.

*—Dean Boyer*

# FLORSHEIM®

Established in 1892, Florsheim is one of the oldest and best-known brands of quality men's dress shoes. In recent years, The Florsheim Shoe Company, a subsidiary of St. Louis-based Interco Incorporated, also introduced a line of casual shoes for men and a line of outdoor shoewear. Florsheim shoes were sold in more than 300 company-owned Florsheim Shoe Shops and 5,000 independent shoe stores. In addition to those sold in the United States, Florsheim shoes were available in Australia, Canada, and Mexico.

## Early Brand History

Sigmund Florsheim was a shoe salesman who opened a shop in Chicago in 1856. In 1892, 10 years after the invention of the shoe-lasting machine that revolutionized the shoe-making industry, his son, Milton S. Florsheim, then 24, founded The Florsheim Shoe Company. In 1894 the company produced 150 pairs of shoes. Milton Florsheim also began branding his name on the sole of every shoe his company produced, creating one of the earliest brand names in the shoe industry.

The brand benefited early in its history from the company's many innovations. In the early 1900s, Florsheim became one of the first nationally advertised brands of shoes, with advertisements running in magazines such as *The Saturday Evening Post.* The Florsheim Shoe Company also became one of the first shoe manufacturers to open its own retail stores in major cities, and introduced the first low-cut shoes for men, which quickly became the standard men's dress shoes. Florsheim stores were the first to put shoes on display rather than having shoe salesman bring out one pair at a time from the back room, so customers could see all the available styles at once.

Milton Florsheim, who had become chairman of the board for The Florsheim Shoe Company, died in 1936. His son, Irving S. Florsheim, was then president of the company, and a second son, Harold M. Florsheim, was vice president. Harold Florsheim later served as chief of the shoe and leather division of the Office of Production Management in the years leading up to U.S. entry into World War II.

In 1953, Irving and Harold Florsheim sold controlling interest in the company their father founded to the International Shoe Company in St. Louis. The International Shoe Co., which later changed its name to Interco Incorporated, dated to 1836 and the founding of the Peters Shoe Company. In the 1950s it was the nation's largest shoe manufacturer; with 55 factories turning out more than 55 million pairs of shoes annually, it contributed about 10 percent of the total production of shoes in the United States. However, the International Shoe Co. had concentrated on the medium-priced market. Florsheim was then producing less than 2.5 million pairs of shoes annually, but was one of the best known brands in the high-quality men's shoe market. Florsheim's line of women's shoes, introduced in 1929, was less successful. The Florsheim Shoe Company continued to operate as a division of the International Shoe Company after the purchase.

## Express Shop

In the early 1980s, most shoe stores were cutting back on inventory to reduce operating costs. The Florsheim Shoe Company, with more than 600 company stores and nearly 5,000 dealer outlets, faced the same financial pressures. However, the company also advertised that its stores carried Florsheim-brand shoes in every possible combination of size, width, style, and color, which meant maintaining an inventory of more than 14,000 pairs of shoes. Not wanting to give up its reputation for wide selection and service, in 1982, Florsheim introduced Express Shop as a way out of its dilemma.

Express Shop was an interactive kiosk with a keyboard and full-color video screen. Customers were able to "window shop" in Florsheim stores by computer, selecting the style and color of

## AT A GLANCE

**F**lorsheim brand of shoes founded in 1892 by Milton S. Florsheim when he created the Florsheim Shoe Company; company sold to International Shoe Co. in 1953; International Shoe Co. changed name Interco Incorporated in 1966.

**Performance:** *Market share*—20% of men's dress shoes.

**Major competitor:** Dexter; also Bass, Rockport, and Hush Puppies.

**Advertising:** *Agency*—Frank C. Nahser.

**Addresses:** *Parent company*—The Florsheim Shoe Company, 130 S. Canal St., Chicago IL 60606; phone: (312) 559-0009. *Ultimate parent company*—Interco Incorporated.

the Florsheim shoes they wanted from all 14,000 available combinations. If the store did not have the exact shoes, the customer could try on another pair of the same style for size. The proper shoes were then delivered within a week to the customer's home or office from a 1-million square foot warehouse in Jefferson City, Missouri. Florsheim picked up the cost of delivery, even though it cost the company about five dollars a pair.

Florsheim later changed the name of its kiosks from the Express Shop to The Florsheim Special Order Center, and the program continued to grow. From a pilot program involving 60 stores in 1982, there were more than 500 terminals in 1992, including several in Sears & Roebuck Co. shoe departments. Company plans called for a nationwide network of 2,000 Florsheim Special Order Centers before 1995.

## Current Marketing

In 1992, responding to a survey that showed many consumers associated the Florsheim brand name with high prices, the company announced that it was reducing prices on four of its most popular styles of men's shoes. Long known almost exclusively for men's dress shoes, Florsheim also introduced several new styles in 1993 that targeted the market for men's casual footwear and expanded the Outdoorsman line of hiker and hunting boots it had

introduced in 1989. Florsheim also became a sponsor of the American Park Network, and Outdoorsman shoes were sold in equipment stores in the national parks.

In 1993, Florsheim also began redesigning its retail outlets. For many years, Florsheim stores reflected a subdued men's club atmosphere with dark paneling and leather furniture. The new store design was brighter and more casual, which the company also hoped would reflect a younger and more casual image for its shoes.

## Further Reading:

"Background on the Florsheim Shoe Company," Chicago: The Florsheim Shoe Company, 1992.

Bermer, Amy, "Customers Go Shopping at a PC," *PC Week,* October 20, 1987, p. 57.

"Biggest Shoemaker Gets Bigger," *Business Week,* February 14, 1953, p. 146.

"Florsheim . . . A Century of Quality and Fashion," Chicago: The Florsheim Shoe Company, 1993.

"Florsheim Steps Boldly into Next Century," Chicago: The Florsheim Shoe Company, 1993.

"Florsheim New Store Concept Positions Company for Next Century," Chicago: The Florsheim Shoe Company, 1993.

*—Dean Boyer*

# FORMULA 409®

Formula 409 brand of all-purpose cleaner revolutionized the cleaning of greasy dirt when it was introduced in 1957. Even though sales of the brand were not stunning under the ownership of the Brian Scott Products & Manufacturing Company of Detroit, Michigan, sales soon increased under the ownership and marketing genius of William L. Harrell. Harrell brought Formula 409 to the attention of consumers and major competitors like the Procter & Gamble Company. Innovative marketing support has proved a necessary ingredient to the sales of Formula 409. Under the ownership of The Clorox Company, Formula 409 continued to be a top selling all-purpose cleaner into the 1990s.

## Brand Origins

Two young Detroit, Michigan scientists are credited with concocting Formula 409 in the late 1950s. The mixture was named after the 409 attempts the scientists made before finding the right balance of ingredients. Formula 409 became a registered trademark in 1959, two years after it had been in use. Formula 409, a mildly alkaline solution containing water, solvent, detergent builder, surfactant and coloring, is a hard surface cleaner that works effectively on greasy dirt. It is not highly concentrated and can be used full strength without rinsing. Formula 409 was not successfully marketed by the Brian Scott Products & Manufacturing Company in Detroit and was sold in 1963 to marketing gadfly and entrepreneur Wilson L. Harrell of Westport, Connecticut.

Harrell, a World War II hero with plenty of stories to tell about how he survived Nazi capture, founded Harrell International in 1959 after a stint as a London-based food broker supplying military commissaries and post exchanges. Once he began his company, he acquired Formula 409 for $30,000 and soon expanded his businesses overseas to include marinas, cattle ranches, shrimp farms, and brokerage firms. Harrell turned Formula 409 into a profitable acquisition. According to Joseph P. Kahn in *Inc.,* "Practically everything about 409 was serendipitous, including the fact that Harrell had firsthand knowledge of the cleaner's popularity—his military customers adored it—even among consumers who never saw any advertising for it."

## Market Strategy

Harrell always had a knack for knowing when to risk it all. The 409 story goes as follows: Harrell runs into a food broker in Hawaii, who suggests and then helps him implement a way to distribute Formula 409 nationally. The plan would be to subcontract advertising, produce commercials in-house, buy air time market-to-market at a discount, hire local personalities with local credibility and cut them in on the deal, wrote Kahn in *Inc.* Harrell approached Art Linkletter to sign him up, but came out of the deal with $85,000 and Linkletter in a ten-percent equity position.

Harrell began to compete with one of the top domestic products companies, Procter & Gamble. Procter & Gamble was ready to roll out its own all-purpose cleaner called Cinch. Harrell knew he could not spend or promote more than Procter & Gamble, so he resorted to another tactic. He told *Inc.* that he "scrambled the numbers by taking Cinch's test markets and ordering all Formula 409 shipments to those cities delayed." He then halted 409 advertising and in-store promotions. Procter & Gamble responded by heavily investing in Cinch's test marketing and national rollout in the face of no competition. Just when Cinch was being unveiled, Harrell began flooding the market with jumbo-size bottles of 409 (enough for a four-month supply), which shoppers immediately purchased over Cinch. It didn't take long for Cinch to disappear completely because of poor sales.

Harrell's gamble proved he could market Formula 409 on a small budget. Procter & Gamble CEO Howard Morgens eventually told Harrell that what he had done (to compete against Cinch) was "one of the finest marketing jobs he'd ever seen." *Inc.* quoted Harrell as recalling that Morgens' statement "meant a hell of a lot to me." Harrell estimated that he probably cost Procter & Gamble $25 million to cancel Cinch.

In its early days, Formula 409 helped make Harrell wealthy. But Harrell soon changed his strategy and ruined his success with the brand. In an *Inc.* article bearing his by-line, he said, he "couldn't leave well enough alone. . . . I became victim of the entrepreneurial disease." He sought advice from other seemingly more professional business consultants. His previous style of innovative seat-of-the-pants marketing gave way to corporate staidness and Formula 409 began to lose market share. "If you want to destroy a small company, just hire a mule driver to manage a bunch of racehorses. I ruined a company that way," Harrell wrote.

His luck changed in 1970, when The Clorox Company paid him $7.5 million for Formula 409. The previous year, The Clorox Company had been spun off from Procter & Gamble as a public

## AT A GLANCE

**F**ormula 409 brand of all-purpose cleaner invented by two Detroit, Michigan scientists in the late 1950s after 409 tries; manufactured by the Brian Scott Products & Manufacturing Company; brand became registered trademark March 31, 1959; trademark and product sold to Wilson Harrell of Harrell International, Westport, CT, for $30,000, 1967; Formula 409 spray cleaner and aerosol bathroom cleaner acquired by The Clorox Company for $7.5 million in 1970.

**Performance:** *Market share*—9.6% of the all-purpose cleaner market; 3.5% of the cleaning solution market; *Sales*—$33.7 million (approx.) in supermarket sales.

**Major competitor:** Dowbrand's Fantastik; also, Procter & Gamble's Cinch.

**Advertising:** *Agency*—Foote, Cone & Belding, San Francisco, CA 1970—. *Major campaign*—"Cuts greasy dirt fast."

**Addresses:** *Parent company*—The Clorox Company, 1221 Broadway, Oakland, CA 94621; phone: (510) 271-7000; fax: (510) 832-1463.

company, with Clorox liquid bleach as its only product. The Clorox Company (which Procter & Gamble had been ordered to divest because its acquisition violated the Clayton Anti-Trust Act) realized that diversification into other areas besides bleach was essential to its survival. Clorox branched out into three areas: nonfood grocery products, food (specialty and institutional), and cleaning products.

## Brand Development

The Formula 409 brand line, which included spray cleaner, bathroom disinfectant, and soap pads marked Clorox's entry into the household cleaner market. The purchase price also included other Harrell International brands: Chemisol, an institutional cleaner, Dif, a specialty hand cleaner, and Soil-off liquid cleaner. Clorox decided to concentrate on Formula 409 spray cleaner and disinfectant bathroom cleaner, phasing out the other brands.

A year after its acquisition, however, Formula 409 sales were below the prior year's level, company reports stated. A national marketing program was expected to shore up sales, although the Formula 409 bathroom cleaner was still not as established a brand at that time.

In 1973, a new, reformulated Formula 409 bathroom cleaner hit the market. Two years later The Clorox Food Service Products Division added an institutional version of Formula 409 all-purpose spray cleaner to its product line. Consumers would not see new packaging until 1980 when the trigger sprayer model of the 409 spray cleaner rolled out nationwide. A 22-ounce replacement bottle appeared on shelves in 1982 after positive test market results, according to documents from The Clorox Company. But later that year, the company decided to pull Formula 409 disinfectant bathroom cleaner entirely to concentrate on marketing the all-purpose spray cleaner. Time spent on reformulating the brand made the all-purpose cleaner much more effective on greasy dirt and stains. The result was record shipments for Clorox and a gain in market share.

Not much would be done to the brand until 1992, when a concentrated refill was test marketed in San Francisco and Boston.

As an environmental measure, the 10-ounce concentrate ended up using 65 percent less plastic than the 22-ounce size. This feature, in addition to The Clorox Company switching to recyclable plastic packaging in the early 1990s, would earn Formula 409 and the company a DuPont special citation in 1992. The DuPont awards have recognized international industry innovations in plastic packaging materials since 1986. Judges called the brand's new packaging an "environmental breakthrough" because bottles were manufactured and filled by one machine, requiring little plastic.

An extension of the Formula 409 brand occurred in 1993 with the introduction of Formula 409 glass and surface cleaner, which is distributed nationally, directly competing with DowBrand's Glass Plus and other multi-purpose glass and surface cleaners. Formula 409 glass and surface cleaner comes in 22-ounce trigger spray bottles and 32-ounce refills in retail outlets and in 32-ounce trigger and 64-ounce refills at warehouse stores. Formula 409 already competes directly with another DowBrands' product, Fantastik. Together Formula 409 and Fantastik dominated the $200 million segment, holding 90 percent of the spray cleaner market by the early 1990s.

## Advertising

Foote, Cone and Belding of San Francisco, California has handled the Formula 409 account since Clorox purchased the brand line from Harrell International. But it was Harrell who used his connections and friendship with celebrity Art Linkletter to sell Formula 409 on its effectiveness as a convenient cleaner.

Foote, Cone and Belding made the brand a star and developed a series of print ads that stress the brand's grease cutting properties. When Clorox decided to move to recyclable plastic, Foote, Cone and Belding launched a program of free-standing inserts with packages. As in all of its packaging, Clorox was careful to note that its cleaning products were encased in partially recycled plastic materials, reported Bradley Johnson in *Advertising Age*.

The firm's strategy often positioned Formula 409 (the 409 in big, blue lettering, with a 'Formula' superimposed in minuscule print) as "the greasy dirt specialist," a "grime buster" that "starts to work before you wipe," and as "no other spray cleans tough kitchen grease better." Ads appearing in the late 1970s depicted people making a mess that was cleaned up with the help of Formula 409 and a sponge. "Formula 409 has a special combination of 4 grease cutters to cut those greasy household messes down to size. And the economy refill is a real money saver. So get Formula 409 Spray Cleaner. Because one greasy dirt specialist deserves another," read a 1977 print ad.

Foote, Cone and Belding also played up the fact that a little bit of Formula 409 went a long way in an advertisement that featured a cook standing amid his grease- and food-smeared kitchen: "Every day Frank's Diner goes through 40 pounds of beef, 2 gallons of oil, 7 quarts of chili, 11 pounds of butter, 19 slabs of bacon, 3,000 french fries, 18 pounds of sausage . . . and 4 ounces of Formula 409." Advertising in the early 1990s stressed how the brand worked on all kinds of dirt and grease.

As part of being a good corporate citizen, The Clorox Company has at times donated Formula 409 products in the wake of natural disasters such as California's Lom Prieta earthquake and the 1992 hurricane damage in Florida, Louisiana, and Hawaii. Other Clorox products were donated to the American Red Cross,

Salvation Army, and other relief organizations to help disaster survivors.

## Performance Appraisal

Formula 409 was a hit before it became a Clorox Company product and remained a top selling cleaner because it fit so well with The Clorox Company's strategy to diversify its line of household cleaners. Supermarket sales for Formula 409 reached $33.7 million by 1990. The product was ranked as the fifth best-selling multi-purpose cleaning brand by *Adweek's Marketing Week,* and tenth best household cleaning brand by *Discount Store News.* Its share in the market ranges from 3.5 percent of cleaning solutions to 9.6 percent of all-purpose cleaners, depending on the category and source. A 1993 Paine Webber *Industry Report* tracked the brand's progress throughout 1992, showing that the brand began the year with 8.7 percent of the all-purpose cleaning market, dipped to 7.7 percent and rebounded to 9.6 percent in the first quarter of 1993. "The approximately $2.3 billion home cleaning products market is seeing a flurry of the new entries. Relative to all-purpose cleaners, dilutable versions of existing brands have been growing and now account for about one-quarter of category sales," the report stated.

Moving into the glass and surface cleaner arena will likely keep Formula 409 a strong, top-selling brand. Formula 409's success has even prompted the return of Procter & Gamble's Cinch glass and surface cleaner in 1991. Whether Formula 409 can weather the new competition remains to be seen. Since it is bolstered by fellow Clorox cleaning brands Clorox Clean Up and Pine-Sol, 409 promises to put up a good fight. "Clorox Clean Up, Pine-Sol and Formula 409 are three of the family of brands which have made the Company the virtual leader in the $2.3 billion hard surface cleaner market," a Clorox Company 1992 *Annual Report* stated. The report went on to mention the other brands that keep the company's cleaner market sales strong. "The others are Liquid-Plumr drain opener, Soft Scrub mild abrasive liquid cleanser, Tackle cleaner disinfectant, and Tilex mildew remover. We are in an excellent position to capitalize further on the growth opportunities in this market."

## Further Reading:

Byrne, Harland S., "Clorox Co., After an Earnings Slowdown, a Rebound Is in Store," *Barron's Investment News & Views,* December 3, 1990, pp. 47–48.

Campanella, Frank W., "Still the Leader," *Barron's Investment News & Views,* March 25, 1985, pp. 57–58.

"Clorox Has Recycled Packaging Plan," *Advertising Age,* November 4, 1991, p. 8.

Fitzgerald, Kate, and Judann Dagnoli, "New Cleaners Mop Up Household Category," *Advertising Age,* September 9, 1991, p. 3.

Harrell, Wilson, "Betting on the Right Horses," *Inc.,* September 1986, pp. 103–104.

Johnson, Bradley, "Clorox Recycles Bottles," *Advertising Age,* November 11, 1992, p. 64.

Kahn, Joseph P., "Portrait of a Compulsive Entrepreneur," *Inc.,* April 1985, pp. 79–88.

Schusteff, Sandy, *International Directory of Company Histories,* vol. 2, Chicago: St. James Press, 1988.

*—Evelyn S. Dorman*

# FRUIT OF THE LOOM®

Show America's shoppers a picture of a brightly colored fruit cluster, and the vast majority of them will recognize it as the Fruit of the Loom emblem. They'll also associate it with medium-priced, good-quality underwear—a once-dull necessity that has recently acquired a much-more-trendy gloss. Show these same customers a picture of the Fruit of the Loom logo at the beginning of its 140-year lifetime, and hardly anyone would be able to place it. Instead of an assortment of fruit, the logo was a single red apple hand-painted against a beige background. Indeed, the emblem in its earliest days was matched to bolts of fine muslin intended for hand-sewing rather than underwear. In fact, this emblem traces its origins not to a company in sophisticated Boston or Washington, D.C., but rather to a little country store operated by Hudson Valley apple farmer Rufus Skeel.

The famous Fruit of the Loom trademark made its debut in 1856 courtesy of Skeel's daughter, who displayed her painted apple against a bolt of the cloth its manufacturer called ''Fruit of the Loom.'' Noting that the cloth sold much more briskly than its unadorned fellows, her father encouraged the budding artist to mark other fabrics in the same way. All of them proved so attractive to Skeel's customers that he showed his daughter's work to the cloth's manufacturer, Rhode Island-based Robert Knight of B.B. & R. Knight Mills, Inc. Impressed with the trademark's drawing power, Knight adopted it, putting copies on all the fabric the company shipped to its New York distributors. Later, the firm took care to register it as soon as the United States Patent Office opened in 1871. Now bearing the number 418, it was the first American trademark ever used for textiles.

Four years later, the Knights re-registered an updated design that featured an assortment of fruit. The logo was redesigned again in 1893 by a company artist commemorating the Chicago World's Fair. After this third remodeling the Knight family was finally content with the trademark, which is still an American institution 100 years later.

## Licensing—a Lucrative Sideline

Until the early years of the twentieth century the Fruit of the Loom trademark symbolized only Knight Mills' fine-quality fabrics. Later, when World War I revolutionized American industry with its urgent demands for huge quantities of mass-produced domestic linens, underwear, and uniforms, the colorful label took on new luster as a marketing tool. Instantly recognizable as a

stamp of high quality to textile trade stalwarts, the fruit cluster offered the company a way to advertise the value of its own wares.

Knight Mills quickly saw the financial advantages of licensing their label to these manufacturers. It gladly took on first a manufacturer of sheets and pillow cases, then, in 1922, a producer of nurses' uniforms, ladies' dresses, and pajamas for men, as well as the underwear that would later become its principal product.

As is so often the case, however, the trademark bonanza was not all good news. The burgeoning demand for mass-produced linens and clothes caused the market for hand-sewing fabrics to plummet. The result was predictable—for the first time since its 1848 organization, Knight Mills lost money.

## A Fresh Start Fails

Once again, the directors looked to their powerful trademark for financial support. In 1930 the company organized Fruit of the Mills Inc. to market its wares on the Pacific coast. The new venture was not a success, so the company liquidated it in 1932, and soon afterwards cut back on other projects by closing its fabric-manufacturing mills in favor of plants devoted entirely to finishing.

This ploy was scarcely more successful, as the dismal sales figures for 1935 showed. While the mills had racked up $4.3 million in sales, their profits were a paltry $33,382, a figure which left them $2.1 million in the red when operating expenses had been paid.

In 1938 the cycle of failure began to break. The first positive step, based on the enduring value of its trademark, was the re-incorporation of Knight Mills as Fruit of the Loom Mills, Inc. Next came yet another lucrative licensing opportunity. The agreement, which spanned 25 years, allowed the use of the logo on the medium-priced men's underwear produced by a Kentucky-based manufacturer called Jacob Goldfarb. At first blandly routine, the new deal between Goldfarb and Fruit of the Loom soon became one of the most profitable partnerships in American industry.

## Enter Jacob Goldfarb

Goldfarb had been in the men's underwear trade since his immigration to the United States in 1926. Originally based in Indianapolis, he had begun by manufacturing only unionsuits, which were then the favored forms of underwear for men. Lacking

## AT A GLANCE

**F**ruit of the Loom brand of muslin founded by Robert and
Benjamin B. Knight, owners of B.B. & R. Knight Mills, Inc. in
Rhode Island, in the early 1850s; in 1850 Robert Knight and his
partner, Zachariah Parker, purchased the mill they had been
leasing; soon after, Parker sold his share to Robert Knight, and
circa 1851 Knight's brother, Benjamin B. Knight, became a
partner in the business; the trademark, which originally appeared as a single apple in 1856, was registered by Knight Mills
in 1871; Knight Mills re-incorporated as Fruit of the Loom
Mills, Inc., in 1938; in 1961 the company was bought by the
Philadelphia & Reading Corporation, which in turn was acquired in 1968 by Northwest Industries; in 1985 Farley, Inc.,
bought out Northwest for $1.4 billion.

**Performance:** *Market share*—40% of Men's and Boys' Underwear category; 13.9% of Women's and Girls' Underwear
category.

**Major competitor:** Hanes Corp.'s Hanes brand; Jockey International Inc.'s Jockey brand

**Advertising:** Leo Burnett Company Inc., Chicago, IL.

**Addresses:** *Parent company*—Fruit of the Loom, Inc., 233
South Wacker Drive, 5000 Sears Tower, Chicago, IL 60606;
phone: (312) 876-1724. *Ultimate parent company*—Farley Industries Inc., 233 S. Wacker Dr., Chicago, IL 60606; phone
(312) 876-1724; fax: (312) 993-1783.

a factory, the resourceful Goldfarb had bought his cloth from a
supplier, and had taken it first to a cutter, and then to convents
scattered around his native Indianapolis, where his underwear was
assembled by nuns before being offered for sale.

At this stage of his life, Jacob Goldfarb's dream was to own a
factory where all operations could be streamlined and undertaken
under one roof. This wish had come true in 1930, by way of an
invitation to move his operations to Depression-damaged Kentucky. Relocation proved to be a smart move—by 1935, Union
Underwear was employing 650 workers and was well on the way
to full vertical integration.

As soon as he was satisfied that his factory was running
smoothly, Goldfarb decided that he was ready to compete with
other manufacturers across the country. He commenced a search
for a trademark to represent "high quality" to any shopper unfamiliar with Union Underwear merchandise. By 1938 Goldfarb was
satisfied that Fruit of the Loom would bring his products the
recognition they needed, and eagerly entered into the aforementioned 25-year licensing agreement.

However, Goldfarb's dream of industry leadership had to wait.
The World War II years, which kept his factory humming with
orders from the army, replaced his personal priority with patriotic
duty. Nevertheless, as soon as hostilities ended, he returned immediately to his dream of building Fruit of the Loom into a national
brand. He advertised extensively and came up with the innovative
idea of packaging his underwear in cellophane three-packs, each
with the Fruit of the Loom logo on the bag. Taking no chances on
incorrect display, he even supplied his distributors with wooden
racks to show off his wares.

All this effort paid such handsome rewards that by 1948 Goldfarb's company was able to expand the line to include knit underwear, which in turn was successful enough to warrant opening

a big Kentucky-based knitting and bleaching plant four years later.
Gaining impetus, the move towards diversity continued in 1951,
when Fruit of the Loom filed serial number 613,810 with the U.S.
Patent Office for use on covers for bowls and appliances made of
flexible plastic material.

### The Serenely Profitable 1950s

By the mid-1950s the company was using television advertising on Dave Garroway's "Today Show" to build its Fruit of the
Loom underwear into a staple with consumers. This big-budget
exposure was boosted with newspaper slicks and banners for
stores, as well as a cooperative advertising program that concentrated on seasonal events like Back-to-School and Father's Day.
Shoppers also found Fruit of the Loom underwear packs in the
mass-merchandising outlets that began to burgeon during the
1950s. Goldfarb was careful to keep his prices in line with their
merchandising strategy, thus carving his wares a market niche
they still occupy 40 years later.

All these successes made Union Underwear a coveted property
for expansion-hungry investors like Philadelphia & Reading Corporation, a hard coal business that bought the company in 1955. In
1961, pleased with Union's steady profits, Philadelphia & Reading
went a step further. Realizing that Goldfarb's original 25-year
trademark agreement with the Knights would run out in a couple
of years, they bought Fruit of the Loom Inc., a surviving subsidiary of now-defunct Knight Mills. This purchase made it possible
for Union Underwear to use the Fruit of the Loom trademark
forever.

By the end of 1968 the Union Underwear product list had
broadened enough to send 14.5 million items flowing down its
assembly lines. Hot new offerings included shirts, sweat shirts,

*Early labels used interchangeably on Fruit of the Loom products.*

and infant wear, a new line of Dacron and cotton underwear for
both men and boys called the "Golden" Fruit of the Loom line. In
addition, the company now had 27 licensees. All this success made
Philadelphia & Reading a juicy investment plum that was plucked
during the year by Northwest Industries.

## A Brand-New Image

Union's new owners immediately instituted a new advertising campaign to pump new potential into the Fruit of the Loom product lines. Acknowledging that their underwear offerings had never fallen into the category of exciting merchandise, they changed its image by linking it to a healthy, outdoor-type lifestyle represented by sportscaster Howard Cosell, who was contracted to star in a series of television commercials over a three-year period. Cosell proved to be the first of many celebrities hired to sing the praises of Fruit of the Loom wares.

By the 1970s Union Underwear was sailing profitably along, buoyed by an impressive list of 350 merchandise classifications carrying the Fruit of the Loom trademark in both domestic and overseas markets. Typical of foreign partnerships was the licensing agreement with the Marubeni Corporation, which brought the company's linens to the attention of Japanese consumers via sophisticated radio and television advertising. The domestic consumer found the familiar cluster of fruit on sheets and towels from Burlington Industries, as well as on women's underwear, infant clothes, and disposable diapers, and even on costume jewelry. Another enduring licensee was the CBS Apparel Corporation, a division of Warnco, Inc. that produced 80 percent of its goods in Asian countries but sold them in America. Fruit of the Loom even had a $7.7 million agreement with the U.S. Army to supply men's underwear. Altogether, the trademark was being used by a grand total of 29 licensees by the end of 1974.

Buttressing their success, the company began to step up its advertising even further. First came the famous "Fruit Guys," four men dressed in costumes to echo the label's appearance. This jolly group was prominently featured in a series of television commercials. So successful was this ad campaign that the live trademark was used to represent Fruit of the Loom for the following 13 years. Next, in 1976, came an advertising program designed to promote the whole Fruit of the Loom line by featuring money-back coupons in leading women's magazines. Galvanized by all these measures, the Fruit of the Loom share of the men's underwear market steadily grew.

## New Owners—Again

In 1985 Northwest Industries was bought by Farley, Inc. for $1.4 billion. The Fruit of the Loom product line subsequently underwent a major facelift. In an effort to rev up a lackluster men's underwear market Farley spent $120 million on modernizing production and boosting capacity. Another $3 million went into a new ad campaign that reflected a new interest in men's fashion underwear, wholesale sweatshirts, and t-shirts for screen-printing.

By 1985 Union Underwear controlled more than 40 percent of the $1.2 billion men's underwear market. Soon, seeking a new market, the company joined Calvin Klein and Jockey in producing underwear for women. Unlike them, however, its target was not department-store sales, but the discount merchandisers like K-Mart that had always been its principal outlets.

Once again the company turned to television advertising to launch this line. This time, however, the new campaign did not feature the Fruit of the Loom figures. Instead, the company opted for the voice of actress Tammy Grimes, who described the evolution of the company's product line into the realm of women's underwear.

Union found the going in the women's underwear market to be unexpectedly choppy. The turbulence came from competing women's underwear producer Hanes Knitwear, a subsidiary of Sara Lee Corporation that had hitherto been a close but not harmful rival. Now the rivalry soared, to culminate, in 1986, in a $15 million television ad campaign launched by Hanes. Hanes claimed in one commercial that its t-shirts shrank 38 percent less than those manufactured by Fruit of the Loom, and in a second advertisement that its line of underwear simply fit better. Hanes found itself in court for "insulting Fruit of the Loom's underwear." Fruit of the Loom lost the court battle, but eventually won the market share war.

The beginning of the 1990s found the country in a stubborn recession that caused retailers to trim their inventory. Though underwear sales began to sag, Fruit of the Loom, Inc., was given an upward boost by sales of recently introduced activewear such as hooded fleece jackets, shorts, and sweatpants. In 1991 the line was augmented by bras from Warnaco with the Fruit of the Loom trademark and also by men's and boys' underwear sold under the Munsingwear and Kangaroo labels. The company closed out the year with sales of $574 million in 1991—a figure that soared to $1.8 billion by the end of 1992.

## Further Reading:

Bauer, Betsy, "New Ads Escalate Undies War," *USA Today,* September 10, 1985, p. B1.

"The Birth of the Fruit of the Loom Name," Fruit of the Loom, Inc.

Bovee, Courtland L., and William F. Arens, *Contemporary Advertising,* Irwin, 1986, p. 55–56.

*Fruit of the Loom Company Annual Reports,* Fruit of the Loom, Inc., 1972–1978, 1991.

"Fruit of the Loom Inc. Sues Rival Over Underwear Ads," *Wall Street Journal,* August 15, 1986, p.16.

"Judge Shrinks From Ban of Underwear Commercial," *Wall Street Journal,* Sept. 2, 1986.

Koshetz, Herbert, "Fruits of Nonproduction," *New York Times,* July 14, 1974, P. F12.

Morgan, Hal, *Symbols of America,* Penguin, 1986, p. 193.

*Moody's Manual of Investments,* Moody's, 1930, p.126; 1942, p. 691.

*Moody's Industrial Manual,* 1956, p. 915.; 1976, p. 2297; 1991, p. 1157.

*Official Gazette,* U.S. Patent Office, August 7, 1923, p. 22; May 6, 1952, p. 41; February 24, 1959, TM 156; March 17, 1959, TM 111; August 25, 1959, TM 147; June 8, 1976, TM 87; January 18, 1983, TM 384.

Oneal, Michael, "Fruit of the Loom Escalates the Underwars," *Business Week,* February 22, 1988, p. 114.

Sloan, Pat, "Different Briefs Seen in Underwear Battle," *Advertising Age,* March 23, 1987, p. 4.

*World's Greatest Brands,* John Wiley, 1991.

—*Gillian Wolf*

# GARANIMALS®

In the mid-1970s, the Garanimals brand broke new ground in the marketing of children's apparel by using an unconventional approach and media. The unique concept harnessed the influential power of television to introduce and promote the brand's pre-matched separates and jungle characters to mothers and children. The brand performed well in the late 1970s and early 1980s, but fell out of favor during the designer-driven mid-1980s. A late 1980s recession, though, revived both consumers' perception of value and branded childrenswear sales.

## Brand Origins

The Garanimals brand of childrenswear was introduced in 1976 by Seymour Lichtenstein, chairman of Garan Inc. As mass merchandisers and discount department stores captured an increasing share of the childrenswear market in the 1970s, Lichtenstein and others at Garan Inc. recognized an opportunity to offer branded kidswear in markets that had previously been dominated by private labels. The Garanimals concept hinged on matching shirts and pants that corresponded to animals on hang-tags. "Hippo" shirts, for example, matched "hippo" pants. The coordinating animal hang-tags established an identity for the brand and reduced the amount of time mothers spent selecting clothing.

The matching animals scheme also permitted children to help in the selection of their own clothes. Since several outfits could be created with a few purchases, Garanimals also appealed to cost-conscious consumers during the recessionary 1970s. As the concept took shape, other benefits came to light. The brand provided Garan with a national identity it had not previously enjoyed. The pre-packaged, coordinated line also eliminated the need for elaborate mix-and-match displays and therefore required fewer sales people.

## Promotional Strategies

Garan utilized television advertising to introduce and position Garanimals. Although using that media was virtually unheard of, Garan reasoned that it could reach its target audience—mothers of young children—in an uncluttered marketplace. The brand's primary competitor on television at that time was Sears' Toughskins brand. Garan aired 30-second spots on all three networks during daytime and early and late fringe hours. The ads emphasized fashion, quality, and competitive pricing. Renowned psychologist Dr. Joyce Brothers even promoted the brand on nationally televised talk shows, emphasizing the psychological value of children being able to match their own clothing. The strategy proved successful; by 1982 Garanimals boasted a 98 percent brand awareness, rivaling that of top childrenswear brand Healthtex. Garan planned to reuse the introductory ads to launch Garanimals in the United Kingdom and Germany in the 1980s.

## Early Obstacles

The initial launch of Garanimals revealed several logistical hurdles. Since shirts and pants were produced in two separate factories, it took a high level of internal coordination to ship the items to stores simultaneously. Some of Garan's customers had different buyers for shirts and pants, and it took time and patience to get them to work together to purchase coordinating sets. At the retail level, sales personnel had to be trained to display Garanimals. Store managers and personnel became more cooperative when, as Garan's president told *Marketing & Media Decisions* magazine, "the cash register started ringing."

## Uneven Performance in the 1980s

Ironically, Garan's success at establishing the Garanimals brand may have backfired in the 1980s. During the late 1970s and early 1980s, children as young as eight years old became brand conscious, as childrenswear began to mimic adult apparel. To take advantage of this trend, Garanimal styles copied the preppy, clean-cut look of the time. For example, Garan offered Izod-like t-shirts for boys. But Garanimals sales were strongest from infant sizes up to children's 6x and 7, when the mother made most of the purchasing decisions. Once children became the primary decision-makers, Garanimals lost sales. The problem was exacerbated as the decade progressed: brand consciousness and demand for high-status clothing intensified overall. Despite these trends, Garan continued its advertising focus on value and targeted mothers as the primary advertising audience.

Garan's sales fell dramatically over the course of the decade, from $175 million in 1984 to $133 million in 1988, as more prestigious labels captured many age categories in the apparel market. But Garanimals bounced back during a late 1980s and early 1990s recession, when an appreciation for value began to take precedence over brand consciousness. The brand was also buoyed by the continued rise of mass and discount merchandisers. By 1992 Garan had regained its $170 million-plus sales record.

## Further Reading:

Dreyfack, Madeleine, "Garanimals Formula: Hang Tags and TV," *Marketing & Media Decisions,* February 1983, pp. 68–69, 179.

Esquivel, Josephine R., "The Pains and Gains of '91," *Bobbin,* June 1992, pp. 50–60; "The Bobbin Top 40," *Bobbin,* June 1993, p. 40.

Sloan, Pat, "Kids' Clothes-Buying Role a Marketer's Dilemma," *Advertising Age,* April 5, 1982, p. 24.

Sobczynski, Anna, "Three Clothiers Tailor Distinct Looks," *Advertising Age,* September 20, 1984, pp. 22–23.

—*April S. Dougal*

## AT A GLANCE

**G**aranimals brand of childrenswear founded in 1976 by Seymour Lichtenstein, chairman of Garan Inc.

**Major competitor:** Healthtex.

**Advertising:** *Agency*—Shaller Rubin Advertising and Leigh Infield Associates.

**Addresses:** *Parent company*—Garan Inc., 350 Fifth Avenue, New York, NY 10118; phone: (212) 563-2000; fax: (212) 695-2488.

# GERITOL®

**GERITOL.**

One of the best-known daily multivitamin and mineral supplements on the market today, Geritol was introduced in 1950 as an iron-based tonic to supplement Americans' daily dietary intake of iron. Manufactured by SmithKline Beecham in Pittsburgh, Pennsylvania, since 1982, Geritol was originally a product of the J. B. Williams Company.

## History of the Brand

The original Geritol, available in liquid and tablet form, made its debut in 1950 as a daily iron supplement for Americans who suffered from a lack of that essential mineral in their diets. Marketed with the famous tag line "for iron poor blood," Geritol's primary ingredient was indeed that element—two Geritol tablets contained twice as much dietary iron as a pound of calf's liver, and (in most people's minds) in a more palatable form. The first Geritol formula also contained some vitamins, but its major attraction to consumers was its high-potency iron content.

The product was the best-selling iron supplement in the country throughout the 1950s and 1960s. Its image as an iron "tonic" led many Americans to try it, thinking its healthful properties would help them combat the day-to-day fatigue they encountered as they worked and played hard in the post-war economic boom. In 1967 Geritol was reformulated to include a wider range of dietary supplements. The new Geritol contained not only iron, but seven essential vitamins as well.

Originally sold as a product for both men and women over the age of 12 who suffered from an iron deficiency, Geritol was marketed as a "woman's product" during the 1970s. Recognizing that women's nutritional needs differ from those of men, the product targeted that specific demographic group. This marketing strategy was boosted by women's growing presence in the workforce. Women's increased visibility as mothers, homemakers, *and* workers brought them to the attention not only of marketers, but of medical researchers as well. During this period, scientists established concretely that women needed more iron, calcium, and other minerals and vitamins than men, and products like Geritol had a new target audience.

Geritol was acquired by SmithKline Beecham in 1982, and underwent a metamorphosis in 1983, when it was reintroduced as "new improved Geritol." The new product still boasted of its high level of iron, but it had increased the number of other vitamins and minerals from seven to nine.

Another reformulation occurred in 1984, when "Geritol Complete " was launched. The new product contained iron as well as 29 vitamins and minerals—more than any other dietary supplement on the market. The new product also contained more vitamins and minerals at 100 percent of the recommended daily allowance set forth by the U.S. government than any other leading brand.

Beta carotene was added to the Geritol Complete formula in 1988. The product was repositioned as a multivitamin and mineral in 1993, when it was reformulated to contain 100 percent of the U.S. recommended daily allowance of iron.

## Product Line Extensions

Geritol Extend was introduced in 1990 as the first multivitamin especially formulated for adults over the age of 50. Again following demographic trends, SmithKline Beecham saw an opening for a product aimed at older adults, a rapidly growing segment of the population.

The company noticed that Geritol Complete was being purchased increasingly by younger consumers. At the same time, the proportion of older Americans to the population as a whole was increasing. In addition, the aging of the baby boomer generation would soon greatly expand a market for such products as vitamin, mineral, and dietary supplements that took the needs of older Americans into account. Hoping to corner the market on both distinct groups—those aged below 50 and those above 50—the company launched its new product. Using guidelines established by the National Academy of Sciences, Geritol Extend was formulated to include the recommended daily allowances of vitamins and iron for adults over age 50.

The current line of Geritol products includes Geritol Complete, sold in tablet form, Geritol Extend, available in caplets, and Geritol Tonic (the original Geritol), sold only in liquid form.

## Advertising Strategies

Geritol's claim to be a product for those suffering from "iron poor blood" was touted by such familiar radio and television

## AT A GLANCE

**G**eritol brand of iron and vitamin supplement introduced by the J. B. Williams Company in 1950; acquired by SmithKline Beecham in 1982; reformulated to include more vitamins and minerals and relaunched as Geritol Complete in 1984; Geritol Extend, for people over 50, introduced in 1990.

**Performance:** *Market share*—4.9% of $500 million adult multivitamin market. *Sales*—$24.4 million.

**Major competitor:** Miles Inc.'s One-a-day; also American Cyanamid's Centrum and Centrum Silver.

**Advertising:** *Agency*—Grey Advertising, New York, NY, 1982—. *Major campaign*—Geritol Complete's slogan, "For the best years of your life," and Geritol Extend's slogan, "To help you act as young as you feel."

**Addresses:** *Parent company*—SmithKline Beecham, 100 Beecham Drive, P.O. Box 1467, Pittsburgh, PA 15230; phone: (412) 928-1000; fax: (412) 928-1080.

voices as Ralph Bellamy and Ted Mack (of Ted Mack's Amateur Hour) throughout the 1950s and 1960s. One of the more familiar advertising tag lines in America, "iron poor blood" was synonymous with the product even in the 1980s, when tennis player Evonne Goolagong became a spokesperson for Geritol.

When Geritol Complete was introduced in 1984, the advertising strategy shifted from solely highlighting Geritol's high iron content to emphasizing its multivitamin formula. The shift in emphasis led to a new campaign in which couples were depicted on an anniversary of a watershed moment of their lives together—their marriage, the birth of their children, or some other important milestone—still feeling as vital and youthful as they had 20 or 25 years earlier. The new slogan introduced with this campaign was "Geritol: for the best years of your life," a tag line that appears not only in the advertising, but also on all the Geritol Complete packaging.

Geritol Extend was launched with a separate campaign in 1990, which extolled the benefits of this product for adults over the age of 50. Using the slogan "Geritol Extend: to help you act as young as you feel," the product was launched with extensive television advertising, coupons, direct mail, and a big-band dance promotion.

### Future Performance

As Americans' awareness of the importance of staying fit and healthy continues to grow, their interest in vitamin and mineral supplements will likewise increase. With Geritol's long heritage and strong brand name, it will undoubtedly keep its strong position in the $500 million adult multivitamin category. Among its strongest competitors are Miles, Inc.'s One-a-day and American Cyanamid's Centrum. Also to be watched, however, are the many private-label products being marketed by supermarkets and drug stores, which are using lower prices to attract consumers. At the same time, Geritol Extend is well positioned to capture a larger portion of the senior adult market. Among its strongest rivals is Centrum Silver. But with an aging population that is growing in number almost daily, there is plenty of room for maneuvering in this lucrative segment.

### Further Reading:

Stern, Aimee L., "Geritol Extend Goes for the Old," *Adweek's Marketing Week*, February 17, 1992, p. 30.

Stipp, David, "Studies Showing Benefits of Antioxidants Prove Potent Tonic for Sales of Vitamin E," *Wall Street Journal*, April 13, 1993, p. B1.

Historical and product information supplied by SmithKline Beecham, Pittsburgh, PA.

*—Marcia K. Mogelonsky*

# GILLETTE®

The Gillette brand of blades and razors, marketed by The Gillette Company, is one of the top selling product lines in the United States. Gillette shaving supplies and toiletries have been offering performance and value to consumers since 1903. Gillette razors and blades have remained market share leaders due to years of quality assurance and innovative advertising. The Gillette Company also manufactures such popular brands as Right Guard Anti-Perspirants and Deodorants, Oral-B Toothbrushes, and Waterman Fountain Pens.

## Brand Origins

As early as 3500 B.C., humans began fashioning razors of bronze and volcanic glass. During the reign of English King Charles II, beginning in 1660, shaving became essential for gentleman. But it was King C. Gillette, who, more than any English potentate, would popularize the clean-shaven male face. One summer morning in 1895 in his home in Brookline, Massachusetts, as Gillette started to shave, he found his razor edge dull and unfit for use without professional sharpening. This incident prompted Gillette's vision of an entirely new razor and blade. He envisioned an extremely thin piece of steel with an edge on both sides, a handle, and a clamp to center the blade over the handle. Certain that this product would be his life's work, he set about trying to perfect the new razor.

The process was not easy. Experienced toolmakers and Massachusetts Institute of Technology (MIT) scientists laughed and admonished him to forget his idea. But, in 1901, William Nickerson, an MIT graduate and successful machinist, agreed to examine the idea more closely. Within a few weeks, Gillette and Nickerson became partners. To raise the $5,000 needed to manufacture the razor commercially, they formed The American Safety Razor Company on September 28, 1901. Gillette sold stock, while Nickerson created machinery in a friend's shop.

## Early Marketing Strategy

In 1903, the year production finally began, Gillette hired a Chicago group, Townsend & Hunt, as sales agents and fixed the price of a razor set, which included 20 blades for five dollars. The 20-blade packages were soon reduced to a more profitable package of 12 blades for one dollar. In October of that year, the first Gillette advertisement, offering a 30-day money-back guarantee, appeared in a business journal called *System Magazine*. By the end of 1903, Gillette had sold 51 razor sets and 168 blades.

Sales increased dramatically in the next few years. Gillette received a U.S. patent on the safety razor, and the company moved to a six-story building on First Street in South Boston in 1904. Management soon hired a full-time driver with a horse and wagon to make deliveries to and from local suppliers, railroads, and wharves. By 1905, production had soared to 250,000 razor sets and nearly 1,200,000 blades.

## First Commercial Success

In 1906, as sales of blade packages exceeded those of razor sets, the company paid its first cash dividends to stockholders. From 1906 to 1916, during which time razor sets continued to sell at a rate of between 300,000 and 400,000 per year, blade sales skyrocketed from 450,000 packages of a dozen blades to seven million packages. In 1913, production capability and employment increased dramatically with Nickerson's invention of fully automated sharpening machines. These sharpening machines, along with the automatic hardening accoutrements Nickerson had invented a few years earlier, greatly reduced costs and improved blade quality.

When American servicemen entered World War I in 1917, their commanders worried about the unsanitary conditions of trench warfare. Learning that French soldiers, who had battled in the trenches for three years, relied heavily on the Gillette safety razor to remain clean-shaven, American commanders asked the government to place an order. More than three million razors and 36 million blades were ordered. To meet the order, the company worked around the clock and hired 500 new employees, and production leaped seven-fold. The government's sales orders not only boosted the company's business but also permanently changed American attitudes toward shaving habits.

## Advertising Innovations

During the boom years following World War I, Gillette conceived a new aggressive distribution approach to build its customer base: premiums. In Gillette's first sales contract with the Wm. Wrigley Jr. Company, each dealer purchasing a box of Wrigley's gum received a free razor set. In excess of one million Silver Brownie razor sets were supplied in this promotion, more

## AT A GLANCE

Gillette brand of razors and blades founded in 1904 by King C. Gillette and William Nickerson, copartners in The American Safety Razor Company, Boston, MA; King C. Gillette's portrait and signature became a registered trademark, 1905; diamond trademark added, 1908; company renamed the Gillette Safety Razor Company, 1902; company incorporated, 1917; company name changed to The Gillette Company, 1952.

**Performance:** *Market share*—66.5% (top share) of the blades and razors category. *Sales*—blades and razors: $264.4 million; Gillette Series products: $1.1 million.

**Major competitor:** Warner-Lambert Co.'s Schick; also Bic Corp.'s Bic.

**Advertising:** *Agency*—BBDO, New York, NY. *Major campaign*—"Gillette: The Best a Man Can Get."

**Addresses:** *Parent company*—The Gillette Company, Prudential Tower Building, Boston, MA 02199; phone: (617) 421-7000.

than the total razor sales during any one of the company's first fifteen years. Banks across the nation, brandishing the motto, "Shave and Save," offered Gillette razor sets to all new depositors. Hotels, restaurants, and service stations gave away razors to opening day customers. One ambitious entrepreneur sold 100,000 boxes of marshmallows by packing a free razor in every box. By 1926, millions of new customers had become acquainted with Gillette razors.

The Gillette Company was a pioneer in the field of sports advertising. By 1939, sports advertising was held in such low esteem that most large companies would not even think of sponsoring a baseball game. But on August 1, 1939, Gillette purchased radio broadcast rights to the 1939 World Series for $100,000 and offered a three-piece razor with five blades as the "Gillette World Series Special." Even though the Yankees trounced the Cincinnati Reds in four straight games, sales of the razor and blades were anything but a disaster. World Series sales more than quadrupled Gillette's estimate for a good return on its investment.

Before long, Gillette was sponsoring the Orange Bowl, the Sugar Bowl, the 1940 World Series, and the Kentucky Derby. In August 1941, Gillette sports programming became known as the "Sports Cavalcade." By January 1942, the name was changed to the "Gillette Cavalcade of Sports," one of the most effective identification tags in the history of sports advertising. During the war, Gillette not only expanded its football and baseball roster but entered the boxing ring as well, with the Joe Louis and Billy Conn rematch attracting the second highest audience rating in radio history. In the autumn of 1944, Gillette began placing its boxing shows on television.

In a newspaper advertisement in late 1945, Gillette's message was, "Look Sharp, Feel Sharp, Be Sharp. Use Gillette Blue Blades with the sharpest edges ever honed," words which became the Look Sharp jingle broadcast during the 1946 World Series. A march version of the jingle, launched during the 1952 World Series, later became the identifying theme of all Gillette Cavalcade of Sports performances. In 1952, the World Series premiered a new animated theme, "How're Ya Fixed for Blades," spotlighting a parrot named Sharpie who became one of America's most beloved cartoon characters.

Gillette may well have been the first company to use testimonials by sports figures as an advertising strategy. In 1910, newspaper ads depicted John McGraw, the feisty manager of the New York Giants, spouting such unlikely statements as, "Gillette makes shaving all to the merry." By the 1950s, stars such as Bob Feller, Warren Spahn, and Willie Mays, among others, testified publicly to the benefits of shaving with a Gillette razor.

## Brand Development

The first packages of blades and razors bore the signature and face of King C. Gillette as the company trademark. However, in 1908, management, thinking that in some instances the portrait and signature were too elaborate, began featuring the name "Gillette" in a diamond trademark along with the portrait and signature mark. This trademark endured until 1967, when the portrait and signature were phased out of the company's packaging and advertising.

## Product Changes

Gillette introduced a long line of product improvements rather than reduce the retail price of a product. In 1921, as Gillette's patent on the safety razor was about to expire, manufacturers of cheaply priced imitation razor sets were preparing to flood the market. But in May of 1921, Gillette surprised its rivals by launching the new improved Gillette razor in a variety of versions, priced from $5.00 to $75.00, and the Silver Brownie razor, an old-style razor with three blades which cost only one dollar, as its entrance into the low-price market segment. In 1923 the company debuted a gold-plated razor, also at the one dollar price.

In 1928, Henry J. Gaisman, the owner of a single-edge blade firm, tried to pitch Gillette his patented idea for a new process of producing double edge blades. Gillette rejected Gaisman's offer, and Gaisman decided to manufacture the blade himself. Shortly thereafter, Gillette debuted a double edge blade of its own. In June of 1932, the Gillette Blue Blade, destined to become one of the most recognizable products in the company's history, premiered in advertising touting its superior quality. The following fifteen years saw Gillette introduce many new products, including in 1934, a One-Piece razor and the Probak Junior blade; in 1936, Gillette Brushless shave cream; and in 1938, Gillette Thin Blades.

The full-scale introduction of the Gillette Super Blue Blade, the company's first coated blade, was in 1960. Challenged in 1961 by the stainless steel coated-edge blade produced by the British Wilkinson Sword Company, Gillette quickly produced its own version, which by 1964 outsold its competitor. The end of the 1960s heralded the arrival of such products as Gillette foamy aerosol lather, the Gillette Adjustable Safety razor, the Lady Gillette razor, the Gillette Techmatic razor with a band instead of a blade, the Super Stainless Steel Injector blade, and the Platinum-Plus blade.

Debuting in 1971, the tandem blade Trac II marked a revolution in the razor business. Just a few months later, Gillette had shipped more than 1.7 million razors and more than five million dual-blade cartridges. Soon, a feminine version of the Trac II Razor became a leader in the women's razor market. So successful was the Trac II Razor that it prompted the development of the Gillette Twinjector in 1973, the Trac II Adjustable cartridge in early 1975, and two disposable razors embodying the twin blade concept: the Daisy Shaver for women and the Good News! razor for men.

Yet another evolutionary product appeared in 1977, when the ATRA (Automatic Tracking Razor Action), a twin-blade razor with a spring which permitted the blade cartridge to adjust to facial contours during shaving, was introduced. Subsequent razors introduced included the MicroTrac, the slimmest twin-blade disposable razor then available, the Good News! Pivot, Atra Plus, Trac II Plus, and Good News Pivot Plus with a lubricating band to prepare the skin for the flick of the blade, and the Daisy Plus with the Lubrasmooth Lubricating strip and the Daisy Slim with the UltraSlim head. In 1990, the Gillette Sensor shaving system was launched, becoming an instant international success. In early 1993, Gillette debuted a 14-item line of male shaving preparations, anti-perspirants/deodorants, and aftershave conditioners, with an advertising approach similar to that used for the Sensor, building a single identity for the products. Called the Gillette Series, the line was an instant success.

## Controversies in Marketing

After Gillette introduced its double edge blade, it merged with the AutoStrip Safety company of Henry J. Gaisman to avoid a patent infringement suit. During 1931, Gaisman was elected chairman of the board, and King C. Gillette resigned. The Gaisman strip-processing method, which efficiently separated the long strips of metal into single blades just before packaging, thereby producing blades of more uniform quality, was quickly installed in Gillette factories. But the Probak blade remained the major Gillette product sold in this country until 1932, when the company premiered the Gillette Blue Blade.

Originally sold in Gillette's familiar green package, the blade became blue when market research indicated that consumers could not distinguish it from the "New Gillette Blade" manufactured during the Probak challenge, a blade which had proved less than satisfactory. In order to distinguish the new blade from its predecessor, management decided to color it blue, market it in a blue package, and introduce it during an advertising campaign so innovative for its era that it became a textbook example of a marketing strategy which told consumers the truth.

Consisting of a series of large, editorial-style ads with headlines such as "A Frank Confession" and "We Made a Mistake," the campaign emphasized the theme that although the company had debuted a disappointing blade in 1930, since then it had acquired a far superior manufacturing system, discarding over $8 million worth of equipment to conform to this new method. The ads carefully pointed out that the "new blades were made under new management with a new process." At first, the ads ran in more than 600 papers nationwide, and then the ads became more conventional, published four times a week for months in nearly 700 papers.

The Blue Blade was expensive and it had rivals. Because of the Depression, competitive blades, cheaply made and retailing for a penny apiece or less, were well liked by consumers. Gillette fought back, stressing "social consciousness" in its advertising and the correlation between being clean-shaven and being successful in romantic as well as employment endeavors. Other ads admonished consumers that "constant irritation from cheap-inferior blades may lead to malicious skin ailments." The company also attempted price-cutting, reducing the retail cost of the Probak and Valet blades from five for 25 cents to ten for 49 cents. By the spring of 1938, the One-Piece razor, which had retailed at $4.00 in

1934, was selling for just 69 cents. In spite of these marketing strategies, sales slumped.

Deciding to emphasize blade quality rather than price in its advertising and marketing campaigns, Gillette developed a manufacturing process which produced a better blade. After years of trying to make blades last, consumers lined up for the razor sets. Satisfied with the blade's results, the public switched its affections to Gillette.

Even though the penny blade war had ended, World War II had not. Servicemen needed razors, which Gillette supplied under government contract. Four years of military sales amounted to some 20 million razors and 1.5 billion blades. The war, having shown 16 million soldiers the benefits of a daily shave, also spurred domestic razor sales.

## International Growth

Gillette took the whole world as its marketplace. Although the first isolated sales abroad occurred in England and Russia in 1904, the Gillette management, weighing the risks of foreign commerce, did not expand its overseas market officially until 1905, when the company opened a sales office in London. Encouraged by soaring sales in Great Britain, Gillette sold a large number of razor sets to a German firm in Hamburg, which marketed the razors in Germany, Austria, and Scandinavia, and to three French wholesalers. In 1905, the company's first overseas manufacturing facility opened in Paris. A Milan wholesaler routed safety razors to Italian merchants in 1906, and similar channels were paved in other European countries, as well as in parts of Asia, Canada, and South America. Though World War I slowed Gillette's overseas expansion, it picked up again following the war.

By opening new markets and aggressively nurturing existing ones, Gillette obtained superlative results. The three years from 1921 to 1923 marked an increase of more than 300 percent in overseas sales. In fact, foreign business accounted for nearly 30 percent of the total volume of Gillette sales in 1923. Gillette further enhanced its foreign persona by being appointed Royal Purveyor to the Prince of Wales in 1922, and to His Majesty King Gustav V of Sweden in 1924. In 1927, the Paris office presented Colonel Charles A. Lindbergh with a Gillette Gold Traveler Set the day after he landed The Spirit of St. Louis in the French capital.

Following World War II, overseas sales grew, and by 1953 company profits were split almost evenly between domestic and foreign markets. Global expansion resulted in new manufacturing facilities in France, England, Mexico, Switzerland, Australia and Canada, and expanded facilities elsewhere. By 1992, manufacturing operations were conducted at 57 facilities in 28 countries, and Gillette products were distributed through wholesalers, retailers, and agents in over 200 countries and territories. Building upon the record results of 1991, Gillette reinforced its worldwide leadership position in the blade and razor business by launching its Sensor for Women Shaving System in mid-1992 and by acquiring established razor and blade factories in India, the former Soviet Union, China, Turkey, and Eastern Europe. Also in 1992, more than 85 million men in Europe and North America used Gillette Series grooming aids.

## Performance Appraisal

From its first year of marketing in 1903, the Gillette brand was a leader. By 1918 annual razor sales passed one million, and blade sales exceeded $120 million. In 1976 Gillette sold over 850 products to more than a billion consumers in over 200 nations and territories, and sales were about $1.5 billion. During the 26 weeks ending in February, 1993, Gillette again proved its superiority in the market place by selling $264.4 million worth of blades and razors, for a top market share of 66.5 percent, a 13.5-percent increase over 1992. The Gillette Series personal care line sold $1.1 million worth of products and earned a 1.2 percent, or ninth-place market share, jumping into the top 10 after only a short period of introductory sales.

## Further Reading:

Ackerman, Lawrence D., "Gillette: Rewriting the Rules," *Management Review,* September 1991, p. 30.

Adams, Jr., Russell B., *King C. Gillette: The Man and His Wonderful Shaving Device,* Boston: Little, Brown, and Company, 1978.

"Back-to-School, Back to Basics," *Discount Store News,* February 4, 1991, p. 67.

Bonney, Joseph, "Gillette International's Edge," *American Shipper,* November 1991, p. 53.

Chakravart, Subrata N., "We Had to Change the Playing Field," *Forbes,* February 4, 1991, p. 82.

Cleary, David Powers, *Great American Brands,* New York: Fairchild Publications, 1981, pp. 120–127.

"Cosmetics Ship Out in Degradable Loose-Fill," *Packaging,* August 1992, p. 2.

"Direct Selling," *Drug and Cosmetic Industry,* June 1992, p. 46.

Di Talamo, Nicholas, "Ceiling in Europe without a Sales Force," *Direct Marketing,* May 1990, p. 22.

Freeman, Laurie, and Patricia Winters, "Franchise Players: Brand Expansion Preferred Route," *Advertising Age,* August 16, 1986, p. 3.

"The Gillette Company," *Gillette News,* 1977.

The Gillette Company 1992 Annual Report, Boston: The Gillette Company, 1993.

Gillette, King Camp, *The People's Corporation, King C. Gillette,* New York: Boni and Liveright, 1924.

"Gillette Sharpens Just-In-Time Delivery," *Packaging Digest,* October 1987, p. 56.

"Gillette," *World's Greatest Brands, An International Review by Interbrand,* New York: John Wiley & Sons, 1992, p. 53.

Guzzardi, Walter, Jr., "The U.S. Business Hall of Fame," *Fortune,* March 14, 1989, p. 142.

Harrington, Lisa H., "Jafra's Quest for Quality Service," *Traffic Management,* August 1987, p. 44.

Holmgren, R. Bruce, "Gillette Efficiency Up; Rejects Down," *Packaging,* January 1988, p. 50.

Koeppel, Dan, "Gillette's Rivals Predict A Razor War," *Adweek's Marketing Week,* October 16, 1989, p. 3.

Liesse, Julie, "Brand Scorecard," *Advertising Age,* April 19, 1993, p. 22.

Manissano, Anthony P., "BBDO Breaks Gillette Sensor Campaign During Super Bowl," *Back Stage,* January 26, 1990, p. 43.

Merline, John W., "A Better Blade," *Consumers' Research Magazine,* December 1989, p. 38.

Sloan, Pat, "Gillette Rolls New Series Line," *Advertising Age,* January 25, 1993, pp. 3, 41.

"Some Machines on SRD'S Razor-Packaging Lines Have Been in Service for Years," *Packaging Digest,* October 1987, p. 57.

Sturken, Barbara, "Continental's Razor Tie In Lets Customers Shave Fares as Well," *Travel Weekly,* August 10, 1987, p. 9.

"What Price A Close Shave?," *Consumer Reports,* August 1990, p. 505.

Whelan, Sean, "Gillette Looks Sharp about Razor Launch," *Marketing,* October 5, 1989, p. 5.

*—Virginia Barnstorff*

# GIORGIO BEVERLY HILLS®

Within four years of its 1981 debut at Giorgio, a small, upscale boutique in Beverly Hills, California, Giorgio Beverly Hills perfume grew to become the best-selling woman's prestige fragrance in the United States. The $150-an-ounce fragrance in the yellow and white striped box started a revolution in the perfume industry by creating a new method of marketing fragrances, and subsequently paved the way for the world's movie capital to become one of the world's fragrance capitals.

By 1985, Giorgio annual sales had reached $75 million (one source says $100 million), putting it at the top of perfume sales charts. It remained there for four consecutive years, to be bumped down to second place only by Red, another Giorgio perfume, which made its debut in 1988. The Giorgio line includes Giorgio for Men, Red, Red for Men, V.I.P. Special Reserve for Men, and Wings; overall sales have surpassed the $200 million mark.

## Origins

Giorgio fragrance is composed of 450 different natural perfume oils, including jasmine, rose, gardenia, orange flower, chamomile, sandalwood, and patchouli. The perfume is the brainchild of Gale Hayman, who along with her husband, Fred, purchased the Giorgio boutique in 1961. Over time the store, with its warm, friendly atmosphere, pool tables, fireplace, and oak bar, grew to become one of Beverly Hills' most famous boutiques.

In 1979 Gale Hayman decided to develop a signature perfume for the boutique. The perfume houses she contacted on the East Coast to help her create her scent were initially skeptical of her plan. "I told them I wanted a floral and they said florals were out," Hayman said in a 1988 *Los Angeles Times* interview. "They told me women wanted 'green' fragrances [which are light, fresh and grassy]. I held my ground and told them the ladies who shopped in my shop would wear florals." Hayman spent two years sampling fragrances before deciding on the one that would bear the Giorgio name. "It was the first fragrance I loved in two years," she said. "Later I found out that the scent had been sitting on the shelf for five years. It had been rejected by Revlon. Yves Saint Laurent turned it down. But I knew it was right for my customers—right for Beverly Hills."

## Early Success

Giorgio Beverly Hills was introduced in November of 1981 at a gala for 1,200 guests held under an enormous yellow and white striped tent, designed to complement the perfume's bright packaging. The product was sold at the Haymans' Rodeo Drive store and by mail order. In the months following its introduction, advertisements appeared in local publications with the tag line, "You Know Who Wears It"; a toll-free number was provided for customers to order the perfume by mail. Giorgio's popularity among the Beverly Hills crowd grew by leaps and bounds.

In August of 1982 Giorgio was introduced at Bloomingdale's flagship store in New York City and soon became the store's best-selling fragrance. Although distribution remained limited to Giorgio's Beverly Hills boutique, Bloomingdale's, and mail order, Giorgio advertisements began appearing in *Harpar's Bazaar*, a national women's magazine, in April of 1983. One month later Giorgio pioneered the use of scent strips, pieces of heavy paper doused with a fragrance, that appeared in *Vogue* and 61 other magazines by the end of the year. This brought the scent of Giorgio into the homes of approximately 30 million potential customers and created a demand for the fragrance that far surpassed its availability.

The demand for Giorgio was so great that retailers bombarded the Haymans with requests for the distribution rights. In one midwestern city, a group of women allegedly went so far as to petition Giorgio, demanding that the perfume be sold in their home town. Giorgio increased its distribution slowly, adding 200 upscale department stores across the United States to its list of retailers. In August of 1984 Giorgio Extraordinary Fragrance Boutique opened on East 57th Street in New York City. In October of that year Giorgio successfully entered its first overseas market when it debuted at Harvy Nichols—London. By Christmas, Giorgio Beverly Hills for Men began appearing in the Rodeo Drive and East 57th Street boutiques. In two years Giorgio sales shot up from $30 million to more than $100 million, breaking all fragrance sales records in the United States and making it the number one product in the industry.

## Early Marketing Strategy

Giorgio's marketing was revolutionary. The Haymans positioned their new perfume as "The Beverly Hills life style in a

## AT A GLANCE

Giorgio Beverly Hills brand perfume founded in 1981 by Fred and Gale Hayman, owners of the Giorgio boutique in Beverly Hills, CA; became a registered trademark, 1981; brand sold to Avon Products, Inc., 1987. Company introduced Giorgio Beverly Hills for Men, 1984; V.I.P. Special Reserve, 1987; Red by Giorgio Beverly Hills, 1988; Red for Men, 1991; and Wings, 1993.

**Performance:** *Market share*—(for Red by Giorgio Beverly Hills) Top share of prestige fragrance category. *Sales*—(for Red by Giorgio Beverly Hills; 1991) $70 million; (for Giorgio Beverly Hills; 1991) $48 million.

**Major competitor:** Obsession, by Calvin Klein Cosmetics Co.; also, fragrances by Estée Lauder, Inc.

**Advertising:** *Agency*—Eisaman, Johns & Laws, 1981—. *Major campaign*—Television campaign for Wings perfume presenting image of a woman on a mythical journey that ends with her taking flight.

**Addresses:** *Parent company*—Giorgio Beverly Hills, Inc., 2400 Broadway, Suite 400, Santa Monica, CA, 90404; phone: (310) 453-7116; fax: (310) 453-4763. *Ultimate parent company*—Avon Products, Inc., 9 West 57th St., New York, NY 10019; phone: (212) 546-6015; fax: (212) 526-9360.

bottle,'' an unusual deviation from traditional marketing techniques of associating fragrances with certain emotions. As Steve Ginsberg, author of the book *Reeking Havoc: The Unauthorized Story of Giorgio,* put it, ''The image of sex, affluence and style equated with Beverly Hills—everybody wanted that life style in the '80s. And when Giorgio came along, it fit right in to the American Dream.'' Giorgio's combination of heavy magazine advertising and limited supply generated an aura of exclusivity around the product that increased its popularity even more.

In the brand's early years, Giorgio's marketing team, led by Gale Hayman, relied on a number of special events to bring the perfume closer to the public. Perhaps the most extravagant was during the first annual Beverly Hills St. Patrick's Day parade: a float containing an eight-foot Giorgio perfume bottle motored down the parade route and sprayed the fragrance on parade-goers as Merv Griffin and Ava Gabor waved from above. Other ploys included spraying the perfume from small jets located just above the door to the Giorgio boutique and delivering inaugural shipments of the perfume to stores in such varied vehicles as armored trucks, flowered cabs, stagecoaches, and gold limousines.

Giorgio can also lay claim to a number of industry ''firsts.'' It was the first fragrance to be marketed by direct mail. It was the first to use scent strips in magazine advertisements. It was the first to employ dramatic in-store visuals as a marketing technique. It was the first American fragrance to be the top-seller at Galeries Lafayette, the largest department store in Paris. And Giorgio was the first fragrance to be banned by a restaurant.

### Tumultuous Times

As Giorgio was making history in the fragrance world, backstage troubles threatened its seemingly bright future. Fred and Gale Hayman divorced in 1985, the same year their perfume captured the number one position in the perfume industry. Shortly after, Fred, who holds the position of chairman and chief executive

officer, fired his former wife and head of Giorgio's perfume business. Not much later, James Roth, Jr., and David Horner, the two Giorgio executives who ran the business with Gale, resigned. More troublesome, however, was the realization that, despite its monumental success, Giorgio's stellar growth was beginning to slow.

Although Giorgio sales continuously held or hovered near the number one position, its growth had hit a plateau. According to industry analysts, sales could grow no further because no new products had been introduced since 1984 when Giorgio for Men hit the market. Horner and Roth had been working with Gale Hayman to develop an extension of the Giorgio line to include products such as skin care lotion and candles based on the fragrance, but after their resignation these plans were put on the back burner. When Fred assumed control of the perfume business, he chose instead to improve sales by expanding the distribution of the fragrance beyond the 350 U.S. outlets and 40 European outlets.

The company announced plans to expand distribution into Australia and ten European countries including Italy, Spain, and the Scandinavian countries, using the same marketing technique of exclusivity that made the perfume so successful in the United States. Average sales were down at each individual Giorgio outlet in 1987; nevertheless, overall sales were up because of the perfume's expanded distribution.

Fred Hayman put the perfume business up for sale in 1985, and his former wife made an offer. The offer was refused, and the cosmetics firm Estée Lauder Inc. bid the same price. Fred negotiated with Lauder for eight months, then announced that Giorgio Inc. was no longer for sale.

The company's turbulent times ended in 1987 when Hayman sold Giorgio Inc. to Avon Products, Inc., for $165 million. Very little in Giorgio's marketing and management changed under Avon's new ownership. Hayman relinquished control of the perfume business but, under the agreement with Avon, repurchased the Beverly Hills boutique and continued to operate it under the Giorgio name. Giorgio's senior management remained intact, with Hayman's hand-picked successor, Michael Gould, staying on as president. Upon its purchase of the fragrance business, Avon announced plans to introduce much-needed new products into the market and to continue expanding Giorgio's international outlets.

### New Products

Although sales of Giorgio's women's fragrance were in a slump, Giorgio for Men continued to show steady growth of about $20 million annually. In April of 1987 Giorgio added another fragrance to its men's line, introducing V.I.P. Special Reserve at the Giorgio boutique, Sak's Fifth Avenue, and later at the Robinson's department store chain in California. V.I.P. Special Reserve was created to be a high-priced, high-quality perfume and was marketed with the advertising slogan, ''Maybe one man in a thousand will wear it.''

More eagerly anticipated was Giorgio's second fragrance for women, which the company spent three years developing and whose debut was delayed due to the complications created by the Haymans' divorce and Avon's purchase of the business. The new fragrance, called Red, was a softer scent than Giorgio, created in response to a consumer survey that found a large segment of the market preferring a more subtle fragrance than Giorgio's powerful floral scent. Red was introduced in November of 1988 through a scented order form that was sent to Giorgio's mail-order customers. The $165 an ounce fragrance hit the Giorgio boutique in January and became available in 450 department stores in the months that followed.

Within 50 days Red sales totaled over $6.5 million, and retailers were calling it the most successful fragrance launch in history. In some stores Red sales posted volumes three to four times higher

*Red perfume made its debut in 1988.*

than Giorgio, the previous number one fragrance. By the end of 1989, Red had captured the number one position in the U.S. fragrance industry, and Giorgio firmly held the number two position.

In 1990 Giorgio made another entry into the increasingly competitive men's fragrance market with Red for Men, using marketing techniques such as Red Car Rallies, raffle drawings for lessons at a professional racing school, and free weekends with a rented red car. In-store visuals included red carpeting and counter samples of the fragrance in a red vial shaped like a car. In an unprecedented move for the company, Red for Men was also introduced through a national television campaign.

Giorgio introduced Wings, its third women's fragrance, in 1993. Like Red, the name and image created for the new floral-based perfume were developed in response to a survey of 2,500 people to determine their lifestyle preferences. The survey found a desire for a lifestyle characterized by freedom, spontaneity, and exhilaration. Wings was introduced through mail order, magazine ads, and a series of television ads in which a woman embarks on a quasi-mythical journey and takes flight from the top of an ancient religious monument. Sales of Wings were $4 million in March of

1993, the first month of national distribution. Company officials said they expected the fragrance to be among the top five in the United States.

## Analysis and Future Predictions

Although Red held the number one position in 1991, Giorgio had slipped in the rankings. Competition from more established perfume houses such as Calvin Klein Cosmetics Inc. and Estée Lauder Inc. was on the rise. Furthermore, Giorgio's exclusive cachet was being tarnished by knock-off fragrances and discount promotions offered through drug stores and other less prestigious retail outlets; also, sales were down in the early 1990s due to the recession in the United States.

When Linda LoRe succeeded Michael Gould as president of Giorgio fragrance in 1990, the company embarked on a new marketing direction. Her strategy was to continue expansion of overseas markets where sales were still strong; to create a Giorgio line of handbags, watches, small leather goods, and eye wear; and to manage Giorgio fragrances differently. "We're no longer in an introduction or growth phase," LoRe told *Women's Wear Daily* in 1991. "We're a fragrance that wants to be here to stay. To our customers, we're considered a classic. To stay in the top ten for so many years is a real good indication of that. Now we have to manage the brands that way. Giorgio needs to get out there and behave like a classic."

Industry observers believe that Giorgio has a large amount of untapped potential to develop into a full-fledged cosmetic company along the lines of its competitors Estée Lauder and Calvin Klein. But Giorgio's continuity depends largely on whether it can successfully make the transition from a 1980s media sensation to a full-fledged fragrance line in the 1990s. With the introduction of Wings in 1993, Giorgio has made a step towards establishing itself as one of the world's premier fragrance houses. However, as the world's economy grows tighter in the 1990s, it seems that Giorgio will have to laboriously climb, rather than fly, to the top.

## Further Reading:

Applebaum, Cara, "Beauty's Big Makeover," *Superbrands 1991* (supplement to *Adweek's Marketing Week*), 1991, pp. 76–77.

Calistro, Paddy, "Eau de L.A.," *Los Angeles Times Magazine*, November 13, 1988, p. 13.

Carson, Teresa, "Selling the Beverly Hills Lifestyle," *Business Week*, May 5, 1986, p. 34.

Ginsberg, Steve, *Reeking Havoc: The Unauthorized Story of Giorgio;* "Giorgio Entry a Rare Item," *Women's Wear Daily*, April 10, 1987, p. 6; "Giorgio's Michael Gould: Now It's His Turn," *Women's Wear Daily*, July 17, 1987, p. 7.

*Giorgio Beverly Hills press releases,* Santa Monica, CA: Giorgio Beverly Hills, Inc.

Glover, Kara, "Sweet Smell of Success: Giorgio CEO Linda LoRe Has a Nose for Winning Fragrances," *Los Angeles Business Journal*, April 20, 1992.

Marlow, Michael, *Women's Wear Daily*, "LoRe's Giorgio: A Global Agenda," October 25, 1991; "Giorgio's New Wings Aiming for $50 Million Flight," October 16, 1992, p. 1.

Rice, Faye, "The Romance Turns Gothic at Giorgio," *Fortune*, June 9, 1986, p. 57.

Silverstein, Stuart, "Success Smells Sweet," *Los Angeles Times*, July 16, 1990, p. D1.

*—Maura Troester*

# GITANO®

To the value-seeking shopper, garments sold under the Gitano label are often associated with quality, style, and affordability. The Gitano Group, Inc.'s apparel lines are comprised of four major divisions: Gitano women's jeanswear, Gitano women's sportswear, EJ Gitano childrenswear, and Gitano menswear. The Gitano Group also markets the upscale Gloria Vanderbilt brand of jeans, a trademark that the company acquired and revived in a 1988 licensing agreement with Murjani Worldwide B.V. Market research conducted by the firm of NPD Research, Inc. in 1991 revealed that Gitano brand women's denim jeans ranked third in sales in the United States and first in women's non-denim jeanswear and bottoms.

Until 1991 Gitano's competitors regarded the company as the undisputed leader in marketing strategy. The key to Gitano's success was the introduction of a "hot" new brand of designer jeans launched with an advertising campaign that associated the jeans with chic and youthful images while specifically targeting mass-market discount retailers like K-Mart, Wal-Mart, and Venture. This was unprecedented at a time when most designer jeans, like Ralph Lauren and Calvin Klein brands, sold their merchandise through department stores. Gitano managed to successfully create its own "downscale" marketing niche—a strategy that paid off handsomely as sales climbed from $30 million in 1980 to $807 million in 1990.

## Brand Origin and History

The Gitano brand was created by Haim Dabah, the eldest of four children from a Syrian Jewish family. After arriving in the United States at the age of 16, Haim enrolled in the Talmudical Academy of Baltimore in Maryland. Following his graduation, Dabah turned down an offer to work at his father's wholesale clothing business and accepted a position with Big D, a New Jersey-based apparel discounter. Dabah quickly rose from stockboy to store manager, but he quit in 1974 to take over his father's floundering business. Later joined by his brother Isaac, Dabah not only rescued the company but transformed it into a national success story through effective advertising techniques that provided Gitano with a youthful and sexy image. More importantly, however, were the solid customer relations Gitano cultivated with large and small discount chains, including the rapidly expanding Wal-Mart chain.

With sales booming by the late 1980s, much of Gitano's long-term debt had been retired. It appeared that the company was poised to engage in further expansion when things began to unravel. As the U.S. economy began to falter in the early 1990s, Gitano's sales took a nosedive. Compounding the problem was the company's failure to maintain a reliable set of internally monitored financial operation controls which might have served as an early warning sign of impending decline. Further exacerbating the company's problems was an alleged managerial rift between Haim and Isaac Dabah and the controversial 1989 acquisition of the Childrens Place, a 130-store retail chain, which shortly thereafter experienced a serious liquidity crunch.

Plans to revitalize the Gitano brand name began in 1991 with the commencement of an extensive long-range restructuring program. The plan called for bringing in non-family member Robert E. Gregory to replace Morris Dabah as the company's chairman and chief executive officer. Prior to coming on board with Gitano, Gregory had been president of another apparel company, VF Corp., where he gained a formidable reputation within the industry

## Product Development and Company Structure

The Gitano Group markets a diverse range of women's jeanswear, intimate apparel, and sportswear. Additional men's and children's clothing lines offer a range of jeanswear and sportswear. Each division is directed by a separate management team to insure a maximum level of flexibility and responsiveness to retailers and consumers. Furthermore, the divisions are organized with distinct design, sales, buying, merchandising, and support teams that specialize in their particular product lines, enabling them to keep abreast of the latest developments in their markets.

Gitano's manufacturing sources, both wholly owned subsidiaries and contracted suppliers, are centrally administrated in order to coordinate matters related to distribution, management information, finance, purchase orders, inventory levels, marketing, and advertising services. By 1992 Gitano-labeled products were purchased by the company from manufacturers operating in approximately 30 countries. These facilities were located throughout areas in the Far East, South and Central America, the Caribbean, the United States, Eastern Europe, and the Mediterranean.

Manufacturer contracts are drawn up on an order by order basis that ensures that no particular manufacturer contributes more than five percent of Gitano's products. Contract terms specify that each manufacturer produce ready-to-wear garments in accordance with samples and patterns approved by Gitano. Garments must be delivered to Gitano distribution centers at the contractually specified time. Depending upon the make of the garment, Gitano may require the manufacturer to purchase the fabric from a particular mill. Gitano employees and agents located abroad monitor production at each manufacturing site to ensure that quality standards and pattern specifications are strictly followed.

The women's jeanswear division accounts for the largest percentage of Gitano brand apparel. The most notable garment types included within this product line are jeans sold in junior, missy, plus, and maternity sizes. The jeanswear apparel collection includes pants, shorts, skirts, vests, jackets, and shirts manufactured from denim and other fabrics. Jeans are usually marketed under "Gitano" and "Gitano Express" labels for junior sizes while missy and plus sizes carry the "Gitano" or "P.S. Gitano" label. The "P.S." abbreviation stands for "proportionately sized," and denotes a special sizing system that Gitano implemented in 1982 to eliminate the problems many women encounter when purchasing jeans. These Gitano jeans incorporate various lengths and rises (the distances between the waistband and the crotch) to fit short, regular, or long waisted women of varying heights.

## AT A GLANCE

Gitano brand clothing originated in New York City in 1974 by Haim Dabah's Gitano Group, Inc.; company went public in 1992.

**Performance:** *Sales*—$781 million (1991). *Market share*—7% of women's apparel market (3rd place).

**Major competitor:** Levi Strauss & Co.; also Lee jeans.

**Advertising:** *Agency*—In-house.

**Addresses:** *Parent company*—Gitano Group, Inc., 1411 Broadway, New York, NY; phone: (212) 819-0707; fax: (212) 786-7758.

Gitano's women's sportswear division markets an extensive line of sportswear such as knit and woven tops, dresses, jumpsuits, along with separates and coordinates designed to appeal to various fashion tastes and social settings. The Gitano childrenswear division offers infant and childrenswear under the "EJ Gitano" trademark for infants, toddlers, and children up to size 14. Children's jeanswear includes basic and fashion jeans, shorts and overalls, and skirts made of denim and other fabrics. During 1991 EJ Gitano introduced "Baby Gitano," an ensemble of basic sportswear in sizes 12–24 months made from 100 percent cotton fabrics.

Gitano menswear manufactures men's woven shirts, knit tops, basic five-pocket denim jeans, casual pants, and shorts in a variety of fabrics. In the fall of 1991, the menswear division created the AmeriCo. division to offer a higher quality line of value-driven, integrated fashion basics made with 100 percent natural fibers. The collection was marketed under the "AmeriCo." trademark and distributed to mass merchant and discount establishments. Menswear also markets a complete line of boyswear that consists of casual pants, denim jeans, woven and knit shirts, shorts, and sweaters.

## Marketing Structure

The Gitano Group, Inc. has been in a state of flux since it entered its crisis period in 1991, and this has affected its marketing network. Gitano's first retail store was opened in 1986, and by early 1992 it operated 101 stores, primarily located in outlet centers throughout the United States. Gitano's outlet stores served to dispose of excess or slow moving inventory in an attempt to prevent the unchecked free fall of gross profit margins. However, by 1993, as part of its restructuring program, Gitano had completely exited the retail store business. The economic recession of the early 1990s and the subsequent slow growth of the apparel industry had an adverse impact on Gitano. For example, Gretchen Morgenson reported in *Forbes* that Gitano was a major creditor to several large bankrupt department stores such as Hill Department Stores, Ames, and Alexander's. Morgenson also reported that Wal-Mart's patriotic campaign urging consumers to buy "American Made Products" left Gitano out in the cold since most of its products were made overseas.

More than 99 percent of Gitano's apparel is sold in the United States and Canada through mass-merchandisers, major department stores, and specialty stores. Close to 56 percent of Gitano's 1991 sales were to its ten largest customers, and approximately 76 percent of sales were to its 60 largest customers. Despite the retailer's "buy American" campaign, fully 26 percent of Gitano's revenues came from Wal-Mart, a chain which *Business Week*'s Ron Stodghill II claimed was notorious for "squeezing its vendors for every penny."

## Marketing Strategy

With Robert E. Gregory at the helm, plans to radically restructure the Gitano Group left no stone unturned. As quoted in *Women's Wear Daily,* Gregory observed that Gitano's survival depends on the company's ability to identify its "core consumer and product segments." With this in mind, Gitano downsized its operations, shedding many marginal clothing lines and reducing its manufacturing and wholesale division workforce from about 5,323 in 1992 to 1,555 in 1993. It also slashed its retail workforce from 1,990 to 550.

For 1991 about 80 percent of Gitano-labeled women's apparel sold was in missy, plus, or maternity sizes. Gitano concluded that women in this age group, roughly 25 years and older, represent the fastest growing market in the United States and will remain Gitano's targeted core consumer segment. Gitano brand apparel designed for these sizes features basic designs that are not subject to the same fleeting trends and fads as is clothing for women aged 15–25. Gitano markets most of it products using a "packaged goods" approach. Attached to Gitano apparel are customized hangtags and pocket flashers that emphasize special product features or suggest ways to coordinate individual apparel items into fashionable ensembles.

In the early 1990s, to bolster the brand's reputation, Gitano launched its "shop-within-the-store" concept. This marketing strategy attempted to differentiate Gitano clothing from its competitors through the extensive use of distinct in-store displays that created a Gitano section within the store. Gitano's experienced field merchandising coordinators would select the featured merchandise and provide point-of-sale visuals. The intent of the program was to increase multiple purchases of Gitano products while simultaneously reducing the need for promotional sales.

## Advertising

Gitano advertisements are typically placed in television, print, outdoor, in-store, and point-of-sale media. These ads originate from the Ad Group, Gitano's in-house advertising organization which is responsible for the conception, development, and implementation of all advertising materials. To perpetuate a consistent image, most of Gitano's mass media advertising designs are replicated in the brand's in-store videos, hangtags, dressing room posters, and point-of-sale displays.

During the early 1990s, in Gitano's effort to align itself with socially responsible causes, the company donated a percentage of its sales to three nationally known environmental groups. In addition, Gitano has sponsored public service announcements starring actor Neil Patrick Harris to promote literacy. Continuing its family values theme, Gitano launched a 1992 promotion with Cheerios that placed $3.00 savings discount coupons in specially marked cereal boxes. The same campaign distributed 1,000 gift certificates in random Cheerios boxes that granted eligibility in a Gitano sweepstakes.

## Future Trends

Since the early 1990s, Gitano has been operating under adverse financial conditions. Despite the results of its restructuring program and massive downsizing, the Gitano Group has continued to draw on outside credit sources to finance its operations. For 1992 the company's working capital deficit was $55.9 million, and its stockholders deficit was $104.2 million; moreover, the company failed to comply with numerous debt covenants. A further problem concerned the unresolved status surrounding the "Multifiber Arrangement." This agreement regulates the degree to which import quotas must be maintained and directly affects Gitano because of the company's reliance on foreign sources. Also, the end of the recession has failed to generate any meaningful increase in Gitano's sales. Downward prices, overcapacity, and increased competition continue to plague the apparel industry; thus, Gitano's future may depend more on economics than fashion.

## Further Reading:

Applebaum, Cara, "Gitano Signs the Denim Diva," *Adweek's Marketing Week,* January 27, 1992, p. 8.

Gordon, Maryellen, "Gregory's Plans for Revitalizing Gitano," *Women's Wear Daily,* March 3, 1993, pp. 5–6.

"Gitano and Cheerio's" *Adweek's Marketing Week,* February 10, 1992, p. 3.

Gitano Corporation Annual Reports and 10K, New York: The Gitano Corporation, 1992–1993.

Morgenson, Gretchen, "Greener Pastures," *Forbes,* July 6, 1992, p. 48.

Stodghill, Ron, "Is This Any Way to Run a Family Business," *Business Week,* August 24, 1992, pp. 48–49.

*—Daniel E. King*

# GLAD®

Glad, which is owned by First Brands Corporation, is the only brand that provides a full line of food protection and disposer products. The brand also has the widest selection of plastic bags with different types of closures. Glad products to protect food include storage, freezer, and sandwich bags. The line of Glad disposer bags features indoor garbage bags and outdoor trash and lawn bags. Closure types include zippers and twist ties for food bags, and twist ties, keys, handle-ties, and drawstrings for disposer bags.

In addition to plastic bags for use with food, the Glad name also appears on Cling Wrap, clear polyethylene that keeps foods fresh in storage. In addition, the wide Glad product line offered to consumers is supplemented by plastic disposer bags for industrial and commercial users. Glad makes trash can and drum liners for industrial markets and commercial can liners for use in offices, restaurants, institutions, motels, and hotels.

Since their introduction, Glad bags have undergone changes and improvements that sought to bring greater quality and convenience to consumers. Using market research to identify consumer interests and needs, the company has both modified existing products and developed new ones through proprietary technology. Bags have become stronger and more durable, pleasing to look at in colors, easier to use and close, and packaged in boxes of varying sizes for greater value and task suitability. In addition to product changes, modifications in marketing strategies have enabled consumers to purchase Glad bags more economically and in new and different types of retailing outlets.

Glad has also sought to project an image of social responsibility by demonstrating the usefulness of Glad disposer bags for cleaning up the environment. With media attention focused on the role of plastic in the solid waste crisis, Glad offered a possible solution. Glad disposer bags were donated to national cleanup programs, and volunteers then filled them with waste. Rather than adding to the solid waste problem that harms the environment, the company was able to suggest that Glad disposer bags could help rid the environment of waste. Also, to reduce the amount of material going into landfills, the company has devoted considerable research and development resources into making Glad bags with less plastic. The Glad disposer bag of the early 1990s had half the plastic of a similar product of ten years earlier, yet was just as strong.

## Brand Origins

The first Glad bags to appear were utility and sandwich bags, test marketed in 1963 then distributed nationally in 1965. The sandwich bags were designed to keep sandwiches moist and were meant for short-term storage. The storage and freezer bags introduced in subsequent years were meant to protect foods during longer-term storage. Storage bags were typically used to keep foods fresh overnight in the refrigerator, while freezer bags were intended to prevent freezer burn and keep foods from drying out while stored in freezers.

The food bags were followed by different types of indoor and outdoor disposer bags. In 1968 Glad Disposer Trash Bags were put on the market, and in 1972, Glad introduced Large Kitchen Garbage Bags. During the 1970s, heavy-weight trash bags and other types of disposer bags, in addition to a greater selection of food bags, were added to the Glad line.

## Early Marketing Strategy

When Glad bags were first marketed in the United States, after having been marketed in Canada, there were some concerns about how they would be accepted. They were a completely new type of product to be used by consumers, and there were some questions about municipalities allowing homeowners to pack their trash in them for pickup.

An educational campaign was implemented in order to inform the public about the role and value Glad disposer bags could play in a community's efforts to contain its trash. The campaign was centered around community cleanup and beautification. Several programs, such as "Community Cleanup Kits," "Stash the Trash" contests involving community cleanup projects, and brochures titled "This Land is Your Land, Keep It Clean," aimed to promote awareness of Glad disposer bags among consumers and municipal figures.

## Brand Development

During the 1980s, product development focused on creating easier-to-use closures and improving the strength and quality of bags. In 1981 Handle-Tie bags were introduced. In the early 1980s Glad test marketed a food storage bag with an interlocking closure called Snap Lock, and then changed the name to Glad-Lock in 1985. Also in 1985, Glad developed blue and yellow locking strips

## AT A GLANCE

Glad brand of food storage and disposer products founded in 1965; acquired by First Brands Corporation, 1986.

**Performance:** *Market share*—Top share in plastic bags, wrap, and related products category. *Sales*—$612.4 million (1992).

**Major competitor:** Ziploc; also Hefty.

**Advertising:** *Agency*—Leo Burnett Co., Chicago, IL, 1961—. *Major campaign*—Television commercials depicting situations where other brands of plastic bags are inferior and using the tagline, "Don't get mad, get Glad."

**Addresses:** *Parent company*—First Brands Corporation, 83 Wooster Heights Road, P.O. Box 1911, Danbury, CT 06813-1911; phone: (203) 731-2300; fax: (203) 731-2518.

on food bags that turned green when closed correctly, to help consumers see more clearly whether or not the bags were sealed properly. Another innovation was storage bags in clear polyethylene, which enabled consumers to write on labels for easy identification of bag contents.

Further technological improvements allowed Glad to develop three-ply trash bags with "Stress Flex" plastic, a revolutionary plastic that helped to make the bags stronger and more durable. The formula came to be used for garbage bags, kitchen garbage bags, and trash bags, since these bags must be strong enough to not burst open while in use. Subsequent additions to the Glad line included freshly scented indoor disposer bags introduced in colors. Small garbage bags were marketed in rose pink, medium garbage bags in beige, and large garbage bags in white. Glad Recycling Bags with handle-ties were introduced in blue. Tall kitchen can liners, some trash bags, and some large trash bags were later made more durable and labeled as Sheer Strength.

Throughout the years, Glad has created different types of closures for different sized bags, for bags used for different purposes, and in order to suit consumer preferences. Only the food bags have zipper locks and are called Glad-Lock. Pleated sandwich bags, however, have Fold-Lock Tops, and storage bags can also be open-mouthed for closing with twist ties.

The wide variety of Glad disposer bags have several different types of closures. The indoor small garbage bags use twist ties; medium garbage bags have notched keylocks and handle-ties; and large kitchen bags have notched keylocks, handle-ties, and drawstrings. Outdoor trash bags and large trash bags each use handle-ties and drawstrings, and lawn bags use drawstrings and notched keylocks.

### Value in Packaging

Glad has always held to the belief that packaging must be convenient for consumers to use. Bags should be easy to remove from the package and easy to open and close. But since they are using them as disposable items, consumers want value as well as convenience. Glad bags are packaged in different sized boxes, and the number of bags enclosed depends upon the gallon size of the bag and the size of the package. Zipper sandwich bags, for example, may have up to 100 bags, while Fold-Lock Top sandwich bags may have up to 300 in a box. Zipper freezer bags might have as few as 15 and as many as 40 bags per box. Indoor and outdoor disposer bags are similarly packaged; small garbage bags can

contain 30 in a box, while "The Heavyweight" trash bags have either 8 or 15 to the box.

To help the value-conscious consumer save money, Glad has bags that are packaged in larger boxes. Glad sandwich, freezer, and storage bags are sold in institutional packs consisting of 3 separate boxes within a box called Warehouse Club Food Package. There are also indoor and outdoor disposer bags sold in Warehouse Club Disposer Packs. In addition, both food bags and disposer bags are sold in giant economy packs.

### Advertising Innovations

The earliest Glad commercials in the 1960s focused on the ability of Glad bags to solve problems for homemakers. A character called "The Man from Glad" appeared first in TV and then in print ads in 1965. The silver haired, secret-agent type man was clad in a white raincoat. He would arrive in some type of unusual vehicle, such as a helicopter or rubber dinghy, just in time to save the day. While the hero initially appeared to be the Man from Glad, the true hero was the Glad bag. The campaign became one of the most memorable and effective in advertising history and continued until 1972.

During the 1970s, Glad conducted a few different advertising campaigns. One centered on the Glad family, a take-off on a successful comedy program at the time, *All in the Family*. The next campaign proved to be another popular, effective series that also featured Glad bags as problem-solvers. The tagline of the commercials was "Don't get mad, get Glad."

In 1979 the advertising campaign featured Tom Bosley, star of the popular television sitcom *Happy Days*, as the Glad spokesperson. Bosley appeared in the commercials as a problem-solver, one who had helpful suggestions for neighbors about the value of using Glad bags. He might tell them that the bags would keep food from leaking in the refrigerator, keep food fresh, or keep refrigerators from getting filled with bad odors.

Mid-1980s ads once again emphasized how strong Glad bags were, using a familiar tagline, "Don't get mad, get Glad." During the late 1980s, the campaign focused on the strength of Glad bags as well as some of its other features. Some TV spots used the demonstration method to show how Glad bags compared to other bags. One commercial was called "Angry Bees" and stressed the bags' zipper closures. The actor tried to prove to an unbelieving woman that of the two bags filled with "killer" bees, Glad would be more effective because she would be assured it was closed simply by looking at the green color-change seal. Another ad, titled "Pigsty," suggested that comic book collectors preserve their collections in Glad plastic bags.

### "Green" Marketing

The growing environmental movement of the 1980s increased public awareness of the solid waste problem. Some studies showed that consumers were making buying decisions on the basis of a product's effect on the environment, or how environmentally friendly a company was perceived to be. As a manufacturer of plastic bags, Glad sought to demonstrate its sense of social responsibility with a national spring cleanup effort, called Glad Bag-a-Thon.

Glad works with retailers in many of the 100 cities where it conducts the annual Bag-a-Thon. The effort involves the public and private sectors joining forces in voluntary cleanup efforts. The program's philosophy was expressed by the Director of Solid Waste Issues for First Brands: "Retailers and manufacturers should build a working coalition that could also include legislators and concerned environmentalists. Such a coalition could work to resolve the solid waste problem in a constructive, positive way."

In addition, Glad worked on environmental issues with such organizations as the Grocery Manufacturers of America, the Food Marketing Institute, and other trade groups. In 1989 Glad created a separate group, including government relations and municipality liaison representatives, to work with municipalities on solid waste issues.

During 1992, in conjunction with Keep America Beautiful Inc., Glad conducted its seventh consecutive Glad Bag-A-Thon, the nation's largest organized community cleanup program. More than 740,000 volunteers in 100 cities across the United States used donated Glad trash bags to collect 14 million pounds of litter and two million pounds of recyclables.

Environmental programs help to give Glad extensive local, state and national media exposure. In addition, public awareness was created through educational materials about Glad bags, which were distributed to more than half a million school children and several million consumers throughout the United States. The value of these programs to the community was even recognized by the federal government in 1992 when Glad Bag-a-Thon was selected by the U.S. Department of Interior as a national winner in the Take Pride in America awards program.

## Performance Appraisal

The wide product line of Glad bags and the diversity of choices available to consumers has enabled the company to post strong sales gains. From 1988 to 1992, sales increased 94 percent, nearly doubling even during a period when the nation was in an economic recession. The strong growth indicated how widely accepted Glad bags had become since their introduction almost three decades before. Throughout its history, Glad has sought to provide quality products that are affordable for consumers. For the future, the company hoped to continue being innovative in product development, manufacturing, and marketing programs.

## Further Reading:

"The Best Ways to Keep Food Fresh," *Consumer Reports,* February 1989, pp. 120–123.
*First Brands Corporation Annual Report,* Danbury, CT: First Brands Corporation, 1992.
"Food Wraps and Bags," *Consumer Reports,* December 1989, pp. 277–282.
"Garbage Bags," *Consumer Reports,* May 1988, pp. 339–341.
"Garbage Bags," *Consumer Reports,* December 1989, pp. 272–277.
*Glad Celebrates 25 Years as No. 1,* First Brands Corporation.
Lippert, Barbara, "Glad Demonstrates How to Keep Advertising Leftovers Fresh," *Adweek's Marketing Week,* August 7, 1989, p. 55.
McMurray, Scott, "Ziploc No Longer Has Its Market in the Bag," *Wall Street Journal,* December 24, 1991, p. 8.
Weinstein, Steve, and Michael Sansolo, "Coping With a Complicated Environment," *Progressive Grocer,* May 1991, pp. 73–80.

—*Dorothy Kroll*

# GUCCI®

# GUCCI

The Gucci brand is an internationally recognized symbol of quality and luxury. Gucci goods range from hand-crafted leather luggage, cases, handbags, and shoes to lines of haute couture men's and women's wear to finely designed accessories such as watches, ties, and scarves. Gucci items have been worn or carried by international trendsetters since the 1930s, and many are design classics. The Gucci moccasin has been worn by presidents and princes, and it is a globally recognized mark of elite status. The Gucci bamboo bag—a handbag with a distinctive arched bamboo handle—has been carried by such famous women as Jacqueline Onassis and Elizabeth Taylor, and Gucci's "Handbag No. 0633" is preserved in the collection of the Museum of Modern Art in New York. The Gucci line is priced out of the reach of the ordinary consumer, with shoes and handbags costing hundreds of dollars. In the 1970s Gucci production surged, and more than 10,000 items bore the linked GG logo or the Gucci red and green stripe. Gucci towels, key chains, and coffee mugs were also widely available, tarnishing the brand's image of prestige. But the Gucci line was cut in half by the end of the 1980s, and new management ensured that the brand represented only the highest end of the consumer market. Nevertheless, Gucci continues to be popular with young people in America, Europe, and Japan. The United States accounts for about 45 percent of Gucci sales, and there are 180 Gucci boutiques worldwide.

## Brand Origins

The Gucci brand was founded by Guccio Gucci, born in Florence in 1881. His family owned a struggling straw hat factory, but Guccio did not enter the family business. When still a teenager, he made his own way from Florence to London, and there found a job at the Savoy Hotel. The hotel was associated with many famous names. It was owned by Richard D'Oyly Carte and managed by the Swiss hotelier Cezar Ritz. Composer Arthur Sullivan was on the board of directors. The chef was fabled French culinary artist Auguste Escoffier. These people of international reputation attracted an equally lustrous clientele. Guccio Gucci worked as a waiter to the rich and famous for three years. He saw what these people wore, what they were happy to spend money on, and the seed of his future business was planted.

When Guccio returned to Italy in 1920, he found work in a leather goods firm called Franzi. He quickly learned the business, and in 1922 he opened his own shop in Florence. The Gucci shop specialized from the first in the highest quality merchandise. Gucci's fine materials and workmanship soon attracted the attention of local customers. Even more important was the tourist clientele. People from all over Europe and America flocked to Florence to view the city's many art treasures. They were eager to buy hand-crafted Italian leathers as well, and Gucci quickly established an international following. At the Savoy in London Guccio had seen what these wealthy travellers preferred in luggage, and he was quite successful in producing luxury articles. Craftsmen worked in the back of the store or did piecework at home, and made exceptionally sturdy cases out of the finest raw materials. The Gucci store also did repair work, and Gucci articles achieved a reputation for durability as well as beauty.

The business expanded little by little. In 1926 the Florence store moved from its original location to a larger facility in a more fashionable district. At first the store had sold mainly luggage and bags, but smaller items such as belts and jewel cases were added to attract women gift shoppers. The approach of World War II meant that Gucci could no longer freely import tanned leather from Scotland, and many designs were adapted so that less leather was used. Leather bags were converted into canvas bags with leather straps and corners. These new designs sparked the creativity of the Gucci craftsmen, and more non-leather accessories became part of the Gucci look.

At some point, Guccio Gucci came up with the linked GG that continues to be the Gucci symbol. It resembled the two-piece snaffle horse bit, and other horse motifs became part of Gucci designs. The signature Gucci red and green stripe was taken from the colors of horse blankets, and a blue and white stripe motif was similarly borrowed from race horse silks. Elements of horse tack were incorporated into Gucci scarves and ties as well. With these consistent design themes, Gucci evolved from simply producing fine leather goods to retailing a Gucci look.

Though World War II brought difficult times for Gucci's business, Guccio's oldest son Aldo insisted on taking a daring gamble. He opened a Gucci shop on the swanky Via Condotti in Rome in September of 1938. This shop stayed open throughout the war, and began to prosper as soon as the war was over. Another of Guccio's sons, Rodolfo, opened the next Gucci expansion, a store in Milan. Rodolfo had been a star of the Italian silent cinema before he joined the family business. He had a taste for high living,

## AT A GLANCE

**G**ucci brand originated in 1922 when Guccio Gucci opened his first leather goods shop in Florence, Italy; trademark was registered internationally in 1953 by Guccio Gucci, S.p.A.; that same year the brand was introduced to America under a U.S. division, Gucci America Inc.

*Performance:* *Sales*—$182 million (worldwide).

*Major competitor:* Louis Vuitton, and other high-end designers.

*Addresses:* *Parent company*—Gucci America Inc., 685 Fifth Avenue, New York, NY, 10022; phone: (212) 826-2600; fax: (212) 644-2954. *Ultimate parent company*—Guccio Gucci S.p.A., Via Tornabuoni, 73/r 50123, Florence, Italy; phone: 055-264011; telex: 571468 GUCCIFI.

and he helped refine the Gucci image of luxury. Aldo was intent on ridding his Rome shop of any vestige of cheap goods that had to be sold during the war. The Gucci stores proved very successful in the post-war years, and soon expanded overseas.

## International Success

In 1953 the Gucci trademark was registered internationally, and the business took a cross-Atlantic leap. Aldo Gucci opened the first New York store in a small space in the Sherry Netherland Hotel. In November of 1953 the store moved to a posh space at 7 East 58th Street. Americans who had bought Gucci while travelling in Italy seemed delighted to have a Gucci boutique on their own soil. The business flourished. Many famous people became regular Gucci customers, and the Gucci designs of the 1950s were the ones that went on to become classics.

Gucci's reputation came from its fine quality, but more than that, it flourished on the reputations of its well-known customers. Princess Elizabeth of England had visited the Gucci shop in Milan before she became Queen, and told Guccio Gucci that England had nothing like his shop. American movie stars also bought Gucci and added to the brand's cachet. Grace Kelly flaunted a particular Gucci floral print scarf, and at her wedding to Prince Rainier of Monaco, she gave copies of this scarf to her guests as mementos. Kim Novak and Audrey Hepburn also wore Gucci scarves, as did Elizabeth Taylor. The Gucci bamboo bag was introduced in 1957, and this particular purse became the favorite of Jacqueline Onassis, Elizabeth Taylor, and many others. The bag had an outline reminiscent of a saddle, and a handle made of bamboo that had been carefully bent into an arch by skilled Gucci craftsmen. A 1990 *Vogue* article recalled nostalgically how women in the 1950s saved up to buy this bag, because it was something "you had to have. . . . If you could only afford one, you bought it in brown. If you could buy two, you bought the other in burgundy." Other Gucci "must-have" items were an ID bracelet, silver chains, hand-stitched gloves, and perhaps the most desired of all, the Gucci moccasin. Though women also wore it, it was a men's loafer style slip-on shoe; President Kennedy, John Wayne, Clark Gable, Frank Sinatra, and Prince Rainier helped make it popular. With the likes of these wearing Gucci goods, hosts of other people bought Gucci as well. Gucci opened stores in other prominent U.S. markets such as Palm Beach, Bal Harbor, Florida, and Beverly Hills, and abroad in London, Paris, and Tokyo.

Founder Guccio Gucci died in 1953, and the worldwide expansion of the firm was carried out by his sons Aldo, Rodolfo, and Vasco. The Gucci reputation seemed unsinkable, and customers were paying more than $1,000 for crocodile handbags and gold mesh belts. By 1968, the Gucci firm's assets were estimated at $28 million, and the company was still expanding into new markets. Gucci goods were still made by hand in and around Florence, with workers turning out as many as 7,000 pairs of shoes each month. The sheer status element of owning Gucci goods fueled sales, but customers also remarked that the shoes were extremely comfortable, and the handbags never wore out. If a repair was needed, a Gucci store anywhere in the world would do the job for free.

## Retail Personality

Gucci had been made popular by its rich and famous patrons, but the brand certainly had more ordinary customers as well. The Gucci shop in New York, however, made a reputation for treating common folk with little politeness. One explanation for this, in an article in *New York* magazine titled "The Rudest Store in New York," claimed that at Gucci "they seem to think that if Americans are treated like dirt, they will buy more." A woman quoted in this article detailed having a Gucci loafer snatched away from her by a clerk as she was waiting to try it on, until she was finally told that her instep was too high and Gucci would never make a shoe in her size. In another incident, an American customer who spoke Italian overheard clerks dubbing customers who failed to buy anything *cafone*—Italian for coarse, vulgar lowbrow. Another Italian speaker overheard the employee who was waiting on her instruct his co-worker, "When I ask you if we have brown in 36, say you know we do not." One Gucci customer was forcibly dragged back into the store after she impatiently flounced out. She had spent $1000 there but was kept waiting more than half an hour for her sales slip to be written up. She sued the store and was compensated $500 in cash and $500 in Gucci gift certificates.

This kind of mistreatment evidently did not stop customers from flocking to the store. Nor did the *New York* magazine exposé worry Gucci management. Aldo Gucci was said to have been so pleased by the publicity that he sent the author a $500 floral bouquet.

Some customers, though, preferred to buy Gucci knock-offs—articles that looked like Gucci but patently were not the real thing. Other people, intentionally or not, bought Gucci fakes, as these began proliferating. Gucci was involved in continuous lawsuits against firms that appropriated the Gucci trademark. A pseudo-Gucci store even operated in Mexico City in the 1970s, selling fake Guccis at low prices. Gucci was able to legally confiscate fake goods when it found them, and it arranged with the courts to liquidate many Italian manufacturers of Gucci copies. But the fakes did not seem to cut into Gucci profits. Gucci opened more branches in the United States, and opened franchises around the world. While the company was reluctant to release sales figures, Roberto Gucci revealed to the *New York Times* in 1978 that sales volume had more than doubled since 1975.

## Brand Proliferation

One reason Gucci's sales climbed so rapidly in the 1970s was that the firm's management had decided to increase production on many of the line's less expensive items. While this strategy brought in profits, the exclusive status of the Gucci brand became watered down. If any one could afford Gucci, it was not so special, and these cheaper items lacked the appeal of the top of the line. A Gucci coffee mug could not carry the reputation for exquisite workmanship and flawless style that a crocodile bag could; the Gucci image consequently sagged.

The Gucci name suffered even more from fakes and knock-offs, but the company found it impossible to prevent these. Gucci opened more stores, and sold its goods through franchises as well, so that by the 1980s there were more than 2,500 Gucci outlets worldwide. Mass marketing led to sharply increased sales, with an

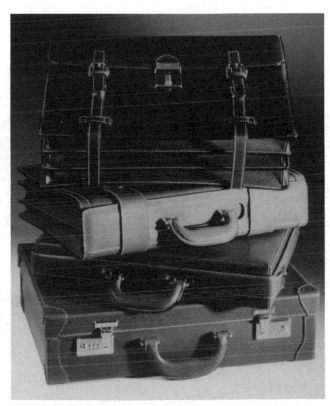

*Leather luggage and cases were the first products to bear the Gucci brand name.*

estimated $11.5 million in profits by 1985. But the cost to Gucci's reputation was great. The president of Louis Vuitton, a French competitor, told *Business Week* in 1987 that ''Gucci shops have become like gift shops.'' And the financial boom did not last long. 40 percent of Gucci's sales were in the United States, and the falling dollar began to eat into the firm's profits. In 1986 overall sales were $175 million, but profits dropped suddenly to only $5 million.

Part of the problem stemmed from a lack of managerial direction. The firm was wholly owned by the Gucci family up until 1989, but the family had started to quarrel. With top management locked in various court battles, the brand was allowed to drift. One of Aldo Gucci's sons, Paolo, wanted to leave the firm and design his own lines, because he felt his father and uncles were ignoring his design suggestions. Paolo sued the Gucci company to gain the right to use his own name, and Gucci sued him for trademark infringement. A boardroom fight that Paolo claimed led to blows made tabloid headlines, and Paolo sued again for assault. These lawsuits were eventually settled out of court, but some of the documents Paolo had entered to support his claims ended up

showing criminal tax evasion by the Gucci firm. In 1986 Aldo Gucci, then 80 years old, pleaded guilty to evading taxes totalling more than $7 million, and he was sentenced to a year in jail. Even as this was going on, Aldo and his sons were suing Maurizio Gucci, son of Aldo's late brother Rodolfo, for obtaining Rodolfo's shares in the company through fraud. Maurizio was eventually cleared of these charges. In 1988 he bought out his relatives' shares in the company and sold them to a Bahrain investment firm called Investcorp International.

## New Direction

With Maurizio firmly installed as president of Gucci, the brand began to recover some of its lost glamour. Maurizio moved to cut the number of Gucci items from over 10,000 to just 5,000. He bought back all 26 U.S. Gucci franchises so that Gucci goods would again be sold only through the firm's own shops. He also hired Dawn Mello, who had been president of New York department store Bergdorf Goodman, to oversee product development. While the company was reorganized financially, Mello took charge of improving the designs. She decided that rather than introduce new products, Gucci would update its classics. She redesigned the GG logo and had it put on the inside of leather goods, so that the brand would sell for its style and workmanship, not just its name. She also gave many of the old Gucci favorites a more youthful look, offering the Gucci moccasin in red and pink, for example, and selling smaller bamboo bags in yellow and green satin. Gucci men's and women's wear leaned towards a more casual look. Both *Vogue* magazine and *Women's Wear Daily* reported enthusiastically on Mello's accomplishments and noted a resurgence in Gucci's popularity among the young and with other fashion designers as well.

It is not clear whether Gucci's financial restructuring will be as successful as its new design outlook. A worldwide recession in the early 1990s caused a slump in the luxury goods market that affected Gucci and many other firms. Though Gucci claimed to break even in 1992 on sales of $182 million, investment bankers following the company estimated Gucci lost between $20 and $30 million, leading to rumors of an impending bank takeover. Problems with cash flow led to delayed payments to Gucci suppliers and interrupted the 1993–94 advertising campaign. Yet the head of Gucci's American branch reported that 1993 sales were ahead of the previous year and denied that the U.S. division had any financial problems. And the brand is still attracting star customers, with recent converts including actor Warren Beatty and model Cindy Crawford. So however Gucci's apparent money difficulties are resolved, the Gucci name still means glamour, and that should ensure Gucci's continuing presence in the luxury market.

## Further Reading:

''Artisans & Art: Gucci,'' *Fortune,* July 23, 1984, p. 49.

Bernier, Linda, ''Crazy for European Luxury,'' *International Management,* December 1987, p. 24.

Costin, Glyn, ''Dawn Mello Revamping Gucci,'' *Women's Wear Daily,* May 29, 1992, p. 6.

Crittendon, Ann, ''Knock-Offs Aside, Gucci's Blooming,'' *New York Times,* June 25, 1978, p. F1.

Forden, Sara Gay, ''Banks Putting Big Squeeze on Gucci Chief,'' *Women's Wear Daily,* April 26, 1993, p. 1.

Friedman, Arthur, ''Aldo Gucci Dies at 84,'' *Women's Wear Daily,* January 22, 1990, p. 8.

''Gucci, A Brief History,'' and press releases, New York: Gucci America, Inc., 1993.

"Gucci on the Go," *Time,* July 25, 1969, p. 72.

"Gucci, Taking Control," *Women's Wear Daily,* January 9, 1987, p. 54.

"Gucci to Go," *Harper's Bazaar,* February 1991, p. 66.

Howell, Georgina, "Gucci Again," *Vogue,* December 1990, p. 322.

McKnight, Gerald, *Gucci: A House Divided,* New York: Donald I.Fine, Inc., 1987.

Orr, Andrea, "Court OK's Limited Use of Paolo Gucci Name," *Women's Wear Daily,* June 20, 1988, p. 2.

Rossant, John, "At Gucci, La Vita Is No Longer So Dolce," *Business Week,* November 23, 1992, p. 60.

Rossant, and Andrea Rothman, "Can Maurizio Bring the Glamour Back?," *Business Week,* February 5, 1990, p. 83.

Sheraton, Mimi, "The Rudest Store in New York," *New York,* November 10, 1975, p. 44.

Wolman, Karen and Elizabeth Weiner, "Can an Outsider Fill Aldo Gucci's Loafers?," *Business Week,* November 30, 1987, p. 52.

*—A. Woodward*

# GUESS?®

Guess? jeans burst on the scene in 1981 and changed the image of jeans in the United States permanently. In the mid-nineteenth century, when blue jeans were introduced by Levi Strauss to American workers, the Marciano family had not yet arrived in the south of France, where the four Marciano brothers of future Guess? Inc. fame would be raised. More than a century later, in December 1981, Georges Marciano, a recent immigrant to the United States, brought a few pairs of the brothers' homemade European-style jeans to the flagship Bloomingdale's store in Manhattan. This marked the beginning of Guess? Inc. The brothers had come to California, where they had been unable to find a suitable outlet for their progressive denim styling. Denim was not popular in the fashion industry at the time, so the Marcianos were elated to find that the first 30 pairs of jeans sold from Bloomingdale's within hours of their placement on the floor.

Each of the four brothers brought his own expertise to the company. Georges was the designer, and came to the United States only after having established himself in his native France. Armand, the eldest brother, took care of shipping, processing, and customer relations. Maurice was the financial leader of the company, and Paul handled the creation of the Guess? image through advertising. That image included the now-familiar Guess? triangle that first appeared on the back pocket of Guess? jeans.

The 1980s were turbulent, with a severe worldwide recession as well as personal difficulties among the brothers affecting the company. Despite these troubles and a long-fought legal battle with the owners of a rival jeans company, Guess? Inc. thrived. Still innovative in the jeans business, Guess also entered several other markets, including athletic footwear, fragrance, and children's clothing among others. In the summer of 1991, when *Consumer Reports* evaluated the basic five-pocket western jean ten years after the brand's founding, Guess? jeans were still among so-called "trendy brands" in comparison with "familiar" Levi, Lee, and Wrangler brands. Beginning with their classically styled jeans and moving into other western-accented clothing and accessories, the Marcianos built a business that found success through fine merchandising, good value, and canny product design and advertising.

## Bold and Provocative Advertising

From the beginning, Guess? jeans and clothing were supported by a striking and unusual advertising campaign. Paul Marciano,

the youngest of the four brothers, led the way. As the principal of his own in-house advertising agency, Paul created an image that attracted buyers across the country. The seductive and glamorous look of the advertisements was intended to reflect on the clothing itself.

Most of the advertising budget went to print ads, which were dominated by fine black and white photographs that featured models with a dramatic flair. Some of the models who gained prominence as "Guess girls" included Claudia Schiffer, Carré Otis, and Eva Herzigova, who started with Guess? as an 18-year-old Marilyn Monroe look-alike. Schiffer moved from print ads to television work for Guess? Fragrance. The common element in these models was the young, provocative, sensual image they conveyed. Star power was also recruited in the mid-1990s with Drew Barrymore.

Among fashion companies, Guess? was known as a major advertiser. The company bought advertising space in a wide range of magazines, from such established fashion magazines as *Glamour, Elle,* and *Vogue* to fresh, untested magazines like *Detour* and *Vibe.* It was also a regular advertiser in regional, national, and international consumer magazines such as *Harper's Bazaar, Chicago Magazine, Los Angeles Times Magazine,* and *L'Uomo Vogue.* Guess? Inc. spent more than $20 million advertising its apparel in 1992.

## Beyond Jeans

The success of the Guess? brand was due only in part to its advertising, of course. The jeans were made to fit. Originally designed for women, the jeans were tailored to women's bodies, and customers enjoyed both the high styling and the comfortable fit. After creating men's lines, Guess? jeans were just the beginning. Sales increased in the retail environment and the management of Guess? lost little time moving the Guess? name and signature style onto various licensed products.

As a small, family-run business, Guess? wanted to expand by giving the name to already established manufacturers to create licensed products. The company chose manufacturers whose goods met with their standards of style and quality. Some of these licensees included manufacturers of knitwear, infant and children's clothes, and fragrances. On the occasion of the tenth anniversary of Guess? and its jeans, Paul Marciano told a trade

## AT A GLANCE

**G**uess? brand founded in 1981 by the Marciano brothers in California; Georges Marciano first brought Guess? jeans to New York in 1981; success brought all four Marciano brothers—Georges, Maurice, Paul, and Armand—into the company; Guess? jeans and clothing still manufactured and sold by Guess? Inc.

**Performance:** *Sales*—$550 million.

**Major competitor:** Levi Strauss & Co.'s Levi's jeans.

**Advertising:** *Agency*—All advertising done in-house. *Major campaign*—Paul Marciano's black and white photos featuring high-profile models.

**Addresses:** *Parent company*—Guess? Inc., 1444 South Alameda Street, Los Angeles, CA 90021; phone: (213) 765-3100, fax: (213) 765-5788.

magazine, *DNR,* "Guess is a brand with name recognition . . . Guess hasn't ever been just a women's brand or a men's brand . . . "

Guess also branched out into other areas by licensing new items that had strong brand identification. One of the licenses that was successful in its early years was athletic footwear. Guess hired a former vice-president for Nike, Jim Moodhe, as the president of the fledgling athletic footwear company. Moodhe stated in the June 1991 issue of *Sporting Goods Business* that "While Guess's name signifies lifestyle and has fashion appeal, and I hope our shoes have fashion appeal, our shoes will be functional." He also noted that Guess? was very careful with distribution and was consciously aiming to create a good price-value relationship. The line included tennis, basketball, casual, rugged, and running shoes for men and women priced from $40 to $90. Its limited 1992 introduction appeared in selected shoe stores and various sporting goods, specialty, and department stores. One popular model, called the Attitude, combined a basketball shoe with a hip hop design.

Other in-house Guess? divisions were the young contemporary, men's, and Boutique Collection lines. Some of the firm's manufacturing licensees in the United States included Charles David of California for leather and rubber footwear; Revlon for fragrances; Callanen Int. for watches; DML Marketing Group for legwear; Day-Lor Creations, Inc. for belts; Pour Le Bebe for Infants and Kids; and Viva International for eyewear, which became a licensee in 1987.

Guess? also used foreign licensees, including sportswear manufacturers in Argentina, Mexico, The Philippines, Brazil, Chile, Korea, Thailand, and Canada. The company also opened a chain of retail stores, called MGA, that sold Guess? jeans and clothing in France.

### Guess Ranch

In late 1992 Guess? jeans and clothing were off in yet another direction with the opening of the 6,000-square-foot Guess Ranch on Rodeo Drive in Beverly Hills, California. The recession had exacted a toll on many of the high-style shops of Rodeo Drive, and the Ranch was a breath of fresh air. Unlike the other Guess? shops in other locations, which have chrome and wood interiors and sleek contemporary styling, the Guess Ranch was reminiscent of a

Hollywood backlot filled with western memorabilia. Speaking in the trade magazine *Women's Wear Daily,* then-chairman and Guess? designer Georges Marciano said that the Guess Ranch would have a wide-ranging effect on the company's lines. "It is going to have a big influence on our fashion," he said. "My guess is the lines are going to be a lot more western because of the store."

Besides the trademark Guess? jeans, the ranch also sold T-shirts, jackets, and western style gear, as well as knick-knacks and souvenirs arrayed along the second floor mezzanine. The dressing rooms were tepees, and a real railcar spilled cowboy boots and vests onto the tracks. Clothing was stacked in slightly unkempt piles, in contrast to the perfectly ordered displays in other Guess retail stores. The ranch was a vision of the Marcianos, who cited a strong connection to the American West. (The old boots that Gene Autry wore were purchased by Georges Marciano at an auction, and are proudly displayed at the ranch.)

Due to the success of Guess Ranch, the company planned to open another Rodeo Drive store next to the Guess Ranch. The new shop was to be about one quarter of the size of Guess Ranch. It was slated to carry signature designer lines in order not to compete with the Guess Ranch in its sale of jeans, shirts, and accessories.

### Seven-Year Legal Battle

The family business suffered from a prolonged and bitter legal dispute with another family—the owners of Jordache Enterprises, Inc. The trouble began in 1983, when Guess? was struggling to keep up with demand for their products. The Marcianos sold half of Guess? Inc. to the Nakash brothers of Jordache for $4.75 million. The Marcianos filed lawsuits in 1984 in the United States and Hong Kong, charging that Guess? designs were being used in Jordache apparel. In 1989 a jury determined that Jordache had acted fraudulently in the 1983 partial acquisition of Guess? The parties agreed to an out-of-court settlement in 1990, in which the Nakash brothers returned their entire stake in Guess? to the Marcianos. The years of acrimony and expensive legal fees were difficult for the company, and the Marciano brothers were relieved to finally regain complete ownership. A lawyer for Guess? told the New York Times that the settlement was notable "particularly where the company has increased in value as Guess Jeans has over the years."

A few years later, the U.S. Labor Department found several Guess? contractors in California to be in violation of the Fair Labor Standards Act. The company quickly made amends, both by donating money to an organization helping Los Angeles area children and by planning clothing donations for other charities. The company eventually reached an agreement with the Labor Department in 1992. In the agreement, Guess? volunteered to monitor labor violations by its contractors. The company used about 100 sewing contractors who made Guess? jeans and clothing by employing more than 7,000 workers. After the riots in Los Angeles in the spring of that year, Guess? general counsel Stanley Levy said, "Recent events in Los Angeles remind us that we must care for the fabric of our society—not just the fabric of our garments. We recognize that it's our moral obligation to monitor our contractors."

The brothers Marciano did not always see eye-to-eye on the future of their jeans and clothing. Georges believed that slow growth in department store sales was hindering the company. He suggested that Guess? clothing be designed for discounters like

Wal-Mart. Maurice, Armand, and Paul preferred to increase their own retail operations while keeping distribution limited to department stores. The disagreement over strategy led to an eventual buyout in August 1993 by Armand, Maurice, and Paul of Georges' 40 percent share in the company.

Plans were made to phase out the Georges Marciano name and trademark over the following year. Company officials speculated that the apparel would carry the new designation: Marciano Collection for Guess? After Georges's departure, Maurice Marciano was chief executive officer, Paul Marciano was president and chief operating officer and head of advertising, and Armand Marciano retained his title of senior executive vice president of Guess? Inc.

In 1993, Guess? Inc., hired Bernard Zeichner to oversee retail operations with an aim to expand its retail business, and to boost sagging sales in existing stores. Nearing the end of the century, Guess? jeans continue to bring a unique fashion sense to the industry. The company hopes that the jeans, coupled with other Guess? clothing and the licensed Guess? products, will propel the company to a bright future.

## Further Reading:

"Blue Jeans," *Consumer Reports,* July 1991, pp. 456–461.

Dang, Kim-Van, "Guess to Inspect, Report to U.S. on Contractors," *Women's Wear Daily,* August 6, 1992, p. 15.

"Guess? Solving Fashion Formula," *Sporting Goods Business,* March 1993, p. 14.

"K-Swiss' Moodhe Exits to Launch Guess," *Sporting Goods Business,* June 1991, p. 12.

Lev, Michael, "Jeans Makers Settle Seven-Year Fraud Case," *The New York Times,* May 31, 1989, p. D5.

Lockwood, Lisa, "Guess Boosts Fall Budgets for Print Ads," *Women's Wear Daily,* June 26, 1992, p. 1.

Marlow, Michael, "Guess at 10: $550 Million And Growing," *Women's Wear Daily,* December 20, 1991, p. 1; "Guess on Rodeo: The Beverly Hills Cowboy," *Women's Wear Daily,* November 24, 1992, p. 13; "Hear Marcianos Readying a Second Rodeo Drive Unit," *Women's Wear Daily,* March 5, 1993, p. 11.

Marlow, Michael, and Kim-Van Dang, "Georges Marciano to Leave Guess and Sell His Stake," *Women's Wear Daily,* August 3, 1993, p. 1.

Ryan, Thomas J., "Marcianos Buy a Piece of Gitano," *Women's Wear Daily,* March 17, 1993, p. 2.

Strom, Stephanie, "Guess Names Specialty Store Chief to Lead its Retail Unit," *The New York Times,* August 31, 1993, p. C4.

Wilson, Marianne, "Guess Ranch Lassos Rodeo Drive," *Chain Store Age Executive,* January 1993, pp. 174–75.

*—Fran Shonfeld Sherman*

# HAGGAR®

In the world of men's dress slacks, the brand name Haggar is closely associated with high quality and innovation. Having consistently outperformed its rivals through the years, Haggar has earned a reputation as the undisputed men's dress slacks leader. In 1991, Haggar held an estimated 20 percent share of the men's dress slacks market in the United States. The brand is designed, manufactured, and marketed by Haggar Apparel Company, headquartered in Dallas, Texas. In addition to men's dress slacks, the Haggar brandname also appears on casual dress pants, men's custom-fit suits and sportcoats, shorts, and shirts.

## Brand History

The Haggar brand was first created in 1926 by J. M. Haggar, an immigrant from Lebanon. Located near Dallas, Texas, the company became a regional, then a national, then an international success story. By 1992 the brand was also produced in such geographically diverse locations as the Dominican Republic, Mexico, Austrialia, Canada, Japan, and India. The principal domestic and export markets for the slacks were located in the United States, Central America, and Europe.

Until 1992, the Haggar Corporation was a privately held company owned by a number of Haggar family members. In December of 1992, in a highly publicized affair that was the talk of Wall Street, Haggar Corporation went public. The initial public offering was well received because, according to Sidney Rutberg in the *Daily News Record,* Wall Street viewed Haggar as a "solid, well-financed company," which just prior to going public had undertaken a "thorough housecleaning" by closing five U.S. operations and liquidating its women's apparel busines. When the dust had settled, the offering left over $30 million in the hand's of several Haggar family members and their favorite trusts and provided the company with $27 million to pay off bank debt. After the offering, Rutberg also reported that the Haggar family still retained 50 percent of the stock.

The sale of the women's apparel division in 1990 was indicative of the business savvy exercised by the brand's parent company. For a number of years the division had been a money-losing venture. In 1990 it lost money on sales totaling an estimated $8.7 million. The division was purchased by an undisclosed buyer for approximately $9.3 million, with Haggar Corporation taking a loss of approximately $2.3 million. However, the new buyer had agreed to a four-year licensing arrangement, specifying their use of the Haggar label through 1994. In addition, the buyer was obliged to make annual royalty payments amounting to 3 percent of total sales or a minimum of $500,000 per year.

## Recent Brand Development

The men's apparel industry took notice when, in October of 1992, Haggar introduced its 100 percent cotton "Wrinkle-Free Slacks." The product's debut was purported to have scored an industry coup in the men's casual slacks category. The new line was intended to compete with the number one casual slacks brand, Levi's Dockers, who first launched the all-cotton slacks in 1986.

The year after Haggar introduced its wrinkle-free line, Brenda J. Gall, a veteran apparel industry analyst with Merrill Lynch, noted the slacks' unexpected popularity among consumers and predicted an eventual narrowing of the market share gap separating Haggar's 9 percent and its rival Levi's Dockers' 22 percent.

The development of Haggar's wrinkle free all-cotton casual slacks's was the outcome of a prolonged research program. As Joe Haggar III, Haggar's president and chief executive officer, explained to the *Daily News Record,* the company had been developing the slacks "for years." Market research undertaken by Haggar concluded that consumers leveled two recurrent complaints against casual all-cotton slacks: the slacks became wrinkled when worn, and, to be worn again, they needed to be either dry cleaned or ironed at home. To overcome these shortcomings, the company developed a way to treat fabric with resin, a process for which a patent was sought. In addition to treating the all-cotton fabric line, Haggar intended to extend the process to its corduroy, canvas, gabardine, and brushed twill fabric lines.

To compete in the lucrative discount slacks mass market, the company initiated the Reed St. James brand in 1983. Since that time the label has become a significant force in a market dominated by 11 major labels. Industry reports indicated that the Wal-Mart discount store chain was the label's largest customer, accounting for 10 percent of the brand's sales in 1993. That same year, the Reed St. James division generated two new labels: Mustang, which had been trademarked by J. M. Haggar back in 1938 and which the company now used for a line of denim jeans, and Taos Country, which Haggar applied to a new Western wear collection of slacks and sportcoats.

## Manufacturing Structure

Haggar has traditionally operated manufacturing sites, both company-owned and contract-sourced, in the United States and abroad. Most foreign production is conducted through licensing arrangements. When a new management team took the reins in 1990, it made increased foreign production a critical component of its strategic growth plan. An emphasis on foreign sources was deemed necessary to accomplish Haggar's objectives of a more flexible and balanced supply network and a reduction in unit costs. Between the years 1990 and 1992, the combined contribution of foreign operations rose from 50 percent to 55 percent.

During the 1980s, Haggar broke new ground in the apparel industry when it unveiled two inventory management systems known as Electronic Data Interchange (EDI) and Quick Response. Haggar's links to its retail network are maintained by these systems. Speaking at the 82nd annual National Retail Federation convention, Bill Howell, chairman and chief executive officer of J.C. Penny, praised Haggar's use of these systems. Howell noted that Haggar's shipments of Penny's orders averaged 18 days, 10 days quicker than the next comparable major supplier. The EDI and Quick Response systems helped reduce retail-level inventory overhead and boost profit margins.

## AT A GLANCE

**H**aggar brand of menswear founded in 1926 in Dallas, TX, by J. M. Haggar; remained a private, family-owned business until 1991; went public in 1992.

**Performance:** *Market share*—20% (top share) of men's dress slacks category; 9% (second-largest share) of men's casual slacks category.

**Major competitor:** Levi's Dockers; also Farah's Savanne.

**Advertising:** *Agency*—Tracy-Locke, Dallas, TX. *Major campaign*—Comedian/stuntman Super Dave Osborne performing stunts and announcing, "The pants still aren't wrinkled."

**Addresses:** *Parent company*—Haggar Apparel Company, 6113 Lemmon Ave, Dallas, TX 75209; phone: (214) 352-8481; fax: (214) 956-0367. *Ultimate parent company*—Haggar Corporation.

Prior to the 1990s, the Mexican retail network system functioned similarly to its U.S. counterparts in the 1940s and 1950s, said Frank Bracken, Haggar's executive vice president of global marketing. Retailers would typically purchase products in large lots and sell their inventory down. But with the introduction of the Quick Response and just-in-time delivery systems, Bracken changed that system. As a result, Haggar's Mexican retailers have been able to boost their profit margins and Mexican consumers were able to select slacks in a far greater variety of sizes and colors than ever before.

In the early 1990s, in an effort to better coordinate the brand's design, manufacture, and marketing operations, Haggar upgraded its computer operations. For its hardware platform, Haggar selected IBM's Application System/400. The company developed software applications through the use of a computer-aided design and engineering package meant to facilitate the integration of the company's existing applications. Tom Sample, senior vice president of Haggar's management information systems, explained that before the AS/400's arrival, most of the company's previous systems were of "various ages" and "not integrated." To complement the AS/400s, Haggar installed a Business Planning and Control System software package. According to Sample, the system was well suited to Haggar's needs since it allowed the complete integration of matters related to forecasting, distribution, and finance.

### Marketing Strategies and Structures

In the early 1990s, garments with the Haggar label were carried by approximately 7000 retail outlets throughout the United States. Among the major department stores, J.C. Penny, Macy's, and Dillards constituted the brand's largest retail customers. Of these, the J.C. Penny account was the largest and responsible for an estimated 22.6 percent of the brand's sales in 1992.

Haggar's corporate marketing division is organized into three different branches-one each for Mexico, the United States, and Canada. Each branch sells directly to their respective retailers. Where trade restrictions apply, the company's merchandise must be sold under a different label. Haggar believes that the expected passage of the North American Free Trade Agreement will eliminate this pratice and eventually strengthen the brand's image and name recognition.

In the spring of 1994, Haggar implemented a new product labeling and packaging design intended to make consumer purchases easier and faster. Founded on consumer research, the new label was thought to better inform prospective buyers about the garment's fit and easy care features. Haggar's characteristic "no iron" phrase was prominently displayed on the labels.

### Recent Advertising

Most of Haggar's United States advertising is conducted through television and magazines. In October of 1992, the company commenced its largest national advertising campaign in 10 years to promote its wrinkle-free all-cotton casual slacks. The estimated cost of the campaign was $10 to $12 million. Although the slacks had been selling at a brisk pace prior to the campaign, Joe Haggar III justified the expense as a means for Haggar to supplant Levi's Dockers as the number one men's casual slacks. He added that a comparable high-cost campaign that Haggar had launched ten years ago for the brand's newly introduced suit separates and sportcoats catapulted Haggar into the number one position in each category.

The wrinkle-free ad campaign featured two television commercials. The first, a 15-second "Wrinkled Label" spot, pictured a pair of wet Haggar slacks going head-to-head with a pair of wet Levi's Dockers. It showed a closeup of the wet label from each brand. As the slacks dried, the Docker label became wrinkled while the Haggar label remained wrinkle-free. A concluding sound-over informed the consumer that "Haggar's new 100 percent cotton pants solve a problem our competition hasn't been able to straighten out."

The second commercial, called "Super Wash & Dry," featured comedian and stuntman Super Dave Osborne dressed in Haggar wrinkle free slacks. Osborne appeared strapped to a rocket sled. In one motion he was launched through high-pressure wash and dry jets of a car wash, then hurled through a brick wall, and came to a rest only to announce that the pants were still unwrinkled.

Haggar uses the same promotional concepts in all three North American countries. Frank Bracken found that the same commercials played just as well in Mexico and, to a lesser extent, in Canada. With thirty-plus years in Haggar Corp.'s sales and marketing operation, Bracken summed up his experience with the quip that, once the appropriate translation is made, "consumers are consumers."

### International Presence

Haggar has always be active in both the foreign manufacture and retailing of its branded products. In 1988, Haggar began exporting into South and Central America. In 1992, a joint-venture with the Mexican firm of Portefino SA de CV, a long-established slacks producer, led to the creation of a new company located in Monterrey, the capital of the northern Mexico state of Nuevo Leon. Named Industrias DAK SA de CV, in 1994 the facility was the largest men's slack producer in Latin America. Domestically, the bulk of its Hagger labeled slacks were distributed through large Mexican department stores such as Liverpool, Placio de Hierro, Sears, and Salinas y Rocha. The plant was also scheduled to begin exporting Haggar slacks to Europe.

The joint-venture was the result of a 20-year courtship between Haggar and Portenfino, reported Jennifer Delson in the *Daily*

*News Record*. Haggar had high expectations that the joint venture would serve as a manufacturing and distribution platform from which the company could dramatically increase the brand's penetration into a rapidly expanding Mexican market. With a retail client list in excess of 1500 outlets, Portefino had a more than adequate customer base, and the company also contributed highly regarded marketing skills, according to Jim Scully, Haggar's international manager.

Under the Maquiladora program, Haggar has a wholly owned plant in Leon Mexico that permits the free import of raw materials to be worked up and then shipped back to the United States for distribution. As mentioned earlier, Haggar also has manufacturing plants in the Dominican Republic, Australia, Japan, India and Canada.

## Future Trends

Like most apparel companies with a global scope, Haggar eagerly anticipated the passage of the North American Free Trade Agreement. If enacted, Haggar was poised to pursue many more joint ventures, which it viewed as more lucrative than restrictive licensing arrangements. Preliminary efforts were also being made to step up the company's production and marketing presence in Europe.

Domestically, Haggar's introduction of wrinkle-free 100 percent cotton casual slacks, along with its aggressive advertising campaign aimed at a Docker's, poses a serious challenge to Levi's number one market share position in the casual slacks category. Such an effort to gain more of the casual end of the market is consistent with overall men's apparel industry trends, which point to a substantial shift toward more comfort and easy-care features in men's clothes.

**Further Reading:**

Cusack, Sally, "Menswear Maker to Build AS/400 Applications," *Computerworld,* March 30, 1992, p. 81.

Delson, Jennifer, "Haggar Poised for Biz in Mexico," *Daily News Record,* August 4, 1992, p. 6.

Farnsworth, Steven, "Haggar Family May Reap $28 Million From Stock Offering," *Daily News Record,* October 6, 1992, p. 10.

Gellers, Stan, "Haggar Jumps Into Jeans," *Daily News Record,* February 5, 1993, p. 10.

Gall, Brenda G., "Haggar Corp.—Company Report," *Merrill Lynch,* January 25, 1993.

"Haggar 93 Sales, Earnings Seen Rising," *Daily News Record,* January 27, 1993, p. 10.

Lloyd, Brenda, "Slack Firms Expand All-Cottons," *Daily News Record,* August 19, 1992, p. 12.

Mhlambiso, Thembi, "Haggar Begins TV Ads For Wrinkle-Free Slacks," *Daily News Record,* October 22, 1992, p. 8.

Palmieri, Jean E., "Haggar Launching New Western Wear Collection," *Daily News Record,* January 14, 1993, p. 4.

"Profiles in Marketing: Franck Bracken," *Sales & Marketing Management,* April 1993, p 10.

Rutberg, Sidney, "Haggar Puts New Wrinkle in Initial Public Offering," *Daily News Record,* January 13, 1993, pp. 4–5.

Spevack, Rachel, "Haggar-J.C. Penney Partnership Spells Success for Both Firms," *Daily News Record,* January 21, 1993, p. 3.

Walsh, Peter, and Jean Palmieri, "Macy's Adding Haggar," *Daily News Record,* June 4, 1993, p. 1.

*—Daniel E. King*

# HALLMARK®

Hallmark brand cards first appeared in the mid-1920s. Since that time they have become one of the most recognized names in greeting cards. The most popular Hallmark card, a sentimental friendship card featuring a cart filled with purple pansies, was created in 1939; it continued to be a part of Hallmark's line into the 1990s, having sold over 27 million copies. The company which first marketed the cards was Hall Brothers, Inc., founded in 1910 by Joyce C. Hall; in 1954 the company name was changed to Hallmark Cards, Inc., with head offices in Kansas City, Missouri. The brand's distinctive trademark, a five-pointed crown and signature, was adopted in 1949 and became a registered trademark in 1950. Hallmark Cards, Inc., which ranks 36th in *Forbes* magazine's 1992 listing of largest privately held American companies, has annual sales of approximately $3.1 billion and a 40 percent market share.

Besides greeting cards, the company produces art supplies, crayons, toys, wrapping paper, holiday ornaments, and related products under various brand names including Crayola, Ambassador, Springbok, Liquitex, and Magic Marker. The domestic leader in the "personal communications" industry, which includes greeting cards, gift wraps, writing implements, and associated products, the company also publishes products in more than 20 languages and distributes them in some 100 countries around the world. In addition, the company has established its position in broadcast media through its sponsorship of "The Hallmark Hall of Fame," an award-winning television series, and it has recently expanded further into television and theatrical projects through Signboard Hill Productions, formed in 1992, and into cable television operations, through Crown Media, Inc., created in 1991.

## Early History

Joyce C. Hall, the founder of Hallmark Cards, arrived in Kansas City, Missouri in 1910 and began operating a wholesale postcard business, the inventory of which was stored in two shoe boxes he kept under his bed in the local YMCA. In an era when communications relied almost exclusively on the written word, the idea of selling picture postcards was profitable. Within a few months, Hall was joined by one of his brothers, and by 1912 Hall Brothers, Inc., their small company, expanded to include greeting cards.

During the next three years, the company flourished. Valentines were added in 1913, and the brothers extended the product line to include cards of their own design. In 1915, however, the company suffered a major setback when its inventory was completely destroyed by a devastating fire. In the reorganization that followed, Hall and his brother bought an engraving firm and began to expand the product line once more. After a third brother joined the firm in 1922, the company grew rapidly, moving from one site to another in the Kansas City area. Among the innovations it introduced was a line of decorated gift wrap to be used in place of mundane brown paper. Anecdotal history suggests that Hall invented the idea of gift wrap when his company ran out of red and green Christmas tissue paper in 1917 and began to use decorated envelope lining paper instead.

The company was incorporated as Hall Brothers in 1923, a year after it developed its first logo, a torch and a shield. The word "Hallmark" appeared on the backs of cards as early as the mid-1920s, but was not adopted officially as the company's name until almost three decades later.

## The Depression Years

Although the greeting card business was hit hard by the Depression, the company managed to expand and flourish. Hall refused to fire his employees, convincing them instead to take across-the-board pay cuts. The company launched its first international venture in 1931, when it entered into an agreement with the W. E. Coutts Company of Canada, which became its Canadian affiliate. During the 1930s, Hall pioneered the point-of-purchase card display, which made its debut in stores in 1936 and allowed his wares to be seen by customers firsthand. Until that time, store owners would simply keep greeting cards in a drawer near the cash desk until someone asked for one, and then an appropriate one would be selected at random by a store clerk. To continue to build consumer awareness, in the late 1930s Hall began to advertise his cards and related products in national magazines and on local radio. His forays into these media gave rise to Hallmark's involvement with network radio in 1941, and with the fledgling medium of television in the early 1950s.

## Innovations at Mid-Century

Throughout the war years, the Hall Brothers continued to produce greeting cards. It was during this period that Hallmark cards were sold with the slogan "When you care enough to send the very best," written by company executive Ed Goodman in

## AT A GLANCE

**H**allmark brand cards were introduced by Hall Brothers Cards, Inc. in 1910; Joyce C. Hall served as president of the company until 1966; the company name was officially changed to Hallmark Cards, Inc., 1954. Hallmark Cards distinctive five pointed crown and signature logo became a registered trademark, 1950.

*Performance:* *Market share*—40% of the personal communications industry (top share). *Sales*—$1.4 billion.

*Major competitor:* American Greetings Corp. (Cleveland, OH); also, Gibson Greetings (Cincinnati, OH).

*Advertising:* *Agency*—Leo Burnett, Chicago, IL, 1988—. *Major campaign*—"When you care enough to send the very best" is Hallmark's best-known slogan. Other campaigns include the Shoebox Greetings' envelope/card giveaway in national magazines.

*Addresses:* *Parent company*—Hallmark Cards, Inc., P.O. Box 419580, Kansas City, MO 64141-6580; phone: (816) 274-5111.

1944, and recognized as one of the most familiar tag lines in America. The famous crown-and-signature logo was introduced in 1949, replacing the torch and shield emblem that previously graced the back of all Hall Brothers cards. The company officially changed its name to Hallmark Cards, Inc. in 1954; shortly thereafter it moved its headquarters to a distinctive inverted-pyramid-shaped building in Kansas City.

By the end of the 1940s, card lines included those with reproductions of works by American artists Norman Rockwell and Grandma Moses. In 1948, Hall launched a line of Christmas cards under the name "Hallmark Gallery Artists." Featuring works by Michelangelo, Rembrandt, and Da Vinci, among others, the cards fulfilled Hall's dream of bringing cultural masterpieces into the lives of those who may not otherwise be exposed to them.

Product lines expanded throughout the 1950s and included a series of cards featuring paintings by statesman Winston Churchill. In 1953, Hallmark designed the first official presidential Christmas card for President Dwight D. Eisenhower. Cartoon characters shared the spotlight with politicians. Disney figures first appeared in the mid-1930s and were eventually joined by Charles Schultz's Peanuts gang in 1960.

In 1951, Hall entered into the television venture that earned him at least as much recognition as his greeting cards. His company sponsored television's "Hallmark Hall of Fame" series, which premiered with *Amal and the Night Visitors,* the first original opera written for television, and the first network-sponsored show to appear in color. The Hall of Fame telecasts, noted for their entertainment quality and intellectual content, included works by William Shakespeare, Bernard Shaw, Noel Coward, as well as modern American dramatists. They have won a number of Emmys and other awards for their fine content and topical messages. The shows continued on an ad hoc basis into the 1990s.

### Developments in the 1960s and 1970s

One of the secrets of Hall's marketing success was his ability to track the trends that affected Americans in their daily lives. By charting shopping habits the company demonstrated that mass-

merchandising channels, such as chain drug stores, supermarkets, and discount stores, represented a lucrative market for greeting cards. In response to this previously untapped source of revenue, in 1959 Hallmark developed its Ambassador line of greeting cards, which was created solely for these outlets.

At about the same time, Americans had begun frequenting suburban shopping malls, reveling in the convenience of being able to select from a wide variety of stores under one roof. As a response to this change in shopping patterns, Hallmark began in 1960 to develop its own retail concept. As more products were added to the Hallmark line, the network of independently owned and operated—not franchised—stores flourished. In 1993, of 21,000 retail outlets, 10,000 are specialty shops selling Hallmark products. Only about 200 of these were company-owned.

During the 1960s and 1970s, new product lines continued to be introduced. Hallmark was one of the first companies to target the ethnic market with its introduction of cards that reflected the country's growing diversity. Both Spanish-language and African-American theme cards were launched in the 1960s. Greeting cards that feature Hispanic themes and Spanish prose are marketed under the *Primor* line, while the works of African-American poets, artists, and writers are showcased in the *Mahogany* line.

### Product Innovations in the 1980s and 1990s

One of Hallmark's most successful and controversial launches was its introduction of Shoebox Greetings (billed as "a tiny little division of Hallmark") in 1986. Shoebox Greetings targeted the alternative-card market, a lucrative segment, providing cards for unconventional situations like "Congratulations on your diet" and unconventional cards for mainstream holidays like "Happy Mother's Day to My Step-Mother."

The alternative-card segment was invented by the Chicago-based Recycled Paper Products in the early 1970s, and has proven to be the most rapidly expanding area of the greeting card industry. Alternative cards have a predicted ten percent growth per year, compared with the one to three percent average for the industry as a whole. Hallmark's entry, which premiered with 540 cards, has expanded to include more than 1,700 choices, featuring such characters as Maxine, artist John Wagner's crotchety senior citizen. The line also includes gift items, humor books, and party ware.

While the card-buying public expressed its enthusiasm for Shoebox Greeting's off-beat humor, Recycled Paper vilified the company in a series of trade-publication ads accusing the "Hallmark Hall of Shame" of plagiarism for copying such familiar images as those by Recycled Paper's artist Sandra Boynton. The dispute was eventually settled out of court, but not before some of Hallmark's perhaps questionable marketing tactics were exposed in the press. The publicity, however, did not dampen the appeal of the Shoebox Greeting products. In 1991, the line was reported to have grossed close to $100 million. If Shoebox Greetings was an independent company, rather than a division of Hallmark, it would be the fifth-largest greeting card company in the country.

Other recent launches include the 1990 introduction of "any day" cards under the "Just How I Feel" line. Comprising some 500 different cards, the line is designed to help people convey personal messages, including those expressing hopes and disappointments about everyday goals and achievements. In 1993 "Just How I Feel" was rolled into the new "Windows" line, and the combined line includes more than 1,000 cards for everyday occasions like birthdays, anniversaries, and weddings. Windows brand cards feature wording that is "warm, and to the point." The "Just for Today" line includes inspirational, motivational cards and gifts for such contemporary situations as addiction, drug-dependency, and serious-illness recoveries.

Hallmark became an industry pioneer when it began its *Personalize it!* system, in which customers can personalize greeting cards in point-of-purchase kiosks located in retail outlets. First introduced on a limited basis in 1986, the kiosks include some 200 Hallmark cards programmed into in-store computers. The interactive system allows customers to insert personal names and messages into prewritten verses. Some 2,000 *Personalize it!* workstations are currently in place in Hallmark Gold Crown stores. *Touchscreen Greetings,* another personalized offering, is in an additional 1,600 locations, including chain drug stores. In mid-1993, Hallmark and its partner Sprint announced Long Distance Greetings, which enable a sender to mail a card that is good for ten minutes of long distance calling in the United States and its territories. In late 1993, Hallmark introduced voice-recorded greeting cards, Hallmark Recordable Greeting Cards, that allow the sender to record a lasting, ten-second message.

## Innovative Advertising Campaigns

Hallmark's reputation for mounting creative advertising campaigns was established as early as 1928, when Joyce Hall wrote his company's first national ad for the *Ladies Home Journal.* While

*Reproduction of an antique greeting card from the Hallmark Historical Collection.*

many of his contemporaries tried to persuade him that people did not consider brand names important when buying greeting cards, Hall persisted, and established Hallmark's reputation.

Ad campaigns of the late 1980s and early 1990s continued to show the same creative flair that marked the earliest forays into the national media. One of the company's most recent successes was a 1990 promotion, in which almost 20 million Shoebox Greetings envelopes were featured in a two-page spread in major magazines. Customers were asked to peel off the envelopes and bring them to their local Hallmark store, where they could be redeemed for a free card. Handled by Hallmark's current primary agency, Leo Burnett, the campaign enjoyed enormous success. Other 1990 campaigns included a test sale of fresh flowers in Hallmark Stores on Valen-

tine's Day, and a cooperative venture between Hallmark and US Sprint Communications Co. for a combined Mother's Day greeting card/free long distance service promotion.

Hallmark's advertising strategy changed dramatically in 1992 to attract recession-weary customers hunting for bargains. For the first time in company history, Hallmark began to convey not only the quality of its products, but their value as well. Among the bargains were a "buy two, get one free" sale of Shoebox Greetings cards, price markdowns on best-selling items, and direct-mail newsletters with cents-off or free coupons for frequent shoppers.

## Future Prospects

While Hallmark holds its first ranked position in the greeting card industry, with an estimated 40 percent of the market, it experienced very slow growth in the early 1990s. In 1991, its revenues grew only one percent, below its target, and also below the growth of Hallmark's two major rivals, Cleveland, Ohio-based American Greetings Corp. and Gibson Greetings of Cincinnati, Ohio.

While the recession is partly to blame for the company's slow growth, analysts point out that another culprit is the growing share of shoppers who buy greeting cards in discount chains, drug stores, and supermarkets, locations in which American Greetings and Gibson have a stronger foothold than Hallmark.

The Greeting Card Association's analysis of card sales by trade channel pointed out that 32 percent of the market is allocated to card and gift shops, while drug stores are a close second, with 26 percent, according to *Supermarket Business.* Supermarkets hold a 17 percent share, while mass merchandisers control 16 percent of the greeting card trade. Supermarkets and drug stores began limiting space for cards, so Hallmark must fight not only with its competitors, but also with retailers of other products for room to display its wares.

Innovative point-of-purchase displays, like Hallmark's Ambassador Cards program, which integrates traditional and alternative cards in a 40-foot section featuring pop-out signs marking cards for a sending occasion, are catching the attention of supermarket card shoppers. At the same time, Hallmark has been experimenting with ways of reorganizing its retail outlets to attract new customers. Among the ideas being tried are special-occasion shops and party-goods stores.

Changes in marketing tactics are also being reflected in Hallmark's investment strategies. The company recently divested its interest in its Spanish-language TV network, and became an active investor in the cable-TV business, with its control of Crown Media, one of the nation's biggest cable companies. By regrouping and by keeping abreast of demographic and social changes in American society, Hallmark will undoubtedly retain its position as the country's leader in the personal communications field.

## Further Reading:

Barach, Arnold D., *Famous American Trademarks,* Washington, DC: Public Affairs Press, 1971.

Bushnell, Victoria, "Harmony's Lieberman Directs Hallmark for Burnett/Chicago," *Back Stage,* December 8, 1989, p. 6.

Butcher, Lola, *Kansas City Business Journal,* "Formula for Future Found in Shoebox at Hallmark," November 8, 1991, p. 1; "Promotion's a

First for Hallmark,'' July 24, 1992, p. 1; ''Hallmark Cards' Agent of Change,'' October 9, 1992, p. 1.

Cleary, David Powers, *Great American Brands: The Success Formulas That Made Them Famous,* New York: Fairchild Publications, 1981.

Fitzgerald, Kate, *Advertising Age,* ''Hallmark Cards Get Personal,'' September 8, 1991; ''Hallmark Scares Up New Ad,'' October 8, 1990, p. 6; ''Hallmark Tries Flower Power to Grow Sales,'' August 13, 1990.

''For the Record . . . '' *Advertising Age,* March 16, 1992, p. 39.

''For the Record . . . '' *Advertising Age,* January 19, 1993, p. 49

''Hallmark Cards Inc. and US Sprint Co. Join Forces to Introduce Card and Long-Distance Call Promotion,'' *Kansas City Business Journal,* November 12, 1990, p. 4.

Hallmark Cards, Inc., press releases, 1992, 1993.

Hallmark Cards, Inc., *This Is Hallmark,* Kansas City, MO: Hallmark Cards, Inc., 1992.

Hammel, Frank, ''Greeting Cards,'' 45th Annual Consumer Expenditures Study, *Supermarket Business,* September 1992, p. 121.

Shore, Harvey, ''To Send the Very Best,'' *Business Quarterly,* March 1987, pp. 16–18.

Stern, Sara E., ''Card Rivals Deal Ads,'' *Advertising Age,* July 27, 1987, p. 28.

''The Envelope, Please,'' *Advertising Age,* July 2, 1990, p. 23.

Voss, Bristol, ''Selling with Sentiment,'' *Sales and Marketing Management,* March 1993, pp. 60–65.

*—Marcia K. Mogelonsky*

# HANES®

The Hanes brand, as part of parent company Sara Lee Corporation's Packaged Consumer Products group, which also includes the well-known L'eggs brand, helps to account for 25 percent of overall corporate sales. By concerted market expansion and differentiation, Sara Lee has parlayed the Hanes brand name far beyond hosiery so that it now encompasses women's and girls' underwear, men's and boys' underwear, bras and other intimate apparel, casual clothing, activewear, socks, gloves, and scarves. The brand-driven strategy has paid off handsomely. For example, Hanes Her Way, a women's panty line introduced in 1986, is now number one in its market. Other new market leaders include Hanes socks and Hanes fleecewear. In addition, Hanes men's and boys' underwear is a strong number two in its market and growing rapidly. Since 1990, all of these Sara Lee Knit Products, Sara Lee Hosiery, and Sara Lee Intimates have benefited from a megabrand advertising campaign that underscores the quality of Hanes products with the phrase ''Nothing Else Feels So Right.'' The highly successful campaign was updated in 1992 as ''Wait'll We Get Our Hanes On You,'' complete with new Hanes logos and such celebrity spokespersons as Phylicia Rashad, Carol Alt, Michael Jordan, and Joe Montana in soft-focus television ads.

## A Family Merger

In 1962 an event unique in American corporate history took place. This was the merger of two North Carolina concerns, P. H. Hanes Knitting Company and Hanes Hosiery Mills Company, a consolidation which brought together for the first and only time two independent, non-competing businesses that shared the same family name. The former company specialized in men's underwear, the latter in women's hosiery. The story of their formation is also unique. During the 1800s, brothers Pleasant Henderson Hanes and John Wesley Hanes launched the P. H. Hanes Tobacco Company and oversaw its development into the third-largest tobacco company in the country. At the turn of the century, due to a serious illness that beset John, the brothers sold the business to R. J. Reynolds Tobacco Company for $175,000. When John recovered, the brothers boldly reentered the business world, this time as autonomous entrepreneurs in the textile industry. John Wesley's business, originally named Shamrock Mills Company, was devoted initially to the manufacture of men's stockings (by 1920, women's hosiery had become the company's sole product). Pleasant's firm (of which his sons, Will and P. Huber, were principals)

concerned itself with the creation of a new type of knitwear, men's heavy-weight, two-piece underwear.

In 1914, the same year in which Shamrock Mills changed names, P. H. Hanes Knitting introduced the red Hanes shield logo on its underwear, arguably creating the first branded product in the industry (Jockey's little-known predecessor was touted in a 1911 national ad campaign as the Kenosha Klosed Krotch, though a brand name was not affixed to the product.) In the decades that immediately followed, the Hanes brand became important to the company's growth, though probably less so than the company's start-to-finish capabilities, which included everything from yarn manufacture to distribution. After the death of Pleasant in 1925, P. Huber assumed control of Hanes Knitting and expanded production to include men's, women's, and children's knitted shirts as well as sleepwear, briefs, and undershirts. According to ''The History of the Hanes Brand Name,'' both Hanes Knitting and Hanes Hosiery ''went to extremes to assure that when customers bought their products, they received the finest quality for a reasonable price. To consumers, the name Hanes meant one company, whether the product was hosiery or underwear.''

## L'eggs' Lift

Thus the creation of Hanes Corporation was the natural, if belated, direction to take. Interestingly, the two Hanes companies were roughly the same in size, with each then enjoying annual sales of approximately $50 million. Much of the first decade of Hanes Corporation was characterized by slow growth and sporadic profits. By 1970, sales had grown to just $157 million. Part of the explanation for this may have stemmed from the company's cautious approach to advertising and promotion, an expense limited to just 5 percent of sales at the time. Then came the introduction of the L'eggs brand.

The brainchild of Hanes executive (and later president) Robert Elberson, the idea for L'eggs pantyhose arose from a need to transform Hanes Corporation from a struggling apparel manufacturer to a top-performing consumer goods firm. When the product was test-marketed in the spring of 1970, the timing could not have been better, for the hosiery market was then highly fragmented and plagued with out-of-stock problems. Because of the brand's phenomenal, instantaneous appeal, the national rollout was quickly accelerated. In the process, Hanes became an aggressive marketer and by 1975 was spending $42 million, or 13 percent of

## AT A GLANCE

**H**anes brand of underwear founded in 1914 in Winston, NC (forerunner of Winston-Salem, NC), by Pleasant H. Hanes, owner of P. H. Hanes Knitting Company; P. H. Hanes Knitting Company merged with Hanes Hosiery Mills Company, founded as Shamrock Mills Company by brother John Wesley Hanes, to form Hanes Corporation, 1962; with development of L'eggs brand pantyhose in 1970, Hanes Corporation moved into consumer goods market; Hanes Corporation purchased by Consolidated Foods, 1979; Consolidated Foods renamed Sara Lee Corporation, 1985.

*Performance:* *Market share*—44% (combined top dollar share with L'eggs) of U.S. hosiery sales to department and specialty stores; 30% (middle share) of men's and boy's underwear category; 19% (top share) of women's and girls' underwear category. *Sales*—$1.3 billion.

*Major competitor:* Fruit of the Loom.

*Advertising:* *Agency*—Lintas/Long, Haymes & Carr. *Major campaign*—"Wait'll We Get Our Hanes On You."

*Addresses:* *Parent company*—Sara Lee Corporation, 3 First National Plaza, Chicago, IL 60602; phone: (312) 726-2600; fax: (312) 558-8567.

sales, on advertising; in essence, the company had risen within a five-year span to the top of the industry in terms of marketing prestige.

Ironically, the resounding success of L'eggs pantyhose served to relegate the Hanes brand name, at least for a while, to secondary status. This gradually changed as the company began to place equal emphasis on its Hanes-label hosiery, which Elberson described for *Advertising Age* in 1977 as "the Cadillac of pantyhose brands." During this period—and, in fact, until the end of the 1980s—Hanes hosiery was supported by the "Gentlemen Prefer Hanes" campaign.

### Hanes Enters the Consolidated Foods Fold

While Hanes was busy refashioning itself, giant Chicago-based Consolidated Foods Corporation was fast becoming a major player in the apparel industry through a number of key acquisitions, beginning with Gant shirts in the mid-1960s. On the whole, Consolidated's apparel group did not perform well during the 1970s. However, in September 1978, *Business Week* reported that the company, under CEO John H. Bryan was "courting women's hosiery leader Hanes Corp. with uncharacteristic ardor" and had purchased 20 percent of Hanes's common stock. The takeover move was initially rebuffed by Hanes, which was nearing the $450-million mark in sales, but ultimately accepted.

With the solid backing of Consolidated Foods (which was renamed Sara Lee Corporation in 1985), Hanes was poised by 1980 to spend more than $100 million on advertising and thus catapult itself into the elite ranks of the nation's top 50 advertisers. Since that time, Hanes has become a megabrand through product differentiation. In 1982 Hanes products, including L'eggs, accounted for $1 billion of Consolidated Foods' $6 billion in sales. Although growth became more difficult in the 1980s due to market share battles and a shrinking demand for hosiery, Hanes brand sales had risen to $1.3 billion by 1992. More significantly, Hanes

and Sara Lee had indisputably become the company's flagship brands.

### Soft Sell Follows Hard-Minded Inspector 12

Although long synonymous with the Hanes name, men's underwear was a company segment that had been largely overshadowed by women's hosiery since the merger. The underwear line was further obscured by the stellar successes of Jockey and Calvin Klein in specialty department stores and Fruit of the Loom in mass merchandise outlets. In 1987 Hanes renewed its men's and boys' market with a feisty, irresistible campaign featuring a grey-haired spokeswoman known simply as Inspector 12. Although conventional wisdom said that underwear for males was primarily a commodity product, the purchase of which was influenced primarily by price, Hanes executives realized that this was becoming less and less true due to the advertising leadership of Jockey. The company needed to take market share away from Fruit of the Loom—still the biggest seller of men's briefs—while upholding the stature of the Hanes brand through mid-pricing and an emphasis on product quality and comfort.

In inimitable fashion, Inspector 12 stressed that Hanes underwear had superior construction, fit better, and shrank less than its competitor. Fruit of the Loom retaliated with its own superiority ads, but not before Hanes was able to increase its market share from 18 percent in 1986 to 23 percent in 1987. A lawsuit by Fruit of the Loom led to an out-of-court settlement and the end of the contentious ads on both sides. The competition, nonetheless, continued to be fierce. As Rebecca Fannin wrote in *Marketing & Media Decisions,* "Both Fruit of the Loom and Hanes promise a duel to the death." In 1988, Hanes acquired the promotional services of basketball hero Michael Jordan and football star Boomer Esiason. Accordingly, Hanes's media buys have centered around major sports events, including the Super Bowl. Periodic price discounting and the introduction of new colors and styles that mimic the department store labels have rounded out the Hanes underwear strategy. Hanes continues to be the fastest-growing major underwear label in the country.

### The Gentleman Prefers

From 1977 to 1989 the "Gentlemen Prefer Hanes" campaign, with its memorable "smooth and silky—sexy, shapely" jingle defined Hanes as a premium brand of hosiery. The campaign was replaced with an updated, 1990s format that unequivocally spotlighted the confident, informed decision-making of women, rather than men. This new campaign, entitled "The Lady Prefers Hanes," was designed to build department store hosiery volume and accent such brand extensions as Hanes Ultra Silk, Silk Reflections, Hanes Alive, and Alive Lights. "Nothing Else Feels So Right" and the "Wait'll We Get Our Hanes On You" Lifestyle series of integrated ads have also helped highlight Hanes' women's and girls' products while intermingling them with the men's and boys' wear.

### Nobody Does It Like Sara Lee

In the fall of 1991, Sara Lee acquired Playtex Apparel, a $480-million powerhouse. According to Karyn Monget in *Women's Wear Daily,* "The merger rattled much of the innerwear community with the dominant position it gave Sara Lee in the field." Since then, Sara Lee has fortified its intimates, knit products, and hosiery groups through big ad spending, other acquisitions, expansion of its European markets, and ongoing brand extensions.

Regarding the last, Sara Lee required that first-year dollar volume for new products be in the $10 million to $20 million range before longer commitments are made. Not all Hanes products meet this test, despite high performance reviews. One such example is Hanes Silk Reflections Lingerie, a line which failed to attract a large enough niche at the department store level. Hanes Her Way Cotton Casuals for girls, on the other hand, were successfully introduced at mass-merchandise outlets in 1992. Consequently, the line will be further expanded in 1993. Perhaps the best news for Hanes, as it looks to the future, is that its parent company is in excellent health. At the end of fiscal 1992, Sara Lee boasted its lowest debt-to-capital ratio in 15 years (29 percent). That means more money for building brand awareness and boosting market share, two areas in which Hanes has long excelled.

## Further Reading:

Baltera, Lorraine, "Hanes Pulls up Its Socks, Strides into Cosmetics," *Advertising Age,* May 16, 1977, p. 44.

Barrett, Amy, "John H. Bryan," *Financial World,* April 3, 1990, p. 76.

Bernstein, Henry R., "Hanes' Plans Will Put It Among Top 50 Advertisers," *Advertising Age,* March 24, 1980, p. 28.

Bird, Laura, "Hanes," *Wall Street Journal,* March 5, 1992, p. B5.

"Consolidated Foods Hungers for Hanes," *Business Week,* September 25, 1978, pp. 54–5.

Curtis, Carol E., "Nothing Beats a Great Pair of L'eggs," *Forbes,* September 29, 1980, pp. 72–3.

David, Gregory E., "Sara Lee: Humbled Pie," *Financial World,* August 3, 1993, p. 16.

Delamaide, Darrell, "Hanes Set to Fashion Smart Profits Comeback," *Barron's,* October 6, 1975, pp. 64–5.

Fannin, Rebecca, "Underwear Inspector 12 Takes on the Fruits," *Marketing & Media Decisions,* April 1988, pp. 55–6, 58, 60.

"Hanes Expands L'eggs to the Entire Family," *Business Week,* June 14, 1976, pp. 57, 61.

"The History of the Hanes Brand Name," Winston-Salem, N.C.: Sara Lee Corporation, 1990.

"A Lift from Hanes," *Barron's,* May 5, 1980, pp. 45, 49.

McGough, Robert, "Icing on the Cake," *Financial World,* October 17, 1989, pp. 22–4.

Monget, Karyn, "Designer Push Clicks at Hanes," *Women's Wear Daily,* May 24, 1990, p. 10; "Sara Lee Intimates: Making It With Mega-brands," *Women's Wear Daily,* May 13, 1993, pp. 4–5.

Moskowitz, Milton, Robert Levering, and Michael Katz, eds., "Sara Lee," *Everybody's Business: A Field Guide to the 400 Leading Companies in America,* New York: Doubleday, 1990.

Newcomb, Peter and Liz Comte, "You Want Michael Jordan? You Gotta Take Boomer Esiason," *Forbes,* November 23, 1992, pp. 96–7, 100–01.

Newman, Jill, "In the Markets: Hanes Hosiery Revamps Sales Effort," *Women's Wear Daily,* June 26, 1992, p. 13.

"Pantyhose Through a Pipeline: Elberson of Hanes Corp.," *Forbes,* May 15, 1975, p. 122.

"Sara Lee Apparel Units Sign Olympic Games Pacts," *Wall Street Journal,* February 8, 1993, p. B2.

"Sara Lee Buys Italian Hosiery Manufacturer," *Women's Wear Daily,* June 2, 1993, p. 15.

"Sara Lee Knit Products: A History of Quality," Winston-Salem, NC: Sara Lee Corporation, 1991.

"Sara Lee: The Master Hand at Branding Global Textiles," *Textile World,* June 1991, pp. 38–40, 43, 45–6.

Sharoff, Robert, "Sara Lee Predicts Huge Growth for Hanes, Champion Divisions," *Daily News Record,* October 30, 1992, p. 2.

Slutsker, Gary, "The Naked Truth," *Forbes,* August 16, 1993, p. 94.

Walash, Eileen R., "New Ad Focus at Hanes: What Do Women Want?" *Women's Wear Daily,* September 21, 1989, p. 6.

Walden, Gene, "Sara Lee Corporation," *The 100 Best Stocks to Own in America,* 2nd ed., Chicago: Dearborn Financial Publishing, Inc., 1991, pp. 28–31.

—*Jay P. Pederson*

# HATHAWAY®

# Hathaway®

Hathaway®

For over 155 years, Hathaway Shirts have been known for their high quality and traditional, classic style. The C.F. Hathaway Company was created in 1837 in the Waterville, Maine parlor room residence of Charles Foster Hathaway, who, when not engaged in the worldly pursuits of his shirt business, was a practicing Baptist preacher. His religious vocation often conflicted with his secular aspirations. For example, though Hathaway forbade his wife, Temperance, to wear buttons on her clothes because they were too ornamental, he designed men's shirts with elaborate frills and ruffles. Despite this tension, Hathaway created what was to become one of the more successful, widely recognized shirt brands in the United States.

Hathaway shirts has survived in a volatile industry renown for its alternating periods of prosperity and decline. Since its creation, the brand has undergone numerous ownership changes; yet the brand has managed to retain its distinctive trade label and reputation for product innovation attuned to the latest in fashion changes. After a turbulent period that left the brand teetering on the brink of bankruptcy, Hathaway was purchased in early 1960 by an investment group headed by Samuel J. Holtzman of the Baltimore Luggage Company. Later that year, Hathaway was purchased by the women's apparel division of Warner Brothers Company. Established in 1874, Warner Brothers Company was renamed Warnaco in 1967. In a highly acrimonious affair, the family-owned and managed Warnaco company was acquired in April of 1986 by an outside investment group and renamed The Warnaco Group Inc.

## Brand History

Charles Hathaway was the second born in a family of ten children. With little or no formal education, he went to work in a nail factory at the age of eleven and was employed as a printer for the publishers of *Webster's Dictionary* by the time he turned fifteen. It is not at all clear where he developed his flair for fashion. However, in 1837 Hathaway began his shirtmaking business in his house in Waterville, Maine. He had previously worked in two shirtmaking operations in Plymouth and Boston, Massachusetts, but left them because of their abominable "sweatshop conditions." Hathaway employed workers from farms in the Waterville area. The workers stayed at Hathaway's home where the sewing and ironing of shirts was performed entirely by hand. The workers typically produced two dozen shirts in a week, and Hathaway

arranged the workload so that the workers could return home in time to observe the Sabbath. Besides seeing to his workers' material needs, Hathaway also administered to their spiritual needs by leading them through hymns and prayers prior to the start of each working day.

Every two or three months Hathaway would deliver his shirts to his own men's furnishing store in Boston. As the shirts gained in popularity, other stores began to peddle Hathaway's merchandise. By 1853 Hathaway had earned enough from shirt sales to finance the purchase of an acre of land for $900 and build a new shirt factory that was to remain in production for over 100 years. It was at this site, on the eve of the Civil War, that Hathaway first installed sewing machines that, shortly thereafter, were put to use making shirts for the Union Army.

Despite his best intentions, Hathaway's quarrelsome personality strained his relationships with those whom he associated with in both religious and secular engagements. He bickered constantly with his employees over wages and with several business partners over finances. He frequently fought with Baptist pastors over spiritual issues, and threatened to leave the Baptist Church and start his own following. From 1872 until his death in 1893, the asset value of Hathaway's shirtmaking operations had risen from $58,000 to $100,000. Hathaway, due to the efforts of his wife, Temperance, reconciled his differences with the Baptist Church and bequeathed his entire business to the Baptist Missionary Society.

Immediately thereafter, the company was sold to Clarence A. Leighton, an entrepreneurial-minded Hathaway salesman. Under Leighton's ownership, the brand's shirts became far more successful. The reason, according to one of Hathaway's biographers, was because Leighton was "more of a salesman and less of a minister." Whatever the case, Leighton proved adept at interpreting the latest fashions and incorporated these into his shirt designs. He discarded the styles featuring frills and ruffles and replaced them with the then fashionable full-length starched bosom and cuff shirt. When Leighton passed away in 1915, his son Edward and Frank Smith began running the company. By 1920, weekly production at the Waterville plant reached seven hundred dozen shirts.

During World War I Hathaway was engaged in the production of work-related, collar-attached khaki military shirts. The com-

## AT A GLANCE

Hathaway brand of shirts created in 1837 by Charles Foster Hathaway, owner of the C.F. Hathaway Company; company bequeathed to the Baptist Missionary Society, 1893; sold to Clarence A. Leighton, 1893; controlling interest purchased by Ellerton Jette and Charles McCarthy, 1933; sold to investment group headed by Samuel J. Holtzman of Baltimore Luggage Company, 1960; resold the same year and became a subsidiary of ultimate parent, Warner Brothers Company; Warner renamed Warnaco, 1967; Warnaco acquired and renamed The Warnaco Group, Inc., 1986.

**Major competitor:** Arrow; also Van Heusen.

**Addresses:** *Parent company*—C.F. Hathaway Company, 90 Park Avenue, New York, NY 10016; phone: (212) 370-8222; fax: (212) 370-0832. *Ultimate parent company*—The Warnaco Group, Inc., 90 Park Avenue, New York, NY 10016; phone: (212) 370-8222; fax: (212) 370-0832.

fortable experience of wearing collar-attached shirts left a lasting impression on the returning veterans. Immediately following World War I the collar-attached shirt, featuring an assortment of colors and stripes, became an instant hit. Almost overnight the traditional stiff-bosom white shirt, which was made with an irritating starched neckband to which the wearer fastened a stiff collar, vanished from the scene. Many of the older shirt companies were slow to recognize this as a permanent change in the men's shirt industry and eventually went out of business. Hathaway, however, seized the day and moved to the industry's forefront by offering the new style in a line of stylish colors.

By the late 1920s and early 1930s the Great Depression reversed Hathaway's climb to success. Total shirt sales fell dramatically, plunging from $600,000 to $125,000, and Edward Leighton gave serious thought to closing up the business. Just when all seemed lost, Ellerton Jette and his partner Charles McCarthy offered to buy the company. The two partners had previously worked as salesmen for the Buffalo Shirt Company and wanted to run their own business. Jette and McCarthy believed that Hathaway's established name and reputation would carry the company through the difficult financial times. Leighton sold the business for a very low price, and Jette and McCarthy agreed to assume all of Hathaway's debts and risks. McCarthy focused on the financial aspects of the business, while Jette developed the brand's styles. Jette's fashion ideas, design innovation and flamboyant salesmanship made him a leading industry figure. Under the guidance of Jette and McCarthy, the company's fortunes were revived and Hathaway shirts regained their position as a leading brand of shirts.

A series of questionable business acquisitions undertaken by Jette left the company with a huge inventory of unsold shirts in 1958. Hathaway's was on the verge of bankruptcy before its creditors intervened to restore order. As a result, Jette was moved outside of operations and given the ceremonial position of chairman. Vincent J. McDermott became president and chief executive officer of the company and, along with the banks, took control of the company's finances. In 1960, with the company back on its feet, Hathaway was sold to an investment group headed by Samuel J. Holtzman. Later that year Hathaway was sold to Warner Brothers Co., which was subsequently renamed Warnaco in 1967. Fol-

lowing a successful hostile takeover bid, the company's name was changed to The Warnaco Group, Inc., in 1986.

## Brand Development and Structure

Despite its popularity, the collar-attached shirt was not without faults. Fashionably, the most striking drawback was the tendency of the shirt's collar points to turn up, regardless of whether they had been fully-starched, soft or fused. Hathaway provided a partial solution when it designed and placed a removable celluloid strip down the front inside edge of the collar. The finishing touch was applied when Hathaway came out with a collar pin that held the points in place. A later invention, the bi-angle collar, introduced by Hathaway, solved the problem and eventually superseded the need for collar pins.

Despite his poor financial investments, Ellerton Jette had an enormous impact on the men's fashion industry. In 1937, Jette and the designer Ashley Logan, brought to the attention of the apparel industry the fact that a man's neck tended to pitch forward from the shoulder and was not round but oval shaped. Their discovery prompted the design of a new collar that was fitted to the natural contours of the neck. This design soon became an industry standard. Jette is also credited with developing the single-needle technique used in manufacturing Hathaway shirts, which, in his expert opinion, produced a shirt of superior quality. Additional innovations attributed to Jette include sleeves made from a single piece of cloth, square-cornered cuffs, and the three-hole button, which proved more durable and was thought to be more fashionable than the industry standard four-hole button. Jette's penchant for travel brought him into contact with many exotic fabrics, which he later incorporated into the Hathaway product line. From India he brought madras, gingham from Scotland, prints from France, Viyella from England, and broadcloth from Japan.

During the late 1960s and early 1970s the iconoclast-influenced "unconventional look" was reshaping the fashion world. New companies were becoming extremely successful in selling clothing with unconventional designs. In response to this trend Hathaway created "Hathaway Other-wear," which featured "offbeat" shirts for men, and a "Hathaway Patch" line for women. By 1976, however, both the Patch and Other-wear labels were struggling and Warnaco ceased their production. During this time Hathaway also introduced a line of apparel in the burgeoning sportswear market. Under its Warnaco parent company, Hathaway produced Jack Nicklaus Golden Bear sportswear and manufactured Christian Dior shirts.

Two Hathaway trademarks, first introduced in the 1930s, could still be found on shirts produced in the 1990s. Jette's aforementioned three-hole button shirt demonstrated greater durability than the more conventional four-hole type because the securing stitch avoided puncturing the fabric twice along the same weave. The other permanent feature came in the form of an embroidered red "H." This was originally sewn onto the gussets, (where the front and back of shirts meet) and was later placed on the extra long tail of every Hathaway shirt. Throughout the 1970s, research and development focused on ways of improving shirt styles, providing a better fitting and comfortable shirt, enhancing shirt durability and using new fabrics, treatments and efficient manufacturing methods.

The actual process of manufacturing a Hathaway shirt begins with the arrival of fabrics to the company's Waterville plant. Given Warnaco's extensive worldwide sourcing network, Hathaway shirts are made from top quality materials supplied by fabric mills located throughout the world. These fabrics are given one final inspection to determine whether Hathaway's standards for high quality, comfort and durability are met. Computer-traced patterns cut by advanced machines are used to produce a precise fit, eliminate waste, and raise productivity. According to a Hathaway company document printed in 1987, a shirt passes through 47 individual operations before its production is completed. Along the way, Hathaway utilizes a single-needle tailoring process for flat, smooth and strong seams. All shirt collars are turned by hand and where collars, cuffs and pockets meet with other fabrics, Hathaway shirtmakers hand-match fabrics to guarantee that pin stripes and check patterns are perfectly aligned.

## Early and Recent Advertising

During the early period of the brand's existence most of the company's advertising efforts were confined to small newspaper ads and retail signage. Typical retail signage was found on store facades, windows and interior walls. The signs featured simply the Hathaway named printed over a contrasting color background. It was the creative genius of Ellerton Jette that dramatically changed Hathaway's low-profile advertising approach and elevated it to a national level. Working in collaboration with David Ogilvy, Jette ran an advertisement which appeared in the *New Yorker* on September 22, 1951. The ad featured a White Russian expatriate named Baron George Wrangell wearing an eye patch accompanied by a headline that read "The Man in the Hathaway shirt." Ogilvy photographed Wrangell in a context meant to invoke an image of culture, wealth and European-styled elegance. For the next four years the ad would only appear in the *New Yorker*. Despite its limited exposure, the ad's unprecedented notoriety served to thrust Hathaway shirts into the national spotlight. According to Hal Morgan in *Symbols of America,* the campaign was largely responsible for tripling sales of Hathaway shirts.

Since then, "The Man in the Hathaway Shirt" campaign has featured popular men who have achieved fortune and fame in business, entertainment, politics, science and sports. The Baron Wrangell ads ceased in 1963 and were followed by ads that featured Colin Leslie Fox, renown for his solo transoceanic sailing voyages. The next "Hathaway man" was Clark Halstead, a wealthy real estate executive. Other subsequent notables included: sportsmen and television mogul Ted Turner; J.W. Marriott Jr., hotel industry magnate; John Connally, Texas businessman and

politician; and Pete Dawkins, whose various accomplishments range from Heisman Trophy Winner, to Rhodes Scholar, to Brigadier General and Wall Street investor. These ads were commonly placed in men's magazines, on outdoor billboards, or as poster displays in large metropolitan airports or commuter stations.

## Future Trends

Since the mid-1980s the men's shirt industry has experienced intense price competition and declining profit margins, downsizing, bankruptcies and leveraged buyouts. At the retail level negative forces were generated as traditional customers, like major department stores, either fell into bankruptcy, were reorganized, or shifted from brand name to private label merchandise.

By 1993 many of these negative pressures were reversed. A sense of stability returned to the apparel industry and analysts issued guardedly optimistic forecasts. The forecast for Hathaway, however, remained slightly questionable as its parent company Warnaco was still feeling the aftershocks of its leveraged buyout status. Since the time of its acquisition, Warnaco has financed its growth with only $70 million per year in working capital while paying out over $600 million in cash for interest, debt principal and preferred stock dividends. The company's limited availability of cash could impair attempts that Hathaway might undertake to gain market share through advertising campaigns.

## Further Reading:

Arnold, Pauline, and Percival White, *Clothes and Cloth: America's Appeal Business,* New York: Holiday House, 1961.

Ciampi, Thomas, "Warnaco Men's Sales Decline 7.9% in 1991," *Daily News Record,* March 12, 1992, p. 12.

Fields, John W., *Fig Leaves and Fortunes,* West Kennebunk, ME: Phoenix Publishing, 1990.

MacIntosh, Jeane, "Warnaco Men's Biz Returns to Black," *Daily News Record,* July 30, 1992, p. 2.

Morgan, Hal, *Symbols of America,* New York: Penguin Books, 1986.

Ryan, Thomas, "Men's Biz a Dynamo at Warnaco," *Daily News Record,* May 15, 1992, p.1.

*The One Hundred Fiftieth Anniversary of the C.F. Hathaway Company,* New York: C.F. Hathaway Company, 1987.

Rappaport, S. E., *Warnaco Company Report,* Morgan Stanley & Co., Inc., July 23, 1992.

Vernon, R. Hutchings, "Mother of All Annual Meetings," *Barron's,* May 6, 1991, p. 32.

—*Daniel E. King*

# HAWAIIAN TROPIC®

In the early 1990s, Hawaiian Tropic was the second best-selling brand of suntan and sun-protection products in the United States and a leading brand in the international market. Hawaiian Tropic brand products, manufactured in plants in five countries, included 90 different formulations of suntan oils and lotions, tanning gels, sunblock lotions, lip balms, and skin moisturizers. Parent company Tanning Research Laboratories also licensed the Hawaiian Tropic brand name for use on swimwear, T-shirts, hats, sunglasses, watches, and other merchandise that was sold through retail stores, and Hawaiian Tropic swimwear was sold by mail order.

## Brand Origins

Ron Rice, the founder of the Hawaiian Tropic brand, Tanning Research Laboratories, and chairman of the company in 1993, may be the only person to know the true story of the origin of Hawaiian Tropic suntan and sun-protection products. According to Hawaiian Tropic promotional material, Rice, a Daytona Beach, Florida, high school chemistry teacher and part-time lifeguard, was inspired to create a new suntan lotion while vacationing in Hawaii. Rice noticed sunbathers using a combination of natural oils to deepen their tans and protect their skin from sunburn. After returning from his trip, he supposedly borrowed $500 from his father and began mixing suntan oil in a garbage-can factory set-up in his garage. However, Rice often omitted the story about the Hawaiian vacation in interviews and offered a more prosaic account of Hawaiian Tropic's beginnings. Although he had visited Hawaii, he once told the *Daytona News-Journal* that he decided to "do something better" while lifeguarding on Daytona Beach, "I thought I would sell a few bottles. That was the extent of it."

According to most accounts, the 25-year-old Rice bought a 20-gallon garbage can in 1966 and hired three neighborhood children to mix batches of coconut, avocado, papaya, guava, and other natural oils and pour it into bottles. Rice peddled the bottles on the beach and at swimming pools, returning to his garage at night to experiment with new formulas based on the suggestions of tourists who used his suntan oil. However, according to *Florida Trend,* one of the original Hawaiian Tropic formulas was developed by a Miami chemist hired by Rice. According to the magazine, Rice asked the chemist to create a mixture that would bring the Hawaiian Islands to mind when it was applied. The chemist used coconut oil to provide a tropical scent.

Rice, a native of North Carolina and graduate of the University of Tennessee, originally called his product Tropic Tan. Since a New Jersey company had already copyrighted the name, Rice renamed the product Hawaiian Tropic and founded Tanning Research Laboratories in 1969. According to Tanning Research Laboratories, Inc., Hawaiian Tropic was the first suntan product to use coconut and banana fragrances in its lotions and oils and was the first to include natural moisturizers.

## Marketing

Selling suntan lotion to beach supply stores near his home in Florida was a sideline for Rice at first, but the business proved to be profitable. Using his contacts as a football coach, Rice recruited other coaches to sell his mixture to high school students, some as far north as Myrtle Beach, South Carolina. A friend from college began selling Hawaiian Tropic at a lake resort in Kentucky, although Rice doubted there was enough sunshine to create a strong demand. He later told *Florida Trend,* "Everyday the guy would call back and increase the order. He had sold $1,000 in two days and didn't even have a sample."

By 1970 Rice had moved his factory out of his garage and into rented space in a Port Orange, Florida, service station, although he continued to employ neighborhood kids to mix the oils and fill bottles. In 1972 Rice's Tanning Research Laboratories, whose only products were Hawaiian Tropic oils and lotions, boasted sales of $4 million, and Rice quit his teaching job to devote himself full time to selling suntan lotion.

A year later Bristol-Myers stopped marketing a suntan lotion called Tanya Hawaii, which it had been advertising heavily. Rice's company, now headquartered in an old building in Daytona Beach, reaped the benefits of people looking for a "tropical" suntan product.

Rice summarized his marketing strategy for Hawaiian Tropic in an interview with *Tampa Tribune* in 1981, telling the newspaper, "Suntan is sex . . . that's what it all boils down to. Sex and vanity." In the 1970s Rice cultivated this image by surrounding himself and his products with bikini-clad young women, carefully nurturing a Hawaiian Tropic mystique. Company literature touted Rice's sybaritic lifestyle, which included fast cars, wild parties, and a $5 million oceanfront home in Daytona Beach that had three swimming pools and a television room with 56 screens.

## AT A GLANCE

**H**awaiian Tropic brand of suntan lotion created in 1966 by Ron Rice; parent company Tanning Research Laboratories, Inc., founded in 1969.

*Performance:* *Market share*—20% of suntan, sunblock, and after-sun product market.

*Major competitor:* Schering-Plough's Coppertone.

*Advertising:* *Agency*—In-house. *Major campaign*—"Escape to the Islands" sweepstakes.

*Addresses:* *Parent company*—Tanning Research Laboratories, Inc., P.O. Box 5111, Daytona Beach, FL 32118; phone: (904) 677-9559; fax: (904) 677-9595.

Hawaiian Tropic also sponsored beauty contests, rock concerts, and sporting events—especially beach volleyball and car races. A controversial billboard in the mid 1970s showed a deeply tanned woman lying on her back; to the viewers eyes it appeared that she was wearing no bikini bottoms. However, her leg was bent to reveal no nudity. The billboard prompted a flood of outraged complaints, but Rice told *Florida Trend* the letters were signed by women with names like Gertrude and Hortense who ''didn't buy my product anyway.'' A bikini bottom was later added to the billboard.

Although Hawaiian Tropic adopted a less steamy image in the 1980s, with products and advertising directed toward families, there were still plenty of beautiful, bikini-clad women in company literature. Hawaiian Tropic also continued to sponsor the Miss Hawaiian Tropic International Pageant. A corporate biography of Rice in 1993 said the 50-year-old ''jet-setting, multi-millionaire'' was ''the epitome of the American Dream [with] palatial home, car races, celebrity ski tournaments, beauty pageants, and much more.'' In the 1980s, Tanning Research Laboratories began paying inclusion fees for Hawaiian Tropic brand products to appear prominently in many youth-oriented movies that included beach scenes.

Hawaiian Tropic also scored early with its distinctive plastic bottles, which sunbathers preferred over the glass bottles then used by most other brands. Stephen Michaels, then Hawaiian Tropic advertising manager, told *New York* magazine in 1983, ''We came out with fancy packaging and eye-catching displays of thatched roofs and island girls and built a tropical image around places people dream of going to. And we came out at the right time.'' Rice originally purchased the shatter-proof bottles from a local supplier. Hawaiian Tropic began producing its own bottles in 1976. In the early 1990s, Tanning Research Laboratories was producing 26 million moulded Hawaiian Tropic bottles per year in more than 30 different shapes and sizes. The colorful Hawaiian Tropic graphics, also produced in-house, were printed in ten languages.

### Suntan Preparations

Tanning is produced by the effect of ultraviolet radiation, an invisible form of light, on normal skin cells. The cells react by producing a dark pigment called melanin, which helps protect the skin from damage. Until the early part of the 20th century, only field laborers acquired deep tans, and white skin was a status symbol for the upper classes. Recreational tanning became popu-

lar in the United States during the 1930s as vacations to the beach became more common and swimsuits began to reveal more skin. By the 1950s a dark tan had become synonymous with youthful health and vigor. However, research in the 1970s proved that tanning was far from healthy. Overexposure to ultraviolet radiation caused wrinkles, premature aging, and skin cancers, including a particularly deadly form of skin cancer known as malignant melanoma. In 1992 the Skin Cancer Foundation estimated that 90 percent of all skin cancer was caused by ultraviolet radiation. Hawaiian Tropic addressed this issue by joining the Skin Cancer Foundation and submitting their products for intense testing. Consequently, all Hawaiian Tropic products with an SPF of 15 and above now carry the seal of the Skin Cancer Foundation.

Dr. Benjamin Green, a Miami Beach physician, created the first commercial suntan preparation in 1944. Green was one of several doctors who worked with the U.S. government in the early 1940s to develop red petrolatum, a petroleum-based sunblock that was issued to Army Air Corps fliers who risked exposure to the harsh tropical sun if they were shot down over the South Pacific. Green also experimented with formulas for a tanning lotion containing cocoa butter, which he mixed on a stove at his home and tested on his own bald head. He named his concoction Coppertone Suntan Cream and promoted the jasmine-scented lotion with the slogan ''Don't be a paleface.'' Thousands of U.S. servicemen in the South Pacific used Coppertone during World War II. The brand was eventually acquired by the Schering-Plough Corporation and was the leading brand of tanning and sun-protection products in the early 1990s.

In 1978 the Food and Drug Administration proposed a rating system, originally developed by Coppertone, for measuring the effectiveness of various oils and lotions to protect a sunbather's skin from damaging ultraviolet radiation. The numbering system, readily adopted by other makers of suntan products, was based on a Sun Protection Factor, or SPF. The higher the SPF rating the more protection the product offered. Theoretically, a person whose skin normally burned after 15 minutes in direct sunlight could stay out for an hour before burning using a product with an SPF of 4. A product with an SPF of 15 or greater allowed almost no tanning. In the 1980s researchers also began differentiating between two types of ultraviolet radiation, known as UVA and UVB. The SPF rating referred only to UVB radiation, which caused sunburns during high intensity summer months. UVA radiation did not cause sunburn, but was relatively constant throughout the year and was considered a cause of premature aging and wrinkles.

Until the late 1980s, the most common ultraviolet-absorbing chemical in suntan lotions, including Hawaiian Tropic, was para-aminobenzoic acid, known as PABA. However, many people were sensitive to PABA, and the chemical was removed from major brands. Hawaiian Tropic eliminated PABA from its products in 1987.

### Brand Extensions

In the early 1990s Tanning Research Laboratories offered a complete line of Hawaiian Tropic brand suntan, sun-protection, and skin-care products. Suntan products included gels, oils, and lotions with SPF ratings of zero to six. The Hawaiian Tropic Plus line of ultraviolet-protection products included gels and lotions with SPF ratings of eight to 45, and three flavors of lip balms with an SPF of 15. Hawaiian Tropic products were the first to offer an

SPF greater than 15. Skin-care products contained aloe vera-based moisturizers for use after exposure to the sun.

Hawaiian Tropic literature urged sunbathers to practice "safe sunning," which meant tanning gradually, using a product with a high SPF rating to start, and gradually reducing the SPF level as the skin increased its natural melanin. The company noted that 90 percent of Hawaiian Tropic's customers "still seek a tan, [so] Hawaiian Tropic has strived to maintain that delicate balance between tanning and good, sound sun protection." But critics complained that Hawaiian Tropic encouraged harmful exposure to ultraviolet radiation by depicting deeply tanned models in its ads.

In 1986 Hawaiian Tropic introduced a line of sunblock products specifically designed for young children and infants, although the company said the nonstinging, waterproof formulas were also suitable for adults who wanted to baby their skin. Hawaiian Tropic Baby Faces included gels and lotions with SPF ratings from 20 to 50, which was the highest SPF available. In late 1993 Hawaiian Tropic also offered a line of self-tanning products and two nonrunning, waterproof products designed for the sports market, Sport Sunblock 30 and Sport Sunblock 15. Another new product introduction was an older children's product named Just For Kids in two formulas—30 SPF and 45 SPF.

Self-tanning products, which created the appearance of a tan without exposing the skin to ultraviolet radiation, were the fastest growing segment of the suntan lotion industry, increasing more than 50 percent from 1991 to 1992. Hawaiian Tropic offered a line of four self-tanning products, including Self Tanning Sunblock with an SPF of 15. Coppertone introduced the first self-tanning product in the 1960s with Coppertone QT, but early products were dyes that often streaked and left the skin with an orange tinge. Newer products used a clear chemical dye that bonded to proteins in skin and changed color gradually.

## Forecast

The outlook for Hawaiian Tropic appeared strong in the early 1990s, especially as the product line was expanded to meet the needs of people who wanted to avoid overexposure to the sun's damaging ultraviolet radiation, as well as those who desired a deep tan. A study conducted by Opinion Research Corporation for the American Academy of Dermatology in the late 1980s revealed that half of all teenagers and a third of all adults intentionally work on getting a tan. However, more than three fourths of all adults also used some protection to avoid overexposure. Products with an SPF rating of five or more accounted for 65 percent of the market for suntan oils and lotions in 1992.

Parents were also buying more suntan or sun-protection products for their children because of heavy advertising and concerns about the effects of ultraviolet radiation. The Skin Cancer Foundation predicted that the incidence of malignant melanoma would increase from about one percent of the U.S. population in 1990 to about 1.5 percent in the year 2040, due primarily to the thinning of the atmosphere's ozone layer that absorbs ultraviolet radiation. However, researchers said that as much as 90 percent of the damage from the sun leading to skin cancer was done by the age of ten. They also estimated that using a high-SPF product regularly during childhood and adolescence could reduce the chance of getting certain types of skin cancer by 75 percent. These warnings call for continued, and perhaps increased, reliance on sun-protection lotions and a steady market for Hawaiian Tropic products.

## Further Reading:

Craddock, John, "The Suntan King Makes Millions Without Getting Burned," *Florida Trend,* June 1985, p. 54.

"Ex-High School Coach Has become Suntan Lotion Entrepreneur," *Tampa Tribune,* July 19, 1981, p. 14B.

Information Sheet, Hawaiian Tropic Tanning Research, Daytona Beach, Florida, 1993.

Jaroff, Leon, "The Dark Side of Worshipping the Sun," *Time,* July 23, 1990, p. 68.

Lazarus, Bill, "Ron Rice: Sunshine Superman," *Daytona Beach News Journal,* March 15, 1987, p. 1E.

Parrett, Tom, "Staying Safe in the Sun," *Money,* July 1982, p. 101.

Press Kit, Hawaiian Tropic Tanning Research Laboratories, Daytona Beach, Florida, 1993.

"Ron Rice: A Biography," Hawaiian Tropic Tanning Research Laboratories, Daytona Beach, Florida.

Russell, Cheryl, "Tall and Tan and Young and Lovely," *American Demographics,* December 1987, p. 19.

Shaw, Anita Hipius, "Sun Scare," *Soap/Cosmetics/Chemical Specialties,* February 1992, p. 38; "The Sunless Tan," *Soap/Cosmetics/Chemical Specialties,* April 1992, p. 50.

"What's New Under the Sun: The Selling of Suntans," *New York,* August 8, 1983, p. 19.

*—Dean Boyer*

# HEAD & SHOULDERS®

Head & Shoulders brand shampoo is one of the top-selling shampoos in the United States. Packaged in its trademarked long-necked plastic bottle, Head & Shoulders shampoo has evolved from its original pyrithione zinc formula in 1961 to its intensive treatment selenium sulfide formula in the 1990s. When salon brands vaulted into the circle of the top-ten selling shampoo brands in the early 1990s, Head & Shoulders consistently snowed would-be competitors. Just one line of personal care goods manufactured by consumer giant Procter & Gamble Company (P&G), which also manufactures such other popular brands as Bounty paper towels, Pringles potato chips, and Comet cleanser, Head & Shoulders shampoo has become a standard item in many U.S. homes.

## Brand Origins

The year was 1961, John Fitzgerald Kennedy was President of the United States, and in P&G's Cincinnati, Ohio, laboratories, a shampoo was formulated that was heralded as a cure for dandruff. A condition characterized by excessive flaking and scaling of the scalp, dandruff required a special treatment that had always eluded researchers. Scientists knew that cell growth in a dandruff-plagued scalp was disorderly and was complicated by hair cells that were shed from the scalp prematurely. This abnormal cell growth combined with sebum (hair oil) secretions caused the cells to bind into large scales 20 to 40 cell layers thick. This cluster of dead cells becomes visible as dandruff, unlike the far greater number of healthy cells which the scalp discards daily and which go unnoticed.

Dandruff presented an unusual problem because, while an individual could keep it under control, researchers could not ascertain its cause. Scientists sought to formulate an anti-dandruff product which would remedy the problem by controlling the growth of the micro-organisms living on the surface of the scalp. As early as 1950, P&G scientists were working on such a product that consumers could obtain over the counter at their local drugstore. P&G screened over 2,000 ingredients, seeking the one compound that possessed the following properties: it would remain active when exposed to scalp oils, it would continue to work even after shampooing, and it would not pose a safety problem in the home.

After five long years, P&G scientists isolated one possible ingredient—pyrithione zinc, developed by the Olin Chemical Company—and commenced extensive testing in conjunction with Vanderbilt University. Pyrithione zinc, whose structural name was zinc-pyridinethiol-1-oxide, was an anti-microbial agent that worked especially well on microbes believed to cause dandruff. P&G's safety and clinical tests included animal studies that determined skin absorption, oral toxicity, and dermatological effects. The series of more than 1,300 clinical studies confirmed the effectiveness of pyrithione zinc in the P&G's new shampoo, which the company launched under the brand name Head & Shoulders.

P&G's long and patient investment in research culminated in three years of test-marketing in limited areas beginning in 1960. Head & Shoulders shampoo rolled out nationally in August of 1963, and by January of 1964 it became a brand in its category. To promote the brand, P&G formed the Professional Services Division, which informed dermatologists about Head & Shoulders. By the late 1970s service representatives were calling almost 4,000 dermatologists annually to encourage them to recommend Head & Shoulders shampoo to their patients. Through word-of-mouth the product's reputation grew.

## Advertising Innovations

P&G's advertising dates back to 1882, when Harley Procter, son of the company's cofounder, formulated the first promotional campaign for Ivory soap. Many of Procter's marketing concepts were so intrinsically well thought out, logically planned, and consumer-oriented that they continued to be utilized into the next century. By 1993 advertising strategies for the Head & Shoulders brand included large point-of-purchase displays featuring refund tear-off forms, coupons in Sunday newspapers, and direct-mail campaigns that distributed trial size Head & Shoulders shampoo to potential customers.

To please the customer, P&G had to get to know its customer. The company achieved this objective through intense market research that relied heavily on mail surveys. P&G also established two-way communication with its consumers by listing toll-free telephone numbers on its products; by the early 1980s every P&G package boasted such a number. In addition to these innovations, P&G pitched Head & Shoulders shampoo to school children—potential customers—by distributing consumer-education materials to teachers free of charge.

## AT A GLANCE

**H**ead & Shoulders brand shampoo and conditioner originated in 1961 at the laboratories of the Procter & Gamble Company, Cincinnati, Ohio; owned by the Procter & Gamble Company.

**Performance:** *Market share*—7.3% (third-place) of the shampoo category (1992). *Sales*—$48.5 million (July 1992 through January 1993).

**Major competitor:** Procter & Gamble's Pert Plus; also Helene Curtis Industries' Suave.

**Advertising:** *Agency*—Tatham/RSCG, Chicago, Illinois.

**Addresses:** *Parent company*—Procter & Gamble Company, One Procter & Gamble Plaza, Cincinnati, OH 45202; phone: (513) 983-1100; fax: (513) 983-7847.

## Brand Development and Product Changes

As times changed, so did the Head & Shoulders brand. In 1982–83 the conditioning formula was launched as an alternative to the regular formula, but was later discontinued due to slow sales. Changes through the years included improved fragrances, formulas, and package variations. In September of 1985 the regular formula was revamped as Head & Shoulders Normal to Oily, the conditioning formula was marketed for normal to dry hair, and a tube form became a concentrate version.

Still not satisfied with the brand's success, P&G researchers developed yet another version: Head & Shoulders Intensive Treatment shampoo—whose main ingredient was selenium sulfide rather than pyrithione zinc—to alleviate persistent dandruff. Beginning in July of 1990, this shampoo premiered nationally in a blue bottle. Two years later, Head & Shoulders Intensive Treatment Dandruff shampoo and Head & Shoulders Seborrheic shampoo and conditioner were introduced as a patented, clinically-proven formula with an amended FDA warning statement. In another attempt to further improve their original product, P&G developed Head & Shoulders in a ZPT formula. ZPT, the active ingredient in the new version, referred to dandruff-controlling platelets in the compound. All Head & Shoulders shampoos are pH-balanced, meaning they are neither too acidic nor too alkaline for the skin.

Since its introduction in 1961, Head & Shoulders consistently cinched a market share by addressing the common problem of dandruff. However, from July of 1992 to January of 1993, the brand's rank slipped from second place to third place in the market, and its sales slid to $48.5 million. It is likely that these losses resulted from the debut of other two-in-one (shampoo and conditioner) brands. In an effort to regain its lost ground, P&G itself soon introduced Head & Shoulders shampoo in a two-in-one formula. In addition to its popularity in the United States, Head & Shoulders shampoo enjoyed strong sales in Europe and the Far East, where advertising strategies mirrored those utilized in the United States—broadcast media, sampling, coupons, and refunds.

## Future Predictions

Born of the belief that an effective dandruff shampoo would produce consumer loyalty, the Head & Shoulders brand for over 30 years remained one of the top-selling brands of anti-dandruff shampoos in the United States, Europe, and parts of Asia. Much of this success was due to P&G's tradition of reacting quickly to the changes and needs of consumers and understanding the importance of constant advertising.

If past performance is a predictor of future success, Head & Shoulders shampoo should continue to keep pace with progress. P&G chemists and marketers continue to query consumers, create new technologies, and retain a high presence in the market. As a P&G researcher once remarked: "It isn't enough to invent a new product. Through constant improvement, we must manage every existing brand so that it can flourish year after year in an ever-changing, intensely competitive marketplace. . . . At P&G, we create the future."

## Further Reading:

*Answers About Marketing,* Cincinnati, OH: Procter & Gamble Company, 1993.

"Anti-Dandruff Shampoo," *Drug & Cosmetic Industry,* December 1991, p. 40.

Christiansen, Suzanne, "A Question of Snow Removal," *Soap-Cosmetics Chemical Specialties,* October 1991, p. 28.

Cleary, David Powers, *Great American Brands,* New York: Fairchild Publications, 1981.

*Facts About Procter & Gamble,* Cincinnati, OH: Procter & Gamble Company, 1993.

"FDA OK's Five Flake Fighters," *FDA Consumer,* April 1992, p. 4.

"Head & Shoulders," Cincinnati, OH: Procter & Gamble Company, 1993.

"Ivorydale—A Procter & Gamble Landmark," Cincinnati, OH: Procter & Gamble Company, 1993.

Lawrence, Jennifer, "P&G Hooks Up Interactive Product-Sampling Hot Line," *Advertising Age,* October 5, 1992, p. 3.

Lief, Alfred, *"It Floats"; The Story of Procter & Gamble,* New York: Rinehart, 1958.

Liesse, Julie, "Brand Scorecard," *Advertising Age,* April 19, 1993, p. 22.

*Procter & Gamble: The House That Ivory Built,* Lincolnwood, IL: NTC Business Books, 1988.

*The Procter & Gamble Company,* Cincinnati, OH: Procter & Gamble Company, 1993.

Procter and Gamble Company 1992 Annual Report, Cincinnati, OH: Procter & Gamble Company, 1993.

Rogers, Jean, "Flake Off: 12 Easy Ways to Shake a Case of Dandruff," *Men's Health,* April 1991, p. 23.

Schisgall, Oscar, *Eyes on Tomorrow: The Evolution of Procter & Gamble,* Chicago: J.G. Ferguson Publishing Company, 1981.

*—Virginia Barnstorff*

# HEALTHTEX™

Founded in 1921, Healthtex children's apparel has become a perennial mainstay in the U.S. childrenswear market. A major reason for the brand's success has been Healthtex, Inc.'s tireless pursuit of a marketing strategy that endeavors to maintain brand loyalty among mothers and grandmothers. During 1991, following a five year period of decreasing sales and continued downsizing, Healthtex was purchased by VF Corporation, a leading manufacturer of approximately 20 popular apparel brands. In 1992 *Fortune* magazine ranked VF 127th on its list of the "500 Largest U.S. Industrial Corporations." While under VF's ownership, Healthtex's apparel line underwent a radical overhaul. The restructuring effort proved to be confidence-instilling, since VF's forecasts indicated that Healthtex was poised to increase its market share and reestablish itself as a force to be reckoned with in the childrenswear industry. Shortly thereafter, such optimism was confirmed when within two years of VF's purchase, increases in Healthtex's total sales were to exceed the 80 percent mark. This permitted Healthtex to secure a second place market share in the category of newborn to 6X/7-sized children's playwear by 1992.

In addition to being known as one of the top industry brand names, Healthtex broke new ground in 1992 when it hired Ellen Rhode to serve as the first female president of one of the nation's largest childrenswear companies. Rhode played a significant part in Healthtex's turnaround; it was under her tenure that Healthtex, Inc., went from a company teetering on the brink of extinction to one regaining its status as one of the major players in the children's apparel industry. In November 1993, Rhode was named president of Girbaud, another division of VF; Gary Simmons, former vice-president of marketing at Healthtex, was named the company's new president.

## Brand Origins

What was to eventually become Healthtex apparel first appeared in New York City in 1921 and was manufactured by a small-scale firm known as Standard Romper Company, Inc. The company's product line consisted of children's flannel pajamas/sleepers, rompers, and creepers, all of which carried the Stantog label. Due in large part to the efforts of company principals Louis Russek and Morse Gould, Standard Romper managed to survive the tumultuous years of the Great Depression and even went on to experience increases in its level of sales.

In 1937 the Healthtex label replaced Stantog, despite the fact that no change was made in company ownership. Over the period from 1937 through 1971, Healthtex brand garments prospered and went on to capture national acclaim. According to company sources, by 1960 Healthtex apparel stood alone as the nation's "largest" and "best known . . . line of young children's clothing."

In 1971 Standard Romper went public and was acquired by Chesebrough-Pond's, Inc., a multi-product firm engaged in the production and marketing of top-selling branded consumer products such as Ragu foods and Vaseline. Under the direction of Chesebrough-Pond's, the upward momentum of Healthtex apparel continued as sales doubled between 1971 and 1978. During the first half of the 1980s, additional impetus was gained with the introduction of the Kidproof, Our Gang, and Our Girl product lines intended for children five years and older.

In 1985 the winds of success stopped blowing into Healthtex sails. Chesebrough agreed to sell its Healthtex division—which at the time numbered 9,000 employees and spread across 16 plants—to a management and private investor group headed by its then-chief executive officer, Robert Blackstone. From 1985 to 1990 Healthtex apparel underwent a period of upheaval. As was the case with many other leveraged buyouts, the financial strains imposed by the debt burden had a debilitating impact that resulted in round after round of downsizing strategies and management changes.

In 1990, just when it seemed likely that the brand might never regain its industry-leading status or could possibly disappear altogether from the childrenswear market, Healthtex's creditors brought it to the attention of VF Corporation. Prior to its purchase of Healthtex, VF was a leading apparel manufacturer and marketer solidly positioned in the jeanswear, casual sportswear, intimate apparel, and occupational product lines. For the year 1991, VF was responsible for the production of 20 apparel brands that included Lee and Wrangler jeanswear, Jansport and Jantzen sportswear, and Vanity Fair intimate apparel. The company's motivation to acquire Healthtex was prompted by a desire to gain entry into the lucrative childrenswear market via the purchase of a well-established brand name label.

## AT A GLANCE

**H**ealthtex brand of childrenswear founded in 1921 in New York by Standard Romper Company, Inc. and originally marketed under Stantog label; brand renamed Health-tex, 1937; Healthtex, Inc., went public and was acquired by Chesebrough-Pond's, Inc., 1971; sold to private investor group, 1985; acquired by VF Corporation, 1991; brand dropped hyphen and became Healthtex, 1992.

**Performance:** *Market share*—Second spot in children's newborn-6X/7 playwear category. *Sales*—$100 million (1993 estimate).

**Major competitor:** Oshkosh B' Gosh; also Carter's and Buster Brown.

**Advertising:** *Agency*—The Martin Agency, Richmond, VA, 1992—. *Major campaign*—Healthtex featured primarily in a print campaign, which began running in 1992.

**Addresses:** *Parent company*—Healthtex, Inc., P.O. Box 21488, Greensboro, NC 27420-1488; phone: (919) 316-1000; fax: (919) 316-1022. *Ultimate parent company*—VF Corporation, 1047 North Park Rd., Wyomissing, PA 19610; phone: (215) 378-1151; fax: (215) 375-9371.

## Brand Development

During the 1990s the operative buzzwords most frequently heard throughout the childrenswear industry were "value factor." Keeping in mind that changes in fashion trends and marketing strategies are a constant in the apparel industry, then, according to manufacturers, value factor generally translates into products whose characteristics include quality, durability, and stylistic detail along with a reasonable price. For the most part, whether a brand prospered or not depended on meeting these criteria. To this end Healthtex has always prided itself on being a consumer-driven apparel company, which explains why the company has typically spent a considerable amount of time and money on research and consumer focus groups.

For some time, the dominant features of the entire Healthtex apparel line have included bright clean colors, young playful prints, and value-added styling. The overall intent of Healthtex designs has been to incorporate a consistently comfortable fit utilizing soft but durable fabrics whose attractiveness is maintained throughout the life of the garment. In addition, the company has always emphasized the ease with which children and their parents could put on and take off the clothes.

Healthtex manufactures everyday playwear for children, sizes newborn to 6X/7. The company's mission is to be the most responsive kidswear company in understanding and meeting the needs of targeted consumers and retailers with basic everyday playwear that lasts. Everyday playwear focuses on comfortable core products driven by bright, clean colors and young, playful prints that meet mothers' performance criteria.

For the spring of 1993 Healthtex introduced a line of clothes made specifically for infants, sizes 12 to 24 months. The one-piece Healthtex Bodyshirt was marketed as an all-in-one shirt complete with a snap crotch, snap shoulders, and finished leg openings designed to ensure comfort and durability. The garments, developed after extensive consumer research, were made available in cheerful fashion solids or prints coming in hot pink and purple for girls, or royal and jade for boys.

Another new product, launched in the fall of 1993, was Healthtex Playwear Denims, available in infant girls and boys sizes 12 to 24 months and boys and girls sizes 2T to 6X/7. These cotton denims are roomy and loose-fitting and feature an earth-friendly organic enzyme wash for extra softness. Additional features include reinforced double knees for durability, elastic leg openings, covered elastic waistbands, and bar tacking at stress points. The denim playwear line was made available in a variety of fun silhouettes such as pull-on pants, jumpers, overalls, shorts, and skirts.

## VF's Influence

One unambiguously beneficial event that resulted from VF's acquisition of Healthtex was the opportunity it offered the brand to gain access to its parent company's sophisticated Market Response System (MRS). Since being implemented in 1988, MRS has systematically transformed how VF's numerous divisions have carried out their business operations. Becoming more complex as it evolved, MRS has led to the integration of a host of components and functions that range from conducting continuous consumer and product research, to reducing production cycle periods and inventory costs, to creating highly successful marketing strategies.

An integral component of MRS emerged with the development of its Flow Replenishment System. Beginning at the point-of-sale, the implementation of the Flow Replenishment System made it possible for Healthtex to bring consumer-driven products more quickly to market and provided immediate feedback about the degree of consumer responsiveness toward new products. Electronic links connecting points-of-sale to VF's Healthtex division allowed for the relatively easy stock replacement of a product according to its exact size and color in as little as one week's time—a process that in 1989 took anywhere from 80 to 90 days.

During the early 1990s Healthtex undertook a number of programs directed at quality improvement. First of all, numerous preferred vendor programs were instituted. In order to qualify, fabric suppliers needed to possess a proven track record in meeting Healthtex's standards of durability and quality. Such quality improvement measures have enabled Healthtex to significantly reduce the time period it had previously devoted to sample testing. Secondly, employees at one of Healthtex's plants in Warrenton, Georgia, attended a quality awareness program offered at a local community college. Based on the quality improvements that resulted from this program, Healthtex was prepared to enroll its remaining plants into similar programs. And, finally, Healthtex took steps to monitor the results of its modular sewing manufacturing units, whose compensation was linked to meeting specific quality standards.

Healthtex, Inc.'s corporate headquarters are located in Greensboro, North Carolina, and the company maintains a showroom in New York City and Dallas. In 1993 it operated manufacturing facilities in Danville, Virginia; Centreville and Luverne, Alabama; and Warrenton, Georgia, while distribution took place through the VF Distribution Center in Reidsville, North Carolina. In 1993 Healthtex apparel was sold in more than 3,500 stores throughout the United States. The brand can be found in middle-market department stores such as May Co., Mercantile, and JCPenney, and in children's specialty chain stores like Kids "R" Us, but has not yet broken into the discount store arena.

## Advertising

Beginning as far back as the Stantog era and stretching well into the Healthtex period, nearly all advertisements heralding the garments' many features were typically located in magazine media and had a common theme—children at play. Usually the children were actively but contently engaged in a number of activities. Following the 1960s, the same theme was played out but ads began to feature children of a variety of ethnic backgrounds.

By the 1990s Healthtex ads contained a large amount of consumer-related information that was stylishly printed and meant to communicate that Healthtex had a sophisticated understanding of which clothing attributes mothers found desirable, along with issues that concerned mothers with infants and young children. At the bottom of the ads was a toll-free number that could be called to find out where the nearest Healthtex dealer was located and to ask questions. Most of the ads were placed in such consumer magazines as *Parents, Working Mother,* and *Child,* which cater mainly to a childrearing female audience.

In 1992 Healthtex's logo was changed; the hyphen that previously separated the words "Health" and "tex" was dropped, and the word "tex" was modified to reflect a chalk-like scrawl as if to suggest that it had been written by a child. The logo also took on a more striking contemporary green color, accompanied by an orange and magenta accent.

## Further Reading:

Applebaum, Cara, "Reinventing Health-tex," *Adweek's Marketing Week,* January 13, 1992, p. 12.

Greenwood, Monique, "Ellen Rhode: Playing for Keeps," *Children's Business,* August 1993, pp. 64-67.

*Healthtex Company History,* Greensboro, NC: Healthtex, Inc.

"Value at Forefront in Children's Wear," *Bobbin,* June 1993.

*VF Corporation 10K and Annual Reports,* Wyomissing, PA: VF Corporation, 1991-92.

"VF Is Rx for Healthtex," *Daily News Record,* March 20, 1992, p. 3.

*—Daniel E. King*

# HEFTY®

Hefty brand plastic bags and foam plates are owned by the Mobil Chemical Co., a unit of the Mobil Corporation. The company's food storage bags, sold under the Hefty Baggies name, control the third-highest share of the market. Hefty Baggies include sandwich, storage, and freezer bags; Hefty also markets a freezer wrap. The Hefty Baggie sandwich bags are designed for short-term storage while the storage and freezer bags are meant to keep foods fresh for longer periods of time, either in the refrigerator or freezer. All of the food bags are designed to keep moisture out so the foods remain fresh. The trash bags, which are the second best-selling brand in their category, are sold under the Hefty label. These bags include medium and tall kitchen garbage bags, large garbage bags, lawn and leaf bags, and a line that is promoted for use in collecting recyclable material. These bags vary in size and strength, according to their intended purposes. Closures include either twist ties or drawstrings. The trash bags are designed to withstand the rigors of collecting different types of location-specific garbage. Throughout the years, Mobil has made a number of product changes and improvements meant to fit changing consumer needs and interests. These changes are designed to make use of the trash bags easier, more convenient, more economical, and even more in keeping with social concerns.

The Hefty brand is maintained by the Mobil Chemical Co., which also has interests in petrochemicals, films, and plastics. Mobil Chemical reported total sales in 1991 of more than $4.03 billion.

## Brand Development

The twist-tie food Baggies for storage and freezer use have become heavier and stronger throughout the years. In addition to Baggies sandwich bags, the storage and freezer bags are sold as Hefty Baggies, Hefty Baggies Super Weight, and Hefty Baggies Freezer.

The trash bags include a variety of Hefty bags designed for different purposes, marketed in different sizes, and armed with different types of closures for consumer convenience. In addition to offering consumers bags of varying size and strength, Hefty developed a deodorized bag for kitchen use, and a larger size bag for collecting recyclable materials.

Hefty Kitchen bags are sold in two sizes, medium and tall. The Medium Kitchen bags include Hefty and Hefty Steel Sak, each

with twist tie closure, and Hefty Cinch Sak, which contains a drawstring. The Tall Kitchen bags include Hefty and Hefty Odor Guard, each with twist tie; and Hefty Cinch Sak and Hefty Steel Sak, each with drawstring.

Large garbage bags are marketed as Hefty Cinch Sak with drawstring, and Hefty with twist tie. Lawn and leaf bags include Hefty Cinch Sak with drawstring and Hefty with twist tie closure. The Hefty Cinch Sak recommended for collecting recyclables is a clear bag with drawstring closure. The Hefty Steel Sak garbage bag was introduced in 1991; made of a high density polyethylene plastic that previously was available only for the institutional market, the bag was promoted as the strongest Hefty bag available. In late 1992, Hefty Basics was introduced, a line of large-pack trash bags that would save costs for consumers. The bags were reportedly stronger, made with a "new concentrated strength" high-molecular weight plastic, and were available in 13, 30 and 33-gallon size rolls.

## Pitfalls of Green Marketing

Many studies suggest that environmentally-conscious consumers make buying decisions based on their perceptions of a company's friendliness to the environment. As the environmental movement heated up in the late 1980s, some manufacturers made environmental claims for their products that were later disputed and even legally challenged.

Hefty bags was one of these products. However, as David Marshall, vice-president of marketing and sales, made clear in a lengthy interview with Jennifer Lawrence of *Advertising Age,* the company did not intend to deceive consumers, and was simply trying to respond to the needs of retailers and its own sales force. Marshall argued that Hefty's competitors were marketing plastic bags that were being promoted as degradable, and retailers were anxious to give shelf space only to those products that consumers deemed environmentally friendly. Hefty was getting pressure from its sales people, who in turn, were getting pressure from retailers. The retailers were getting the heat directly from consumers.

So in 1989 Hefty introduced a trash bag with a degradable claim. The fact was that Mobil's environmental position was actually more in line with the Environmental Protection Agency, namely that a waste management program should include source

## AT A GLANCE

**H**efty brand products, including foam plates, trash bags, and Baggie food storage bags, are produced by the Consumer Products Plastics Division of Mobil Chemical Co., a unit of Mobil Corporation.

**Performance:** *Market share*—Hefty Baggies rank third in food storage bag category; Hefty trash bags line ranks second in plastic trash bag category; Hefty foam picnic plates rank first in disposable foam plate category.

**Major competitor:** First Brands' GLAD Bags.

**Addresses:** *Parent company*—Mobil Chemical Co., Plastics Division, Consumer Products, 1169 Pittsford-Victor Road; phone: (716) 248-5700; fax: (716) 248-5949. *Ultimate parent company*—Mobil Corporation, 3225 Gallows Road, Fairfax, VA 22037-0001; phone: (703) 846-3000; fax: (703) 846-4669.

reduction, recycling, incineration, and selective landfilling. Explaining the reasoning behind the company's claim, Marshall said, "Principally, the pressure was felt in two areas—from consumers and legislators. At one time 35 states were considering legislation with regard to plastics. We started to feel a lot of heat. Some states were saying that unless a product is degradable, you may not be able to sell the product in that marketplace."

Further describing the retailers' position, Marshall stated that "the consumers started to be vocal even to our trade (retailers). It was a natural evolution for the trade to say to us and other suppliers that we better do something with an environmental product. In some cases, it wasn't even as gentle as that. It was unless you have an environmental product, you won't be able to sell the product in this store." Marshall claims that the company had to offer a degradable product "to survive in the marketplace."

Mobil reformulated Hefty with an additive that would hasten degradation of the bags by 25 percent to 40 percent when exposed to the sun. However, only the product's labeling, rather than an advertising campaign, touted the claim. All Hefty boxes had a new design depicting a pine tree and a sunbeam with an eagle. The word "degradable" was followed by an asterisk that explained elsewhere on the package that degradation would be "activated by exposure to the elements."

Although Hefty had not lost sales to competitors before it marketed the bag with the degradable claim, after its introduction no major sales growth took place. However, Marshall believes that ultimately sales would have fallen off. Marshall reports, "I can tell you that had we not responded, the damage in our consumer products division would have been considerable. Our share would have dropped significantly. The pressure was on us, and we would have lost tremendous market position, in my opinion."

In the meantime, the Environmental Defense Fund called for consumers to boycott products that allegedly made false degradability claims, although Hefty sales were seemingly not adversely affected by this. The Federal Trade Commission also asked for Hefty's claims to be substantiated. In early 1990 a task force convened to investigate Mobil and some of its competitors.

Hefty removed the claim from its packages in March 1990 but kept the additive in the product. But it was too late. On June 12, 1990, seven states in separate lawsuits sued Mobil, charging deceptive advertising and consumer fraud for its degradability claims.

## Performance Appraisal

Various Hefty brand products have enjoyed positive reviews in several consumer tests. An investigation of trash bags by *Consumer Reports,* reported in May 1988, found that Hefty Steel Sak didn't burst apart in its lab test. The test consisted of lifting and carrying bags until they were positioned above a concrete "sidewalk" and then dropping them to see how strong they were. The bags of several other competitors fell apart but Hefty's Steel Sak stayed "essentially intact."

Another study by the same magazine, in February 1989, examined food bags. The report included a finding that while most bags tested kept moisture in only Hefty Baggies Freezer bags "were an effective barrier to oxygen."

Hefty's foam plates, the leading brand in the country, enjoyed sales growth of more than ten percent in 1992.

## Further Reading:

"The Best Ways to Keep Food Fresh," *Consumer Reports,* February, 1989, pp. 120–123.

Fisher, Christy, "Mobil Avoids Hefty Green Claim," *Advertising Age,* April 1, 1991, p. 4.

"Food Wraps and Bags," *Consumer Reports,* December, 1989, pp. 277–282.

"Garbage Bags," *Consumer Reports,* May, 1988, pp. 339–341.

"Garbage Bags," *Consumer Reports,* December, 1989, pp. 272–277.

"Hefty Review a Tale of Four Cities," *Adweek,* December 21, 1993, p. 28.

Lawrence, Jennifer, "Mobil," *Advertising Age,* January 29, 1991, pp. 12–13.

McMurray, Scott, "Ziploc No Longer Has Its Market in the Bag," *Wall Street Journal,* December 24, 1991, p. 8.

"Mobil Rolls Out Large-Pack Hefty," *Supermarket News,* February 1, 1993, p. 20.

Warner, Fara, "Hefty"s Got a New Sack," *Adweek's Marketing Week,* May 6, 1991, p. 7.

*—Dorothy Kroll*

# HUGGIES®

Kleenex Huggies, the best-selling diaper brand in the United States, struggles to maintain the top position in the fiercely competitive disposable diaper market. Introduced by Kimberly-Clark in 1977 as a premium-priced diaper, the Huggies brand was one of the first disposable diapers to feature an hourglass shape and elasticized legs. The brand's quality and Kimberly-Clark's marketing expertise enabled Huggies to steadily acquire market share and eventually outsell long-time leader Pampers.

## Brand Origins

In the early 1960s only one percent of all diaper changes in the United States involved disposable diapers. Ten years later, due largely to the popularity of Procter & Gamble's (P&G's) Pampers brand, over half of those changes utilized disposable diapers. For years the Pampers brand dominated the market without any serious competition, until Kimberly-Clark recognized the opportunity to capture a percentage of this market by introducing its own brand. By the late 1970s Kimberly-Clark had attempted to break into the booming disposable diaper market with several different brands but had yet to succeed nationally

In 1977 just months after they introduced Kleenex Super Dry diapers, Kimberly-Clark test-marketed Kleenex Huggies in Wisconsin and northern Michigan. Patterned after Procter & Gamble's new brand, Luvs, the Huggies brand sported an hourglass shape and elastic leg gathers. It also featured stronger and wider waist tapes than other diapers and a new polypropylene liner that Kimberly-Clark claimed would allow wetness to pass through to the diaper's absorbent material immediately. The diaper was to be sold in the same premium-priced segment of the market as Luvs, with a price approximately 30 percent higher than market-leading Pampers.

## The Early Competition

The Huggies brand faced stiff competition from the Luvs brand. However, P&G spent two and a half years test-marketing Luvs, which gave Huggies diapers a chance to establish itself. Market analysts speculated that P&G conducted the unusually long test to be sure their new product would not interfere with the company's sales of Pampers. As a result, Huggies and Luvs brands were introduced on the east coast at the same time.

Huggies diapers were selling well in Illinois, Michigan, and Wisconsin by the time Kimberly-Clark introduced them in Boston in 1978. At that time the Luvs brand was moving into the New York/New Jersey area and both began sales in Philadelphia at approximately the same time. Fiercely competing for consumers' attention, the parent companies heavily advertised their respective brands in television and print advertisements and with coupons.

For the most part, however, the competing brands were introduced in different cities across the country, with Huggies concentrating on the Midwest and the West. By 1980 the two brands competed directly in only a few cities, and the market advantage seemed to fall to whichever brand had first introduced elastic leg gathers to the area. The real test came when both brands completed their national expansions. Luvs was the first to achieve this goal, with its final introduction on the west coast in 1980. At the time, Huggies was available in only 60 percent of the country, mainly in the North and West.

Despite Luvs' wider distribution, the Huggies brand trailed its market share by only a half of a percentage point. The two brands sales' figures were almost identical until Kimberly-Clark completed its own national rollout of Huggies diapers in 1982. Within a year, Huggies had surpassed Luvs to become the second-best-selling diaper in the United States.

In the early 1980s the Huggies brand claimed slightly over 21 percent of the market; competing brand Luvs claimed 21 percent, and Pampers claimed 40 percent. This was not good enough for Kimberly-Clark, which had already set its sights on surpassing the best-selling Pampers brand. Richard Bowers, Kimberly-Clark's product manager for infant care products, revealed this goal in *Advertising Age* but acknowledged that "We still have a long way to go."

## Product Innovations

In 1983 Kimberly-Clark added refastenable tapes to Huggies diapers. Uncharacteristically, however, they did so without first test-marketing the new feature. The company's research had indicated that over 80 percent of mothers interviewed thought that refastenable tapes would be the most valuable product improvement. Huggies brand was the first of the top three brands to add refastenable tapes nationally, although both Pampers and Luvs were test marketing their own versions in certain areas of the

## AT A GLANCE

**K**leenex Huggies brand of disposable diapers founded in 1977 by the Kimberly-Clark Corporation.

**Performance:** *Market share*—30.1% of the disposable diaper category. *Sales*—$749.7 million (1991).

**Major competitor:** Procter & Gamble's Pampers and Luvs.

**Advertising:** *Agency*—Ogilvy & Mather, New York. *Major campaign*—Huggies Pull-Ups slogan, "I'm a Big Kid Now."

**Addresses:** *Parent company*—Kimberly-Clark Corporation, P.O. Box 619100, Dallas, TX 75261; phone: (214) 830-1200; fax: (214) 830-1490.

country. Certain that P&G would eventually offer the improvement nationally, Kimberly-Clark skipped the testing in order to give their brand an advantage of six to nine months lead time in the market.

Initial advertising for Huggies diapers with refastenable tapes included two national television commercials that highlighted the improvement. However, Kimberly-Clark soon returned to emphasizing the product's more general benefits of stopping leaks and providing absorbency. Bowers told *Advertising Age,* "We have so much to say about product superiority that there isn't enough time in a thirty-second TV·spot to talk about secondary benefits," referring to the refastenable closures.

In 1986 Kimberly-Clark introduced a line extension called Huggies UltraTrims, superabsorbent diapers that replaced Huggies regular fluff-pulp filling with a granular polymer. The filling turned into gel-crystals when wet and absorbed almost twice the moisture as the original diapers which allowed them to be thinner. Kimberly-Clark introduced the new Huggies UltraTrim in certain parts of the country in 1992; P&G was still testing their version in early 1993.

Huggies diapers again followed in the footsteps of the Pampers brand when it introduced different diapers for boys and girls, a concept P&G had introduced a year earlier. Pampers Phases, diapers designed to accommodate successive stages of a baby's development, were first marketed in 1991, and Kimberly-Clark followed in 1992 with Huggies Baby Steps.

### Advertising Heats Up

Huggies' market share steadily increased throughout the 1980s, causing rival P&G to defend its brands. Although both companies put great effort into luring customers with improved diapers, they also intensified their advertising campaigns. By 1985 Kimberly-Clark was spending $19 million a year to advertise Huggies diapers, and P&G was spending $40 million a year to promote their Pampers and Luvs brands.

In addition to the typical advertising mediums of television and print, Kimberly-Clark formulated several other promotions to boost their brand's visibility. A particularly successful campaign allowed consumers to exchange proofs-of-purchase for items offered in the "Huggies Shopper" catalogue. The catalogue's most popular item was a t-shirt for babies emblazoned with the phrase "I Love Huggies" that could be acquired for buying approximately a month's worth of diapers. Other items in the catalogue included Huggies sneakers and a stuffed bear.

In 1986 Kimberly-Clark initiated another successful promotion in which parents collected scratch-off game cards from packages of Huggies diapers. Consumers could win prizes three different ways: by instantly winning coupons for free diapers or twenty dollars, by saving up the rubbed-off squares to win up to one thousand dollars in savings bonds, or by entering a sweepstakes to win a fifty thousand dollar U.S. savings bond.

Kimberly-Clark also began to focus more of its advertising energy on direct marketing techniques. Although the company had used direct marketing since the introduction of the Huggies brand, it rarely did more than send coupons to prospective buyers. Targeting the specific consumer segment that might be interested in the product was the next step. Dudley Lehman, Kimberly-Clark's director of marketing for infant care products, explained to *Advertising Age* that "Reasonably good new-mother lists have existed for some time, and since only 10 percent of households have children in diapers it was natural to target [them]." In the early 1980s Kimberly-Clark hired Ogilvy & Mather Direct to broaden its direct marketing promotions for Huggies brand diapers. Ogilvy & Mather developed a series of informational mailings organized in a magazine format that, according to Lehman, "[gave] meaningful information on development and, hopefully, [created] a positive image for the brand." William Morrissey, president of Ogilvy & Mather Direct, explained the value of the campaign to *Advertising Age:* "There has been a continuing series of new product innovations in disposable diapers, but this adds a dimension of service: 'The people at Huggies understand you and are there to help you.' " Though Kimberly-Clark continued the campaign for over four years, they had difficulty measuring exactly how many purchases the mailings had prompted.

In 1988 Kimberly-Clark achieved their goal of making their Huggies brand the best-selling diaper in the United States. The brand's steady increase in market share peaked in 1991 at 32.4 percent of the disposable diaper market, and even when its share dropped to 30.1 percent a year later, it was still ahead of the 29.2 percent share held by the Pampers brand.

### Expanding the Line

In the late 1980s and early 1990s Kimberly-Clark turned their attention toward expanding the Huggies' product line. The company's first brand extension was Huggies Baby Wipes, disposable paper cloths used to clean a baby during a diaper change. Huggies Baby Wipes entered the established baby wipes market with the advantage of a recognizable brand name. With the slogan "Huggies Clean Like a Washcloth," the product's advertising emphasized the wipes' thickness and durability. Kimberly-Clark sought to distinguish their Huggies brand wipes from others by assuring consumers that their wipes contained no alcohol and therefore would not dry out babies' skin.

Kimberly-Clark's next expansion of the Huggies line pioneered an entirely new product—disposable training pants. Huggies Pull-Ups diapers combined features of disposable diapers with underwear to create a disposable product that absorbed moisture and could be pulled on and off like underwear. The advantage to parents attempting to toilet train their children was clear—kids could be introduced to the idea of underwear without the risk of soiled clothes. Advertising for the product emphasized children's pride in being able to wear underwear and pull them on and off themselves. The slogan "I'm a Big Kid Now!" summarized that idea.

Kimberly-Clark began rolling out Pull-Ups diapers in 1989, and within the first year sales reached $125 million. By the end of 1992, with sales topping $350 million, they were still the only company manufacturing disposable training pants. Weyerhaeuser Company, the largest private label diaper manufacturer in the United States, was preparing to sell its own version under store brand labels, and Drypers Corporation, a regional diaper manufacturer, was expected to introduce gender-specific training pants in 1993. However, chief competitor Procter & Gamble had still not introduced a competing product by mid-1993, leaving the Huggies brand to dominate the market. Although Kimberly-Clark enjoyed profits from the sale of its training pants, Huggies Pull Ups were probably eating into diaper sales due to parents' switching over from diapers a month or two earlier than they would have otherwise.

### International Expansion

By the early 1990s Huggies brand had only a small presence outside the United States. With approximately $360 million in European sales for 1992, Huggies diapers trailed far behind sales of Pampers diapers overseas. However, Kimberly-Clark saw their chance to grab sales and attention away from the competition by introducing their disposable training pants in Europe. The company built a plant in Barton-upon-Humber, England, that was expected to be fully operational by 1993. The initial expense required for European expansion was expected to hurt Kimberly-Clark's short-term earnings.

Although the Huggies brand had fought its way to the top of the disposable diaper heap, the battle to retain that position proved fierce. Sales of low-priced store brand diapers were on the rise, and even cloth diapers were making a comeback. Kimberly-Clark received a serious blow in April of 1993 when Procter & Gamble cut Pampers' brand price by five percent and slashed the Luvs' brand price by 16 percent. Because a large portion of Kimberly-Clark's profits came from Huggies diapers, the company's stock fell almost two points upon the news of P&G's price cuts. Whether or not the Huggies brand could sustain its market share and profits through the price war remains to be seen.

### Further Reading:

Bittman, Mark, "Huggies Wraps Diapers in Dialog," *Advertising Age,* October 27, 1986, p. S2.

Edwards, Larry, "Huggies Now K-C's Second Diaper Under Kleenex Label," *Advertising Age,* December 12, 1977, p. 1; "Premium Diapers Gear for Eastern Clash," *Advertising Age,* September 25, 1978, p. 136; "Luvs Beats Huggies Across U.S.," *Advertising Age,* June 16, 1980, p. 3.

Freeman, Laurie, "Diaper Marketers Pin Hopes on Promotions," *Advertising Age,* May 2, 1985, pp. 37 38; "K-C Game Backs Regular Huggies," *Advertising Age,* October 13, 1986, p. 77.

Giges, Nancy, "K-C's Huggies Claims Grip on Second Place," *Advertising Age,* October 31, 1983, p. 2.

"High and Dry," *Economist,* September 28, 1991, p. 74.

"Kimberly-Clark to Enter Europe Market for Disposable Diapers, Training Pants," *Wall Street Journal,* February 15, 1993, p. B4.

Lawrence, Jennifer, "Kimberly, P & G Rev Up to Market Latest Twist in Disposable Diapers," *Advertising Age,* June 29, 1992, p. 3; "Rivals Readying First Challenges to Huggies Pull-Ups," *Advertising Age,* October 12, 1992, p. 4.

"100 Leading National Advertisers," *Advertising Age,* September 23, 1992, p. 42.

Rice, Faye, "The Battle for Bottom Share," *Fortune,* February 13, 1989, p. 9.

Schiller, Zachary, "A Rash Decision?" *Business Week,* April 26, 1993, p. 36.

Warner, Fara, " 'Pull-Ups' Are a Hit, But Where's P & G?," *Adweek's Marketing Week,* August 5, 1991, p. 10.

*—Susan Windisch Brown*

# HUSH PUPPIES®

Hush Puppies is known as the "world's most comfortable shoe brand" in more than 60 countries. The comfortable pigskin shoes have endured a 36-year legacy accomplished from 120 patents and a pledge to manufacture footwear in a diverse range of sizes. The melancholy, yet cuddly, basset hound logo has remained familiar to 97 percent of adult consumers in the United States. The "breathable" Hush Puppies casual shoes met a demand of increased leisure activity in post-war America. By 1965 Hush Puppies, made by Wolverine World Wide, Inc., had become a leader in the casual footwear market and have remained popular with consumers due to strong management and aggressive world-wide marketing. The company also produces other core brands, including Wolverine Work Boots & Shoes, Wolverine Wilderness (rugged outdoor shoes and boots), Bates uniform footwear, Tru-Stitch slippers, Coleman outdoor footgear, and Wolverine Leathers (pigskin tannery).

## Brand Origins

The Hush Puppies Shoes brand was created in 1957, after much trial and error with the experimentation of pigskin processing by Victor Krause, one-time chairman of Wolverine. Pigskin, although plentiful in the 1950s, posed two major disadvantages for shoe leather manufacturers. First, pigskin was not durable enough for work shoes. In addition, skinning equipment couldn't separate pigskin from muscle without tearing the skin or decreasing the yield of salable pork. Krause believed so strongly in the future of pigskin shoes that he resigned as chairman of the board to devote all his time to the pigskin processing dilemma. He worked as a consultant without salary for two years. Within those two years, engineers appointed by Krause patented a machine to skin pigs effectively—a major innovation. In the meantime, Krause designed a pair of prototype shoes out of pigskin. Despite mixed reactions by Wolverine's board, market research was initiated, and the search for a brand name was begun.

## The Hush Puppies Hound

As the story is related by Ellen Pulda in *Footwear News Industry Directory,* the well-known canine logo was inspired by southern cooking. In 1957, Jim Muir, then-sales manager at Wolverine World Wide, partook of a fried fish dinner at the home of one of his customers. After the meal, Muir asked his host why the tiny fried balls of corn dough were called "hush puppies." Muir

was told that "the fried dough was used by farmers to quiet their barking dogs." Muir decided that "Hush Puppies" would be a perfect brand name for Wolverine's prototype pigskin shoes because they "could soothe a customer's aching feet, a.k.a. their 'barking dogs.' " Adolf Krause, president of Wolverine in 1957, officially chose the name "Hush Puppies" for the shoes.

Hush Puppies shoes were test marketed in 1957. The following year the brand was introduced nationally with an all out advertising blitz, departing thoroughly from traditional shoe merchandising strategies. Newspaper ads were the medium of choice for promoting the brand, a pioneering way for a shoe maker to reach major markets. Within two months Hush Puppies shoes were retailing in 35 main markets across the United States. By 1965 the Hush Puppies brand had made Wolverine a leader in the casual footwear business.

## Marketing Strategy

The dual benefits of comfort and quality in leather continued to be the marketing anchor for the Hush Puppies brand in the 1960s and the 1970s. A shift in demographics of the U.S. population, however, resulted in a leveling off of sales for the pigskin suedes. Although Hush Puppies were still popular among older consumers, younger purchasers were shying away from the brand, particularly women. In 1972, reorganization of upper level management at Wolverine produced an aggressive, long-term marketing plan to attract younger buyers with contemporary styles. Besides quality and comfort, style had become an important consideration in revitalizing the Hush Puppies brand.

In the latter part of the 1980s, Hush Puppies introduced "Bounce technology" to consumers. As reported in *Footwear News,* "The Bounce technology propels the foot forward as the heel compresses and absorbs energy. As weight moves to the ball of the foot, the sole redistributes the pressure to key areas of the foot." In addition to Bounce technology, Hush Puppies established the Italian Design Center in 1988, promoting "fashion-right styling," yet maintaining strict guidelines for comfort. Hush Puppies capitalized on the two innovations by introducing new styles into the line from 1990 to 1992, including the sporty "Boulder" walking shoe and the upscale "Bel Air" wing-tip. The Hush Puppies Comfort Curve design for increased flexibility was also expanded into the "Cripple Creek" boot and the "Plateau" lace-ups. The line, called the Signature Collection, featured combined patented technologies with scuff, stain, and water resistant leather. Trilogy, introduced in 1991, brought together the Weathertight patent with pigskin uppers and direct-attach soles. A special advertising portfolio appearing in an issue of *Gentlemen's Quarterly* featured the new styles of Hush Puppies shoes as befitting the active lifestyle of men in the 1990s.

Wolverine World Wide developed specialty stores under the name "Little Red Shoe House" in the 1980s to increase retail sales, particularly in children's shoes. Half the brands carried in the stores were Hush Puppies, while the other half included such well-known brands as Keds, Mitre, Toddler University, and L.A. Gear. Several innovations in children's shoes created by Hush Puppies were sold in the Little Red Shoe Houses. The Pre-Lacing System, Wear In The Water safety footwear, machine-washable suede shoes, and Whale Tail built-in shoe horn were patented by Hush Puppies. In 1992 the Little Red Shoe Houses were converted into Hush Puppies Direct Outlets.

In spring of 1992 Hush Puppies debuted a new line of "Duty shoes," combining three of the brands top-selling features—Bounce, Supreme Comfort, and Comfort Curve. The Hush Puppies Professionals line was retail priced from $50 to $75 a pair. To promote the new line, Hush Puppies advertised in popular nursing publications and gave out free consumer information through its 1-800-433-HUSH line. The new line was distributed in standard shoe stores and specialty uniform shops.

### International Growth

In 1959 Greb Shoes, Ltd. of Canada became the first international licensee to manufacture Hush Puppies Shoes. By the summer of 1992, there were 27 international Hush Puppies licensees that marketed the brand throughout 160 specialty stores and leading distribution channels in 15 countries.

In 1988 a Hush Puppies store was opened in Sophia, Bulgaria, and as reported by Julie A. Cohen in *Management Review*, experienced such "phenomenal success" that 30 other stores were created by Pirin, the Bulgarian licensee. An aggressive and heavy advertising campaign has been mainly credited for this success.

According to *Management Review*, "The image of the Hush Puppies' mascot could be seen on television, in the print media and on the streets." The Bulgarian connection later broke ground in June of 1991 for the final approval of the ten-year licensing agreement with Kirov, a Russian tanning and shoe manufacturing concern, after two years of negotiations.

The Hush Puppies brand has remained steadfast in character and quality. For instance, as stated in Wolverine's 1991 annual report, the Hush Puppies mascot became an "international advertising and promotional star" among 30 licensees, who adapted the U.S. advertising logo to local cultures, adding that "more than 70,000 Britons took Hush Puppies toys home as part of a two-week 'Give A Dog A Home' promotion." In the United States, Best of Industry awards were won for specialty advertising of Hush Puppies Washers and a Hush Puppies Children's Doghouse point of purchase display.

Cultural differences, however, produced variances in marketing strategies for the brand. In Chile, for example, Hush Puppies was targeted toward trendy young women, whereas in England, the market has remained more traditional, consisting of older consumers. The marketing plan in Japan has been a "two tiered one, offering Hush Puppies as well as Hush Puppies 525, aimed at a younger consumer," as reported by Ellen Rooney in *Footwear News*. Cultural differences between customers in the U.K. and America have changed the way Hush Puppies are retailed in England. As Rooney stated, "Americans want to know more about the individual features of a shoe, while British consumers want to know the overall benefit of buying a particular style."

### Performance Appraisal

From 1958 to 1965, sales of Hush Puppies had increased five times, making the brand a leader in the casual footwear arena. New products and global markets contributed to the brand's meteoric success. A slump in the late 1960s and early 1970s led to a modernization of the product line to reflect younger consumer tastes. By 1992 approximately 35,000 pairs of Hush Puppies were sold in any given day around the world. In August of that year a famous designer from Macy's, Maggi Mercado, was hired to revitalize the Hush Puppies line of shoes for women. As reported by Kathryn M. Welling in *Barron's*, Wall Street investor Neal Goldman praised the brand revitalization of Hush Puppies, stating, "The image is changing and now the style is changing. They are in the right place at the right time."

According to Wolverine's 1992 annual report, "In June, 1992, all marketing, retailing and licensing activities for the Hush Puppies brand in the U.S. and 60 other countries, were consolidated into one division of the Company, called the Hush Puppies Company." Hush Puppies adopted a key business plan to reposition and revamp the men's and women's lines of shoes. According to the *Value Line Investment Survey*, Hush Puppies, Wolverine's core brand, "is on the rebound." Although the popularity of the pigskin bucks has been decreasing, the revamped line has revealed more contemporary fashions while maintaining patented comfort features. A new strategy has targeted Hush Puppies in buyer-oriented, casual lifestyle areas in synch with the brand's tradition of comfort. *Footwear Market Insights* forecasted that the casual shoe market will run abreast of the athletic shoe market for the rest of the 1990s. With its emphasis on quality, comfort and styling in the global market place, Hush Puppies should continue to keep in step with the ever-changing needs of the consumer.

## Further Reading:

"Bounce-y ads to run," *Footwear News,* September 10, 1990, p. 33.

Cohen, Julie A., "Soviets Do The Shuffle—American Style," *Management Review,* March 1990, pp. 42–43.

"Hush Puppies' new duty shoe combines 3 comfort features," *Footwear News,* April 20, 1992, p. 19.

"Hush Puppies tests retail plan," *Footwear News,* September 3, 1990, p. 20.

Lassiter, Dawn, "Hush Puppies to start barking in Bulgaria," *Footwear News,* May 11, 1987, p. 28.

Pulda, Ellen, "What's In A Name," *Footwear Industry News Directory,* November 1988, p. 13.

Rooney, Ellen, "WWW putting Bounce tech in sandals," *Footwear News,* August 5, 1991, p. 52.

Rooney, Ellen, "WWW eyes global Hush Puppies promo," *Footwear News,* August 17, 1992, p. 41.

"Wolverine W.W.," *Value Line Investment Survey,* May 28, 1993.

"USSR: Wolverine," *Business Eastern Europe,* November 23, 1987, p. 376.

Welling, Kathryn M., "No-Name Stocks: Bearish Neal Goldman Still Finds Things to Buy," *Barron's,* December 14, 1992, pp. 12–13.

*A Tradition of Success* (100th Anniversary Book), Rockford, MI: Wolverine World Wide, Inc., 1983.

Wolverine World Wide, Inc. Annual Reports, Rockford, MI: Wolverine World Wide, Inc. 1991, 1992.

"WWW's Russian pact gets final OK," *Footwear News,* June 17, 1991, p. 20.

*—Kim Tudahl*

# IVORY®

Virtually synonymous with purity, the Ivory brand of products is one of the topselling families of products in the United States. Packaged in a trademarked red, white, and blue wrapper, Ivory soap has offered purity and mildness to consumers for more than a century. Including other products such as Ivory dishwashing liquid, Ivory Snow, and Ivory shampoo and conditioner, the Ivory family has maintained product integrity while keeping up with the times. Ivory soap has changed from merely a white bar soap that floated and served a variety of uses in 1879 to a the non-aerated moisturizing soap in the 1990s. Ivory Snow, a flaked soap product introduced in 1930 and marketed primarily for baby laundry, evolved into Liquid Ivory Snow in 1989, designed for cleaning both baby and adult clothing. Ivory dishwashing liquid, which debuted in 1957, responded to consumers' demands by becoming available in a "clear" version in 1993. Manufactured by the Procter & Gamble Company, Ivory brands have remained market-share leaders due to years of quality assurance and innovative advertising.

## Brand Origins

In 1879 a new soap was born at a factory in Cincinnati, Ohio, owned by the Procter & Gamble Company. Procter & Gamble was a thriving business, having been awarded contracts by the government to supply soap and candles to the Western Union Army. Previously, Procter & Gamble had been manufacturing a soap created by chemist James N. Gamble, son of a cofounder, known simply as the White soap. After the company's first chemist was hired in 1875, a makeshift laboratory was erected in the corner of the plant machine shop. One day in 1879, during the mechanical crutching, or stirring, process which mixed and blended the boiled soap mass before it hardened, a worker neglected to turn off the crutcher. As a result, a sizable amount of air was added to the mixture. Duly packaged, shipped, and sold by the prosperous company, this particular batch elicited repeat orders from customers who requested "more of that floating soap." Once James N. Gamble discovered the cause of the soap's aeration, he improved crutchers to replicate the conditions that produced the popular soap.

Harley Procter, son of Procter & Gamble cofounder William Alexander Procter, was determined to make the White soap a huge success. During a church service, the words of the scripture struck him: "And thy garments smell of myrrh, aloes, and cassia, out of the ivory palaces whereby they have made thee glad." The following Monday morning Procter & Gamble's family council unanimously approved his suggestion for the new name of the White soap.

## Early Marketing Strategy

Determined to design a distinctive wrapper, Harley Procter decided upon a black checkerboard pattern with the name printed, in large print, in a panel. Ads in trade papers proclaimed that "The IVORY . . . is the only Laundry Soap that successfully answers for Toilet Use" and showed two feminine hands holding a "stout thread" to divide the large cake. The soap sold well, but Harley Procter was not satisfied. He channeled $11,000 in 1882 into touting his pet product. Favoring ads in periodicals as opposed to the "business card" approach to advertising then in style, Harley Procter placed the first Ivory ad in December of 1882. His "stout thread" ads were headlined: "The 'Ivory' is $99\frac{44}{100}$ percent pure," and added, "The 'Ivory' will 'float.' " (Consumers liked the idea of a floating soap that eliminated the need to fish for the product in dishpans, wash pails, and bath tubs.) Later, Harley Procter personally canvassed cities in the Midwest to open up new outlets.

The origin of the "$99\frac{44}{100}$ percent pure" slogan also rested with Harley Procter. He asked prominent chemical consultants, college chemistry professors, and independent laboratories to analyze the three leading brands of castile soap along with Ivory. One chemist defined pure soap in tabular form as fatty acids and alkali combined; anything else was "foreign and unnecessary substance." Harley Procter scrutinized the chemist's reply that noted the impurities in Ivory Soap: uncombined alkali, 0.11 percent; carbonates, 0.28 percent; and mineral matter, 0.17 percent. He therefore concluded that Ivory was $99\frac{44}{100}$ percent pure. The "It Floats" was added to Ivory's slogan in 1891 and eventually became so identified with the product that it was registered as a trademark with the U.S. Patent Office.

Later ads urged readers to purchase Ivory Soap a dozen bars at a time and to keep a cake handy in every room—since the soap wouldn't yellow. To emphasize the Ivory brand's mildness and suitability for washing fine fabrics, Harley Procter introduced the Ivory baby and gave every grocer a life-sized cardboard cutout to display. Procter also used pre-printed color inserts in magazines that only had color on the covers; he pioneered the use of outdoor

## AT A GLANCE

**I**vory brand of bar and liquid soap, dishwashing liquid, powdered and liquid detergent, and shampoo and conditioner founded in 1879 at Procter & Gamble Company, in Cincinnati, OH, by James N. Gamble and Harley Procter, sons of the cofounders; Ivory name became a registered trademark in 1879.

**Performance:** *Market share*—8.3% (fourth-place share) of the personal soap category.

**Major competitor:** (Personal bar soap) Lever Brothers' Dove and Lever 2000; also Greystone/Dial's Dial; (personal liquid soap) Jergens and Dial; (dishwashing liquid) Colgate-Palmolive's Palmolive; also Lever Brothers' Sunlight; (fine fabric care detergent) Boyle-Midway's Woolite; (shampoo) Procter & Gamble's Pert Plus; also Helene Curtis's Suave.

**Advertising:** *Agency*—(Ivory bar and liquid soap, Ivory Liquid dishwashing detergent) Saatchi & Saatchi Advertising, New York, NY; (Ivory Snow laundry detergent) D'Arcy Masius Benton & Bowles, New York, NY; (Ivory shampoo and conditioner) N. W. Ayer, New York, NY. *Major campaign*—(For original Ivory bar soap): "It's 99 and $^{44}/_{100}$ pure—it floats"; and, "Baby your skin with Ivory."

**Addresses:** *Parent company*—Procter & Gamble Company, One Procter & Gamble Plaza, Cincinnati, OH 45202; phone: (513) 983-1100; fax: (513) 983-7847.

posters (previously utilized only in advertising theaters and the circus); he commissioned artists to paint babies and children for his ads and then offered reproductions suitable for framing in exchange for Ivory soap labels; he gave consumers free soap to sample before purchase; he offered consumers extra bars free when they purchased a large quantity of the soap. A poetry lover, Procter sponsored contests—with prizes—for the best verses about Ivory soap for use in Ivory ads. One competition alone attracted 27,388 entries.

Toward the end of 1883, Procter & Gamble realized that Harley Procter's advertising was working extremely well—several million cakes of Ivory had been sold. Ivory was a leader, and Harley Procter meant to keep it one with large advertising budgets, a more aggressive sales force, and stricter trade policies.

### Advertising Innovations

Harley Procter first advertised Ivory in 1882, but many of his marketing concepts showed such foresight that they proved useful for a century. When radio moved into the American home, "Mrs. Reilly" in Ivory commercials discussed baby care. When market researchers discovered that listeners wanted mirth, not messages, Procter & Gamble introduced radio's first daytime serials, affectionately dubbed "soap operas" because of the sponsorship of Ivory and other brands. Ivory was among the first products advertised on television. Procter & Gamble filmed a weekly 30-minute television show, *Fireside Theater*. Procter & Gamble would only advertise the Ivory brand on "wholesome" television programs that embodied family values, a policy it continued into the 1990s. William Cooper Procter, grandson of the co-founder, instructed the company to begin marketing directly to retail stores on July 1, 1920, heralding the beginning of direct factory-retailer-consumer marketing in the United States.

Ivory was the first Procter & Gamble brand to benefit from Harley Procter's concepts of product image, brand promotion, and consumer orientation. By the 1990s Procter & Gamble would become the nation's largest advertiser, allocating monumental amounts of time and money to marketing and promotions, which included personal selling, media and direct-mail advertising, and sales promotion. Procter & Gamble also introduced new ways of handling communication with customers. In the late 1970s, already answering hundreds of questions a day about its products, the company decided to include toll-free telephone numbers on its packages. By the early 1980s, every Procter & Gamble package boasted a toll-free number.

An example of Procter & Gamble's approach was the national introduction of Ivory clear dishwashing liquid. After a consumer was given a free product sample by an ActMedia representative in the store, he or she could call a special interactive product-sampling hot line. Different from the regular consumer hot line, which was staffed by "real people," the sampling hot line was automated and interactive. Using a touch-tone phone, the consumer could press buttons in response to oral menu options to comment on the product or to speak with a human representative. In addition to telecommunicative advertising, Procter & Gamble pitched Ivory to schoolchildren—future customers—by distributing consumer education materials free to teachers.

October of 1991 saw the advent of a new marketing strategy for Procter & Gamble—the Everyday Low Price (EDLP) policy that covered all Procter & Gamble products. While this lowered the store's cost for Procter & Gamble products, it also eliminated the marketer's generous trade allowances. A reflection of Chairman/CEO Edwin L. Artzt's vision of a new Procter & Gamble, this "value pricing" program was not welcomed by retailers. As a trade-off, one of Procter & Gamble's advertising agencies, J. Brown and Associates in New York City, developed the Bonus Media Program in which specially tagged television spots mentioned the local retailer's name at the end of the commercial.

One of Procter & Gamble's most important advertising approaches was that of promoting brand identity. Procter & Gamble had always been leery of using a single name to advertise a family of products. While the Ivory name adorned several types of products, each was marketed in a separate sales category and had a different brand manager. Each Ivory product had to survive on its own merits. This advertising approach would later extend to other Procter & Gamble brands.

### Brand Development

As detergent technology advanced, so did the Ivory brand, beginning with the introduction of Ivory Flakes in 1919. Procter & Gamble had been gaining strength in the commercial laundry market, selling Ivory Soap Chips industrially on a small scale since 1902. The chips were rather thick and not completely soluble. When power laundry machines were invented, Procter & Gamble produced flakes. "Safe Suds in a Second! A 'chip off the old block'!" proclaimed the ads. To preserve product identity, the design of the package was an imitation of the old soap wrapper. In 1926, though, the wrappers changed. The checkerboard was eliminated in favor of an elegant scroll, dark blue ink was substituted for black, waterproof paper was restored, and a larger typeface was placed on the front panel. The flakes were also refined to achieve "tissue thinness" ($^{3}/_{1000}$ inch) for quicker dissolving action, and their name was changed from Ivory Soap Flakes to Ivory Flakes.

By 1920, engineers at Procter & Gamble's laboratories were experimenting with spray-drying a paste of puffed granules. When tested, the granules proved suitable for washing light laundry, dishes, and glassware. Furthermore, the granules sudsed freely and left no residue. Ivory Snow, one of the Company's first synthetic detergents, quickly became a popular soap for baby laundry and hand laundering delicate fabrics. Like the Ivory bar, Ivory Snow was made from natural ingredients—pure soap (tallow and vegetable oil) for cleaning and softening—but had small quantities of fabric whiteners and perfumes added. The onset of laundry detergents—synthetic cleaning agents—and automatic washers after World War II signaled the decline in popularity of laundry soaps. Debuting in 1989, Liquid Ivory Snow was a liquid laundry detergent that also offered Ivory mildness. (It also helped baby's clothes retain their flame-retardant qualities.)

In 1982 Liquid Ivory soap was launched. Packaged in a convenient pump dispenser, the liquid soap was mild to the skin, yet provided superlative cleaning and lathering benefits. Liquid Ivory offered convenience at the sink for washing the hands and face. Ivory dishwashing liquid, the first Ivory product which was not a soap, debuted in 1957. Used primarily for dishes and hand washing fine fabrics, it was a light-duty liquid detergent. In 1993 Ivory Clear made its appearance in response to the clamor of consumers for products with a "crystalline" content. Ivory shampoos and conditioners were introduced in 1983 and contained only the high-quality ingredients "normally" found in premium-priced products. Ivory shampoos and conditioners contained only mild, biodegradable surfactants.

## Product Changes

The first Ivory was a white bar soap that could clean practically everything. By 1887 it was available in two sizes, laundry and toilet, and by 1921 it was the top-selling bath and toilet soap in the United States. However, when perfumed toilet soap rose in popularity, salesman Richard Deupree came up with the idea to manufacture a five-cent size of Ivory for the washstand, to be called Guest Ivory. Launched in 1923 by couponing (two cakes free with the purchase of one package of Ivory Soap Flakes), it came wrapped in light blue paper with a white colonial doorway design.

In the early 1930s, Ivory underwent a drastic improvement. Procter & Gamble scientists learned to minimize the soap's tendency to yellow and warp while also controlling moisture content and promoting better lathering. A novel device, the hydrolyzer, was employed in the new process of aerating and freezing the soap during production. Patented in 1942, this process speeded production considerably. During World War II, Procter & Gamble, along with other soap manufacturers, had to stretch its supplies of soap. A formula calling for 75 percent coconut oil and 25 percent tallow was revised with a ratio of 15 to 85. The soap performed yet did not produce suds very quickly.

Personal Ivory, introduced in 1939, was a result of Procter & Gamble scientists' crystalline-structure studies, the hydrolyzer, and the aerator-freezer. Lever Brothers sued Procter & Gamble over a manufacturing process used in New Ivory (and Procter & Gamble won the case, but the decision was reversed in 1943) and Procter & Gamble sued Lever Brothers over Swan's collocation of features identifying Ivory (Procter & Gamble lost this one). But even though Lever won, its soap did not. The public still preferred Ivory.

In 1954 a newly-designed bar in the shape of twin cakes was introduced. It was easy to snap apart—a concept directly descended from Harley Procter's "stout thread." Perhaps the most dramatic improvement in Ivory occurred in 1992 when New Ivory underwent a facelift to become a non-aerated, moisturizing form called New Ivory Ultra Safe Skin Care Bar. The new product competed with complexion bar Dove and deodorant bar Lever 2000 and quickly gained impressive sales.

## Public Relations Incidents

The first negative exposure relating to the Ivory name occurred in September of 1944, when a woman in Springfield, Massachusetts sent in a cake of Ivory Soap which sank. "Sinkable? Unthinkable!" chemists had always claimed. News of the incident quickly spread, and the story became a national media event. Procter & Gamble's chemists refuted the woman's claims by explaining that in storage this one particular cake might have been compressed and its tiny air pockets crushed. Nonetheless, company researchers inspected the manufacturing process and made an adjustment to avoid future claims.

Rachel Carson's 1962 book, *Silent Spring,* brought more controversy to Procter & Gamble. The company had utilized a cleaning agent called alkyl benzene sulfonate (ABS) in Ivory dishwashing liquid. Although the effectiveness and the lower cost of the ABS rendered it useful to manufacturing, it was not completely biodegradable during sewage treatment. Occasionally the residues of the compound left white foam along the banks of some rivers and streams. Even though Procter & Gamble proved in Congressional investigations that problems with ABS were aesthetic, the company voluntarily changed its surfactant to linear alkyl sulfate (LAS). But the suds along waterways persisted, and environmentalists pushed for government intervention.

About this time at a European Procter & Gamble facility, enzymes were discovered. Thomas Bower, a Procter & Gamble supervisor abroad, reported that enzymes could eradicate a host of stain-causing substances. By the late 1960s, most of Procter & Gamble's detergents contained enzymes. However, when a few workers in European and American detergent plants reported allergic reactions to enzyme dust, opponents prompted the FTC to commence a nonpublic investigation in 1969. The investigation became very public when newspapers across the nation carried headlines declaring that enzymes were unsafe. Despite reassurances by the National Academy of Sciences that enzymes were effective, non-hazardous, stain-removing agents, the uproar continued. In 1971 Procter & Gamble decided to remove enzymes from its detergents in the United States.

In the 1960s, an international commission composed of representatives of Canada and the United States was appointed to study phosphate builders in detergents used in Canada and the Great Lakes basin. The commission concluded that lake quality was dangerously declining due to "accelerated eutrophication" caused by the over-fertilizing of algae, whose decay consumed oxygen in the water that normally sustained fish and other marine life. The commission's report stated that although eutrophication was common, detergent phosphates accelerated the process and threatened important water sources and should be banned. Procter & Gamble scientists maintained that phosphate was a safe ingredient (it is commonly found in food), and that the source of water pollution was improperly treated city sewage and factory water. But environmentalists remained adamant and consumers cut back on their usage of Ivory dishwashing Liquid and Ivory Snow. Seeing the sharp decline in sales, Procter & Gamble replaced the ill-fated phosphate with a safer substance, NTA (sodium nitrilotriacetate). In testing, however, government scientists found that NTA was hazardous when it interacted with other materials in lakes and streams. In December of 1970, the United States Surgeon General asked Procter & Gamble to "voluntarily cease" using NTA in detergent products manufactured for use in the United States. Procter & Gamble's research and development department spent years trying to find a suitable phosphate substitute. In 1980, however, the U.S. Environmental Protection Agency concluded that NTA should not be prohibited for use as a detergent builder.

Consumers demanded phosphate-free detergents, but Procter & Gamble, proud of its roster of superlative products, believed that phosphate-free detergents did not clean so efficiently as did phosphated ones and that non-phosphated detergents, at that time relying on highly alkaline and corrosive ingredients, could be hazardous to the eyes or mouth. Company shareholders could not understand why Procter & Gamble resisted changing its formula in the face of consumer protest. The principle of the founding fathers was never to sell "shoddy goods," and the company reluctantly decided to withdraw its detergents from the market place for a time rather than sell ineffective products. Eventually, Procter & Gamble researchers did find and use phosphate alternatives. In 1979 the joint Canadian-U.S. commission investigated conditions in the Great Lakes area again and found that, as proper sewage treatment had been expanded over the years, the quality of Great Lakes water had improved. Moreover, it found that 53 percent of all phosphorus entering the Great Lakes came from groundwater runoff, with sewage accounting for 24 percent; airborne dust, 19 percent; and detergents, only two percent. Phosphates were back in vogue, and Ivory Dishwashing Liquid and Ivory Snow became stronger brands than ever because they had not compromised on quality.

## International Market

Early on Procter & Gamble had found a market for its products overseas. In 1897 Ivory was introduced in England. Procter & Gamble acquired Sabatés, S.A., a soap-perfume-candle factory in Havana in 1931 and the Philippines Manufacturing Company in Manila in 1935 (which included an existing business in soap and vegetable products). In 1940 Procter & Gamble constructed three new facilities—a soap factory in Quincy, Massachusetts, a third plant for the English subsidiary in London, and a soap plant at Surabaja (Java) Indonesia. That same year, Procter & Gamble added a soap production unit to the shortening and oils plant in Dallas. Federal officials pointed out that Procter & Gamble's expertise in packaging soaps could easily be transferred to the packaging of powdered and granulated explosives in steel containers. Thus, Procter & Gamble did its part to help win World War II.

By the end of the war, heavy-duty detergents such as Tide were sweeping the nation in popularity, and the company looked to expand its detergent market. Prior to the war, Procter & Gamble's foreign plants had been primarily in England and Canada, with ancillary factories in Cuba, the Philippines, and Indonesia. In 1948 Procter & Gamble launched its new detergent formula through existing facilities in Canada, Great Britain, and Cuba. Satisfied

with success in these channels, Procter & Gamble decided to penetrate Mexico and constructed a detergent plant near Mexico City.

Venezuela was the next venue, with factories opening in 1952. Ivory products were now available in most of the Western Hemisphere. Procter & Gamble broadened its overseas operations by studying consumers' preferences, washing conditions, language, customs, and kind of government of each foreign country. Realizing that Ivory would be a competitor with foreign brands on unfamiliar territory, Procter & Gamble tailored products to fit the demands of foreign consumers. Frequently, Ivory product names changed to adapt to the new language. By advertising, distributing free samples, couponing, and refunding, Procter & Gamble was able to introduce international consumers to the Ivory family.

In 1954 Procter & Gamble leased a detergent plant, owned by the Fournier-Ferrier Company, in Marseilles—a plant that the company later purchased. Expansion into Belgium soon followed, and a Malines facility opened in 1956. The foreign scene was not always calm, however. When rumors surfaced of an impending takeover of American-owned plants by Fidel Castro and his rebels, Procter & Gamble sold its Cuban facilities. Havana's industrialists paid $4.5 million in cash for the plants, but the remaining balance was in notes that Castro refused to recognize when he assumed power. Indonesia, too, proved a risky market when political conditions there grew too volatile to warrant plant operations. In 1964 facilities were closed.

Between 1956 and 1981, total net earnings of the foreign subsidiaries soared from $8 million to $149 million and Ivory brands became available in 24 nations. Since the early 1970s, Procter & Gamble had treated Europe as one market both conceptually and organizationally. In 1992 European sales of Procter & Gamble products accounted for more than one-quarter of Procter & Gamble's total annual sales of $29.4 billion. So impressed were Procter & Gamble vice-presidents with the performance of the foreign subsidiaries that they broke out Europe as a separate business division, approaching research, marketing, sourcing, manufacturing, distribution, and organizational development on a European regional basis, without regard to national boundaries.

## Performance Appraisal

Since its birth in 1879, the Ivory brand reigned far above the competition. Early rivals such as Pears, the English import, and Fairbank's Fairy could not compare in versatility. In 1921 Ivory was the top-selling bath and toilet soap in the United States, because of the product's quality and Procter & Gamble's clever, creative advertising. In the late 1930s, Lever Brothers debuted Swan, an aerated soap developed specifically to compete with Ivory, but the public still preferred the Ivory brand.

In the 1990s, as complexion and deodorant soaps became family favorites, Ivory began to dip in popularity. In the 52-week period which ended on June 13, 1992, Lever Brothers' Dove reigned as number one, with a 16.5 percent market share; Dial soap followed with a 12 percent share; Lever 2000 gleaned an 8.7 percent share; and Ivory came in with an 8.3 percent share, a 0.6 point loss from the same period the previous year. Procter & Gamble scientists decided that Ivory needed a slight facelift to compete with Lever 2000. The result was New Ivory Ultra Safe Skin Care Bar, test-marketed during the second half of 1992 with excellent response. Non-aerated, moisturizing New Ivory made a big splash in the soap market, although original Ivory was still available.

In the hair care market, Ivory shampoos and conditioners did not fare so well. Probably the reason Procter & Gamble's own Pert Plus skyrocketed to the head of the shampoo category was the trend of the times toward two-in-one products which combined a shampoo and conditioner in one bottle, an innovation which was roundly applauded.

## Future Predictions

The Ivory brand is truly an American phenomenon, born of Procter & Gamble's belief that consumers counted on and deserved the best—a product that was pure, multifunctional, and economical. Procter & Gamble chemists and marketers continue to ensure the future success of Ivory by querying consumers, sampling and advertising, creating new technologies, welcoming new members into the Ivory family, and improving—but not deviating from— basic formulas.

## Further Reading:

*Answers About Marketing,* Cincinnati, OH: The Procter & Gamble Company, 1993.

Cade, Peter, "Formulating Shampoos with New Ingredients," *Drug and Cosmetic Industry,* December 1989, p. 26.

Carson, J. C., "Deposition of Quaternary Compound from Shampoo Systems Containing Amphoteric Surfactants," *Drug and Cosmetic Industry,* May, 1990, p. 30.

Cleary, David Powers, *Great American Brands,* New York: Fairchild Publications, 1981, pp. 172–181.

"Dishwashing Liquids," *Consumer Reports,* December, 1986, p. 51; March, 1988, p. 196; December, 1988, p. 71; December, 1989, p. 270; September, 1991, p. 592.

"Effectiveness Ratings," *Mediaweek,* March 11, 1991, p. 27.

*Facts About Procter & Gamble,* Cincinnati, OH: The Procter & Gamble Company, 1992.

"Hand and Bath Soaps," *Consumer Reports,* December, 1986, p. 158.

Helioff, Michael W., and Marsi, K. Scott, "Shampoo Innovation Via A New Surfactant [Surfadone LP-300]," *Drug and Cosmetic Industry,* April, 1988, p. 38.

Hibler, Michelle, "Laundry, Soil, and Stain Removers," *Canadian Consumer,* August–September, 1987, p. 41.

"Ivory," *World's Greatest Brands, An International Review by Interbrand,* New York: John Wiley & Sons, 1992, p. 2.

*The Ivory Family, Ivory Snow,* and *Ivory Soap,* Cincinnati, OH: The Procter & Gamble Company, 1993.

*Ivorydale—A Procter & Gamble Landmark,* Cincinnati: The Procter & Gamble Company, 1993.

"Laundry Detergents," *Consumer Reports,* December, 1988, pp. 33, 72.

Lawrence, Jennifer, "Procter & Gamble Hooks Up Interactive Product Sampling Hot Line," *Advertising Age,* October 5, 1992, p. 3; "Procter & Gamble Plans Big New Ivory Push," *Advertising Age,* November 23, 1992, p. 12; "Procter & Gamble Customizes Ads to Plug Retailers," *Advertising Age,* February 8, 1993, p. 38; "Will Procter & Gamble's Pricing Policy Pull Retailers Over to Its Side?" *Advertising Age,* April 19, 1993, pp. 1, 42–43.

Lief, Alfred, *"It Floats": The Story of Procter & Gamble,* New York: Rinehart, 1958.

Liesse, Julie, "Brand Scorecard," *Advertising Age,* April 19, 1993, p. 22.

Morgan, Hal, *Symbols of America,* New York: Steam Press, 1986, p. 185.

*The Procter & Gamble Company* and *The Procter & Gamble Company Annual Report,* Cincinnati: The Procter & Gamble Company, 1993.

*Procter & Gamble: The House That Ivory Built,* Lincolnwood, IL: NTC Business Books, 1988.

Reed, Cecelia, "A Classic's Redesign," *Advertising Age,* August 20, 1987, p. 114.

Schisgall, Oscar, *Eyes on Tomorrow: The Evolution of Procter & Gamble,* Chicago: J. W. Ferguson Publishing Co., 1981.

*—Virginia Barnstorff*

# IZOD LACOSTE®

The Izod Lacoste brand of sportswear began in the early 1950s as a collaboration between two separate brands. Vincent Draddy, CEO of David Crystal, Inc., bought the Izod name from a men's clothier in Saville Row, London, and soon after joined with the French tennis star Rene Lacoste to market an extended line of Izod sportswear named Izod Lacoste. The line's innovative style—some thought it downright peculiar—benefited from Draddy's marketing savvy. Soon the brand's distinctive stitched alligator logo became synonymous with quality sportswear. In the 1970s and early 1980s, Izod Lacoste became a market fad, generating record sales for knit shirts. By the end of the 1980s, however, rising competition and saturated markets contributed to profit losses. General Mills, Inc., who had acquired the brand in 1969, allowed Crystal Brands, Inc., to take Izod Lacoste when they spun off in 1985. Initial gains backfired in the early 1990s, and in 1992 Crystal Brands sold its 50 percent interest in Lacoste Alligator S.A. and its exclusive distribution rights. Unable to sustain its alligator, Crystal Brands had to give it up.

## Brand Origins

The early history of Izod Lacoste involves the histories of two separate brands, Izod and Lacoste, which were eventually fused by the marketing mind of Vincent Draddy, CEO of David Crystal, Inc. In its early years, the company was primarily a maker of women's dresses, suits, and other apparel. The David Crystal Womenswear Company, formed in New York in 1905, had started as a manufacturer of skirts, moving into dresses after World War I. By the 1920s the brand had become so well known that comic strip character Winnie Winkle claimed to wear Crystal dresses. By the 1950s, under Draddy's direction, the company moved toward diversification into men's clothing. On a business trip to London, Draddy found a shop called "Jack Izod's" in the Saville Row district, an area famed for fine custom tailoring houses. The name Izod and the shop's statement, "By appointment—Shirtmaker to the King," seemed a perfect fit for Crystal's nascent men's line. Discovering that the proprietor was planning retirement in the near future, Draddy negotiated the right to the Izod name and its statement of royal appointment. Before long, David Crystal dresses were accompanied by names like Izod, Izod Haymaker, and Izod JG Childrenswear.

In the early 1950s, Draddy and French tennis star Rene Lacoste began negotiations to produce an innovative sports shirt developed by the athlete. In 1933 Lacoste had changed the look of tennis by wearing a short sleeve knit shirt in place of the customary white dress style. Indeed, the player's reputation afforded him room for such flair: Between 1925 and 1928 Lacoste had won multiple victories in the French, British, and U.S. Singles Championships. He also played on the French team that won the 1927 and 1928 Davis Cups. This scorecard lent credibility to the whimsical fashion statement and contributed to its growing success in French markets by the mid-1930s. Not until Lacoste's tennis heyday had passed, however, did he try his hand at mass production of his tennis wear. U.S. tennis champion Bill Talbert introduced Vincent Draddy to Lacoste, who suggested Draddy introduce his innova-

tive shirt to the U.S. market. "The Lacoste shirt was funny looking," recalled Draddy in a brief company history, "knit with a long tail and it had an animal sewn on it. I really didn't want to hurt Bill Talbert's feelings so I said I'd buy a couple thousand." What seemed a pittance to Draddy was a windfall to the French tennis pro *cum* shirtmaker. "He almost fell over in a dead faint," Draddy added. "I guess he thought I might buy a dozen or so." Nor was the surprise limited to Lacoste. Draddy, too, would be stunned by the shirt's acceptance, which grew into a veritable craze by the 1970s.

## Early Marketing Strategy

At first Lacoste's shirts were unwelcome oddities in the New World: "I couldn't get rid of them," Draddy later remembered. "They were about $8.00 too expensive and strange looking. I figured I might as well give them away." And give them away he did, but very selectively. Presented to such personalities as Ben Hogan, Bob Hope, Bing Crosby, and Dwight Eisenhower, the shirts made their way into tennis and golf tournaments and other sporting events, gaining visibility and appeal among highly visible celebrities. Once Eisenhower appeared on television playing a round of golf clad in an alligator shirt, the style began to get noticed. Where there had originally been no demand for the product, Draddy made sure that a demand was created.

By the end of the 1950s, the Lacoste shirt had gained public exposure, and Draddy began to improve the product to insure wider market appeal. After convincing Lacoste that the fashion world was rediscovering color and that the alligator shirt had a future beyond the white fashions of the tennis courts, a full line of color variations was introduced. To further widen the shirts' market appeal, Draddy combined the Lacoste name with Izod, thereby drawing on both the sports renown of Lacoste and the Izod reputation for quality garments. The Izod Lacoste brand combined innovation and tradition.

Innovation and tradition both contributed to a double knit fabric of dacron polyester Izod Lacoste introduced for the holiday line of 1968. The combination of easy-care fabric with the customary pique stitch and distinct Izod Lacoste tailoring translated into tremendous growth for the brand. Just as Lacoste had deviated from tradition on the tennis court, Izod Lacoste deviated from traditional tennis wear in sports fashion at large.

## Rising Competition

Izod Lacoste's popularity soared to tremendous heights by the late 1970s and early 1980s. At the height of the preppy fashion trend, sales reached $596 million. Saks Fifth Avenue, the exclusive retail chain, enjoyed $10 million in annual sales of Izod Lacoste merchandise, according to Roger Farah, senior vice president of the chain, in a 1987 *Crain's New York Business* article. The brand appeal was so strong that any product bearing the telltale alligator (which was originally designed to resemble a crocodile) was in high demand. Richard Kral, chairman of Crystal Brands,

## AT A GLANCE

Izod Lacoste brand of sportswear founded in the early 1950s by Vincent Draddy, CEO of David Crystal, Inc., when he bought the Izod brand name from an established men's clothier, Jack Izod, in Saville Row, London, and combined the name with a brand of shirts produced by renowned French tennis star Rene Lacoste; in 1969 David Crystal was acquired by General Mills, Inc. and joined the General Mills Fashion group as Crystal Brands, Inc.; spun off from General Mills in 1985; in July 1992 Crystal sold its 50 percent interest in Lacoste Alligator S.A. to Sporloisirs S.A. and as of June 30, 1993, terminated its exclusive license in the United States, Canada, and the Caribbean to produce, market, and sell products bearing the Lacoste alligator trademark.

**Performance:** *Market share*—4.5% of the apparel industry in 1991, includes all Crystal Brands labels; *Sales*—Approximately $827 million, counting all Crystal Brands products.

**Major competitor:** Ralph Lauren's Polo shirts.

**Advertising:** *Agency*—HDM, New York, NY, 1988—; prior to 1988 all advertising was done in-house.

**Addresses:** *Parent company*—Crystal Brands Inc., Southport, CT 06490; phone: (203) 254-6200; fax: (203) 254-6252.

pointed out in *Crain's* that Lacoste had evolved into more than a brand: "It's a religion," he remarked.

However, if Izod Lacoste bordered on religion, it attracted its share of false converts and institutional corruption. Rising success was paired with rising competition, including a slew of imitation and counterfeit brands. In August of 1982 inspectors from the Department of Consumer Affairs joined with Izod Lacoste representatives to conduct an alligator hunt of sorts in New York City's lower east side. Seeking out counterfeit garments with Lacoste labels and alligator trademarks, the department found that 5 out of 20 stores visited on Orchard Street had sold its inspectors counterfeit items. Dozens of shirts and sweaters later, the commission concluded that consumers faced a serious problem, often paying for goods that they weren't really receiving.

In addition, other legitimate brands rode on the coattails of Izod Lacoste's success, offering quality merchandise in similar styles but with different emblems—horses, unicorns, foxes, dragons, and sheep—and often more attractive prices. Riding an antipreppy fashion wave, one company, Mad Dog Production, Inc., played off the Izod Lacoste emblem with a "Croc O'Shirt," featuring a belly-up crocodile with Xs for eyes and its tongue hanging out. After alleging trademark infringements, Izod Lacoste arranged an out-of-court settlement with Mad Dog. Despite its victory against imposters and lampooners, the brand lost old support. Lisa Birnback, editor of *The Preppy Handbook*, complained of lagging quality under the auspices of General Mills. "For a while they made blended ones with polyester and ugly sleeves," she told *Crain's New York Business* in 1987.

By 1984 Izod Lacoste sales had lost their glamorous shimmer. From 1982 to 1983, the brand saw a 35 percent drop in operating profits, from $75.9 million to $49 million. "What they failed to see was the rapid proliferation of look-alikes," explained John Bierbusse, an analyst at Duff & Phelps in Chicago, in a November 1984 *New York Times* article. "There was a rapid saturation of the

market. They were premium-priced emblem shirts. Many of the others were discount."

## New Marketing Efforts

General Mills took steps to resuscitate Izod Lacoste in the face of slipping market share. Crystal Brands expanded both the Izod and Izod Lacoste brands into men's, women's, and children's lines. Instead of increasing sales, however, that strategy diluted the brands' focus in a market increasingly parceled out to specialized competition. By 1984 the company was defining its brands by usage categories, with the Izod brand representing its "spectator" wear and Izod Lacoste for its "active sportswear." In addition, Crystal Brands continued to develop promotional campaigns, such as representation in the $500,000 Buick WCT Finals. In both 1984 and 1985, Izod Lacoste was chosen to bear the official WCT logo as the "official clothier" of the tournament.

The company also recruited new marketing specialists to give Izod more bite. Robert Tutnauer was named president of Izod Ltd. in 1983. Richard Baker was named president of the men's division in May of that year. In August General Mills named Richard F. Kral corporate executive vice president in charge of the fashion group, which included Izod, Izod Lacoste, and other key brands.

## Brand Revitalization

Despite General Mills's efforts to enliven its alligator, business continued to belly-flop into 1985. That year, according to *New York Times,* La Chemise Lacoste, the French company that originally sold the alligator emblem to David Crystal Inc., expressed interest in buying all the properties associated with the Lacoste trademarks. Wanting to stop short of selling out, General Mills arranged an alternative move with Richard Kral. The plan involved the formation of a spin-off company, Crystal Brands, Inc., that would move toward dividing apparel lines into categories— menswear, womenswear, and youthwear—as opposed to brands. The alligator would be relegated to sportswear and other casual clothing.

In 1985 the proposed spin-off went into effect, with Crystal Brands controlling private-label womenswear for J.C. Penney Co. and Sears, Roebuck & Co.; Monet, Evoke, and Yves Saint Laurent jewelry; and such key brands as Ship 'n Shore, Haymaker, and Izod Lacoste. To cut costs, Kral moved operations from Manhattan to Southport, Connecticut, in 1986. He then began an aggressive program to revitalize Izod Lacoste after years of market decline. In a March 1987 article for *Advertising Age,* Kral noted that "We're in a unique situation here. Here's a company doing $450 million in volume that lost $80 million when it was part of General Mills . . . now analysts are saying we'll make money."

Crystal paid special attention to restoring Izod Lacoste. In an initial move to recapture some of the reptile's lost snob appeal, the line was reestablished in Bloomingdale's, one of the finer and more status-minded retailers. But the ascent to elitism would not be easy. "It's hard to become exclusive again once you've been nonexclusive," said Jay Meltzer, a Goldman, Sachs & Co. analyst specializing in textiles. Using a price, quality, and image hierarchy to suggest exclusivity, Crystal created three brand lines, each aimed at a different segment of the men's market. Izod was a price-sensitive, main-floor line of updated traditional sportswear; Lacoste provided a full line of sport-specific activewear geared for tennis, golf, fitness, and running, as well as active-inspired sportswear; and Chemise Lacoste, the highest priced line, was positioned as a premium, active-inspired sportswear collection. By 1988 Izod Lacoste had recovered to a point where Meltzer applauded Crystal's completed success. "We have seen a fallen angel—namely the alligator—rise from the dust and become a viable category again," he said in a September 1988 *Women's Wear Daily* article. In 1989 Crystal moved its advertising out of house, assigning the Izod Lacoste account to HDM, New York.

## Product Changes

Though Izod Lacoste "rose from the dust," in Meltzer's terms, to become a viable category again, the category proved volatile, and the brand suffered a new round of losses in the early 1990s. Recession caused consumer demand to contract, leaving retailers in financial straits. Attempting to expand sales, the company offered greater than normal discounts and returns and allowances, severely compressing margins. In 1991 Crystal sustained a net loss of $71,394,000, or $7.84 per share, and in 1992 a net loss of $75,256,000, or $8.25 per share. In his 1992 letter to shareholders and employees, Gordon E. Allen, CEO, noted that the "company faced more serious challenges in 1992 than at any other time in its seven years as an independent publicly-owned corporation." In June of 1991, Jay Meltzer, the Goldman, Sachs & Co. analyst who had applauded the revival of Izod Lacoste just three years earlier, lowered his full-year estimate, excluding the restructuring charge, to $2.10 a share from $2.50. Financial duress paired with the decreasing popularity of Izod Lacoste began to transform the brand from an asset into a liability.

Crystal tried bold strategies to reverse declining sales of Izod Lacoste. In 1991, the company exited the high-end collections business in its Izod Lacoste boyswear division. That same year, a new embroidered crest—without alligator—was designed for the company's classic cotton knit shirt. And in 1992, the reptilian logo was removed from Izod Womenswear and replaced with two new labels, Picone Sport and EP Pro. In a 1992 *Women's Wear Daily* article, Lawrence M. Mathe, president of Izod Womenswear, explained the name change. First, Izod Lacoste brand identity was grounded in men's shirts, making it difficult to define it as a viable women's product. In addition, the women's line distracted from the exclusivity of the men's line. In an attempt to re-establish the brand's success, Crystal was trying to focus its identity on specific, successful markets.

## A Partnership Ends

Cumulative profit losses from the early 1990s led to company credit problems, which, in turn, further pressured Izod Lacoste. In 1991 the company fell into default and began restructuring, hoping to arrange longer-term financing, implement a turnaround strategy, and reduce debt. Citing a cash shortage, on July 23, 1992, Crystal sold its 50 percent share of Lacoste Alligator S.A. to Sporloisirs S.A. for $31.5 million and terminated, effective June 30, 1993, its exclusive license in the United States, Canada, and the Caribbean to produce, market, and sell products bearing the Lacoste alligator trademark.

In November of 1992 Kral resigned as chairman and chief executive of the company, retaining his post as director, but passing his executive duties on to Gordon E. Allen. Though the company declined to give a reason for Kral's resignation, analysts cited the plunge of Crystal's stock and its losses, including the loss of the Lacoste brand name. With the breakup of a brand alliance that had lasted over thirty years, Izod and Lacoste went their separate ways. But before the last Izod Lacoste clothes wear out, the two brands will no doubt produce their own replacements.

## Further Reading:

Ciampi, Thomas, "1,000 to Lose Jobs in Major Restructuring at Crystal Brands," *Women's Wear Daily,* July 2, 1991, p. 7.

Crystal Brands Annual Report, Southport, Conn.: Crystal Brands, Inc., 1992.

"Crystal Brands Forms Special Markets Group," *PR Newswire,* August 31, 1987.

Crystal Brands News Release, Southport, Conn.: Crystal Brands, Inc., July 23, 1992.

"Crystal Brands to Sell its Stake in Lacoste Alligator," *New York Times,* July 14, 1992, p. D4.

Hartlein, Robert, "Izod Women's Changes and Drops Croc," *Women's Wear Daily,* April 29, 1992, p. 6.

"An Historic Look at Izod Lacoste Sportswear" and "The Story Behind Izod," Southport, Conn.: Crystal Brands, Inc., 1993.

Hollie, Pamela G., "Izod's Fall From Vogue a Drag on General Mills," *The New York Times,* November 15, 1984, p. D4.

Kerr, Peter, "Counterfeit Sweaters and Shirts," *New York Times,* August 28, 1982, Section 1, p. 12.

Lebow, Joan, "Can Kral Put Bite Into Crystal Gator?" *Crain's New York Business,* February 23, 1987, p. 1.

Schechter, Dara, "Jay Meltzer: SA Soothsayer; Apparel and Textile Analyst," *Women's Wear Daily,* September 8, 1988, p. 12.

*—Kerstan Cohen*

# JANTZEN®

A highly respected name in swimwear since 1913, Jantzen maintained the leading share of the women's swimwear market almost eight decades later. As popular as Jantzen swimwear has been throughout the twentieth century, the product itself has been overshadowed at times by its well-known trademark, the "red diving girl," a graceful female figure in a curved diving position. The figure, clad in a brilliant red suit, red bathing cap, and red knee-high stockings, had been drawn to promote the company's one-piece, rib-stitch suits. The suits were developed by Carl Jantzen, part owner of Portland Knitting Company, the Oregon concern that eventually took his name. Jantzen's lightweight, elasticized suits transformed the apparel industry and changed the product designation from "bathing" to "swimming" suit. The Jantzen Inc. of the 1990s, a maker of swimwear and sportswear, is a division of VF Corporation, the world's largest publicly held apparel company.

## Brand Origins

The brand name Jantzen, used to describe a type of swimsuit produced by Portland Knitting Company, was in common use about five years before the company changed its name to Jantzen and about seven years before the "red diving girl" was officially adopted in 1920 as Jantzen's trademark. Within five years of the 1910 founding of Portland Kitting, the company had outgrown its original trademark, PK, according to *Great American Brands.* Prospective customers were beginning to clamor for Carl Jantzen's stretchy new rib-stitch swimsuits, which were often referred to as "Jantzens."

Jantzen had developed the first elasticized suit for a member of the Portland Rowing Club who was looking for a pair of trunks to combat the chilly Oregon mornings. He was so pleased with the trunks that he ordered a full suit for swimming. Jantzen's first one-piece suits were produced using the same rib-stitch equipment designed for sweater cuffs.

Based on the success of the new product, John A. Zehntbauer, an owner and founder, decided that the company's name should be changed to Jantzen Knitting Mills. The company already had its trademark diver, which had been drawn by Portland free-lance artists Florence and Frank Clark for a catalog illustration. "The Clarks had recommended against showing a young woman posed realistically in a dive," according to David Powers Cleary in *Great American Brands.* "Instead they favored a female figure in a graceful, curved position, just diving through the air."

## Early Marketing Strategy

Jantzen and Zehntbauer first realized that their diver emblem was a hit in 1915, when a young man stopped by the company's shop for a dozen catalogs. He told the sales clerk that he had pasted the picture of the red diving girl on the windshield of his car and now all his friends wanted to do the same. The partners wisely decided that the diver should be the focal point of their first national advertising campaign. They put their entire 1914 advertising budget of $400 into promoting the red diver.

The diver logo made its first national appearance in a *Vogue* magazine ad in 1920, the same year it was registered as Jantzen's official trademark. The red diver soon became one of America's first pin-up girls. By 1922 the acclaimed illustrator McClelland Barclay was drawing her for the *Saturday Evening Post.* During that same period, Jantzen launched a national Learn-to-Swim Week.

In 1923 Jantzen and Zehntbauer went to a convention in Washington, D.C., and took along a batch of decals with the diver logo. They put a few on their train window, did some promoting at the convention, and started an actual fad. Upon their return, they decided to produce several thousand cutouts of the diver for store displays and give out stickers to everybody who asked for them. That first summer, they sent out 400,000 stickers. The red diver sticker eventually appeared on the windshields of about four million cars. The popularity of the stickers as a car ornament was so great that it prompted police chiefs in some cities to ban the stickers in the interest of public safety. The chief of police in Rockford, Illinois, for example, decided that "keeping one eye on the figure of the bather and the other on the road is an impossibility," according to Hal Morgan in *Symbols of America.* He set a fine for "persistent offenders."

Buyers of the suits were soon asking for a diving girl emblem they could apply. Jantzen provided them with a 14-inch felt cutout, which the company then began stitching across the chests of all suits they produced. The company later reduced the size of the emblem to 10 inches. The logo in varying sizes was sewn or embroidered on Jantzen swimwear for almost 60 years. The red diving girl also appeared on billboards in New York's Times

## AT A GLANCE

Jantzen brand of swimwear developed in 1911 by Carl Jantzen and John A. Zehntbauer, owners of Portland Knitting Company; "red diving girl" logo officially registered, 1920; company renamed Jantzen Knitting Mills, 1918; later renamed Jantzen Inc., 1947; merged with Blue Bell, Inc., owner of Wrangler brand jeans, 1980; Jantzen Inc. acquired by VF Corporation, 1986.

**Performance:** *Market share*—17% of women's swimwear category. *Sales*—More than $200 million (1993 estimate).

**Major competitor:** Speedo; also LaBlanca.

**Advertising:** *Agency*—Bozell Inc., New York, NY, 1991—. *Major campaign*—"Keep Our Beaches Beautiful" and "Clean Water," a revival of a 1926 campaign, the focus of which is to preserve and clean up beaches and waterways.

**Addresses:** *Parent company*—Jantzen Inc., P.O. Box 3001, Portland, OR 97208-3001; phone: (503) 238-5000; fax: (503) 238-5067. *Ultimate parent company*—VF Corporation, 1047 North Park Road, Wyomissing, PA 19610; phone: (215) 378-1151; fax: (215) 375-9371.

Square, the Boardwalk in Atlantic City, and Mexico City's Paseo de la Reforma, among other places. During the 1930s and 1940s, artists George Petty and Andrew Vargas gave the diver a still more sensual image for her appearance in national ads and on billboards.

### Advertising Innovations

While Carl Jantzen's development of the world's first elasticized swimsuit was certainly an important accomplishment, the company's effective use of a trademark as the driving force behind an outstanding marketing and advertising campaign was equally innovative. The red diver not only became the first memorable apparel logo, it contributed greatly to the product's success. "The Jantzen diver is an example of a trademark that led its company to fame and prosperity," noted Hal Morgan in *Symbols of America.*

The use of the red diver, however, was not the only innovative advertising strategy employed by the Jantzen company over the years. In the early 1930s a widespread revival of interest in nude bathing had management worried. But they promptly responded with an ad for "molded-fit swimming suits." One Jantzen ad of the time was headlined, "The Answer to Nude Bathing." The copy read: "New molded-fit Jantzen gives a thrilling sensation of swimming with no suit on at all—yet assures a fashionable and modest appearance."

More than 50 years later, Jantzen launched another swimwear industry first by distributing more than 13 million advertising inserts in department store statements. Consumers who held credit card accounts with any of four major department stores across the country received the inserts. Jantzen supported the inserts with billboards to create awareness of its swimwear and sportswear lines.

In 1990 Jantzen revived its 1926 advertising and marketing campaign entitled "Clean Water." The campaign was originally launched to create cleanliness standards for public pools and

beaches. In its updated campaign, Jantzen donated money to organizations that helped clean up beaches. Also, when shoppers bought clothing with specially marked tags, the company and the retailer each donated a dollar to the cause. Roger Yost, Jantzen's vice-president of advertising and sales promotion, was quoted in the *New York Times* as saying the company was committed "to clean up the places where our products are worn and to restore and preserve recreational waters." The ad campaign's slogan was "We're not trying to save the world. Just three-fourths of it." Both campaigns featured the diving girl trademark.

Jantzen was responsible for yet another swimwear industry innovation in 1993, when, along with J.C. Penney and Revlon, it sponsored Indianapolis 500 driver Lyn St. James in the 1993 races. The announcement was made in Phoenix, Arizona, where St. James and members of the Dick Simon Racing Team were preparing St. James's "Spirit of the American Woman" Lola Ford car for the first race of the season. The company also returned to Times Square with an illuminated bilboard promoting its Clean Water campaign—the first environmental statement to be seen on "The Great White Way."

### Brand Development

Portland Knitting Company might have remained an obscure producer of sweaters, socks, caps, and mittens if not for Carl Jantzen's tinkering. He had been working in the early 1900s with the knitting machinery to develop a trimmer, stretchier sweater cuff when he received that fateful order from the rowing club member that changed forever the direction of the company. The club member told Jantzen that the resulting swimsuit, made with the same equipment used for sweater cuffs, was warmer and better-fitting than any suit he had worn before but was too heavy when wet. He asked Jantzen if he could make a lighter-weight version of the suit.

Jantzen responded by putting together a small test team to help him develop a lightweight, rib-stitch swimsuit. They tested suits in a local YMCA pool and the Willamette River. Soon, they developed a suit so springy that the Jantzen salesperson was illustrating the suit's elasticity by pulling it on over his street clothes during sales presentations. The early designs were identical for men and women—including the obligatory tasseled hat—although women were expected to wear long black stockings under the suits.

The production crew at the company continued to improve their knitting technology over the years, inventing new machines as needed. To reduce the seasonality of its business, Jantzen management diversified its line to include sweaters, foundation garments, and sportswear. World War II put a temporary halt to the company's diversification plans but also helped Jantzen expand its technology. Jantzen turned to wartime production of such utilitarian items as sleeping bags and gas masks. The experience taught the company new volume techniques, new woven and knitted technology, and such innovative scientific processes as how to combine natural and synthetic fibers.

After World War II, Jantzen was ready to put its newfound expertise to work in the casual wear market. The company changed its name to Jantzen Inc. and established five separate divisions: Misses, Men's, Children's, Intimate Apparel—which was eventually discontinued—and International. Jantzen became the first garment manufacturer to blend synthetic and natural fibers and would later become the pioneer of doubleknit fabrics, according to *Great American Brands.*

In 1988–89 swimwear sales sagged, along with sales for the rest of the retail industry, according to *Advertising Age.* Leading manufacturers, including Jantzen, decided to combat the trend by designing one-piece swimsuits that would appeal to women aged 20 to 40. Typical suits of the period featured "figure-contouring darts, silhouette-softening ruffles, and high-cut leg openings intended to draw the eye upward, making legs look longer and thighs slimmer."

Jantzen's sales began climbing in the 1990s after the company began reducing its cycle time from design to delivery as part of a VF Corporation Market Response System. The system en-

*Film star Dick Powell models a Jantzen swimsuit for the company's 1933 catalog.*

abled Jantzen to tap into sales figures at stores throughout the country and match its manufacturing and deliveries to consumer demands.

To further enhance its responsiveness to consumer wants and needs, Jantzen opened its first store devoted exclusively to Jantzen swimwear and sportswear in 1992. The store was operated under license by the Portland clothing store chain Made in Oregon and sold apparel for both sexes. Menswear, including T-shirts, tank tops, swimsuits, and surf shorts, accounted for 35 percent of the store's merchandise. According to *Women's Wear Daily,* Jantzen used the venue as a means to test its products.

In 1993 Jantzen planned to redesign its men's sweater line to appeal to a wider range of consumers. Different styles of sweaters,

from the company's basic sweaters to Denim Blues, would be marketed in a variety of ways.

## International Growth

From the time Jantzen and Zehntbauer established their business, they had been dreaming of international growth. "Portland, Oregon, whose population had just passed 200,000, was too small to support its many present knitting mills in any kind of style, and was isolated from America's largest markets—but Portland, the port, could make the whole world their market," observed Cleary in *Great American Brands.* Jantzen's new swimsuit helped move the partners toward their goal.

The company began exporting its products to Japan and China as early as 1922. A Canadian subsidiary was established in 1924, and by 1925 the Jantzen sales force had entered Europe and Africa. A new sales representative in Vienna, as quoted in *Great American Brands,* reported, "Our method of dramatizing the elasticity of the Jantzen swimsuit by putting it on over our jacket and pants to show how this tightly knitted suit expanded to fit size 36, 38, or 40, etc. was really the talk of the town wherever we went to introduce the garments." In 1928 Jantzen became the first U.S. apparel company to achieve true worldwide distribution by establishing a second international subsidiary in Australia. The company prided itself on responding promptly to the wants and needs of individual markets. In Sweden, for example, the little knitted cap was very popular, so all woolen remnants at the Portland mill were made into "beaners."

In the early 1990s, Jantzen products were being sold in approximately 7,500 retail stores in the United States and Canada and in some 100 other countries through export or licensing arrangements with companies based in Mexico, Europe, Africa, South America, Japan, and Hong Kong. A worldwide version of the "Clean Water" campaign was rolled out at the company's international meeting in Tokyo in 1993.

## Performance Appraisal

Before Jantzen's swimsuit made a worldwide splash, Portland Knitting Company produced and sold about $7,000 of knitwear annually. By the time of the postwar boom, Jantzen had an annual sales volume of approximately $125 million. Over the years, Jantzen experienced some ups and downs, often the result of general economic conditions. Swimwear sales sagged in 1930, 1984, and again in 1989. Although the company does not release sales figures, analysts estimated that Jantzen revenues in 1993 were $200 million. Jantzen also suffered a 1990 loss of $10 million on sales of $150 million, its first profitless year since the 1930s. VF Corporation's casual/sportswear division, which also includes Bassett-Walker and JanSport, accounted for roughly 19 percent of the company's total $2.6 billion in 1990 apparel sales.

The company showed a profit in 1991 with the same sales volume it had the previous year. VF Corporation's 1992 annual report stated that Jantzen recorded improved sales in 1992, driven by double-digit sales increases in the swimwear and casual wear categories and overall operating cost reductions. Net sales for 1992 in VF's casual wear division were $652,571,000.

## Future Predictions

While Jantzen's first rib-stitch swimsuit certainly revolutionized the apparel industry, the company was following a more conservative path in the 1980s and 1990s. As company management was quoted as saying in *Great American Brands,* published in 1981, ''We can assure you that good fashions are evolutionary, not revolutionary.'' The opinion of industry analysts in the early 1990s was that VF Corporation wanted Jantzen ''to secure profits with simple alterations instead of daring designs,'' according to the *Business Journal.* While Jantzen had experienced some slumps over the previous few years, Robert Lindley, president of Jantzen Inc. predicted more prosperous times ahead. ''We want a better position in the marketplace,'' he told the *Business Journal.* ''I want to take them to the next level.''

Jantzen took several initiatives to help the company better gauge customer wants and needs—from opening the first stand-alone store to adopting a sophisticated system to measure market response. These efforts have helped Jantzen get a better idea of what consumers are looking for, and the company is redesigning its clothing lines accordingly. ''Based on extensive consumer research, Jantzen is in the process of positioning both men's and women's products to capitalize on its favorable image and the youthful attitude of its target customers,'' as outlined in VF Corporation's 1992 annual report. ''The new marketing approach has already had an impact on the women's swimwear business. It will also influence product and program development in women's casual wear, as well as in the men's sweater and activewear groups.''

## Further Reading:

''Accounts,'' *New York Times,* September 4, 1991, p. D5.

Cleary, David Powers, *Great American Brands,* New York: Fairchild Publications, 1981, pp. 182–191.

Hartlein, Robert, ''On the Comeback Trail,'' *Women's Wear Daily,* July 8, 1992, p. S50.

*Jantzen: A Brief History,* Portland, OR: Jantzen Inc., September 1, 1992.

''Jantzen and Bozell Revive '28 Campaign,'' *New York Times,* April 14, 1992, p. C18.

''Jantzen Revives Ads to Clean Up Water,'' *Sporting Goods Business,* July 1992, p. 18.

Magiera, Marcy, ''Swimwear Makers Aim for 'Older' Women,'' *Advertising Age,* April 21, 1986, p. 4.

Morgan, Hal, *Symbols of America,* Penguin, 1986, p. 193.

Smith, Matthew, ''Jantzen Slimming Down to Fit Into New Corporate Suit,'' *Business Journal,* September 23, 1991, p. 3.

Spector, Robert, ''Jantzen Sticks a Toe in Retailing,'' *Women's Wear Daily,* September 23, 1992, p. S14; ''Jantzen's Portland Store Showcases New Ideas,'' *Daily News Record,* September 23, 1992, p. 3.

*VF Corporation Annual Report,* Wyomissing, PA: VF Corporation, 1992.

Walsh, Peter, ''Jantzen Aims for Bigger Chunk of Sweater Biz,'' *Daily News Record,* March 16, 1993, p.8.

*—Pam Berry*

# JERGENS®

# Jergens®

For the better part of the twentieth century, Jergens lotion led all products in the U.S. hand lotion market and helped make its parent company, Andrew Jergens Company of Cincinnati, Ohio, a leader in the soap and lotion industry. Faced with increased competition in the late 1960s, most notably from Chesebrough-Ponds's Vaseline Intensive Care lotion, Jergens lotion lost its dominant market position, and the company scrambled to develop strategies to diversify its product line and retain market share. Once known for its top two products—Jergens lotion and Woodbury's Facial Soap—Andrew Jergens Company branched out into shampoos, conditioners, and other bath products in the 1970s, often marketing these products without the Jergens name.

Jergens products retained steady though diminished market share in the soap and lotion markets throughout the 1970s and into the 1980s, but the acquisition of the company by the Japanese Kao (pronounced "cow") Corporation promoted rapid development in the 1990s. Under Kao, company management has revitalized the Jergens brand name, paid increased attention to customer needs, and encouraged aggressive research and development of new products. Jergens held 20 percent of the market share in the highly competitive lotion market in 1991, just behind Vaseline, but company executives insisted that Jergens would soon regain the number one spot.

## The Andrew Jergens Company

In 1882 Andrew Jergens invested $5,000 in a partnership with Charles H. Geilfus and W. L. Haworth to form Andrews Soap Company, a one-kettle soap works in Cincinnati, Ohio. Working together to produce, package, and market the soap, the young entrepreneurs soon developed a profitable business. Andrew Jergens brought his brothers Herman and Al into the business in 1894, renaming the business Andrew Jergens & Company. On June 28, 1901, the company was finally incorporated as Andrew Jergens Company, with initial stock of $1.25 million. The year 1901 also marked the beginning of the company's dramatic growth, as it acquired the two products that would ensure its success: Woodbury's Facial Soap and Jergens lotion.

"The origin of Jergens Lotion was more accidental than intentional," Paul F. Erwin recounted in *With Lotions of Love*, a history of the first 80 years of what became Andrew Jergens Company. When Andrew Jergens Company bought the Robert Eastman Company in 1901, it was more interested in Eastman's line of perfumes than in its lotions and creams. However, former Eastman employee Charles Conover had developed a smooth white lotion that Andrew Jergens Company decided to market as "Jergens Benzoin And Almond Lotion Compound." The lotion soon became the company's top seller, and its formula was kept secret for more than 50 years.

## Early Advertising

Although Andrew Jergens Company had advertised its various Woodbury products for years, it was not until 1922 that it began national advertising of Jergens lotion. Prior to 1922, wrote Erwin, "the only advertising that had been done consisted of the distribution of samples in a more or less haphazard fashion." The first Jergens lotion ad appeared in *Ladies' Home Journal* and promoted Jergens lotion as "a product which softens and freshens the skin, yet does not overload it." Sales jumped after the ad appeared, and soon Jergens lotion was being advertised in a number of national magazines. The early ads featured women in evening gowns, and the copy promoted the healing properties of the Benzoin and Almond contained in the product. In 1923 Andrew Jergens Company spent $84,000 in magazine advertising alone.

Beginning in the 1930s, Andrew Jergens Company began advertising its lotion on radio, most notably through its 16-year sponsorship of the Walter Winchell radio program. Winchell's trademark sign-off—"With lotions of love"—helped to make Jergens a household name; it possessed a generic connection to skin lotion akin to that which Kleenex bears to facial tissue or Scotch to transparent tape. Winchell "won Jergens lotion a loyal following of millions of women," Erwin observed, "and was the start of a strong consumer franchise of glamour for the lotion through its association with Hollywood stars." Andrew Jergens Company also pursued innovations in distribution to boost product popularity. It was one of the first toilet goods companies in the 1920s to sell its products in chain stores as well as drugstores; it later placed its lotions and creams on grocery store shelves.

Riding the crest of its as yet unchallenged dominance of the U.S. lotion market, Andrew Jergens Company initiated overseas distribution of Jergens lotion in 1963 through Andrew Jergens Company (U.K.) Limited. One year later, in 1964, the company introduced Jergens Extra Dry Skin Formula and increased expenditures on advertising and promotion. Jergens lotions were advertised on many popular prime-time television programs, and the

## AT A GLANCE

Jergens brand of lotion developed in 1901 by Charles Conover, an employee of Andrew Jergens Company, which was founded in 1882 by Andrew Jergens, Charles H. Geilfus, and W. L. Haworth as the Andrews Soap Company; incorporated as Andrew Jergens Company, 1901; became subsidiary of American Brands Company, 1970; became subsidiary of Kao Corporation, 1988.

*Performance:* *Market share*—20% (second spot) of lotion category; 6% of bar soap category. *Sales*—$136 million in lotion sales.

*Major competitor:* Chesebrough-Ponds's Vaseline Intensive Care; also Lubriderm.

*Advertising:* *Agency*—Bloom FCA, New York, NY 1992—. *Major campaign*—"Jergens: Science you can touch," a $25 million 1992 advertising campaign in print sources only.

*Addresses:* *Parent company*—Andrew Jergens Company, 2535 Spring Grove Ave., Cincinnati, OH 45214; phone: (513) 421-1400; fax: (513) 421-1590. *Ultimate parent company*—Kao Corporation of America, Inc., 2711 Centerville Rd., Wilmington, DE 19808-1643; phone: (302) 992-0188; fax: (302) 992-0184. *Ultimate ultimate parent company*—Kao Corporation, 14-10, Nihonbashi Kayabacho, 1-chome Chuo-ku, Tokyo, 103, Japan; phone: 03-3660-7111; fax: 03-3660-7044.

Jergens Company was a sponsor of ABC-TV's coverage of the 1964 Olympic games. With heavy advertising, effective distribution, and a high-quality product, Jergens lotions captured over 35 percent of the U.S. lotion market throughout most of the 1960s.

### The Challenge of Competition

"Early in the 1970s," noted *Advertising Age* contributor Jennifer Alter, "Jergens had the misfortune to suffer through a marketer's nightmare." A number of factors contributed to Jergens's nightmare. The popularity of skin lotions had boomed in the 1960s, inviting the entrance of strong competitors in the market. At the same time, Andrew Jergens Company relied on the popularity of its two lotions and its Woodbury and Jergens brand soaps rather than diversifying its product base. In 1968 Chesebrough introduced Vaseline Intensive Care lotion on the market, and five years later that product had swept to number one, reducing Andrew Jergens's sales from $61.3 million in 1968 to $55.1 million in 1973.

Vaseline's entry into the lotion market forced a number of changes at Andrew Jergens Company. *Advertising Age* interviewed an unnamed Jergens executive who said that before there was competition the company had no reason to develop and market new products. The company was not exactly "running scared," he continued, but it was "scrambling." Guy Chandler, vice-president of marketing at Andrew Jergens, told Alter "It was unusual that any one brand had so much share. Maybe we were on borrowed time."

Andrew Jergens Company responded with what many analysts thought was long overdue diversification. By 1980 the company was producing four new products, two bearing the Jergens name: Jergens Aloe & Lanolin lotion and Jergens Lotion Enriched soap. While the products not bearing the Jergens brand name—Gentle Touch soap, Gee Your Hair Smells Terrific shampoo, Spring

Feeling shampoo, and Pre-Heat protective conditioner—were less successful commercially, Andrew Jergens's sales had rebounded to $98.2 million by 1980.

### Changing Ownership, Changing Strategies

The year 1970 saw change of another kind for Andrew Jergens Company, as it was purchased by American Brands Company. American Brands was a holding company with interests in tobacco (Carlton, Lucky Strike, Pall Mall, and other cigarettes), distilled spirits (Jim Beam bourbon, DeKuyper liqueurs, Gilbey's Gin, and others), as well as financial services, office products, hardware, and home products. Under American Brands' ownership, Andrew Jergens Company was "something of an orphan," commented *Cincinnati Enquirer* contributor Patricia Gallagher. "As long as the soap and lotion firm met its sales and profit targets, American Brands pretty much left it alone." While such corporate control allowed the company autonomy, it failed to provide the strong financial and developmental support needed to expand the company as it prepared to enter its second century.

Despite the benign neglect of its parent company, Jergens continued to thrive in the 1980s, even if it did consistently place second behind the immensely successful Chesebrough-Ponds products. In the early 1980s, Jergens lotions commanded just 12 percent of the lotion market, while its soaps captured approximately six percent of the bar soap market. The late 1980s saw a number of changes that boded well for the company's future: in 1988, under the leadership of newly appointed President and Chief Executive Officer Rodger V. Reed, Jergens boasted sales of $199 million—up 15 percent from the previous year—and a 13.5 percent share of the lotion market.

The aggressive growth that Reed fostered for Andrew Jergens Company attracted the attention of Kao Corporation, a Japanese household products concern that had sales of $4 billion in 1988. Kao purchased Andrew Jergens from American Brands in the spring of 1988. Company insiders and industry analysts viewed the acquisition as a good foundation for the future growth of Andrew Jergens Company. While Andrew Jergens retained its name, employees, and facilities, "the only thing the company will likely be asked to give up," Gallagher claimed, "is any fondness for the status quo."

### Kao's Influence

Kao Corporation recognized that if its acquisition of Andrew Jergens Co. were to be an effective entrance into the American market it would have to look to long-term market and product development rather than quick profits. In 1989, under the leadership of Kao, Andrew Jergens took a number of steps to ensure its future success. The company sold an industrial soap subsidiary, made plans to develop a new research and development facility near its Cincinnati headquarters, and sped up its new product development timetable. Tim Zimmerman, senior vice-president of marketing at Jergens, described Kao's investment philosophy to *Supermarket News* contributor Marc Millstein: "They didn't just want to make a lot of money immediately; they were willing to invest in the future of the company. They were interested in where we would be five years down the road." The objective, noted Zimmerman, "is to lead the [lotion] category, to be the initiator of new ideas, and to respond to what consumers are telling us they want in the business."

Under Kao's leadership, changes appeared in Andrew Jergens Company before consumers began to see changes in Jergens brand products. In 1990 Andrew Jergens Co. restructured its marketing department, creating three product groups—the soap division, the hand care division, and the bath additive division—where previously there were only lotions and soaps. In 1991 the company opened its $7 million, five-story, 50,000-square-foot research and development center. President Rodger Reed told the *Cincinnati Enquirer* that "our new research center will give our researchers the opportunity to become more closely involved with consumers and give them an environment which will promote innovation." Such a research center was consistent with Kao's overall corporate structure, which dedicates more than 25 percent of its employees to research and development. Out of the research center would come Jergens' leading products for the 1990s.

In 1992 Kao Corporation turned its attention to reshaping the management of its subsidiary. Rodger Reed, president and CEO since 1988, left the company in May of 1992 and was replaced by Toshio Hoshino, who had been serving as the liaison between Kao and Jergens. "I could never consider leaving if the business wasn't in good shape," Reed told *Cincinnati Enquirer* contributor Gallagher upon his departure. Hoshino introduced sweeping changes in management style, opening up the decision-making process to those most actively involved in production and encouraging teamwork among all levels of workers. Employees interviewed by Gallagher expressed their satisfaction with the changes. "Most of the people here were ready," one employee said. "They wanted to move forward."

### Products for the 1990s

Even though both Kao Corporation and Andrew Jergens Company were spending a great deal of energy preparing for future success, the early 1990s also saw a number of new product introductions and a prominent refocusing of brand identity. Early in 1991, Andrew Jergens introduced a reformulated, repackaged version of its famous lotion, renamed New Improved Jergens Advanced Therapy lotion, in Original Scent, Extra Dry Skin Treatment, Aloe & Lanolin, and Vitamin E & Lanolin versions.

The new lotions contained a patented ingredient called ISCE, which *Dermatology Times* described as "a pure synthetic form of the skin's own moisture-retaining lipids," which allows the lotion to "bond with and recondition the intercellular lipid complexes" in the skin. The new Jergens lotion also got a new white bottle that plays up the Advanced Therapy name, ships easily, and allows more product to fill less retail space. The new product cost Jergens $41 million, reported Gallagher in the *Cincinnati Enquirer,* with $39 million for advertising and promotion and $2 million for adapting production facilities. In 1992 the product was also made available in a refill pouch. The pouch is said to reduce waste of the lotion by 78 percent, be more economical for the consumer, and reduce solid waste in landfills. Jergens Advanced Therapy lotion promised to be the company's flagship product, and it boosted Jergens share of the lotion market to 20 percent in 1991, just behind Chesebrough's 24 percent.

Jergens Aloe & Lanolin and Vitamin E & Lanolin Skin Conditioning bars received new packages with a "New & Improved" label in 1991. Jergens Anti Bacterial Plus liquid soap, benefitting from the technical innovations churned out by Andrew Jergens Company's new research center, boasted its ability to kill the stubborn odors of fish and onions left on the hands. In 1993 the company introduced Jergens Refreshing Body Shampoo, a liquid cleanser accompanied by a soft sponge for use in the shower. The product was targeted at consumers who were changing their minds about using liquid soaps only for their hands.

The most important innovation in products not bearing the Jergens brand name was the Actibath bath additive tablets. The tablets are dropped into the consumer's bathtub, where they release a combination of carbonated bubbles, moisturizers, and scent that are touted for their ability to relax and soothe tired or sore muscles. The company hoped that Actibath might one day contribute up to 10 percent of overall sales, and early market testing indicated that Actibath could be a market leader.

### Superbrand

Perhaps the biggest factor behind Jergens success in the 1990s was the re-emphasis on the Jergens brand name. In the 1970s and 1980s, the company had developed many new products, but few were identified with the Jergens name. "Correcting that situation," Zimmerman told Gallagher, "has been one of our major thrusts. We now are restaging our brands much more aggressively around the Jergens name." In 1992 Andrew Jergens Company launched a major new advertising campaign with advertising agency Bloom FCA. The $25 million dollar campaign—led by the slogan "Jergens: Science you can touch"—was devoted entirely to magazine advertisements, many of which were attention-grabbing gatefolds or two-page foldouts. Bloom FCA CEO George Guimaraes called the campaign a "grand gesture" in *Adweek Midwest Edition,* and Senior Vice-President and Media Director Bonnie Barest claimed that the ads would reach 80 percent of the intended market in the first month of their run. With aggressive advertising, strong corporate support for research and development, and a reinvigorated brand name, Jergens seemed poised to achieve its goals: leadership in the lotion market category and growth in the bar and liquid soap categories.

### Further Reading:

Alter, Jennifer, "Broader Line at Jergens Creating Momentum," *Advertising Age,* November 23, 1981, pp. 4 and 12.

Appelbaum, Cara, "Three Years Later, Kao Remakes Jergens," *Adweek's Marketing Week,* July 29, 1991, p. 11.

Cebulski, Cathy, "Jergens Plans Big Splash With Actibath," *Cincinnati Business Record,* August 13, 1990.

Erwin, Paul F., *With Lotions of Love,* Cincinnati, OH: News Gazette Printing Company, 1965.

Freeman, Laurie, "Jergens Bubbly Over New Soap," *Advertising Age,* July 2, 1984, pp. 2 and 38; "Jergens Tries on Sports Tie," *Advertising Age,* October 8, 1990, p. 40.

Gallagher, Patricia, "Jergens 'Anxious to Move Ahead,'" *Cincinnati Enquirer,* February 19, 1990; "Jergens to Focus on New Products," *Cincinnati Enquirer,* November 28, 1990, p. F4; "Jergens' Research Center Opens," *Cincinnati Enquirer,* November 13, 1991, p. B10; "Jergens Smooths Path to Change," *Cincinnati Enquirer,* March 28, 1993, p. I1.

Goldman, Debra, "Jergens Putting 1992 $25 Million Ad Budget Into Magazines," *Adweek Midwest Edition,* June 15, 1992, p. 5.

Groon, Amy C., "Jergens Teams With Local Sports," *Adweek's Marketing Week,* November 5, 1990, p. 14.

"Jergens EverSoft Concentrated Skin Cream," *Lookout (Non Foods Edition),* October 24, 1988.

"Jergens Refreshing Body Shampoo," *Lookout (Non Foods Edition),* March 23, 1993.

"Jergens Smooths Way for EverSoft Intro," *Advertising Age,* September 19, 1988, p. 37.

"Jergens to Have New Product," *Cincinnati Enquirer,* September 10, 1988, p. C5.

"Lotions Work With Skin's Own Lipids," *Dermatology Times,* February 1992, p. 81.

McCarthy, Michael, "Jergens Looks to Lift Sagging Skin Care Biz," *Adweek Eastern Edition,* November 11, 1991, p. 6.

Millstein, Marc, "Technology's an Absorbing Subject," *Supermarket News,* January 25, 1993, p. 26.

*—Tom Pendergast*

# JOCKEY®

Jockey, a name long associated with style and comfort, is the leading U.S. brand of men's underwear. For over a century, Jockey's classic Y-front design has proven so popular with men that the term ''Y-front'' can now be found in the *Oxford English Dictionary* as a synonym for men's briefs. The relatively new introduction of a line of women's undergarments, Jockey for Her, has boosted corporate earnings to record levels, and the privately held company has also capitalized on ventures into men's sportswear and a number of licensing agreements. Products bearing the Jockey name are sold in more than 14,000 department and specialty stores throughout the world; internationally, the logo is licensed to 135 different companies in over 100 countries worldwide. Although Jockey possesses neither the ''hot'' brand status of Calvin Klein (thanks to rapper Marky Mark) or the whimsical appeal of Joe Boxer, it is nonetheless an industry front-runner with a rich tradition for innovation and brand promotion.

## Brand Origins

In 1876 S. T. Cooper of Ludington, Michigan, purchased six hand-operated knitting machines. With his sons, Cooper began producing woolen socks that he sold locally. From socks, the business soon grew to include the manufacture of the one-piece ''union suit,'' a practical long-legged, long-sleeved undergarment that buttoned up the front. The manufacture of the union suit, the only undergarment available during this period, helped the young company to flourish and eventually move its growing manufacturing operation west to Kenosha, Wisconsin, a developing industrial center.

After the turn of the century, Cooper's Underwear Company, as it was now known, made a change to the classic union suit that would revolutionize the design of men's clothing. The ''Kenosha Klosed Krotch'' was introduced in 1910—the front was constructed so that two layers of fabric overlapped like an X over the crotch so as to eliminate the need for cumbersome buttons. The freedom that this gave the wearer was obvious; public reception of the new, trademarked design was uniformly positive.

Confident in the success of the Kenosha Klosed Krotch, the company commissioned J. C. Leyendecker—famous for his stylish illustrations for Arrow Shirts—to create a series of colored advertisements featuring its new product. The ad appeared in the *Saturday Evening Post* on May 6, 1911, and is notable as the first national advertising campaign to promote men's underwear. In the years that followed the introduction of the Kenosha Klosed Krotch, consumer preferences were shaped, among other factors, by the advent of central heating at home and in the workplace, which eliminated the need for heavy undergarments. During World War I, American troops were issued woven shorts for use under their uniforms during the summer months in lieu of one-piece knitted undergarments. Men found these ''boxer'' shorts to be more comfortable and provide more freedom than the union suit, and continued to wear the abbreviated undergarments even after their return stateside. By 1920, the union suit had relinquished its position as the most popular men's undergarment.

In an effort to address this change in consumer taste, Cooper's introduced its ''Jockey Singleton,'' a sleeveless, body-hugging, one-piece garment made of Durene yarn that captured much of the sales lost by the declining sales of Jockey's union suits. The name ''Jockey'' was chosen by a think-tank of Cooper's executives because of its athletic connotation and the relationship that existed between sports, flexibility, and protection.

## From the Klosed Krotch to the Y-Front

In 1934 Cooper's developed a new undergarment inspired by the scanty bathing suits then being sported on the French Riviera. The senior vice-president of Cooper's saw in the risque French bathing costume the potential for a garment that could not only be attractive and comfortable, but provide support as well. The style 1001 ''brief'' was produced in a small quantity in September of that year, and despite the competition denouncing the design as a mere fad, Cooper's applied for and was granted a patent on its construction. The patent served to eliminate copying of the distinctive Y-front design, and the company continued to defend its patent rigorously against duplication of what would become a classic design in men's underwear.

Style 1001 briefs were packaged in clear cellophane and sold for 50 cents per pair. While younger men were quick to break free from the confines of a one-piece undergarment, Cooper's needed to educate more conservative consumers about the benefits of the radically altered undergarment. In its advertising, the company stressed the ease of laundering and the comfort of a lighter garment with shorter legs and elastic waist: ''No buttons, no gaping, direct tension for masculine support, scientifically styled in a fabric which absorbs perspiration.''

## AT A GLANCE

Jockey brand underwear founded as the Kenosha Klosed Krotch in 1910 in Kenosha, WI, by S. T. Cooper; S. T. Cooper and Sons incorporated as Cooper's Underwear Company, 1896; renamed Jockey International, 1972; later developers included J. C. Leyendecker, Harry Wolf, Howard Cooley, and Donna Wolf Steigerwaldt.

**Performance:** *Market share*—30% (top share) of men's underwear category. *Sales*—$300 million.

**Major competitor:** Calvin Klein brand underwear; also, Sara Lee Corporation's Hanes brand.

**Advertising:** *Agency*—Thorobred Advertising (in-house agency), 1987—. *Major campaign*—Spot TV and print ads, in such magazines as *Rolling Stone*, promoting new products (i.e., Lycra Jockey Pouch underwear) with male models striking relaxed poses, accompanied by the phrase, "Feels Great."

**Addresses:** *Parent company*—Jockey International, Inc., 2300 60th Street, Kenosha, WI 53140; phone: (414) 658-8111; fax: (414) 658-8111.

Style 1001 was quickly refined into Style 1007, which made its debut at a company meeting in January of 1935, and a window display in downtown Chicago's Marshall Field & Co. department store prompted consumers to purchase over 12,000 of the new undergarments in less than a day. More notable was the formal unveiling of the new "Jockey Classic" inverted "Y-front" brief, as well as the "midway" style boxer short, at the National Association of Retail Clothiers and Furnishers Convention, held in Chicago in February of 1938. In what was most likely the first fashion show for undergarments, Cooper's hired a male model to don the newly designed "Jockey Classic" beneath a half-transparent cellophane wedding tuxedo. At the "groom's" side was the "bride," exposing through the cellophane half of her fashionably-cut wedding gown the latest in feminine undergarments. The unconventionality of the fashion show brought Cooper's into the national spotlight, as pictures of the Cellophane Wedding party appeared in major newspapers and magazines around the globe. Underwear had become fashion, and Cooper's Underwear Company was leading the way.

### Innovation in Textiles

As American troops returned from World War II, and manufactured goods became readily accessible once again, the country was filled with a new vitality. Cooper's entered the 1950s with the same spirit of innovation with which it had been founded more than 70 years before. With the Y-front design a success, Cooper's turned to the fabric from which its popular briefs were made. Silk tricot, a non-stretching, warp-knit fabric that had originated in France, was translated into a new, nylon version of the Jockey Classic. Cooper's found that the fabric held color well and soon the standard white line bloomed an array of striking colors.

Next came the creation of novelty print undergarments. Tricot, with its lustrous silken drape, was ideal for what Cooper's marketed as "Animal Pants." Leopard, tiger, and zebra printed briefs were worn under conservative business suits shortly after their introduction in 1953, and Valentine's Day-inspired patterns appeared two years later. As underwear became more fashionably sexy, it also became more revealing. "Scants," a smaller cut brief,

was marketed by Cooper's in 1959. Underwear was now making a personal statement.

When clothing styles changed in the early 1960s, Jockey briefs became more snug-fitting, and the company once again looked at how they could adapt a successful product to a changing marketplace. Cooper's turned to textiles for the answer. In 1964 the company introduced a fiber with the trade name "Suprel." A blend of polyester and combed cotton, the new fabric provided more stretch and comfort than tricot. New styles continued to be generated as consumer tastes changed. In the 1980s the "Jeans Brief," a low-riding undergarment in denim blue with orange stitching, became popular with wearers of designer jeans. In 1964 so-called "fashion" underwear accounted for only three percent of sales, with most customers opting for the more conservative, classic white brief rather than Animal Pants and colored undergarments. However, by 1990, the market of fashion underwear for men accounted for more than half of all the company's sales.

### Jockey Becomes a Household Word

In the early 1970s Cooper's Underwear Company underwent several important changes. Harry Wolf, a consultant to Cooper's, was impressed with how popular the company's product was with American men. He assembled enough capital to make the Cooper family an offer to purchase the business. The family accepted, and Cooper's Underwear Company became Jockey International in 1972. Jockey remained privately owned into the 1990s. After Wolf's death in 1978, ownership in the company was divided between his three children. Wolf's son sold his share of the company to his two sisters in 1983; Donna Wolf Steigerwaldt held a controlling interest and became chair and CEO, while her sister retained the remainder of the company's stock.

### Athletic Appeal

"Take away their uniforms, and who are they?," asked a 1976 ad campaign featuring winning Baltimore Orioles pitcher Jim Palmer and eight other athletes. Four years later Palmer became the official Jockey spokesperson. In addition to modeling the company's product in both promotional literature and advertisements, Palmer's celebrity status allowed him to make personal appearances to promote the Jockey line; on an episode of the *Mike Douglas Show,* Palmer recounted the history of underwear for the edification of the television viewers, in addition to modeling Jockey underwear and the company's new line of sportswear, called Man in Motion.

In 1980 Palmer began appearing in print advertisements for Jockey Elance briefs, a fashionable variation of the classic Y-front. The public's reaction boosted underwear sales. As CEO Steigerwaldt told Bess Gallanis in *Forbes:* "Women buy 70% of men's underwear. They think Jim Palmer is sexy—incredibly sexy." Palmer's popularity propelled the company into making a poster-sized version of the ad available, and the proceeds of the poster sales were donated to the Cystic Fibrosis Foundation where Palmer served as National Sports Chairman. By 1982, the company had increased its hold on the men's fashion underwear market to 65 percent.

### Jockey—Not Just For Him Anymore

In 1981 cotton panties made up 20 percent of the women's panty market, but by 1983, cotton garments would account for almost 30 percent. Part of the upward trend in the popularity of cotton undergarments was Jockey for Her, a line of all-cotton women's bikinis, hipsters, and full panties that Jockey began test-marketing in Dallas, Milwaukee, and Los Angeles in the fall of 1982. By the holiday season of the following year, the line of panties was available in a wide variety of colors and patterns. Packaged in distinctive clear plastic tubes, the underwear appeared in upscale department stores throughout the United States. Like that for its men's underwear, the Jockey for Her logo was woven into the garment's unique white elastic waistband: "A touch not lost on Mr. Klein," noted Pat Sloan in an article comparing Calvin Klein's line of Women's underwear introduced to compete with Jockey for Her.

At the same time, Jockey introduced a string bikini, camisole top, and ribbed, sleeveless athletic t-shirts. As with the manufacturer's panties, the new garments in the Jockey for Her line were available in 20 colors, carried the Cotton Inc. trademark signifying that the products were made from 100 percent quality cotton fiber, and were moderately priced at two-thirds the cost of the competing Calvin Klein line. As the brands each battled for market share in the $866 million women's panty market, Jockey expanded its line to include the popular "french cut" panty, a line of "Queen-sized" underwear, and all-cotton undergarments for boys and girls, which were introduced in 1987.

The initial advertising campaign for Jockey for Her consisted of TV and magazine ads proclaiming, "Look who's wearing Jockey now." In addition, 1984 saw the start of a $4.5 million coupon program to entice women to try Jockey for Her for free. Howard Cooley, then president of Jockey International, devised the marketing strategy. Cooley told Kevin Brown of *Advertising Age* that marketing research showed Jockey that they had a superior product and they wanted to encourage women to try it. "It's the same thing the soap people do. When they want you to try their product, they put it in your mailbox." The company sent coupons for free panties to 25,000 gynecologists and obstetricians informing the medical community of the health benefits of wearing undergarments of 100 percent cotton; in addition, coupons were inserted into product samplers given to women enrolling at over 400 colleges, stressing not only the health benefits of the undergarments but their fashionable appearance. Additional advertising was done in national magazines aimed at both young women and health-conscious women; these included *Seventeen, Health, Cosmopolitan, People, Self,* and *Glamour.* The program proved successful when revenues from Jockey for Her increased company sales volume by 20 percent in the first two years following its introduction.

In 1988 Jockey purchased Nantucket Mills, a hosiery manufacturer, and began test-marketing a line of women's hosiery with the phrase: "At last! Pantyhose that fit!" Jockey for Her hosiery—pantyhose, thigh-highs, stockings, and knee-highs in both sheer and opaque tones—appeared on upscale department-store shelves the following year. Advertising featured a "real people" theme that had proved successful in previous ad campaigns. Jockey's marketing strategy was to compete with Hanes, considered the front-runner in the race to corner the women's hosiery market with 25 percent of the $2.2 hosiery business. According to Cooley, Jockey is striving to be a "strong number two," which will necessitate bypassing such popular brands as Round the Clock, Evan Picone, and Christian Dior on its way to the second spot.

## Advertising Innovations

From its early print ads in *Saturday Evening Post* to the novelty of the Cellophane Wedding, Jockey has approached advertising with a view to the creative. A prime example of this occurred after Jockey for Her women's undergarments elicited thousands of letters praising the line. *Love Letters to Jockey for Her,* a compilation of those letters, aided the company in persuading retail store owners to give the line valuable retail space—especially important in the case of Jockey's new line due to the fact that it is packaged and sold in a free-standing store display unit. In addition, the ad campaign for Jockey for Her received several awards

*Models appeared in cellophane clothing to show off their Jockey underwear at a 1935 menswear tradeshow.*

for depicting "real people"—mothers, working women, students, women of many ages and backgrounds. Women Against Pornography's Ms. Liberty Award for "A Step in the Right Direction" was presented to Jockey in 1985 for advertising that "does not exploit or disgrace the woman and positions her in a positive role." Two years later, Jockey's "real women" theme was once again rewarded, in this case with a citation from *Plus Magazine* for depicting a banker/grandmother and thus offering a "creative, attractive solution to marketing to the 'mature' audience."

In the early 1980s the company began to focus on sports and athletics to market its products: Jim Palmer was joined in 1987 by Olympic Gold Medalist Bart Conner in Jockey ads. In addition,

Palmer's ad campaign brought the element of sex-appeal directly before the underwear consumer, and other companies were quick to follow. In 1991 Jockey combined sex-appeal and a focus on athletics in advertising Jockey for Women in a "teaser" ad campaign—a form of advertising that has a proven ability to catch a consumer's attention and hold it for an extended period of time. In May of that year, an image of Jim Palmer that had graced a billboard in New York City's Times Square was replaced by that of a mystery woman. Under the headline "So Comfortable! Jockey for Her," was a reclining female figure wearing Jockey brand underwear. The woman's face was veiled at the beginning of the billboard campaign, but people's suspicions were confirmed later that summer when the veil was removed to reveal Olympic Gold Medalist Nancy Hogshead, already a model for Jockey's print ad campaign. Hogshead, who lives within walking distance of the billboard, was pleased with the campaign and her position as Jockey's first celebrity spokeswoman. She noted in *Sports Illustrated,* "The point of the whole campaign is to show real women. That's one of the things I like about it."

The women's underwear line experienced an overall growth of 14 percent in 1991, partially due to the Hogshead ad campaign. As Cooley told *Women's Wear Daily,* the ads are carefully designed to depict "everyday people in lifestyle environments that consumers can relate to." Hogshead's reputation as a successful, attractive, and active woman—as opposed to a young, anorexic-looking model—reflects many women's growing interest in reconciling good health with beauty. Throughout its history, Jockey has clearly allied its brand name with that movement.

## International Growth

In 1936 Jockey became the first U.S. company to license its product outside the country when Cooper's began dealing with a Canadian firm. For several years this was the extent of the company's international growth. However, with the overseas coverage of the Cellophane Wedding, the Jockey brand began to get recognition outside the United States. In response to such foreign interest, Cooper's Underwear licensed the English firm of Lyle & Scott to manufacture and sell the Jockey Classic in Great Britain. The relationship between the two companies has proven to be successful: at the close of the 1980s, 70 percent of British men still preferred the Y-front brief to boxer shorts and other styles of undergarments. The Jockey brand is a common sight in British department stores and has achieved recognition in numerous other markets throughout the world where the company has licensed its trademark design and logo. Jockey for Her has also found its way overseas; in 1985 the line was introduced in such European cities as Zurich, where it has continually gained in popularity.

## Performance Appraisal

In 1982 underwear accounted for 50 percent of the $240 million in annual sales posted by Jockey International. By 1986 production had increased to the point where the company had to construct two additional plants to keep up with demand for Jockey brand undergarments. In the succeeding decade, Jockey accelerated its diversion into such related areas of production as men's sportswear, and both fashion and athletic socks for men, women, and children. To increase its profitability, Jockey has begun licens-

ing agreements with Yves St. Laurent, a prominent name in the designer category, and Wrangler, a recognized standard in the mass merchandise category. It also plans to compete with Izod and Polo with the St. Laurent line.

In the $900 million men's underwear market of the 1990s, Jockey holds a 30 percent share, with yearly growth anticipated at the rate of 1-2 percent. While Jockey's success has created profits for its owners, it has also spawned competition and repeated threats to its trademarked innovations. The successful ad campaign featuring Jim Palmer encouraged Calvin Klein to compete for a share of the $1 billion year men's underwear market by producing his own line of underwear. Klein copied Jockey's distinctive waistband design by printing his brand name at the elastic edge.

## Looking to the Future

As Jockey's Y-front celebrated its first half-century of popularity in 1988, Noelle Britton noted in *Marketing,* "There are not many brands which can celebrate a 50 year birthday and boast that their lack of product innovation is a key factor in their success." Through a shrewd blend of conservatism and creativity, the company predicts that the women's underwear line will soon overtake the men's line as the bulk of Jockey International's sales. In the larger market for women's underwear, Jockey is finding a wider niche to fill with its well-made line of fashionable undergarments, and past history can only suggest that steady progress towards aligning public demand with quality will stand the company in good stead.

## Further Reading:

Bloomfield, Judy, "Jockey for Her," *Women's Wear Daily,* January 13, 1992, p. 5.

Brashler, William, "The Rise of Beefcake," *Chicago,* November 1982, pp. 22, 24.

Britton, Noelle, "The Y's the Limit: Holding on to Success in a Delicate Business," *Marketing,* April 28, 1988, pp. 20–21.

Brown, Kevin, "Jockey Finds Giveaway Campaign Fits," *Advertising Age,* May 2, 1985, p. 40.

Elliott, Stuart, "Jockey's Faceless Approach to a Times Square Teaser," *New York Times,* June 10, 1991, p. D11.

Gallanis, Bess, "Understatements," *Forbes,* June 21, 1982, p. 143.

"Jockey to Solve Big Mystery Today," *New York Times,* September 11, 1991, p. D16.

Marx, Linda, "Audubon Never Saw One Like Him: Jim Palmer Is the Oriole with the Colorful Underwear," *People,* October 4, 1982, pp. 110–12.

Parr, Jan, "The Woman's Touch," *Forbes 400,* October 27, 1986, pp. 332–33.

Schmidt, Beth, "Whose Head?," *Sports Illustrated,* July 8, 1991, p. 12.

Sloan, Pat, *Advertising Age,* "Palmer Goes the Distance for Jockey," April 25, 1983, p. 63; "Briefly Speaking, There's No Shortage of Shorts," October 17, 1983, p. 85; "Going In-House: Jockey Pulls Account from Warwick," April 6, 1987, p. 12; "Jockey Jumps into Hose," August 21, 1989, p. 62; "Underwear Wants to Be Outgoing: Shorts Become a Fashion Statement," February 8, 1993, p. 6.

"Why Jockey Switched Its Ads from TV to Print," *Business Week,* July 26, 1976, pp. 140, 142.

—*Jay P. Pederson*

# JOHNSON'S® BABY PRODUCTS

*Johnson's*

The Johnson's brand of baby-care products from Johnson & Johnson has been the choice of mothers for decades. Johnson's baby powder was introduced in 1893, and has become one of the company's most enduring products. Inspired by its success with baby powder, the company went on to develop an entire line of Johnson's baby products, beginning with baby soap in 1917. The company also added Johnson's baby oil (1935), Johnson's baby lotion (1943), and Johnson's baby shampoo (1953). Johnson's baby-care products were often the market leader in baby toiletries, but also proved popular for adult use.

## Brand Origins

In 1890 a physician complained that a medicated plaster sold by Johnson & Johnson was irritating his patient's skin, and he asked the company how to remedy it. Pharmacist Frederick B. Kilmer, who had joined Johnson & Johnson as scientific director in 1888, suggested that the doctor try talcum powder. Talcum powder is made from talc, a soft mineral that is found in many areas of the world. The suggestion worked so well that Johnson & Johnson began including small tins of talcum powder with several of its medicinal preparations. After customers repeatedly asking for just the powder, the company introduced Johnson's toilet and baby powder in 1893. The name was changed to Johnson's baby powder in the 1930s.

## Advertising Innovations

Early ads for Johnson's toilet and baby powder often focused on the benefits of a good night's sleep. One ad, showing a mother and two children, said, "[T]he greatest gift a baby can have is a wonderful mother—a mother who knows that hours and hours of restful sleep are essential to baby's future . . . . Do you realize that Johnson's Baby Powder was the suggestion of a famous physician who knew that skin comfort is the surest path to sounder sleep?" Johnson & Johnson also stressed that its powder was made "especially for babies in laboratories that prepare hundreds of articles for the medical profession. . . . The difference between Johnson's Baby Powder and ordinary talcums appeals to a mother."

In the early 1930s, Johnson & Johnson launched what was then the largest ad campaign in its history to promote Johnson's baby powder. Four-color ads appeared in magazines showing a line up of smiling babies and declared: "The Jury of Babies Does Declare Johnson's Baby Powder The Best For the Toilet." The ads also

were used as window displays in thousands of drugstores. Inside the stores, the company placed placards that read: "Your baby deserves the best . . . Only the best is good enough for the health and happiness of the little darling. By the way, are you using Johnson's Toilet and Baby Powder . . . Best for baby, Best for you."

In the 1960s, the focus of advertising for Johnson's baby powder began to shift to the physical bonding between mothers and their babies. Lawrence G. Foster, former vice president of public relations at Johnson & Johnson and the author of *A Company That Cares: One Hundred Year Illustrated History of Johnson & Johnson,* wrote, "The more this relationship was understood, the more obvious it became that the most important function of baby toiletries was the facilitation of a mother's need to physically demonstrate love to her child." Johnson & Johnson ran ads showing mothers tenderly holding their babies. The text read, "Your touch tells him everything. That's why we make our baby powder so pure and soft and soothing. It feels like love." Johnson & Johnson also became a major sponsor of seminars and legitimate scientific research into maternal nurturing and the importance of touching to a child's healthy development.

## Brand Development

The familiar white plastic container of Johnson's baby powder was introduced in 1963. In its *Annual Report* for 1980, Johnson & Johnson said of its baby powder, "Very few products have ever attained the long-term universal acceptance and engendered such pleasant thoughts." According to a study by *American Baby* magazine in the late 1980s, baby powder was the third most-used product in the baby toiletries category, behind baby shampoo and cotton swabs. In the early 1990s, Johnson's baby powder held about a 60 percent share of the market.

Like Johnson's baby powder, Johnson's baby oil, introduced in 1936, consisted of one basic ingredient—in this case mineral oil—and added fragrance. Mineral oil, made from petroleum, was used in many medicinal and cosmetic preparations. In 1987 Johnson & Johnson introduced baby oil mousse, which the company said provided the same moisturizing benefits of its regular baby oil in a less greasy, easy to apply formula. That was followed in 1990 with Johnson's creamy baby oil.

## AT A GLANCE

Johnson's brand of baby powder introduced in 1893 by Johnson & Johnson; Johnson's baby oil introduced in 1936; Johnson's baby lotion debuted in 1943; Johnson's baby shampoo introduced in 1953.

*Performance:* Market share—63% of baby powder category.

*Major competitor:* Mennen Company's Baby Magic; also Fisher-Price and S.C. Johnson & Son brands.

*Advertising:* Agency—Young & Rubicam, New York. *Major campaign*—"Everything you do to your body you do to your baby."

*Addresses:* Parent company—Johnson & Johnson, One Johnson & Johnson Plaza, New Brunswick, NJ 08933; phone: (908) 524-0400.

Johnson's baby lotion was introduced in 1943. Initially, it was sold primarily to hospitals and physicians. Then in 1948, the *Journal of Pediatrics* reported on a two-year study by eight hospitals that showed that regular use of Johnson's baby lotion significantly reduced diaper rash and other skin irritations. Johnson's baby lotion also was credited with ending an epidemic of impetigo in one hospital. In 1950 Johnson & Johnson launched a nationwide advertising campaign based on the results of the study.

Headlined "science takes greatest step in infant skin care!" one ad proclaimed that Johnson's baby lotion was "hospital-proved" to be the most effective preparation known to prevent impetigo, raw buttocks, diaper rash, and heat rash. The ad also suggested that Johnson's baby lotion was "promising" in the treatment of adult skin irritations such as acne and eczema. The text of another ad began, "Mother! You can minimize the danger of your baby's suffering from the four most common skin irritations of infancy—with regular daily use of new Johnson's Baby Lotion." The ad said Johnson's baby lotion "actually kills the germs that commonly cause impetigo and diaper rash" and also "prevents that unpleasant odor" of wet diapers.

Johnson's baby lotion changed little over the next 40 years, although in 1991 Johnson & Johnson announced a "longer lasting protection formula." Johnson & Johnson held about a 40 percent share of the market for baby lotions.

Johnson's baby shampoo was introduced in 1953, followed in 1954 by the well-known "No More Tears" formula. But, according to the *New York Times,* product development began 20 years earlier. In a story about Johnson & Johnson's research center in 1954, the *Times* reported that a chance remark about crying babies at bath time led researchers to begin experimenting with shampoo formulas. By 1950, the company had developed a formula that cleaned well without irritating the eyes. However, it took several more years to perfect a formula that also lathered well, which was important for consumer acceptance. The *New York Times* reported that Johnson & Johnson spent more than $1 million in 1954 to promote Johnson's "No More Tears" baby shampoo, "the most it has ever spent for advertising and promotion of a new product," and added "further funds are being spent to improve the product despite ready acceptance by mothers and babies."

According to *American Baby,* baby shampoos were the most often used product in the baby toiletries category, with 79 percent of new mothers using some brand of baby shampoo. Until the

early 1990s, Johnson's baby shampoo dominated the market, accounting for more than half of all sales. However, in 1992, *Financial World* reported that Mennen's Baby Magic shampoo had passed Johnson's baby shampoo in market share. Ralph Larsen, then chairman of Johnson & Johnson, told *Financial World,* "Right now, our [baby care] products are targeted to mother and baby. So we're bringing out a J&J line of children's products . . . to strengthen that line by segmenting it to children as well as infants."

Ironically, Johnson's baby shampoo had been targeted not only for babies but for the entire family since its introduction. In the 1970s, Johnson & Johnson launched a television campaign that stressed that if Johnson's products were good enough for infants they were good enough for adults. Temporarily, the campaign helped make Johnson's baby shampoo the number one shampoo in the country. The shampoo was especially popular with adults who shampooed frequently because of its gentle formula. However, by the late 1980s, Johnson's baby shampoo's share of the total market had fallen from a high of about 4.5 percent to about 3.5 percent. In 1990 the company launched an advertising campaign, "Take Good Care of My Baby," that continued to target all ages. According to *Soap/Cosmetics/Chemical Specialties* magazine, more than half of the baby shampoo sold in the United States was used by adults.

Over the years, the Johnson's brand name has been used with many other baby-care products. Products still on the market in 1993 included Johnson's baby cream (1921), Johnson's baby corn starch and Johnson's baby wash cloths (1980), Johnson's baby bar (1982), Johnson's medicated diaper rash ointment and Johnson's baby bath (1990).

### Performance Appraisal

Birth rates began to climb in the United States in the mid-1980s, fueling an increase in the market for baby-care products. In 1990, the baby toiletries category grew by as much as 15 percent. Established companies responded with renewed advertising and by introducing brand extensions, such as Johnson's creamy baby oil. Other companies also entered the market, including S.C. Johnson & Sons, which introduced a line of baby-care products with its respected Fisher-Price brand. Fisher-Price baby toiletries quickly became the number three brand behind Johnson & Johnson and Baby Magic from the Mennen Company. Mennen, which was the leader in baby bath products, introduced baby powder and baby shampoo products in 1990.

More stores also were beginning to stock baby toiletries not only with other baby-care products but also along side adult products, since more baby-care products were being purchased by adults who seldom went down the baby-care aisle. In 1991 *Soap/Cosmetics/Chemical Specialties* suggested that companies would soon begin marketing baby-care products specifically to older adults. "As the population matures, the need for gentler products, no-tears formulas and products made from natural formulas continues to grow. Many adult versions of hair and skin products are too harsh for the older adult and few products are currently available that cater to their needs."

These trends suggested that the market for baby toiletries would continue to grow, and most likely would become even more competitive than in the past. Although baby-care products had become a small part of Johnson & Johnson's immense product line, new product introductions in the late 1980s and early 1990s indicated the company would continue to be a dominate force in the market for baby toiletries.

In 1992, in keeping with its tradition of promoting infant health, Johnson & Johnson launched a public service ad campaign focusing on prenatal care rather than selling baby-care products. One television commercial showed scenes of pregnant women drinking alcohol, smoking, and taking drugs. Meanwhile, an announcer warned, "Everything you do to your body you do to your baby."

## Further Reading:

*Johnson & Johnson Annual Report,* New Brunswick, NJ: Johnson & Johnson, 1980, p. 8.

Brucato, Patricia S., "Oh, Baby!" *Soap/Cosmetics/Chemical Specialties,* June 1991, p. 36.

Foster, Lawrence, *A Company That Cares: One Hundred Year Illustrated History of Johnson & Johnson,* New Brunswick, NJ: Johnson & Johnson, 1986.

"Health & Beauty Aids: Baby Care," *Progressive Grocer,* August 1989, p. 70.

Linsenmeyer, Adrienne, "No Band-Aid Solution," *Financial World,* January 21, 1992, pp. 25–27.

"Prescription for Growth," *Forbes,* June 26, 1978, pp. 97–99.

Sloan, Pat, "Baby Boom in Toiletries Hits J&J," *Advertising Age,* January 21, 1991, p. 15.

*—Dean Boyer*

# JOHNSON'S® WAX

The wide name recognition of Johnson's Wax is based more on the product's long history than on its current use. As more women entered the work force in the latter half of the twentieth century, time-consuming methods of floor waxing drew less and less interest. The owner and creator of Johnson's Wax established his product and reputation on a solid base, however, which allowed succeeding generations to diversify the family business. In the early 1990s S.C. Johnson & Son, Inc., more commonly known as SC Johnson Wax, maintained its stature as one of the largest privately held companies in the United States.

## Founder Background

Samuel Curtis Johnson, creator of Johnson's Paste Wax and founder of S.C. Johnson & Son, Inc., was born the eldest of 11 children in Elyria, Ohio, on December 24, 1833. The family moved to Chicago, then Rockford, Illinois, continuing on to Elkhorn, then Grafton, Wisconsin. Johnson's first job was in the Milwaukee office of the Chicago, Milwaukee & St. Paul Railroad. Though his early education was scattered due to the family's many moves, Johnson enrolled in Ohio's Oberlin College in 1857. He left after a year to become secretary for the Kenosha, Rockford, & Rock Island Railroad in Kenosha, Wisconsin. Within several years he married Caroline Fisk and decided at this time to invest half of his $100 monthly salary in the company, a policy he continued for some time.

S. C. Johnson lost all his savings when the railroad company went bankrupt. He spent the next 30 years working in a variety of positions, including becoming a partner in a Kenosha stationery store that failed. In 1886 Johnson took a job selling parquet flooring—a decorative style using various colored woods laid in geometric patterns—for the Racine Hardware Company. Johnson bought his employer's company the same year, leased a second floor shop, and with a staff of two men and two boys, began selling and installing parquet flooring. S. C. Johnson's son Herbert F. Johnson joined the company in 1888 at age 20.

## Enter Johnson's Wax

Customers soon wrote for advice on caring for their floors. Johnson knew that some European parquet floors had been maintained for up to 300 years when polished with beeswax. With that information in mind, the entrepreneur mixed his own waxes and in 1888 settled on a product he called Johnson's Prepared Paste Wax.

Johnson included a can of wax free with each floor his company installed.

Although competing waxes and polishes were introduced, Samuel Johnson's company gained a reputation as wood-finishing experts. By 1898 Johnson's sales of wax, wood fillers, and finishes soon outstripped contracts for new flooring. This was a fortunate development, as the demand for parquet flooring decreased significantly by the turn of the century. Since the simpler styles of maple and oak floors required similar maintenance as the parquet floors, business remained steady for the 12-year-old company.

In 1906 Herbert F. Johnson became a partner in the business, and the company was named S.C. Johnson & Son. By 1910, growth in S.C. Johnson's wax and wood finishing business prompted the company to add new buildings. SC Johnson Wax had a staff of 92.

## Manufacturing and Packaging

Early manufacturing of Johnson's Paste Wax was similar to the method S. C. Johnson first employed at home: batches were mixed up in large kettles. The wax was then poured into cans that were filled by hand with the use of a sprinkling can. After the cans of wax were cooled on a table, the lids had to be pressed onto the cans. In the early years employees literally walked over the tops of the lids to close them tightly. As described in the *JonWax Journal: 75th Anniversary Issue,* published in 1961, the "hand-filled cans" were then "hand-packed 100 to a hand-made wooden box and hand-trucked to the shipping room where they were hand-loaded into cars or horse drawn drays." In the early 1900s, a daily average of 8,000 cans of Johnson's Paste Wax were produced by this method.

Perhaps due to the nature of the ingredients, wax continued to be melted in large kettles and stirred with wooden paddles until the early 1930s. And while other parts of the manufacturing process were gradually being improved, hands-on work was still necessary. Early production line machines for Johnson's Semi-Gloss Enamel required that an employee stand ready to catch the can as it came off the line and check that the label adhered. Similarly, both Johnson's Traffic Paste and Liquid Wax, introduced in 1933, were packaged in oblong cans that required hand-labeling. In 1935 cans of various wax products were packed in wooden crates closed shut by a hammer and nail.

## AT A GLANCE

Johnson's brand of wax founded in 1898 as Johnson's Prepared Paste Wax by Samuel Curtis Johnson, president of S.C. Johnson & Son, which began in 1888 and sold parquet floors; wax sales exceeded flooring sales by 1906; S.C. Johnson & Son., Ltd., established in England, 1914; company incorporated as S.C. Johnson & Son, Inc., 1932; extended brand name to include insecticides in the 1950s and personal care products in the 1970s.

*Advertising:* Agency—Foote Cone Belding, Chicago, IL.

*Addresses:* Parent company—S.C. Johnson & Son, Inc., 1525 Howe Street, Racine, WI 53403-5011; phone: (414) 631-2000; fax: (414) 631-2133.

As the market for Johnson's Wax and other products grew, more specialized equipment was needed to meet the demand. SC Johnson Wax engineers designed production facilities, including a magnetized conveyor, an automatic code-dater, a can cleaner, a vacuum purger, a labeling machine, and an automatic carton loader. The company was an innovator in the creation of filling machines, palletizing equipment—machines that supply cans to a production line—and automatic packing for oblong cans.

### Sales Strategies

In 1914 salespeople traveled by street car from Racine to Kenosha and called on stores, door to door; later, they traveled by surrey. By 1917 Johnson's Wax had a sales staff of 12. Emphasis was placed on the company, the quality of the products, and the profit opportunity for the retailer.

To begin to sell his wax products in different markets, S. C. Johnson looked to the early automobile market. It was decided that a company car would not only serve as transportation for the salespeople, but could also be used as a demonstration model. Salespeople drove around in a 1911 Mitchell, polishing the baked enamel fenders and hoods as part of the effort to sell Johnson's Wax.

By 1916 S.C. Johnson & Son branched into the grocery and drugstore market, sending sales representatives with the original paste wax, as well as newer developments such as a carbon remover, stop squeak oil, and a product called Black Lac used specifically for the fabric tops of automobiles. All of these items were grouped into Johnson's Car Saver products, which were to form the base of the company's automotive line.

In 1922 the sales objective was increased by 50 percent. Some of the slogans the SC Johnson Wax used to energize its staff were "Sell the right customer right" and "Sell them on the new Products, resell them on the old." Before the development of supermarkets, the challenge to Johnson's Wax sales staff was to sell to one-line stores. Thus, hardware or paint store owners had to be convinced that products for floor and furniture waxing would appeal to their customers. As supermarkets became common, part of selling included providing retailers with special events displays to catch the consumer's eye. SC Johnson Wax's sales staff also had to provide the merchandiser with a diversified line of wax products which the company was continuously developing.

### SC Johnson Wax Branches Out

Although Johnson's Wax was the company's flagship brand, product diversification was an early goal. SC Johnson Wax concentrated in wood finishing products and various wax cleaners until World War II. At that time, automobile waxes and oils as well as liquid wax were introduced. Throughout the 1920s the company introduced a variety of products designed to assist in the waxing process, such as a lambs wool wax applying mop, an electric floor polisher, and polishing mitts. The focus remained on encouraging the many uses of Johnson's Wax. Two significant products, though, were developed during the late 1920s and early 1930s: Johnson's Prepared Wax for Airplanes and Glo-Coat.

### Airplane Promotions

In 1928 SC Johnson Wax research laboratories studied the benefits of waxing the surfaces of airplanes. Tests showed that drag was reduced on a waxed airplane. The following year a newly acquired company plane, the Johnson Waxbird, flew to St. Louis, Missouri, with four cases of liquid wax. Due to widespread publicity, the air-shipped products sold out quickly at area department stores.

Another promotion was planned in 1931 with the company's second plane, the Johnson Waxwing. A pilot and a young woman billed as "Johnson's Wax Doll" toured the United States, presenting Johnson's Electric Floor Polishers to winners of a national contest in various cities. In 1936 H. F. Johnson made a 20,000 mile air journey to South America to study the carnauba palm and its wax derivatives. Such widely publicized events helped make Johnson's Wax a household name.

One of H. F. Johnson's great accomplishments was the development of Glo-Coat, a self-polishing floor wax, in 1932. Taking over in 1928 as president and chairman of the board upon the death of his father, H. F. Johnson, Sr., the 28-year-old grandson of the founder faced a challenge. During the Great Depression of the 1930s, Johnson refused to lay off workers even though by 1932 sales were at a historical low. Instead, in addition to such products as Carnu, an automobile cleaner and polish, and Cream Wax, the first Johnson furniture polish, he introduced Glo-Coat, the first and highly successful one-step floor polisher, which gave the company the boost it needed.

### The Johnson Wax Building

In 1936 work began on a new Administration Center in Racine, Wisconsin. Though certainly conceived for utilitarian purposes—a May 6, 1939, *Business Week* story was titled "Office Building Goes Functional"—the headquarters building designed by Frank Lloyd Wright must be named as a factor in the development of SC Johnson Wax. Completed in 1939, the structure became known as the Johnson Wax building and drew many visitors from outside Racine. As stated by a contributor to *JonWax Journal: 75th Anniversary Issue,* a company-published book, "There is no question that the striking modern architecture of our Administration Center had done much to enhance the public image of Johnson's Wax as a dynamic, forward-looking company."

### Service Products and R & D

Firmly established in the household products market beginning in the 1930s, SC Johnson Wax turned some focus to the service sector. The company packaged popular products in large containers for use in building maintenance. Users discussed their special needs concerning floor care in heavy traffic areas. Johnson Wax reciprocated by developing longer-lasting finishes, floor buffing and polishing machines, and a whole line of furniture polishes and even insecticides.

As SC Johnson Wax worked with more users, industrial needs were communicated, and the company began working on products unrelated to floor upkeep but technologically analogous to wax and polishes. A Research and Development Division was founded in 1946. The company subsequently developed a wax product to prevent metal corrosion, an antistatic wax for plastics manufacturers, and wax coatings to protect vegetables and fruits during shipping.

### Early Advertising

While new products and sales strategies were constantly being developed, the growth of SC Johnson Wax in the early twentieth century had as much to do with advertising and promotion as any other factor. As listed in the book *JonWax Journal: 75th Anniversary,* the first advertisement recorded was a two-inch ad placed in the November 1888 issue of *Century* magazine. In 1893 an ad appearing in *Cosmopolitan* carried a clear message: "Johnson's Prepared Wax Saves Labor." By 1920 the company had advertised in *Scribner's, Everybody's, McClure's, Carpentry and Building,* and the *Saturday Evening Post.* SC Johnson Wax devoted $1 million to its advertising budget for the years 1926 and 1927, branching into color ads in *Ladies Home Journal, Women's Home Companion, McCalls, Good Housekeeping, Better Homes & Gardens,* and *American Home.*

It was the use of radio advertising in the 1930s, though, that made SC Johnson Wax an even more familiar company. Sponsoring orchestras, poetry reading, and even broadcasting its own show, S.C. Johnson & Son, Inc., had its name mentioned frequently on the airwaves.

Late in 1934 SC Johnson Wax's William Connolly and Jack Louis toured the country and discovered a couple from Peoria, Illinois, named Marion and Jim Jordan. Together with scriptwriter Don Quinn, SC Johnson Wax put together a show with the Jordans playing the characters Fibber McGee & Molly in a show of the same name. Broadcast continuously from April of 1935 to May of 1950, the show competed for first place in ratings with performers such as Jack Benny. In its later years, the show reached a network of 135 radio stations nationwide.

From 1952 through 1954 S.C. Johnson & Son, Inc., sponsored a news broadcast for the Mutual Broadcasting System on 550 stations, reaching audiences five times a day, six days a week. The company went on to sponsor 20 shows through 1961. Later, from the 1960s to the present, television commercials became the medium of choice for advertising.

### International Development

Johnson's Wax was introduced in England in 1914 with the establishment of S.C. Johnson & Son, Ltd. In a dramatic development, the first shipment of wax to England was lost when the ship carrying it was sunk by a World War I submarine. Three years later S.C. Johnson & Son, Inc., entered Australia with a subsidiary in Sydney. In 1920 another S.C. Johnson & Son subsidiary was opened in Canada.

Herbert F. Johnson died within a decade of his father in 1928, leaving his son H.F. Johnson, Jr., to take over as president and

chairman of the board at age 28. International expansion continued, with the establishment of a French subsidiary in 1931. On the heels of H. F. Johnson's highly publicized flight to Brazil in 1936, a subsidiary was established in Fortaleza, Brazil, where Johnson researchers sought to improve the quality of carnauba wax.

The establishment of international headquarters slowed during World War II, but by 1957 SC Johnson Wax had incorporated in Germany, and subsidiaries were opened in Mexico, the Philippines, and Venezuela. By 1961 Johnson's Wax and other products were being produced in Argentina, Chile, Italy, New Zealand, Switzerland, Sweden, and the Union of South Africa.

Howard M. Packard, named president of S.C. Johnson & Son in 1958, was the first person outside the Johnson family to hold the post and was followed in later years in that capacity by other non-family members. Samuel C. Johnson was named new products director in 1955, a year after he joined the company. The founder's great-grandson became chief executive in 1966.

By 1968 SC Johnson Wax's foreign affiliates numbered 30. The company continued to broaden its European business bases, and through the 1970s and 1980s moved into Eastern Europe, Asia, and the Middle East. Using its experience in developing products based on specific customer needs—a skill that had established the company in the United States in the early 1900s—S.C. Johnson & Son, Inc., did well in Japan when other American companies were faltering. An SC Johnson Wax joint venture in Kiev in the Ukraine led the company to look for further expansion in Poland and Hungary in the early 1990s.

### Wax Wanes

While the S.C. Johnson & Son, Inc., was successfully generating income abroad in the 1950s, its core wax and polish products were becoming less necessary as new hard-surface vinyl floor coverings replaced wood and linoleums. As new products director, Samuel Johnson steered the company into other markets.

SC Johnson Wax, known for packaging and marketing success, combined these skills with the technical and research expertise it had developed to enter brand new markets. As reported in the June 10, 1985, issue of *Advertising Age,* H. F. Johnson wasn't very keen on the idea of expansion when Samuel Johnson first broached the concept in 1955: "You know we don't make products without wax in them," the elder Johnson had said.

Nevertheless, in 1956, two aerosols were introduced at the urging of Samuel Johnson: Raid insecticide and Glade air freshener. Off! insect repellant followed in 1957 and Pledge furniture polish came out in 1958. The decades following brought more and more non-wax products; in the 1970s the company entered personal products with Edge shaving cream and Agree hair conditioner. Quoted in the February 14, 1977, *Business Week,* Samuel Johnson explained, "We looked around the house and found we were running out of markets to conquer. We were already polishing the floors and furniture, cleaning the rugs, killings the bugs, sweetening the air, and waxing the old man's car."

Continuing the family business begun with Johnson's Paste Wax more than a century ago, the fifth generation of the Johnson family is in active management of the S.C. Johnson & Son, Inc., at various levels. The president and chief executive of the early 1990s, William D. George, Jr., is not a family member. Home Care is the largest division in the company, according to overall sales figures, which is appropriate, since SC Johnson Wax originally made its name in the floor polishing business.

## Further Reading:

"A Family Company Keeps Its Verve," *Business Week,* July 6, 1968, p. 60.

"Corporate Dynasties: Defying the Odds," *D&B Reports,* March/April 1992, p. 16.

Freeman, Laurie, "S.C. Johnson Shines with New Products," *Advertising Age,* June 10, 1985, p. 4.

Ingham, John, "Herbert Fisk Johnson," *Biographical Dictionary of American Business Leaders,* 1985.

"Incubator for New Products," *Business Week,* June 10, 1950, p. 56.

"Johnson of Johnson's Wax," *Fortune,* November 1966, p. 51.

*JonWax Journal: 75th Anniversary Issue,* Racine, WI: S.C. Johnson & Son, Inc., 1961.

"Office Building Goes Functional," *Business Week,* May 6, 1939, p. 24.

Robinson, Duncan, "Johnson Wax's Venture Surmounts Ukraine Woes," *Journal of Commerce and Commercial,* October 28, 1991, p. 1A; "Johnson Aims to Expand in Europe," *Journal of Commerce and Commercial,* October 28, 1991, p. 10A.

"S.C. Johnson Tries Again on Personal Care," *Business Week,* February 14, 1977, p. 54.

*S.C. Johnson Wax Profile,* Racine, WI: S.C. Johnson & Son, Inc., 1991.

Simmons, Tim, "Industry Needs to Ride the Waves of Change," *Supermarket News,* March 18, 1991, p. 10.

Skur Hill, Julie, "Japan Hatches New Brands for Johnson," *Advertising Age,* September 2, 1991, p. 36.

*—Frances E. Norton*

# K-SWISS®

Although relatively unknown outside of tennis and still tiny compared to industry giants Nike and Reebok, K-Swiss was one of the fastest growing brands in the $4.8 billion U.S. market for athletic shoes in the late 1980s and early 1990s. Sales increased more than 500 percent between 1986 and 1992, when they reached $126 million. K-Swiss's share of the market more than tripled from approximately .5 percent to nearly 1.6 percent.

Marketed by K-Swiss Inc., the K-Swiss line includes the company's highly regarded Classic tennis shoes and its increasingly popular shoes for hiking and other rugged outdoor activities. K-Swiss, based in Chatsworth, California, also markets shoes for basketball and nautical activities as well as a line of athletic apparel.

## K-Swiss Inc.

Art and Earnest Brunner were brothers and ski instructors who perfected the design for the K-Swiss Classic tennis shoe in their native Switzerland. In 1966 they immigrated to the United States and founded K-Swiss Inc.—short for Kompany Swiss—Pacoima, California-based importer of athletic equipment. Executive offices would be moved to Chatsworth in 1992.

For 20 years, the company's only product was the K-Swiss Classic, which developed a loyal clientele among tennis professionals and dedicated amateurs. Then in 1987, Steven Nichols, former president of Stride-Rite Children's Group, Inc., formed an investment group that purchased K-Swiss for $20 million. Before resigning as president of Stride-Rite's footwear manufacturing division, Nichols had tried unsuccessfully to convince Stride-Rite to buy K-Swiss. He later said he was amazed at the response he received as he sought financial backers: "I'd sit down in a room full of highly successful people and time and again I'd find that more than half of them wore the Classic. It blew me away."

Nichols's surprise stemmed from the fact that he recognized K-Swiss's potential for further market success. *Footwear News* named K-Swiss Company of the Year in 1990, the same year the athletic shoe maker went public. K-Swiss was cited by *Business Week* as one of the nation's Hot Growth Companies in both 1991 and 1992 and was on the *Forbes* list of 200 Best Small Companies in 1992. And Nichols, then president of the company, was named Marketer of the Year by *Footwear News* in 1993.

## K-Swiss Classic

The K-Swiss Classic was one of the first all-leather tennis shoes sold in the United States. It was introduced at the All-England Championships at Wimbledon in 1966 and immediately found favor with tennis professionals. The upper part of the shoe was sewn from just three pieces of leather, which increased the shoe's comfort and durability. Five white strips of a tough, mountaineering fabric on each side helped provide stability. The shoe also had an inner sole of polyurethane foam and a high-quality rubber outer sole with a herringbone pattern developed by a Swiss tire manufacturer to provide a firm grip on a number of surfaces. The Classic also sported two small D-rings above the last eyelets that allowed the shoe laces to adjust as the foot moved, which provided a snug, comfortable fit. The five white stripes became a company trademark, as did the red, white, and blue shield sewn on the shoe. The shield logo was emblematic of the Brunners' home canton, or state, in Switzerland.

The Classic remained virtually unchanged into the 1990s and still accounted for nearly 40 percent of K-Swiss sales in 1992. That year, Nichols told *Racquet Magazine* that the stable Classic model shoe "will always be the personality of this company." He also remarked in *California Business,* "If I had to bet, [the Classic] will make it to 50 years without a change." Many of the Classic's features, in fact, including the D-rings, were carried over to other K-Swiss shoes.

## Brand Expansion

K-Swiss began to expand its line of shoes after the company was purchased by Nichols in 1987, ultimately adding more than 70 new models by 1994. The first move Nichols made was to introduce a line of children's shoes. Then in 1988, K-Swiss introduced a second tennis shoe, known as the Gstaad. That was followed in 1989 with shoes for basketball, boating, and alpine hiking.

In 1993 K-Swiss introduced a line of walking shoes for women that was designed with input from two female podiatrists who served on the company's Walking Advisory Staff. K-Swiss promotional materials predicted that walking would "become the activity sport of the '90s." For the following year, K-Swiss planned to come out with a line of men's and women's sandals—the company's first non-sports shoes. Other than its Surf and Turf canvas boating shoes, most K-Swiss shoe designs carried Swiss-

## AT A GLANCE

**K**-Swiss brand of athletic shoes founded in 1966 by K-Swiss Inc.; originally manufactured in Switzerland; K-Swiss Inc. purchased in leveraged buyout by an investment group, 1986.

*Performance: Market share*—1.6% of athletic shoe category. *Sales*—$126 million.

*Major competitor:* Nike; also Reebok.

*Advertising: Agency*—Kresser/Craig, Santa Monica, CA, 1993—. *Major campaign*—"Crafted with Passion."

*Addresses: Parent company*—K-Swiss, Inc., 20664 Bahama St., Chatsworth, CA 91311; phone: (818) 998-3388; fax: (818) 998-6179.

sounding names, such as the Ontré men's tennis shoes, the Grancourt Gstaad women's tennis shoes, and the Bria walking shoes.

## Marketing

With only a single product to market during its first 20 years, K-Swiss rarely advertised, relying primarily on word-of-mouth among tennis players to sell the Classic, which was available in specialty shoe stores and tennis club pro shops. Even after K-Swiss began to expand in the late 1980s, the company shied away from the cutthroat advertising wars that generally characterized the athletic shoe industry in the United States. In 1989, for example, LA Gear, another athletic shoe brand with a similar share of the market, spent $70 million on advertising, but K-Swiss spent just $3.2 million. In 1992 the advertising budget had grown to about $7 million. Instead of television and high-priced endorsements by sports heros, though, K-Swiss relied on relatively low-cost radio, billboards, and specialty magazines that delivered a targeted audience. Preston Davis, then-K-Swiss vice-president of marketing, told *Forbes* in 1990, "Our campaigns focus on what we call the shoe as hero."

K-Swiss also became a major sponsor of the junior tennis circuit, providing shoes and K-Swiss brand sports apparel to about 500 top junior tennis players, 200 college teams, and more than a thousand teaching pros. Robert Larsen, who succeeded Davis as vice-president of marketing, explained in 1992, "We could have signed an endorsement agreement with one or two big-name players, but for the same amount of money we've been able to establish a real grass-roots level loyalty in the tennis world." In 1993 K-Swiss was selected as the official footwear and apparel sponsor of the prestigious International Tennis Academy in Atlanta, Georgia, run by former tennis pros Dennis Ralston and Tom Gorman. K-Swiss also signed an endorsement agreement that year with Peter Burwash International, a sports management firm that represented more than 90 professional tennis players.

When K-Swiss did occasionally hire a "celebrity" to endorse its products, it was often an unlikely choice. For example, Bud Collins, then a balding, middle-aged TV sports commentator, was hired as a spokesperson for K-Swiss tennis shoes. Although Collins was perhaps best known for covering Wimbledon, he was also was once voted the game's worst announcer by readers of a tennis magazine. Marketing VP Davis told the *Los Angeles Times* that most people do not remember what shoes athletes wear, except for a few superstars that are out of K-Swiss's price range. By signing

unlikely people to endorse its products, "It's a little bit of what we call guerrilla warfare. It makes you stop and think."

K-Swiss also signed lesser known players to endorse its basketball shoes, such as David Rivers in 1989, then a little-used rookie for the Los Angeles Lakers and backup to superstar Magic Johnson. In 1993 K-Swiss signed former tennis star Virginia Wade, then a coach and TV broadcaster, to promote its tennis shoes and apparel.

K-Swiss's most effective marketing has perhaps been its sponsorship of prestigious sporting events that fit its particular product mix. In 1992 K-Swiss' Surf and Turf nautical shoes were named the Official Footwear of the America's Cup races, the most publicized sailboat competition in the world. K-Swiss also was the Official Footwear of both the International Orienteering Federation and the United States Orienteering Federation in the early 1990s. The company's products were displayed prominently at the U.S. Orienteering Championships and the World Orienteering Championships, which were held in the United States for the first time in 1993. K-Swiss Marketing Vice-President Larsen said the company's association with orienteering, a sport developed in the early 1900s as part of the Swedish army's outdoor training program, "has proved to be very successful in designing a line of top quality outdoor shoes. [We] had our shoes tested by the best U.S. orienteers under the most rugged conditions."

## Distribution

Rather than attempt to compete with industry leaders, K-Swiss also established itself as a prestige brand by selective distribution. For nearly 20 years, the K-Swiss Classic had been available only in athletic shoe stores and tennis club pro shops; by 1987, though, the shoes were offered at discount prices in many department stores. When Nichols purchased the company, however, he pulled the shoes from high volume outlets and again concentrated distribution through specialty stores. The decision restored the brand's cachet with tennis players. In 1992 the Foot Locker chain of athletic shoe stores accounted for approximately 15 percent of K-Swiss sales.

In the early 1990s K-Swiss shoes were also available in Europe and the Far East with about $29 million in foreign sales in 1991. K-Swiss's entry into the Far Eastern market was a natural expansion since nearly all of its shoes were made in South Korea, Taiwan, Indonesia, or China. In 1988 the company formed an ill-fated partnership, K-Swiss Japan Ltd., with a Japanese company that was responsible for distribution. The brand became popular quickly, but K-Swiss became disenchanted with the partnership because its shoes were being sold at steep discounts in large retail stores. K-Swiss withdrew from the partnership in 1991 and signed a new agreement with a Japanese distributor. Similar to what it had done in the United States when Nichols purchased the company, K-Swiss pulled its shoes in all but a few specialty stores, which pushed up the retail price and improved the brand's image without significantly affecting sales. According to *California Business*, the K-Swiss Classic was the best-selling athletic shoe in Japan in the early 1990s.

The company's experience introducing the K-Swiss brand in Europe was similar to that in Japan. K-Swiss formed a joint venture, with C&J Clark International Inc., a longtime London-based European shoemaker, in 1990. However, Clark began struggling financially, and K-Swiss ended the agreement by purchasing Clark's stake in K-Swiss Europe Ltd. K-Swiss also had distributors in other countries throughout the world.

In a fashion-crazed industry where styles often change every few months, K-Swiss has endeared itself to customers and retailers by refusing to continually change its shoes to keep up with the latest fads. Such continuity of style has resulted in strong repeat sales to customers who could consistently find the same shoes they liked. Shoe stores also appreciate NTOs, or no-try-on, sales, and K-Swiss was the athletic shoe industry's NTO leader in the early 1990s. K-Swiss's supplier return rate of less than one percent was among the lowest in the industry.

### Trends

In the early 1990s K-Swiss was attempting to establish a reputation as an environmentally conscious company. In addition to becoming the Official Footwear of the U.S. and international orienteering federations, K-Swiss established the K-Swiss Environmental Challenge Awards in 1993 for retailers selling its shoes. The retailers could win trips to U.S. national parks by initiating in-store programs to protect the environment or preserve natural resources. K-Swiss also joined with the National Parks Service to produce a music video about the need to preserve natural resources. "Conviction of the Heart"—also the name of the recording artist Kenny Loggins's song featured on the video—was scheduled to be shown at all National Parks in 1994.

In 1993 K-Swiss unveiled an athletic shoe made from recycled materials at the National Sporting Goods Association trade show. The upper portion of the shoe—called "The S.H.O.E." for "Start Healing Our Earth"—was made of a polyester derived from plastic soft-drink bottles. K-Swiss planned to introduce The S.H.O.E. in retail stores in 1994, along with displays showing how the shoes were made. The company also planned a promotional

tie-in with the National Arbor Day Foundation's Rain Forest Rescue project.

K-Swiss was also banking on a situation comedy launched by ABC-TV in 1993. The show, *Phenom,* focuses on a 15-year-old tennis prodigy played by Angela Goethals. K-Swiss signed an agreement for its products, including tennis shoes, socks, polo shorts and posters, to be featured on the show. The agreement also called for the K-Swiss brand name to be shown prominently during the opening of each episode and for the company to receive mention in the closing credits.

An advertising campaign, "Crafted with Passion," also launched in 1993, included the first K-Swiss commercials for television. The black and white commercials feature ordinary athletes and attempt to capture emotional moments in a photo-journalistic style. K-Swiss also received nationwide exposure from an unusual source in 1993, when Pope John Paul II, in Denver for World Youth Day, sent three representatives to a local Athletes Foot store to buy a pair of tennis shoes. Their choice was a pair of white K-Swiss Classics—with gold laces, specially requested—that the pope wore during religious services and a trip to Cherry Creek State Park.

### Further Reading:

*K-Swiss Inc. 1992 Annual Report,* Chatsworth, CA: K-Swiss Inc., 1993.

Lee, Don, "K-Swiss Dips a Toe in Europe," *Valley Business,* Nov. 3, 1992, p. 3.

Schlax, Julie, "The Shoe as Hero," *Forbes,* August 20, 1990, p. 76.

Smith, Elliott, "K-Swiss in Korea," *California Business,* October 1, 1991, p. 76.

Stewart, Mark, "All the Right Moves: The Emergence of K-Swiss," *Racquet Yearbook,* 1992.

*—Dean Boyer*

# KEDS®

The Keds brand of footwear, boasting a 95 percent rate of brand recognition, has been a household name for most of the twentieth century. The dominant sneaker trademark of the 1950s and 1960s, Keds was pummeled by competition from high-performance athletic shoe brands in the 1970s and early 1980s. The brand, held by Keds Corporation, regained some of its sales in the late 1980s and early 1990s by concentrating on classic styling for women and children. In the early 1990s, women accounted for two-thirds of Keds' sales, while men made up only four percent of the total; children's sneaker sales provided the balance. The brand was also licensed for a line of casual clothing.

## Brand Origins

When rubber was first discovered in the jungles of the Amazon, natives used the substance to make durable footwear. It was brought to America, and shoes were the first product developed and manufactured from rubber. Charles Goodyear discovered and patented vulcanization, a process that used heat to bond rubber to cloth and other materials, in the early nineteenth century. Goodyear organized the Goodyear Metallic Rubber Shoe Company in the 1840s in Naugatuck, Connecticut, and applied his process to the manufacture of rubber-soled shoes with canvas uppers.

In 1892 international merchant, financier, and negotiator Charles R. Flint coordinated the consolidation of nine small rubber companies, including Goodyear, to form the U.S. Rubber Company. When the company was created, management appointed a committee that was charged with selecting an umbrella brand that would replace the individual companies' trademarks. By the turn of the century, the corporation commanded approximately 70 percent of the U.S. rubber footwear business, worth $25 million in sales, but still sold shoes under a variety of brands. Shoes constituted about half of the country's rubber consumption during that pre-automobile period.

By 1913 U.S. Rubber's brand committee still had not decided on a common corporate brand of footwear. By this time, the company operated 30 plants and held just as many separate brand names, a configuration that translated into higher costs and diluted market influence. U.S. Rubber narrowed its scope and provided the five most important brands with promotional support but still did not achieve the desired impact on the market.

In the latter half of the 1910s, after over two decades of indecision, the brand committee settled on "Peds," from the Latin for foot, as a trade name. But Peds had already been trademarked, so in 1916 the choices were narrowed down to "Veds" or "Keds." The stronger sounding Keds made the final cut. U.S. Rubber dropped its other trademarks in favor of the new label, despite some hesitation among the corporation's member companies. Some of the individual companies had invested 60 years of time and support into the various brands. The Keds brand was applied to U.S. Rubber's canvas-upper, rubber-soled footwear. The Keds trademark would eventually become one of the company's most valuable properties.

## From Difficulties to Dominance

During the early years of Keds' history, footwear sales depended on the weather: a hard winter generally meant strong sales, while mild winters resulted in low sales. Balmy winters during the late 1920s and early 1930s combined with intense competition from imported shoes to result in tough years for Keds. U.S. Rubber responded with its first emphasis on fashion. Updated styles fueled planned obsolescence: consumers learned to buy new shoes when styles changed, as opposed to waiting until the shoe wore out. Keds' sales increased, and the brand soon achieved industry leadership that would last more than three decades. Keds canvas sneakers, first in basic white, then in colors and novelty patterns, began to replace more formal leather shoes as the basic everyday footwear of American boys and girls. The brand soon became, as Cara Applebaum observed in a 1991 *AdWeek's Marketing Week* article, "the unisex uniform of the 1950s and 1960s."

With over 50 percent of the industry's sales, Keds dominated the American sneaker market, and its only competition throughout the first half of the century came from Converse and P.F. Flyers. The Keds name became "damn-near generic," as a Young & Rubicam executive told *Advertising Age* in 1978. Although each brand had its own style, all three earned reputations as basketball, tennis, or all-purpose shoes. As long as these sports dominated young adults' activities, Keds controlled the sneaker market.

## Market Segmentation Left Keds Behind

In the 1970s Keds and especially its parent, Uniroyal, failed to recognize and react to the segmentation of the sneaker market into individual sports, especially the 1970s sensation, running. Com-

## AT A GLANCE

**K**eds brand of footwear founded in 1916 by U.S. Rubber Company; U.S. Rubber renamed Uniroyal, 1960; Keds brand purchased by Stride Rite Corporation, 1979.

**Performance:** *Market share*—5.9% (fourth spot) of women's canvas tennis shoe category. *Sales*—$150 million.

**Major competitor:** Nike; also Reebok, L.A. Gear, and Converse.

**Advertising:** *Agency*—Leonard Monahan Saabye & Lubars, Providence, RI, 1988—. *Major campaign*—Television commercials in which actress Demi Moore declares, "Keds. They Feel Good."

**Addresses:** *Parent company*—Keds Corporation, 5 Cambridge Center, Cambridge, MA 07101; phone: (617) 491-8800; fax: (617) 491-8402. *Ultimate parent company*—Stride Rite Corporation, 5 Cambridge Center Cambridge, MA; phone: (617) 491-8800.

petitors Adidas, Puma, and Nike utilized high-visibility celebrity endorsements and slick, expensive advertising to propel themselves to fame and fortune, while the Keds brand floundered under Uniroyal's weak marketing commitment. While other shoemakers updated their production methods, Keds stayed with obsolete factories. Although Keds' sales peaked at $350 million in 1975, the erosion of the brand had already begun. Keds' share of the expanding sneaker market had plunged from half to less than 17 percent by mid-decade. The brand suffered from poor—some would say nonexistent—brand management, which resulted in an out-of-date line of shoes with inadequate advertising and promotion. Some analysts also noted that Keds' strongest sales were in the Northeastern and Southern regions of the United States, while the new high-tech shoe trend was fueled by sales on the West Coast.

Uniroyal made a half-hearted, last-ditch effort to revive the brand in 1977, when it replaced advertising agency McCann-Erickson with Young & Rubicam and purged the Keds management team. Still, in 1978, the brand's ad budget stood at only $1 million. Despite the changes, Keds lost a astonishing $22 million on sales of $100 million in 1978, and lost $11 million on sales of $125 million in 1979. Uniroyal sold the brand to Stride Rite Corporation for a mere $40 million in 1979.

Stride Rite hoped to combine its 60 years of expertise in marketing children's shoes with Keds manufacturing strengths. Stride Rite Chief Executive Officer Arnold Hiatt initiated the brand's turnaround by slashing Keds' sales force by 40 percent and contracting out production to cheaper facilities in Korea. The modifications met with modest success: whereas Uniroyal expected Keds to lose $22 million in 1979, Stride Rite made the brand earn a profit of $500,000. But reorganization of the business did not change the brand's fortunes. Keds lost a total of $7 million on sales of $149 million in 1980 and 1981.

Stride Rite attempted to parlay Keds' brand equity into a position in the expensive men's athletic shoe business when it launched the Keds Millenium, a $50 running shoe that featured replaceable, pop-out wear plugs in the sole. Stride Rite was forced to withdraw the shoe within a few months due to manufacturing problems and inadequate advertising and promotion. The company then tried to enter Keds into the high-performance market

through tennis and basketball but failed to make inroads into the field. Stride Rite simply could not match the advertising muscle of its larger rivals, and some analysts questioned whether the Keds name would ever connote high-performance.

### Repositioning Fuels Comeback

Finally, in the mid-1980s, Keds decided to abandon the lucrative and attractive high-performance market to concentrate on its traditional strengths, women's and children's footwear. Barbara Scott, who joined the Keds marketing team in 1984, has been credited with the brand's stunning late 1980s turnaround. Her formula for success was to target women by emphasizing classic styling and distribution at department and specialty stores. She capitalized on Keds' attractive combination of brand familiarity and moderate pricing. The price encouraged consumers to purchase multiple pairs, especially when Keds began to offer a variety of colors and patterns in the late 1980s. Keds also successfully reentered the children's sneaker market by reviving classic barnyard and novelty patterns, such as shoes that glow in the dark. Keds continued its winning streak with the introduction of a leather sneaker in 1988. The shoes were priced lower than competitors' bottom-of-the-line pairs.

The repositioning of the Keds brand was supported by advertising that jumped from a low of $2 million, when the brand was still with Uniroyal, to about $14 million by 1989. Keds' sales climbed 67 percent in fiscal 1988 and 43 percent in 1989, which helped Stride Rite's volume to nearly double by 1990. With eight percent of the sneaker market, Keds quickly became the company's largest profit source: three-fourths of Stride Rite's revenue growth from 1985 to 1990 came from Keds.

At the turn of the decade, however, several factors worked to slow Keds' rebounding sales growth. First, the brand became entangled in Campeau Corporation's disastrous purchase of Federated Department Stores and its flagship Bloomingdale's. Stride Rite was compelled to cut its contracts with the bankrupted chain of upscale department stores. Some analysts estimated that the retail contracts may have accounted for 10 percent of Keds' volume. To compound the situation, Keds' market share was eroded by knock-offs from both ends of the price spectrum. Cheap imports and pricey imitations from such designers as Liz Claiborne and Ralph Lauren took a bite out of the down-to-earth market Keds had recreated. Then, in the early 1990s, styles began to move on to more rugged, hiking-type foot fashions, and Keds' share dropped to five percent.

Keds' flattening sales also reflected a market that grew just 14 percent from 1989 to 1990. Competition for a piece of the relatively stagnant market grew tougher, as top brands raised spending and launched new promotions. Keds responded to the higher level of competition with the 1990 introduction of washable leather sneakers and new ads featuring voice-overs by the sultry actress Demi Moore with the tagline, "Keds. They Feel Good." The new product boosted sales by 22 percent in 1990. Then in 1991, the brand marked its 75th anniversary with an attempt to break into the men's fashion sneaker market. Stride Rite launched its Pro-Keds high-top revival shoe, which went up against old nemesis Converse's reborn Chuck Taylor model, which had been in circulation since the mid-1980s. Keds urged retailers to "Consider the Pros instead of the Cons" in trade advertisements. The three-quarter-century mark was also promoted with a "Show Us Your Keds" contest, which asked for photos in five categories:

Oldest Keds, Family in Keds, Friends in Keds, Traveling in Keds, and Potpourri. The new products and special promotions helped Keds' sales grow by 21 percent in 1991 to $345 million, and the brand's market share rebounded almost a full percentage point, to 5.9 percent.

## Licensing

Next, Stride Rite hoped to parlay Keds' powerful brand loyalty into increased sales in the high-margin apparel category. The brand was licensed to sportswear manufacturer Signal Apparel Corp. of Chattanooga, Tennessee, in 1991. The branded line of basic clothing, or activewear, included such items as denim jeans, T-shirts, sweatshirts, pants, hats, and KedSkins, a line of tights and leggings. Like the shoes, Keds apparel was targeted primarily at women, but also included men's, young men's, and juniors' sizes. The extension was inaugurated as a showcase brand in 35 department stores, including Dayton-Hudson's and Marshall Fields sites in the fall of 1992.

After more than 80 years in branded footwear, Keds held fourth place, with 5.9 percent of the 1991 athletic shoe market. Although market leaders Nike and Reebok accounted for over half of the United States' sneaker sales, the increasingly fashion-oriented market left room for continued competition. Keds hoped to broaden its brand appeal through increased visibility in apparel and close attention to fashion trends.

**Further Reading:**

Applebaum, Cara, "Keds—in Spandex—Takes on The Gap," *AdWeek's Marketing Week,* December 9, 1991, p. 6.

Bayor, Leslie, "Shoe Marketers Prep for Workout," *Advertising Age,* March 11, 1991, p. 12.

Grimm, Matthew, "Keds Revives Pro-Keds with a Soft Touch," *AdWeek's Marketing Week,* March 4, 1991, p. 12.

*The History of Keds,* Cambridge, MA: Keds Corporation, 1992.

"Keds History," *Keds Standards,* Cambridge, MA: Keds Corporation, April 1993.

Jereski, Laura, "Back in the Game," *Forbes,* October 31, 1988, pp. 148–149.

Magiera, March, "Small Rivals Leap as L.A. Gear Stumbles," *Advertising Age,* June 8, 1992, p. 12.

Palmer, Jay, "Moving Right Along: Stride Rite Puts Its Best Foot Forward," *Barron's,* October 15, 1990, pp. 18-19.

Reda, Susan, "Keds Debuts Apparel Line: Selected Retailers Showcase Collection," *Stores,* May 1992, pp. 92–93.

Sloan, Pat, "Keds Runs After Market Share with Bigger Budget and Style," *Advertising Age,* February 27, 1978, pp. 3 and 62.

"Stride Rite Steps Out," *Financial World,* December 1–15, 1980, pp. 24–25.

"Stride Rite: Still Trying to Use Keds to Grow out of Children's Shoes," *Business Week,* August 9, 1982, pp. 51–52.

Vila, George R., *The Story of Uniroyal: 75 Years of Progress,* New York: The Newcomen Society, 1967.

*—April S. Dougal*

# KIWI®

The Kiwi brand of shoe polish has survived a long, sometimes tumultuous history: two world wars, numerous other world conflicts, and the decline in popularity of dress shoes in favor of athletic shoes, sandals, and suede. Nevertheless, the company has managed to adjust to both changes in world order as well as changes in footwear preference and maintain its position as the number one shoe polish in the United States and many foreign countries. Kiwi Brands Inc. is part of the Sara Lee Corporation's household and personal care division, the most global of the company's lines. The division also includes such brands as Ambi-Pur air fresheners; Bloom, Catch, Ridset, and Vapona European insecticides; Biotex detergents; and Sanex skin care products. In addition, Kiwi sells Cavalier and Esquire shoe polishes.

## Brand History

Although William Ramsey was an Australian and founded his shoe polish company in Australia, he named it after New Zealand's national bird in honor of his New Zealand-born wife. Ramsey started the company in 1906 after he developed a boot polish of unusually high quality. In addition to paying tribute to his wife, Ramsey also felt that the kiwi bird and name looked attractive on the polish's round tin and would be easy to remember.

During the early part of the twentieth century, Kiwi became popular in Australia and England, especially with members of the military who felt the Kiwi brand produced the best shine on their boots. When the number of soldiers serving in World War I increased, the need for polish also increased proportionately; members of the British Army became walking advertisements for Kiwi among their fellow Allied troops. All of the troops who fought with the British quickly became loyal Kiwi customers. Ten years after the polish was introduced in Melbourne, 30 million tins had been sold.

Because Kiwi had new customers throughout the world who liked its long-lasting "parade shine," the company needed to expand. In 1940 Kiwi was produced in four factories in Australia, New Zealand, France, and England and was sold in 115 countries. Naturally, World War II produced a similar increase in demand for the polish among the military and the four factories were unable to keep up. On March 15, 1948, Kiwi opened its fifth factory and first U.S. manufacturing site, in Philadelphia.

## Changes in Parent Company

In 1981 the Kiwi company merged with the Nicholas Aspro group to become Nicholas Kiwi. In 1984 Sara Lee—then called Consolidated Foods—paid $241 million for the equivalent of 75 percent of Nicholas Kiwi, which represented all of the company's business outside of Australia, including Europe, North America, Africa, and Asia. According to the *Chicago Tribune,* Sara Lee's purpose in buying Kiwi was to "increase its access to developing countries." Because of investment laws in Australia, Sara Lee was unable to buy the remainder of Kiwi until 1986 and then paid $130 million. In that same year, Sara Lee divested Kiwi of all business in the Republic of South Africa. Because of Sara Lee's acquisition of Kiwi, it was forced to divest itself of the Cherry Blossom polish line it had acquired from Reckitt & Colman in 1992. England's Monopolies and Mergers Commission felt that the acquisition would impair competition and give Sara Lee the ability and incentive to increase prices unfairly.

## Advertising and Promotions History

Although the advertising history of Kiwi shoe polish remains largely undocumented, it is clear that advertising has been unnecessary for most of the brand's lifetime. With the armies of most of the Western world as customers, Kiwi has had more than enough business. And Kiwi's business with armies did not end with World War II. The Soviet Army reportedly ordered one million tins of boot polish for its troops in Afghanistan, and in 1991 Kiwi supplied soldiers participating in Operation Desert Storm in the Middle East with three million tins of polish and 100,000 pairs of shoe laces. In addition to providing an attractive shine to boots, Kiwi polish was also held in high regard because of its ability to protect boots from the effects of the intense desert sun and heat.

Despite army patronage, Kiwi eventually had to face the realities of the market place in the late twentieth century. As London's *Financial Times* pointed out in April of 1992, the end of national service 30 years prior "had contributed to a long-term decline in the shoe polishing habit." In the 1960s, the advent of sandals and a generally more casual style of dress was detrimental to the polish industry. Then, in the 1980s and 1990s the prevalence of athletic shoes was the culprit.

Market research conducted by Sara Lee in 1988 confirmed the suspicion that people under 40 were less likely to make a habit of

## AT A GLANCE

**K**iwi brand of shoe polish founded in 1906 by William Ramsey; brand merged with Nicholas Aspro in 1981; company renamed Nicholas Kiwi then bought by Consolidated Foods, which was later known as Sara Lee Corporation; Nicholas Kiwi renamed Kiwi Brands Inc.

**Performance:** *Market share*—90% of shoe polish category (1990).

**Major competitor:** Turtle Wax shoe polish.

**Advertising:** *Agency*—Shaeffer & Associates. *Major campaign*—"Kiwi lets your pride shine through."

**Addresses:** *Parent company*—Kiwi Brands Inc., 447 Old Swede Rd., Douglassville, PA 19518; phone: (215) 385-9347; fax: (215) 385-6177. *Ultimate parent company*—Sara Lee Corporation, 3 First National Plaza, Chicago, IL 60602; phone: (312) 726-2600; fax: (312) 558-8567.

polishing their shoes than their elders. Nevertheless, this younger generation was still concerned with their appearance, and Kiwi was prompted to launch its first public relations campaign in 1989 with the help of Schaeffer & Associates of Philadelphia. At the time, Kiwi held an enviable 90 percent market share and had no competition. As a result, Sara Lee had spent only $151,800 on advertising the previous year, and it was obvious that growth would not be achieved by stealing market share from competitors.

Sara Lee saw public relations as a more cost-effective means of achieving its goals for Kiwi than advertising. The campaign focused on an "Image Index," a test that allowed customers to measure their success potential based on the first impression they made, polished shoes playing a significant role. Media mailings were focused on the company's home base of Philadelphia but also targeted women's magazines and publications in the shoe, apparel, and leather industries. College students were the prime target for the effort, and Kiwi set up free shoe shine booths at college job fairs.

A *Christian Science Monitor* contributor noted that "Kiwi hasn't advertised on television for 20 years—there has been no need to." But 1983 brought another compelling reason to promote Kiwi: competition. When Turtle Wax, a leading car wax producer, decided to enter the shoe polish market, Sara Lee took the threat to Kiwi's number one status seriously, especially since Turtle Wax spent ten times more on advertising than Kiwi.

In the early 1990s Kiwi began compiling lists of the "Shoe Care Top 10," recognizing those who were "demonstrating an exemplary commitment to footwear." Although the awards were somewhat tongue-in-cheek, they garnered media attention by featuring newsworthy winners like George Bush, Bill Clinton, Michael Jordan, and Cybill Shepard. The common element among the winners was of course their shoes.

In 1990 Kiwi launched a major advertising campaign, its first in 20 years. The campaign featured polished television commercials with music and was test marketed in St. Louis and New York City. Some ads featured the jingle, "Kiwi lets your pride shine through," while others had a "Twist and Shine" theme.

## Brand Expansion

At the time of Sara Lee's initial purchase of 75 percent of Nicholas Kiwi—1984—the shoe polish company had expanded to include household products, personal care products, and over-the-counter medicines. Brands under the Kiwi umbrella included Bloo toilet cleaner, Endust and Behold furniture care products, Ambi skin care, Aspro analgesics, and Rennie antacids, leading brands in Europe. In the early years of Sara Lee ownership, the company focused on expanding Kiwi's non-polish brands. After completing its purchase of Nicholas Kiwi in 1986, Sara Lee sought to increase market share, enact cost-containment efforts, and integrate manufacturing facilities and distribution networks.

In 1987, although Kiwi was still the number one shoe polish brand in the United States, it managed to increase market share by introducing Kiwi Elite liquid polish. Liquid polish was gaining popularity because of its ease of application. Old-fashioned paste polish requiring three steps did not fit the lifestyles of a new generation. By 1989 Sara Lee proclaimed Kiwi to be its "most international brand," and reported that the brand held a 92 percent share in the United States, a 27 percent share in the United Kingdom, a 24 percent share in France, a 57 percent share in Australia, a 90 percent share in Thailand, and a 95 percent share in Indonesia.

Kiwi Twist and Shine was introduced in 1989 and offered a compact soft wax shoe polish. The Kiwi Sport line debuted the same year as an effort to retain customers who were following the trend toward wearing more athletic shoes. The sport line consisted of 14 products specifically intended for cleaning and protecting all types of athletic shoes. Nevertheless, in 1990 Sara Lee's annual report noted a declining market for Kiwi in the United States. Overall growth was still realized that year, assisted by a strong increases in Canada, Australia, Denmark, and France. Kiwi was also gaining ground in the developing markets of Thailand, the Philippines, Indonesia, and Kenya. In addition, 1990 brought Kiwi polish to South Korea, and Sara Lee reported "good initial results" in its 1990 Annual Report.

Sara Lee also attributed overall growth of the Kiwi brand to the continuing popularity of the new product lines: Twist and Shine, Kiwi Elite, Kiwi Sneaker Shampoo, and Kiwi Sport. In 1991 double-digit sales growth was attributed indirectly to the Persian Gulf War and increased sales to Kiwi's most loyal customer, the military. Athletic shoe care products were also introduced in Europe and the Pacific Rim. In 1992 Kiwi Liquid Cream was introduced in the United States, while Kiwi Sport Powder Deodorant was making its debut in France. Also in 1992, Australians were buying the new Kiwi Kid's Scuff, a liquid polish, while the Japanese were responding favorably to a shoe care item for women's shoes called Kiwi 5th Avenue. The summer of 1992 brought to the United States Kiwi Scuff Zapper for light- to medium-colored shoes and handbags.

## Predictions

Kiwi shoe polish has held the number one position in its market category for almost as long as the product has been around. Not only has the brand been on top for many years, but it has led by a considerable margin. As part of Sara Lee, the future of Kiwi also seemed secure. Marvin Roffman of Roffman Miller Associates was quoted in the June 29, 1993, *USA Today* as saying, "Sara Lee is one of the best-managed companies in America, and [CEO] John Bryan is one of the top five managers in the country." The same article contained a quote from Bob Messenger of *Food*

*Trends* newsletter regarding Sara Lee's business mix: "Non-food businesses are the stars of the portfolio."

The Kiwi brand also seems to be leading the shoe care industry in the most profitable direction. A 1991 *Footwear News* article concluded from interviews that the "future of shoe care products lies in creating specialized products targeted at a well-defined market." Kiwi's successful introduction of convenience and athletic shoe care products demonstrates the brand's awareness of current trends and its ability to move quickly to capitalize on them. In addition to athletic shoes, Kiwi also believes that the golf industry represents a largely untapped market and estimates that 3.2 million pairs of golf shoes are purchased annually.

Another benefit for Kiwi is that shoe polish seems to be a recession-proof product. In times of prosperity it flourishes, and in times of economic downturns, when people take care of the shoes they own rather than buying new ones, it maintains its market.

## Further Reading:

McGough, Robert, "Icing on the Cake," *Financial World,* October 17, 1989, p. 22.

Oberlaender, Michaela, "Kiwi's First Ever Public Relations Effort Shines," *Public Relations Journal,* January 1, 1989, p. 5.

Rosato, Donna, "Staying on Top an Art for Sara Lee CEO," *USA Today,* June 29, 1993, p. 6B.

*Sara Lee Corporation Annual Reports,* Chicago: Sara Lee Company, 1985–92.

Scott, David Clark, "Shoe-Polish Makers Are Going Toe to Toe to Capture Greater Share of Mass Market," *Christian Science Monitor,* December 6, 1983, p. 26.

*The Story of the Kiwi,* Douglassville, PA: Kiwi Brands Inc.

*—Kate Sheehan*

# KLEENEX®

Kimberly-Clark Corporation's Kleenex is not only the top-selling brand of facial tissue in the United States, but internationally as well, with a trademark that is among the most recognized in the world. In 1924, when Kimberly-Clark & Company developed the technology and material to make tissue, the company literally started a new industry—one for disposable tissues. The strong acceptance of this completely new type of product took hold so firmly that consumers insisted on using the Kleenex brand name as a generic term for all types of facial tissues. The early packaging innovation of a dispenser box that enables tissues to "pop-up" added to the brand's distinction for consumers.

Since its debut the Kleenex brand of facial tissues has undergone changes in name, product, quality, package design, advertising, and market strategy. Many of these changes and improvements have been the result of market research that identified consumer uses and perceptions of the product. The objective was to keep Kleenex tissues competitive with other brands, keep them unique, and make them convenient for consumers to use. In addition, Kimberly-Clark has sought to demonstrate its social responsibility. When the environmental movement of the 1980s became a strong influence on consumer buying habits, the company began including recycled materials in its packaging.

## Brand Origins

In 1914, during World War I, Kimberly-Clark developed a substitute for hard-to-get cotton called Cellucotton, which was used by the U.S. Army for surgical dressings in wartime hospitals and first aid stations. In the later years of the war, an improved version was used as a gas mask filter. When the war ended, Kimberly-Clark was left with a surplus of the material and began developing products in which the Cellucotton could be used. In 1920, the company introduced Kotex sanitary napkins, the first consumer product to include Cellucotton and the company's first consumer product trademark. The idea for Kotex came from nurses who used Cellucotton for feminine hygiene during the war. Then in 1924, after several years of testing, the company developed Kleenex facial tissues using the material, which is made from cellulose, a derivative of wood pulp. The pulp is processed into creped wadding or tissue, and then converted into tissue.

The derivation of the name, Kleenex, is not recorded. However, it is generally believed that Kleenex was derived from the word "cleansing," the purpose for which the tissue was chiefly promoted from 1924 to 1930. This word was shortened and the distinctive capital letter "K" was then added to form Kleen. The suffix, "ex" was tacked on most likely to align the brand with the company's other sanitary consumer product, Kotex.

## Early Marketing Strategy

A war-weary nation was moving into the Roaring Twenties, and women all around the country began to use cosmetics and cold cream. Theorizing that there would be a market for a more convenient way of wiping off the cold cream than the use of facial towels, the company produced the thin sheets of Cellucotton. Packages of Kleenex tissues were labeled "Sanitary Cold Cream Remover," and advertising promoted the product's use for makeup removal.

Initially the tissues were sold in boxes containing 100 Kleenex Kerchiefs and priced at 65 cents. Sales were slow because women perceived it as a luxury item. Magazine and newspaper ads claiming the tissues were the "scientific way to remove cold cream" showed the tag line against a background of Hollywood studios. The aim was to give Kleenex tissues some cachet by associating the product with glamour and class, particularly since it was priced high. Later, Hollywood celebrities were featured in the ads to reinforce the message. Such stars as Helen Hayes, Ronald Colman, and Gertrude Lawrence endorsed the use of Kleenex tissues for makeup removal.

The boost in sales came when the company decided to heed the many letters written by consumers who asked why ads never mentioned how Kleenex facial tissues were really being used—as handkerchiefs for blowing their noses. Consumers had been writing to Kimberly-Clark, questioning why Kleenex tissues were not promoted as handkerchiefs. In order to determine how widespread this usage was, the company decided to investigate whether more of their customers were indeed using Kleenex tissues as handkerchiefs rather than for removing makeup.

In February of 1930, full-page ads were run in two competing newspapers in Peoria, Illinois. Both ads had the same size and layout, and both offered respondents a free box of Kleenex tissues for their participation. But each ad had a different headline asking respondents how they used the tissues. One ad said, "We pay to prove there is no way like Kleenex to remove cold cream." The other ad said, "We pay to prove Kleenex is wonderful for hand-

## AT A GLANCE

**K**leenex brand of facial tissues was developed in 1924 by Kimberly-Clark & Company; originally intended for use as a makeup and cold cream remover, later marketed as a disposable handkerchief based on consumer feedback; company name changed to Kimberly-Clark Corporation, 1928.

**Performance:** *Market share*—46% (top share) of U.S. facial tissue market. *Sales*—$1.012 billion in worldwide sales (1992), including $553 million in international sales.

**Major competitor:** Procter & Gamble's Puffs.

**Advertising:** *Agency*—Foote, Cone & Belding, Chicago, IL, 1983—. *Major campaign*—(for Kleenex Ultra facial tissues) Children talking about how the tissues help their noses when they have a cold.

**Addresses:** *Parent company*—Kimberly-Clark Corporation, P.O. Box 619100, DFW Airport Station, Dallas, TX 75261-9100; phone: (214) 830-1200; fax: (214) 830-1490.

kerchiefs.'' The results tallied at the end of four weeks showed that 61 percent of the respondents were using Kleenex as handkerchiefs.

When Kimberly-Clark realized that more consumers were using Kleenex as disposable handkerchiefs than for makeup removal, the company changed its advertising strategy. Full-page ads suggested that mothers send their children to school with Kleenex tissues in order to avoid spreading germs. The same message was directed toward working people, who were encouraged to take tissues to the office using the headline "Don't put a cold in your pocket." This ad campaign was so effective that within one year, sales of Kleenex tissues doubled. Then in the following year, they doubled once again. These strong sales were all the more surprising because at the time the nation was mired in the Depression.

In 1932 the company offered a 35-cent boudoir-size box of what were now called Kleenex Absorbent Kerchiefs to reflect the products actual usage. Later the tissues were renamed—for the third time in six years—Kleenex Cleansing Tissues. Further price drops took place in 1934 when the tissues cost 18 cents a box, eventually selling for as little as 13 cents or two boxes for a quarter.

### Innovative Package Design

The change in marketing strategy for Kleenex tissues was aided by the development of a convenient new type of package. The Serv-A-Tissue Pop-Up box was introduced in 1929 after Kimberly-Clark's packaging engineers developed a technique that enabled two separate rolls of tissue to be mechanically interfolded. When one tissue was pulled up through the dispenser slot in the top of the box, the next would automatically be pulled up ready for use. The new package allowed the company to promote usage in such places outside the home as the office and car.

The "quadrant design," adopted by the company in 1938 has remained a distinguishing characteristic of the pop-up box. In fact, the high degree of consumer recognition led to a federal trademark registration in 1965, one of the few ever issued for an overall package design. In 1949, letters from consumers once again brought about a marketing change. Tissues were made even easier

to carry away from home due to another packaging innovation—the Pocket-Pack. This pop-up paper package could more easily fit into a purse or on a dashboard.

The blue and white box was used until 1980, when the company redesigned it in different colors. Other tissue companies were introducing boxes in different colors to match or blend with colors in consumer bathrooms and bedrooms. Kimberly-Clark followed with its own colored versions of Kleenex tissues, but retained the familiar pop-box dispenser design.

### Product Changes

Throughout the years, changes to Kleenex tissues have focused mainly on marketing the tissues in different-sizes of pop-up boxes and creating different levels of softness by selecting tree species that contain thin wood fibers which add to the desirable qualities of softness, absorbency, and strength.

By 1989, there were ten varieties of Kleenex tissues, marketed in various shapes, sizes, and packages, including Kleenex Man Size, a three-ply tissue larger than the standard size at 11 x 11½ inches, and Kleenex Little Travelers, which measured 6 x 8½ inches. In 1991 Kleenex Ultra was introduced to compete with a new type of tissue marketed by Procter & Gamble, makers of the brand's major competitor, Puffs. Kleenex Ultra is treated with an oil-free lotion for extra softness. Ultra also has improved thickness, consisting of three layers of tissue combined with the lotion instead of the usual two-ply. Jean Allen, director of corporate communications at Kimberly-Clark stated in *Advertising Age* that "the product won't leave a residue or trace elements." Ultra was first marketed in a family size box, and then in a cube-shaped box in 1992. The embossed Kleenex Softique with improved softness was introduced in 1992.

### Advertising Innovations

Recognizing that Kleenex tissues could be used for new and different purposes, while further expanding sales, in 1936 Kimberly-Clark offered $5 for each new use reported by consumers. By this time, the product had undergone still another name change, becoming Kleenex Disposable Tissues, in keeping with its new product image. A package insert already listed 48 uses that consumers had cited, such as using the tissues for cleaning tools, draining fried foods, wiping windshields and cleaning out pans.

Three years later, another attempt to learn how consumers were using tissues was initiated. A new ad campaign called "Kleenex True Confessions" asked consumers to "confess" to other uses for Kleenex. This pattern of asking consumers for feedback, then using the information to make improvements and changes in product or marketing was a key strategy used in later years as well.

Advertising and promotional activity also increased during slow economic times, as was the case during the recession of the late 1980s and early 1990s when sales of facial tissues dropped slightly. Tissues are said to be recession-resistant rather than recession-proof. Industry observers noted that the away-from-home market particularly suffered because people stayed home more to save money as confidence in the economy slipped.

### "Green" Marketing

The environmental movement of the 1980s made consumers increasingly aware of packaging in the waste stream, and there were demands for more recycling and use of recycled materials in packaging. Market research indicated that consumers were making buying decisions based on environmental-friendliness of packages. Some consumers stated that they stopped buying certain branded products because the companies were viewed as environmental polluters.

According to spokesperson Jean Allen, the company's goal "is to use recycled and recyclable components whenever supply and performance allow." In 1990, the company made several changes in packaging, which included the use of recycled paperboard in Kleenex tissue boxes. When discussing whether the tissues could also incorporate recycled paper, Allen noted that "only virgin fiber provides the necessary level of softness."

## International Expansion

The company saw foreign markets, especially Europe, as the segment with the strongest growth for the 1990s. International marketing of Kleenex facial tissues began as early as 1925. In the 1950s, companies were operated for the first time under Kimberly-Clark's ownership in the United Kingdom, Mexico, and Germany. In the 1960s, 17 international operations were begun. By the early 1990s, there were 150 operations outside the United States, with manufacturing plants in 21 foreign nations. A new tissue plant began operating in France in 1991, and other mills were due to be built or expanded in North Wales and Britain by 1992.

## Further Reading:

"Facial Tissues," *Consumer Reports,* December 1989, pp. 39–41.

Fong, Diana, "Brand-name Burnout," *Forbes,* January 8, 1990, pp. 306–307.

Forest, Stephanie Anderson and Mark Maremont, "Kimberly-Clark's European Paper Chase," *Business Week,* March 16, 1992, pp. 94–96.

Freeman, Laurie and Judann Dagnoli, "Green Concerns Influence Buying," *Advertising Age,* July 20, 1990, p. 30

Kimberly-Clark Corporation Annual Report, Dallas: Kimberly-Clark Corporation, 1992.

"Kleenex Gets Ultra Version," *Advertising Age,* November 26, 1990, p. 4.

"Markets Turn 'Squeezably' Soft in Recession," *Pulp & Paper,* July 1991, pp. 35–37.

"U.S. Paper Industry Earnings Down 54%," *Pulp & Paper,* June 1991, pp. 23–25.

Winters, Patricia, "Cola Giants Take Packaging Lead," *Advertising Age,* December 17, 1990, p. 30.

*—Dorothy Kroll*

# KOTEX®

Kotex was the first successful brand of sanitary napkins and remains one of the United States' top feminine hygiene products. This pioneering brand brought women's products out of a world of secrecy and into mainstream advertising. Due to heavy competition, Kotex has declined from its early dominance of the industry from the 1930s to the 1960s. Kotex is one of a large line of products offered by the Kimberly-Clark Corporation that includes Kleenex tissues and Huggies diapers.

## Brand Origins

Kotex was created during a time when women's hygiene in general and menstruation in particular were such taboo subjects that many women would not discuss "that time of the month" with their own daughters. Before Kotex was introduced, women used linen cloths that they washed each month, providing the origins of the cliche, "let's not air our dirty linen in public." Health and hygiene giant Johnson & Johnson had attempted to introduce a disposable napkin in 1896, but the product was soon discontinued for lack of places that would allow advertising.

In the early 1910s, Kotex's parent company, Kimberly-Clark, developed an absorbent wood pulp product that improved on the cotton wadding used for surgical dressings at the time. "Cellucotton," introduced commercially in 1914, had five times the absorbency of cotton, more effectively prohibited infection, and cost half as much as cotton wadding. Dressings made from Cellucotton also needed to be changed less frequently, making the product even more cost-effective. Kimberly-Clark began that year supplying the Red Cross and War Department with Cellucotton at cost, and by the time the United States became involved in World War I in 1917, demand for the product had quadrupled.

Cellucotton was used primarily for medical purposes, but some nurses in France adapted the material for menstrual use. This rudimentary disposable pad caught on so quickly with service women that several asked Kimberly-Clark to market Cellucotton commercially as pads. At war's end, Kimberly-Clark (K-C) was forced to purchase surplus Cellucotton back from the Red Cross and Army or face the prospect of them undercutting K-C's price. The war surpluses, added to K-C's own overproduction, stuck the company with massive amounts of product and a dramatically diminished market.

Despite the huge surpluses and the untapped market, Kimberly-Clark, now a 49-year-old company, was very reluctant to enter the sex-charged arena of women's sanitary protection. In order to protect the company's reputation in case of a backlash, Kimberly-Clark carefully distanced itself from the product by creating a second company, International Cellucotton Corporation, to produce and market pads. The product was manufactured in 1920 and marketing efforts began in 1921. The pads were first called "Cellunap," an abbreviation of "Cellucotton napkins." While the name made sense, it did not indicate the product's purpose in any way. Cellucotton hired Charles F.W. Nichols Company as the brand's first advertising agency. Nichols's first suggestion was to change the trade name to Kotex. Conflicting reports say the name stood for either "cotton textile" or "cotton texture," and although the name was logical, it still did not suggest specific uses for the product.

The first Kotex pad was nine inches long and three and a half inches wide. Though the product was very bulky, it proved that Cellucotton could serve its purpose. Tabs that extended five and a half inches in front and seven and a half inches in back attached to undergarments with safety pins to hold the napkin in place. The pads were packaged 12 to a box with a blue end label for identification.

The first Kotex print campaigns were vague and largely ineffective, primarily to avoid any appearance of impropriety. A headline, "To Save Men's Lives Science Discovered Kotex (Cotton Textile) A Wonderful, Sanitary Absorbent," on the first advertisement suggested the wartime uses of Kotex, but not the menstrual application. The second advertisement was not much of an improvement. Featured in women's service magazines, the ad depicted two nurses flanking a wheelchair-bound man, another unidentified woman, and the obscure headline, "At stores and shops that cater to women." Small type at the bottom left of the ad proffered twelve napkins postpaid for 65 cents and a short list of shops that carried Kotex.

The over $181,000 spent on these earliest ads did little to bring Kotex into the decidedly disinterested public eye: two years after marketing for the sanitary napkin began in 1921, most stores still refused to stock or display it. In one instance, when a San Francisco Woolworth's displayed Kotex in its window, a men's organization protested and had it removed. In addition, women's

## AT A GLANCE

**K**otex brand of feminine sanitary products founded as Cellunap in 1920 in Neenah, Wisconsin, by International Cellucotton Corporation; Kimberly-Clark Corporation purchased International Cellucotton, 1955.

**Performance:** *Market share*—26% of sanitary napkin category (1991); 6% of tampon category (1991). *Sales*—$117.3 million (1991).

**Major competitor:** Procter & Gamble Company Company's Always; also Stayfree.

**Advertising:** *Agency*—Ogilvy & Mather, New York, NY, 1983—.

**Addresses:** *Parent company*—Kimberly-Clark Corporation, P.O. Box 619100, Dallas, TX 75261; phone: (214) 830-1200; fax. (214) 830-1490.

magazines refused to run the ads, and women themselves were still very uncomfortable with the subject.

### First Commercial Success

Kotex's declining fortunes changed in 1923, when International Cellucotton hired Albert D. Lasker, president of the ad agency Lord & Thomas (now Foote, Cone & Belding), and copywriter Claude Hopkins. The team had earned a favorable reputation through their involvement in several brand promotions, including Palmolive soap, Pepsodent toothpaste, Lucky Strike cigarettes, and Goodyear tires. Their early successes publicizing patent medicines led Lasker and Hopkins to emphasize the hygienic qualities of Kotex. By positioning menstruation, a natural function, as a medical problem, Hopkins hoped to capitalize on the public's trust in the medical profession.

The agency's first ad for Kotex, headlined "The Safe Solution of Women's Greatest Hygiene Problem," was signed by real-life graduate nurse Ellen J. Buckland, who seriously and professionally discussed menstrual issues. Packaging featured a white cross on a light blue background to extend the medical metaphor. As Lasker and Hopkins hoped, women began to solicit Kotex from nurses, and International Cellucotton initiated a large-scale sampling program through medical professionals. Lord & Thomas's more forward ad style continued through 1927 and earned Kotex an overwhelming share of the market it created.

Lasker also came up with marketing schemes that made purchasing Kotex less embarrassing for women. Cellucotton convinced retailers to feature Kotex in large, easily spotted, unmarked packages that would not divulge the contents. The self-service display allowed any woman who wished to buy Kotex to drop 50 cents in a box near the pile of packages, take one, and leave without incident. The brown wrapper promotion was short-lived, however, because competitors soon adopted the packaging. International Cellucotton also distributed Kotex through pharmacies that offered home delivery and ladies' room vending machines, further lessening the embarrassment factor.

Despite the more widespread acceptance of Kotex, Lord & Thomas still had trouble convincing Edward Bok, editor of the United States' leading women's magazine, *Ladies' Home Journal,* to publish Kotex ads. After years of coaxing, corporate folklore recounts that Lasker dared Bok to let his secretary decide whether the ads were tasteful enough to appear in the magazine. Her affirmative answer supposedly opened the magazine industry to feminine hygiene product ads. In 1924 Kotex ads appeared in 20 different magazines, including *McCall's, Redbook,* and *Good Housekeeping.*

When competition first appeared on the scene in 1924, Kotex offered free samples of a new deodorant napkin to retain brand loyalty. By that year, Kotex claimed over five million users and boasted that eight out of ten women in "the better walks of life" used Kotex. The ad team kept up a constant stream of ads, with insertions in magazines and newspapers, especially in the women's or society section. Advertisements touted Kotex's comfort, low price (12 for 60 cents), and the end of "the laundry problem." Kotex had earned the support of several large department stores by 1925: Chicago's Carson Pirie Scott promoted Kotex with displays in the corset department, and Montgomery Ward featured the product in its catalog the following year.

### Early Competition

By the mid-1920s, an estimated 300 brands had entered the new and growing sanitary napkin industry. Kotex learned that some dealers had been substituting cheaper brands for Kotex, so it undertook a vigorous trade and consumer brand campaign, urging women to "Take no chances . . . be sure to specify Kotex." Price wars began in the late 1920s and extended into the Great Depression years of the 1930s. When market research revealed that by 1928 Kotex had lost a good deal of its 65 percent share to cheaper brands, it cut its price by almost one-third, from 65 cents for a box of twelve to 45 cents. Cellucotton took a loss of $1.5 million that year, but Kotex enjoyed extraordinary brand loyalty for quite some time thereafter.

Ellen J. Buckland was Kotex's spokeswoman until 1928, when Mary Pauline Callender, an imaginary advice columnist, replaced her. Callender reminded cloth-napkin holdouts that "80 percent of better-class women [had] discarded ordinary ways for Kotex" by that time. Within just a few years, the pitch had evolved from health to fashion concerns: Kotex introduced Phantom Kotex, a less noticeable pad. Ads for the product featured attractive women in close-fitting gowns to illustrate the improvement.

Johnson & Johnson, through a subsidiary, Personal Products Co., began to advertise its Modess sanitary napkin in 1929, inaugurating decades of intense competition with Kimberly-Clark. By this time, there were an estimated 560 napkin brands, and competition throughout the 1930s was fierce. In 1932 Kotex was forced by market pressure and the Depression to reduce its price of a standard box of twelve napkins to 35 cents. The undercutting reached its nadir the following year, when Modess met the off-brands' unbelievably low price of two boxes for 25 cents. Kotex followed suit, and prices held at that level until April of 1934, when Kotex raised its price to 20 cents per box. The price held at that level until 1941.

Kotex targeted preteen girls very early in its marketing. In 1931 a booklet titled *Marjorie May's 12th Birthday* was introduced in Great Britain as an educational and promotional tool. Kotex brought the idea to the United States and Canada in 1932 and started its well-known education program. The booklets were published and distributed through mothers and teachers in the hopes that a young girl's first brand of pad would be her lifetime choice. In 1933 Kotex set up its first Consumer Testing Board, which was made up of 600 women. Consumer Board tests showed that women wanted a smaller pad for days of lighter flow, so Kotex introduced a ''Junior'' size in 1935.

## Competition with Modess Intensifies

During the 1940s and 1950s, Kotex was occupied with trying to respond to Modess's aggressive advertising, marketing, and promotional efforts. By the end of the 1930s, Modess's advertising budget was triple that of Kotex, and Modess had entered grocery outlets in four southern states. Although Kotex had limited itself to drugstore sales up to this time in order to maintain druggists' brand loyalty, marketers felt compelled to expand distribution to groceries. Kotex answered Modess's barrage of ads with all-type ads that presented ''Straightforward Facts for Women,'' and fashion ads that declared, ''The Days of Don'ts Are Over.'' Moddess ads in the 1940s hit even harder, attacking the ''stiff, papery layers'' in Kotex pads, as opposed to Modess's fluff-type filler. Kotex, in turn, began its ''Ever Pack a Suitcase?'' campaign, claiming that the pad's folded construction was better than the competitor's wadded material.

Kotex marketers realized that Modess had siphoned off its younger, more active customers, so the brand intensified its pursuit of women who were just coming into the market. The outdated *Marjorie May* booklet was replaced in 1941 with *As One Girl to Another.* The free publication topped distribution of 2 million by the end of the year. ''Are You in the Know'' ads asked timely

*A 1942 advertisement using a wartime theme for Kotex sanitary napkins.*

questions about grooming, dating, and etiquette. The ever-changing ads attracted more magazine readers than almost all other print ads. This successful series with the tag line, ''More women use *KOTEX* than all other sanitary napkins put together'' ran until

1956. In 1946 *The Story of Menstruation,* and educational film shown in schools and women's group meetings, was commissioned from Walt Disney. It would be seen by more people than any film but *Gone with the Wind,* until *The Godfather* took that distinction.

By the beginning of World War II, approximately 80 percent of the United States' menstruating women were using commercial sanitary napkins. Cellucotton put Kotex machines in factories, thereby capturing the majority of the market of women workers by the end of the conflict. The brand had led the disposable napkin revolution: nearly 100 percent of the women in the target market used sanitary napkins.

But despite all of Kotex's efforts, Modess had eroded the dominant brand's market share to about 72 percent by the end of the 1940s. In 1949 Modess introduced ''petal soft Modess'' and fired two volleys in the marketing and promotion war that would mark the 1950s. The rival brand's ''Let us buy your first box of Modess'' refund campaign coincided with the introduction of its very successful, long-running ''Modess . . . because'' ad series, which featured models in haute couture to visually emphasize the importance of protection against leakage.

Modess also started offering premiums to encourage sales. Free perfume, silk scarves, and even a tiny sewing kit were offered in the first five years of the decade. Finally, with the support of now-outright owner Kimberly-Clark Corporation, Kotex responded with its first premium offer, a discount on stockings in 1955. The brands exchanged blows with offers of purses, simulated pearl earrings, and sweepstakes over the next several years. In 1958 Kotex changed its logo to a more feminine script, which was incorporated the following year into a pastel packaging design with a symbolic white rose. The end of the decade, however, still saw Kotex's share of the sanitary napkin market dwindle to less than 60 percent.

Kotex tried to recapture the sales it had lost with a newsy ad campaign that replaced the long-running ''Are You in the Know'' series. The ''protects longer—protects better'' campaign promoted a new, non-absorbent Kimlon (rayon) core that forced moisture to the ends of the pad, making it more absorbent. But neither Kotex nor Modess had made a truly groundbreaking improvement to sanitary napkins. Then, in 1960, Scott Paper Co. introduced its Confidets triangular pad to limited markets. The napkin measured two inches at the front and just three-quarters of an inch at the back, and was ushered in with a high-fashion introduction.

Kotex responded to the threat with Kotex Slenderline pads, which measured two inches wide and just three-quarters of an inch thick. Modess copied Confidets with its Vee-Form line of tapered pads. Although Confidets were never able to capture more than ten percent of the market for feminine napkins, Johnson & Johnson's Modess continued to eat away at Kotex's leading share. By the mid-1960s, Modess held about one-third of the market; Kotex had fallen to barely 55 percent. While Kotex still clearly dominated, Modess had shown that the giant was vulnerable.

## A Revolution Leaves Kotex Behind

Johnson & Johnson's Personal Products Co. was finally able to unseat Kotex in the early 1970s, not with Modess, but with a truly revolutionary change in sanitary napkins. Stayfree adhesive-backed napkins, introduced in 1969, eliminated the need for a bulky, itchy sanitary belt or safety pins. The belt had been used since 1930, when Kotex introduced it to provide a more stable, comfortable fit than pinned pads. With the help of ultimate parent Johnson & Johnson's "deep pockets," Stayfree quickly gained market share from Kotex's old-fashioned belted pads. The competition prompted Kimberly-Clark to float another brand of pads, New Freedom. In 1975 alone, Stayfree's advertising budget topped $5 million, and Kimberly-Clark's budget for New Freedom and Kotex combined was just over half that amount, $2.7 million.

In an attempt to turn its fortunes around, K-C pulled the feminine products account from 59-year veteran Foote, Cone & Belding (successor to Lord & Thomas) and awarded it to Kelly, Nason of New York. In 1975 the company launched Kotex Lightdays Pantiliners with $3 million in ad support, and the feminine napkin line received an additional $5 million campaign the following year.

## Toxic Shock Syndrome

First introduced in the United States in the 1930s by Tampax Incorporated (now Tambrands), tampons had gradually captured a portion of the feminine protection market until 1980, when they accounted for about 40 percent of total menstrual care sales. Kimberly-Clark would not come out with a Kotex tampon until 1960, once again following trends rather than setting them.

But in 1980 toxic-shock syndrome, or TSS—a disease linked to a bacterium that occurs mostly in menstruating women using tampons—rocked the industry. When Procter & Gamble's superabsorbent Rely brand tampons were linked with two dozen reported deaths from TSS, 16 percent of women switched from tampons to pads. Though tragic, the event put Kotex, as the oldest and still a prominent brand, in a position to recapture the rebounding sanitary napkin market.

Unfortunately, Kotex marketers reacted slowly to the development, perhaps assuming that consumers would return to the brand without coaxing. Johnson & Johnson, Tambrands, and ironically, Procter & Gamble, quickly developed new, thinner varieties to entice the pad converts. Some analysts surmised that these much larger companies could afford the massive research and advertising budgets it took to capture and maintain market leadership. Johnson & Johnson grabbed the leading share—50 percent in 1983—with Sure & Natural pads, and Tambrands introduced a thin pad, Maxithins, in 1981, that quickly moved into third place with about 10 percent of the market.

In 1984 alone, the four top producers introduced eight new brands of pads with 26 variations, bringing the total selection of beltless pads to 88 types, excluding private-labels. That year, Procter & Gamble launched its Always line with a promotional assault surpassing $100 million that emphasized "revolutionary" dryness technology. By the end of 1984 Always owned 15 percent of the market, and Sure & Natural had slipped to 40 percent.

Part of Always's success came at Kotex's expense: the brand's share fell from one-third to less than one-quarter by the mid-1980s. In addition, Kotex's thick pads, like its belted products of the 1970s, quickly fell behind the times. By 1983, thin pads had claimed an estimated 20 percent of the market for external feminine protection. Rather than change the positioning of Kotex, Kimberly-Clark Corporation introduced a thin version of its New Freedom pad. Since that time, the company has concentrated most of its new product introductions on the New Freedom line, but Kotex continued to capture a higher share than New Freedom. Ad spending for the Kotex line ran slightly over $3.5 million annually in the late 1980s, and Kotex maintained its share of the sanitary napkin market.

## Further Reading:

Alter, Jennifer, "K-C Picks Anyday to Fight J&J Lead," *Advertising Age*, August 11, 1980, pp. 1, 74; "A Delicate Balance: Not Everything Goes in the Marketing for Unmentionables," *Advertising Age*, July 12, 1982, pp. M2–M3, M8.

Edwards, Larry, "Rely Wins No. 2 Test Market Spot; Kimberly-Clark May Be Big Loser," *Advertising Age*, July 1, 1974, pp. 1, 46.

Gershman, Michael, *Getting It Right the Second Time*, Reading, MA: Addison-Wesley, 1990.

Hume, Scott, " 'Most Hated' Ads: Feminine Hygiene," *Advertising Age*, July 18, 1988, p. 3.

"J & J Gears up Stayfree Pads for Challenge From Kimberly," *Advertising Age*, May 12, 1975, pp. 2, 80.

"Promote Interest in Sanitary Protection," *Drug Topics*, November 25, 1991, pp. 60–61.

"A Risky Bid in Feminine Hygiene," *Business Week*, May 16, 1983, pp. 35–36.

Schiller, Zachary, and Jo Ellen Daily, "How Toxic Shock Galvanized a Market," *Business Week*, April 15, 1985, p. 90.

Schnorbus, Paula, "Personal Appeal," *Marketing & Media Decisions*, October 1987, pp. 125–126+.

*—April S. Dougal*

# L.A. GEAR®

The L.A. Gear brand burst into the burgeoning world of athletic footwear in the 1980s via a curious and circuitous path and was an instant success. Founded by entrepreneur Robert Y. Greenberg, a onetime hairdresser, L.A. Gear, Inc. dove foot first into a marketplace already dominated by such well-established brands as Reebok and Nike. Early results were spectacular. Sales rose from $11 million in 1985 to $617 million in 1990, vaulting L.A. Gear firmly into third place in terms of market share in the footwear arena, and company stock took a meteoric rise. Product lines were diversified, moving from primarily fashionable young women's shoes to men's and children's shoe markets as well as casual attire. Billboards, television commercials and magazine ads featured well-known celebrities touting the brand.

The balloon of L.A. Gear's success soon burst, however, largely due an economic recession, the fickleness of the marketplace, and what might be deemed marketing and product mishaps. As market share dramatically declined, a new investor arrived on the scene in 1991 with an infusion of cash to purchase a one-third stake in the company. An entirely new management team followed and embarked on a massive restructuring plan; the L.A. Gear brand appeared well on its way to regaining market share.

## Brand Origins

The L.A. Gear brand did not become a reality until 1985, after what might be termed "checkered" beginnings. Founder Robert Y. Greenberg claimed he had acquired an entrepreneurial bent from his father, a vendor of fresh produce in Boston. Dubbing himself as someone who seeks out trends and rides them to success, Greenberg, a former hairdresser, launched his entrepreneurial career in 1979 with a roller skate rental shop that he named Good Times, Inc. Recognizing that a rental business was temporary at best, he gradually converted the business to a skate manufacturing entity that he named United Skates of America.

When skate sales ebbed, Greenberg turned his attention to novelty shoelaces and sold some $3 million worth of them in just three months. Three years after his initial foray into skating, in 1982, he opened a store in Los Angeles that sold brand name clothing, accessories, and shoes. It was in this shop that he began his own branded clothing line, and the name, according to Greenberg, was submitted in a contest he held among his employees. L.A. Gear was first used in November of 1985 on labels for casual clothes, shoes, and sandals and became a federally registered trademark two years later.

## Early Marketing Strategy

Trend picker Greenberg decided two years later, in 1984, that a retail store was not the way to grow and felt that he should concentrate his efforts on wholesale shoe sales. Against the advice of his then business partner, Ernest Williams, who did not believe another athletic footwear company could compete in the marketplace, Greenberg closed the retail shop, and the partners split. Greenberg turned to the Orient to find sources capable of producing and distributing shoes according to his designs and introduced his first product, the Canvas Workout shoe, in 1985. It was an instant success.

Greenberg honed in on his selected target audience, fashion-conscious females between the ages of 12 and 35, 80 percent of whom, according to Kathleen Kerwin of *Business Week,* "rarely set foot on a tennis or basketball court." The buyers were looking for stylish shoes that were also comfortable, and L.A. Gear responded by offering new and trendier styles every year as sales skyrocketed.

When the company went public in 1986, raising the money to diversify, it turned its sights on sportswear and casualwear for men, women, and children while retaining footwear as its main business. From its success with the Canvas Workout shoe for women, it expanded to spangles, gold lamé, pastel colors, and fringe. It created flashy hightop basketball shoes for men and black and white checkerboard and cow spots designs for children's shoes. L.A. Gear even created a line called Street Hikers, street shoes that offered the comfort of sneakers.

Sales continued to soar, increasing 200 percent in 1986 and doubling the following year. In both 1988 and 1989, L.A. Gear was selected by *Business Week* as one of the best small companies in the United States. Four prestigious publications—*Fortune, Wall Street Journal, Business Week,* and the *Los Angeles Times*—noted that L.A. Gear was the best performer on the New York Stock Exchange in 1989. While some in the Wall Street community were skeptical of the company's success, citing weak sales in sporting goods stores, which were traditionally the best outlets for athletic shoe sales, others lauded the company's marketing strategy in seeking mass merchandisers and department stores as pri-

## AT A GLANCE

L.A. Gear brand of men's, women's, and children's athletic shoes founded in 1979 by Robert Y. Greenberg, owner of Good Times, Inc., a roller skate rental shop; company evolved into a skate-manufacturing business known as United Skates of America and eventually emerged in 1985 as L.A. Gear, Inc.; Trefoil Capital Investors LP purchased a controlling 34 percent interest in L.A. Gear, which restructured as a designer, developer, and marketer of a broad range of athletic and casual footwear.

*Major competitor:* Reebok; also Nike and Keds.

*Advertising: Agency*—Ogilvy & Mather, New York, NY, 1993—. *Major campaign*—"Get in Gear" theme featuring professional sports superstars Joe Montana, Karl Malone, and Hakeem Olajuwon.

*Addresses: Parent company*—L.A. Gear, Inc., 2850 Ocean Park Boulevard, Santa Monica, CA 90405; phone: (310) 822-1995.

mary outlets. At the end of 1990, the company's sales had reached an incredible $818.8 million, from $11 million just four years before.

### Synonymous with Show Business

L.A. Gear operated in a manner as flamboyant and glitzy as that of founder Greenberg and his executive vice-president, Sandy Saemann, who was not only a friend but had been a colleague in the roller skate business. Greenberg was the shoe designer, while showman Saemann ran the marketing. A former advertising executive, Saemann acted as creative director of L.A. Gear's in-house advertising agency and spent money lavishly on television commercials, print advertising, and publicity stunts. The L.A. Gear image was virtually synonymous with the L.A. and Southern California image—blonde, sexy, sunny and sizzly. Ads featured attractive young blonde women wearing little more than their L.A. Gear shoes. Saemann also turned to celebrity endorsers, including actress/businesswoman Priscilla Presley, glamorous actress Heather Locklear, and singers Belinda Carlisle and Paula Abdul.

Such endorsements were acceptable for the women's line, where style and fashion were the rule. The male sports enthusiast market, however, was an entirely different matter. This market looked for heros to emulate, so in order to create credibility and a market for L.A. Gear's men's performance athletic footwear, Saemann reached out for endorsers. He signed as one spokesperson Joe Montana, then the star quarterback for professional football's San Francisco 49ers. Montana, considered by some as the finest quarterback in the history of football, had already been selected three times as the most valuable player in the Super Bowl and was a highly regarded and very visible "hero."

Saemann also attempted to counter Nike's endorser Bo Jackson, at the time a young superstar of sports, by hiring retired Los Angeles Lakers basketball star Kareem Abdul-Jabbar to launch a line of basketball shoes to be called "Jabbars." The advertising campaign featuring Montana and Abdul-Jabbar met with questionable results. Matthew Grimm, writing in *Adweek's Marketing Week,* reported, "under Saemann's creative hand, their endorsements came off as corny and gratuitous."

But possibly the most questionable move by Saemann was to sign pop music icon Michael Jackson to a deal some speculated to be worth $20 million to have him design and endorse a line of shoes and clothes. The plan, predicated on maintaining L.A. Gear's fashion image, called for coordinating the rolling out of the Jackson line of shoes and clothes with the release of a collection of his greatest hits, to be entitled "A Decade," under a Saemann-inspired umbrella theme "Unstoppable." According to *Business Week*'s Kathleen Kerwin, "The choice of Jackson seems odd. He was hot in 1984, when he did a TV spot for Pepsi. But since then, teens seem more interested in reports of Jackson's plastic surgery." What followed was a disaster. The album was never released, and the heavy black buckled shoes designed by Jackson sold poorly. The line and his endorsement were brought to an end, but the several million dollar cost to the company was a significant set-back.

There were other factors contributing to the L.A. Gear downward slide. The company's decision to enter the highly competitive men's market, in which technology and not fashion determined sales, seemed ill-advised. Where men's athletic shoes accounted for 70 percent of the competition's total sales, they only accounted for 20 percent of L.A. Gear's. Furthermore, while the competition opted for high tech shoes, L.A. Gear continued to hype style with bold and brash hightops named Street Slammers, Hot Shots, and Brats.

This dedication to fashion and style led to another marketing error—introducing too many new shoe styles—which in turn created problems of increased inventories and diminishing profits. Sales projections reached monumental proportions resulting in inventory stockpiling and a subsequent move to discount virtually all styles to enable the company to reduce inventories. The discount policy angered retailers, whose prices seemed exorbitant by comparison, and also downgraded the L.A. Gear brand image. As a result, many stores refused to give L.A. Gear products shelf space. Sales in 1991 declined, and the company suffered a net loss. Despite this, the brand achieved its highest market share.

### The Agonies of Growth

Growing pains, questionable marketing decisions, and a recognition that fashion would not work in the men's athletic shoe market contributed to L.A. Gear Inc.'s move into the men's technical shoe market. The company introduced a basketball shoe, without the brand name, in 1991. Named Catapult, the $100 high-tech shoe, featuring a fiberglass and graphite heel supporting an air cushion, was marketed to distance it from L.A. Gear's young and low-priced image. A strategic marketing decision called for selecting an endorser with whom the market could identify, and the company chose Karl "The Mailman" Malone, a star performer with the Utah Jazz professional basketball team. Initial sales, unfortunately, were negatively affected by an incident that aired on national television. The company had provided Catapult shoes to the Marquette University basketball team and during a televised game, one player fell when his shoe fell apart. Although the team continued to wear the shoes and the company announced it was improving the quality, the mark was indelible.

Other problems, stemming from the company's failure to differentiate its technology from that of the competition, arose for L.A. Gear in the technical shoe area. Suits were filed by both Nike and Reebok, one of which was settled out of court in 1992, and while the company continued in the early 1990s to be a defendant in certain legal actions, management stated that the disposition of these actions is not expected to have an adverse effect on the company's financial position.

## New Ownership, New Management, and a Turnaround

Marketing setbacks affected L.A. Gear's financial position, and the company sought capital infusion. In 1991 a $450 million partnership known as Trefoil Capital Investors LP paid $100 million for a one-third stake in the company, and then-President Saemann resigned. Trefoil is an investment fund managed by Shamrock Advisors, Inc. Trefoil assumed control of L.A. Gear's Board when President Robert Greenberg resigned in January of 1991 and hired former Reebok marketing executive Mark R. Goldston as president and chief operating officer. Goldston recruited some of his former colleagues while encouraging Chairman and CEO Greenberg to direct key operations in the company. The company conducted an advertising agency review and hired Ogilvy & Mather in New York in 1993.

Trefoil's increased control and massive restructuring plans led to Greenberg's resignation in January of 1992, and Trefoil replaced him with Disney's turnaround expert, Stanley P. Gold, who was chosen as one of the "25 Executives to Watch" from among the companies of the 1992 *Business Week 1000.* All together, the Trefoil shakeout resulted in 24 of the top 25 people at L.A. Gear being replaced. The company also found a new sourcing agent in the Far East, one highly regarded throughout the footwear industry. The new agent was charged with supervising production—in Indonesia, South Korea, Taiwan, and the People's Republic of China—scheduling, all foreign shipping, and inspecting the quality of finished products. In addition, according to *Adweek's Marketing Week,* L.A. Gear "retooled its product line, paring down from more than 400 styles to 150." The magazine continued, "Now L.A. Gear ships its sneakers like the rest of the industry, on the basis of advance orders," as opposed to its former practice of warehousing product for instant shipment and being overwhelmed by inventory when a model became passe.

Other changes were instituted after the new management took hold. From November of 1991 through October of 1992, a Kidder, Peabody research report found, L.A. Gear Inc. "reduced staff by 45 percent, or 613 employees" and "reduced office space from 200,000 square feet in five buildings to 116,000 square feet in two buildings." Further cost reductions were achieved by closing the company's apparel production and marketing facilities and instead licensing the L.A. Gear name to a limited number of manufacturers.

Restructuring was most apparent, reported *Advertising Age,* in the decision to separate operations into two distinct divisions—lifestyle and athletic shoes—that "will run as stand-alone companies in the marketplace." The diamond-shaped L.A. Gear logo was designated for the lifestyle shoes; and the square L.A. Tech logo for the athletic shoe line. The company also opted to market children's shoes separately using a Bendables logo that features a drawing of a baby. Implicit in all elements of the restructuring was the objective of reclaiming the confidence of retailers and regaining more shelf space for L.A. Gear products.

## Looked Confidently to the Future

L.A. Gear's new advertising strategy—led by Ogilvy & Mather—was simple: update the dated "sexy blonde women at the beach" theme. The new agency introduced the umbrella theme, "Get in Gear," in January of 1992 at the Sporting Goods Manufacturer's Association Super Show in Atlanta, Georgia. President Goldston told *Advertising Age,* "Our strategy is for athletic lifestyle and the theme line is one that can be used for years and years."

L.A. Gear Inc. also dramatically reduced its enormous budgets for endorsers. A three-year endorsement budget of $8 million was established, according to the *Los Angeles Magazine,* and the previous lengthy list of endorsers was set at three—basketball stars Hakeem Olajuwon and Karl Malone and football star Joe Montana, all of whom would be specifically involved with the men's line of technical sport shoes. While international business continued in 60 countries—where products were marketed through agreements with independent distributors—the restructuring program called for the company to begin to sell products directly abroad in selected markets in order to reduce its reliance on independent distributors and thereby more closely control retail prices in those markets.

The introduction of new products held promise for the future. Light Gear and L.A. Lights, which feature interesting and well-accepted patented elements "should appeal to night runners and athletes and consumers seeking that exciting new look," according to the Kidder, Peabody report. The report indicated that the company's light products were included in the *Fortune* magazine feature "Innovation: Products to Watch."

The financial market, which had closely followed the roller coaster path of L.A. Gear and had reacted accordingly, seemed to reflect a belief that the new management is clearly focused on a return to solid growth through dynamic cost cutting, restructuring, inventory reduction and a return to marketing to full-margin retailers and away from mass discounters. As L.A. Gear management stated in the 1992 Annual Report, "Although this is a difficult period in which to effect a turnaround, we believe that the accomplishments of the past year have laid the groundwork upon which we can build to achieve our ultimate objective—to make L.A. Gear a leader in the footwear industry and one of the most admired companies in America."

## Further Reading:

Barrett, Amy, "L.A. Gear Still Looks Like an Also-Ran," *Business Week,* December 21, 1992, p. 27.

Bayor, Leslie, "Shoe Marketers Prep for Workout," *Advertising Age,* March 11, 1991, p. 12.

Brown, Jim, "New Nets Put L.A. Gear on Right Foot," *Network World,* January 22, 1990, pp. 15–16.

Grimm, Matthew, "Gearing up for the Long Run," *Adweek's Marketing Week,* February 3, 1992, pp. 12–13.

Jacobson, Gary M., *Kidder Peabody Company Report,* August 19, 1993, pp. 1–12.

Jefferson, David J., "Don't Walk a Mile in His Shoes: Can Disney Magic—and Money—Put Former L.A. Gear Shoe King Robert Greenberg Back on the Fast Track?," *Los Angeles Magazine,* December 18, 1991, sec.1, p. 114.

Karp, Richard, "The Home Run Hitters," *Institutional Investor,* March 1990, pp. 51–55.

Kerwin, Kathleen, "L.A. Gear is Going Where the Boys Are," *Business Week,* June 19, 1989, p. 54; "L.A. Gear is Tripping Over its Shoelaces," *Business Week,* August 20, 1990, p. 39; "L.A. Gear Calls in a Cobbler," *Business Week,* September 16, 1991, pp. 78, 82; "25 Executives to Watch," *Business Week,* 1992, pp. 74–86.

Kibler, Mark, "Shoes Step in Time to Special Orders," *Transportation & Distribution,* September 1991, pp. 76, 78.

*L.A. Gear Annual Reports,* Santa Monica, CA: L.A. Gear, 1989 and 1992.

"L.A. Gear's Refrain: Turnarounds Take Time," *Brandweek,* February 1, 1993, p. 14.

Lazzareschi, Carla, "L.A. Gear CEO Greenberg Says He'll Step Down," *Los Angeles Times,* January 27, 1992, p. D1.

Magiera, Marcy, "L.A. Gear Toughens Up," *Advertising Age,* January 30, 1989, p. 76; "Nike Edges Reebok, L.A. Gear Sprinting," *Advertising Age,* September 25, 1989, p. 93; "Rebound Team: L.A. Gear Relies on Montana, Jackson," *Advertising Age,* July 2, 1990, pp. 2, 30; "Gary Patrick—Brash L.A. Gear VP Pumps Up Media Strategy," *Advertising Age,* September 10, 1990, p. 72; "L.A. Gear Creative Review Ahead," *Advertising Age,* June 17, 1991, p. 48; "L.A. Gear Looks for New Image," *Advertising Age,* November 4, 1991, p. 2; "L.A. Gear Shifts Ahead," *Advertising Age,* December 23, 1991, p.26; "Small Rivals Leap as L.A. Gear Stumbles," *Advertising Age,* June 8, 1992, p. 12; "L.A. Gear's Comeback Plan: Fashion, Fitness Shoes to Get Separate Identities," *Advertising Age,* June 29, 1992, p. 12.

"New Shoes Race to Store Shelves," *Advertising Age,* February 15, 1993, p.46.

Paris, Ellen, "Rhinestone Hightops, Anyone?," *Forbes,* March 7, 1988, p. 78, 80, 84.

Pereira, Joseph, "Sneaker Makers, Hearing Clomp-Clomp of Competition, Launch 'Rugged' Lines," *Wall Street Journal,* September 14, 1993, p. B1.

*—Michael Finn*

# LAVA®

The Lava brand of bar and liquid soap, in its original volcanic pumice formula, is one of the most enduring grime fighters in the United States. For a full 100 years, Lava soap, packaged in its trademark bright red wrapper depicting a volcano, has been offering effective cleaning action to consumers, pleasing the purse as well as the palm. Lava has gone from the utilitarian gray hand cleaner of the 1890s to the fashionable green fresh-scented bathroom bar of a century later. Just one product manufactured by the Procter & Gamble Company (P&G), which also produces such other popular brands as Jif peanut butter, Secret anti-perspirants and deodorants, and Charmin toilet tissue, Lava soap has remained a venerable product due to years of quality control and innovative reformulation.

## Brand Origins

In St. Louis Missouri in 1858, when the U.S. flag brandished 32 stars, a soap company was founded when a German immigrant, William Waltke, bought a horse and wagon and collected fats from houses in the city. One of the toilet soaps the Waltke Company developed was composed of volcanic pumice and vegetable oils and was named Lava to remind consumers of its content.

## First Commercial Success

With the onslaught of the Spanish-American War and World War I, factory and munitions work boomed. Soldiers as well as factory workers needed a tough soap to remove grit and grime from greasy hands, and Lava was there to do the job. After the wars, the same soldiers and factory laborers remembered the soap and asked for it by name at their local country stores. Lava became a family favorite when housewives saw it could clean the stove as well as the shed.

Over the years, ownership of the Waltke Company was passed on to the founder's sons and eventually grandsons. In December of 1927 the Procter & Gamble Company—established in 1837—with its Cincinnati factories strained by heavy sales and its executives looking to buy another soap factory (preferably in the Midwest), purchased the Waltke firm for cash plus approximately $6.7 million in six percent preferred stock issued expressly for this purpose.

## Early Marketing Strategy

Early marketing of Lava, under the auspices of Procter & Gamble as well as the Waltke Company, took place primarily through the distribution of free samples. All that remained to boost the soap's popularity after Procter & Gamble's acquisition in 1927 was a hefty dose of advertising, which the company readily provided. And with P&G's expanding North American empire stretching as far east as Port Ivory on Staten Island in New York, the soap's basic ingredients—pumice (imported from the Italian island of Lipari) and coconut oil (shipped from the tropics)—could be much more easily transported to Cincinnati.

In 1932, however, marketing widened when P&G began advertising on radio and George, the Lava Soap Man, premiered with his own evening show. The first of the P&G-sponsored radio entertainers, George was a singer whose melodies not only trumpeted the company's more extensive use of radio but also heralded P&G's debut into evening programming for the entire family. Lava's sales soared.

## Advertising Innovations

P&G's advertising dated back to 1882, when Harley Procter, son of the cofounder of the company, formulated the first promotional campaign for Ivory soap. Many of his marketing concepts proved so intrinsically well thought out, logically planned, and consumer-oriented that they continued into the next century. Sampling, a significant part of Harley's marketing strategy, formed the basis of Lava's advertising campaign and made the soap a household name, even though the product's versatility was limited.

To garner more sales for Lava, P&G had to get to know its customer. The company achieved this objective through intense market research, mail surveys especially. One example of P&G's sensitivity to consumer concerns lay in the handling of communications. In the late 1970s, P&G, already answering hundreds of letters a day about its products, became one of the first companies to display toll-free telephone numbers on its packages. By the early 1980s, every P&G package boasted a toll-free number.

An outgrowth of the toll-free telecommunication practice premiered in 1992, when another P&G brand, Ivory Clear Dishwashing Liquid, was rolled out nationally. After a consumer was given a free product sample by an ActMedia representative in the store, he or she could call a special interactive product-sampling

## AT A GLANCE

Lava brand of bar and liquid soap founded in 1893 by William Waltke, president of the William Waltke Company; brand sold to the Procter & Gamble Company, 1927.

**Performance:** *Market share*—0.5% of toilet soap category (1991).

**Major competitor:** Lever Brothers' Dove and Lever 2000; also Greystone/Dial's Dial.

**Advertising:** *Agency*—Leo Burnett, Chicago, IL. *Major campaign*—"Don't need no Lava soap . . . Nope."

**Addresses:** *Parent company*—Procter & Gamble Company, One Procter & Gamble Plaza, Cincinnati, OH 45202; phone: (513) 983-1100; fax: (513) 983-7847.

hot line on the bottle. Different from the regular consumer hot line, which was staffed by "real people," the sampling hot line was automated and interactive. All a customer had to do, using a touch-tone phone, was to press buttons in response to oral menu options to comment on the product or to speak with a human representative. Lava would be sure to follow Ivory's lead.

### Brand Development and Product Changes

In 1956, after consumer research findings were examined, Lava's abrasive was changed to whitened pumice and its dark gray color was reformulated into a creamier white color in a successful attempt to expand the soap's customer base. No longer was Lava viewed as just a heavy-duty cleaning soap; it was then also considered a superlative hand soap for the whole family. In 1976 the soap underwent another metamorphosis: its color was changed to an attractive shade of green and the soap was given a fresh scent. Thus, Lava could function not only in America's laundry rooms and kitchens but in its bathrooms as well.

In 1993 the main ingredients in Lava were coconut soap, to provide cleaning and lathering; finely-ground pumice, to aid in removing tough soil and stains abrasively; coconut oil, to make lather last longer; water, to make the soap malleable enough to be molded and stamped into the desired shape without breaking; perfume, to give Lava its fresh fragrance; salt, to make the bar firm and easy to hold; and colorants, to give Lava its inviting green color. At that time, Lava was sold nationally in both bar and liquid form. The bar form was available in two sizes—large (5.75 ounces) and regular (4 ounces). Packaging, consisting of a bright red wrapper depicting a volcano, reminded the consumer that Lava contained pumice. Both forms could be found in grocery, drug, variety, and department stores.

### Performance Appraisal and Future Predictions

Introduced as a grime guerilla in 1893, Lava has remained a stable soap standby for 100 years. Whereas other faddish soaps became sudden stars and then slowly sank into a sea of poor sales, Lava, through Procter & Gamble's astute marketing, endured for several reasons. First, P&G placed its greatest emphasis in marketing on consumer preferences. Second, through the years, the company kept the personality of the Lava brand consistent in advertising. And, finally, P&G always insisted that *Lava,* not the company, be the star of its advertising. By focusing on the grit and grime cleaning abilities of Lava, P&G maintained the soap's strong market share.

If longevity were any indicator of worth, Lava is sure to endure into the twenty-first century. P&G chemists and marketers maintain a focus on the brand's future by querying consumers, sampling and advertising, and updating Lava soap in an effort to improve, but not deviate from, its basic formula. Factory laborers will always need a tough dirt-cutter at the end of a hard day's work, and no doubt Lava would be there to do the job.

### Further Reading:

*Answers About Marketing,* Cincinnati: Procter & Gamble Company, 1993.

Diamano, Nancy, "Soaping Up," *Canadian Consumer,* March 1991, p. 15.

*Facts About Procter & Gamble,* Cincinnati: Procter & Gamble Company, 1993.

"Hand and Bath Soaps," *Consumer Reports,* December 1986, p. 158.

"Ivory," *World's Greatest Brands, An International Review by Interbrand,* New York: John Wiley & Sons, 1992, p. 2.

"Ivorydale—A Procter & Gamble Landmark," Cincinnati: Procter & Gamble Company, 1993.

*Lava,* Cincinnati: Procter & Gamble Company, 1993.

Lawrence, Jennifer, "P&G Hooks Up Interactive Product-Sampling Hot Line," *Advertising Age,* October 5, 1992, p. 3.

Lawrence, and Pat Sloan, "P&G Plans Big New Ivory Push," *Advertising Age,* November 23, 1992, p. 12.

Lief, Alfred, *"It Floats"; The Story of Procter & Gamble,* New York: Rinehart, 1958.

*Procter & Gamble and Prices,* Cincinnati: Procter & Gamble Company, 1993.

*The Procter & Gamble Company,* Cincinnati: Procter & Gamble Company, 1993.

*Procter & Gamble Company Annual Report,* Cincinnati: Procter & Gamble Company, 1993.

*Procter & Gamble: The House That Ivory Built,* Lincolnwood, IL: NTC Business Books, 1988.

Schisgall, Oscar, *Eyes on Tomorrow: The Evolution of Procter and Gamble,* Chicago: J. W. Ferguson Publishing Co., 1981.

*—Virginia Barnstorff*

# LEE®

Lee brand of jeans has been vying for first place in the category with Levi's brand for decades. Henry David Lee, the founder of H.D. Lee Mercantile Company, began making denim overalls and dungarees in 1911 to supply his mercantile business. The company's tradition of product innovation began in 1913 when Lee developed a one-piece work garment that slipped over regular clothing to keep it clean. Over the years, Lee has introduced a number of other successful products, including a denim cowboy pant—the predecessor of Lee Riders—in 1924. Lee, along with other jeanswear manufacturers, prospered in the 1960s and 1970s as baby boomers adopted jeans as their uniform of choice. Acquired by VF Corp. in 1969, Lee has remained a market share leader. In the 1980s, as baby boomers aged and their tastes in clothing changed, sales of jeans plummeted. Lee responded by expanding its product line, introducing state-of-the-art technology, and launching inventive advertising campaigns.

## Brand Origins

The Lee brand was created in 1889 when Henry David Lee was granted a charter by the state of Kansas to establish the H.D. Lee Mercantile Company, a wholesale grocery business. Before the company's tenth anniversary, it was firmly established as the dominant wholesale grocer in the Midwest and had expanded its operation to include notions, furnishings, stationery, and clothing.

Aggravated by unreliable deliveries of workwear items, Lee decided to build his own garment factory in Salina, Kansas (where his mercantile business was located), in 1911. Two years later, he developed a one-piece workwear garment, Union-All, that changed the company's direction. Essentially a jacket and dungarees sewn together, Union-All could be slipped over regular clothing to protect it from dirt and debris. (Some people believe that the Union-All was the brainchild of Lee's chauffeur, who spent a great deal of time servicing his boss' new automobile.) By 1915 a second garment factory, devoted exclusively to production of Union-Alls, was opened in Kansas City. The product was so successful that the U.S. Army adopted it as the official doughboy fatigue during World War I.

The 1920s were notable because of several new product developments. A cowboy pant made from 13-ounce denim was introduced in 1924. A series of merchandising firsts arrived in 1926: jeans with zippers, work clothes with slide fasteners, the U-shaped saddle crotch, and tailored sizing, in which the rise and seat proportions were based on waist and inseam measurements. By 1939 the company was the largest manufacturer of work clothes in the United States. In recognition of the company's increasing involvement in apparel manufacture, the company name was changed to H.D. Lee Company in 1943. Two years later, the Lee brand, with its strong Western flavor, was added to the pants. With some thickening and roughening, the brand mark is still used.

## Advertising Innovations

Lee became the first national advertiser in the apparel industry in 1917 when it placed a full-page ad for its Union-Alls in the *Saturday Evening Post.* The firm added a zipper to its Union-Alls in 1927 and then organized a consumer contest to name the new garment. The newly christened "Lee Whizits" were introduced in print ads featuring the cast of the "Our Gang" comedies. The wonders of Lee's Jelt Denim—an 11½-ounce cloth with twisted yarns for unsurpassed durability—were proclaimed in a series of Ripley's "Believe It or Not" ads.

After World War II, full-page color ads for Lee Riders appeared in *Life,* emphasizing the "authentic Western" flavor of the merchandise. Lee introduced its Leesures casual line in 1954 as "comfort clothes for work and play." Beginning in 1961, Lee's ads featured the slogan "the clothes you need for the life you lead."

Joining forces with the Fallon McElligott advertising agency in 1986, Lee moved to consolidate its position with consumers in the 18- to 34-year-old age bracket, rolling out award-winning advertising that sought to emulate real-life situations. In 1988 the agency introduced a trio of spots that director Joe Pytka considered his "best 30-second work to date," according to *Back Stage.* Titled "Laundromat," "Highway," and "Vacation," the spots used the ragged, jerky camera technique that the director first employed for Nike and Michelob. "The spots consist of brief fragments of impressions and purposefully go for informational overkill," Pytka was quoted as saying in *Back Stage.* The product did not become the focus of the spots until the final frames when the logo appeared.

The following year, Fallon McElligott created three new 30-second spots for Lee that were "bound to put its farmer image out to pasture," wrote Susan Shahoda in *Back Stage.* Once again directed by Joe Pytka, the spots were unconventional ads. "Road Trip," for example, showed two men stopping at a diner on their

## AT A GLANCE

The Lee brand was launched in 1889 when Henry David Lee started a wholesale grocery business, the H.D. Lee Mercantile Company. He began manufacturing clothing, including dungarees, to supply his business in 1911. The Lee brand was acquired by VF Corp. in 1969.

**Performance:** *Market share*—10.9% of jeanswear market. *Sales*—Approximately $800 million (1990).

**Major competitor:** Levi Strauss & Co.'s Levi's; also Wrangler.

**Advertising:** *Agency*—Fallon McElligott, Minneapolis, MN, 1986—. *Major campaign*—"Maybe it's a better fitting jean."

**Addresses:** *Parent company*—VF Corp., 1047 North Park Rd., Wyomissing, Pennsylvania 19610; phone: (215) 378-1151; fax: (215) 375-9371.

way out West. When they inquired about the rhubarb pie, an old-timer launched into a lengthy discussion about rhubarb. Nowhere in the spot were viewers given any information about Lee jeans. "What we are trying to do with these commercials is build a brand image," copywriter Bill Miller was quoted as saying in *Back Stage.* "[These commercials] are moments in time and space that people can look at and say, 'I recognize myself in that situation or that's happened to me before.' "

As the number of teens dwindled in the 1990s, jeanswear manufacturers began targeting aging baby boomers in their advertising. Lee positioned its product as the brand that fits the lifestyle of today's consumer. Television spots featuring Lee's Easy Riders took a humorous jab at "men who are trying to squeeze today's body into yesterday's jeans," said Kevin Berrigan of Fallon McElligott in *Marketing News.* Lee continued to take a humorous approach in a series of ads that appeared in 1993. "On Superbowl Sunday, Lee Apparel introduced the latest middle-ager too plump to squeeze into his jeans," wrote Bernice Kanner in *New York.* "He inhales so deeply that the clothes fly out of his dresser and a canary is sucked from its cage into his mouth. In another spot a man watches through a shade-covered window as his trim date struggles into her jeans, then collapses on the floor with a dress dummy, which from his vantage point looks alarmingly like another suitor." Such clever advertising helped to increase Lee's sales by 35 percent from the previous year.

### International Growth

Lee launched its international division in New York City in 1959 and opened its first overseas factory five years later in Sint Niklaas, Belgium. The company received two presidential citations for its outstanding export record, first in 1959 and again in 1970. Lee's international growth was spurred after 1969 when the company was acquired by VF Corp. The acquisition enabled Lee to enter into several joint ventures, including business arrangements in Scotland, Belgium, Spain, Australia, Brazil, and Hong Kong. By 1991, Most of Lee's international sales were to Western European markets, although business in Latin America, Asia, and the Pacific Rim markets has continued to expand. Lee jeans have been made in Northern Ireland for more than 40 years.

### Brand Development

H.D. Lee's development of the Union-All in 1913 signalled the start of a series of product innovations that has spanned decades.

The 1920s saw an impressive series of firsts, including jeans with zippers, work clothes with slide fasteners, the U-shaped saddle crotch, and tailored sizing. Lee also introduced the predecessor of Lee Riders, a denim cowboy pant, and launched color-fast herringbone twills. Lee entered into the women's jeans market in 1949 with Lady Lee Riders, lauded as the best-fitting jeans in the industry. One of the firm's manufacturing facilities in Chetopa, Kansas, lent its name to workwear clothing made from a tough new fabric dubbed Chetopa Twill, launched in 1953. Lee entered the leisure sportswear market in 1954 with the introduction of Leesures and established a position in boys wear when it launched "Double Knees" in 1957. Dressy white jeans and jackets arrived in the form of the Lee Westerner in 1959, with such features as center creases and narrower legs (added two years later). In 1964 Lee introduced stretch denim and permanent press slacks, which it marketed under the "Lee Prest" banner. Leisure suits, a sporty interpretation of the business suit, were introduced by Lee in 1972. Lee launched the Ms. Lee label the following year, emphasizing a "new fit" for women, and formed its youthwear division in 1979.

The 1980s, a challenging decade for the jeanswear industry, were marked by intense competition and changes in consumer tastes. Lee responded by implementing new technologies and expanding its product lines. When the "baby boomlet" hit, Lee added infant and toddler apparel to its offerings. The company also developed Dress Blues, which featured superior color retention, Denim-Cable stripes, and Ultra Cords. The second half of the decade saw the addition of big and tall products for men, new relaxed-fit and pleated products under the Relaxed Riders and Easy Riders labels. Stonewashed jeans also helped revitalize the sluggish jeanswear industry in the 1980s. (The stonewashing process involved washing jeans with bleaches, chemicals, softeners, and pumice stones to make them softer and faded looking.) Lee introduced its first stonewashed jeans, Frosted Riders, in 1986, followed by Glacier, a frosted fabric made from a denim woven from twisted yarns, and Pepper jeans, featuring denim with a nubbed surface.

Hoping to capitalize on the public's demand for sweat attire, Lee launched Lee Sweats, a line of sweatshirts and pants, in 1990. A $2 to $3 million ad campaign promoted the suitability of sweats for almost any activity. In 1992 the company split its Riders line off as a line of men's and women's jeans and knitwear to be marketed in discount stores.

### Performance Appraisal

H.D. Mercantile Company, the forerunner of H.D. Lee Company and the Lee Apparel Company, was launched in 1889 with an initial capitalization of $100,000. By 1990 Lee Apparel, a division of VF Corp., had sales of approximately $800 million. VF Corp.'s jeanswear group, which includes Lee, Wrangler, Rustler, and Girbaud, commanded about 25 percent of the jeanswear market. Sales had been disappointing in the 1980s, largely due to problems with the Lee division and a sluggish jeans market, according to *Hoover's Handbook of American Business.* The company responded by streamlining Lee's management and refocusing the division on basic jeanswear rather than high fashion garments. The approach apparently paid off. Sales in VF Corp.'s jeanswear product group increased by 14 percent in 1991, largely attributable to changes at Lee. "Operating profit increased substantially over 1990 due to the recognition in 1990 of restructuring expenses, high provisions for excess inventories and inefficiencies from plant downtime, particularly at Lee," the *VF Corporation 1991*

*Annual Report* stated. "Conversely, the most significant increases in 1991 operating profit resulted from improvements at Lee."

Lee reported increased sales and profits for the year, with growth driven by all three segments of the division's business—women's, men's and youths. Lee is the only jeans brand to have a major share in all three markets and is the number one brand in women's and girl's jeans, according to the annual report. Lee was ranked the top brand in ladies apparel by upscale discount chains in 1986. The company was the number three jeanswear manufacturer in 1991 with 10.9 percent of market share.

## Future Predictions

While tastes in fashion are difficult to forecast, Lee has already begun to structure its business for the remainder of the century and beyond, according to *One Hundred Years of Excellence,* a Lee Apparel Company publication. A major step in the company's preparation for the future was the construction of a 225,000-square-foot distribution center in Mocksville, North Carolina. The state-of-the-art facility replaced two older facilities, allowing for greater operating efficiencies and speedy service to Lee's retail customers.

A highly effective restructuring play introduced in 1990 resulted in financial recovery at Lee and underscored management's commitment to ensuring long-term competitive success. Lee took steps to reduce product development cycle times, inventories, and costs. The company also restored its traditional focus on core products by offering classic styles recognized for value, quality, fit, and comfort. This initiative has been supported by consumer marketing programs and advertising tailored to the brand's image. "Momentum achieved by the brand in the marketplace points to the divisions' continued growth," the *VF Corporation 1991 Annual Report* stated.

## Further Reading:

"Big Ads Back on Super Bowl," *Advertising Age,* February 17, 1992, p. 1.

Kanner, Bernice, "Jean Genies," *New York,* March 8, 1993, p. 24.

"Lee Plans Separate Riders Effort," *Advertising Age,* September 14, 1992, p. 8.

"Lee Scores as Top Ladies' Brand with Upscale Discounters," *Discount Store News,* October 13, 1986, p. 1.

Magiera, Marcy, and Sloan, Pat, "Basic Jeans Shine for Levi's, Lee," *Advertising Age,* February 17, 1992, p. 22.

Meyers, Janet, "Lee Sweats New Category," *Advertising Age,* October 22, 1991, p. 12.

Miller, Cyndee, "Jeans Marketers Look for Good Fit with Older Men and Women," *Marketing News,* September 16, 1991, p. 1.

Morgan, Hal, *Symbols of America,* New York: Penguin Books, 1986.

*One Hundred Years of Excellence,* Merriam, Kansas: Lee Apparel Company, 1989.

Shahoda, Susan, "Lee Jeans Launches New Image Campaign," *Back Stage,* June 16, 1989, p. 8.

Smith, Lisa M., "Fallon, Pytka Create New Ads for Lee Jeans," *Back Stage,* June 3, 1988, p. 1.

—*Pam Berry*

# L'EGGS®

L'eggs pantyhose, in its familiar oval-shaped container, has been the best-selling brand of pantyhose in the United States for more than two decades. The story behind its success is a study of basic marketing strategies. The leaders at L'eggs built a brand based on three simple marketing premises: unique packaging that distinguished the brand from its competition; efficient distribution networks to drugstores, supermarkets, and mass merchandisers; and attention to consumer needs and preferences.

## Brand Origins

As the 1950s drew to a close, more and more American women gave up their positions as homemakers and entered the outside workforce. The hosiery of the day was cumbersome and uncomfortable; girdles, stockings, and garterbelts were required apparel for women who worked in offices and similar settings. By the mid 1960s, women began replacing some of these uncomfortable items with pantyhose. At the time, however, the available brands were rife with fit and durability problems.

When first introduced, pantyhose were expensive—approximately $8.00 per pair—and were available only through department and specialty stores. Toward the end of the 1960s prices had dropped to more affordable levels, and distribution had spread to drugstores, supermarkets, and mass merchandisers, who now comprised 16 percent of the hosiery market. In 1968 Robert E. Elberson joined the Hanes Corporation, a textile and apparel manufacturer based in Winston-Salem, North Carolina. Elberson's common sense approach to marketing contributed directly to the success of the L'eggs brand. When the company developed a stretchable, non-sagging pantyhose, marketing studies showed that it fit nearly 90 percent of all women. Despite the fact that the new product was more expensive to produce than high-end department store brands, Elberson realized the potential of the versatile material.

Originally, Hanes executives were divided over the best way to market the new pantyhose. Some wanted to position it as a high-end item, raising the price and targeting women with disposable incomes in order to secure a high profit margin. However, Elberson, president of the hosiery division, disagreed. The product met the needs of a mass market, and Elberson noted the success of Lady Brevoni, a West German brand that was sold through supermarkets and drug stores in ready-to-display cartons. Despite its price of a mere 79 cents, Lady Brevoni offered the retailer a 40 percent profit margin. Elberson decided to follow this volume sales strategy rather than rely on high margins to make the new product profitable.

Elberson solicited the help of a young marketing analyst who was assigned the task of studying the competition, and his findings were daunting. The supermarket and drugstore pantyhose market was highly fragmented—nearly 600 brands were in production, the largest of which held no more than a two or three percent market share. For Hanes to make the leap from department store hosiery to mass merchandised hosiery, the company needed a leader with extensive packaged goods experience. Elberson appointed David Harrold, formerly with General Foods, to successfully introduce Hanes pantyhose to drugstores and supermarkets. In a move that shook up the conservative hosiery industry, Harrold hired two marketing research firms and paid them an unprecedented $400,000 to find a way to break into the market.

The firms' findings were illuminating; the most basic problem was product availability. Most retail hosiery displays were typically under-stocked. In addition, they found a rampant consumer distrust of inexpensive brands. Fit and durability problems still plagued the market, and as a result most women preferred to purchase pantyhose in department and specialty stores.

Thus, the Hanes company needed to create a national market for a product regarded as low-quality. Moreover, it had to differentiate itself from hundreds of other brands. The new product's criteria for success was evident; it needed to be consistent in quality, easy to keep in stock, have a recognizable brand name, and be displayed in such a way that it grabbed the consumer's eye.

Harrold assigned the advertising responsibilities to Dancer-Fitzgerald-Sample, and he assigned packaging responsibilities to Smith, Carnse, and Ferriter. After crushing a sample pair of hose in his hand, Roger Ferriter decided on "nature's most beautiful package"—the egg. He combined the concept of the egg, legs, and a twist of European innuendo with an apostrophe, and created the brand name L'eggs.

To meet the point of purchase needs of Ferriter's innovative packaging, a Hanes engineer designed a free-standing display rack. The eye-catching rack made the L'eggs brand stand out from the competition in the supermarket aisles, and—at a mere two feet high—it held two dozen pairs of pantyhose in many colors, sizes,

## AT A GLANCE

**L**'eggs brand of pantyhose founded in October, 1970, in Winston-Salem, NC, by Hanes Corporation employees Robert Elberson and David Harrold; the Hanes Corporation was acquired in 1974 by conglomerate Consolidated Foods; later Consolidated Foods became Sara Lee Corporation.

**Performance:** *Market share*—42% (top share) of drugstore/supermarket-sold hosiery category. *Sales*—$924 million.

**Major competitor:** Kayser-Roth Corporation's No Nonsense.

**Advertising:** *Agency*—Saatchi & Saatchi Advertising, New York, NY. *Major campaign*—"Our L'eggs fit your legs"; also "Nothing beats a great pair of L'eggs."

**Addresses:** *Parent company*—L'eggs Products Incorporated, 5660 University Parkway, Winston-Salem, NC 27105; phone: (919) 744-2011; fax: (9191) 744-8594. *Ultimate parent company*—Sara Lee Corp., 3 First National Plaza, Chicago, IL 60602; phone: (312) 726-2600; fax: (312) 558-8567.

and styles. The rack also had space for promotional materials and coupons.

To solve the problem of running out of stock, Hanes executives decided to distribute L'eggs pantyhose to retailers on consignment. This method provided skeptical retailers with a no-risk opportunity to earn a 42 percent profit margin on every pair of pantyhose sold through their stores. This was seven times the average return-on-square-foot. Hanes would own the units and the inventory. The retailer needed only to provide in-store space.

Finally, L'eggs management developed a novel approach to stocking its units by hiring 450 "route girls" to serve as sales representatives and stocking agents. Attired in red, white, and blue hot pants, the route girls stocked shelves, distributed and arranged promotional literature, collected sales data, and reported retailers who were discounting Hanes' fair trade pricing policy. According to retailers, these route girls were the topic of a great deal of positive in-store conversation.

### Brand Introduction

Because the hosiery industry relies so much on brand-name recognition, Harrold, Elberson, and the other Hanes executives knew they needed to support the introduction of L'eggs pantyhose with a solid investment in advertising. Before Elberson had joined Hanes, they company's entire media budget was only $250,000 annually. With the new L'eggs brand roll-out alone, expenditures rose dramatically to $10 million. By 1980 the Hanes advertising budget skyrocketed to $75 million—$30 million of which was devoted entirely to the L'eggs brand.

L'eggs pantyhose premiered in May of 1970 in Milwaukee; Kansas City; Sacramento; and Portland, Maine, behind the advertising slogan, "Our L'eggs fit your legs." Six months later Hanes executives launched the product in cities nationwide. The effort paid off magnificently. The brand's appeal, convenience, price, and availability convinced many women to select the brand regularly. Six months after its debut in major cities, a quarter of all women surveyed identified L'eggs as their regular brand. First-year sales soared to $9 million. Second-year sales grew 500 percent to $54 million, and the following year they reached $112 million. By 1973 the L'eggs brand held a 30 percent market share

of all pantyhose sold through supermarkets and drugstores. Its closest competitor, Kayser-Roth Corporation's No Nonsense, held only a nine percent market share.

The rapid rise of L'eggs pantyhose to industry leader and its ability to maintain that position for over twenty years is due to more than its unique packaging and efficient distribution. Corporate officials pride themselves on the company's response to consumer needs and preferences. Through the years, Hanes has added a wide variety of sub-brands to meet seasonal needs, satisfy color choices, and fit a wider range of sizes. These extensions include Sheer Energy (support pantyhose), Sheer Elegance and Sheer Elegance Silken Mist (high-end, sheer pantyhose), Just My Size (queen-sized), and Underalls (pantyhose and underwear in one).

### Continued Growth

Over the next fifteen years, sales of L'eggs pantyhose grew at three times the industry average. Though such brisk sales fueled the success of the brand, it also presented management challenges for Hanes executives. As sales rose and product offerings multiplied, management requirements became increasingly complex. The inventory control system, for example, was straining under a tenfold increase in stock volume. In light of these challenges, in 1989 company officials implemented a major restructuring of manufacturing, distributing, and production planning based on a new business strategy.

After examining the manufacturing processes, product managers found several problems. First, style-based production facilities relied on month-old marketing data from the field to produce sales forecasts. This heavy dependence on traditional forecasting led to drastic fluctuations in each facility's production plan, frequent stockouts, excessive inventory levels, and a lack of current information in planning production.

The L'eggs brand's competitive advantage was due to its ability to respond rapidly to consumer demand, while keeping inventory levels at a minimum and manufacturing costs low. To maximize these advantages, Hanes switched its L'eggs plants from a style-based system to a steady-stream based system contingent on a baseline demand level. To better anticipate market demand, production planning was switched from its forecast-driven method to a demand-driven, safety stock concept based on current information. Using this new approach, the Hanes salespeople could survey weekly consumer buying habits and send the information immediately to headquarters via hand-held computers. This enabled the company to be more responsive to changes in demand and shorten the distribution pipeline for the product. By the end of the 1980s, the L'eggs brand was able to meet 98 percent of its weekly production targets, and it completely eliminated the need for inventory in warehouses and distribution centers. L'eggs pantyhose now controlled 42 percent of the $2.2 billion market—four times the share held by the No Nonsense brand.

In 1990 a new challenge faced the L'eggs brand team. As Americans gained awareness of environmental issues pertaining to solid waste, consumers began to question the need for the product's ubiquitous plastic egg container. After an extensive market research study, L'eggs officials decided to replace the package that gave the company instant brand recognition with an environmentally-friendly recycled cardboard package. While the new container maintained the classic egg-shaped silhouette, it reduced the amount of packaging material in the L'eggs pantyhose box by 33 percent. Although the company needed to spend millions of dollars to convert the brand's production, merchandising, and distribution systems, officials were determined to maintain the product's affordable consumer price. Once again, the L'eggs brand positioned itself as a champion of consumer responsiveness while retaining its 42 percent market share.

## Further Reading:

*Focused Manufacturing and Inventory Control (FMIC) System,* American Management Systems Project Description Report, 1991.

"L'eggs to Scrap Plastic 'Egg' Package," *Marketing News,* August 19, 1991, p. 20.

McGough, Robert, "Sara Lee: Icing on the Cake," *Financial World,* October 17, 1989, pp. 22–24.

McKenzie, Phillip E. and Kincey Potter, "Getting a 'L'egg' Up on the Competition," *Manufacturing Systems,* May 1989, pp. 58–61.

Therrien, Lois, "This Marketing Effort Has L'eggs," *Business Week,* December 23, 1991, pp. 50–51.

*—Wendy Johnson Bilas*

# LEVI'S®

**QUALITY NEVER GOES OUT OF STYLE.**

"Guaranteed to shrink, wrinkle and fade," Levi's jeans are one of the most famous consumer brands. Known worldwide by his first name, Levi Strauss invented what has become the American "folk costume," worn by miners and movie stars, farmers and hippies. The continued success of the Levi's brand since the mid-19th century can in large part be attributed to Levi Strauss & Co.'s consistent commitment to quality products. Patented rivets and strong fabric, snaps, and thread provide the durability guaranteed by the "Levi's Promise" card attached to each of the 2.5 billion pairs of Levi's jeans sold. Although overall sales of jeans in the United States declined during the 1980s, Levi Strauss and Co.'s innovative advertising contributed to revitalizing the jeans market towards the end of the decade. The ailing economy also attracted consumers back to basic jeans apparel, which was more practical and affordable than designer clothing. Throughout the early 1990s, Levi Strauss & Co. maintained its lead in the domestic market share of jeans products, though the VF Corporation's Wrangler and Lee brands narrowly edged out the Levi's brand in jean production.

## Brand Origins and Founders

Levi Strauss, like countless other adventurers, headed West to try to capitalize on the Gold Rush of 1849. In 1853 the 24-year-old Bavarian immigrant boarded a clipper ship in New York and set off for California, where his brother-in-law, David Stern, had established a dry goods business. At Stern's invitation, Levi sailed to San Francisco, supplied with various fabrics, including plenty of heavy brown canvas-like material, intended for tents and Conestoga wagon covers.

Upon arrival, however, the prospectors who looked over his merchandise were unimpressed. Legend has it that a tattered old miner told Levi Strauss, "You should've brought pants. Pants don't wear worth a hoot up in the diggin's. You can't get a pair strong enough to last no time." The enterprising Levi brought the canvas to a tailor and thus were created the first pair of "jeans." Rumor quickly spread around town of the superior durability of "those pants of Levi's," and soon the supply of canvas was depleted. After some experimentation with various materials, including local sailcloth, Levi Strauss opted for a heavy, cotton fabric from the French town of Nimes, called *serge de Nimes,* which was later abbreviated to *denim.* He then chose the deep indigo dye that would become the definitive color of blue jeans.

In the early 1870s Levi Strauss added the hallmark copper rivets for extra strength. A Carson City tailor, Jacob W. Davis, had written to Levi Strauss, describing how he had stumbled upon the idea of reinforcing pants with rivets. Davis had asked a harness maker to rivet a pair of pants for a client of his, a miner, who incessantly complained that his pockets would rip from the weight of gold nuggets and tools. These durable pants were heartily welcomed by the miner, and Davis's riveting became a popular tailoring technique with his clientele. And so, in 1873, with the cooperation of Davis, Strauss obtained a patent for the rivets. In that same year the double arcuate stitching was designed for the hip pockets, a pattern which, according to the company, is the oldest apparel trademark in use in the United States.

In 1886 another distinguishing feature added to the pants was the "two horse brand" patch, which depicts two horses trying to pull apart a pair of Levi's jeans in a mock game of tug-of-war. The leather patch was affixed to the back of the waistband and has remained essentially unchanged for over a century. In 1890 the year Levi Strauss & Co. was formally incorporated, the company designated "lot numbers" to their products. "501" was assigned to the "waist-high overall," which was the name Levi preferred to "jeans," a French derivation ("genes") of the cotton slacks worn by Genovese sailors ages ago. Not until several decades after Levi Strauss's death in 1902 did the company freely use the term jeans.

## Product Changes

The first Levi's product to be marketed nationwide, in 1912, was the new one-piece playsuit for children, Koveralls, designed by Jacob Davis's son, Simon. Although the success of this product allowed Levi Strauss & Co. to expand their geographic base, the core jeans market remained the manual workers of the West. Ten years later the 501s were slightly updated with the addition of belt loops, although the suspender buttons were not removed until after World War II. Another addition, the Red Tab, was attached to the right-hand hip pocket, and became a world-famous trademark.

A few other minor changes have been made since then, including, in 1937, covering the rivets on the back pockets with denim after complaints about scratched saddles and school chairs. And the crotch rivet, unpopular with cowboys, was eliminated by "executive order." As the company story goes, Walter Haas, Sr., president of Levi Strauss & Co., had the rather uncomfortable experience of stooping next to a raging campfire in crotch-riveted

## AT A GLANCE

Levi's brand jeans founded in 1850 in San Francisco, CA, by Levi Strauss & Co. owners, including Levi Strauss and David Stern; later developers include Sigmund Stern, Walter A. Haas, Sr., Daniel Koshland, Walter Haas, Jr., and Robert Haas; leveraged buyout in 1985 by Levi Strauss Associates, Inc.

**Performance:** *Market share*—19% (top share) of jeans category. *Sales*—$5.6 billion (1992).

**Major competitor:** VF Corporation's Wrangler brand (with 15.4% share of the market); also, VF Corporation's Lee (with 10%) and Rustler (with 6%) brands.

**Advertising:** *Agency*—Foote, Cone & Belding, San Francisco, CA 1930—. *Major campaign*—Young men discussing life in the 501 campaign, "Got To Be Real"; also, "A loose interpretation of the original," with athletic men on a beach in the 550 and 560 looser-fitting jeans.

**Addresses:** *Parent company*—Levi Strauss Associates Inc., Levi Strauss & Co., 1155 Battery Street, San Francisco, CA 94111; phone: (415) 544-6000; fax: (415) 544-6134.

jeans. Cowboys' complaints of the heat-conducting rivet were finally heeded, and the feature was removed. In 1955, in order to appease Eastern consumers, Levi & Strauss & Co. made jeans available with zippers.

It was around the 1950s that the company began to actively expand into new product lines. In an attempt to appeal more to East Coast tastes, Levi's "Lighter Blues" casual slacks were introduced in 1954. Then in 1960 "White Levi's" jeans, the beige-colored variant of the original 501s, made their debut. Shortly thereafter, stretch corduroy jeans and Sta-Prest permanent press were added to the Levi's roster, in 1961 and 1964 respectively. It was not until 1968, a century after the founding of the Levi's brand, that the company designed a product for the other half of the population, and "Levi's for Gals" were born. By the 1990s, Levi Strauss & Co. included the brand names Brittania, Dockers, Little Levi's, the Silver Tab and Orange Tab, as well as the traditional 501 jeans and the 550, 560, and Levi's 900 series, among others.

### Early Marketing Strategy

During the 1880s Levi Strauss & Co. prospered as a wholesaler of jean products, including the standard button-fly 501s, work shirts, and riveted coats. At the beginning of the decade the company reached over $2 million in sales, according to the *International Directory of Company Histories*. After the death of Levi in 1902, however, the company, inherited by Levi's four nephews, faced serious hardships in the next few decades. The San Francisco Earthquake of 1906 destroyed the company headquarters, and the following year a recession swept across the country. By the early 1920s Levi Strauss & Co. came close to liquidation.

But a few changes in management salvaged the business. Walter Haas, brother-in-law to the company president, Sigmund Stern, joined the business. Among his contributions to the company were modernizing operations and increasing productivity. He also increased spending on advertising, which was a rather radical idea at the time. By the end of the 1920s, jeans accounted for 70 percent of the company profits.

The 1930s, ironically, proved to be a propitious time for the Levi's brand. As the Depression set in and the agriculture industry weakened, the West turned to tourism. Cattle and horse ranches, converted into "Dude ranches," attracted Eastern visitors, who quickly took a liking to the authentic Western clothes, including the rugged Levi's blue jeans. Furthermore, western movies, with actors such as Gary Cooper and Roy Rogers, also popularized blue jeans, adding a romantic aura of adventure to the Levi's brand.

### Changes in Marketing Strategy

Levi Strauss & Co. took advantage of this new Western mystique and redefined its markets. Toward the end of the 1930s, the typical jeans consumer was no longer strictly a manual laborer. The Levi's brand was gaining national status. As jeans became fashionable among college students, Levi Strauss & Co. found the marketing niche—young men between the ages of 15 and 24—that would become the core Levi's jeans consumers.

During World War II the U.S. government declared jeans an "essential commodity"; consequently scarce, the jeans became all the more coveted by consumers and more prestigious to wear. In the wake of several years of rationing jeans, the company reconsidered its marketing strategies. Consumer demand seemed insatiable, so the company pursued the twin strategy of geographic expansion and diversification.

During the 1950s Levi Strauss & Co. finally abandoned the wholesaling of other dry goods and focused entirely on manufacturing clothing. With the post-war baby boom and the rising popularity of Levi's jeans, nationwide sales increased dramatically. Pop culture also had an enormous impact on the allure of Levi's jeans. When actors James Dean and Marlon Brando appeared clad in blue jeans in the highly popular films *Rebel Without a Cause* and *The Wild One,* respectively, Levi's jeans were destined to be the uniform of the new generation. Soon the casual denim pants would serve as a symbol for anti-establishment views among the younger members of the population. At the close of the 1950s, some ten million pairs of jeans were sold each year.

At the same time, the Levi's brand was introduced into the international market. At first, Levi's jeans were exported to foreign countries, but by 1965 Levi Strauss & Co. began manufacturing and marketing operations in some of the countries themselves, namely in Europe and Asia.

Despite continued growth and expansion of the firm throughout the 1970s, in the early 1980s Levi Strauss & Co. experienced a considerable decline in profits. The company realized that baby boomers—those 77 million individuals who were born between 1946 through 1964—were beginning to mature out of their jeans. So it pursued the double strategy of marketing certain jeans as high fashion apparel, while also introducing a new casual-wear line in 1986, called Dockers. During this time, advertising expenditures increased considerably, and several new finishing techniques were developed, including stonewashing and bleaching. By the early 1990s the Levi's brand had regained its stature as one of the world's most prestigious clothing products, with the Levi's trademark registered in over 150 countries.

In the early 1990s Foote, Cone & Belding, the longtime advertising agency for the Levi's brand, devised a new strategy for marketing called "brand architecture," which called for increased involvement of the ad agency in the entire marketing process. Richard Ward, the executive vice president and general manager of Foote, Cone San Francisco, told Stuart Elliott of the *New York Times* that the "greatest advertising will have limited effectiveness if it doesn't pull through to the point of sale." The intention was to develop more cohesive presentations of the products by tying in the media messages with the more mundane aspects of sales, such as store displays and clothing hang-tags. Levi Strauss & Co., which has had a working relationship with the ad agency since 1930, sees the logic in this strategy, saying that "the idea of lone rangers, solving problems with hip shots, is as illogical outside the company as it is inside the company."

## Noteworthy Advertising

Levi Strauss & Co. directed the bulk of its advertising dollars toward the promotion of the flagship 501 jeans to the core consumer group of young males in 1984. During the early 1980s, when the company experienced declines in earnings, an enormous advertising campaign was launched for the 1984 Olympics. The $40 million investment, however, did not salvage the flagging profits. But after major company reorganization, and a leveraged buyout of the company in 1985 by the Haas family, the Levi's brand finally regained momentum with the groundbreaking ad campaigns "501 Blues" and "501, U.S.A.," which ran between 1984 and 1989. These vibrant and emotional ads were so successful that they contributed to reviving the popularity of basic jeans in the late 1980s.

Beginning in 1990, filmmaker Spike Lee directed several quirky Levi's commercials during a two-year campaign that featured unusual hobbies of "real" people. Later, another strong ad campaign was developed for 501 jeans with the theme "Got To Be Real," in which young men engaged in conversations about the meaning of life.

Although these advertising campaigns were successful, they were primarily aimed at the younger male population. Meanwhile, Levi Strauss & Co. was concerned that the baby boomers were shying away from Levi's slim-cut 501s, which led to more aggressive advertising for the 550 and 560 series of men's looser-fitting jeans. The theme for these ads was "A Loose Interpretation of the Original," and they depicted handsome and agile young men running along a deserted beach, performing acrobatic stunts. At the same time, the campaign was directed toward another consumer group, the younger "hip-hop" set, among whom the baggy look was becoming fashionable. To finance the campaign, the advertising budget was increased in 1992 to an estimated $75–80 million, including about $30 million specifically targeted for the baggy jeans. In contrast, the annual 501 ad budget was estimated at $20 million between the mid-1980s to early 1990s.

While the bulk of the advertising for the Levi's brand was for men's jeans, advertising for women was rather sporadic and met with limited success. Although Levi's for Gals were introduced in 1968, a 1991 survey conducted by Levi Strauss & Co. indicated that 70 percent of women were uncertain whether Levi's jeans were even made for women. So in 1991 Levi Strauss & Co. invested $12 million in an ad campaign inspired by painter Henri Matisse to promote women's jeans and to capture more of the $2 billion-a-year women's jeans market.

## International Market

In the late 1950s the company began granting operating licenses overseas. In 1971, in order to finance some of the expansion, Levi Strauss & Co. sold stock to the public for the first time in its history. Within a few short years, the company as a whole had reached record sales of $1 billion. Levi Strauss & Co. continued more cautious expansion. In the early 1990s the company had affiliates in 23 countries, licensing agreements with 15 countries, and sales in over 70 nations.

Throughout the 1990s Levi Strauss & Co. planned to expand operations in the former Soviet republics of Eastern Europe. Existing Levi Strauss & Co. facilities in the Central and Eastern European region include a plant in Poland and a joint venture in Hungary.

The largest international market in sales and profits during the early 1990s was Europe, and the Asian Pacific was in second with robust sales in Japan and Australia. The company credited this favorable performance to the strong demand for denim basics, especially the family of 501 products. The increasing demand for Levi's jeans, however, also led to increased counterfeiting of the brand. In 1991 over 1.3 million pairs of Levi's imitations were confiscated.

Overall, the company reported record dollar sales in the overseas operations, topping $2 billion in 1992, a ten percent increase from 1991. Unit sales, however, increased at a slower rate. Between 1990 and 1991 sales increased seven percent. Much of this increase was attributed to higher product prices and favorable foreign exchange rates as compared to a weaker dollar.

## Performance Appraisal

In the first few decades of Levi Strauss & Co., the profits derived from the sale of jeans were far less than from the sale of the company's other dry goods. But by 1929, 70 percent of the company's profits were attributable to jeans sales, according to *International Directory of Company Histories*. After the World War II boom in the demand for jeans, the company profits exceeded $1 million from the sale of four million pairs of jeans in 1948, and *International Directory of Company Histories* further states that by the end of the 1950s, ten million pairs of Levi's jeans were sold annually.

Sales continued to increase, and the Levi's brand remained a market share leader. However, after the global expansion during the 1960s and 1970s of the largest U.S. jeans companies, including Levi Strauss & Co. and Wrangler, the companies retrenched and returned to private ownership. And yet, in the beginning of the 1980s, the U.S. jeans market suffered a decline as sales decreased from 500 million pairs in 1981 to 430 million in 1985. The European market also slipped from 250 million in 1981 to 150 million in 1985.

By the early 1990s, though, the jeans industry experienced a slight rebound as consumers opted for the practical and relatively affordable Levi's jeans. Though total jeans sales were only 386 million, that amount was up from 350 million in 1989. A 1993 disclosure from Levi Stauss Associates, Inc. stated that worldwide sales of the basic 501 products accounted for 23 percent of company sales, or $1.3 billion, in 1992, and increased 9 percent from the previous year. Other Levi's jeans products, such as the Silver Tab and Orange Tab series, also experienced increases in sales, thereby contributing to an overall growth in dollar and unit sales for the company's jeans products. Levi Strauss & Co. attributes these positive trends in part to a strong worldwide demand for jeans products.

In 1990 the Levi's brand led the overall jeans market with 22 percent, but the following year Levi Strauss & Co.'s slipped to 19.2 percent while Wrangler increased a percentage point to 15.4 percent in 1991. Lee remained at about 11 percent during this period. By 1992, the VF Corporation, which owns Wrangler, Lee, and Rustler, captured 31 percent of the $6.8 billion jeans market, up from 26 percent in the previous year and ahead of Levi Strauss. In the women's category, Lee led the market with 15.4 percent in 1990, and Gitano was second with 11.4 percent.

## Future Growth

The Levi's brand will probably remain among the leaders in the global jeans market, due to its commitment to quality products and its knack for innovative advertising and marketing strategies. Forecasts for the mid-1990s predicted some growth in demand in the U.S. and foreign markets for jeans products. Unit sales were also expected to increase, though only slightly because of uncertain economic conditions and consumer caution in spending.

## Further Reading:

Barach, Arnold B., *Famous American Trademarks,* New York: Public Affairs Association, 1971.

Beckett, Jamie, "Levi, B of A Focus on Feelings in Latest Campaigns," *San Francisco Chronicle,* August 3, 1992, p. C3.

Cleary, David Powers, *Great American Brands,* New York: Fairchild Publications, 1981.

Cray, Dan, "Levi's Ups Budget," *Mediaweek,* May 6, 1991.

Elliott, Stuart, *New York Times,* "The Media Business: Levi's Two New Campaigns Aim at Who Fits the Jeans," July 27, 1992, p. D7; "The Media Business: Going Beyond Campaigns and into Sales and Marketing," November 18, 1992, p. D6.

"Fashion Statement," *San Francisco Business Magazine,* October 1992, sec. 1, p. 30.

Horovitz, Bruce, "New Levi's Campaign Looks for Good Fit in Women's Jeans Market," *Los Angeles Times,* July 30, 1991, p. D1.

*International Directory of Company Histories,* Volume 5, Detroit: St. James, 1992.

Interbrand, *World's Greatest Brands,* New York: Wiley, 1992.

*Levi Strauss Associates Inc., Disclosure,* 1993.

Magiera, Marcy and Pat Sloan, *Advertising Age,* "Levi's, Lee Loosen up for Baby Boomers," August 3, 1992, p. 9; "Basic Jeans Shine for Levi's, Lee," February 17, 1992, p. 22.

Miller, Cyndee, "Marketers Tap into Rap as Hip-Hop Becomes 'Safe,'" *Marketing News TM,* January 18, 1993, p. 10.

Moore, Martha T., "Jeans Stretching to Fit All in Flat Market," *USA Today,* August 16, 1991, p. B8.

Morgan, Babette, "Just Call Them Consumer Boomers," *Newsday* (Nassau and Suffolk Edition), March 8, 1993, p. 25 (business section).

Morgan, Hal, *Symbols of America,* New York: Penguin, 1986.

Rawsthorn, Alice, "Shrinking to Fit as Times Get Tight," *Financial Times,* October 25, 1988, p. I29.

Simpson, Blaise, "Levi's Makes Push in Women's Wear," *Women's Wear Daily,* March 2, 1988.

"Spike Lee Runs for His Life," *PR Newswire,* August 29, 1991.

*Superbrands* (supplement to *Adweek's Marketing Week*), 1991, p. 44.

"Top 100 Entry Price: $114 Million in Ads," *Advertising Age,* September 25, 1991, p. 45.

*—Audra Avizienis*

# LISTERINE®

# LISTERINE®

If any social faux pas claimed to be the "the gaffe of the century," halitosis would be the hands-down winner. Living in fear of offending others with their bad breath, many consumers arm themselves with all the breath-aid artillery available. Toothpastes promise fresh, clean breath; sprays offer similar protection when toothbrushes are absent; and candy serves as a last resort to screen others from the spices of one's lunch. For the manufacturers of these items, halitosis is big business, and Listerine brand mouthwash has long been a staple item in many U.S. medicine cabinets.

It started in St. Louis, Missouri, with a physician named Dr. Joshua Lawrence. Lawrence not only rounded out his practice by editing a magazine on practical medicine, but he even found time to experiment with pharmaceuticals. Keenly aware of the latest trends in his field, Lawrence was particularly impressed by "Listerism," a form of antisepsis first developed in 1865 by British surgeon Joseph Lister.

## Listerism Finds a Disciple

In 1879 soon after Lister had visited the United States on a promotional tour, Lawrence decided to market an antiseptic of his own. He made a solution from thymol, eucalyptol, methyl salicylate, and menthol. Then in honor of the surgeon's original product, he forever linked his invention with Dr. Joseph Lister by calling it Listerine.

While Listerine's fame as a bad-breath blaster was still years away, Lawrence enthusiastically trumpeted the medical versatility of his new product. He told his colleagues it was a powerful antidote against dandruff. It soothed insect bites. Athlete's foot disappeared when dabbed with Listerine. Perhaps best of all, it could be used most effectively as an antiseptic that cleaned cuts and abrasions.

But marketing the Listerine brand required more time than a busy doctor could manage. In 1881 Lawrence sold his formula to Jordan Wheat Lambert, who established the Lambert Pharmacal Company for the purpose of selling the solution as a surgical antiseptic. A prudent businessman, Lambert took the precaution of registering his new formula's name as a trademark on August 2, 1881.

Lambert was so optimistic about his product's chance of success that he had no hesitation about entering into a royalties contract with Lawrence. In an agreement so simple that it has proved impossible to break, Lawrence used one sheet of notepaper to promise Lawrence or his heirs a monthly payment of $20 per gross of Listerine sold. Four years later, though the company had been formally incorporated, an agreement just as amiably casual and just as watertight reduced the royalty payment to $6 monthly.

Despite the healthy royalty payments, Lambert made steady progress. Soon he was prosperous enough to invest in custom-made glass bottles stamped with both "Listerine" and "Lambert Pharmacal Company," a touch that impressed dentists in 1895, when they were introduced to Listerine as a new oral antiseptic.

## Listerine Goes Over-the-Counter

Listerine was available only to doctors and dentists until 1914, when the lucrative over-the-counter trade beckoned. The Lambert Company plunged eagerly ahead in the new direction. The round glass bottles were spruced up for consumers with brownish-green wrappers that became the company's calling-card. By the 1920s Listerine had become a steady if unspectacular seller; its 25 percent alcohol content made it a popular beverage in Prohibition-era America. But nobody actually gave it the breath of life until 1926, when Jordan Lambert's two sons, Gerard and Marion, began to take a serious interest in the company their father had founded.

## Hail to Halitosis!

The Lamberts began by taking Listerine Antiseptic back to the drawing board to look for the one distinctive feature that would make it indispensable to every household. The company chemist, Dr. Deacon, was asked for details about what the mixture could actually accomplish. Deacon obligingly listed its benefits for the Lambert brothers, mentioning delicately, that it could remove "halitosis." The brothers latched on to the term—a word fringing on the medical, yet suggesting a dreaded condition familiar enough to scare consumers into buying their product. So they persuaded a newly formed New York advertising company, Lambert & Feasley, to use the word "halitosis" frequently when promoting the brand. The result was an advertisement written primarily by a former calliope player named Gordon Seagrove that became one of the longest-running advertising campaigns of all time.

## AT A GLANCE

**L**isterine brand mouthwash invented by Dr. Joseph Joshua Lawrence, in 1879; formula sold to entrepeneur Jordan Wheat Lambert in 1881, as a cure-all for several different minor ills; available only to medical professionals until 1895, then available also to the dental professionals; in 1914 Listerine became available for over-the-counter sale.

**Major competitor:** Procter & Gamble Company's Scope.

**Advertising:** J. Walter Thompson, New York, NY.

**Addresses:** *Parent company*—Warner-Lambert Company, 201 Tabor Road, Morris Plains, NJ 07950; phone: (201) 540-2000.

Stalwart women's magazines like *Ladies Home Journal* carried the advertisements for years. "Often a Bridesmaid, But Never a Bride," blared the headline that never varied through the 1930s and the 1940s, pointing out the dilemma of "Edna," the feminine misfit whose unchecked halitosis prevented her from achieving her life's mission—marriage.

While Edna's best friend was unwilling to tell her about her bad breath, Wall Street was less reticent about Lambert's solution. In 1954 Listerine sales boosted the company's annual figures to $35 million, thereby spurring a merger offer from a large manufacturer of ethical drugs, cosmetics, and hair-care preparations named Warner-Hudnut.

### Successful Merger

By March 31, 1955, the merger had become reality and had triggered substantial changes for both partners. Sealing the new union was a change of name, the former Lambert Pharmaceutical Company and the former Warner-Hudnut merged to become Warner-Lambert. In addition, the aging St. Louis factory was closed in favor of spacious new quarters in Morris Plains, New Jersey.

Even before these basics were settled, the merger was regarded as such a success that Lambert shareholders benefited to the tune of almost $4 million. From the companies' viewpoint, the advantages were just as hefty. Warner, which had been rescued from lackluster obscurity in 1945 to become a formidable player in foreign pharmaceutical markets, was now able to introduce Lambert's Listerine to overseas areas which had formerly seemed tantalizingly unreachable. In turn Listerine provided a streamlined sales system that gave Warner's home permanents and other cosmetics a badly needed entry into domestic supermarkets and revved up existing niches in both drug and department stores.

All these innovations gave the former Lambert Company a stake in the 1881 royalty agreement that reached $3 million by the end of the 1950s. However, even the most adroit attorneys were unable to break the original contract, even though a 1950 sale of half the original estate had mitigated it considerably. At that time, the Salvation Army and Wellesley College had each purchased a share, but the principal purchaser had been a New York realty company named John J. Reynolds, Inc., which had firmly held them ever since for several religious charities. Since there was no way to break the watertight contract, the matter rested until 1966 when one of Jordan Lambert's great-granddaughters decided to sell half of her portion. This one-eighth share alone yielded 1965

royalties totalling $382,000 after increasing steadily at a rate of almost ten percent annually.

### A New Promotional Era

As the 1960s began other companies began marketing their own brands of mouthwash and competition increased. First came Colgate-Palmolive's Colgate 100, which was soon followed by Procter & Gamble's Scope. But Listerine, now firmly established as the nation's favorite mouthwash, was securely buttressed by three new stablemates, all introduced in the mid-1960s. Toothpaste, breath freshener tablets, and throat lozenges, all bearing the Listerine name, played key roles in keeping the company at the top.

A generous advertising budget also helped a great deal. In 1964, 99 years after Lister's first use of surgical antisepsis, a big slice of the company's promotional funds went into an educational movie called *The Story of Dr. Lister,* which was shown to schoolchildren throughout the United States. In 1965 an $8,000 promotion marked the same anniversary with a mailing of 120,000 first-day issue stamps to stockholders and regular customers. By 1967 the Listerine advertising budget had soared to $80 million, of which about half was used for television advertising. So effective were the television commercials that Listerine sales rose by nine percent that year in the $175 million mouthwash market.

Nevertheless, the competitors gained enough ground by the 1970s to leave Listerine brand with a bitter taste. Aware that the newcomers were trying to undermine Warner-Lambert's industry leadership by referring to Listerine's bitter taste, the company turned a minus into a plus with its 1971 television ad stating, "The taste you hate. Twice a day." This campaign was a small consolation in 1974, when Procter & Gamble's Scope referred to Listerine in its advertisements as the "medicine breath" mouthwash. To further ad insult to injury, the Council of Better Business Bureaus' National Advertising Division ruled that Procter & Gamble's research indeed proved Listerine to be "mediciney."

Procter & Gamble continued their attempts to steal Listerine's market share. In September of 1975 they rolled out another competing mouthwash called Extend. This time, Warner-Lambert was ready to fight for the dollars of their longtime loyal consumers with a new promotion, a dual-coupon deal saving Listerine customers an eventual $1.00 per bottle of mouthwash.

### Listerine and the Law

Other litigation revolved around a problem that had lain dormant since the 1930s, when the company had suggested that Listerine might cure the common cold. The Federal Trade Commission had first challenged this claim in 1940, but had conceded that "the truth was probably undiscoverable" after 105 hearings failed to come to a satisfactory conclusion.

The debate concerning Listerine's effectiveness in fighting the common cold was rekindled in 1972 after a company-sponsored study showed that 60 percent of the consumers surveyed believed that Listerine was effective in fighting both colds and sore throats. A determined Federal Trade Commission official seized on this claim and held onto it until 1978, when Warner-Lambert lost their final legal appeal. Victorious, the Trade Commission ordered the company to provide revised statements on all advertising for two full years. Warner-Lambert bowed to the will of the court at a cost of $10 million.

The cold-cure claim was not the only legal hassle of the 1970s. Another face-off involved new Listerol, a Warner-Lambert spray disinfectant that was launched as a challenge to long-established Lysol. Lysol's manufacturer, a division of Sterling Drugs, charged Warner-Lambert with trademark infringement, partly because Listerol's spray-can packaging was similar to theirs. Warner-Lambert changed the color of their spray can and spent $5 million to promote their disinfectant, but the product was not of a high enough quality to break the Lysol monopoly and was withdrawn in late 1975.

Through the rest of the decade and into the mid-1980s, Listerine maintained its lead in the $350 million mouthwash market without making any further claims. That changed in 1984 when the company claimed that Listerine could help prevent gingivitis and plaque buildup on teeth. This statement was picked up by *Consumer Reports,* which cautiously mentioned in March of 1984 that the American Dental Association was developing guidelines for such claims. Warner-Lambert, however, had no qualms about spending $16 million in 1987 to publicize Listerine's new role as a plaque and gingivitis blocker. The following year, company confidence was reinforced by the American Dental Association, which concluded its extensive research by endorsing plaque-fighting claims and issuing a seal of acceptance.

Although the American Dental Association had placed Listerine's plaque-protection ability second only to a preparation available by prescription, the Food and Drug Administration questioned the claim in 1989. Along with other companies making identical claims for their mouthwashes, Warner-Lambert received a warning letter threatening that products could be removed from store shelves if advertising was not amended. This did not prevent other makers from applying for the ADA plaque-fighting seal, even though FDA requirements seemed to split the claim into parts separating the cosmetic claims (plaque-fighting ability above the gum-line) and the dental claims (gingivitis-curing ability occurring below the gums).

## Back to Basics

By 1992 there was another issue gaining top priority with *Consumer Reports.* Concerned with products' claims of removing halitosis, *Consumer Reports* set out to answer the question by gathering a list of 15 mouthwashes and a test panel of 20 garlic-eating volunteers. After all tests, the consumer magazine concluded that no mouthwash could totally eliminate halitosis, and the longest protection was about one hour, after which a best friend's services might well be required, especially if the afternoon promised important events.

If "Edna," the perpetual bridesmaid of the 1940s, were around today, this *Consumer Reports* revelation probably would not disturb her in the slightest. Like her, other consumers showed their faith in the 113-year-old Listerine brand between May of 1992 and May of 1993 by spending $221.1 million on the product in a mouthwash market totaling $670.9 million. A further $80.1 million was spent on Cool Mint Listerine, introduced in June 1992 to provide a "less mediciney" alternative.

**Further Reading:**

American Dental Association, "Council on Dental Therapeutics Accepts Listerine," *Journal of the American Dental Association,* September, 1988.

"The Contract that Left the Lawyers Breathless," *Business Week,* August 20, 1966.

Elliott, Stuart, "Listerine, a Venerable Brand of Mouthwash, Has Been Rejuvenated by its Minty Extension," *New York Times,* July 9, 1993.

"FDA Attacks Dental-Rinse Firms' Claims That Products Fight Plaque, Gingivitis," *Wall Street Journal,* June 12, 1989.

*Heritage: A Brief History of Warner-Lambert and the Entrepreneurs Who Shaped It,* Morris Plains, NJ: Warner-Lambert Company.

"Listerine Now Says It's More than a Mouthwash," *Advertising Age,* December 29, 1975.

"Listerine Sales Climbed 9% in 67, Stockholders Told," *Advertising Age,* April 29, 1968.

"Listerine Slips in Disclaimer," *Advertising Age,* September 11, 1978.

"Merger-Minded Warner-Lambert," *Fortune,* October, 1955.

"Mouthwashes," *Consumer Reports,* March, 1984.

"Mouthwashes," *Consumer Reports,* September, 1992.

"The Newest 'Miracle' Dentifrice," *Consumer Reports,* October, 1953.

"P&G's Scope Pushes Competitors Hard in Mouthwash Market," *Advertising Age,* April 4, 1968.

"Recent Merger Seen Spur to Net of Warner-Lambert," *Barron's,* June 27, 1955.

"Warner-Lambert Marks Centennial of Lister's Antisepsis Find with Massive Stamp Mailing," *Advertising Age,* September 13, 1965.

"Warner-Lambert Distills Higher Net from Merger," *Barron's,* June 4, 1956.

"Warner-Lambert Dropping Listerol Spray," *Advertising Age,* September 15, 1975.

"Warner-Lambert Says Scientific Data Will Back Up Ad Claims," *Advertising Age,* September 28, 1970.

"Warner-Lambert Told by FTC Aide to Alter Listerine Advertising," *Wall Street Journal,* December 10, 1974.

Watkins, Julian Lewis, *The 100 Greatest Advertisements: Who Wrote Them and What They Did,* New York: Dover, 1949.

*—Gillian Wolf*

# LIZ CLAIBORNE®

Since its inception in 1976, the Liz Claiborne brand of clothing, accessories, shoes, jewelry, and cosmetics has become one of the most powerful brands in the business. In 1992—its best year ever—sales reached $2.19 billion, amid the deepest retailing slump since the Great Depression. Liz Claiborne has actually profited from the recession to become the top brand in the women's apparel market. Just one of the brands designed and marketed by Liz Claiborne, Inc., which also distributes the Elisabeth, Dana Buchman, and Liz & Co. lines, Liz Claiborne has remained a market share leader due to the company's attention to style, quality, fit, and value.

## Brand Origins

The Liz Claiborne brand was created in 1976 when fashion designer Liz Claiborne realized that the working woman needed more wardrobe options. She was unable to sell the concept of stylish, sporty, and affordable clothing for working women to her employer, Jonathan Logan's Youthguild dress division. Claiborne left the company and along with her husband, Arthur Ortenberg, and two other partners, Leonard Boxer and Jerome A. Chazen, founded Liz Claiborne, Inc. They pooled $50,000 in savings and borrowed an additional $200,000 from friends and family to launch the women's apparel company, whose focus was on fashions that were both functional and affordable.

Claiborne's timing was perfect; her company provided clothes to women as they started entering the work force in record numbers. Other designers had not yet tapped this fast-growing segment of the population. Liz Claiborne clothing was manufactured for six selling periods: pre-spring, spring I, spring II, summer, fall, and holiday; the company ignored the traditional industry seasons of spring and fall. This provided consumers with new styles every two months. In addition, these short cycles allowed more frequent updates of new styles and put clothes on the racks in the appropriate season. By adding cycles, stores cut their inventory costs and overseas suppliers operated more efficiently with the two extra cycles filling their slack periods.

## Brand Diversification

During the 1980's the Liz Claiborne name was no longer seen only on sportswear. A petite sportswear division as well as a dress division were introduced in 1982. However, a 1984 foray into girls' clothes under the Liz Claiborne label failed within several years. A line of petite dresses was launched in 1985 as well as an accessories division, which had previously been a licensee. Some components of this line included leather handbags, small leather goods, and jewelery. The company also expanded into men's clothing that year after discovering that 70 percent of its women customers purchased clothing for men.

The company further extended the Liz Claiborne line with the introduction of its signature scent in September of 1986. The cosmetics division began as a joint venture with Avon, and in 1988 the company regained full rights to the line. The division has since marketed two other fragrances, Realities and Claiborne for Men In fall of 1993, the division offered Vivid, its third women's fragrance under the Liz Claiborne brand name.

In 1988 the company moved into the retail apparel business when it opened its first retail stores. These stores, called First Issue, did not offer the Liz Claiborne brand of clothing. Despite this the stores were extremely successful, especially when considering the risk and expense involved in retail apparel start-ups. When the venture proved prosperous, the company opened its first Liz Claiborne stores in 1989. These 18 stand-alone stores were placed in suburban malls and served as laboratories for the company to test new Liz Claiborne brand designs and product presentations. They provided the company with immediate information regarding market trends through state of the art bar coding and other electronic data interchange systems.

The greatest challenge to the company occurred in 1989 when Liz Claiborne and Arthur Ortenberg announced their resignation from active management in order to pursue philanthropic interests. Industry insiders wondered if the business could survive without Liz herself, but their fears proved unfounded. A broad array of new products under the Liz Claiborne label was introduced, including jewelry in 1990, and sport shoes and Liz Claiborne tailored suits for the working woman in 1991. Although the company already sold sportswear separates that could pass for suits, Liz Claiborne could now compete with lines like Kasper, Tahari, and PSI, which offered fitted business suits for career women. The Liz Claiborne suits featured ornamental trim, jewelry-like buttons, and elegant fabrics. The look was feminine and fashionable. The suit division was expected to generate sales of $100 million by 1996.

Jewelry became a strong division—sales increased 195.2 percent in 1992 to $18.3 million. As a result of design changes and

## AT A GLANCE

Liz Claiborne brand of women's apparel and accessories founded in 1976 in New York City by Liz Claiborne, Inc. founders Elisabeth Claiborne Ortenberg, Arthur Ortenberg, Leonard Boxer, and Jerome A. Chazen.

**Performance:** *Market share*—3% (top share) of publicly held manufacturers of women's apparel. *Sales*—$2.19 billion (company wide) in 1992.

**Major competitor:** JH Collectibles; also Bernard Chaus, Inc., Leslie Fay Companies, Inc., Ellen Tracy, Evan Picone, and DKNY.

**Advertising:** *Agency*—Attschiller ReitzFeld/Tracy-Locke, New York, NY, 1991—. *Major campaign*—Print campaign only, consisting of multiple-page spreads in a variety of magazines.

**Addresses:** *Parent company*—Liz Claiborne, Inc., 1441 Broadway, New York, NY; phone: (212) 354-4900; fax: (212) 719-9049.

improved quality, market share increased, the line expanded into more stores, and stores gave the line more space. The Monet brand, which has long been the dominant name in department store costume jewelry, has recently weakened and this could benefit the Liz Claiborne brand further. In addition, the company's shoe division, formerly a licensee which was acquired from U.S. Shoe in mid-1990, should make further inroads into the footwear market with its sports, casual, and career shoes marketed under the Liz Claiborne name. The Liz Claiborne brand name could also be found on women's and men's optical frames and women's hosiery.

## Advertising

Sales for the entire company increased 9.3 percent in 1992 to a record $2.19 billion, up from $2.0 billion in 1991, while the company's ten percent return on net sales remained one of the highest in the apparel industry. However, while the number of working women between 25 and 54 grew 43 percent in the 1980s, this demographic group was expected to increase only about 25 percent in the 1990s. The brand needed to increase its visibility in order to maintain market share. The combination of economic recession, increased competition in moderately priced sportswear, and the push into new markets led Liz Claiborne, Inc. to seek a higher profile. In October of 1991, the company launched its first print advertising campaign for apparel and accessories. The six million dollar advertising blitz debuted in the November 1991 issues of 15 consumer publications, including *HG, Vanity Fair,* and *Elle.*

Liz Claiborne, Inc. realized that cooperative advertising with retailers and domination of department store floors was not enough to promote its brand name; it also needed to solidify its fashion image and create a global corporate image. Advertising is crucial in preserving its strong relationships with consumers and retailers, and Liz Claiborne, Inc. could not expect to gain a foothold in Europe with an unadvertised fashion brand. Since floor space in Europe is much more limited, companies must aggressively advertise their images just to get into stores. Liz Claiborne, Inc.'s advantage is its commitment to quality, value, and fit—exactly the standards of the Europeans and Japanese.

## Brand Clout

The Liz Claiborne brand has dominated the selling floors of many major department stores—sometimes occupying more than half the allotment for women's apparel. Because profits and volume have increased for Liz Claiborne, Inc., so has its influence at the manufacturing and retail ends of the business. The company does not own any factories; all of its merchandise is made through contracts with independent factories in 50 nations. The company has reduced its reliance on Hong Kong, South Korea, and Taiwan in favor of countries like Malaysia, China, and Sri Lanka, where labor is less expensive. Less than ten percent of Liz Claiborne's products are made in the United States. To ensure that the items are produced to the high standards consumers expect, Liz Claiborne, Inc. employs an overseas staff of almost 700 who regularly visit the factories.

At the retail end, Liz Claiborne, Inc. commands extensive clout. The company adheres to a rigid noncancellation policy, which means that if spring merchandise does not sell well in stores, retailers cannot cut summer orders. In addition, the Liz Claiborne brand generates strong "sell through." The clothes are rarely marked down—about five percent of its merchandise versus the industry norm of 15 percent. To reduce the risk of markdowns, the company produces fewer goods than the level of demand forecasts. Thus, retailers obtain better profit margins from the brand than from competing labels and allow the Liz Claiborne line more floor space.

## International Expansion

In 1988, sales and marketing efforts began in Canada. By January of 1991, the Liz Claiborne brand entered Great Britain, and later the same year it was introduced into Spain when the company began shipping to five of the Gallerias Preciados department stores. The brand is also sold to stores in the United Kingdom, Ireland, and Switzerland. The company realized that it had to tailor its strategies when marketing the Liz Claiborne label outside the United States. In some United Kingdom stores, for example, the company leases space and sells the product itself. In Japan the company markets the brand through a mail-order catalog, and through a joint venture in Singapore and Hong Kong, Liz Claiborne stores have been granted licenses. American looks, especially in petite sizes, sell well in these countries. The strategies seem to be working well as international sales totaled $101.8 million in 1992, while six years ago only $1.4 million of sales came from outside the United States.

In anticipation of the unification of the European Economic Community, Liz Claiborne relocated its European distribution center from Manchester, England, to Rotterdam, the Netherlands—the second largest container port in the world after Singapore. With this distribution setup, Liz Claiborne will be able to ship its products directly from its various offices around the world to the European continent without paying stiff tariffs.

Very few American companies have been able to expand abroad successfully and profitably while continuing to increase their business at home. The process by which a collection evolves from conception to sale is highly complex; for example, The Limited, Inc. has had many problems getting its brand to stores outside the United States. Liz Claiborne is one of the few merchandisers who have been successful in expanding rapidly without sacrificing quality or timeliness of deliveries.

## Future Direction

How far can Liz Claiborne go? Much depends on its new direction. The company is not likely, however, to venture into heavily promoted goods, such as swimsuits, coats, and bed linens, because these frequently become sale items in many stores. The Liz Claiborne brand name stands for quality and value, and the company does not want to give consumers the wrong impression by placing its name on items that are promptly marked down. Although the company has created other lines, the Liz Claiborne brand continues to be its most recognizable and profitable. By continuing its current marketing strategy, the label hopes to retain its freshness and the loyalty of the many consumers who shop exclusively for the Liz Claiborne line.

## Further Reading:

Agins, Teri, "Liz Claiborne Seems to Be Losing Its Invincible Armor," *Wall Street Journal,* July, 1993, p. B4.

Deveny, Kathleen, "Can Ms. Fashion Bounce Back," *Business Week,* January 16, 1989, pp. 64–70.

Gannes, Stuart, "America's Fastest-Growing Companies," *Fortune,* May 23, 1988, pp. 28–40.

Graham, Judith, "Claiborne Opens its Own Sites," *Advertising Age,* June 5, 1989, p. 55.

Hass, Nancy, "Like a Rock," *Financial World,* February 4, 1992, pp. 22–24.

Liz Claiborne, Inc. Annual Reports, New York: Liz Claiborne, Inc., 1991–92.

Morris, Michele, "The Wizard of The Working Woman's Wardrobe," *Working Woman,* June 1988, pp. 74–80.

Sellers, Patricia, "The Rag Trade's Reluctant Revolutionary," *Fortune,* January 5, 1987, pp. 36–38.

Sloan, Pat and Gary Levin, "Claiborne Attire Tries On Ads . . . ," *Advertising Age,* June 10, 1991, p. 20.

*—Carol Kieltyka*

# LONDON FOG®

London Fog is the best-selling brand of men's and women's raincoats in the United States with more than 60 percent of the market. The brand enjoyed extraordinarily high recognition among consumers, with 97 percent of men and 99 percent of women aware of the London Fog name.

Ironically, London Fog raincoats are manufactured by an American company, the Londontown Corporation of Eldersburg, Maryland. Although the brand and corporate logos picture the famed Big Ben clock tower over the English Houses of Parliament, and commercials often used London as a setting, London Fog was unavailable in the United Kingdom until 1992. In addition to men's and women's raincoats, Londontown manufactured a line of outerwear, knitwear, and sportswear under the London Fog, FOG, and Towne by London Fog brand names, respectively. The London Fog brand name was also licensed to other apparel and accessory manufacturers.

## Brand Origins

The Londontown Clothing Company was founded in 1922 in Baltimore, Maryland. The company failed eight years later at the beginning of the Depression, but an employee, Israel Myers, purchased the Londontown name and the physical assets of the men's clothing manufacturer in 1931. Forty years later, Myers, who had gone to work for Londontown in 1923 at age 16, commented in *The Baltimore News American,* "If I [had] had a good job offer, I probably would have taken it. But there were no jobs available, [and] I had worked hard and saved my money."

Under Myers' direction, Londontown continued to manufacture men's clothing until the start of World War II. During the war, Londontown switched to making synthetic rubber coats for enlisted men under contract to the Navy. When the war ended, Myers changed the company name to Londontown Manufacturing Company. He decided to continue making raincoats, but using more fashionable fabrics and the fine tailoring that had gone into Londontown clothes. According to *How to Make Raincoats and Weatherproofs,* published by the Apparel Institute in the 1960s, "What impressed [Myers] at the time was the lowly position of the raincoat in the minds of manufacturers and the buying public. Rainwear was simply considered as anything that would shed water. It held no status as a part of the wardrobe."

The task that Myers took on was formidable. He found that conventional fabrics could be made waterproof, but the coats were heavy, hot, and uncomfortable. Myers then tried a promising new fabric that was a blend of cotton and Dacron, a synthetic polyester created by E. I. du Pont de Nemours & Company. Unfortunately the sewing machines used by Londontown created so much friction that the synthetic fibers melted during sewing.

Working with Du Pont, the fabric maker, Reeves Brothers, Inc., eventually developed a blend of Dacron and cotton that would stand up to Londontown's sewing process. Du Pont also developed a chemical treatment that was used to increase water repellency. In 1954 Londontown was ready to introduce a fashionable, light-weight raincoat that was machine washable.

A friend reportedly suggested the name London Fog as the label for Londontown's new line of raincoats. Myers, however, initially rejected the name, believing that London Fog was not sellable. But when no better name was suggested (Scottish Mist was also considered and rejected), London Fog was accepted. Londontown sold its first 100 London Fog raincoats to Saks Fifth Avenue in New York. Saks put the coats on sale for $29.95, almost twice the price of other men's raincoats, and sold out in a few days.

In the March 13, 1954, "Advertising and Marketing Fields" column in *The New York Times,* London Fog was called the perfect name: "Every once in a while a name comes along for a product that is exactly right. It describes the product exactly and does a selling job that even the legendary 10,000 words cannot do. Such a one is London Fog." A 1954 newspaper ad was headlined, "Introducing the 'London Fog' weather coat in the new Dacron and cotton fabric. . . ." The ad went on to describe the coat as, "The perfect answer to everything a man can ask for in a raincoat. Remarkably lightweight and wrinkle-free . . . it actually resists creasing even after packing."

The traditional raincoat design, with its epaulets and sleeve straps, grew out of the military "trench coats" of World War I, but as the Apparel Institute reported, "Londontown feels that as a result of its efforts, it has contributed to elevating the position of raincoats in the minds of retailers, consumers, and the trade in general to the point where today the raincoat is a respected part of the wardrobe." In 1973, the *News American* stated that Myers had "done probably more than any one individual in changing the

## AT A GLANCE

London Fog brand of outerwear introduced in 1954 as a label for a line of men's raincoats manufactured by the Londontown Manufacturing Company; company name changed to Londontown Corporation, 1971; Londontown Corporation acquired by Interco Incorporated in 1976; acquired by Eldersberg Acquisitions Group, 1988; 90% equity ownership purchased by Merrill Lynch Capital Partners, Inc. in 1990; London Fog Corporation, a holding company, created in 1993.

**Performance:** *Market share*—60% of men's and women's raincoats. *Sales*—$300 million.

**Major competitor:** Misty Harbor; also Burberry's.

**Advertising:** *Agency*—Martin Agency, Inc., 1992—. *Major campaign*—"The New Generation of London Fog."

**Addresses:** *Parent company*—Londontown Corporation, 1332 Londontown Boulevard, Eldersburg, MD, 21784-5399; phone: (410) 795-5900. *Ultimate parent company*—London Fog Corporation. *Ultimate ultimate parent company*—Merrill Lynch Capital Partners, Inc.

raincoat from an inexpensive, shapeless piece of clothing into one of today's most versatile, attractive garments.''

### London Fog Innovations

The first major change for London Fog raincoats came in 1955 when John Wanamaker's, the leading department store in Philadelphia, asked Londontown to create a raincoat for women, who had been buying the men's design for their own use. The company moved the buttons to the left side and added two darts across the chest. It then delivered 90 of the redesigned coats to Wanamaker's, which sold out almost immediately. Londontown has made London Fog coats for both men and women ever since.

Londontown was also the first company to use full zip-in linings, which made London Fog raincoats usable year-round. Other innovations attributed to London Fog include the use of an inner "mini cape" to improve water repellency and a patented Bachelor Buttons process that helps prevent buttons from falling off by placing a small rubber ring around the thread to absorb stress and reduce fraying. London Fog coats were also the first to come with replacement buttons.

In the 1960s, Londontown began sewing instructions for washing to the inside of its London Fog coats, the first major company to do so. Most manufacturers at the time were sewing instructions to the outside of a sleeve, where they were removed and discarded before wearing. Londontown's consumer-oriented innovation even received notice in the *Congressional Record.*

### Changes in Ownership

After growing steadily for 15 years, sales of London Fog coats suddenly fell by 25 percent in 1968. Jonathan P. Myers, Israel Myers' son, who became president of the company in 1969, later attributed the decline to Londontown's failure to understand a changing market for women's fashions. By the mid 1960s, women's coats accounted for about half of Londontown's sales. But while other manufacturers were bringing out coats designed especially for women, Londontown stayed with its traditional male-oriented lines. Myers told *The Daily Record* in 1979 that

"the women's movement, women's liberation, started with clothes. [I]t was in the mid-60s that women started to say, 'I don't want man-tailored clothes. I'm not going to be dictated to'.''

It took Londontown about five years to regain its share of the market for women's raincoats, and by 1975 London Fog accounted for approximately two-thirds of all raincoats sold in the U.S. in the mid-priced category and above. The company also launched a line of London Fog winter coats, golf jackets, and clothes for camping and boating in the early 1970s. The first London Fog Outlet Store was opened in 1972.

In 1976 Londontown agreed to be acquired by Interco Incorporated, a St. Louis-based conglomerate whose other subsidiaries made products ranging from Ethan Allen furniture to Florsheim shoes. Over the next 12 years, sales of London Fog coats more than tripled, from $71 million in 1976 to $226 million in 1988. However, in 1988 Interco found itself fending off a hostile takeover attempt, and decided to sell its apparel companies. A senior management team at Londontown, led by then-President Mark Lieberman, formed the Eldersberg Acquisition Corporation (the name Eldersburg was misspelled on the hastily drafted legal papers) and purchased the company in December for $178 million. Lieberman, who retired in 1993, said in a press release, "The

*An advertisement from 1954 introducing the London Fog raincoat.*

buyout will allow us to preserve the integrity and heritage that has become synonymous with the London Fog name.''

In 1990, Merrill Lynch Capital Partners purchased a 90 percent equity ownership in the company. The management group retained control of day-to-day operations. A holding company, the London Fog Corporation, was created in 1993 to capitalize on the strength of the brand name.

## Marketing Strategy

In 1990, Lieberman stated in *Women's Wear Daily* that Londontown's strategy would be to make the London Fog brand as prominent in wool coats and active outerwear as it was in raincoats. Pursuing that strategy, in 1992 Londontown introduced a line of wool coats for women with the FOG label, which was also used for raincoats and other outerwear that sold for slightly more than the traditional London Fog line. The company reported that the FOG brand was "for the customer who demands more updated fashion with quality. For the fashion conscious." Londontown also created a lower-priced line of raincoats and outerwear with the Towne by London Fog label, a line it described as "backed with all the tradition and quality from London Fog for a price sensitive customer."

That year also marked London Fog's introduction to the United Kingdom. Ads that ran in the London press were headlined: "After 38 years in America, we're coming home." In 1993 the company announced plans to expand distribution throughout the United Kingdom. In a press release, Lieberman said, "It makes great sense for us to increase our presence in the United Kingdom, where rainwear and outerwear are essential wardrobe elements."

Another element of Londontown's strategy was to increase brand awareness by licensing the use of the London Fog name by other manufacturers. In 1991, Monterey Fashions signed an agreement with Londontown to produce a line of fake furs under the London Fog label. Other licensees manufactured children's outerwear, hats, umbrellas, luggage, and eye glasses under the London Fog brand name. In 1993 London Fog Corporation announced that Streets Ltd. Design Group would manufacture a line of Teflon-coated, stain- and water-repellant silk neckwear for men, called the Hydrofuge Neckwear Collection, which would also carry the London Fog name.

An advertising campaign launched in the late 1980s also emphasized the fashion and variety of London Fog clothing. One typical print ad showed an American family in London with Big Ben in the background. The text read: "Heritage and style from London to L.A., London Fog keeps you and your family in fashion with rainwear and outerwear, hats, umbrellas, shirts, ties, sweaters, eyewear, luggage and children's outerwear. Wherever you travel . . . there's a lot of your life in a London Fog."

## Further Reading:

D'Innocenzio, Anne, "Londontown pins growth to fashion," *Women's Wear Daily,* February 25, 1992, p. 9.

Friedman, Arthur, "Monterey inks licensing pact with London Fog for fake furs," *Women's Wear Daily,* February 5, 1991, p. 12.

*How to make raincoats,* Great Neck, NY: Apparel Institute, Inc.

"Interco Sells Londontown," *New York Times,* December 30, 1988.

"London Fog Holds 60 Per Cent Of U.S. Raincoat Market," *Daily Record,* June 27, 1979.

"Londontown Corporation," Eldersburg, MD: Londontown Corporation, 1972.

Merrill Lynch wraps Londontown purchase," *Women's Wear Daily,* June 29, 1990, p. 11.

Pogoda, Dianne M., "Londontown: After the buyout," *Women's Wear Daily,* March 21, 1989, p. 1; "Londontown: Refinanced and Ready to Grow, " *Women's Wear Daily,* August 21, 1990, p. 6.

Rosenthal, David, "London Fog's Big Deal," *The Baltimore Sun,* March 6, 1989, p. 19; "Staying dry and in style: London Fog updates image," *The Baltimore Sun,* March 6, 1989, p. 20.

Schechter, Dara, "Londontown holds major market share, peak sales," *Women's Wear Daily,* June 13, 1989, p. 9.

Sloan, Pat, "Seeking heat in cold: London Fog tests women's wool coats," *Advertising Age,* December 4, 1989, p. 26.

*—Dean Boyer*

# L'ORÉAL®

# L'ORÉAL

"Because I'm worth it." These words, self-confidently proclaimed by beautiful models, have come to represent the high quality yet general accesibility of L'Oréal hair colorings. L'Oréal is one of approximately 50 brand names used by L'Oréal S.A., one of the world's largest cosmetic companies and producer of such brands as Lancome, Ambre Solaire, and Cacharel. As the company's mass-market line, L'Oréal encompasses a wide variety of hair care products, cosmetics, nail enamel, and skin creams. L'Oréal's markets cover the United States and Europe, and the brand has become the world leader in professional hair care products. Its mass-market cosmetics line, founded in the late 1970s, is considered a high-quality brand in the mass-market cosmetic industry. It holds the fourth-largest market share in the United States and has made strong inroads into Italy, Spain, Belgium, and France.

## Brand Origins

L'Oréal's history stretches back to early twentieth century France, when the fashion among women of the demimonde (mistresses of wealthy men, actresses, and women who had "fallen" from society) was to dye their hair. Their choices at that time, however, were restricted to either an unnaturally harsh jet black or fiery red. In 1907 chemist Eugene Schueller devised a synthetic dye that produced a much more natural looking hair color. He manufactured the product by night in his Paris kitchen, and during the day he peddled the new dyes to local hair salons under the brand name Aureole. The new dyes caught on, and within two years Schueller outgrew his kitchen and founded the Societe Fracaise des Teintures Inoffensives pour Cheveux. Schueller soon changed the company and brand name to a more easily recognizable L'Oréal. Sales continued to rise throughout France, and by 1912 L'Oréal hair colorings were available in salons throughout Austria, Holland, and Italy.

Much of Schueller's early success can be attributed to a change in lifestyle and fashion following the end of World War I. The Jazz Age was blossoming and women were celebrating a new-found sense of freedom by shortening both their hair and their hemlines. New hairstyles emphasized shape and color. During the 1920s as the number of hair salons in France grew to over 40,000, L'Oréal's new coloring products O'Cap, Imedia Liquide, and Coloral were positioned to tap into the growing market. By 1920 L'Oréal employed three research chemists and ten salesmen, and the brand's market covered 17 countries, including the United States, Brazil, Chile, Peru, Euqador, Bolivia, and the Soviet Union.

## Product and Marketing Innovations

Throughout its history, L'Oréal's growth has been propelled by scientific research and an ability to provide a rapidly changing French society with desirable new products. In 1929 the company developed a breakthrough method of simultaneously lightening and coloring hair that remains the basis of permanent hair coloring today. When Jean Harlow and Mae West dominated the movie screens of the 1930s, L'Oréal capitalized on the popularity of platinum blonde hair with L'Oréal Blanc. When the Front Populaire won the 1936 national elections and made paid vacations available to all French workers, L'Oréal responded with Ambre Solaire, the world's first line of mass-market suntan lotions. L'Oréal also introduced Dop, the first mass-market shampoo, as well as new salon products such as cream developer, powder bleach, color-compatible permanent wave solutions, instant setting lotions, and styling mousse.

During the 1930s L'Oréal expanded its market—previously restricted to hair salons—by offering products such as Ambre Solaire and Dop through pharmacies and perfumers. L'Oréal also expanded internationally, establishing subsidiaries in Italy, Belgium, and Denmark.

Schueller was a master at promoting his new products. In 1933 he hired popular artists to design eye-catching posters, and he founded his own women's magazine, *Votre Beaute,* to serve as a publicity vehicle for the growing line of L'Oréal products. Schueller also brought his mass-market products directly to the purchaser by promoting such events as children's "hair-lathering competitions" (using Dop shampoo, of course) at the popular French circuses. By 1938 L'Oréal radio jingles could be heard throughout the land. Schueller continued to produce innovative advertising over the decades and was rewarded not only with increased name recognition and rising sales for his brand, but also with an advertising Oscar in 1953.

L'Oréal managed to survive the economic hardships wrought by World War II. Despite Schueller's right-wing, anti-Semitic beliefs, and fascist political ties, sales of L'Oréal in Europe continued at a healthy pace. Women were turning to cosmetics and hair products as a means of lifting their spirits during a time of

## AT A GLANCE

Originally marketed under the brand name Aureole, L'Oréal brand of hair colorings and cosmetics formulated in Paris in 1907 by chemist Eugene Schueller, who founded the Societe Francaise des Teintures Inoffensives pour Cheveux in 1909 to market his synthetic hair dyes; shortly after Schueller changed company name to L'Oréal, S.A.; sales extended to Italy, Austria, and Holland by 1920; to United States in 1953; sole U.S. licensee: Cosmair Inc.

*Performance:* Market share—10% of mass-market cosmetic sales. Sales—Approximately $4 billion in 1992.

*Major competitor:* Cosmetics market—Revlon, also Maybelline; hair coloring market—Clairol.

*Advertising:* Major campaign—"More beautiful by design" series of print ads for the cosmetics line, focusing on specific products rather than a lifestyle or cover girl; "Because I'm worth it" slogan for hair colorings.

*Addresses:* Parent company—Cosmair, Inc., 575 5th Ave., New York, NY 10017; phone: (212) 818-1500. *Ultimate parent company*—L'Oréal S.A., 14 Rue Royale, Paris, Ville de Paris 75008, France; phone: (1) 40 20 60 00; fax: (1) 47 56 86 42.

strict rationing. Schueller was able to expand distribution to the United Kingdom, Argentina, and Algeria, and the L'Oréal research team grew to include 25 chemists. In 1945 L'Oréal made another hair care breakthrough with Oreol, the first cold permanent wave product.

The 1950s brought further expansion to L'Oréal as consumers' disposable income increased greatly and two other blonde movie stars, Marilyn Monroe and Brigitte Bardot, made blonde hair popular once again. In just five years, L'Oréal's research team had grown from 25 to 100 and a number of "firsts" were introduced in hair salons worldwide, including Imedia D, the first lightening tint, and Colorelle, the first coloring shampoo. In 1953 L'Oréal began importing its hair colorings to the United States through privately owned Cosmair, Inc. Within a year, Cosmair was making inroads into the vast United States market by manufacturing and distributing L'Oréal hair care products on American soil.

### Mass-Market Products

L'Oréal's growth continued through the 1960s, fueled by cultural and consumer interests that were increasingly youth-oriented. L'Oréal hair colorings appealed to consumers who desired to retain—or obtain—a youthful appearance. New products in the early 1960s included Recital hair colorings and Ellenet hair spray. New boutiques, supermarkets, and chain stores sprouted up across the United States and Europe in the 1960s and filled the growing consumer demand for beauty products. Sensing a customer demand for in-home hair dyes and permanents, L'Oréal created a retail division in 1966, and began selling products formulated for in-home use through drug, food, and mass-merchandise retail outlets.

One of L'Oréal's most successful mass-market introductions was its Preference hair color. Introduced in 1970 with the tag line, "Because you're worth it," Preference became a top seller, and its familiar slogan was translated into numerous languages.

By the mid-1980s, although it held a 20 percent market share in the United States, L'Oréal's mass-market hair dye business had hit a plateau. In response, L'Oréal reformulated and repackaged its Preference hair coloring and introduced New Performing Preference in 1985, followed shortly by Advantage, a semipermanent hair coloring formulated with no ammonia or peroxide aimed at aging baby-boomers. In 1986 L'Oréal made a comeback with its Studio line of styling gels, mousses, and sprays. Smartly packaged in bright yellow, red, and blue containers, the Studio line appealed to a younger market with the tag line "Sculpt your hair any way you like it."

### Mass-Market Cosmetics

L'Oréal expanded into the fiercely competitive United States cosmetics market in the late 1970s, introducing another line of cosmetics for nails and lips. Its visually striking ad campaigns emphasized the product without a tie-in to a famous model or a particular lifestyle. Initially, sales of L'Oréal cosmetics were slow, placing fifth among U.S. cosmetic brands. However, with financial support from its strong hair product division, L'Oréal reformulated its nail and lip colors, added a line of eye shadows and mascaras, and staged a relaunch in 1983. Sales picked up enormously, aided by the introduction of L'Oréal Visuelle in 1984. The line, which included L'Oréal's first foundation, pressed powder, and powder blush, was introduced through a $10 million dollar, six-month advertising blitz.

By 1985 L'Oréal offered a full line of mass-market cosmetics that allowed it to compete directly with giants Revlon, Noxzema, and Maybelline. Its national ranking moved up one notch to fourth place, with L'Oréal nail enamel taking the third position in some regions. L'Oréal positioned its new line as a high-end version of mass-market cosmetics. Priced slightly higher than its competitors, L'Oréal sought to create an image of quality that tied in with the "Because I'm worth it" idea behind its hair colorings.

L'Oréal S.A. committed 3.3 percent of its cosmetic sales to research and development in the 1980s—twice the amount spent by the Revlon Group and three times that of Avon Products Inc. The results paid off well; the company was able to reformulate its Lancome Nisome Daytime Skin Treatment into a series of mass-market products to be sold as L'Oréal Plentitude. The liposome-based treatment for aging skin, destined for the prestige market under the Lancome brand name, translated well into mass-market products under the L'Oréal name.

Plentitude was launched in Europe and Australia in the late 1980s and in the United States in 1989. Capitalizing even further on L'Oréal's high-quality image, the Plentitude launch resembled department store introductions of more expensive cosmetics, with on-site representatives discussing skincare with customers and local models offering samples of the product. The U.S. launch rang up at $35 million with a media campaign based on the themes "Living with time" and "Helps reduce the signs of aging." By 1993 Plentitude held a 15 percent share of the U.S. skin care market, threatening the Procter & Gamble Company's best-selling Oil of Olay.

### Battling over the World Market

By 1990 certain L'Oréal products were sold in Italy, Spain, and Australia. Having proven themselves in the U.S. market, L'Oréal color cosmetics were introduced under the name L'Oréal Perfection in France and Belgium during the summer of 1992. L'Oréal thus initiated a fierce battle with the Procter & Gamble Company for dominance of the world wide cosmetic business.

Although Procter & Gamble held the number one worldwide position with 25 percent of all mass-market cosmetic sales and L'Oréal held position number four with ten percent, L'Oréal seemed well positioned to enter battle. Sales in May of 1992 were up 19 percent over the previous years to an estimated $250 million. L'Oréal nail enamel continued to hold a number one position with 15.1 percent of the nail polish category, estimated at $39 million in sales.

Cosmair Inc. began beefing up its marketing in the United States during 1992, increasing its advertising budget for color cosmetics by 15 percent and for Plentitude by a whopping 50 percent. "More Beautiful by Design" became the tag for L'Oréal's new print ad campaign, which presented a sleek image of a woman's face shadowed by a large-brimmed hat, except for her bright red lips. The ad was in keeping with L'Oréal's philosophy of focusing on the product and its image and was noteworthy because it did not feature model Andie MacDowell, a longtime L'Oréal model.

L'Oréal also armed itself with a series of new products: Lightness light natural makeup, Hydra-Renewal day cream, and Dry and Go Nail Enamel Quick Dry Lotion. In addition, the company dramatically restructured its in-store merchandising with a concept labeled "System 2000," a user-friendly display system that groups products according to skin type and product function.

## Performance Appraisal

Although the hair coloring market was considered a no-growth category during the 1980s, L'Oréal wisely used its steady stream of profits to build its cosmetic division into a formidable world player. In 1992 worldwide sales for L'Oréal S.A. totaled FF39 billion (U.S. $7.1 billion). L'Oréal's mass-market sales contributed half of that figure and continue to climb with each new product introduction.

The L'Oréal line has benefited from strong research and development and from judicious borrowing of marketing strategies from some of L'Oréal S.A.'s prestige lines. Its image as a high-quality brand in the mass-market cosmetic industry is well supported by innovative new products and advertising. Continual product development and foreign expansion are key to the growth of the L'Oréal brand. L'Oréal seems to have built a solid marketing strategy which will serve it well in the future.

## Further Reading:

Applebaum, Carla, "L'Oréal Unlocks Its War Chest," *Women's Wear Daily,* May 22, 1992, p. 17.

Berss, Marcia, "On the Scent," *Forbes,* March 12, 1994, p. 88.

Slogan, Pat, "P&G, L'Oréal to Face Off in Cosmetics," *Advertising Age,* January 4, 1993, p. 4.

*—Maura Troester*

# LYSOL®

Lysol brand disinfectant has been one of America's leading cleaning products for over 100 years. The original Lysol brand disinfectant kills germs on surfaces and eliminates odors and continues to be sold in its original concentrated form. Lysol disinfectant was one of the first products offered by Louis Lehn and Frederick Fink via their company Lehn & Fink Products. The company (now L&F Products) was founded in 1874 as a marketer of pharmaceutical chemicals and botanicals. Originally imported from Germany, the product was first sold under the name Liquor Cresolis Compositus. Lysol brand disinfectant grew to be a top-seller, but the true success of the brand name was secured in 1963 with the introduction of Lysol Disinfectant Spray, which continued to be the brand's biggest seller into the 1990s. The strength of the Lysol brand name led to ten line extensions by 1993. Lysol brand extensions include Lysol Disinfectant Spray, Lysol Toilet Bowl Cleaner, Lysol Deodorizing Cleaner, Lysol Basin Tub & Tile Cleaner, Lysol Direct Multi-Purpose Cleaner, Lysol Cling, Lysol Pine Action, Lysol Hard Water Stain Cleaner, Lysol Sanitizing Bleach, and Lysol Bathroom Touch-Ups.

## Early Advertising

Originally sold in the drug and health-aid section of stores, Lysol disinfectant had maintained a top-selling position since its introduction, but sales had stagnated by the mid-1950s. To explain the lack of product growth, *Printers' Ink* noted that "people thought of it as a drug item rather than a household helper; they used it for many specific germ-killing jobs around the house." Indeed, L&F's advertising campaign for the disinfectant supported the public's perception of the product. Until the early 1960s, Lysol brand advertisements used scary warnings about germs and various epidemics. The ads were modeled after newspaper headlines. One announced "Warning: Help protect babies and new mothers against dreaded staph germs," and went on to say that Lysol should be used regularly because it kills "disease germs, including staph, on contact."

Even though the introduction of a pine-scented version of Lysol disinfectant increased the product's sales, it did not foster the continued growth L&F thought was available to the brand. To create a long-term growth pattern for the Lysol brand, L&F's executives decided to revamp the disinfectant's image. The company discovered that the Lysol brand's strong core of customers was growing older and that the product was not being used

regularly by younger housewives. The reason for the brand's difficulty in winning new customers, according to retired L&F executive Roger Kirk in *Sales Management,* was that "for a housewife to identify herself as a Lysol prospect, she had to have just come through a flood, hurricane, or be in the middle of an epidemic." As a result, all media support for Lysol disinfectant was discontinued while the company searched for a new advertising campaign, and in the six-month interim, sales of the product actually rose.

## Repositioning for More Growth

The new marketing approach L&F unveiled in July of 1961 expanded opportunities for Lysol brand sales without dropping the brand's core customers, appealed to housewives of all ages, focused on all the product's features, and featured Lysol disinfectant as a product for daily use. To enhance the brand's new multi-use message, it was moved to the household section of stores. Television was chosen as the best medium to illustrate the many uses for Lysol disinfectant. The commercials said that the product was a necessary part of everyday cleaning without insinuating that housewives were lax in their duties. The announcer stated that "even the most careful mothers can't completely protect their families from household germs," and the commercials went on to demonstrate Lysol disinfectant's helpfulness in doing regular cleaning like the laundry or cleaning the bathroom.

By using a "scatter plan," the company estimated that the television campaign reached more than 90 percent of American homes with televisions, according to *Advertising Age.* The scatter plan rotated commercials on 11 television shows in what *Printers' Ink* called "the most powerful night-time TV campaign in the product's history." *Printers' Ink* reported that the plan resulted in a 40 percent rise in sales.

In addition, L&F expanded its advertising schedule to include the summer months. The Lysol brand had not been previously advertised in the summer because the company did not think women worried about germs and sickness as much during the hot months. Lysol disinfectant, however, was found to be an effective killer of molds and mildews that plague households in hot, humid weather. The television summer spots started by announcing that "no matter how careful you are, summertime brings problems. . . . "

## AT A GLANCE

Lysol brand disinfectant imported from Germany by Lehn & Fink Products under the name Liquor Cresolis Compositus in 1874; Lysol Disinfectant Spray introduced, 1963; other line extensions include: Lysol Toilet Bowl Cleaner, Lysol Deodorizing Cleaner, Lysol Basin Tub & Tile Cleaner, Lysol Direct Multi-Purpose Cleaner, Lysol Cling, Lysol Pine Action, Lysol Hard Water Stain Cleaner, Lysol Sanitizing Bleach, and Lysol Bathroom Touch-Ups; Lehn & Fink Products acquired by Sterling Drug, Inc., 1966; Sterling Drug purchased by Eastman Kodak Company, 1988; Lehn & Fink Products changed name to L&F Products, 1990.

**Performance:** *Market share*—Lysol brand products hold 13.5% of the cleaning solution market (Investext, Thomson Financial Networks, January 24, 1992). *Sales*—$83.2 million (according to *Superbrands: America's Top 2,000 Brands* [supplement to *Adweek's Marketing Week*], September 1991).

**Major competitor:** Dow Chemical's Dow brand bathroom cleaner and Tough Act; also, Procter & Gamble's Spic and Span, Mr. Clean, and Cinch; Clorox's Formula 409, Clorox Clean Up, and Pine-Sol.

**Advertising:** *Agency*—Lintas, New York, NY, 1963—.

**Addresses:** *Parent company*—L&F Products, 225 Summit Ave., Montvale, NJ 07645; phone: (201) 573-5700. *Ultimate parent company*—Eastman Kodak Co., 343 State St., Rochester, NY 14650; phone: (716) 724-4000.

### Lysol Spray

The 1963 introduction of Lysol Disinfectant Spray met with immediate success and further strengthened the Lysol brand name. Lysol Disinfectant Spray had a "stranglehold" on the spray segment of the disinfectant market by the 1970s, according to *Advertising Age*. To foster such quick growth, the company supported Lysol Disinfectant Spray with a formidable advertising budget. In 1966, with Lysol spray already leading its market, L&F unrolled a newspaper campaign in 100 of its top markets. Written in newspaper article format, the ads carried the headline "Lysol spray kills major known cause of common cold." The same headline was used in 20-second commercials on NBC and ABC, airing during the same period the newspaper ads were released. In addition, the television spots were positioned in areas that the U.S. Public Health Service had deemed flu-infested. The theme used for flu-infested areas was "Lysol brand disinfectant kills flu virus wherever you clean, so it helps you protect your family. Lysol kills flu virus that babies can pick up." Lysol spray was also promoted in color ads in magazines such as *Family Circle, Good Housekeeping, House and Garden, American Home, Ladies' Home Journal,* and *Woman's Day.*

The ad's claim that Lysol spray kills cold germs and flu viruses was supported by the Environmental Protection Agency, but the EPA noted that the product's germ fighting ability is effective only on surfaces. Even though the ads were literally true, the Federal Trade Commission filed a suit against the company, arguing that the advertisements' statements were deceptive. The FTC said that Lysol spray's ability to kill cold and flu germs on surfaces "has nothing to do with human colds and flu because these germs were generally absorbed from the air," according to *Advertising Age*. As a result, the ads were discontinued.

### More Sales from a Similar Theme

Advertising for Lysol liquid refocused attention on its myriad uses in the 1970s because, as Nancy Giges wrote in *Advertising Age*, "where specialty products boomed in the late '60s and early '70s, cleaning aids that can do more than one job are now showing more growth." The company had discovered that Lysol disinfectant was in 60 percent of homes but was used for specific disinfecting jobs rather than daily cleaning. A radio campaign was launched that tried to reach women when they were doing their daily chores. One spot started by saying, "Monday, so what are you doing?" A woman responded that she was doing her laundry. The announcer went on to say, "Let's talk about getting that wash a lot more than clean. Cutting down on germs. That's basic. That's Lysol brand disinfectant, probably right there in your cleaning closet . . . brown bottle in the red and yellow box." The announcer would then suggest that the disinfectant be used in the washing machine. Other spots focused on the benefits of using the product to do various regular cleaning routines. In addition, television spots touted Lysol disinfectant as "one of the few things left that does a lot for a little."

L&F has used advertising not only to boost sales but as an effective weapon against competitors. L&F traditionally spent more than its competitors, concentrating its advertising thrust on competitors' test markets to skew their test results. One competitor tested its disinfectant spray in Dallas and Memphis, but Giges noted that the Lysol brand was advertised with $30 million "to muddy the results in those markets." "The company had used this method," she continued, "to protect Lysol against competitors in the past." By 1974, Lysol disinfectant held 85 percent of the supermarket sales and had warded off six different competitors.

### Symbol of Confidence

In the hospitality industry, the Lysol brand has captured market share by using the Lysol "Symbol of Confidence" program. Started in the late 1980s, the program provided hotels free dispensing equipment, training for housekeeping staff, and use of Lysol door hangers or amenity cards that let the visitor know the room had been cleaned and disinfected with Lysol products. Nick Baker, general manager of the Hilton in Pearl River, New York, emphasized the amount of brand recognition the Lysol brand had with his guests, telling *Lodging and Hospitality* that "once we told them that we were using Lysol brand products, it was incredible to see the jump in how much cleaner the guests perceived the rooms as being." The program was used in 2,700 hotels in 1992 and continued to expand into nursing homes and hospitals.

### Parent Company

L&F Products became a division of Sterling Drug, Inc. (now Sterling Winthrop Inc.) in 1966, where it grew to acquire many more successful products. The Eastman Kodak Company's 1988 acquisition of Sterling Drug, however, included a restructuring that allowed L&F Products to function as an independent operating unit, reporting directly to Kodak by 1989. Kodak was one of the top 100 advertisers in 1991, mostly because of its ad spending on Kodak film and photo products and the Lysol brand. Kodak spent over $19 million advertising Lysol disinfectant, over $11 million promoting Lysol bath products, and almost $9 million advertising Lysol cleaners, according to *Advertising Age*. Though L&F's profits are tied to those of Kodak, L&F president Michael Gallagher told *New Jersey Business* contributor James T. Prior that L&F Products' $1 billion in sales would make it "a member of the Fortune 500 as a stand-alone company.'' Gallagher went on to emphasize L&F's focus on international development in the early 1990s. He said, ''Through the use of global strategies, we are maximizing the value of our products and expanding into new markets on a country by country basis for maximum return. These markets include Australia, Thailand, Taiwan, the Philippines, Hong Kong and New Zealand. We'll also increase our foothold in markets where we've had a presence such as Canada, France, England, Ireland, Puerto Rico and Japan.'' The Lysol brand was marketed in more than 40 countries by 1987.

Household products like Lysol disinfectant account for 70 percent of L&F's sales, with do-it-yourself products, such as the Minwax line of wood-finishing products and Ogilvie hair-care products, making up the remaining 30 percent. L&F's continued focus on household and do-it-yourself products has allowed it to acquire many respected, profitable brands since its founding. Peter Benario, executive vice-president of L&F's former broker, Sayres Co., told *Crain's New York Business* that L&F are ''either the No. 1 or No. 2 brand in every category they compete in.'' Some of L&F's other products include Thompson's exterior waterproofing, Formby's wood finishing, Resolve carpet cleaner, Chubs baby wipes, and RID-X septic additive.

Lysol brand products remained strong in the marketplace into the 1990s. According to *Thomson Financial Networks,* Lysol disinfectant held the leading position of the all-purpose cleaners category with 8.9 percent in the fourth quarter of 1992. Adding in the sales of Lysol Pine Action, Lysol Direct Multi-Purpose Cleaner, and Lysol Bathroom Touch Ups, L&F had 14.6 percent of that category, ranking it third behind Procter & Gamble and Clorox. Lysol disinfectant and Lysol Bathroom Touch Ups combined sales gave L&F 18.3 percent of the bathroom cleaner category, just behind Dow Chemical. Continued strong consumer brand recognition and advertising support with the ''a little goes a long way'' theme seem to promise Lysol brand products a secure future.

## Further Reading:

''Cosmetics & Household Products Industry Report,'' *Thomson Financial Networks,* April 8, 1993.

''Expect Settlement Soon in FTC's Lysol Ad Case,'' *Advertising Age,* December 31, 1973, p. 2.

''FTC Challenges Lysol Flu Prevention Claims,'' *Advertising Age,* March 6, 1972, p. 8.

Giges, Nancy, ''Listerol Makes Inroads, but Lysol Still Big Gun,'' *Advertising Age,* June 17, 1974, pp. 3, 126.

Giges, Nancy, ''100 Years Young, Lysol Revitalized as Marketing Success,'' *Advertising Age,* August 11, 1975, pp. 3, 48.

''Lysol Ad Budget Restored to '60 Level in Renewal,'' *Advertising Age,* July 22, 1963, p. 8.

''Lysol Brand Name Rates at Hotel,'' *Lodging Hospitality,* September, 1990.

''Lysol Disinfects Its Image,'' *Sales Management,* September 20, 1963, pp. 89–91.

''Lysol Puts the Shine on Mackinac,'' *Lodging Hospitality,* August, 1992, p. 84.

''Marketing Is Expanded for Two New Lysol Products,'' *Advertising Age,* March 7, 1966, pp. 3, 36.

O'Connor, John, ''Lysol Fights New Listerol with Lawsuit,'' *Advertising Age,* November 19, 1973, pp. 1, 8.

Prior, James T., ''L&F Products on Growth Track,'' *New Jersey Business Magazine,* January 1, 1991.

Rigg, Cynthia, ''The Hidden Gem in the Sterling Setting,'' *Crains New York Business,* November 26, 1990, sec. 1, p. 3.

''70-Year-Old Lysol Met 20th Century Television,'' *Printers' Ink,* August 17, 1962, pp. 38–41.

''Winning a Broader Market by Consolidating Product Lines,'' *Printers' Ink,* October 22, 1965, pp. 55–57.

*—Sara Pendergast*

# MAALOX®

**Maalox**

Indigestion and heartburn, conditions caused by excess hydrochloric acid in the stomach, afflict millions of people each year. As a result, the drugs most commonly used to neutralize stomach acid, antacids, have grown into a billion dollar industry worldwide. Historically, antacids contained only a handful of ingredients, each with their own drawbacks. For example, one of the most common antacid foundations, magnesium hydroxide (milk of magnesia), has a laxative effect when taken in sufficient amounts. Another common antacid, aluminum hydroxide, can induce constipation. William Rorer, Inc. solved these problems with its Maalox antacid by combining both magnesium hydroxide and aluminum hydroxide, which effectively cancelled out each other's side effects. Consequently, Maalox has been one of the most successful antacids on the market for over thirty years.

## Brand Origin and History

William Rorer, Inc., a pharmaceutical company founded in 1910, introduced Maalox in 1949. It quickly became the company's leading product and provided a majority of the company's profits until William Rorer, Inc. began diversifying in the late 1960s. Sales of the product have consistently increased annually, except for short periods in the 1970s and 1980s. While competing brands have reduced Maalox's market share from around 40 percent in the 1970s down to about 15 percent in the early 1990s, profits have continued to be strong due to the product's vigorous promotion and advertising in both the United States and internationally.

Maalox originated as an ethical product—one that was promoted only to members of the medical profession. While it has always been available without a prescription, marketing and advertising efforts targeted physicians, pharmacists, hospital personnel, and government purchasers. Following its introduction, Maalox quickly became the most frequently recommended antacid in the United States. In July of 1969 Rorer-Amchem produced their 25th million gallon of Maalox suspension and estimated that they had manufactured approximately 6 billion individual doses of antacid since 1949. By 1984 the company had sold 550 million 12 ounce bottles of Maalox, and three years later sales of Maalox reached $100 million within the United States and $200 million worldwide.

The product has not been without its problems, however. In August of 1963 Maalox and William Rorer, Inc. received a mild blow to sales when the breakdown of their preservation system resulted in the formation of carbolic acid in roughly one percent of its bottles. Although some consumers complained of discomfort, no one became seriously ill. The company recalled the affected lots and no legal action was taken. During the late 1960s shortages of magnesium hydroxide, one of the two main ingredients, severely curtailed promotional programs. The company solved their supply problem the following year by opening its new subsidiary plant in Delaware that manufactured both magnesium hydroxide and aluminum hydroxide, the major ingredients in Maalox.

## Brand Product Development

In the years following the introduction of the original Maalox liquid in 15 ounce glass bottles, William Rorer, Inc. also introduced liquid Extra Strength Maalox and a tablet form of the original Maalox. In 1967 the company introduced two new package designs geared towards consumer convenience. To aid their ethical market comprised of hospital personnel, the company created Maalox Suspension Unit Dose in pre-measured packages; improved flavor followed in 1970. William Rorer, Inc. also introduced individually wrapped Maalox Tablets in Strip 80s as well as plastic five ounce bottles of the original liquid form "for the convenient use by the ambulatory patient," according to the 1970 annual report.

In the mid-1970s, sales of the original Maalox antacid began to level off for the first time since its introduction in 1949. To counteract this slump the company continued to add line extensions such as Maalox Plus. The "plus" was the addition of Simethicone to relieve stomach gas. Maalox Plus proved to be Rorer's most successful new product to date, with $5 million in sales in the first years. In response to the development of new types of non-antacid ulcer drugs by other manufacturers, William Rorer marketed a new high potency formulation, Maalox Therapeutic Concentrate in 1978. The company's studies showed that the new Maalox TC was as effective as the ulcer drug cimetidine. In February of 1984 Rorer Pharmaceutical, Inc. introduced Maalox Plus tablets in rolls, hoping to attract a new group of antacid users. They also phased out the 12 ounce amber glass bottle in favor of more convenient break-resistant plastic bottles that had the added benefit of reducing the company's production and distribution costs.

## AT A GLANCE

**M**aalox brand of antacid founded in 1949 by Gerald Rorer, president of William Rorer, Inc.; became a registered trademark, 1951; company changed name to Rorer-Amchem in 1968, Rorer Pharmaceutical Corporation in 1976, and Rhone-Poulenc Rorer in 1990.

**Performance:** *Market share*—14.7% of antacid category in 1989. *Sales*—$253 million worldwide in 1991; $100 million in U.S. sales in 1992.

**Major competitor:** SmithKline Beecham's Tums; also Johnson & Johnson's Mylanta, Warner Lambert's Rolaids, and Procter & Gamble's Pepto-Bismol.

**Advertising:** *Agency*—Angotti, Thomas, Hedge Inc., New York, NY, 1992—. *Major campaign*—"Maalox Moment" television commercials depicting stressful situations compounded by indigestion.

**Addresses:** *Parent company*—Rhone-Poulenc Rorer, Inc., 500 Virginia Dr., Fort Washington, PA 19034; phone: (215) 628-6000.

One product development that failed to catch on was the 1987 introduction of Maalox Whip—the first antacid in an aerosol can. Marketed on the premise that the aerosol eliminated the chalky taste normally associated with antacids, the product received the widest publicity of any new product in Rorer Pharmaceutical Inc.'s history. Despite the advertising blitz, as Janet Novack reported two years later in *Forbes* magazine, "it bombed." The company returned to existing products and developed Extra Strength Maalox Plus, which boasted "the highest acid neutralizing capacity of any antacid on the market," and became the company's "flagship product" according to their 1988 annual report.

When the Food and Drug Administration appointed a review panel in 1972 to analyze marketing claims of antacids, Rorer Pharmaceutical conducted clinical studies to demonstrate Maalox's medicinal value. In addition, the development in the mid-1970s of new ulcer drugs such as Cimetidine, Tagamet and Zantac, which inhibited the secretion of stomach acid rather than neutralizing it, also posed a threat to Maalox sales that they sought to overcome by research that proved Maalox's effectiveness. Long-term clinical study results were reported in 1985 and 1986 that showed that Maalox products were effective in preventing the recurrence of ulcers. The 1986 studies compared Maalox with both Tagamet and Zantac, and found Maalox Tablets to be just as effective in preventing duodenal ulcers as the acid inhibitors.

Rorer Pharmaceutical, part of the larger Rhone-Poulenc Rorer, Inc., has continued to develop new Maalox antacid products. In the early 1990s, they introduced flavored formulas. In 1991 they introduced Maalox GRF, or Gas Relief Formula. The following year, with much fanfare and a large advertising budget, they introduced Maalox HRF—heartburn relief formula. This new product sought to prevent stomach acid from traveling into the esophagus (a function called refluxing), one of the most painful and distasteful parts of indigestion. "The new product boasts a patented formula that includes a foam barrier to prevent stomach acid from refluxing into the esophagus," claimed Rhone-Poulenc Rorer's 1992 annual report. Maalox HRF tablets and Maalox caplets also became available that year.

## Advertising History

William Rorer, Inc. maintained Maalox as an ethical product for over two decades, during which the marketing and sales departments concentrated their efforts on physicians, pharmacists, and hospital personnel. Company representatives attended conventions to present studies and demonstrations of Maalox's effectiveness. Through the late 1960s, the drug was sold only to wholesalers, retail pharmacists, physicians, hospitals, and government agencies.

In 1970 Rorer-Amchem introduced Camalox, a formula described in their annual report as a "superior antacid" in a smoother suspension. This became the company's ethical product, and they began to move Maalox into the consumer market. Soon special drugstore displays promoted Maalox suspension and tablets directly to the consumer. Rorer-Amchem continued to promote Maalox directly to the physician, however, with a thirty-minute color film entitled *Peptic Ulcer,* which featured physicians discussing the effectiveness of Maalox to other medical personnel.

In 1972 Rorer-Amchem launched a more aggressive Maalox campaign in its attempt to break into the consumer antacid market. Though Rorer-Achem already dominated the $100 million ethical antacid market, they sought to increase their presence in the $300 million total antacid market. Their 1972 annual report stated that "for the first time we decided to capitalize on [our presence in food stores and mass merchandisers]. . . . We are capitalizing on the growing Maalox consumer franchise as more people become aware of it and tend to purchase it as a result of our cultivation of the consumer market." Within a few years Rorer Pharmaceutical began to advertise nationally. In the late 1970s and early 1980s, a series of television ads for Maalox antacid featured actor E.G. Marshall.

In 1988 Rorer cut their advertising budget for Maalox, and the sales staff was prohibited from handing out free samples to medical professionals. "We thought we had such a solid franchise that we could sustain our share with a lower level of support," company representative Ralph Thurman told *Forbes* magazine in 1989. This proved not to be the case, and sales dropped. The following year, in response to their slipping sales and market share, Rhone-Poulenc Rorer initiated a $20 million advertising campaign. The "Maalox Moment" television commercials were based on actual letters from Maalox users which described somewhat comical but stressful situations that were overcome with the help of Maalox. One popular ad depicted a family dinner interrupted by the unannounced arrival of the teenage daughter's disheveled date, which causes her father to have a "Maalox moment." Each television spot included the company's address and requested viewers to send in accounts of their own "Maalox moments." The slogan proved effective and the brand enjoyed record share increases. A few years later, Rorer took this effective campaign to the local level on radio with the Local Marketing Corporation. The revised campaign shared spots with local retailers and traffic reports—rush hour traffic being a reliable supplier of Maalox moments. The campaign won the advertising industry's coveted Reggie Award for 1992.

Competition among antacids became fierce in the 1990s with total advertising spending rising 27.1 percent in 1990 to the record amount of $101.2 million. In 1991 Rorer moved their Maalox account from Grey Advertising Inc., the creator of "Maalox moments," to another agency, BBDO, a decision impacted by corporate restructuring. BBDO's first campaign was for the new

Maalox HRF. Television commercials released in 1992 depicted the discomfort of heartburn and indigestion as menacing flames; a voice-over warns that "it could start in your office, in your home, over lunch" and suggests Maalox HRF to alleviate the situation.

## International Market

William Rorer, Inc. expanded into the international market in the early 1960s by briefly distributing the U.S.-made Maalox brand abroad before licensing overseas companies to manufacture it. By doing this, Rorer circumvented heavy freight charges and tariffs. This licensee arrangement proved unsatisfactory, however, because it limited the company's profits and because they were forced to rely on other companies for quality control. The company's 1967 annual report explained that despite the availability of Rorer products in 74 countries, Maalox was entering the world market very slowly. "Because we have been reluctant to permit the manufacturing of Maalox in plants we do not own or control," the report stated, "this product accounts for only a small part of our foreign business. With our rapidly expanding network of worldwide Rorer companies, however, we can expect greater Maalox sales [worldwide]." To expand their network, Rorer bought foreign companies in order to gain control of all production and marketing processes.

By 1965 William Rorer, Inc. owned several foreign subsidiaries including Rorer-Philippines, Rorer de Mexico, and Rorer-Berk in England, all of which produced and distributed Maalox. Other markets were added in the following years, including Italy and Japan in 1966 and Germany, France, Iran, and Canada in 1967. Overseas sales of the product grew faster than domestic sales. By 1977 Maalox had captured almost 30 percent of the antacid market in Italy and more than 20 percent of the market in France. In 1985, Maalox grew from a three percent to 11 percent market share in the United Kingdom. Other countries in which Maalox had established a substantial market share included Austria, Belgium, Brazil, Canada, Central America, Chile, Colombia, Germany, Ireland, Japan, Korea, Mexico, the Middle East, Netherlands, Peru, Philippines, Puerto Rico, Southeast Asia, Spain, Sweden, Switzerland, and Venezuela.

## Performance Appraisal and Future Growth

The Maalox brand has remained a profitable product for its parent company, despite fluctuations in the market. Sales increased consistently in the first two decades of the product's existence, and various line extensions debuted with similar success. However, with increased competition in the late 1980s from Johnson and Johnson's Mylanta and Warner Lambert's Extra Strength Rolaids, Maalox began to lose market share. To counteract these consumer opponents, the Rorer Group sought to attach themselves to the promotional power of Procter & Gamble (P&G). In 1990 Rorer attempted to sell the Maalox marketing rights to P&G, putting themselves "in the hands of a giant," as their spokesman Jeffrey C. Richardson told the *New York Times*. This

merger fell through when the United States Justice Department threatened to block the deal for violating antitrust laws. The companies canceled the deal rather than risk a legal fight.

This failed deal may have been a fortuitous event for the Rorer Group, since its 1991 global sales were up 14 percent to $253 million. Despite a decline of seven percent the following year, The company estimated that by 1994, sales will reach $275 million. The company estimates that most of this growth will be in the world market. While the United States accounts for more than two-thirds of 1992 Maalox sales, international sales should increase when the product is introduced as an over-the-counter item in other countries. As of the early 1990s, Maalox remains an ethical market prescription drug in much of the world. In their 1992 annual report, Rhone-Poulenc Rorer reported that "once Maalox is available as a non prescription product its price can be increased at a higher percentage than governments allow for prescriptions products."

## Further Reading:

Freemen, Laurie, "Rorer Gives P&G Its Maalox Moment," *Advertising Age*, March 19, 1990, p. 60.

Freudenheim, Milt, "Procter & Gamble Acquires Rights to Distribute Maalox," *New York Times*, March 14, 1990, p. D1.

Freudenheim, Milt, "Agreement on Maalox Is Canceled," *New York Times*, August 24, 1990, p. D3.

Gannon, Kathi, "Maalox HRF Helps Take the Burn out of Heartburn," *Drug Topics*, March 9, 1992.

"Incentive Marketing: And the Winner Is . . . ," *Incentive*, April 1992, p. 47.

Lipman, Joanne, "Maalox Moments," *Wall Street Journal*, July 6, 1989, p. B4.

"Maalox Moved from BBDO," *New York Times*, September 22, 1992, p. D25.

"Maalox Moved from Grey to BBDO," *New York Times*, October 15, 1991, p. D20.

"New Campaigns," *New York Times*, February 2, 1992, p. D5.

Novack, Janet, "Please Pass the Maalox," *Forbes*, August 7, 1989, p. 114.

Rhone-Poulenc Rorer, Inc., Annual Reports, Fort Washington, Pennsylvania: Rhone-Poulenc Rorer, Inc., 1990–1992.

Rorer Amchem, Inc. Annual Reports, Fort Washington, Pennsylvania: Rorer Amchem, Inc., 1968–1975.

Rorer Group, Inc. Annual Reports, Fort Washington, Pennsylvania: The Rorer Group, Inc., 1977–1989.

Schlossberg, Howard, "Local Radio Tie-ins Break through Promotional Clutter," *Marketing News*, May 11, 1992, p. 12.

Sloan, Pat, "Maalox Readies Heartburn Cure," *Advertising Age*, February 17, 1992, p. 12.

Swasy, Alecia, "P&G May Face Maalox Moment Over Antitrust," *Wall Street Journal*, August 6, 1990, p. B1.

William Rorer, Inc. Annual Report, Fort Washington, Pennsylvania: William Rorer, Inc., 1964–1967.

"The World According to Maalox," *Medical Advertising News*, October, 1992, p. 18.

*—Robin Armstrong*

# MAIDENFORM®

# MAIDENFORM®

Made famous by the "I dreamed" advertising campaign, which ran from 1949 to 1969, Maidenform bras and undergarments hold a large share of the U.S. intimate apparel market, with annual sales of $150 million. Parent company Maidenform Worldwide, Inc. is the largest privately held intimate apparel company in the United States and has been controlled by the same family for the 71 years of its existence. Through consistent marketing, advertising, and careful attention to the ever-changing trends in the fashion industry, the brand has managed to remain a giant in the intimate apparel industry. Maidenform's market spans 70 countries where distribution is primarily through department stores.

## Brand Origins

Dubbed "the mother and father of the bra," Ida and William Rosenthal took a novel idea and built it into an industry. The time was 1922, a fashion era dominated by the flapper look with its bobbed hair and boyish figures. To achieve that look, women wore boyish form bandeaux, tight-fitting undergarments that flattened the bustline. At that time, Ida had a custom dress business called Enid Frocks on Manhattan's fashionable 57th Street. Her business partner, Enid Bissett, was a curvaceous woman, proud of her figure, and also well suited to the shapely dress styles sold at their shop. One day she took her own boyish form bandeau, cropped it, and gathered it in the middle to form two cups. Trying it on for size, she found that it provided support while also enhancing her curves, but as the story goes, the product itself wasn't very appealing.

Ida took her partner's invention to her husband William, who made it more attractive by adding a covered elastic center. They named it the Maiden Form Brassiere, and began giving the brassiere as a free gift with each dress purchased. Demand for the brassiere (then called an "uplifting garment") grew quickly, however, and the partners began to sell separate Maiden Form Brassieres at one dollar each. By 1925 the Rosenthals and Enid Bissett had formed the Enid Manufacturing Company, which produced the Original Maiden Form Brassiere exclusively. In 1930 the company changed its name to the Maiden Form Brassiere Company, in recognition of the success of the Maiden Form brand.

The Rosenthals worked as a team, with Ida managing sales and finances and William controlling design and manufacturing. In 1925 manufacturing was moved to Bayonne, New Jersey. At that time, there were few direct competitors in the brassiere business,

and business grew steadily. Production was limited, however, because one seamstress could only produce two or three brassieres a day. Taking his cue from the industrial efficiencies that began in the 1930s, William Rosenthal created an assembly line—an industry first—to boost productivity. By the end of its first decade, the Maiden Form Brassiere Company had sold over one million brassieres, and William had designed a few other industry "firsts," including a brassiere for fuller figures and one for nursing.

## Second Generation Management

Like many American companies, Maiden Form supported the U.S. effort during World War II, supplying brassieres for the WACs, parachutes for the U.S. Army Signal Corps, and vests for carrier pigeons. Many U.S. factories employed women during that time and Maiden Form was no exception. Among the growing number of female employees was Beatrice Rosenthal, the daughter of Ida and William, who joined the company in 1938, first sewing bra cups together, then moving through a variety of administrative positions. When the war ended, Beatrice's husband, Dr. Joseph A. Coleman, decided to give up his medical practice and join Maiden Form. Beatrice offered to quit—"That was the way things were then," she stated in *Working Woman* magazine in 1987, adding that "when the boys came home, the girls went home"—but Coleman countered that he wouldn't join the company if she quit, and the two stayed on together.

Sales grew steadily during the 1940s, fueled by the enormous popularity of "Chansonette," a structured white cotton broadcloth bra with circular-stitched cups, which accounted for 25 percent of Maidenform sales. While her husband was in charge of advertising, Beatrice moved to the design department in the mid-1940s, eventually becoming design coordinator in the 1950s. One of her responsibilities was to oversee product development, "trying to get designs away from designers," as she put it in *Working Woman*. Her ability to successfully transfer innovative design concepts to new products is credited with the enormous success Maidenform—as the name now appeared—enjoyed during the 1950s, an era when it rose to dominate the market.

## Early Advertising

Maidenform had marketed and advertised its products nationally since the late 1920s and internationally since the early 1930s. It was, in fact, one of the first intimate apparel manufactur-

## AT A GLANCE

**M**aidenform brand of undergarments was created in 1922 by Enid Bissett and William Rosenthal as the Original Maiden Form Brassiere in New York, NY; Enid Manufacturing Company founded in 1925; brassiere was patented in 1926; company name changed to Maiden Form Brassiere Company, 1930; Maiden Form trademark registered internationally by the early 1930s; in 1960 the company became Maidenform, Inc.; name was later changed to Maidenform Worldwide, Inc.

**Performance:** *Market share*—18.5% of department store undergarment category. *Sales*—$150 million.

**Major competitor:** Warner's; also Playtex.

**Advertising:** *Agency*—Ogilvy & Mather, New York, NY, 1992—. *Major campaign*—(Historic) "I dreamed"; "If you've got something to say, now's the time to get it off your chest."

**Addresses:** *Parent company*—Maidenform Worldwide, Inc., 90 Park Avenue, 38th Floor, New York, NY 10016; phone: (212) 856-8900; fax: (212) 983-5834.

ers to invest in national print advertising. Maidenform hired the William Weintraub agency (later Norman, Craig & Kummel), which created the long-running "I Dreamed" campaign in 1949. The campaign had an element of daring: it appealed to women through the enactment of a fantasy which could be portrayed in a number of ways. The first full-color print ad pictured a woman shopping at the chic John Frederic's hat salon, with nothing on top but her Maidenform bra. The caption read, "I dreamed I went shopping in my Maidenform bra." During its 20-year lifetime, the campaign helped triple Maidenform sales.

The imaginative ads appeared with over 150 variations in over 70 countries. Women dreamed they swayed the jury, barged down the Nile, and lived in a castle in Spain, all while wearing their Maidenform bras. The "I dreamed" format provided continuity. Bra styles and the image of the woman changed with the times, but the women were always dreaming and always wearing Maidenform. In earlier versions, women were perfectly coiffed, and some even wore hats and fur coats. By 1967, women wore entire lines of Maidenform undergarments (illustrating how the brand had grown), their hair blew in the wind, and the copy, which appeared in psychedelic letters, said such things as "I dreamed I held the world on a string in my Maidenform bra."

The "I dreamed" campaign was retired in 1969. Rebellious young baby boomers were coming of age and rejecting the products and advertising to which their mothers had responded. Maidenform began manufacturing free-form stretch bras and in 1971 began advertising them to this new generation primarily through television.

### The Maidenform Woman

Eleven years later, the "I dreamed" campaign reemerged with slight variations as the "Maidenform woman." The new campaign created by the Daniel & Charles ad agency, depicted a beautiful woman standing aloof in such chic locations as a theater lobby, an antique store, a cafe, or a helicopter pad. A man stood nearby, oblivious to her presence. She wore elegant shoes, jewelry, makeup, and a coat was draped gracefully over her shoulders,

revealing the latest line of Maidenform undergarments. The caption read, "The Maidenform woman. You never know where she'll turn up." Coupled with Maidenform's popular new "Sweet Nothings" underwear line, the new ads had a tremendous impact on Maidenform sales. Such retailers as Macy's and Lord & Taylor reported sales growth of as much as 200 percent in 1980.

Intended to celebrate the freedoms brought about by the women's movement, the ad created waves when it first appeared in the pages of women's magazines such as *Mademoiselle, Ladies Home Journal, Bride,* and *Working Woman.* In 1982 Maidenform received a plastic pig from Women Against Pornography who considered the advertising exploitive and degrading. Others wrote letters to Maidenform complimenting the elegant tone set by the ads. The following year Maidenform replaced the relatively daring "Maidenform Woman" campaign with a softer, more romantic series of print ads created by Wyse Advertising. "The Maidenform Woman Dares to Dream" was the headline that combined both earlier campaigns. Each ad featured shots of a model wearing a bra, at times with matching lingerie. One photo in each ad showed the fully-dressed model with a man.

Maidenform adjusted its advertising based on market research findings that stated 65 percent of women preferred lacier, more romantic underthings. This was also the beginning of the huge growth in sales of romantic novels, and the ads seemed to reflect this aura of romance. "Femininity, frills, the desire to be a woman have all come back into vogue," said Lois Wyse, the campaign's creator.

In 1987 Maidenform asked for a bolder, more attention-getting approach from the company's new agency Levine, Huntley, Schmidt & Beaver. Defying the conventions of the category, the television and print ads showed neither the product nor a woman.

*Two historical Maidenform logos.*

Instead the ads featured such romantic leading men as Omar Sharif, Michael York, Corbin Bernsen, Christopher Reeve, and Pierce Brosnan. Over a three-year period, each male celebrity discussed how he felt about women and women's lingerie.

## No More Fantasy

For the sober, back-to-basics decade of the 1990s, Maidenform dropped the element of fantasy that had characterized its advertising since 1949. They also dropped the "middle man" as spokesperson and began to speak directly to women in a controversial series of television and print ads which some lauded as progressively feminist and others claimed upheld sexist stereotypes of women. The $6 million campaign developed by Levine, Huntley, Schmidt & Beaver started with "Lassie." This TV spot featured quick cuts of women's torsos through the ages, each era exaggerating either bust, waist, or hips. The child's song "Have you ever seen a lassie go this way and that way" runs underneath, while a voice over asks, "Isn't it nice to live in a time when women aren't being pushed around so much anymore?" The Maidenform logo appears at the end. Two other commercials with similar themes ran in concert with "Lassie."

Maidenform's philosophy behind the advertising was to communicate that the company understands and supports women. They extended the "women's advocacy" campaign in 1992 with the company's first cause-related advertising, created by its new worldwide ad agency, Ogilvy & Mather. The television commercial consisted of a series of quick cuts of women's torsos, each featuring a different statement button representing a wide range of social issues and political causes. The music underneath was "Yankee Doodle Dandy"; the voice over said, "If you've got something to say, now's the time to get it off your chest." The final shot was of a "Vote" button followed by a Maidenform logo. The highly praised commercial ran intensively for the three weeks prior to November election day.

## Performance Appraisal

Bra customers are both brand and style loyal. Maidenform conducts ongoing qualitative and quantitative research to determine consumer preferences for this core business. Its sleepwear line, founded in 1980, was phased out in 1988 after it was determined that sleepwear could not develop into a growing branded business. Maidenform has shifted its target audience over the years in order to follow the age curve of the baby boomers—from 18 to 44 years of age in the 1970s to the present target audience of women between the ages of 25 and 64. In keeping with this marketing target, the company introduced the Full Figure Fashion Collection for full-busted women and the Brava! by Maidenform Collection. The latter was designed for the "generation of baby boomers whose tastes and bodies have changed throughout the years."

Maidenform's 18.5 percent share of the foundations market is second only to Warner's. The company views its consistently innovative and occasionally controversial brand advertising as its greatest asset in generating public awareness of Maidenform. Marketing efforts continue to emphasize value rather than low price, both domestically and throughout Maidenform's international operations, which the company is aggressively expanding. This privately held company projects sales of $360 million by the year 2000.

## Further Reading:

Armour, Lawrence A., "Underworld Pay-Off," *Barron's*, March 16, 1965, p. 3.

Dougherty, Philip H., "Advertising: Years of Maidenform Dreams," *New York Times*, September 10, 1967.

Ettorre, Barbara, "The Maidenform Woman Returns," *New York Times*, June 1, 1980.

Kanner, Bernice, "The Bra's Not for Burning," *New York*, December 12, 1983, p. 26; "Sending Up the Bra," *New York*, December 17, 1990, p. 19.

Monget, Karyn, "In the Markets: Maidenform: Shaping Its Own Future," *Women's Wear Daily*, November 5, 1992, p. 8.

Morris, Michele, "The Mother Figure of Maidenform," *Working Woman*, April 1987, p. 82.

*—Maura Troester*

# MAX FACTOR®

# MAXFACTOR

Max Factor International is one of the largest and most widely recognized cosmetics companies in the world. The Max Factor line, sold in more than 90 countries, includes cosmetics, fragrances, clothing, and treatments for skin, hair, and nails. What began as a small beauty shop grew into a cosmetics company of national renown as the founder's numerous innovations became the driving force behind the company's rise to fame during the early 1900s. For decades, Max Factor was considered the authority on cosmetics research and development for the theater, motion picture, and television industries, and the company is credited with such cosmetics creations as pan-cake makeup, lip gloss, concealer, and waterproof makeup. Max Factor was a family-owned business until the 1970s, when it was sold to Norton Simon, Inc. (NSI). The company changed hands three times during the 1980s and was purchased in 1991 by the Procter & Gamble Company, a multinational company that produces a variety of foods and beverages, household and personal care products, and chemicals and pharmaceutical preparations. Procter & Gamble also owns Noxell Corporation, the immediate parent of Cover Girl Cosmetics.

## Brand Origin

Max Factor & Company, as it was originally known, was established in 1909 in California by Russian immigrant Max Factor, a makeup artist who sold his hair products and cosmetics to theatrical groups. In addition to selling his own creations, Factor distributed theatrical makeup for two other manufacturers. The most frequently used makeup by theater performers of the time was greasepaint, a thick mixture of either grease or melted tallow and coloring that was produced in stick form. The makeup was heavy and difficult to apply evenly. It was also not particularly sanitary.

With the advent of the motion picture came new challenges for makeup artists, and Factor's dominance as a cosmetics creator was established. One of the first things discovered by movie makers was that theatrical greasepaint made screen actors look unnatural. Factor refined the theatrical greasepaint, producing a thinner base that was easier to apply and that looked more natural on film. Factor's greasepaint came in a cream rather than a stick form and was available in a variety of graduated shades. The company's creation was heralded as a major breakthrough in cosmetics development and thereafter was used throughout the film industry. Max Factor's second innovation was to offer greasepaint in a tube, a method of packaging that eliminated many of the sanitary problems associated with using greasepaint sold in either a jar or stick form. Again, Factor's creation earned the company accolades as well as a reputation as the authority in creating beauty products for the silver screen.

## Brand Development

During the 1920s, the company expanded its product line, introducing Color Harmony, a new concept in the art of makeup. Factor recognized that the variations of performers' skin, hair, and eye color required different color combinations in makeup—a shade that flattered one actor's complexion might make another look unnatural. Color Harmony included makeup and complexion charts that actors could use to determine which shades would best complement their coloring. The concept, again developed for the film industry, was later introduced to the general public in 1927 as Max Factor's Society Make-up line. This line included a wide variety of shades and colors and was also accompanied by a Color Harmony Prescription Make-up Chart and a Complexion Analysis Card that a woman could use to determine the appropriate shades of makeup for her particular coloring. Color Harmony proved extremely successful, and the basic concept is still used by many modern manufacturers. While Max Factor continued to design and create cosmetics primarily for specialized markets such as the theater and film industries, from that time forward, the company also produced many of its beauty products for mass market sales.

In 1928 the motion picture industry introduced a major advancement in film technique, Panchromatic film. Unlike existing film, Panchromatic film was highly sensitive to variations of light, which produced subtle shading. This completely changed the look of motion pictures and with the change in film technique came the need for new makeup. Max Factor responded by creating Panchromatic Makeup, a makeup line that included a wider spectrum of shades and was more effective in properly reflecting light variations on screen. The company's latest effort was so successful that Max Factor received an Academy Award for the effort. By 1930 Max Factor had become an internationally renowned company with sales of its products in more than 80 countries. The company continued its research into new product development and that same year introduced the first lip gloss.

By 1935 the company was so successful that it opened the Max Factor Hollywood Makeup Salon and expanded its scope to in-

## AT A GLANCE

**M**ax Factor brand of cosmetics founded by Max Factor, owner of Max Factor & Company, in Los Angeles, CA, 1909; company was family owned and operated until 1973 when it was purchased by Norton Simon, Inc.; sold to Esmark Company in 1983, which was acquired by Beatrice Companies, 1984; Beatrice placed Max Factor under its International Playtex Division; International Playtex Division sold Max Factor to the Revlon Group, Inc., 1986; Revlon later sold Max Factor along with German cosmetics company, Betrix, to Procter & Gamble Company, 1991; Max Factor & Company was renamed Max Factor International in 1993.

*Performance:* Market share—5% of 1991 U.S. mass market cosmetics sales. Sales—$690 million worldwide in 1992, $185 million U.S.

*Advertising:* Agency—(United States) Lotas Minard Patton McIver, New York, NY, 1991—; (Europe and Japan) Leo Burnett Company, Chicago, IL, 1991—. Major campaign—"Impact—for the woman who has it and the woman who wants it."

*Major competitor:* Revlon; also Maybelline and Cover Girl Cosmetics.

*Addresses: Parent company*—Max Factor International, 1 Procter & Gamble Plaza, Cincinnati, OH 45202; phone: (513) 983-1100; fax: (513) 562-4500. *Ultimate parent company*—Procter & Gamble Company (address same as above).

clude hair pieces. The company's Hair Department became famous for its contributions in developing hair products and wigs. Max Factor produced the first wig made of human hair to be used in the movies and also invented hairlace wigs—wigs that created a natural-looking hairline. For each movie star who needed a hair piece for a film, the Hair Department created a wooden mold of the actor's head, which could then be used to custom fit wigs without the lengthy fitting sessions at the salon that had previously been necessary. Max Factor later expanded its offerings to the general public with Flatter Wigs for women and a self-measurement hairpiece chart with which a man could order a custom-made toupee through the mail. Factor's mail-order hairpieces were accompanied by an unconditional guarantee of satisfaction.

One of Max Factor's most important contributions to the cosmetics industry occurred during the mid-1930s in concurrence with the introduction of color film. Makeup that had been used successfully in black and white films made actors look unnatural on color film, frequently causing their faces to reflect the colors surrounding them. This meant an actor might end up blending in with the set or his or her clothing. In response to this problem, Max Factor created Pan-Cake makeup. Pan-Cake makeup had a matte finish that closely reflected natural skin tones and helped eliminate the problem of actors' faces reflecting the colors around them. Called Pan-Cake because of its flat, round container, the makeup was so popular among actresses that they began wearing it outside the studio. As Pan-Cake makeup became the standard throughout the industry, the general public began clamoring for Max Factor's latest creation. The company introduced its newest cosmetic through full-color print ads that featured various movie stars. Max Factor recognized its great success with Pan-Cake makeup and registered it as a trademark in 1937. The company later modified Pan-Cake makeup and in 1948 introduced a stick form called Pan-

Stik makeup. Pan-Cake makeup continues to be one of the largest selling items in the cosmetics industry.

The invention of television led to new challenges in cosmetics development for Max Factor. The company consulted with the industry to determine its requirements and then introduced a line of products designed specifically for the unique eye of the television camera. In 1954 the company introduced a line of cosmetics designed for color television that became the standard product line for the industry. The most popular of these new products was Erase, the first concealer.

## Sales and Acquisitions

After the death of Max Factor in 1938, Factor's four sons assumed control of the company, maintaining the founder's innovative traditions throughout the 1940s and 1950s. In the early 1960s, however, tentative plans were made to merge family-owned Max Factor with two other corporations, first with Lanvin-Parfums, Inc. in 1963, then American Cyanamid Company in 1964. Profits of $6.3 million on sales of $73 million in 1963 had made the company a worthy investment, but after lengthy negotiations, both merger attempts were terminated. Company sales continued to climb, and Max Factor reported net sales of $187.5 million with a net income of $16.5 million for 1969. Two years later the company introduced the first waterproof mascara, yet another industry breakthrough.

During the early 1970s, Max Factor held the number three spot in cosmetics in the United States. The company's focus was predominantly overseas, however, where approximately 60 percent of net income from sales was generated. In late 1972 Max Factor again considered a merger and in 1973 was acquired by Norton Simon Inc. (NSI) for $480 million. This sale marked the beginning of serious problems for the company, including numerous changes in management and a substantial, long-term decline in both sales and reputation.

## Brand Expansion

Following the acquisition, Max Factor developed several new products and product lines. While sales continued to flourish in Factor's overseas markets, its U.S. sales suffered. The Just Call Me Maxi fragrance line, introduced in 1977, proved unpopular and cost the company over $10 million in product development and advertising. NSI had reassigned funds from other Max Factor brands to promote the new fragrance, and the company's other product lines suffered as a result. The failure of this latest creation was reflected in Max Factor's gross profits, which slipped from $34.1 million in 1977 to just $12.6 million in 1978. One industry observer, quoted in *Advertising Age,* deemed Just Call Me Maxi "the biggest industry bomb ever."

The failure of the fragrance line resulted in changes in top management at the company. A new long-range plan to revitalize the company was developed and put into place in 1979. Two advertising campaigns were launched to rejuvenate Max Factor's reputation and encourage brand loyalty among women in the 18- to 45-year-old age range. The first campaign, designed for 18- to 30-year-old women, centered on the slogan "Take Your Face to Maxi." The second was targeted at wealthier women who were between the ages of 25 and 44. This campaign carried the slogan "Don't You Love Being a Woman?" The company's efforts proved successful, and sales and profits increased steadily between 1980 and 1982.

The new campaigns were accompanied by the introduction in 1979 of Colorfast, a long-wearing lipstick, and the Epris fragrance in 1980. Hoping to capitalize on the success of Epris, which was promoted with advertisements featuring actress Jaclyn Smith, Max Factor created Le Jardin de Max Factor perfume in 1983. Actress Jane Seymour was contracted to serve as spokesperson for Le Jardin de Max Factor in advertisements that emphasized the romance of the scent. NSI earmarked $6 million for launching the fragrance. While both perfumes—particularly Le Jardin de Max Factor—earned respectable market shares, the company lost money in 1983 due to a recession that affected many of its strongest overseas markets.

As a result of 1983 losses, NSI sold Max Factor to Esmark Company. This acquisition marked the first of three such corporate ownership transitions in approximately three years. Sales continued to decline and Max Factor claimed only ten percent of the U.S. mass market for cosmetics, having fallen from third to fourth place behind Revlon, Maybelline, and Cover Girl Cosmetics. The following year Esmark, along with Max Factor, was acquired by German manufacturer Beatrice Companies. Beatrice placed Max Factor into its International Playtex Division, but did not invest enough resources or capital to greatly revitalize the company. While Max Factor sales increased slightly in 1984, the company was still spending five to ten times less on advertising than its top competitors.

In 1985 Max Factor introduced its Light and Natural makeup line using a "heritage" advertising campaign that featured long-time brand spokeswoman Jaclyn Smith complimenting Max Factor's contributions to the industry in creating some of Hollywood's most famous faces. The ads concluded with Smith saying "The glamour goes on" and "Thanks Max." Again, while International Playtex increased the company's advertising budget, promotional spending for Max Factor was still far below that of the leading mass-market cosmetics companies, and the new product line was not overly successful.

In 1986 negotiations were completed by International Playtex to sell Max Factor, along with its Almay and Halston lines, to the Revlon Group, Inc. for approximately $300 million. This acquisition amount reflected the general decline of Max Factor, which had sold in 1973 for $480 million. The acquisition of Max Factor boosted Revlon back into the top spot in mass-market makeup sales, a position it had relinquished the prior year.

In conjunction with the acquisition, Max Factor introduced "The California look," a new line of fragrances ranging from a mass-market eau de cologne to a limited edition perfume priced at $200. The advertising budget for the line was set at $10 million and featured Jaclyn Smith in print and television advertisements with the slogan "The fragrance that captures the dream." The California line was based on the company's hunch that American women wanted to be "California girls."

In the years following its acquisition of Max Factor, Revlon experienced numerous financial difficulties. As a result, Max Factor and Betrix, a German beauty products company, were sold to the Procter & Gamble Company in 1991 for over $1 billion. Procter & Gamble, which also owns Cover Girl Cosmetics and Clarion, sought Max Factor to increase its U.S. share of mass market cosmetics and to strengthen its international position in European and Asian cosmetics markets (eighty percent of combined Max Factor and Betrix sales were outside the United States). Procter & Gamble made plans to increase sales of Max Factor in the United States and utilize Betrix as a vehicle for promoting the Cover Girl line overseas. Sales of Max Factor in 1991 accounted for only five percent, or $80 million, of the U.S. mass market cosmetics industry.

## Procter & Gamble Encourages Growth of Brand

Procter & Gamble began its expansion and revitalization of Max Factor by assigning the U.S. cosmetics line to the New York advertising agency Lotas Minard Patton McIver. Plans were made to relaunch Max Factor as Max Factor International in a campaign that focused on promoting it as the premier cosmetics brand worldwide. This relaunch included completely overhauling the Max Factor line from products and packaging to advertising and store displays. According to a report in *Women's Wear Daily,* new color palettes were created using "the colors that exist around the world." Prices for the new "global" Max Factor were set at eight to twenty percent above existing prices, and Procter & Gamble set aside $20 million in 1993 and $25 million in 1994 for advertising and promotion. The Max Factor line was standardized across markets, and the same television and print advertisements were used internationally. Procter & Gamble estimated that its expanded line would increase worldwide sales of Max Factor by roughly $50 million in the first year alone.

The global roll-out of Max Factor International was plagued with problems, however, as the company underestimated the amount of time necessary to transfer the product line from Revlon to Procter & Gamble plants. Shipments of the new line were months behind schedule, leaving many retailers angry and without stock. Procter & Gamble cleaned up the production problems associated with the corporate transition, and the new Max Factor International cosmetics line was launched in 1993.

Despite this initial setback, Max Factor is well positioned in the 1990s to recoup its losses in sales and reputation and to expand both in the United States and overseas. As evidenced by a strong investment of capital and resources, Procter & Gamble has shown its commitment to reestablishing Max Factor's reputation as *the* name in cosmetics.

## Further Reading:

Brookman, Faye, "Stores Rate the Delivery Factor," *Women's Wear Daily,* January 8, 1993, p. 8.

Kagan, Cara, "Procter & Gamble Puts a Global Spin on Max Factor," *Women's Wear Daily,* February 19, 1993, p. 8.

"The Max Factor in Mahoney's Life," *Business Week,* November 18, 1972, pp. 22–3.

"Max Factor Company History," New York: DeVries Public Relations.

Ramirez, Anthony, "Asset Sale by Revlon Called Near," *New York Times,* April 10, 1991, pp. D1, D4; "P&G Gets Revlon's Max Factor," *New York Times,* April 11, 1991, pp. D1, D5.

Schiller, Zachary and Larry Light, "Procter & Gamble Is Following Its Nose," *Business Week,* p. 28.

Sloan, Pat and Jennifer Lawrence, "What P&G Plans for Cosmetics," *Advertising Age,* April 15, 1991, p. 3, 46.

Stroud, Ruth, "Max Factor Tries to Make Up Lost Ground," *Advertising Age,* April 1, 1985, pp. 4, 80.

—*Shannon Young*

# MAYBELLINE®

Few brands can claim the kind of enduring success that the Maybelline brand of cosmetics can. From its humble beginnings in a Chicago boarding house in the early 20th century, through changes in parent company, to the highly competitive 1990s, Maybelline remained a leader in the U.S. cosmetics market. Perhaps the most telling aspect of Maybelline's success is that its top product is the same one that started the company: mascara. In the early 1990s Maybelline was owned by Wasserstein Perella Management Partners, Inc., as part of Maybelline, Inc., an umbrella that also covers Maybelline International and Yardley. The brand continues to have fresh appeal with its target group, 18- to 34-year-old female consumers, and with women of all ages, who find the products accessible and affordable.

## Brand Origins

In 1915, when Mabel Williams applied a homemade petroleum jelly-based concoction to her eyelids and lashes, her brother T. L. Williams took note. Thinking that this inexpensive makeup might be a profitable addition to his mail-order business, he took the idea to a chemist friend. The mix of jelly and black pigment was packaged in small tins. Although the original name for the mascara was Lash-Brow-Ine, Williams renamed it Maybelline (after his sister) and copyrighted the name in 1920. The success of the product through Williams's mail-order business led to its sales in dime stores. Williams's original philosophy still drives Maybelline. According to the company, he felt that his product should "perform as promised; ensure customer satisfaction and repeat sales; be easy to use; create an instant, observable beauty transformation; have universal appeal to women of all ages and backgrounds."

## Brand Development

For most of the company's early years, it concentrated on eye makeup. In 1970 Maybelline introduced its now-famous Great Lash mascara, which is the largest single-selling mascara in the world. In 1973 the company expanded beyond its successful line of eye makeup into other categories such as blush, lipstick, and nail polish. During the 1970s, the company also introduced Great Lash, Fresh Lash, and Ultra Big Ultra Lash, which dominated the mascara category into 1993. The company introduced the Shine Free line of products for teens in 1982, the Shades of You line for

women of color in 1991, and the Revitalizing Face collection in 1993, extending its reach to all age and ethnic groups.

In 1975 Maybelline opened a 300,000-square-foot manufacturing facility in North Little Rock, Arkansas, only 150 miles from its research, sales, and administrative offices in Memphis, Tennessee. In 1993 the company described the plant as state-of-the-art after having increased the size to 800,000 square feet, adding high-tech machines for moving merchandise and for computerized inventory control and order fulfillment. Quality control was also a high priority at the plant, which boasted a minimum of 25 quality checks per batch.

Maybelline also claimed to be one of the first cosmetics companies to devise general requirements for hypoallergenic testing and counted itself among the first to add sunscreen protection to makeup. Maybelline introduced the claim that all of its mascaras were contact lens and sensitive-eye friendly in 1988. In addition, the company stated that all facial cosmetics were non-comedogenic (would not clog pores), hypoallergenic, and dermatologist-tested.

By the late 1980s declining sales indicated that it was time to infuse new energy into Maybelline. In 1986 Maybelline found itself number two to rival Cover Girl for the first time. As a result, seven new products were introduced in 1987 to combat disappointing sales in 1986. The new products were in the eye makeup category, the company's strongest. Gary M. Mulloy, then senior vice-president of marketing, advertising, and market research, felt that Maybelline had rested on its laurels in the early 1980s. "I think we stopped innovating and creating excitement and exciting new products and shade promotions," Mulloy was quoted as saying in *Women's Wear Daily*.

## Advertising Strategies

Although advertising was still in its infancy in the early part of the 20th century, T. L. Williams believed in its future. Williams's first ad for Maybelline ran in popular magazines and encouraged women to "Beautify your lashes with Lash-Brow-Ine; send 25 cents." Response was encouraging enough that Williams believed that advertising would play a significant role in his new product's sales. From the early days of Williams's magazine advertising through the 1990s, not a single month has gone by that Maybelline has not been advertised. Maybelline's was the first cosmetic ad-

## AT A GLANCE

**M**aybelline brand of cosmetics founded in 1915 by T. L. Williams; became a registered trademark in 1920; brand sold to Plough, Inc. in 1967; company changed name to Schering-Plough, Inc. when it merged with Schering Corporation. Maybelline brand sold to Wasserstein Perella Management Partners, Inc. in 1990.

**Performance:** *Market share*—Approximately 18% of cosmetics category (1992). *Sales*—Approximately $307 million (1992).

**Major competitor:** Procter & Gamble Company's Cover Girl.

**Advertising:** *Agency*—Lintas, Inc., 1991—. *Major campaign*—"Maybe she's born with it. Maybe it's Maybelline," featuring supermodel Christy Turlington.

**Addresses:** *Parent company*—Maybelline, Inc., 3030 Jackson Ave., Memphis, TN 38112-2010; phone: (901) 324-0310; fax: (901) 320-4950.

vertised on radio and television, and the company also pioneered advertising on Hispanic television.

Advertising for Maybelline has historically relied on celebrity tie-ins and endorsements. Hedy Lamarr promoted the products in movie magazines of the 1940s, and Joan Crawford's ads declared she "would never be without" Maybelline. Although these early ads seemed to imply that Maybelline was glamorous, the company has touted its affordability and practicality throughout the years. For many years Maybelline used the slogan "fine makeup, sensibly priced" as its primary advertising tag line.

In 1980 the company signed actress Lynda Carter, known primarily for playing "Wonder Woman" on the television series of the same name, to a long-term contract as its primary spokeswoman. Carter was given the title beauty and fashion director and acted as a consultant on new product development and marketing. Carter was featured in ads for Moisture Whip skin care and cosmetics and during the first three years of her tenure increased sales for the company by 200 percent. Carter remained a Maybelline spokeswoman for more than ten years.

After buying Maybelline in 1990 from Schering-Plough, Wasserstein Perella Management Partners revamped its advertising strategy by dramatically increasing the advertising budget—from $35 million to $50 million—and replacing Carter. (Besides being associated with a tired campaign, Carter's credibility as a spokeswoman was compromised by husband Richard Altman's involvement in the BCCI banking scandal.) In addition, the new owners were "seeking to infuse its plain and practical cosmetics line with generous helpings of glamour and glitz," according to a *New York Times* article.

The influx of advertising dollars was part of a four-part strategy that included new packaging, product formulations, and products. Robert N. Hiatt, Maybelline president and chief executive officer, declared the new strategy to be "a rebirth of a classic," and hoped it would "fundamentally change the way the customer thinks about Maybelline." Along with introductions of new products, the company also dropped 150 poorly performing products from a line that had totaled 560. Longtime agency DDB Needham was replaced with Lintas, Inc. (which had been Cover Girl's agency until its acquisition by Procter & Gamble). Supermodel Christy Tur-

lington was signed, and the tag line "Maybe she's born with it. Maybe it's Maybelline" was introduced. Scheduled to run throughout 1992, the campaign was intended to reach 90 percent of all U.S. women between the ages of 18 and 49 at the rate of 4.7 times per month. The company purchased commercial slots on prime-time television, daytime soap operas, cable television, and print ads in *Vogue*, *YM*, *Cosmopolitan*, and *Glamour* magazines.

### Changes in Parent Company

Founder T. L. Williams and his family owned Maybelline as a private company until 1967 when he sold it to Plough, Inc. of Memphis, Tennessee. In 1971 Plough merged with Schering Corporation to become Schering-Plough, a multinational pharmaceutical company. Maybelline's new parent was eager for the brand to grow. The company expanded the line, increased advertising spending, and updated the look of the line. Under the ownership of Schering-Plough, Maybelline made great strides in line extension, visibility, advertising, and product innovations. Schering-Plough intended to position Maybelline as "the cosmetics authority," according to the company's 1980 annual report. To realize this goal, instructions were highlighted and featured in packaging and in booklets in women's magazines. Nevertheless, the late 1980s saw a return by large companies to their core businesses and Schering-Plough was no exception. Just as the Eli Lily and Squibb pharmaceutical companies were selling their cosmetics divisions, Schering-Plough announced in 1989 that it would sell Maybelline.

According to a 1989 article in *Reuter Business Report,* Schering-Plough sought to "shed its financially unpredictable beauty-products arm" and reported that Maybelline had been a "drain on the pharmaceutical company's bottom line because of low profit margins and rocky sales." Proceeds from the sale also strengthened the company and helped it brace itself against takeover attempts. According to the company's 1989 annual report, the decision to seek offers for Maybelline reflected its new focus on prescription and over-the-counter pharmaceuticals, and personal care and vision care products. The company had already sold its two foreign cosmetics companies, Rimmel and Chicogo, the previous year.

Although analysts predicted that Maybelline could bring between $420 and $560 million when the initial announcement was made, the company was actually sold for a disappointing $300 million. After an initial deal with MBP Acquisitions Corporation (which also owned Playtex) fell through, Maybelline was acquired by Wasserstein Perella Management Partners, Inc. in July of 1990. In July of 1992 Wasserstein announced the sale of over $83 million in stock (in excess of 20 percent of the company) to the public.

### Market Segmentation

Although Maybelline has traditionally counted women from 18 to 34 as its strongest customers, it has always attempted to appeal to women of all age groups and races. Because of its price and easy availability in drug stores and supermarkets, Maybelline has been the first makeup for many young girls, thus establishing strong brand loyalty.

In keeping with the original wishes of T. L. Williams that Maybelline have "universal appeal to women of all ages and backgrounds," in February of 1991 the company introduced Shades of You. This line of cosmetics was intended for women of color and soon became number one in its category. In 1993 the company launched a national advertising campaign for its Revitalizing line, for women 35 and older. Shine Free products were aimed at young women from 12 to 20 whose primary cosmetic problems were controlling oily skin and blemishes.

## The Industry Environment

The cosmetics industry in the United States is generally divided into two large categories, known in industry jargon as "class and mass." In the class category are the upscale brands sold exclusively in department stores and featuring a significantly higher price point. Mass refers to brands sold through drug stores, supermarkets, and beauty outlets. In 1967 when Maybelline was bought by Plough, Inc., it became one of the first cosmetics companies in newly created mass-market outlets. While the class cosmetic producers have a higher profit margin, they are much more vulnerable to economic downturns. By the mid-1980s the percent of cosmetics purchased in department stores was declining while at the same time the mass-market cosmetics industry was changing the look of its products to more closely mirror its high-end competitors.

The department store environment has also proven to be a significant drain on the profits of the high-end cosmetics companies. A large percentage of sales must be shared with the stores while the companies must still pay their own promotional costs and pay 100 percent commission to their salespeople. Companies like Maybelline have stepped up the competition by creating more upscale packaging and using the same terminology in describing its products as the class marketers. A *Forbes* contributor pointed to the trend away from high priced makeup and noted that "in this new world of cosmetics, there will be winners and losers. The likely beneficiaries in the mass market arena are all publicly traded companies: Maybelline. . . . "

## Performance Appraisal

Roughly from its introduction in 1915 until 1986, Maybelline has been the market leader in cosmetics. In 1986 longtime rival Cover Girl eclipsed Maybelline for the first time and claimed the top spot, although Maybelline mascaras still outsold all other brands. Maybelline fought hard to regain its position, and though changes in ownership and marketing philosophy made it difficult, a dramatic increase in advertising spending in the early 1990s helped close the gap. In 1993 Maybelline was still attempting to overtake Cover Girl.

## Future Predictions

Wasserstein Perella's aggressive plans for Maybelline may well place the brand back on the throne as reigning cosmetics queen. In addition, the company's revival of Maybelline, Inc.'s Yardley North America has already shown a return on their investment. Maybelline's attempt to expand its primary customer base beyond 18- to 34-year-olds reflects a realization that the number of younger women will decline from 12.3 million to 10.3 million by the year 2000. A new introduction of an existing line for baby-boomer women, called Maybelline Revitalizing, began in March of 1993 as a result of Maybelline's continuing market and demographic research.

The industry itself is also growing and, according to *Going Public: The IPO Reporter,* "the segment, which consists of mass merchandisers, drug stores and food stores, is the largest and fastest growing segment of the $3.4 billion domestic color cosmetics market." Maybelline's long history, large consumer base, strong presence in all mass market retail outlets, understanding of fashion trends, growing international presence, and high level of brand recognition indicate that the brand will continue to be a major force in this growing industry well into the future. In January of 1993 Robert Hiatt noted, "Our strategic business plan has proved to be right on track, and for 1993 we will continue to increase consumer demand for Maybelline cosmetics, build the recently-acquired Yardley brand, and expand distribution in international markets."

## Further Reading:

Allen, Margaret, *Selling Dreams: Inside the Beauty Business,* New York: Simon and Schuster, 1981.

Ellis-Simons, Pamela, "A Model Makeover; Cosmetics Industry Winner Maybelline the Top Marketing Success of 1988," *Marketing & Media Decisions,* March, 1989, p. 64.

*Schering-Plough Annual Reports,* Madison, NJ: Schering-Plough Corp., 1980–1990.

Shaffer, Marjorie, "Schering-Plough to Sell Maybelline Cosmetics Business," *Reuter Business Report,* December 12, 1989.

—*Kate Sheehan*

# MEAD® SCHOOL AND OFFICE PRODUCTS

Mead School and Office Products is the largest manufacturer of school supplies in the United States, marketing over 3000 items. The company also produces stationery products for use at home and in the office. Mead School and Office Products is a division of the Mead Corporation, a large paper, wood, and electronic publishing company with annual sales of $4.6 billion. Mead has developed and marketed many of the all-time best sellers in the retail school supply and stationery markets, including the Spiral brand of school supplies.

## Brand Origins

Mead Corporation's division of School and Office Products was formed by a merger between Mead Corporation and Westab Inc., a stationery manufacturer based in St. Joseph, Missouri. Founded in 1906 under the name Western Tablet Company, Westab manufactured paper tablets, loose-leaf paper, greeting cards, and stationery. In 1927 the firm merged with Miami Tablet Company, Kalamazoo Stationery Company, Hopper Paper Company, and Smith Tablet Company. The new company, Western Tablet and Stationery, was headquartered in Dayton, Ohio, and operated plants in Ohio, Missouri, Michigan, Virginia, and Massachusetts. Western Tablet and Stationery later acquired J. C. Blair Company in 1929 and the Montag Stationery Company in 1961.

In 1964 Western Tablet was renamed Westab Incorporated. Under the direction of president Paul Allemang, Westab Inc. merged with Mead Corporation in 1966. Allemang assumed an executive administrative position with Mead Corporation under president George Pringle in 1967. The following year, James W. McSwiney, who had been pushing Mead to diversify and had been responsible for Mead's acquisition of Westab, became president and CEO of Mead. By the end of the 1960s McSwiney had steered Mead into a dozen different markets such as cement, limestone, computerized legal research, and school and office products. The Westab division of Mead retained its name until 1976, when it became Mead School and Office Products.

## Brand Development

Mead began replacing the standard blue canvas loose-leaf binders in the 1960s. The company developed the Spiral line of school supplies in the early 1970s, pioneering the method of binding loose-leaf paper together with wire and establishing the

company as a leader in school supply and stationery design. The wire-bound notebook has developed into a number of related products, including the Spiral Organizer notebook, which was introduced in 1974. The Organizer features a tri-fold wire-bound notebook with pockets. The Spiral and the Spiral Organizer are top selling items during the back-to-school season.

### Further Product Introductions

Since the 1970s Mead has featured a number of new wire-bound products. The Flex 3 notebook consists of three expandable pockets with velcro tabs. The Five Star line of products includes wire-bound notebooks and laminated portfolios on heavyweight paper with long lasting covers. In 1987 Mead began marketing the Wireless Notebook, which features perforated tear seams that provide a smooth edge when the page is removed from the notebook, eliminating the ragged edges of paper torn from a spiral notebook. The Trapper Keeper line of binders and portfolios feature a vertical pocket for loose papers and a closure flap with a velcro tab. Introduced in 1989, the Mead Grad is geared toward the older student. Mead Grad products include a wire-bound notebook with pressboard covers and black wire, as well as portfolios with two cut vertical pockets.

During the 1980s Mead began using licensed characters for the covers of notebooks and other school supplies. Characters licensed for use on Mead products include Garfield, the Sophisticats, and Critter Sitters. Mead has also offered a portfolio folder with a mirror on the front, which is embellished with drawings of beauty products like mascara and lipstick. The Safari Party is a line of pre-school activity items first introduced in 1990. These brightly colored items such as junior organizers and drawing pads are marketed for children between three and seven years old. Mead introduced a line of products made from recycled paper in 1992.

New back-to-school items introduced by Mead in 1993 include the Major League Baseball Upper Deck collection of school supplies and an update of the Five Star line of products. The Upper Deck Collection features binders and folders that include baseball cards and statistical information on current players. Mead also offers memo pads and portfolios that feature color reproductions of popular players. The Five Star Day Planner contains academic sections and places for class and activity schedules.

## AT A GLANCE

**W**estern Tablet Company founded in 1906 in St. Joseph, Missouri; merged with Kalamazoo Stationery Company in 1927; company changed name to Westab Incorporated, 1964; became a division of Mead Corporation, 1966; division changed name to Mead School and Office Products, 1976.

**Advertising:** *Agency*—Partners & Shevack, New York, NY; also Sive Associates, Cincinnati, OH.

**Addresses:** *Parent company*—Mead Corporation, Courthouse Plaza, NE, Dayton, Ohio, 45463; phone: (513) 222-6323.

## Marketing Strategy

Traditionally, the back-to-school season is the peak sales period for Mead. In 1970 Mead began advertising their school and office products on national television, and eventually became one of the largest television advertisers during the back-to-school season. The company introduces anywhere from 10 to 15 new designs each year, based on the responses of test market groups which measure the preferences of students, teachers, and parents. Mead School and Office Products Division has surveyed up to 2,000 children in primary and high schools, soliciting suggestions and asking their preferences in design and color for various items.

## Quick Response Distribution System

Mead School and Office Products markets more than 3,000 items through its national sales group. Some school and office products are sold through distributors and wholesalers, while a large portion of Mead products are sold directly to department, drug, and convenience chain stores by the Mead sales force. Mead has established electronic connections with 40 of the nation's leading retailers, creating an information sharing network through which data from each Mead purchase is recorded through optical scanning and provided to both Mead and the retailer. Retailers can electronically upgrade their receiving and inventory databases, and items are automatically reordered to maintain inventories, enabling Mead to cut down the turnaround time for customer orders. The company has invested heavily in the new system, which "requires a large amount of information sharing between customer and supplier," according to Dave Reinhart, Mead's manager of the Quick Response system.

## Sales

Sales figures for Mead School and Office Products are combined with those of Zellerbach Co., a Mead distribution company that distributes paper, machinery, packaging materials, and commercial and industrial supplies to a large number of regional markets in the United States. Zellerbach and the School and Office Products division make up the Distribution and School and Office Products segment of the Mead Corporation.

Sales figures for the segment for 1992 were down two percent over 1991, to $1.95 billion. Sales for the segment were $1.99 billion in 1991, which was a nine percent decline from the record $2.18 billion in 1990. Mead attributes the decline in sales to lower prices and lower volume during a sluggish economic period.

The Mead School and Office Products division is the largest manufacturer of school supplies in the United States. The division is headquartered in Dayton, Ohio, but operates sales offices and manufacturing plants at various locations around the United States. Mead School and Office Products operates major manufacturing plants in the following locations: Garden Grove, California; Atlanta, Georgia; Kalamazoo, Michigan; St. Joseph, Missouri; Salem, Oregon; Alexandria, Pennsylvania; and Garland, Texas.

For the past 25 years Mead School and Office Products has been a leader in school and office supply manufacturing. The company is beginning to focus on boosting sales during periods other than the back-to-school season. Mead will then be able to staff its manufacturing plants more efficiently, which should increase revenues. In a move to maintain its leadership position, Mead School and Office Products has made significant investments in the automation of its order processing and inventory control systems. The Quick Response System will provide clients with faster service, cut down on paperwork, and help control inventory costs, all of which should help Mead maintain its leadership role in the school supply and retail stationery markets.

## Further Reading:

Carr, William, *Up Another Notch: Institution Building at Mead,* New York: McGraw-Hill, 1989.

Cohen, Shara, "Array of Supplies Put Students in a Daze," *Los Angeles Times,* September 3, 1992, p. E3.

Gellene, Denise, "Teen Buying Spree: Retailers Study up for School Days," *Los Angeles Times,* September 9, 1986, p. A1.

*A History of Mead School and Office Products,* Dayton, Ohio: Mead, 1990.

"Mead Corp. to Lay Off 1,000," *New York Times,* July 3, 1992, p. D3.

*Mead Corporation and Consolidated Industries Annual Report,* Dayton, Ohio: Mead, 1992.

Moss, Marie, "Earthly Delights: It's Time to Put Your Greenbacks Where Your Eco-Heart Is," *Chicago Tribune,* April 22, 1992, p. 19.

Shapiro, Eben, "Retail Sales Look Weak for August," *New York Times,* September 3, 1991, p. D1.

Sherman, Beth, "It's the Back to School Show," *Newsday,* August 23, 1990, p. 3.

Sporkin, Elizabeth, "A Trend of Note: Composition Books," *USA Today,* December 4, 1989, p. D1.

*—William Tivenan*

# MENNEN®

# MENNEN

Mennen personal care products have been offered in the United States for over 100 years. Health and beauty aids marketed under the umbrella brand include: Afta, Sof' Stroke, and Skin Bracer shaving products; Speed Stick, Lady Speed Stick, and Teen Spirit deodorants and antiperspirants; Baby Magic baby care products and other skin, hair, and foot care products. The brand's moderately priced line is offered in supermarkets, drug stores, and mass merchandise outlets in over 100 countries throughout the world. The family-owned Mennen Company was purchased by Colgate-Palmolive Co. in 1992 and has been strengthened by the new parent's worldwide presence.

## Brand Origins

Mennen was founded in 1878 by Gerhard H. Mennen, a German pharmacist who immigrated to the United States at the age of 15. After graduating from the New York School of Pharmacy, Mennen purchased a corner drug store in Newark, New Jersey. Like many other marketers of the nineteenth century, Mennen offered products bearing his name and image as a personal endorsement of their quality. The first product marketed under his namesake brand, Mennen's Sure Corn Killer, was hand-packed at the back of the pharmacy. In 1889 Mennen broadened his product line and became the United States' first marketer of baby products with the introduction of Mennen's Borated Talcum Powder. The likeness of a baby on the package was meant to appeal to mothers and hint at one of the product's many uses. The Mennen baby was actually the child of a proud supply salesman who happened to show the pharmacist a photo during the product's development.

Gerhard Mennen has been touted as a naturally talented marketer. He recognized the importance of advertising, and declared that he would stay ahead of the competition by devoting half of Mennen's profits to advertising. Mennen utilized local advertising and promotions to expand distribution of the branded products from local retailers to regional, and eventually national, outlets. His personal endorsement must have impressed consumers, because he was soon overwhelmed with the talcum powder trade and moved to a larger headquarters.

## Product Innovations

Mennen's packaging innovations brought the brand increasing success and set standards that were hard to keep up with in later years. Baby powder packaging evolved from a cardboard container to a metal can with a shaker top. The innovation kept the product drier and made it easier to dispense. Later packaging included a rotating sifter top and a container with double seams to prevent leakage. Known as the "Mennen seam," the packaging improvement was adopted by many competitors. Mennen was also the originator of shaving cream in a tube.

When Gerhard Mennen died during the first decade of the twentieth century, his wife, Elma, took the reins until son William G. Mennen graduated from Cornell University in 1908. William, who directed Mennen for more than five decades, went on to expand the brand to include "Baby Magic by Mennen." The Baby Magic line included lotions, liquid bath soaps, and oils that were specially formulated to be gentle to babies' skin. Grey Advertising of New York launched Baby Magic in 1950, just as the postwar baby boom was getting underway. The line soon outsold Mennen's original array of baby products.

Mennen continued under family control throughout most of the twentieth century, and private ownership meant that its sales figures were closely guarded. William's son, George S. Mennen, took over in 1963 and oversaw several product innovations and line extensions during his 18-year presidency. The brand's Speed Stick antiperspirant, introduced in 1958, was the first stick deodorant in a market then dominated by cream competitors like Arrid and Mum. Although aerosol delivery enjoyed market domination over most of the next decade, Speed Stick began to gain market share in the mid-1970s. Rising public health concerns over both the ingredients in aerosols and their impact on the ozone layer combined with economic pressures that made sticks a more thrifty delivery method than sprays. Mennen's Skin Bracer was one of the first aftershave lotions. Mennen was able to boost sales by creating this new category of men's toiletries. Both products maintained top positions in their markets into the 1990s.

## Flops Mark Mid-Century

The weight of a historically innovative company may have proven too heavy for Mennen in the 1970s. Some of its new product launches suffered misguided marketing, while others were thwarted by outside forces. Protein 21 shampoo was launched in 1971 and achieved unprecedented initial market share and strong performance in diverse markets around the world. It was touted as a healer of split ends, but sales suffered when the product didn't deliver.

## AT A GLANCE

**M**ennen brand founded in 1878 in Newark, NJ, by pharmacist Gerhard H. Mennen; headquarters later moved to Morristown, New Jersey; introduced first shaker talcum powder and first stick deodorant; purchased by Colgate-Palmolive Co. in 1992.

**Performance:** *Market share*—Speed Stick 17%, top individual brand of antiperspirant/deodorant; Baby Magic 20%, second ranked brand of baby toiletries; Lady Speed Stick, fourth ranked brand of women's antiperspirant/deodorant. *Sales*—$450 million (all personal care products combined).

**Major competitor:** Procter & Gamble's Sure (10% of antiperspirant/deodorant market), Johnson & Johnson Baby Powder (57.8% of baby toiletries market), Procter & Gamble's Secret (14% of women's antiperspirant/deodorant market).

**Advertising:** *Agency*—For Speed Stick: McCann-Erickson Worldwide, New York, NY, 1985—; for Baby Magic, Skin Bracer, Real: Lowe Marschalk, Inc., New York, NY, 1985—. *Major campaign*—The tag line, "By Mennen."

**Addresses:** *Parent company*—The Mennen Company, Hanover Avenue, Morristown, NJ 07960; phone (201) 631-9000; fax:(201) 292-6117. *Ultimate parent company*—Colgate-Palmolive Co., 300 Park Avenue, New York, NY 10022; phone (212) 310-2000.

In 1972 Mennen made a revolutionary discovery that it hoped would set its deodorant products apart from all others and make it demonstrably superior. Dr. Harold Schwartz and Dr. Robert Suffis, of Mennen's research department, found that Vitamin E, among other attributes, prevented underarm odor from developing. Mennen set out to develop a product that would take advantage of this breakthrough. The research and development department and marketing team worked quickly to create, test market, and launch the product. Time was of the essence because Vitamin E, as a natural element, could not be patented; the door was thus wide open to competition.

During the product's development, the U.S. government seemed to give "Mennen E" even more of an edge by compelling the removal of hexachlorophene, a germicide and the active ingredient in most deodorants. Many deodorants switched to a formulation with aluminum salts, which constrict the pores to prevent perspiration, as an active ingredient. Mennen E was felt to be superior in that it prevented odor without pore constriction or clogging.

After hasty, "simulated" market tests and carefully released articles announcing the scientific discovery of Vitamin E's deodorant qualities, Mennen E was launched with a $1.3 million campaign that featured a series of 30-second television commercials and print ads. The brand's market share for its first three months outperformed any other deodorant entry to date, garnering 2.2 percent of the total marketplace with distribution in only half of the supermarkets and 75 percent of drug and mass merchandising businesses.

But this exciting initial performance was followed by a Federal Trade Commission investigation of all Mennen E's product claims. Although Mennen was able to support its health and deodorizing claims, the Food & Drug Administration reported receipt of about 50 letters complaining of irritation from Mennen E, and this second government agency forced the removal of the product from the market without further testing. The stinging rebuff may have impacted Mennen's rate of new product introductions in the decades to come.

## International Expansion

Mennen International's operations started with headquarters in Paris, France, in 1965. Long-term joint venture agreements with L'Oréal S.A. helped Mennen establish its men's "green line" in France and Italy, then throughout Europe. The line's liquid aftershaves, pre-shaves, and colognes were distributed in the United Kingdom, Finland, Sweden, Holland, Denmark, and Norway by the end of the decade. Mennen's aftershaves quickly achieved market leadership in France, Italy, Greece, Finland, and Norway, and occupied second place in Sweden, Holland, Spain, and Belgium by 1972. The brand employed one concept throughout its international promotions, making only slight adaptations in approach and copy from country to country and culture to culture. In late 1971 Mennen moved its overseas headquarters from Paris to Brussels, the seat of the European Common Market.

Since 1929 Mennen has been shipping to Central and South America. By 1992 Mennen Speed Stick had captured 17 percent of France's men's deodorant market, and strong market positions had been gained in Canada, Chile, Costa Rica, Mexico, and Venezuela. Competition from such global giants as Unilever PLC, Gillette Co., Johnson & Johnson, and Procter & Gamble Company, who had seemingly unlimited advertising and research and development budgets, prevented family-owned Mennen from earning a commanding presence elsewhere.

## Segmentation and Competition Force Change

A latecomer to the women's segment of the antiperspirant/deodorant market, Mennen introduced Lady Speed Stick in 1983. Lady Speed Stick rose to the number four spot in this highly competitive segment by the end of the decade, when it was joined by Mennen Real, an ill-fated cream antiperspirant. Feeling that its product sales were skewed towards men, Mennen hoped to capture more of the women's toiletries market with the product. Real was introduced in 1986 with a $14 million print and television campaign, but its phallus-shaped container, unfamiliar applicator, and vague name brought an abrupt end to its sales, and eventually, its marketing support. The product remained in limbo in the early 1990s, but reportedly may launch a comeback under a new name, "Lady Speed Smooth-On."

In late 1989, Mennen's leading position in the men's antiperspirant field was threatened by two new products from Helene Curtis Industries and Unilever. Unilever hoped to break into the American antiperspirant market and thereby increase its leading 18 percent share. The international giant's Powerstick men's deodorant was positioned in direct competition with Mennen's Speed Stick, and shaved 1.5 percent off the leading brand's 16.5 percent market share by the end of 1990.

The challenge was met with $16.7 million in advertising in 1990 and plans for an increased push for 1991. Mennen also employed several promotions that helped its family of sub-brands, but heated competition diminished Mennen's advertising budget in comparison with the global giants. Industry-wide consolidation, combined with a lack of leadership among the youngest members of the Mennen family, prompted Mennen's 1992 sale to Colgate-Palmolive for $670 million.

Mennen's sales increased steadily after the change in ultimate ownership, based on couponing and Colgate's immediate doubling of the brand's advertising budget. Mennen hoped to parlay its brand equity with Colgate's worldwide distribution and marketing influence to make strong advances in global markets. A saturated American market prompted the company's attempt to segment and expand the market with the introduction of Teen Spirit antiperspirant/deodorant, the first brand made exclusively for teens, in 1990. Mennen also joined the new "clear" marketing movement with the introduction of its "Crystal Clean" deodorant, which targeted the 40 percent of American women who considered themselves light perspirers. The clear deodorant gave users the advantage of insuring little or no residue on clothing, but had not yet been formulated to stop perspiration.

In mid-1992, Mennen Speed Stick led the $1.7 billion U.S. market with a 17 percent share, but low pricing by high-volume Procter & Gamble (whose combination of brands led the antiperspirant/deodorant market) kept the level of competition up. New technologies, such as non-aerosol pump delivery and a clear antiperspirant formula, may keep this market in flux through the mid-1990s. Mennen may need to revive its innovative roots to keep up with its global rivals.

Mennen's Baby Magic, however, has enjoyed a resurgence. After losing its hold on baby toiletries in the 1970s, Baby Magic shampoo moved ahead of chief rival Johnson & Johnson in 1990, and the entire line, long stuck at number two, staged a comeback. Competition in this arena was also expected to rise in the 1990s, as products from S.C. Johnson & Son's Fisher-Price, The William Carter Co.'s Carter's Naturals, and Walt Disney Co.'s Baby Mickey & Co. entered the fray.

## Performance Appraisal

Gerhard Mennen founded his namesake brand with a strong focus on marketing and product innovation. His ideals propelled the trademark products to market dominance that went virtually unchallenged for decades. But as competition from publicly owned rivals heated up in the waning decades of the twentieth century, family-owned Mennen's advertising budget seemed to dwindle in comparison. Buttressed by the financial support of the Colgate-Palmolive Co., Mennen is expected to remain a leading member of the crowded antiperspirant/deodorant field.

## Further Reading:

Chase, Charles W., Jr. "Short-range production based forecasting at the Mennen Company," *Journal of Business Forecasting,* winter 1988/1989, pp. 2–5.

"Drugstores meeting tougher competition for deodorants; niche marketing drives deodorant sales," *Drug Topics,* August 19, 1991, pp. 65–67.

Landey, Martin H. "Mennen E," *Advertising Age,* October 15, 1973, pp. 55–58.

Linsenmeyer, Adriene. "No Band-Aid solution," *Financial World,* January 21, 1992, pp. 25–27.

Loffredo, Douglas. "Cosmetic Chemicals '92—Antiperspirants: Price and Value," *Chemical Marketing Reporter,* August 10, 1992, pp. SR8, SR10.

"Mennen, reorganized abroad, sees lower costs in Mart," *Advertising Age,* July 31, 1972, pp. 33.

"Mennen Yesterday & Today," Morristown, NJ: The Mennen Company.

Miller, Elaine B. "Non-aerosol deodorants gaining in market share," *Advertising Age,* November 3, 1975, p. 42.

Morgan, Hal. *Symbols of America,* New York: Steam Press, 1986.

Nayyar, Seema. "Colgate mulls a repositioning," *AdWeek's Marketing Week,* June 8, 1992, pp. 1, 5; "Colgate buys its way back into the game," *AdWeek's Marketing Week,* February 17, 1992, pp. 4–5.

Poole, Claire. "Sweating it out," *Forbes,* October 16, 1989, p. 274.

Rosendahl, Iris. "Drugstores Meeting Tougher Competition for Deodorants; Niche Marketing Drives Deodorant Sales," *Drug Topics,* August 19, 1991.

Sloan, Pat. "Mennen up for sale; Japan's Kao in lead," *Advertising Age,* November 11, 1991, pp. 1, 70; "Mennen sale to rock shops," *Advertising Age,* February 17, 1992, pp. 3, 62; "Baby boom in toiletries hits J&J," *Advertising Age,* January 21, 1991, p. 16.

Sloan, Pat and Laurie Freeman. "Degree makes leaders sweat," *Advertising Age,* December 10, 1990, p. 16.

*—April S. Dougal*

# MONET®

Monet brand of jewelry was the first line of high quality costume jewelry in the world. Owned by Crystal Brands, Inc., the Monet jewelry division is the largest in the world and the company's most important section. Monet necklaces, bracelets, earrings, and other fashion jewelry items are moderately priced, between 20 and 60 dollars, and are sold in major department stores throughout North America and in Europe. Based on timeless fashion, quality workmanship, and affordable prices, Monet has become a world leader in the costume jewelry industry.

## Brand Origins

The Monet brand of jewelry had its beginnings when brothers Jay and Michael Chernow established Monocraft, Inc. in New York in 1929. Both men were Russian immigrants of considerable culture and education, and 1929 was one of the most prosperous years of the Roaring Twenties, with New York City the locus for the luxury trade. Monocraft, Inc. manufactured and marketed beautifully crafted monograms for women's handbags. Even during the worst years of the Depression that followed, the firm stayed in business, its monograms admired increasingly by the retailers who marketed them. Many such retailers encouraged the Chernow brothers to lend their talents to jewelry design. In 1937 the Monet jewelry line made its first tentative appearance. It was the first quality costume jewelry in the world, resembling real gold and silver jewelry. Chic adornments were no longer the prerogative of the rich. The brand name ''Monet'' conveyed an aura of exclusivity and European sophistication that made the unique jewelry instantly popular.

## Product Innovations

High quality gold and silver jewelry and gems in that era were imported from western Europe, and Europeans cornered the market. Endowing a line of fashion jewelry with a very prestigious French name like Monet, and crafting it to look like the famous European brands, was a slap in the face to the major European jewelry manufacturers. World War II, however, was a propitious time for an American firm to come out with an American line of jewelry. Patriotism was dominant, and if America was a cultural backwater compared to Europe, it did have Hollywood. The Monet jewelry line came out with accessories that often matched the kind of jewelry worn by Hollywood film stars. Popular Monet items in the 1940s were coordinated sets, such as large pins with

matching earrings and bracelets, as well as equestrian theme jewelry pieces.

Monet jewelry in the years following World War II closely reflected fashion clothing trends. The 1950s ushered in full hoop skirts, box hats, and gloves, and Monet's bow pins billowed out like the skirts of the day. Also popular were Monet's very feminine, highly polished bead pins and earrings that complemented the prim, ladylike fashion of the day.

Fashion altered radically in the early 1960s when Jackie Kennedy set the tone with simple, A-line skirts and single strand pearl necklaces. Monet caught the fashion mood with its single strand pearls. In the late 1960s, along with the mini-skirt and bell bottom trousers, came Monet's popular hoop earrings; at the same time, the over-40 generation was catered to with elegantly designed pendants and brooches.

Natural fibers and the ''preppy'' look were popular in the 1970s; earrings were being worn by nearly all young and middle-aged women for the first time in fashion history, and gold chains were the rage. Monet's sculpted gold pieces and beautifully finished faux rings were timely innovations. In the 1980s, when accessories were an indispensable complement to fashion, innovative Monet pearls came in all different shapes and sizes, adorned with stones and often in multiple strands. Monet reintroduced and popularized its big hoop earrings once more. In the 1990s, Monet branched out into fashion wristwatches, a first for the company.

## Advertising

Since its inception, Monet jewelry was advertised in the same glossy fashion magazines in which clothing and cosmetics were promoted. For decades after its inception, Monet had few competitors and therefore could maintain its number one market position from print advertising and in-store promotions.

As late as the spring of 1990, Monet was the unchallenged leader in the costume jewelry business with its numerous competitors trailing far behind. However, the severe recession that affected the domestic economy took its toll. For the first time, Monet was advertised in direct-mail campaigns and on television. The television advertisements stressed the theme, set to classical music, "The Beautiful Endures," a theme echoed in all of Monet's promotions. Advertising expenditures for in-store and television promotions climbed to $3 million. Direct-mail and in-store promotional advertising of Monet closely imitated the advertising of cosmetics. With the waning of the recession, television advertising as well as all print advertising were eliminated in favor of radio and direct mail, still stressing the ageless theme, "the Beautiful Endures."

## International Growth

While exports of jewelry in the United States account for only 15 percent of total jewelry sales, there is much potential for growth as trade barriers all over the world are collapsing in favor of free trade zones. Monet has been exported for decades, and in the early 1990s, vigorous efforts are being made to sell Monet in department stores in Europe, with considerable success. Over the years, Monet has established factories offshore, since the crafting of Monet jewelry is labor intensive and highly paid.

## Future

Monet jewelry is still the most popular costume jewelry in North America, with a long history of success and quality, despite the growing competition. Historically, Monet jewelry has adapted itself rapidly to changing fashion and has maintained its moderate prices. With the growth in international market activity, Monet will most likely enjoy successful growth and expansion.

## Further Reading:

Longley, A.B., "Crystal Brands—Company Report," *Donaldson, Lufkin & Jenrette Securities,* January 20, 1992.

Meadus, Amanda, "Crystal's Jewelry Units Merge (Crystal Brands Jewelry Group, Monet, Trifari, and Marvella)," *WWD,* April 9, 1993, p. 9; "Taking on the World: Six Fashion Jewelry Firms Explore the Potential of International Business," *WWD,* April 26, 1993, p. S14.

"New Approach Tried for Monet Jewelers," *New York Times,* February 21, 1990, pp. C15, D17.

Newman, Jill, "Monet Slates $2 Million for Spring Ads (Monet Jewelers)," *WWD,* March 2, 1990, p. 10.

Sloan, Pat, "Fending Off Foreign Faux: Costume Jewelry Leader to Double Ad Budget (Monet)," *Advertising Age,* June 25, 1990, p. 49.

*—Sina Dubovoj*

# MR. CLEAN®

The battle between Procter & Gamble Company (P&G), Colgate-Palmolive, and Lever Brothers for market supremacy in consumer products first erupted in the mid-1950s. Recognizing weaknesses in its competitors' brand promotions, P&G adopted a kind of "supply side formula," fortifying its distribution network to ensure that the company's products would be available in every city, town, and village in America. Backing this strategy were massive advertising campaigns that made P&G brands familiar to everyone who came into contact with an information medium. Meanwhile, the company was investing heavily in new product development, creating undeniably superior formulations of toothpaste, soap, detergent, bleach, and other products.

## Brand Origins

In the 1950s, based on the success of the Crest and Comet brands, P&G decided to enter the all-purpose cleaner market. Against such well-known competition as Lysol, Pine-Sol, and Adell Chemical's Lestoil, the company launched Mr. Clean in 1958. The brand was conceived well before the product was even formulated. P&G was concerned with the time-consuming process of putting together a winning promotion. Creating the cleaning compound was the easy part.

In order to create for consumers the association of Mr. Clean with power and strength, Procter & Gamble chose to represent him as a capable, "all-purpose" muscle man. An exotic cartoon physiognomy that was based loosely on actor Yul Brynner and the character Djinn, the genie in *Aladdin's Lamp,* was created for Mr. Clean. A single sailor's earring was then added to the figure.

Mr. Clean was one of Procter & Gamble's few cartoon personalities. As such, he could produce a larger-than-life wink, which became a trademark for the character. With few exceptions, the company's advertising had consistently been defined by real-life characters, usually depicted as housewives, who testified in the most honest terms about the superior qualities of Procter & Gamble products.

## Brand Development

After an initial test marketing period in 1958, Mr. Clean was rolled out nationally the following year. Mr. Clean entered a market dominated by powders and fractionalized by limited regional distribution of such competing liquid brands as Pine-Sol and Lestoil. Thanks to the product's strong qualities—it was an easily-diluted liquid, it was a safe and effective cleaning agent, and it could be used to clean anything from soiled kitchen sinks to weathered attic floors—and clever advertising, Mr. Clean made a universal impact, quickly becoming the top-selling all-purpose cleaner in the United States.

In defense of their franchises, Lever Brothers and Colgate-Palmolive improved the formulations and redoubled promotion of their own brands. The most serious backlash to Mr. Clean, however, came in October of 1961, when Colgate-Palmolive created a new all-purpose cleaner with ammonia as an extension of its Ajax cleanser brand. Backed by distinctive advertising that featured a kitchen-cleaning white tornado and benefiting from the promotion of other products with the Ajax brand name, the cleaner overtook Mr. Clean in only nine months.

P&G responded in 1963 with a reformulated Mr. Clean and advertising that quipped, "It's better in the bucket." The battle against Ajax was expanded with new promotions for Spic & Span, whose franchise remained solid, and with a new all-purpose, ammoniated cleaner called Top Job. Supported by a hugely expensive ad campaign, Top Job surpassed Ajax as the leading seller. In the process, however, Mr. Clean fell yet another notch, to third, and then fourth place.

A second reformulation, "Clean and Shine" Mr. Clean, was created in 1966 especially for cleaning floors. This was followed in 1970 by an extension created as an alternative to pine-scented cleaners. Lemon Mr. Clean would "get the dirt but leave the wax shining." In search of another niche in a thoroughly segmented market, in 1976 P&G developed "Sunshine Fresh" Mr. Clean to "make everything you clean shine like the sun and smell sunshine-fresh."

## Advertising

A clever jingle can make ad campaigns particularly memorable, so Mr. Clean's early advertising was accompanied by a catchy song: "Mr. Clean gets rid of dirt and grime and grease in just a minute, Mr. Clean will clean your whole house and everything that's in it." In later campaigns Mr. Clean became more aggressive with the grime. In one series he was featured as a "two-fisted" cleaner that knocked out dirt with one hand and left a shine with the other.

## AT A GLANCE

**M**r. Clean brand of cleaning solution developed by Procter & Gamble Company in 1958; introduced nationally in 1959; improved formulation developed in 1963; "Clean and Shine" formula launched in 1966; Lemon Mr. Clean introduced in 1970; "Sunshine Fresh" Mr. Clean added in 1976.

**Performance:** *Market share*—3.5% of cleaning solution market. *Sales*—$40.7 million.

**Major competitor:** Pine-Sol; also, Lysol and Ajax.

**Advertising:** *Agency*—Tatham, Euro RSCG. *Major campaigns*—"Better in the Bucket"; "The Grimefighter"; "Leaves a sheen where you clean"; "Moving In"; "Old Friend."

**Addresses:** *Parent company*—Procter & Gamble Company, 1 Procter & Gamble Plaza, Cincinnati, OH 45202; phone: (513) 983-1100; fax: (513) 562-4500.

Remade again as a "grimefighter," Mr. Clean was dressed as a police officer who "arrested your dirt problem." Other notable tag lines proclaimed, "Mr. Clean leaves a sheen where you clean and a shine behind." In one television commercial Mr. Clean was given a black eye, an allusion to being a floor "shiner." In order to dispel concerns that Mr. Clean might be a harsh chemical, a series of ads used the phrase, "Babies love Mr. Clean."

The promotions were playful, but effective in keeping the viewing audience from getting bored. In an effort to heighten consumer interest in the character, a special contest was held to give Mr. Clean a first name. Thousands of responses were collected, and P&G settled on "Veritably" as the functional winning entry.

### Performance Appraisal

Since his inception in the late 1950s, Mr. Clean has been one of America's best-known and most recognizable commercial characters. In fact, some observers claimed that Procter & Gamble concentrated too heavily on promoting the cartoon representative, at the expense of selling the product. While it is debatable whether Mr. Clean the man overshadowed the cleaning solution he represented, he did gradually lose impact, despite attempts to keep the bald muscle man fresh. By the mid-1970s, the product was battling a dozen other all-purpose cleaners for supremacy in its segment. Procter & Gamble allowed Mr. Clean to settle into the middle of a field that included Ajax, Top Job, Pine-Sol, and to a lesser extent, Lysol and Lestoil.

Procter & Gamble had tried to resuscitate the brand several times by introducing several variations, including the Lemon Scented and Sunshine Fresh formulas. A true brand extension was never launched, however. Though such products as a Mr. Clean cleanser or Mr. Clean bleach may have helped to revitalize the brand, these items would have infringed on existing franchises occupied by other Procter & Gamble brands. Instead, Mr. Clean remained essentially the product it was invented to be, a safe and effective liquid all-purpose cleaner. This identity remained unchanged through the 1980s and into the 1990s.

Procter & Gamble did try and give Mr. Clean a brief promotional jolt in the 1980s by running a contest to find a real live Mr. Clean. Hundreds of bald body builders sporting a single earring entered the competition, and many looked very much like the animated character. Unfortunately, the contest received more attention than the eventual winner. In the end, Procter & Gamble did not pursue a campaign featuring a human Mr. Clean. While the product no longer dominates the market as it did in 1960, Mr. Clean is able to hold his own in a strong field of competitors.

### Further Reading:

"Any Number Can Play," *Sponsor*, March 15, 1965, pp. 31–33.

"Colgate vs. P&G," *Forbes*, February 1, 1966, pp. 26–35.

"Comet Leads Ajax in Hot Cleanser Clash," *Printers' Ink*, March 18, 1960, pp. 11–12.

"Does Ajax Surge Mean Closer Race Between Colgate and P&G?," *Printers' Ink*, September 28, 1962, p. 24.

"Mr. Clean," Cincinnati, OH: Procter & Gamble Company.

"Mr. Clean Muscles Past Lestoil," *Printer's Ink*, p. 16.

"The Screen and Mr. Clean," *Advertising Age*, August 24, 1959, p. 74.

"Why Ajax Vanquished Mr. Clean," *Broadcasting*, January 31, 1966, pp. 48–49.

*—John Simley*

# MYLANTA®

**MYLANTA®**

ANTACID/ANTI-GAS

The history of Mylanta antacid demonstrates the dependance of sales success on marketing strategy. For the first ten years after it was introduced, Mylanta was marketed aggressively with impressive results. Then for almost twenty years under indifferent ownership, Mylanta performed indifferently. In 1989 Johnson & Johnson-Merck acquired the product and initiated the strongest campaign yet, with spectacular results. In just a few years, Mylanta jumped from fifth to first place in the antacid market.

## Brand Origin and History

Mylanta antacid, equal parts aluminum hydroxide and magnesium hydroxide with the anti-gas ingredient methylpolysiloxan, later called simethicone, was developed by the Stuart Company and introduced in 1961. The Stuart Company, incorporated in 1941, manufactured pharmaceuticals and dietary supplements including vitamin and mineral supplements, laxatives, and Mylicon, an anti-gas preparation consisting solely of the anti-gas ingredient used in Mylanta.

In 1961, the same year Mylanta was introduced, the Stuart Company merged with Atlas Chemical Industries, a manufacturer of plastic molding compounds, ammonia compounds, and explosives. The merger was the first foray into pharmaceuticals for Atlas, and would prove to be very profitable. Over the next decade, Atlas's aggressive marketing tactics tripled Stuart's sales of gastro-intestinal products. By the time the British-based Imperial Chemical Industries acquired Atlas in 1971, Mylanta was the fastest-growing antacid in the country.

Imperial Chemical Industries (ICI) is an industrial chemical conglomerate whose pharmaceutical division focused on high-technology research and development of prescription drugs. They marketed Mylanta with no spectacular results until 1989, when the company divested themselves of their United States over-the-counter (OTC) products in an agreement with Johnson & Johnson-Merck, one of the most successful OTC companies in the country.

Johnson & Johnson had been in the health care field since the founders developed sterile bandages in the late nineteenth century. Johnson & Johnson entered the pharmaceutical market in the middle of the twentieth century; their consumer division, which handled over-the-counter medications, was their largest. In the late 1980s, many prescription drug companies began to align themselves with over-the-counter companies. Johnson & Johnson entered into a 50-50 joint venture agreement to develop and market OTC medications with the pharmaceutical company Merck. When Johnson & Johnson–Merck Consumer Pharmaceutical Company acquired the United States OTC business of ICI, they were well prepared to apply their combined drug marketing expertise to Mylanta and Mylicon. The money they invested in the marketing of these products not only increased sales, but eventually cornered the largest market share for their antacid.

## Marketing and Advertising History

For much of its history, Mylanta was an ethical pharmaceutical marketed to physicians only. After acquiring the Stuart Company, Atlas initiated an aggressive marketing policy for all of their ethical pharmaceuticals by increasing the size of their sales staff and investing in training. Marketing strategy involved personal visits with physicians rather than advertising. Stuart products prospered, with sales of all ethical pharmaceuticals increasing 60 percent in the first five years and continuing to grow by 15 to 20 percent per year.

By 1971 sales had increased for the Stuart division by 350 percent. Every year sales increased, with Mylanta setting the pace. In 1961 vitamins and other dietary supplements were the best-selling product for the Stuart Company, and gastrointestinal products accounted for only 12 percent of sales; by 1971 Mylanta and Mylicon had become 62 percent of the Stuart division's total sales. In 1970 Atlas Chemical's Annual Report stated that Mylanta was ''the fastest growing major product in its field.'' ICI also relied heavily on promoting the product to health care professionals, although as antacids gradually became consumer rather than ethical products, Mylanta followed suit.

Johnson & Johnson-Merck began an aggressive new marketing strategy immediately upon its acquisition of the product. Under the direction of the advertising firm Saatchi & Saatchi of New York, they launched the campaign ''My doctor said Mylanta,'' which proved very successful. In the first year sales increased 13 percent, and the product moved into fifth place in the antacid market with a 12 percent share. In 1992 Mylanta had moved up to third place, and by the beginning of 1993, it had captured the market to become the number one antacid in the United States.

Mylanta's rapid rise in market share apparently earned the antacid the animosity of several of the other major antacid compa-

## AT A GLANCE

**M**ylanta brand of antacid founded in 1961 by the Stuart Company; brand sold to Atlas Chemical Industries Incorporated (in merger with The Stuart Company) in 1961; sold to Imperial Chemical Industries in 1971; sold to Johnson & Johnson–Merck Consumer Pharmaceuticals in 1989.

**Performance:** *Market share*—Top share of antacid category. *Sales*—$85 million in wholesale sales (1991).

**Major competitor:** SmithKline Beecham's Tums; also Rhône-Poulenc Rorer's Maalox, Warner Lambert's Rolaids, and Procter & Gamble's Pepto-Bismol.

**Advertising:** *Agency*—Saatchi & Saatchi Advertising, New York, NY. *Major campaign*—"My Doctor said Mylanta. . . ."

**Addresses:** *Parent company*—Johnson & Johnson-Merck, Camp Hill Road, Fort Washington, PA, 19034. *Ultimate parent company*—Johnson & Johnson, One Johnson & Johnson Plaza, New Brunswick, New Jersey, 08933; phone: (908) 524-0400; fax: (908) 214-0332.

nies, who developed advertisements comparing their products directly with Mylanta. Rhône-Poulenc Rorer produced an ad maintaining that their Extra-Strength Maalox Plus had stronger capacity to neutralize acid than the strongest Mylanta product. SmithKline Beecham ran an ad for Tums that suggested that calcium-based antacids such as Tums were healthier than aluminum- and magnesium-based products. Johnson & Johnson-Merck attempted litigation against both advertising campaigns but was unsuccessful.

In addition to employing aggressive advertising, Johnson & Johnson-Merck developed and extended their product and brand name, adding new flavors and lending the Mylanta name to new products.

### Brand Development

Stuart originally offered Mylanta in a liquid form in 5-ounce and 12-ounce bottles, and in pills in packages of 100. During its decade of ownership, Atlas also offered smaller packages of the same dosage in both the liquid and tablet form. When Mylanta came under the direction of ICI, numerous variations in packaging were introduced, including hospital packs, special packages for the military, and many variations for consumers. ICI also developed a stronger formula, and in 1973 began marketing Mylanta II, which offered twice the amount of active ingredients.

When Johnson & Johnson-Merck acquired the product, development and extension became a powerful marketing tool. In 1993 *Drug Topics* magazine discussed the growing trend among OTC companies to created line extensions to build revenues and capitalize on widely known brand names. For Johnson & Johnson-Merck, this strategy helped Mylanta to corner the biggest share of the antacid market.

The company's first action was to change the name of Mylanta II to Mylanta Double Strength, presumably to accentuate its difference from the original product. The following year, the company changed the name of Mylicon to Mylanta Gas, and, for the strongest dosage, Maximum Strength Mylanta Gas. In 1991 new flavors were introduced: in addition to the regular flavor, consumers could purchase Mylanta tablets and liquid in both Cherry Creme and Cool Mint Creme. The following year the company introduced a completely new antacid product, the Mylanta Gelcap, which was the first tablet that could be swallowed without chewing. Unlike the original Mylanta, whose active ingredients were aluminum hydroxide and magnesium hydroxide, the new Mylanta Gelcap was a calcium-based antacid, with neither of the other ingredients.

In 1993 Johnson & Johnson-Merck sought to further capitalize on the Mylanta name and reputation by replacing its previous brand of bulk laxative with Mylanta Natural Fiber Supplement. Advertising for this product, which is available in sugar-free and orange flavors, touts its natural ingredients, as contrasted with chemical stimulants. Initial sales were helped by special introductory retail promotions.

### International Stature

Johnson & Johnson is a global company. As J&J's management stated in its 1993 annual report, "A measure of our diversity is our stature in major health care markets. The latest estimates show our pharmaceutical business to be the fifth largest in the U.S., and eighth largest in the world. . . . We believe we are well positioned to continue our growth in the future as the world's best and most comprehensive health care products company." In 1993 Johnson & Johnson had subsidiaries in about 55 countries, and their consumer products were sold in over 150 countries in Europe, South America, Africa, and Asia.

### Further Reading:

"Ads for Tums Upset a Rival," *New York Times*, February 13, 1991, p. D6.

*Atlas Chemical Industries Incorporated Annual Reports, 1961–71*, Wilmington, Delaware: Atlas Chemical Industries Incorporated.

DeNitto, Emily, "Maalox, Mylanta Challenge P&G's Metamucil Laxative," *Advertising Age*, June 21, 1993, p. 3.

Gannon, Kathi, "Shelf Busters: Analyzing Nonprescription Drug Trends," *Drug Topics*, January 25, 1993, p. 34.

"J&J-Merck's Mylanta Is Number One Antacid in U.S.," *F-D-C Reports Prescription and OTC Pharmaceuticals: The Pink Sheet*, February 8, 1993, p. 25.

"J&J-Merck OTC Marketing Muscle Puts Mylanta on Track to Overtake Antacid Market Leader Maalox," *F-D-C Reports Prescription and OTC Pharmaceuticals: The Pink Sheet*, March 25, 1991, p. 18.

*Johnson & Johnson Annual Reports, 1989–93*, New Brunswick, New Jersey: Johnson & Johnson.

*Moody's Industrial Manual*, New York: Moody's Investor's Service, 1961–91.

*Physicians Desk Reference*, Oradell, New Jersey: Litton Industries, 1993.

*Physicians Desk Reference for Nonprescription Drugs*, Montbale, New Jersey: Medical Economics Data Production Company, 1993.

"SmithKline Beecham's Tums Comparative Ad to Mylanta," *F-D-C Reports Prescription and OTC Pharmaceuticals: The Pink Sheet*, October 7, 1991, p. T&G–11.

"SmithKline Beecham's Tums v. J&J-Merck's Mylanta," *F-D-C Reports Prescription and OTC Pharmaceuticals: The Pink Sheet*, April 6, 1992, p. T&G–14.

Winters, Patricia, "Mylanta Antacid Sold," *Advertising Age*, October 23, 1989, p. 113.

—*Robin Armstrong*

# NEUTROGENA®

# Neutrogena®

Neutrogena Corporation has developed the profitable niche it built around its distinctive transparent golden-amber glycerine soaps into a complete line of hair and skin care products that command premium prices for their perceived purity and effectiveness. Neutrogena has garnered attention for its products by cultivating the support of the dermatological community and has maintained a "golden" image for its products. The brand's advertisements are targeted at affluent consumers and most often appear in print rather than on television. *Forbes* magazine has consistently ranked the Neutrogena Corporation as one of America's best small companies in terms of financial performance.

## Brand Origins

The company that became Neutrogena Corporation, Natone Company, was launched in 1930 by Emmanuel M. Stolaroff. One of Natone's most successful products, Lip Life Lipstick, was still being produced in the 1990s. The soap that became Neutrogena was developed in 1954 in Belgium by Dr. Edmond Fromont, a cosmetic chemist, who spent several years working on a soap that would not irritate the skin and would rinse away cleanly. This soap was also less alkaline than other soaps and had little effect on the skin's pH balance. Stolaroff began importing this soap—called "Neutrogena"—and sold it in Los Angeles department stores for $1 per bar. The new soap was extremely successful in spite of—or perhaps because of—its price. At that time, the average price of a bar of soap was between 10 and 15 cents.

Lloyd Cotsen, chairman and chief executive officer of Neutrogena, joined the operation in 1957, when sales of Neutrogena soap were $80,000 per year. A trained archeologist, Cotsen "couldn't get a job" with his degree in history from Princeton and his Harvard M.B.A., so he went to work for his father-in-law, Emmanuel Stolaroff, in the soap-making industry. After joining the team, Cotsen bought manufacturing rights from their European source and in 1959 began making the product in America. The soap's formula was rather simple—Neutrogena soap contained only 11 ingredients—but the manufacturing process was quite time-consuming. Cotsen believed that their complicated manufacturing process discouraged competition from larger-scale operations like Procter & Gamble Company.

When Cotsen joined the company in 1957, Neutrogena soap accounted for less than 10 percent of Natone's sales. By 1962, however, the product had become so important (Cotsen called it "our Panzer tank") that the company changed its name to Neutrogena Corporation. In 1981, the soap accounted for 62 percent of the company's sales.

## Marketing Strategy

The Neutrogena marketing philosophy has always been niche-oriented. Stolaroff found a niche with the affluent housewives of Los Angeles who wanted a mild soap that wouldn't irritate the face. The transparency of the soap was emphasized in marketing the product to connote purity, with bars packaged in clear cellophane embossed with the Neutrogena name in script or in a Roman type. Print advertising also focused on the theme of purity. Lloyd Cotsen reached the upscale consumer by selling samples to resort hotels. The samples made their way into the hands of businessmen's wives and captured some of the prestige associated with the resorts.

Cotsen worked on developing the Neutrogena beneficial, even therapeutic, reputation by developing a relationship with dermatologists and allergists. Part of the company's sales force has been dedicated solely to visiting these doctors, developing rapport and supplying samples. This is an expensive and time consuming sales strategy, but it is one way that Neutrogena has outmaneuvered such competitors as Procter & Gamble and Bristol-Myers that dominate television advertising. Later, Neutrogena included plastic surgeons and gerontologists in this marketing program and advertised in trade journals. Other soap manufacturers have also begun advertising in medical journals. A separate division, Neutrogena Dermatologics, was created in 1977 to develop and market pharmaceutical products.

Not only have physicians become familiar with Neutrogena products, but Neutrogena has become receptive to doctors' preferences. When Neutrogena Vehicle/N compounding solution came out, doctors preferred it over Procter & Gamble's comparable product, which was pre-mixed with an antibiotic. Cotsen noted that doctors "resented being told what antibiotic they had to use," and Neutrogena was seen as a neutral, even utilitarian, product.

After the company went public in 1973, the Neutrogena product line was streamlined to focus on mild skincare products that would supplement the original Neutrogena soap. One such product was Neutrogena Norwegian Formula Hand Cream, based on a recipe Cotsen picked up in Norway. Variants of the original

## AT A GLANCE

**N**eutrogena brand of cosmetics and toiletries developed in Belgium by Dr. Edmond Fromont; first marketed in the United States in 1954; later developed by Emmanuel M. Stolaroff of Natone Company; renamed Neutrogena Corporation in 1962.

**Performance:** *Market share—2% of cosmetics and toiletries category. Sales—$267.4 million.*

**Major competitor:** *Estée Lauder's Clinique; also Jergens, Lever Brothers' Dove, Colgate-Palmolive's Softsoap, Biersdorf's Basis, L'Oréal's Plenitude, and Palmolive.*

**Advertising:** *Agency—Carlson & Partners, New York, NY, 1991—. Major campaign—"For skin with the healthy Neutrogena glow."*

**Addresses:** *Parent company—Neutrogena Corporation, 5760 West 96th Street, P.O. Box 45036, Los Angeles, CA 90045; phone: (310) 642-1150; fax: (310) 337-5564.*

formula soap for different skin types were also introduced. In the 1980s the following products came on the market: Neutrogena Moisture, Liquid Neutrogena, Neutrogena Conditioner, Neutrogena Rainbath, Neutrogena Night Cream, Neutrogena Emulsion, and Neutrogena Sunblock. The dermatological division introduced such products as T/Sal Shampoo and Melanex, a depigmenting agent available only by prescription. Neutrogena pharmaceutical products included Vehicle/N, a medium for dermatological treatments.

In 1980, Neutrogena introduced two shampoos to the hair care market. Neutrogena Shampoo was marketed through the same outlets as Neutrogena soap and T/Gel Shampoo was targeted at the medical community. T/Gel Shampoo, developed by the Neutrogena Dermatologics division, featured a mild tar formula designed to be therapeutic for certain skin disorders. This shampoo was preceded by T/Derm Therapeutic Tar Body Oil designed to relieve psoriasis and eczema. Neutrogena Conditioner was introduced in 1986 to provide a "clean" system for hair when used with the shampoo.

Neutrogena Moisture Pure Facial Moisturizer, with a sun protection factor (SPF) of five, was first introduced in 1983. In 1989, Neutrogena Rub-Proof Sunblocker SPF15 was introduced and priced at $7 for 2.25 ounces, about $10 less than Estée Lauder's Advanced Suncare products which were introduced at about the same time. A "chemical-free" version containing titanium dioxide—said not to react chemically with the skin—was introduced in 1993. Neutrogena Moisture was introduced in 1988 and featured both an SPF of 15 and a "hint of color" to impart a sun-washed look. Neutrogena came out with its alcohol-free Antiseptic Cleanser in 1989, touting its superior antibacterial properties and mildness.

The company continued to create new products designed for special niches within the skin care market. By 1990, the Neutrogena soap line included Neutrogena Original, Neutrogena Original Fragrance Free, Neutrogena Cleansing Bar for Acne Prone Skin, Neutrogena for dry and oily skins (with a fragrance-free version for dry skin), Neutrogena Baby Cleansing Formula, Liquid Neutrogena Facial Cleanser, and Neutrogena Cleansing Wash. The facial cleanser is a liquid version of the Original soap; unlike most liquid soaps, it does not contain detergents. Neutrogena Cleansing

Wash was designed for skin irritated by treatments such as Retin-A. Though the soaps contain different ingredients, they all have the brand's familiar transparent look.

In 1992 Neutrogena introduced Rainbath Spray-On Dry Oil, Rainbath Splash-On Silkener, Neutrogena Intensified Day Moisture, and Neutrogena Antiseptic Cleansing Pads. In 1993 Neutrogena expanded its Rainbath line of shower products to include a spray-on lotion mist, a sponge, and exfoliating body bar. Neutrogena also eliminated animal testing for its cosmetic products in early 1992.

## Performance

In 1990, sales for all of Neutrogena's products were $209.8 million, up 3 percent from 1989. However, profits fell 36 percent to $17.23 million. A separate division, Neutrogena International, has been created to market Neutrogena products abroad. In 1992 the company's sales exceeded $267 million, and Neutrogena products were sold in over 50 countries. The company had branches in Great Britain and Germany and a subsidiary in France. The source of the formula and name for Neutrogena soap, Fromont Laboratories, continued to market its own products in Belgium and other countries.

In a 1992 report to stockholders, chief executive officer Lloyd Cotsen expressed disappointment in Neutrogena earnings and attributed the disappointing performance to heavy expenditures in television advertising and the general downturn in the U.S. economy. Cotsen planned to revive earnings by spending less on television, introducing fewer products, and distributing fewer promotional items.

## Packaging

There is a clinical, understated aspect to Neutrogena packaging. The very name itself suggests not only newness and rebirth in "neu" and "gen," but also "neutr"ality. The final "a" in "Neutrogena" gives the name both a Latin and feminine feel. The company name is featured on the packages in a classic Roman typestyle with the characters elongated and spaced closely together to form a distinctive logo.

The company's packaging of its shampoo is unusual in that it in a sense justifies the product's price. Information on packaging and in advertising explains in an up-front, no-nonsense manner that the product is designed to be used only as a supplement to one's regular shampoo. The product's selling pitch centers on the claim that it will cleanse residue from a consumer's previous shampoo within two weeks.

## Advertising

Neutrogena advertising campaigns have traditionally relied on print ads, heavy product sampling, and doctors' recommendations. However, in 1981, Neutrogena tried a major television campaign for its soap, using the theme, "For pure, beautiful skin, Neutrogena is pure necessity." The campaign was handled by Eisaman, Johns & Laws. In 1990, Neutrogena spent $27 million on print advertising. In 1991, a new advertising strategy was initiated and Neutrogena increased television spending from $3 million in 1990. This campaign used the theme, "Neutrogena shampoo. A breath of fresh air for your hair." Utilizing both print and television, the company also started a $6 million image campaign for Neutrogena skincare products that featured the slogan, "For skin with the healthy Neutrogena glow." In 1990 Neutrogena rivals Plenitude by L'Oréal and Oil of Olay by Procter & Gamble spent $16 million and $25 million respectively on network television advertising.

### Value Controversy

The most prevalent criticism of Neutrogena products has centered on their high prices. *Consumer Reports* found in 1990 that Neutrogena Original was one of the most expensive soaps yet it gave the fewest washes. The report compared the Neutrogena brand with Pear's, an English brand based on a two-hundred-year-old glycerin formula, and found that Pear's offered more washes than the Neutrogena bar. *Forbes* magazine pointed out that Neutrogena costs five times as much as the average bar of soap (down from the one dollar to fifteen cent ratio of the 1950s) and lasts a fifth as long.

These reviews have not questioned the high quality of the Neutrogena products; their criticism has focused solely on the high cost of the products. However, there are many more expensive soaps on the market, such as the ones associated with fashion designers and sold through department stores. These include Estée Lauder's Clinique and a host of others. No doubt chief executive officer Cotsen has expected this kind of criticism. The company has stated that its pricing policy "denotes quality." As Cotsen told *Forbes* in 1989, "If we just sell commodities, we're going to get waxed."

### Further Reading:

Baskerville, Dawn M., Sheryl Tucker, and Donna Whittingham-Barnes, "21 Women of Power and Influence in America," *Black Enterprise,* p. 74.

"CW 300," *Chemicalweek,* May 8, 1991, p. 27.

Darconte, Lorraine, "Soap Wars," *Soaps/Cosmetics/Chemical Specialties,* December 1990, pp. 24–26.

"FYI," *Cosmetics & Toiletries,* October 1992, p. 24.

Harris, William, "If I Have the Doctor . . . ," *Forbes,* March 30, 1981, pp. 63–64, 67.

Heins, John, "Neutrogena Defends Its Turf," *Forbes,* June 26, 1989, pp. 80–88.

"How We Define 'Best'," *Forbes,* November 13, 1989, p. 220.

Kagan, Cara, "Neutrogena Turning On the Shower Power," *WWD,* April 16, 1993, p. 7.

Kintish, Lisa, "Updating Old Standards," *Soap/Cosmetics/Chemical Specialties,* December 1991, pp. 26–28.

Kretchman, Laurie, "A True-Life Soap Opera," *Fortune,* March 9, 1992, p. 152.

Marcial, Gene G., "This Stock Could Make You Feel Pretty Slick," *Business Week,* September 9, 1991, p. 84.

"A McKinsey-Type Consultant Would Charge a Lot for This Advice," *Forbes,* June 25, 1990, p. 20.

*Neutrogena Corporation Annual Report,* Los Angeles: Neutrogena Corporation, 1992–93.

"Neutrogena Refocuses on Print," *Advertising Age,* January 13, 1982, p. 6.

"Neutrogena Sales Go Flat," *Soap/Cosmetics/Chemical Specialties,* February 1991, p. 74.

"Neutrogena Sees Better, More Attractive Soap Wrap in Switch to 'Opaque White' Film," *Soap/Cosmetics/Chemical Specialties,* October 1983, pp. 77, 86.

"Neutrogena Shuffles Shops," *Advertising Age,* January 6, 1992, p. 8.

"Neutrogena Soap to Launch First Major TV Blitz," *Drug Topics,* September 4, 1981, p. 2.

"Neutrogena Soaps up TV Spending," *Mediaweek,* June 10, 1991, p. 26.

"Neutrogena: Specialist in the Care of Sensitive Skin," *Cosmetics and Toiletries,* November 1978, pp. 34–36.

"News," *Soaps/Cosmetics/Chemical Specialties,* May 1992, p. 74.

"The 100 Best Stocks," *Fortune,* February 1, 1988, p. 30.

Schiro, Anne Marie, "Patterns," *New York Times,* January 26, 1993, p. B7.

Sloan, Pat, ". . . As Neutrogena Boosts Use of TV," *Advertising Age,* June 10, 1991, p. 56.

"Soaping Up," *Consumer Reports,* October 1990, pp. 644–647.

"Sunscreens," *Consumer Reports,* June 1988, pp. 370–374.

"Up Front," *Drug Topics,* January 16, 1984, p. 48.

—*Frederick Ingram*

# NIKE®

In two short decades the Nike brand rose up from obscurity to become the top-selling athletic shoe in the world. Nike, Inc., maintained this position throughout the late 1980s and early 1990s largely because of its commitment to quality and innovation and its ability to respond quickly to changes in market behavior. Nike's dynamic advertising campaigns also greatly enhanced the brand's popularity. Nike's world-famous "swoosh" logo has come to represent not only high performance sports shoes, but also a distinctive personality associated with the brand name.

## Brand Origins and Founders

In 1962, after graduating from Stanford Business School, Phillip (Buck) Knight, took a fateful trip to Japan. Knight believed that Japanese athletic shoes could do well in the U.S. market. So he fabricated a front company, Blue Ribbon Sports, and arranged to distribute Japanese athletic shoes in the U.S. through Onitsuka Tiger Company. In 1964 he began selling the Tiger shoes at track meets from the trunk of his car. His mother's laundry room served as storage space.

That year Knight teamed up with Bill Bowerman, his former track coach at the University of Oregon. Each invested $500 and formally incorporated Blue Ribbon Sports. While Knight concentrated on business matters, Bowerman worked on shoe design and performance, working closely with athletes in perfecting his designs. Because he had been unable find a firm to manufacture his shoes, Bowerman had been making running shoes by hand, using his kitchen as a work shop. In 1966, two years after Blue Ribbon Sports was formed, Bowerman developed his first commercially successful athletic shoe, the Cortez. The following year the company developed the first athletic shoe with a fully cushioned mid-sole.

Meanwhile, the company expanded its distributing operations to the East Coast. In 1971 Knight established a credit line with a Japanese trading company called Nissho Iwai. That same year Blue Ribbon Sports began manufacturing athletic shoes under its own brand name, Nike, the name of the mythological Greek goddess of victory. Also that year, Carolyn Davidson, an undergraduate student at Portland State University, designed the "swoosh" logo and was paid $35 for it. According to Dori Jones Yang of *Business Week,* "Knight's initial reaction to the now ubiquitous checkmark logo [was]: 'I don't love it. But I think it will grow on me.' "

## Early Marketing Strategy

In 1972 Nike severed its ties with Onitsuka Tiger after a dispute about distribution rights. Nike then began to actively promote its own brand. During the 1972 Olympic Trials in Eugene, Oregon, several marathon runners agreed to try out the Nike brand, and Knight and Bowerman quickly capitalized on the event with advertisements boasting that "four of the top seven finishers" were wearing Nike shoes. And thus began the Nike marketing strategy of establishing close relationships with prominent athletes through grassroots promotions. As Diana B. Henriques wrote in the *New York Times,* these informal endorsements were "the first step in a process that ultimately came to define the company and, indeed, the entire industry," in which athletic shoe manufacturers contracted professional as well as amateur athletes and coaches.

Initially, these relationships were important for Nike not only for their promotional value, but also for experimenting with design and establishing contacts with competitive athletes. Direct feedback allowed Nike to quickly respond to the athletes' comments and requests and thus develop superior athletic shoes. As Nike continued to grow, it remained responsive to consumers by developing strong market segmentation. Throughout the early 1990s Nike remained a formidable force in the athletic shoe industry because of its continued commitment to innovation and improvement.

## Product Development

One of the most important breakthroughs in athletic shoe design occurred one morning in 1972 at Bowerman's breakfast table. Bowerman was having waffles, when it suddenly occurred to him that the waffle texture might make outsoles that would provide excellent traction. So he put some rubber latex into the waffle iron and created the first Waffle sole. With that innovation he made the Moon Shoe, a strong, light-weight shoe for distance running.

In 1979 the company developed another important shoe design, the Nike-Air cushioning system. The air-cushioned insoles reduced the stress of impact. Nike continued to improve its shoe technology throughout the 1980s with the introduction of Visible Air in 1987, the same year cross-training took off. In 1991 Nike offered 50 percent more air cushioning with the introduction of

## AT A GLANCE

**N**ike brand shoes founded in 1964 in Eugene, OR, by Phillip Knight and Bill Bowerman, owners of Blue Ribbon Sports; company renamed Nike, Inc., in 1978 and went public in 1980.

**Performance:** *Market share*—33% (top share) of U.S. athletic footwear; 21% (top share) of worldwide athletic footwear. *Sales*—$3.7 billion (for Nike brand only).

**Major competitor:** (Domestic) Reebok brand, with 23% of market, and L.A. Gear brand, with 8% of market; (worldwide) Reebok, with 16%, Adidas, with 10%, and L.A. Gear, with 5%.

**Advertising:** *Agency*—Weiden & Kennedy, Portland, OR, 1986—. *Major campaign*—Athletes featured in "Just Do It" advertisements.

**Addresses:** *Parent company*—Nike, Inc., One Bowerman Drive, Beaverton, OR, 97005; phone: (503) 671-6453.

Air 180. Beginning in 1993 Nike-Air technology was offered in different shapes, sizes, pressures, and locations. A new Air Max series provided, according to the company, 35 percent more cushioning than ever before in running, basketball, and cross-training shoes. Another innovation, Flexible Air in the forefoot, brought flexibility and cushioning to aerobic shoes. Walking shoes also gained a new technology, a low-pressure Air unit in the heel for extra comfort. Nike continues to research methods to enhance cushioning and to develop even lighter-weight shoes.

During the early 1990s the product engineers at Nike concentrated on improving shoe design in four basic categories: cushioning, fit, stability, and light weight. In 1991 Nike unveiled a light, form-fitting running shoe, Air Huarache, made with a neoprene and Lycra spandex upper. The design was such a success that Nike integrated the Huarache technology into its other athletic shoes, setting a precedent for the whole industry.

Environmental concerns about an increasing shortage of landfill space prompted Nike to develop Nike Regrind. The Nike Regrind process allows otherwise discarded materials from the manufacturing process to be recycled into outsole material for new shoes. The results are reduced demand on non-renewable resources, reduced impact on landfills, and reduced production-based pollutants. The company emphasizes that recycled does not mean reduced durability or performance, and that Nike Regrind outsoles are designed to last. First introduced on the Nike Air Escape Lo in the spring of 1993, the Nike Regrind technology is now used in the company's entire line of outdoor cross-training shoes and in the best-selling Caldera trail series. According to Julie Hatfield of the *Boston Globe*, Nike said that although the method was still expensive, the end product was a more durable shoe. Recycled packaging was also used for a number of Nike shoes. The next environmentally correct step for Nike is to establish a post-consumer recycling program, wherein consumers trade in their old shoes; this program is being tested in Seattle and Fort Meyers.

### Shifts in Marketing

Throughout the 1970s Nike continued its general marketing strategy of gaining recognition by supporting sporting events and by asking top U.S. athletes, such as Jimmy Connors and America's best middle-distance runner, Steve Prefontaine, to wear Nike

products. Nike was also prominent at the 1976 Olympic Trials. And within a few years Nike signed a formal endorsement contract with tennis great John McEnroe.

Towards the end of 1970s, when jogging had become a popular sport in the United States, Nike quickly capitalized on the market, capturing close to 50 percent of domestic share in running shoe sales. As revenues increased, the company began to diversify into other products lines, developing children's athletic shoes and creating an athletic apparel division in 1978, the same year the company officially changed its name to Nike, Inc. (even though Nike brand shoes had been sold since 1972). In 1980 the company went public and used the revenues for further expansion, especially in Europe.

In the early 1980s the jogging craze began to wane, and in order to boost its domestic shoe sales, Nike launched its first national campaign in 1981. But profits continued to decline, so the company scaled back the number of shoe products by 30 percent—there were over 200 different lines at the time. In further efforts to boost sales, Nike in 1985 signed a contract with basketball superstar Michael Jordan to endorse the basketball shoe named after him, Air Jordan. The campaign was a success, and sales for Nike-Air products quickly rebounded.

However, other Nike shoe products suffered declines in sales during the late 1980s. Nike had been slow to respond to the shifting trends in the sports industry, in particular, the rise in the popularity of aerobic dancing. While Nike tried to grapple with the changing market, Reebok edged out Nike as the top-selling brand of athletic shoes in 1986. But sales of the Visible Air products launched in 1987 were strong, and by 1989 Nike once again took the lead in market share. In 1988 Nike diversified further, making the foray into the casual and formal shoe market when it purchased Cole Haan.

In the early 1990s Nike focused more attention on the sports and fitness categories dominated by women, especially aerobics, walking, and cross-training. Nike's women's products went on to represent about 20 percent of all sales, fueled by a successful three-year "Dialogue" print campaign that depicted sports as empowering for women. The campaign generated more than 250,000 letters and phone calls to Nike's consumer hotline phone number. In 1991 the women's print campaign won the Stephen E. Kelly Award, the most prestigious award in U.S. print advertising, given by the Magazine Publishers of America; the ad also won the National Women's Political Caucus "Good Guys" award. When the campaign repeated in 1992, it captured the Kelly Award for the second time. Nike continued developing its women's division with an $8 million television campaign in early 1993. Nike clearly has realized the power of the female consumer, resulting in an increase of 40 percent in Nike's women's business in the early 1990s.

### Noteworthy Advertising

Although Nike was devoted to producing top performance products, Nike's advertising strategies shied away from "hokey displays of product," as Rob deFlorio, divisional advertising manager, told *Footwear News*. Instead, Nike began promoting its own "personality," to create an emotional bond between the consumer and the company. As chairman Phillip Knight said in an interview with *Harvard Business Review*, "People at Nike believe in the power of emotion because we feel it ourselves."

In 1986 Nike changed its advertising agency to Wieden & Kennedy, which developed the fitness "Revolution" commercial. The agency used the Beatles' song of the same title, and though they had paid a rights fee to use the song, Wieden & Kennedy and Nike were sued nonetheless. But the ensuing publicity generated by the lawsuit was a considerable advantage for Nike. "That commercial helped turn the company completely around," said Scott A. Bedbury, Nike's advertising director, to the *New York Times.*

The $10 million "Just Do It" campaign, which began in 1988, was also a tremendous hit, and remained a major Nike slogan through the early 1990s. In the late 1980s filmmaker Spike Lee appeared in and directed the "Spike and Mike" ad campaign, and a few years later he was featured in "Spike's Urban Jungle Gym" campaign, in which Lee promoted racial harmony. Ironically, the campaign was filmed just a few weeks before the L.A. riots and in the same area. The "Bo Knows" campaign was another popular series of ads, which continued even after baseball/football player Bo Jackson's hip injury, when the ads specifically addressed his recovery. With the success of these ad campaigns, Nike's advertising budget increased steadily; spending only $20 million in 1987, the company in the early 1990s spent $150 million on advertising in the United States alone.

## Controversies Associated with Nike

In 1990 the Rev. Jesse Jackson and the civil rights group Operation PUSH proposed a boycott of Nike shoes. In addition to complaining that Nike exploited African American children by enticing them to buy the company's expensive sneakers, which can cost upwards of $100, Jackson argued that the company was not doing enough for the African American community. The boycott forced Nike to realize that, as the leading corporation in its industry, the public had an interest in Nike's minority hiring practices. During this period, Nike went from a minority population amongst its employees of 14.3 percent (6.5 percent African American) in July of 1990 to 22.4 percent minority population (13.2 percent African American) in July of 1993. Nike attributed the rise of minorities in its workforce to the overall growth phase the company experienced during this time.

In 1991 Nike experienced problems with the women's footwear line, Side 1, when the company Sideout Sport filed a trademark infringement suit against Nike. But Nike persisted with the product line, committed to expanding Nike's women's division. Side 1 was reintroduced the following year after designing a new oval logo and scaling back the campaign from the original $8 million. In 1993 Side 1 came to represent a dance-funk apparel and footwear collection.

In another controversy, this time in 1992 during the Olympics in Spain, the Spanish constitutional court ruled that Nike could not advertise or sell its clothing in Spain because of a conflict with a Spanish apparel firm, also called Nike, which had registered its trademark in 1932. Nevertheless, the U.S. team wore their Nike uniforms when they accepted their medals. A different controversy ensued at the 1992 Olympics when members of the U.S. basketball "Dream Team," including Michael Jordan, David Robinson, Scottie Pippen, and Charles Barkley—all of whom had contracts with Nike—threatened not to appear at the ceremony in the official uniforms, because they had the Reebok logo emblazoned on them. The problem was resolved by turning over the collars and draping an American flag over their shoulders, thereby covering the logos.

In still another conflict, in the fall of that year a Maryland lobbying group, Made in the USA, attacked Nike for manufacturing the bulk of its products overseas. Nike responded that over 1,000 of its 6,200 U.S. employees work in manufacturing. Moreover, as Nike spokesperson told Jamie Beckett of the *San Francisco Chronicle,* "We can't make shoes here and sell them at prices consumers want to pay. . . . The technology to make athletic footwear in the U.S. is not here."

## International Status

In 1973 Canada became Nike's first foreign market, and the next year Nike expanded to Australia. In 1981 Nike International, Ltd., was formed in order to further develop Nike markets in Europe, Asia, Latin America, and Africa. From its beginnings in the early 1970s, Nike had established an elaborate network of subcontractors overseas to manufacture its products, with operations in China, South Korea, Taiwan, and Thailand. While the cost of making the Air Jordan in Asia was $30—about $100 less than the suggested retail cost in the United States—Nike has consistently invested more in research and development than any other athletic shoe firm; for example, it funds and operates the Nike Sports Research Laboratory, the only full-scale, in-house research lab in the industry.

In 1991 Nike led the $11.3 billion international athletic shoe market with 21 percent of sales. Reebok was a close second with about 20 percent. That year, Nike spent about $30 million on advertising in over a dozen foreign countries. The investment paid off, as Nike's international footwear sales increased 80 percent in fiscal year 1991, to $862 million; Asian demand increased by 76 percent, while German demand increased by 59 percent. The following year Nike's international footwear revenues jumped an additional 32 percent, to more than $1.1 billion. Nike's largest international market remained Europe, and despite the sluggish economy, European retailers increased their orders for Nike products for the first half of 1993 by 21 percent.

## Performance Appraisal

In 1972, the first year of Nike brand distribution, Blue Ribbon Sports grossed close to $2 million. By 1974, sales had more than doubled, to $4.8 million. Revenues continued to increase dramatically, doubling in 1977 to $28 million and reaching $867 million by 1983. The following year, although revenues grew 6 percent to $920 million, earnings declined for the first time in the company's history. Nike had surpassed Adidas in worldwide sales but faced a new threat from U.S.-based Reebok International. By capitalizing on the growing women's aerobic market, Reebok was able to overtake Nike by the end of 1986, a year in which Nike's U.S. footwear revenues fell 22 percent. Nike responded in 1987 by aggressively streamlining operations, refocusing its marketing efforts on innovative performance products, and launching the first national television advertising campaign ("Revolution").

In 1988 revenues rebounded to a record $1.2 billion, and the following year Nike regained its number one position, with total sales of $1.7 billion. By 1993, U.S. sales alone had surpassed $2.3 billion, and worldwide sales stood at $2.7 billion. Nike's U.S. market share continued to grow, reaching 33 percent, while Reebok, after increasing to 24 percent in the early 1990s, fell back to 22 percent. Nike's dominance in the United States was best illustrated in the $1 billion basketball market, the largest and fastest-growing shoe category during the late 1980s and early 1990s. In 1993 Nike's market share stood at over 60 percent, while Reebok held only 15 percent.

## Future Growth

Nike has established strong global media links and predicts that international sales would account for at least 50 percent of its total revenues by the end of the 1990s. Nike's dedication to quality and innovation, as well as its dynamic advertising campaigns, should contribute to keeping the Nike brand at the forefront of the athletic footwear industry. Nike's domestic sales should continue to see gains in the fast-growing categories of basketball, outdoor, cross-training, and women's products.

## Further Reading:

Beckett, Jamie, "Dunk Nike Is Theme of New Ad Campaign," *San Francisco Chronicle,* November 2, 1992, p. C3.

Berger, Warren, "They Know Bo," *New York Times,* November 11, 1990, sec. 6, p. 36.

Bloomberg Business News, "Saving Battered Soles; Sneakers Find an Afterlife as Nike Starts Recycling," *New York Times,* July 25, 1992, sec. 1, p. 37.

"The Business of the Olympics," *Los Angeles Times,* August 8, 1992, Business sec., p. 1.

Hatfield, Julie, "Environmentally Smart and Stylish," *Boston Globe,* August 24, 1992, Living sec., p. 34.

Henriques, Diana B., "They Just Did It," *New York Times,* February 2, 1992, sec. 7, p. 9.

Lazarus, George, "New TV Ad Shows Adidas' Street Smarts," *Chicago Tribune,* August 17, 1992, Business sec., p. 4.

Magiera, Marcy, *Advertising Age,* "Nike Readies Third Launch for Side 1," July 6, 1992, News sec., p. 10; "Spike Lee Gets in Front of Camera for Nike," May 25, 1992, News sec., p. 3; "Nike Takes Global Steps; Air 180 Shoe to Get Worldwide Introduction, Campaign," January 14, 1991, News sec., p. 3.

"Nike Announces Third-Quarter Earnings Rise 7 Percent," *PR Newswire,* March 15, 1993, Financial News sec.

"Nike Sees No Olympics Impact from Dispute," *Reuters,* July 23, 1992.

Rabin, Phil and Carolyn Myles, "Celebrity Soda Endorsements May Be Losing Their Pop, *Washington Times,* April 3, 1991, p. C3.

Rifkin, Glenn, "All About/Basketball Shoes; High Tops: High Style, High Tech, High Cost," *New York Times,* January 5, 1992, sec. 3, p. 10.

Schwartz, Jerry, "Aiming Sports Apparel at Women," *New York Times,* February 8, 1992, sec. 1, p. 35.

"Sideout Sport Alleges Nike Withheld Information and Seeks Contempt of Court," *PR Newswire,* January 9, 1992, Financial news sec.

Strauss, Gary, "Women Sport New Clout," *USA Today,* February 9, 1993, p. B1.

Wieden, Dan, "A Sense of Cool: Nike's Theory of Advertising," *Harvard Business Review,* July/August 1992, p. 97.

Wilner, Rich, "Anatomy of an Ad Campaign," *Footwear News,* October 12, 1992.

Yang, Dori Jones, "How Nike Blasted Off," *Business Week,* April 6, 1992, p. 10.

*—Audra Avizienis*

# NIVEA®

Invented in Hamburg, Germany, in 1912, the non-greasy Nivea brand of creams and lotions helped revolutionize the cosmetics industry. Until then, the only way people moisturized their skin was by rubbing fatty creams on themselves. Although available in the United States in the early part of the twentieth century, Nivea was more widely known and used in Europe. It wasn't until the mid-1970s, when parent company Beiersdorf Inc. established a U.S. subsidiary in Norwalk, Connecticut, that the brand started establishing itself in the American marketplace. The Nivea brand of creams and lotions—distinguished by its cobalt blue and white packaging—ranks among the top ten hand and body lotions in the United States.

## Brand Origins

In 1911, Dr. Isaac Lifschutz, a chemist at the toiletries and pharmaceutical firm of C.P. Beiersdorf & Co. in Hamburg, Germany, used his patented method of emulsifying oil in water to launch a line of beauty products. He had made his discovery nine years earlier and called the formula "Eucerite," which became the basis for Nivea Moisturizing Creme in 1912, the first thoroughly modern skin cream. A year later, Nivea became a registered trademark in the United States. Eucerite is highly water absorbent, thus making Nivea a "non-greasy" moisturizer.

The Nivea name did not originate with the launch of a skin cream line. Nivea was the name of a Beiersdorf & Co. soap and dentifrice that had been discovered after Carl P. Beiersdorf, a Hamburg pharmacist, founded the company to produce ointments and bandages in 1882. Beiersdorf, who joined forces with "Father of Dermatology" Paul Gerson Unna, developed a company devoted to solving health care problems. Unna founded the first Hamburg skin hospital and recruited Lifschutz to join Beiersdorf & Co.

Beiersdorf & Co. has prided itself on a history of promoting therapeutic skin care. Company scientists developed the first adhesive tape and invented a treatment for hyperkeratoses (a skin ailment). In 1884, the company developed and introduced a super fatted soap and a glycerin-gelatin combination known as "Unna's Boot," for the treatment of various ulcers and skin diseases. Nivea stands as the company's most significant scientific development, company sources say, because the addition of water to ointments helps cool and treat the skin. Nivea Moisturizing Creme is also

Beiersdorf's best-known trademark worldwide. In the United States, the company owns the Basis soaps, and Eucerin Therapeutic moisturizer trademarks as well as a line of Aquaphor pharmaceutical products.

## Early Marketing Strategy

Nivea, at least in Europe, had marketing appeal for the entire family and was used by both men and women. Men applied Nivea Moisturizing Cream as an after-shave balm. Women used it as an all-over moisturizer; for children, it was positioned as a pure, fresh-scented moisturizer appropriate for tender skin. Through posters and advertisements, Nivea Creme was advertised as "providing the right degree of moisture to preserve a smooth complexion." In the summer of 1925, Beiersdorf added a new slant to its ad campaign, anchoring a huge mock-up of the Nivea Creme tube off Germany's Baltic Sea coast to inspire swimmers to view the creme as the perfect protection against the drying effects of the sun, wind, and surf. It was at this time that the familiar blue and white tin packaging was developed.

By the 1930s, tanning became a fad and Nivea had become the German sunbather's staple. In 1931, Beiersdorf added Nivea Oil to the product line and positioned it as a tanning lotion. Beiersdorf company press kit materials state that by the 1940s, Nivea had "become the cream of the crop" of moisturizers and was synonymous with "superior skin care all over Europe and America."

During World War II, however, the brand was no longer distributed throughout the United States. Its familiar blue and white tins and tubes were discontinued and replaced by glass jars, but the change may not have been very noticeable as supplies were only sporadically available. Nivea made a resurgence after the war; however, the brand was taken over by a British company, Smith and Nephew PLC. The company has operations in Ireland, Australia, New Zealand, Canada, and South Africa and cooperates with Beiersdorf on new product development. According to *World's Greatest Brands,* the dual ownership of many of Germany's popular brand names resulted from the country owing war reparations after both world wars. Germany used the overseas rights to many of its famous brands to pay off these debts. There is little information available on the brand's success throughout the Cold War. The following events, however, were important to the development and sales success of the Nivea line: in the 1950s, Nivea's

## AT A GLANCE

**N**ivea brand of skin cream and lotion created in 1912 in Hamburg, Germany, by Isaac Lifschutz, a chemist at the toiletries and pharmaceutical firm of C.P. Beiersdorf & Co.; product was developed from Lifschutz's non-greasy "Eucerite" formula; became an American registered trademark, 1913; many products manufactured in United States through Beiersdorf Inc.-licensed Duke Laboratories, which merged with Beiersdorf in 1973; U.S. subsidiary located in Norwalk, CT.

**Performance:** *Market share*—Approximately 7% of hand and body lotion category. *Sales*—$52 million (estimate).

**Major competitor:** Unilever's Vaseline Intensive Care Lotion; also Jergens, S.C. Johnson's Soft Sense, Warner Lambert's Lubriderm, and Helene Curtis's Suave.

**Advertising:** *Agency*—TBWA, New York, NY, 1990—. *Major campaign*—Print ads featuring the tagline "Europe's Number One Moisturizer."

**Addresses:** *Parent company*—Beiersdorf Inc., P.O. Box 5529, Norwalk, CT 06856; phone: (203) 853-8008; fax: (203) 838-7525.

classic tin package returned and in 1958 Beiersdorf introduced Nivea Suntan Spray in Europe; in the 1960s, the Nivea brand line of sunning products was extended; and in 1967, Nivea Milk, a creamy, white moisturizing lotion, was introduced in Europe.

Nivea products gained a foothold in the United States in the 1970s. Carl Herzog, a German-born chemist and international pharmaceutical businessman, brought many of Dr. Unna's medicinal products to the United States for manufacture through the Beiersdorf-licensed Duke Laboratories. In 1973, Duke Labs merged with Beiersdorf, returning the therapeutic inventions and discoveries of Unna to their original manufacturing name. Beiersdorf, Inc. was established in Norwalk, Connecticut and one of the products it brought to the U.S. market was Nivea "Milk." The product featured a lighter formulation than the European "Milk" to meet America's different consumer and climactic demands.

### Product Changes

For the next 20 years, the brand continued to establish its solid position in the U.S. market. The Nivea product line was expanded as the company introduced products that appealed to American consumers' concerns about sensitive skin and preservatives in cosmetics. The company launched its Nivea Sun skin care line in the 1980s and introduced its Nivea Extra Enriched Formula Moisturizing Lotion in 1986.

A year later, Nivea Visage, a leading brand of facial nourishing cream and lotion in France, was introduced in the United States. Nivea Visage was unique because it contained sun-filtering properties. In the early 1990s, Nivea Visage (visage means face in French) was further expanded to include a variety of facial cleansers, anti-wrinkle and restorative creams, and an alcohol-free moisturizing facial toner. Products with liposomes—fatty compounds which surround droplets of water-based emollients—were launched in 1992. These products include Eye Contour Gel, Firming Gel Creme, and Creme with Vitamin E.

In an attempt expand its Nivea moisturizer line, Beiersdorf in 1989 entered the bath market with Nivea Bath Silk in 1989. Bath Silk, which was the leading European bath brand, was initially advertised separately from the Nivea cream and lotion line, but the marketing strategy was changed to capitalize on the Nivea trademark. Additionally, the bath line, in addition to all the Nivea and Beiersdorf-related moisturizing and cleansing products, was positioned in the skin care section of supermarkets.

Beiersdorf used "live test markets" in Chicago and Seattle at the end of 1988 to try strategies for products described as "nichey," according to Leslie Brennan in *Sales & Marketing Management.* Bath Silk was also used to help boost sales of Nivea lotions by appealing to loyal consumers. Bath packets were included in lotion packages, and samples with coupons were distributed to encourage customers to purchase lotion and bath products at the same time. Customer surveys determined that 80 percent of current Nivea lotion users were "happy to see a new product from" Beiersdorf, according to *Sales & Marketing Management.*

In early 1993, Beiersdorf created a Nivea brand of lotion for sensitive skin to be sold in more than 50,000 retail outlets. Company officials told *Women's Wear Daily* that they projected Nivea Sensitive would grant the Nivea brand an additional 1 to 2 percent of the market in that year. Beiersdorf stated it would spend $10 million in advertising for Nivea Sensitive in the fourth quarter of 1992. "We've been watching the sensitive skin trend for the last several years," Irena Vallas, director of business development for Nivea told *Women's Wear Daily.* "Just about everyone has come out with a product for it." Fritz Hoffer, senior vice president of marketing and sales at Beiersdorf's consumer products division, also commented: "People are becoming more conscious of the environment and chemicals in skin care products and are looking for products they think are safer to use."

### Performance Appraisal

Beiersdorf has grown to 50 subsidiaries and 82 licenses worldwide. Nivea products were sold in 148 countries and were recognized as the number one moisturizer brand in Europe. Nivea controls a 6.5 percent to 8 percent share of the U.S. hand and body lotion market, ranking seventh behind the following competing brands: Vaseline Intensive Care, Jergens, Soft Sense, and Lubriderm. The brand's leadership position in European markets is often attributed to cultural differences. Europeans reportedly learn to guard their complexions from an early age and are "quite deliberate about it." "American women often wait until the first wrinkle appears before they use moisturizer," according to company press kit information.

Consequently, Beiersdorf has taken the initiative to educate American audiences about proper skin care. In 1986, Beiersdorf hosted an international symposium in Hamburg attracting leading American beauty editors who attended sessions on skin care, chronobiology, and fragrances used in skin care formulations. In the early 1990s Beiersdorf invited beauty writers and editors to explore the future of skin care under company auspices in Berlin and Hamburg. The company also offered consumers free guides on the ABCs of skin care, titled "Beauty by Definition," in 1993.

## Further Reading:

Allen, Margaret, *Selling Dreams,* New York: Simon & Schuster, 1981, p. 162.

Appelbaum, Cara, "Nivea Offers Six New Items for the Face," *Women's Wear Daily,* September 12, 1992, p. 16.

Blumenthal, Deborah, "Preserving Skin Without Preservatives," *New York Times,* January 4, 1992, pp. 14(N), 48(L).

Brennan, Leslie, "Meeting the Test," *Sales & Marketing Management,* March 1990, pp. 57, 89.

Kagan, Cara A., "Nivea's Sensitive Solution," *Women's Wear Daily,* November 6, 1992, p. 7.

*World's Greatest Brands,* New York: Wiley, 1992, p. 54

*—Evelyn S. Dorman*

# NORTHERN®

Northern bathroom tissue, the third-best-selling brand of bathroom tissue, was one of the first brands in national distribution. Northern is considered a premium brand in a competitive market that includes numerous national, regional, and store brands. The total U.S. bathroom tissue industry is estimated to be about $3 billion per year, a figure accounted for by the fact that some kind of tissue is used in nearly every household in the country. Research studies show that the average American uses bathroom tissue about eight times each day, or almost 75 rolls each year. Consumers have transformed tissue into a versatile household product with uses as diverse as removing makeup and nail polish, cleaning eyeglasses and jewelry, and wiping around the sink.

The Northern brand was established at the dawn of the twentieth century. Full-service indoor plumbing had begun to be installed in some affluent American homes only twenty years earlier, resulting in an increased consumer demand for toilet paper. Northern's subsequent survival and growth was due to its product improvements and line extensions in a highly competitive market. The company strategically used market research to determine consumer needs and concerns in regards to bathroom tissue. Product changes have included enhanced softness, absorbency, and strength as well as changes in product and packaging design and sizes.

## Brand Origins

The Northern name was adopted in 1902. The previous year, seven men from Wisconsin built a small paper mill on the Fox River in Green Bay. With one machine they produced a product called Sanitary Tissue, although in 1904 a second machine that could also produce newsprint was added, and for years the mill also manufactured the paper for the Sears Roebuck catalog. The tissue was first packaged as a roll of 1,000 sheets, four inches wide by ten inches long. Each bundle had a wire loop cutting through it so that the consumer could hang it on a nail.

The challenge for Northern as an early entrant into this new product area was to develop a process that would remove the paper's splinters. When ordinary logging wood was ground with water to create pulp which dried into paper sheets, the splinters remained. In addition, many manufacturers also used chemicals and dyes in their tissues; these were further sources of discomfort. In the 1920s Northern successfully created technology that not only removed the splinters but also created a softer product. The

process was called "Linen-izing," and it involved cooking the log chips until the splinters disappeared and the paper became softer. This was followed by sterilization, during which the paper was cooked under a steam heat of 302 degrees Fahrenheit. Northern tissue was originally marketed in single rolls. The four-roll pack debuted in 1956. By the 1990s the Northern package had expanded to include six rolls, and even the nine-count Big Roll.

During the 1950s, manufacturers sought to make bathroom tissue fluffier. Northern tissue incorporated cotton-soft pure cellulose to do the trick. Another post-war development was the introduction of colored tissue to match the new pastel bathroom fixtures that were becoming popular in homes. In the 1970s Northern marketed its first line of tissue that employed an embossed pattern of flowers. Consumers found that this new variation also enhanced the comfort of the tissue. This same method of embossing was featured in the 1993 Quilted Northern brand, designed for softness, absorbency, and strength. The two-ply tissue featured a plush design embossed with cross-stitching and flowers reminiscent of a quilt. Quilted Northern was initially available in pastels and soft prints. Each roll contained 280 two-ply sheets, and each sheet was 4.5 inches x 4.4 inches.

## Market Research Strategy

Quilted Northern was developed after company researchers conducted a study with 1,200 respondents. The study found that softness in a bathroom tissue was the top priority for consumers. Over 50 percent of the respondents associated softness with two-ply and quilting. As important factors, softness was mentioned by 66 percent of the respondents, strength by 63 percent, two-ply by 57 percent, and fluffiness by 51 percent. According to Quilted Northern's brand manager, "We knew that doing our homework would be the key to delivering a superior product. When consumers told us they wanted softness more than anything, we took 'soft' to a higher level with a plush, quilted design that makes Quilted Northern the most comfortable bathroom tissue on the market."

Regarding Quilted Northern's other attributes, the brand manager continued: "We've always known that softness is the primary motivator in choosing a particular brand of bathroom tissue. But the research showed that absorbency and strength also were key factors. Our new quilted product combines all three benefits in one package to deliver the truly ultimate product." Accompanying

## AT A GLANCE

Northern brand of bathroom tissue introduced in 1902, a year after seven Wisconsin men began production of the tissue at their Green Bay mill; Northern, Dixie, and Marathon lines purchased by American Can Corporation (later Primerica Corporation), 1957; these operations were sold to the James River Corporation, 1982; Quilted Northern bathroom tissue launched, 1993.

**Performance:** *Market share*—15–18% (third place) of toilet tissue category. *Sales*—(estimated U.S. sales for 1992) $540 million.

**Major competitor:** Procter & Gamble's Charmin; also Scott Paper Company's ScotTissue.

**Advertising:** *Agency*—DDB Needham Worldwide, New York, 1992—. *Major campaign*—Northern Kids and the Northern Girl.

**Addresses:** *Parent company*—James River Corporation, Consumer Products Business, 800 Connecticut Ave., P.O. Box 6000, Norwalk, CT, 06856; phone: (203) 854-2000; fax: (203) 854-2184. *Ultimate parent company*—James River Corporation of Virginia, 120 Tredegar St., Richmond, VA 23219; phone: (804) 644-5411; fax: (804) 649-4428.

this product introduction was a national advertising promotional program.

Northern's market researchers also investigated various consumer practices in regards to bathroom tissue. Wondering if consumers preferred the roll to dispense tissue over or under, the researchers discovered that 75 percent preferred it over the top. When asked if they tore the tissue from right to left or left to right, 42 percent of respondents reported that they tore it right to left while 35 percent tore left to right. The remaining percentage pulled it straight down. The researchers also wondered what consumers did with the tissue once they pulled it off the roll. The study termed 30 percent of the consumers "wrappers" because they wrapped the tissue around their hands. Another segment of 30 percent folded their tissue into a multi-layered packet. The largest group of 40 percent, however, just crumpled it up for use.

### Advertising Innovations

In an early promotional effort, a free sample roll of Northern bathroom tissue reportedly was shot from a spring-loaded cylindrical gun during a 1922 parade in downtown Green Bay. More traditional advertising was being utilized by the early 1950s as ads began to emphasize the product's superior softness qualities with the headline, "Snowy-Soft . . . made with Fluff." This ad featured a cartoon-type lamb combing his hair while standing in a snowy field. The single roll pine forest logo was altered in the 1950s to depict three pine trees under the brand name.

The earliest Northern package featured the brand name above a design of a pine forest, which was altered in the 1950s to depict three pine trees under the name. A major advertising development took place in 1958 when illustrator Frances Hook designed the first "Northern Kids." The fresh-faced children appeared on billboards and packages of Northern tissue, and they received such wide consumer recognition that in 1959 the company commissioned a series of art prints to commemorate the kids. By the time the offer expired in 1964, 30 million sets had been sold at 25 cents

apiece. That same year packages of Northern bathroom tissue began featuring the "Northern Girl." Based on one of the early Northern Kids, a Northern Girl doll was introduced in 1987, and more than 350,000 were sold. The Northern Girl continued to appear on packages into the 1990's and she was shown cuddling a quilt to her face on Quilted Northern wrappers.

When Quilted Northern bathroom tissue was introduced, 30-second TV commercials emphasized the link between the comfort of a quilt and the comfort of the bathroom tissue. A jingle emphasized the qualities of a quilt and suggested that consumers could take comfort in new Quilted Northern tissue. Accompanying shots depicted a young girl snuggled under a quilt with her teddy bear. Another 30-second teaser campaign asked viewers if their toilet paper was quilted. With romantic violin music in the background, viewers were told that they would be given a minute to find out before they were informed about new Quilted Northern.

Market studies have shown that just about every cart in a grocery store has one or more rolls of bathroom tissue. However, the wide range of prices and brands offers consumers choices. In slow economic times, some consumers trade down from premium brands to lower-priced brands. In order to retain market share, some manufacturers slash their prices in an effort to retain consumers' brand loyalty. Such was the case during the recession of the early 1990s, when the James River Corporation, which had acquired the Northern brand in 1982, followed other makers' strategies and cut its prices.

### "Green" Marketing

In 1992 Northern introduced a 100 percent recycled bathroom tissue for environmentally conscious consumers. Recognizing that some consumers based purchasing decisions on a product's impact on the environment, the company sought to demonstrate its friendliness to the environment. The Northern line also included Northern table napkins, and like the bathroom tissue, included one product made with 100 percent recycled paper.

The increasing success of Northern is apparent from its production statistics. When the Northern brand originated, 800 tons were

*A Northern tissue advertisement, circa 1950, promoting the softness of the brand.*

produced annually by one machine. By the time Northern celebrated its 90th anniversary at the Green Bay Mill in 1992, 87,000 tons or 6.8 million cases were produced annually with six machines. When accounting for the tonnage from other mills that produced Northern tissue, production rose to about 20.4 million cases per year.

The company will continue to rely on market research studies to determine the preferences and interests of consumers. Throughout the years, changes have been made to satisfy a broad range of consumer tastes in order to gain a leading share of the bathroom tissue market. It can be further expected that the company will strive not only to maintain a leading position among various national and regional brands but also to be the top brand of bathroom tissue.

Studies conducted by the company found that consumers had high regard for the quality and performance of Northern products. The company's objective was stated in a 1951 Northern publication, "Our biggest purpose and our constant goal is to satisfy the consumer. Obviously, we have done so to a great degree, for Northern is one of the top toilet tissue brands in the United States.

But until Northern is the top brand, we know there is room for us to grow and we shall have to continue our search for better ways of making better products."

## Further Reading:

Feldman, Amy, "Consumer Nondurables," *Forbes,* January 6, 1992, pp. 126–128.

*Introducing New Quilted Northern,* Norwalk, CT: James River Corporation.

James River Corporation Annual Report, Norwalk, CT: James River Corporation, 1992.

"Northern Bathroom Tissue Celebrates 90 Years in Business, 1902–1992!," *Tissue Talk,* August 6, 1992.

*Northern Rolls Out New Quilted Bathroom Tissue,* Chicago, IL: Bozell Public Relations, April 1993.

"Toilet Paper," *Consumer Reports,* August 1986, pp. 440–442.

*Toilet Paper Through Time,* Chicago, IL: Bozell Public Relations.

*—Dorothy Kroll*

# NOXZEMA®

The Noxzema brand medicated skin-cream, a product of Procter & Gamble Company, was first marketed by George Avery Bunting in Baltimore, Maryland, in 1914. It was sold initially in small blue glass jars, and later in plastic jars. Skin cream versions include Noxzema Original (1914), Noxzema Plus (1992), and Noxzema Sensitive (1993) and are available in jars and pumps. Other Noxzema products include Noxzema astringents, a line of acne medications, and Noxzema shaving cream.

## Brand Origins

Born in Bishopville, Maryland, in 1870, Dr. George Avery Bunting was a teacher and school principal who went back to college as a post-graduate in the late 1890s to study pharmacy. After graduating from the University of Maryland in 1899, Bunting opened a small drug store in Baltimore and began experimenting with formulas for a medicated skin cream in the back room. Sometime around 1914, he developed Dr. Bunting's Sunburn Remedy. He heated and mixed the white cream in a huge coffee pot before pouring it into little blue glass jars.

Bunting's customers jokingly complained about poor service because he was always busy mixing up batches of his skin cream. Bunting's formula became extremely popular with his customers, and Bunting soon decided to devote his attention to marketing his discovery. However, since the concoction was more than a sunburn remedy, Bunting needed a new name for his skin cream before he went into business. According to company lore, a customer who had tried the skin cream on his eczema, an inflammation that leaves the skin scaly and itchy, came into Bunting's pharmacy and announced, "Doc, your cream sure knocked my eczema." Bunting was apparently inspired by this unsolicited testimonial, and renamed his sunburn remedy "Noxzema." Bunting kept the blue jars, which came to be as widely recognized as the brand name.

In 1917, Bunting founded the Noxzema Chemical Company, which he ran out of his pharmacy. Bunting was also secretary of the Maryland Board of Pharmacy, and many of his colleagues began recommending Noxzema to their customers and investing in Bunting's company. By 1920, Bunting had moved out of the drug store and into the first Noxzema "factory," a small house in Baltimore that he rented for $27 a month. Bunting hired a one-man sales force, while he and a bookkeeper continued to mix and pour Noxzema by hand. He paid himself $50 a week as president of the company, and had become a well-known and highly respected member of the pharmaceutical community. In 1949 Dr. Robert L. Swain, editor of *Drug Topics* and past president of the Maryland Pharmaceutical Association, commented on the 35th anniversary of Noxzema, "I have known no one to whom friendship was so real and lasting as to Dr. Bunting."

## Brand Expansion

On the verge of bankruptcy during its first six years of operations, the Noxzema Chemical Company finally made a small profit in 1923. By 1925, annual sales had reached $100,000, although Bunting still paid himself only $50 a week. It was then that Bunting decided to expand beyond Baltimore, and going against the counsel of friends, he picked New York as his next target market.

As he had in Baltimore, Bunting put every available dollar into advertising Noxzema in the New York market as a multipurpose cream that was good for soothing tired feet, softening hands, and relieving the pain of sunburn. In one early ad, a nurse, called the Angel of Mercy, praised the healing qualities of Noxzema. Bunting's small sales force also canvassed the city, and the results were overwhelming. Demand for Noxzema rose so rapidly that Bunting was forced to build his first large scale factory, which he kept in Baltimore. Bunting began distributing Noxzema in Chicago and other Midwestern markets in 1928, and in the Southern and Pacific Coast states in 1930. Also in 1930, Bunting established the Canadian Corporation in Toronto to manufacture and market Noxzema. By 1938, Noxzema was being distributed nationally, with sales approaching $1 million.

In late 1938, Noxzema began sponsoring "Professor Quiz," a nationally broadcast radio program, and sales jumped 40 percent in one year. Noxzema later sponsored "Quiz of Two Cities" and "Mayor of the Town," which starred Lionel Barrymore. By 1944, the Noxzema brand product line had expanded to include shaving cream, suntan oil, and medicated cold cream, and company sales in the United States and Canada exceeded $3 million.

Noxzema's popularity continued to grow during World War II, despite wartime restrictions that made it impossible for the company to expand production facilities. In addition to meeting civilian demand, the company produced more than 63 million little

## AT A GLANCE

**N**oxzema brand of cosmetics, cleansers, and shaving creams founded as Dr. Bunting's Sunburn Remedy in 1914 in Baltimore, MD, by George Avery Bunting; product name changed to Noxzema, 1914; Noxzema Chemical Company founded in 1917; company renamed Noxell Corporation, 1966; company and brand name sold to Procter & Gamble Company, 1989.

**Performance:** *Market share—9% of shaving cream category.*

**Major competitor:** (Shaving cream) S.C. Johnson's Edge; (acne medication) Procter & Gamble's Clearasil.

**Advertising:** *Agency—Leo Burnett, Chicago, IL, 1990—. Major campaign—"Noxzema face moments."*

**Addresses:** *Parent company—Procter & Gamble Company, One Procter & Gamble Plaza, Cincinnati, OH 45202; phone: (513) 983-1100; (513) 983-7847.*

blue jars of Noxzema for the Armed Forces. After the war, with sales having reached $4 million, the company began work on a new 44,000-square-foot plant. By 1949, the company sold more than $5 million worth of Noxzema products.

### Postwar Developments

Following the war, the skin cream market became increasingly competitive, and Bunting's son, George Lloyd Bunting, became president and general manager of Noxzema Chemical. Under his direction, Noxzema Chemical expanded its distribution as well as its product line. Noxzema Medicated Soap and Nozain Medicated Cream were introduced in the 1950s, along with Nox-Ivy, a poison-ivy medication. By 1959, Noxzema products were available in 39 countries.

Lloyd Bunting also continued his father's extensive use of advertising. In the early 1950s, print advertisements relied on testimonials from average consumers. These ads pointed out that "letters from women all over America praise Noxzema's quick help for oily skin and externally-caused blemishes." Television commercials for Noxzema were also seen on a regular basis by an estimated 50 percent of the 45 million homes in the United States that had televisions. Noxzema continued to be one of the top brands advertised on television until the company began focusing more on its cosmetics lines in the late 1960s.

### Cover Girl "Makeup by Noxzema"

In 1961, Noxzema Chemical Company introduced Cover Girl cosmetics, which initially traded on the Noxzema brand name with the tag "Make-up by Noxzema." Cover Girl was endorsed in print ads and on television by superstar models such as Jennifer O'Neill, Christie Brinkley, and Cheryl Tiegs. Despite the advertising, however, Noxzema never pretended to be a chic or upscale cosmetic. Norbert A. Witt, who became president of the company in 1963, once told a meeting of The Newcomen Society that the strategy was to "make Noxzema products available wherever and whenever the consumer shops." This meant that Noxzema was available in supermarkets and drug stores, and from low-priced retailers like F. W. Woolworth and other discount chains. But even

with its cosmetics, the company shied away from upscale department stores and specialty shops where the Noxzema brand would have competed with flashier products. "From the start then, Cover Girl was run more like a toiletries business than a fashion-oriented cosmetics business," according to a 1983 *Forbes* article. The Cover Girl brand was especially successful in appealing to young women and teenagers, and became the leading brand of cosmetics, representing about 60 percent of the company's revenues.

In 1966, the Noxzema Chemical Company changed its name to the Noxell Corporation. About the same time, Noxzema shaving cream was reintroduced in aerosol cans. The commercials that accompanied the product launch were among the most risque on television. While "stripper music" played in the background, Gunilla Knutson, a former Miss Sweden, encouraged men to "Take it off, take it all off."

### Acne Medications

In 1981, Noxell introduced Noxzema 12-Hour Acne Medicine to accompany its Noxzema Antiseptic Skin Cleanser, which had been introduced in 1978. At the time, the company clearly repositioned Noxzema as a product for teenage consumers by advertising Noxzema along side its brand-name acne medicines in magazines such as *Seventeen* and by sponsoring television shows such as *Happy Days* and *Laverne and Shirley*. Noxell later introduced Noxzema Clear-Ups Medicated Pads, another acne medication. Robert W. Lindsey, then Noxell vice president and secretary, claimed in an interview with *Business Week* that Noxzema "already [has] the older customer," but the magazine noted that "critics [believe] Noxell should have expanded Noxzema into night or eye creams."

### Future Directions

In 1989, Noxell was purchased for $1.3 billion by the Procter & Gamble Company, giving the consumer products company an entry into the cosmetics market. In 1992 Procter & Camble introduced Noxzema Plus Cleansing Cream, which contained a moisturizer and was positioned for older women. Noxzema Sensitive Cleanser was added to the line in 1993.

### Further Reading:

Bernstein, Aaron, "Time to Make a Move," *Forbes,* February 14, 1983, p. 90.

Campbell, Hannah, "Why Did They Name It . . . ?," New York: Fleet Publishing Corporation, 1964, p. 120.

"Heft Isn't Everything," *Forbes,* January 23, 1978, p. 63.

"Noxell Glows in the Mass Market," *Business Week,* February 14, 1983, p. 148.

Rice, Faye, "Making Millions on Women Over 30," *Fortune,* May 25, 1987, pp. 75–78.

Shapiro, Eben, "'$1.3 Billion P&G Deal for Noxell," *New York Times,* September 23, 1989, p. 17.

Sullivan, Raymond F., "Four Noxzema Homes Picturize 35 Years of Progress," *35th Anniversary Souvenir Program,* Baltimore, MD: Noxzema Chemical Company, 1949.

Witt, Norbert A., *The Noxzema Story,* The Newcomen Society in North America, New York, 1967.

*—Dean Boyer*

# OFF!®

### INSECT REPELLENT

Ever since Off! was introduced in 1957 by S.C. Johnson and Son, Inc. (commonly known as Johnson Wax), it has been the undisputed leader of the insect repellent market. With just a few major line extensions— Deep Woods Off! , Ticks Off!, and Off! Skintastic—and an advertising budget that reached over $2 million in 1991, Johnson protected Off!'s market share to the point where it consistently held 50 percent of the market in the late 1980s and early 1990s. When Off! was introduced in 1957, it was much more effective than anything else on the market. Off! was the first insect repellent offered to the public that contained a highly effective chemical developed by the United States Department of Agriculture just after World War II to protect U.S. soldiers. This chemical, which Off! still uses, is N,N-diethyltoluamide (commonly known as "deet," but also called "jungle juice" by American soldiers in Vietnam).

Off!'s speed to the market and status as the first commercial repellent equipped with deet help explain its initial success, but this early advantage was soon lost when Miles Inc. introduced the Cutter brand of deet-based repellent just three years after Off! appeared. Since then, Cutter has consistently offered Off! its fiercest competition (Cutter held 30 percent of the market in 1991). Yet Off! has managed to maintain its dominance over Cutter and other brands since the late 1950s. Certainly Off!'s name—simple and easily associated with the product's purpose—has been a key. Furthermore, Off! has benefited from many successful ad campaigns run by Johnson's longtime ad agency, Foote, Cone & Belding of Chicago.

Off!'s longest running and perhaps most effective ad campaign was the one that appeared from the late 1950s to the early 1970s. It vividly demonstrated that an arm coated with Off! would remain unbitten—even in a cage full of hungry mosquitoes. Other reasons for Off!'s success, however, can be traced to S.C. Johnson & Son, Inc.'s response to the specific challenges to success in the insect repellent market, including fluctuating demand for varying types of repellents and negative publicity surrounding repelling chemicals.

## Responding to Sudden Demands

The demand for Off! and all other insect repellents fluctuates, sometimes quite predictably because of the shift in seasons. At other times, however, these market shifts can be dramatic and unpredictable, predicated on such factors as fear of insect-spread disease and meteorological trends (such as floods or droughts) that promote or restrict the reproduction of insects. For instance, in the late 1980s and early 1990s, sales of insect repellents increased as much as 30 percent in regions experiencing outbreaks of equine encephalitis (spread by mosquitoes) and Lyme disease and Rocky Mountain spotted fever (both spread by different kinds of ticks). Because the outbreak of Lyme disease during this period received so much press attention, the demand for insect repellents increased dramatically.

Johnson responded to this growing demand in 1989 when it spent most of the $3 million it had budgeted for Off! that year on an advertising campaign to sell Deep Woods Off! as a tick repellent; the company had previously marketed Deep Woods Off! almost strictly as a mosquito and fly repellent. But even with all the new marketing, Johnson came to realize, according to company spokeswoman Barbara Jorgensen in the *Los Angeles Times,* that there was "a great deal of consumer confusion that existed" over which Off! products to use against ticks. Johnson then attempted to correct this confusion in 1990 by introducing Ticks Off!—a more specialized tick repellent than Deep Woods Off!—which it distributed to regions especially affected by tick-borne diseases.

## Targeting The Marketplace

In order to take advantage of such demands successfully, Johnson has done more than just promote its products through the standard media of magazines and television. Off! has been featured in several clever marketing strategies designed to target likely consumers. For instance, in the mid-1980s Johnson effectively used a merchandising strategy in which it recommended that retailers feature Off! alongside such product tie-ins as paper plates and charcoal. In the early 1990s Johnson reached one of its most consistent consumer groups—campers—through such methods as the inclusion of product samples within promotional kits distributed at campgrounds. These methods proved "highly successful" for Off! according to a Johnson spokeswoman quoted in *Advertising Age* in 1993. Indeed, as Nancy Levine, president of the promotions company CampSamps, explained in *Advertising Age,* "Camping is a less costly way to travel, but many families who camp are actually very affluent and therefore they're a sought-after audience."

## AT A GLANCE

**O**ff! brand founded in 1957 in Racine, Wisconsin, by Samuel C. Johnson, head of New Products Department for S.C. Johnson & Son, Inc.; Off! was the first insect repellent offered to the public that contained N,N-diethyltoluamide (or "deet"), a chemical developed by the United States Department of Agriculture just after World War II to protect soldiers.

*Performance:* *Market share*—50% (top share) of insect repellent category. *Sales*—$43 million.

*Major competitor:* Miles Inc.'s Cutter.

*Advertising: Agency*—Foote, Cone & Belding, Chicago, IL, 1957—. *Major campaign*—Print ads selling Off! Skintastic with slogan "feels great on, keeps bugs Off!."

*Addresses: Parent company*—S.C. Johnson & Son, Inc., 1525 Howe Street, Racine, Wisconsin 53403-5011; phone: (414) 631-2000; fax: (414) 631-2632.

Another way in which Johnson reached campers in the early 1990s was through promotions within or for nearly all of the U.S. national parks. The National Park Service (NPS) allowed Johnson to advertise Off! in national parks, or with the name of national parks, in exchange for much-needed financial support from Johnson. For one such cooperative effort, Johnson paid for and distributed an NPS brochure that detailed the insects found in the parks and suggested means by which park guests could repel those insects. Johnson also promoted Off! with in-store displays that urged concerned individuals to join the "Green Team" by donating to the National Park and Conservation Association.

Johnson's search for ways to market Off! to park visitors backfired somewhat when it used an actual Florida state park ranger and the seal of Florida's Department of Natural Resources (DNR) in a print ad instructing people to "Take Off! to Florida State Parks." Although Johnson had gotten prior approval for the ad from Florida's DNR by promising to donate 50 cents of each Off! can sold in Florida (up to $10,000) to Florida's state parks during the summer of 1990, this and future cooperative efforts were jeopardized when Governor Bob Martinez and Attorney General Bob Butterworth found out about the ad after it had been printed and voiced their severe disapproval. The attorney general, as quoted in the *St. Petersburg Times,* objected to the "exploitation of the state's good name for the benefit of product promotion." The governor agreed, stating that "the public's business is represented through its government, and therefore the symbols of government should not be used for commercial purposes."

### Contending with Product Health Concerns

The Off! insect repellent line increased in popularity as a result of public fear over the outbreak of Lyme disease, but it also had to face some adverse effects from the attention health experts and officials began to pay to the sudden widespread use of maximum strength repellents like Maximum Strength Deep Woods Off!, which contains 95 percent deet. With the dramatically increased use of such repellents came several case studies on the effects of deet published by several major medical journals. These journals concluded that applying deet excessively or in high concentrations may be hazardous to a user's health, with the potential to cause slurred speech, confusion, and even seizures and comas among children.

On the opposite side of this controversy—that is, on the side of producers such as S.C. Johnson and Son, Inc.—is the Chemical Specialties Manufacturers Association (CSMA). CSMA claimed that after conducting 22 studies over seven years, it reached the confident conclusion that deet poses no health threats, even to children. The president of CSMA, Dr. Ralph Engel, has consequently charged in the *Boston Business Journal* that any regulators who argue otherwise are "wrong" and "just picking up rhetoric." Nevertheless, because of the growing health concerns about deet, New York state health officials in 1992 instituted a regulation that would ban insect repellents with concentrations of deet greater than 30 percent. Though Johnson filed a joint lawsuit with other insect repellent manufacturers to overturn the regulation, and succeeded in getting a temporary restraining order on the ban, Johnson still faced the growing prospect that other states—and perhaps the Environmental Protection Agency (EPA), which didn't yet control levels of deet—would soon follow suit and adopt their own bans.

Faced with this growing opposition to deet, Johnson had to respond. Johnson couldn't immediately alter its product line to satisfy those apprehensive about high levels of deet, so the company first attempted to allay public fears by defending deet. Johnson vehemently argued that deet is safe if used properly and reminded consumers to be sure to read Off!'s warning labels. "Deet has been around for over 30 years and has been used by millions of people," said Marilyn Blood, a spokeswoman for Johnson, in the *Orlando Sentinel Tribune.* "Our products have varying levels of deet to meet different needs. If people use the product according to label directions, it's fine."

Although deet may indeed be safe if used according to these label directions, "there are people using deet repellents and not reading the labels," as Carl Schreck of the U.S. Agricultural Research Service stated in the *Orlando Sentinel Tribune.* "I've seen parents take their children and spray them with repellent from head to toe. That's crazy." Opinions differ regarding the suitability of providing repellents with lower concentrations of deet. Such repellents were certainly available when health concerns first arose about deet, and manufacturers like Johnson began producing repellents with even lower concentrations of deet because of the negative publicity. But the increased use of these low concentrations led some health experts—those who still insisted that high concentrations are safe if applied properly—to express fears that the popularity of these weaker repellents might allow a greater spread of Lyme disease, since these low concentrations might not be effective against deer ticks.

Despite all the efforts to defend deet, the substantial negative publicity surrounding the substance continued to be a serious threat to Johnson's Off! line, which had dominated as much as 80 percent of the deet-based repellent market in the early 1990s. There is no known substance more effective than deet at repelling insects, although Johnson engages in research to discover just such an alternative. Even though deet was developed just after World War II, it has long been considered the most effective active ingredient in insect repellents. As Roger Grothaus, director of insect research at Johnson, explained in *Advertising Age* in 1989, "What's most fascinating is that deet has been so difficult to top. Since 1957, we've been looking for that 'factor X' that improves upon deet as much as deet improved on what came before. We're still looking."

## Maintaining Success Despite Deet

Johnson was thus faced with the dilemma of having to contend with negative publicity and regulatory restrictions against deet at the same time as it knew that it still needed to rely on deet, especially as fear over such insect-borne diseases as Lyme disease increased. This increasing fear, and the increasing demand it created for effective repellents, prompted Johnson in 1990 to introduce a new product called Ticks Off! specifically designed to repel disease-spreading ticks. This product contained 40 percent deet, a level of deet warned against by some health experts, but a level which Johnson nonetheless argued was necessary to protect against ticks. Johnson decided to introduce Ticks Off! on a limited scale and only in regions most affected by Lyme disease. Moreover, Johnson didn't even advertise the introduction of this extra-strength deet-based product. In stark contrast, when Johnson developed a repellent the very next year with only 7.5 percent deet content—called Off! Skintastic—the company spent $2 million in advertising and conducted its biggest sampling effort ever (distributing ten million samples) to launch this new product.

Besides selling Off! Skintastic as safer for children and those concerned about higher levels of deet, Johnson made the product even more appealing by selling it as a skin moisturizer. Because of common complaints that deet-based repellents leave the skin sticky or greasy, Johnson combined the deet with a moisturizing formula of aloe vera and glycerine. Actually, consumer complaints were not the only reason Johnson innovated this combination.

Much to Johnson's dismay, Off! experienced significant competition in the late 1980s from a non-repellent source: a bath oil and lotion called Skin So Soft, made by Avon Products, which many consumers believed could be used as an effective insect repellent—even though Avon doesn't market the product as such. "It's snake oil. Avon must be laughing all the way to the bank," declared Richard Pollack, a medical entomologist at the Harvard School of Public Health, in *The Boston Globe*. Though Skin So Soft's 1990 sales of $40 million were due primarily to its skin lotion properties, the product posed a threat to Off!'s sales. Johnson produced Off! Skintastic to blunt the Skin So Soft threat, though Off! Skintastic was also attractive to consumers because it was thought to contain a safe level of deet and at the same time did not leave their skin sticky or greasy like other deet-based repellents.

In addition to the maddening competition Off! Skintastic continued to receive from Skin So Soft, Johnson's low-concentration deet repellent soon also had to face what would become its biggest competitor in this new category: Skedaddle! (with 10 percent deet), created by the LittlePoint Corp., in 1992. Though Skedaddle! actually contained more deet than Off! Skintastic (10 percent vs. 7.5 percent), Skedaddle! was still attractive to the health-conscious consumer because of its use of founding technology that protects the body from overexposure to deet by preventing the chemical from being absorbed into the skin.

## Protecting Off!'s Market Share

Johnson has managed to protect Off!'s market share extremely well, especially considering all of the potential threats to that market standing that Johnson has faced. Increased competition,

coupled with negative publicity and regulatory restrictions against deet, have all challenged Off!'s market leader stature. Opposition to deet came as a threat to the entire repellent industry, but the makers of Off! proved able to adjust to the rapidly changing situation. Johnson shrewdly backed off from promoting its more potent deet repellents and heavily pushed the low-deet-content Off! Skintastic product. With Off! Skintastic, Johnson had a response to three major threats to market share: health concerns about overexposure to deet, Avon's Skin So Soft, and LittlePoint's Skedaddle! Still, Johnson cannot rely strictly on Off! Skintastic to protect Off!'s market share. There is still a need for stronger repellents. As Johnson itself acknowledges in a promotional sheet, Off! Skintastic is designed simply "for those who are traditionally non-repellent users and for those with lighter repellency needs." The rest of the Off! product line, however, remains a formidable one that shows no sign of weakening.

## Further Reading:

"Ad Growth Sluggish for 100," *Advertising Age*, September 24, 1987, p. 4.

Beam, Alex, "Deet, Skeeters and Skin So Soft; T. G. I. W.," *The Boston Globe*, June 19, 1991, p. 69.

"Butterworth Says Parks Should Off! Endorsement," *Orlando Sentinel Tribune*, August 28, 1990, p. B4.

Daniels, Cora, "A Repelling Business; Products to Fend Off Insects Do $50 Million a Year in Sales," *The Houston Chronicle*, August 16, 1992, p. 7; "All About Insect Repellents; Companies Grapple with the Bugs in Repellents," *The New York Times*, August 16, 1992, sec. 3, p. 12.

"Deet-Laden Products Are Best Bet to Keep Summer from Bugging You," *Chicago Tribune*, July 13, 1986, p. 3.

Fitzgerald, Kate, "Repellent Bzz-ness Booming," *Advertising Age*, June 24, 1991, p. 3.; "Sampling Efforts Find Campsites a Friendly Place," *Advertising Age*, June 21, 1993, p. 31.

"Focus on Summer Selling," *Supermarket News*, February 25, 1985, p. S4.

Freeman, Laurie, "Repellent Sales See Uptick," *Advertising Age*, July 24, 1989, p. 50.

"Insects Pay Homage to National Park Service 75th Anniversary," *PR Newswire*, June 20, 1991.

"Johnson Wax Introduces Off! Skintastic; Insect Repellent in Moisturizing Lotion Form Product Announcement," *Cosmetics International*, 15, September 10, 1991, p. 8.

"Kiddie Bug Repellent Boasts Less Chemicals," *Boston Business Journal*, July 13, 1992, p. 9.

Meier, Barry, "In Battle of the Bugs, Is Stronger Better?," *The New York Times*, July 20, 1991, p. 46.

"New Campaigns," *Advertising Age*, June 17, 1991, p. 45.

*The Off! Family of Insect Repellents*, Racine, WI: S.C. Johnson & Son, Inc., 1992.

Rovner, Sandy, "Beware of Biting Insects That Don't Buzz Off," *The Washington Post*, May 8, 1990, p. Z11.

Sutton, Charlotte, "Attorney General Irate about Off! Commercial," *St. Petersburg Times*, August 28, 1990, p. 4B.

"Top 100 Entry Price: $114 Million in Ads," *Advertising Age*, September 25, 1991, p. 44.

Villarreal, Luz, "There's More Than 1 Way to Swat a Mosquito," *Orlando Sentinel Tribune*, August 6, 1992, p. I1.

Wesley, Joya L., "Not Much Net Profit in Anti-Lyme Disease Line," *Los Angeles Times*, September 23, 1990.

—*Jeffrey E. Mash*

# OIL OF OLAY®

Oil of Olay is the world's best-selling brand of facial moisturizer. Now owned by consumer goods giant Procter & Gamble, Oil of Olay began as the product of a South African company so small it had no advertising budget for years. Despite this, the "mysterious fluid" soon became popular among women around the world who used it to make their skin look younger. The brand has grown over the years into a diversified product line that includes a beauty fluid for extra sensitive skin, moisturizers with sunscreen, a bath bar, and an array of facial cleansing products.

## Brand Origins

South African chemist Graham Gordon Wulff formulated Oil of Olay during World War II as a topical skin treatment intended to prevent dehydration of burn wounds on British Royal Air Force pilots. Sensing his creation's possible appeal as a beauty treatment, Wulff refined the product after the war and recruited Shaun Adams Lowe to help him market it. The two partners founded Adams National in 1949 and began selling the product door-to-door in South Africa.

Wulff and Lowe devised the original name, Oil of Ulan, to give the impression that the product was made with an extract from a rare and exotic plant. Not only did the Ulan plant never exist, but Adams National modified the name of the product in each country in order for it to sound more pleasing and realistic to the consumers. Thus, the product is now called Oil of Olay in the United States, Oil of Ulay in England, Oil of Olaz throughout most of Europe, and Oil of Ulan in South Africa.

## Early Marketing Strategies

Wulff and Lowe's small budget prevented the widespread advertising of Oil of Olay in its early years. In fact, they launched the product with no advertising whatsoever, relying instead on public relations efforts they hoped would gain them editorial coverage. Capitalizing on the unusual name, they presented the product as something mysterious and exotic, and in keeping with this strategy, they would not reveal the formula or any of the ingredients. Wulff and Lowe even refused to define the purpose of the product—a flagrant contradiction of traditional marketing practices. Instead, they described a variety of characteristics of the "oil," such as its smoothness, silkiness, ease of absorption, and ability to refresh dry skin. Each woman was to see in it what she needed.

The strategy worked. As sales increased and budget restrictions loosened, Adams National decided to continue their secretive advertising style. Because South Africa allowed no commercial television at the time, the company chose print as their primary medium for advertising. The advertisements' editorial style was so convincing that it was difficult to distinguish the ads from editorial writing. The product's image as something secret and mysterious and its unusually discreet advertising intrigued journalists, who promoted the product by giving it press coverage.

The public relations program later expanded to include a consumer advice service. At first Adams National offered this service in the company's traditional manner, through press releases and other editorial means, but later the consumer tips were incorporated into Oil of Olay's advertising. The name of the beauty advisor, Margaret Merril, created some confusion when Adams National was bought in 1971 by Richarson Merrill. Although it was never revealed whether Margaret Merril was a real person or not, the new company continued to to utilize the advice tips in Oil of Olay's advertising around the world.

## International Market

Oil of Olay expanded internationally upon its debut in Australia in 1957, followed by its unveiling in the United States and England in 1962. The product was also introduced to the Netherlands in 1964, Canada in 1965, Germany in 1966, and Mexico in 1967. Although the name was tailored to each new market, marketing tactics remained the same. Restrained advertising and a mysterious image were key strategies in each country. Even press releases were identical; South African press releases that referred to skin becoming "dried out on the veldt" or "dry from long days in the sun" were used almost word for word in countries throughout the world, regardless of climate or geography. These references added to the product's exotic appeal, and soon Oil of Olay was enjoying strong international sales.

Oil of Olay's successful international development attracted interest among several major consumer products companies in the late 1960s. Richardson Merrill (later renamed Richardson-Vicks) prevailed and acquired Adams National in 1971 for what was at the time a considerable amount of money. Richardson-Vicks's substantial resources fostered Oil of Olay's continued growth. Wider distribution and heavy advertising expenditures, including television advertising, fuelled the product's rise in popularity.

## AT A GLANCE

**N**ame originally Oil of Ulan Beauty Fluid; marketed as Oil of Ulay in England, Oil of Olaz in most of Europe, and as Oil of Olay in the United States; formulated in South Africa during World War II by Graham Gordon Wulff as a treatment for burn wounds; marketed by the Adams National (founded by Wulff and marketer Shaun Adams Lowe in the early 1950s); Adams National bought by Richardson Merrill in 1970; company later renamed Richardson-Vicks; Richardson-Vicks acquired by Procter & Gamble in 1985.

**Performance:** *Market share*—28% (top share, 1990) of the facial moisturizer category.

**Major competitor:** Noxell Corp.'s Noxzema; also Unilever's Pond's, Cosmair's Plentitude.

**Advertising:** *Agency*—Wells Rich Greene BDDP, New York, NY. *Major campaign*—"Oil of Olay. Younger looking skin is proof that it works."

**Addresses:** *Parent company*—Richardson-Vicks USA Inc., 1 Far Mill Crossing, Shelton, CT 06484; phone (203) 925-6000; fax: (203) 925-6822. *Ultimate parent company*—Procter & Gamble Company, 1 Procter & Gamble Plaza, Cincinnati, OH 45202; phone: (513) 983-1100; fax: (513) 562-4500.

Richardson-Vicks continued to introduce the product to other countries, launching it in France in 1973 and in Italy the following year.

### Image Continuity

Although Richardson-Vicks applied its own mass marketing strategy to Oil of Olay after the company acquired the brand, it strove to maintain the mysterious image of the beauty fluid. Refusing to specifically define the product or reveal its formula, Richardson-Vicks wanted women to find that the formula suited their particular needs. However, the company broke from the product's formerly subdued advertising strategy and vastly increased its advertising expenditures. This effort to increase the product's visibility through television and print media led to steady sales growth for Oil of Olay.

Despite this success, the company did not abandon the mainstays of the product's early growth: public relations and beauty advice. In addition, Richardson-Vicks preserved the original formula of the product for the entire fourteen years it owned Oil of Olay. Although a new formula had been developed in Europe, Richardson-Vicks had not authorized the local management to use it by the time they sold the company in 1985.

### Brand Development

Although department stores had long offered extensive lines of skin care products, mass-market brands sold in grocery and drug stores were usually limited to single product lines. When Richardson-Vicks acquired Adams National, the Olay product line fit the standard picture of a mass-market brand; it consisted of only Oil of Olay and Olay Vitalizing Night Cream. When the brand's growth began to slow in the late 1970s, Richardson-Vicks hoped to increase sales volume by introducing Night of Olay in the United States. However, weak promotional support and the product's similarity to Olay Vitalizing Night Cream resulted in a disappointing reception.

Oil of Olay maintained a strong hold on the mass-market facial moisturizing category through the early 1980s. Capitalizing on this strength, Richardson-Vicks introduced the Olay Beauty Bar in 1983. After some initial distribution difficulties, the cleansing bar achieved a respectable $6 million in sales in 1984. Although that figure was only a small fraction of the Oil of Olay brand's $100 million total for that year, the company expected Olay Beauty Bar sales to more than double the following year. In 1984 the company extended Olay's cleansing line with Olay Beauty Cleanser, a facial cleanser that distinguished itself from the comptetition with its pump format packaging. Richardson-Vicks invested a great deal of money in the new products' launch and supported them with continued advertising in hopes of establishing them in the competitive market.

By the mid-1980s Oil of Olay was entrenched as the leading mass-market facial moisturizer. Richardson-Vicks hoped to further increase the product's sales by enticing customers away from department store brands as well. Peter Wilson, former vice president of marketing for Richardson-Vicks' personal care department, told *Advertising Age* that "there's some difference in our products, but it's minimal. Oil of Olay is just as good as, if not better than, department store brands. Consumers are paying for the fragrance, image, packaging, and service of department stores."

### Procter & Gamble Redirects Brand

Procter & Gamble (P&G) acquired Richardson-Vicks in 1985, and shortly thereafter the company redesigned Oil of Olay's marketing strategy. With their philosophy of capturing consumers while they were young in hopes that it would initiate brand loyalty, P&G was dissatisfied with Oil of Olay's general advertising thrust, "makes you look younger," because it limited their market to women over the age of 35. For this reason and because they felt that Oil of Olay was being threatened by Pond's younger image, P&G aimed for a wider range of consumers and relaunched the brand with a new advertising campaign.

Within two years of acquiring the brand, P&G introduced a new "enriched" formulation of Oil of Olay in the United States. A 15 percent year-on-year sales increase followed, along with a simultaneous increase in advertising expeditures. Originally, the brand's management hesitated to introduce the new European formula without assurances that American consumers would like it. Thus, several months of research and development were necessary before P&G introduced the enriched formulation in the United States.

In an article for *MarketScope*, Nicholas Hall, a former marketing manager for Oil of Olay at Procter and Gamble, pointed to a weakness in the company's usual marketing strategy as it applied to Oil of Olay. "P&G prefers to operate in markets where brand differences, features, and benefits can be measured in quantitative not qualitative terms," Hall stated. "This is diametrically opposed to the skin care market, where the greatest advances in recent years have been made by prestige and specialist brands, particularly those active in the anti-ageing or anti-cellulite categories. If ever there were products where the benefit was in the mind rather than in the eye, it is these, and yet this is where recent growth has come from." Hall saw another disadvantage in the company's typical approach to marketing in that P&G attempts to create one or two megabrands in each category worldwide, as seen in their efforts with Pampers brand diapers and Crest brand toothpaste. This approach, according to Hall, is difficult to succeed with in the skin care market, where consumers tend to experiment with different products and brand loyalty is low.

However, over the next several years P&G combined their strategy of creating megabrands with consumers' desire for specialty skin care products. The company abandoned Oil of Olay's long-standing efforts of allowing women to define the product and began segmenting consumers by needs and preferences. In 1988 they introduced their highly successful Sensitive Skin Beauty Fluid which they followed in 1989 with their Intensive Moisture Complex. In 1990 they introduced the Oil of Olay Cleansing Collection, which added Foaming Face Wash, Water-Rinsable Cold Cream, and Refreshing Toner to the existing Facial Cleansing Bar and Facial Cleansing Lotion. In 1991 Oil of Olay entered the bath bar market with a conditioning bath bar designed to compete with the market leader, Unilever's Dove. Although P&G already held nine percent of this market with their Ivory bath bar, they hoped to capture more of the beauty segment of this category with the Oil of Olay product. Ads challenged Dove with the statement that the Olay bar provided "younger feeling skin all over because it's not a soap."

P&G succeeded in bettering the 21 percent share of the moisturizer market that Oil of Olay held in 1984 when it was owned by Richardson-Vicks. By 1990 Oil of Olay had stretched its lead as the number one facial moisturizer to 28 percent of the market. In 1991 Oil of Olay's extended product line also ranked first in the mass-market facial skincare category with more than a 20 percent share.

In 1992 P&G announced its plans to introduce another new series of Oil of Olay skincare products. Described as more efficacious and technologically advanced than their current products, the new line was scheduled to be released in 1993. Advertising for the line was being handled by Wells Rich Greene BDDP, New York, who released the name of one of the future products: Hydro Gel Advanced Moisturizer. No longer relying on the appeal of an oil extracted from an exotic plant or a mysterious formula, the company apparently felt that consumers wanted products improved by the latest scientific advances. Banking on Oil of Olay's respectable history its own ample resources, P&G aims to strengthen its hold on the skin care market.

## Further Reading:

Gibb, Robina N., "What P & G Sees in Vicks's Medicine Chest," *Business Week,* October 14, 1985, pp. 41–42.

Hall, Nicholas, "A Secret that Was Never Revealed," *MarketScope,* Spring 1989, pp. 8–12.

"P&G Developing New Oil of Olay," *Advertising Age,* October 26, 1992, p. 20.

"Repair," *Advertising Age,* February 21, 1985, pp. 13, 30.

Sloan, Pat, "Night of Olay Support Still Awaited by Stores," *Advertising Age,* April 30, 1979.

Sloan, Pat, "Oil of Olay to Add 2nd New Cleansing Line," *Advertising Age,* October 15, 1984, pp. 3, 93.

Sloan, Pat, "Skincare Surges in Mass Market," *Advertising Age,* July 30, 1990, p. 18.

Sloan, Pat, "Olay Bath Bar Takes Aim at Dove," *Advertising Age,* February 4, 1991, p. 9.

*—Susan Windisch Brown*

# OLD SPICE®

The Old Spice line of men's grooming products includes the world's best-selling men's fragrance brand and one of the most enduring aftershave lotions in the United States. Packaged in cream-colored bottles brandishing a clipper ship (which was changed to a yacht in 1993), Old Spice products have offered a masculine, clean-scented deodorant protection for over 50 years. When other men's toiletries faded from the market, the Old Spice brand endured by adapting to consumers' changing needs and tastes. Just one line of many personal care products owned by the Procter & Gamble Company, Old Spice toiletries have remained a market share leader due to their tradition of product innovation and astute advertising.

## Brand Origins

The year was 1934, Franklin Delano Roosevelt was President of the United States, and in a crowded New York City loft, William Lighthouse Schultz formulated his Early American Old Spice fragrances and soaps for women. In 1936 the line rolled out nationally, but success was not immediate. Undaunted, Schultz received a trademark for the name in 1937 and added the Old Spice men's fragrance line. The early American motif that Schultz developed was adapted for the packaging as well.

## Early Marketing Strategy and First Commercial Success

Unlike other men's toiletries which were advertised exclusively around holidays, the Old Spice brand was advertised year-round in drugstores and supermarkets. The scent and the image created a powerful impact on the great middle market of consumers who thought that Mennen Skin Bracer and Aqua Velva were too cheap and designer aftershaves too expensive. Men liked it not only because the aftershave, soap, and deodorant were refreshing, but because the sweet and spicy scent appealed to the women in their lives as well. Women gave their husbands, fathers, brothers, and boyfriends Old Spice products on birthdays and holidays.

Schultz's canniest marketing maneuver came when he convinced the U.S. Army to put Old Spice aftershave in soldiers' toiletry kits during World War II. In this manner thousands of young men were introduced to the brand overnight. The marketing strategy enhanced Old Spice's macho image at a time when many men thought that using an aftershave or a cologne was unmanly.

When the soldiers returned home, they continued using Old Spice products.

Manufacturing facilities grew as quickly as the brand name. Schultz's burgeoning business grew exponentially, and his company, Shulton, Inc., relocated across the river to Hoboken, New Jersey. When that plant became inadequate, Shulton moved again to nearby Clifton, New Jersey, and established the company's first permanent home there in the autumn of 1946. In 1971 Old Spice was purchased by the American Cyanamid Company, of Wayne, New Jersey, and in 1990 the brand was acquired by consumer products conglomerate Procter & Gamble Company (P&G) of Cincinnati, Ohio.

## Advertising Innovations

Under Shulton, Inc. most of Old Spice's advertising budget was allocated to network prime-time and daytime television, with a small share directed toward ads in *Cosmopolitan, Glamour, Good Housekeeping,* and *Family Circle* to reach female gift-givers. In the 1990s under Procter & Gamble, Old Spice made full use of all these avenues of advertising as well as other print media. P&G advertising dated back to 1882, when Harley Procter, son of the co-founder of the company, formulated the first promotional campaign for Ivory Soap. In 1993 health and beauty aids sections of retail stores regularly received large cardboard displays for Old Spice featuring refund tear-off forms. In addition, color inserts in Sunday newspapers continued to extol the virtues of Old Spice, and potential consumers periodically received trial sizes of Old Spice products via direct mail.

To please the customer, P&G had to get to know its customer. This objective was attained through intense market research—mail surveys in particular. One example of P&G's sensitivity to consumer concerns lay in the handling of communications. In the late 1970s P&G became one of the first companies to include toll-free telephone numbers on its packages to facilitate two-way communication with its consumers, and by the early 1980s every P&G package boasted such a number.

October of 1991 saw the advent of an adventurous new marketing strategy for P&G—the EDLP (Everyday Low Price) policy which lowered the store's cost for P&G products and also eliminated the marketer's generous trade allowances. A reflection of CEO Edwin L. Artzt's vision of a new P&G—a more profitable

## AT A GLANCE

**O**ld Spice brand of men's toiletries was founded in 1934 by William Lightfoot Schultz in New York City; Shultz formed Shulton, Inc. as the brand's parent company; trademark registered in 1937 by Shulton, Inc.; brand sold in 1971 to American Cyanamid Company, Wayne, NJ; brand acquired in 1990 by Procter & Gamble Company, Cincinnati, OH.

*Performance:* *Market share*—4.3% of the deodorant category; 1.6% of the men's and women's shaving cream category. *Sales*—$28.3 million in the deodorant category; $1.6 million in the men's and women's shaving cream category (August 1992 to February 1993).

*Major competitor:* Deodorant category—Mennen's Speed Stick, Carter-Wallace's Arrid, Procter & Gamble's Sure; shaving cream category—S.C. Johnson & Son's Edge, Gillette Company's Foamy, Pfizer Inc.'s Barbasol; men's fragrance category—Mennen's Skin Bracer, Coty's Stetson.

*Advertising:* *Agency*—Tatham/RSCG, Chicago, IL. *Major campaign*—"Old Spice . . . isn't just for fathers."

*Addresses:* *Parent company*—Procter & Gamble Company, One Procter & Gamble Plaza, Cincinnati, OH 45202; phone: (513) 983-1100; fax: (513) 983-7847.

company driven by lower costs and higher brand loyalty derived from streamlined manufacturing operations, more control over trade promotions, and consumer-oriented advertising—initially this "value-pricing" program was not well-regarded by retailers. As a trade-off, one of P&G's advertising agencies, J. Brown and Associates in New York City, developed the Bonus Media Program, in which some TV spots appeared to promote a specific retailer.

### Brand Development and Product Changes

As trends changed, so did Old Spice. In June of 1989 the Liquid Stick Anti-Perspirant/Deodorant was discontinued, as well as less preferred anti-perspirant/deodorant scents. Procter & Gamble also changed the formulation of the existing Old Spice Anti-Perspirant/Deodorants in an attempt to improve the fragrance and changed the packaging from the familiar red and beige to red on red. Other fine-tuning of the product line followed with the premiere of the three-ounce Anti-Perspirant/Deodorant Solid in the original, fresh, and musk scents and the discontinuation of the Leather-Scented Cologne, Classic Sport Scent, Island Breeze, and the smaller-size musk scents. In January of 1993 Soap-on-a-Rope, the Shave Mug Refill, and the Lime Anti-Perspirant/Deodorant Aerosol were reformulated to comply with the California Clean Air Standards Act which sought to control smog. The High Endurance Glycol-Based Wide Stick in original, fresh, and musk scents debuted in April of 1993. In May of 1993 a new Spray Cologne rolled out nationally. Also in May the shape of the bottle was changed on the Traveler After-Shave Lotion and Pre-Electric Shave. Sensitive Skin After-Shave Splash was introduced nationally in a patented nonalcoholic formula in packaging that brandished green and silver bands (signifying that the product was alcohol-free). In July of 1993 the principal Old Spice plant location was moved to Greensboro, North Carolina, from Memphis, Tennessee.

In an attempt to attract a younger segment of the market to its flagship Old Spice After-Shave, Procter & Gamble dry-docked the

whistling mariner and clipper ship in favor of more modern images. Television commercials for 1993 featured young, athletic characters, though the sea motif was preserved with closing shots of ocean images. The classic clipper ship was replaced by a sleek new yacht in television and print advertisements.

### Environmental Controversy

In 1975 and 1976 the use of aerosol sprays became controversial when studies conducted by the Food and Drug Administration suggested that the sprays' chlorofluorocarbon propellants might be responsible for damage to the earth's ozone layer. When Procter & Gamble acquired Old Spice from American Cyanamid Company in 1990, at least a quarter of Old Spice's research and development expenditures were allocated to satisfying governmental regulations. Old Spice was continuously examined by P&G for possible formula, packaging, and graphics modification.

By the time the Old Spice brand was ready for overseas marketing, P&G manufacturing facilities could be found worldwide. P&G's international expansion started in 1897 when Ivory soap was introduced in England. By 1937, the centennial of P&G's founding, the company had acquired plants in Canada, Europe, and the Pacific Rim. By 1993 Old Spice products were sold in more than 50 countries worldwide, from Canada to the Far East.

### Performance Appraisal

Through the years, Old Spice shaving toiletries and anti-perspirant consistently retained hefty market shares in their respective categories. For instance, during the 26 weeks ending on February 20, 1993, Old Spice Shaving Cream sold $1.6 million worth of goods, down 11.9 percent from the previous year's sales, for a 1.6 percent, or seventh-place, market share. During those same 26 weeks, in the deodorant category, Old Spice products sold $28.3 million worth of goods, a three percent increase over the previous year, for a market share of 4.3 percent, or a ninth-place ranking. Old Spice continued to present a strong brand image and maintained its niche on the charts.

### Future Predictions

Since its debut in 1937, the Old Spice brand has remained a market share leader in the competitive markets of deodorant and men's shaving cream products. When Procter & Gamble acquired the brand, the brand was boosted by the company's aggressive marketing philosophy. If past performance proved any predicator of subsequent success, Old Spice would continue to keep pace with progress. Procter & Gamble chemists and marketers are always thinking of tomorrow by querying consumers, by sampling and advertising, and by creating new technologies, improving, but not deviating from, Old Spice's basic formulas. As a P&G researcher once remarked: "Through constant improvement, we must manage every existing brand so that it can flourish year after year in an ever-changing, intensely competitive marketplace. . . . At P&G, we create the future."

### Further Reading:

*Answers About Marketing,* Cincinnati: The Procter & Gamble Company, 1993.

"Coming Clean in America," *U.S. News and World Report,* June 26, 1989, p. 74.

"Deodorants at a Glance," *Adweek's Marketing Week,* April 10, 1989, p. 12.

*Facts About Procter & Gamble,* Cincinnati: The Procter & Gamble Company, 1993.

"Gender Marketing Dominates Deodorant Market," *U.S. Distribution Journal,* October 1989, p. 12.

Lawrence, Jennifer, "P&G Customizes Ads to Plug Retailers," *Advertising Age,* February 8, 1993, p. 28.

Lawrence, Jennifer, "P&G Hooks Up Interactive Product-Sampling Hot Line," *Advertising Age,* October 5, 1992, p. 3.

Lawrence, Jennifer, "Will P&G's Pricing Policy Pull Retailers Over to Its Side?" *Advertising Age,* April 19, 1993, pp. 1, 42–43.

Lief, Alfred, *"It Floats"; The Story of Procter & Gamble,* New York: Rinehart, 1958.

Liesse, Julie, "Brand Scorecard," *Advertising Age,* April 19, 1993, p. 22.

Muirhead, Greg, "Getting Deodorants a Little Closer," *Supermarket News,* January 6, 1992, p. 21.

"Old Spice 'Freshens Up,' " Sunday *Star-Ledger* (Newark, NJ), Section 3, p. 7.

The Procter & Gamble Company 1992 Annual Report, Cincinnati: The Procter & Gamble Company, 1993.

*Procter & Gamble: The House That Ivory Built,* Lincolnwood, IL: NTC Business Books, 1988.

Schiller, Zachary, "P&G Is Adding New Spice to Old Spice," *Business Week,* July 9, 1990, p. 32.

Schisgall, Oscar, *Eyes on Tomorrow: The Evolution of Procter & Gamble,* Chicago: J.G. Ferguson Publishing Company, 1981.

Schnorbus, Paula, "Vial Strategies," *Marketing & Media Decisions,* June 1987, p. 125.

Shields, Jody, "*Vogue* Beauty: Sweat," *Vogue,* June 1991, pp. 111–112, 114.

Sloan, Pat, "Old Spice Liquid Stick Rolls Out," *Advertising Age,* October 24, 1988, p. 86.

Trachtenberg, Jeffrey A., editor, "The Sweet Smell of Success," *Business Week,* August 10, 1987, pp. 92–93.

*—Virginia Barnstorff*

# OSHKOSH B'GOSH®

OshKosh B'Gosh, "The Genuine Article Since 1895," is the industry leader in casual clothes for kids. A classic, household brand name, OshKosh stands for durable casual clothing that in a fairly short time has become a prominent symbol of American culture. The publicly held, family-run Oshkosh, Wisconsin, company that owns the brand did not begin aggressively marketing children's wear—which accounts for 95 percent of total sales—until the mid-1970s, more than three-quarters of a century after the clothes manufacturer was founded. Well into the 1950s, in fact, the company was known almost exclusively for its line of highly durable work apparel geared toward men and boys. A reorientation of the company and the brand occurred when a mail-order house featured a pair of children's overalls in its national catalog. When Bloomingdale's, Lord & Taylor, and Saks Fifth Avenue all began selling the "pint-sized" OshKosh clothes, the brand enjoyed a national rebirth and became linked not simply with quality but with cuteness, kids, and upscale chic.

Since that time, the story of OshKosh's growth has read, more often than not, like a fairy tale. One critical point did arrive with OshKosh's plunge into mid-level retailing (i.e. J.C. Penney, Sears, and Kids "R" Us), a controversial move that elicited pronouncements of the brand's decline. However, through premium pricing and family-oriented advertising, OshKosh has retained its prestige appeal while attracting a far broader, middle-class following. The brand now garners 28 percent of the market for children's wear, despite stiff competition from less expensive children's labels, including Healthtex and Carter's. OshKosh's biggest challenge now is convincing retailers, parents, young adults, and older children that the brand can be all things to all ages: that OshKosh need not be limited by its dominant "baby brand" status.

## Why "B'Gosh"?

OshKosh B'Gosh, Inc., was founded as Grove Manufacturing Co. in 1895. At that time, there was a particularly high demand by farmers, railroad workers, and tradesmen for clothing that was rugged, durable, and reasonably priced. The hickory-striped denim bib overalls produced by Grove Manufacturing satisfied these demands perfectly. The original garment was so successful that it quickly spawned a broadened line of work clothes that included pants, jackets, and shirts. In 1896 the company renamed itself Oshkosh Clothing and Manufacturing; then in the early 1900s, one of the owners, William Pollock, embarked on a fabric-buying trip to New York City. There he saw a vaudeville act in which the phrase "Oshkosh b'gosh" was used in a humorous sketch. Pollock immediately recognized the value in the town's unusual name (a Menominee Indian word that means "brave") and added the "B'Gosh" to OshKosh products.

Pollock was far from alone in his appreciation of the name. Through the years, the town has been the subject of light-hearted fun for numerous comedians, from Milton Berle to Henny Youngman. Now, said a Milwaukee advertising executive quoted in *Working Woman*, "the name alone is worth millions of dollars in advertising. . . . It's been like opening a can of gasoline under a match. The market was ready to embrace it."

## Dressing up Overalls

In accordance with Pollock's early intuition, OshKosh B'Gosh (the brand name became the company name in 1937) became a manufacturer known for its creative advertising and forward-thinking promotion. As Jerry Jakubovics stated in *Management Review,* "Not everyone looks at a bib overall and sees a glamour product. But OshKosh B'Gosh has made every effort to treat it this way through the effective use of promotion." In the 1930s the company sponsored daily radio contests with $5 prizes for the most creative ad slogan; similar contests were held around the country at state and county fairs. Consumers vied against each other to coin jingles proclaiming the superiority of OshKosh B'Gosh products and, in the process, spread the company's name among their neighbors. For a relatively small investment, OshKosh B'Gosh received a great deal of advertising.

In addition to the contests, the company sponsored radio host Pat Butram, who was accompanied by the "OshKosh B'Gosh Radio Boys," and then hired actor Andy Devine as its radio spokesperson. The firm also garnered considerable publicity from its tradition of presenting political figures and celebrities with sample overalls. During their presidential campaigns, Dwight Eisenhower and John Kennedy were photographed wearing OshKosh B'Gosh products, and talk-show host Johnny Carson modeled a pair of bib overalls made of gold lamé on *The Tonight Show*. Later large-scale promotions have included the Picture Perfect Photo Contest, which in its first year attracted well over 130,000 entries.

## AT A GLANCE

**B**rand founded in 1895 in Oshkosh, WI, by the Grove Manufacturing Co.; company name changed to Oshkosh Clothing and Manufacturing Co., 1896, then to Oshkosh Overall Co., then to OshKosh B'Gosh, Inc., 1937; developers include William Pollock, Earl Wyman, Charles F. Hyde, and Douglas W. Hyde.

**Performance:** *Market share*—28% of children's wear branded business. *Sales*—$346.2 million (1992).

**Advertising:** *Agency*—Laughlin & Constable, Milwaukee, WI, 1979—. *Major campaign*—Various nostalgic, lighthearted print ads featuring children in casual clothes with the blue and gold logo and the slogan "The Genuine Article Since 1895"; one ad features a father and daughter sharing a laugh, with the word sequence "Freckles," "Sniffles," "Sticky Fingers," "Ghost Stories," "Snow Angels," "Kids," "OshKosh B'Gosh," "As Genuine As Ever."

**Major competitor:** Healthtex brand children's clothing.

**Addresses:** *Parent company*—OshKosh B'Gosh, Inc., 112 Otter Ave., Box 300, Oshkosh, WI 54902-0300; phone: (414) 231-8800; fax: (414) 231-8621.

### Entering the Children's Market

While OshKosh's reputation for providing well-fitting, rugged, sensible work clothes at competitive prices was untouchable, it was also self-limiting: save for longstanding but quiet sales of novelty bibs for children and a modest foray in the 1950s into young men's sportswear, the company was single-mindedly devoted to expanding and satisfying its original market. In fact, in 1968, it was considering dropping children's clothing altogether. That year, however, Wisconsin-based mail-order firm Miles Kimball Co. added children's overalls by OshKosh B'Gosh to its Christmas catalog. Orders for 15,000 pairs of the bib overalls caused OshKosh B'Gosh to begin rethinking its strategy. As Charles F. Hyde (then president, now chairman) explained to William Harris in *Forbes,* company executives began wondering, "if overalls are that popular for Miles Kimball customers, why shouldn't retailers find some sort of response for them? Maybe our traditional outlets—men's and boy's clothing stores—are the wrong outlets."

Through direct mail, OshKosh B'Gosh began promoting to hundreds of children's clothing specialty stores around the country (until then, some 90 percent of sales were drawn from within a 600-mile radius of the company's headquarters). Its brochure advertised the seven items then constituting its children's line, including overalls, coveralls, and painter's pants. The plan, first championed by Hyde's son and current CEO, Douglas, hardly constituted a strategy that would launch the company to the first ranks of clothing manufacturers for kids. Nonetheless, that was the ultimate result.

Existing customers saw a name they recognized being sold through a different outlet; they knew the men's overalls had a reputation for durability and assumed that they would be just as rugged for children. As Jerry Jakubovics noted in *Management Review,* the company's timing and promotional strategy was perfect: "Apparently, children dressed in overalls conjured up for many the image of the kind of clothing worn by Tom Sawyer. And in the mid-1970s, when overalls were the fashion rage, these

garments got an additional boost." By the 1980s, OshKosh B'Gosh was positioned to become, as Charles Paikert put it in *Adweek's Marketing Week,* "the strongest force in the children's clothing market."

### Beyond Denims

Much of OshKosh's success was based on the company's decision in the early 1980s to expand its children's line beyond the plain, striped denim look that had been its hallmark since the turn of the century. It adopted what the industry refers to as a "fashion forward" look: multiple fabric choices in a variety of prints and brightly colored solids. In essence, they took their bib overalls upscale. Young parents appreciated the durability of the garments as well as the appeal of the OshKosh look, well suited to the rapidly evolving, trendy "yuppie" lifestyle of the 1980s.

Although the expanded line of overalls—rugged, colorful, and unisex—sold incredibly well, the company elected not to rest on its success. The decision was made to move further into the children's clothing market with a full complement of jackets, jeans, jumpers, shorts, skirts, sweaters, sleepwear, and swimwear. Eventually the firm licensed out the manufacturing of such items as shoes, hats, mittens, and gloves, all with the blue and gold OshKosh B'Gosh logo prominently displayed.

### New Retail Outlets

When economic recession brought difficult times for retailers, the effects were soon felt by manufacturers, including children's clothing manufacturers. The upscale reputation that helped OshKosh B'Gosh achieve its remarkable growth threatened to work against it in the increasingly cautious retail market. As one young parent told Julia Flynn Siler in *Business Week:* "I want [my son] to be trendy-looking. But I don't want to spend lots of money." In June of 1991 the company announced its plan to begin selling OshKosh products through more accessible chain stores. "We believe eventually it will hurt their brand name," a buyer for Dayton Hudson and Marshall Field's told Siler in *Business Week.*

Fortunately, the company had predicated its move on thorough research. In particular, corporate analysts studied the experience of Levi Strauss & Co., another long-time marketer of garments through limited suppliers that expanded into the chain stores in the early 1980s. While Levi's lost a few customers (for example, Macy's quit carrying Levi's jeans because it thought the company's image had suffered), it more than made up for the loss by increased overall sales. In fact, J.C. Penney became Levi's biggest customer.

In light of this and other data, OshKosh B'Gosh decided to move into mass merchandisers, but with the goal of retaining its customer base in the upscale stores. In order to accomplish this, the company began preparing to sell unique, high-margin items to the pricier department stores. It also planned to broaden the company's line of adult products, expanding beyond work clothes into the sportswear market.

Results of such strategies are, as yet, inconclusive. Overall sales for 1992 dropped 5.2 percent, from the 1991 level of $365 million to $346 million. Ironically, sales in most of the company's subsidiaries and divisions were actually up for this period. For instance, its Retail, International, and Domestic Licensed Products divisions, as well as its Essex Outfitters and OshKosh B'Gosh Europe subsidiaries, saw higher sales in 1992 than in 1991. Only the domestic wholesale division—the largest division and life-blood of the company—experienced a decline in sales. It is

*A 1992 magazine advertisement for OshKosh B'Gosh.*

unclear, however, how much of this change may be attributed to the economy and the resulting decline in retail sales.

## Into the Future

The company's 1992 annual report stated that the "goal is to restore both the operational and financial performance of our core children's business." To help further this plan, OshKosh B'Gosh underwent some corporate restructuring, including the replacement of top managers. In addition, the company updated its basic line, introducing OshKosh "sweats" in the fall of 1993, and placing considerable emphasis on its partnership with French clothing maker Poron.

"Overall," reported Charles Paikert in *Adweek's Marketing Week,* "analysts see a bright future for OshKosh." He quoted one expert as saying: "There will be enough births in the 1990s to

sustain their basic market. Plus they have room to expand geographically, especially in the South and West. There are still substantial opportunities for growth." In the end, wrote Julia Flynn Siler in *Business Week,* the company's future may depend on the very feature that established its reputation almost a century ago, the quality of its core products. Through the years OshKosh B'Gosh has obsessively maintained quality and durability in its garments, carefully monitoring the manufacture of even those items produced under license by other firms. Added Siler, "As long as the goods are durable . . . , so will be the demand."

## Further Reading:

Abelson, Reed, "Investing One's Way out of Trouble," *Forbes,* June 11, 1990, pp. 88–92.

Byrne, Harlan S., "OshKosh B'Gosh Inc.: It's on the Mend after a Costly Distribution Snarl," *Barron's,* June 19, 1989, p. 54.

Connole, Jon, "Hyde Leads Oshkosh B'Gosh to National Stature," *Business Journal—Milwaukee,* September 16, 1985, p. 10.

Fenner, Elizabeth, "A Baby's First Words: 'Buy-Buy' (OshKosh B'Gosh)," *Money,* July 1991, pp. 60–61.

Freeman, Laurie, "OshKosh Out to Cover Adult Market," *Advertising Age,* April 28, 1986, p. 69.

Harris, William, "Fashion Is Fickle," *Forbes,* June 22, 1981, pp. 102–03.

Jakubovics, Jerry, "OshKosh's Upward Climb," *Management Review,* September 1987, pp. 14–15.

Kosnett, Jeff, "Star-Spangled Investments: OshKosh B'Gosh," *Changing Times,* July 1990, p. 33.

Kretchmar, Laurie, "On the Rise: Douglas W. Hyde, 40," *Fortune,* May 20, 1991, p. 136.

Miller, Cyndee, " 'Brands Are Extremely Important': Parents Make Fashion Statement by Dressing Kids in 'Status'," *Marketing News,* June 8, 1992, pp. 1, 14–15.

"OshKosh B'Gosh, Inc.," *Wall Street Journal,* April 27, 1993, p. B4.

*OshKosh B'Gosh, Inc., Annual Report 1992,* Oshkosh, WI: OshKosh B'Gosh, Inc., 1993.

"OshKosh B'Gosh, Inc. Posts 40% Drop in Net for Its Third Quarter," *Wall Street Journal,* October 22, 1990, p. B2.

"OshKosh Will Drop Children's Wear Line," *Wall Street Journal,* February 7, 1992, p. B10.

Paikert, Charles, "OshKosh B'Gosh's Britches Are Getting Bigger," *Adweek's Marketing Week,* September 19, 1988, pp. 30, 32.

Perlick, Gail, "B'Gosh, It's OshKosh," *Working Woman,* August 1987, pp. 39, 41, 42.

Siler, Julia Flynn, "OshKosh B'Gosh May Be Risking Its Upscale Image," *Business Week,* July 15, 1991, p. 140.

Trachtenberg, Jeffrey A., "The Threads Business," *Forbes,* December 16, 1985, pp. 202, 204.

Wiener, Daniel P., "OshKosh B'Gosh Inc. (Companies to Watch)," *Fortune,* June 24, 1985, p. 68.

*—Jay P. Pederson*

# PALMOLIVE®

One of the best-known names in soap, Palmolive has a reputation as an effective washing agent that is gentle to the skin. The Palmolive brand was introduced as a bar soap for facial and other cosmetic applications, and was later extended to include shaving cream and dishwashing liquid. Under the direction of parent company Colgate-Palmolive, Palmolive liquid continues to be promoted as a gentle general use soap that is less likely than other brands to cause the dreaded condition "dishpan hands."

## Brand Origins

Palmolive was introduced in 1898 by the B. J. Johnson Soap Company, a manufacturer of soap, candles, and cheese in Milwaukee. From its founding in 1864, Johnson Soap sought to create cleaning agents that were gentler to the skin than homemade soaps, which were notoriously harsh and left the skin red, dry, and chapped. Johnson created a line of mild detergent soaps that were less caustic and a clear improvement over domestically manufactured lye, potash, and even tree oil soaps. In the years following the Civil War, Johnson built a large enterprise whose distribution covered much of the Midwest.

In the 1890s, Johnson's son Caleb established a chemical laboratory to investigate the composition of new cleaning agents. In this lab, the first industrial research facility of its kind in America, Caleb Johnson created soap from vegetable oils rather than from the harsh fatty acids and oils then in use. His research led him to formulations made by the ancient Greeks, who made effective soaps from vegetable oils. He experimented with palm and olive extracts, and later perfected a formula that was so mild it could be used on sensitive facial skin. Due to the nature of its ingredients, the soap had one curious quality: it would float.

The new brand, which the younger Johnson named "Palmolive," was difficult and expensive to manufacture. As a result, sales and distribution of the soap were initially limited. In 1909, however, Johnson attended an exhibit of French soap-making machinery in St. Louis. One device on display could mill hard soaps similar in composition to Palmolive. Johnson immediately ordered the French machinery for his company, and the following year began mass production of his Palmolive soap.

## Early Marketing Strategy

In 1910 Johnson's advertising manager, Charles Pearce, made the acquaintance of Claude Hopkins, then a leading proponent of strategic advertising. Pearce and Johnson met with Hopkins's agency, Lord & Thomas, and laid out a plan for national promotion of Palmolive soap.

Lord & Thomas developed a campaign for nationally distributed magazines that centered on the soothing, almost medicinal qualities of Palmolive soap. The earliest promotional copy established Palmolive as a luxury product. Advertisements depicted Greek maidens at elegantly appointed marble baths with captions such as, "The luxury-loving Greeks equipped the bath with extravagant accessories, *but* they lacked Palmolive Soap."

Later promotions in the art nouveau style of the 1920s portrayed Palmolive as a "Queen's secret." Additional ad copy noted, "Historic ingredients produce its smooth creamy lather—the famous palm and olive oils that Cleopatra prized." Later, sales manager Edward H. Little invented a more modern approach. Little framed Palmolive as "Nature's simple rule to keep that *schoolgirl* complexion." Leading with such phrases as "Natural Loveliness," Palmolive ads claimed the soap could clean skin pores, adding that "the world's leading specialists on skin care agree to this."

A common form of promotion in the early decades of the century was the coupon. Palmolive coupons promising two bars for the price of one were printed in newspapers and magazines. To keep grocers and druggists from padding their margins, the company prominently displayed Palmolive's retail price, which was ten cents. The company also included 36 two-for-one postcard coupons with each gross of Palmolive soap. The retailers' instructions were to send the cards to their best customers. This improved retailers' relations with their customers and established Palmolive as a featured product.

## Brand Development

Shortly after Palmolive bar soap was introduced, Johnson developed a shampoo that claimed the same qualities as the soap. In fact, the two products were advertised in tandem as complementary products: soap for the skin, shampoo for the hair. Sales of Palmolive soap and shampoo doubled every few years. This led Johnson to adopt the brand name for his company, and in 1917 he reincorporated as the Palmolive Company. The enterprise relocated to Chicago, where it occupied the Palmolive Building on the city's Gold Coast.

The rapid growth of the brand and the company led Johnson to investigate better distribution of his popular soap. In 1927 he concluded a merger with the Peet Brothers Company, a soap manufacturer with facilities in Kansas City and Berkeley, California. The combined Palmolive-Peet company covered several additional markets and economized both freight and warehousing costs.

The following year the company merged with another leading soap manufacturer, the Colgate Company. As a result, the Palmolive brand gained manufacturing facilities in Jersey City and Jeffersonville, Indiana. Over the years, Colgate-Palmolive-Peet made room for increased production of Palmolive products by eliminating other existing lines. In addition, more efficient manufacturing equipment was installed, helping to further reduce production costs.

The company's attempt to establish a consumer products conglomerate was destroyed by the 1929 stock market crash, and the company was forced to ride out the Depression on the strength of Palmolive soap and Colgate toothpaste and shaving soap. As the economy recovered during the 1930s, sales of Palmolive gradually rose. Much of the brand's growth during this period came at the

## AT A GLANCE

**P**almolive brand developed by Caleb Johnson of the B. J. Johnson Soap Company in 1898; company name changed to the Palmolive Company, 1917; company merged with Peet Brothers Company in 1927 to form Palmolive-Peet; merged with Colgate in 1928 to form Colgate-Palmolive-Peet. Palmolive shampoo introduced in 1914, Palmolive dishwashing liquid in 1964, Palmolive Automatic dishwasher detergent in 1986, Palmolive Sensitive Skin in 1993.

*Performance: Market share*—19.2% of dishwashing liquid category; 9.1% of dishwasher detergent category; .07% of soap category (1992).

*Major competitor:* Lever Brothers' Sunlight; also Procter & Gamble's Cascade and other brands of soap, dishwashing liquid, and dishwasher detergent.

*Advertising: Agency*—FCB/Leber Katz Partners, New York. *Major campaign*—"You're soaking in it"; also "For that schoolgirl complexion," "You cook, we'll clean."

*Addresses: Parent company*—Colgate-Palmolive Company, 300 Park Avenue, New York, NY 10022; phone: (212) 310-2000; fax: (212) 310-3284.

expense of smaller, weaker competitors, but some was also attributable to an expanded distribution network that brought Palmolive to hundreds of locales where it had not been available before.

The brand experienced some difficulties during World War II, when soap and the raw materials used to make it were strictly rationed. Other cheaper and more basic soaps received more favorable access to resources and markets, while Palmolive, hampered by its reputation as a luxury product, continued production under difficult market conditions throughout the war.

After the war sales of Palmolive regained their earlier rates of increase, boosted by a growing economy. During the 1950s the brand began encountering strong competition from Procter & Gamble, whose numerous brands were direct alternatives to those of Colgate-Palmolive. As the company entered the 1960s a combination of strong competition from better-formulated brands and a series of marketing and advertising blunders caused Colgate-Palmolive's earnings to decline steadily. Even the Palmolive Building was sold, to become the Playboy Building.

Chairman G. H. Lesch ordered the development of new compounds and manufacturing processes that would enable the company to lower its production expenses. Palmolive was reformulated to stretch the brand's margins and keep its retail price low. Despite the efforts, Palmolive continued to lose ground, both as a bar and shaving soap and now as a dishwashing liquid, to brands from Procter & Gamble and Lever Brothers. Colgate-Palmolive spent only about a sixth as much as its competitors on new product development. While the Palmolive name was very valuable, the company had few products under development for extension of the name.

Market share losses stabilized during the 1970s, mainly through effective, relentlessly repetitive advertising. By the mid 1980s the formula was successful in propelling Palmolive dishwashing liquid past Procter & Gamble's Dawn, which had been the market leader. At the time, the company also introduced the liquid with a lemon-lime fragrance. In 1986 the company introduced an automatic dishwasher soap with the Palmolive name. Test marketed as Bright Side, the new soap went up against Cascade and Calgonite, but ultimately failed.

### Advertising

Colgate-Palmolive launched one of its most successful advertising campaigns after the introduction of Palmolive dishwashing liquid. Drawing heavily on the "gentleness" equity, Palmolive focused on the prevention of chapped, dishpan hands. The company chose to feature a testimonial from the highest authority on beautiful hands, a manicurist. Madge, a fictional manicurist played by the actress Jan Miner, was shown preparing a woman for her manicure by soaking her fingers in a dish of Palmolive. When queried about the liquid, Madge revealed that it was Palmolive. The shocked client pulled her fingers out and exclaimed, "Dishwashing liquid?" "Relax," Madge replied as she pressed the fingers back into the dish, "it's Palmolive."

This advertisement was updated to keep pace with fashions, make-up, and hairstyles and was repeated for nearly 20 years. The occasional re-shoots of precisely the same script suggested that Madge soaked every one of her client's fingers in Palmolive, and continued the practice for years on end. The ad didn't show how well Palmolive cleaned dishes, but it didn't have to. Palmolive's cleaning ability had already been well established; the product being sold was mildness. Interestingly, in an example of life imitating art, the ads created some misguided demand for Palmolive as a manicure preparation. The Madge ads were dropped in 1991, but remain indelibly marked in the minds of millions of consumers. The ad even inspired a good-humored parody by A&W in which Miner, in her role as Madge, soaked her fingers in a glass of root beer.

### Packaging

Palmolive soap was formulated with a green dye that became the brand's signature color. The bar soap's package consisted of a green paper wrapper with the Palmolive name printed across a dark band in bold white capital letters. When the liquid shampoo was formulated, the same shade of dye was used to give the liquid an enticing visual quality. The shampoo was packaged in an exotic clear bottle, with a diagonal name band on the label.

The shampoo packaging scheme was used for Palmolive dishwashing liquid, and remained unchanged with the introduction of plastic bottles and their retractable squirt nozzles. The label underwent a gradual set of changes, evolving into a simple white design with the Palmolive name printed in olive blue.

The bar soap is packaged in a clean white box and adorned with the brand name in an elegant pastel shaded script. The shaving soap container is considerably more stark: a white tube box with Palmolive written in bold black capital letters.

### International Development

Palmolive made an early and bold move into foreign markets under the direction of Ed Little, who was responsible for building a European franchise for the brand during the 1920s. He established production licensing agreements with a number of manufacturers in France, Britain, and Germany. During the 1930s he began a campaign to acquire of European manufacturers.

By 1938 it had become apparent that war in Europe was inevitable. The company ran up against strong opposition for wartime production quotas from Unilever, which lobbied to keep Palmolive's imports from Canada out of domestic consumption figures. Colgate-Palmolive prevailed, and purchased the Goodwin & Sons company to make soap for the impending hostilities. The factory was later destroyed, as were the other European operations. After the war, these facilities were rebuilt, and the markets in which they operated recovered.

After the war Palmolive expanded into markets including the Philippines, Malaysia, Thailand, and Latin America. Palmolive enjoyed its highest sales growth rates in international markets, where advertising often featured Madge speaking in the country's native language. In 1990 the company began to focus its advertising toward the specific countries in which it was sold. The Palmolive name had been extended to a full range of beauty care products, including shampoo (which had been discontinued in the United States), conditioner, and skin cream. In addition, Palmolive-branded toiletries, deodorants, styling aids, and other body care products were test marketed.

While the Palmolive name had been more widely extended overseas than in the United States—and had better growth—these brands experienced strong competition from Procter & Gamble brands that were newcomers to foreign markets. Learning from Colgate-Palmolive's own experience, Procter & Gamble made great use of its successful Ivory soap brand by extending the name into a full range of liquids, shampoos, and conditioners in the United States. The move enabled P&G to cross-utilize advertising and avoid having to support a range of different brand identities.

## Future Predictions

Palmolive has one of the most thoroughly established identities in the business, and its recognition is international. As a result, Palmolive's best prospects for expansion are probably in brand extension. The company could revive Palmolive shampoo domestically, and add such products as Palmolive cleanser, glass cleaner, stain remover, detergent, and even fabric softener.

Through innovative advertising of Palmolive, the company has proven its ability to "overcome housewife resistance through advertising." This phrase, drawn from a speech on the company's history, aptly illustrates the original task of weaning consumers away from their homemade soaps, and the more current task of luring them away from competing brands. In the process, Colgate-Palmolive has built the Palmolive brand name into a venerable and valuable franchise that it cannot afford to leave under-utilized.

## Further Reading:

"Colgate Axes Global Ads, Thinks Local," *Advertising Age,* November 26, 1990, pp. 1–59.

"Colgate Works Hard to Become the Firm It Was a Decade Ago, *Wall Street Journal,* November 23, 1981, pp. 1–8.

Foster, David R., *The Story of Colgate-Palmolive,* New York: Newcomen Society in North America, 1975.

"How to Be Happy Though Number Two," *Forbes,* July 15, 1976, pp. 36–38.

"Is Efficiency Enough?" *Forbes,* March 18, 1991, pp. 108–09.

"No Madge or Manicures in Palmolive Campaign," *New York Times,* October 1, 1991.

"Palmolive Liquid Goes Automatic," *Advertising Age,* June 2, 1986, pp. 3–89.

Sims, W. I., *150 Years and the Future,* New York: Newcomen Society in North America, 1956.

"Updating Old Standards," *Soap/Cosmetics/Chemical Specialties,* December 1991, pp. 26–28.

*—John Simley*

# PAMPERS®

# Pampers

Pampers is one of the world's most popular brands of disposable diapers. Holding 29 percent of the U.S. market, it vies for the leading position with Kimberly-Clark's Huggies, which holds 30 percent. Introduced in 1961, Pampers has been credited with creating the market for disposable diapers in the United States. Although disposable diapers existed, they were little used before Procter & Gamble created their own dramatically improved version. After dominating the market for years, Pampers has gradually lost ground to other disposable diaper brands and even to cloth diapers. P&G has fought to maintain their market position, relying in great part on improvements to the product to hold their customers. The company has introduced many versions of Pampers over the last three decades, the most recent being Ultra Dry Pampers Thins, a superabsorbent diaper in two sizes for crawlers and walkers.

## Brand Origins

The idea for Pampers originated in 1956 when Procter & Gamble's director of exploratory development, Vic Mills, experienced the joyless task of washing his grandchild's diapers. Realizing that most mothers must not like cleaning diapers any more than he did, Mills felt that there was a huge untapped market for disposable diapers. At his suggestion, P&G began to investigate the practicality of marketing a disposable diaper.

Building on research done by recently acquired Charmin Paper Company, P&G discovered that fifteen billion diaper changes were performed each year in the United States. The labor involved in rinsing, soaking, washing, drying, and folding those diapers was considerable, and the expense of avoiding it by hiring a diaper service was not insignificant. In addition, most consumers had serious criticisms of cloth diapers: they bunched and sagged when wet, making the babies uncomfortable; they kept wetness against the babies' skin, causing diaper rash; and they were unpleasant to wash or, if a diaper service was used, to store when soiled.

Disposable diapers did exist, such as Chux, Drypers, and Kleinerts, but they accounted for less than 1 percent of the country's diaper changes. Consumers felt they controlled wetness even more poorly than cloth diapers and that their expense made them impractical for everyday use. Parents bought them mostly for use when traveling.

However, many mothers who were interviewed said they would like a dependable disposable diaper. Combined with the other data P&G had collected and P&G's experience in manufacturing absorbent disposable products like Bounty paper towels, the company felt confident enough to create a full-time diaper research team in 1957.

## Initial Design Fails

Six months of development resulted in a product similar to one marketed successfully in Scandinavia: a highly absorbent, pleated pad that was placed inside a specially designed plastic panty. Free samples were given to parents in Dallas for testing. Although parents found them absorbent and comfortably shaped, they almost unanimously rejected the diaper. With average maximum temperatures at 93 degrees, the plastic pants made the babies too uncomfortable and caused rashes even more frequently than the plastic pants that were used with cloth diapers.

Almost ready to abandon the project, the vice-president of research was convinced to continue by new samples created by Mills's research team. The new diaper replaced the plastic pants with a thin plastic outer layer that kept moisture in but allowed air to circulate more easily. The diaper's absorbent material spread the moisture throughout the diaper, helping avoid soggy spots that would sag. In addition, the researchers had developed a porous sheet that rested between the baby and the diaper's absorbent material. Called a "moisture barrier" by P&G, the sheet allowed fluid to pass through and be absorbed by the diaper's inner layer, but kept the wet wadding from resting against the babies skin, thus helping prevent diaper rash.

The final design was approved for testing in 1959. The research staff assembled 37,000 diapers by hand to be used in a test in Rochester, New York. Both a tape-on and a pin-on design were tested, and parents favored the pin-on version. More importantly, two-thirds of the test participants found the product as good or better than cloth diapers.

The next hurdle P&G had to overcome was designing machinery that could make the new diaper efficiently. Oscar Schisgall, in his book *Eyes on Tomorrow* quoted one engineer as saying, "I think it was the most complex production operation the company had ever faced. . . . It seemed a simple task to take three sheets of material—plastic back sheet, absorbent wadding, and

## AT A GLANCE

**P**ampers brand of disposable diapers founded in 1961 by Vic Mills, director of exploratory development of Procter & Gamble Company.

**Performance:** *Market share—29.2% of disposable diaper category. Sales—$54.65 billion.*

**Major competitor:** *Kimberly-Clark's Huggies; also Procter & Gamble's Luvs.*

**Advertising:** *Agency—D'Arcy Masius Benton & Bowles, New York.*

**Addresses:** *Parent company—Procter & Gamble Co., 1 Procter & Gamble Plaza, Cincinnati, OH 45202; phone: (513) 983-1100; fax: (513) 562-4500.*

water repellent top sheet   fold them in a zigzag pattern and glue them together. But glue applicators dripped glue. The wadding generated dust. Together they formed sticky balls and smears which fouled the equipment. The machinery could run only a few minutes before having to be shut down and cleaned.'' P&G had filed for a patent on July 17, 1961, but it was an entire year before engineers completed a small production line.

### Combating Entrenched Views

P&G learned in their research and the Rochester test some problems caused by consumers' habituation to cloth diapers. Accustomed to square diapers, some consumers stretched the rounded disposable diapers too far, causing them to rip and then leak. P&G solved the problem by printing detailed instructions on the first packages of their machine-made diapers.

More difficult to change were mothers' attitudes about what constituted good care for their children. According to P&G research, some women felt that the amount of time they spent caring for their babies reflected the amount of love the babies were receiving. Using disposables made these women feel guilty because they spent less time caring for their babies' physical needs.

P&G attempted to alter consumers' view that disposable diapers were merely a convenience that parents used at the expense of their babies' welfare. Although several names for the new diaper were considered, including Tads, Solos, Dri-Wees, Larks, Winks, and Zephyrs, P&G chose the name Pampers to emphasize that the product was good for babies. Later, the company changed its marketing strategy, de-emphasizing Pampers's convenience and focusing instead on the product's benefits for the baby, namely, increased dryness and comfort.

Pampers began its first full test market in Peoria, Illinois, in December, 1961. The results again disappointed Procter & Gamble product developers. Advertised as flushable, Pampers often stuck in pipes, certainly negating the convenience of not having to wash cloth diapers. A much more serious problem soon became apparent: consumers felt that the diapers cost too much. At ten cents a diaper, Pampers cost slightly less than cloth diapers and a diaper service, but the price was not low enough to induce people to change the way they were accustomed to caring for their babies.

Disappointed but not defeated, P&G set about reducing costs. Production costs were targeted first: the package was simplified, including cutting back from three- to two-color printing, speeding

up the assembly lines, and reducing the costs of certain raw materials. However, nothing could reduce costs enough to lower the price of Pampers by several cents per diaper except vastly increasing the volume sold. If the volume was doubled, P&G felt it could sell Pampers at six cents a diaper.

### Finally, the Right Formula

P&G conducted a second test, marketing Pampers in Sacramento for eight cents a diaper. The lowered price was enough to convince consumers to buy them for everyday use. The enthusiastic consumer response and, more importantly, the numerous reorders led to new P&G plants being built in Pennsylvania, Missouri, Georgia, and California. P&G continued to drop the price as sales increased, eventually reaching their goal of six cents a diaper.

By the late 1960s Pampers had established the market for disposable diapers, changing their image from a convenience to be used only when traveling to a legitimate option for everyday diapering. In the product's more established markets, 25 percent of the diaper changes were done with Pampers. In addition, Pampers held almost complete control of the market. By the mid-1970s, half the babies in the United States wore Pampers. Taking advantage of their head start, P&G had cornered the market on disposables: in 1975, 75 percent of disposables sold were Pampers.

### International Market

In the 1970s Procter & Gamble made great efforts to market Pampers internationally. The company's strategy for expanding their cleaning products internationally had been to laboriously research each market, a process necessary because of the widely various cleaning methods and needs throughout the world. When it came to researching the disposable diaper markets, however, P&G decided that separate evaluations were unnecessary because ''a baby is a baby.'' The company also decided that U. S. plants, operating seven days a week, could supply the diapers until plants could be built abroad.

P&G concentrated initially on marketing Pampers in Canada and Puerto Rico. Pampers were welcomed enthusiastically in Puerto Rico, where many families had no access to washing machines or driers. Not only was washing diapers by hand an unenviable task, but the area's high humidity made drying diapers on a clothesline difficult. Puerto Rico soon became one of Pampers's best markets.

Procter and Gamble built several Pampers plants to better supply their growing international market. By the end of the decade, they had a plant in Canada, two in Germany, and plans for one in Japan. These necessary additions helped supply the seventy-five countries Pampers were being sold in by 1979.

### The Competition Intensifies

Pampers had always had other disposable diaper brands to contend with, but it wasn't until the late 1970s that it met with serious challenges to its market share. Procter and Gamble decided to compete with its own product by introducing another disposable diaper brand: Luvs. More expensive than Pampers, Luvs featured an hourglass shape, extra padding, and elasticized legs to contain leaks. Another challenger emerged from the pack of disposable brands: Kimberly-Clark's Huggies. Also designed for the upper end of the market, Huggies had many of the same features as Luvs.

Although both cost up to 30 percent more than Pampers, many parents happily paid more to avoid messes. From 1979 to 1983 Huggies and Luvs gained market share at a rate of 29 percent a year.

As Pampers's market share dwindled, hitting about 40 percent in 1983, P&G fought back by increasing their advertising and luring consumers with promotions. By 1985 P&G's combined budget for Pampers and Luvs was approximately $40 million. The same year, Pampers launched a highly successful promotion in which customers could exchange proofs-of-purchase for Baby Muppets stuffed dolls. Timed to coincide with the release of the movie *The Muppets Take Manhattan,* the promotion generated a great deal of interest. However, Huggies attempted to match Pampers's efforts with a $19 million budget and a highly successful promotion of its own. It had already surpassed Luvs as the country's second most popular diaper and was steadily gaining on Pampers.

## The Features War

P&G came out with frequent improvements to Pampers in an attempt to maintain its top position, even encroaching on the territory it had staked out for Luvs. In 1983, the company added "stay-dry gathers" to Pampers, putting it in more direct competition with the premium-priced Luvs, whose elasticized legs were a major selling point. When industry analysts speculated that the improved Pampers would hurt the sales of Luvs, P&G asserted that there was room in the market for both. A Procter and Gamble spokesman told *Advertising Age* that Luvs provided "premium fit and containment" whereas Pampers was marketed toward consumers who want "improved containment at a lower cost." *Advertising Age* also quoted an industry observer as saying, "P&G has been smart enough through the years to compete with themselves before someone else does it."

Pampers also lost market share during this time to generic and store-brand disposables. Although these brands usually lagged behind the industry leaders in introducing innovations such as elasticized legs and waist gathers, their low price was winning an increasing proportion of the diaper customers. However, Huggies remained Pampers's main concern; by 1984 Huggies held about 23 percent of the market, while Pampers held about 35 percent. *Fortune* quoted former P&G executive Hercules Segalas as saying, "Kimberly-Clark stole a page right out of Procter's manual of how to succeed: get an excellent product and execute well."

By 1986 Pampers had moved up to the premium-priced segment, sporting such features as a shaped fit, refastenable tapes, high absorbency, double elastic gathers, a waist shield, and breathable leg cuffs. P&G continued to distinguish their two brands by promoting Luvs as the most comfortable diaper and Pampers as the best at keeping baby dry.

The features war continued throughout the 1980s and into the 1990s. In 1985 Pampers made a significant advance in diaper performance when it switched to a superabsorbent filling. However, its advantage was short-lived since Huggies introduced its own superabsorbent version in 1986. The three leading brands struggled to be the first to introduce features such as sex-specific diapers with more padding in front for boys and more padding in the center for girls or shapes tailored to babies' specific developmental stages.

## Loses Number One Spot

Pampers's efforts could not stop their gradual loss of market share. In 1988 Huggies became the top-selling diaper in the United States By 1991 they held 30 percent of the market, while Pampers held only 28 percent. Store brands, usually made by Weyerhaeuser, Pope & Talbot, or Johnson & Johnson were also gaining ground with low-cost products.

Pampers tried again in 1992 to win with a superior product by developing a new superabsorbent material, allowing a thinner, more comfortable diaper. But Huggies managed to come out with its own version, Huggies UltraTrim, months ahead of Pampers's scheduled introduction. P&G hoped the new Pampers would at least grab market share from store brands, which are relatively slow in catching up to innovations by the big name brands.

## International Lessons

In the early 1980s, Pampers held 90 percent of the Japanese disposable diaper market. By 1985, it held only seven percent. In 1982 Pampers's virtual monopoly was threatened when Japan's Uni-Charm Corporation introduced a diaper filled with a highly absorbent granular polymer that soaked up wetness and held it in the form of a gel. P&G continued to sell their diapers filled with paper pulp while Uni-Charm and other Japanese competitors gained on and then surpassed Pampers's market share. Uni-Charm also did extensive market surveys and responded to consumers' complaints by adding leg gathers and reusable adhesive closures. According to *Business Week,* "P&G's biggest mistake was its complacency." Pampers's sales began to improve after P&G brought out its own polymer-filled version in 1985. However, great damage had already been done. Although four-fifths of the babies in the United States and Europe wore disposable diapers, only 30 percent did in Japan. Some estimated that Japanese disposable sales would grow by 30 percent a year. Pampers unfortunately had lost the chance to capitalize on their initially huge market share in a rapidly growing market.

P&G apparently learned that one had to be proactive in the international market. The company introduced Pampers in Hungary in 1991, much sooner than they had originally planned. Wolfgang C. Berndt, president of P&G Eastern Europe, told *Advertising Age,* "In the early months of 1990, we changed our strategy to reflect the much faster reform that was happening in Eastern European countries." The company also departed from the usual formula for international product expansion by introducing Pampers Phases within months of the product's introduction in the United States. Lynne Hyman, an analyst at First Boston, explained to *Advertising Age,* "In the past, a product would be introduced in the home market. If it was successful, overseas companies would copy it for their markets before the originator entered their market. P&G is moving so fast that it doesn't allow the competition to see what it's doing. Foreign competition can't react. This is very aggressive and smart."

## Environmental Concerns

In the late 1980s and early 1990s other disposable diaper brands were not Pampers's only problem. For the first time in years, Pampers had to concern itself with competition from cloth diapers. The growing environmental movement targeted disposable diapers as a wasteful, polluting single-use product that should be eliminated, especially since a reusable option (cloth diapers) already existed. Disposable diaper manufacturers defended themselves by contending that cloth diapers are as environmentally destructive as disposables, pointing out the pesticides used to grow the cotton, the detergents needed to wash them, and the energy used to wash and dry them. Although studies had been done to determine which product was worse for the environment, the results contradicted each other—not surprising since they had been commissioned by diaper manufacturers like Procter and Gamble or by the National Association of Diaper Service Industries, neither objective parties.

P&G tried to alleviate environmental concerns by doing research on diaper composting and then airing a national television ad that seemed to confront the problem head-on. The commercial depicted a mother holding her baby, who explained that she was concerned about both her baby's health and the environment. She chose Pampers because they kept babies drier and their skin healthier, and then mentioned that some disposables were now composted. Although an announcer admitted that municipal solid-waste composting wasn't widely available, the commercial sidestepped questions about composting's effectiveness or feasibility for this type of product.

The gradual decline in Pampers's market share belied its steady improvement in quality. *Consumer Reports* rated Pampers as the best disposable diaper, although Huggies was not far behind. In 1993, when the features war seemed to have exhausted its possibilities, a price war took shape. Pampers cut its prices three times in a twelve-month period, once by 5 percent. It was unclear whether Pampers would soon regain the top market position. Although P&G has the honor of knowing that Pampers changed the way a nation's parents care for their babies, they will still have to fight for every baby's bottom they want to cover with Pampers.

## Further Reading:

Alter, Jennifer, "P&G's Pampers Tries Elastic Legs at a Lower Price," *Advertising Age,* March 15, 1982, p. 80.

Buell, Barbara, "How P&G Was Brought to a Crawl in Japan's Diaper Market," *Business Week,* October 13, 1986, p.71.

"Diaper Decisions," *Consumer Reports,* August 1991, pp. 551–56.

Freeman, Laurie, "Diaper Marketers Pin Hopes on Promotions," *Advertising Age,* May 2, 1985, p. 37.

Gershman, Michael, *Getting It Right the Second Time,* Reading, MA: Addison-Wesley Publishing, 1990, pp. 245–49.

Giges, Nancy, "P&G Pampers Diaper Brands," *Advertising Age,* January 21, 1985, p. 78.

"High and Dry," *Economist,* September 28, 1991, p. 74.

"100 Leading National Advertisers," *Advertising Age,* September 23, 1992, pp.53–4.

Lawrence, Jennifer, *Advertising Age,* "P&G Ad Argues for Disposable Diapers' Merits," August 26, 1991, p. 4; "P&G Marches into E. Europe," September 30, 1991, p. 10; "P&G Rushes on Global Diaper Rollout," October 14, 1991, p. 6; "Kimberly, P&G Rev Up to Market Latest Twist in Disposable Diapers," June 29, 1992, p. 3.

Rice, Faye, *Fortune,* "Trouble at Procter & Gamble," March 5, 1984, p. 70; "The Battle for Bottom Share," February 13, 1989, p.9.

Schiller, Zachary, *Business Week,* "P&G Tries Hauling Itself Out of America's Trash Heap," April 23, 1990, p. 101; "A Rash Decision?," April 26, 1993, p. 36.

Schisgall, Oscar, *Eyes on Tomorrow: The Evolution of Procter & Gamble,* Chicago: J. G. Ferguson Publishing, pp. 216–20, 290–91.

*—Susan Windisch Brown*

# PAPER MATE®

**PAPER ♡ MATE.®**

Paper Mate was one of the first and most successful ball-point pen companies in the United States and continues to be a leader in the market. Paper Mate today is part of The Gillette Company's Stationery Products Group which also includes the upscale Waterman and Parker brands, Liquid Paper correction products, and Helit, a German maker of desk accessories. With the acquisition of Parker Pen Company in 1993, Gillette became the world's largest writing instrument company.

## Brand History

As ubiquitous as ball-point pens are today, it is hard to imagine a time when they were shunned by serious professions like banking and teaching. Such was the case, however, when the first ball-point pens were sold in 1945 and thousands of people lined up at Gimble's department store in New York City to buy them. The ball-point was invented by Laszlo Joszef Biro, a Hungarian proofreader working in Paris in the 1930s. Frustrated with the shortcomings of conventional fountain and quill pens, Biro developed the ball-point, using a more viscous ink that was fed past a small ball bearing held by a small socket. Biro then moved to Buenos Aires to manufacture his new product. The British Royal Air Force and the United States Army Air Corps quickly realized the advantages of the ball-point and their large purchases during World War II helped create a civilian interest.

The Reynolds International Pen Company was the first to mass produce the pens and originally sold them for $12.50. Their wide acceptance encouraged many other manufacturers, and soon the price of the pens ranged from 25 cents to $25. Despite their popularity, ball-point pens were not without drawbacks. The ink smelled bad, leaked unexpectedly, smeared, and faded. Bankers would not accept checks written in ball-point, claiming that they were subject to easy forgery. Lawyers feared legal documents would become invalid as the signatures faded. Many teachers prohibited the use of ball-point pens in their classrooms because of the smears and smudges they produced. Into the fray stepped Patrick Joseph Frawley, Jr.

Frawley had entered his father's import/export business in San Francisco and had also lent money to a ball-point pen company. Frawley took over the company and set out to find a way to make disposable ink cartridges for his product. He located a chemist who had formulated an ink that was immune to fading and transferring. To convince his sales force of this, Frawley provided them with samples to use for one week. He also convinced two local banks to accept checks written with his pens and named the company Paper Mate to stress its superior qualities. To further stress the improvements made to his brand, Paper Mate's initial advertising proclaimed that the pens were "banker approved." The company grew quickly, and by 1951 sales were more than $1 million, soaring to more than $9 million the following year. According to Russell Adams in his book *King Gillette: The Man and His Wonderful Shaving Device,* "Paper Mate had become the overnight, indelible standard for ball-point pens."

Success and sales of this magnitude did not go unnoticed, and The Gillette Company soon became interested in Paper Mate. Neison Harris, then president of Gillette's Toni division, thought Paper Mate would be an especially appropriate acquisition for Gillette because of their similar merchandising and distribution techniques. Harris recommended the purchase in 1952, suggesting that Paper Mate might be acquired for $650,000. Gillette passed on the opportunity at that time in order to weigh carefully other acquisition options. When they were ready to consider the purchase again the following year, however, the price had risen to $2 million and was climbing weekly. Frawley proposed selling a half interest in Paper Mate to Gillette for $1.5 million, with the condition that he be named chief executive officer. Gillette officials resisted this offer, preferring to buy the company outright. The deal was finally completed on September 30, 1955, and Patrick Frawley received $15.5 million in cash. Although Frawley was named president of Paper Mate, he remained for only three months. The entrepreneurial spirit that had helped him build Paper Mate would not allow him to be content in the corporate environment. Neison Harris took over Frawley's position and immediately set out to make sense of the complicated web of companies and facilities that comprised Paper Mate. Russell Adams noted that by 1962 Paper Mate was "contributing a relatively comfortable ration of profits."

## Brand Expansion

When Gillette purchased Paper Mate in 1955 the line consisted of three ball-point pens and a refill. Gillette quickly introduced a 98 cent pen and the Piggy Back refill. In the 1960s the company launched the Paper Mate Powerpoint, which could write upside down, and in 1964 the brand expanded to include slim, regular, and husky versions of its popular ball-point pens. In 1968 a new

## AT A GLANCE

Paper Mate brand of pens founded in 1949 by Patrick Joseph Frawley, Jr.; sold to The Gillette Company in 1955.

**Performance:** *Sales*—$520 million (product line).

**Major competitor:** Bic.

**Advertising:** *Agency*—In-house.

**Addresses:** *Parent company*—The Gillette Company, Prudential Tower Building, Boston, MA 02199; phone: (617) 421-7000.

plant was opened in Santa Monica to keep up with demand. In the mid-1980s Paper Mate faced a bold new competitor: Bic. Also a maker of razors, Bic had entered the disposable pen market with a vengeance. In an effort to become more competitive, Paper Mate developed the Write Brothers line.

In 1989 Paper Mate introduced one of its most successful line extensions: the Eraser Mate pen with erasable ink. William H. Holtsnider, then president of Paper Mate, noted in the *New York Times,* "We hadn't anticipated the demand. We've had to cut down on advertising while we build up a bigger capacity." This revolutionary technology relied on special ink, more like tar, that didn't bond with paper for hours or even days. To eject this special ink from the pen, a special pressurized cartridge was required. Ironically, the banking and legal professions once again raised objections to erasable ink for obvious reasons, requiring that Eraser Mate pens carry a package warning that they not be used to write checks or sign legal documents. The Gillette Company's 1980 annual report stated that Eraser Mate doubled its share that year and became the top-selling ball-point pen in the United States.

Early in 1981 the company introduced Eraser Mate 2, a disposable version of the popular pen. The timing of the introduction of the Eraser Mate line was fortuitous, because its high sales figures helped the division maintain financial strength through the challenging early years of the 1980s. Gillette's 1982 annual report explained that "The writing instrument business . . . was affected by the depressed state of worldwide economic activity to a greater degree than most of the Company's product lines." The same report stated that "ball-point pen sales declined moderately in the United States," but there was category growth and "much of this growth was attributable to the Eraser Mate 2 brand, which significantly expanded its share of the market."

Although sales in the stationery products division continued to decline slightly throughout the mid-1980s, Gillette continued introducing new products under the Paper Mate brand name. In 1984 the Accu-Point roller ball pen was presented to the United States market after favorable response from European consumers. The

company's first disposable mechanical pencil, the Paper Mate Sharpwriter, also debuted in 1984, and initial response encouraged extended distribution to Africa and the Asia-Pacific markets. The following year the Paper Mate Advancer, a refillable mechanical pencil, was added to the line. In 1987 sales and profits in the stationery products division finally turned a corner and began an upswing. The premium priced Flexgrip stick pen was introduced during that year, and the Flexgrip Roller pen in 1990. In 1991 the Flexgrip Retractable and the Dynagrip, which featured a patented rubber grip for comfort, were added. Also in 1991, an "improved line of Paper Mate markers was introduced successfully." The Flexgrip Highlighter was introduced the next year in North America and Europe. The Paper Mate Rubberstik pen was added in 1993. The Rubberstik is a stick ball pen with a rubberized barrel meant to provide writing comfort.

### Predictions

Gillette seems to have positioned itself well in the pen market. By augmenting the purchase of Paper Mate with the acquisition of the Waterman Pen Company—with price points as high as $400—and Parker Pen, which represented the mid-price point, the company now covers virtually the entire range of writing instruments. In addition, the global presence of these brands has enabled Gillette to realize profits domestically when foreign markets are depressed, and to succeed in foreign markets during times of domestic economic downturns.

The Gillette Company is the worldwide sales leader in writing instruments with its Paper Mate, Parker, and Waterman brands. The company also is the leader in correction products under the Liquid Paper brand name. It is expected that these brands will continue to enjoy a comfortable position among the leaders in their markets.

### Further Reading:

Adams, Russell B., *King Gillette: The Man and His Wonderful Shaving Device,* Boston: Little, Brown and Company, 1978.

Apodaca, Patrice, "Schick Centers Seeking a Financial Cure; Addictions: Patrick J. Frawley Jr.'s Hospitals are Struggling Despite the Boom in Drug- and Alcohol-Treatment Services," *The Los Angeles Times,* December 7, 1989, p. 2.

Chakravarty, Subrata N., "We had to Change the Playing Field," *Forbes,* February 4, 1991, p. 82.

The Gillette Company Annual Reports, Boston: The Gillette Company, 1980–1992.

"The Gillette Company 1901–1976," *Gillette News,* 1977.

Ramirez, Anthony, "A Radical New Style for Stodgy Old Gillette," *The New York Times,* February 25, 1990, p. 5.

Strange, Julia, "The Way it was Meant to Be: Some Office Supplies Immune to Technology," *Indianapolis Business Journal,* September 16, 1991, p. 1.

*—Kate Sheehan*

# PARKER® PENS

A leader in what is now a multi-million dollar industry, the Parker brand of fountain pens has had a reputation for quality, innovation and superb craftsmanship since its creation over a century ago. Though the fountain pen was invented by American L.E. Waterman in 1884, it was George Safford Parker who made the pen an efficient and popular writing instrument.

## Brand Origins

George Safford Parker, a teacher of telegraphy in Janesville, Wisconsin, moonlighted as a salesman for Ohio-based John Holland pens in 1888. Parker gave pens to his students but found that the ink in these pens often leaked or clogged. Frustrated with the poor performance of these pens, Parker soon began spending more time fixing the pens and less time teaching. As he learned more about the intricacies of pen craftsmanship, he set out to "build a better pen." On December 10, 1889, Parker patented his Parker fountain pen design. Two years later, Parker and a local insurance man, W.F. Palmer, decided to become business partners. They would incorporate their business in 1892 as the Parker Pen Company.

Parker never ceased trying to improve upon his fountain pen's functions. As David Powers Cleary describes in his book, *Great American Brands,* Parker "made a fetish of building it to exacting new standards." Pen making was becoming a sophisticated science, and Parker had his technicians working on the fountain pen's capillary action, vacuum, surface energy, osmotic pressure, porosity, and viscosity.

In 1891, Parker patented a system that controlled a pen's ink flow. Parker refined this system further, patenting his "Lucky Curve" system in 1894. The Lucky Curve ink feed system solved the problem of unstable ink flow and became the foundation for the company's future success. Prior to Parker's invention, a pen carried in a pocket retained ink in the feed tube; as the ink warmed from body heat, it would expand and be forced to the pen's point. When the pen cap was removed, excess ink would flow out— usually all over a person's hands. Parker's Lucky Curve was a curved rubber feed bar that used capillary action to drain ink back into the pen reservoir and prevent such excess.

Four years later, as he was successfully selling pens to the mass market and the American Armed Forces, Parker created the slip-on cap. In 1899, Parker introduced the "Jointless" Fountain Pen, which featured an improved Lucky Curve design. The peace treaty signed in Paris on December 10, 1899 by the United States and Spain, marking the end of the Spanish-American War, was inked with a Parker Jointless Fountain Pen. Parker's next challenge was to convince Americans to use pens for everyday writing.

## Marketing Strategy

Parker pen use by the following famous erudite personalities helped popularize the brand and kept the company at the forefront of the American pen industry: Giacomo Puccini used a Parker Lucky Curve pen to write *La Boheme* in 1896; Sir Arthur Conan Doyle wrote his Sherlock Holmes stories with a Parker; much later, George Bernard Shaw used a Parker pen to stage *Pygmalion;* Robert L. May used one to write "Rudolph the Red Nosed Reindeer"; and Ernest Hemingway employed a Parker pen to write *For Whom the Bell Tolls.*

At the end of the nineteenth century, pens were used primarily by people who were educated in reading and writing. People wanted their pens to be noticed, as they were a visible sign of a person's education and social status. So Parker, between 1900 and 1915, launched a line of pens that were gold, silver, gold-filled, and mother of pearl that became status symbols (and hot collector's items decades later) among the social elite. A memorable design was Parker's Snake Pen, a hard, black rubber, eyedropper-filled pen with a sterling silver or gold-filled, green-eyed snake winding its way around the pen barrel and cap.

During this period, Parker made the following improvements to fountain pen design: a spear-head feed, the first safety pen cap (called the Jack Knife), a new Lucky Curve, gold rings on the top of "lady sized pens," and the level lock clip. He was also expanding his business by establishing distributorships. He opened his first distributorship in 1903, when he convinced a Copenhagen shopkeeper to carry his pens. In 1906 he introduced the Parker Emblem Pen that featured the emblems of secret societies such as the Knights of Columbus and the Masons.

World War I initiated a boom in letter writing and record keeping and, Parker capitalized on it by being granted the U.S. War Department contract to produce the Parker Trench Pen for the American soldiers. The Trench Pen, launched in 1917, featured black pigment pellets that could be converted into ink with water. The Trench Pen was extremely popular and received wide exposure overseas. By 1918, Parker had exceeded $1 million in pen

## AT A GLANCE

**P**arker brand pens invented by George Safford Parker in 1888 in Janesville, WI; patented in 1889; Parker Pen Company incorporated in 1892; Lucky Curve ink feed system patented in 1894; patented the slip-on cap and the George S. Parker Jointless Fountain Pen in 1899; company acquired Wahl-Eversharp Writing Instrument Division in 1957 and Manpower Inc. employment services in 1976; Writing Instrument Group of Parker Pen acquired in a leveraged buyout, 1986; Parker Pen Ltd. acquired by The Gillette Company in 1993 for $561 million.

**Performance:** *Market share*—53% of pen category in the United Kingdom; 25% of prestige pen category and 10% of $3 pen market in the United States. *Sales*—(Parker Pen USA Ltd.) $84 million.

**Major competitor:** Schaeffer; also Cross and Mont Blanc.

**Advertising:** *Major campaign*—Individual campaigns, developed by in-house advertising department, for each pen line.

**Addresses:** *Parent company*—Parker Pen Ltd., Parker House, Newhaven East Sussex, England BN9 0AU; (U.S. distributor) Parker Pen USA Ltd., 1400 North Parker Drive, Janesville, WI 53545; phone: (608) 755-7112; fax: (608) 755-7227. *Ultimate parent company*—The Gillette Company, Prudential Tower Bldg., Boston, MA 02199; phone: (617) 421-7000; fax: (617) 421-7123.

sales. Business success was reflected in the construction of a five-story manufacturing and administrative facility in Janesville, Wisconsin in 1919. The operation was run by several Parker family members including his sons Russell and Kenneth and grandsons George and Dan. In 1928, business partner Palmer sold out his 75 percent stake in the company to an investment banking house, which, in turn, sold the shares in the Chicago Stock Exchange. This marked the first public offering of Parker's shares.

When World War II began, the Parker brand pen was an established industry leader. At this time the company introduced its innovative Duofold pen, described as an over-sized, bright red-orange fountain pen with a gold nib—the only non-black pen on the market. The Duofold stood out, not just because of its flamboyant color, which Parker actually patented, but also because of its $7 price tag, which was almost three times more than the price of competing fountain pens.

Chicago was the test market for the new pen and Parker selected the *Chicago Tribune* to advertise Duofold. The aggressive marketing strategy for the pen included a 10-member sales force that canvassed the city armed with product samples, color posters, testimonial letters and a 25-year guarantee for the pen. Within a week, gross sales of Duofolds exceeded the cost of the three-month ad campaign; five months later, Parker launched Duofold Pens nationwide.

The Duofold's elegance was not the only attractive aspect that appealed to customers. The pen had double the ink capacity and "its large, flexible gold point make it an immediate favorite of penmanship buffs who favored the distinctive Spencerian and Palmer styles of handwriting," according to David Powers Cleary in *Great American Brands.* Cleary also notes that only five percent of the U.S. population owned fountain pens and the Duofold's "electrifying" appearance set off creative attempts to meld color and pen design.

Within four years, sales had quadrupled, vaulting Parker Pen into the top-selling position of the high priced pen market in 1926. Duofold was continually improved and its brand line expanded to include new sizes, finishes, and such colors as "Jade Green, Mandarin Yellow, True Blue, Lapis Blue." A Lady Duofold was introduced in 1923, and student Parker DQ (Duofold quality) entered the mass market in 1926. Duofolds made of a plastic called Permanite were also launched that year. Plastic enabled Parker to offer an unlimited guarantee. The use of plastic also made for such interesting sales promotions as dropping Duofolds from airplanes into the Grand Canyon to prove the pen's durability. Imperial Duofolds (later Duofold DeLuxe) debuted for upscale consumers in 1928 in black and pearl. Desk sets also became popular at this time and Parker formed the Pen Desk Set Company. Vest Pocket Duettes appeared in 1930.

### Research and Development in the Golden Era

Extensive research and development helped Parker Pens release successful products that kept the company prospering during the Great Depression and after George S. Parker's death in 1937. Most product development focused on fountain pen and ink improvements.

One such innovation was Quink, the first pen cleaning ink—a formula that has remained unchanged since the 1930s. Three years later, the company promoted its new improved sac-less filling mechanism in a "see through" Vacumatic Pen, which met with instant success. This pen was considered safe on commercial airlines because it would not explode under pressure.

The Parker Vacumatic's barrel was made from a laminated plastic with alternating layers of black and silver pearl and came with a new Arrow pocket clip, designed by New York artist Joseph Platt. The Vacumatic became Parker's most widely recognized product trademark and was a best seller until 1940, according to company literature. The Vacumatic pen's capacity was also 102 percent greater than that of the Duofold.

### Setting New Standards

The next Parker Pen set a new standard for pen workmanship. Instead of making a pen that would hold more ink than a competitor's, Parker unveiled in 1941 a completely different type of fountain pen called Parker 51. Made of alkali-resistant lucite, (the ink's alkali content often corroded pen interiors) the Parker 51 was slimmer and came with a hooded nib. It used a quick drying ink and was named "51" because it was developed in Parker's 51st year. This pen was so different that Parker promoted it as being "like a pen from a different planet."

The Parker 51 was so extraordinarily successful that the company ran out of the pens and actually had to take out advertising apologizing for the shortage. However, the company apparently had enough Parker 51s on hand during the peace treaty signings at the end of World War II and the Korean War. General Dwight D. Eisenhower insisted that two of his Parker 51 pens be used to sign the Armistice on the European Front, and General Douglas MacArthur signed the Japanese surrender aboard the Battleship Missouri using his own 20-year-old Parker Duofold. On July 27, 1953, General Mark W. Clark used a Parker 51 Flighter pen to witness the armistice that ended the Korean War.

Between 1947 and 1949, the celebrated Parker pens (most notably the Parker 51) became the noted pens used at ceremonies.

Parker pens were used in the following historical treaty and contract signings: the agreement between the United States and Britain to share costs of the Anglo-American zone of Western Germany, the economic agreement establishing closer cooperation between the United States and Turkey under the Marshall Plan, and the contract between the Ford Motor Company and Detroit autoworkers. Parker 51 pens were also given to the King and Queen of England as Silver Wedding gifts. The pens were mounted with the royal ciphers—the king's in gold and enamel and the queen's in platinum and diamonds.

In 1948, the company introduced the Parker 21, a lower priced "51" version, which earned 60 percent of the market of pens priced over $5. The next year, a solid 24-karat gold Parker Presidential debuted. The Parker 51 was awarded the Fashion Academy Award for exceptional styling, precision and craftsmanship in 1950. According to *Great American Brands,* the " '51' pioneered new materials and would write with new ease for half a mile between refills."

Though the "Parker 51 was voted one of the five best-designed products of modern times," according to *Great American Brands,* the company wasn't about to rest on its laurels. However, Parker wasn't going to jump onto the ball point pen bandwagon. Parker waited ten years for design, price, and market fluctuations to stabilize before unveiling a superior quality ball point pen called the Jotter in 1954. The Jotter came with a choice of point sizes and a high capacity cartridge. It was revamped in 1957 with a textured tungsten carbide ball point that was as porous as a sponge and as hard as a diamond. This "T-ball Jotter" exceeded industry expectations; Parker sold 3.5 million Jotters in its first year and introduced an International Jotter in the late 1950s.

Meanwhile, Parker was still launching new and improved fountain pens like the Parker 61, the first self-filling fountain pen in 1956, the Parker 61 Jet Flighter in 1958, followed by the Parker 45 (the first ink cartridge pen) and the Parker VP in 1962. Between 1976 and 1979, the company introduced the Parker 180, a dual-line nib, Parker 25, Parker 50, Ms. Parker, a women's designer pen, and a novelty neck fountain pen, called the Swinger.

## Happy Anniversary

The year 1963 marked the Parker Pen company's 75th anniversary, and the introduction of the solid sterling silver Parker 75 luxury pen with a 14-karat gold nib to commemorate the company's 75 years of success. Since the 1960s, Parker has endeavored to sell more upscale models made out of rare or antique materials to mark historical moments.

One such brand was the 75 Spanish Treasure Fleet Edition (1965) that was made from silver recovered from the Spanish treasure ships sunk off the coast of Florida in 1715. Only 4,821 of the pens were made. To celebrate ten years of the American space program, Parker introduced a special edition of the 1967 classic line of slim-contoured writing instruments, made from the booster rocket that propelled the first American in space.

Other one-of-a-kind Parker pens included: T-1, made of titanium (1970); Big Red ball point and soft tip versions of the Duofold (1972); the Parker 75 Keepsake Pen (1973) used in the signing of the Vietnam Peace Agreement; Arrow line gift pens with engravable pocket clips (1981); Sterling Silver Parker 75s (1987) that witnessed the signing of the Intermediate Nuclear Forces Treaty between then President Ronald Reagan and Soviet General Secretary Mikhail Gorbachev; a Duofold Centennial edition (1987) that encompassed a fountain pen, ball point versions; and an expanded Duofold Collection (1990).

## Variations Upon the Same Theme

If the ball point Jotter pen expanded the Parker Pen brand line into the next generation of the modern pen, the roller ball took pens into a new realm. A roller ball combined the smoothness of the fountain pen with the convenience of the ball point. Parker had introduced its own line of roller balls with Systemark in 1975 that featured interchangeable soft tips and plastic tip stylus refills. In 1982, the Vector Roller Ball was introduced in the United Kingdom and a Vector Vogue in fashionable pastel colors targeted to the teen market appeared in 1985. Other brand names would also come in a roller ball version, such as the custom Parker 75 plated with 22-karat gold and crowned with a red star sapphire. This particular pen was used when former President George Bush and Mikhail Gorbachev signed the 1991 Strategic Arms Reduction Treaty. Duofold Orange Roller Ball pens were also used by Bush and Russian President Boris Yeltsin in 1992 to seal important intercontinental agreements. A roller ball pen was also employed to sign the agreement freeing the American hostages in Iran.

## Company Expansion, Decline and Rebirth

In 1988, the Parker Pen Company celebrated its centennial anniversary, but it had just undergone the first of two management buyouts and disastrous sales losses. The company had lost $22 million in its U.S. pen business in 1985, after focusing on selling to foreign markets and trying to sell more convenient, lower-priced ball point pens in the United States. Up until that point, the company had steadily grown from a family business into a conglomerate and was experiencing sales gains every year.

Heavy growth in the 1950s spurred the development of manufacturing facilities in France and Mexico and the installation of state-of-the-art equipment at its Janesville, Wisconsin-based Arrow Park facility, which later became company headquarters. In 1957, Parker acquired Wahl-Eversharp's Writing Instrument Division to maintain a presence in the low-priced end of the market, while still promoting its upscale and higher priced products. In 1976, Parker purchased Milwaukee-based Manpower Inc. (and renamed itself after this company), an employment services company, in an effort to stabilize the business. Manpower sales tripled shortly after its acquisition, but the pen business in the United States began to slide, according to a 1980 *Dun's Review.*

In the early 1980s, 75 percent of the company's writing instrument revenues came from international markets, further weakening Parker's position in the United States. A.T. Cross Co. began capturing the corporate upscale pen market just as Americans began returning to fountain pens as their pen of choice. The company's European officials attempted to rejuvenate the pen division of Parker. In 1986, Parker United Kingdom managers and investors acquired the company in a $100 million leveraged buyout from Manpower Inc.; Parker became privately held and its headquarters moved to Newhaven, England. North American headquarters remained at Parker offices in Janesville, Wisconsin. Led by Jacques G. Margry, the new Parker Pen refocused its marketing strategy, cut production and staff costs, raised U.S. prices 30 percent and increased advertising spending by 60 percent over 1985 levels to target the "style conscious and the affluent," according John Marcom Jr. in *Forbes* magazine.

In addition to the Parker Duofold Collection of luxury writing instruments, Parker launched European-styled Parker 88 Place Vendome fountain and ball point pens, the Insignia line of pens and mechanical pencils, World Memorial Pens, and personalized pens for the five living U.S. presidents. In 1993, the company was purchased for $561 million by The Gillette Company. Parker officials told the Associated Press that they had been seeking ''an international products company that could enhance the strength of its brand names and their international distribution.''

## Advertising Strategy

Individual Parker pen brands are promoted separately in an effort to maintain each pen's personality, style and uniqueness. However, Parker Pen Ltd. has always used the same format in its copy and graphics; each advertisement ''must offer the reader some reward in return for his time and attention—news, benefits, or service,'' according to Cleary in *Great American Brands.* Taglines have depicted Parker as ''superior to all others,'' ''a good pen,'' ''the only ball point that won't skip,'' ''the world's most wanted pen,'' and ''mightier than the sword.'' In 1958, Norman Rockwell created a series of popular print ads that featured famous people using their favorite Parker pens. According to *Great American Brands,* Parker advertisements often focused on ''developing a gift concept.''

After the 1986 management buyout, Parker abandoned global advertising by centralizing the advertising budget and increasing it by about 50 percent. Company officials downplayed cheaper pens and targeted four key markets: the United States, Japan, France and Germany. Ads differed widely from country to country and were printed in more than 40 languages. For example, German ads showed an upscale Parker pen writing the headline ''This is how you write with precision,'' while British advertising emphasized the exotic procedures used in making Parker pens—gold nibs being polished gently by walnut chips for 56 hours, for example.

To capitalize on the resurgence of the fountain pen in the late 1980s and early 1990s, Parker spent $4.4 million on advertising (twice as much as competitors Mont Blanc, Waterman, and A.T. Cross) to promote its fountain pen's historical origins. Duofold advertising used news photos of Dwight D. Eisenhower and Douglas MacArthur using Parker pens to sign World War II surrender documents. Other print ads stressed Parker's witnessing of other famous treaty signings, and often featured the following tagline: ''The pen is mightier than the sword, and some pens are mightier than others.'' During this period, ads also featured more photos of famous signers. Lowe Tucker Metcalf of New York had been assigned to design and place these ads in business magazines and upscale consumer print media, and sales grew 40 to 50 percent annually.

In addition to convincing pen users to consider luxury as well as convenience, the company also appealed to consumers' global consciousness. In 1991, Parker offered pens made of metal from dismantled American and Soviet missiles (a result of treaties between the two countries which were signed with Parker pens). Half of the proceeds of these pen sales were given to the worldwide Memorial Fund for Disaster Relief.

## International Presence

George S. Parker said that his pens ''will write in any language,'' and his pioneering work establishing company distributorships led to its vast network of 19 operating subsidiaries and 100 independent distributors worldwide. Parker alone traveled to Europe, Asia, and Australia during the early 1920s to establish an international network of distributors for his products. He also succeeded in establishing manufacturing facilities in Toronto, Canada, and England in 1924. Parker's presence in England has been especially enduring. In fact, the pen maker controls 53 percent of United Kingdom's pen market. In the early 1990s, the company—which held two royal warrants by appointment to Her Majesty the Queen and His Royal Highness the Prince of Wales—had manufacturing bases in Meru, France; Newhaven, England; and Janesville, Wisconsin. Production facilities exist in Argentina and pens are assembled in Columbia and Mexico. Parker was producing more than 50 million finished writing instruments and accessories annually in the early 1990s.

## Performance Appraisal

Throughout its history, Parker has pioneered new techniques in precision engineering and automated production. Its manufacturing expertise has led the industry in developing new products and technologies. Its strategy of focusing on the higher end of the pen market has proven extremely successful. Consumer preferences for prestige items were reflected in Parker's revival in the early 1990s. By the time of the Gillette buyout, 20 percent of Parker's unit sales were generated by the more expensive pens, compared with 5 percent in 1985. According to the Associated Press, the company was expected to make an operating profit of $61 million on revenue of $322 million in 1992, compared to a pre-tax loss of $17.9 million on revenue of $206 million in 1985.

Parker's pen line was expected to aptly complement Gillette's low-end Paper Mate and higher end Waterman brands. In the United States, Parker controlled about 10 percent of the $3-pen market and enjoyed a 25 percent share of the prestige pen market in the early 1990s. Its competitors in the high end were Schaeffer, Cross, and Mont Blanc.

## Further Reading:

Brown, Christie, ''Power Pens,'' *Forbes,* September 2, 1991, pp. 150–151.

Cleary, David Powers, *Great American Brands,* New York: Fairchild Publications, 1981, pp. 223–231.

Cote, Kevin, ''Parker Pen Finds Black Ink,'' *Advertising Age,* July 13, 1987, p. 49.

Fuccini, Joseph J., and Suzy Fuccini, *Entrepreneurs, the Men and Women Behind Famous Brand Names and How They Made It,* Boston: G.K. Hall & Co., 1985, p. 226.

''Gillette Co.,'' *Advertising Age,* September 14, 1992, p. 73.

''Gillette Inks Deal for Parker Pens,'' *USA Today,* September 11, 1992, sec. B, p. 3.

Levine, Joshua, ''Pen Wars,'' *Forbes,* January 6, 1992, pp. 88–89.

Marcom, John, Jr., ''Penmanship with a Flourish,'' *Forbes,* April 3, 1989, pp. 152–154.

McGrath, Molly Wade, *Top Sellers, U.S.A.,* New York: William Morrow and Co., 1983, p. 159.

''Parker Pen Is for Sale,'' *Wisconsin State Journal,* February 4, 1992, p. 1.

''Parker Pen UK Says It Seeks an Acquirer 6 Years After Buyout,'' *Wall Street Journal,* February 4, 1992.

''The Pen is Still Mighty at Parker—But,'' *Dun's Review,* October 1980, pp. 45–46.

Walker, Robert, ''How Parker's Past Became Its Future,'' *AdWeek's Marketing Week,* June 12, 1989, pp. 58–59.

''Writing off the Weapons,'' *Time,* October 28, 1991, p. 81.

—*Evelyn S. Dorman*

# PENNZOIL®

## Performance. Protection. Quality.™

Speculative organizations, acquisitions, and mergers clutter the history of the oil business. Pennzoil motor oil's parentage is no exception. While the Pennzoil Company traces its roots to the South Penn Oil Co., which was organized on May 27, 1889, as a producing unit of Standard Oil Co., the origins of the motor oil brand are more accurately traced to two marketing companies with a common interest. The Oil City Oil and Grease Co. of Pennsylvania marketed its branded products under the "Merit Oil" trademark in the east; a similar company in the west, Panama Lubricants Co., of California, used the trademark "Panama" (because of the canal). Neither name generated the sales the companies wanted, so they tried to come up with a better name. What they arrived at was "Pennsoil," which was an abbreviation for William Penn's oil and also reflected the brand's "100% Pure Pennsylvania" grade oil content. But the companies still had a problem. They found that their customers pronounced the word "Pennsoil" instead of "Penn's oil." Someone at the California company solved the problem with the suggestion to change the "s" to "z."

Pure Oil was the only obstacle to the companies' adoption of the Pennzoil name as their trademark. Although it no longer used the brand name, Pure had the rights to the word "Pennoil." However, Pure sold the rights for the original cost to register the trademark—$65. Oil City Oil and Grease and Panama Lubricants thus introduced the Pennzoil trademark by the end of 1915. It was legally registered in the U.S. Patent Office on August 1, 1916. The Liberty Bell became part of the design that became the well-known Pennzoil emblem.

In 1921 the marketing companies changed their names to emphasize their Pennzoil brand. Panama Lubricants Co. became The Pennzoil Co. (a California Corp.) and Oil City Oil and Grease Co. became The Pennzoil Co. (a Pennsylvania Corp.). In the same year, Pennzoil marketed lubricating oil in Detroit, Toledo, Cleveland, and Pittsburgh. A marketing division launched in 1922 in Buffalo became Pennzoil Co. of New York. J. Paul Getty's South Penn Oil Co. purchased a controlling interest in Pennzoil in 1925. Pennzoil became a South Penn division in 1955.

J. Hugh Liedtke, his brother Bill, John Overbey, and oil field equipment salesman George Bush founded Zapata Petroleum in 1953. In 1962 Hugh Liedtke became president of South Penn and the following year, Zapata Petroleum and Stetco Petroleum were merged into South Penn Oil Co. and the corporate name was changed to Pennzoil Company. According to *Pennzoil—The First 100 Years,* "The new name was designed to cash in on the name recognition of South Penn's big product, a yellow can of lubricant oil."

### "Handi" Containers

Pennzoil altered packaging over the years to meet customer demands. Pennzoil offered metal containers of varying sizes to early motorists to haul oil in their cars. The automobiles of the era consumed large amounts of oil (it was common for the cars to need a quart every 200 miles) and often service stations were not easy to reach. In a mid-1920s advertisement, the company promoted its "Handigallon" metal container that "provides the last word in stow away convenience for your take along reserve supply of Pennzoil." The container featured a long, leak-proof swing spout.

Other Pennzoil containers included the "Handican," a flat one-quart can that "disappears into the door pocket" and the "Handitank," which held ten gallons and "looks good in anybody's garage." Additionally, Pennzoil sold a five-gallon container with a pelican spout designed to fit on the running board of a car, which might have a crank case capacity of up to ten quarts of oil.

The Handi containers were relatively expensive to manufacture and fill and the odd shapes made stacking difficult, so the company explored other types and means of packaging their motor oil. In 1931 Pennzoil became one of the first companies to incorporate sealed containers in its operations when it installed a canning line at its refinery near Oil City, Pennsylvania. The company used equipment originally developed for the food industry and began to utilize yellow metal cans that could be easily stacked for delivery and retail display. Composite cans made of foil and cardboard replaced the metal cans in 1964. The company also bottled oil in glass containers during the 1940s and 1950s.

Following the lead of competitor Quaker State motor oil, Pennzoil introduced a yellow plastic bottle container in 1985. Unlike Quaker State's container, which was round and hard to stack, Pennzoil's was square in shape, which allowed retailers and gas stations to put more product on shelves. The company's latest "handican" combined a pour spout with a reusable, tamper-proof twist-off cap. Due in part to the new container, Pennzoil motor oil

## AT A GLANCE

**P**ennzoil brand of motor oil founded in 1915 by two oil marketing companies, Oil City Oil and Grease Co. in Pennsylvania and Panama Lubricants Co. in California; originally Pennsoil (named for William Penn's oil), customers pronounced it Penn-soil, so "z" replaced "s"; marketing companies purchased rights to the word Pennoil from Pure Oil; Pennzoil became a registered trademark, 1916; both marketing companies changed their names to The Pennzoil Co., 1921; South Penn Oil Co. acquired controlling interest in Pennzoil Co., 1925, and merged, 1955; South Penn merged with Zapata Petroleum to create Pennzoil Company in 1962.

**Performance:** *Market share*—21% (number one share) of motor oil category. *Sales*—$1.6 billion (January through September 1993).

**Major competitor:** Quaker State Corp.'s Quaker State; Valvoline Inc.'s Valvoline.

**Advertising:** *Agency*—Eisaman, Johns & Laws Advertising, Inc., Houston, TX, 1957—. *Major campaign*—"We Owe You One" promotion features Arnold Palmer as spokesperson.

**Addresses:** *Parent company*—Pennzoil Company, Pennzoil Place, P.O. Box 2967, Houston, TX 77252-2967; phone: (713) 546-4000; fax: (713) 546-6314.

soon took over the number one share position from Quaker State. It has retained the top spot through the early 1990s.

### "Sound Your Z"—Advertising Through the Years

Pennzoil advertisements have historically followed national advertising trends and highlighted Pennzoil's involvement in current events of human interest. The company launched its first national advertising campaign in the 1920s to promote its products, reputation for quality, and the Pennzoil name. Motorists who read such magazines as *The Saturday Evening Post* and *Harpers* became familiar with the "Sound your Z for Pennzoil" slogan.

The early Pennzoil ads featured pencil-sketched vignettes at the top of the ad with dialogue at the bottom espousing the superiority of Pennzoil products. A 1920s full-page ad in *The Saturday Evening Post* told about an Army airplane's nonstop East to West Coast flight on Pennzoil. A 1926 ad in the same magazine described the cross-country endurance drive by Ab Jenkins, during which his Pennzoil-lubricated Studebaker smashed every coast-to-coast record. Jenkins covered 3,471 miles in 86 hours of "merciless driving without a change of oil." His car used only 11 quarts of oil, an average of 1,262 miles per gallon.

Pennzoil was established as a well-known and highly respected lubrication name from the company's earliest years. By the end of the 1920s, only three airplanes had flown nonstop across the United States, and all three had been lubricated with Pennzoil. The oil was important in automobile racing, too. In 1927 Pennzoil-protected vehicles set these records: Ab Jenkins, in a Studebaker Commander, crossed the country in 77 hours, 40 minutes; a Duesenberg won the half-mile race on a dirt track in Harrisburg, Pennsylvania, in 28.4 seconds; and an automobile using Pennzoil won the Pike's Peak Climb (for the first of four consecutive years).

When Pennzoil-lubricated cars finished eighth and tenth at the 1930 Indianapolis 500, it was clear that a car lubricated with mineral oil could complete the grinding pace. Prior to that race

only cars with castor oil in their crankcases had lasted the 500 miles. The racing circuit was used frequently to promote Pennzoil motor oil, the sponsorships as a supplement to the company's use of traditional advertising media. Pennzoil-lubricated and identified cars also won the Indianapolis 500 in 1951, 1980, 1984, 1985, 1987, and 1988.

During the 1930s the company sponsored The Pennzoil Hour network radio show, which showcased the Pennzoil Orchestra and announcer Pennzoil Pete. Pete told a Depression-weary America that quality Pennzoil products were a better bargain for their money. Pennzoil also enlisted Hollywood to promote its motor oil. Jean Harlow's 1930 movie *Hell's Angels* featured World War I airplanes lubricated with the company's products. Harlow appeared in Pennzoil ads, too, as did screen star Mary Astor, shown signing a Pennzoil motor oil guarantee.

South Penn and Pennzoil grew into a modern production and marketing organization in the 1930s and 1940s. Product research and development, aggressive sales promotion, and complete advertising campaigns combined to make the company's products among the country's most respected. The company strove to keep ahead of the demands made by modern automobiles and machinery. It experimented with oil additives that cleared the way for later developments in high performance lubricants, including the development of a "double refining" vacuum distillation process that gave its oil longer life with less consumption. Until the fall of 1931, double-refined "Tough Film Pennzoil" motor oil represented the highest standard of lubrication then available. Monogram and Oilzum were Pennzoil's biggest competitors at the time.

Pennzoil continued to research and improve its motor oil after the successful introduction of double refined oil in 1930. In 1935 Pennzoil introduced its first solvent-extracted oil for internal combustion engines. The oil involved three extra steps in its refining and produced an oil without undesirable sludge-forming elements. As shown by impartial laboratory tests, the oil was 133 percent superior to the former Pennzoil motor oil on points such as wear, oil consumption, carbon, and sludge. The 1930s advertising slogan "Flows fast and stays strong" highlighted Pennzoil improvements. The slogan referred to the oil's capability in the current automobile engines that had a compression ratio of about 4-to-1 and burned 60-octane gasoline (compared to 9-to-1 compression ratio and an octane rating of more than 85 in the 1990s).

Around 1936 the Pennzoil "Safety System" became a favorite of new car dealerships. The system displayed Pennzoil products—along with the Pennzoil owls—and advised customers to "be oil wise." A 1940s advertising slogan told motorists that Pennzoil "Wakes up lazy engines. Don't be a Nero at Zero!" In the 1950s Pennzoil made an effort to expand its market position by targeting such special interests as motorboat enthusiasts, the new do-it-yourself market, and racing fans. The company used the slogan "You can FEEL the power difference as you drive." After the company introduced additives to its motor oil with its "Z-7" protective package, motorists were advised to "Switch to Pennzoil" by Penny Pennzoil in 1959.

Pennzoil sponsored drag racer Don Garlits in "Swamp Rat" in the early 1960s. In the 1970s it ran the "Underground Hero" racing promotions, and in the 1980s Indy Car racer Rick Mears became a popular Pennzoil spokesperson. In the early 1990s, the company found that a program of NASCAR racing, drag racing, and Indy Car racing contributed to strong sales volumes.

"The Lonely Oil" campaign ran in the 1960s and gave the company an opportunity to advertise Pennzoil products on national television. The tag line "Ask for Pennzoil" assured customers they would get quality Pennzoil protection. Print ads in

*A can of Pennzoil motor oil as it used to appear, featuring an endorsement by United Airlines.*

demographically researched markets, including newspapers and magazines like *Cosmopolitan, Woman's Day,* and *Field & Stream,* supplemented television and radio spots in the 1970s and 1980s.

Other slogans Pennzoil used over the years were "Gives your engine an extra margin of safety," "The oil that goes farther, faster, safer," "Protection and Pennzoil; Get them together in your car," "Quality in every extra mile," "Quality protection; Ask for it," and "5/50 warranty; Pennzoil keeps it running."

Golfing legend Arnold Palmer first served as the Pennzoil motor oil spokesman in 1979; he has continued in that capacity through the early 1990s. With Palmer as the spokesperson, the company in 1993 used the theme "We Owe You One" to advertise and market a message that emphasized Pennzoil quality and

gratitude to customers who kept the motor oil brand number one. Advertising was primarily through national network, cable, and spot television and radio.

All these factors—the racing program, the push to fill the shelves of mass marketers, the introduction of the plastic bottle, and canny marketing strategies—helped make Pennzoil a leader in motor oils. In 1980 sales of Pennzoil Products Co. passed the $1 billion mark for the first time.

### Keeping Market Share

Pennzoil motor oil became the nation's top seller in 1986, a position it has held ever since. The company introduced its first synthetic motor oil, Performax 5W-50, in 1992 to round out its premium line of motor oil for automotive vehicles, outboard motors, motorcycles, chain saws, and lubricants. The company's efforts to extend its reach in the motor oil market will be difficult, however, as the domestic motor oil market is considered a mature one, with an anticipated growth of only one to two percent a year for the foreseeable future. Most of that growth is expected to take place in the installed market (fast lubes, service stations, and automobile dealers). As the owner of Jiffy Lube International, Inc., the world's largest franchisor of fast oil change centers, Pennzoil is in a good position to tap into the growth.

The company's reputation as a dependable distributor also positioned Pennzoil to maintain its market share. Pennzoil has built a nationwide distribution system centered around 75 company-owned distribution centers and 157 authorized distributors; the company usually delivers products within 48 hours anywhere in the country. Pennzoil has also forged partnerships with the nation's top retailers. In addition, Pennzoil has increased its international presence, marketing products in 58 countries.

### Further Reading:

Hannon, Kerry, "Run Over by the Competition," *Forbes,* September 5, 1988.

Ivey, Mark, "Pennzoil's Trip Down a Slippery Slope," *Business Week,* July 22, 1991, p. 53.

Jaffe, Thomas, "Texaco vs. Pennzoil II?" *Forbes,* March 15, 1993, p. 21.

Moskowitz, Milton, Robert Levering and Michael Katz, eds., *Everybody's Business: A Field Guide to the 400 Leading Companies in America,* New York: Doubleday, 1990, p. 489.

*Pennzoil—The First 100 Years,* Houston, TX: Pennzoil Company, 1989.

*Pennzoil Company Annual Report,* Houston, TX: Pennzoil Company, 1992.

Sharp, Harold S., *Advertising Slogans of America,* Metuchen, NJ: The Scarecrow Press, Inc., 1984, p. 361.

—*Doris Morris Maxfield*

# PEPSODENT®

Although no longer among the market leaders in the early 1990s, Pepsodent remained one of the oldest and best-known brands of toothpaste in the United States. The Pepsodent brand, owned by Chesebrough-Pond's USA Company, a subsidiary of Unilever United States Inc., held about 1.7 percent of the U.S. toothpaste market in sales. This was compared to 36 percent for Crest, the number one toothpaste from the Procter & Gamble Company, and 12 percent for SmithKline Beecham's Aquafresh.

Pepsodent was the leading brand of toothpaste during much of the 1920s and 1930s, and again in the 1940s. In the 1950s Pepsodent was the second best-selling brand of toothpaste with the classic advertising jingle "You'll Wonder Where the Yellow Went When you Brush Your Teeth With Pepsodent." During its 75-year history, Pepsodent was promoted by such show business celebrities as Amos and Andy, Bob Hope, Lucille Ball, Dick Van Dyke, and Lena Horn.

## Brand Origins

Pepsodent toothpaste was developed by Douglas Smith, a Chicago businessman who purchased the original peppermint-flavored formula from a chemist in Lincoln, Nebraska. Smith founded the Pepsodent Company in 1916, and Pepsodent quickly became the best known brand of toothpaste in the United States, thanks to a fortuitous meeting between Smith and Albert Lasker, then head of the Lord & Thomas advertising agency.

Toothpastes had been sold in the United States since before the Civil War. However, toothpaste did not begin to outsell tooth powder until the 1890s, when Dr. Washington Sheffield, a Connecticut dentist, began packaging toothpaste in collapsible food tubes imported from Europe. Other companies, including industry leader Colgate Company, soon began selling toothpaste in tubes. By 1916 Dr. I. W. Lyon's Tooth Powder, introduced in 1874, was practically the only powder still advertised nationally.

However, as late as 1916 an estimated 60 percent of the U.S. population still had never used a tooth brush. When Lasker met with Smith he recognized the enormous market potential for toothpaste and agreed to invest $300,000 of his own money to advertise Pepsodent in return for a 25 percent share of the company. Lasker gave the Pepsodent account to Claude Hopkins, an advertising copywriter who created the slogan "shot from guns" for the Quaker Oats Company's puffed cereals. Hopkins read up on dental science and came across the term "mucin plaque," the filmy mucous build-up found on teeth. He also decided that people were less interested in healthy teeth, which most toothpastes then promised, than they were good-looking teeth. The advertising campaign Hopkins developed focused on Pepsodent's ability to remove the mucus film from teeth, enhance the user's appearance, and lead to success in love and commerce. The advertisements, launched in 1917, were eventually printed in 17 languages.

### Amos 'n' Andy

From 1929 until the mid-1930s, Pepsodent sponsored *Amos 'n' Andy*, a comedy about two black men and perhaps the most popular radio program of all time. AT&T once claimed that telephone calls practically stopped when the program was broadcast. Theaters interrupted their movies and played the show set up on stage so moviegoers would not miss an episode. At the end of every broadcast, announcer Bill Hay would remind an estimated 40 million listeners to "use Pepsodent twice a day, see your dentist twice a year."

The show not only boosted sales of Pepsodent, it demonstrated for the first time the tremendous power of radio to reach an audience. *Amos 'n' Andy* initially aired at 11 p.m. Eastern time. However, NBC switched the 15-minute program to 7 p.m. when East Coast parents complained that their children would not go to bed until after *Amos 'n' Andy*. This then prompted a rash of complaints from listeners in the West. Angry fans threatened to stop buying Pepsodent and the Secretary of State of Colorado wrote a letter to the Pepsodent Company asking that *Amos 'n' Andy* be broadcast later so state employees could enjoy the program when they got home. NBC eventually asked Freeman Gosden and Charles Correll, who played Amos and Andy, to do their live show a second time at 10 p.m. to satisfy fans on both sides of the country.

Fans associated *Amos 'n' Andy* so closely with Pepsodent that the company received thousands of letters and telegrams in response to various story lines. A "Name the Baby" contest when Amos was about to become a "father" resulted in more than two million entries, each with a flap from a Pepsodent toothpaste box. In 1931, when Amos was falsely accused of murder, the Parent Teacher Association even threatened to boycott Pepsodent if he was convicted. For several episodes it looked as if Amos would be found guilty. Then, just as the jury was about to deliver its verdict,

## AT A GLANCE

**P**epsodent brand of toothpaste developed by Douglas Smith who founded the Pepsodent Company, 1916; Pepsodent Company purchased by Lever Brothers & Company, a subsidiary of Unilever Group, Ltd., 1944; another Unilever Group, Ltd. subsidiary, Unilever United States Inc., purchased Chesebrough-Pond's USA Company and brand was transferred to that company, 1987.

**Performance:** *Market share*—1.7% of toothpaste category. *Sales*—$25.5 million.

**Major competitor:** Procter & Gamble Company's Crest; also Colgate-Palmolive Company's Colgate brand.

**Advertising:** *Major campaign*—"You'll Wonder Where the Yellow Went When You Brush Your Teeth With Pepsodent."

**Addresses:** *Parent company*—Chesebrough-Pond's USA Company, 33 Benedict Place, Greenwich, CT 06830; phone: (203) 661-2000. *Ultimate parent company*—Unilever United States Inc., 390 Park Ave., New York, NY 10022; phone: (212) 888-1260; fax: (212) 752-6365. *Ultimate ultimate parent company*—Unilever Group, Ltd.

an alarm clock sounded and the show revealed that Amos had been dreaming. Correll admitted later that it "was a dirty trick but we had to do it. We had to get out of it someway."

## Fair Trade Laws

Despite the popularity of *Amos 'n' Andy,* sales of Pepsodent began to fall in the early 1930s when independent druggists throughout the country began refusing to sell the toothpaste. Druggists in Brooklyn went so far as to string banners across their storefronts declaring, "We do not carry Pepsodent products." At issue was the question of minimum retail prices.

Almost all toothpaste was then sold in drugstores. Chain drugstores often sold the most popular brand-name products, including Pepsodent, as "loss leaders," dropping the price below cost to attract customers. Independent druggists, who made up the bulk of the industry, could not afford to match the price cuts, and encouraged manufacturers to sign chain stores to minimum price contracts. Theoretically, minimum price contracts violated antitrust laws against price fixing. However, California passed the first fair trade law legalizing minimum price contracts in 1931, and other states soon followed suit. Independent druggists took Pepsodent to task for not signing chain stores to minimum price contracts.

In 1935 Pepsodent hired Charles Luckman, a young district sales manager for Colgate-Palmolive, as national sales manager to solve the price-cutting problem and stop Pepsodent's declining sales. In his autobiography, *Twice In A Lifetime,* Luckman said he had been on the job less than a day when he learned that the independent druggists were determined to declare a full-blown boycott of Pepsodent at their national convention, which started in two days. He also learned that the boycott movement was headed by the California delegation, which would pass through Chicago that night en route to the convention in New York.

An organized boycott by 100,000 independent druggists, who accounted for 75 percent of Pepsodent's sales, would have destroyed the company. Instead, Luckman convinced Kenneth Smith, who had succeeded his father as president of the company,

to give him a check for $25,000, made out to the National Retail Druggists Association. Luckman also made plans to be aboard the same train taking the California delegation to New York.

Aboard the train, Luckman wrangled a meeting with the California druggists in the mail car. He asked them to forego the boycott and promised to work with them to find a solution to the problem. He also told them the check was to back the fight for a national fair trade law, regardless of their decision. Luckman wrote, "The next three hours can best be described as sheer bedlam. In the last half hour the discussion became more rational and unemotional. At that point, the issue was finally reduced to a division between 'Let's murder Pepsodent,' and 'Give the kid a chance.' ''

Luckman got his chance. Instead of calling for a boycott at the convention, the California delegation introduced Luckman, who presented the $25,000 check. He also promised to spend 50 of the next 52 weeks traveling across the country to build a better relationship between Pepsodent and the independent druggists.

In 1936 Pepsodent began refusing to sell direct to any chain drugstore that sold its toothpaste below a minimum retail price. Pepsodent also changed its relationship with wholesalers, delivering toothpaste on consignment, which allowed Pepsodent to confiscate unsold stock from dealers who sold to blacklisted drugstores. The ensuing war between Pepsodent and the National Chain Drugstore Association centered around the influential Katz Drug Stores, based in Luckman's hometown of Kansas City, Missouri. Initially, the minimum-price program cost Pepsodent more than a million dollars, but with the backing of the independent druggists, sales began to increase. Before the year was over, the National Chain Drugstore Association agreed to support Pepsodent's minimum prices.

The following year Congress passed the Miller-Tydings National Enabling Act, which suspended anti-trust laws to legalize minimum pricing contracts in interstate trade. However, it took Pepsodent almost a decade to regain its position as the country's leading toothpaste. Most fair trade laws were repealed in the 1960s. Congress abolished the rest by withdrawing the exemption from antitrust laws in 1975.

## The Pepsodent Show

*Amos 'n' Andy* was still one of the most popular shows on radio in 1938 when Luckman was promoted to vice president of sales and advertising. One of his first decisions was that *Amos 'n' Andy* was not reaching a young enough audience. Luckman later said, "As I traveled around, I began to see that the people buying Pepsodent were old. . . . I went in to see [Pepsodent president] Ken Smith and said, 'I think we ought to drop *Amos 'n' Andy.*' It was a big shock to them, but I said . . . 'If we want to sell toothpaste, it better be to people whose teeth aren't put in with some kind of glue or something.' ''

The advertising agency, Lord & Thomas, suggested that Luckman see a show then playing in New York called *Red, Hot & Blue,* which co-starred a wisecracking comedian named Bob Hope. Luckman offered Hope a radio show sponsored by Pepsodent if the comedian occasionally would tell jokes at his own expense to gain the audience's sympathy. At first, according to Luckman, Hope declined. But after two short-lived radio programs for other sponsors, Hope called Lord & Thomas and said, "Now what the hell was that young punk trying to say again." To clinch the deal,

Hope was invited to dinner aboard Smith's yacht. According to Arthur F. Wertheim in *Radio Comedy,* as the comedian was boarding the boat, a Lord & Thomas account executive told Hope, "I want you to remember one thing: Amos and Andy built that boat." Hope replied, "When I finish with Pepsodent, Mr. Smith will be using the yacht for a dinghy."

*The Pepsodent Show,* starring Bob Hope, debuted in September of 1938. It quickly became popular with listeners as Hope delivered a fast-paced opening monologue on current events and performed self-effacing skits with guest stars. Hope also delivered Pepsodent's commercial messages and wove the Pepsodent name into the show's theme song, "Thanks for the Memories," which he had sung in the movie *The Big Broadcast of 1938.* On the first show, Hope finished the song with, "Now we are sorry to leave you. It's just for a week we'll be missin'. To show Pepsodent that you listen, mail in the doors from four drug stores."

Hope often began his shows with, "Hello ladies and gentlemen, this is Bob 'Pepsodent' Hope." He closed with such lines as, "This is Bob 'Pepsodent' Hope saying that if you brush your teeth with Pepsodent you'll have a smile so fair that even [Bing] Crosby will tip his hair." When Pepsodent sponsored Hope's tour of U.S. military bases during World War II, Hope entertained the soldiers with lines like "Use Pepsodent and the girls will always give you eyes right because you'll always have your teeth left."

In 1943 *The Pepsodent Show,* which by then was known as *The Bob Hope Show,* was the most popular program on radio with more than 40 percent of all radios in the United States tuned in every week. Pepsodent was back on top of the toothpaste market by 1944 with a dominating 45 percent share. The radio program ended its run in 1950 when Hope left to do movies and television. Luckman, who became president of Pepsodent in 1943, once said he could tell the show's ratings "by the tone of Hope's voice when he phones me for a raise."

## Brand Extensions

Tooth powders made a brief comeback in the 1930s, when both Colgate-Palmolive, Pepsodent, Listerine and other companies launched products to compete with Dr. Lyon's Tooth Powder. Pepsodent Tooth Powder was introduced on *Amos 'n' Andy* in 1935. In 1942, Pepsodent Tooth Powder was the number one brand in the country. However, the use of tooth powders fell sharply after World War II and the product was dropped.

Two other Pepsodent products were also introduced in the late 1930s: a Pepsodent-brand toothbrush and Pepsodent mouthwash. The Pepsodent toothbrush, which came with a small sample tube of toothpaste, was the first toothbrush to use nylon bristles instead of hog bristles. Like Pepsodent Tooth Powder, it quickly became the leading brand of toothbrush. The mint-flavored mouthwash, however, was less successful. Luckman blamed Listerine mouthwash, then the market leader, which had a strong medicinal taste. Listerine was marketed with the idea that the bad taste meant it was effective, and according to Luckman, "Consumers at the time would not believe anything that tasted good could be good for you."

## Lever Brothers

In 1944 Lever Brothers & Co., a subsidiary of the multinational Unilever Group Ltd. and the second-largest retailer in the United States, surprised the business world by buying the Pepsodent Company for $10 million cash. Former president Smith had been the majority stockholder; retired advertising executive Lasker, who had risked his own money on the unknown toothpaste in 1917, owned about 30 percent, and Luckman held about 15 percent. Pepsodent's sales were then about $50 million annually. Pepsodent continued to operate as a division of Lever Brothers, which turned all of its drug and personal-care products over to the marketing organization created by Luckman. Luckman, who stayed on to run the division, became president of Lever Brothers in 1946, although he quit in 1950 in a dispute over the slow pace of new product introductions.

After Luckman left, Lever Brothers switched the Pepsodent account to a new advertising agency. Lord & Thomas, which had been renamed Foote, Cone & Belding after Lasker retired in 1944, had been the Pepsodent brand's advertising agency for almost three decades. However, a new advertising manager had taken over and decided it was time for a change. In 1956 the Pepsodent account was returned to Foote, Cone & Belding. But by then Pepsodent toothpaste not only had fallen from number one, it was well back in the pack.

## You'll Wonder Where The Yellow Went

Soon after regaining the Pepsodent account, Foote, Cone & Belding created an advertising campaign that would establish Pepsodent's identity for years to come. Unfortunately the toothpaste never regained anywhere near the market prominence it had enjoyed in the 1930s and 1940s.

In *With All Its Faults,* Fairfax M. Cone, a principal in the advertising agency, said that he found the first line of the new slogan while rummaging through a pile of discarded layouts on the office floor. The agency added a second line, prepared a sample newspaper ad, and recorded a mock radio commercial with the complete jingle "You'll wonder where the yellow went, when you brush your teeth with Pepsodent." Cone then presented the campaign to Lever Brothers's management. He later said, "I made the shortest presentation of my life. When I played the record, and before I could unfold the newspaper advertisement, [the marketing manager] said, 'How soon can you get it on the air?'"

The advertising campaign, reminiscent of the early Lord & Thomas campaign created by Claude Hopkins, ran from 1956 until 1960. For a while it seemed that consumers everywhere were whistling the Pepsodent toothpaste jingle, and sales of Pepsodent nearly doubled. Unfortunately, just as the Pepsodent brand was beginning to regain market share, the American Dental Association (ADA) announced in 1960 that clinical studies had proved that Crest, a new toothpaste marketed by Procter & Gamble with a fluoride additive, was effective in reducing cavities in regular users. With the ADA's first-ever endorsement of a brand-name toothpaste, Crest rocketed to market dominance, more than doubling its market share from about 12 percent before the announcement to 26 percent only a few months afterward.

## Fluoride

Lever Brothers introduced Pepsodent Fluoride toothpaste in 1962 with the tag line, "Delivers more of what you buy a fluoride for." A new advertising agency also revived "You'll wonder where the yellow went" from 1963 to 1964 in an animated commercial showing how Pepsodent breaks up yellow tooth film and "yellow mouth." However, the real battle for market leadership was being waged between Crest and Colgate. By the end of the 1960s, Crest held a 40 percent share of the market, compared to 23 percent for Colgate. Pepsodent, in the meantime, had fallen out of the top five.

Advertising for Pepsodent continued to emphasize whiter teeth, including a celebrity campaign with such TV stars as Mary Tyler Moore, Lucille Ball, and Andy Griffith endorsing Pepsodent for "teeth that need to be white." But it was believed that consumers had come to like other flavors of toothpaste better than the Pepsodent brand's candy-like peppermint taste. In addition, Lever Brothers still focused marketing efforts on drugstores, continuing the close relationship nurtured by Luckman in the early 1940s. However, by the 1960s, supermarkets had begun to replace drugstores in sales of personal care items.

## Value Pricing

Lever Brothers stopped all consumer advertising of Pepsodent in 1987 and adopted a value-pricing strategy, positioning Pepsodent as a low-cost, brand-name toothpaste for the entire family. There was a brief attempt in the late 1980s to relaunch Pepsodent as a major brand, including the introduction of a pump dispenser and a new fluoride formula.

In 1987 Unilever United States Inc., the U.S. subsidiary of Unilever Group, purchased Chesebrough-Pond's USA Company, a personal-care products company founded in 1880. The Pepsodent brand was assigned to the new subsidiary, and in the early 1990s Chesebrough-Pond's redesigned Pepsodent toothpaste's packaging and introduced a baking-soda formula. As of 1993 the Pepsodent brand was available only in 6-ounce tubes in "regular" and "baking soda" formulas, regularly selling at about 60 percent of the cost of other national brands of toothpaste.

## Further Reading:

Cone, Fairfax M., *With All Its Faults: A Candid Account of Forty Years In Advertising,* Boston: Little, Brown & Company, 1969.

"Coup de Toothpaste: Lever Bros.' Purchase of Pepsodent Points to P&G-Colgate Battle," *Newsweek,* July 10, 1944, p. 64.

"Dentists endorse Colgate formula," *Business Week,* October 11, 1969, p. 46.

Firestone, Ross, ed., *The Big Radio Comedy Program,* Chicago: Contemporary Books, Inc., 1978.

"Flack Ack-Ack," *Newsweek,* October 30, 1961, p. 62.

"Irium-Plated Alger," *Time,* April 10, 1944, p. 79.

"Lever Bros. Buys Pepsodent Co. For About $10,000,000 in Cash," *New York Times,* June 30, 1944, p. 25.

"Lever's New Bid," *Business Week,* July 8, 1944, p. 58.

Luckman, Charles, "Hope Delivered the Pepsodent 'Pitch,' " *Advertising Age,* June 18, 1990, p. 54.

Luckman, *Twice In A Lifetime: From Soap To Skyscrapers,* New York, W.W. Norton & Company, 1988.

"Merger of Champions," *Time,* April 10, 1944, p. 86.

"Pepsodent in Comeback," *Business Week,* May 13, 1944, p. 86.

Ramirez, Anthony, "Growth Is Glacial, but the Market Is Big, and So Is the Gross," *New York Times,* May 13, 1992.

"Toothpaste Ad Battle Looms," *Business Week,* August 6, 1960, p. 28.

"Toothpastes: The Hot Commercial," *Newsweek,* August 8, 1960, p. 48.

Vinikas, Vincent, *Soft Soap, Hard Sell: American Hygiene in an Age of Advertisement,* Ames, IA: Iowa State University Press, 1992.

Wertheim, Arthur Frank, *Radio Comedy,* New York: Oxford University Press, 1979.

Wharton, Don, "Why We Brush Our Teeth," *Readers Digest,* February 1949, p. 139.

*—Dean Boyer*

# PEPTO-BISMOL®

## Pepto-Bismol®

The Pepto-Bismol brand of gastrointestinal remedies is a top-selling antacid/digestion aid in the United States. Packaged in bottles with the trademark yellow and maroon label and in yellow cardboard boxes with maroon highlights, Pepto-Bismol has been offering performance and value to consumers for almost a century. Pepto-Bismol has gone from being a mere digestion aid in the early 1900s to the highly sophisticated heartburn, upset stomach, and diarrhea remedy in the 1990s. Through the years, Pepto-Bismol has consistently outmuscled such formidable competitors as Rolaids, Mylanta, Maalox, and Alka-Seltzer. Just one product put out by the Procter & Gamble Company, which also manufactures such popular brands as Max Factor cosmetics, and Bounty paper towels, Pepto-Bismol has remained a market share leader due to years of performance and innovative advertising.

### Brand Origins

In 1901 in Norwich, New York, a gastrointestinal remedy was born at the laboratories of the Norwich-Eaton Pharmaceutical Division of Morton-Norwich Products. The new remedy helped alleviate stomach problems including gastroesophageal reflux, a condition in which a burning sensation occurs in the chest after meals or in the middle of the night. The liquid concocted at the Norwich-Eaton facility was composed primarily of bismuth and was called Bismosal. In 1918 Norwich-Eaton began marketing the product, whose brand name it changed to Pepto-Bismol in 1919 when the company discovered that a competitor's product bore the same name.

Early marketing took place primarily when Norwich-Eaton's detail men left samples with pharmacists, who recommended it to walk-in patrons. The product worked so effectively that it became a stellar success. Few formula changes occurred until 1964, when Pepto-Bismol became available in tablet form. In 1982 Norwich-Eaton was acquired by Procter & Gamble.

### Marketing

Under the aegis of Procter & Gamble, Pepto-Bismol sponsored family-oriented TV programs and made full use of the print media. Health and beauty aids sections of retail stores regularly received large cardboard displays for Pepto-Bismol featuring refund tear-off forms. Color inserts with vendor coupons in Sunday newspapers extolled the virtues of Pepto-Bismol, and customers received samples of the product via direct mail.

In the 1980s, P&G, like many companies, began questioning some of its fundamental mass marketing principles and began investigating micro-marketing initiatives to reach special "mosaic minority" segments of the population. Experiments included sponsoring local promotional events, such as the Pepto-Bismol Chili Cooking Contest. To please the customer, P&G had to get to know its customer. The company conducted intense market research, often through mail surveys.

### Brand Development

After Pepto-Bismol's acquisition by Procter & Gamble, many changes were made to the brand. In 1984 the company began printing a toll-free number on Pepto-Bismol's packaging. In 1988 Maximum-Strength Pepto-Bismol, with a darker pink liquid, improved flavor, and a maroon label was introduced. In 1988 the glass bottle was replaced by plastic. In 1989 benzoic and sorbic acids were added to the line, and FD&C Red #27 replaced FD&C Red #3 in the original tablets. 1990 witnessed the addition of benzoic and sorbic acids to the rest of the sizes, a change in the shape of the tablets from triangular to circular, the replacement of

FD&C Red #3 and Red #40 by FD&C Red #22 and Red #28 in the Original and Maximum-Strength formulas, and the premiere of cherry-flavored tablets.

Packaging and graphics kept pace with modifications in product formulation. In 1983 tamper-evident packaging was introduced, and in 1988 a plastic dose-cup was added. In 1990 the label was changed for Maximum-Strength Pepto-Bismol and the plastic over-wrap was removed from the tablets; the product was instead hung on J-hooks on supermarket shelves. Cherry-flavored tablets soon became available in 30- and 42-count packages and 12-count roll packs.

Pepto Diarrhea Control (Loperamide Hydrochloride Caplets) was introduced in 1992. In 1993 liquid Pepto-Bismol in its Maximum-Strength formula contained 500 milligrams of bismuth subsalicylate and benzoic and sorbic acids as active ingredients, had no sugar, and was low in sodium.

## Medical Boost

In 1983 Pepto-Bismol received an unexpected marketing boost when clinical studies conducted at Stanford and other universities indicated that ulcers, stomach cancer, and various other stomach problems were not caused by stress but by a mysterious, spiral-shaped bacterium called *H. pylori*. As a result of these findings, some doctors started to treat ulcers, gastritis, and many types of indigestion with antibiotics rather than with traditional drugs. A two-week regimen of antibiotics and bismuth, a substance found in Pepto-Bismol, proved especially helpful in alleviating gastrointestinal distress.

Since its debut in 1901, Pepto-Bismol has remained a market share leader in the gastrointestinal products category due to its emphasis on performance and value. P&G chemists and marketers continue to query consumers, devise innovative advertising strategies, and create new technologies to improve Pepto-Bismol and expand its market. As a P&G researcher once remarked: "Through constant improvement, we must manage every existing brand so that it can flourish year after year in an ever-changing, intensely competitive marketplace. . . . At P&G, we create the future."

## Further Reading:

*Advertising Age,* Editors of, *Procter & Gamble: The House That Ivory Built,* Lincolnwood, Illinois: NTC Business Books, 1988.

"Answers about Marketing," Cincinnati: The Procter & Gamble Company, 1993.

Carey, John, "What Barry Marshall Knew in His Gut," *Business Week,* August 10, 1992, pp. 68–69.

"Coping with Symptoms," *Consumer Guide Magazine,* April 1986, p. 24.

Cramer, Tom, "A Burning Question: When Do You Need An Antacid?" *FDA Consumer,* January–February 1992, pp. 18–22.

*Facts about Procter & Gamble,* Cincinnati: The Procter & Gamble Company, 1993.

Gannon, Kathy, "Rolaids Heartburn Index: Eureka Is Hot; El Paso Is Not," *Drug Topics,* July 23, 1990, p. 30.

Goldfinger, Stephen E., "Cooling It," *Harvard Health Letter,* July 1992, p. 4.

"Heartburn: Antacids Are Only One Line of Defense," *Mayo Clinic Nutrition* Letter, June 1988, p. 7.

Holland, Lisa, "Heartburn: Causes and Cures," *Good Housekeeping,* May 1988, p. 221.

"Ivorydale—A Procter & Gamble Landmark," Cincinnati: The Procter & Gamble Company, 1993.

Kleinmann, Susan, and Cynthia Carney Johnson, "Gut Feelings," *Parents Magazine,* May 1992, p. 243.

Lawrence, Jennifer, "P&G Hooks Up Interactive Product-Sampling Hot Line," *Advertising Age,* October 5, 1992, p. 3.

Lief, Alfred, *"It Floats": The Story of Procter & Gamble,* New York: Rinehart, 1958.

Maxwell, Tracey, "Understanding Gastric Discomfort," *Drug Topics,* October 4, 1991, p. 32.

Moskowitz, Milton; Robert Levering; and Michael Katz, eds., *Everybody's Business: A Field Guide to the 400 Leading Companies in America,* New York: Doubleday, 1990.

*Procter & Gamble Company Annual Report, 1992,* Cincinnati: The Procter & Gamble Company.

Schaeffer, Charles; Suzan Richmond; and Sherri Miller, "Spelling Heartburn Relief," *Changing Times,* April 1988, p. 104.

Schiller, Zachary, "Can P&G Commandeer More Shelves in the Medicine Chest?" *Business Week,* April 10, 1989, pp. 64, 67.

Schisgall, Oscar, *Eyes on Tomorrow: The Evolution of Procter & Gamble,* Chicago: J. G. Ferguson Publishing Company, 1981.

"Stalking the New Consumer," *Business Week,* August 28, 1989, pp. 54–62.

Stern, Gabriella, "P&G's Pepto Shown Effective to Treat Diarrhea in Young," *Wall Street Journal,* June 10, 1993, p. 87.

Thomas, Patricia, "Gut Feelings: How to Quit Your Bellyaching," *Health,* April 1990, p. 76.

Tyler, Aubin, and Anne Dowden, "Managing Heartburn," *McCall's,* April 1988, p. 69.

Winters, Catherine, "The Perils of Pigging Out," *Ladies Home Journal,* December 1992, pp. 76–85.

*—Virginia Barnstorff*

# PHILLIPS'® MILK OF MAGNESIA

Phillips', now known almost solely for its milk of magnesia, originally earned its reputation as a provider of tonics and nutrient medicaments, including Phillips' Wheat Phosphates, Phillips' Digestible Cocoa Compound, and Phillips' Phospho-Muriate of Quinine Compound. One of the country's first brand names, Phillips', marketed by Sterling Winthrop Inc., established its enduring fame when Charles Phillips created milk of magnesia in the 1870s. This gentle treatment for constipation has proven its effectiveness by continuing to be sold well over a century after its introduction.

## Brand Origins

Charles Henry Phillips was a chemist, as pharmacists were known in the 19th century, who came to the United States from England and went into the retail drug business in Elizabeth, New Jersey. Like many chemists, he dreamed of originating and manufacturing his own products. That dream came true when he established laboratories in Glenbrook, Connecticut, in 1849.

The first products manufactured in Phillips' laboratory were superfine white wax, refined camphor, and a high grade of essential oils. Phillips' Palatable Cod Liver Oil Emulsion and Phillips' Phospho-Nutritive followed these products. The latter was a solution containing phosphates similar to those in wheat; thus, the product was soon renamed Wheat Phosphates (Acid). At the time, there was a growing demand for phosphate preparations, which physicians were freely prescribing for the treatment of wasting diseases such as tuberculosis. Besides Wheat Phosphates, the laboratories marketed a syrup of wheat phosphates; Phillips' Digestible Cocoa Compound, a phosphated cocoa nutrient medicament; and Phillips' Phospho-Muriate of Quinine Compound, introduced to the medical profession before tonic compounds containing iron, quinine, and strychnine became the vogue.

The "product that marked a milestone in the course of pharmacal specialties," according to Forde Morgan in his bulletin for the Chas. H. Phillips Chemical Co., "was the invention of 'Milk of Magnesia' for which the United States Government granted a patent to Chas. H. Phillips in 1873." Although people knew for centuries that magnesia was useful as a laxative, it was not a popular product because of the impurities found in commercial preparations and the difficulty of administering magnesia in powder form. Milk of magnesia aptly described Phillips' formulation of a white suspension of magnesium hydroxide in water. The

name was registered in the *Trade Marks Journal* in 1880 by Phillips.

## Marketing Strategies

When Phillips' laboratories introduced products, they did not advertise them to the public nor did they publish medical testimonials about them. Products gained favor and prestige through their merit alone. Morgan states, "The utility of Phillips' Milk of Magnesia is attested not only by the unqualified endorsement of physicians and dentists, which carries with it tremendous weight, but also by its favorable reception as a trusted member in the med[i]cine cabinet of discriminating households."

Charles H. Phillips died in 1882. His four sons, Dr. A.N., Dr. C.E.H., W.D., and J.B. Phillips, carried on their father's work by incorporating The Chas. H. Phillips Chemical Company in 1885. Sterling Products acquired the company in 1923. After the acquisition, the Glenbrook Laboratories developed Phillips' Dental Magnesia in 1925, described as "a superior tooth paste representing more than 75 percent of Phillips' Milk of Magnesia," and Phil-

---

## AT A GLANCE

**P**hillips' brand of milk of magnesia founded in 1872 by Charles Henry Phillips, a manufacturing chemist with laboratories in Glenbrook, Connecticut; became a registered trademark, 1880; Phillips' sons incorporated The Chas. H. Phillips Chemical Company in 1885; sold to Sterling Products company, 1923; successor Sterling Drug and its Glenbrook Laboratories acquired in 1988 by Eastman Kodak Company, which formed Sterling Winthrop Inc., the parent company of Phillips'.

**Performance:** *Market share*—7% of laxative category. *Sales*—$52 million.

**Major competitor:** Metamucil; also Ex-Lax and Correctol.

**Advertising:** *Agency*—Ammirati & Puris, New York, NY.

**Addresses:** *Parent company*—Sterling Winthrop Inc., 90 Park Ave., New York, NY 10016; phone: (212) 907-2000; fax: (212) 907-2723. *Ultimate parent company*—Eastman Kodak Company, 343 State St., Rochester, NY 14650; phone: (716) 724-4000; fax: (716) 412-3516.

lips' Milk of Magnesia Tablets in 1931, "each containing the equivalent of one teaspoonful of Phillips' Milk of Magnesia liquid."

Milk of magnesia is a saline laxative that works by increasing water content within the colon and thus increasing bulk and promoting bowel action. Since it does not use stimulants or irritants, it does not affect the cells lining the bowel wall. Phillips' slogans and product claims emphasized the product's gentleness and effectiveness: "so gentle for children, so thorough for grown-ups"; "stay fit for fun with Phillips' "; "to fly high in the morning, take Phillips' at night"; "in the best of regulated families"; "the same effective yet gentle overnight action many hospitals rely on"; "effective overnight relief"; and "doctor recommended." One of the brand's most memorable slogans was "America's true blue friend," which underscored its reliability and provided a mental picture of the blue bottles that contained Phillips' Milk of Magnesia. Phillips' Milk of Magnesia tablets used the line "no water needed."

## Brand Improvements and Outlook

Few changes were made to Charles Phillips' formula over the years, and even those focused on producing new flavors. Sterling introduced a mint-flavored liquid in the 1950s and added a concentrated formula of milk of magnesia in orange vanilla and strawberry flavors in 1990. Now consumers not only had a greater chance of finding a flavor they could tolerate, but they also only had to swallow half as much as the regular formula. Sterling also improved Phillips' Milk of Magnesia and introduced new cherry flavor Phillips' Milk of Magnesia in 1992. The company marketed mint-flavored Phillips' Milk of Magnesia chewable tablets. Phillips' Gelcaps competed in the pill segment of the overnight laxative market, but that product do not contain milk of magnesia.

Eastman Kodak Company acquired Sterling Drugs and its Glenbrook Laboratories in 1986 and incorporated them as the subsidiary Sterling Winthrop. As part of Eastman Kodak's new Life Sciences Division, Sterling was to help reach the goal of $1 billion in sales by the early 1990s. Through its acquisition of Sterling Drug, Eastman Kodak also acquired a well-established position in the worldwide pharmaceutical market and experience in how to channel new drugs through the complicated federal regulatory process. The subsidiary created afterward, Sterling Winthrop Inc., included as part of a mission statement that it was "committed to creating distinctive solutions for the needs of mankind in pharmaceutical and consumer health products." The company subsequently introduced the new and improved milk of magnesia products described above, and continued to support the Phillips' brand.

## Further Reading:

Garfield, Bob, "Phillips' Milk of Magnesia Rolls Out Effective, Inoffensive Effort," *Advertising Age,* January 8, 1990, p. 46.

Goldbaum, Ellen, "Kodak Finds a Good Fit with Sterling Drug," *Chemical Week,* February 3, 1988, pp. 9, 12.

Morgan, Forde, *Chas. H. Phillips and The Chas. H. Phillips Chemical Company: Their Origin and Progress,* Bulletin No. 4, The Chas. H. Phillips Chemical Company: 1934.

Room, Adrian, *NTC's Dictionary of Trade Name Origins,* Lincolnwood, IL: NTC Business Books, 1991, p. 122.

Sharp, Harold S., *Advertising Slogans of America,* Metuchen, NJ: The Scarecrow Press, Inc., 1984, p. 366.

Urdang, Laurance, Editorial Director, and Ceila Dame Robbins, Editor, *Slogans,* Detroit: Gale Research Company, 1984, pp. 124, 126, 128.

*—Doris Morris Maxfield*

# PINE-SOL®

Pine-Sol, manufactured by The Clorox Company, is the nation's leading brand of pine oil multi-purpose cleaner. But unlike other products whose formulations are merely scented with lemon, pine, or potpourri, Pine-Sol actually derives its cleaning capabilities, and henceforth its name, from the so-called "tall oils" extracted from pine trees.

Pine trees, common in various forms throughout North America, yield an unusually harsh sap. Unlike the sweet, edible saps of maple and other trees, pine sap is an extremely thick and repulsive tasting effluent. This is due to the fact that its main constituents are turpentine and pine tar. While these sap extractions may be used as additives to paint, varnish, and roofing tar, they also are effective in dissolving thicker oil-based substances. In fact, turpentine, one of the most effective cleaning agents in common use, is derived almost exclusively from pine trees.

## Brand Origins

The formula for Pine-Sol was developed in 1929 by an amateur inventor, Harry A. Cole, Sr. A resident of Jackson, Mississippi, Cole had access to numerous pine harvesting operations that sprang up along the many river systems in his home state. While the trees were cut primarily for their wood, much of the byproduct was reduced to pulp for use in making paper and other wood products. In the steam distillation process, numerous rosin acids and fatty acids were extracted. These acids exhibited powerful capabilities in dissolving grease, breaking up oils, and removing dirt. As a result, they were commonly incorporated into a wide variety of soaps, emulsions, and lubricants.

When Harry Cole stumbled upon the idea of mixing some of these pine acids with a detergent, it was hardly a scientific breakthrough—others had been doing precisely the same thing for many years. But Cole's innovation was to concoct a mixture that was neither too harsh for daily cleaning nor too weak to be effective.

## Early Marketing Strategy

Cole delivered his first case of the detergent solution to a Walgreen Drug Store in Jackson, where he intended it to be sold in bulk to area janitors. Workers from local banks regularly patronized the store for cleaning supplies and were directed to Cole's new liquid. Carting it off in their own jugs, the janitors diluted the solution in water and used it to mop floors. In addition to cutting through the myriad of stubborn floor stains—including motor oil, railroad creosote, and even animal droppings—the cleaner left a fresh pine scent that immediately drew the attention of one of the bankers. A vice-president of the Deposit Guaranty Bank, his identity now lost, suggested that Cole package the solution in bottles for distribution to housewives. The banker suggested that the organically derived cleaning liquid would appeal to women who had grown weary of using such monstrous cleaning agents as lye, turpentine, acids, and even gasoline.

Cole decided that, if he was going to merchandise his cleaner, it should have a catchy name. But he wanted to avoid using a name that did not specifically identify the origin of his product. After ruminating upon the term "pine solvent" for a few days, he eventually settled upon the truncated version, Pine-Sol. While reinforcing the strong odor of his cleaning solution, the name Pine-Sol also provided stark differentiation with Lysol, whose name was apparently drawn from "lye solvent."

## Brand Development

Pine-Sol was sold only within a limited number of small markets during the 1930s. Sales of the brand were stunted by the Great Depression. However, as Mississippi was already burdened by a depressed local economy, Pine-Sol could scarcely have been hurt more.

Undiluted, Pine-Sol would kill salmonella and staphylococcus bacteria. It was safe for use on eating surfaces and was perfect for cleaning and deodorizing garbage cans and musty bathrooms and basement floors. Just as the government promoted the use of bleach for health reasons, consumers began to search out other cleaning agents. Cleanliness had become a public campaign. But while Pine-Sol was popular with janitors, grocers were unable to move the product among housewives. The brand's label featured only a single skinny pine tree and the Pine-Sol name. Even many grocers weren't sure what the product was or how to use it.

Cole, who had built the Magnolia Chemical Company around his pine cleaner, went broke trying to break into the household market. The company remained a privately run six-man operation until 1949, when the company went broke and was acquired by Robert Ernest Dumas Milner in lieu of a debt repayment. Milner changed the name of the company to Milner Products and began a campaign to broaden Pine-Sol's distribution. He placed Howard Cohoon, a 25-year veteran of the detergent industry, in charge of building the brand. Cohoon hired the Best agency to query everyone related with the product, from employees in pine mills to customers, and designed a new green label with simple service copy that clearly explained the product. Borrowing an idea from bread bakers, he added such tidbits as "Five cents off!" to the label.

He reintroduced Pine-Sol in Birmingham, Alabama, in February 1949. Encouraged by the success of the label, Milner later added paper bands to bottle collars with even more information, because "they get 100 percent distribution without extra work by grocers, brokers or salesmen." As a premium, Milner attached a second small bottle of Pine-Sol to the large bottle. To discourage grocers from selling the premium, the label on the small bottle was marked "free goods."

Milner bottled the solution in stock clear glass bottles that were adorned with glued-on green labels that featured the Pine-Sol name in large white narrow helvetica type. At the time, most competing cleaners were packaged in amber glass bottles. As a

## AT A GLANCE

**P**ine-Sol brand cleaner invented by Harry A. Cole, Sr., in Jackson, Mississippi, in 1929; marketed for household use later that year; company and brand purchased by Robert Milner in 1948, company renamed Milner Products; acquired by American Cyanamid Company in 1963; brand distributed nationally in early 1970s; reformulated in 1989 to include broad spectrum disinfectant capability; acquired by The Clorox Company in 1990.

**Performance:** *Market share*—20% (second-best-selling multipurpose cleaner).

**Major competitor:** L & F Products' Lysol; Procter & Gamble's Spic & Span and Mr. Clean.

**Advertising:** *Agency*—Foote Cone and Belding, Chicago, IL.

**Addresses:** *Parent company*—The Clorox Company, 1221 Broadway, Oakland, California 94612; phone (510) 271-7000.

result, the yellowish Pine-Sol appeared lighter and cleaner, and less like it had something to hide. In addition, Pine-Sol was the only cleaner to exhibit what chemists may call a "blush," or "bloom." When diluted in water, it produced an opaque solution. This was caused by the fact that the pine oils in Pine-Sol were not water soluble. But rather than separating completely, like oil and water, Pine-Sol would become fully distributed, creating an even solution.

Pine-Sol gained a reputation for versatility during the 1940s, when many new applications were discovered for the solution. Unlike other floor cleaners and disinfectants, Pine-Sol was mild enough in diluted form to be used as a pre-soak treatment for laundry. In fact, Pine-Sol was one of the few cleaners capable of muscling grimy stains out of the cotton flannel work clothes commonly worn by blue-collar laborers. The cleaner's unique utility in clothes washing evaporated, however, after the emergence of new detergents containing enzymes and other active ingredients.

### Advertising

Entering Birmingham, Pine-Sol was occasionally featured in full-page advertisements in daily papers. Each ad prominently displayed the brand and carried such heavy copy as "Forty-three vital home uses" for Pine-Sol. As the primary market for Pine-Sol was housewives, ever concerned about keeping a spotless kitchen and fresh bathroom, advertising for the brand was intended specifically to suggest that a home was only really clean if it was cleaned with Pine-Sol. Through years of advertising and promotion, the company sought to make the pine scent of Pine-Sol synonymous with the highest standard in home disinfecting and deodorizing. Ads proclaimed how the "magic" product kept "baby's things hospital fresh," and featured a cartoon strip called "The Rescue of Ruth . . . by Pine-Sol." Pine-Sol also proved to be an effective complement to other harsher chemicals.

These unique and useful qualities were prominently featured in Pine-Sol advertising, particularly after 1950, when the brand's distribution was expanded. From Birmingham, the brand was introduced to Shreveport, Houston, Dallas, Fort Worth, and Memphis. From these bases, distribution was expanded regionally (by

the early 1970s, Pine-Sol had emerged as a national brand). Accordingly, Milner began using radio ads to gain greater coverage and keep the impressions from occasional newspaper ads fresh. These were later complemented by contests and, with the advent of television, the use of TV commercials.

### Performance Appraisal

The formula and trademark of Pine-Sol were acquired by the American Cyanamid Company in 1963. The new parent company had an effective nationwide marketing network in place that substantially strengthened Pine-Sol's distribution. No longer confined to regional markets, Pine-Sol was now a direct competitor to major brands from household product giants such as Procter & Gamble and Colgate-Palmolive.

Other manufacturers scrambled for an angle that would enable their own brands to compete with the pine-scented cleaner. While pine brands such as Fels entered the market, many other cleaners became available in extensions that included lemon extracts. None were able to break Pine-Sol's exclusive association with pine oils. Some observers claimed that consumers were weary of the lemon scent, which was simply not natural in many homes. In addition, Pine-Sol's odor dissipated gradually, while the perfume of lemon-scented brands often lingered. In any event, Pine-Sol grew in popularity outside of its traditional markets.

Pine-Sol's ascension during the 1960s helped it to an impressive market share by the 1970s. In order to protect the franchises of existing products, many competitors were forced to finally introduce their own pine-scented extensions. But these proved only marginally successful in stealing away market share from Pine-Sol.

### Future Growth

With its "pine fresh" identity fully intact, Pine-Sol remains the quintessential pine-scented cleaner. But having largely saturated the market, the only avenue for growth open to the brand was extension. Pine-Sol, which had been available in the familiar clear glass bottle and bold green label, had long been offered in a wide variety of sizes. But the emergence of Formula 409 all-purpose cleaner, a competitor brand, inspired the introduction of a Pine-Sol spray cleaner. Later, the Pine-Sol identity was extended to a line of moist household wipes called Spruce-Ups.

In 1989 Pine-Sol was reformulated for the first time. The solution was given a broader spectrum of disinfectant capability than before, although it maintained its previous level of cleaning capability.

In 1990 Clorox purchased the Pine-Sol brands, including Spruce-Ups, from American Cyanamid. Clorox, long limited to the bleach market where it was dominant, had failed miserably with detergents. Thus it simply acquired the successful Pine-Sol brand in a financial transaction. In fact, the acquisition may prove to be of extreme strategic value to Clorox. The company now has the ability to leverage two well-known brand names into the creation of new products.

### Further Reading:

"Clorox's Identity Crisis," *Advertising Age*, May 6, 1981, p. 1.

"Clorox Dumps Its Detergents and Sticks to Its Core Brands," *Adweek's Marketing Week*, May 27, 1991, p. 6.

"From Scratch to $3,000,000 Volume in Six Years: Pine Sol Did It," *Sales Management*, January 15, 1955, pp. 82–88.

"Fels Expands Marketing of its Pine-Scent Cleaner," *Advertising Age*, February 10, 1964, p. 9.

"History of Pine Sol Cleaner," Clorox Company.

"Pine Sol Profile," American Cyanamid Company.

*—John Simley*

# PLAYTEX® TAMPONS

Even though use of the tampon can be traced to Egypt in the 15th century B.C., the disposable tampon with an applicator was not "invented" and mass marketed until 1936. By industry standards, International Playtex, Inc. was a latecomer. It was not until 1967 the company became the first manufacturer to introduce a tampon with a plastic applicator. And even then, the product was not a "hit with women who were used to a completely flushable" tampon, according to Nancy Friedman in *Everything You Must Know About Tampons*. But the Playtex brand has been a key innovator in the market and, in the 1990s, was the second top-selling tampon behind Tambrand's Tampax.

## Brand Origins

In 1936 Tampax Incorporated (now Tambrand) marketed what it called a "civilized solution to the problem of sanitary protection." At that time, most women still used rags or sanitary napkins. There is evidence of tampon use throughout history: Roman women used wool tampons; women in ancient Japan made them out of paper and held them in place with a bandage; Hawaiian women used the furry part of a native fern called hapu'u; grasses and mosses were used by Native American, African, and Asian women.

Tampons also were used covertly at the turn of the century. Women made them at home out of surgical cotton, or they used natural sea sponges that could be washed out and used again. But these women tended to be actresses, models, athletes, or prostitutes. Tampons were perceived as something used by less respectable women, because "respectable" women did not touch themselves in the area of tampon insertion. Thus, the tampon made its entry into the marketplace much later than that of sanitary napkins.

In 1933 Dr. Earle Haas invented the modern tampon in response to his wife's complaints. Myrtle Haas, a Denver nurse, found sanitary napkins uncomfortable because they were chafing. Most women also found sanitary napkins and the belts that held them in place a nuisance—any kind of physical activity was awkward. They demanded more convenience. Dr. Haas adapted a device that was commonly used after surgery to absorb bleeding in body orifices. Haas' tampon was made by compressing cotton and stitching a heavy waterproofed cord to the bundle. He also made a two-part applicator out of spiral strips of cardboard held together with nontoxic glue. Tampax Incorporated bought Haas' patent and brought the modern day tampon into commercial use.

The public response to tampons was mixed. Women loved them. *Everything You Must Know About Tampons* stated that "in June 1937, Tampax could boast in a Good Housekeeping ad that 'hundreds of letters of praise and gratitude had poured in to the company'. . . . the product was 'accepted for advertising by the *Journal of the American Medical Association.*' " But clergymen, doctors, and most men in authority rushed in with criticism. Tampons were "agents of defloration and general wickedness," a "menace."

Bad press did not dissuade tampon use. By 1942 *Consumers Reports* (later *Consumer Reports*) reported there were nine major brands on the market. Studies about the health benefits of tampons were nonetheless mixed. A 1942 Tampax study found the "tampon method of menstrual hygiene is safe, comfortable and not prejudicial to health." *Consumers Reports* tested nine tampons for "all-round utility," and found that "no thorough clinical study of the safety of tampons has yet been reported," but hinted that tampons could "dam up the menstrual flow, possibly causing uterine and tubal infections."

Tampons gained more acceptance during 1950s. Medical studies concluded that tampons were "innocuous, comfortable and adequate." One doctor even claimed in 1956 that tampons helped women with vaginitis and that tampons were a successful treatment for sterility. Throughout this time, Tampax had always been a major brand leader. Then, in the mid-1960s, new products such as the applicator-less and the purse-size tampon appeared. What tampons had initially given women was freedom. The newer brands made life even more convenient. The Carefree purse-sized tampon was innovative because it was made of rayon, not cotton, which helped increase its absorbency.

## Product Development

International Playtex, Inc. entered the market with the first plastic, petal-tipped applicator in 1967. Ads described this new tampon applicator as "soft and gentle," "its smooth, satin finish acts like a self-lubricator." Advertising claimed that Playtex tampons were 45 percent more absorbent on the average than the leading tampon because of its tampon blossomed out (often depicted by photos of unfolding tulips) to fit a woman's "inner figure." International Playtex claimed its brand of tampon expanded along its radius versus lengthwise (as does Tampax), therefore serving as a better vaginal plug than its competitors.

## AT A GLANCE

**P**laytex brand of tampon introduced in 1967 by International Playtex, Inc.; became a registered trademark in 1966; in 1971 Playtex introduced "deodorant" tampons; Playtex brand reformulated in 1980 for greater absorbency; International Playtex, Inc. purchased in 1985 by Esmark, Inc.; Playtex Ultimates with rounded cardboard applicator introduced in 1991.

*Performance: Market share*—30.8% of the $690 million market (1993). *Sales*—$96.5 million (1993).

*Major competitor:* Tambrand Inc.'s Tampax; also Kimberly-Clark's Kotex; also Johnson & Johnson's o.b.

*Advertising: Agency*—Grey Advertising, New York, NY 1987—; *Major campaign*—"Dare to Be More Comfortable."

*Addresses: Parent company*—Playtex Family Products Corp., 700 Fairfield Ave., Stamford, CT 06904; phone: (203) 356-8000.

Playtex was able to fight off other brands that developed plastic applicators such as Johnson & Johnson's Meds by innovating once again. In a move that was responsible for launching Playtex as a major player, the company unveiled the Playtex tampon with a deodorant line in 1971. According to *Everything You Must Know About Tampons,* "There was no deodorant in Playtex tampons—only a heavy, cloying fragrance (which in the ads was called a 'fresh, delicate, scent.')" Playtex included a warning advising women to see their physicians if irritation occurred. And many women did develop allergic reactions to the new tampon. Playtex officially declared its product safe, but also paid the medical bills of women who complained.

Ill side effects did not hamper marketing of the brand. Playtex heavily advertised the deodorant tampon, appealing to women's need to feel clean and odor free in their "feminine areas." One 1972 magazine ad featured a woman at a party with a look of anguish on her face. The tag line suggested that women had to worry about smelling bad during their periods: "When you're wearing a tampon you don't worry about odor. But should you?" Actually, menstrual fluid only produces an odor after it is exposed to the air and begins decomposing. But Playtex succeeded in selling deodorant tampons regardless.

## Advertising History

The National Association of Broadcaster's lifting of the ban on television advertising of tampons, sanitary napkins, and douches in 1972 greatly benefitted Playtex tampons. Ads were more graphic and displayed photos of tampons expanded in water. Brands hyped their security, protection, and confidence. Television advertising spending on tampons alone doubled from 1975 to 1978. Playtex's competitor Tampax did not advertise on television until 1978 and lost market share, which fell from 90 percent to about 70 percent.

Between 1968 and 1978, sales for tampons increased 244 percent, compared to sanitary pad sales, which only grew 86 percent. By 1980, 70 percent of American women used tampons at some time. Playtex ranked as the number two tampon brand behind Tampax by the early 1980s and has held on to this position for more than ten years, despite competition from such up and coming

brands as Procter & Gamble Company's Rely tampon and Johnson & Johnson's o.b. brand.

But then something happened that changed the feminine hygiene market forever—a potentially fatal disease that attacked women when they were menstruating. The Toxic Shock Syndrome of the 1980s—with it symptoms of high fever, a sunburn-like rash, sore throat, headache, diarrhea, low blood pressure and shock—was directly related to tampon use. The disease was traced to the staphylococcus aureus bacterium that produced a toxic infection. Some of the women afflicted suffered organ failure; others died. Researchers agreed that tampons were involved, but could not explain why. According to *Everything You Must Know About Tampons,* the first company to be sued and linked to the majority cases was Procter & Gamble for its Rely tampon brand. Rely was eventually taken off the market. Eventually every manufacturer would be sued. International Playtex was sued for $10 million by a Los Angeles woman who claimed she contracted toxic shock while wearing a Playtex tampon. The final verdict regarding tampon use and Toxic Shock Syndrome was that any tampon, if left in the body long enough, could breed bacteria. Synthetic tampons scratch the vaginal membranes and provide a route into the bloodstream for the staphylococcus aureus toxins; thus, the more absorbent a tampon, the greater the risk a woman faces of getting Toxic Shock Syndrome.

The medical establishment and the Federal Drug Administration, along with some tampon makers including Playtex, recommended that women use sanitary napkins when their flows were light, that they change their tampons frequently, and that they consider not using them when they slept. The marketplace changed overnight. Women were encouraged to and switched to using sanitary pads. Sanitary pad manufacturers heeded the call and produced different brands of maxi, mini, thin, and super-thin pads to meet demand. According to Mary Ann Hogan in a *Los Angeles Times* article, industry analysts estimated the number of women who used tampons exclusively dropped by 40 percent. Tampon makers stopped using super absorbent rayon and synthetic materials and returned to using surgical cotton.

## Strategy After the Storm

In 1980 the company discovered through market studies that its deodorant brand was losing market share—from 35 percent to 31.5 percent from 1978 to 1979. Also, Playtex tampons had been associated by the Centers for Disease Control with about 20 percent of toxic shock syndrome cases studied, according to Friedman in *Everything You Must Know About Tampons.* Playtex had revised its brand for more absorbency in 1980, but as cases of Toxic Shock Syndrome mounted, International Playtex had to change its strategy. In the same year, the company joined with Johnson & Johnson to conduct a public service advertising campaign informing consumers about toxic shock. Playtex also worked with other manufacturers to print and distribute leaflets warning about toxic shock that were placed in drugstores and supermarkets. These warnings stressed that women would eliminate their risk by not using tampons. Playtex, in a massive television campaign featuring Brenda Vaccaro, stressed this message along with explaining why "Playtex Tampons were the intelligent choice." Playtex began listing the ingredients of its tampons and toxic shock cautions on tampon packages. Boxes also advise consumers to choose the "minimum absorbency needed to control your menstrual flow in order to reduce the risk of getting TSS."

Playtex' strategy during the mid-1980s was to pitch its product to all menstruating women by looking for television shows that had the largest audience of women aged 18 to 38. Advertisements designed by Grey Advertising of New York were of the "snapshot approach," reported *Marketing & Media Decisions*. These ads depicted "women on the move."

## Environmental Concerns

In response to environmental concerns about plastic applicators, Playtex Family Products Corp. extended its brand to include Playtex Ultimates in 1991. Ultimates contained a rounded petal-tipped cardboard applicator to challenge market leader Tampax. Tambrand asserted in a 1992 company report that "over the next few years, Tambrand should be well-positioned to gain share domestically, since its major tampon competitor, Playtex, has not been successful with its cardboard applicator, Ultimates." Tambrand went on to say that Playtex Ultimates' demise supported the thesis that "tampon brand loyalty is exceptionally high" for Tampax.

Playtex was expected to spend at least $7 to $10 million to launch the new line. Grey Advertising handled the account with a cable television campaign, freestanding inserts, and direct mail. Playtex stressed environmentalism by urging consumers to throw away their applicators in the trash and not the toilet because "flushing the applicators can cause household plumbing problems, and the applicators can eventually appear on beaches and shorelines," *Advertising Age* reported. Indeed, some reports state that plastic applicators have washed up on the shores of Hawaii and Tahiti.

Judann Dagnoli in *Advertising Age* estimated that the Playtex product change would help make retailers' profits from Tampax more competitive with those earned from Playtex sales. Playtex planned to reduce the quantities in boxes (20 tampons in a box for example, instead of 24) and offer price reductions. At the same time, Tambrand restaged Tampax to include Tampax Comfort Shaped tampons that resembled Playtex Ultimates and promoted their product as "kind to the earth" and "biodegradable since 1936." Tambrand officials told *Supermarket News* that the switch to cardboard would help save about 350,000 pounds of plastic.

## Performance Appraisal

The Playtex brand of tampons has maintained its second place standing while sales and market share continue to fluctuate. At one time, sales for Playtex Tampons were an estimated $190 million in the United States. Recent reports indicate sales are approximately $96.5 million. Tampax is still a market leader at about 50 percent. Financial difficulties attributed to the breakup of Playtex into separate units—Playtex Family Products Company (personal hy-

giene products) from the division that makes bras and girdles—and debt incurred from leveraged buyouts of former parent companies Esmark and Beatrice, continue to plague the company with a debt burden.

Gerri Willis, in a *Wall Street Journal* article, wrote, "There could be few better times to test women's loyalties to tampon brands. . . . High debt from several leveraged buyouts in the 1980s has created lingering problems for Playtex FP Group, a private company." Willis quoted First Boston Corp. analyst Lynne Hyman as saying that "from a competitive standpoint, it's a good time [for Playtex to challenge Tambrand cardboard applicator.]" In fact women may change their habits despite their loyalty to Tampax, she wrote.

## Future Growth

The toxic shock scare has not stopped tampon sales. Some industry analysts believe the issue has faded from women's consciousness; others say women are aware and take necessary precautions like changing their tampons more frequently. Still another theory, as explained by Paula Schnorbus in *Marketing & Media Decisions,* states that the plethora of sanitary pad brands has confused women so much that they have turned to tampons.

Product innovations—such as Playtex switching to comfortable rounded cardboard applicators—have helped generate sales increases in the tampon category. Yet competition remains fierce between the top brands. Marketing blunders by top-selling Tampax may erode enough of its market share to catapult Playtex into the lead position.

## Further Reading:

Dagnoli, Judann, "Tampons Go for the Green," *Advertising Age,* July 2, 1990, pp. 1, 32; April 15, 1991, p. 4; "$25M tampon boost; Tambrand, Playtex hike spending for launches," *Advertising Age,* September 30, 1991, p. 46.

Friedman, Nancy, *Everything You Must Know About Tampons,* New York: Berkley Books, 1981.

Hogan, Mary Ann, "The Super, Ultra, Maxi Revolution," *Los Angeles Times,* March 4, 1993, p. E1.

Muirhead, Greg, "Green Trend May Doom Plastic in Ttampon Lines," *Supermarket News,* August 26, 1991, p. 49; "Tampon Changes Raise Sales," *Supermarket News,* September 30, 1991, p. 54.

*Marketing & Media Decisions,* October 1987.

Sloan, Pat, "Tampons Stress Environment, Price," *Advertising Age,* February 15, 1993, p. 50.

Sloan, Pat, "Tambrand's Strategy Strays; Share Drops," *Advertising Age,* June 21, 1993, p. 20.

Willis, Gerri, "Tambrand Plans to Challenge Playtex Using Paper vs. Plastic in Similar Item, *Wall Street Journal,* February 1, 1993.

*—Evelyn Dorman*

# PLEDGE®

Pledge has dominated the furniture polish market since its introduction in 1958. The invention and marketing of Pledge reflects an ongoing effort on the part of S.C. Johnson and Son, Inc. (better known as S.C. Johnson Wax) to research and develop new products. Developed in the Johnson Wax laboratories in Racine, Wisconsin, Pledge immediately captured the lion's share of the furniture polish market when it was introduced as a "new aerosol spray" that would provide "instant waxed beauty as you dust." Pledge has since gone through several changes in packaging and marketing strategies. The most important development in Pledge's history was the addition of lemon scent to the furniture polish. Although Pledge has since been marketed with several different scents, lemon Pledge is by far the most popular version of the brand with consumers. Scent changes notwithstanding, the basic nature of the product has remained consistent and Pledge continues to enjoy the top market share and widespread brand name recognition.

## Brand Origins

Johnson Wax credits one researcher, E. L. Muoio, with the invention of Pledge. In a 1993 interview with Hilary Gopnik, Muoio, then retired after forty-seven years with Johnson Wax, discussed his role in the development of the product. An integral part of the company's philosophy had been to encourage researchers to develop ideas for what they called "products plus." According to S.C. Johnson in his book on the history of his family-run company, these were products which would not only improve existing performance but would add a significant new component, allowing the product to open up new marketing sectors. In the mid-1950s Muoio responded to this challenge with his idea for Pledge, a one-step furniture wax system.

Johnson Wax had already marketed a furniture polish, Pride, for a number of years. Pride, and all other furniture polishes then on the market, required a two-step application. The user first had to apply the polish with one cloth, wait for it to dry to a matte finish and then buff the surface to a shine with a separate cloth. This time-consuming process meant that homemakers polished their furniture relatively infrequently, using only dry-cloth or feather dusting to maintain the shine of their furniture on a daily basis. Sales for furniture polish had declined steadily after World War II as women spent less time engaging in labor intensive chores. Research conducted by Johnson Wax in the late 1950s showed that less than 50 percent of homemakers polished their furniture on a regular basis. Muoio reasoned that if a polish could be developed that required only one cloth and only one application then dusting and shining could be combined into a single easy-to-perform task. The ease of shining and dusting simultaneously would not only boost the sales of the new Johnson Wax polish, but would also open up a whole new market for the product as a dusting aid, and a dusting aid would be used much more frequently than traditional polish.

While working on possible solutions to the problem of a "wipe-to-shine" finish, Muoio recalled from his days in the army that servicemen, faced with the task of keeping their gear ready for inspection at a moment's notice, had used a fast but effective trick for shining their boots. Known in the army as "spit shining," this technique involved the use of comparatively little polish topped with a small amount of water (or spit when circumstances required it). Muoio realized that if he could devise a way of emulsifying the Johnson furniture polish with the right amount of water he would be able to reproduce this effect. After experimenting with a variety of components and delivery systems for a year, Muoio came up with a water-based solution in a pump sprayer that he felt was ready to be field tested.

Initial response to the product by a group of homemakers near the company headquarters in Racine, Wisconsin, was mixed. They were reluctant at first to use any water-based product on their wood furniture. They had always believed that water would damage wood finishes, and researchers found it difficult to convince them that water mixed with the wax ingredients would clean the surface but not penetrate the wood. To make matters worse, the pump sprayer systems then available produced a fairly coarse spray and clogged easily with the emulsified wax. After a series of further field tests on a variety of woods and finishes, Muoio decided to continue to refine the solution. Even more importantly, he decided to experiment with a new delivery technology—aerosol.

Pressurized spray cans had been available since the 1920s, but only after World War II had they became inexpensive and reliable enough to be used widely in consumer products. As aerosol technology improved, its use spread, and in the late 1950s and early 1960s, aerosol cans flooded the market, delivering products that ranged from hairspray to oven cleaner. Although it meant a

## AT A GLANCE

**P**ledge brand of furniture polish founded in 1958 in Racine, Wisconsin, by researcher E.L. Muoio of S.C. Johnson & Son, Inc. (commonly known as S.C. Johnson Wax).

**Performance:** *Market share*—43% (top share) of furniture polish category. *Sales*—$101 million.

**Major competitor:** Drackett's Endust and Behold.

**Advertising:** *Agency*—Foote, Cone & Belding Communications, Chicago, IL, 1988—. *Major campaign*—Mother and child at a piano with a "touchable shine."

**Addresses:** *Parent company*—S.C. Johnson & Son, Inc., 1525 Howe St., Racine, WI 53403; phone: (414) 631-2000; fax: (414) 631-2000.

higher price tag on the supermarket shelf, Muoio realized that an aerosol system would greatly improve the performance of the product. The fine mist that aerosol cans could deliver would make it easier to apply the small, even quantities of wax that the single application system required. Not only would aerosol be the perfect vehicle for the one-step polish, but Muoio was fairly certain that other companies were trying to produce an aerosol wax as well. If his one-step system could beat them to the market, Johnson Wax would be able to take advantage of two new features at once. Working 14-hour days in the rush to be first on the market, Muoio put together 25 aerosol cans of his new formula and once again conducted field tests among the homemakers of Racine. This time the product was very favorably received, and in 1957 Muoio was able to present Johnson Wax with a marketable "product-plus."

### Brand Development

Pledge was an immediate success in the furniture polish category. By the early 1960s it did not merely control the top share of the market, it had completely redefined the category. Now all furniture polishes had to match the one-step application process of Pledge. In addition, although furniture polishes had always cleaned as well as shined, the cleaning properties of the polishes now became a major selling point. Following the example set by Pledge, new products were being promoted as cleaning and dusting aids to be used on a regular basis. Their ability to clean therefore became an issue for both the consumer and the researchers trying to improve the product.

During the initial development of Pledge, Johnson Wax researchers had believed that a water-based formula would be most effective for cleaning. The original formula Pledge was good at cleaning sticky messes like jelly and light oils like fingerprints, but was less efficient with stains caused by heavier greases. In response to major challenges to their dominance of the market by such new brands as Drackett's Behold, researchers at Johnson Wax began work on improving the cleaning properties of Pledge. They soon realized that an oil-based product not only cleaned more effectively but actually improved the surface shine and required less polishing. In 1967 Johnson Wax introduced this new formula Pledge, adding a lemon scent to compete with Drackett's increasingly popular lemon-scented Behold. The new lemon Pledge remained the number one selling furniture polish into the 1990s.

Although the essential formula for Pledge was established in the 1960s, the researchers at Johnson Wax have continued to modify the product in response to new consumer demands. Responding early to consumer concerns over the threat to the environment caused by chlorofluorocarbons (CFCs) in aerosol cans, Johnson Wax converted Pledge and all its other aerosol products to a non-CFC aerosol system in 1974, some two years before the government introduced regulations restricting CFCs in pressurized containers. Although the new aerosols did not contain the ozone-destroying CFCs, by the late 1980s they were still perceived as environmentally unfriendly by some consumers, prompting Johnson Wax to add a pump sprayer to its Pledge line. A spokesperson at Johnson Wax acknowledges, however, that the formula used in the pump sprayer does not produce as high a shine as that in the aerosol format.

In the late 1980s and early 1990s two new product features were introduced. Advertised as "the touchable shine," the new Pledge claimed to reduce the appearance of fingerprints on shiny surfaces. In response to increased awareness of allergies caused by interior environments, the researchers at Johnson Wax also introduced a dust-repellant formula that claimed to reduce the accumulation of dust on surfaces treated with the product. Where this airborne dust would settle instead was not made clear, but presumably it was hoped that it would land on surfaces such as carpeting where it could be vacuumed away. Two new scents, Potpourri and Spring Fresh, were also added to the Pledge line of products, although these have not become as popular as the lemon-scented formula. In the early 1990s, Johnson Wax introduced a wood and surface cleaner under the Pledge brand name.

### Marketing Strategy

When Pledge was first introduced to the American consumer in 1958, S.C. Johnson & Son, Inc., already had an efficient marketing and advertising strategy. As sponsors of the popular *Red Skelton* television show, Johnson Wax used simple but effective demonstration commercials to promote their line of home care products to a wide audience. When Pledge was introduced, the company simply fit the new product in among the host of their other established successes.

Fearing that other companies were also working on aerosol furniture polishes, Johnson Wax rushed Pledge onto the market after its development in 1957. The Benton & Bowles advertising agency, responsible for the launch of Pledge, undertook some quick market research and decided that rather than advertise Pledge as an aerosol furniture wax, it should simply be called an "aerosol spray" that would provide "waxed beauty every time you dust." The agency felt that if Pledge could avoid being indentified as a furniture wax, it would be able to escape the declining sales of the furniture polish category. This approach was remarkably effective; Pledge not only rose to the top of the furniture polish sector but actually caused the previously declining overall sales of furniture polish to increase by $2.5 million in one year.

The company maintained this simple approach to marketing and advertising into the early 1960s. By the mid-1960s, however, the sponsorship of television shows by one company or brand became less feasible as the television industry became more competitive and diversified. Major sponsors, such as Johnson Wax, had to change the way that they spent their advertising dollars. The first challenges to Pledge's dominance of the furniture polish market coincided with the more competitive atmosphere in the electronic media.

Through the 1970s and 1980s Johnson Wax maintained a fairly consistent approach to the marketing of Pledge. Although a series of advertising agencies were used, including J. Walter Thompson (Chicago), HDM Dawson, Johns and Black (Chicago), and Foote, Cone and Belding Communications (Chicago), the basic theme of the print and electronic media ads remained constant. As a product strongly associated with the upkeep of traditional wood furniture, Pledge advertisements have always stressed reliability and trust. Like ads for most cleaning products, they tended to be aimed at, and most often featured, women. The ad campaign of the early 1990s, produced by Foote, Cone and Belding, was typical. The "piano series" featured a child and grandmother at a piano. As the child reaches up to touch the lid, the grandmother gently chides her, fearing that she will leave fingerprints. The girl's mother intervenes, explaining that the new Pledge resists fingerprints. A brief demonstration is capped with the motto "Pledge, the touchable shine." These ads have run principally during traditionally female dominated daytime television hours. Johnson Wax has also tried to expand their target audience by increasing their use of such alternative advertising media as direct mail.

## Major Competitors

Since its initial success Pledge has been forced to ward off aggressive attacks from competitors. The most significant of these have been the Drackett's furniture polishes, Behold and Endust. In a series of television commercials developed and executed by Young & Rubicam in the early 1970s, Drackett attempted to demonstrate the superiority of their aerosol furniture polish Behold over Johnson Wax's Pledge. The commercials used a demonstration showing the two products cleaning an oily stain to claim that Behold was better at cleaning and was cheaper to use than Pledge. Johnson Wax challenged the television campaign on both claims, insisting that Pledge could be demonstrated superior to Behold in cleaning water-based stains and was competitive in cost as well. In 1975 *Advertising Age* reported that the self-regulating advertising boards NAD (National Advertising Division of the Council of Better Business Bureaus) and NARB (National Advertising Review Board), upheld Drackett's claim to a lower price but found in favor of Johnson Wax on the cleaning issue. Both boards stated that even though Drackett had successfully proven that Behold was better in cleaning oil-based stains, the advertisements implied overall product superiority and this claim was unsubstantiated. Although Drackett registered "strong disagreement" with the decision, they agreed to abide by it and withdraw the ads.

In their second entry into the furniture care market, Drackett introduced Endust, a product advertised as a wax-free dusting aid that would not promote "wax buildup." From its inception, the marketing strategy for Pledge had been to encourage regular use of the product as a dusting and cleaning aid. This meant that homemakers would be waxing their furniture much more frequently than they had in the past. Although Johnson Wax has always maintained that each application of Pledge removed the old wax as it cleaned, many consumers believed that frequent use of a wax-based product might lead to a dull accumulation of residue wax. The Drackett company's wax-free Endust was marketed directly towards this concern.

Endust was an instant success, picking up a significant market share at Pledge's expense. Johnson Wax responded quickly with a series of demonstration ads showing that even very frequent applications of Pledge could not create a buildup of wax. Pledge's slogan was also changed from "waxed beauty instantly as you dust" to "natural beauty every time you dust." In 1988, Foote, Cone and Belding, newly assigned to the Pledge account, ran a series of advertisements directly comparing Pledge and Endust. Although Pledge soon returned to their more conservative advertising approach stressing reliability and tradition, Endust remained a considerable threat to Pledge's dominance of the market throughout the 1980s. Johnson Wax introduced a waxless dusting aid of their own, Duster Plus, but it failed to gain an appreciable share of the new market. The very success of Endust has made it difficult to determine its exact effect on Pledge's market share since the introduction of Endust created an entirely new market sector. With Endust categorized as a "dusting-aid" and Pledge as a "furniture polish," both products are able to claim the leading position in their respective sectors.

Ironically, for a brief period of time in 1993, the onetime rivals Behold, Endust, and Pledge were all part of the same family. In January of 1993, S.C. Johnson & Son, Inc. purchased Drackett from parent company Bristol-Myers Squibb. The Federal Trade Commission, however, stipulated as a condition of sale that Johnson Wax must sell Endust and Behold as soon as a buyer could be found in order to avoid creating a monopoly in the furniture care market.

## International Presence

An important part of S.C. Johnson and Son's success has been their ability to expand into foreign markets. Soon after its introduction into the U.S. market as Pledge, Johnson Wax's aerosol furniture polish was introduced in Europe. Using the more international sounding brand name Pronto, the aerosol wax quickly gained a sizable market share in every country in which it was introduced. By 1962 Pronto was being marketed in 13 countries worldwide, selling 6 million cans annually in England alone. Different patterns of housekeeping in each country meant that a separate advertising campaign had to be devised for each national market. Handled by J. Walter Thompson Co., the introductory campaigns of the 1960s included British ads stressing the polish component of the product, French campaigns emphasizing its silicone content, and German ads promoting Pronto's cleaning properties.

Pledge has managed to maintain the top share in its category since its introduction in 1958. After an initial soaring success, their market share leveled off between 40 percent and 50 percent in the 1960s when serious competitors began to appear on the market. Pledge has held this proportion of the market for most of the 35 years since its introduction, only occasionally nipping above the 50 percent mark or dipping below 40 percent. The introduction of Pledge in 1958 gave a major boost to the furniture care market, which had been on the decline in the 1950s. In 1959 the total sales of furniture polish jumped from $14 million to $16 million and has risen steadily ever since. By 1993 it had risen to $206 million, up five percent from 1992. With Pledge controlling almost half of this market, prospects look good for sales to the end of the century.

The major challenge to the furniture care category is likely to come from new developments in wood finishing technology. Many new furniture makers claim that their finishes do not require polishing at all. Certain manufacturers have even recommended against the use of silicone-based products such as Pledge, because of possible problems in refinishing silicone-treated surfaces. The researchers and marketers at Johnson Wax will have to continue to modify their product in response to these developments in the furniture industry.

## Further Reading:

Deveny, Kathleen, "As More Americans Declare War on Dirt, Cleaning-Product Firms Make Tidy Sums," *Wall Street Journal,* April 6 1993, p. B1.

"For Growing Band of Shoppers, Clean Means Green," *Wall Street Journal,* April 6, 1993, p. B1.

Freeman, Laurie, "New Household Products Bow," *Advertising Age,* November 25, 1985, p. 3.

"Furniture Polishes," *Consumer Reports,* January 1986, pp. 45–47.

"How They Knew Pledge Would Sell," *Printers' Ink,* November 11, 1960, p. 70.

Johnson, S.C. *The Essence of a Family Enterprise: Doing Business the Johnson Way,* Indianapolis, IN: Curtis Publishing Co., 1988.

"Johnson Shifts Pronto Appeal in German Campaign," *Advertising Age,* April 16, 1962, p. 131.

Leaversuch, Robert D., "Pledge Packaging," *Modern Plastics,* July 1992, p. 20.

"Lemon Gives New Twist to Polish Marketing," *Advertising Age,* October 30, 1967, p. 1.

"NARB Toughens Comparative Ad Rules," *Advertising Age,* December 1, 1975, p. 1.

"100 Leading National Advertisers," *Advertising Age,* September 4, 1986, pp. 119–22; September 24, 1987, pp. 120–23; September 23, 1988, pp. 98–106; September 27, 1989, pp. 81–88.

"S.C. Johnson Drops All Fluorocarbons in its Aerosol Products," *Advertising Age,* June 23, 1975, p. 1.

Thomas, Dana L. "Pay Dirt: For Makers of Cleaning Products, Prospects Have Never Been Brighter," *Barron's,* December 12, 1960, p. 3.

*—Hilary Gopnik and Donald McManus*

# POLO®/RALPH LAUREN®

American designer Ralph Lauren has parlayed his name into one of the most distinctive and pervasive brands in America. The first products to bear Ralph Lauren's name were wide ties in the early 1970s, but he soon created an entire line of menswear called Polo by Ralph Lauren and a line of Ralph Lauren brand womenswear. Over the years his name has come to grace fragrances and accessories for men and women, clothing for young boys and infants, and a wide variety of housewares, shoes, furs, jewelry, leather goods, hats, and eyewear. The extension of the Ralph Lauren brand name into such a diverse array of products has led observers to credit the designer with the creation of a American aesthetic based on tradition, family, and manners. Alessandra Stanley, writing in the *New Republic,* described the proliferation of Ralph Lauren products as the "Laurenification of America"; others called the 1980s the decade of Ralph Lauren. "Lauren's lasting contribution to fashion," wrote Fred Ferretti in the *New York Times Magazine,* "is not that he is a great designer, or even a great stylist, but that he is skilled in translating romantic American dreams into items of quality and timelessness." The popularity of Ralph Lauren brand products has turned the Polo/Ralph Lauren Corporation into a multimillion-dollar private business and led *Forbes* magazine to name Ralph Lauren one of corporate America's most powerful people in 1992.

## A Sense of Style

Ralph Lauren was born Ralph Lifschitz in 1939, and grew up in the Mosholu Parkway section of the Bronx, New York. Lauren's father, Frank Lifschitz, was an Orthodox Jew who had immigrated from the Soviet Union and worked as a painter, creating murals when he could and painting houses when he needed the money. Lauren and his siblings, two brothers and a sister, all had an artistic bent that was encouraged by their parents. Lauren told *New York* magazine that his childhood was characterized by "a very nice life-style, very happy, very good home, very nice values in terms of not being frivolous." That sense of values has always been important to Lauren, who is known for shunning the fast-paced world of the fashion industry for the simpler pleasures of domestic life.

Growing up in the same neighborhood as designer Calvin Klein, Lauren never imagined himself working in fashion. "My dreams were of how many shots I was going to hit over the fence," he related to a *Vogue* reporter, "of making spectacular catches, landing on my backside and still holding the ball. . . . I didn't dream of a certain life, I wasn't obsessed. I was a happy middle-class Jewish kid in the Bronx." But as a teenager, Lauren began to develop a sense of style: he designed satin warm-up jackets for his baseball team when he was fifteen, and was known in his neighborhood for his flair in choosing clothes. "I was the preppiest kid you ever saw!," remembered the designer in *New York.* "When I was eighteen I was preppy, even before preppy came the first time!"

When Lauren was sixteen, he and his brother Jerry—who runs the menswear division of the Polo/Ralph Lauren company—changed their name from Lifschitz to Lauren, a decision that has earned him accusations of cultural insecurity and pretentiousness. But the designer insists that his brother suggested the idea for good reasons. "The name was a problem," Lauren explained in *New York.* "Kids would laugh. If my name had been Bernstein, I never would have changed it. I went to yeshiva. I go to synagogue. I don't pretend to be something I'm not. There's no embarrassment. Totally the opposite." Part of the problem with his adopted name is that people typically mispronounce it as Lo-RENN, making it sound fashionably French. A company spokesperson pointed out in *Mademoiselle,* however, that the name is pronounced LOR-rin.

Lauren's education did little to prepare him for his eventual career. He attended Yeshiva University, the largest Jewish university in the United States and a training center for rabbis, took business classes at City College of New York, and spent six months serving in the Army. Instead, Lauren learned fashion by living it. At sixteen he hung clothes in a department store, and later he worked as a glove salesman, roaming New York City in custom-made suits and an English sports car, and as a salesman for Brooks Brothers suits. Finally, Lauren became the New York representative for Abe Rivetz, a Boston necktie manufacturer. It was there that Lauren decided to design ties of his own. In 1967, he went to Abe Rivetz with his proposal to design a line of ties, but Rivetz told him "The world is not ready for Ralph Lauren." Lauren decided that it was, and he left the company to try to sell his ties to someone else.

## Birth of a Brand

In the late 1960s, men's ties were two-and-a-half inches wide; Lauren broke with tradition and designed ties that were nearly

## AT A GLANCE

**R**alph Lauren brand ties created in 1967 by designer Ralph Lauren, followed by an entire line of menswear in 1968; Lauren and his brother Jerry formed Polo Fashions, Inc., in 1968; Ralph Lauren womenswear introduced 1971; Polo Fashions, Inc. became Polo/Ralph Lauren Corporation, 1972; Polo by Ralph Lauren and Lauren fragrances introduced 1978; Ralph Lauren Home Collection introduced 1983; various other products bearing the Polo or Ralph Lauren brand names include shoes, eyewear, scarves, hosiery, leathergoods, and jewelry.

**Performance:** *Sales*—Approximately $1 billion dollars annually.

**Major competitor:** Calvin Klein, Anne Klein, Liz Claiborne, Adrienne Vittadini.

**Advertising:** *Agency*—Carlson & Partners, New York, NY.

**Addresses:** *Parent company*—Polo/Ralph Lauren Corporation, 650 Madison Ave., New York, NY 10022; phone: (212) 319-7000; fax: (212) 888-5780. *Major licensees*—Ralph Lauren Womenswear, Bidermann Industries, 550 Seventh Ave., New York, NY 10018; phone: (212) 704-9507; fax: (212) 704-9525; Ralph Lauren Fragrances, Cosmair, Inc., 575 Fifth Ave., New York, NY 10017; phone: (212) 818-1500; Ralph Lauren Home Collection, 1185 Avenue of the Americas, New York, NY 10036; phone: (212) 642-8700.

four inches wide. "I didn't know how to make a tie," Lauren confessed in *Vogue* in 1982. "I didn't know fabric, I didn't know measurements. What did I know? That I was a salesman. That I was honest. And that all I wanted was quality." Lauren convinced the Beau Brummel clothing company to produce his ties, and he and his brother Jerry named their fledgling tie company Polo, choosing the name because it sounded English and vaguely aristocratic. The ties sold quickly in small menswear stores and, buoyed by his success, Lauren was soon knocking at the door of Bloomingdales, New York City's preeminent department store. Lauren resisted the store's request to make the ties narrower and sell them under the store label, and soon the ties were selling for the unheard-of price of fifteen dollars. "I used to take my ties home and knot them, and they were *perfect*. They represented what I stood for: quality, realness, specialness," Lauren recalled. "I *loved* them, and everything I did from then on, I loved. Because I made what I loved; my life was there." Lauren's single-minded dedication to quality and insistence on controlling the integrity of the products that bear his name were to become characteristic of his future endeavors.

From wide ties, the Polo collection of clothing designed by Ralph Lauren soon blossomed to include shirts, suits, and sportswear. In 1968, the Lauren brothers formed Polo Fashion, Inc., with financial backing from Norman Hilton Clothing Company. The company designed, manufactured, and distributed the Polo collection, which met with the approval of department stores that featured the clothes and the fashion critics who praised their style. In 1970 Lauren received the coveted Coty Award for menswear. In a rare move, Lauren then began designing clothes for women as well as for men. His first designs—men's dress shirts cut for women—met with great success in 1971, and soon sales topped $10 million.

## Design Comes First

The rapid growth of Polo fashions proved hard to manage for the young entrepreneur, who had succeeded in crafting a brand identity but not in managing his business. Lauren was unique among clothing designers in that he designed, manufactured, and distributed all his clothing, rather than designing clothes and licensing their manufacture and distribution to other companies. The difficulties of "doing it all" soon caught up with the company. "I almost blew my business," Lauren told a *Forbes* correspondent. "I wasn't shipping on time and had problems delivering." As he remembered in *New York*, "It was probably . . . one of the darkest moments in my life." Scrambling to survive, Lauren invested $100,000 of his savings in the business and convinced Peter Strom to leave his job with the Norman Hilton Clothing Company and become his partner. The Lauren brothers and Strom made changes to the structure of the company that set the stage for over two decades of unparalleled success.

Lauren's first step was to license the manufacture of Ralph Lauren brand womenswear to Stuart Kreisler, an experienced manufacturer who set out to build the reputation of the Lauren brand name. Strom insisted that those retailers who sold Lauren's clothes make a commitment to selling the entire line, which meant they had to carry the $350 Polo suit. "That eliminated two-thirds of our accounts," Strom told *Vogue*. "But those who stayed with us experienced our commitment to them, and it wasn't long before we felt their loyalty in return." With his business once again secure, Lauren was able to turn his attention to crafting a brand image as distinctive as any in America.

## The Brand, the Man, and the Image

The interconnection of brand identity and personal style that Ralph Lauren has created is a marvel of marketing. His advertising, his public persona, his clothes, and every product that bears his name presents a seamless image. For over twenty years, journalists and fashion critics have sought to describe this image, using words like integrity, elegance, tradition, sophistication, WASPy, mannered, pseudo-English, sporty. Lauren himself claimed in *New York* to be interested in "style but not flamboyance, but sophistication, class, and an aristocratic demeanor that you can see in people like Cary Grant and Fred Astaire." Although the actual clothes change every season, the image has remained the same for over twenty years.

Brand and man began to be intertwined in 1974, when Lauren appeared in a newspaper advertisement run by the Saks Fifth Avenue department store. Standing among his suits and sports clothes, Lauren wore blue jeans and a tweed jacket. "That ad caught people's imagination," Lauren told *Forbes*. "Why didn't he get dressed up, is he married, who is he? So it built something. It's nice to know that there is a living, breathing person behind the clothes instead of the company." That image—casual sophistication—has been replicated dozens of times since then, in profiles in *Time, People,* and *Life* magazines, in numerous features in fashion magazines, in the multi-page lifestyle advertisements that Lauren pioneered and appeared in, and in a 1992 television ad for a new Lauren fragrance, Safari for Men. Lauren added to the mystique by designing the costumes for two popular 1970s movies, *The Great Gatsby* and *Annie Hall*.

Though Lauren presents himself as casual, he surrounds his products with sophistication. Lauren has typically used print advertising to present his products, because the medium allows him greater control over the context in which his products are viewed. "TV is a fast sell, and that isn't the way we promote our products," he told *Forbes*. "You've got to hit the customers very hard on TV. But ours isn't a Seventh Avenue, bang-'em-out business." Instead, Ralph Lauren products appear in a world that seems lifted out of time. His multi-page ads catch wealthy, attractive people during a weekend at their country estate or on safari in Africa. In a *Vogue* article, the ads were described as a kind of "home movie," with a cast of "faintly sorrowful but wildly attractive people. The women are always between childhood and thirty; the men are sometimes old." Lauren lavishes huge amounts of money on these ads, as much as $15 and $20 million a year, though his licensees share some of the cost by returning two to three percent of sales into the advertising budget. An ad director for a major fashion magazine commented in *Time*: "Ralph has some of the best advertising in the business because it sets a mood, it evokes a life-style."

Lauren strives to maintain the same air of controlled sophistication in the retail atmosphere. As his clout in the clothing business has grown, he has been able to demand that retailers devote space and money to displaying his products in lavishly detailed Polo shops. The in-store shops surround the products in luxurious hardwood and carefully selected accessories, providing a Polo/Ralph Lauren oasis amid the bustle of a busy store. "Once stores commit so much space to Lauren's products," it was noted in the *New York Times Magazine,* "they must back it up by advertising them liberally. All of which contributes to Lauren's phenomenal success."

Ralph Lauren was rumored to be contemplating the ultimate extension of his image late in 1992, when *Advertising Age* reported that the designer was working with Hearst Magazines on "an up-scale consumer magazine that insiders think will revolve around the 'lifestyle of the Ralph Lauren look.'" The magazine, with potential titles of *Polo* and *Lauren,* would provide Lauren the control that he is known to crave over the advertising environment. An anonymous advertising executive pointed out in *Advertising Age* that "Ralph has a very strong view about where his advertising should be placed and the environment in which it appears, and the only way to accomplish that [control] is to have his own magazine."

## Complete Control

In 1971, Jerry Magnin opened the first Polo shop independent of a department store, beginning an important chapter in the development of the Polo/Ralph Lauren Corporation. Since that time, the company has franchised over 150 independent Polo/Ralph Lauren stores worldwide and has opened its own stores in New York, London, and Paris. The stores provide Lauren with the rare opportunity to exercise complete control over the environment in which his products appear. Moreover, the company operates a number of factory outlet stores located some distance from the retail outlets. The outlet stores allow the company to control the distribution of irregulars and items that have not sold by the end of each season, thereby preventing Ralph Lauren products from appearing in discount stores. Their distance from retail outlets insures retailers that the outlet stores do not steal business from them.

The flagship of the Polo/Ralph Lauren retail enterprise is the refurbished Rhinelander mansion on Madison Avenue in New York City. Opened in 1986, the 20,000-square-foot mansion features mahogany woodwork, hand-carved balustrades lining marble staircases, and sumptuous carpeting. "While men who look like lawyers search for your size shirt and ladies who belong at deb parties suggest complementary bags and shoes, you experience the ultimate in lifestyle advertising," wrote Lenore Skenazy in *Advertising Age*. "Instead of seeing Polo pomp in print or TV, you're free-sampling it. This is the *life!* And, of course, this is the pitch." Naomi Leff, who designed the interior of the Polo palace, called it "a marker in retailing history. It tells manufacturers that if they're willing to put out, they'll be able to make their own statement, which is not being made in the department stores."

Establishing a brand-focused retail outlet made perfect sense for Polo/Ralph Lauren because it allowed the company to increase profits by eliminating the middleman and controlling the environment in which their products appeared. In fact, other designers have since followed Polo/Ralph Lauren's lead, including his old neighbor Calvin Klein, Liz Claiborne, Adrienne Vittadini, and Anne Klein. But the move caused tension between the designer and his traditional retailers, the large department stores. A *Forbes* feature on Lauren's strategy claimed that "a lot of people in business think it is in bad taste to compete with your own customers. Lauren clearly does not agree. And such is his pull at the cash register that he may get away with this piece of business heresy."

Indeed, the strategy paid off for most of the 1980s, as an economic boom created a new class of consumers—Yuppies—who yearned for the old-money sophistication that Ralph Lauren clothing and products provided. Polo/Ralph Lauren opened dozens of stores in the 1980s, the increased exposure fueled brand growth, and everyone selling items bearing the Ralph Lauren name profited. By the end of the decade, analysts estimated Polo/Ralph Lauren's sales at $1 billion a year. "From wardrobes to home furnishings, the 1980s could be described as the 'Ralph Laurening' of America," wrote Robert Parola in the *Daily News Record*. "In one way or another, this highly focused image is responsible for helping launch more fashion trends and product lines in the American market and abroad than any other American designer. Ever." Alessandra Stanley theorized in the *New Republic* that George Bush's ability to identify himself with the Ralph Lauren image earned him the Presidency of the United States. In such a positive climate no store owners were willing to refuse Ralph Lauren's products simply because he opened a few retail stores. In fact, Ted Marlow, an executive at Marshall Field & Co. department store, told *Wall Street Journal* reporter Terry Agins that "It may sound hard to believe, but [the stores have] actually helped our business."

## Brand Expansion

When Ralph Lauren reorganized his young company in the early 1970s, he set the stage for years of brand expansion. With the exception of Polo by Ralph Lauren menswear, which after 1978 was manufactured in a Lawrence, Massachusetts factory owned by the company, every other product bearing the Ralph Lauren name has been licensed to an outside manufacturer. Under a licensing arrangement, a designer contracts with a manufacturer to produce and distribute goods that he or she has designed in exchange for a share of the profits. Strom told *Forbes* in 1986 that "Lauren's cut is usually 5% to 8% of wholesale revenues." Licensing has allowed Lauren to concentrate on establishing and designing products to fit his brand image.

Lauren developed his brand identity with clothing in the early 1970s, enticing those "who [thought] high-fashion . . . too faddish and traditional business garb . . . not quite sporty enough," wrote *Time* contributor Stephen Koepp. He quickly developed a reputation for quality, elegance, and durability. Grace Mirabella, former editor in chief of *Vogue* magazine told Koepp: "He doesn't do one thing that is out of character, whether it is comforters or jackets or men's ties."

After establishing a solid brand identity, Lauren began to branch out in the late 1970s. Important additions to his adult clothing line included a collection of casual sportswear called Chaps and a line of clothes for young adults called University Club. In 1978 he introduced Polo by Ralph Lauren cologne and clothing for boys; in 1981, when his daughter was seven, he introduced a girlswear line; in 1982, Ralph Lauren luggage and eyeglasses appeared, followed in 1983 by home furnishings, and in 1985 by women's handbags. Later brand extensions included shoes, furs, and underwear. The company expected to introduce its collection of apparel for newborns, infants, and toddlers in 1994. The variety of Lauren's products is not as indiscriminate as some might think. He has turned down offers to design telephones, autos, and chocolates, preferring instead to design those items which he enjoyed most and which fit his image. "I have visions, and I go at it," Lauren asserted in *Life*. "Everything I've done, I've done because I loved it and saw a need."

### Polo, Anyone?

If there is a single item that most people associate with Polo/ Ralph Lauren it is the Polo shirt, the company's version of the cotton-knit, soft-collar, short-sleeved shirt with the floppy tail. Lauren updated the shirt with his trademark—a polo player poised in mid swing—and sold millions. By 1986, with the shirt well established as a mainstay in the wardrobes of many American consumers, the company was selling four million Polo shirts a year. In 1991, the *Wall Street Journal* reported the decline of the logo-bearing shirts, but noted that "the only exception to the no-logo look seems to be Ralph Lauren's signature polo shirts." Polo/ Ralph Lauren added to its Polo shirt line in 1991 with the Polo Big Shirt. Jerry Lauren, senior vice-president of men's design, commented in the *Daily News Record*, "We feel a certain movement towards loungier, easier-fitting shirts." The polo player remained on the new shirt, though it was moved from the left chest to the right hem.

In 1978 Ralph Lauren introduced his first two fragrances: Polo by Ralph Lauren for men and Lauren for women. The designer's entrance into the fragrance field surprised some industry analysts, but as Lauren maintained in the *New York Times Magazine,* "My philosophy about fashion, about anything, is simple. If the best doesn't already exist, create it." Lauren licensed these fragrances to Warner Communications, and they proved steady though unspectacular sellers into the mid-1980s.

In 1984 Cosmair, Inc. acquired the licensing for Ralph Lauren Fragrances and, in 1990 the licensee began a series of fragrance introductions that took the market by storm. That year, Cosmair introduced Polo Crest, a complement to Lauren's original Polo fragrance. According to *Chemist & Druggist,* Polo Crest combined "the classic elements of the original Polo with fresh, green and citrus notes." The new fragrance was available in an eau de toilette spray, an eau de toilette bottle, and an aftershave bottle. Also launched in 1990 was Lauren's Safari for women, an accom-

paniment to Lauren's popular Safari collection of clothing. *Cosmetic Insiders' Report* called Safari the "Fragrance of the Year" after it recorded sales as high as $11,000 a day at some Bloomingdale's department stores. Cosmair hoped to sell between $25 and $30 million wholesale by the end of the fragrance's first year.

Two years later Lauren and Cosmair launched their biggest fragrance ever: Safari for Men. Ralph Lauren promoted the fragrance and accessory line in an uncharacteristic television commercial in which he rode a horse bareback on a beach, and Cosmair backed the launch with an advertising and promotion budget estimated at $20 million. Consumers could purchase a host of Safari for Men items, ranging from an $85 pewter hair brush to a $75 shaving mug to a $15 shaving gel. Patty Payne, an executive at Federated Merchandising, told a *PR Newswire* correspondent that Safari for Men was "breaking many women's fragrance launch records; it's a great name, a great package, a great fragrance, and a balanced launch campaign." According to *Women's Wear Daily,* Cosmair hoped to sell $28 million in wholesale at the end of six months, and top $50 million by the end of two years. In 1992 Polo/Ralph Lauren and Cosmair added to the Safari lines with the Safari Climate Response Collection, which included tanning, bathing, and skin care products.

### Coming Home to Ralph Lauren

Ralph Lauren made one of the boldest moves in his design career in 1983 when he decided to "dress the home." Lauren designed an entire line of products for the home—from sheets and towels, to hand-blown wine goblets, to stainless steel flatware—that numbered over 2,500 items in all. *House & Garden* called the collection "the most complete of its kind conceived by a fashion designer," and according to David M. Tracy, vice-chairman of the licensee for the line, the J.P. Stevens Company, "It is the next plateau of life-style marketing." Lauren, as usual, claimed that the collection was simply the logical extension of the Lauren brand image. "People live different lives," the designer maintained in *Vogue*. "They dress for different occasions. They wear roughwear, active-wear, dress clothes. I felt the home was very similar to that. The collection is perceived as a total life-style." And, Lauren added, "As I went into the stores over the years, I realized what they call 'designer sheets' were horrible; they were rip offs." Lauren vowed that his home collection would provide quality.

The Ralph Lauren home collection initially suffered a number of problems, however. J.P. Stevens experienced difficulties getting the products to retail outlets on time and, having themselves licensed elements of the line to other companies, had trouble maintaining quality control. In addition, Stevens demanded that stores that wanted to show the collection construct $250,000 freestanding, wood-paneled boutiques to display the items. Polo/ Ralph Lauren vice-chairman Peter Strom told *Time* that the introduction was "a disaster!"

Polo/Ralph Lauren quickly took control of the home collection management, weeded out the troublesome items, and put the collection back on the right track. Strom had estimated that by 1986 sales would reach $20 million. Top selling items were towels, sheets, pillows, and blankets. Lauren has added to his original collection with a set of fine sterling silver, silver plate, and stainless steel flatware manufactured by Reed & Barton Silversmiths, and by offering a youth-oriented bed and bath collection to complement his University Club line of clothing for young adults.

## The Benefits of Being Laurenized

Clothing, fragrances, and home furnishings are the most noticeable items bearing the Ralph Lauren brand name, but the designer has placed his Midas touch on many other items that fit into his carefully conceived world. In 1989 the designer introduced a golf apparel line for men and women that included shirts, trousers, rain jackets, and shoes. The hand-made shoes sold for between $395 and $430 retail, according to *Golf Pro Merchandiser,* and were sold only at top country clubs and destination resorts. In 1990 licensee Tugallo River Boxer Co. began distribution of Polo/Ralph Lauren underwear. The underwear, a mid-rise brief, was packaged simply and expected to reach sales of $3 million for 1991. Also in the early 1990s, Lauren created a line of clothing for the America 3 America's Cup sailing team, and designed a line of ski accessories, including a boot bag and a ski case. In a survey of Lauren's first twenty-five years as a designer, *Mademoiselle* contributor Janet Siroto commented that "there seems to be no object that can't benefit from being Laurenized."

Lauren's high-profile brand image has allowed him to branch out into an astonishing array of products, but it has also attracted imitators. In 1991, according to *Detroit Free Press* reporters David McHugh and Joanne Muller, federal agents investigating trademark rip-offs arrested two men who were preparing to sell $1.4 million in counterfeit Polo/Ralph Lauren shirts. In the same year, Polo/Ralph Lauren brought suit against a San Antonio, Texas-based retail chain for selling shirts with a polo player symbol remarkably similar to Ralph Lauren's. Philip Gottfried, trademark counsel for Polo/Ralph Lauren, said in the *Houston Business Journal* that the fake shirts could have fooled a regular buyer, but warned "If Polo goods are sold at a price too good to be true, it probably is."

Lauren's competitors have not hesitated to take swipes at the designer when they could. In 1990 Ralph Lauren Womenswear lowered prices in an attempt to increase sales volume. Howard Rosenberger, president of licensee Bidermann Industries Corp., told *Women's Wear Daily* that the move was made in reaction to "the market being so competitive and retail being so dramatically down." Analysts expected Lauren's competitors to follow suit, but instead they questioned Lauren's motives. "When someone cuts their prices by 25 percent, you have to ask if it was overpriced to begin with, or are they trying to increase profit margins and will quality suffer?," asked Richard Catalano, president of Adrienne Vittadini, in *Women's Wear Daily.* Another competitor, the small Boston Preparatory Co., took a shot at Ralph Lauren and other designers in advertisements with copy that read, "Apparently some designers think Americans look better in their clothes, than in their factories." A spokeswoman for Ralph Lauren insisted in the *Wall Street Journal* that the ad is "inaccurate and misleading . . . the majority of our products are produced domestically."

## Adjusting to a New Decade

The Polo/Ralph Lauren company rode its expertly crafted brand image to remarkable heights in the 1980s, as sustained economic growth and the United States' fascination with Lauren's image fueled an unparalleled expansion in products bearing the Ralph Lauren name. But retail expansion slowed dramatically with the economic downturn early in the 1990s, and some stores that once thrived on the sales of Ralph Lauren's high-priced products complained that the company was unable to adjust to changes in the market. Robert Parola, writing in *Daily News Record,* noted that many clothing manufacturers lifted their designs from Ralph Lauren and sold them for less. One department store owner told Parola that Lauren is "in a bind because he has a traditionalist image. But traditionalism is over as fashion."

Peter Strom acknowledged the difficulties of adjusting to the changing retail market, and told Parola that the company planned to stop opening new stores and lower prices. But he also insisted that "traditionalism is what we do, and it's what we do best. It's what Ralph believes in." As Lauren himself pointed out in *New York* magazine, "The things I do are not about novelty. They're things I love and can't get away from. There are some things in life that, no matter what the times are, keep getting better and better. That's really my philosophy." This attitude has allowed Lauren to create some of the most distinctive and popular consumer items of the last decades, and it seems unlikely that American consumers as well as consumers in growing markets in Europe and Japan will soon overcome their fascination with the sophisticated, quality goods bearing the Ralph Lauren name.

## Further Reading:

Agins, Terry, "Clothing Makers Don Retailers' Garb, Manufacturers Open Stores, Irk Main Outlets," *Wall Street Journal,* July 13, 1989.

Agins, Terry, "Izod Lacoste Gets Restyled and Repriced," *Wall Street Journal,* July 22, 1991, p. B1.

Aronson, Steven M. L., "High Style in Jamaica," *House & Garden,* October 1984, pp. 127–137, 230.

Barns, Lawrence, "J. P. Stevens Takes the Designer Route," *Business Week,* September 19, 1983, pp. 118–119.

"Beyond the Name Game: New Design World from Halston and Ralph Lauren," *Vogue,* September 1983, pp. 550–552.

"A Big Time Safari for Ralph Lauren," *Women's Wear Daily,* October 27, 1989, pp. 1, 14.

Born, Pete, "Polo Crest Takes Fashion Approach to Fragrance," *Daily News Record,* July 26, 1991, p. 3.

Born, Pete, "Lauren Hits TV Trail for Men's Safari," *Women's Wear Daily,* August 21, 1992, p. 5.

Born, Pete, "New Men's Lauren Fragrance to Debut," *Daily News Record,* March 6, 1992, p. 4.

"Bunkhouse Bed Fashions," *Madison Avenue,* October, 1983, pp. 16–18.

Cocks, Jay, "Born and Worn in the U.S.A.," *Time,* June 16, 1986, pp. 96–97.

Donaton, Scott, and Pat Sloan, "Hearst, Lauren at Work on Lifestyle Magazine," *Advertising Age,* April 27, 1992, pp. 1, 54.

Donaton, Scott, and Pat Sloan, "Ralph Lauren Sets Magazine Test," *Advertising Age,* November 2, 1992, p. 3.

Dowling, Claudia Glenn, "Ralph Lauren," *Life,* May 1989, pp. 136–141.

Ettorre, Barbara, " 'Give Ralph Lauren All the Jets He Wants,' " *Forbes,* February 28, 1983, pp. 102–103.

Ferretti, Fred, "The Business of Being Ralph Lauren," *New York Times Magazine,* September 18, 1983, pp. 112–113, 124–133.

Gellers, Stan, "1992: The New American Evolution," *Daily News Record,* October 28, 1991, p. 14.

Goldman, Kevin, "More Made-in-the-USA Claims, Surprisingly, Are Showing Up," *Wall Street Journal,* January 15, 1993, p. B5.

Gross, Michael, "The American Dream," *New York,* December 21, 1992, pp. 71–72.

Koepp, Stephen, "Selling a Dream of Elegance and the Good Life," *Time,* September 1, 1986, pp. 54–61.

Kohn, Bernie, "Chaps of South Hills Owner Says Polo Lawsuit Is Unfounded," *Poughkeepsie Journal* (New York), December 4, 1986.

Kornbluth, Jesse, "Ralph Lauren: Success American Style," *Vogue,* August 1982, pp. 263–265, 306–307.

Kudelka, Bob, "Myrtle Beach Club Wins Fight Over Shirt Emblem," *State* (Columbia, SC), November 14, 1989.

Lafayette, Jon, "Ralph Lauren Drops WRG," *Advertising Age,* September 18, 1989, pp. 1, 84.

Langway, Lynn, with Linda R. Prout, "Lauren's Frontier Chic," *Newsweek,* September 21, 1981, p. 115.

"Lauren," *New York,* October 21, 1985, pp. 40–47.

"Lauren Price Cuts Don't Spark a Trend," *Women's Wear Daily,* June 14, 1991, p. 17.

Ling, Flora, "Ralph Lauren's Polo Game," *Forbes,* June 26, 1978, p. 88.

Lockwood, Lisa, "Ralph Lauren's Sales Go Up as Prices Fall," *Women's Wear Daily,* June 11, 1991, p. 1.

Mander, Lois, "Safari for Men by Ralph Lauren Off to a Powerful Start," *PR Newswire,* September 18, 1992.

McHugh, David, and Joanne Miller, "Sales Team had Designs on $1.4 Million," *Detroit Free Press,* September 12, 1991.

Moin, David, "Ralph Lauren Is Back at Saks in a Big Way," *Women's Wear Daily,* October 14, 1992, p. 3.

Parola, Robert, "Polo/Ralph Lauren," *Daily News Record,* October 17, 1990, p. 3.

Parola, Robert, "Polo/Ralph Lauren: At the Crossroads," *Daily News Record,* October 29, 1990, p. 10.

"Polo/Ralph Lauren Adding Store in California," *Women's Wear Daily,* October 29, 1990, p. 11.

"Ralph Lauren: The Dream Maker," *U.S. News & World Report,* February 8, 1988, p. 78.

"Ralph Lauren, the Seventh Avenue Designer Known for His Sportswear, Is Taking a Major Swing at the Golf Market," *Golf Pro Merchandiser,* 1989, p. 37.

"Reed & Barton/Ralph Lauren Ties: Flatware from Resource to Add New Dimension to Noted Designer's Home Collection," *HFD,* February 18, 1991, p. 55.

Rosen, Pat, "Phony Pony?: Polo Player Rides to Court in Logo Lawsuit," *Houston Business Journal,* May 6, 1991, sec. 1, p. 1.

Siroto, Janet, "Ralph Lauren—Looking Back," *Mademoiselle,* May 1992, pp. 156–159.

Skenazy, Lenore, "Lauren Gets Honorable Mansion," *Advertising Age,* October 20, 1986, p. 56.

Sohng, Laurie, "Polo Partners Ralph Lauren Footwear Always Plays to Win," *Footwear News,* October 14, 1991, p. Sa4.

Spevack, Rachel, "Polo and Izod: Adding New Luster to Knit Logos," *Daily News Record,* March 12, 1991, p. 5.

Talley, Andre Leon, "Everybody's All-American," *Vogue,* February 1992, pp. 203–210, 284.

Trachtenberg, Jeffrey A., "You Are What You Wear," *Forbes,* April 21, 1986, pp. 94–98.

Wohlfert, Lee, "What do Woody, Bob and Diane Have in Common? Money, Yes, but Designer Ralph Lauren Too," *People,* February 6, 1978, pp. 82–84.

Zutell, Irene, "Ralph Lauren's Summer Home Theme," *HFD,* November 26, 1990, p. 42.

*—Tom Pendergast*

# POND'S®

# POND'S

Some of the world's most beautiful and glamorous women—among them three European queens and six princesses—have touted the benefits of using Pond's Cold Cream as a facial cleanser superior to soap. Their endorsements and Pond's tradition of providing quality products has made Pond's Cold Cream the top face cream in America. The Pond's brand, after nearly a century and a half of success, recently expanded to include a line of moisturizers and related skin care products.

## Brand Origins

The founder of one of the oldest brand names in the United States, Theron T. Pond began his career as a chemist in Utica, New York. In 1846 he extracted from the bark of a witch hazel shrub a "pain destroying and healing" potion that became known as Pond's Extract. The application of the extract on wounds was thought to help alleviate pain in minutes and quickly heal wounds better than any other topical remedy. Pond set up a small distillery in the rear of his apothecary and began producing Pond's Extract. Although he was not the first to recognize witch hazel's medicinal properties and healing qualities, he was among the first to preserve it and commercially distribute it. Pond prepared his product by combining distilled extract with a pure grain alcohol and aging it in oaken barrels for three to five years. Patients, physicians, and apothecaries soon endorsed the extract.

In 1849 Pond formed the T. T. Pond Company with partners Edmund Munson and Alexander C. Hart of Utica, New York. By 1852, Pond sold out to his partners because of ill health and died shortly thereafter, unable to profit from his company's future successes. The company opened branches in London in the late 1850s, and after the Civil War the T. T. Pond Company opened in New York City and established a factory in Brooklyn. The company then began to diversify its products by adding a line of toilet articles, toilet creams, lip salve ointments, and a veterinary remedy based on Pond's Extract.

After fires destroyed company witch hazel distilleries, the Clinton, Connecticut, plant—also known as the Whittemore Soap Factory—was established. In 1903 the company developed an antiseptic cream and a massage cream based on the extract, which became the forerunners of Pond's Cold Cream. In 1907 the company developed a vanishing cream to protect the skin and introduced the official Pond's Cold Cream. The company incorporated in 1914 as the Pond's Extract Company.

The roots of Pond's Cold Cream date to the first century when ointments made out of plants were used as beauty aids. Cold cream, according to Ruth Winter's *A Consumer's Dictionary of Cosmetic Ingredients,* was originally developed by a Greek physician named Galen. The term cold cream got its name from how it was originally stored. Early in the 20th century, druggists kept the product on ice, thus keeping it fresh and giving the consumer a "cooling" sensation when it was applied. T. T. Pond produced a cold cream formula that was more refined and did not need to be chilled to maintain its freshness. Pond's Cold Cream is described by the company as a rich facial cleanser formulated to remove dirt and makeup that soap leaves behind. Using it, the company claims, leaves a person's skin soft and smooth.

## Early Marketing and Advertising Strategy

The T. T. Pond Company did not have many avenues for advertising open to it in the mid-1800s. Its products were promoted mainly with advertising cards and product booklets placed in apothecary shops. In 1892 testimonials were added to the booklets: in addition to describing the use of Pond's Extract, a booklet contained excerpts of letters received from grateful users. In 1886, Pond's embarked on a national advertising campaign as one of J. Walter Thompson Advertising Agency's first clients. The 1904 Pond's Girl ad campaign won first place at a national advertising convention. The Pond's Girl was the focal point of this 1910 ad: "Avoid Sunburn, Freckles and Chaps. The Out-of-Doors Girl can easily avoid the unpleasant effects of sun and wind on her delicate skin by always using Pond's Extract Company's Vanishing Cream." This and similar advertisements urged customers to test Pond's products at the company's expense. Customers who sent the company their name and the name of a drugstore dealer would be sent samples of either the vanishing cream or Pond's Extract.

Pond's Cold Cream—packaged in white glass jars that were later adorned with Pond's famous flower logo—gained notoriety in the 1920s. At the time, American heiresses and European nobility (including Princess Matchabelli whose husband's perfume business would be sold to the company 33 years later) promoted the product, raving about it as an excellent beauty aid. A 1948 *Good Housekeeping* advertisement featured Mrs. Nicholas R. du Pont and proclaimed, "She uses Pond's!" Mrs. du Pont was quoted: "I can't imagine using a finer face cream," and the ad

## AT A GLANCE

**P**ond's brand of cold cream introduced in 1907 by the Pond's Extract Company in Clinton, CT; became a registered trademark in 1926; the brand name Pond's first used for Pond's Extract, a pain-killing potion extracted from the bark of witch hazel shrub, developed by Theron T. Pond in 1846; Pond founded the T. T. Pond Company in 1849; incorporated in 1914 as the Pond's Extract Company; in 1955 merged with the Chesebrough Manufacturing Company to form Chesebrough-Pond's; company acquired by Netherlands-based Unilever, Inc., in 1987.

*Performance:* Market share—13% of face cream and lotion category; 1.0% of hand and body lotion market; 20.3% of facial cleanser market.

*Major competitor:* Procter & Gamble's Noxzema and Oil of Olay; also L'Oréal's Plentitude, Biersdorf AG's Nivea, KAO's Jergens, and S. C. Johnson's Soft Sense and Curel.

*Advertising:* Agency—Ogilvy & Mather, New York, NY, 1993—. Major campaign—"The Pond's Institute for the latest discoveries for beautiful skin. Toll-free number provided for free skin care guides."

*Addresses:* Parent company—Chesebrough-Pond's USA, 33 Benedict Place, Greenwich, CT 06836-6000; phone: (203) 661-2000; fax: (203) 625-1602. Ultimate parent company—Unilever USA, 390 Park Ave., New York, NY 10022-4698; phone: (212) 888-1260; fax: (212) 906-4411.

copy read: "Pond's is used and beloved by more women than any other face cream. Get yourself a big jar of snowy Pond's Cold Cream—today!"

## Company Evolution

At the advent of World War II, Pond's Extract Company was the world's largest producer of face creams, selling its products in 96 countries around the world. As part of the war effort, Pond's manufactured two-tone camouflage cream and insect repellent, and packed POW packages and K-rations for the U.S. troops. Pond's flagship product suffered: production of witch hazel was curtailed during the war because of the shortage of manpower and alcohol. Advertising and promotion ceased, and by 1950 the production of witch hazel was entirely discontinued, according to company documents.

A 1955 merger with the Chesebrough Manufacturing Company (inventors of Vaseline Petroleum Jelly) saved the day. The merger was hailed as the "marriage of Aristocrats," by the American Stock Exchange. The new Chesebrough-Pond's Company diversified further with the Prince Matchabelli line of perfumes and cosmetics, Aziza eye makeup, and Cutex nail polishes. These additions strengthened the company as a leader in the cosmetic industry. Chesebrough-Pond's continued success made it attractive to other companies, and in 1987 the company was purchased by the British- and Dutch-owned Unilever, one of the world's largest consumer product manufacturers.

## Product Changes

The Pond's brand, whose fame came to rest almost entirely on its cold cream, changed little for most of the second half of the 20th century. Medicinal benefits, a focus for Pond's products since

that first concoction of witch hazel extract, continued to find a place in the cold cream advertising. Pond's Cold Cream packaging states that the product is "suitable for sensitive skin, is hypoallergenic and won't clog pores." The brand expanded little, for years adding only cold cream variations, including Water Rinsable Cold Cream in late 1988, Pond's Dry Skin Cream, and Pond's Lemon Cold Cream. The big break with the past came in 1992, when Chesebrough-Pond's repackaged the entire line and added cleansers and moisturizers. Pat Sloan in *Advertising Age* reported that the introductions were to be positioned as "sophisticated entries in mass-market skincare, using upscale packaging and advanced ingredients."

Pond's, which had held the majority of the facial cleanser market with about a 20 percent, began trailing facial cleansers such as Procter & Gamble's Noxzema and L'Oréal's Plentitude in the early 1990s. This slip prompted company officials to launch a $30 million network television, print, and promotional campaign by McCann Erickson Worldwide of New York in 1992. *Advertising Age*'s Sloan wrote that the campaign was to "help the entire brand by further distancing Pond's from its old-fashioned cold cream image."

The line, advertised as the "New Face of Pond's," offered Pond's Dramatic Results Skin Smoothing Capsules, Cleansing Lotion & Moisturizing in One, Clarifying Astringent, Foaming Cleanser & Toner in One, Moisturizing Cleansing Bar and Oil Controlling Cleansing Bar. The new "soap-free, oil-free, hypoallergenic, and non-pore clogging" line performed "two functions in one, in less time and can cost less than two separate products." Meanwhile, the new collection of facial moisturizers included: Pond's Dramatic Results Skin Smoothing Capsules, Pond's Nourishing Moisturizing Lotion, Pond's Nourishing Moisturizer Cream, Pond's Revitalizing Eye Gel with Vitamin E, Pond's Nourishing Lotion with Sunscreen SPF 15, and Pond's Overnight Nourishing Complex.

Chesebrough-Pond's executive vice president of marketing and sales, Peter England, was quoted as saying the move was "a demonstration of our continued commitment to growth." Backed by a $48 million marketing budget, Pond's Cold Cream was repackaged in early 1992 to make it look more like a cosmetics line. The Pond's transformation used the company's "Master Brand" strategy to capitalize on the reputation of trusted major Chesebrough-Pond's brands while bolstering them with new products and a unified marketing campaign. The new packaging incorporated the classic Pond's white jar (albeit plastic) and identified products with either a green (cleansers) or pink (moisturizers) flower logo.

To advertise the new products, television and print ads featured the "Pond's Institute," where one can try the latest discoveries for beautiful skin. These ads were prominently placed and offered consumers a free skin care guide to be obtained by calling a toll-free number.

## Future Performance

By refurbishing the Pond's Cold Cream brand, Chesebrough-Pond's can only stand to gain in the facial cleanser market, which is projected to grow eight to ten percent through new product introductions. The company asserted in a 1992 *Discount Store News* advertising supplement that Pond's has maintained its leadership by "consistently setting the pace for product innovations designed to meet the evolving needs of facial cleanser users." In terms of advertising voice, the brand garners 48 percent share, compared to Noxzema at 47.4 percent and Procter & Gamble's Oil of Olay at 4.5 percent.

The restaging of its cold cream line did boost Pond's share in the cleanser market by one point, raising it to 14 percent, Pat Sloan wrote in a 1992 *Advertising Age* article. The magazine cited industry observers as "expecting the increases to continue in 1993 with the help of more than $15 million in advertising for these products alone." Chesebrough-Pond's in mid-1993 switched from McCann-Erickson Worldwide (which continued to handle such company accounts as Vaseline Intensive Care) to Ogilvy & Mather, New York. Their mission was to help bring Pond's into the 21st century and to advertise the brand worldwide as part of Unilever's strategy to expand its global markets in Asia, India, and South America.

**Further Reading:**

"The First 100 Years," Greenwich, CT: Chesebrough-Pond's, 1980.

Frankenstein, Diane, *Brandnames: Who Owns What,* Facts on Filc, 1986, pp. 147–48.

Moskowitz, Milton, *Everybody's Business,* New York: Doubleday, 1990, pp. 137–39.

"100th Anniversary," Greenwich, CT: Chesebrough-Pond's, 1988, pp. 1–20.

"Pond's New Initiatives Drive Face Care Sales," *Discount Store News,* May 18, 1992, pp. 62–64.

Sloan, Pat, "Chesebrough Puts New Face on Its Brands," *Advertising Age,* January 27, 1992, p. 3; "Pond's to Spend $30 Million for Launch of Moisturizers," *Advertising Age,* September 28, 1992, p. 49.

Wilson, Mitchell, *American Science and Invention,* New York: Simon & Schuster, 1954.

*—Evelyn S. Dorman*

# POST-IT®

# Post-it

Post-it brand of reattachable adhesive notes evolved from a failed adhesive to become a necessity in offices worldwide. Minnesota Mining & Manufacturing Company (3M) invented the market for reattachable note paper, and its product dominates the category. Post-it notes stand as a prime example of how 3M turned a mistake into a money maker.

## Brand Origins

In 1973 Dr. Spencer Silver, a researcher at 3M in St. Paul, Minnesota, discovered a new type of adhesive. He showed Geoffrey Nicholson, one of many technical directors, his new adhesive even though it had failed internal tests. Nicholson, however, could not find an application for the product. Yet 3M Corporate Scientist Arthur Fry, whose job was to find business applications for the new materials being developed in the research department, finally did.

Fry was in search of the perfect bookmark for his church choir hymnal—pieces of paper kept falling out of it. After one frustrating Sunday at St. Paul's North Presbyterian Church in 1974, Fry realized that he needed a bookmark that could both stick to its place and be lifted off without damaging the page. Such a marker would require a new kind of adhesive, one that Fry described as "permanently temporary." Remembering Dr. Silver's failed adhesive, Fry obtained a sample and dabbed it on a piece of paper to create a makeshift "permanently temporary" note. In *Getting It Right the Second Time,* Fry recalled that he "realized very quickly that this was a systems approach to note taking. It had the means of attaching it and the means of removing it built right into it."

Fry presented his idea to the product manager of 3M's commercial tape division and was granted authority to continue researching the product under the company's "15 percent rule." This rule stipulated that company employees could spend up to 15 percent of the workweek on anything they wanted to as long as it pertained to a product. Getting a product such as his sticky bookmark and notepad prototypes to market was fraught with obstacles. Marketing officials at 3M even questioned the need for sticky notepads. Fry, however, viewed his idea as "something that could eventually grow into something as useful as Scotch tape." Bob Molenda, product manager for the commercial tape division, agreed and allowed Fry to use money allocated for other projects (a 3M system known as bootlegging) to fund his research.

Another problem was that Fry's notes were based on a different concept than most 3M products. The company had successfully produced products that came in rolls, and company machinery was not able to create padded forms. Fry's notes were packaged as tear-off pads. According to Fry was that "no one knew how to stack sticky sheets of paper in perfect alignment to make the pads. We had a lot of people looking at the problems, both inside and outside of 3M. I had an idea about how to do it, but little time was left. I built the machine in my basement, dismantled the door frame and part of a garden wall myself to get it out and installed it in the Pilot Plant (no construction crew involved). It worked from the start and allowed us to make the pads."

## Early Marketing Strategy

Fry first marketed his Press'n'Peel notes by giving samples to 3M employees. Nicholson also did his part by passing out the pads to 3M executives. Soon there were so many requests that "my office started resembling a supply depot," Nicholson noted in *Getting It Right the Second Time.* Internal demand proved so great that in 1977 3M marketing personnel decided to test the Press'n'Peel pads in 1977 in Denver, Tulsa, Tampa, and Richmond, Virginia. Company representatives first visited test markets, offering both 1½ by 2-inch and 3 by 5-inch notepads. They also placed advertising inserts in local and regional issues of office supply trade publications and sent subscribers product brochures and 3M catalogs.

The Press'n'Peel notepads performed poorly in test markets because customers were not sure how to use them. Therefore 3M marketing officials, who made cold calls on customers, began demonstrating the product to office employees and were "writing orders along the way." Joe Ramey, 3M Commercial Tape Division vice-president, told the *Corporate Report,* "My reaction when I went out into those markets was that we probably had a dead duck on our hands, and it just wasn't going to make it. . . . I didn't frankly think that it was a product that people would buy. I didn't think it was a product we could sell in volume."

Before long, Ramey understood that the notepads had potential but were mismarketed. In *Getting It Right the Second Time,* he explained, "Our communication package was put together very badly, and the consumers didn't really understand the product. To get people motivated to buy this product, we had to get a sample

## AT A GLANCE

**P**ost-it brand of self-stick note paper invented in 1974 by 3M engineer Arthur Fry as Press'n'Peel notes; product renamed Post-it notes in 1979 and became a registered trademark of Minnesota Mining & Manufacturing Company (3M).

**Performance:** *Market share*—Majority share of self-stick notepad market. *Sales*—$500 million (est.) in 1990.

**Major competitor:** Avery; also Barton Nelson.

**Advertising:** *Agency*—Martin Williams, Minneapolis, MN, 1976—. *Major campaign*—Focuses on promoting Post-it tape flags and fax notes.

**Addresses:** *Parent company*—Minnesota Mining & Manufacturing Company, 3M Center, St. Paul, MN 55144; phone: (612) 733-1110; fax (612) 733-9973.

into their hands." The company tried a new tact when infiltrating the Boise, Idaho, market. In 1978 3M launched its "Boise Blitz" campaign where the Press'n'Peel notes were advertised in inserts in the *Idaho Statesman*. The notepads were promoted throughout the city with enticing window, counter, and ceiling displays. 3M also hired Manpower temporaries to conduct live demonstrations in Boise offices. "We just literally bombarded the city with everything we could," stated marketing director Jack Wilkins, in the *Corporate Report*. "And when we went back in and checked out the intent to repurchase, I think it was up over 90 percent. That's absolutely unheard of—in any field."

### First Commercial Success

Renamed Post-it notes in 1979, the notepads were introduced on the West Coast, followed by national distribution in 1980. By 1983, the *Wall Street Journal* reported that sales were up to $45 million a year and rising—although 3M officials never confirmed or denied that figure. 3M did report that in 1983 Post-it notes had a unit growth of 85 percent and that sales were 185 percent of forecast, according to George Dixon in *Corporate Report*. A year later, Post-it notes became 3M's most successful new product in its history. According to *Getting It Right the Second Time*, Post-it notes ranked as one of the top five office supply products, joining fellow 3M brand Scotch tape, Liquid Paper, file folders, and copy paper. 3M would later award Fry with its higher scientific honor, the Carlton Society Award. According to a 1984 *Corporate Report* article, "Word is that Post-it notes have become the successor to Scotch Tape as the commercial tape division's most profitable product line, as well as perhaps the entire company's most signal recent product."

### Advertising Innovations

The Martin Williams advertising agency of Minneapolis created a campaign focusing on the simplicity and facility of using Post-it notes. Early advertising was targeted to high potential users such as law firms. One ad read "Law and Order" and showed Post-it notes stuck on legal textbooks, reported Debbie Seaman in *Adweek's Marketing Week*. In 1987 the agency released a print campaign targeted at a wider audience. A subsequent ad, titled "I Love You Mom," showed a child's drawing on a large Post-it note. The campaign underscored the brand's theme of "when people count on you, count on Post-it notes."

The print series often consisted of only a handwritten note on a Post-it note to demonstrate the simplicity and ease of leaving a message for someone. Martin Williams' Bill Zabowski told *Adweek's Marketing Week* that "3M invented the product, and one of the jobs of the campaign is [to make sure] that people make no mistake in calling Post-it notes by [another] name. The ads don't take up a lot of your time, but they communicate the strengths of Post-it notes. That's why there's no body copy in them."

### Brand Development

Post-it notes were originally marketed to the office supply industry as light yellow adhesive notepads—to contrast with most office correspondence. Sizes ranged from $1\frac{1}{2}$ by 2 inches to 3 by 5 inches. A 3 by 3-inch size was developed before the brand was marketed nationally. (Ten years later, Post-it notes came in sizes up to 5 by 8 inches.) In 1981 3M introduced a Post-it Note Tray because customers were losing the notepads on their desks. The brand line expanded in 1985 to include multi-colored and neon color pads and pads printed with standard office headings—"Rush," "Please Copy," "F.Y.I."—once 3M overcame printing obstacles by forming its own Quality Note Printers in Mankato, Minnesota. A fan-folded Post-it note package called Pop-up note dispensers joined the line in 1990. In the early 1990s, the Post-it brand line included a full line of Post-it notepads, Post-it recycled paper notes, Post-it preprinted notes, tape flags, correction and cover-up tape, memo boards (corkboard with the Post-it adhesive on it), glue sticks, and desk organizers.

### International Market

Approximately 47 percent of 3M's sales and 43 percent of its profits are derived from foreign markets. Under Chairman Desi DeSimone the company has been content to "wait a generation for foreign business to succeed," according to *Forbes*. Patience paid off in Japan where 3M made considerable profit in that seemingly closed market with Japanese-style Post-it notes. Japanese Post-it notes are long and thin so each person in a hierarchical chain of command could write on them. 3M international strategy also has been to engage competitors on their home turf. Most company employees overseas are natives and 70 percent of the foreign company's products are made in the countries in which they are sold, according to Jason Zweig in *Forbes*.

### Future Growth

By 1990 Post-it notes had garnered more than $100 million in annual sales and by the mid-1990s industry analysts estimated the figure at $500 million, although 3M has never revealed specific sales figures. Company official stated that 30 percent of its $13 billion of annual revenue comes from products developed in the past five years. Post-it notes have been a strong performer for 3M, and the product's widespread applications in offices make it probable that it will maintain its impressive market share and sales.

### Further Reading:

Dixon, George, "How 3M Almost Scotched its Best-Selling Office Product," *Corporate Report*, July 1984, p. 47.

Gershman, Michael, *Getting It Right the Second Time*, Reading, MA: Addison-Wesley, 1990.

Kovaleski, Serge F., "These Innovators Discover New Products—And Profits," *Money*, April 1991, p. 57.

Mitchell, Russell, "Masters of Innovation," *Business Week,* April 10, 1989, p. 58.

"Post-it Inventor Still Sticking to It," *Fortune,* February 12, 1990, p. 10.

"Post-it Notes Celebrate 10th Birthday," *Modern Office Technology,* March 1990, p. 30.

"Post-it Notes Click Thanks to Entrepreneurial Spirit," *Marketing News,* August 1984, p. 21.

Seaman, Debbie, "Simple Message for Simple Way to Message," *AdWeek's Marketing Week,* August 3, 1987, p. 22.

"3M: 60,000 and Counting," *The Economist,* November 30, 1991, p. 70.

Zweig, Jason, "Making the World Stick Together," *Forbes,* January 7, 1991, p. 100.

*—Evelyn S. Dorman*

# PRELL®

The Prell brand of shampoo and conditioner is one of the most enduring lines of hair-care products in the United States. Introduced in 1946 by the Procter & Gamble Company, the Prell brand has earned customer loyalty due to its performance and price.

## Brand Origins

By 1946 Americans had access to improved sanitation facilities and were bathing and taking showers more frequently. Many people wanted to use shampoo into the shower stall, but the glass bottles in which the shampoos of the time were packaged were prone to slip out of wet, soapy hands and crash to bathroom floors. Addressing consumers' calls for a non-breakable shampoo container, the Procter & Gamble Company drew upon the knowledge and resources of Ivorydale, its Cincinnati research laboratory, to produce one. Because Ivorydale was overcrowded with projects, Procter & Gamble constructed a laboratory on the outskirts of Cincinnati devoted exclusively to toiletry products. This was the building in which the Prell formula was finally perfected. In 1946 the product, a concentrated green synthetic shampoo in a metal tube, was launched nationally.

## Early Marketing Strategy

The brand was an instant hit. Easy to apply, it lathered luxuriantly into thick suds under the spray of the shower head. At that time, Prell seemed to appeal more strongly to men. Taking advantage of the potential of radio to reach consumers, Procter & Gamble immediately advertised Prell. One commercial had a song with the lyrics, "I'm Tallulah, the tube of Prell, I've got a little something to tell. Your hair can be radiant, oh, so easy, All you've got to do is take me home and squeeze me." A famous actress named Tallulah Bankhead was enraged and sued the company, its advertising agency, and the networks for $1 million, citing distress and humiliation. Both she and Prell derived over $10 million worth of free publicity from the suit. Newspapers ran the story and had great fun with headlines: "Shampoo Ad Gets in Her Hair," "Foaming Tallulah . . . ," ". . . in Lather," ". . . in Froth." The suit was quietly settled out of court for $2,500. But by then, every man, woman, and child who had access to a radio or newspaper knew the saga of Tallulah the Tube and had heard of Prell. Publicity for the product continued when a telegram arrived at Procter & Gamble Company headquarters, purportedly from a dog named Prell, also threatening suit.

On July 23, 1948, Procter & Gamble first advertised Prell on television with its sponsorship of DuMont's WABD *Fashions on Parade*. The company employed models from the Harry Conover Agency to demonstrate step-by-step a Prell shampoo. Fed up with the problems of live advertising, Procter & Gamble executives decided to film all commercials in advance. On Sunday nights, Prell and Tide jointly sponsored *A Letter to Loretta*. Prell also sponsored the ever-popular *This Is Your Life!* hosted by Ralph Edwards. Prell received additional publicity when Mary Martin, portraying nurse Nellie Forbush in the Broadway production of Rodgers and Hammerstein's *South Pacific*, used Prell shampoo as she sang "I'm Gonna Wash That Man Right Out of My Hair."

In addition to the Prell brand's sponsorship of radio and television programs, Procter & Gamble utilized other media to make the public aware of the shampoo concentrate. In 1993 health and beauty aids sections of retail stores regularly received large cardboard displays of Prell featuring refund tear-off forms. Color inserts in Sunday newspapers contained vendor coupons, and consumers could receive premiums in exchange for proofs-of-purchase.

## Brand Development

Since its introduction in 1946, Prell has undergone many transformations. In 1985 Prell conditioner premiered. In May of 1986, a flip cap was used to crown the concentrate. In November of 1987 a "new and improved" Prell in an original, more modified package debuted. In March of 1991 Procter & Gamble introduced three new formulas, all with trace amounts of conditioner—balanced, for normal hair; extra body, for oily or fine hair; and moisture-replenishing, for dry or damaged hair. In 1991 Prell's green color was discontinued and replaced by a pearlescent shade. Later that year, the liquid green variety was discontinued, but the concentrate was retained. April of 1992 saw the reintroduction of original green Prell in a normal to oily formula. In 1993 Prell concentrate in a tube (with no conditioning agents) and Prell liquid were available.

## Future Predictions

Over the years, Prell shampoo has prevailed in the marketplace because of its unique characteristics. In the late 1980s and early 1990s, when shampoo and conditioner in one gained popularity, the Prell brand did lose some sales. Procter & Gamble chemists and marketers ensured the success of the brand by querying consumers, sampling and advertising, creating new technologies, and by updating Prell concentrate—improving, but not deviating from, the basic formula. As a Procter & Gamble scientist once observed: "It isn't enough to invent a new product. Through constant improvement, we must manage every existing brand so that it can flourish year after year in an ever-changing, intensely competitive marketplace. . . . At P&G, we create the future."

## Further Reading:

"Answers About Marketing," Cincinnati: The Procter & Gamble Company, 1993.

Cleary, David Powers, *Great American Brands,* New York: Fairchild Publications, 1981.

*Facts About Procter & Gamble,* Cincinnati: The Procter & Gamble Company, 1993.

Liesse, Julie, "Brand Scorecard," *Advertising Age,* April 19, 1993, p. 22.

Manly, Lorne, "P&G Says Bag This: Sunday Newspapers Will Deliver Shampoo Samples," *Mediaweek,* July 22, 1991, p. 1.

McMath, Robert, "New Shapes Are Turning Heads in the Shampoo Aisle," *Brandweek,* January 18, 1993, p. 30.

*1992 Annual Report,* Cincinnati: The Procter & Gamble Company, 1993.

*The Procter & Gamble Company* and *Procter & Gamble and Prices,* Cincinnati: The Procter & Gamble Company, 1993.

*Procter & Gamble: The House That Ivory Built,* Lincolnwood, IL: NTC Business Books, 1988.

Schisgall, Oscar, *Eyes on Tomorrow: The Evolution of Procter & Gamble,* Chicago: J. G. Ferguson Publishing Company, 1981.

*—Virginia Barnstorff*

# PUFFS®

Procter & Gamble's Puffs was the second best-selling brand of facial tissues in the United States in 1991, commanding a 20 percent share of the market. Facial tissues were considered a staple of American daily life. In fact, many industry insiders claimed that tissues were recession-resistant because even during an economic downturn sales did not fall noticeably.

The Puffs brand of facial tissues represented a full line of products that encompassed a wide variety of choices and preferences for consumers of different income levels, tastes, and interests. There was a Puffs product that focused on each quality that consumers identified as desirable in a facial tissue.

Softness was a key feature considered in the purchase of facial tissues, and Puffs products were manufactured in varying degrees of softness. The premium line extensions, like Puffs Extra Soft, were marketed as being particularly soft, while other Puffs products incorporated consumers' needs for attractive, convenient boxes.

In addition, according to *Consumer Reports* consumers wanted facial tissues to have "wet strength," or remain intact despite getting wet from a runny nose, and to be "sneeze-resistant," or strong enough to withstand the violence of a strong sneeze. Puffs products were developed to respond to both of these consumer needs with increased absorbency and strength.

### Brand Origins and Changes

Procter & Gamble Company came into existence in 1837 through the merger of candlemaking and soapmaking businesses. The company's initial product, Ivory soap, became one of the first brands advertised directly to consumers and began a long history of marketing success for the company. Procter and Gamble grew quickly to become the largest producer of packaged goods in United States. In 1991 the company marketed over 160 products worldwide.

Procter & Gamble first introduced the Puffs brand of facial tissues in 1960. Although Kimberly-Clark controlled the market with its Kleenex brand, Puffs was marketed as a luxury tissue and captured some market share. In addition, Procter & Gamble used a heavy discounting and couponing strategy during the introduction of the brand to induce more price-conscious consumers to try it, with the hope that they would appreciate its softness and continue

to purchase it. During the 1970s, Procter & Gamble introduced Posh Puffs, which was packaged in designer boxes, and later added Puffs Ultra Soft. In the late 1980s and early 1990s the Puffs brand was extended further to include three new varieties: Puffs Plus with Aloe, Puffs Extra Strength, and Puffs-to-Go.

Puffs Plus with Aloe was a revolutionary idea in the making of facial tissues. The aloe lotion was incorporated into the tissue as a moisturizer and created a very soft tissue without adding a scent. In addition, it helped soothe and heal sore noses. Kimberly-Clark soon imitated the idea of a lotion-added tissue by introducing Kleenex Ultra in 1990.

### Marketing Strategy

Puffs products were marketed both to affluent consumers interested in a premium facial tissue and to price-conscious consumers. Prices for the Puffs line often varied by as much as 50 cents from the high end to the low end. As the price increased, the consumer received a more absorbent and/or stronger facial tissue.

Puffs facial tissues were offered in packages that brought convenience as well as appealing designs to consumers. The boxes were color-coded to match the color of the tissues so that they could blend in with the decor of a bathroom or kitchen. All Puffs

## AT A GLANCE

**P**uffs brand facial tissue introduced in 1960 by Procter & Gamble Company; later brand extensions include Posh Puffs, Puffs Ultra Soft, Puffs Plus with Aloe, Puffs Extra Strength, and Puffs-to-Go.

**Performance:** *Market share*—20% (second place) of U.S. facial tissue category. *Sales*—$204.3 million (U.S., 1991).

**Major competitor:** Kimberly-Clark's Kleenex.

**Advertising:** *Agency*—N.W. Ayer, New York, NY, 1983—. *Major campaign*—Puffs Plus provide "First Aid for Sore Noses."

**Addresses:** *Parent company*—Procter & Gamble Company, One Procter & Gamble Plaza, Cincinnati, OH 45202-3315; phone: (513) 983-1100; fax: (513) 983-7847.

products were available in cube or family-size boxes except Puffs-to-Go. This product was intended for away-from-home use and was marketed in a resealable package that held 12 full-size sheets. The compact package fit easily into a pocket, handbag, or glove compartment of a car.

The number of tissues included in a box differed depending on the product as well as the size and shape of the box. For example, Puffs Plus with Aloe contained 144 2-ply tissues. The box differentiated this product from other Puffs products with a banner saying ''with soothing lotion,'' and with a green aloe plant on which yellow letters read ''with aloe.'' Posh Puffs contained 100 tissues in a cube-shaped dispenser box where tissues popped up because they were interfolded. Puffs Family Pack was a larger-size box that contained 250 tissues.

Advertising for Puffs facial tissues focused primarily on their softness. When Procter & Gamble introduced three new Puffs varieties, print ads depicted the Statue of Liberty holding a tissue to her nose. The tag line was, ''New York Is Getting Soft.'' Puffs and Puffs Plus were introduced as America's softest tissue and the two boxes were shown in the picture. Puffs Plus with Aloe was promoted as extra-soft and extra kind to noses, providing ''first aid to sore noses.''

## Performance Appraisal

Sales for facial tissues in the U.S. were about $1 billion each year, and the Puffs brand had an estimated 20 percent market share compared to 50 percent held by the Kleenex brand. A study by *Consumer Reports* in 1989 determined that Puffs Plus was the softest tissue among some 30 brands tested. An estimated 80 to 90 percent of the facial tissue industry was dominated by three major brands, Puffs ranking second among them. With the potential for sales so high, it was expected that Procter & Gamble would continue to develop products that effectively competed with the other market leaders.

One type of change that was predicted to occur was in packaging, in order for the company to appear to be an environmentally friendly manufacturer. Surveys suggested that some consumers were making buying decisions based upon their perception of the company's environmental responsibility. If a company was viewed as a polluter, which meant that their manufacturing process added too many hazardous materials to the waste stream and contributed to overflowing landfills, consumers turned away from buying that company's products. Procter & Gamble addressed these concerns by manufacturing their Puff's boxes from recycled materials.

## Further Reading:

''Facial Tissues,'' *Consumer Reports,* December, 1989, pp. 39–41.

Freeman, Laurie, and Judann Dagnoli, ''Green Concerns Influence Buying,'' *Advertising Age,* July 20, 1990, p. 30.

''Kleenex Gets Ultra Version,'' *Advertising Age,* November 26, 1990, p. 4.

''Markets Turn 'Squeezably' Soft in Recession,'' *Pulp & Paper,* July 1991, pp. 35–37.

''P&G Thumbs Nose (Achoo!) at No. 1 Kleenex,'' *Adweek Marketing Week,* February 13, 1989, p. 38.

*—Dorothy Kroll*

# Q-TIPS®

An observation made at home led to the invention of a machine that could wrap cotton on a stock to produce cotton swabs. First called Baby Gays, Q-tips Cotton Swabs became the largest selling brand of cotton swabs in the world as well as the largest selling baby product. Although they originally developed as a baby care product, consumers soon discovered the usefulness of the swabs for numerous personal care, household, and hobby applications. Today the Chesebrough-Pond's USA brand is a staple of many households in America.

After a visit to the United States, Polish-born Leo Gerstenzang decided he wanted to become a U.S. citizen. He served in the U.S. Army during World War I and became associated with the fledgling Red Cross Organization. Ex-President Herbert Hoover tapped Gerstenzang's knowledge of Europe and languages, asking him to assist in the Relief Administration's rehabilitation activities. Gerstenzang also worked with other war rehabilitation agencies and briefly entered into the banking business before returning to the United States in 1922. There he founded the Leo Gerstenzang Infant Novelty Co., which sold accessories essential to baby care.

A year later, as Gerstenzang watched his wife care for their baby daughter during her daily bath, an idea sparked. He saw Mrs. Gerstenzang put a wad of cotton on a toothpick to use as an applicator. "The Fascinating Story of Q-tips Brand Products," a corporate account of the brand's beginnings, notes that because Gerstenzang was "mechanically minded and a man who loved to 'make things,' he conceived the idea of manufacturing a ready-to-use cotton swab by automatic machine."

Gerstenzang experimented and researched several years before he had a fully functional machine that could take a stick of carefully selected and cured nonsplintering birchwood with blunt ends and wrap cotton uniformly at each end. The machine packaged the swabs in a sliding tray type of box that enabled the consumer to open the box and extract a single swab with one hand and, in a further step, sterilized and sealed the boxes with an outer wrapping of glassine (later cellophane). According to "The Fascinating Story," "The entire operation was accomplished entirely by machine, so that the phrase 'untouched by human hands' became widely known in the production of cotton swabs from manufacturing to packaging."

Gerstenzang's company introduced the cotton swab applicators in 1925, calling them Baby Gays after considering and discarding several names. In 1926 the name became Q-Tips Baby Gays. Eventually the company removed Baby Gays from the product name and Q-Tips became the identifying mark for its brand of cotton swabs. The brand name became a perfect tie-in to the slogans "Q for Quality" and "a swab by any other name is not the same." The Leo Gerstenzang Infant Novelty Co. subsequently became Q-Tips, Inc.

## Just the Thing

Q-tips proved to be a popular product and sales increased steadily. The product was the only cotton swab on the market until 1941 and it remained the leader in the category into the 1990s, with more than a 60 percent market share. Perhaps much of that success is attributable to the versatility of the applicators. They were, as a slogan said, "Just the thing."

As when the product was first introduced, a primary use for Q-tips Cotton Swabs was for baby care. Parents could clean their infant's ears, nose, and mouth, oil their tender skin, and apply baby lotions. "The safe swab" slogan reinforced the idea that Q-tips were safe to use on children.

However, consumers found hundreds of other uses for the little swabs. Hobbyists and others used them in the workshop to apply liquid cement or glue to small, hard-to-reach places, to oil tools and machine parts, to clean fishing reels and firearms, to touch up furniture, and to color portraits by applying paint with one end of a swab and blending in color with the other end. The swabs also became essential in first aid treatment, as beauty and grooming aids, and in pet care.

## Product Improvement

Q-Tips, Inc., significantly expanded its manufacturing operations over the years. It formed Q-Tips S.A. in Paris in 1946 and Q-Tips (Canada) Ltd. shortly afterward. In 1958 Q-Tips, Inc., acquired a company that manufactured paper sticks for the confectionery trade, Papersticks Ltd. of England. Q-Tips brought the Papersticks machinery to the United States and adapted it to manufacture paper stick swabs. The innovation made Q-tips Cotton Swabs available in biodegradable paper and wood sticks. (The brand's competing Johnson & Johnson swabs have plastic sticks.)

Chesebrough-Pond's added Q-tips to its product line in 1962 and more than doubled its profits from the line in the first two

## AT A GLANCE

**Q**-tips brand of cotton swabs (originally known as Baby Gays) founded in 1925 by Leo Gerstenzang; Leo Gerstenzang Infant Novelty Co. subsequently became Q-Tips, Inc.; name of swabs changed to Q-tips Baby Gays, 1926; Q-tips became registered trademark; brand sold to Chesebrough-Pond's, 1962; Chesebrough-Pond's acquired by Unilever in 1986.

**Performance:** *Market share*—65% of cotton swabs category.

**Major competitor:** Johnson & Johnson swabs.

**Advertising:** *Agency*—J. Walter Thompson, New York, NY, 1992—present. *Major campaign*—50% More Cotton At The Tip Than Any Other Swab.

**Addresses:** *Parent company*—Chesebrough-Pond's USA, 33 Benedict Place, Greenwich, CT 06830-6000; phone: (203) 661-2000; fax: (203) 625-1602. *Ultimate parent company*—Lever Brothers, 390 Park Ave., New York, NY 10022; phone: (212) 688-6000; fax: (212) 906-4416. *Ultimate ultimate parent company*—Unilever PLC, P.O. Box 68, Unilever House, Blackfriars, London EC4P 4BQ United Kingdom; phone: (071) 822-5252; fax: (071) 822-5898. Unilever N.V., P.O. Box 760, 3000 DK Rotterdam, Netherlands; phone: (10) 464-5911; fax: (10) 217-4798.

years of ownership. The company introduced Q-tips Cotton Balls in 1970, which could clean a greater surface area and had hundreds of household uses, and added Q-tips Cosmetic Applicators in 1984 and Q-tips Manicure Sticks in 1987.

### Brand Outlook

Chesebrough-Pond's USA, a manufacturer and marketer of personal products, derives from the company founded by Robert A. Chesebrough, a chemist who developed a method to refine the rod wax obtained during petroleum drilling to make petroleum jelly. Chesebrough sold Vaseline from a truck until the product's popularity grew so much he incorporated his company in 1880. A year later Standard Oil, Chesebrough's supplier for petroleum, bought the company. When the Standard Oil Trust was dissolved

in 1911, Chesebrough became an independent company again. The merger with Pond's occurred in 1955, and Chesebrough-Pond's became part of the Lever Brothers operating unit of Unilever in 1986, one of the world's leading manufacturers of consumer branded products and packaged goods.

During the early 1990s, Chesebrough-Pond's sought to strengthen its presence in the beauty industry by innovating and renovating its brands and giving them more marketing attention. Q-tips received its first major product improvement in more than 20 years. While the packaging kept its blue and white color scheme, the new contemporary graphics included a special logo reading "50% More Cotton At The Tip Than Any Other Swab" (the brand's exclusive product claim) and more stylish lettering and fine, light-blue pinstripes. The new package became available nationwide in April 1993. The brand re-launched with its first advertising since 1989 in various family magazines and with a special promotion.

The interest by Chesebrough-Pond's USA in repositioning Q-tips should only further secure and enhance the brand's already comfortable position in its category.

### Further Reading:

"Classic Q-tips Package Gets a New Look; New Ad Campaign to Launch This Summer," Chesebrough-Pond's USA, press release, 1993.

"The Fascinating Story of Q-tips Brand Products," Chesebrough-Pond's USA, n.d.

McGrath, Molly Wade, *Top Sellers, U.S.A.; Success Stories Behind America's Best-Selling Products From Alka-Seltzer to Zippo,* New York: William Morrow and Company, Inc., 1983, pp. 53–54.

Moskowitz, Milton, Robert Levering, and Michael Katz, eds., *Everybody's Business: A Field Guide to the 400 Leading Companies in America,* New York: Doubleday, 1990, pp. 137–38.

Sharp, Harold S., *Advertising Slogans of America,* Metuchen, NJ: The Scarecrow Press, Inc., 1984, 384.

*The Story of Chesebrough Pond's Inc.,* Greenwich, CT: Chesebrough Pond's, 1965, p. 9.

Urdang, Laurance, and Ceila Dame Robbins, *Slogans,* Detroit: Gale Research, 1984, p. 348.

—*Doris Morris Maxfield*

# QUAKER STATE®

When Colonel Edwin L. Drake drilled the world's first oil well in 1859 in Titusville, Pennsylvania, he not only opened up a new industry that would forever impact civilization, he opened up the oil patch that held the world's choicest crude oil. Pennsylvania Grade became the standard by which all crude would be judged and the hallmark of an oil that used only 100 percent Pennsylvania Grade—Quaker State Motor Oil.

Colonel Drake's discovery led to much speculation. Oil businesses sprang up all along the famed Pennsylvania Grade Oil Field spanning New York, Ohio, Pennsylvania, and West Virginia. Activity was particularly intense near the Titusville site; dozens of companies formed or redirected their interest to become drillers, refiners, or marketers of oil. The early oilmen knew they had a fine oil from which to make products for lubricating steam engines, machinery and wagons, and for illuminating homes and shops, but it wasn't until the automobile entered production that they found a use for the byproduct that would become known as motor oil. Pennsylvania Grade proved to be excellent for lubricating engines. The grade had a paraffin base that was relatively free of sulfur, tar, asphalt and other impurities; had little affinity for chemical reaction or change, giving it greater stability; and had a high natural lubricity and viscosity index. Nearly one-third of Pennsylvania Grade crude oil could be converted to lubricating oil as opposed to three percent of oil from other fields.

Marketer T. G. Phinny was one of the oilmen who successfully built a business out of Pennsylvania Grade motor oil. He worked for the Phinny Brothers Oil Company located in Oil City, Pennsylvania, just sixteen miles from Titusville. Phinny originated the trade name "Quaker State" in 1912 to distinguish his motor oil from others. The Phinny Brothers Oil Company purchased their oil from the Eastern Refining Company, a subsidiary of both Emlenton Refining Company and Berry Co.

## Product Endorsements

In 1913, the Franklin Motor Car Company of Syracuse, New York, put out a call for help. The air-cooled Franklin engines ran extremely hot, and they needed an oil that could simultaneously cool and lubricate. Phinny responded to the call by sending samples of Quaker State Motor Oil to Franklin for testing. The motor oil solved the lubrication problems that had plagued Franklin cars since 1902 and worked so well that the company immediately advised all Franklin car owners to use Quaker State. In July of 1914, Franklin signed a contract with Phinny Brothers and Eastern Refining to guarantee a continuing supply of Quaker State Motor Oil for their cars. The company also began to equip each new car leaving the factory with a five-quart can of Quaker State Motor Oil fitted under the seat.

The Franklin endorsement was the beginning of the Quaker State quality image that became the keystone of the parent company's operations, advertising, and efforts to "refine and market the highest quality motor oils." The engineers of the Rolls Royce and Willys car companies also endorsed Quaker State. Ten years after the Franklin endorsement, Eastern Refining Company acquired the Quaker State trade name from Phinny Brothers Oil Company and renamed itself the Quaker State Refining Company. The following year a separate Quaker State company was formed in California to service accounts on the West Coast. In 1931, Chicago stockbroker Charles Pape brought together nineteen companies and subsidiaries to form Quaker State Oil Refining Corporation. From a small marketing company, Quaker State grew into the largest independent refiner and marketer of Pennsylvania Grade motor oils.

## Demand for Quality

The word quickly spread about the quality of Quaker State Motor Oil and its ability to adequately lubricate an engine's vital working parts. In 1936, Standard Oil of Indiana (now Amoco) signed a contract to become Quaker State's exclusive sales agent in thirteen midwestern states. The company later distributed the brand nationwide through its stations.

Because of its superior quality, Quaker State was very nearly the only motor oil specified for the military at the beginning of World War II. However, the company lacked the capacity to meet the needs of the military and its regular Quaker State customers. The great wartime pressures to increase supplies led Quaker State to buy Forest Oil Company's crude oil properties; thus, the company expanded from manufacturing, compounding, and distribution of refined and semi-refined petroleum products into drilling and production. For a time, Quaker State supplied as much as 24 percent of its crude oil needs. Later, Quaker State Corporation would diversify into non-motor oil product lines, too.

The brand's quality was unquestioned, the Quaker State had a research program in place that was developing and using additives

## AT A GLANCE

**Q**uaker State brand of motor oil founded in 1912 by T. G. Phinny of the Phinny Brothers Oil Company; brand sold to Eastern Refining Company, 1924; Eastern Refining Company changed name to Quaker State Oil Refining Corporation, 1925.

**Performance:** *Market share*—13% of motor oil category. *Sales*—$327.9 million (lubricants).

**Major competitor:** Pennzoil; also Valvoline.

**Advertising:** *Agency*—Grey Advertising, New York, NY, 1986—. *Major campaign*—"High tech, high quality, high performance."

**Addresses:** *Parent company*—Quaker State Corporation, Oil Marketing and Refining Division, P.O. Box 989, Oil City, PA 16301; phone: (814) 675-7676; fax: (814) 676-7030.

to make improved and special blends. The first improved product, created in 1940, increased chemical stability and was called "Stabilized Quaker State Motor Oil." In 1941, the company introduced Quaker State HD, a high detergency oil. By 1954, Quaker State motor oils contained a combination of antiwear, antirust, anticorrosive, and high detergency properties. The company introduced Quaker State DeLuxe Motor Oil in 1961.

A daring decision made by management in the mid-1950s to market motor oil in all mass merchandise and discount stores, while retaining the garage mechanics, automobile dealers, and service stations that had sold and used Quaker State products for decades, resulted in increased sales and the need for extra capacity. Quaker State sales increased eight-fold after thirty years to hover around $50 million annually in the 1960s. Sales climbed 150 percent in the decade and reached $120 million in 1970. In the early 1970s, the company built a refinery that provided an additional twelve thousand barrels per day capacity, a company-wide increase of 75 percent, to meet the rapidly increasing demand. It also increased capacity through the purchase of motor oil blending and packaging plants. Sales volume approached $300 million by 1975 and have since exceeded $1 billion. Although Quaker State was the market leader in motor oil between 1978 and 1988, its market share was becoming vulnerable. During this period, Americans started to drive smaller, hotter-running automobiles. While Quaker State continued to make a fine motor oil for all cars, the competition perceived a need on the part of the public for a motor oil for smaller cars and started marketing their quality oil and high-tech additives.

When Quaker State eventually responded to the changing market with new products, it found it difficult to compete with the other industry giants that were spending heavily on packaging and advertising, offering rebates to retailers and consumers, and slashing prices. The price wars of the late 1980s and early 1990s cut into Quaker State's operating profits and market share. Its financial position improved when motor oil prices increased 18 percent after Saddam Hussein invaded Kuwait in 1991. Even though retail customers balked at the price when it went over one dollar per quart, the company held firm and profits rose to ten times what they were at the height of price cutting in 1988. By the next year, however, competitor Pennzoil and other vendors cut motor oil prices again, dashing Quaker State's chance to regain the number one market share position.

## Advertising and Marketing

Since Phinny Brothers and Eastern Refining extended marketing nationwide by placing the first national advertisement in the March 15, 1915 issue of the *Saturday Evening Post,* quality has been the key theme in Quaker State marketing efforts. In his address to The Newcomen Society, Quentin Woods repeated the text of that first ad which highlighted the association with Franklin, "Quaker State is *certified* and *guaranteed* to be the highest quality oil suitable for every engine purpose. It prolongs the life of the motor. Will not burn before lubricating. Gives practically double mileage. Prevents engine overheating. Cuts oil bills." The ad also made the research claim, "Latest test—100 miles, nonstop, on low gear, throughout the U.S."

A decade later, an ad (perhaps inspired by the five-quart container in every Franklin car) claimed Quaker State's purity "actually adds an extra quart of lubricant to every gallon of Quaker State Medium." By the 1940s, ads advised drivers to "Quaker State your car." In the mid-1950s, a Quaker State ad pictured the product's purity in an illustration of a woman holding a champagne glass filled with motor oil. The copy read: "Our picture is purest fantasy. We do not suggest that you drink Quaker State. But it is definitely one of the finer things of life—for your car."

Quaker State has used the following tag lines over the years: "Engine life preserver"; "An extra quart of lubrication in every gallon"; "The first choice of experience"; "It's a lucky day for your car when you change to Quaker State Motor Oil"; "Trust your car to the oil of character"; "We put it in writing; No one else does"; and, "You need an oil this good." In 1993 the company discontinued "the tough motor oil" campaign, which used actor Burt Reynolds as spokesperson. The new slogan "High tech, high quality, high performance" complemented the use of the brand as the hero. Besides advertisements and commercials, Quaker State promoted its motor oil by sponsoring a stock car running in the NASCAR racing circuit and by supporting NHRA and Indy 500 race teams.

In 1984, Quaker State introduced a marketing innovation when it decided to package all retail motor oil in plastic, easy-pour, no-drip bottles. The move helped Quaker State's 10W-40 grade motor oil become the best selling automotive product marketed in stores like Kmart and Woolco; for products of all types, it was second only to a name-brand paper towel. Eighteen months after Quaker State introduced its round plastic cans, it lost shelf space when Pennzoil came out with a square container that retailers and gas stations could fit easier on their crowded shelves. Quaker State retained the round bottles, but switched the color from yellow to green in 1993 to make them more distinguishable from the competition.

Quaker State capitalized on its brand name recognition with many different products. It produced Quaker State Sterling, DeLuxe, Super Blend, HD, and H.D.X. motor oils; Quaker State Dexron II, F-L-M transmission fluids; Quaker State High Performance, Super Quad, and Quadrolube gear oils; Quaker State greases; Quaker State antifreeze; Quaker State brake fluid; Quaker State silicone oil; Quaker State racing oil; and Quaker State 2-Cycle oil and 4-Cycle oil. Quaker State began to change the name of its franchised quick-change oil and lube shops from Minit-Lube to QLube in 1991 to increase visibility of the brand name.

## Brand Outlook

Despite stiff competition within a market that is sensitive to fluctuations in crude prices, Quaker State Motor Oil has maintained a competitive advantage. That edge in the lubricant business is its position as one of the nation's most recognized brand names in the automotive aftermarket. Over the years, Quaker State availed itself of opportunities to leverage its brand name into a growing number of products and services, without compromising its high quality standards. This focus on quality is expected to contribute to the future success of Quaker State Motor Oil in both domestic and international markets.

## Further Reading:

Dubashi, Jagannath, "Quaker State: Oh What a Lovely War!" *Financial World,* March 31, 1992, p. 17.

Hannon, Kerry, "Run Over by the Competition," *Forbes,* September 5, 1988, p. 80.

Marcial, Gene G., "Two Suitors Are Tailgating Quaker State," *Business Week,* December 17, 1990, p. 50.

Palmer, Jay, "Aroused Quaker; A Drive to Turn Around Earnings Hits Pay Dirt," *Barron's,* June 8, 1992, pp. 15–18.

Rosow, Jerome M., *Made in America,* New York: Facts On File, Inc., 1984, p. 214.

Sharp, Harold S., *Advertising Slogans of America,* Metuchen, NJ: The Scarecrow Press, Inc., 1984, p. 384.

"The Story of Quaker State," Quaker State Oil Refining Corporation.

Urdang, Laurance, and Ceila Dame Robbins, *Slogans,* Detroit: Gale Research Company, 1984, pp. 267, 269.

Wood, Quentin E., "Quaker State Roots Go Deep into the World's First Oilfield," address presented at 1986 Lake Erie Meeting of The Newcomen Society of the United States, Erie, PA.

*—Doris Morris Maxfield*

# RAID®

The Raid brand has long dominated the insecticide market. S.C. Johnson & Son, Inc. (commonly known as S.C. Johnson Wax) introduced Raid House & Garden Bug Killer on the *Red Skelton* show in 1956 as the first insecticide consumers could use indoors. This innovative new bug killer—featuring a water-based formula which neither smelled up the house nor hurt household plants—was the result of nine months spent in the laboratory by new employee Samuel C. Johnson (great-grandson of the founder) and the recently established New Products Department he headed. S.C. Johnson & Son continued this commitment to innovation through its Raid Center for Insect Control—the world's largest entomological research facility. This research allowed the company to produce many effective and competitive Raid line extensions, and these product innovations help explain how the company managed to remain competitive and to increase and protect the market share of its Raid brand. Indeed, because the company consistently innovated its insecticides and gave them focused and hefty advertising support, always insisting that every new Raid product "kills bugs dead," Raid became Johnson Wax's best-selling line of products—and that is something for a company whose name has been virtually synonymous with floor and furniture wax ever since its inception in 1886.

## Innovating Raid to Diversify beyond Wax

Until S.C. Johnson & Son introduced Raid in 1956, the company had been devoted exclusively to parquet flooring and floor and furniture wax. It was Samuel C. Johnson, having recently completed his chemistry studies at Cornell and having attended Harvard Business School, who urged his father, the company president, to diversify. The young Johnson, who 12 years later was to become the fourth-generation Johnson to run the company, contributed to this new commitment to diversification soon after joining the company in 1954 as an aide to his father. When the New Products Department was created in 1955, Sam Johnson became its first director. He focused on developing an insect spray as the company's first non-wax product, despite the fact that his father voiced definite resistance to diversifying beyond the company's traditional product lines. S. C. Johnson & Son, like some other family-owned, family-run businesses, was resistant to change because of the family's deep-seated values and each generation's long tenure of leadership. However, with Raid S.C. Johnson & Son dramatically departed from a 70-year family tradition of wax.

But even though the young and less-traditional Johnson had the business sense to diversify, his father had the business experience to check his son's enthusiasm by requiring that any diversification be an innovation. When Samuel Johnson's first attempt produced an insecticide that was effectively no different from those currently on the market, the elder Johnson refused to manufacture the prototype and insisted that he return to the lab. Nine months later, Samuel Johnson, with the help of his chemists, innovated a water-based solution which, unlike the competing products of the time, was friendly to the home environment, neither giving off a noxious odor nor harming household plants. The product was Raid House & Garden Bug Killer, and it contained—as do many other Raid products still on the market—natural active ingredients called pyrethrins, drawn from Chrysanthemum flowers. Pyrethrins are thus natural and biodegradable, features which continued to make it a good selling point among the more environmentally conscious consumers and regulators of the 1980s and 1990s. "Pyrethrins are unlike many synthetic compounds," stated Dr. Keith Kennedy of the Raid Center for Insect Control in the *U.S. Distribution Journal.* "They are among the safest insecticides known and they control many types of bug problems effectively without posing a threat to us or the environment."

## Keeping Up with the Unbeatable Bug World

Important to the success of the Raid brand was not only innovation but the basic fact that, as Samuel C. Johnson himself said in the *Business Journal of Milwaukee,* "The insecticide business is a growing business because the bugs of the world are winning." Johnson vice-president and general manager at the time, Beth Pritchard agreed with Johnson's view, acknowledging in the same article that "bugs continue to outstrip our ability to kill them. Not only that, but there are always new infestations that are cropping up." In other words, as long as insects continued to develop resistance quickly to new insecticides, Johnson Wax could always count on a worldwide market for the Raid brand—assuming the company could continue to innovate effective Raid products and convince consumers that Raid products were more effective than the competition.

To further urge innovation, Johnson Wax conducted research in its Raid Center for Insect Control, affectionately known among entomologists as the Bug Farm. Johnson Wax valued this facility so much that it not only made this Bug Farm the world's largest, housing over 15 million creepy crawlers from more than 30 different species, but it also spent more on research and development at this facility than all its competitors combined. The work done by Raid scientists resulted in the production of more than 24 line extensions, including Raid Ant & Roach Killer, Raid Flea Killer Plus, Raid Roach Baits, Raid Fumigator, and Raid Roach & Flea Fogger.

With so many products to sell, Johnson Wax had to help consumers decide which products to buy and convince consumers that Raid brand specialized insecticides were better than the competition. For many years, this advertising challenge was not too difficult for Johnson Wax, which was content to let its longtime advertising firm—Foote, Cone & Belding (FCB) of Chicago—continue to use the same successful keys to its worldwide marketing strategy that it had been pushing since the Raid brand's inception: the Raid name was easy to remember; the Raid slogan, "kills bugs dead," was equally memorable; and the familiar animated bugs from Raid commercials were the result of the "strategic concept that says a light-hearted treatment of a serious problem can be an effective way of selling an insecticide," as Carl Behr, FCB worldwide account director, explained in *Marketing & Media Decisions.* Despite the long-term success of this marketing strategy, Johnson Wax significantly modified its approach in the late-1980s in response to two main factors: a new and formidable competitor and the rise of the environmentally conscious consumer.

### Combating Combat

In 1985 American Cyanamid's Shulton Inc. subsidiary introduced cockroach baits called Combat into the home insecticide market. These baits were unusual because their poisoned food killed roaches slowly enough to allow them to carry the food back to the nest to poison the other roaches. By 1989 the Combat brand had more than a 20 percent market share, while the Raid brand's market share had dropped from an estimated 55 percent to about 40 percent. And in 1991 when American Cyanamid sold the Combat brand to the Clorox Company, a company with more advertising muscle, Raid received even greater competitive pressure. According to industry analysts cited in *Advertising Age,* Combat baits caught Johnson Wax by surprise. Julia Hodge, a consultant with Kline & Co., observed that the makers of Combat

"hit the timing perfectly. People perceive bait trays as being safer, and Combat trays went like gangbusters." Johnson Wax's first response to Combat—and it was a long-expected response—came in 1987 when it introduced its Combat-style Raid Roach Controller.

In addition to directly combating Combat with similar roach baits, Johnson Wax took several other approaches to protect its market share which marked a shift away from its consistent marketing strategies of the past. Unwilling to phase out its roach sprays, Johnson Wax decided to take advantage of the fact that many consumers felt more assured when they saw their insecticide take immediate action and kill the offending bugs before their very eyes. The Combat-style baits worked without any immediate demonstration. Instead, consumers only knew the baits had worked when they no longer saw roaches. In 1988's response to the competitive pressure from Combat, Johnson Wax adopted two new strategies. One strategy was to introduce a new formula for Raid roach spray which more dramatically killed roaches so that the consumer would develop even more confidence in the effectiveness of the spray. This new formula attacked the central nervous system, causing roaches to race around in circles before dying. Johnson Wax's other new strategy was to introduce a multimillion-dollar ad campaign which for the first time in the history of the Raid brand vividly demonstrated the spray's effectiveness by showing it kill actual living bugs dead rather than the more benign and amusing animated "insectus deadicus."

Exerting its incredible advertising might in the face of the competition offered by Combat, Johnson Wax spent over $16 million that year (up 23 percent) to promote its Raid products, especially its sprays. All this despite the fact that sprays clearly were not the most effective method of attacking insect problems. For every roach consumers saw and happened to spray, there were an estimated 500 hiding in their walls. The ABC News television show *20/20* did a story in 1990 on how the desire of consumers "to see roaches die now" allowed the Raid spray products to enjoy continued success despite the fact that "every expert *[20/20]* spoke to said if you want to kill roaches, what works best is bait" for long-term control. Johnson Wax realized baits were more effective, but the company banked its advertising on the idea that sprays would be more popular because of their visible results.

Besides shifting from animated to live bugs, Johnson Wax further altered its traditional marketing strategy (as part of its effort to counter the growing success of the Combat brand and to respond to the perceived demand for more effective insecticides) by introducing an extra-strength line extension called Raid Max. Raid Max changed the long-standing slogan from "kills bugs dead" to "when Raid Max attacks, you win." However, since Johnson Wax kept the "kills bugs dead" slogan for the standard Raid line while at the same time selling Raid Max as a more effective option, the veracity of the slogan was implicitly called into question. As one industry executive cynically asked in *Advertising Age,* "If Raid kills bugs dead, then what does Raid Max do?"

In order to overcome such questions about the need for this new, premium-priced "ultimate solution," Johnson Wax launched Raid Max in 1989 with a $10 million ad campaign. This campaign included print ads in women's and home magazines for the Raid Max Roach Killer which continued the company's move away from cartoon crawlers by providing vivid visual support for its new TV claim that Raid Max Roach Killer could kill 300 roaches in a matter of just 10 seconds. To convince retailers that these extra-strength products would sell, Johnson Wax assured them that the Raid Max products were so powerful that consumers would turn to Raid Max rather than professional exterminators. But with the deployment of such strong chemicals came concern about their impact on public health and the environment.

## It's Not Easy Going Green

Some of the Raid Max products were involved when Johnson Wax was fined $300,000 by the New York State Department of Environmental Conservation (DEC) for violating state pesticide laws in 1990. The company agreed to the fine and admitted that it had failed to wait for the required product approvals—though it did apply for registration—from the state's DEC before distributing seven pesticide products over a three-year period. These products included Raid Max Ant Bait and Raid Max Roach Bait, which were the two of the seven products which Johnson Wax agreed to recall statewide.

Though such violations of environmental law were rare for the Raid line, Johnson Wax still felt pressure from other sources to allay consumer fears about the chemicals in Raid. For instance, a family in California filed a lawsuit against Johnson Wax in 1988 claiming that three years earlier their then four-year-old son suffered burns over 80 percent of his body because the canister of Raid Professional Strength Ant & Roach Killer which he sprayed over a fire (and leaked on himself) caused the fire to engulf his body. In 1990 one man gained publicity when he claimed that his family had become ill from the combination of his DuPont Stainmaster carpet and a Raid insecticide. Although Johnson Wax denied responsibility in these cases, the publicity could only have worsened public concerns about the chemicals in Raid. Johnson Wax, like so many companies during the late-1980s, needed to demonstrate to health-minded consumers that it had become more responsive to their interests.

Actually, some Raid products had been friendly to the environment for a long time. Indeed, the very first Raid product—Raid House & Garden Bug Killer—contained safe and natural ingredients called pyrethrins. This fact may not have meant much to consumers in 1956, but it did to environmentally conscious consumers in the early-1990s; and consequently, Johnson Wax called new attention in 1991 to pyrethrins to promote two new products—Raid Liquid Roach & Ant Killer and Raid Multi-Bug Killer. These two products also featured adjustable triggers designed to allay fears about the health risks in handling insecticide canisters (the triggers allowed the handler greater directional control when spraying).

To industry observers, seeing such efforts from Johnson Wax was not at all surprising. Indeed, Samuel C. Johnson, who ran the company from 1965 to 1988, was referred to by *Fortune* as "corporate America's leading environmentalist." In the mid-1970s, when it was first reported that chlorofluorocarbons (CFCs), which are found in aerosol sprays, might deplete the earth's ozone layer, Sam Johnson took the report seriously and stated as much in *Fortune:* "There was no pressure on us, and we couldn't prove that CFCs were hurting the ozone layer, but based on the concern of our customers, I banned CFCs from all our products worldwide." This was a ban Sam Johnson enforced three years before the United States banned CFCs in all aerosols. Although this early ban cost the company several million dollars, Johnson continued to hold his company to strict environmental standards, setting ambitious goals for limiting the use of toxic chemicals, reducing excess in packaging, and using recycled materials.

However, for all the steps the company took to make Raid insecticides more friendly to the environment, many consumers still held negative perceptions of the products. For instance, even though Johnson banned CFCs in 1975, research revealed that consumers in 1991 still believed that Raid sprays were harmful to the ozone layer. In response to such beliefs, Johnson Wax began making a concerted effort in TV spots and in product labeling to correct misperceptions consumers had about the environmental effects of Raid. As Cynthia Georgeson, environmental communications manager for Johnson Wax, explained in *Advertising Age,* "We realized we'd been too quiet for too long on the subject, and it was time to . . . explain to consumers that we aren't using CFCs—along with other environmental initiatives we've taken on." And so, besides protecting the Raid brand's market share from such competitors as Combat, Johnson Wax's toughest challenge for the continued success of Raid—a line of products which must depend on chemicals to kill bugs dead—was the challenge of convincing consumers that Raid harmed only insects.

## Further Reading:

Brown, Kevin, "National Ad Spending by Category," *Advertising Age,* September 27, 1989, p. 8.

Brown, Kevin and Kristine Stevens, "From Past Issues of Advertising Age; 30 Years Ago—1956," *Advertising Age,* May 26, 1986, p. 68.

*A Century of Progress,* Racine, WI: S.C. Johnson & Son, Inc., 1986.

"Creative Advertising from around the World," *Advertising Age,* May 22, 1989, p. 45.

Debenport, Ellen, "Household Hazard or Myth? Chemicals in Carpet, Home Blamed for Range of Illnesses," *St. Petersburg Times,* March 4, 1990, city edition, p. 1A.

Doden, Daniel L., "Selecting a Brand Name that Aids Marketing Objective," *Advertising Age,* November 5, 1990, p. 34.

"Everybody Hates Me," *20/20* television show, ABC News, November 9, 1990.

Fitzgerald, Kate, "S.C. Johnson Aims at 'Misperceptions,' " *Advertising Age,* July 8, 1991, p. 16.

Freeman, Laurie, "FCB Reaps Windfall from Johnson Wax," *Advertising Age,* May 15, 1989, p. 69.

Freeman, Laurie, "Johnson Takes Raid to the Max," *Advertising Age,* March 6, 1989, p. 41.

Freeman, Laurie, "Johnson To Battle Roaches, Combat," *Advertising Age,* December 15, 1986, p. 78.

Freeman, Laurie and Patricia Winters, "Extra! Extra! Read All about It; Marketers Embrace New, Improved Claim," *Advertising Age,* May 22, 1989, p. 12.

Glionna, John, "It's Been 6 Years since a Devastating Fire Scorched 80% of Jimmy Nute's Body. Now, He's Trying To Be a Kid Again; Learning To Live," *Los Angeles Times,* November 14, 1991.

Huth, Jane E., "Insecticides for Household Use Challenge Industry To Develop Safer, More Effective Products while Satisfying Heavy Government Requirements," *Soap, Cosmetics, Chemical Specialties 63,* November, 1987, p. 28.

Jereski, Laura Konrad, "Foote, Cone Lets the Client Lead," *Marketing & Media Decisions 19,* December, 1984, p. 54.

Levin, Gary, "Hot Raisins and More; FCB Turns On Its Creative Brainpower," *Advertising Age,* July 6, 1987, p. 24.

"Makers of Raid Fined for Violations of Pesticide Laws," *United Press International,* May 21, 1990.

"Making Sense of the Insecticide Shelf," *PR Newswire,* May 2, 1991.

Nulty, Peter, "The National Business Hall of Fame," *Fortune,* April 5, 1993, p. 108.

Oneal, Michael, "Zap! Splat! It's War in the Business of Battling La Cucaracha," *Business Week,* May 16, 1988, p. 81.

"Raid Restages Insect Killers; Environmentally-Safe Insecticides," *U.S. Distribution Journal 218,* July 15, 1991, p. 69.

"S. C. Johnson & Son," *Advertising Age,* September 26, 1990, p. 88.

Slutsker, Gary, ed., "Adios, La Cucaracha," *Forbes,* September 21, 1987, p. 174.

Stoffels, Kenneth, "Beth Pritchard Sells a Little Corporate Wax and Has Fun," *Business Journal* (Milwaukee, WI), April 28, 1986.

"Stopping the Greasies," *Forbes,* July 9, 1979, p. 121.

"Top 100 Eke Out 2.7% Ad Increase," *Advertising Age,* September 4, 1986, p. 3.

*United Press International,* November 11, 1986.

Ward, John L. and Craig E. Aronoff, "Make Change Your Tradition; Family Businesses," *Nation's Business 78,* September, 1990, p. 46.

Witt, Linda, "Coat of Family Philosophy Keeps Johnson Shining," *Chicago Tribune,* November 18, 1985.

*—Jeffrey E. Mash*

# RAY-BAN®

Ray-Ban sunglasses carry one of the most widely recognized trademarks in the sunglass market: in the early 1990s, surveys indicated that about 80 percent of sunglass wearers in the United States, Europe, and Asia could identify the name. That recognition translated into unit and dollar volume sales greater than that of Ray-Ban's next four largest competitors combined. Once a practical solution for U.S. Air Force pilots, this accessory has become a much-copied status symbol with several lines of styles. The brand's original "Aviator" design has been an icon of American fashion and the best-selling sunglass model in history.

## Brand Origins

Ray-Bans were developed by the Bausch & Lomb Optical Company, which had been established in 1853 and became America's first producer of optical quality glass in the 1910s. In the 1920s, Bausch & Lomb, which later came to be known as Bausch & Lomb Incorporated, was asked by the U.S. Army Air Corps to create an optical quality glass to resist the harsh glare endured by fighter pilots. The bright sunlight often left airmen with severe headaches and nausea, and absorptive glass that had been developed up to that time distorted the pilots' vision.

Bausch & Lomb's scientists worked throughout the late 1920s and early 1930s to develop the green-tinted glass that exceeded the Army's specifications by not only cutting glare, but also inhibiting ultraviolet and infrared rays. The "Anti-Glare goggles" were introduced to the public in 1936. Some skeptics balked at the retail price of $3.75, which was extremely high when compared to the average 25-cent price of most other plastic-framed sunglasses on the market.

By 1937, Bausch & Lomb felt confident in the new product line, and took steps to shore up its burgeoning sunglass market. The company knew that Anti-Glare was not distinctive enough to be protected as a trademark, so they changed the name to the straightforward Ray-Ban. The brand name was registered in March of 1937 and first appeared in a magazine advertisement two months later.

The company introduced its "Aviator" style in 1937 and "Shooter" sunglasses the following year. Both styles offered metal frames, but consumers could now choose between two lenses: original Ray-Ban Green or Kalichrome, a bright yellow glass designed for hazy conditions.

First named "Skeet" glasses, the "Outdoorsman" model was introduced in 1938. Both the Outdoorsman and Shooter models offered impact resistant lenses. During this period, the optical-quality eyewear offered by Bausch & Lomb was purchased primarily by sportsmen and professionals whose jobs called for sharp vision and protection from the sun: commercial pilots, police, yachtsmen, hunters, and fishermen.

During World War II, Ray-Bans were part of the armed forces' standard government issue uniform. The sunglasses achieved fame when General Douglas MacArthur was photographed wearing his Aviators. Many soldiers returned from the front with the aviator or, as they were sometimes known, "MacArthur" sunglasses that had become a valued possession.

Bausch & Lomb's development of Ray-Ban sunglasses continued to be driven by the armed forces during the postwar period. Dark sunglasses were developed in the late 1940s to help pilots improve their night vision. Military doctors had discovered that fliers were losing visual purple, a chemical required for night vision. Bright sunlight bleached out the chemical, which the body replaced with time. Research demonstrated that wearing dark sunglasses improved dark adaptation by 40 to 50 percent. The dark lenses developed by Bausch & Lomb were introduced in 1951. They had an absorption level of 85 percent and were significantly darker than the standard green and yellow sunglasses of the period. Although Bausch & Lomb worried that consumers would balk at sunglasses that masked their eyes, they were pleasantly surprised that customers appreciated the comprehensive protection and comfort that the new glass provided.

The Ray-Ban "Wayfarer," a style that has remained popular, was introduced in 1952. The model was valued for the classic simplicity of its design, its sturdy construction and superior fit. Wayfarer sunglasses have maintained a steady sales record for more than four decades.

## Marketing Innovation

Up until the mid-1950s, Bausch & Lomb perceived its line of eye protection as more utilitarian than fashionable. However, in 1956, the company recognized the growing consumer perception of sunglasses as a fashion accessory, and began expanding the Ray-Ban sunglass line to include a variety of new styles each year.

## AT A GLANCE

**R**ay-Ban brand of sunglasses developed in the 1920s in Rochester, NY, by Bausch & Lomb Optical Company; originally named Anti-Glare goggles; introduced to U.S. Army Air Corps fliers, 1930s; Ray-Ban trademark registered, 1937; company became legally known as Bausch & Lomb Incorporated, 1960.

**Performance:** *Market share*—40% of worldwide premium sunglasses category. *Sales*—$675.9 million.

**Major competitor:** Vuarnet.

**Advertising:** *Agency*—Grey Advertising, Inc., New York, NY. *Major campaign*—Olympic sponsorship.

**Addresses:** *Parent company*—Bausch & Lomb Incorporated, One Lincoln First Square, Rochester, NY 14601-0054; phone: (716) 338-6000, or (800) 344-8815.

Unlike some competitors' models, which often mimicked prescription frame styling, Ray-Ban glasses were offered in more advanced shapes, decorations, and colors. Since then, the company has developed and introduced many new styles each season. In 1957, the "Caravan" squared goggle style offered an alternative metal-framed model to the standard aviator shapes. Ray-Ban's design leadership earned Bausch & Lomb an award for outstanding contributions to fashion from the Council of Fashion Designers of America in 1965.

## Product Changes

Although it seems that Bausch & Lomb has worked continually to improve its Ray-Ban line of sunglasses, the 1960s, 1970s, and early 1980s found lens researchers especially active. During that time, Ray-Ban worked to refine the technological aspects of its products and, at the same time, enhance their form. By 1962, all Ray-Ban sunglasses featured impact-resistant lenses, an innovation that came a full decade before the U.S. Food and Drug Administration's requirement. Ray-Ban introduced a new metal finish in 1970: the company's specially-treated "Black Chrome" was an option for consumers who preferred metal frames, but didn't like the gold "Arista" finish.

Two new light-sensitive lenses, Changeable Gray and Ambermatic, were launched in 1974 and 1978, respectively. Changeable Gray lenses adjusted to the sun's brightness, and Ambermatic all-weather lenses changed both color and density to accommodate light and weather conditions. Under overcast skies, they were a light to medium shade of amber/brown that cut haze, improved contrast and sharpen details. As skies brightened, they darkened to deep shades of gray-brown to block glare. In 1981, Constant Density brown lenses that cut glare, improved contrast, and sharpened details by absorbing blue light were offered.

Larger versions of many Ray-Ban styles were introduced throughout this period. In 1965, the Olympian I and II models and the Balorama style joined the Wayfarer line of sunglasses. In 1973, Large Metal II, a bigger version of Large Metal aviator sunglasses hit the scene, and in 1980, a larger rendition of the Outdoorsman style was introduced. These technological and stylistic changes enhanced the brand's position as a fashion accessory as well as a performance article for sportsmen.

## Commercial Success

During the 1980s, Ray-Ban reached into its stylistic past to make substantial sales gains. Several factors came together during the first half of the decade to push sunglasses in general, and Ray-Bans in particular, to the forefront of the fashion industry. The combination of subtle celebrity "endorsement," new research indicating that the sun's ultraviolet rays can harm the eyes, and the entry of several prominent fashion designers into the sunglass industry created a sunglass "boom."

The 1981 release of the movie *The Blues Brothers,* which featured actors John Belushi and Dan Akroyd wearing Ray-Ban Wayfarers, was the first of a series of media "cameos" for Ray-Ban eyewear. Publicity in *GQ* and *Mademoiselle* magazines pushed the retro-shades into even higher recognition, and when Tom Cruise wore them in the movie *Risky Business,* sales skyrocketed. Don Johnson, star of the weekly television series *Miami Vice,* made Wayfarers an integral part of his on- and off-camera image. The exposure kicked off a retro movement in the industry that saw Ray-Ban revive and revamp some of the brand's most enduring shapes and styles.

In 1982, "fine English bridle leather" was offered as an optional trim for many of Ray-Ban's classic metal-framed styles. The new set of frames was introduced as the Ray-Ban Leathers collection. In 1984, tortoise shell frames were introduced in the Tortuga Classic Metals collection. The popularity of Wayfarer sunglasses spurred a renewed interest in the fashions of the 1950s and 1960s. Soon other Ray-Ban sunglass styles, including the Balorama and Olympian I and II were revived, and retro-look Drifter and Clubmaster models were developed. Sunglasses made especially for driving were also introduced that year.

Tom Cruise subtly promoted another classic Ray-Ban sunglass, the Aviator, in 1986 when he wore them for his role in the movie *Top Gun.* U.S. Ray-Ban sales jumped by over one-third, and worldwide sales grew by 40 percent that year. "The General," a high-performance version of the 1937 original that recalled the historic association between Ray-Ban sunglasses and General Douglas MacArthur, was released in 1987 to commemorate Ray-Ban's fiftieth anniversary and capitalized on the revitalized popularity of the style. In 1989 alone, Ray-Ban sunglasses were apparent in over 110 movies. That year, the brand received a special Woolmark award for enduring influence on men's fashion in the United States.

Unit sales of Wayfarers in 1986 doubled those of the previous year, and dollar revenues were fifty times greater than in 1981. Ray-Ban's sales outpaced the U.S. sunglass industry by 10 percent in 1986. That year, designer Liz Claiborne joined a growing list of fashion moguls who launched lines of sunglasses. Ray-Ban had started to focus on women as a separate consumer group in 1979, and further segmented its market in 1988 with the introduction of Bausch & Lomb's Donna Karan DKNY EYES and the short-lived Levi's brands of sunglasses. Over the course of the decade, the non-prescription sunglass market had doubled to over $1.7 billion.

## International Market

Bausch & Lomb's international sales of Ray-Bans also grew dramatically in the 1980s. The company had placed subsidiaries and independent distributors in Europe, the Middle East, and Asia by 1980, but its international division was hindered by a bureaucratic organization that treated foreign subsidiaries as "sales adjuncts to the U.S. divisions," as Ronald Zarella, senior vice-president of the international division, admitted in a May 1992 *Fortune* article.

In 1984, Bausch & Lomb's international sales comprised about one-fourth of total sales. At that time, production and marketing policies originated at the Bausch & Lomb headquarters in Rochester, New York. Although international markets appreciated the uniquely American Ray-Ban styles, Europe's high-fashion markets wanted more innovative designs. The subsequent decentralization of Ray-Ban's international operations brought immediate success: worldwide sales increased 30 percent from 1985 to 1986. Of course, part of that dramatic increase was due to the explosion of Wayfarer sales worldwide: unit turnover for the style doubled during the same period.

By 1991, more than half of the new Ray-Ban products were developed for international sale. Europeans preferred flamboyant, more progressive styles, and the brand's Asian representatives redesigned many standard Ray-Ban models to better suit Asian facial characteristics. By 1992, Ray-Ban had captured 40 percent of the world's premium-priced sunglass market, and revenues outside the United States increased by more than 20 percent that year. Also in 1992, international sales comprised 56 percent of worldwide sales. In the early 1990s, Bausch & Lomb continued to concentrate on the rapidly-expanding markets outside the United States to keep the sunglass division the fastest-growing segment of the company. Ray-Ban also gained worldwide exposure through Bausch & Lomb's sponsorship of the 1988 and 1992 Olympics, when the company paid Olympic athletes to wear its sunglasses on television for additional promotion.

## Performance Appraisal

The Ray-Ban brand enjoys extraordinary customer loyalty: 1991 figures showed that 77 percent of the tradename's consumers did not consider purchasing another brand, 85 percent would buy Ray-Ban sunglasses again, and more than two-thirds of the brand's customers "would go elsewhere if they could not buy Ray-Ban sunglasses at the retail outlet they visited." But in some ways, the phenomenal success of the mid-1980s created two problems for the brand: knockoffs and discounting. In 1991, Bausch & Lomb closed down eighteen distributors who discounted heavily, because their bargain-basement prices and seedy sales locations eroded Ray-Ban's prestigious image. From 1987 to 1992, Bausch & Lomb's worldwide sunglass business grew at a compounded rate of over 25 percent annually; but in 1991, growth slowed to 14 percent due to market saturation and discounting. During 1991 and 1992, Bausch & Lomb stopped supplying 35 distributors who were suspected of "diversion," a tactic wherein merchandise sold to wholesalers in the United States was resold in other markets.

## Further Reading:

*Bausch & Lomb Incorporated Annual Reports,* Rochester, NY: Bausch & Lomb Incorporated, 1978–1992.

Jacob, Rahul, "Bausch & Lomb: Trust the Locals, Win Worldwide," *Fortune,* May 4, 1992, pp. 76–77.

Pouschine, Tatiana, "Cruising on Ray-Bans," *Forbes,* August 3, 1992, pp. 53–54.

*Shedding Light on a Legend: Understanding Ray-Ban Sunglasses,* Rochester, NY: Bausch & Lomb Incorporated, 1993.

*World's Greatest Brands,* New York: John Wiley & Sons, 1992.

*—April S. Dougal*

# RED WING® SHOES

Since the brand was founded in 1905, Red Wing shoes have enjoyed a reputation as durable and comfortable footwear tailored for specific occupational and recreational activities such as farming, hunting, and hiking. Until the 1970s, Red Wing's reputation rested primarily on a wide variety of footwear marketed as "work shoes," which emphasized functionality in the workplace. This focus shifted as American workers increasingly moved out of industrial and agricultural sectors into service-related jobs in the 1980s. Under the direction of president William J. Sweasy, Jr., and a new generation of management, Red Wing shifted emphasis from "work shoes" to "shoes for work"—a slight semantic change that underlined a much greater change in Red Wing's business. Innovative lines of lighter, more comfortable footwear were developed to accommodate new work-oriented and recreational needs. Recent Red Wing products include a lighter, more fashionable line of Lady Red Wings, walking shoes, steel toe athletic shoes, redesigned hiking boots for adults and a special line for children, and sports sandals. Red Wing Shoe Company, Inc. expanded its presence in international markets to over 80 countries by 1992.

## Brand Origins

Red Wing shoes originated in 1905, when German immigrant Charles Beckman closed his retail shoe store and organized the Red Wing Shoe Company with 14 other investors. On January 26th of that year, the daily newspaper in Red Wing, Minnesota, reported that the new factory would employ roughly 100 people at the outset, and forecasted that the figure would increase before long. The Red Wing Shoe Company's initial output was 110 pairs of shoes per ten-hour day. By the 1990s, Red Wing's workforce had grown to over 1,400 employees, and the company was selling over 12,000 pairs per day worldwide. In the United States, the products were sold through 400 Red Wing shoe stores—of which 40 percent were company owned—and through approximately 4,800 privately owned shoe stores.

The brand's steady growth stemmed from its fundamental dedication to quality, functionality, and diversity. When Beckman conceived of his company, farming, logging, mining, blacksmithing, and railroading were booming industries waiting to be serviced with suitable footwear. Red Wing tailored its footwear to the demands of specific occupations and offered a wide range of shoe sizes and widths to ensure fit.

Growing diversity of Red Wing products in the company's early years reflected efforts to appeal to widening markets. In 1908 the brand offered welt-constructed shoes featuring a leather strip attached to the shoe upper and sewn onto the sole. The enhanced comfort and durability of the shoes particularly appealed to farmers, Red Wing's primary customers at the time. Continued demand justified the construction of a four-story factory with a daily output of 450 pairs, four times the 1906 capacity. In 1912 Red Wing added the black and brown "Chief" line, commonly known as "the farmer's shoe." In addition to the traditional welt construction of earlier farming shoes, the "Chief" featured specially tanned and manure-proof leather designed for longer durability.

At the onset of World War I, Red Wing contributed to the war effort by manufacturing the regulation Munson U.S. Army Last, designed to "fit all feet" with maximum comfort and durability. After the war, the Munson remained a top seller for Red Wing and influenced shoe designs for years to come. In the 1930s Red Wing initiated a line of steel-toed boots that provided added protection in high-risk jobs. The innovation was especially successful, and steel toes were designed into numerous models. The steel toe construction retained its popularity through the years and even became a fashion statement of the punk-rock movement of the 1970s—an emblem of tough-footedness on the streets. Oil field workers of the 1930s adopted Red Wing's "Oil King" boot, made from an oil-resistant leather. For slightly more elite circles of the era, Red Wing introduced a men's dress or riding boot dubbed the "Aristo," which was later adopted into a women's line of shoes and boots.

## Early Product Innovation

Though innovative and functional designs contributed to Red Wing's success in its early decades, the company's use of rubber in its shoes proved to be a windfall. In the early 1930s, company president J.R. Sweasy introduced the rubber cord sole as a replacement for the leather standard. His gamble with the new material was trend setting and lucrative. The Gro Cord soles and Goodyear heels used in Red Wing shoes set a new industry standard, and synthetic materials became key components in many types of footwear shortly thereafter. In addition to providing added durability, synthetic materials also lowered Red Wing's costs. During the Great Depression, synthetic materials made for extremely cost-

## AT A GLANCE

**R**ed Wing brand shoes and boots founded in 1905 in Red Wing, MN, by German immigrant Charles Beckman and 14 investors; the Red Wing Shoe Company catered primarily to workers in farming, logging, mining, blacksmithing, and railroading; in the 1980s Red Wing Shoe Company, Inc. developed walking shoes, steel toe athletic shoes, multi-terrain hiking boots, children's hiking boots, and sports sandals; by 1992 U.S. distribution had expanded to 400 Red Wing shoe stores (40% company owned) and new emphasis on international markets placed Red Wing in over 80 countries.

**Performance:** *Sales*—$186.00 million (1992).

**Major competitor:** Dunham Shoes; also Georgia/Durango Boot Co., Sheboygan Footwear, Inc., and Timberland.

**Advertising:** Agency—In-house.

**Addresses:** *Parent company*—Red Wing Shoe Company, Inc., Riverfront Centre, 314 Main Street, Red Wing, MN 55066; phone: (612) 388-8211; fax: (612) 388-7415.

effective shoes. Model No. 99, named after its price of 99 cents, kept the factory in production and the community employed during a financially unstable period.

Though Red Wing continued to grow steadily, the brand did not gain national and international recognition until World War II. During the war, the U.S. government contracted with Red Wing to produce hundreds of combat shoes manufactured to regulation specifications in 239 different sizes and widths. By the time William D. Sweasy took over as company president in 1949, Red Wing had proven its reliability in meeting urgent demand under tight guidelines. Sweasy turned that strength to civilian ends and reorganized the company to place greater responsibility on department heads and to develop teams of management specialists. Sweasy also envisioned opening Red Wing retail stores from coast to coast across the United States.

The new management method paid off quickly. The company's record profits for 1952 were largely attributed to the No. 877 Irish Setter Sport Boot, which assured Red Wing's foothold in the boot market. Red Wing expanded its boot line in 1965 with the formation of the Vasque Outdoor Division, which capitalized on the hiking boot craze of the 1970s. The division maintained its presence in this area in later years with its introduction of light-weight hiking books and walking shoes.

### Brand Development

In order to gauge consumer demand for its products, Red Wing depended on marketing tools such as census tracking and focus groups. In the early 1980s these devices revealed fundamental changes in the work shoe market, prompting Red Wing to change its brand lines and marketing techniques. In an article for *Footwear News*, Red Wing product manager Tom McConnell identified three social trends that impacted the company's business: A shift from a rural to a metropolitan workplace, the replacement of a manufacturing workforce with a service-related one, and rising numbers of women in the workforce. To service these new markets, Red Wing changed its emphasis and its motto from "work shoes" to "shoes for work." "By identifying ourselves as a manufacturer of work shoes, we had a limited sales potential of about 5 million pairs a year," McConnell explained in *Footwear*

*News.* "Yet by distinguishing our product line as 'shoes for work,' we have expanded that potential market to about 36 million pairs per year," he added. While the brand continued to offer work and sports boots, product development and marketing efforts in the 1980s increasingly focused on markets that promised the most growth—professions such as computer operations, food service, health care, and security.

Red Wing's shift in marketing strategy paralleled the company's shift to a newer and younger generation of management. In 1985 William J. Sweasy, Jr., assumed the role of president after Arlo "Ole" Jensen retired from the post. Sweasy marked the third generation of Red Wing executives from the same family—his father, William Sweasy, remained CEO, and his grandfather had been president in Red Wing's formative years. The 33-year-old president ushered in an era of active strategic planning, greater communication, increased line diversity, and new personnel. "Before, the upper management team operated intuitively; they shot from the hip, so to speak," noted one company spokesperson in *Footwear News*. The company's new direction favored unique approaches in light of changing and emerging business opportunities.

### Product Changes

Red Wing devoted special attention to women's comfort footwear. While over 40 million women held jobs involving substantial standing or walking by the 1980s, McConell commented in *Footwear News* that "most resources have simply remade men's styles on a scaled-down last [shoe mold]." To that end, Red Wing introduced Lady Red Wings and incorporated their trademark safety toes and lightweight urethane soles into shoes without a clunky appearance. McConnell projected sales of approximately 250,000 pairs, retailing at $40 and up.

Red Wing's sister brand, Vasque, developed aesthetically appealing walking shoes shortly thereafter. Early walking shoes often sacrificed style for hi-tech features used in running shoes—evas, rubbers, bottoms packages, heel counters, and lacing systems. Art Kenyon, divisional manager for Vasque, stressed in *Footwear News* that "the consumer today really is concerned with cosmetically fine footwear, boots that can function and still look nice. That has really forced people in the walking shoe market to consider cosmetics more seriously." For Red Wing that translated into new emphasis on casual, multi-use shoes.

In order to meet the demands of consumers who wore athletic shoes outside of work, Red Wing introduced steel toe athletic shoes in a black and white lowtop style. In addition, their work shoes incorporated lighter materials and softer leather. "Our consumers are saying, make it soft but tough," explained Andy Thompson, advertising and promotions manager of Red Wing in *Footwear News*. "They want comfort, but also the durability they have gotten from shoes," he added. Red Wing also developed a group of barnyard acid-resistant shoes geared for the farm industry and a sole "decathlon," a material featuring light weight, shock resistance, durability, and oil resistance.

Red Wing also introduced product changes in its recreational shoe lines. Capitalizing on renewed popularity of hiking boots, the Vasque division became the fastest-growing segment of the Red Wing Shoe Company, Inc. in the early 1990s. After their popularity in previous decades, hiking boots sales declined in the fashion-conscious 1980s until Vasque redesigned boots for different purposes; heavy hiking boots for wilderness excursions and a variety of lighter styles for casual walkers and fashion customers. When the hiking trend took off again, Vasque was ready: "We came from the mountain down to the mainstream," said Art Kenyon, president of Vasque, in a *Chicago Tribune* article. "The others came up from the gymnasium," he added, referring to competition from such athletic footwear companies as Nike, Reebok, and New Balance. In 1993, Vasque returned to the mainstream again when it launched its first line of sport-sandals, further tightening the straps in Red Wing's reputation and financial security.

## Marketing Innovation

Red Wing boosted new products with innovative marketing efforts. Lady Red Wings, for example, appeared in a television ad campaign that was second only to Acme Boot in terms of market saturation, according to McConnell. Premiering in October of 1984, the commercials' computer animation lent a contemporary feeling to the line. Red Wing also ran a series of print advertisements featuring a top model in *McCalls, Women's Day* and *Mademoiselle* magazines, thus updating the image of Red Wing.

In the late 1980s the company began restructuring its retail division in order to gain more exposure and further penetrate the market. Wes Thies, retail division manager, outlined Red Wing's two-fold strategy in *Footwear News.* The object was to expand the existing specialty store concept by introducing three prototype stores geared toward various consumer demographics. The first prototype store targeted small markets with populations between 30,000–60,000. Catering to Red Wing's blue-collar consumers, the stores would have a sales area in the front and a shoe repair shop in the back. Red Wing also emphasized the use of a company newsletter as a marketing tool. The monthly "Red Wing's Shoe News & Views" helped the company's 40-member sales staff communicate product news and company policies to more than 6,000 stores that carried the Red Wing brand.

While the Red Wing newsletter addressed retailers, the company sought to develop more effective means of communicating brand awareness directly to consumers. With the advent of desktop computers and database marketing, age-old advertising techniques were losing their effectiveness. Stan Rapp, president of CRC Consulting Group in New York, told attendees of the 1992 All-Industry Marketing (AIM) Conference that marketing efforts had to be increasingly individualized since mass advertising was rapidly becoming obsolete. He noted that shoe companies needed to micromarket and draw consumers into a feedback loop by fostering two-way, relationship marketing. In its own variation on such techniques, Red Wing launched a television campaign that provided a toll-free number in order to establish direct communication with consumers. The commercial's catch-phrase—"our shoes don't wear out"—was accompanied by consumer testimonials and the phone number. Customers who ordered shoes over the phone received a thank-you note and were asked to rate their salesperson. Six months later each customer received another form to rate the shoes' performance, thus strengthening a personalized, two-way marketing dynamic.

## International Growth

Red Wing's efforts to adapt to changing markets emphasized international growth. From its original market of Minnesota farmers, the brand was distributed in more than 80 countries by 1990. Despite the intricacies of dealing with currency fluctuations and of identifying elusive, foreign trends, the market for American

footwear exports offered substantial growth potential for Red Wing. Palmer Beebe, one executive instrumental in setting up Red Wing's international department, moved on to run Team America, an export business handling footwear for a consortium of U.S. companies. "U.S. footwear is underexported," Beebe claimed in a July, 1991 *Footwear News* article.

As early as 1984 Red Wing reported that just 2–3 percent of overseas laborers in supervisory positions were company customers, thus identifying a large, untapped market. The company projected 25 percent growth over the next few years, citing a wider distribution base and increased technology as means of lowering prices to raise foreign sales. By 1990, Census Bureau statistics indicated that the best European countries for American footwear were West Germany, France, Italy, the United Kingdom, and Spain. Other large importers of shoes and boots included Canada, Japan, Mexico, Hong Kong, and Saudi Arabia.

## Future Predictions

The uncertain outcome of a Common Market in Europe and of the North American Free Trade Agreement (NAFTA) overshadowed Red Wing's international activity in the early 1990s. European growth would depend largely on import regulations and incentives drafted in Brussels. Closer to home, the congressional stalemate on NAFTA set many business analysts on edge and frustrated long-term plans for Red Wing in markets south of the Rio Grande. Supporters of NAFTA argued that its approval would stimulate industry and employment, yielding 400 to 3,500 new jobs in Minnesota over the next decade. They also argued that rejection of the agreements would close valuable markets between Mexico and the United States in the future. "The price of the defeat of NAFTA is a revival of Mexican protectionism," said Hector Garcia, executive director of Minnesotans for NAFTA, in the *Star Tribune.* Opponents of NAFTA, on the other hand, warned that as many as 103,000 manufacturing jobs in Minnesota would be endangered by the agreement and that Mexican workers may be exploited and subjected to environmental hazards. In one year, the brand had sold fewer than 20,000 pairs of shoes in Mexico, representing less than half of one percent of that year's sales. Nevertheless, plans to open the first Red Wing retail stores and distribution centers in Mexico depended heavily the success of NAFTA. Without the treaty, Red Wing faced tariffs adding as much as 19 percent to imported shoe prices, according to the *Star Tribune.* By the late fall of 1993, however, President Bill Clinton had garnered enough congressional support to guarantee NAFTA's passage.

The decisive factor in Red Wing's continued success remains its exploitation of new markets as it shifts from "work shoes" to "shoes for work" in an increasingly service-oriented economy. With William Sweasy, Jr., presiding over new initiatives in marketing and brand development, Red Wing will likely shod the ever-growing population with quality shoes to outlast and out-step its competitors.

## Further Reading:

Francis, Lorna R., "Work and Safety Shoes Make Nick in Fashion Scene; Boot Industry," *Footwear News,* November 3, 1986, p. 26; "Strong Gains Reported in Steel Toe Athletics; Work and Safety Shoes," *Footwear News,* November 14, 1988, p. 4.

"How the Once Ugly Duckling Was Turned Into a Swan; Walking Shoes," *Footwear News,* April 11, 1988, p. 52.

Howard, Tammi, "Red Wing Shifts Marketing to Service-Related Fields," *Footwear News,* October 1, 1984, p. 17; "Footwear Sources Jump on Newsletter Bandwagon; Marketing Tools," *Footwear News,* May 26, 1986, p. 12; "Red Wing Giant Waking Up To Get Place in the Sun," *Footwear News,* May 26, 1986, p. 52.

Meyers, Mike, "Proving a Negative Positively Impossible, Especially When It's About NAFTA Impact," *Star Tribune,* May 31, 1993, p. 1D.

*Red Wing Shoe Co. Attributes 87 Years of Success To One Word: Service,* News Release, Red Wing: The Red Wing Shoe Company, spring, 1992.

Rooney, Ellen, "Vasque to Celebrate Silver Anniversary," *Footwear News,* October 9, 1989, p. 15.

Seckler, Valerie, "Micromarketing Puts Focus on Individuals; Footwear Marketing," *Footwear News,* May 18, 1992, p. 2.

St. Anthony, Neal, "Worker's Comp Irks Blue-Collar Employers; Above-Average Rates Frustrate Companies," *Star Tribune,* November 30, 1992, p. 1D.

Underwood, Elaine, "The Competition Is Stepping Up for Hiking Boots," *Chicago Tribune,* September 9, 1991, p. C6.

"Vasque Debuts Line of Kids' Hiking Boots," *Footwear News,* November 12, 1990, p. 23.

Watters, Susan, "Makers Hedge Dollar Bets to Build Export Business; Fluctuating Foreign Currency Deters U.S. Footwear Companies From Exporting," *Footwear News,* July 8, 1991, p. 30.

Wilner, Rich, "Resources Set to Put Sport Sandals in Overdrive," *Footwear News,* November 9, 1992, p. 1.

—*Kerstan Cohen*

# REEBOK®

Reebok holds the number two position in U.S. athletic shoe sales (23.7 percent of the $12 billion industry), trailing only behind arch-competitor Nike as the two battle it out for diminishing shares of the already mature U.S. market. Riding the crest of the 1980s fitness wave, Reebok recorded remarkable sales growth in its early years—from $900,000 in 1980 to $1.8 billion by 1989. Sales took off in 1982 when Reebok introduced its "Freestyle" and "Princess" women's aerobic workout shoe. The women's fitness market accounted for more than 50 percent of Reebok sales during those years, with sales of tennis, walking, running, and cross-training shoes filling in the gaps. In 1986 Reebok beat Nike for the number one position in athletic shoe sales by capitalizing on its fashionable image. Nike took the lead in 1989 as the aerobics craze died down, and consumers became more interested in high-performance shoes. Reebok has since focused its marketing efforts on introducing a wider variety of styles and capitalizing on its already strong presence in the international market, where it holds the number one brand position in such countries as Canada, Australia, Great Britain, New Zealand, Hong Kong, and Singapore.

## Brand Origins

Reebok's ancestry dates back to the 1890s, when a British athlete named Joseph W. Foster invented running shoes with spikes in the soles. In 1895 he founded J. W. Foster & Sons, Inc., reportedly the world's first manufacturer of athletic shoes, to hand-stitch his running shoes for many of Britain's top runners. Over time his running shoes became popular with an international cache of world class athletes. In 1958 Joseph and Jeffrey Foster, grandsons of the founder, started a companion company, giving it the name Reebok, after an African gazelle admired for its swiftness and dexterity. Eventually, J. W. Foster & Sons was absorbed by the new company.

Reebok's presence in the United States was minimal until 1979, when Paul B. Fireman, a partner in a U.S. sporting goods distributorship, spotted Reebok at an international sales conference and negotiated for the rights to distribute the shoes in the United States. That year, Reebok U.S.A. introduced three new running shoes priced at $60, the highest on the market.

Reebok's sales grew to over $1.8 million in 1981, but the running shoe market was highly saturated by established competitors, and furthermore, the recreational running boom was starting to slacken. Fireman was forced to get a cash infusion by selling 60 percent of Reebok U.S.A. to another British shoe company, Pentland Industries PLC. Together with his new partner, Fireman contracted production of the shoes to facilities in South Korea —a move that significantly lowered costs and made Reebok shoes more viable on the U.S. market.

## First Major Success

In 1982 Reebok decided to tap into the growing aerobic dance market and introduced its "Freestyle" and "Princess" shoes, the first athletic shoes designed especially for women. With this introduction, Reebok both anticipated and encouraged three trends that fueled the athletic footwear industry in the 1980s: the growing popularity of aerobic exercise, the influx of women into the world of health and fitness, and fashion trends that made athletic shoes an acceptable alternative for street and casual wear.

Fireman's marketing targeted instructors of the new exercise routine, based on the reasoning that aerobic students would strive to emulate their teachers or would at least ask them questions concerning proper shoes. Reebok also sponsored certification programs for aerobic trainers and funded studies on aerobic-related injuries. By 1983, Reebok possessed an almost 100 percent share of the aerobic shoe market, and sales rocketed to $13 million in 1983. One year later, sales jumped even higher to $66 million.

Another important factor behind Reebok's success has been the use of color in its shoe design. Reebok shoes were marketed not just as exercise gear, but as fashion accessories. The shoes were made of supple leather and were offered in a variety of colors or in white with bright trim, elements that also garnered them large amounts of department store display space and customer attention.

This strategy of marketing athletic shoes as a fashion accessory was an industry first and contributed greatly to Reebok's early success. Although Reebok continued to sell running shoes, aerobic shoe sales grew to such an extent that by the mid-1980s, 75 percent of the company's customer base was female. The shoe's popularity as a fashion item was sealed in 1985 when actress Cybill Shepherd wore a pair of orange Reebok shoes under her black evening gown at the annual Emmy Awards. Across the United States, women could be seen wearing them with their business suits as they walked to work, while working out, or doing

## AT A GLANCE

**R**eebok brand shoes founded in 1958 in Bolton, England, by brothers Joseph and Jeffrey Foster, heirs to J. W. Foster & Sons, Inc., the world's oldest manufacturer of athletic shoes; Joseph and Jeffrey's Reebok company absorbed J. W. Foster & Sons, and company name was changed to Reebok International, Ltd.; U.S. rights to sell Reebok purchased by Paul B. Fireman in 1979, and Reebok U.S.A. was incorporated; 60% of Reebok U.S.A. sold to Pentland Industries PLC in 1981; Pentland and Reebok U.S.A. purchased Reebok International, Ltd., in 1984; Reebok International stock offered publicly in 1985.

**Performance:** *Market share*—23.7% of athletic shoe market. *Sales*—$3.02 billion (footwear and apparel in the United States and abroad; 1992).

**Major competitor:** Nike.

**Advertising:** *Agency*—Chiat/Day. *Major campaign*—"Planet Reebok" international campaign with tag line, "What's life like on Planet Reebok?"

**Addresses:** *Parent company*—Reebok International, Ltd., Reebok Brands, 100 Technology Center, Stoughton, MA, 02072; phone: (617) 341-5000; fax: (617) 341-5087. *Ultimate parent company*—Reebok International, Ltd. (address same as above).

such mundane things as grocery shopping. By 1986, Reebok was part of a full-fledged fad, with sales of $307 million.

### Brand Development

Anticipating that the aerobics fad would ultimately peak and decline, Reebok began diversifying its product offerings. It entered the tennis shoe market in 1984, followed by forays into the basketball and children's shoe markets. Also in 1984 Reebok running shoes were given a marketing boost when Steve Jones set a world marathon record wearing his Reebok shoes to complete a 26.2 mile course in 2:08:05. In June of 1986 Reebok threw an unprecedented $500,000 advertising budget into the introduction of its Instructor 5000 series of aerobic shoes, partially in response to growing competition in that market.

Reebok sales tripled in 1986, with aerobic shoes making up only 33.2 percent of sales. Children's shoe sales were growing well, as were sales of its tennis shoe lines, which had captured 40 percent of the market within three years. Despite this rapid growth, Reebok was slow to give its name to new products, rejecting as many as 50 requests for licensing agreements in one year. "The easiest way for a hot name to grow is to stick it on everything. We've chosen not to grow that way," said Reebok's Chief Financial Officer Paul Duncan in a 1987 *Working Woman* article. But grow they did, doubling sales in 1987 to $1.4 billion. By 1987, Reebok's 350 different models held 30 percent of the $8.1 billion athletic shoe market. Nike, its closest competitor, held 20 percent, with third place Converse holding 4.2 percent.

### Advertising and Marketing

Reebok's 30 percent market share in 1987 indicated that the brand was well on its way to maturity and could no longer expect the phenomenal growth of its early years. Perhaps as an acknowledgement that the glory days of its youth were fading, Reebok spent $65 million on advertising in 1988, its biggest budget up to

that point. Perhaps it heard the footsteps of Nike, Inc., which was quickly gaining on its rival. Either way, Reebok put $35 million of that budget behind its "Reeboks let U.B.U." campaign, which put the message forward that Reebok shoes were "basically about freedom of expression." The television and print ads were developed by the advertising agency Chiat/Day and featured a variety of eccentrics—a fairy princess, a set of odd-looking triplets, a nerdy looking fellow—cavorting about in their Reebok shoes.

Continuing within its "freedom of expression" theme, Reebok took a number of politically minded promotional tactics to keep on top of the game. The company renovated inner-city playgrounds, gave shoes away to celebrities whom it considered trendsetters, and sponsored South African activist Nelson Mandela's trip to Boston in 1988 and Amnesty International's Human Rights Now music tour, which featured such big names as Bruce Springsteen, Peter Gabriel, and Sting.

But the U.B.U. campaign was a disaster. By fiscal year end 1988, earnings (on sales of $1.79 billion) dropped one-fifth, and Nike had captured the top market share through an advertising campaign for its basketball shoes. The following year, Reebok responded with an entirely new $30 million advertising campaign. Targeting Reebok's historically strong sales base among women, the campaign, titled "The Physics Behind the Physiques" drew upon themes that united working out with notions of sex and narcissism. Following so quickly on the heels of the playful U.B.U. campaign, the series reportedly served to confuse Reebok's image in the minds of its audience. Reebok's sales continued to slip, and by 1989, Reebok's market share had fallen to 24.1 percent, while Nike's continued to rise.

### New Products, New Image

In November of 1989 Reebok introduced the revolutionary Pump line of basketball shoes, which featured a chamber built into the upper portion of the shoe. By pressing a button on the tongue, the chambers could be inflated and thus mold to the wearer's foot. Reebok also chose to return to its original marketing concept: emphasizing performance and style as opposed to a life-style.

The Pump proved to be a formidable player in the battle against Nike. Its advertising took a direct hit on Nike Air, the top-selling basketball shoes in the United States at that time. "Pump up, and Air out," the ads declared. Reebok contracted as spokesperson for the shoe Boston Celtic's forward Dee Brown, who gave the shoes a serendipitous bit of publicity when he wore them for a nationally televised slam-dunk competition and reached down and pumped up his shoes before each run to the basket. The combination of a high-performance shoe, celebrity endorsement, and slick style paid off well: 12 million pairs of Pump shoes had been sold by April of 1993.

The following year Reebok applied the same concept with equally impressive results. Sensing an opening in the tight basketball shoes market, Reebok developed the Blacktop shoe line, with thicker soles that could better withstand the wear and tear of urban asphalt courts. Reebok named the first three lines after famous urban blacktop courts: the Battleground in Harlem, the Boulevard in Boston, and the Settlement in Detroit. The company hired African-American comedian Sinbad as spokesperson for the shoe. Within two months of its introduction, over two million pairs of the shoe were sold—an almost unheard of figure in the shoe industry. Revenues grew 18 percent that year, and Reebok's market share edged up to 24.3 percent. In 1992 Reebok introduced its football and baseball lines. Over 200 players in the Major League and the National Football League sported Reebok shoes. Marketing momentum increased as Notre Dame's football team won the Cotton Bowl, wearing shoes supplied by Reebok. "After two years of stops and starts," declared an industry analyst in 1991, Reebok "is clearly back on the footwear scene."

## International Expansion

Nationwide athletic shoe sales grew a mere 9 percent in 1992, down from 18 percent in 1990, with the majority of growth divided between giants Reebok and Nike. Manufacturers began looking for niches in which to expand. Both Reebok and Nike targeted the women's market for further growth, and both gave a lot of attention to expanding overseas markets. Twenty-five percent of Reebok sales were from foreign markets, primarily in Europe, Australia, and Japan. In 1991 overall European sales had grown by 86 percent. Reebok expanded distribution to approximately 140 countries, holding the top sales position in nine of those.

In 1993 Reebok solidified its marketing strategy and premiered a new campaign designed to position it globally for the next decade. Although Europeans had traditionally disdained wearing athletic shoes for anything other than the sport for which they were intended, Reebok and Nike both made strong inroads during the early 1990s by spending heavily on advertising that promoted American style.

Reebok's foreign target was the teen market, considered more open to new fashion ideas than their elders. During the 1993 Superbowl, Reebok introduced a new advertising campaign designed to carry Reebok's performance message to the international teen market. The spot, titled "Planet Reebok," opened with the question, "What is life like on Planet Reebok," followed by a series of quick takes of different sports in action, such as heli-skiing, football, rock climbing, and other sports. The Reebok message accompanies the shots: "No stopping. No fear. No mercy. No fat. No Beauty pageants. No excuses. No lawyers. No winners. No losers."

The ad ran simultaneously on Music Television's global network, which aired in some 70 different countries. It was supported by an integrated marketing program that tied in with advertising for established shoe lines, retail merchandising materials such as videos, radio programming, as well as sponsorship of the Russian Olympic Committee and other sporting events.

## Performance Analysis

Reebok's growth since the early 1980s has been phenomenal, due primarily to its ability to accurately spot and capitalize on consumer trends. Despite some clumsy advertising ventures during the late 1980s, Reebok continues to have strong brand recognition among consumers, thanks to the introduction of new high-performance, high-style footwear lines in the early 1990s.

Although Reebok held a strong 20.3 percent of the already mature U.S. athletic shoe market in 1993, holding more promise is the international market, which grew by 86 percent in 1991. Despite the European recession slowing growth for Reebok and its competitors, the brand's 1993 sales in Europe alone are up ten percent. Reebok is firmly entrenched in the battle with Nike for world market domination, with both predicting that half of their sales will be in overseas markets by 1996. With its "Planet Reebok" advertising campaign, the brand seems possibly to have settled into a suitable image and marketing program that should be a potent tool for reaching new consumers.

## Further Reading:

Benoit, Ellen, "Lost Youth," *Financial World,* September 20, 1988, p. 28.

"Bouncing with Reebok," *Economist,* July 18, 1986, p. 55.

Dubashi, Jagannath, "Reebok: The 'Round Mound of Rebound,' " *Financial World,* August 6, 1991, p. 16.

Grimm, Matthew, *Brandweek,* "Deft Reebok Strides into Women's Walking," August 24, 1992, p. 4; "Reebok's Big Idea," January 25, 1993, p. 3; "Reebok Joins Bally's Health Clubs," February 15, 1993, p. 4.

Meeks, Fleming, "The Sneaker Game," *Forbes 400,* October 22, 1990, p. 114.

Pereira, Joseph, "Off and Running: Pushing U.S. Style, Nike and Reebok Sell Sneakers to Europe, *Wall Street Journal,* July 23, 1993, p. A1.

*Reebok International Ltd. Corporate Backgrounder,* Stoughton, MA: Reebok International Ltd.

"Reebok Puts $2 Million in Aerobic Shoe Drive," *Footwear News,* June 16, 1986, p. 26.

Rowland, Mary, "Keep on Walking," *Working Woman,* May 1987, p. 87.

Sloan, Pat, "Reebok Takes Off around the Planet," *Advertising Age,* January 25, 1993, p. 3.

"The Sneaker Wars," *Forbes,* March 29, 1993, p. 132.

*—Maura Troester*

# REVLON®

# REVLON

Revlon cosmetics ranks among the top five brands of cosmetics in America. The Revlon name has represented quality and fashion since 1932 and is one of the most respected and valuable names in the industry. Revlon was the first brand offered by parent company Revlon, Inc., which has developed and purchased such notable brands as Almay, Bill Blass, Charles of the Ritz, Etherea, and Halston.

## Brand Origins

Revlon was created in the midst of the Great Depression by the eccentric, abrasive, and fabulously successful Charles Revson (who would become famous for his "We sell hope" quote, among others). A New York City native, Revson went to work for his cousin's Pickwick Dress Company after graduating from high school. His keen sense of color soon earned him a position as a piece goods buyer working with fabrics. Legend has it, however, that Revson was fired in 1930 for buying too much of a particular pattern that he liked. Revson moved to Chicago and began work with a business that sold sales motivation plans, but the early years of the Depression crushed the business. Revson returned to his parents' home in New York and started selling nail polish for Elka, a New Jersey company.

Elka's product was revolutionary for the time. Its opaque reds were different from other companies' transparent nail enamels, and Charles saw great potential in this difference. Other products were made with dyes and thus were limited to three shades of red. Revson felt that nail enamel made to really cover the nails, and offered in a wide variety of shades, would seize the market. At the time, consumers were largely limited to actresses and women of "ill-repute": Revson hoped to bring cosmetics into the mainstream.

Charles and his brother opened an Elka nail enamel sales office and began to make the rounds of New York beauty salons, where Charles learned all he could about nail enamel and its customers. During this early period in his career, Revson also honed his customer service skills, asking women what they liked and didn't like about the product and its competitors.

In 1932, when Revson felt confident enough to ask Elka to expand into nationwide distribution, the management refused. Revson joined with two brothers, Joseph and Martin, and a partner, Charles Lachman—who had married into a chemical business

that just happened to manufacture nail enamel for many brands—to start a separate new business. The partners decided to brand their product, and casted about several combinations of the two family names, including "Revlac," before arriving at Revlon.

During the brand's first nine months in circulation, sales were $4,055. Early sales were predicated upon Charles's salesmanship: he even wore the nail enamel himself to test and demonstrate it. Once people bought the enamel, they reordered, and early business was built on positive word of mouth. Demand grew so quickly that nearly every other brand was shut out of the market.

In 1933, sales rose to $11,246, and by 1937, Revlon was well-established. Sales had multiplied 40 times in four years, and Revson plowed $62,000 into advertising by Batten, Barton, Durstine & Osborn that year. The company nearly tripled its sales in 1938 on the advertising momentum. That year, Revlon started sending out Christmas manicure sets, including all the supplies needed to do an at-home manicure: bottles of enamel, tweezers, an orange stick, and an emery board, etc.

From 1932 to 1937, Revlon dealt exclusively with the beauty trade. When the brand was promoted in "selected" department stores, Revlon could then add the phrase, "Used by the Professionals," to give its product even more authority. The idea was to make Revlon almost as accessible as other nail enamels, yet preserve the aura of exclusivity.

## Early Marketing Strategies

Before Revlon came into being, women normally used an entire bottle of nail polish before purchasing a new one. Offering a wider variety of colors, Revlon introduced the element of fashion to the industry. Following the lead of mass producers like General Motors, Revlon paved the way for planned obsolescence through the introduction of new colors each fall and spring. According to Revson biographer Andrew Tobias, "by the mid-1940s, the brand's semi-annual shade promotions were as much an event to women as Detroit's new-car introductions were to men." Unlike previous nail enamel marketers that simply numbered their shades, Revlon gave its colors attractive, evocative names, like "Cherries in the Snow" or "Fifth Avenue Red." The brand competed on quality, not price, and relied on heavy advertising to give the impression that the business was a larger concern than it really was.

## AT A GLANCE

**R**evlon brand of cosmetics founded as a nail enamel in 1932 in New York, NY, by Charles Revson, his two brothers, Joseph and Martin, and a partner, Charles Lachman; product line extended to wide variety of cosmetics; purchased by Mac-Andrews & Forbes Inc. in 1985 and renamed Revlon, Inc.

**Performance:** *Market share*—15% (third-largest share) of mass market cosmetics category (1990 estimate). *Sales*—$15.23 million (1990).

**Major competitor:** Maybelline; also, Avon, L'Oréal, Estée Lauder, and Noxell Corporation's Cover Girl.

**Advertising:** *Agency*—Revlon Creative Workshop Inc. (in-house), 1987—. *Major campaign*—"The most unforgettable women in the world wear Revlon," featuring high fashion models and celebrities.

**Addresses:** *Parent company*—Revlon, Inc., 767 Fifth Avenue, New York, NY 10153; phone: (212) 572-5000. *Ultimate parent company*—Revlon Group Incorporated, 555 Southwest 12th Avenue, Pompano Beach, FL 33069; phone: (305) 785-4334. *Ultimate ultimate parent company*—MacAndrews & Forbes Group.

Revlon added lipstick to the product line in 1940 with its "Matching Lips and Fingertips" campaign. The promotional effort featured Revlon's first full-color, two page ads. "Matching lips and fingertips" was an ingenious way to enter the lipstick, and eventually, color cosmetics, business. The only way to coordinate your lipstick with Revlon nail enamel was, of course, with Revlon lipstick. Interestingly, the campaign was not an original Revlon concept. Another company had used the theme in its ads a few years previously, but Revson had much greater success with it.

During World War II, Revlon was stymied by government rationing. Glass bottles were in short supply. Lipsticks were seen as important for morale, but their metal cases had to be replaced, first with plastic, then with paper. Despite these setbacks, however, distribution was extended and sales grew.

### International Market

World War II saw the beginning of Revlon's overseas distribution, which was first handled through United States government post exchanges. "Duty free" shops carried Revlon products that American soldiers gave to their European girlfriends. Revlon opened operations in England and Mexico and exported to independent distributors, but had low sales early on. Foreign sales were instituted in earnest in 1960, and went up to $20 million in 1962. After ten years, international sales had grown to $200 million. Revlon did not have a particularly innovative international marketing scheme: brand support was usually just translated from English into the target language. However, American products were in strong enough demand during the 1950s and 1960s that the country of origin itself was a strong draw. The strategy even worked in Japan, the world's second largest cosmetics market.

### Revlon's Celebrated Shade Promotions

Near the end of the war, Revlon promotions concentrated entirely on the brand's colors. These semi-annual promotions focused on the introduction of each season's new colors. In 1945,

it was "Fatal Apple—the most tempting color since Eve winked at Adam." In 1949, the shade was "Plumb Beautiful," which earned Revlon's nail enamel eight panels loaded with furs in Bergdorf Goodman's window display. The new color for 1950 was introduced with a full-page teaser in the *New York Times* that featured a black hole, smoke, and the headline, "Where's The Fire?" Days later, Revlon introduced the shade "Where's the Fire?"

But in the fall of 1952, Revlon kicked off a promotion that would be renowned as "one of the most effective ads in cosmetics history," according to a *Business Week* article published that year. The two-page spread for "Fire and Ice" featured redheaded model Dorian Leigh in a sparkling silver-sequin dress with a crimson cape and the tagline: "Are you made for 'Fire and Ice'?"

Response to the promotion was unprecedented. Nine thousand window displays were devoted to "Fire and Ice." It was referred to in newspapers and magazines and on the radio, and "Fire and Ice" beauty contests were held across the country. Twenty-two hotels, from the Plaza in New York to the Cornhusker in Lincoln, Nebraska, staged "Fire and Ice" preview parties. The "Fire and Ice" promotion was named best ad of the year by *Advertising Age* magazine in 1952. Revlon managed to organize all of these campaigns despite very stormy agency relations. It has been reported that Revlon used nine separate advertising agencies between 1947 and 1957. Grey Advertising was contracted by Revlon in 1959, and the agency managed the account until 1987.

### The Revlon Girls

Revlon helped propel several young models to fame during the height of the brand's dominance in the 1950s and 1960s. Candice Bergen was a student in Philadelphia when Revlon splashed her image across the pages of *Vogue* magazine. Barbara Feldon, later "Agent 99" of television's *Get Smart,* was also signed to an exclusive contract. However, four young models—Dorian Leigh and her sister Suzy Parker, Barbara Britton, and Lauren Hutton—came to be so closely identified with Revlon over the middle decades of the twentieth century that they were, collectively, "the Revlon girl."

Dorian Leigh was already a leading model when she did her first Revlon promotion, "Fatal Apple," in 1945. After that, Revson used her in one shade campaign after another. Suzy Parker became so well-known that *Life* magazine devoted a cover to her in 1957. During the 1950s, Barbara Britton performed in nine commercials each week for Revlon: three each on *The $64,000 Question, The $64,000 Challenge,* and *The Walter Winchell File.* She became famous for the line, "If it's the finest of its kind it's by Revlon—Revlon London, Paris and New York," which opened *The Ed Sullivan Show* every week.

Although Charles Revson had a natural bias against television's black and white offerings (color was a key to Revlon's sales), he agreed to produce *The $64,000 Question,* a game show that first aired June 7, 1955. Within four weeks the show was number one in the ratings, and some of the Revlon products it featured enjoyed 300 percent and 500 percent sales growth. One shade of lipstick sold out in ten days. At its peak, a remarkable 82 percent of the nation's television sets were tuned to emcee Hal March, the famous "isolation booth," Revlon spokeswoman Barbara Britton, and the latest Revlon campaign.

*The $64,000 Question* catapulted Revlon to complete dominance of American cosmetics. Up until this time, Revlon had risen to the level of its competitors, but dominated only the nail polish market. It was these game show advertisements that raised Revlon sales, profits, and consumer awareness and gave the brand its lead position in the market. Sales, which had been growing at approximately 10 percent to 20 percent a year in the first half of the 1950s, suddenly shot up 54 percent in 1955—even though *The Question* was only on the air for the last six months of the year. Profits for the year tripled. In 1956, sales rose yet another 66 percent, to $85 million, and profits more than doubled. Competitors Helena Rubinstein, Max Factor, Coty, and Hazel Bishop, which had all been at least within striking distance of Revlon before the show went on the air, were left far behind. Revlon came up number one in lipstick, number one in hair spray, number one in nail products, and number one in makeup.

By 1957, however, a slew of competitive quiz shows had begun to dilute the question craze, and Revlon was compelled to raise the top prize money from $64,000 to $256,000 to keep audience's attention. Within a year, quiz shows had become old news, and worse, were the subject of federal hearings that revealed that *The Question* and other shows were fixed. *The $64,000 Question* was terminated, but not before it had boosted Revlon sales by over 100 percent.

## Competition with the Core Brand

During the mid-1960s, competition in the cosmetics industry heated up, and drew Charles Revson's attention from the basic Revlon brand to more upscale offerings. The company's Moon Drops dry-skin line, Etherea hypoallergenic line, and especially its Marcella Borghese and Ultima II prestige lines were enmeshed in hot competition with such names as Max Factor, Helena Rubinstein, Hazel Bishop, L'Oréal's Lancome and particularly Estée Lauder.

Estée Lauder came out with a hypoallergenic line before Revlon could, and gained an edge in the prestigious department store trade as well. Revson tried to promote the Revlon brand as a high-end competitor, yet released other upscale brands as well. The competition continued after Revson's death in 1975, when he was replaced by Michel Bergerac.

Revlon was unprepared to defend its 20 percent market share when growth in cosmetics demand fell in 1981. More versatile rivals began to chip away at Revlon's share, and retailers, tired of Revlon's heavy-handed merchandising tactics, began to offer more display space to other brands. Revlon also missed new beauty trends, like skin-care treatment. In addition, the brand's foreign beauty operations were plagued by weak management and successive losses. The negligence had a price: in 1981, earnings fell for the first time since 1968, by 9 percent.

During the early 1980s, the base of the Revlon brand's dominance in the mass-market was also attacked from both ends of the cosmetics industry. Paris-based L'Oréal and Avon Products cut into the brand's market share until Revlon came up second in sales in 1984, sandwiched between Avon at number one and L'Oréal in third. The overall slowdown in cosmetics use in the early 1980s compounded the impact of company management that allowed Revlon's basic beauty business to languish in favor of health care acquisitions.

To turn the basic beauty group around, Bergerac tried to refocus on the ailing Revlon brand. He devoted more spending to the brand, started a program to improve trade relations, and reorganized the sales department. By the mid-1980s, a revitalized creative department had brought "Custom Eyes" interchangeable eye shadow compacts to market, as well as a new line of skin-treatment products.

Custom Eyes was supported with a glamorous campaign featuring high fashion models like Iman, Jerry Hall, Rachel Hunter, and Claudia Schiffer. Later, the umbrella campaign that promoted the only brand straddling both mass market and popularly priced department stores utilized celebrities like Liza Minelli, Brooke Shields, Oprah Winfrey, and Frank and Barbara Sinatra.

Revlon was taken private in 1985 by corporate raider Ronald O. Perelman, owner of MacAndrews & Forbes Inc., a holding company. Perelman sold off the company's health care businesses to concentrate on cosmetics and worked to free up Revlon's creative department by simplifying the product development process. The changes cut the time it took to introduce a new product in half. By 1989, Revlon had introduced new products like "No Color" mascara made of a clear gel, and Electric Youth, a fragrance designed especially for teens that featured high-tech packaging and ads starring clean-cut teen rock star Debbie Gibson.

## Agency Juggling

During the late 1980s, Revlon was also plagued with agency shakeups that kept promotions off-balance. After 27 years with Revlon, Grey Advertising dropped its contract in December of 1987 to work for Procter & Gamble Company. Within a week, another agency, Bozell, Jacobs, Kenyon & Eckhardt left to promote Elizabeth Arden. Both houses claimed that their Revlon accounts had grown unprofitable when Revlon had started to shift much of its business to its in-house agency, The 50th Floor Workshop, Inc. Then, in 1989, Revlon hired Dick Tarlow as vice president of advertising, and purchased his agency, Tarlow Advertising. The shift allowed it to let agencies Hill Holliday, Connors, Cosmopulos and Sudler & Hennessey out of their assignments, and "hire" the proprietary agency to save on commissions.

## Refocus on the Mass Market

By 1991, Revlon's share of the upscale department store market had dropped to less than 8 percent, putting it in fourth place. That year, the company decided to refocus on its core brand and its relatively strong performance in that market. By this time, the mass market comprised 68 percent of cosmetics sales, or $1.37 billion. The company sold off several of its prestige brands, including Princess Marcella Borghese and Alexandra de Markoff, and used a sweeping reorganization of its North American operations to concentrate on selling Revlon in broad distribution and specialty stores. The move has helped Revlon hold its top position in drugstore sales, and has boosted the brand up to the number three position in mass-merchandising and supermarket sales.

## Performance Appraisal

Revlon was established with an innovative concept by a strong-willed founder. Charles Revson helped bring cosmetics out of the realm of taboo and into the mainstream. The brand's ingenious marketing schemes led it to dominance in the 1950s and 1960s, but when the cosmetics market was later segmented into department store and mass categories, Revlon's commanding lead was diluted by the introduction of upscale brands like Ultima II and Marcella Borghese and competitors like Estée Lauder. The death of Revlon's ambitious founder in 1975 also marked a break in the brand's advancement. Though the Revlon brands suffered due to company reorganization in the 1970s and increased competition in the 1980s, the company's renewed focus on its historical (and lucrative) stronghold may help the brand to recapture a larger share of the cosmetics market.

## Further Reading:

Bagot, Brian, "Beautiful Schemers," *Marketing & Media Decisions,* February 1990, pp. 59–66.

Benway, Susan Duffy, "Hey, Charlie's Back! Or at Least There's Fresh Allure to Revlon," *Barron's,* May 13, 1985, p. 34.

Berss, Marcia, "On the Scent," *Forbes,* March 12, 1984, pp. 88–89.

Davis, Donald A., "Whither Revlon?," *Drug & Cosmetic Industry,* April 1986, pp. 32, 102; "The Changing Face of the Cosmetic Industry," *Drug & Cosmetic Industry,* July 1992, pp. 8–16.

Freeman, Laurie, and Adrienne Ward, "Animal Uproar; Consumers at Odds with Animal Testing," *Advertising Age,* February 26, 1990, pp. S1–S2.

Lafayette, Jon, "Tarlow Cuts Shops," *Advertising Age,* August 14, 1989, pp. 45.

Nayyar, Seema, "Trade to Revlon: Lighten Up!," *AdWeek's Marketing Week,* June 8, 1992, p. 5.

Roman, Monica, "The Changes at Revlon Are More Than Just Cosmetic," *Business Week,* November 20, 1989, pp. 74, 76.

Sloan, Pat, "Revlon Shops on Edge: Makeup Shake-Up," *Advertising Age,* January 11, 1988, pp. 1, 58; "Revlon Redistributes to Win Wider Appeal," *Advertising Age,* August 19, 1991, p. 12.

Tobias, Andrew, *Fire and Ice: The Story of Charles Revson—The Man Who Built the Revlon Empire,* New York: William Morrow, 1976.

"Tracking Leading Marketers Becomes More Complicated; Establishing Leader List Entails Considerable Stretching," *Drug & Cosmetic Industry,* June 1992, pp. 30–35.

*—April S. Dougal*

# REYNOLDS WRAP®

Reynolds Wrap was the leading brand of aluminum foil in the U.S. consumer market in the early 1990s. The Reynolds Metals Company of Richmond, Virginia, also manufactured a variety of related kitchen products under the Reynolds brand name.

## Brand Origins

Reynolds Wrap was introduced by Reynolds Metals Company in 1947. It was the first aluminum foil to be marketed successfully for use in the kitchen, although aluminum foil for commercial purposes had been developed more than two decades earlier by the United States Foil Company, the predecessor to Reynolds Metals Company.

The history of Reynolds Wrap dates back to the founding of the United States Foil Company in 1919 by R.S. Reynolds, Sr., the nephew of tobacco tycoon R.J. Reynolds. For several years, U.S. Foil, with a single plant in Louisville, Kentucky, struggled along making tin foil for the inside wrappings of cigarette packages. At the time, the aluminum industry was in its infancy, but managers at U.S. Foil began to wonder if they could make a better protective foil, at less cost, using lighter weight aluminum instead of tin. U.S. Foil produced its first aluminum-foil wrappings in 1926. Two years later, the company built a plant exclusively to produce aluminum foil, and changed its name to Reynolds Metals Company.

For the next 14 years, Reynolds was content to be a modestly successful maker of foil for commercial packaging, buying its aluminum from the Aluminum Company of America (Alcoa), the only aluminum producer of any size in the United States at the time. In 1940 with Europe at war and the United States promising strategic materials to the Allies, Reynolds decided to begin producing its own aluminum. The company borrowed $15 million to build an aluminum-smelting plant near Sheffield, Alabama, and poured its first aluminum ingot on May 18, 1941. The U.S. government also built several aluminum plants during the war and commissioned Alcoa to run them. After the war, to break up Alcoa's near monopoly, the government sold its wartime plants to Alcoa's competitors. Reynolds purchased six of the wartime facilities. However, the added aluminum smelting capacity created a postwar glut of aluminum, inspiring Reynolds Metals to create a demand for an entirely new consumer product, Reynolds aluminum foil.

## Early Marketing

According to corporate lore, the idea of using aluminum foil for home cooking had actually been around since 1932, when a senior Reynolds Metals executive, Clarence Manning, was roused from a nap on Thanksgiving Day because his wife could not find a pan for roasting the turkey. Figuring he had little hope of borrowing a turkey roaster on such short notice, the executive gave his wife some aluminum foil samples that were being tested by a local meat packer for baking hams. The turkey was done to perfection, and Reynolds Metals began testing aluminum foil for a variety of home-kitchen uses.

However, the Depression and then World War II delayed the introduction of aluminum foil for the consumer market. Ironically, Alcoa, which would become Reynolds Metals' chief competitor, had marketed aluminum foil for home use in the 1930s, but only briefly. After the war, David P. Reynolds, one of the founder's four sons, would be credited with reviving the idea of selling aluminum foil as a consumer product. Because Reynolds Metals had no experience in the consumer market, it hired Charles Mapes, who had been with the Scott Paper Company, to develop the concept that would become Reynolds Wrap aluminum foil, including length of roll and packaging. He settled on a 25-square foot roll and a coral box with blue lettering. The package was later changed to a predominately blue box with white lettering, but the coral was retained on one end.

Mapes also was in charge of test marketing the new product in Richmond, Virginia. Until Reynolds Wrap was introduced in late 1947, the only other product sold almost exclusively for wrapping food was waxed paper. Therefore, the challenge facing Mapes was to educate the public to the many uses of aluminum foil. That process started with ads in the Richmond newspapers proclaiming, "New Kitchen Miracle Hits Richmond." The ads went on to explain that Reynolds Wrap was "The Perfect Food Wrap that you Bake and Cook in, too . . . 1001 Kitchen Miracles in every roll."

The marketing campaign also included in-store demonstrations on how to use Reynolds Wrap and an extensive lobbying effort to get local food editors and cooking schools to try the new product. David Reynolds, then vice president of sales and director of advertising and later chairman of the board, once recalled, "They called it 'silver paper' or 'tin foil,' and they didn't know what it could be used for. We showed them."

## AT A GLANCE

**R**eynolds Wrap brand of aluminum foil was introduced in 1947 by Reynolds Metals Company, Richmond, VA.

**Major competitor:** Store brand aluminum foil.

**Advertising:** *Agency*—J. Walter Thompson, 1972—. *Major campaign*—"New Tricks" recycling commericals.

**Addresses:** *Parent company*—Reynolds Metals Company, 6601 West Broad Street, Richmond, VA 23230; phone: (804) 281-2000; fax: (804) 281-4160.

The introduction of Reynolds Wrap in its hometown of Richmond proved successful, and Reynolds Metals soon expanded distribution of Reynolds Wrap to Philadelphia, Baltimore, Washington, DC, and New York, with each city receiving the same intensive marketing effort. Other early ads promised that women would become better cooks with Reynolds Wrap, and also promoted the use of aluminum foil by men for outdoor barbecuing. Sales representatives would actually set up barbecue grills in front of grocery stores, drug stores, hardware stores, and other places where Reynolds Wrap was sold, demonstrating how to line the grill for easy clean-up and how to wrap potatoes and corn-on-the-cob in aluminum foil for easy cooking. Meanwhile, home economists hired by Reynolds Metals continued to mail out a steady stream of recipes and new uses for Reynolds Wrap to food editors at newspapers and magazines.

Expansion, however, was put on hold when the Korean War broke out in 1950 and increased the government's need for aluminum. In response, Reynolds Metals ran an ad in national magazines headlined "Return Flight Guaranteed," and explaining that Reynolds Wrap had "gone to war." Reynolds Wrap remained available in limited quantities in the 33 markets where it had already been introduced.

Although the Korean War would not end until mid-1953, ads proclaiming "Reynolds Wrap Is Back" appeared in 1952, and Reynolds Metals resumed distribution of Reynolds Wrap. However, this time other aluminum companies were also entering the market. Reynolds Metals countered with national television advertising campaigns, magazine ads printed on aluminum foil, a door-to-door sales campaign by employees of its Louisville plant to boost sluggish summer sales, and by stepping up its consumer education programs.

In 1967 Reynolds published a cookbook, "Creative Cooking with Aluminum Foil," and in the late 1970s, the company produced a film entitled *Outdoor Cooking Adventures* that showed campers using Reynolds Wrap to fashion ovens, frying pans, soup bowls, and other cooking utensils. The 1970s also saw the creation of the Reynolds Wrap kitchens—modern, homelike testing facilities where home economists developed new uses for Reynolds Wrap in cooking and decoration. In addition to recipes, the Reynolds Wrap Kitchens produced brochures on using aluminum foil for freezing, gardening, and outdoor cooking. In 1974, *Forbes* said, "More than anyone else, [Reynolds Metals] changed aluminum from an exotic industrial raw material into a fabricated end product."

## Brand Extensions

In 1952 the company introduced a 75-square foot economy roll and a heavy duty Reynolds Wrap for freezer storage. The line expansion continued in 1955 with a 200-square foot roll, and in 1959 with Reynolds Aluminum foil gift wrap and Reynolds Wrap in colors, called Reynolds Wrap Jr. But probably the most welcome innovation in the 1950s was the serrated metal cutting edge on the Reynolds Wrap box. The 1960s saw the addition of Reynolds Wrap textured foil and a special foil for broiling.

In 1970 Reynolds Metals introduced its first non-aluminum consumer product, Brown-In-Bag cooking bags for the oven, later renamed Reynolds Oven Bags. Another non-aluminium product followed in 1977, Eskimo Freezer Paper, a plastic-coated freezer wrap that was later renamed Reynolds Freezer Paper. In 1982 Reynolds Metals introduced Reynolds Plastic Wrap, and in 1989 Reynolds Crystal Color, a line of colored plastic wraps. Although these products did not carry the "Reynolds Wrap" brand name, the company redesigned its packaging in 1993, reflecting the familiar graphics of the Reynolds Wrap cartons. The Reynolds emblem, resembling a heraldic crest, is a representation of the legendary St. George battling a dragon. Richard S. Reynolds reportedly chose the symbol in 1940 when he decided to begin refining aluminum, which would put his foil-making company in competition with the mighty Aluminum Company of America. The emblem was carried on boxes of Reynolds Wrap from its introduction.

In 1989 *Business Week* reported that Reynolds was considering brand-name trash bags, plastic cups, and other items that would be carried on shelves alongside Reynolds Wrap. William O. Burke, then chairman of Reynolds Metals, told *Business Week,* "We want to own that aisle" in the supermarket.

## "1001 Kitchen Miracles"

The first box of Reynolds Wrap promised that consumers would find "1001 Kitchen Miracles" inside, and although nobody at Reynolds Metals has kept track, the company is sure that that early marketing claim has come true, although not every use has been found in the kitchen. Over the years, Reynolds took pleasure in publicizing many of the unique uses people have found for aluminum foil, from covering windows at home to keep out the hot summer sun to wrapping hot dogs and cooking them on the exhaust manifold of a car during family vacations. The product is useful in crafts and decorations, and for emergency repairs—one family wrote Reynolds to tell how they had wrapped the wheel bearings of their camper with aluminum foil and "Reynolds Wrap . . . brought us all the way home."

During a performance of *Macbeth* at the Arena Stage in Washington, D.C., the entire theater-in-the-round was covered with Reynolds Wrap, which was then painted black and scrubbed with steel wool to give it the stark look of armor plate. In the 1960s artist Andy Warhol threw a party and covered his entire warehouse-sized studio in Reynolds Wrap, from the ceiling pipes to the walls; things that could not be wrapped in aluminum foil were painted silver, from the telephone to the commode. Also during the 1960s people were making dresses, bathing suits, and other fashions from Reynolds Wrap.

In addition to the consumer market, Reynolds Metals actively promoted aluminum foil for commercial packaging, and by the mid-1950s, more than a hundred food manufacturers were using aluminum foil from Reynolds Metals. Many of their packages also displayed the same Reynolds Metals corporate emblem that consumers were used to seeing on the Reynolds Wrap box.

### Recycling

Beneath the advertising line "1001 Kitchen Miracles" on the first Reynolds Wrap package designed by Charles Mapes in 1947 were the words "rinse and use it over and over." Although reusability was always important in marketing Reynolds Wrap, recycling aluminum foil became a major campaign for the company in the early 1990s. In one popular television commercial, a dog was shown eating off of a sheet of Reynolds Wrap, then rinsing it under the kitchen faucet, and finally depositing it in a bin with aluminum cans. An unseen announcer explained that "Recycling is easy when you use Reynolds Wrap. So use it for everything." Schools also were encouraged to compete for cash prizes in the "Great Balls of Foil!" recycling contest. In 1992 the competition in 33 cities resulted in the collection of more than 36 tons of aluminum foil, a substantial portion of the 246 tons of aluminum foil Reynolds Metals said it recycled in 1992.

### Further Reading:

"Can Reynolds Wrap Up the Kitchen Market?" *Business Week,* May 19, 1989, pp. 68–69.

*Happy 40th Anniversary: Reynolds Wrap,* Richmond, VA: Reynolds Metals Company, 1987.

*The Reynolds Wrap Story,* Richmond, VA: Reynolds Metals Company, 1977.

"Two More Reynolds Creations," *Forbes,* December 1, 1971, p. 36.

"Voyage into the Unknown," *Forbes,* December 1, 1971, pp. 30–41.

*—Dean Boyer*

# RIGHT GUARD®

**RIGHT GUARD®**

The Gillette Company's Right Guard brand deodorants and antiperspirants have ranked among market leaders from their introduction in 1960. Originally positioned as a men's deodorant, Right Guard was later marketed to both men and women. The brand quickly captured over 20 percent of the U.S. deodorant/antiperspirant market, a share it held until 1973, when it began to lose market share as a result of consumers' revolt against the use of fluorocarbons in aerosol sprays. Although unable to regain its dominance of the market, Right Guard maintained a respectable market share throughout the 1970s and 1980s; by the fourth quarter of 1992, Right Guard products had captured 8.5 percent of the $1.46 billion U.S. market. With a strong brand identity, sure corporate backing, and innovative advertising, Right Guard promises to retain a comparable share through the 1990s.

## Origins

The Gillette Company worked its way into the top echelons of American business on the success of one product: razors. Founded by the flamboyant entrepreneur King C. Gillette, the Gillette company name became nearly synonymous with razor blades, and the company captured 64 percent of the U.S. shaving market by 1989. Like most modern corporations, however, Gillette diversified its product offerings over the years. In addition to razors, blades, and shaving creams, Gillette makes men's and women's toiletries, writing implements (PaperMate), coffee makers (Braun), and dental products (Oral-B). Right Guard underarm deodorant began as just one addition to a rapidly expanding product line, but its immense popularity soon made it the leader of Gillette's toiletries and cosmetics division, which also includes Dry Idea deodorants and antiperspirants, White Rain hair care products, Foamy shaving creams, and Jafra skin care and cosmetics.

In the late 1950s, Gillette executive Vincent Ziegler pursued a strategy of broadening the Gillette product base. According to Russell B. Adams, Jr., author of *King C. Gillette: The Man and His Wonderful Shaving Device,* Ziegler posted this encouragement over his conference-room blackboard: "Nothing will ever be attempted if all possible objections must be first overcome." The first objection to introducing a new deodorant was that Gillette's initial entry into the women's deodorant market, Hush, was a dismal failure. But Ziegler and others favoring new product development pointed to the example of Mennen, which had introduced a deodorant for men that quickly captured half the market. Surely there was room for another entrant in the rapidly expanding men's deodorant market. "Surveying the wide range of squeeze sprays, roll-ons, sticks, and other types of available products," wrote Adams, "Gillette hit on the still-novel aerosol method of application, then featured in only about 1 percent of the deodorants on the market." After strenuous testing, Gillette introduced its new product to a consumer test panel which concluded that it was as good as or better than all its potential competitors. Newly christened as Right Guard, the deodorant was introduced on a trial basis in four cities. After capturing 20 percent of the market in the test cities, Right Guard was introduced nationally in mid-1960.

## Early Advertising

Right Guard's early marketing stressed its appeal to men: the product was promoted on Gillette-sponsored World Series games and on *Cavalcade of Sports* television programs. "Gillette's studied advertising strategy," noted Adams, "had been to position Right Guard unequivocally as a men's product, an aim that was accomplished primarily by television commercials featuring sweating athletes and deep-voiced announcers who spoke of 'Right Guard, the convenient deodorant made especially for men.' " This strategy landed Right Guard an immediate 11 percent market share, which grew to 27 percent by 1963. Although Gillette marketers could not help but be pleased, the men's deodorant market accounted for only 27 percent of the $130 million U.S. market. If they wanted real success in the deodorant market, they would have to sell their product to women as well.

Many within Gillette resisted marketing Right Guard to both sexes, arguing that men would object to using a product that was also marketed to women, and that the company could ill afford the costs of the big advertising campaign needed to reposition the product. But Ziegler overrode the objections, launching an advertising campaign that set important precedents for the brand. The commercials depicted a teenage girl in a bathroom asking her brother where their mom keeps her deodorant. "All I see here is Right Guard," she says. "That's it, Sis," Jimmy replies. "The whole family uses it now." "But I thought it was a man's deodorant," says his sister. "Right Guard *is* a man's deodorant," Jimmy answers, "but Mom and Betty found out how great it is. Give it a try." An announcer then reminded viewers that "Gillette Right Guard power spray is just right for the whole family . . . because nothing touches you but the spray itself." Those who shuddered at

## AT A GLANCE

**R**ight Guard brand deodorants and antiperspirants introduced in 1960 by the Gillette Company; Right Guard Sport introduced in 1987.

**Performance:** *Market share*—8.5% (second place) of the deodorant and antiperspirant category. *Sales*—$120 million (estimate).

**Major competitor:** Procter & Gamble's Secret; also Procter & Gamble's Sure and Old Spice, Colgate-Palmolive's Mennen, Helen Curtis's Degree, Carter-Wallace's Arrid, Bristol-Myers's Ban.

**Advertising:** *Agency*—N. W. Ayer, New York, NY, 1987—. *Major campaign*—"Sports Animals" commercials featuring notoriously wild sports figures Marvin Hagler, Charles Barkley, Hulk Hogan, Chuck Norris, and others.

**Addresses:** *Parent company*—Gillette Co., Prudential Tower Building, Boston, MA 02199; phone: (617) 421-7000; fax: (617) 421-7123.

the thought of using someone else's roll-on or stick deodorant could easily share an aerosol. With this campaign, which ran on more family-oriented programs, Right Guard succeeded in winning over the entire family and became a major player in the market. By 1965, Right Guard had captured over 20 percent of the $200 million deodorant/antiperspirant market by stressing the benefits of its aerosol product. Gillette's reliance on the aerosol medium, however, would come back to haunt them a decade later.

### Adjusting to a Regulated Marketplace

Right Guard enjoyed nearly ten years of dominance in the U.S. deodorant/antiperspirant market before the roof fell in. In 1974, according to the *Wall Street Journal,* researchers reported that "the fluorocarbon gases used in aerosol sprays could impair the atmosphere's ability to screen out excess ultraviolet radiation. The Food and Drug Administration said it would ban fluorocarbon aerosols, consumers began to turn away from them, and Gillette, like many manufacturers, announced plans to discontinue them." Roll-ons quickly became the underarm product of choice for most Americans, and Bristol-Myers' new product, Ban roll-on, soon captured the leading market share. In 1977 Gillette responded with a new advertising campaign promoting its non-aerosol Right Guard "power pump," in which football players Garo Yepremian and Dave Casper told television viewers, "You can spray twice as much Ban Basic and still not match the power of Right Guard." *Advertising Age* reported that Gillette invested $5 million in the campaign, but to no avail. Bristol-Myers' Ban products claimed 16.7 percent of the market by 1977, compared to Right Guard's 15.4 percent. Another result of the aerosol scare was Gillette's development of a new deodorant/antiperspirant line called Dry Idea, which it introduced in 1979. The new brand allowed Gillette to retain strength in the market, but it also cut into Right Guard sales, which declined by the early 1980s to less than 9 percent of the market.

Adding to the difficulties of Right Guard's second decade of existence were the efforts of the Federal Trade Commission (FTC) and consumer groups to ensure the validity of product claims made in advertising. In 1973, the FTC demanded that eight deodorant and antiperspirant makers document their advertising

claims. Gillette was asked to provide substantiation for its claim that Right Guard is the product with "the best wetness fighter in any antiperspirant spray," reported the *Wall Street Journal.* Two years later, the FTC questioned a Right Guard advertisement that touted the product as an "antistain, antiperspirant . . . so effective it helps prevent wetness AND stains." Gillette provided evidence of extensive testing—it had provided white shirts to six "heavy antiperspirant stainers," asked them to use several different products, and eventually concluded that perspirers using Right Guard Powder Dry stained substantially less—and in both cases no action was taken.

Gillette had anticipated one potential regulatory disaster in 1973, when it removed two products from the market because tests had shown "mild inflammatory" reactions when the product was tested on animals, according to the *Wall Street Journal.* The products—Right Guard Extra Strength Anti-Perspirant and Soft & Dri Extra Strength Anti-Perspirant—had passed all necessary medical tests, but were withdrawn at the insistence of Robert P. Giovacchini, head of Gillette's Medical Evaluation Laboratories. The recall cost Gillette over $1.5 million, but Giovacchini later became a hero within the company, for the ingredient that had caused the irritation—zirconium—was later banned from all aerosol antiperspirant use. "Consumer advocates hailed the company's move," wrote Adams, who added that "Gillette's action was surely a rare instance of a manufacturer's withdrawing a product before being told to do so by the government agency."

### Reinvigorating Right Guard

In 1982, Gillette responded to what had been almost a decade of market share decline for its Right Guard brand products with what the *Wall Street Journal* hailed as a "major relaunch." The company poured over $28 million—more than it had ever used to launch a new product—into television commercials, print advertising, promotion, and packaging. Under the theme "The Changing of the Guard," Right Guard appeared in new black containers with bold graphics and color coding to distinguish the new varieties of deodorants and antiperspirants. More than just the container was changed, however. Aerosol, stick, and roll-on applications of Right Guard had all been reformulated, and a new scent was added to the stick version. Seeking to protect its own declining market share, Mennen quickly filed suit against Gillette and its advertising agency, Young and Rubicam Inc., charging that Right Guard's new package infringed on the Mennen package design and was misleading to consumers. A federal judge in New York ruled in favor of Gillette, however.

Gillette's relaunch of Right Guard failed to have the desired effect, as Procter & Gamble's Secret and Sure brands dominated a market divided among an ever-changing and growing number of products. *Advertising Age* contributor Judith Graham attributed Right Guard's stagnant growth to the very nature of the deodorant/antiperspirant market, which she said is driven by "consumers' tendency to buy shapes and forms rather than brands." The most popular products in the market in the early 1980s were solids and sticks, and Gillette was still overly reliant on its sprays. By 1987, however, Gillette took steps to reassert itself in the changing market.

"We don't intend to remain in second place," announced Gillette vice-president of finance Milton Glass in 1987, as Gillette launched a strategy designed to boost all of its deodorant/antiperspirant products. Carole Johnson, marketing manager of Gillette's personal-care division, told *Advertising Age:* "Now that we've spent time building our roll-on and aerosol business, we feel it's time to turn our attention to the sticks/solids business." It was high time: in the previous 18 months, 65 new aromas, shapes, and sizes of deodorant and antiperspirant had been introduced in response to consumer desire for "twist-up" products. Right Guard Sport, aimed at men between the ages of 18 and 34, was introduced in solid, stick, and aerosol applications, and was supported by a $12 million advertising and promotional campaign designed by N. W. Ayer.

Right Guard's distinctive new campaign, featuring notoriously rough sports figures touting the civilizing aspects of Right Guard, proved enormously successful and was still running in 1993. The initial commercial featured tough boxer "Marvelous" Marvin Hagler; other 1980s commercials featured baseball player Kirk Gibson and football player Brian Bosworth, who noted that anything less than Right Guard would be "uncivilized." Jan Keeler, senior vice-president at N. W. Ayer, reported that the commercials helped to increase Right Guard's market share 69 percent between 1988 and 1989. The campaign worked, noted Keeler in *Advertising Age,* because it "allowed us to present torture-test advocacy: That if the meanest, toughest guys in sports are using the product, it must work." N. W. Ayer executive Jeanne Chinard added: "We're lucky that the whole concept depends on these sports figures being wild. There's always some risk, but generally the wilder they are the better because we're using the product to tame them." The campaign continued into the 1990s. Notable commercials featured burly professional wrestler Hulk Hogan painting a delicate seascape and proclaiming, "A true artiste should be remembered for inspiration, not perspiration," and martial artist and actor Chuck Norris advising that "the best defense is not to offend."

## Changing in the 1990s

The early 1990s saw Right Guard brand deodorants and antiperspirants face new opportunities and unique challenges. In 1992, Right Guard was "relaunched" in Great Britain, with the aim of capturing the number one market position in a country which saw significant increases in usage of deodorants and antiperspirants in the 1980s. Leading the relaunch is Right Guard Drive, aimed at a similar market segment to that held by Right Guard Sport in the United States. In 1993, Gillette added Right Guard Rapide for Men and Right Guard Azure for Women, both newly scented products designed to appeal to consumers between the ages of 15 and 24.

At the same time that Right Guard was meeting with success overseas, it faced a number of challenges in the U.S. market. Helene Curtis's new Degree antiperspirant, introduced in 1990, immediately stole market share from all other products because of its superior technology. The unisex Degree has a unique body-heat activation formula that promises all-day protection. *Advertising Age* contributors Pat Sloan and Laurie Freeman predicted that other manufacturers would have to invest in new deodorant/antiperspirant technologies to remain competitive.

Another competitor came from within Right Guard's parent company, as Gillette announced the introduction of its new "Gillette Series" line of products in the fall of 1992. Designed to capitalize on the success of Gillette's razor business, the new line of personal products share the theme, "Gillette: The best a man can get." The Gillette Series products benefitted from Gillette's

renewed commitment to improved technology, as did Gillette's other brands, including Right Guard, Dry Idea, and Soft & Dri. But sources within the company indicated to *Wall Street Journal* reporter Lawrence Ingrassia that the new line seemed sure to steal market share from Right Guard. This tradeoff—advancing a Gillette "superbrand" at the expense of the old standbys—was deemed acceptable to the company. "We're already the worldwide leader in blades," Gillette chairman and chief executive Alfred M. Zeien told Ingrassia. "Will we be the world-wide leader in other toiletries or not? That's our goal." It remained to be seen in 1993 whether the Right Guard brand would be lifted by the rising fortunes of its parent company.

## Further Reading:

Adams, Russell B., Jr., *King C. Gillette: The Man and His Wonderful Shaving Device,* Boston: Little Brown, 1978.

"All about Deodorants," *New York Times,* August 12, 1990.

"Antiperspirant Makers Ordered to Document Advertising Claims," *Wall Street Journal,* May 25, 1973.

"Brand Report 35: Deodorants and Anti-perspirants," *Marketing & Media Decisions,* November 1978.

"Chuck Norris Gets Civilized," *Adweek Eastern Edition,* July 6, 1992.

"Corporate Album: Gillette Co.," *Boston Business Journal,* April 23, 1993.

"Deodorants," *Progressive Grocer,* August 1991.

Fannin, Rebecca, "Brand Report 62: Deodorants," *Marketing & Media Decisions,* February 1981.

Fitch, Ed, "Tough to Argue With: Being a Sports Animal Has Its Advertising Perks," *Advertising Age,* August 21, 1989.

"Gillette and Others Give Data to FTC on Underarm Stains," *Wall Street Journal,* July 7, 1975.

*Gillette Company Annual Reports,* Boston: Gillette Co., 1968-1991.

"Gillette Co. to Call Back 2 New Anti-Perspirants," *Wall Street Journal,* October 2, 1973.

"Gillette Co. to Spend $28 Million in Push for New Right Guard," *Wall Street Journal,* March 8, 1983.

"Gillette Wins Round in Suit by Mennen Co. on Deodorant Package," *Wall Street Journal,* May 31, 1983.

Graham, Judith, "Gillette Fights Back: Major Push for Antiperspirants," *Advertising Age,* October 26, 1987.

Grimm, Matthew, "Gillette Back Heavy in Sports," *Brandweek,* March 15, 1993.

Ingrassia, Lawrence, *Wall Street Journal,* "Face-Off: A Recovering Gillette Hopes for Vindication," September 29, 1989; "Marketing: Gillette Ties New Toiletries to Hot Razor," September 18, 1992; "Taming the Monster—How Big Companies Can Change," *Wall Street Journal,* December 10, 1992.

Lippert, Barbara, "Adweek Critique: The Hulkster Gets Civilized for Right Guard," *Adweek Eastern Edition,* January 14, 1991.

Nayyar, Seema, "Gillette Takes Old New," *Brandweek,* September 21, 1992.

"No Worries for Right Guard as It Heads for the Top," *Chemist & Druggist,* March 14, 1992.

O'Connor, John J., "New Pump Sprays Aim at Ban Basic: Right Guard, Arrid Join Antiperspirant Trend," *Advertising Age,* July 11, 1977.

"Right Guard Gets Young Appeal Variants," *Chemist & Druggist,* May 15, 1993.

Shore, A., "Cosmetics and Household Products Industry Report," Paine-Webber, Inc., April 8, 1993.

Sloan, Pat, "Heat's on Gillette," *Advertising Age,* March 30, 1992.

Sloan, Pat, and Laurie Freeman, "Degree Makes Leaders Sweat," *Advertising Age,* December 10, 1990.

"Sweating It Out: Time, Risk, Ingenuity All Go Into Launching New Personal Product," *Wall Street Journal,* November 17, 1978.

*—Tom Pendergast*

# ROBITUSSIN®

America's leader in over-the-counter cough and cold remedies, the Robitussin line of products has expanded from one cough syrup formula introduced more than 40 years ago to include some dozen syrups, soft-gel caplets, and cough drops for adults and children. Manufactured by the A. H. Robins Company, now a division of American Home Products, Robitussin has a 43.6 percent share of the cough syrup market with approximately $214 million in annual consumer sales, according to July 1993 Nielsen survey data.

## History of the Brand

The flagship product of the A. H. Robins Company, based in Richmond, Virginia, Robitussin was introduced and trademarked in 1949 as an "ethical over-the-counter" drug. In other words, the product was recommended by physicians and could be obtained from a pharmacist without a prescription.

In 1954 Robins produced the current Robitussin formula, the active ingredient of which is guaifenesin. An expectorant, guaifenesin works to loosen phlegm and thin bronchial secretions to make coughing more productive. It is the only expectorant sanctioned by the U.S. Food and Drug Administration as being safe and effective in over-the-counter products.

A. H. Robins was acquired by American Home Products Corporation in December 1989. The parent company of a host of prescription and non-prescription pharmaceuticals, it is also a leader in infant product, medical supply, and other health-related industries as well as animal health care products. American Home Products is the parent company of such food lines as Chef Boyardee prepared pasta products, Pam cooking spray, and Gulden's mustard. Within American Home Products' corporate structure, A. H. Robins and Whitehall Laboratories share the lucrative over-the-counter drug division.

## Line Extensions

The original Robitussin formula was patented in 1954. In 1965 another cough syrup, Robitussin DM, was introduced as a product to control cough and relieve chest congestion. A third cough syrup, Robitussin PE, formulated to clear nasal stuffiness and loosen and relieve chest congestion, was introduced in 1967. In that year, the first Robitussin cough drop, Robitussin DM Cough Calmers, was also launched. Robitussin CF, a syrup to relieve

nasal stuffiness, control cough, and loosen and relieve chest congestion, came on the market in 1974.

Only one Robitussin product, Robitussin Night Relief, was introduced in the 1980s. In the early 1990s, a number of new Robitussin line extensions were launched, including Robitussin Pediatric, the first non-prescription Robitussin formula targeted exclusively toward children. Maximum Strength Robitussin, Robitussin Pediatric Cough & Cold, and Robitussin Cough Drops were introduced in 1991, and Robitussin Maximum Strength Cough & Cold hit the market in 1992.

In 1993 the company launched a number of products that offered not only higher concentrations of guaifenesin but also a new way of taking cough and cold medications. These new formulations were manufactured in capsule form, in which a clear liquid medication was surrounded by a seamless gelatin capsule. In this way, consumers who preferred not to swallow syrups could instead ingest cold and cough medication in an easy-to-swallow form. Among the products in this new format are Robitussin Severe Congestion Liqui-gels and Robitussin Cough & Cold Liqui-gels. Also introduced in 1993 were Robitussin Pediatric Night Relief and Robitussin Liquid Center Cough Drops.

## Sales

Robitussin is the leader in the cough syrup category, with a 43.6 percent share of the $490 million industry, according to July 1993 data provided by Nielsen. Among its rivals vying for market position are Procter & Gamble's Nyquil, Richardson-Vicks's Vicks, and Miles Inc.'s Alka Seltzer Plus.

In the $350 million cough drop category, Robitussin's share amounts to slightly over 10 percent, according to Nielsen. Warner Lambert Co.'s Halls, Vicks, and F & F Laboratories' Smith Brothers compete for market share with a number of private-label brands. With the introduction of its liqui-gel products, Robitussin anticipates major inroads in the cold treatment category, which currently amounts to some $2.3 billion in annual sales.

## Advertising

Among the strong advertising and promotional efforts that support the Robitussin line of products are national television commercials, free-standing inserts, mail-in rebates, and in-package coupons. The advertising agency for the brand, Scali, McCabe & Sloves, is responsible for such well-known television spots as the "Dr. Mom" series, in which the slogan "Recommended by Dr. Mom" is the familiar tag line. The commercials show a mother dispensing Robitussin cough remedies to her children with the assurance that they are recommended more than any other brand by doctors and pharmacists.

## Further Reading:

*Superbrands 1991,* "OTC Drugs: An Industry Reaches to the Converted," pp. 108–12.

Other information supplied by A. H. Robins/Whitehall Labs.

*—Marcia K. Mogelonsky*

# ROLEX®

The Rolex brand of wristwatches has been a status symbol for decades. In 1948 Rolex Watch U.S.A., Inc., a subsidiary of Geneva, Switzerland-based Montres Rolex S.A., opened its doors for the first time. Ever since, Rolex wristwatches have found their biggest market in the United States. (There are also more counterfeit Rolex watches sold illegally in the United States than anywhere else in the world.) The universal success of the Rolex brand has been due to the watch's unsurpassed quality, international marketing, and patronage of ''prestigious'' sports such as polo, horse racing and yachting. Although Rolex has always disdained the mass market approach of American watchmakers such as Timex and Bulova, the company has been on the cutting edge of watchmaking; Rolex was the first company to develop the waterproof watch in 1926, and was the first to make the fully automated watch in 1931.

## Brand Origins

Until the late nineteenth century, the pocket watch was universal for both sexes. After that, many realized the utility of a watch on the wrist rather than a cumbersome pocket watch. Hans Wilsdorf, the founder of the Rolex watch, moved from Germany to Switzerland as a young man to master the watch trade. A talented entrepreneur, Wilsdorf headed for London when he finished his apprenticeship. There, in 1905, Wilsdorf established the Wilsdorf & Davis Company, sensing the possibilities of the wristwatch. Although the company initially made watch cases and only marketed wristwatches, it was establishing a reputation as an innovator by producing a compact travel clock and an impressive ''portfolio'' watch.

Hence when the company started selling wristwatches, the incentive was there to make them unusual. Unlike competitors, Wilsdorf's firm sold its wristwatches in a variety of cases, including rugged sports cases and more elegant, formal ones. The market for wristwatches prior to World War I was small but growing, and Wilsdorf's products sold well. He dubbed his wristwatches with a unique name that could be pronounced in virtually all languages: Rolex. (It was also a short enough name to be inscribed on the dial.) In 1908 the Rolex wristwatch was launched, and, two years later, the watch won an award for precision timing. In 1914 the Kew Observatory in Great Britain distinguished the Rolex watch with a Class A certificate, the first brand of wristwatch ever to be so honored. Superior performance would be the foundation of the

Rolex watch's enviable success. Subjecting every watch to time consuming and costly precision tests also meant that the watch would cater to the affluent.

Demand for wristwatches exploded during the long years of World War I. More and more watch firms were latching on to wristwatches, giving their brands military names such as tank and aviator. One firm even created a watch dial that would light up in the dark. Thereafter, the popularity of the wristwatch was assured, especially among the young, the sports-minded, and women.

## First Commercial Success

At the end of the war in 1919, many European countries erected high tariff barriers. This affected Hans Wilsdorf's firm in London, since all Rolex watch parts were imported from Switzerland. When the British government raised the import tax 33 percent in 1919, Wilsdorf could not stay in business. That year he moved back to Geneva, where he established Montres Rolex S.A., retaining the London office as a branch.

A knotty problem for his firm, which depended on the international market for success, was creating a moisture-proof watch. Many Rolex watch shipments, especially those to Asia and Africa, were being damaged by fierce humidity and water. Company researchers focused on the problem throughout the 1920s and found the solution in 1926. That year, the Rolex watch received a patent for its waterproof solution. The improved watch—the first of its kind—was subsequently named the Oyster. For precision timing and waterproof protection, Rolex wristwatches were setting the industry standard.

While business was good in the years following World War I, it was not until 1927 that Rolex experienced radical success. That year young British stenographer Mercedes Gleitze became the first person to swim the English Channel. She wore the Rolex Oyster watch during the entire 15-hour ordeal. When she emerged from the frigid waters, the watch was undamaged and kept perfect time. Rolex quickly touted this triumph of engineering. While other watch firms raced to introduce their own waterproof watches, Rolex was the acknowledged beneficiary of the swimming feat.

## Product Development

The Rolex Oyster remained as the basic Rolex model, but improvements were continuously added. The 1928 Rolex Prince

## AT A GLANCE

**R**olex brand of wristwatch introduced in 1908 by Hans Wilsdorf, founder of wristwatch firm Wilsdorf & Davis Company, London; in 1919, firm moved to Geneva, Switzerland, where it adopted the name Montres Rolex S.A.; in 1948 U.S. subsidiary Rolex Watch U.S.A., Inc. was established in New York City.

**Performance:** *Sales*—$100 million.

**Major competitor:** Omega Warch Corp.'s Omega; also Rado Watch Co., Inc.'s Rado; also Seiko Corp. of America's Seiko.

**Advertising:** *Agency*—J. Walter Thompson, New York, NY, 1967—. *Major campaign*—Glossy, full page magazine ad featuring photograph of smiling golfer Arnold Palmer with silver trophy accompanied by slogan, "Rolex and the Senior Open: the Classics Endure."

**Addresses:** *Parent company*—Rolex Watch U.S.A., Inc; Rolex Building, 665 Fifth Avenue, New York, NY 10022-5383; phone: (212) 758-7700; fax: (212) 980-2166. *Ultimate parent company*—Montres Rolex S.A., Rue Francois-Dussaud, 1211 Geneva, Switzerland; phone: 011-41-22-30-82200; fax: 011-41-223-002255.

featured a rectangular watch case and dual dialing. With the development of the waterproof watch in 1926, Rolex watches were fully dustproof and shock resistant. The next challenge for Rolex was creating an automatic, or self-winding, Oyster wristwatch. Attempts to manufacture such a watch had been made as far back as the mid-19th century, but the constant movement of the wrist negated the engineering methods of the day. In 1931 the head of Rolex's technical division in Geneva, successfully devised a rotating mechanism in the watch that resulted in the first ever self-winding wristwatch. Hence the Rolex Perpetual was born. It was shock resistant, dustproof, and waterproof, and although it was self-winding, the hand winder was retained on the watch to avoid alienating the more tradition-minded customer.

Rolex received numerous first-class awards from observatories in England, France and Switzerland after this innovation, heightening Rolex's formidable reputation for superior workmanship. The World War II years ground Rolex innovations and sales virtually to a halt. However, during the last year of the war, Rolex came out with the Datejust, the first wristwatch to display the date on the dial. Style variations followed, especially in the watch bracelet. In 1955 an aviator's watch, the Rolex GM-Master, allowed the pilot to gauge exact time in different time zones. By then, a special Rolex watch for deep sea divers had been introduced that enabled them to wear a Rolex to a depth of 330 feet (in 1971 this capacity was enhanced to 20,000 feet). While Rolex was not the inventor of the Quartz watch, which gained popularity in the 1970s, it came out with its own version.

In the 1990s, annual production of less than one million Rolex watches per year scarcely kept up with the demand. Throughout the 20th century, Rolex has been synonymous with high or rising status and superior, rather than merely good, performance and engineering. In the early 1990s, Rolex manufactured several types of watch products, from the stainless steel Tudor watch—priced at the lower end of the scale at approximately $1,000—to the 18-karat gold watches, including the Cellini line or Oyster brand, that cost more than $10,000.

## The Counterfeiting Problem

Because of the high prestige of Rolex watches and the company's adherence—despite variations—to one basic model, counterfeiting of Rolex watches was relatively easy and became a serious problem in the 1970s and 1980s. With the refinement of counterfeiting techniques, astonishingly good look-alikes could be sold abroad for a fraction of the real cost of a Rolex—and in some cases, for the same cost to unwary purchasers. The most lucrative black markets for such items were in Los Angeles, New York, Miami, Houston, and Chicago. In these cities, local business people with ties to Asian port cities—where many counterfeiters were based—often obtained hundreds of thousands of fake Rolex watches for illegal sales, usually via street vendors. Sometimes they merely procured the machinery to convert cheap watches into Rolex look-alikes, and only a highly trained eye could catch the dissimilarities. Because Rolex feared a cheapening of its image as a result of the illegal use of its trademark, they called the FBI. By 1990, an ingenious anti-counterfeit label was developed for the watches which slowed down, but by no means solved, the problem of fake Rolex watches.

## Advertising

From the inception of the Wilsdorf & Davis watch company in London, advertising was extremely important in the firm's marketing strategy. All advertising means of the day were used, especially the print media. Even before Mercedes Gleitze's channel swim made Rolex renowned, the company had launched a massive advertising campaign in the print media to announce the Rolex Oyster, its waterproof watch. The ads, which generally displayed several styles of watches, were always careful to note that these masculine looking wristwatches were "for men OR women." In 1925 the firm also had made sure that the Rolex trademark name was stamped on the case and dial of all of its wristwatches.

The Gleitze triumph, or rather, the triumph of the Rolex waterproof watch she was wearing, was advertised for all it was worth. The heroine's photo appeared in all Rolex ads, and advertising gimmicks in jewelry stores featured the Rolex Oyster watch in an aquarium along with live fish. Any feat that involved a Rolex watch, such as the 1930s flight from London to Melbourne, Australia by Lieutenant Cathcart Jones, who wore a Rolex watch that kept perfect time during the grueling flight, was seized upon by adroit Rolex advertising executives. A 1930 advertisement in the London *Watch & Clock Maker* stressed the fact that Rolex wristwatches were "waterproof, dustproof, sandproof, perspirationproof."

Radio personalities in the 1930s endorsed the Rolex brand, and the use of celebrities subsequently became an important advertising ploy. After World War II, country clubs found Rolex a willing sponsor, as did most high-profile, prestige sporting events such as polo, yachting, golfing, horse racing, and tennis tournaments. Always the image of Rolex as the ultimate prestige wristwatch has been carefully cultivated.

## International Growth

The jewelry business, to which one could include luxury watches, depends heavily on an international clientele, because only a small segment of the public can afford real jewels, gold, and silver. The luxury watch trade in the United States is only approximately six percent of the wristwatch business overall. After World

War I, Rolex watches were exported to Asian and African markets, which provided the incentive to come up with a waterproof, and hence rustproof, wristwatch. In the 1930s, exports to the Far East, before the outbreak of the Sino-Japanese war in 1937, were increasingly lucrative. Immediately following World War II, Rolex strove to re-establish itself in the Far East and Japan. In 1948 the Swiss company established a branch, Rolex Watch U.S.A., in New York City. Since then, North America has become Rolex's most important market. In the 1970s and 1980s, sales of Rolex watches in the United States rose 20 percent annually.

The success of Rolex is beyond dispute, and with the fall of trade barriers worldwide, there will be lucrative markets for the ''Rolls Royce'' of wristwatches well into the 21st century.

## Further Reading:

Bremner, Brian, ''Stalking the Wild—and Phony—Rolex Watch,'' *Crains Chicago Business,* March 7, 1988, p. 3.

Forden, Sara Gay, ''China Embraces New Revolution: Designer Fashion,'' *WWD,* May 21, 1993, p. 1.

Fuhrman, Peter, ''Jewelry for the Wrist,'' *Forbes,* November 23, 1992, pp. 173–178.

Gordon, George, *Rolex, Timeless Elegance,* Hong Kong: Zie Yongder Co., Ltd., 1989.

Jardine, Cassandra, ''Timeless Mystique of the Rolex,'' *Business-London,* February 1988, pp. 114–117.

Merina, Victor, ''Watch Thieves Put the Arm on Wearers of Costly Rolex,'' *Los Angeles Times,* July 9, 1990, p. A1.

Seymore, Kelly Bishop, ''Time Watches as Rolex Flees,'' *Mediaweek,* May 6, 1991, p. 5.

*—Sina Dubovoj*

# S.O.S®

S.O.S brand of scouring pad stood as the leading soap-filled scouring pad on the market in 1993, with sales of nearly $48 million. Owned by Miles Inc., the brand accounted for about 60 percent of the market, compared to 25 percent for Dial Corporation's Brillo soap pads, its primary competitor.

## Brand Origins

In the early 1900s, women in the United States began replacing heavy, black cast-iron pots and pans with shiny new aluminum cookware. Coal stoves quickly covered the aluminum pots with grime, and even gas stoves left the cookware blackened. The need arose for a product that would keep aluminum cookware looking new.

Erwin W. Cox, a door-to-door salesman of aluminum cookware in San Francisco, was very familiar with the problem. He also needed a gimmick to help him sell his wares. Cox dreamed up the idea of soap-filled pads of steel wool and, initially, offered them as free gifts to housewives who let him demonstrate his pots and pans. When customers began calling his house asking for more soap pads, Cox decided to go into business as a manufacturer. He also needed a name for his product and, according to folk lore, his wife suggested ''S.O.S.,'' the international distress signal mistakenly believed to stand for ''Save Our Ships.'' She reasoned that these initials could also stand for ''Save Our Saucepans.'' The name was later changed to S.O.S—with two periods—to protect the trademark.

Cox applied for a patent on his soap-filled steel-wool pad in 1917, four years after another peddler of pots and pans had founded the Brillo Soap Pad Company in Brooklyn, New York. S.O.S pads, however, were significantly different. Brillo came with a cake of reddish polishing soap in a box of steel wool pads. Cox, on the other hand, had devised a method of impregnating soap into S.O.S pads by repeatedly hand-dipping steel wool into liquid soap and then allowing them to dry. (Brillo did not begin infusing soap into its pads of steel wool until 1930, and for several years afterward offered Brillo with or without the soap inside the pad.) The S.O.S Company introduced the familiar oval-shaped pad in 1938.

## Brand Ownership

Cox manufactured S.O.S soap pads in the basement of his home in San Francisco until 1919. He then sold the rights to his patent on a geographical basis. Cox retained the right to manufacture S.O.S in the Midwest, and in 1920 he moved to Chicago and established the S.O.S Company. Later that year, a California group that had purchased the S.O.S patent rights for the western United States bought out Cox. The group also acquired the East Coast rights, creating a national S.O.S Company. After three years of manufacturing S.O.S in both San Francisco and Chicago, all operations were moved to Chicago in 1923.

The S.O.S Company continued to manufacture S.O.S brand scouring pads until 1957. That year the company was purchased by the General Foods Corp., the largest producer and distributor of prepared foods and household products in the United States. In 1966 the Federal Trade Commission ruled that the purchase of S.O.S had violated the Clayton Antitrust Act (prohibiting mergers that lessen competition) and ordered General Foods to sell the S.O.S business. The Supreme Court upheld the ruling in 1968, and later that year, General Foods sold S.O.S and several other household brands to Miles Inc.

## Competition

S.O.S was marketed heavily in the 1950s and 1960s, a period of rapid expansion for consumer items. During that time, S.O.S and Brillo captured nearly the entire market for soap-filled scouring pads. Ads during the period promoted S.O.S, the "magic scouring pad," as "interwoven to hold its shape, hold its soap. That's why women say nothing else cleans, scours and shines as fast." Colgate-Palmolive Company attempted to enter the market in the early 1960s with Ajax Powder Pads, yet the product was able to gain only about a three percent share of its test markets and was soon dropped. By the mid-1980s, S.O.S and Brillo were both considered established brands in a mature market and neither did much advertising. However, there was speculation in 1993 that a new product, Scotch Brite Never Rust from the Minnesota Mining & Manufacturing Company (3M), could result in increased advertising.

## Further Reading:

"Big Food Concern Plans Expansion," *New York Times,* October 5, 1957, p. 21.

*Brief History of S.O.S,* Chicago, IL: Miles, Inc.

*A Brilliant Idea Continues to Shine,* The Greyhound Corporation, 1988.

"General Foods Is Ordered To Sell S.O.S Co. in a Year," *New York Times,* March 18, 1966, p. 56.

"General Foods Must Sell S.O.S," *New York Times,* May 21, 1968, p. 63.

Goldman, Kevin, "Scouring-Pad Rivals Face 3M Challenge," *Wall Street Journal,* January 11, 1993, p. B8.

"The Idea Was Brilliant," *Go Greyhound,* Greyhound Corporation, fall, 1985.

"Ruling Against General Foods," *New York Times,* March 19, 1966, p. 35.

"Sale of S.O.S Set By General Foods," *New York Times,* July 9, 1968, p. 49.

—*Dean Boyer*

# SARAN WRAP®

Saran Wrap brand plastic film, marketed by DowBrands, the household product affiliate of Dow Chemical Company, has remained the most impermeable, puncture-resistant plastic wrap on the market since it invented the household plastic wrap category in 1953. Saran Wrap, made of a polyvinylidene chloride film with an acetyl tributyl citrate plasticizer for added stretch, resists moisture and oxygen to keep food fresh in the refrigerator or freezer, and tolerates heat and hot oils to protect food in the microwave. Because of these qualities, it remains one of the most versatile plastic wraps on the market. In 1990, Saran Wrap shared the second largest market share with Mobil's Hefty brand plastic wrap, each with 20 percent of the market, while First Brand's Glad plastic wrap held a 30 percent share.

## Invigorating an Old Invention

In 1933 while Dow researcher Ralph Wiley worked on chlorinated dry cleaning solvents, he became intrigued by a cloudy plastic by-product. After analyzing it, he and his colleagues realized it was monomeric vinylidene chloride, a substance that had been discovered a century earlier by a French chemist named Regnault but had never been used commercially. For five years Dow researchers studied ways to make the substance versatile and profitable. They found ways to manipulate it for use in the heaviest of tasks, such as making it into a heavy cable, or in the most delicate of jobs, such as stretching it into a strong silklike thread. Originally, Dow dubbed the substance VC Plastic, but by 1940 the substance was called Saran. John Steadman, a sales representative for Firestone Tire & Rubber Company, had submitted the name via telegram to Dow. He remembered the word from the time he spent working in India where saran was the name of a tree. The new name met Dow's requirements of a word with no more than five letters and no negative connotations. According to Don Whitehead's history of the company, *The Dow Story*, the sales department felt Saran's lack of meaning was its "greatest virtue." The company felt strongly about the name change and warned its employees in *Dow Diamond*, a company magazine, that "from now on, in fact, any one caught referring to Saran by any of its former names will be tried for heresy, and if found guilty will suffer the usual penalty."

At first Saran had myriad uses in the domestic market. Saran made suspenders, belts, handbags, and seat covers for buses, trains, and subways strong and durable. It also proved useful as a material for pipes and tubing that would carry corrosive chemicals, oils, and waste material, noted Whitehead in *The Dow Story*. It was during World War II, however, that Saran began attracting attention. Saran tubes, bags, and film protected weaponry and other defense equipment while in transit to forces overseas, effectively sealing the expensive equipment from the damaging effects of saltwater, sand, and corrosion.

Saran's protective qualities proved so useful during the war that, when the war ended, Dow decided to produce a Saran film to protect food in the home. Saran's consistency was changed from a greasy yellowish product to a clear, dry film. After patenting Saran Wrap in 1948, Dow employees test marketed the product by selling it door-to-door in Midland, Michigan. The limited introduction proved so successful that Dow unveiled Saran Wrap to the national consumer market in 1953 with help from Dow's first retail sales campaign. The campaign included radio and television commercials and local newspaper advertisements in the test cities of Cincinnati, Columbus, Dayton, and Toledo, Ohio. Pleased with the sales in the test cities, Dow "launched what was up to that time the greatest single-product promotion in the company's history," according to Whitehead. The promotion spanned popular NBC television shows like the *Today* show, the *Kate Smith Hour*, and the *Show of Shows*, and was carried in *This Week* magazine, which had a distribution of over one million copies. Whitehead noted that the successful campaign "established Saran Wrap as one of the leading household products in the country."

## Production and Improvements

The production of Saran Wrap is a multi-step process. First, the polyvinylidene chloride is heated and then pushed through an extruder, which transforms it into a long narrow bubble that is four times thicker than the final Saran Wrap. Next, the resultant bubble is pressed into a thin, six-foot wide film. The finished Saran Wrap is then rolled for sale in 50, 100, and 200 square foot rolls, as well as an extra wide 65.5 square foot roll.

Although the ingredients of Saran Wrap have not changed since its introduction, its thickness and package have been modified in response to consumer suggestions. Consumers had complained that Saran Wrap stuck to itself too easily and was hard to unroll out of the package. In 1964 Dow unveiled an improved Saran Wrap that alleviated those grievances and gave the consumer an added bonus. The new version was 15 percent thicker,

## AT A GLANCE

**S**aran Wrap brand of plastic film introduced by Dow Chemical Company in 1953; marketed by Dow's household product subsidiary DowBrands.

*Performance:* *Market share*—20% (tied for second place with Mobil Corporation's Hefty brand plastic wrap) of the plastic wrap category.

*Major competitor:* First Brand's Glad; also Mobil's Hefty.

*Advertising:* *Agency*—Campbell-Mithum-Esty, Minneapolis, MN, 1991—.

*Addresses:* *Parent company*—DowBrands, 9550 Zionsville Road, Indianapolis, IN 46268; phone: (317) 873-7000; fax: (317) 873-7968. *Ultimate parent company*—Dow Chemical Company, 2030 Willard H. Dow Center, Midland, MI 48674; phone: (517) 636-1000.

which reduced its tendency to cling to itself, came in a new package that included a starter tab to open the package and an easy restart strip, and contained 50 feet of product for the price of the old 25 foot roll. *Printers' Ink* reported that the improvements were not "entirely altruistic," adding that Dow commented that people "had a tendency to skimp in using the shorter roll of the wrap; now they use twice as much Saran Wrap." Indeed, more people did use the wrap. By 1977 Dow manufactured the largest amount of vinylidene chloride in the United States, producing 150 million pounds of it annually to make Saran Wrap.

Though Saran Wrap is a difficult product to recycle, Dow initiated a waste-saving program to reduce landfill use, which subsequently opened Saran to new markets. Production of Saran Wrap creates hundreds of pounds of waste each day when bubbles break or the film, having been flattened too much, needs to be trimmed back to a six-foot width. Scrap Saran Wrap is turned into pellets that Dow sells to a weaving company, which prepares the pellets for use in the soles of military boots and other heavy-duty products. Dow production supervisor Edward L. Rule told *Saginaw News* writer Geri Rudulf that in 1992 "the recycling effort saved Dow up to $75,000 in hauling and landfill costs." To further reduce waste, wrinkled or damaged rolls of Saran Wrap are sent to the Arnold Center, a vocational rehabilitation facility in Midland, Michigan, where workers fix the wrinkled wrap and broken cartons. After being repaired, the center coordinates the distribution of the rolls to food pantries, rescue missions, and other organizations for the poor, according to Rudolf.

### Performance

*Consumer Reports* compared brands of plastic wrap in 1989 and found that any plastic wrap would keep a refrigerated sandwich fresh overnight or keep food fresh in the freezer for weeks. But Saran Wrap was a "standout" in the tests, which found that Saran Wrap was as good at retaining moisture as aluminum foil and almost as strong as the extra-heavy-duty Reynolds Wrap foil. It was also the only oxygen-impermeable plastic wrap. Saran Wrap out-performed Glad Cling Wrap, Kroger's Home Pride, Albertsons, A&P, Arrow, Lady Lee, Handi-Wrap II, Safeway, Borden Sealwrap, and Reynolds Wrap in moisture retention, resistance to bursting, and resistance to puncturing.

*Consumer Reports* also put to rest consumer concerns that the plasticizer in Saran Wrap was harmful. DowBrands claimed that

"there is no evidence that polyvinyl chloride or polyvinylidine chloride wraps, used properly, pose any significant health risks." Furthermore, Dow told the Johnstown, Pennsylvania, *Tribune-Democrat* that Saran Wrap "complies with the requirements of the Federal Food Drug and Cosmetic Act and is safe for use in the microwave oven." The Saran Wrap package touted the product as the "best wrap for food protection and microwave cooking, too," noting that it "keeps food fresher," and "won't melt, shrink or dissolve at high temperatures like other plastic wraps," and that it "promotes fast, uniform cooking."

In fact, Saran Wrap is sold with a "Freshness Guarantee," which states that if the consumer does not feel Saran Wrap "holds in freshness best," Dow will refund their money. Saran Wrap packages advise consumers to perform a simple test—wrapping a piece of bread in Saran Wrap and two other leading wraps—to help prove that Saran Wrap does keep food the freshest. Indeed, Saran has long been thought of as a wrap that insured freshness. In 1961 for example, Tee-Pak, Inc., wanted to switch from wrapping its beef in cellophane to Saran because of "saran's protective properties." *Chemical Week* added that Saran "is capable of extending the shelf-life of the meat up to seven days. In comparison, conventionally wrapped hamburger loses its freshness after a few hours."

### Advertising Support

Saran Wrap advertising expenditures increased 340.4 percent in 1991 to over $6 million dollars, up from almost $1.5 million in 1990. This expenditure amounted to only a small portion of the $127.1 million Dow spent to support all its brands, especially Ziploc food storage bags and Seldane allergy medication. The advertising company of Campbell-Mithum-Esty in Minneapolis, Minnesota, handled Saran Wrap in addition to Ziploc food storage bags and Perma Soft and Style shampoo. The account was estimated at $25 million, according to *Adweek-Eastern-Edition*. Advertising supported Saran Wrap through in-store promotions, television commercials, and print campaigns in magazines like *Ladies' Home Journal, Reader's Digest,* and *McCall's.* Coupons were also used in magazines, following a tradition that Saran Wrap began in 1964 when coupons were distributed in bags of General Mills, Inc.'s Gold Medal flour.

Saran Wrap's uniqueness in the marketplace has given it strong staying power. It has continued to thrive in the plastic wrap market, despite its consistently higher price. Dow supports it by diligently striving to find new uses for Saran Wrap. Even though the plastic wrap market had declined 1.5 percent in 1992, Dow continued to expand its advertising budget for Saran Wrap. The northeastern United States was targeted for in-store promotions, according to Scott McMurray in the *Wall Street Journal.* Saran Wrap had been vacillating among the top few shares of the plastic wrap market in the early 1990s; its sales and Dow's continued support suggest that it will continue to be one of America's leading plastic wraps.

### Further Reading:

"The Best Ways to Keep Food Fresh," *Consumer Reports,* February, 1989, pp. 120–23.

"Cents-Off Coupons for New Saran Wrap Inundate Market," *Advertising Age,* May 25, 1964, p. 2.

"Council to Sell Saran," *Chemical Week,* December 9, 1961, pp. 41–42.

"DFM Loss: Dow Fingers C-M-E for Ziploc," *Adweek-Eastern-Edition,* July 1, 1991, p. 5.

''Dow Heeds Advice, Improves Saran Wrap,'' *Printers' Ink,* March 20, 1964, p. 15.

McMurray, Scott, ''Ziploc No Longer Has Its Market in the Bag,'' *Wall Street Journal,* December 24, 1992, p. 8.

''100 Leading National Advertisers,'' *Advertising Age,* September 23, 1992, p. 28.

''Preliminary Test Results Linking Vinylidene Chloride to Cancer in Mice Have Started a Controversy Over the Chemical's Safety,'' *Chemical Week,* March 2, 1977, p. 171.

Raj, D. D., ''First Brands Corporation—Company Report Investext,'' *Merrill Lynch,* March 5, 1990, pp. 1–5.

Rudolf, Geri, ''Dow Makes Progress Recycling Saran Waste,'' *Saginaw News,* January 17, 1993.

Wu, Pei-Tse, ''Saran Wrap Not Toxic, Dow Says,'' *Tribune-Democrat* (Johnstown, PA), February 15, 1990.

*—Sara Pendergast*

# SCOPE®

Procter & Gamble has become one of the strongest consumer products marketing companies in the world. Several of its products serve as excellent case examples of how Procter & Gamble earned that reputation. Scope, a mint-flavored green mouthwash, is one such example.

Typically, Procter & Gamble concentrates only on mass-market products—things which everyone may have a reason to use. Having chosen an appropriate commodity, the company develops a product with unique characteristics. Finally the product is aggressively marketed with the single aim of capturing a leading share of the market for that commodity.

Procter & Gamble introduced Crest toothpaste this way in 1955, and eventually overtook the perennial market leader Colgate. The company's experience with Scope followed a slightly different path.

## Brand Origins

After their success with Crest toothpaste, Procter & Gamble marketing strategists decided in the early 1960s to attempt another fresh market entry, this time into the mouthwash market, which was dominated by Warner-Lambert's Listerine brand. Listerine, which had been in existence since 1880, had a well-established reputation as an antiseptic mouthwash that could help prevent the common cold. During the 1940s it was even promoted as a hair tonic.

Listerine held more than half of the $600 million mouthwash market in 1965. As the market leader, the brand naturally became a model for Procter & Gamble. First, the company closely studied the experience of another newcomer to the mouthwash market from archrival Colgate-Palmolive. In 1964 that company introduced a red mouthwash called Colgate 100. This brand captured a small market share but failed to make the slightest dent in Listerine's commanding position.

Procter & Gamble then set out to create a completely new kind of mouthwash. It formulated a powerful liquid, consisting of about 19 percent alcohol, a mild detergent, mint flavoring, and a green coloring agent. The flavor and color made the liquid easily distinguishable from the harsh-tasting yellow Listerine. Unlike Crest toothpaste, the new mouthwash did not contain fluoride, a chemical believed to help strengthen tooth enamel. This may have been due to concern that too much fluoride exposure can turn teeth brown.

The new brand was called Scope. It was test marketed in late 1965 in Cincinnati, parts of Illinois, Denver, Pittsburgh, and Syracuse. In those markets, Scope tested very highly, ostensibly appealing to people who wanted an alternative to medicinal-flavored Listerine.

## Early Marketing Strategy

A year after test marketing, the Scope brand was introduced nationwide. The key to Procter & Gamble's marketing strategy for Scope was its advertising. The first ads for the brand stressed long-lasting breath protection and fresh mint flavor. The campaign was enormous, consuming $12 million in promotional funds. This was more than Warner-Lambert had spent on Listerine. Procter & Gamble also gave away 20 million 1.5-ounce bottles of Scope in markets of more than 100,000 people.

Building on the approval Crest toothpaste had gained from the American Dental Association and its strong reputation with dentists, Procter & Gamble developed detailed information packages for dentists. These materials provided the results of testing that indicated the dental benefits of using Scope.

Certain mouthwashes claimed antiseptic qualities and even the ability to fight plaque and gingivitis, a gum disease. Several dentifrice manufacturers were cited for scurrilous or poorly supported claims of protection against plaque and gingivitis by the Food and Drug Administration in 1988. Scope, however, never carried such claims and so was not mentioned. Scope labels indicated a single unique ingredient, "T25." No explanation was available on the composition, qualities, or benefits of T25, and it has never been expressly promoted in advertising.

Scope immediately gained a small but important share of the mouthwash market. This so alarmed Warner-Lambert that it was forced to rush out its own minty mouthwash, a blue concoction called Reef. This brand failed to stem the growing popularity of Scope and was later discontinued.

## Brand Development

The core of Procter & Gamble's effort to replace Listerine as the mouthwash market leader with Scope centered on differentia-

## AT A GLANCE

**S**cope brand of mouthwash introduced in 1965, rolled out nationwide in 1966; Peppermint Scope first marketed in 1986, DuraCool and Red Mint in 1992.

**Performance:** *Market share*—30% (second-highest after Listerine) of mouthwash category.

**Major competitor:** Warner-Lambert's Listerine.

**Advertising:** *Agency*—D'Arcy Masius Benton & Bowles, New York, NY. *Major campaign*—"Bad Breath Anonymous," imploring consumers to report people with bad breath to Procter & Gamble; "Medicine breath," implying that Scope tastes better than Listerine.

**Addresses:** *Parent company*—Procter & Gamble Company, 1 Procter & Gamble Plaza, Cincinnati, OH 45202; phone: (513) 983-1100; fax: (513) 983-7847.

tion. Because Scope was not an antiseptic, the primary selling point of the brand reverted to social confidence. Scope was simply more palatable and refreshing.

In 1974 after exhausting the possibilities of pushing the Scope brand's minty flavor, Procter & Gamble turned to a comparative campaign in which Listerine left people with "medicine breath." As may be expected, this put Warner-Lambert's lawyers into action. They complained that Procter & Gamble's characterization was unfairly disparaging (a so-called "slam" ad) and asked the National Advertising Division to review the campaign. Procter & Gamble supported its case with market research in which people were asked to blindly describe the mouth odor of someone who had used Listerine. The most popular reaction was "mediciney/antiseptic." This was good enough for the NAD, which allowed the Scope ads.

However, Procter & Gamble later voluntarily softened the ads, dropping the direct reference to Listerine and describing the market-leading brand more precisely as "mediciney," as its research had indicated. This was an act of good faith that was intended to keep Warner-Lambert from slamming the Scope brand.

As a result of this successful new campaign, the percentage of the mouthwash market held by Scope began to climb rapidly. By 1975 the brand claimed more than 20 percent. The market share held by Listerine, meanwhile, declined to just over 40 percent.

### Advertising

The first advertisements for Scope claimed the brand was a ground-breaking "new mouthwash discovery." These ads said using Scope "once in the morning helps keep your breath fresh even in the afternoon." This lofty claim was successful with consumers, but drew criticism from competitors who charged Procter & Gamble with stretching the truth. Eventually a compromise was worked out in which morning use of Scope mouthwash could "help you feel safe for hours." The softer approach lessened the impact of the brand's advertising, but only slightly.

In a memorable campaign that began in 1968, consumers were asked to take action on someone else's breath problem. In television ads, people backed down from attempts to confront someone about their bad breath. Later ads showed a person speaking to the camera, saying, in effect, "You have bad breath." The person was then hit in the face with a pie or doused with spaghetti. "It is often embarrassing and unrewarding to tell someone he has bad breath," the announcer then admitted. "What can be done to make it easier? Sign up the guilty party in Bad Breath Anonymous, Box 121, New York, New York."

Procter & Gamble collected several thousand names of people with bad breath. Keeping the informers anonymous, Procter & Gamble sent the offenders cents-off coupons for Scope mouthwash. The promotion was very successful, but became tiresome after a short while and was discontinued.

In ads intended to illustrate the unpleasant flavor of the Listerine brand, Procter & Gamble began a campaign in 1974 that capitalized on the market leader's "mediciney" taste. In one vignette, a woman told a man to go use some Scope mouthwash. He used his own brand instead, and when he returned to collect his kiss he was greeted with, "Now you smell like a medicine chest. You didn't use Scope." The subject objected, "But my mouthwash fights bad breath." To which the woman retorted, "Scope fights bad breath, too. But your breath smells minty fresh, not *mediciney.*" The ads closed with a voice-over in which the announcer said, "Scope doesn't give you medicine breath."

### Packaging

As part of the effort to differentiate Scope mouthwash from Listerine, Procter & Gamble produced a special container of unusual shape that would show off the brand's deep green hue. The bottle was shaped something like a spade, narrow on top but wide on the bottom. The bottle was also flattened, so that its base was oval rather than round. This presented a larger face upon which to place a label, and made the product look larger than it was. The front of the bottle featured a unique oval flange which served only to frame the paper label. The label design was simple, a bordered oval with Scope spelled out across it in large letters.

The cap of the bottle was also unusual. Rather than a small, shallow black cap like Listerine, Scope had a large white cap that could be used to measure a gargling dosage. The cap also featured several vertical indentations to provide a gripping surface for fingers. This was intended to keep the cap from slipping out of a wet hand.

While distinctive and attractive, the bottle proved impractical. In order to withstand breakage during shipping, the bottle was cast thickly. This increased the shipping weight, which added to distribution costs. As part of a campaign to reduce packaging, Procter & Gamble introduced a much lighter plastic bottle for Scope mouthwash in 1981. This enabled Procter & Gamble to retain the trademark Scope bottle shape and drastically reduce shipping weight. In addition, plastic bottles were virtually unbreakable during shipping.

In July of 1985 the company rolled out a large 32-ounce bottle, and in February of 1992, the Scope brand became available in a 48-ounce bottle with a flip-cap dispenser.

### Extensions

In 1975 Procter & Gamble became convinced that a "sweet-tasting mouthwash," as the Scope brand was described in ads for Listerine, could garner only so much of the market. A significant number of consumers continued to believe that only a bad-tasting mouthwash could be effective.

The company developed a new mouthwash which was technically an extension of Scope, but marketed it under the name Extend. The new brand was given an amber color (matching Listerine) and flavored with spices. This gave Extend a natural breath-freshening equity that could compete well against the Listerine brand. Having witnessed the loss of Listerine's market share to Scope and Extend, Warner-Lambert introduced its own spicy amber mouthwash called Depend. Market analysis indicated that neither brand was winning market share from its competitor's flagship brands, however, and both were later phased out.

Warner-Lambert later mounted a more serious challenge to Scope with a mint-flavored extension of the Listerine brand called Listermint. In June of 1986, Procter & Gamble countered the entry of Listermint with yet another brand. Where Extend was given a separate name and identity, Procter & Gamble decided to lend the Scope name to a new peppermint-flavored mouthwash. Test marketed in Seattle, the blue-colored peppermint Scope mouthwash went into national distribution in February of 1987. By the end of that year, the Listerine brands held 38 percent of the mouthwash market, while the Scope brands held 23 percent.

In June of 1992, Procter & Gamble began test marketing in Denver for DuraCool Scope, an upgraded version of the flagship brand with a more intense and longer-lasting effect. In October the company introduced a novelty extension, Red Mint Holiday Flavor Scope. Distributed only between October and December, this brand was intended to commemorate the Christmas holiday season.

## Performance Evaluation

The market for mouthwash grew out of the myth that all bad breath was chronic and common. In fact bad breath typically results from plaque-based oral bacteria. While significant germ and bacteria reduction occurs with the use of mouthwash, physical processes such as brushing and flossing are necessary to counter both breath odors and tooth decay.

Scope's ability to capture nearly a third of the mouthwash market from a thoroughly entrenched market leader was a tremendous achievement, even if it took nearly 20 years to accomplish. Having extended into virtual versions of each other's products, Procter & Gamble and Warner-Lambert eventually reached a fairly balanced position in the market. While Listerine's lead was trimmed in recent years, it remained fairly solid. Any further growth in Scope at Listerine's expense was likely to come from marketing innovations (such as the red Christmas Scope), and further extensions.

Any play in market share was mainly attributable to advertising and promotion. Whether the Scope brand would eventually regain its higher growth rates and overtake Listerine became more a matter of winning mouthwash non-users over to the practice of using Scope.

## Further Reading:

Edwards, Larry, "How W-L Won Key Product Battle," *Advertising Age,* August 20, 1987, p. 112.

Giges, Nancy, "NAD Okays Scope's Listerine Research; 'Mediciney' Can Stay," *Advertising Age,* December 15, 1975, p. 2.

Lazarus, George, "Scope Challenges No. 1 Mouthwash," *Adweek's Marketing Week,* February 23, 1987, p. 30.

"Now Your Best Friend Has a Way to Tell You, *Advertising Age,* September 23, 1968.

"P&G's Mouthwash Entry Intensifies Battle for Market," *Advertising Age,* September 26, 1966.

"P&G's New Scope Mouthwash Enters More Test Markets," *Advertising Age,* November 15, 1965.

"P&G's Scope Pushes Competitors Hard in Mouthwash Market," *Advertising Age,* April 4, 1966.

*—John Simley*

# SCOTCH® TAPE

The invention of Scotch brand adhesive tape epitomized an era of entrepreneurial growth in the United States. "It was a time when almost every small invention promised a better life, when seemingly crude experiments provided the roots for modern technology," according to *Office* magazine. When Richard Drew, a Minnesota Mining and Manufacturing Company (3M) lab technician, created Scotch masking tape to solve an automobile painter's problem of marking a straight line between colors on two-tone cars in 1925, he shifted the focus and profits of 3M from abrasives to coating and bonding technologies. Although Drew's first tape proved to be only a mild improvement on the gummed Kraft paper the auto body shops originally used, the 1930 refinement of Scotch tape—using cellophane to make a waterproof seal—was the beginning of the household identification of 3M products. The 1961 addition of Scotch brand Magic transparent tape further insured 3M's domination of the market. Scotch tape has since become a symbol of American ingenuity and has continued to hold the world's largest tape market share into the 1990s.

## Inventing a Legend

In 1929 Drew was searching for a watertight backing to make a moisture-resistant sealant for insulation used in refrigerated railroad cars and considered the DuPont Chemical Company's newly invented cellophane. Drew thought that cellophane would make a good watertight backing for tape, but it was heat-sensitive and adhesive-resistant. He initiated a series of experiments to make cellophane a practical tape backing. Meanwhile, many food-packaging firms, who had heard about the original Scotch masking tape used in auto body shops, contacted 3M in their efforts to find a waterproof seal for food wrappers. In 1930, after what 3M called the "longest and most discouraging months in 3M's history," one of the food-packaging firms, Shellmar Products Corp., tried the first roll of cellophane tape. The company was thrilled with the results and encouraged 3M to produce the tape. *Our Story So Far,* 3M's history of its first 75 years, quoted Shellmar Products Corp.'s prophetic reaction to the new product: "You should have no hesitancy in equipping yourself to put this product on the market economically. There will be a sufficient volume of sales to justify the expenditure."

3M was cautious in its initial efforts at marketing the tape. The company's explanation of the product in its 1930 annual report was brief: "During the year, a new product known as 'Scotch'

Cellulose Tape was introduced. It consists of a cellophane coated with a transparent pressure-sensitive adhesive." The report further speculated that "the [packaging] market appears to have large possibilities." Indeed, the first year sales for the tape did not warrant much fanfare—only $33 worth of Scotch tape was sold. However, its low sales may have been the result of the product's quality. "We can admit now that some of the tape was pretty awful," former 3M executive Hal B. Kosanke told *Office* magazine. "It would refuse to unwind . . . I can remember sending out a team of men . . . to do nothing but replace those crummy rolls. That cost money, but it earned us all sorts of goodwill and it got people into the habit of using tape." Though the tape did not work as a sealant for insulation as Drew had intended, the food-packaging industry provided an ample source of sales.

## Early Marketing

Grocers, meat packers, and bakers comprised Scotch cellophane tape's first market. To boost tape sales, 3M persuaded these companies to package food in cellophane wrappers which required tape closures. The use of these wrappers was so crucial to the success of cellophane tape that 3M marketed the wrappers until they were widely used. Even though 3M successfully reached its target market with Scotch tape, the use of cellophane tape within the food-packaging industry proved to be short-lived. DuPont invented a convenient heat-seal method for closing packages that soon replaced cellophane bags and tape.

To continue to make a profit from their product, 3M marketed Scotch tape to consumers for the first time just as the Great Depression began. Although the tape was originally conceived as a luxury item, people soon found a myriad of practical uses for it and sales increased steadily. It was used to extend the life of worn objects, to mend clothing, toys, and letters, to remove lint, and even to hold together cracked eggs. People found more uses for the tape than 3M had ever envisioned. Moreover, the use of tape was made more convenient by former 3M sales manager John Borden's 1932 invention of the tape dispenser. The dispenser allayed customer complaints about unwieldy tape rolls and made it easier to find the tape end and cut it without scissors.

Scotch tape had become such an integral part of American life by the World War II that 3M ran advertisements apologizing for its shortage during rationing. The ads appeased consumers by explaining that "of course, for a while yet there's not going to be

## AT A GLANCE

**S**cotch cellophane tape introduced in 1930; Scotch brand masking tape invented in 1925 by Richard Drew, a lab technician at Minnesota Mining and Manufacturing Company; tape sales improved with the introduction of the first heavy-duty tape dispenser, 1932; began to be sold internationally, 1951; improved Scotch brand Magic transparent tape introduced, 1961.

*Performance:* Market share—85% of the world cellophane tape market.

*Advertising: Agency*—Martin Williams Advertising, Minneapolis, MN. *Major campaign*—Television commercials depicting a Scotch tape testing laboratory in which women demonstrate the convenience and effectiveness of Scotch tape.

*Addresses: Parent company*—Minnesota Mining and Manufacturing Company, 3M Center, Saint Paul, MN 55144-1000; phone: (612) 733-1110; fax: (612) 733-6557.

nearly enough for everybody who needs it—but we're being mighty careful about seeing that everyone gets a fair share.'' Another ad promised that ''when victory comes. 'Scotch' cellulose tape will be back again in your home and office.''

### Improvements and Productions

By 1961, 3M engineers improved the tape so that it would no longer ooze adhesive, dry up, or turn yellow. This new tape seemed to disappear when applied to a surface and was dubbed Scotch Magic transparent tape. Scotch Magic transparent tape's uniqueness is its backing, which consists of cellulose acetate, a ''space-age'' plastic, and its adhesive, a polymer that sticks without the use of the original tape's combination of rubber, resins, and oils.

Producing Scotch Magic transparent tape required three different processes: producing the cellulose acetate film backing, mixing the pressure-sensitive synthetic adhesive, and then combining them to make the finished tape. To make the cellulose acetate, the cellulose fibers of wood pulp or cotton linters are chemically reduced to their most basic structure. The resulting fibers are combined with acetic acid and acetic anhydride to form triacetate. The triacetate is then treated with water to produce cellulose acetate. The water is removed from the cellulose acetate, and the substance is made into pellets. Finally, the pellets are melted into sheets that are one-fifth the thickness of typing paper. The sheets of film are rolled and ready for adhesive application. The adhesive is a hydrocarbon solvent made by a proportionally-exact combination of alcohols, acids, and water. The recipe for the adhesive must be followed so carefully that the adhesive's 29 ingredients must pass 60 quality checks before they are deemed suitable for production.

After the film backing and the adhesive are produced, the film is prepared to accept the adhesive. One side of the film is treated with a ''release coating'' that will allow the tape to unroll easily, and the other side is primed to ensure that the adhesive will stick. The film is then dried in heated drums called ''hot cans.'' When dry, the film is coated with the adhesive, which in turn is dried in long, high-temperature ovens. Finally, the tape is wound into what 3M calls a ''jumbo roll,'' which is in turn cut into half- or three-

quarter-inch strips and wound into many sizes of tape rolls on individual cores.

### Selling Strategies

The ingenuity of 3M's Scotch tape customers seemed to guide the company's marketing strategy. It was noted in a *Forbes* company profile that 3M successfully grasped a ''very basic fact of marketing: that what may be a single product from the manufacturing point of view may be many different products as far as marketing is concerned.'' 3M diversified its sales forces to cover all the potential markets for the tape. The Retail Tape and Gift Wrap division, for example, had two sales forces, both of which called on department stores. One sales force sold Scotch tape for in-house department store use, and the other sold tape for retail sale. The reason 3M sales forces are so vast, explained former 3M president Harry Heltzer in *Forbes,* is that ''most of our products are of the disposable kind that lend themselves to systems marketing. That is why our salesmen work so closely with the end customer.'' Heltzer emphasized the importance of 3M salespeople's commitment to knowing their market and creatively solving their market's problems.

The 3M sales force's intimate knowledge of many small markets generated more sales opportunities for the entire company. The company's 37 divisions produced products that could be useful to many of the same customers. In 1981 corporate management implemented a sales program to cross 3M's diverse market sectors: health care; transportation-equipment manufacturing and maintenance; electronics/electrical manufacturing; safety and security; voice, video, and data communications; office, training, and business; consumer; communication arts; industrial production; and construction and maintenance. The program required that salespeople be familiar with all the products that ''serve their sectors so that they can identify sales opportunities for other divisions,'' according to Sally Scanlon in *Sales and Marketing Management.* Scanlon noted that management wanted salespeople to ''[raise] their sights above narrow divisional demands.'' Also in *Sales and Marketing Management,* John M. Pitblado added that salespeople ''are not the order taker, they are the solver of business problems.'' To supplement the salespeople's efforts, a corporate advertising campaign by Batten, Barton, Durstine & Osborn (BBDO) of New York was launched to reinforce the many facets of 3M's products.

As market share slipped from 90 percent to 85 percent in 1988, Scotch tape advertisements returned to television after a ten-year hiatus. The commercials depicted a Scotch tape testing lab that showed a woman pulling tape from a dispenser with the announcement that ''Scotch brand Magic tape is as easy to dispense as it is to use. Scotch brand Magic Tape. Stick with the one you know.'' Another vignette showed a woman sticking a piece of tape on her finger and being dunked into a tank of water. The announcement was: ''Scotch brand Magic Tape resists moisture, so it sticks around a long time.''

### A Company of Many Products

Founded in 1902 as a mining company in rural Two Harbors, Minnesota, 3M became profitable after it abandoned mining in favor of manufacturing sandpaper. The company's first revolutionary product was ''Wetordry '' sandpaper in the early 1920s. Interested in broadening the scope of its business, 3M encouraged the type of experimentation among its employees that led to the invention of Scotch brand tape. A continuing dedication to research has allowed 3M to diversify into a multi-billion dollar company. Until World War II, the company focused its expansion on products that involved coating, bonding, or abrasives. After the war, 3M diversified its product line to include fluorochemicals, cameras, sound and video tape recorders, photographic film, plastic film, electric connectors, and thermoelectric power units. Over one thousand products have been introduced by 3M through the years, including surgical tapes, printing supplies, office copying machines, copying paper, decorative ribbons, video tapes, and sound recording tapes. By 1984 3M had produced more than 100 types of pressure-sensitive tapes. Many Scotch brand products, including video tapes, held leading market shares in their product categories into the 1990s.

## The Scotch Brand Name

The Scotch brand name was coined by an auto painter while using 3M's prototype masking tape. After the first coating of paint, the tape fell off the car. The angry painter advised the salesman to "take this tape back to those Scotch bosses of yours and tell them to put more adhesive on it," according to 3M. Despite the ethnic slur, 3M has continued to use Scotch as the product's brand name, and in the 1940s the packaging incorporated a tartan design to make the tape more easily identifiable to consumers.

Most of 3M's major consumer product lines used the Scotch brand name. Still other products used the related Tartan brand name, which was derived from the original Scotch tape name and package design. 3M developed four different plaid designs to differentiate its products in order to present a unified marketing message so that the customer could easily identify 3M's products. For example, Scotch cellophane tape was sold with a red plaid dispenser, and Scotch Magic transparent tape dispensers sported green plaid. Because 3M's product base is so large and because the company sought to establish an all-encompassing visual image, 3M insisted that its plaid designs "show equally well on metal dispensers, containers, paper packages or other applications."

## Continuing Domination

Scotch tape has "changed the habits of a nation" and has become an indispensable part of everyday life in both home and office, stated 3M's promotional material. It has been sold around the world, including France, Germany, the United Kingdom, Australia, and Canada, since 1951, and has continued to be the "bread and butter" item for many of 3M's international companies into the 1990s. Even though Scotch tape lost market share in the 1980s, its continued domination of the marketplace has allowed 3M to capitalize on the variety of related products the invention has spawned.

## Further Reading:

Garfield, Bob, "Scotch Tape Shines in Sticky Situations," *Advertising Age,* November 21, 1988, p. 62.

Huck, Virginia, *Brand of the Tartan,* New York: Appleton-Century-Crofts, Inc., 1955.

Minnesota Mining and Manufacturing Company, *Our Story So Far: Notes from the First 75 Years of 3M Company,* St. Paul, MN: Minnesota Mining and Manufacturing Company, 1977.

Scanlon, Sally, "Try Patching That Copier with Our Scotch Tape, Sir," *Sales and Marketing Management,* May 18, 1981, pp. 38–44.

"The Tale of the Tape—50 Years of Innovation at 3M," *Office,* September, 1980, pp. 101–104.

"3M: Little Drops of Water, Little Grains of Sand," *Forbes,* September 1, 1969, pp. 30–36.

"3M's Way: Patents Plus Labs," *Business Week,* October 4, 1958, pp. 114–125.

*—Sara Pendergast*

# SCOTT®

# SCOTT

The first company in the nation to market toilet paper, Scott Paper Co. is the leading maker of sanitary tissue products in the world. By 1993 the company operated more than 60 manufacturing plants in the United States and 18 foreign nations, and its paper products were sold in more than 60 countries worldwide.

## Brand Origins

Originally, Scott Paper Co. made "coarse" paper goods such as bags and wrapping paper. However, in the late nineteenth century there was an increasing awareness of personal hygiene on the part of the public, due in part to the advent of sanitary plumbing and a rising standard of living. The Scott brothers saw an opportunity to manufacture and sell a paper product that would be known as "toilet tissue."

When Scott first marketed its toilet paper, nineteenth-century mores did not permit the advertising of such a product. Instead of marketing their product directly, the Scott brothers bought "parent rolls" of paper, which they converted into toilet paper. Then they sold the paper to independent merchants who put on their own private labels. At the height of this venture, Scott produced over 2,000 different brands for these merchants.

The company began to make paper towels in 1907. According to company legend, the paper towel was created to meet the need of a Philadelphia school teacher who wanted to replace the unsanitary cloth towel used daily by her students with some other type of product. The ScotTowels brand name was first introduced in 1931.

## Product Innovations

Throughout the years, the company sought to develop technology that would enhance the properties of its toilet paper, paper towels, and facial tissues in order to satisfy consumer demands and remain competitive. Consumers wanted these products to be soft, have wet strength, and absorb moisture quickly. ScotTissue was made safer for consumers with septic systems, and the roll was made more convenient to use by attaching a small starter tab. ScotTowels were made to separate easily and cleanly at the perforations so that the user didn't pull off too much or too little.

## Advertising and Marketing

Arthur Scott, son of co-founder Irvin, created the advertising slogan for the company's toilet paper, "Soft as old linen." It was Arthur who at the turn of the century first perceived a change in public attitudes toward toilet paper. He suggested that the company market some brands under its own name rather than maintain its private label policy. Arthur's business plan was to make just a few products that were of the highest possible quality, to manufacture and market them at the lowest possible cost, and to use extensive advertising to inform the public about the products.

Scott's aggressive marketing tactics were in evidence when the company introduced its Mega Rolls. Included in newspaper inserts was a coupon for 75 cents, reportedly the highest amount for a coupon to be used with a product that had a suggested retail price of $1.29. In any event, 75 cents was the biggest coupon saving for paper towels, and one supermarket chain operator said the Mega Rolls were "blowing out of here." An additional bonus was a 20-cent coupon included in the package to entice customers to make a repeat purchase. To woo retailers into giving the product shelf space, Scott hired a magician to entertain them during a special show.

---

## AT A GLANCE

**S**cott brand bathroom tissue, facial tissue, and paper towels founded by brothers E. Irvin and Clarence E. Scott of Scott Paper Co., founded in 1879.

**Performance:** *Market share*—6% (third place) of facial tissues category; 20% (second place) of bathroom tissue category; 12% (second place) of paper towels category. *Sales*—paper towels: $202.9 million; bathroom tissue: $626 million; facial tissue: $63 million (1991 estimates).

**Advertising:** *Agency*—Weightman Advertising Agency, Philadelphia, 1988—.

**Major competitor:** Procter & Gamble's Charmin bathroom tissue and Puffs facial tissues; also Bounty paper towels and Kimberly-Clark's Kleenex facial tissues.

**Addresses:** *Parent company*—Scott Paper Co., Scott Plaza, Philadelphia, PA 19113; phone: (215) 522-5000; fax: (215) 522-5129.

## Performance Appraisal

In May 1988, *Consumer Reports* magazine tested 34 brands of paper products and found that Scotties gave consumers the best value for its price. The magazine rated Scotties its "Best Buy." ScotTowels was similarly honored in January 1992 when the magazine reported that the product "combined modest price with decent performance." An earlier study in September 1987 found that the towels were among the less expensive brands that were good enough to handle most heavy-duty cleaning chores.

## International Markets

Before World War II, the Scotts' international business was conducted through a network of sales agents based in foreign countries. In the 1950s, the company set up manufacturing affiliates abroad by sharing ownership with local businesses that had established markets. Later Scott focused on investing in international businesses in which it could hold majority ownership and management control. A wholly owned subsidiary, Scott Worldwide, is responsible for marketing Scott products both in the United States and abroad. The company sees overseas markets as having greater sales potential than the saturated U.S. market: in some countries, per capita consumption of sanitary paper is less than 25 percent of that in the United States. In the early 1990s, Scott's European ad budget was about $30 million for its toilet paper and about $20 million for its paper towels and facial tissues. Scott's marketing strategy has been similar in the United States and abroad. The company has sought long-term growth by serving markets with high growth potential, and by developing and improving products to give it an edge over competing brands.

## Further Reading:

"Bathroom Tissues," *Consumer Reports,* September 1991, pp. 606–09.

"Facial Tissues," *Consumer Reports,* May 1988, pp. 332–34.

Lazarus, George, "The Mega Fanfare for Scott's Mega Roll," *Adweek's Marketing Week,* December 3, 1990, p. 38.

"Paper Towels," *Consumer Reports,* September 1987.

"Paper Towels," *Consumer Reports,* January 1992.

"Scott Realigns European Brands," *Adweek,* February 1, 1993, p. 13.

*—Dorothy Kroll*

# SECRET®

The Secret brand of anti-perspirants and deodorants, in all its varieties and fragrances, is one of the top-selling underarm-odor fighters in the United States. Packaged in trademarked containers that feature a blue background on which tiny, pale-blue flowers surround a dainty pink or blue lotus-like flower, Secret Anti-Perspirants and Deodorants have been offering comprehensive underarm-odor protection to consumers since 1956. The Secret brand marked the Procter & Gamble Company's (P&G) first entrance into the deodorant market. Through the years, by constantly improving its products, Secret has consistently disarmed such hefty competitors as Arrid and Right Guard. Just one line of items put out by Procter & Gamble, which also manufactures such popular brands as Folger's Coffee, Charmin Toilet Tissue, and Tide Detergent, Secret Anti-Perspirants and Deodorants have remained a market share leader due to years of performance assurance and innovative advertising.

## Brand Origins

When perspiration emerges from the pores, it is a colorless, odorless, complex mixture of compounds. However, when it emerges from the underarm, the secretions of the billions of bacteria which thrive on moist skin produce a characteristic odor. In the eighteenth century, society recognized the need to mask certain natural odors of the body, among them underarm perspiration, by using intensely strong animal scents such as musk, ambergris, and civet, which were thought to purify the surrounding air. By the mid-1750s, more subtle, sweet florals replaced the animal scents. When sweat glands were discovered and city sanitation improved at century's end, body odor became less socially acceptable. Still, almost 100 years would elapse before the first deodorant would be created.

Although bathing removes some of the bacteria that cause perspiration odor, deodorants and anti-perspirants are required to complete the operation. Technically, a deodorant is a deodorizer, a substance which removes bad odors or changes them to pleasant ones. Applied to the underarms, deodorants mask the natural odor of perspiration by absorbing it. In the twentieth century, when aluminum chloride or zirconium—which actually stops perspiration for a time and reduces it by at least 25 percent—was added to the petrolatum base, the resulting deodorant was reclassified by the FDA as an anti-perspirant. Research indicated that aluminum chloride and zirconium worked so well because molecules in sweat glands carry a slightly negative charge, whereas anti-perspirant compounds are slightly positive; anti-perspirants, then, actually "plug" the pores.

Trademarked in 1888, Mum, the first commercial deodorant, contained bacteria-fighting zinc oxide and was offered in a cream form that had to be applied with the fingers. Until the introduction of Mum, the subject of body odor was never talked about in the polite ladies' circles of Victorian times; women discreetly scrubbed their underarms with a solution of ammonia and water.

In the 1900s ammonia and Mum were eclipsed by Everdry Anti-Perspirant, which could be applied with a cotton swab. In spite of its genteel mode of application, Everdry stung the skin and often damaged clothing. Hygiene-minded ladies of the 1920s were told by deodorant manufacturers that an astringent would shrink the pores in the armpit, thereby arresting the flow of perspiration. In 1933, slow-drying "liquid non-perspirants" were the vogue. Users had to wait fifteen minutes for the solution to "set," but the products would restrict perspiration for up to three or four days. Even in the 1930s, deodorant application continued to be a sticky, messy process. However, in the 1940s, an innovation was introduced—icy-cold and slow-drying deodorant sprays. In the 1950s, ballpoint-pen manufacturing opened the door for another innovation, the roll-on deodorant. Roll-ons have long been considered the most effective applicators because they deliver ingredients directly to the underarm.

As supermarkets and self-service stores opened in the mid-1950s, opportunities in toiletries manufacturing seemed infinite. The variety of products displayed in department as well as drug stores appeared to offer new avenues of retailing in addition to some radical changes in merchandising techniques. Shopping malls began to spring up in the suburbs, bringing innovations of their own and attracting an affluent clientele. Prior to World War II, most toiletries had been retailed through department stores, beauty shops, and full-service drugstores. However, by the mid-1950s, grocery supermarkets had added departments to handle toilet articles, and a new breed of discount self-service outlet had come on the scene. These large-volume, self-service stores were rapidly capturing a mushrooming portion of toiletry sales (and would go on to handle over 16 percent of all toiletries by the early 1970s).

## AT A GLANCE

Secret brand of anti-perspirants and deodorants developed in 1956 in Cincinnati, OH, at the laboratories of the Procter & Gamble Company.

**Performance:** *Market share*—8% (second-largest share) of deodorant category. *Sales*—$77.3 million.

**Major competitor:** Mennen's Lady Speed Stick; also Arrid and Right Guard.

**Advertising:** *Agency*—Leo Burnett, Chicago, IL. *Major campaign*—"Strong enough for a man, but pH-balanced for a woman."

**Addresses:** *Parent company*—Procter & Gamble Company, One Procter & Gamble Plaza, Cincinnati, OH 45202; phone: (513) 983-1100; fax: (513) 983-7847.

Perceptively recognizing the trend away from personal advice and guidance by beauty counselors and druggists, Procter & Gamble realized that the new self-service sections would require new attention to packaging, advertising, and merchandising. Consequently, the company concentrated its growing technological ability in these areas of all of its high-volume product lines. Toothpaste was the largest-selling category, followed by shampoos, deodorants, and home permanents.

### First Commercial Success

The introduction of Secret in 1956 represented the company's entry into the skyrocketing deodorant market. At this time, Procter & Gamble was also enhancing its research facilities to give its marketing people wide latitude to study, experiment, and investigate consumer preferences, without being distracted by existing business. The first marketed version of Secret came in a cream form in a glass jar. The packaging consisted of a cardboard box brandishing a pink flower, representing femininity, on a blue background, connoting coolness. The words "ice blue" were later added to the product description. From its inception, Secret was gender-specific, aimed at women. Its name harkened back to Victorian times—how a woman handled underarm perspiration was her own private affair. The cream was composed primarily of petrolatum, which absorbed odors. Later, aluminum chloride, which actually *stopped* odor for a time, was added to the brand's formula. At that point, Secret was designated as an antiperspirant.

### Early Marketing Strategy

Procter & Gamble continued to perform product research vigorously in the late 1950s. Its Winton Hill Technical Center, a spacious campus-style conglomerate of laboratories begun in 1959 on the outskirts of Cincinnati, was rapidly expanding. By 1973, a new site at Sharon Woods was added to the company's research facilities.

One important finding of researchers' investigation of the buying habits of American women indicated that while the housewife was still a major toiletry customer, teenagers purchased 50 percent more deodorants than their mothers. From this one report, the brand's advertisers were able to formulate a campaign targeted at teenagers. In the 1950s, when television took up permanent residence in the American living room, Secret was advertised on such family programs as *The Donna Reed Show.* These early commercials featured Secret spokesperson Katy Winters (her sur-

name symbolizing the cooling effectiveness of the product) extolling the virtues of ice-blue Secret and maternally advising a teenaged girl to apply some of *her* ice-blue "secret" before going on a date.

Coupons, samples, premiums, and other promotional devices spurred Secret's sales by stimulating trial and re-trial. Coupons offered Secret at a reduced price or frequently for free, while premiums induced consumers to try it at no cost. Promotional tools such as the point-of-purchase displays and price features made Secret stand out in the store. Based on the premise that consumers would like Secret and buy it again, these promotional devices built sales volume and were the cornerstone of the brand's success.

### Brand Development and Product Changes

Secret Cream, introduced in 1956 and first packaged in a glass jar, was swiftly introduced in other forms. In November of 1964, Secret Deodorant Spray premiered, followed by Secret Anti-Perspirant Spray in September, 1967. Secret Solid debuted in 1978, while 1983 witnessed the introduction of a silicone-based formula and the packaging of the cream in a plastic jar. New shaker instructions for the roll-on, still considered the most effective applicator, appeared in April of 1986, and in May of that year the Powder Scent premiered in all forms of Secret except the deodorant spray and the cream products. September of 1986 marked the updating of package graphics for all forms of the line and the introduction of the wide solid, although the round stick was still available. In March of 1987, the Spring Breeze scent debuted in all forms of the product except the cream and the deodorant spray. In September of 1989, the Sporty Clean scent was introduced, its name changing to Shower Fresh in 1993. The three-ounce round solid was discontinued in October of 1989; in the spring of 1990, all round solids were discontinued and all roll-ons and solids were improved. In the early 1990s the brand was available in a wide variety of fragrances. The roll-on, wide solid, and anti-perspirant deodorant spray were offered in Regular, Unscented, Powder Fresh, Spring Breeze, and Shower Fresh, while the deodorant spray and cream both showcased the original scent. On January 18, 1993, polydecene was added to all forms of the product to lessen the white residue on skin and clothes.

### Innovations in Advertising

Procter & Gamble's innovative advertising dates back to 1882, when Harley Procter, son of the co-founder of the company, formulated the first promotional campaign for Ivory Soap. Many of his marketing concepts proved so successful that they were used into the next century. In 1993, Health and Beauty Aids sections of retail stores regularly received large cardboard displays for Secret featuring refund tear-off forms. Sunday newspapers offered coupons, and free trial size packages of Secret were available via direct mail. Twin packs of Secret, which offered a nearly 50 percent saving to consumers, were also available at many retailers.

Procter & Gamble performed intense market research, most notably through mail surveys, in order to keep abreast of their customers' needs and preferences. One example of the company's sensitivity to consumer views lay in the handling of communications. In the late 1970s, Procter & Gamble, already answering hundreds of letters a day about its products, became one of the first companies to include toll-free telephone numbers on its packages. By the early 1980s, every Procter & Gamble package boasted a toll-free number. An outgrowth of this telecommunication practice debuted in 1992, when another company brand, Ivory Clear Dishwashing Liquid, rolled out nationally. In addition to telecommunicative advertising, P&G indirectly pitched Secret to school-children—future customers—by distributing free consumer-education materials to teachers.

October, 1991 saw the advent of a startling new marketing strategy for Procter & Gamble—the EDLP (Everyday Low Price) Policy which, while it lowered retailers' costs for P&G products, also eliminated a marketer's generous trade allowances. A reflection of Chairman and CEO Edwin L. Artzt's vision of a new P&G—a more profitable company driven by lower costs and higher brand loyalty derived from streamlined manufacturing operations, more control over trade promotions, and consumer-oriented advertising—this "value pricing" program was not well regarded by retailers. As a trade-off, one of P&G's advertising agencies, J. Brown and Associates in New York City, developed the Bonus Media Program, in which specially "tagged" television spots mentioned the local retailer's name, gratis, at the end of the commercial.

### Environmental Controversy

In 1975 and 1976, aerosol sprays were challenged by the Food and Drug Administration when studies suggested that chlorofluorocarbon propellants had damaging effects on the ozone layer of the atmosphere. Secret survived when P&G switched to an alternate propellant. Thereafter, at least 25 percent of the brand's research and development expenditures were allocated to ensure compliance with government regulations. In the late 1970s, as consumer concern about the environment heightened, an increasing number of products, previously thought to be safe, were determined to pose long-term threats to the environment and consumers' health. Among these products, Secret Anti-Perspirants and Deodorants were singled out because one of their active ingredients, zirconium, was linked to cancer in laboratory research. Though used safely for years, it was suddenly being attacked because of hypothetical long-term health effects, and it received widespread publicity. P&G sweated out the crisis by simply reformulating the chemical additive into a safer derivative which evolved into the aluminum zirconium trichlorohydrex gly still used in 1993.

### Performance Appraisal

From its inception, Secret was a leading seller, always retaining a top share of the deodorant market. In 1992 and 1993, for example, the brand held steady at the number two slot. However, sales did suffer; for the 26 weeks which ended in February, 1993, it sold $77.3 million worth of goods, down 5.5 percent from the previous 26 weeks, and its market share slipped from 12.7 percent in 1992 to 11.8 percent in 1993. Yet, the brand managed to trounce such rivals as Arrid, Right Guard, Ban, and P&G's own competing brand, Sure. In both 1992 and 1993, only Mennen outsold the brand—probably because Secret had become a gender neutral product ("Strong enough for a man, yet pH-balanced for a woman."), whereas Mennen sported specific varieties for men, women, and teenagers.

### Future Predictions

Debuting as a simple deodorant in 1956, Secret, for more than 30 years, remained a market share leader in the volatile deodorant market largely because P&G focused intently on consumer prefer-

ences and kept the personality of the Secret brand consistent in advertising through the years. Most importantly, of course, Secret effectively prevented odor and controlled perspiration.

Performance and value have been the marketing foundations of Secret. The Secret brand belonged to a company that believed in recruiting, developing, and retaining quality professionals by an approach called P&G College. The program offered employees externally-directed, marketplace-focused education about P&G's methods of doing business. With P&G managers as professors, P&G College enabled the company to pass on the knowledge and expertise of one generation of management to another.

The future development of the Secret brand is entrusted to P&G chemists and marketers who continue to perform market research, create new technologies, and update Secret Anti-Perspirants and Deodorants, by improving, but not deviating from, the basic formula. As a P&G researcher once remarked: "It isn't enough to invent a new product. Through constant improvement, we must manage every existing brand so that it can flourish year after year in an everchanging, intensely competitive marketplace. . . . At P&G, we create the future."

### Further Reading:

"Answers About Marketing," Cincinnati: Procter & Gamble Company, 1993.

Appelbaum, Cara, "HBA's Healthy Performance (Health and Beauty Industry)," *Adweek,* September 23, 1991, p. 598.

Bird, Laura, "Hygiene Crusades Drive Sales," *Adweek's Marketing Week,* September 17, 1990, p. S122.

Boyer, Pamela, "Sweet Success: *Prevention's* Guide to Stay Fresh and Dry During Emotional Heat and Hot Weather," *Prevention,* August 1991, p. 87.

Brian, Sarah Jane, "All's Well That Smell's Well," *Science World,* January 11, 1991, p. 3.

"Coming Clean in America (Soap and Deodorant Spending)," *U.S. News and World Report,* June 26, 1989, p. 74.

Conkling, Winifred, "Disarming the Armpit: Researchers Have Found the Culprit in Underarm Odor," *American Health: Fitness in Body and Mind,* December 1990, p. 16.

Crown, Judith, "Helene Curtis's Degree Makes Competitors Sweat," *Advertising Age,* October 29, 1990, p. 20.

"Deodorants at a Glance," *Adweek's Marketing Week,* April 10, 1989, p. 12.

Disapio, Alfred J., "Assessing the Potential of the European Underarm Market," *Drug and Cosmetic Industry,* September 1991, p. 32.

Editors of *Advertising Age, Procter & Gamble: The House That Ivory Built,* Lincolnwood, IL: NTC Business Books, 1988.

*Facts About Procter & Gamble,* Cincinnati: The Procter & Gamble Company, 1992.

"Gender Marketing Dominates Deodorant Market," *U.S. Distribution Journal,* October 1989, p. 12.

Greene, Eva-Lynne, "Decoding Deodorants," *American Health: Fitness of Body and Mind,* December 1992, p. 26.

Groeneveld, Benno, "Dare to Be Different (Deodorants and Anti-Perspirants)," *Chemical Marketing Reporter,* July 22, 1991, p. SR38.

"Health and Beauty Aids (Sales Statistics: 1989 Non-Foods Sales Manual)," *Progressive Grocer,* August 1989, p. 69.

"Heavyweight Deodorants to Clash," *Brandweek,* September 28, 1992, p. 1.

Kanner, Bernice, "No Sweat: Keeping America Dry (Deodorants and Anti-Perspirants on Madison Avenue)," *New York,* November 23, 1992, p. 28.

Lawrence, Jennifer, "P&G Customizes Ads to Plug Retailers," *Advertising Age,* February 8, 1993, p. 28; "Will P&G's Pricing Policy Pull

Retailers Over to Its Side?'' *Advertising Age,* April 19, 1993, pp. 1, 42–43.

Licf, Alfred, *''It Floats''; The Story of Procter & Gamble,* New York: Rinehart, 1958.

Liesse, Julie, ''Brand Scorecard,'' *Advertising Age,* April 19, 1993, p. 22.

Loffredo, Douglas, ''For Anti-Perspirants, Niche Growth No Sweat,'' *Chemical Marketing Reporter,* July 23, 1990, p. SR30; ''Price and Value: Strong Competition Has Anti-Perspirant and Deodorant Producers Watching the Bottom Line,'' *Chemical Marketing Reporter,* August 10, 1992, p. SR8.

McMath, Robert, ''Did Remedies Inspire New Products?'' *Adweek's Marketing Week,* July 1, 1991, p. 33.

Merrefield, David, ''Analgesics and Deodorants: Sales Growth's in Store,'' *Supermarket News,* January 23, 1989, p. 11.

Millstein, Marc, ''New Deodorants Look for Sweet Smell of Success (HBC Pharmacy),'' *Supermarket News,* May 13, 1991, p. 30.

Muirhead, Greg, ''Getting Deodorants A Little Closer; Unboxed and Reduced-Package Anti-Perspirants Are Making Room on the Shelf for the Bevy of New Products (HBC Pharmacy),'' *Supermarket News,* January 6, 1992, p. 21; ''Clear Choice: New and Popular Clear Deodorants Are Replacing Slow-Selling Sprays and Roll-Ons on Store Shelves,'' *Supermarket News,* January 4, 1993, p. 17.

*The Procter & Gamble Company,* Cincinnati: Procter & Gamble Company, 1993.

*Procter & Gamble Company 1992 Annual Report,* Cincinnati: Procter & Gamble Company, 1993.

Roach, Mary, ''Underarmed and Dangerous,'' *Health,* July–August, 1992, p. 24.

Rosendahl, Iris, ''Drugstores Meeting Tougher Competition for Deodorants,'' *Drug Topics,* August 19, 1991, p. 65.

Shields, Jody, *''Vogue* Beauty: Sweat,'' *Vogue,* June, 1991, pp. 111–114.

Sloan, Pat, ''Unilever Powers Up Deodorant,'' *Advertising Age,* September 25, 1989, p. 10.

Sloan, Pat, Laurie Freeman, and Jon Lafayette, ''Degree Makes Leaders Sweat,'' *Advertising Age,* December 10, 1990, p. 16.

Schisgall, Oscar, *Eyes on Tomorrow: The Evolution of Procter & Gamble,* New York: J. G. Ferguson Publishing Company, 1981.

Snyder, Glenn, Marjorie Wold, Stephen Bennett, Paula McDonagh, and Tricia Janicki, ''Deodorants,'' *Progressive Grocer,* August, 1991, p. 52.

Snyder, Glenn, Jo-Ann Zbytniewski, and Stephen Bennett, ''Health and Beauty Aids (The 1992 Non-Foods Sales Manual),'' *Progressive Grocer,* August, 1992, p. 75.

*—Virginia Barnstorff*

# SEIKO®

# SEIKO

Seiko Corporation of America began marketing its famous wristwatches in the United States in the late 1960s. As of 1992, Seiko wristwatches constituted the largest market share of mid-priced watches (starting at $125) in the United States, although Seiko watches and clocks were by no means the only brand produced by the Seiko Corporation. Seiko products were named the official timekeepers at numerous major sporting events, such as the 1964 Tokyo Olympics and the 1992 Barcelona Olympics. Seiko was the first brand to come out with a revolutionary departure in timepieces, the quartz watch, in 1969. The name "Seiko" in Japanese conveys an image of precision and craftsmanship.

## Brand Origins

The wristwatch was invented in Europe in the early 1900s as a result of changing conditions and lifestyles that would characterize the twentieth century: mass transportation, growing leisure time, the mass appeal of sports, and the arrival of "modern" warfare. Until the late nineteenth century, the pocketwatch was universal for both men and women. Modern warfare demonstrated the impracticality of the pocketwatch, however, especially for officers in command with little or no time to pull out a pocketwatch. That inspired the search in Europe for a more practical watch, and by the turn of the century the market for wristwatches was no longer limited to the military; it included working women and those who were beginning to participate more frequently in sports.

Since wristwatches were a European invention and there was no domestic watch industry in Japan, all watches and clocks were imported until well into the nineteenth century. The Japanese market for watches and clocks was slow to grow. In Japan, the military and business worlds were the biggest consumers of pocket and wristwatches, as well as clocks. Factories and shops also began to run according to a rigid time clock. Not surprisingly, the Japanese learned to make watches from westerners, and soon made them even better.

A twenty-one-year-old clockmaker and energetic entrepreneur, Kintaro Hattori, became the founder of the Seiko brand of watch when he opened a tiny clock shop on the edge of the Ginza district in Tokyo in 1881. The shop marketed imported pocketwatches and clocks and was named after its founder, K. Hattori & Co., Ltd. Business was good, and eleven years later the firm, with fewer than eleven employees, began manufacturing its own clocks. The

same year the Hattori company established the Seikosha clock supply factory, which would in time become another member in the giant Seiko group of companies. With the establishment of the Seikosha company, Japan's domestic clock industry was born.

Destroyed by the devastating Kanto earthquake that struck Japan in 1923, the Hattori Co. recuperated its losses and in 1924 came out with the first Seiko brand watch, which still had to compete fiercely with many imported clocks in Japan. Two other important divisions of the Seiko group of companies were formed to assist distributor K. Hattori & Co. and clockmaker Seikosha. The Daini Seikosha Co., predecessor of today's Seiko Instruments, Inc., was established in 1937 in Tokyo, and Suwa Seikosha Co., predecessor of today's Seiko Epson Corporation and located some 125 miles from Tokyo, were acquired in 1942 at the height of the Allied bombings of Japan. These firms became the manufacturers for Seiko watches, which grew popular during World War II because of the Japanese military government's strict limits on imports. Daini Seikosha manufactured wristwatches for women and Suwa Seikosha for men, which the Hattori company in turn marketed and distributed. Seikosha continued to produce Seiko clocks.

Nearly destroyed during the World War II, the Seiko group of companies averted dissolution under the firm rule of General Douglas MacArthur. With the recovery of the Japanese economy in the 1950s, demand for watches rose precipitously. The Japanese had not been renowned for research and innovation (waterproof, shock-resistant, and automatic-winding watches were Swiss inventions of the 1920s and 1930s), but this would change in the postwar years as the government loosened its control of the economy and the huge *zaibatsu,* or prewar Japanese conglomerates, were destroyed.

## Product Development

From being a follower of watch and clock trends, the Seiko companies became an acknowledged leader in the late 1960s with the development of the first quartz watch. Seiko developed the world's first-ever quartz wall clock in 1968, and followed this product a year later with the Seiko Astron, the world's first quartz wristwatch. Quartz electronic watches were a revolutionary breakthrough in the watch industry, allowing for great accuracy. Electronic movements regulated the watch according to the vibrations of a quartz oscillator which was embedded in every quartz watch,

## AT A GLANCE

Seiko brand timepieces first marketed in 1924 in Japan; original marketer of Seiko watches and clocks was K. Hattori & Co., Ltd., founded in Tokyo by Japanese clockmaker Kintaro Hattori in 1881; in 1983 K. Hattori & Co. Ltd. was renamed the Hattori Seiko Company, Ltd., which changed its name again in 1990 to the Seiko Corporation; headquarters of Seiko Corporation in Tokyo; Seiko Corporation of America, a wholly owned, private subsidiary with headquarters in Mahwah, New Jersey, established in 1970.

*Performance:* Market share—50% of mid-priced domestic watch category.

*Major competitor:* Citizen Watch Co. Ltd.'s Citizen brand.

*Advertising: Agency*—AC&R Advertising, Inc., New York, NY, 1967—. *Major campaign*—TV commercials with the slogan: "Now the forces of nature can move the hands of time," referring to the new watch's ability to operate without a battery.

*Addresses: Parent company*—Seiko Corporation of America, 1111 MacArthur Blvd., Mahwah, NJ 07430; phone: (201) 529-5730; fax: (201) 529-1124. *Ultimate parent company*—Seiko Corporation, 6-21, Kyobashi 2-chome, Tokyo 104, Japan; phone: (03) 3563-2111; fax: 3-5250-7065.

producing the most accurate timepieces to date. The explosion of watch sales as a result of the invention and marketing of this new technology by Seiko opened up new markets and, most importantly, provided the incentive for ever more sophisticated innovations.

Several years after introducing the Seiko brand quartz watch, Seiko produced the world's first quartz LCD (Liquid Crystal Display) watches, capable of displaying up to six digits. Later line extensions included Seiko quartz watches for women (1972), the world's first fashion quartz watch (1974), and the world's first quartz alarm clock (1976). These Seiko brand watches and clocks were technologically superior to other timepieces already on the market.

In the 1980s the Seiko companies branched out into wrist instruments so technologically advanced that initially Seiko executives feared that there might be little market demand for them. They were wrong. In 1982 the Seiko TV watch became the first on the market, with a back pocket receiver that could pick up UHF and VHF channels as well as FM radio stations. This was followed only one year later with the world's first watch with sound recording functions, and in 1984 by a watch with computer functions. In the same year Seiko introduced the "Pulsemeter" watch, which measured the wearer's pulse in addition to telling time. In 1985, Seiko introduced the world's first wall clock with a ten-year battery. Several years later, the Seiko AGS (Automatic Generating System) wristwatch heralded yet another breakthrough development, in that it dispensed with batteries altogether and generated its own energy source via the world's tiniest generator. The AGS technology has been significantly developed and refined. Since 1992 the batteryless quartz watches have been sold under the name of Seiko Kinetic Quartz.

A few other technological marvels of the early 1990s included the Seiko Perpetual Calendar watch, with the world's first built-in millennium-plus (1,100 years) calendar; the Seiko Scubamaster, which incorporated a computerized dive table; and the Seiko

Receptor Message Watch, with paging functions and built-in antenna that allowed messages to be displayed on the watch face. Such technological feats made the Seiko brand a global leader in the watch industry.

### Early Marketing Strategy

Throughout the 1950s and 1960s, the Seiko watch and clock brand was known primarily in Japan. By then Seiko watches were widely advertised in sporting events, so much so that Seiko was selected as the official timekeeper for the Tokyo Olympics in 1964. Nevertheless, not until the late 1960s did Seiko executives decide to market their watches and clocks aggressively abroad.

The United States represented potentially the most lucrative market. In the late 1950s, a tiny Seiko sales office opened in Manhattan, selling watches and clocks mainly to Japanese jewelry and department stores in the United States, and watch parts to U.S. manufacturers. Even when Seiko watches were on display in the Japanese pavilion in the 1964 World's Fair in New York, they were an unfamiliar brand to Americans.

Rather than build a national sales force from the ground up, as competitors were doing, Seiko Corporation in 1969 decided to earmark more than a dozen U.S. distributors (who were in the wholesale jewelry business) to market Seiko watches exclusively. Using this unique strategy that created a firm distribution network, Seiko set the stage for the biggest leap in watch sales in the company's history in the 1970s.

### First Commercial Success

In 1969 Seiko's development of the world's first quartz watch created the possibility of huge new markets. As a result, the company's advertising expenditures shot up from $75,000 in 1967 to over $600,000 a few years later, merely to advertise its quartz watches on U.S. television. By 1977 two million Seiko quartz watches were sold in the United States, garnering the brand 20 percent of the mid-priced wristwatch market. Meanwhile, U.S. electronics companies rushed to produce cheap quartz-based digital watches, or LEDs (light-emitting diodes, which flashed the time only when the wearer pushed a side dial), while Seiko contented itself with targeting the middle- and upper-priced watch market with its quality analog quartz wristwatches.

After the market became saturated with the cheap digitals, Seiko entered that market itself with technologically superior models such as the hugely popular six-digit display LCD quartz watches, which dispensed with the side button. All the companies that had an enormous stake in the LEDs were overwhelmed by the new LCDs.

### Advertising

Meanwhile, enroute to becoming a top-selling brand, Seiko engaged an advertising agency in Manhattan to create Seiko watch ads. The resulting barrage of 30-second commercials (on local rather than national TV), all of which listed local jewelers who carried Seiko watches, was an unheard of strategy in the highly conservative watch industry. Because of the technical innovations of Seiko watches, the theme of these commercials was "The Automation Age Watch."

When the quartz wristwatch appeared on the U.S. market in early 1970, in an unusual departure from its TV advertising, Seiko Time put out a full-page ad in the *New York Times* announcing the revolutionary new watch. Heavy advertising produced the desired heavy demand. By 1977 Seiko Time's advertising budget exceeded $12 million, mainly for television commercial time.

Another important advertising medium for Seiko watches was sporting events, a marketing approach dominated for so many years by Swiss watchmakers. Seiko became official timekeeper at the 1964 Tokyo Olympics, the 1972 Sapporo Olympics, and the 1992 Barcelona Olympics, and also sponsored the World Soccer championship games in Argentina in 1978, Spain in 1982, and Mexico in 1986. A year before the Olympic Games in 1992, Seiko came out with a special U.S. Olympic Team collection of watches and clocks, as a reminder of the brand's association with world-class athletes.

## The Future

Seiko Corporation's international expansion took place after World War II. Seiko watches were introduced in Hong Kong in 1968, where American G.I.s on leave from the Vietnam War bought them in great quantity and succeeded in spreading their popularity by word of mouth in the United States when they returned. The establishment of the Seiko Corporation of America in the United States in 1970 took place at the same time that Seiko was introduced in Australia. Also in the 1970s, Seiko watches were introduced in western Europe and Latin America, and in 1989 they appeared in Thailand. The international marketplace was expected to be vital to the brand's future growth.

By the 1990s Seiko watches were produced in a wide variety of styles to fit the most exotic taste, from high-fashion to high-tech. The future of the watch industry appeared to be headed toward the high-tech, low-energy timepieces in which Seiko excelled. While the Seiko Corp. manufactured other watch brands, such as Lorus, Pulsar, and Lassale, it was the Seiko brand upon which the company's reputation and prestige rested. The image of precision and craftsmanship which the name conveyed in Japanese became widespread throughout the world.

## Further Reading:

Davis, Riccardo A., "Seiko, Citizen Set Big Sports Watch Campaigns Timed to Holiday Season," *Advertising Age,* December 21, 1992, p. 27.

*Seiko,* Mahwah, NJ: Seiko Corporation of America, 1992.

"Seiko's Smash: The Quartz Watch Overwhelms the Industry," *Business Week,* June 5, 1978, pp. 86–92.

"Seiko to Make All Its Watches Nickel-Free," *American Metal Market,* April 22, 1993, p. 1.

"Seiko Unveils Travel Alarm with Photo Frame," *HFD—The Weekly Home Furnishings Newspaper,* March 9, 1992, p. 43.

Thompson, Joe, "The New World of Seiko," *Modern Jeweler,* April 1990, pp. 51–58.

Thompson, Joe, "The Selling of Seiko," *Jewelers' Circular-Keystone,* August 1981, pp. 217–236.

Thompson, Joe, "Seiko's Olympic Gamble," *Modern Times, A Monthly Review of the Watch and Clock World,* November 1992, pp. 43–49.

*—Sina Dubovoj*

# SLIM-FAST®

# Slim·Fast®

Slim-Fast is the top selling brand in the liquid meal replacement category and has become synonymous with weight loss to one-fourth of 50 million dieting Americans. The Ultra Slim-Fast weight loss program is a 1,200 to 1,300 calorie low-fat, high-fiber meal plan that combines two highly nutritious milk-based shakes with a regular well-balanced meal and up to three snacks. The program encourages permanent weight reduction through both regular exercise and behavior modification in conjunction with a nutritious meal plan. Average weight loss that may be expected on the program is approximately 3–4 pounds the first week and 1–2 pounds each week thereafter.

Slim-Fast is one of the greatest consumer brand success stories of the last decade, but customer interest in this type of program seems to be leveling off. While only three years ago, in 1990, liquid meal replacements reigned as the nation's number one weight-control craze, sales in supermarkets, drugstores and mass-merchandise outlets have since dropped noticeably. Nearly every major brand of the liquid meal replacements experienced a sharp decline, but the Slim-Fast Foods Company's brand still dominates the category with an 88 percent share. Slim-Fast Foods Company also manufactures the Slim-Fast Nutrition Bar.

## Brand Origins

Fresh out of the U.S. Army in 1945, S. Daniel Abraham longed to be in business for himself. He read an ad in a trade publication for the maker of San-Cura itch-relieving ointment and ended up buying the company for $5,000. That company became Thompson Medical Company, Inc. As early as 1956, Abraham introduced his first diet product, Slim-Mint gum, a benzocaine-based product that dulled hunger. Four years later he came out with his own diet capsules, called Figure-Aid. Then, in 1976, he brought out Dexatrim, his first really big product. Dexatrim is a diet pill formulated with the powerful appetite suppressant phenylpropanolamine or PPA. This heavily advertised diet pill became the best-seller in its category.

The Slim-Fast brand was created in 1977 when Abraham first introduced the Slim-Fast powdered drink mix to the market. That same year, however, customers grew wary of weight-loss aids when 59 dieters died after using an unrelated product, a liquid diet consisting of as little as 300 calories per day. Slim-Fast was in no way associated with the deaths, but its sales disappeared all the same. In the early 1980s, as the faddish diet market changed again,

Abraham reintroduced Slim-Fast. As a result, Thompson Medical's sales boomed between 1983 and 1984.

## The Diet Craze

Consumers' interest in liquid meal replacements took off in late 1988, after talk-show host Oprah Winfrey boasted of her 67-pound weight loss to television viewers. Winfrey used the Optifast Program, made by a Sandoz Ltd. unit, a prescription product marketed only through hospitals. But the program's cost—up to $3,000 for six months—sent waist-watchers scrambling for cheaper alternatives.

About the same time, Slim-Fast began recruiting such larger-than-life celebrities as Tommy Lasorda, and television personality Cristine Ferrare to hawk its diet program. Thompson Medical then spun off the Slim-Fast Foods Company division. Popularity of the products reached a peak after Slim-Fast recruited six formerly flabby National Football League coaches to provide testimonials.

Since then, however, millions of viewers have watched as Ms. Winfrey gradually returned to her former girth. The reverse testimonial only seemed to underscore the most glaring weakness of all diet products: They are rarely a lasting solution to being overweight. Weight-loss experts say 90 percent to 95 percent of all dieters on any plan regain any weight lost within five years.

## Advertising Innovations

In 1992 Slim-Fast launched a campaign to show how residents in the aptly named hamlet of Pound, Wisconsin, gave Slim-Fast six weeks and took off (almost) a ton. The testimonial spot from Grey Advertising caught 160 Pound residents midway through their "No Hunger" Slim-Fast diet. It posed the question "What if an entire town decided to eat healthy and lose weight?" The answer, according to the commercial, is that they'll lose 1,738 pounds in six weeks, or some 11 pounds apiece.

Slim-Fast's binge on Madison Avenue is an attempt to reverse the tough times all merchants have had in recent times. Slim-Fast's elaborate publicity stunt in the heart of dairy country was also part of an attempt to remake the image of Slim-Fast from a staple of crash dieters to "America's healthy way to lose weight," as the campaign's new tag line proclaimed. The company reportedly ditched its "Give us a week, we'll take off the weight" pledge because consumer research found that dieters wanted to eat

# AT A GLANCE

**U**ltra Slim-Fast Weight Loss Program founded in 1977 in New York by S. Daniel Abraham, owner of Thompson Medical Company, Inc.; brand owned as of December, 1990 by Slim-Fast Foods Company.

*Performance:* *Market share*—88% (top share) of liquid meal replacement category (according to *Advertising Age* magazine). *Sales*—$242.4 million (according to *Advertising Age* magazine).

*Major competitor:* Nestle Food Co.'s Sweet Success.

*Advertising:* *Agency*—Grey Advertising, New York, NY, 1987—. *Major campaign*—Various celebrities and sports personalities touting the Slim-Fast weight loss program.

*Addresses:* *Parent company*—Slim-Fast Foods Company, 919 3rd Ave., New York, NY 10022; phone: (212) 688-4420; fax: (212) 415-7171.

nutritiously, not just lose weight. The company wanted consumers to realize that Slim-Fast is real food as much as cottage cheese and cereal.

To drive that point home, another spot starred veteran Slim-Fast booster and talk-show host Kathie Lee Gifford. Gifford noted that an Ultra Slim-Fast chocolate shake has half the fat and over 100 fewer calories than a lunch of fruit and low-fat cottage cheese. Slim-Fast also used others to promote the ad campaign, including former New York Mayor Ed Koch, actress Kim Fields, singer Mel Torme, actor Peter DeLuise, sports commentator Dan Dierdorf, 1988 Miss USA Courtney Gibbs, actress Shari Belafonte, Elizabeth Ashley, and singer and actress Ann Jillian.

## Marketing Strategy

Founder S. Daniel Abraham heavily involves himself in the company's marketing. He buys his company's raw materials and visits retailers like Sam Walton, whose Wal-Mart stores sell an estimated $100 million worth of Slim-Fast every year. Abraham is lavish with money for advertising and promotion. He personally signed Tommy Lasorda, the Los Angeles Dodgers' manager, to appear in Slim-Fast's ads in 1989, promising that the company would contribute to Lasorda's favorite charity if the ballplayer stuck to the diet. Lasorda lost some 30 pounds in three months on the diet and the Sisters of Mercy, a Nashville group of nuns, got a new convent. Two years after the Lasorda campaign and a subsequent campaign using the overweight NFL coaches, Slim-Fast sales grew to an estimated $650 million, while the percentage of male customers grew from ten to 35 percent of the total. In 1992 the company reported that it would spend about $100 million promoting Slim-Fast and the new, thicker shake with extra fiber called Ultra Slim-Fast, according to Judann Dagnoli in *Advertising Age.*

## Brand Development

Slim-Fast brand liquid diet meal replacement drink has undergone little change since first introduced in 1977. A thicker shake with extra fiber called Ultra Slim-Fast was introduced in 1988 and currently holds the majority of the market share for Slim-Fast. A Slim-Fast mix that works with fruit juice rather than milk entered the market in 1990. Ultra Slim-Fast Plus, a powder that mixes with

12 ounces of milk rather than eight, was introduced in 1992 and holds a very small percentage of Slim-Fast's total share.

Slim-Fast then decided to further expand its product line under the Slim-Fast brand. The first Slim-Fast food product was the Ultra Slim-Fast Nutrition Bar in 1984. This bar can be eaten as a snack or a meal in itself, if taken with a glass of skim milk. But the product introductions began to heat up in earnest in 1990 when Ultra Slim-Fast pudding mix was launched, and later Ultra Slim-Fast Lite 'N' Tasty popcorn and cheese curls salty snacks.

Because Slim-Fast realized that people not only wanted to lose weight but to eat healthy, the company instituted its new lifestyle ad campaign in January of 1991 to reposition the meal replacement marketer as a full-scale diet plan. One month prior, Slim-Fast Foods Company split off from its parent Thompson Medical Company, Inc. to become and independent entity. Slim-Fast began a series of commercials focusing on a group of well-proportioned people having a good time at the beach, playing games, and, of course, exercising. These spots were intended to serve as an umbrella campaign for the new line of reduced-calorie foods the company planned to introduce under the Ultra Slim-Fast name. Because Slim-Fast has had much success with its weight-loss testimonial campaign, the new commercials also feature cameo appearances of well known people who have demonstrated in previous ads how they shed excess pounds using Slim-Fast. These commercials have launched new products such as pretzels. The company also plans to introduce canned soft drinks, single-serve juices, spaghetti sauce, and spaghetti.

The new Slim-Fast meal plan aims at getting a dieter to spend $25 to $30 a week on Ultra Slim-Fast products, rather than the $80 per week or more on some weight-loss system programs. Slim-Fast also offers pre-mixed Ultra Slim-Fast in a can. It is offered in vending machines as well as wherever the powder is sold.

Slim-Fast Foods Company, in a joint venture with Welsh Publishing Group, launched *Slim-Fast Magazine* in June 1991 as a quarterly. The magazine, aimed at Slim-Fast users, focused on fitness, health, and nutrition. The magazine was loaded with Slim-Fast testimonials and success stories. Before launching the magazine, the company received 3,000 letters a day from customers. But the publication ran for only one year.

## Competition

With an 88 percent market share, Slim-Fast has little to worry about concerning the competition. But competition in the market has intensified. Marketing powerhouse and the world's largest food company, Nestle Food Company, has launched Sweet Success, a powdered chocolate diet meal replacement aimed at chocolate lovers. The company claims it products' superior taste will attract the disgruntled customers of competitors. Although sales of meal replacements in supermarkets and drugstores have skidded, Nestle still sees opportunities. The company feels that the diet market is one that thrives on new products. Advertising spending for Sweet Success rivals the Ultra Slim-Fast brand. Sweet Success is targeted at women and sells for close to the same price as Ultra Slim-Fast. The product is offered in five chocolate flavors, including chocolate raspberry truffle.

Nestle Food, successor to Carnation Company, isn't new to dieting. It experimented with a chain of retail weight-loss centers in the early 1980s, and it's marketed Slender diet drink since the 1960s. Nestle pulled Slender from the market as it rolled out Sweet

Success. Of course, there are copycat products being offered also. Meijer, Inc. distributes a powdered diet drink mix named Extra Thin Quick. Its price is about one-third that of Ultra Slim-Fast.

## Regulation Needed?

Dieters and government officials are starting to scrutinize diet practices, and the industry may well have only its own heavy marketing to blame. Representative Ron Wyden (D-Oregon) opened a series of hearings in 1990. Their focus: the hype in the industry and the need for regulation. Reporters and spectators jammed Wyden's committee room on Capitol Hill to hear testimony on many aspects of the diet craze. Hearings were also scheduled to discuss the problems users of clinic-administered and mass-market powders have in keeping off weight.

In 1991 the Federal Trade Commission began a broad probe into the diet industry's ads. In its first action, the FTC charged marketers of three liquid diet brands—Optifast 70, Medifast 70 and Ultrafast—with making deceptive claims about the long-term safety and effectiveness of their products. Jenny Craig, Inc. and Weight Watchers International, two industry heavyweights, have petitioned the commission to issue advertising regulations for the entire industry.

Slim-Fast hasn't gotten into any trouble, but with its various commercials it could expose the tendency of dieters using liquid meal replacements to regain pounds as quickly as they shed them, the very issue at the heart of the FTC's investigation. The focus of the FTC's investigation is on long-term, sustained weight loss. The agency may require diet companies to disclose in their ads the probability of regaining weight.

## Beyond Good Health

Slim-Fast Foods is proud of its position as a leader in the industry. The company is committed to helping people everywhere lose weight and stay slim through good nutrition. Slim-Fast food products are available in Canada, the United Kingdom, France, Germany, Israel, and many other countries worldwide.

Slim-Fast Foods Company has been a major contributor to such causes as the Miami Project to Cure Paralysis, the 1990 March of Dimes WalkAmerica, the Actors Fund of America (AIDS help and research), Tomorrow's Children (cancer research) and Camp Simcha (a camp for terminally ill children).

## Performance Appraisal

Because Slim-Fast Foods Company is privately held, sales and market share information is difficult to obtain. Various sources state that the market for liquid replacement meals declined by 45 percent to $274.5 million over the 12 months ending June 1992. Slim-Fast has an 88 percent market share or $242.4 million. Despite dwindling consumption in the liquid diet category, Slim-Fast continues to benefit. Competition poses little threat to the market leader as it continues to show superior performance.

Many weight-loss programs are of here-today-gone-tomorrow variety, including the grapefruit and Scarsdale diets. Slim-Fast Foods Company's Ultra Slim-Fast Weight Loss Program has seemed to survive the faddish diet market. With top market share and continuous line extensions, the company is constantly repositioning itself to be a provider of nutritious health food.

## Further Reading:

Dagnoli, Judann, "Slim-Fast Beefs Up Menu of Food Items," *Advertising Age,* May 27, 1991, p. 10.

Dagnoli, Judann, and Julie Liesse, "Kraft, ConAgra Go Head-to-Head In Healthy Meals," *Advertising Age,* October 22, 1990, pp. 58–59.

Donaton, Scott, "Magazine Floodgate Opens," *Advertising Age,* December 16, 1991, p. 3.

Endicott, R. Craig, "The Top 200 Brands—AT&T Pushes Past McDonald's," *Advertising Age,* November 19, 1990, p. 27.

Foltz, Kim, "Slim-Fast to Sell Itself As 'A Way of Life,' " *New York Times,* December 31, 1990, p. 35L.

Freeman, Laurie, "Ultra Slim-Fast," *Advertising Age,* July 6, 1992, p. 58.

Johnson, Bradley, "Nestle Targets Dieters With New Chocolate Fix," *Advertising Age,* August 24, 1992, p. 1.

Liesse, Julie, "Frozen Novelties Look for Hot Summer," *Advertising Age,* May 13, 1991, p. 6.

*Slim-Fast Foods Company Background,* New York: Slim-Fast Foods Company.

Winters, Patricia, "Diet Aid Goliath to Fatten Up on Slim-Fast Foods," *Advertising Age,* February 12, 1990, p. 3.

Winters, Patricia, "Slim-Fast Dishes Up New Foods," *Advertising Age,* January 7, 1991, p. 38.

*—Carol Kieltyka*

# SMITH BROTHERS®

Manufactured by F&F Laboratories, Inc., in Chicago, Illinois, Smith Brothers Cough Drops are one of America's most familiar products, having been marketed continuously for more than a century. The distinctive Smith Brothers logo, which features two bearded gentlemen known as "Trade" and "Mark," first appeared on jars and envelopes of cough drops in the late 1870s. That famous trademark has remained unchanged in the last century, although the product line has expanded to include a variety of different flavors and a range of packaging types.

## Early History

James Smith, a carpenter from the Quebec town of St. Armand, established a restaurant in Poughkeepsie, New York, in 1847. Given the "secret recipe" for cough candy by a restaurant customer, Smith began to manufacture batches of the product, which his sons William and Andrew sold throughout the town. After their father's death in 1866, the two sons continued to sell the product under the name of "Smith Brothers Cough Drops." The product became well known throughout the Hudson Valley, and was promoted as an aid to "all afflicted with hoarseness, coughs or colds" in early print ads. Since its introduction, the brand has faced stiff competition. A number of similar products, sold under such names as "Schmitt Brothers," "Smythe Sisters," and even under the identical name, were also popular in the market.

The Smith Brothers expanded their cough drop business by establishing a factory on the outskirts of Poughkeepsie. They also persuaded other retailers to sell the cough drops, which were displayed in glass jars bearing the Smith Brothers name and dispensed in similarly marked envelopes. To make sure that theirs was the only product sold under that name, they developed cough drop molds which incorporated the initials "SB" into the actual cough drop. Beginning in 1877, Smith Brothers cough drops were sold in boxes imprinted with the likenesses of the two brothers. The box was intended to show that "Smith Brothers Cough Drops" was a registered trademark, through the placement of the word "Trade" under the image of William and the word "Mark" under the image of Andrew.

The first Smith Brothers cough drops were manufactured in two flavors: wild cherry and black licorice. Other early product line extensions, some of which have been discontinued, included menthol cough drops (1922), a cough syrup (1926), and assorted fruit cough drops and smokers drops (both 1958). The Smith

family continued to manufacture the cough drops until 1967, when the business was sold to F&F Laboratories, Inc. Smith Brothers Cough Drops continue to be manufactured today by F&F Laboratories in Chicago. Still one of the most popular non-prescription cough and throat drops on the market, the product is currently sold in bags, boxes, and rolls. There are four flavors on the market today—black licorice, wild cherry, menthol-eucalyptus, and honey-lemon. The company also launched its first sugar-free cough drops in its most popular flavor, wild cherry.

Although Smith Brothers is one of the most popular over-the-counter cough and throat drops on the market, the brand faces stiff competition—primarily from Halls Cough Drops, as well as Vicks, and Ludens.

## Advertising Strategies

Some of the earliest print ads for Smith Brothers cough drops appeared in Poughkeepsie newspapers with the following copy: "James Smith & Sons Compound of Wild Cherry Cough Candy for the Cure of Coughs, Colds, Hoarseness, Sore Throats, Whooping Cough, Asthma, &C, &C." Current advertising strategies include national radio campaigns and television ads in ten major metro markets, featuring the following slogan: ''Smith Brothers: The name you can trust since 1847.''

## Further Reading:

Barach, Arnold D., *Famous American Trademarks,* Washington, DC: Public Affairs Press, 1971.

Campbell, Hannah, *Why Did They Name It?,* New York: Fleet Publishing Corporation, 1964.

Morgan, Hal, *Symbols of America,* New York: Penguin Books, 1986.

*—Marcia Mogelonsky*

# SPEEDO®

Speedo International is one of the world's largest manufacturers of swimwear. Since the company's inception in the late 1920s, more than 250 million Speedo swimsuits have been sold. Brandishing a lightning flash logo, the sleek Speedo suits have been top-sellers in competitive swimwear, worn by more Olympic gold medal winners and world record holders than any other swimwear brand. Speedo has generally specialized in performance swimwear, but beginning in the late 1980s, when ownership of Speedo International changed hands, the Speedo brand name began to extend to a broader variety of water-related products. The North American distributor of Speedo, Authentic Fitness Corporation, actively pursued expansion and also promoted the Speedo brand by opening retail stores that featured Speedo brand name products. Although Speedo is no longer Australian-owned, during the 1990s Australians still considered Speedo "cossies" as inherently their own.

## Brand Origins and Ownership

The Speedo brand was founded in Sidney, Australia, in 1929 by the McCrea family. Speedo first came to prominence at the 1956 Olympics in Melbourne, when Speedo sponsored the Australian swim team. Shortly thereafter, Speedo International Ltd. was formed and the company expanded operations worldwide through licensing and manufacturing agreements. In 1956 Speedo entered the U.S. market and five years later, Hirsch Weis, a subsidiary of Warnaco Inc., became Speedo's U.S. distributor and licensee. In 1983 the marketing activities were also transferred to Hirsch Weis.

In 1986 Speedo was sold and restructured. By 1990 the Pentland Group had acquired Speedo International and Speedo Australia from the Linter Group receivership for $47.5 million in August, marking the end of Australian ownership of one of the country's few international brands. British-based Pentland also purchased the European branch of Speedo and about 40 percent of the Authentic Fitness Corporation, which became the sole distributor of Speedo brand products in the United States. Authentic Fitness was formally incorporated in 1990 when an investment group headed by Warnaco CEO Linda J. Wachner purchased the active-wear division at Warnaco Inc. for $85 million. Warnaco Active-wear held the Speedo license in the United States, Canadian, Mexican, and Caribbean markets in perpetuity. Authentic Fitness went public in June of 1991 and raised about $42 million for restructuring and improvements. The Pentland subsidiary, Speedo

Holdings BV, continued to own its worldwide rights to the Speedo brand name and to receive royalties from Authentic Fitness and its other licensees.

## Shifts in Marketing Strategy

Speedo has designed swimwear for countless Olympic Games and world competitions. Throughout its history Speedo remained largely in the active swimwear category. Beginning in the 1980s, however, Speedo developed a series of new product lines, including men's watershorts, T-shirts, and various swimming accessories such as goggles and Speedo Surf Walker footwear. Within a few years Speedo made plans to expand into surfwear, beachwear, and fashion swimwear. By 1991, Authentic Fitness Corporation, the Speedo distributor in North America, developed a new line of active fitness apparel for year-round sports; at an Atlanta trade show the company launched the "Speedo Aquatic Fitness" program and related products. In December 1992 Authentic Fitness opened its first retail store featuring Speedo brand products at the Beverly Center in Los Angeles. The dramatic interior design included a seven-foot waterfall, with mannequins in Speedo suits diving into the waterfall, and a ceiling that resembled a tiled swimming pool.

During the late 1980s and early 1990s, Speedo focused on increasing its manufacturing capacity, raising it by nearly 50 percent in 1990. Much of the time saved came from improving design and making it less complicated to manufacture. Another of Speedo's goals was to decrease merchandising time, whereby the Speedo catalogue could reach the trade buyers quicker than those of the competition. At the same time, Speedo involved itself more in the promotion of its products at the point of sale. Besides improving product displays, Speedo wanted to provide better customer service by ensuring that retailers had an adequate amount and variety of products and proper changing facilities.

During the early 1990s Speedo's strategies involved not only improving existing Speedo products and developing new categories, but also expanding the worldwide distribution base. At this time, the company pursued more varied promotional strategies. Rather than rely exclusively on visibility garnered at major sports events like the Olympics, Speedo signed a three-year contract with Tom Jager, the American record-holding swimmer, an agreement that included personal appearances, advertising, and endorsements.

## AT A GLANCE

Speedo brand founded in 1929 in Sydney, Australia, by the McCrea family; entered U.S. market in 1956; in 1961 Hirsch Weis, a subsidiary of Warnaco Inc., became Speedo's U.S. distributor and licensee; in 1986 leveraged buyout by Warnaco CEO Linda J. Wachner and a group of investors; in 1990 Authentic Fitness was incorporated for the acquisition of the Activewear Division of Warnaco. In 1986 Speedo International and Speedo Australia were bought by Crowther Group from Linter Group; in 1990 Speedo Europe purchased by Pentland Group; in 1991 Pentland acquired Speedo International and about 40% of the Authentic Fitness Corp. in Van Nuys, CA.

**Performance:** *Market share*—59% (worldwide) of competitive swimwear. *Sales*—$68.2 million (worldwide).

**Major competitor:** Tyr; also Finals and Arena.

**Addresses:** *Parent company*—Speedo International, Pentland Center, Lakeside, Squires Lane, Finchley N32QL London, England; phone: (011) 346-2600; fax (011) 349-4543.

## Noteworthy Advertising

Since Speedo's world debut at the 1956 Melbourne Olympics, Speedo has always taken advantage of publicity possibilities at high profile sports events. In the 1988 Olympic Trials, more than three-fourths of the finalists appeared in Speedo swimsuits. And during the Olympic Games, nearly two-thirds of the U.S. swim team wore the Speedo brand and several of the team members had promotional contracts with Speedo, including diver Greg Louganis and swimmers Janet Evans and Tom Jager. Occasionally, endorsements would conflict, as for instance, during the 1988 Games. Speedo was the official sponsor for the U.S. team, but swimmer Matt Biondi had a contract with Arena. Biondi resolved the dilemma by wearing Arena trunks and a Speedo swim cap.

During the 1992 Barcelona Olympics, Speedo was once again a ubiquitous presence: 34 teams appeared in Speedo brand swimwear. That year, Speedo also received some free publicity from an unlikely source, the Democratic presidential race, when candidate Paul Tsongas appeared in one of his political advertisements doing the breaststroke in his Speedo swimming trunks. In an interview with CNN anchorman Bernard Shaw, Tsongas explained that he would step down from the presidential race, but jokingly added, "I am pleased to announce that I've agreed to accept the presidency of the Speedo Bathing Suit Company."

## Product Development and Innovations

Swimsuit designs have experienced dramatic changes throughout the twentieth century. Prior to the 1930s, women's suits resembled "swim dresses" or "swim bloomers with camisoles" according to Iona Monahan of *The Gazette (Montreal)*. Men's suits, on the other hand, were of simpler and more practical designs. During the 1930s, when fitness was becoming fashionable, new fabrics such as Latex and woven elastic materials led to a snugger fit and a smoother appearance for swimwear. At the same time, swimsuits became increasingly more revealing, a trend that continued throughout the following decades.

Meanwhile, at Speedo, design innovations centered around improving the performance of competitive swimwear. In 1962 Speedo Australia hired Gloria Smythe as the head designer of men's swimsuits. At that time Speedo still sewed skirts into the men's racing suits and discussion on how high to raise the thighline was quite controversial. Smythe oversaw the gradual transition to the streamlined version of men's Speedo suits. But despite Smythe's insistence that women's swimsuits should also be modernized, it was not until the 1976 Montreal Olympics that the women's suit appeared in a major competition without the little skirt around the thighs. With time, Speedo swimsuit designs became even lighter, sleeker, and more form-fitting.

After several years of research and development, Speedo revealed a new competition swimsuit in 1991, the year after Smythe's retirement. The suit was unveiled just in time for the 1992 Barcelona Olympics. The revolutionary new S-2000 fabric was made of a polyester and polyurethane blend and was said to create less water resistance than human skin, reducing frictional drag and thereby increasing the swimmer's speed. The unisex, torso-covering suit was designed with a high neck, was cut high on the leg, and came with a zipper. Until this "long suit" was developed, the trend in women's swimwear design had been just the opposite, towards increasingly more exposed skin.

During the Barcelona Olympics, swimmers chose from a variety of Speedo suits, including the new paper-thin Lycra suit—dubbed the "paper suit"—and the S-2000. Jeff Dimond, U.S. Swimming's information services director, told *The Times* that the U.S. swimmers would have been "crazy not to take advantage" of the state-of-the-art S-2000 suit, which he helped design and which he believed could reduce swim time by 0.3-0.4 seconds. German officials protested the suit, claiming the outfit provided an unfair advantage to Speedo endorsers. Nonetheless, the suit was worn by Olympic swimmers who set four world records and won 19 medals. Also in 1992, at a French sports exhibition, the S-2000 suit won the Sisel D'Or award as the most original new product. Speedo provided the S-2000 fabric for its manufacturers worldwide. In North America all competitive suits were cut and sewn by Kentucky Textiles, which made over two million suits a year.

Speedo's casual swimwear products during the early 1990s included square cut suits, similar to the volleyball shorts popular at the time. Speedo increased the square cut model to 40 percent of its spandex swimwear in 1991. As Jamie Madden at Speedo told the *Los Angeles Times*, "It's a very forgiving fabric and style," especially attractive to slightly overweight men. The square cut suits were made in a number of fashionable patterns, including the popular holograms, mini-checks, and Balinese batik.

In the early 1990s, Speedo also introduced the Surf Walker watersport shoes, which were meant for both athletic use and casual wear. The shoes were made of mesh and neoprene and were designed in four different styles of high-tops and low-cuts. Promotion of the shoes included advertisements in swimming magazines with endorsements by professional swimmers. Speedo also designed floor displays and posters for retail stores to promote the Speedo brand image.

## International Status

By the early 1990s, the Speedo brand was available in over 120 countries, with 23 licensees and distributors worldwide. Although Speedo was the global market share leader in competitive swimwear, the brand did not fare as well in the overall swimwear industry. In the United Kingdom, for instance, Speedo's share of competitive suits was upwards of 60 percent, whereas in overall swimwear it had only 10 percent of the market. Moreover, it possessed a mere one percent of the continental European market.

Arena was in second place after Speedo in European competitive swimwear with 40 percent of sales. European Speedo sales, however, did increase to record levels in the early 1990s, in part because of extensive internal restructuring designed to improve productivity and reduce overhead costs. In the early 1990s, the European and North American markets accounted for 70 percent of total worldwide sales of Speedo. Speedo sales were also strong in Japan, where it dominated three-fourths of the competitive market.

## Future Growth

One of Speedo's long-term goals for the 1990s was to increase its share in the overall swimwear market. While Speedo had more than 65 percent of the performance swimsuit market in the United States during the 1990s, it had only about five percent of the overall swimwear market. The Tyr brand, which had only entered the market in 1986, came in second after Speedo with 14 percent of the U.S. competitive swimwear market by 1991. Other notable competitive swimwear brands included the Finals brand, with ten percent of the market, and Arena, with a five percent market share.

Speedo's success in the future depends on its ability to diversify into new markets of active apparel and develop a strong brand image for such categories as men's shorts, T-shirts, footwear, and swimwear accessories. In the early 1990s, Speedo was showing strong gains in the swimwear accessory category and had plans to open several Authentic Fitness retail stores featuring the Speedo brand. Speedo also planned to continue to utilize the endorsements of professional and amateur athletes as part of its marketing philosophy.

## Further Reading:

Bagwell, Sheryle, "Australia: Swimming Against the Tide," *Australian Financial Review,* January 5, 1993.

Authentic Fitness Corporation Disclosure Statement, AFC, 1993.

Huck, Peter, "Speedo - The World's Cossie," *Australian Financial Review,* September 6, 1991.

Kelleher, Kathleen, "Fish Wanna-Bes," *Los Angeles Times,* August 5, 1992, p. 5A.

"Key Note Market Review UK Sports Market," *Full-text ICC Keynote Market Reports,* January 15, 1993; 1991–1992.

LaFavre Yorks, Cindy, "The Company Store Muscles into Retail," *Los Angeles Times,* February 26, 1993, p. E2.

Lord, Craig, "One-Piece Swimsuit Cuts a Dash," *The Times,* July 9, 1992.

"Management Buyout of Warnaco Activewear Division," *PR Newswire,* May 15, 1990.

Monahan, Iona, "Well Suited to the Times; Swimwear evolves through the Century," *The Gazette (Montreal),* July 28, 1992, p. D2.

Morganthau, Tom, and Todd Barrett, "Piling Up the Gold," *Newsweek,* June 22, 1992, p. 56.

"Pentland Group 2," *Extel Examiner,* June 26, 1992.

Smith, Liz, "Watertight Stream Lines," *The Times,* August 29, 1992.

"Speedo's Casual Line a Watersport Spinoff; Watersport Shoes Athletics/ Active," *Footwear News,* January 28, 1991, p. 68.

"Subsidiary Participates in Acquisition of Activewear Business," *S&P Daily News,* Pentland Group PLC, May 17, 1990.

"Warnaco Unit Buys Speedo Marketing Rights," *PR Newswire,* May 4, 1983.

*—Audra Avizienis*

# SPIC AND SPAN®

The Spic and Span brand of household cleaning products, marketed by Procter & Gamble, is one of the top-selling household cleaners in the United States. Packaged in the trademark orange box and bottle, Spic and Span has been offering performance and value to consumers for more than 60 years.

## Brand Origins

In 1933 in Saginaw, Michigan, Elizabeth P. MacDonald successfully recreated her grandmother's recipe for a wall cleaner with the aid of her aunt, who was a chemist. The recipe, which included no fat in its formula, called for a mildly alkaline material combined with glue sizing and was extremely effective on woodwork. During the Great Depression, Elizabeth's husband, Glen, lost his job when his employer went out of business, and in 1933 the MacDonalds decided to go into business with Harold and Naomi Stenglein to market the wonder woodwork cleaner, which the foursome called Spic and Span.

Employing glue as a basic foundation, Spic and Span differed from any cleaning product then on the market. Elizabeth MacDonald and Naomi Stenglein found that a water solution of glue, when applied to a wall or to a woodwork surface, exhibited an unusual tendency to draw any water-soluble or loose foreign surface material into the solution and away from the surface. If any appreciable amount of the solution remained on that surface, the two women discovered, the drying glue would form a protective film over the surface and impart a transparent lustre to it which would not discolor the surface. To the glue sizing they added borax, sodium carbonate, and trisodium phosphate, and with the help of Elizabeth's aunt, the chemist, manufactured the cleaner in powdered form. All a consumer had to do, then, was to dissolve the powder in water.

## Early Marketing Strategy and First Success

The four entrepreneurs prepared the powdered cleaner in their own homes, put it in brown paper bags, and peddled it in Saginaw to support their families. They employed girls to go from house to house cleaning a patch of front door and then ringing the doorbell to sell a package of the cleaner. This marketing maneuver evoked more delight than displeasure, and soon, unable to keep up with demand for the product, the two couples moved their operation into a factory, where they employed a staff of seven laborers and an equal number of nationwide sales representatives, turning dis-

tribution over to brokers who sold to the grocery trade. In 1937 alone, The Spic and Span Products Company sold $50,000 worth of goods; in 1938 it sold $60,000. In 1945 Procter & Gamble bought out the concern and its brand for approximately $2 million.

## The P&G Era

P&G immediately set out to improve the product's formula to change it from a woodwork cleaner to an all-purpose cleaner. A few years later, Spic and Span received a concentrated sampling throughout the country. Slogans and sample packages directed attention to the spring cleaning jobs it could perform, which induced wall washing and other chores on the part of homeowners who had never before done any housecleaning.

The "do-it-yourself" movement had arrived in America. P&G's aggressive promotion quickly enhanced sales, while complaints and suggestions brought improvements to the brand. For example, complaints that the product was harsh on hands prompted improvements by the company to remedy the situation.

During the early 1950s television was taking up permanent residence in the American living room, and P&G, recognizing the advertising potential of this new medium, became a regular sponsor. Frequently as many as four P&G products were associated with a single show, as in the case of *Search for Tomorrow,* which accommodated not only Cheer, Joy, and Shasta Cream Shampoo, but Spic and Span as well. Both Spic and Span and Gleem later assumed sponsorship of *The Jackie Gleason Show* when this top-rater entered the list of P&G evening favorites. Spic and Span, along with Tide, a new shortening, and a new toothpaste, sponsored *The Edge of Night.* In early 1956 P&G introduced another household abrasive, Comet, as a companion to Spic and Span, the King of Cleaners. Both products thrived.

## Environmental Controversy

In 1962 Rachel Carson's book *Silent Spring* helped to spark consumer awareness of environmental concerns in the United States. P&G had been using a cleaning agent called alkyl benzene sulfonate (ABS) which was not completely biodegradable during sewage treatment, and the residues of the compound left white foam along the banks of rivers and streams. In response to concerns, P&G changed its surfactant to linear alkyl sulfate (LAS),

## AT A GLANCE

**S**pic and Span brand of household cleaners founded in 1926 by Elizabeth P. MacDonald and Naomi W. Stenglein in Saginaw, Michigan; acquired by the Procter & Gamble Company, Cincinnati, Ohio, in 1945.

**Performance:** *Sales*—$58 million (1991).

**Major competitor:** *Texize's Pine Power; also White Cap's Real Pine, Clorox's Pine Sol and Formula 409 Glass and Surface, S.C. Johnson's Windex, and Lehn & Fink's Lysol.*

**Advertising:** *Agency*—Spic and Span Franchise: Saatchi & Saatchi Advertising, New York, NY. *Major campaign*—"It's not clean till it's Spic and Span clean!"

**Addresses:** *Parent company*—Procter & Gamble Company, One Procter & Gamble Plaza, Cincinnati, Ohio 45202; phone: (513) 983-1100; fax: (513) 983-7847.

but the suds along the waterways persisted, and activists pushed for governmental intervention.

Also in the 1960s, an international commission composed of representatives from Canada and the United States was appointed to study phosphate builders in detergents used in Canada and the states of the Great Lakes Basin. The commission's conclusion was that lake quality was declining dangerously due to "accelerated eutrophication" caused by the over-fertilization of algae, whose decay consumed oxygen in the water that normally sustained fish and other marine life. The commission's report went on to state that although eutrophication had always gone on, detergent phosphates had accelerated the process and were threatening important water sources, and they should be banned. P&G, like other manufacturers, was forced to comply with the new regulations.

## Brand Development

When Procter & Gamble purchased Spic and Span in 1945, the small specialty product was sold primarily through hardware stores, and its principal use was to clean painted wall surfaces. P&G chemists improved the formula, and, with a more attractive package and enhanced advertising, the sales department began marketing it to grocery stores. America was switching from papered to painted walls during those postwar years and new linoleum and asphalt tiles were widely used on floors. Spic and Span, effective on such surfaces, quickly became a leading brand.

In 1949 an improved version of Spic and Span was introduced. The product was odorless, sudsier, and milder and had a white appearance, as opposed to the product's original salt-and-pepper look. In 1959 the King of Cleaners acquired green print on its package and a cedar pine fragrance and was advertised as having germicidal properties. In 1981 the 32-ounce package was introduced and the 96-ounce package discontinued. April 1983 heralded the national introduction of Spic and Span's modern formula, which offered consumers grease-cutting action, safety for no-wax floors, a high-impact pine fragrance, and a pour spout added to the box. June 1985 marked the premiere of No-Rinse Spic and Span in certain areas of the United States. This product dissolved better and left less film and streaking than did its predecessors; furthermore, since many American floors were then of the no-wax variety, the ingredient in Spic and Span that took off the wax was removed. The 6-, 32-, and 64-ounce cartons were modified to 8-, 16-, and 27-ounce packages. Usage instructions ap-

peared on the package, and the powder became available in a pine fragrance. Test-marketing completed, new No-Rinse Spic and Span debuted nationally in November 1985. In October 1987, an 8-ounce plastic shaker and 22-ounce carton appeared; these in turn metamorphosed into 8-, 16-, and 27-ounce packages test-marketed in St. Louis, Missouri. In 1989 the 8-ounce box was discontinued in the Southwestern division. November 1991 marked the testing of Ultra Spic and Span Powder which, in 1992, was introduced in more regions of the United States in a smaller, reclosable box containing a scoop and in phosphate and no-phosphate formulas, depending upon the area in which the King of Cleaners was being sold.

Spic and Span Cinch, for glass and multi-surface cleaning, was test-marketed in August 1990, expanded in April 1991, and introduced nationally in September 1991. This product offered streak-free cleaning on surfaces ranging from glass to greasy stove tops.

Test-marketed in the United States in April 1983, Spic and Span Pine Liquid, which cleaned and deodorized kitchens and bathrooms, went national in September 1984. In August 1986, in keeping with concern for the environment, a PETE break-resistant bottle replaced the PVC bottle. In December 1986, the orange screw cap was replaced by a green flip cap, and in 1987, the green label was replaced by an orange one.

Other forms of Spic and Span available in 1993 included Spic and Span Bathroom Cleaner and Spic and Span Basin-Tub-Tile Spray, which cleaned soap scum and hard water stains anywhere in the bathroom, and Spic and Span Multi-Surface Liquid Cleaner, which tackled tough scouring jobs throughout the house. Because of varying water conditions overseas, Spic and Span was marketed only in the United States.

## Advertising Innovations

In 1991 P&G introduced a marketing strategy called the Every Day Low Price Policy, or EDLP. While lowering the store's cost for P&G products, the program also eliminated the marketer's generous trade allowances. The policy was a reflection of Chairman and CEO Edwin L. Artzt's vision of a new Procter & Gamble: a more profitable company driven by lower costs and higher brand loyalty, streamlined manufacturing operations, more control over trade promotions, and consumer-oriented advertising.

The "value pricing" program was not well-received by retailers. As a trade-off, one of P&G's advertising agencies, J. Brown and Associates of New York, developed the Bonus Media Program, in which specially "tagged" TV spots mentioned the local retailer's name, gratis, at the end of a TV commercial. These spots, inviting consumers to come into the store, appeared to be directly from the retailer.

## Performance Appraisal

In rigorous tests conducted in 1988 by Consumers Union, Spic and Span Pine Liquid was topped only by Texize's Pine Power in overall spot-cleaning effectiveness. Pine Power was composed of 20 percent pine oil, a relative of turpentine, as opposed to Spic and Span Pine Liquid's six percent pine oil. Spic and Span matched Pine Power on crayon and pencil, but fell a bit short on grease. Nevertheless, it earned its right to be called a disinfectant because of its pine oil content. In 1993, however, Consumers Union ranked Spic and Span Pine as the number one pine liquid overall for the third consecutive year in the all-purpose cleaners category.

## Further Reading:

"All-Purpose Cleaners," *Consumer Reports,* August 1988, pp. 519–21.

"All-Purpose Cleaners," *Consumer Reports 1989 Buying Guide,* December 1988, p. 93.

"All-Purpose Cleaners," *Consumer Reports 1990 Buying Guide,* December 1989, p. 338.

*Answers About Marketing,* Cincinnati, Ohio: The Procter & Gamble Company, 1993.

"Bathroom Cleaners: Who Needs Them?" *Consumer Reports,* September 1991, p. 603.

*Facts about Procter & Gamble,* Cincinnati: The Procter & Gamble Company, 1993.

*Ivorydale—A Procter & Gamble Landmark,* Cincinnati: The Procter & Gamble Company, 1993.

Lawrence, Jennifer, *Advertising Age,* "P&G Hooks Up Interactive Product-Sampling Hot Line," October 5, 1992, p. 3; "P&G Customizes Ads to Plug Retailers," February 8, 1993, p. 28; "Will P&G's Pricing Policy Pull Retailers Over to Its Side?" April 19, 1993, pp. 1, 42–43.

Lief, Alfred, *"It Floats": The Story of Procter & Gamble,* New York: Rinehart, 1958.

*Procter & Gamble: The House That Ivory Built,* Lincolnwood, Illinois: NTC Business Books, 1988.

*Procter & Gamble Company Annual Reports,* Cincinnati: The Procter & Gamble Company, 1992–93.

Schisgall, Oscar, *Eyes on Tomorrow: The Evolution of Procter & Gamble,* Chicago: J. G. Ferguson Publishing Company, 1981.

*—Virginia Barnstorff*

# STAYFREE®

*Stayfree*®

Stayfree, by Personal Products Co., is the third-best-selling brand in the sanitary napkin category. Stayfree Maxi Pads are in a fierce competitive battle to maintain market share in the $1.9 billion sanitary protection market, which now offers women as many as 175 kinds of products.

## Brand Origins

Stayfree's ultimate parent company, Johnson & Johnson, had tried as early as 1896 to sell a gauze-covered cotton disposable pad. The product was unsuccessful, largely due to the advertising taboos of the times. It wasn't until World War I that French nurses discovered that cellulose surgical gauze used for bandages also served as more efficient menstrual pads than the flannel rags they used and re-used during their periods. The gauze was more absorbent and was cheap enough to be disposable, according to Nancy Friedman in her book *Everything You Must Know about Tampons*.

The first commercial sanitary napkin was marketed by Cellucotton Products Co. (Kimberly-Clark, Inc.) under the name of Kotex in 1921. In 1927 Johnson & Johnson introduced its Modess napkin line through a subsidiary, Personal Products Co. Sanitary napkins did not undergo major changes until 1969, when Johnson & Johnson rolled out its ''revolutionary'' Stayfree Mini Pad—the first slim, beltless pad that could be attached to underwear with an adhesive strip, designed for women who experienced lighter menstrual flows. Mini pads could also be used as a supplement to tampons. Stayfree's Mini Pad won wide acclaim and shortly thereafter other manufacturers launched their own mini pad versions.

In 1971 Personal Products Co. introduced the Stayfree Maxi Pad—a bulked up version of the mini pad with adhesive strips. These new sanitary napkins of the 1970s were a breakthrough, freeing women from the hassle of belts, which could also show through clothing.

The basic sanitary napkin is made to enable fluid to pass through a cover that acts as a 'wicking' agent into an absorbent core. This core could be made of wood pulp or super absorbent polymers. Adhesive strips were intended to keep pads from slipping and thus were meant to offer better protection; in reality however, pads would often bunch up, slip, and cause chafing. Pads also carried the risk of bacterial infection. By being in contact with air, pads become the perfect medium for bacteria growth and odor.

## Marketing

For years advertising for feminine hygiene products was limited to women's magazines and was often obscured, sometimes appearing on a magazine's last page. Product packages were often wrapped in brown paper during the 1940s. Strict controls on advertising weren't lifted until 1972 when the National Association of Broadcasters relaxed its policy regarding feminine products advertising. Johnson & Johnson undertook an aggressive ad campaign in an effort to increase profits from its consumer products division and squash Kimberly-Clark's domination in the category. Advertising took a more open approach with the topic of menstruation (for example, the word 'period' eventually was allowed to be used on television) and the company advertised Stayfree and sister brand Carefree on television. By 1978 Johnson & Johnson had captured half of the market.

The NAB's codes of industry self-regulation were eventually ruled unconstitutional by the U.S. Justice Department in 1982. Even so, networks would only broadcast sanitary protection commercials during daytime soap operas and game shows and then again later at night. Johnson & Johnson aired 30-second TV spots during this time, in addition to running print ads in women's magazines and placing free-standing inserts in newspapers. Stayfree was targeted toward women between 12 and 49 years old; mini pads and thin maxi pads are more appealing to teens. In addition to print and TV advertising, Stayfree sponsored a telethon for the Children's Miracle Network, which raised funds for local children's hospitals; the brand also backed Shelter Aid for victims of domestic violence.

Advertising nonetheless was often stereotypically feminine. In a ''hearts and flowers setting,'' women in ruffled dresses talked about the benefits of sanitary napkins. When Johnson & Johnson used former Olympic gymnast Cathy Rigby to demonstrate how effective her Stayfree pads were while she performed a balance beam routine, the commercial, reported Paula Schnorbus in *Marketing & Media Decisions,* was considered ''too graphic'' by viewers.

## Brand Development

A big boost for the sanitary napkin industry came in 1981 in the form of Toxic Shock Syndrome, a mysterious and potentially fatal disease that was linked to tampons. Until that time, sanitary nap-

## AT A GLANCE

**S**tayfree brand sanitary protection products founded in 1969 by Personal Products Co., a subsidiary of Johnson & Johnson.

**Performance:** *Market share*—14% (third place) in the sanitary napkin category. *Sales*—$69.3 million (1992).

**Major competitor:** Procter & Gamble's Always; also Kimberly-Clark's Kotex.

**Advertising:** *Agency*—Saatchi & Saatchi, New York. *Major campaign*—"Does your maxi pad let you down?"

**Addresses:** *Parent company*—Personal Products Co., Van Liew Ave., P.O. Box 900, Milltown, NJ 08850; phone: (908) 524-0400; fax: (908) 524-0024. *Ultimate parent company*—Johnson & Johnson, Van Liew Ave., Milltown, NJ 08850; phone: (908) 524-0500; fax: (908) 214-0332.

kins had been steadily losing ground to tampons: between 1968 and 1978, sales for tampons increased 244 percent, compared to sanitary napkins sales, which grew by about 86 percent, according to Nancy Friedman. The emergence of Toxic Shock Syndrome caused many tampon makers to withdraw their super absorbent brands, revert to using cotton instead of synthetic fibers, and back mass media campaigns educating consumers about proper tampon use to avoid Toxic Shock. Consumers were advised to discontinue tampon use during days when their menstrual flows were light and when they slept. Tampon use declined dramatically—as much as 40 percent some industry analysts estimated—and pad manufacturers repositioned themselves with new products that were reliable.

Tampons eventually regained some of the lost market share by the 1990s, but what really changed were women's habits. Toxic Shock influenced women to use a combination of tampons, maxi pads, mini pads, and panty shields during their periods, instead of just one type of product or brand.

## Product Changes

In 1983 Johnson & Johnson launched Stayfree Silhouettes. The brand's hour-glass shape enabled the pad to be thicker in the middle and thinner on the ends, and Silhouettes were advertised as fitting the natural contours of the body. Silhouettes did not prove to be enough of a draw against the introduction of Procter & Gamble's Always brand of "winged" sanitary pads, which provided more protection with the added plus of fitting undergarments more snugly. A thinner Stayfree maxi pad was introduced in 1985 and advertised heavily on cable television; a thin Stayfree Silhouette debuted a year later. Johnson & Johnson also was the first to incorporate baking soda as a deodorant in its Stayfree sanitary napkins. Advertising spending increased to $18 million from $14 million between 1986 and 1987, in part, industry analysts speculated, to launch Silhouettes. In addition, Johnson & Johnson fought Always presence by reducing prices on its Stayfree line in addition to heavily promoting the brand. Competition had heated up considerably. By 1989 the number of types of pads had increased by 18 percent, reported Mary Ann Hogan of the *Los Angeles Times*. A Johnson & Johnson consumer survey noted that 70 percent of the women questioned complained about the effectiveness of their maxi pads.

Johnson & Johnson launched another revolution in 1991, introducing Stayfree Ultra Plus Ultrathin Maxi Pads, which were 80 percent thinner than regular maxi pads. These ultra thin maxi pads were paper-thin, but more capable of absorbing many times their weight in fluid. The Stayfree brand came in Maxi and Night Super wing-shaped versions, with the latter variation being longer for overnight protection.

Unique to this brand category was the absorbent material. In the new Stayfree Ultra Plus brand, a natural sphagnum moss core captured and held much more fluid. Sphagnum had been used by Native American women in its raw form for sanitary protection and for diapering babies. During both World Wars nurses and physicians used it to dress wounds in the field. Stayfree's patented process uses only the top honey-colored layers of the sphagnum moss bog, which is harvested from cool water, purified, and compressed into an ultra thin core material. To make Stayfree, the unbleached moss is then sandwiched between a soft fiber layer and white polyethylene backing. The sphagnum core pulls moisture away from the body and into tiny hollow chambers throughout the pad.

Johnson & Johnson had already launched the Ultra Plus line in Canada (where sphagnum moss grows) a year earlier to much success. The American introduction was supported by an extensive ad and consumer education campaign, in-pack leaflets, trade promotions, direct mail, and consumer brochures with a toll-free number. In hot pursuit were Johnson & Johnson's main competitors: Procter & Gamble added its own "Ultra Plus" thin maxi pads to the Always line, with an absorbent gelling material; Kimberly-Clark entered its Kotex Ultra-Thin Maxi Pad.

## International Market

Johnson & Johnson's marketing strategy, like that of its two main competitors, has always been internationally oriented. That is, each company designs new products that are launched worldwide with minor modifications according to the market demands. While the U.S. market has reached the saturation point, European and Asian markets appear to promise a bigger payoff. The same can be said for Latin America, where there is sharp growth in demand, industry analysts say.

According to *Nonwovens Industry Journal,* the worldwide consumption of sanitary napkins for 1991 was approximately 43 billion units, up 1.9 percent over 1990. The 1991 market was valued at $4.1 billion. Johnson & Johnson is still number one in the world, with 24 percent of the international market. The company formed a joint venture in France with Kayserberg S.A. called Vania Expansion and introduced Vespre Silhouette Plus, a sanitary napkin with wings, in the United Kingdom; Serenity in Switzerland and Italy; Ruby Ultra in France; and Serena Ultra in Austria and Switzerland.

Johnson & Johnson is the leading player in the South African market, while in Latin America the company has a 21 percent share behind Kimberly-Clark and Procter & Gamble. An enormous untapped market exists in Eastern Europe, where 400 million women lack basic feminine hygiene products.

## Future Growth

Market share between Johnson & Johnson and its main competitors is likely to continue fluctuating throughout the 1990s and beyond, although Procter & Gamble has been the market leader since the mid-1980s when it added the brand Always. The Stayfree brand has dropped from first place in the 1970s, to second in the mid-1980s, to third place in the 1990s. Product innovation in response to the pressure from private label brands will continue to prompt the big three companies to devise strategies to stay ahead in a saturated American market. Harvin Smith, director of the International Center for Textile Research and Development in Lubbock, Texas, stated to the *Los Angeles Times:* "Companies will add this feature or that, argue over a strap here or there, but in the end," he noted, "most of the product cost is in advertising and marketing—convincing the consumer that this is the product that'll take care of everything."

In a 1993 Johnson & Johnson company report, officials said they believed sanitary protection products, with baby toiletries, accounted for much of their consumer sales growth. Johnson & Johnson had increased prices approximating 11 percent for sanitary protection products and these increases appeared to be holding. However, international sales continued to be hurt by the weak economies in Europe and South America. International sales for Johnson & Johnson were down 1.5 percent to $519 million for the quarter and up 2.3 percent to $2.12 billion for the year. Johnson & Johnson was expecting growth of approximately 4 percent in 1993.

## Further Reading:

Friedman, Nancy, *Everything You Must Know about Tampons,* New York: Berkley Publishing Co., 1981.

Goldstein, Guy, "A Worldwide Overview of the Sanitary Protection Market," *Nonwovens Industry Journal,* April 1993.

Hogan, Mary Ann, "The Super, Ultra, Maxi Revolution," *Los Angeles Times,* March 4, 1993, p. E1.

Moskowitz, Milton, *Everybody's Business,* New York: Doubleday Dell, 1990.

Muirhead, Greg, "Thin's In," *Supermarket News,* March 30, 1992, pp. 19–30.

Reicin, G., *Johnson & Johnson Company Report,* Oppenheimer & Co. Inc., February 4, 1993.

Schnorbus, Paula, "Personal Appeal: Brand Report No. 146—Feminine Hygiene Products," *Marketing & Media Decisions,* October 1987, p. 125.

Shore, A., "Cosmetics & Household Products—Industry Report," Paine Webber Inc., April 8, 1993.

*—Evelyn S. Dorman*

# STRIDE RITE®

Stride Rite has been the leading brand of high quality children's shoes in the United States for decades. Through the early 1990s, Stride Rite was one of the most trusted and respected brands in children's footwear. Its classic black patent dress shoes and white walkers were the trademark styles of the company. Despite its solid reputation for superior quality and fit, during the 1980s, The Stride Rite Corporation had to adjust its product designs to a new age of fashion-conscious consumers. Stride Rite Children's Group, Inc., addressed these challenges by updating and expanding the selection of their shoes to include athletic and casual shoes, as well as dress shoes, in a variety of new styles and brighter colors.

## Brand Origins

In 1892, the 17-year-old Jacob A. Slosberg began his shoe manufacturing career at the John M. Noyes Company in Lynn, Massachusetts. For three decades, Slosberg, known as J.A., worked in the shoe industry, familiarizing himself with all aspects of the business. Once he had saved enough money, Slosberg and his partner, Philip Green, established their own children's shoe company, the Green Shoe Manufacturing Company. The first Green Shoe production facility was a converted stable in Boston, where the company employed nearly one hundred people and produced upwards of 800 pairs of shoes each day. In November of 1919, Slosberg and Green sent out their first shipment of Green stitchdown children's shoes.

The partnership, however, was short-lived because the two men had fundamentally conflicting views regarding product development. While Jacob A. Slosberg opted for manufacturing high quality shoes, his partner Philip Green preferred a lower grade product. With no foreseeable compromise, Green sold his interest of the business while Slosberg continued running the operation.

By 1924, Green Shoe relocated to a larger facility in Boston and gradually expanded operations through the 1930s. In 1933, Slosberg acquired the rights to the brand name Stride Rite from a company salesman who previously had been a children's shoe manufacturer. Initially, the company used the brand name only for its support shoes, but within four years it was applied to all Green shoes. The Stride Rite brand soon established itself as one of the foremost names in children's footwear. Eventually, Slosberg earned the reputation as one of the "deans" in American shoe-making because of his commitment to producing high quality products.

When J.A. Slosberg died in 1953, the business was passed on to his three sons and son-in-law, who maintained the Green Shoe commitment to superior quality. They strove to improve their products with better manufacturing techniques and greater efficiency in quality control and warehousing. Green Shoe continued expansion throughout the 1960s by acquiring a number of smaller shoe firms as well as developing its market internationally. In 1966, the company changed its name to Stride Rite.

During the 1970s, Stride Rite remained a leading brand in quality children's shoes. Capitalizing on the structural changes occurring in the footwear industry Stride Rite entered the retail business and opened its first Bootery in 1972. By 1992, Stride Rite operated 650 Booteries, 132 corporate owned, and leased 41 children's shoe departments. During the 1980s, consumer preferences for children's apparel began to shift toward more trendy styles, and Stride Rite responded by providing a greater variety of new styles. In 1988, Stride Rite also established the Children's Group, a consolidation of the children's wholesale and retail shoe departments, in order to improve organizational efficiency and to be more responsive to consumers and retailers.

## Shifts in Marketing Strategy

During the 1980s, although sales were increasing annually, Stride Rite management recognized that some adjustments needed to be made in response to changing consumer demands. One of Stride Rite's strategies of the mid-1980s was to view the market as three segments according to the age of the children: ages 0–3, 3–6, and 6–10. Stride Rite believed that parents' control over choosing their children's shoes progressively decreased as children grew older. With that in mind, Stride Rite focused their more fashionable looks on the older children's segment, with styles like Cruisers, Spiders, and Snakes, to capture the child's imagination. Promotional giveaways included teddy bears, sunglasses, and various toys. The Children's Group also redesigned the packaging with eye-catching graphics and matched the tissue liners to the individual products. The new Stride Rite slogan was "the best fit with the most fun," according to the August 31, 1987 issue of *Footwear News*. Part of Stride Rite's marketing strategy in the late

## AT A GLANCE

**S**tride Rite brand of footwear acquired in 1933 by Green Shoe Manufacturing Company, which was founded by Jacob A. Slosberg and Philip Green in Boston, MA, in 1919; Green Shoe Manufacturing Company changed name to Stride Rite, 1966; company adopted name The Stride Rite Corporation, 1972; Stride Rite Children's Group, Inc., established, 1988.

**Performance:** *Market share*—11.6% of infant shoe category; 4.6% of girls' shoe category; 3.1% of boys' shoe category. *Sales*—$80 million.

**Major competitor:** Brown Group's Buster Brown; Wolverine World Wide's Hush Puppies.

**Advertising:** *Agency*—Grey Advertising, New York, NY, 1991—. *Major campaign*—"For the way kids really play," which features children walking on walls.

**Addresses:** *Parent company*—Stride Rite Children's Group, Inc., 5 Cambridge Center, Cambridge, MA 02142; phone: (617) 491-8800; fax: (617) 864-1372. *Ultimate parent company*—The Stride Rite Corporation.

1980s and early 1990s included the development of different promotional themes such as "Outer Space" and "Field and Stream." In 1989, Stride Rite also created a brighter design for their logo.

Also during this period, The Stride Rite Corporation streamlined the organization and developed a more coherent brand image. A number of sub-brands, such as Zips and First Steps, were discontinued. Stride Rite also concentrated more efforts on promoting the six-year-old and younger market, and planned to expand the infant shoe division by 30–50 percent over several years.

Stride Rite also began to focus increasingly on presentation at the point-of-sale, instructing its retail managers how to make more innovative use of store space and improve store displays. The booteries were redesigned to accommodate children, providing child-sized seating, and making the shoe purchasing experience more fun, by adding funhouse mirrors, toys, and books. Additionally, new computerized cash registers were installed at the booteries and a new phone system was established for quicker ordering and improved efficiency.

Stride Rite also offered a direct mail program to enhance consumer convenience. One of Stride Rite's goals in the 1990s was to respond to consumer demands more efficiently. In 1992, Stride Rite constructed a new distribution center in Louisville, Kentucky in order to improve customer service and modernize operations. The company also introduced new retail outlets, featuring a combination of two Stride Rite brands in the Stride Rite/Keds stores for children.

### Changes in Advertising

In the late 1980s, after thoroughly researching on changes in consumer tastes and preferences in the children's shoe industry, the Children's Group expanded the Stride Rite Sneaker Line and improved the durability of the shoes. Marcia Morris, president of the Children's Group wholesale division, commented in a September 26, 1989, article in *Business Wire,* "real kids play real games—they run, swing, slide and tumble''; consequently, she

noted, parents must purchase children's shoes "at an alarmingly high rate." This prompted the slogan, "For the Way Kids Really Play." The comprehensive advertising campaign for 1990, which featured this phrase and cost more than $2 million, included print, television, and in-store promotions.

In the late 1980s, the Stride Rite Children's Group increased its emphasis on advertising; its media budget at that time was one of the largest of any children's footwear company. Stride Rite's television advertisements promoted the message that children were top priority for the company. One commercial depicted children walking on walls who were asked, "Is the shoe for your Dad?" The answer was a decisive "No way!"

In the early 1990s, Stride Rite Children's Group adopted as the company mascot a green dinosaur named Dino Dave. The company had plans to develop a life-size Dino Dave that would make special appearances at the booteries. Yet another new strategy to attract customers was a Frequent Buyer Program which offered the thirteenth pair of Stride Rite shoes free of charge. Stride Rite aggressively promoted these new programs in the media.

### Product Innovations

In addition to the classic Stride Rite white walkers and black patent leather dress shoes, Stride Rite introduced new styles of dressy and athletic shoes in brighter prints and eye-catching patterns. Some of Stride Rite's new sporty designs, which included moccasin-style shoes in washed bright colors, were influenced by European fashions. In 1990, Stride Rite introduced a new athletic collection, which featured Munchkin shoes and new hightop designs in a variety of colors and patterns. The five new sporty styles were made with Baby Tuff leather, which was resistant to water, stains, and scuffs. These shoes also featured a Dri-lex lining which soaked up perspiration from the feet. The greatest volume of sales, however, remained with the company's core classics. Stride Rite's general goals for the 1990s included improving technology to create more comfortable and functional shoes, as well as providing a variety of fashionable styles.

### Promotional Programs

The Stride Rite Children's Group established the Learning Path Program, which offered educational toys with their children's footwear. Each pair of Learning Path sneakers came with a special Kid Kit that included an activity booklet and toys related to the year's theme. For instance, the 1991 series "Field and Stream," which promoted environmental awareness, included a trust fund for saving the Humboldt penguin. The Kid Kit provided information pamphlets, toys, stickers and stencils related to the theme. One gift package series featured Dino Dave, the Stride Rite mascot, and offered collectable cards of animals. Stride Rite maintained that the purpose of the Learning Path Program was not only to promote a positive image of the company as socially responsible, but also "to make a child's trip to the shoe store more of an adventure," according to marketing manager Harle Perkins in *Footwear News.*

### Guarantee Program

The Stride Rite Children's Group demonstrated its confidence in the durability, fit and quality of its products by establishing the Guaranteed Sneaker Line in 1988. In 1989 Stride Rite invested $2 million on a promotional campaign that advertised the company's promise to replace any pair of sneakers that wore out before the child outgrew them. The guarantee applied mainly to the Super Series athletic shoes, which were offered in a wide selection of designs and colors, including neons, glow-in-the-dark colors, and pastels. In the early 1990s, Stride Rite did not plan on expanding the guarantee program to more dressy shoes, arguing that certain styles were purchased precisely because of their more delicate features.

In the July 29, 1991 of *Footwear News,* Lou Nagy, vice president of marketing, consumers, and retailers, commented that the guarantee was viewed not as a "hassle-free return but rather as a corporate stand behind a brand name." The guarantee program has been successful as Stride Rite witnessed a yearly increase of about 10 percent in pairage since its introduction. Moreover, the percentage of returned products has remained consistently low; for instance, in the first year only two percent of the shoes were returned.

## Special Distinctions

Stride Rite footwear was awarded the coveted Seal of Acceptance by The American Podiatric Medical Association (APMA) for a number of styles of Stride Rite baby shoes, the first infant shoes in the industry to receive the distinction. The APMA has awarded the Seal to over two dozen styles of Stride Rite footwear, the bulk of them in the infant category. For instance, the Baby Tech series, constructed in a unique direct-inject process without cements or adhesives, was noted for its highly flexible and comfortable design. In 1993, *Working Mother* magazine also praised Stride Rite, as one of the 100 best companies for working mothers.

## International Status

Beginning in the 1970s, foreign competition was undermining the domestic producers in the footwear market. Stride Rite responded to these changes by manufacturing shoes overseas and by expanding marketing and retailing operations as early as 1971. According to an October 21, 1985, article in *New England Business,* Assistant Treasurer William E. Dawson noted that the larger manufacturing firms were evolving more into marketing concerns. By the early 1990s, Stride Rite established several distribution centers in Europe, Asia, and South America.

## Performance Appraisal and Future Growth

Stride Rite was the leading brand of quality children's shoes in the infant shoe category in the early 1990s, with an 11.6 percent market share. Stride Rite also captured 4.6 percent of the girls' shoes market, and 3.1 percent of the boys' shoes segment, and company sales averaged between $75 million and $85 million in the early 1990s. In 1992, net sales declined by $5 million, or 7 percent, although 40 percent of that loss was due to the closings of Stride Rite retail locations. In the early 1990s, Stride Rite closed over 90 retail stores, approximately 8 percent of its retail stores, which were not performing well.

In 1993, the outlook for future growth was positive as the company continued its commitment to quality and customer service. Additionally, the Children's Group was developing the "Store 2000" program, which would attempt improve the retailing of the children's footwear. The project objectives are to create better merchandising techniques, quicker reordering systems, and more efficient communications systems for providing product information.

## Further Reading:

Ash, Jennifer, "Stride Rite Seeks Fashion Edge, Deeper Customer Awareness," *Footwear News,* August 31, 1987, p. 28.

Pulda, Ellen, "Stride Rite Is Enhancing Product Look, Store Image," *Footwear News,* February 13, 1989, p. 2.

Rooney, Ellen, "Shoe Execs Told to Eye Global Markets for Growth," *Footwear News,* November 23, 1992, p. 2.

Sender, Isabelle, "Hullo-o-o . . . There's a Dino at Your Door," *Footwear News,* June 7, 1993, p. 38.

Sohng, Laurie, "Guarantees Used to Designate Value," *Footwear News,* July 29, 1991, p. 13.

"The Stride Rite Corporation," *S & P Corporate Descriptions,* Standard & Poor's Corporation, 1993.

"Stride Rite to Premiere Television Ads," *Business Wire,* September 26, 1989.

Tedeschi, Mark, "Stride Rite Enters World of Aquatic Animals," *Footwear News,* July 30, 1990, p. 54; "Stride Rite to Mix Store Trips, Adventure," *Footwear News,* January 28, 1991.

Warrock, Anna M., "Shoemakers Feel the Pinch," *New England Business,* October 21, 1985, sec. 1, p. 62.

*—Audra Avizienis*

# SUAVE®

Suave brand of shampoos, conditioners, and styling aids are the number one selling hair cleaning products in the United States. Helene Curtis Industries, which manufactures and markets the brand, literally invented shampoo and hair sprays, in 1937 and 1950 respectively. Shampoos still constitute Helene Curtis's primary strength; besides Suave, the company produces several other highly successful brands, including Finesse, Salon Selectives, and Vibrance. Like the proliferation of its shampoo offerings, there also has been notable product differentiation within the Suave shampoo line: not only has Helene Curtis marketed a variety of Suave shampoos and conditioners, it has also introduced Suave styling aids, lotions, and facial care products.

## Brand Origins

Two young energetic Chicago entrepreneurs, Gerald Gidwitz and Louis Stein, founded the National Mineral Company in 1927. With President Calvin Coolidge, a business-friendly politician, in the White House, the time seemed propitious to start a new business. But even in that era of low taxes and scant government regulation, competition was intense and many businesses failed. The two men therefore intended to venture into the relatively new and unique cosmetics and personal care business. They established their company in the heart of Chicago and launched their first product—the Peach Bloom Facial Mask, a facial mud pack (or facial "clay") that promised youthful looks and a reinvigorated complexion. However, in an age when cosmetics had become acceptable in public (society no longer considered "painted" women disreputable), there was little demand for a product that had been popular in the 19th century, when a good complexion was all a woman could hope for. With the onset of the Depression, it seemed that mud packs could hardly keep the company afloat.

The Depression years, ironically, turned out to be among the company's most successful. Gerald Gidwitz sensed opportunity in hair care; fortunately, no one else did. The straight hair of the flapper era was giving way in 1930 to a rage for waves. Every female seemed to crave them and few possessed them naturally. The cumbersome electric waving machines took hours to create permanent waves and proved to be expensive; thus, the beauty hair care business was confined to the rich.

Researchers at the National Mineral Company opened the market when they invented "machineless" waving pads, and constructed a machine that could mass produce them. The com-

pany created a revolution in the hair care industry by making the beauty parlor experience one that all women could afford. Because of the company's close ties with the salon industry and desire to satisfy its loyal customers, Gidwitz became aware of the tremendous mass market for a soap formulated especially for hair. The few available hair shampoos were harsh, overpriced substances that did not cater to the mass market. Beauticians preferred to melt soap chips to form a sudsy mixture that left a film on hair. Most people washed their hair with the same detergent used for laundry or with plain soap.

Accompanied by the advertising slogan "Don't launder hair—shampoo it!" Lanolin Creme Shampoo entered the market in the mid-1930s. Available only in beauty salons, the demand for it was so tremendous that in 1937 the product was followed by another popular hair care item, "Suave Hairdressing." This first Suave brand product also was available only in beauty parlors. Discovering that beauticians often filled small containers with the Suave conditioner from their own stocks, and then sold it to their customers, Helene Curtis began producing small bottles that could be sold in retail stores. The success of its hair care products was so great that in 1938 the National Mineral Company launched a shampoo for the mass market, also dubbed Suave, which is still one of the best-selling shampoos in the industry.

## Product Development

Though Suave had been one of the most popular shampoos in the country on the eve of World War II, the war disrupted its manufacture as the National Mineral Company discontinued production of personal care products in favor of wartime goods, especially radar and electronic motor equipment, aircraft gun turrets, and other military products.

After the war, civilian production returned, and with it the production of Suave. In the meantime, the National Mineral Company had decided to change its name to Helene Curtis, go public, and diversify into an array of products. As part of this diversification, the company invented hair spray in 1950, and launched such highly successful products as the first viable dandruff shampoo, Enden, and the first ever spray deodorant, Stopette, both introduced in the mid-1950s. Suave shampoo and conditioner still were being produced and marketed and continued to be profitable. But compared to Helene Curtis's other new products, Suave was consigned to the back burner.

## AT A GLANCE

**S**uave brand of shampoo introduced in 1938 by the National Mineral Company; company changed name to Helene Curtis Industries, Inc. shortly after World War II.

**Performance:** *Market share*—8% of shampoo category. *Sales*—$100 million (1992).

**Major competitor:** Procter & Gamble Company brand shampoos, including Pert Plus.

**Advertising:** *Agency*—Bayer, Bess, Vanderwarker, Chicago, IL, 1987—. *Major campaign*—Television commercials featuring the slogan: "When Suave works this well, why pay more?"

**Addresses:** *Parent company*—Helene Curtis Industries, Inc., 325 N. Wells Street, Chicago, IL 60610-4791; phone: (312) 661-0222; fax: (312) 661-2250.

With the baby boom generation maturing into the most prosperous generation of young adults in history, plenty of room existed in the market for new shampoos, and new products were continually being introduced. In the early 1970s, therefore, Helene Curtis relaunched Suave shampoo with new advertising and a new, more sophisticated image. So successful was the Suave marketing pitch that the brand quickly gained the largest market share in the country.

The "new" Suave shampoo was really a whole product line of shampoos, with different formulas for different hair types and in a variety of scents, from herbal to fruit and flower essences. Scented varieties were appropriately colored and bottled in plastic see-through containers. The health conscious consumer could select Suave "protein" shampoo or even "egg" shampoo. Glamorizing the shampoo with this proliferation of colors and essences created a trendy image, all part of the manufacturer's savvy sales strategy.

Another aspect of the sales strategy was Suave's low price—it was usually the least expensive shampoo on the market—which encouraged consumers to purchase other similarly low-priced Suave brand hair care products. The company wished to create a loyal consumer base and a complete product line of hair care and personal care products. Hence, after the successful launch of the shampoos there came Suave conditioner and hair styling aids, and eventually skin care products such as lotions and facial moisturizers and cleansers. Suave "cologne shampoos," Suave Baby Shampoo, Suave Shampoo Plus Conditioner, Suave roll-on deodorants, and hair spray followed.

## Advertising

The state of the economy was also important in relaunching the Suave shampoo line in the early 1970s. A recession had hampered consumers' income, and Suave's immense appeal, particularly to the young and middle-aged generations, lay in the product's image as a premium quality shampoo at a discount price of up to 25 percent below premium shampoo costs. The advertising slogan: "Suave does what theirs does at half the price!" proved to be highly effective. The barrage of television ads in the 1970s and 1980s constantly made comparisons between Suave shampoo and premium brands; not unexpectedly, sales rose until Suave became the leading shampoo in America.

Similar themes and advertising pitches were made to relaunch Suave shampoo in newspaper ads and on radio. Radio was an especially important advertising medium with which to reach young consumers, especially teenagers, the heaviest users of shampoo. Advertising on popular teen radio stations helped sales of Suave rise precipitously.

This skillful use of advertising was demonstrated again in 1988 during Suave's fiftieth anniversary. To celebrate this occasion, the company launched a major promotional campaign encouraging consumers to purchase Suave with discount coupons as well as through point-of-purchase promotions. A year later, Helene Curtis laid out $15 million in advertising to introduce Suave's completely new packaging, formulas, and skin care products. A reworking of the perennial Suave advertising pitch, "Looks like you spent a fortune on your hair" to "Beautiful hair doesn't have to cost a fortune" added to the brand's newly polished image. In 1990 the company even reduced the price of Suave hair care products by ten percent, to reemphasize its powerful selling point: premium quality for a low price.

Restaging Suave periodically, with accompanying store promotions and huge advertising blitzes focuses renewed attention on Suave, which has nearly 200 shampoo competitors. So far the expensive strategy has maintained Suave on the top of the list of popular shampoos nationwide, along with several other Helene Curtis hair care products. In fact the principal reason for the success of Helene Curtis, a relatively small company in a business that is dominated by a few giant corporations, has been the lavish,

*An early version of the Suave logo.*

effective advertising of its products. By using 25 to 30 percent of its total revenues for advertising, Helene Curtis has been able to reach those consumers who want the luxury of premium hair and body care products, but are unable or unwilling to pay premium prices.

## The International Market

By the early 1990s, many of Helene Curtis's products were being marketed in over one hundred countries worldwide, and international sales made up at least one third of the company's total sales revenues. However, the Suave product line is not marketed abroad. The low price strategy works primarily in the United States, but has little appeal overseas. Instead, the company has aggressively and successfully marketed its Finesse and Salon Selectives shampoos in foreign countries, and has been content to maintain the Suave brand's popularity in the United States.

Suave's greatest strength lies in the fact that it has been profitable in this country for over fifty years. Moreover, Helene Curtis has a reputation for innovation and creative marketing that ensure the Suave product line's future well into the 21st century. Given the fact that consumers have little or no brand loyalty for shampoos—a typical household usually buys several different shampoo brands—Helene Curtis has established strong ties to discount retailers such as Kmart, Wal-Mart, and Target, which cater to a very broad spectrum of shoppers. Efforts to instill brand recognition among ethnic groups is also a strategy that should prove effective in the future.

## Further Reading:

Annual Report: Helene Curtis Industries, Inc., Chicago: Helen Curtis, 1992, 1993.

Crown, Judith, "Selling Brands Abroad," *Crains Chicago Business,* February 24, 1992, p. 13.

Dubashi, Jagannath, "Shampoo (Helene Curtis Industries)," *Financial World,* December 8, 1992, p. 68.

"Helene Curtis: Beauty Innovations Around the World Since 1927," Chicago: Helene Curtis, 1978.

"Helene Curtis Industries, Inc.," *The Market for Toiletries and Cosmetics,* New York: Business Trends Analysts, Inc., 1989, pp. 515–19.

"Helene Curtis in a Lather Over Suave," *Advertising Age,* July 1, 1991, p. 8.

Raj, D.D., "Helene Curtis—Company Report," *Merrill Lynch Capital Markets,* October 20, 1992; "Global Cosmetics and Household Product Industry," *Merrill Lynch Capital Markets,* December 1, 1992.

Schellhardt, Timothy D., "Tossing Its Head at P&G, Helene Curtis Styles Itself No.1 in the Hair-Care Market," *The Wall Street Journal,* November 19, 1992, p. B1.

"Skin Care Market Shows New Signs of Vitality," *Drug & Cosmetic Industry,* August 1992, pp. 28–29.

Wurdinger, Victoria, "Hair Care Report: Quest for Value Buys and 'Healthy' Hair Spur Aggressive Promotion," *Drug & Cosmetic Industry,* April, 1993, pp. 26–30ff.

—*Sina Dubovoj*

# SUCRETS®

# **SUCRETS**®

Sucrets, the individually wrapped analgesic tablets in the metal box, is the top-selling sore throat lozenge brand in the United States. Assembled in the trademark, snap-top metal tin, Sucrets lozenges have, for more than 60 years, been providing long-lasting soothing relief for sore throats of consumers. Sucrets lozenges were initially made from corn syrup, sugar and hexylresorcinol. Besides the medicinal benefits of Sucrets, its famous tin box has endured as a popular memento, containing an eclectic gamut of odds and ends, from buttons to the crown jewels of Britain. Sucrets are part of SmithKline Beecham Consumer Brands, which also markets such well-known brands as Brylcreem men's hair cream, Contac cold pills, Geritol vitamin supplements, Sominex sleep aids, Tums antacids, Vivarin stimulant tablets, and Aquafresh toothpaste. Sucrets has maintained a major share of the throat lozenge market by emphasizing product enhancement and innovative advertising.

## Brand Origins

The Sucrets brand was originated in 1932 in a pharmacist's shop in Baltimore, Maryland, by Sharp & Dohme (S&D). S&D was issued a patent for hexylresorcinol, a new anesthetic. S&D's Dr. Dohme formulated the hexylresorcinol solution and marketed it as S.T.-37, "a new, powerful, non-poisonous antiseptic for the mouth, nose, throat and all open wounds," as reported in the *Sucrets Gazette: A History Of Sucrets*. Soon afterwards the lozenge form was developed and given the name Sucrets by S&D's Dr. Krall. The sales department created the now familiar metal tin boxes to house the Sucrets Regular Formula lozenges. Salesman August A. Smith distributed the tins of Sucrets to apothecaries in his district. Each tin contained two rows of a dozen wrapped, shiny green lozenges. Smith predicted that the lozenges would sell well, and they did. As reported in the *Sucrets Gazette,* Smith wrote back to his home office, "Everybody from the boss down to the soda clerk wants a lick." Spring 1932 debuted a brisk business that in the 1990s has expanded worldwide.

## Early Advertising & Promotions

The sole marketing device for Sucrets lozenges during the 1930s was the pharmacist's counter. Originally, sales representatives, such as August Smith, dispersed Sucrets lozenges in person to pharmacists. Sharp & Dohme's sales force quickly realized that sampling encouraged druggists to purchase Sucrets. Capitalizing on sampling, S&D featured a special edition box of 50 lozenges. Sales representatives refilled the metal tins of 24 lozenges from the larger containers. The ease of dissemination and the appealing taste of Sucrets lozenges favored sampling as a routine marketing method. This sampling technique was also successfully employed through dentists and doctors. Another prosperous marketing strategy was mailing the brand to nurses. Nurses were already knowledgeable about the active ingredient in Sucrets, hexylresorcinol, through S.T.-37, and ordered them from pharmacists. Children loved the taste of Sucrets, which made the job of giving them out easier for school nurses.

During the 1940s, life-size window ads were placed in numerous pharmacies. The effect of such displays on sales volume was monitored. The first marketing survey conducted by the brand revealed that window displays increased sales by 76 percent. World-renowned Viennese artist Joseph Binder created an award-winning window display promoting Sucrets lozenges. Binder designed the image of "The Ostrich"—the recognizable long-necked bird with the dotted neck scarf—afflicted with a sore throat. Binder's scarves also adorned turkeys, snowmen, snow birds, and even the actors from the popular musical "Oklahoma." In the spring of 1943, "The Ostrich" won the coveted Art Directors Club Medal at the 23rd Annual National Exhibit of Advertising Art. Sucrets was first introduced to television viewers in 1949. As reported in the *Sucrets Gazette,* musical conductor Fred Waring debuted his CBS-TV show chewing something in his mouth. Waring started the show with the endorsement, "I guess you're wondering what I'm chewing. It's a Sucrets for my throat."

The early 1960s debuted the selling of Sucrets in grocery and convenience stores at just "35 cents a tin," as reported in the *Sucrets Gazette*. A "four-spacing" display rack was designed to conserve valuable shelf space. The brand's signature metal tins were loaded at an incline so shoppers could easily detect them. Promotions focused on the winter season, the most popular time for sore throats. Slogans pervasive at the time included "Ready for Ice, Snow and Sore Throat" and "When Winter Weather Gets Your Throat, Try Sucrets."

## Brand Development and Product Changes

The years 1962 to 1969 were characterized by product expansion in the Sucrets line. Variations included Cough Control, Cold Decongestant, and cherry flavored Children's Sucrets. The great-

## AT A GLANCE

Sucrets brand of sore throat lozenges founded in 1932 by Sharp & Dohme (S&D) in Baltimore, MD; the same year Sharp & Dohme's Dr. Krall registered the trademark and coined the name Sucrets for the lozenges sold in a tin; brand sold in 1953 to the Merck Company, changing the company name to Merck, Sharp & Dohme of Rahway, New Jersey; Merck, Sharp & Dohme consumer products division formed the Quinton Company in 1962; Quinton introduced Cough Control, Cold Decongestant, and Children's Sucrets; Merck purchased Calgon in 1969 and organized the Calgon Consumer Products Division, Pittsburgh, PA, new marketer of Sucrets; Calgon Consumer Products sold in 1977 to Beecham of London; Beecham consolidated in 1989 with SmithKline Beckman Pharmaceuticals, changing the company name to SmithKline Beecham PLC; Sucrets marketed in 1992 by SmithKline Beecham Consumer Brands, Pittsburgh, PA.

**Performance:** *Market share*—30.1% of the sore throat lozenge segment, 1992. *Sales*—$25.7 million.

**Major competitor:** Procter & Gamble Company's Chloraseptic brand.

**Advertising:** *Agency*—Grey Advertising, New York, NY, 1972—. *Major campaign*—Television commercial with a warm neck muffler embodying the "Wraps Your Throat In Soothing Relief" slogan, reinforcing Sucrets as a "medicine chest staple."

**Addresses:** *Parent company*—SmithKline Beecham Consumer Brands, 100 Beecham Drive, P.O. Box 1467, Pittsburgh, PA 15230; phone: (412) 928-1000; fax: (412) 928-5864. *Ultimate parent company*—SmithKline Beecham PLC, One Franklin Plaza, P.O. Box 7929, Philadelphia, PA 19101; phone: (215) 751-4000, (800) 366-8900; fax: (215) 751-7632.

est enhancement of the composition of Sucrets lozenges, however, took place in 1982. In that year, Beecham released Maximum Strength Sucrets lozenges with a fresh active ingredient, dyclonine hydrochloride, once available only by prescription. As reported in the *Sucrets Gazette,* "The Sucrets brand was the first throat lozenge to receive FDA approval to use dyclonine hydrochloride." The introduction of dyclonine was significant to the brand's improvement, since it provided an effective anesthetic that desensitized the throat. While the original hexylresorcinol paired better with mint flavorings, the new substance worked better with fruit flavors. Up until the 1990s, different versions of Sucrets containing dyclonine hydrochloride included Maximum Strength Wintergreen, Maximum Strength Vapor Black Cherry, Wild Cherry, Children's Cherry, Vapor Black Cherry, Vapor Lemon and Cherry Spray (the less popular Sucrets liquid variant). Original Mint Sucrets, which accounted for approximately 25 percent of total brand sales in 1992, has retained the hexylresorcinol formula.

### Packaging and Trademark

For 60 years the metal tins have not only kept Sucrets lozenges fresh, but they have also traditionally filled in as storage containers for consumers. SmithKline Beecham has received letters and phone calls from loyal Sucrets users, detailing the utilitarian function of the tins. Household items that have been stored in the trademark metal boxes include stickpins, buttons, needles, bobby pins, jewelry, and fish hooks. Soldiers in World War II were mailed sewing kits in Sucrets tins from back home. Sucrets

containers have also fulfilled some extraordinary roles. For instance, in 1954 Sucrets tins were employed to protect the precious stones of Queen Elizabeth II during the restoration of her Imperial Crown of State. In another case, in post-World War II Japan, scrap metal was used to create a small, metal car toy, emblazoned with the Sucrets brand logo.

The popular heritage of the signature tins has been deeply entwined with the brand's image. When a steel strike in the late 1960s forced Sucrets to resort to cardboard instead of the traditional tins for packaging, Sucrets enclosed a letter of apology in every cardboard box. The tins have been manufactured for the past 26 years by J. L. Clark Company in Lancaster, Pennsylvania. As noted in the *Sucrets Gazette,* "Between 1965 and 1990, an estimated 400 million tins rolled off the line, containing almost 10 billion lozenges." In 1992 a special commemorative tin was made to celebrate the 60th anniversary of Sucrets lozenges.

### Later Advertising and Promotions

In the early 1970s, the medicinal benefits of the Sucrets brand were emphasized in advertising. "Aspirin and Sucrets" as a tagline signaled that Sucrets lozenges were a legitimized method of relieving sore throat discomfort. Television ads in the 1980s for Maximum Strength Sucrets referred to the *Physicians Desk Reference,* a pharmaceutical directory for the general public, as an endorsement of authenticity. Sucrets lozenges were recorded in the guide as a recommended brand, offering "Soothing medicine for sore throat pain."

Marketing strategy in the 1990s has aimed at spurring consumer use of Sucrets throat lozenges over competing brands, such as chief rival Chloraseptic, produced by the Procter & Gamble Company. In 1990 between $5 and $10 million was allocated for media expenditures to encourage consumers to switch from less costly cough drop brands to Sucrets, the "medicine chest staple." Television commercials stressed the "soothing relief" offered by Sucrets lozenges. For example, a popular "Skating Rink" ad was produced showing a family man after taking Sucrets swathed in a warm neck muffler, accompanied by the slogan "Wraps your throat in soothing relief."

In addition to television media, the Sucrets brand has used print advertising sources, such as coupons. For example, a January 1993 free-standing insert reached a 46 million-coupon distribution. A free Sucrets scarf was also part of the promotion, with the slogan, "Get Wrapped Up In Our Free Offer!"

### Performance Appraisal

In the 1960s Sucrets had total sales of $1.2 million annually. Sucrets had also become the top-selling throat lozenge brand in food stores. By 1977 the brand's sales had exploded to $30 million a year. Total sales ending 1992 have leveled off to $25.7 million. Sucrets' intensive advertising and marketing strategy has outsold major competitor, Chloraseptic, by two-to-one. In 1992 Sucrets held 30.1 percent of the market share for sore throat lozenges, followed by Chloraseptic at 15.4 percent market share. Sucrets remains the only throat lozenge brand to contain the active medicine, Dyclonine. As reported by the company in a summary of the brand, "over half of cough cold consumers have used Sucrets in the past year (1992)."

## Further Reading:

Chai, Alan, Alta Campbell, and Patrick J. Spain, *Hoover's Handbook of World Business 1993,* Austin, TX: The Reference Press, 1993, pp. 446–47.

"Cough Drop/Throat Lozenge: Category Review," Pittsburgh, PA: SmithKline Beecham Consumer Brands, 1992, pp. 1–4.

SmithKline Beecham Annual Review and Summary Financial Statement, Philadelphia, PA: SmithKline Beecham, 1992.

"Sucrets: Brand Summary," Pittsburgh: SmithKline Beecham Consumer Brands, 1992, pp. 1–6.

*Sucrets Gazette: A History Of Sucrets,* Pittsburgh: SmithKline Beecham Consumer Brands, 1992.

Teitelman, Robert, "Reverse English," *Financial World,* November 15, 1988, pp. 24–27.

*—Kim Tudahl*

# SURE®

Sure, marketed by Procter & Gamble, is one of the top-selling deodorant and anti-perspirant brands in the United States. Although bathing removes some of the bacteria that cause perspiration odor, deodorants and anti-perspirants are designed to complete the operation. Technically, a deodorant is a deodorizer, a substance that removes bad odors or changes them to pleasant ones. Applied to the underarms, deodorants mask the natural odor of perspiration by absorbing it. In the twentieth century, when aluminum chloride or zirconium—which actually stops perspiration for a time and reduces it by at least 25 percent—was added to the petrolatum base, the resulting deodorant was re-classified by the FDA as an anti-perspirant. Research indicated that aluminum chloride and zirconium work well because molecules in sweat glands carry a slightly negative charge, whereas anti-perspirant compounds are slightly positive. Anti-perspirants, then, actually "plug" the pores.

## The First Anti-Perspirants

In 1933 slow-drying, liquid "non-perspirants" were the vogue. After application, the user had to wait fifteen minutes for the solution to "set" before restriction of perspiration would ensue for three or four days. Application was a sticky, messy, hands-on affair. In the 1940s, an innovation appeared—icy-cold and slow-drying deodorant sprays. In the 1950s, ballpoint pen manufacturing opened the door for another innovation—the roll-on deodorant, long thereafter considered the most effective because it delivered ingredients directly to the underarm.

As supermarkets and self-service stores opened in the mid-1950s, opportunities in toiletries manufacturing seemed infinite. The variety of products displayed appeared to offer new avenues of retailing in addition to some radical changes in merchandising techniques. Shopping malls began to spring up in the suburbs, bringing innovations of their own and attracting an affluent clientele. Prior to World War II, most toiletries had been retailed through department stores, beauty shops, and full-service drugstores. However, by the mid-1950s, grocery supermarkets had added departments to handle toilet articles, and a new breed of discount self-service outlet had appeared. These large-volume, self-service stores were rapidly capturing a mushrooming portion of toiletry sales, and would go on to handle more than 16 percent of all toiletries by the early 1970s.

## Brand Origins

Recognizing the trend away from personal advice and guidance by beauty counselors and druggists, Procter & Gamble realized that self-service purchasing would require new attention to packaging, advertising, and merchandising, and the company concentrated its growing technological ability on high-volume products. Toothpaste was the largest-selling category, followed by shampoos, deodorants, and home permanents.

Secret brand anti-perspirants and deodorants represented the company's entry into the deodorant market. At this time, P&G was also enhancing its research facilities in order to give its marketing staff wide latitude to study, investigate, and experiment with consumer preferences. Buoyed by the success of Secret, in the early 1970s P&G executives decided to expand their deodorant line. While Secret was marketed toward women, Procter & Gamble developed Sure to give the brand a counterpart for male customers.

Sure was advertised on television, and coupons, samples, premiums, and other promotional devices encouraged customers to try and re-try the brand. Promotional tools, such as point-of-purchase displays and price features, made Sure stand out in the store. Based on the premise that consumers would like the advanced formulation of Sure and buy it again, these promotional devices built sales volume. Repeat sales were the cornerstone of Sure's success.

## Safety and Environmental Controversy

In 1975 and 1976, aerosol sprays were challenged when studies conducted by the Food and Drug Administration (FDA) suggested a possible effect on the ozone layer of the atmosphere by certain chlorofluorocarbon propellants. Sure survived when P&G switched to an alternate propellant. In the late 1970s, as consumer concern about the environment intensified, many products previously thought safe were questioned as state-of-the-art technology revealed new information. Sure anti-perspirants and deodorants were singled out because one of their active ingredients, zirconium, was linked to cancer. Under pressure from widespread publicity, P&G reformulated the chemical additive into a safer derivative, which evolved into the aluminum zirconium trichlorohydrex gly still used in 1993.

## Brand Development

As trends changed, so did Sure. Having debuted nationally as a spray in 1972, it premiered as a roll-on in 1975 and as a solid in 1978. September 1986 marked the updating of package graphics for all forms of the line and the introduction of the wide solid. The 3-ounce round solid was discontinued in October 1989; in the spring of 1990, all round solids were discontinued and all roll-ons and solids were improved. In September 1991, Sure Roll-Ons and Solids shed their boxes, not only for environmental reasons but also to cut production costs in a time of recession. In January 1993, polydecene was added to the roll-on formulas of Sure to lessen the white residue that the product left on skin and clothes.

In 1993 many varieties of Sure were available, including a 6-ounce aerosol deodorant in Regular and Unscented formulas. Among the 1.7- and 2.7-ounce roll-on fragrances on store shelves were Regular, Unscented, and Powder Dry. Scents of wide-solids included Regular, Unscented, Desert Spice, and Outdoor Fresh. Sure Pro-Stick, marketed specifically for men, featured Classic, Fresh, Musk, and Spice fragrances. As of 1993, although France supplied most of the fragrances for the manufacturing of the product in the United States, Sure was not marketed abroad.

## Performance Appraisal

From its inception, Sure was a solid seller, always garnering a top share of the deodorant market. In 1993 and 1992, for example, the brand held fourth- and third-place ranks, respectively. Sales did fluctuate during that period: for the 26 weeks that ended in February 1993, Sure sold $54.8 million worth of goods, down 9.6 percent from the previous 26 weeks, and its market share slipped from 9.4 percent in 1992 to 8.4 percent in 1993. Yet, it managed to disarm such rivals as Gillette's Right Guard and Soft & Dri and Bristol-Myers' Ban. In both 1992 and 1993, Mennen outsold it—possibly because Sure was overtly marketed as being gender-neutral ("Be Sure to be dry"), whereas Mennen sported specific varieties for men, women, and even teenagers.

## Further Reading:

"About Deodorants and Anti-Perspirants," Cincinnati: Procter & Gamble Company, 1993.

*Advertising Age,* Editors of, *Procter & Gamble: The House That Ivory Built,* Lincolnwood, Illinois: NTC Business Books, 1988.

"Answers about Marketing," Cincinnati: Procter & Gamble Company, 1993.

Bird, Laura, "Hygiene Crusades Drive Sales," *Adweek's Marketing Week,* September 17, 1990, p. S122.

Cleary, David Powers, *Great American Brands,* New York: Fairchild Publications, 1981.

"Coming Clean in America," *U.S. News and World Report,* June 16, 1989, p. 74.

Conkling, Winifred, "Disarming the Armpit: Researchers Have Found the Culprit in Underarm Odor," *American Health: Fitness in Body and Mind,* December 1990, p. 16.

"Deodorants at a Glance," *Adweek's Marketing Week,* April 10, 1989, p. 12.

*Facts about Procter & Gamble,* Cincinnati: Procter & Gamble Company, 1993.

"Gender Marketing Dominates Deodorant Market," *U.S. Distribution Journal,* October 1989, p. 12.

Kanner, Bernice, "No Sweat: Keeping America Dry," *New York,* November 23, 1992, p. 28.

Lawrence, Jennifer, *Advertising Age,* "P&G Hooks Up Interactive Product-Sampling Hot Line," October 5, 1992, p. 3; "P&G Customizes Ads to Plug Retailers," February 8, 1993, p. 28; "Will P&G's Pricing Policy Pull Retailers Over to Its Side?" April 19, 1993, pp. 1, 42–43.

Lief, Alfred, *"It Floats": The Story of Procter & Gamble,* New York: Rinehart, 1958.

Liesse, Julie, "Brand Scorecard," *Advertising Age,* April 19, 1993, p. 22.

Muirhead, Greg, "Getting Deodorants a Little Closer: Unboxed and Reduced-Package Anti-Perspirants Are Making Room on the Shelf for the Bevy of New Products," *Supermarket News,* January 6, 1992, p. 21.

"Procter & Gamble and Prices," Cincinnati: Procter & Gamble Company, 1993.

"The Procter & Gamble Company," Cincinnati: Procter & Gamble Company, 1993.

*Procter & Gamble Company Annual Report, 1992,* Cincinnati: Procter & Gamble Company.

Schisgall, Oscar, *Eyes on Tomorrow: The Evolution of Procter & Gamble,* Chicago: J. G. Ferguson Publishing Company, 1981.

Shields, Jody, *"Vogue* Beauty: Sweat," *Vogue,* June 1991, pp. 111–12, 114.

*—Virginia Barnstorff*

# SWATCH®

Innovative in both their design and marketing strategy, Swiss-made Swatch watches captured the imaginations of young consumers worldwide with an ever-changing line of affordable, brightly colored plastic watches. Within ten years of its introduction in the early 1980s, over 100 million units of Swatch watches were sold, making it the fastest-selling model in the history of watchmaking. Priced between $40 and $80, the durable plastic Swatches are a major force in the inexpensive watch category, with markets stretching across five continents and 65 countries and worldwide sales of 27 million units in 1992. Swatch USA is a division of SMH Swiss Corporation for Microelectronics and Watchmaking Industries, Ltd., of Biel, Switzerland, formerly known as Asuag-SSIH.

## Origins

Swatch entered the market in the early 1980s as the top contender in Switzerland's fight to regain the world watch market from Japan and Hong Kong. For almost three decades, Swiss watch firms had enjoyed a virtual monopoly on the watch market, fueled by a centuries-old reputation for producing quality time pieces. The seemingly indomitable Swiss watch industry crumbled during the 1970s, however, battered by intense competition from Japan and Hong Kong.

While the Swiss continued manufacturing traditional time pieces, Asian firms were perfecting quartz technology (a Swiss invention). By the mid-1970s, world markets were flooded with digital quartz watches. The popularity of these inexpensive new watches spelled disaster for the Swiss watchmaking industry. Between 1970 and 1985 almost two-thirds of Swiss firms went out of business. The number of watchmaking companies dropped from 1,620 to less than 200; employment dropped from 90,000 in 1970 to 32,000 in 1985.

Enter Swatch, the brainchild of Dr. Ernst Thomke, president of ETA, a subsidiary of the ailing Swiss watch giant Asuag. In 1981 Thomke won fame in the watch industry for making the world's thinnest watch. Named the Concord Delirium, the revolutionary watch contained only 51 individual components, far less than the standard 91 components in most watches.

Despite this success, Asuag teetered on the brink of bankruptcy. To avoid this, Asuag merged with SSIH, another vulnerable Swiss watchmaking giant, in 1982. The banks that were

orchestrating the merger called in management guru Nicolas Hayek to streamline operations and make the new company, known as Asuag-SSIH, competitive in the changing world market. Key to the company's success was strength in the inexpensive watch category. Using the Concord Delirium technique, Hayek and Thomke began working together to develop an inexpensive watch that would compete directly with Japanese watches.

The result was a watch that could be manufactured at impressively low costs and minimal labor. Highly durable and water resistant down to 30 meters, the new watch was made with a plastic casing that could not be opened for repairs. The battery inside would run for three years, after which time the battery could be changed or the watch could simply be thrown away. The company coined the name Swatch—a combination of Swiss and watch—and made plans to sell them for approximately $40, with a one-year guarantee.

## Early Marketing

After Swatch performed poorly in a U.S. test market during 1982, Asuag-SSIH hired Max Imgruth, an independent Swiss marketing consultant, to stage a relaunch. Imgruth didn't like the product at first: ''The brown was too dark; it looked like dirt,'' he spoke of the watch's color in *Fortune* magazine in 1985. ''And the green was frog green. Who wants frog green?''

Imgruth convinced Asuag-SSIH to implement a radical new marketing scheme. He hired a team of designers to brighten up Swatch's image and began positioning the watches as fashion accessories, targeting consumers in the 12- to 24-year-old group. Swatch watches were originally sold by jewelers; Imgruth repositioned them in department stores. The watches were also originally intended to compete directly with quartz watches, but under Imgruth's direction Swatch became the sole competitor in what became known as the ''fashion watch category.'' Imgruth positioned Swatch as a fashion accessory and introduced a new collection of watches every time the fashion industry introduced a new season of clothing.

Swatch was relaunched in the United States, the United Kingdom, Switzerland, and Germany in 1983. More that 400,000 Swatches sold in Switzerland alone that year, four times the projected figures. Sales were equally impressive in the United States, United Kingdom, and Germany, and by 1984, Swatch's

## AT A GLANCE

**S**watch brand watches invented in 1981 by Swiss watchmakers Dr. Ernst Thomke and Nicolas Hayek of Asuag-SSIH in Biel, Switzerland; company name changed to SMH Swiss Corporation for Microelectronics and Watchmaking Industries, Ltd.

**Performance:** *Sales*—27 million units (1992).

**Major competitor:** Seiko brand watches; also, Guess? brand fashion watches.

**Advertising:** *Agency*—Saatchi and Saatchi Advertising, New York, NY, 1990—.

**Addresses:** *Parent company*—Swatch USA, 35 East 21 Street, New York, NY, 10010; phone: (212) 505-4054; fax: (212) 505-9236. *Ultimate parent company*—SMH Swiss Corporation for Microelectronics and Watchmaking Industries, Ltd., Biel, Switzerland.

market had expanded to include France, Holland, Belgium, Luxembourg, Austria, Finland, Norway, Sweden, the Middle East, Hong Kong, Australia, Canada, Columbia, and the Canary Islands. Worldwide sales of 100,000 units per month outstripped production capacity. Swatch was introduced in Japan in 1985 and in Italy in 1986, as the market heated up through the introduction of numerous copycat brands such as Fiorucci, Tiq, Radiant, and Guess. By 1988, five years after its debut, over 50-million units of Swatch watches were sold, and annual sales hovered around $125 million.

### Swatch Styles

Important in the Swatch sales scheme were new designs, introduced twice a year with styles varying from clear plastic watches to watches with black bands and faces emblazoned with bright Japanese characters.

The size and shape of every Swatch watch remained consistent, while designs on the surface were left entirely up to the fancy of a team of artists, architects, and industrial designers at the Swatch Design Lab in Milan, Italy. Very early Swatch watches were given reference numbers and had no names. Themed and named series—inspired by fashion trends and world events—were introduced in the 1983 spring/summer collection. Swatch also created limited edition themed series such as Breakdance, 1985, of which only 9,999 models were produced for sales in the U.S. market. Other series featured scented straps, and some, such as the Aqua Love Series, captured images from the California surfing/body building craze. Still others focused on the sophisticated elegance of European cities.

In 1985 Swatch broke from its philosophy of creating inexpensive watches when it introduced the Limelight watch (named after a famous nightclub), which had four diamonds set in the face and cost $100. Swatch also began producing limited editions designed by famous artists. In 1986 New York subway artist Keith Haring was commissioned to design a series of four Swatch Art Specials, some of which were resold at auctions during the 1990s for over $5,000. In 1989 Swatch commissioned Mimmo Paladino to design a Swatch watch that was then produced in limited editions of 120. Two years later the Paladino Swatch sold at an European auction for $24,500.

Swatch was becoming a collector's item. In 1990 Swatch formed the Swatch Collectors of Swatch Club in Switzerland. Swatch designs were shown at galleries such as Aaron Faber Galleries in New York and auctioned by prestigious houses such as Sotheby's International. In 1992 Swatch launched the Swatch Collectors of Swatch Club in the United States and also developed a global communications link to allow Swatch collectors worldwide to exchange information.

### Advertising

Most of Swatch's print advertising and promotional programs were developed in-house, although in 1983 the company hired McCann-Erickson to coordinate its worldwide advertising and development of European print advertisements. A typical Swatch launch was heralded by hanging a fully functional giant Swatch (500 feet high and weighing 13 tons) from skyscrapers in cities such as Frankfurt, Manhattan, and Tokyo.

Swatch's advertising was as varied as its watch styles, but its message was consistent: trendy. Swatch's first U.S. television commercial ran just in time for the 1983 Christmas season, and appeared regularly on MTV during 1984. One early commercial featured the Fat Boys, a then up-and-coming rap group, which also headlined a Swatch-sponsored music tour in late 1983. At each concert, Swatch distributed flyers that featured pictures of more than a dozen Swatch styles as well as names of local retailers. According to one Swatch sales representative, after the group toured Philadelphia, most of the area retailers had sold their entire supply of Swatch watches within two days. Swatch also sponsored a world breakdancing contest in September, 1984, to promote its Breakdance collection, in addition to sponsoring ski competitions and windsurfing events.

In 1985 Swatch spent $8 million on advertising in the United States alone, with print ads appearing in publications as varied as *GQ, Vanity Fair, New York Times, Glamour, Seventeen, Interview, Campus Voice Biweekly,* and *Skiing.* The average advertisement featured trendy young people all wearing more than one Swatch. Many ads featured playful copy, including the 1985 ad for scented Swatches, which had a tag line reading, "The only watch that makes scents." One slightly unusual series in 1984 incorporated the "Swatch Family," featuring a freshly scrubbed family dressed in 1950s clothing with odd-ball headlines such as, "Since we got Swatch, it's been our best Christmas ever, and the acne cleared up too." The tag line read, "The family that ticks together sticks together."

### Spin-off Products and Marketing Changes

A number of Swatch brand extensions were introduced by Swatch USA during the late 1980s. In 1985 Swatch debuted the Cosmic Cowboy line of clothing, which consisted of shorts decorated with cartoon drawings of cowboys lassoing planets, and matching shirts displaying the Cosmic Cowboy logo in the shape of a sheriff's badge. Swatch also introduced an inexpensive line of accessories. These included the successful Swatch Guard, a colorful plastic band that stretches across the crystal to protect it from scratches. Other Swatch extensions included eyeglass cords, a Swatch army knife, and "Swatch Parafernalia," an Italian-designed line of key chains, razors, pens, and notebooks. The company also produced Swatch lines of sunglasses and sweatshirts.

Swatch's U.S. sales declined during the later half of the 1980s. Analysts attribute the decline to an inability to meet increased demands for the product worldwide, and to the sale of cheaper Swatch accessories that damaged the appeal of Swatch watches. In 1990 Swatch embarked on a minor marketing shake-up. The company boosted worldwide production by 15 percent, switched its advertising account to Saatchi and Saatchi Advertising in New York, and began to implement a new marketing strategy.

Swatch stopped selling cheap accessories and began focusing on attracting an older, more upscale clientele by introducing high-quality specialty watches. In 1990 Swatch launched the Scuba 200 series of plastic watches, waterproof up to 656 feet (200 meters); these were followed quickly by the Swatch Chrono, billed as the world's first StopSwatch. By 1992 demand for Swatch scuba watches and chronographs had outstripped production, and Swatch had regained a share of its declining market.

Swatch also branched into some unexpected territories. Perhaps most unusual for a watch company was the development of the Swatch Solar Car, which won the 1990 Australian World Solar Challenge. In 1989 Swatch introduced the Twin Phone, a telephone that allows two people to simultaneously use the same telephone. According to industry observers, sales of the Twin Phone were slow. "It is successful where introduced, but some markets still don't accept it," one analyst told the *Wall Street Journal* in 1992. Another innovation, Swatch Piepser—the world's smallest wrist paging device—was launched in Los Angeles in 1992 in a joint venture with MobilComm, the largest supplier of paging services and products in the United States.

## Performance Analysis

Swatch was designed to recapture the inexpensive watch category, and has performed very well in that position. Almost single-handedly, Swatch rebuilt the Swiss position in the world watch market. In 1989 Swiss watch sales accounted for more than 50 percent of revenues worldwide. Sales of Swatch in Japan alone for that year soared by 70 percent to $295 million. By 1992, SMH was running neck and neck with Hattori Seiko Co. of Japan for the top watchmaking position in the world.

As it enters its tenth year, Swatch's image is perched somewhere between a collector's item, a trendy throwaway, and a quality Swiss timepiece. In 1985 the average customer owned three different Swatch watches. Its ever-changing image keeps the product fresh, and its three-year average life span insures a large pool of potential second customers. But the generation that made Swatch the most popular watch of the 1980s has grown older. Swatch's 1992 shift in marketing focus takes this change into account. New products capitalize on the Swiss reputation for precision and accuracy. Plans for 1993 include the introduction of the Swatch Stop Watch, two watches in one, and the limited edition Swatch Platinum Case, made with solid platinum and sold at a higher price. By adding high quality, upscale products, Swatch is sending the message that it is more than just a fun trend. Its continued success will depend, in part, on how well that message is received.

## Further Reading:

Deveny, Kathleen, "Swatch Says It's Time to Reach Older Crowd," *Wall Street Journal,* July 2, 1992, p. B1.

Hawkins, William J., "Swiss Ingenuity Creates a Throwaway Quartz Swatch," *Popular Science,* March 1984, p. 116.

Phillips, Lisa, "Swatch Cuts Wide Swath," *Advertising Age,* August 26, 1985, p. 1.

Skolnik, Rayna, "Swatch: The Watch Whose Time Has Come," *Sales and Marketing Management,* March 11, 1985, p. 59.

Sloan, Pat, "Watch Swatch Hatch Batch," *Advertising Age,* May 20, 1985, p. 3.

Specht, Marina, "Swatch a Holiday Hit for European Retailers," *Advertising Age,* December 16, 1985, p. 40.

Studer, Margaret, "SMH Leads a Revival of Swiss Watchmaking Industry," *Wall Street Journal,* January 20, 1992, p. 1.

"Swatch Press Releases," New York: Swatch USA.

Taylor, William, "Message and Muscle: An Interview with Swatch Titan Nicolas Hayek," *Harvard Business Review,* March–April 1993, p. 99.

Tempest, Rone, "Just Watch the Swiss Go—Again," *Los Angeles Times,* February 14, 1990.

Tully, Shawn, "The Swiss Put Glitz in Cheap Quartz Watches," *Fortune,* August 20, 1984, p. 102.

*—Maura Troester*

# TAMPAX®

**TAMPAX®**

Tampax brand tampons have led the market they created since 1936, when they were introduced nationally in the United States. The only product marketed by Tambrands Inc., Tampax tampons are available in more than 150 countries worldwide. The brand holds 60 percent of the U.S. tampon market and accounts for 48 percent of global tampon sales.

## Brand Origins

In 1931 Dr. Earle Cleveland Haas, a general practitioner, developed a product that could be worn internally to absorb menstrual flow. The country doctor was inspired by the women he knew who had to wear bulky and chafing pads. Homemade tampons had been used since ancient times, when Egyptian women made them from softened papyrus, but Haas envisioned a tampon that could be mass produced and sold commercially.

Two years later Haas applied for a patent for what he called a "catamenial device"—a term derived from the Greek word for "monthly." The tampon was made from compressed cotton and a string that allowed the consumer to withdraw the product without touching it. Haas also developed the disposable telescoping cardboard tubes that allowed for sanitary insertion.

Haas also came up with a snappy name for his new product that combined "tampon"—a term used to refer to a plug inserted into a cavity to absorb secretions—and "vaginal pack": Tampax. Haas's wife, a nurse, tested the product, as did other nurses in hospitals around the country. After receiving a trademark for the Tampax name and a patent for the tampon's design, Haas sought a manufacturer for the product in 1933. He sold a six-month licensing option to one prospective manufacturer, but in the depths of the Great Depression, the businessman could not secure financial backing. Haas even attempted to arrange a deal with health products giant Johnson & Johnson but was turned down.

## Early Marketing Strategy

Within a month of the patent grant, Haas was contacted by Gertrude Tenderich, a Denver doctor and entrepreneur who was interested in the new product. Haas sold his tampon patents to Tenderich and her small group of investors for $32,000. Thus, Haas was excluded from Tampax's eventual financial success, but he was ultimately recognized in the London *Sunday Times* as one of "1000 Makers of the 20th Century." Tenderich's group of investors became the Tampax Sales Corporation early in 1934 and proceeded to manufacture and market the tampons. Tenderich made the company's first products herself with a household sewing machine and hand-operated compressor. A manufacturing facility with more automated processes was organized in a second-floor loft in Denver shortly thereafter.

Tenderich's first assignment was to get the tampons into the retail market. She hired salesmen who traveled to Colorado and Wyoming drugstores trying to convince druggists to stock and display the blue-and-white Tampax brand boxes. Although feminine napkins had been available at drugstores for over a decade, many retailers balked at carrying the more personal tampons. Women of the day often did not discuss menstruation with their own daughters, and pharmacists were even more uncomfortable with discussing an internally worn menstrual device. In addition, several religious leaders denounced the product as immoral, suggesting that tampons destroyed physical evidence of virginity and encouraged masturbation.

Under these circumstances, it was not surprising that most newspapers refused to advertise the tampons. However, Tenderich persevered and finally convinced the *Denver Post* to carry a display ad. The medical profession also gave Tampax tampons a promotional hook when Tenderich placed ads in the *Journal of the American Medical Association* (*JAMA*). Educational lectures about the tampon's advantages encouraged sales, and saleswomen canvassed door-to-door to introduce the new product to housewives. Sales expanded into California and other neighboring states, and production increased to meet the slow but growing demand. Limited funds, however, forced the small company to investigate outside sources of financial support for the massive advertising campaign necessary to launch Tampax tampons nationwide. By the end of 1934, Tenderich sold a license for the manufacture and sale of Tampax brand tampons in Canada and the United Kingdom for $25,000. In mid-1935 she sold a limited license for manufacturing in the United States for $50,000, but by the end of the year there still was not enough money to finance the national marketing and education campaign that would make Tampax Sales Corporation profitable.

## The "Mann" Behind Tampax

Tenderich traveled to New York City to solicit financing for her fledgling company. There she met Ellery Wilson Mann, a

## AT A GLANCE

**T**ampax brand tampons invented in 1931 by Dr. Earle Cleveland Haas in Denver, Colorado; rights to product and brand purchased by Dr. Gertrude Tenderich, who formed the Tampax Sales Corporation in 1934; reorganized as Tampax Incorporated, a public company, in 1936 and brand launched nationally that year; company name changed to Tambrands Incorporated in 1984.

**Performance:** *Market share*—48% of worldwide tampon market, 55% of United States tampon market. *Sales*—$684.11 million (1992).

**Major competitor:** Johnson & Johnson's Personal Products Co.'s Playtex.

**Advertising:** *Agency*—BBDO Worldwide, New York, 1991—
.

**Addresses:** *Parent company*—Tambrands Inc., 777 Westchester Avenue, White Plains, New York 10604; phone: (914) 696-6000; fax: (914) 696-6758.

marketer who had specialized in personal products such as laxatives and douches. Mann's career up to that point had included a stint with the H.K. McCann advertising agency, a precursor of McCann-Erickson. Mann joined forces with Robert McInnes, the holder of the U.K. and U.S. Tampax licenses, and along with Tenderich formed Tampax Incorporated, a public company financed with 300,000 shares of common stock with a par value of $1. The new company was headquartered in New York City.

Mann played a critical role in creating the advertising and marketing that would catapult the Tampax brand to market dominance. Mann had high hopes for the brand, with its potential market estimated at 42.5 million women, and he predicted that the Tampax tampon would "largely replace the external type of sanitary napkin."

By the time Tampax Incorporated was formed, the brand already had at least six competitors. Mann was undaunted by this threat and felt that Tampax's patented applicator, compressed cotton construction, and string removal device gave the brand an edge. He was more worried that women who tried inferior tampons would give up on the new product altogether, and he sought to assume industry leadership through aggressive marketing. His plan targeted three primary audiences: physicians, the drug trade, and consumers.

Doctors were deemed important to the campaign because of the authority they would lend the product. Mann emphasized that Tampax tampons were invented by a doctor and announced on the brand's boxes and letterhead that it was "accepted for advertising by the American Medical Association." Although somewhat specious, the statement gave the product a more trusted air. Advertising directed at the medical profession in *JAMA* featured anatomical drawings and technical descriptions to enlighten professionals about the new product so that they, in turn, could advise their female patients about tampon use and hopefully recommend the Tampax brand.

Tampax Incorporated's contacts with the drug trade were made with wholesalers, independent drug agents, and selected retailers. When a company salesman contacted a wholesaler or drugstore owner for the first time, he typically asked for a glass of water.

When the prospective customer brought the glass, the salesman would pull a Tampax tampon from his pocket and drop it into the glass to effectively illustrate its absorptive properties. The company supported retail sales with "point-of-sale" materials like posters, educational brochures and display items. Advertising in such trade journals as *Drug Store Retailing* stressed Tampax brand tampons' profit-making potential.

### National and International Launch

Tampax tampons were introduced nationally in 1936. Although the brand utilized some newspaper advertising, Mann decided that the most effective medium would be magazines with national circulation. He employed a small New York advertising agency, J.M. Mathes Inc. to produce the brand's first national print campaign. The agency had shown its faith in the product by buying a significant block of stock in Tampax Incorporated. The first ad, entitled "Welcome this new day for womanhood," appeared in the *American Weekly,* a Sunday newspaper supplement that professed the "greatest circulation in the world"—11 million. The ad employed a fashion-oriented approach that incorporated illustrations and photographs depicting active, stylish women. Models dressed in white outfits played tennis, swam, and danced, in an attempt to emphasize that tampons removed the fear of staining. The ad highlighted Tampax's advantages over external pads: they were compact, easy to carry, invisible, and eliminated chafing, odor, and staining. The benefits were summed up in three short sentences that the company used in its promotions for years: "No belts. No pins. No pads." By the end of 1936, Mann had committed over $100,000 for advertising in such monthly magazines as *Woman's Home Companion, Good Housekeeping, Ladies Home Journal, McCall's,* and *True Story,* with combined circulation that topped 22.5 million.

This barrage of advertising did not have an immediate effect on brand sales, which actually dropped near the end of the year, and the company posted a $157,000 loss for 1936. The entire sales team was fired, and Fred Ewald, the brand's western sales manager, was forced to cover 28 states on his own. Mann tried to cancel some of the advertising contracts, but the magazines would not allow it. J.M. Mathes, Inc. even sold its Tampax Incorporated stock.

Sales of Tampax tampons began to recover in 1937. Even though the company registered a loss of over $25,000 for the year, it took solace in the fact that the second half of 1937 showed a profit of $39,000. The turnaround was credited entirely to advertising, but Mann fired J.M. Mathes for selling its shares in the company. McCann-Erickson won the account, thereby creating a partnership that would span more than 40 years. Copywriter Leo G. Firth teamed up with Mann to create a series of one-column black and white ads that maximized the advertising budget by allowing the brand to appear in more magazines, including *Life, Look, Modern Screen,* and *True Romance.* By the end of the decade, Tampax tampon ads appeared in 47 magazines and reached a total of 45 million people.

As soon as the Tampax brand began to show a profit, Mann launched the product in England under the terms of the brand's first licensing agreement. Tampax Incorporated also bought the rights from Tampax Sales to manufacture and distribute Tampax tampons outside the United States and the United Kingdom, and in 1937 the product was exported to over 30 countries, including such exotic locales as Singapore and Shanghai. A European subsidiary was formed late in 1938. The expansion more than doubled Tampax's sales and made 1938 its first full year in the black. By the spring of 1940, Tampax tampons were available in 100 countries.

## Educational Campaign

Tampax Incorporated's first educational department was created in 1941 under the direction of Mabel Mathews, a former X-ray technician. Mathews hired and trained "Tampax ladies," who visited schools and colleges to teach young women about the safety and convenience of Tampax tampons and to dispel old myths. The "Tampax ladies" cited medical research released in the early 1940s that virtually endorsed tampon use.

World War II drastically reduced Tampax sales in Western Europe, Asia, and the Pacific Rim. Ironically, World War II proved to be a contributing factor in the brand's widespread acceptance in the United States. Wartime prosperity and the entry of millions of women into military, factory, and volunteer war work propelled Tampax sales. More and more women began to identify with the active women typified in Tampax brand advertising campaigns. Advertising reflected the times, with depictions of Women's Army Corps volunteers and the tag line, "No time for 'time-out.'" Sales skyrocketed during the war years: 11 percent in 1942 to $975,000, and almost 50 percent in 1943 and 1944 to $1,840,000. Wartime sales grew rapidly in Great Britain as well, and Mann worked diligently at the war's end in 1945 to rebuild Western European sales and distribution channels.

## Dominance and Complacency

The unprecedented growth that took place during World War II continued uninterrupted for the next decade under Mann until his death in 1956 when Tom Casey took over. Annual increases in both net dollar sales and unit shipments exceeded ten percent during the postwar years. Sales were boosted again when the postwar "baby boom" generation reached physical maturity.

During the 1950s and 1960s, 90 percent of the tampons sold in the United States carried the Tampax name. This overwhelming share led the brand's marketers to believe that the product would "sell itself," as president Casey was quoted in the Tambrands history, *Small Wonder.* Marketers undertook virtually no market surveys, and while other brands of tampons had moved into supermarket distribution, the Tampax brand was still sold primarily in drugstores.

Kimberly-Clark launched its tampon line in 1960, and Johnson & Johnson soon followed with its o.b. brand. Esmark Inc.'s Playtex brand entered the market in 1968 and eroded Tampax tampons' dominance with innovations like deodorant tampons, plastic applicators, and super-absorbent materials. These innovations enabled Playtex to capture one-fourth of the market, thereby cutting into the Tampax brand share. Then in 1974 consumer products giant Procter & Gamble began six years of test marketing its new Rely brand extra-absorbent tampons. Tampax's unit shipments declined in the late 1970s, and the brand's market share slipped to under 50 percent for the first time in 1979. In classic fashion, Procter & Gamble launched their Rely brand nationally with heavy advertising and sampling. By 1980 the rival brand had acquired 12 percent to 18 percent of the market. Although still the number one tampon brand, Tampax's share plunged to 42 percent.

## Toxic Shock Syndrome Shakes Tampon Market

Disaster struck the industry in June of 1980 when a rare and sometimes fatal new disease called Toxic Shock Syndrome (TSS) was linked to tampon use. News of the illness, symptoms of which included high fever, vomiting, diarrhea, a rash, dizziness, muscle aches, and fainting, threatened the entire tampon industry. Tampax Incorporated executives who wondered how the disease could have been overlooked during the 44 years Tampax tampons had been on the market got their answer in September of 1980—extra-absorbent rival brand Rely was implicated in 71 percent of TSS cases associated with tampon use.

Procter & Gamble pulled their Rely brand from the market within days of the news, and Tampax Incorporated launched an educational campaign about TSS. Total tampon unit sales in the United States dropped almost 11 percent in 1980, and foreign distributors stopped buying tampons entirely. Overseas markets did not resume normal sales until early 1982. In the United States, Tampax Incorporated re-introduced its original all-cotton tampon to provide an option to ultra-absorbent all-rayon varieties. Tampax tampon sales rebounded strongly due to two factors: the Rely market vacuum and Tampax's campaign to educate consumers about TSS and to re-establish consumer confidence in the Tampax product. In 1982 the Tampax brand had reclaimed its 60 percent market share and it gained five additional points the following year.

## A Renewed Commitment

Tampax tampons' plummeting market share of the 1970s was a wake-up call for brand support. William Esty Co., New York, replaced McCann-Erickson as the company's advertising agency in 1980, and Edwin Shutt Jr., a brand manager with experience at Procter & Gamble, became Tampax Incorporated's president in 1981. Shutt encouraged product improvements like the rounded cardboard applicator tip and the introduction of a plastic applicator. In 1984 the company's name was changed to Tambrands Inc.

Tambrands began to target younger consumers in the 1980s by theorizing that a young woman's first brand would be her lifetime choice. Studies released late in the decade showed that consumers who tried both pads and tampons thought tampons were more comfortable, easier to use, and more reliable. The research also found that tampon users have high brand loyalty. Ads for Petal Soft Tampax tampons encouraged teens to switch from pads to tampons. But Playtex snatched away almost three percent of the Tampax brand's market-leading share in 1989 when it introduced a collapsible, pocket-size tampon. Tambrands awarded the advertising account to another New York agency, Ally & Gargano, in 1989, and set a goal to increase its market share to 65 percent by 1994.

Many tampon brands, including Tampax, employed an environmental advertising strategy in the "green" 1990s. Ads emphasized that Tampax tampons, with their flushable applicator, had been "biodegradable since 1936." "Kind to the earth" promotions included the distribution of a booklet, *50 Simple Things You Can Do to Save the Earth.* Packaging incorporated recycled board, and the plastic overwrap was eliminated.

The environmental theme continued when Tambrands switched advertising agencies once again in 1991. BBDO Worldwide was awarded the account and asked to promote the improvements. Tampax Comfort Shaped and Satin Touch tampons were promoted as incorporating the comfortable features of plastic applicator tampons with the convenience of a flushable applicator. A 20-count box was introduced in 1993 to offer a lower priced package.

## International Strategy Propels Future

By the early 1980s, the company had expanded its distribution to over 135 countries, with strong sales in France, Ireland, and the United Kingdom. But with heavy competition and other corporate distractions in the United States, some international markets had been neglected. Tambrands executives compared the market in many developing countries to that of the United States before World War II, when women needed to be educated about sanitary protection before they could be persuaded to use tampons. The company targeted its 800 million potential customers worldwide with advertising that increased by over two-thirds from 1987 to 1988. Tambrands hoped to expand the overall tampon markets of Spain, Portugal, Greece, and Italy through heavy sampling and increased educational spending. The brand was also introduced into the Soviet Union (now Russia), as well as Latin America and China—two regions where most women still used homemade pads. The strategy in these locations was to build strong marketing and distribution networks augmented by education and advertising. Tambrands estimated that if these emerging markets were developed to the extent of the North American markets, the worldwide tampon market would increase from $1.5 billion to $7 billion

annually. In the 1990s Tambrands hopes to nurture these markets and increase Tampax tampons' worldwide share to 50 percent.

## Further Reading:

Bailey, Ronald H., *Small Wonder,* Lake Success, New York: Tambrands Inc., 1986.

Dagnoli, Judann, ''Tambrands Plans Overseas Growth,'' *Advertising Age,* March 14, 1988, p. 24.

Dunkin, Amy, ''They're More Single-Minded at Tambrands,'' *Business Week,* August 28, 1989, p. 28.

Levin, Gary, ''More CME Blues: Tambrands Consolidates at Ally,'' *Advertising Age,* September 18, 1989, p. 6.

Moog, Carol, ''Facing Complexities,'' *Advertising Age,* September 12, 1985, p. 30.

Siegel, Sherry, ''Tambrands Survives in Market 'Jungle','' *Advertising Age,* November 5, 1984, pp. 4, 74.

''Tambrands to Stick to the Basics,'' *Advertising Age,* October 23, 1989, p. 111.

''Tampons Go for Green,'' *Advertising Age,* July 2, 1990, p. 32.

''Tampons Going for the Green,'' *Advertising Age,* April 15, 1991, p. 4.

''Turnabout at Tampax; the Once Stodgy Company is Aggressively Changing Its Ways,'' *Barron's,* November 15, 1982, pp. 59–61.

''$25M Tampon Boost: Tambrands, Playtex Hike Spending for Launches,'' *Advertising Age,* September 30, 1991, p. 46.

Winters, Patricia, ''Tampon Sales Recover from Toxic Shock,'' *Advertising Age,* June 2, 1986, p. 12.

*—April S. Dougal*

# TIDE®

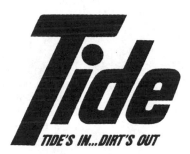

Tide, the first heavy-duty synthetic detergent and the most popular brand-name laundry product in history, was introduced in 1946 by the Procter & Gamble Company. In 1993 the Tide family of detergents included regular Tide, Liquid Tide, Tide with Bleach, Liquid Tide with Bleach Alternative, and the superconcentrated Ultra Tide powder, Ultra Tide Liquid, Ultra Tide Free, and Ultra Tide Free Liquid. As a group, Tide products accounted for 38.5 percent of all laundry detergents sold in the United States. The second-leading brand was Wisk, from Lever Brothers Company, in both liquid and superconcentrated powder formulas, which accounted for about 11 percent.

## Synthetic Detergents

Procter & Gamble created Dreft, the first synthetic detergent for household use in 1933, based on a molecular process developed and licensed by I. G. Farben Research Laboratories in Germany. During World War I, Farben identified a chemical in cattle bile that acted as a natural "wetting agent," allowing dyes to penetrate cloth evenly. After the war, Farben began producing the chemical, which it sold in paste form to the textile industry. The chemical also acted as a detergent, allowing dirt to be washed away. It was used as an industrial cleaner, but it was considered too harsh for household use.

In 1931 Robert A. Duncan, a scientist for Procter & Gamble on assignment in England, heard about the Farben discovery. For years, soap companies had been trying to create a laundry product that worked well in hard water and did not leave behind a soapy scum. Duncan believed the Farben process could be used as the basis for such a product. He bought 200 pounds of the chemical paste and had it shipped to Procter & Gamble's laboratories in Cincinnati for analysis.

The paste was what is now known as a surface-active agent, or "surfactant," then a relatively new chemical discovery. Surfactants reduce the surface tension between the molecules of water in which they are dissolved. This allows water to more easily and evenly penetrate cloth. In addition, surfactants consist of highly complex molecules with very unique characteristics. Procter & Gamble's analysis showed that one end of a surfactant molecule naturally attachs itself to surrounding water molecules, while the other end is repelled by water and attaches itself to other surfaces. In laundry products, these "miracle molecules" attach themselves to grease or oils and allow them to be washed away. All synthetic detergents are based on various surfactants.

Procter & Gamble was encouraged by the cleaning properties of the surfactant manufactured by Farben, and obtained the exclusive rights to market it for laundry purposes in the United States. In addition to developing Dreft, which proved to be good for washing dishes and lightly soiled fabrics, Procter & Gamble also introduced Drene, a liquid shampoo, based on the same formula. Ironically, Drene cleaned hair too thoroughly, removing all the natural oils, and Procter & Gamble was forced to add a conditioning agent to its shampoo.

## The Development of Tide

After introducing Dreft, Procter & Gamble continued working to develop a heavy-duty detergent that would be mild enough for household use. As often happens, when the breakthrough came, it was quite by accident. In the early 1940s the company's commercial customers, who had been using a harsh but effective detergent based on the Farben surfactant for several years, began complaining about lime buildup in their automatic dish-washing equipment. To remedy the problem, Procter & Gamble added a newly discovered chemical compound, sodium tripolyphosphate, which had been shown to eliminate lime precipitate in hard water. Surprisingly, the phosphates also increased the cleaning power of the commercial-strength detergent.

The results were so impressive that Procter & Gamble's researchers began experimenting with household formulas that actually contained more phosphate "builders" than they did surfactants. According to Duncan, quoted in *Eyes On Tomorrow: The Evolution of Procter & Gamble,* "The results of further tests were truly remarkable. Here was a new synthetic detergent formula that could wash clothes visibly cleaner, leave colors brighter, produce better suds, make clothes look whiter, and even eliminate the major problems of washing in hard water." Procter & Gamble named its new detergent Tide.

Procter & Gamble applied for a patent on Tide in 1944, but wartime restrictions on raw materials delayed commercial production for two more years. In 1946 Procter & Gamble began test-marketing Tide, advertised as "The Washday Miracle," in six cities: Springfield, Massachusettes, and Albany, New York, chosen for soft-water conditions; Evansville, Indiana, and Lima,

Ohio, for medium water; and Wichita, Kansas, and Sioux Falls, South Dakota, for hard water. An in-store advertising poster proclaimed "TIDE IS IN . . . Procter & Gamble's Post-War Washing Wonder . . . Gets clothes cleaner—yet actually leaves colors brighter!" Boxes of Tide were distributed door-to-door in the test communities.

The consumer response was overwhelming, which actually delayed national introduction of Tide until 1947. Early radio commercials promised that "Tide gets clothes cleaner than any soap," and millions of homemakers agreed. As late as 1948, Procter & Gamble was barely able to keep up with demand. By 1949, Tide was the best-selling laundry product in the United States—a preeminence it has never once relinquished in more than 40 years.

## Competition

Procter & Gamble patented the formula for Tide in 1949, receiving one of the few patents ever issued in the detergent industry, but other companies quickly followed with their own surfactant-based detergents to challenge Tide. Lever Brothers introduced Surf, advertised to eliminate odors as well as dirt; the Monsanto Chemical Company created "all," a low-suds detergent specifically formulated for top-loading automatic washers, which became popular in the 1950s; and the Colgate-Palmolive Company introduced Fab. Procter & Gamble countered by tinkering with the formula for Tide, adding perfumes, additional surfactants, and fluorescent brighteners, and switching from coconut oil to tallow to create richer suds. Procter & Gamble also modified the Tide formula to appeal to local preferences, creating Daz, a detergent with bleach that was sold in Great Britain, where fabrics were often boiled for greater whiteness, and Ace, which was sold in Mexico, where much of the laundry was still done by hand.

In *The House That Ivory Built,* Laurie Freeman wrote that Procter & Gamble always saved its best technological advances for Tide. But the company also created new detergents that competed with Tide, and perhaps more importantly, competed for the niche markets being staked out by other detergents. From 1947 to 1957, Procter & Gamble invested as much in construction and new equipment as it had during its first 100 years, due largely to the popularity of Tide and the family of detergents it gave rise to. These included Cheer, introduced in 1950 and formulated to clean in cooler water, and Oxydol, an early soap brand that was reformulated as a detergent in 1952.

By 1955 the United States was using nearly 2.5 billion pounds of synthetic detergents, and all these new products and improved formulations set off an advertising war of words that would continue for the next four decades as companies attempted to overtake Tide.

## Advertising

Procter & Gamble helped pioneer the "soap opera" on radio in the 1930s, producing shows such as *Oxydol's Own Ma Perkins.* In 1949 the company created a subsidiary, Procter & Gamble Productions, and in the 1950s, the company began to create soap operas for television, including the company's first network soap opera, *The First Hundred Years.*

Procter & Gamble liked to associate each of its shows with a particular product, and Tide sponsored *Life Can Be Beautiful,* in which Papa David doled out advice about life to his ward Chichi from his "Slightly Read Bookshop." Tide also sponsored the *Musical Comedy Time,* an hour-long show of Broadway musicals. Procter & Gamble enlisted the aid of popular television personalities to advertise Tide, such as Ozzie and Harriet Nelson, who had one of the first sitcom shows in the 1950s, and even Kukla, a puppet on the children's show *Kukla, Fran, and Ollie,* also in the 1950s. By 1955, 80 percent of Procter & Gamble's advertising was by television.

Tide also received major promotional help from the makers of automatic washing machines. At the start of the 1950s, only 3 percent of American homes had automatic washers. By the end of the decade, that figure had risen to more than 30 percent, and many of those washing machines came with a box of Tide inside. In 1956 Procter & Gamble was able to boast that "the makers of 25 automatics recommend Tide."

Throughout the years, the central theme in all of Tide's advertising has been its ability to get out dirt. For example, in the mid-1960s, Procter & Gamble used the advertising line, "Dirt Can't Hide from Intensified Tide. A television commercial of the time showed a dirty towel being sewn inside two other towels. When the wash was done, even the inside towel came out clean. A decade later, Procter & Gamble was using the tag line, "Tide's In. . . . Dirt's Out," and ads proclaimed, "Good ol' everyday ground-in, ground-through, dried-on, tough-to-get-out dirt. That's the kind of dirt Tide cleans best."

## Environmental Concerns

In the early 1960s, environmentalists began campaigning against laundry detergents, which were seeping into rivers and foaming up for all to see. After considerable public debate, manufacturers switched to surfactants that were biodegradable, which all but eliminated the sudsing problem in the nation's waterways. However, environmental concerns about detergents and water pollution were far from over.

In 1967 Stewart L. Udall, then Secretary of the Interior, called upon U.S. detergent makers to eliminate the use of phosphates, which studies showed contributed to eutrophication, the process in which fresh water lakes eventually become clogged with organic material, especially algae, causing fish and other marine life to die. While many companies began selling phosphate-free or reduced-phosphate detergents, Procter & Gamble refused, arguing that it would not market inferior or dangerous products. Phosphate-free detergents were clearly not as effective as detergents with phosphates, and many of the phosphate substitutes were caustic and potentially harmful.

When several communities and even states banned phosphates outright, Procter & Gamble pulled Tide and its other detergents from the shelves in a few areas. The outrage over Procter & Gamble's action was so great that the company was forced to address the issue in its annual report for 1971. Howard J. Morgens, then chairman of the company, wrote, "We did not introduce nonphosphate detergents because we felt strongly that it would be irresponsible for us to do so. The present nonphosphate detergents, as we view them, fall into two general classes. There are those that just won't get dirty clothes clean, and we feel housewives will quickly recognize their ineffectiveness. Then there are those that are dangerous to use in the home."

The uproar over phosphates eventually died down as the detergent industry developed safe and effective substitutes, and environmental scientists came to agree that sewage and other chemicals were probably more to blame for eutrophication than phosphates anyway. In 1993 about a third of the United States still banned phosphates, while other states set limits on the amount of phosphates that was allowed in detergent formulas. The amount of phosphate in Tide was also reduced as new phosphate substitutes became available, although never eliminated. In the 1990s, Tide powder contained varying amounts of phosphate, from less than .5 percent to 6.5 percent, depending on where it was being distributed. Liquid detergents never contained phosphates.

## Liquid Detergents

Early liquid detergents generally lacked the cleaning power of powdered detergents, primarily because they did not contain phosphates, which would not stay dissolved. They also cost more on a per-wash basis. However, they were convenient, and they appealed to consumers' environmental concerns because they did not contain phosphates. The makers of liquid detergents also continued to improve their products, so that by the 1980s, liquid detergents were the fastest growing segment of the market. By the mid 1980s, liquids accounted for about one third of the market for detergents. Wisk, the first liquid laundry detergent, was introduced by Lever Brothers in 1956 and was the leading liquid detergent for almost three decades, eventually capturing about 9 percent of the market for all laundry detergents.

Procter & Gamble entered the market for liquid laundry detergents in the 1970s with Era and Solo, but neither of those brands ever gained much popularity. Then in 1985, Procter & Gamble introduced Liquid Tide. Stephen Donovan, then vice-president of soaps and detergents for Procter & Gamble, told *Fortune* that Liquid Tide was "the first liquid product we've developed that's had the quality of cleaning performance that we felt comfortable putting the Tide name on." *Consumer Reports* backed up Procter & Gamble's lofty claims. In 1987 the magazine reported that "liquids never did a load of laundry as well as phosphate-containing powdered detergents. Liquid Tide was P&G's attempt to make a liquid that could. And, our tests show, it does."

Procter & Gamble reportedly spent 400,000 hours of research and $30 million to develop Liquid Tide, which the company said contained 12 separate cleaning agents and a new "miracle molecule" that trapped dirt in the wash water. Packaged in a bright orange bottle resembling a box of regular Tide, Liquid Tide quickly supplanted Wisk as the liquid leader. By 1987 Liquid Tide was second only to Tide powder.

## Super Concentrates

In January 1993 the *Wall Street Journal* reported, "In the past two years, U.S. consumers have fundamentally changed the way they go about performing one of life's perpetual chores: washing their clothes. For four decades, people spilled powdery soap out of giant-sized boxes into their washing machines. In recent years, many consumers switched to liquid detergents. But now, most are flipping up the top of a small cardboard cube and measuring out a prudent dose of concentrated granules with a recyclable scoop." The superconcentrates, originally developed for the Japanese market, had arrived.

Colgate-Palmolive introduced the first concentrated powder, Fresh Start, in 1980, but it was not well received. However, by the 1990s, washday habits were changing. Consumers were washing bigger loads and less often. In addition, environmental concerns had shifted from phosphates to wasted packaging. In 1990 Lever Brothers introduced a superconcentrated powdered detergent under the Wisk brand name, Wisk Power Scoop. Ultra Tide and an unscented formula, Ultra Tide Free, were introduced the same year. Ultra Tide quickly became the best-selling detergent in the United States. Although sales of regular Tide powder fell to less than 2 percent of the market by 1993, Ultra Tide accounted for almost 21 percent. Ultra Tide Liquid and Ultra Tide Free Liquid were introduced in 1992.

In 1993 superconcentrated powders accounted for more than half the market for laundry detergents. Liquid detergents accounted for another 38 percent, while the original powders had fallen to about 7 percent. Tide was the leading brand in each of those categories.

## Further Reading:

"Back to Enzymes," *Newsweek,* November 29, 1971, p. 62.

"Back to Phosphates," *Newsweek,* September 27, 1971, p. 123.

Bird, Laura, "Detergent Industry Spins into New Cycle," *Wall Street Journal,* January 5, 1993, p. B1.

"Cleaner, Faster, Freener?" *Consumer Reports,* February 1991, pp. 105–06.

Donohue, Janet, "Laundry Detergents Continue to Grab Industry and Consumer Attention with Strong New Product Activity and Heavy Marketing Support," *Soap/Cosmetics/Chemical Specialties,* January 1987, pp. 30–32.

Freeman, Laurie, *Advertising Age,* "The House that Ivory Built," August 20, 1987; "Wisk Rings in New Ad Generation, September 18, 1989, p. 1; "New Surf's Up: Lever Tries to Fight off Tide," March 26, 1990, p. 48.

"Label Claims: The Science behind the Sell," *Consumer Reports,* July 1987, pp. 415–18.

"Memorable Years in P&G History," Cincinnati: Procter & Gamble, 1987.

Ramirez, Anthony, "High Stakes for Product Managers," *New York Times,* December 4, 1989, p. D1.

Rice, Faye, "The King of Suds Reigns Again," *Fortune,* August 4, 1986, pp. 130–34.

Rukeyser, William Simon, "Fact and Foam in the Row over Phosphates," *Fortune,* January 1972, pp. 71–75.

Schisgall, Oscar, "Eyes On Tomorrow: The Evolution of Procter & Gamble," Chicago: J. G. Ferguson Publishing Co., 1981.

Shapiro, Bill, "Procter & Gamble's Comeback Plan," *Fortune,* February 4, 1985, pp. 30–34.

"Soap Opera," *Consumer Reports,* July 1987, pp. 413–14.

"Sudsy Dilemma," *Newsweek,* January 17, 1972, pp. 62–63.

Walley, Wayne, "Genesis of the 'Soaps'," *Advertising Age,* August 20, 1987.

"Why Detergent Makers Are Turning Gray," *Business Week,* February 20, 1971, pp. 64–65.

—*Dean Boyer*

# TIMEX®

# TIMEX®

Less than half a century after its founding, the Timex brand has become a giant in the watch industry. Although the rise of Swatch watches during the 1980s threatened to topple Timex's hold on the market, the superbrand managed to retain a solid grip on mass market watch sales. In the early 1990s the Timex brand's Ironman Triathlon became the best-selling watch in the United States and more Timex watches are sold in drugstores than any other brand. Timex watches' popularity is due in part to their dual reputation for durability and reasonable prices. Its series of unforgettable torture-test commercials featuring commentator John Cameron Swayze and the catch-phrase "takes a licking and keeps on ticking," underscored the brand's image of durability for years. Though these ads served the Timex Corp. well, the fluctuating watch industry and sound brand management have dictated that the company also emphasize technology and styling. Consequently, the 500-model Timex watch line of the 1990s strives to appeal to everyone. From sports watches and classic styles to watches featuring Walt Disney or Star Trek characters, Timex continues to keep abreast of consumer trends. In addition, the Timex Corp.'s acquisition of the Guess, Monet, and Nautica brands further insures that its products reach a mass audience. The company has apparently succeeded in making its name a household word. A 1992 Gallup survey found that 98 percent of consumers polled recognized the Timex name. Rival Seiko brand came in second with 87 percent consumer recognition.

## World Wars and Watch Wars

The Timex story begins with the German invasion of Norway in 1940 that prompted two Norwegian entrepreneurs, shipbuilder Thomas Olsen and engineer Joakim Lehmkuhl, to seek refuge in the United States. Shortly after their arrival, they purchased the nearly bankrupt 84-year-old Waterbury Clock Company in Waterbury, Connecticut, in order to aid the Allied war effort by producing bomb fuses made of clockwork components. The precedent for this had been set in World War I when the Waterbury Company had been one of the first manufacturers of the wristwatch, a device originally designed for artillery gunners. When World War II ended in 1945, Olsen, the majority shareholder, returned to Norway while Lehmkuhl remained to run the company.

Lehmkuhl decided to convert the plant into a mass-production facility for affordable timepieces. The Waterbury Clock Company had accomplished this before in the early 1900s with its Ingersoll

Yankee, a one-dollar pocket watch. Lehmkuhl's new watches would contain alloys and long-wearing bearings that would make them more rugged and less expensive than existing Swiss watches which used jeweled bearings. For his sturdy design and mass-production methods, Lehmkuhl soon won a reputation as "the Henry Ford of the watch industry."

Although the first watches of the new plant rolled off the assembly line in 1949, the Timex brand name was not introduced until 1951. At the time most watches were sold by jewelers, who typically marked up prices by 50 percent. To keep his prices low, Lehmkuhl insisted on only a 30 percent markup. Predictably, jewelers refused to sell his watches because of this pricing strategy. Robert Mohr, head of the company's marketing operation, opted to bypass the jewelers and sell directly to consumer outlets, including drugstores, hardware stores, and tobacco stands. Throughout the 1950s and 1960s, Mohr built a distribution network that reached nearly 250,000 outlets. By 1961 sales had reached $71 million, with after-tax profits of $2.9 million. By 1970 half of all watches sold in the United States sported the Timex brand name; sales had reached $200 million, and profits had exploded to $27 million. Timex was clearly a front-runner in the watch industry.

## Moments of Torture, Years of Returns

During the Timex brand's early years, advertising played a minimal role in development and was limited to simple countertop displays. However, as revenue increased the Timex Corp. sought wider exposure through magazine ads featuring such sports heroes as Mickey Mantle and Ben Hogan. The torture concept began to emerge when Hogan claimed that his Timex watch had withstood 100,000 of his golf swings and when Mantle strapped one to his baseball bat. In 1954 the company capitalized on Timex watches' growing reputation for durability with unique point-of-purchase displays. One showcase outfitted with levers allowed a Timex watch to be submerged in water and have an anvil dropped on it. Two years later, following a rapid rise in sales due to such marketing, Timex commercials debuted on television. Within a few short years the product achieved renown worldwide due directly to a series of ads starring journalist John Cameron Swayze. Exotic locales, death-defying feats, and a perpetually ticking Timex watch were the hallmarks of these spots.

## AT A GLANCE

**T**imex brand watches founded in 1951 in Waterbury, CT, by Waterbury Clock Company owner Joakim Lehmkuhl; company renamed Timex Corporation, 1969; later developers included Frederick Olsen and C. Michael Jacobi.

**Performance:** *Market share*—30% of overall U.S. wristwatch market.

**Major competitor:** Seiko; also Citizen, Fossil, and Swatch.

**Advertising:** *Agency*—Fallon McElligott, 1987—. *Major campaign*—"Timex. It takes a licking and keeps on ticking."

**Addresses:** *Parent company*—Timex Corporation, Park Road Extension, P.O. Box 310, Middlebury, CT 06762; phone: (203) 573-5000; fax: (203) 573-5143.

One of the earliest torture commercials featured a Timex watch affixed to a spinning outboard engine propeller. Unexpectedly, the watch slipped off the propeller during filming but was later recovered—intact and ticking. This mishap became the final commercial, and the "Timex—It takes a licking and keeps on ticking" campaign hit the airwaves. One of the most stunning and memorable of the Timex torture test commercials, devised by the Warwick and Legler agency, was entitled "Timex High Dive at Acapulco." Directed by Hal Tulchin, the commercial required state-of-the-art video engineering and precise crew teamwork because Raoul Garcia's treacherous 150-foot cliff dive into a narrow gorge fed by surging currents was to be shot with no cuts. In the words of Tulchin: "It was all designed so the camera never left the Timex watch from the beginning of the action until it was brought close up, to the lens, still ticking away! The watch was wonderful. It actually could take all kinds of punishment. This was really truth in advertising at work." The landmark spot eventually won its due. In 1984 it garnered the first ever Videotape Production Association's Monitor award for best achievement in classics and best direction in a classic.

### The Times They Are A-Changin'

During the 1960s and 1970s the Timex Corp. expanded its product line, introducing both jeweled and electric watches. However, wrote Chris Roush in *Business Week,* "When digital technology revolutionized watches in the 1970s, Timex stuck to analog timepieces, losing money and market share." Despite the fact that Timex began cautiously manufacturing digital watches with LCDs (liquid crystal displays) in 1974, the company was at a critical point. Persistent management problems left the company especially vulnerable to competition. *Fortune* writer Myron Magnet recorded that "By 1976, when digital watch prices tumbled straight into the company's market niche, there was 'an absolute flat panic,' as one ex-employee puts it." In 1979 Timex lost $4.7 million on sales of $600 million. At this time the Timex Corp. began to diversify its product line; in early 1980 the company announced that it would begin manufacturing a new type of 35-millimeter camera. Although for a while the Timex Corp. continued to grab publicity for its new ventures—including a Timex beginning personal computer priced under $100—the company refocused itself on the watch business under new CEO Fred Olsen, son of founder Thomas Olsen.

By 1983 watches accounted for 90 percent of the company's business and Timex was still the world's best-selling watch brand. The technology bullet that threatened to overturn the company had been successfully dodged. Timex's new slogan, "We Make Technology Beautiful," alerted consumers to the fact that the company was reshaping its product and image. Yet the Timex Corp. was about to encounter another obstacle which would prove to be "a big blunder," according to Timex president C. Michael Jacobi. In 1982 a Swiss firm approached the Timex Corp. with a plan to market a new line of watches worldwide. According to Chris Roush in *Business Week,* "Timex executives passed, believing the garish plastic timepieces wouldn't sell." Regrettably, the "garish" timepieces were Swatch watches.

Though Timex Corp. had updated its product line to meet the needs of the electronics age, it had overlooked the possibility that fads and fashion could exert extraordinary influence on watch trends. The Swatch brand singlehandedly captured the "watch as fashion" market of the mid-1980s, leaving Timex wondering how to recapture its market share. By 1993, however, the Guess and Fossil brands had relegated Swatch to second place in the fashion watch market. In response the Timex Corp. developed the Ironman Triathlon. A durable, high-tech watch named after the grueling annual sports competition, the Triathlon watch boasted a bevy of features useful to swimmers, runners, bikers, and other outdoor

*Disney's Seven Dwarves as interpreted by Timex.*

enthusiasts. Debuting during an Olympic year in a fitness-conscious era, the Triathlon's timing was fortuitous. Some 400,000 Triathlons were sold at $34.95 apiece during the product's first year. Timex brand watches targeting skiers, divers, and others quickly followed.

## Big Recovery

Despite stiff competition by Swatch, Seiko, and other mass market brands, Timex retained its dominance thanks to an increased advertising budget and a heightened emphasis on fashion and consumer research. To complete the circle in 1988, the company revived its legendary torture test campaign which had become defunct in the mid-1970s. Under the creative direction of the Minneapolis-based Fallon McElligott agency, the new Timex "Takes a Licking" commercials served the dual purpose of reconnecting the time-honored slogan with the product and infusing humor into the staid Timex brand image. In the spot called "Piranha," "a native tribesman uses a Timex Diver's watch wrapped around a chicken drumstick as bait in the piranha-packed Amazon River," summarized *Advertising Age*'s Alison Fahey. After the piranhas' feeding-frenzy, the strap is tattered but the watch remains intact and ticking.

In another commercial, the Timex Titanium is used as a guitar pick by a heavy-metal musician. In yet another Clio-winning ad entitled "Psychic," a Timex watch withstands the psychokinetic powers of a crazed-looking psychic, but a fork and a key become mangled. This ad was unsuccessfully challenged in court by real-life psychic Uri Geller, who claimed the commercial's actor bore a striking resemblance to him. Perhaps the most memorable of the six spots filmed during the 1980s was the one featuring a Timex watch taped to the rotund stomach of a Sumo wrestler in competition. The ad was honored with a premier gold award at the International Advertising Festival following its release.

## Timex Keeps on Ticking

In 1990 Timex launched its "extraordinary people" campaign, which focused on strange and dangerous adventures that Timex watch owners have survived to tell. In one such story a scuba diver was helplessly sucked into a water intake pipe of a nuclear power plant. Like the other extraordinary people featured, the diver was not wearing a Timex watch, but the story served to demonstrate the parallel with the brand's durability. Following this Fallon McElligott series, the Timex Corp.'s advertising agency sought to define the product with humor and nostalgia. In 1991 Timex spokesperson Susie Watson told *Adweek's Marketing Week* that "The 1990s is all about a return to the simple life. The pendulum is swinging back to the older brand names that have always represented quality at moderate prices. They tend to make people feel more anchored."

In 1993 Timex concentrated on magazine advertising for its Indiglo line, so named for its patented luminescent technology. A typical full-page Indiglo ad prominently displayed a glowing blue Indiglo watch accompanied by copy that appealed to various market sectors, such as "The first watch you can read at all hours.

(Perhaps you should give one to your teenage son.)," and "Like to get up and run before the crack of dawn? Here's your watch, sicko." The Indiglo watch received attention in February of 1993 from a real-life "extraordinary people" situation following the bombing of the World Trade Center in New York City. An Indiglo owner led a group of people to safety by leading them down 34 flights of stairs in a pitch-black stairwell, guided only by the glow from his Timex watch. Of all the perilous situations the Timex Corp. had portrayed through its advertising over the years, this perhaps best demonstrated the brand's usefulness and versatility.

## Further Reading:

"Act-Alike Suit Dismissed," *Wall Street Journal,* April 23, 1992, p. B3.

Appelbaum, Cara, "High Time for Timex," *Adweek's Marketing Week,* July 29, 1991, p. 24.

Barrett, William P., "Selling Nostalgia and Whimsy," *Forbes,* November 8, 1993, pp. 224–25.

Brown, Christie, "Sweat Chic," *Forbes,* September 5, 1988, pp. 96, 101.

"Dick Tracy Meets the Beeper," *Business Week,* August 14, 1989, p. 89.

"Facial Scrub," *Advertising Age,* January 13, 1992, p. 6C.

Fahey, Alison, "Timex Will Keep Tickin' With New Ad Executions," *Advertising Age,* September 25, 1989, p. 31; "Timex Marks Shift to Image Ads," *Advertising Age,* July 30, 1990, p. 15.

Fierman, Jaclyn, "Timex Retreats," *Fortune,* April 2, 1984, p. 121.

Hwang, Suein L., "And If It Matters, They Also Tell Time," *Wall Street Journal,* September 20, 1991, p. B1.

King, Thomas R., "Timex Hopes 'True Story' Ads Will Keep Watch Sales Ticking," *Wall Street Journal,* October 30, 1990, p. B6.

Mabry, Marcus, "Remembrance of Ads Past," *Newsweek,* July 30, 1990, p. 42.

Magnet, Myron, "Timex Takes the Torture Test," *Fortune,* June 27, 1983, pp. 112–20.

Marbach, William D., "A $100 Home Computer," *Newsweek,* May 3, 1982, p. 63.

Reed, Cecelia, "Timex, Grey Take the Plunge," *Advertising Age,* February 6, 1986, p. 38.

Roush, Chris, "At Timex, They're Positively Glowing," *Business Week,* July 12, 1993, p. 141.

Schwartz, Judith D., "Timex Springs into Action and Winds Up with a New Audience," *Adweek's Marketing Week,* December 12, 1988, pp. 62–3.

Thompson, Joe, "Don't Let Cameras & Computers Fool You—Watches Are Still #1 at Timex," *Jewelers' Circular-Keystone,* August 1982, pp. 260–61, 264.

"Timex Corp. (New Products)," *Advertising Age,* April 27, 1992, p. 10.

Toor, Mat, "Timex Attacks Swatch," *Marketing,* February 27, 1992, p. 7.

"Uri to Timex: Do You Mind?" *Time,* August 12, 1991, p. 49.

Wascoe, Dan, Jr., "What Makes Timex Tick?" *Back Stage,* June 22, 1990, p. 70.

"Wristwatch Pagers," *Fortune,* January 1, 1990, p. 97.

*—Jay P. Pederson*

# TOTES®

Since its founding in 1961, Totes has become one of the rainwear industry's most visible brands, helping consumers deal with inclement weather with its slip-on rubber boots, umbrellas, raincoats, eye wear, and luggage. In the 1970s the company's collapsible umbrellas sold well in upper-end department stores, and its growing line of accessories enjoyed healthy growth—a 20 percent increase per year between 1980 and 1983. By the late 1980s, however, the retail industry shifted toward mass-marketing in discount stores, forcing Totes, Inc. to adapt to new marketing and distribution strategies. The company cut costs, reduced its workforce, lowered prices, and created new products for a changing marketplace. In the face of tough economic times, Totes, Inc. found new ways of protecting consumers from the elements of nature.

### Brand Origins

The Totes brand was born in 1961, when Bradford Phillips sold his house and two cars and borrowed $20,000 from his grandmother to buy the So-Lo Marx Rubber Manufacturing Company. The small company manufactured an eclectic array of products ranging from meat tenderizer to instant gravy, fishing boats, and scuba-diving equipment. Though Phillips had worked as a district sales manager for an industrial products manufacturer, he recalled in an August 8, 1983 *Wall Street Journal* article that "my industrial sales background wasn't good enough for selling products on the retail market." Thus, Phillips set out to learn marketing techniques and was inspired by a book written by Alfred Steele, chairman of Pepsi-Cola Co. Phillips combined good business sense with optimism and humor, as illustrated by an anecdote from the company's early days that was reported in the *Wall Street Journal*. Word had it that one of the company's freshly made boots contained a dead moth molded into the toe. When told of the defect, Phillips remarked that if profit could be made from such low-quality items, then production of high-quality items would no doubt be even better for the company. In truth Phillips was greatly focused on manufacturing quality rubber boots that would create a brand identity for Totes. Once this goal was achieved in 1970, product diversification made the Totes name a leader in the protective rainwear and accessories market.

### Brand Development

Though exact figures are unknown, Totes, Inc. claimed that its size more than quadrupled from the early 1970s to the early 1980s. This growth reflected the company's successful marketing strategies. Deciding in 1970 that "it was time to protect the head as well as the feet," Phillips acquired the patent for a collapsible umbrella. Before long the Totes brand was linked with umbrellas.

Totes launched its women's apparel and accessories division in 1978, introducing affordable and fashionable raincoats and scarves to consumers. Ironically, the rain scarves became a popular Totes item because of Phillips' activities as a board member of the Cincinnati Symphony. "Many rainy evenings I would go to the symphony," he told the *Wall Street Journal* in 1983, "and see

beautifully dressed women wearing these silly little plastic things on their heads." In response Totes began manufacturing fashion-oriented rain scarves, which yielded $25 million in sales in their first three years.

Totes, Inc. also introduced a line of men's accessories in the 1970s, including a rain-resistant version of the Irish tweed hat that Patrick Moynihan, then U.S. representative to the United Nations, had helped make fashionable. The success of Tote's tweed hat prompted new designs in multiple colors that became strong-selling items for Totes, Inc. in the 1980s. One of Totes' less successful ventures into men's accessories was the stainproof necktie that failed to catch on with consumers. "People thought the ties were made of plastic," remarked Phillips.

In an attempt to foster further change within his company, Phillips consulted his friend Howard Morgens, retired chairperson of the Procter & Gamble Company. The alliance led to the formation of a product-manager organization wherein each Totes product had its own manager. With the introduction of new products into the 1990s, this management scheme helped maintain the order and focus needed for Totes, Inc.'s continued success.

### Product Changes

In 1983 the women's apparel division graduated from designing unconstructed, lightweight spring raincoats into creating coats appropriate for more severe weather—"serious raincoats," in the words of Bob Fumento, the division's general manager. The new coats sported removable linings for year-round use and designs intended to be attractive and fashionable. "Just because we became serious . . . didn't mean we had to become dull," explained Fumento in a 1988 *Women's Wear Daily* article. Totes offered their coats in a wide range of colors and styles in hopes of triggering an impulse-buying decision among consumers. From hooded swing coats to the traditional-looking trench coat, prices ranged from $50 to $130 retail, thus appealing to a broad spectrum of consumers. By the late 1980s the division exceeded sales of $10 million.

In 1984 Totes began marketing luggage. Initial market research indicated that consumers perceived Totes luggage as very portable, versatile, and of high quality. According to Totes marketing manager Karen Fritz in a 1987 *Cincinnati Business Courier* article, "We have been in the travel business for a long time with our rubber footwear and expanding bag, and the luggage business is an area we have thought about for a very long time. It is a good product line that goes along with our name." While many retailers doubted that the new luggage would offer any benefits over key competitors Atlantic, American Tourister, and Samsonite, Totes, Inc. insisted that its highly portable products would enhance its overall image of portability and quality. The line was produced primarily in China, Korea, and Taiwan and imported through established channels.

In 1988 Totes acquired the Jones Optical Company of Boulder, Colorado, for approximately $1 million and added sunglasses and

## AT A GLANCE

The Totes brand originated in 1961 when Bradford Phillips bought the So-Lo Marx Rubber Manufacturing Company and renamed it Totes, Inc.; in 1970 after years of manufacturing only rubber slip-on boots, Totes, Inc. added umbrellas, women's raincoats and scarves, ties, hats, and other accessories to its product line; in 1992 Ronald Best became company president and CEO.

*Performance:* *Market share*—82% market share in rain protection accessories.

*Major competitor:* Morlee Corporation; also J Jay Rainwear Products, Gore-Tex Rainwear.

*Advertising:* *Agency*—Sive/Young & Rubicam, Cincinnati, OH 1992—. *Major campaign*—print ads aimed at retailers promoting Chromatics umbrellas: "Here's a New Way to Think about Your Umbrella Sales".

*Addresses:* *Parent company*—Totes, Inc., 10078 E. Kemper Rd., Loveland, OH 45140; phone: (513) 583-2300; fax: (513) 683-8679.

goggles to their repertoire. Jones offered a trademark lens material developed by its founders, Mara and James Yehl. The virtually unbreakable Carbonite 360 was 65 percent lighter than glass, filtered 100 percent of the sun's harmful rays, and was free of optical distortion. While 85 percent of Jones' sales came from sunglasses, the company also marketed T-shirts, soft-sided bags and an eyeglass holder called "Jones Jaws." Anticipating a boost from Totes' marketing, packaging, and distribution resources, Jones launched a new line of hand-painted sunglass frames resembling Hawaiian tropical fish. Dubbed "Aqua-Line" and marketed as "art for your face," the new products added yet another facet to the Totes brand image.

While expanding its product line throughout the 1980s, Totes, Inc. consolidated its advertising by assigning its entire account to Fahlgren & Swink of Cincinnati, Ohio, in August of 1986. From 1983 to 1986 Fahlgren had worked on new product campaigns while Sive Associates was assigned the balance. The 1986 move tripled Fahlren's Totes billings to $1.1 million. Seven years later, however, Totes re-awarded the account to Sive/Young & Rubicam Cincinnati as Totes' advertising budget passed the $2.5 million mark.

### Reorganization

Before further growth could become a reality, Totes, Inc. had to adjust its business strategies to adapt to changes that were sweeping the retail industry. Under the pressures of a sluggish economy and slow wage growth, American consumers increasingly turned to discount stores and outlet malls in search of bargains in the early 1990s. Having firmly positioned itself as a higher-end department store brand in the 1980s, Totes was not prepared for the competition from mass-market businesses such as wholesale clubs. In 1991 Totes failed to reach its goal of $200 million, and sales declined fifteen percent the next year. "We have to do more to appeal to the value-oriented consumer," stressed Ronald Best, who became the company's CEO in 1992.

In March of 1992 Best refocused the company's energy on its core business of umbrellas, rainwear, and other key accessories that had remained profitable. By the end of the year, the teams that

Best had set up throughout the company had identified cost-cutting measures that would save the company over $1.8 million in areas ranging from travel costs to communication, and merchandising displays. In addition, the Totes' workforce was reduced by nearly 25 percent from about 1,250 to 900 employees, and a distribution facility in Lancaster, Pennsylvania, was closed.

### Mass Marketing Strategies

Stores like Wal-Mart helped change consumers' habits from shopping for prestigious brand names at department stores to old-fashioned bargain hunting. As retail analyst Kurt Barnard remarked in the *Cincinnati Business Courier,* "The consumer of the 1990s has Neiman Marcus taste levels with a K Mart pocketbook." Indeed, huge retailers routinely introduced lower-priced "knockoff" products designed to draw attention away from brand-name products on their shelves. "You're constantly faced with a decision: Can I afford to deal with these guys? The brutal truth: You can't afford not to," remarked Best in a 1992 *Business Week* article.

To deal with these marketplace changes, Best organized teams to manage products—one team for umbrellas, galoshes and assorted rain gear; another for Totes Toasties slippers and other casual footwear; and a third team for a rapidly growing line of gift items. Comprised of managers from marketing, production, sales, and procurement domains, the teams oversaw the entire process of product development from design to production.

The teams wasted no time in unveiling a new Totes product line dubbed "Chromatics," which featured a wide spectrum of playful and stylish umbrellas, slippers, scarves, animal-shaped ear muffs, and cosmetic bags in a wide range of patterns and colors. By late 1993 Chromatics were stocked in discount retailers, including SupeRx, Bigg's, Thriftway, Drug Emporium, and Van Launen's. To remain competitive in the new marketplace, Totes reduced prices on roughly two-thirds of its products. The retail price for Totes Toasties, slipper-socks featuring no-skid treads, was reduced from $8.00 to $5.99, and another line of even lower priced slipper-socks called Snuggles were to be introduced in 1993. Umbrella prices were also reduced significantly, despite declining sales and increasing production costs.

In addition to adjusting prices, Totes had to accommodate new distribution requirements in the discount retail market. Discount retailers increasingly formed partnerships with manufacturers to establish electronic ordering and distribution systems. Under the guidance of Best, Totes, Inc. moved to develop quicker order response systems and to increase its distribution and logistics staff. The company also joined the factory outlet trend, operating 48 outlet stores by June of 1992 with plans to expand to a total of 75 within three years.

Mass-market retailers also put pressure on Totes, Inc. to provide services that department stores had never requested. Some big retailers, for example, charged Totes for the cost of putting price stickers on individual packages. One retailer threatened to fine Totes $30,000 for errors in bar-coding, prompting Totes to revamp its inventory systems and automate its bar-coding procedures, according to a 1992 article in *Business Week.*

### Advertising Strategies

Totes' foray into discount retailing was accelerated by aggressive advertising efforts designed to make rainwear and accessories impulse items. "If you treat the category like a commodity and just stick a dozen black umbrellas on an endcap, that's what you're going to sell," explained John Catt, marketing manager for Totes in an October, 1992 *Discount Merchandiser* article. "But if you get proactive and aggressive," he continued, "a lot of people are finding the sky's the limit." Catt emphasized that marketing, not weather, sold umbrellas: 26 percent of respondents to a Totes survey bought umbrellas during a rainstorm, while 30 percent bought them as gift items.

In some instances, emphasis on weather protection proved to be bad business. In March of 1992 Totes, Inc. was temporarily barred from advertising its golf rain suits as waterproof and windproof because the claims were found to be false. Totes developed a golf suit made of Tech-Tex, a material the company described as water-resistant and breathable. Totes ads touted its suit as "guaranteed waterproof yet very breathable, allowing seven times more air and sweat to pass through the rain suit than suits produced from Gore-Tex [a rival brand]." A federal judge in Wilmington, Delaware, decided that the claims were false.

### International Growth

From its Loveland, Ohio, origins in 1961, Totes expanded to Canada in 1973 and Great Britain in 1981. Twenty-six years after its beginning, the Totes brand was available in more than 25,000 retail outlets across the United States, and the company maintained operations in Hong Kong, Seoul, Taipei, the United Kingdom and Canada. Anticipating new markets in a unified Europe prompted expansion to Germany, where Totes Inc. acquired Jagra-Haus Gmbh, a German distributor of umbrellas. Renamed Totes

Deutschland, the firm began distributing a full line of Totes umbrellas, boots, footwear and other products in early 1991. Totes, Inc. anticipated further growth into the developing markets of Eastern Europe, the former Soviet Union, and Asia throughout the 1990s.

### Further Reading:

Bryant, Adam, "Totes Hangs Its hat At Sive/Y&R," *New York Times,* December 17, 1992, p. D19.

Corwin, Pat, "That Rainy Day Arrives," *Discount Merchandiser,* October, 1992, p. 72–5.

Gallagher, Patricia, "Best Making Changes at Totes," *Gannett News Service,* January 15, 1993.

John J., "Totes Awash in Controversy," *Cincinnati Enquirer,* March 21, 1992, p. C4.

Mrowca, Maryann, "Weather-Gear Firm Prospers On Idea of Handier Products," *Wall Street Journal,* August 11, 1983, p. 23.

Paul, Gail L., "Totes to Buy Public Company," *Cincinnati Business Courier,* May 2, 1988, Sec. 1, p. 1.

Pogoda, Dianne M., "Totes: Fairing Well For Foul Weather; Totes Inc., Women's Raincoats," *Women's Wear Daily,* April 19, 1988, p. 8.

"Retooling For a New Consumer," *Cincinnati Business Courier,* June 1, 1992, Sec. 1, p. 1.

" 'Right-Sizing' Program Continues at Totes Incorporated," *PR Newswire,* September 3, 1993.

Schiller, Zachary and Wendy Sellner, Ron Stodghill, and Mark Maremount, "CLOUT!; More and More Retail Giants Rule the Marketplace," *Business Week,* December 21, 1992, p. 66.

Werff, Jan, "Totes Inc. Poised to Launch Luggage Line," *Cincinnati Business Courier,* November 30, 1987, Sec. 1, p. 11.

—*Kerstan Cohen*

# TROJAN® CONDOMS

Trojan condoms, the best-selling brand of prophylactics in the United States in 1993, have long been recognized as a barrier for contraception and the prevention of sexually transmitted disease. In 1992, unit sales of Trojan condoms in drug stores and supermarkets totalled 21.7 million, claiming a 59.7 percent share of the market. Youngs Rubber Corporation, the manufacturer of the brand from its inception in 1916 until 1985, fought hard to upgrade the product's image and change laws that prohibited open condom sales, advertising, and physician prescription. Trojan was one of two brands to achieve national distribution early on, becoming so popular that well into the 1990s many consumers insisted on using the Trojan brand name interchangeably with the generic word "condom."

In September of 1985 the Trojan brand was acquired by Carter-Wallace, Inc., a manufacturer, marketer, and researcher of contraceptive devices, pharmaceuticals, diagnostic reagents, test kits, and pet products. Carter-Wallace was built on Carter's Little Pills, originally known as Carter's Little Liver Pills. In the 1990s consumer products accounted for approximately 52 percent of the company's business, while health care products represented 48 percent. Trojan condoms have been marketed through the Carter Products Division, Carter-Wallace's consumer and health products branch.

Henry Hoyt, part of Carter-Wallace's founding family and managing director of Carter-Wallace, Inc. from 1929 until his death in 1990, believed in investing in research and development and cutting edge products. A 1992 *Forbes* article estimated that the Hoyt family's holdings in Carter-Wallace totalled $610 million in October of that year. Hoyt was quoted as saying in *Forbes,* "I believed in the axiom that a business cannot stand still." Hoyt realized that public awareness of the AIDS virus and the rising number of sexually transmitted disease (STD) cases would prove to be a boon to the condom market.

## Brand Origins

Trojan condoms were first introduced by the Youngs Rubber Corporation, located in New York City. Merrill Youngs, president of the corporation, was an aggressive businessman who recognized that the future of the Trojan brand required breaking down the formidable barriers to birth control. The Comstock Laws, federal laws passed in 1873, prohibited physician prescription of contraceptive devices, and made it illegal to sell across state lines any products which could be used as contraceptives.

Youngs realized that many Americans, particularly those who did not support the use of condoms as contraceptives, were sympathetic to the marketing of condoms for disease prevention. He embarked on a strategy to promote the condoms solely as high quality prophylactics for disease prevention and marketed them exclusively through drug stores and pharmacies. Youngs believed that pharmacy distribution would reinforce the image of condoms as aids for the prevention of disease. Unlike many other condom brands that were made of poor quality rubber and sold illicitly (often in gas stations and barbershops), Trojan condoms were made of durable rubber and promised to function reliably.

Youngs first registered the Trojan brand name with the U.S. Patent Office in 1926, hoping to protect the trademark before competing brands flooded the market. In 1927 he filed a trademark infringement suit against C.I. Lee and Company of Chicago, Illinois, who had begun to package and sell condoms under the Trojan name. When the case first went to court, C.I. Lee and Company argued that the Trojan trademark was illegal since condom distribution was prohibited across state lines under the Comstock Laws. The case was initially dismissed in U.S. District Court, but Youngs filed an appeal, and the final decision in his favor made it a landmark case in the history of birth control.

Judge Thomas Swan not only ruled in favor of protecting the Trojan trademark, but used the case to rule in favor of a reinterpretation of the national laws which prohibited dissemination of information and materials for contraception. Swan ruled that the sender's purpose of marketing the condom was paramount. In this case, the condom was being sold to prevent disease, which could be construed as a legal use of the product as could the prevention of conception in those states that permitted contraceptives. Thus the sale of Trojan condoms through drug stores was ruled as a legitimate use. A more sweeping decision by Judge Augustus Hand granted doctors new discretion, by permitting prescription of contraceptives for ends that doctors deemed medically proper (i.e. to prevent disease or enhance health). This case proved to be an enormous victory for the birth control movement in allowing the dissemination of birth control information and contraceptives. The decision prompted widespread marketing of Trojan condoms and other contraceptives in drug stores across the nation.

## AT A GLANCE

**T**rojan brand of condoms introduced circa 1924 by Merrill Youngs, president of Youngs Rubber Corporation, when he began packaging and distributing rubber latex condoms manufactured by Frederick Killian in Akron, OH, using a process developed by the Goodyear Rubber Company; in 1926, first Trojan trademark registered through U.S. patent office, with several more trademarks to follow; in 1927, Youngs filed patent infringement suit against C.I. Lee and Co. for making prophylactics using the Trojan name; in 1930, suit settled on appeal in landmark decision; Youngs obtains rights to manufacture Trojan condoms, 1934; in 1985, Youngs Drug Products Corporation, with subsidiaries Youngs Rubber Corporation and Holland-Rantos Company, Inc. acquired by Carter-Wallace, Inc., with Trojans marketed through Carter Products Division.

**Performance:** *Market share*—59.7% (top share) of U.S. condom market (October 31, 1992). *Sales*—21.7 million units annually.

**Major competitor:** LifeStyles; also Ramses.

**Advertising:** *Agency*—Backer Spielvogel Bates, 1985—. *Major campaign*—"In control. Trojan helps reduce the risk"; also "You're more in touch with Trojan."

**Addresses:** *Parent company*—Carter Products Division, Carter-Wallace, Inc., 1345 Avenue of the Americas, New York, NY 10105; phone: (212) 395-5000.

Youngs Rubber continued to aggressively market the Trojan brand throughout the years. When condom usage was second only to douching as a contraceptive method between the 1930s and 1950s, Youngs promoted the product as a reliable alternative, and Trojan condoms became the leading brand. When the Army was concerned about venereal disease, the company sponsored a highly successful slide show, later made into a videocassette, that promoted condom use among U.S. servicemen.

### High Quality Manufacturing

The superior manufacturing process used by Youngs Rubber produced a far more durable condom than many of his competitors. A 1949 FDA study of condom manufacturing defects revealed that only condoms made by Youngs Rubber Corporation and Julius Schmid Inc. met FDA quality standards for size, elasticity and elongation, thickness, and strength.

Youngs originally bought, packaged, and resold rubber latex condoms that were manufactured by Frederick Killian, of Akron, Ohio, using a hand-dipping method. This manufacturing process was originally developed by the Goodyear Rubber Company and was believed to be superior to other methods used for condom manufacture. Youngs eventually purchased the rights to manufacture the Trojan brand using this process.

### Product Lines

There were few innovations in the early years when Youngs Rubber had fought for open marketing of Trojan condoms, but as the product gained visibility and acceptance, new product lines were introduced to meet burgeoning demand. The original Trojan condom was plain and nonlubricated, with a rounded end. Receptacle ends were introduced in 1935, when the Trojan-Enz condom was launched. Lubricated Trojan condoms were not introduced until 1953. Texture, sensitivity, and mutual pleasure became more

of a concern in the late 1960s and 1970s. Product innovations included ribbed, specially contoured, natural lamb condoms and condoms specially designed for women's sensitivity.

After the brand was sold to Carter-Wallace, further product improvements were made. In the mid-1980s, when AIDS and sexually transmitted diseases became nationwide public health concerns, condoms, particularly those with the spermicide Nonoxynol-9, were believed to be effective against transmission of AIDS and some sexually transmitted diseases. Carter-Wallace was quick to market condoms with Nonoxynol-9, and by 1993 nearly half of the Trojan line used Nonoxynol-9.

By the early 1990s most Trojan condoms were made with latex rubber which provided a solid barrier; less than 10 percent were made from lamb cecum, a pouch forming part of the animal's large intestine. In 1992, when laboratory testing revealed that both the HIV and hepatitis-B viruses penetrated the porous lambskin condoms, the Food and Drug Administration questioned the effectiveness of natural lamb condoms in protecting against sexually transmitted diseases. The FDA required a warning statement on all packages of non-latex condoms, that only latex rubber condoms could protect against sexually transmitted diseases. By 1993 natural lamb condoms represented a very small segment of the Trojan condom line. Carter-Wallace began to aggressively promote their Extra Strength Trojan brand, a latex condom introduced in 1989 that provided increased strength without sacrificing sensitivity. By 1993 Carter-Wallace was producing twelve condom lines under the Trojan name as well as Mentor and Magnum condoms. As condoms became an acceptable accessory to safe sex in the 1990s, Carter-Wallace looked to convenient packaging and began to market a three-pack variety.

### Trojan Advertising Restrictions

Condom advertising was strictly forbidden when the Trojan brand was initially introduced, and advertising restrictions have persisted well into the 1990s. The media have long viewed condom advertising as highly controversial and not worth taking on because it might jeopardize future advertising and sponsorship. In the 1990s, there was still a taboo in many media on open advertising of condoms as contraceptives; the only acceptable message was one of disease prevention. By 1993 the three major television networks were still not allowing condom commercials to be aired, arguing that the disease prevention issue could best be dealt with in news programs and series.

In November of 1991 the Fox Broadcasting Company became the first national network to permit condom advertising. Fox's new policy allowed condom ads to run after 9 p.m. if they dealt only with disease prevention and not contraception. The change in policy was publicly disclosed just four days after professional athlete Magic Johnson held a press conference to announce his retirement from basketball because he had tested positive for the virus that causes AIDS.

Trojan was the first brand to advertise on the Fox network. Carter-Wallace upstaged Schmid's Ramses brand at the last minute. The Ramses commercial was rejected by Fox because the word "spermicidal" was featured on the Ramses box; Fox argued that this did not meet guidelines that only permitted disease prevention messages. A 15-second Trojan spot portrayed a young man talking about the way bad things have been happening to nice people. It ended with an announcer suggesting the use of Trojan condoms "to help reduce the risk." Many local broadcast and cable stations began to allow condom ads, usually with the proviso that sex and contraception were not to be discussed. Nonetheless, condom brand advertising on television occurred infrequently in the early 1990s.

Print advertising, however, expanded in the 1980s and 1990s, especially in women's, ethnic, and health magazines, including *Vogue, Essence, Parents, Shape,* and *Prevention.* The ads were targeted toward women, who purchased between 20 and 40 percent of the condoms sold in the 1990s according to estimates by industry analysts. The ads in women's magazines emphasized shared responsibility for contraception as well as a prevention message. By contrast, ads appearing in men's magazines promoted more of a disease prevention message.

Restrictions on advertising may have actually prevented newer rivals from eroding the Trojan brand's market share, according to James S. Murphy, author of *The Condom Industry in the United States.* Murphy argued that given the controversial nature of the

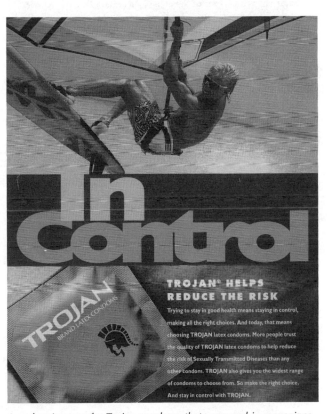

An advertisement for Trojan condoms that appeared in magazines in 1992.

product, advertising may inadvertently offend consumers. He did, however, allow that a highly successful ad campaign by a new rival might prompt a switch to a new brand.

Trojan condoms have also benefited from free publicity in the 1980s and 1990s in the form of public health advisories and celebrity endorsements of condom use to prevent the spread of AIDS and other sexually transmitted diseases. Although such promotions have been generic campaigns, they have proved to be a less potentially controversial substitute for expensive brand advertising.

## Trojan Sales Trends

A 1986 *Fortune* article reported that by the 1970s the public had come to view condoms as "a has-been product on its way to oblivion." Indeed, condom sales had flattened between the 1930s and 1970s, and *Fortune* estimated that sales had declined by 50 percent between 1976 and 1986. This slide was attributed to the widespread availability of more modern solutions to birth control in the 1970s, including the birth control pill, diaphragm, and spermicides. In addition, effective antibiotics were being prescribed for sexually transmitted diseases. By this time, condoms seemed to be primitive and old-fashioned.

With the advent of AIDS and sexually transmitted diseases that were resistant to conventional treatment, Trojan and other condom brands experienced an increase in popularity in the 1980s. The condom market was the first segment of the medical device industry to see growth as a result of AIDS. The publishing of the 1986 Surgeon General's report recommending condoms for the prevention of STDs, including AIDS, is well-recognized as the single most important event spurring condom sales. Between 1986 and 1988 condom sales in drug stores rose from 240 million to 299 million, with the highest sales for latex condoms with spermicide.

While the *Wall Street Journal* reported that condom sales experienced 40- to 50-percent annual increases after the publication of the Surgeon General's report, this growth slowed to 9 percent in 1991 and 5 percent in 1992. Industry analysts argued that the American public had been saturated with the AIDS prevention message by the 1990s. As explained by Fred Kroger, Director of AIDS Information for the Center for Disease Control, in the *Wall Street Journal,* "the most responsible [consumers] were early converts to regular condom use." However, in 1991 the rising number of new AIDS cases in women suggested that the female segment of the market might be further tapped. In addition, information on the risk of viral STDs was much less visible by 1993, and Felicity Barringer reported in the *New York Times* that one in five people in the United States had viral sexual diseases. This untapped market may prove to be a source of further sales opportunities.

In this climate, the Trojan brand continued to have the highest sales of condoms in 1992, achieving sales of 21.7 million units for a 59.7 percent of the market according to Information Resources Inc. data in the *Wall Street Journal.* LifeStyles, the number two brand made by Ansell-Americas, trailed far behind, claiming only 11.1 percent.

Trojan condoms have benefited from increased acceptability in the 1990s. In addition, condoms were no longer sold exclusively in drug stores, but food stores, discounters, vending machines, and mail-order catalogs as well. By 1993 condoms were prominently displayed, often near the cash register in order to take advantage of impulse purchases from that location. Although mired in public debate, school condom distribution increased, particularly in such large cities as New York and Los Angeles, and condom vending machines began to appear on college campuses. In 1993, as cures for AIDS and the viral sexually transmitted diseases eluded researchers, condoms remained the leading growth product in the preventive health segment. Therefore the outlook was good for Trojan brand condoms, which would likely continue to be an important part of the public health agenda.

## Further Reading:

Barringer, Felicity, "Viral Sexual Diseases are Found in 1 in 5 of U.S.," *New York Times*, April 1, 1993, pp. A1, B9.

"Barriers to Entry," *The Economist*, November 30, 1991, p. 71.

"Carter-Wallace: Founding Family's Holdings are Worth $610 Mil +," *Forbes*, October 19, 1992, p. 228.

"Chains Get 51% of Condom Sales," *Chain Drug Review*, January 1, 1992, p. 16.

"Condom Ads Tap Fear Factor," *Advertising Age*, August 4, 1986, pp. 1, 8.

"Condom Makers See Big Potential in the Teen Market," *Drug Store News*, May 18, 1992, p. 19.

"Contraceptive Use to Rise," *Chain Drug Review*, January 1, 1992, p. 16.

Conway, John A., "Protection Money," *Forbes*, February 23, 1987, p. 8.

Deveny, Kathleen, "Despite AIDS and Safe Sex Exhortations, Sales of Condoms in the United States are Lackluster," *Wall Street Journal*, November 24, 1992, pp. B1, B5.

Dienes, C. Thomas, *Law, Politics and Birth Control*, Urbana, IL: University of Illinois Press, 1972.

Elliott, Stuart, "The Media Business: Advertising; The Sponsor is the Surprise in Fox's First Condom Ad," *New York Times*, November 19, 1991, p. D19.

Lowe, J. Thomas, LaWayne R. Stromberg, and Norman F. Estrin, "The AIDS Epidemic: Its Impact on Manufacture and Use of Medical Devices," *The Medical Device Industry*, New York: Marcel Dekker, Inc., 1990, pp. 495–500.

Moran, John S., Harlan R. Janes, et al., "Increase in Condom Sales following AIDS Education and Publicity, United States," *American Journal of Public Health*, May 1990, pp. 607–8.

Muirhead, Greg, "Condoms Get an Assist: Magic Johnson's HIV Announcement has Helped Fuel an Increase in Condom Sales," *Supermarket News*, March 2, 1987, p. 1(3).

Murphy, James S., *The Condom Industry in the United States*, Jefferson, NC: McFarland & Co., 1990.

"Network Shows Deal With Condom Use," *Broadcasting*, February 9, 1987, p. 110.

*Plain Talk About VD: Venereal Disease* (videocassette), Fort Sam Houston, TX: Academy of Health Sciences, 1972.

Ryley, George Scott, *Male Methods of Birth Control*, London: Cobham House, 1937.

Silverman, Edward R., "Condom Sales Lag, but Carter-Wallace Healthy," *Crain's New York Business*, May 15, 1989, p. 34(1).

Waldman, Steven, "The Selling of Safety: After Years of Resistance Madison Avenue now Sees it as a Way to Court Baby Boomers," *Newsweek*, March 12, 1990, p. 64(2).

"Warning of Possible Hazards of Lambskin Condoms Spreads," *Drug Topics*, November 11, 1991, p. 96.

Wilson, Marianne, "New Image for Old Product: Resurgence of Condom Sales Spurred by Fear of Sexually Transmitted Disease: Almost Half of the Purchases are made by Women," *American Druggist*, January 1987, p. 80(2).

Winters, Patricia, "AIDS Fear Poses Crisis for Some, Market for Others," *Advertising Age*, February 3, 1986, p. 1.

*—Laura Newman*

# TUMS®

Tums brand antacid, one of the most popular brands in the antacid category, was founded by Lewis-Howe Company in the mid-1920s. The company used the slogan "taste as good as they make you feel" to advertise the product. In 1978 the Revlon Group Inc. acquired Lewis-Howe and the Tums brand. Revlon was attempting to reduce its dependence on the crowded cosmetics market. Tums next became a Norcliff-Thayer Inc. brand, which used the slogan "for the tummy." To become more of a presence in the U.S. market, a British Beecham company bought Norcliff-Thayer in 1985. In 1989 SmithKline Beecham PLC was formed through the acquisition and merger of SmithKline Beckman Corporation of Philadelphia into Beecham. SmithKline grew to be a leader in clinical laboratories, antacids, and acne remedies.

## Repositioning

Nancy Giges wrote in the March 10, 1986, *Advertising Age* that "until several years ago, tablet stomach remedies were a pretty ho-hum business, the static segment of the total antacid category of $625 million when liquids, tablets and effervescents are included. But Tums added new life to the segment, first with a sodium-free pitch and more recently with its calcium claims." With the new positioning, SmithKline closed the several point gap between Tums and the competing Rolaids brand, mainly at the expense of smaller brands.

Most of the growth came not from increased demand for stomach remedies, but from "the latest rage in nutrients," calcium supplements. Doctors were recommending that women patients take extra calcium to diminish bone loss. A whole new market opened up in calcium supplements. Tums fit into the category because its main ingredient was calcium carbonate. Always watchful of current products and their health claims, *Consumer Reports* in 1984 reviewed the various types of calcium replacement products, including those specifically marketed for people at risk of osteoporosis. The publication's medical consultants found that calcium carbonate, the main component of chalk, was the best choice as a supplement because it was the most easily absorbed form of calcium. They noted that calcium carbonate antacids such as Tums were a good source of easily absorbed calcium because they neutralized acid and had no added ingredients except sweeteners and flavorings, also found in supplements marketed to people with osteoporosis. Tums contained calcium carbonate obtained

from pure limestone via a chemical process that produced a high degree of purity. Additionally, Tums was a calcium supplement that people who could not tolerate dairy products could take.

Norcliff-Thayer jumped at the opportunity and started to advertise Tums as "an inexpensive way to prevent calcium deficiency and osteoporosis" and claimed that "thousands of women are following their doctors' advice and taking Tums daily to avoid this brittle bone disease." The stakes were high; an estimated 20 million women had osteoporosis and an additional 35 million were at risk and were being encouraged to take supplements. The market for calcium supplements shot up in the six years ending in 1986 from $18 million in retail sales to $125 million. Marketers of straight calcium supplements, which cost considerably more than Tums and were at risk of losing sales to the brand, attacked Tums on the calcium claims it was making. Lederle Laboratories and Ayerst Labs filed a complaint with the industry's self-regulatory body, the National Advertising Division of the Council of Better Business Bureaus. They said the claims made in the Tums ads were unsubstantiated. However, the Tums campaign held up under NAD review.

Sales of the Tums brand increased dramatically with the calcium-benefit claims. Although Warner-Lambert at first tried to keep its Rolaids brand from losing more market share to Tums by stating in advertising that doctors preferred Rolaids as an antacid over Tums, it eventually started to mention that Rolaids contained calcium and also came out with a calcium-enriched tablet. Warner-Lambert later presented more direct competition by introducing Theracal, a mint-flavored chewable tablet that was priced at about half the cost of leading bottled calcium supplements.

Tums advertising successfully defended another challenge in 1991. Johnson & Johnson, which marketed Mylanta (a major antacid brand) through a joint venture with Merck Consumer Pharmaceuticals, charged that SmithKline Beecham's Tums antacid ads contained misleading messages about Mylanta's safety and that the ads violated the law by promising a nutritional benefit because Tums contained calcium. A U.S. District Court judge in New York threw out the case.

Tums antacid continued to be advertised as a preventive medicine for use against osteoporosis into the 1990s. SmithKline also kept using a head-on approach to advertising. The company positioned its extra-strength formula against Rolaids, indicating how it was better with the theme "twice as strong, twice as fast." Other Tums commercials featured the booming chant, "Tum Ta Tum Tum Tummmms."

## Brand Extensions and Outlook

It was expected that the already large antacid market would see new growth in the 1990s as marketers of prescription ulcer drugs introduced over-the-counter versions. Manufacturers whose patents were about to expire scrambled to get Food and Drug Administration approval for less potent versions of their drugs to continue earning revenue from the basic formulations. In 1992 SmithKline Beecham and Marion Merrell Dow formed a partnership (90 percent owned by SmithKline) called SmithKline Beecham Consumer Brands to develop and sell nonprescription drugs. One of the venture's first spin-off products was to be Tagamet, which would be a competitor of SmithKline's own Tums brand.

In 1993 SmithKline marketed Tums Antacid Tablets (assorted and peppermint flavors); Tums E-X Tablets (assorted, peppermint, wintergreen, and cherry); and Tums Anti-gas/Antacid Tablets (assorted). The rectangular Tums logo had the words *Tums Antacid* in white letters on a medium blue background. Each end of the rectangle had green vertical bars separated by a thinner blue line. Since Tums products were available for varying degrees of heartburn and stomach irritation as well as being established as a source of absorbable calcium, it appeared the brand would hold onto market share in the antacid and calcium supplement categories.

## Further Reading:

"Ads for Tums Upset a Rival, *New York Times,* February 13, 1991, sec. D, p. 6.

"Beckerman Prevents Disease with Tums," *Back Stage-SHOOT,* June 5, 1992, p. 18.

"A Chalk Talk on Calcium Tablets," *Consumer Reports,* October 1984, p. 579.

"For the Record; SmithKline Beecham," *Advertising Age,* October 7, 1991, p. 65.

Freudenheim, Milt, "Company News; 2 Companies Join in Selling Medications," *New York Times,* August 19, 1992, p. D4.

Giges, Nancy, "Rolaids, Tums Go Belly-to-Belly," *Advertising Age,* March 10, 1986, p. 4.

Moskowitz, Milton, Robert Levering and Michael Katz, editors, *Everybody's Business: A Field Guide to the 400 Leading Companies in America,* New York: Doubleday, 1990, pp. 168–70.

Sharp, Harold S., *Advertising Slogans of America,* Metuchen, NJ: Scarecrow Press, 1984, p. 482.

*SmithKline Beecham Consumer Brands,* typescripts.

"Suit against Tums Rejected," Associated Press, October 2, 1991, sec. D, p. 6.

Urdang, Laurance, editorial director, and Celia Dame Robbins, editor, *Slogans,* Detroit: Gale Research Company, 1984, pp. 123, 126.

Winters, Patricia, "Boning Up On Calcium; Supplements Marketed to Women," *Advertising Age,* January 6, 1986, pp. 1, 68.

Winters, Patricia, "Bristol Pops Up in Surging Antacid Market," *Advertising Age,* October 1, 1990, pp. 3, 55.

*—Doris Morris Maxfield*

# TURTLE WAX®

Turtle Wax, packaged in a turtle-green container, is the top-selling automobile wax worldwide, maintaining a market share of 40 percent or more during the 1980s and 1990s. Continually produced since the early 1950s as Turtle Wax, the wax's predecessor, Plastone Liquid Car Polish, was first produced in 1941. Founder Ben Hirsch maintained close control of both his product and his company, Turtle Wax, Inc., until his death in 1966.

## A Family Business

After leaving his undergraduate studies in chemistry during the Depression to earn a living in positions as diverse as magician and professional wrestling manager, Ben Hirsch invested $500 to open a Chicago business in the early 1940s. He began by mixing up batches of car wax formulas in a bathtub at a small storefront at Chicago and Western Avenues. From the start, the company was a family business: with the help of his wife and business partner Marie, the Hirsch team bottled their first product, Plastone Liquid Car Polish.

Except for a brief period of reorganization following the death of Ben Hirsch in 1966, the founder's family has remained in active management of Turtle Wax, Inc. Joining the company as vice-president of public relations upon her father's death, Sondra (Hirsch) Healy became chairman of the board in 1971.

## Early Marketing Skill

In the early days of the business, Ben Hirsch traveled by streetcar to introduce his automobile wax to gas station and garage owners in the city of Chicago. In a hands-on marketing tactic, Hirsch polished car fenders outside Wrigley Field, waiting for the owners to return to point out the results of his product's use.

Operating out of various storefront locations in the late 1940s and early 1950s, the young company introduced Plastone into the Canadian market by the late 1940s. It was on a sales call closer to home, however, that Hirsch was inspired to change the name of both his company and its primary product. While walking along Turtle Creek in Beloit, Wisconsin, Hirsch made a mental connection between the hard shell of a turtle and his product. Thus, as stated in a 1986 company-published pamphlet, "Plastone Liquid Car Polish became Turtle Wax with the hard shell finish."

Established at the intersection of Madison, Ashland, and Ogden Avenues in the late 1950s, Turtle Wax proclaimed itself to local passersby in an unusually effective manner. A giant "Turtle in the Sky" combination clock-and-weather-forecaster was erected atop the building which, at roughly nine stories, towered above the surrounding businesses.

## Product Experimentation

After being in business for a decade and seeking new product possibilities, Ben Hirsch "jumped hard on the plastics bandwagon," according to Mark Jannot Chicago magazine. Family history recounts that Hirsch decided to manufacture plastic car floor mats during the 1950s. A major rubber manufacturer apparently got wind of the innovation and used their technological expertise to mass-produce the plastic mats and retail them at a lower price than Hirsch could afford to offer. Hirsch took a major economic hit as a result.

In another effort at product diversification, Hirsch experimented with a spray-on shoe polish. The entrepreneur didn't have the ability to test the product, but decided to run with it anyway. "Within months," the Chicago magazine article detailed, "pair after pair of shoes marched into [Hirsch's] Clark Street storefront, shoes that had apparently cracked as a result of progressive shoeshine buildup." Undaunted, Ben had his employees scrub off the coating and shine the shoes the old-fashioned way—by hand.

Attempting to gain wider recognition through supermarkets, Hirsch developed rug shampoo, floor wax, and a line of dessert toppings called Party Day. Hirsch continued to experiment in broadening his market base, though it did cost him. "There were several times my dad nearly went bankrupt," Sondra Healy told the Chicago Tribune. "There were times that he borrowed money from his employees and repaid them in stock—just to keep the business from going under."

## A Leadership Change

By the mid-1960s Turtle Wax began to make inroads in the automotive and household cleaning markets, and relocated to a large factory in an industrial district on North Clybourn Avenue in Chicago. A new factory was opened in England, and sales remained steady in established Canadian markets.

Bigger changes were in store for Turtle Wax in 1966, however, when company founder Ben Hirsch died from heart-related problems. As his death was sudden, no plans for succession had been made. Marie Hirsch was quickly named chairman of the board and the couple's daughter Sondra, employed as a drama teacher in a Chicago suburb, joined the company at 27 as vice-president of public relations. For the next four years conservative management at Turtle Wax eliminated most, if not all, non-automotive products from production.

Attending a Florida specialty chemicals industry convention in 1970, Sondra Hirsch met Denis Healy, a delegate from the Barr Company, a contract packager of aerosol and liquid products based in Niles, Illinois. Healy had previously worked in product development for the Colgate-Palmolive and Mennen companies. The couple found they had much in common, and married within eight months.

In 1971 Marie Hirsch passed away, and Sondra Healy was named chairman of the board, replacing her mother. Denis Healy joined Turtle Wax that same year as vice-president.

"People used to say, 'Vice-president of what?'" Healy commented in an interview with Chicago magazine. "I'd say, 'Vice-president of the company.' I didn't come in to be vice-president of research. Or vice-president of sales, or vice-president of marketing. There was a lot to be done."

## AT A GLANCE

**T**urtle Wax brand automobile wax (originally Plastone Liquid Car Polish) founded by Ben Hirsch in 1941; brand renamed Turtle Wax in the early 1950s.

**Performance:** *Market share*—40-60% (top share) of automotive wax and polish category. *Sales*—$44 million.

**Major competitor:** Products by Armor All Corp.

**Advertising:** *Agency*—Lou Beres & Associates, 1982—. *Major campaign*—High-tech lab environment featured in television ads promoting new products "Finish 2001" and "Formula 2001."

**Addresses:** *Parent company*—Turtle Wax, Inc., 5655 West 73rd Street, Chicago, IL 60638; phone: (708) 563-3600.

Having spent most of his career developing new products, Denis Healy was not ready to accept Turtle Wax as merely an automotive aftermarket supplier. And as the new leader of the company, Sondra Healy had her father's vision in mind; she knew her father's goals for Turtle Wax. Ben Hirsch—according to the daughter who had witnessed his product experimentation first-hand—had never intended to stop developing new products.

Turtle Wax was once again buoyed by the plans of husband-and-wife team Sondra and Denis Healy, like Ben and Marie Hirsch before them. The change in management and philosophy prompted a resurgence in the company's image which attracted potential buyers to Turtle Wax Inc. through the early 1980s. The Healys, however, were not interested in selling.

### New Facilities, New Products

The company moved to its present location in Bedford Park on Chicago's southwest side in 1973. With 400,000 square-feet of total space, Turtle Wax set up administrative and manufacturing operations in one building; across the street, another structure housed Turtle Wax's car wash division, developed in the 1980s. By mid-1988 the company bought three established car washes in the Chicago area. The plan was to operate them for at least six months before committing the Turtle Wax name to the project.

The Healys worked to expand Turtle Wax's reach into new product areas. By 1983 the company was ready to once again diversify into non-automotive markets through supermarkets and larger merchandisers like Kmart.

The first item out of development was the distinctly non-automotive Turtle Wax Creme Shoe Polish. The shoe polish industry, dominated by Sara Lee Corporation's Kiwi Polish Company, was definitely not a growth market. Entering a low-priced category (Kiwi's polish was priced at 95¢, with a 50¢ margin), Turtle Wax decided to price its shoe polish at $2.49, giving retailers a hefty $1.12 margin. The company invested $2 million in television advertising, a record amount for a shoe polish producer. Denis Healy hoped to eventually carve out a 20 to 30 percent share of the market, denting Kiwi's entrenched 80 percent share. Industry records showed Turtle Wax shoe polish, by year-end 1984, with only a three percent share.

Next came Clear Guard, a vinyl automobile-interior protectant intended to compete with Armor All, which claimed $100 million of the $115 million sales in the automotive appearance-chemicals

category. As reported in *Advertising Age,* "packaging and ad copy for Clear Guard stress[ed] the product's many uses 'inside and outside your car and home.' " Bolder language contrasted Armor All's "cloudy" spray to Clear Guard's formula, which, according to ad copy, "Lets the natural beauty shine through."

With television advertising and a consumer-rebate program, Turtle Wax continued adding new products to its foundation business, automotive waxes and polishes. Other products unveiled in the early 1980s included Clear Coat, a non-abrasive polish for new cars which carry a layer of clear paint over a base coat; Color Back, an original formula designed to restore or revive the finish on older cars; and Minute Wax, a silicone-based spray requiring no rubbing or buffing.

Turtle Wax continued its new product blitz. In 1986 it introduced Wash & Wax, a single formula which both washes and waxes in one step; and Sudden Shine, described as an instant finish-restorer for older cars. Both products were directed at the increasing convenience-seeking market. New Turtle Wax entries into the home-care market included carpet and upholstery cleaners, and copper and silver polishes. In August 1986, household products accounted for less than five percent of total sales, but the company envisioned that number growing to 30 percent.

A force in the new product spurt was Chuck Tornabene, who joined Turtle Wax in 1985 as vice-president of marketing. Tornabene had experience in home cleaning products, having worked for the Texize unit of Morton Thiokol Inc., maker of Fantastik and Spray 'n Wash. He saw Turtle Wax's new emphasis as sensible. Quoted in *Crain's Chicago Business,* Tornabene stated that Turtle Wax had been making various car-cleaning products "for years, so the household market is a natural extension for us."

### Candid Consumer Reports

Several Turtle Wax household products were judged by the December 1982 *Consumer Reports.* The company's velour cleaner was judged an effective and versatile product, while Turtle Wax Leather Vinyl Fabric cleaner was placed lower in overall quality than three competing products. In similar tests conducted on carpet cleaners for the year 1990, Turtle Wax's entry in that category was ranked ninth in effectiveness out of twelve chemical cleaners listed.

In the August 1986 *Canadian Consumer* article entitled "None Lasted as Long as Their Claims Might Have You Believe," car finish products were tested for longevity, life of finish, and shine improvement on both moderately faded and faded paint. While the cost per coat and estimated annual cost were listed, the editors stated that overall ratings were based on performance without regard to price; buying recommendations were based on performance in relation to price. With all these categories taken into consideration, Canadian-made Turtle Wax products fared well overall, with Turtle Wax Clear Coat gel, Turtle Wax Metallic (in liquid and paste forms), and Turtle Wax Super Hard Shell ranked satisfactory. In contrast, seven other car finishes ranked higher; Reed Union's Nu Finish liquid was ranked very good, and Borden Rain Dance, good. To remove the least paint when finishing a nearly new car, the magazine recommended Turtle Wax Clear Coat, Minute Wax Silicone spray, and Super Hard Shell paste. Since the mid-1980s many of the Turtle Wax products rated in these studies have been discontinued or reformulated and improved. As of 1993, no current studies were available rating new

Turtle Wax products, but based on the brand's outstanding market share, it seems clear that consumers are satisfied with Turtle Wax products.

## Upping the Advertising Ante

In an attempt to attract new users into the car wax category, Turtle Wax increased its advertising budget to $8 million for 1987, a $3 million increase from the previous year. In a history-making move, the company decided to launch its first television campaign in decades for its tried-and-true product, Super Hard Shell car wax. "Although the product accounts for approximately one-quarter of the company's total sales and one out of every five car care products currently sold in the U.S.," *Crain's Chicago Business* reported, "[Super Hard Shell] hasn't been marketed on TV for 35 years." Tests conducted in Indianapolis and Memphis markets in early 1986 showed a 97 percent increase in sales. Turtle Wax planned to run the ads from April through July, known as prime season for car care product sales.

By June 1987 another new Turtle Wax product was launched. With Scratchguard, a nonabrasive bath and kitchen cleaner, the company took on industry giants such as the Clorox Company (Soft Scrub), Dow Chemical Company (Dow Bathroom Cleaner), and Procter & Gamble (Mr. Clean Cleanser with Soft Abrasives). Distribution went well upon introduction, with Scratchguard in over 70 percent of the market. The company invested several million dollars to advertise Scratchguard; its chief competitors committed anywhere from $3 million to $10.2 million on their cleaners.

Getting back to the basics of Turtle Wax's business—car wax—was necessary for the company in 1988. Armor All, with a more than 80 percent share in the automobile protectant market, introduced its first car wax. The introduction by heavy hitting Armor All could not be expected to help the car wax market grow. Instead, industry suppliers, aware that car wax sales had been flat for several years, predicted that smaller wax-producers would lose shelf space in discount, hardware, and department stores.

Armor All's entry into automobile wax, however—backed by $5 million in advertising the first year—did cause a slight increase in the market overall, which rose from approximately $175 million in 1988 to close to $200 million within two years. By 1990 Armor All had positioned itself to become a serious threat with the purchase of Borden Inc., based in Columbus, Ohio. The Borden acquisition brought Rain Dance, Turtle Wax's biggest competitor in the car wax market, into the Armor All fold.

One way Turtle Wax maintained its lead over competition was to keep a number of car-care products on the shelves of supermarkets and automobile, hardware, and discount stores. The company also stayed on top of changing trends. In the late 1980s, for example, Turtle Wax management noted two separate changes in the market. The first was that autumn, contrary to industry belief, could be a good season to sell car wax. The second change Turtle Wax noticed was that the number of women waxing their cars was increasing. "[Women] account for a sizable segment, it's maybe 40 percent in some cases," stated Chuck Tornabene, as quoted in *Automotive Marketing*. "[In] developing our media plan, we're going to have to take women into consideration," he added. By January 1991 Tornabene had become vice-president and general manager, then president, of consumer products for Turtle Wax, Inc.

## Packaging

The original Plastone Liquid Car Polish was packaged in a squat glass bottle with a small, narrow neck for pouring. The label featured an automobile glowing from its wax job—lines emanated out in circular fashion from the car, like sun rays. In the early 1950s when the product, like the company, was renamed Turtle Wax, the bottle shape stayed the same. The label was changed, however, to feature a happy top-hatted turtle strutting across it, with the word "brilliant" encased in a splash of white, partially covering the shell. Various permutations followed, resulting in the green bottle we see today displaying the familiar turtle in a top hat and the words "hard shell finish" following the curve of the shell.

By 1987 approximately 70 percent of Turtle Wax's business was based on products introduced in the previous six years. The company's Chicago headquarters concentrated on liquid and paste wax packaging, farming out aerosols and specialty products. Company innovations included the industry's first plastic container for Super Hard Shell paste wax, custom-designed bottles for Clearguard, and a new pouch-within-a-pouch wax applicator. The Super Hard Shell plastic container featured an easy snap-on cap; previously, all manufacturers had packaged paste wax in metal cans requiring a screwdriver to open. Super Hard Shell liquid wax was redesigned as well, from a rounded bottle, which stacked four deep on a shelf, to an oval shape which stacked six bottles deep. The Clearguard customized "beaker bottle" was designed to highlight the clear consistency of the product, while being taller and wider than competing products.

As the Turtle Wax product line grew, so did the variation in color and theme. The 1993 company catalog displays an array of car-care products, with a wide variety of packaging styles. In 1990 Liquid Crystal, packaged in sleek black and gold, was introduced. The label touted the product as "The Ultimate 'Stop and Stare' Automobile Polish." Specialty waxes like Carnauba Soft Paste and Turtle Wax Plus with teflon were available. In 1991 another polish was introduced. Finish 2001—presumably designed to take car waxers into the twenty-first century—was packaged in bright lime-green, with a red label and black printing. Spin off products included Finish 2001 car wash, and both a tire cleaner and super protectant for vinyl and leather interiors under the Formula 2001 label.

In December 1990 Turtle Wax began labeling its paste wax cans in house, saving time and money. Previously, the polypropylene cans were molded and fitted with lids, allowed to set, then labeled, arriving back at Turtle Wax in roughly seven days. Once the company applied its own labels, the turn-around time dropped to two to three days, and company response time to retail orders was shortened commensurately. As Roger Gustafson, director of manufacturing, commented in *Packaging Digest:* "With the advent of electronic data interchange, [retailers] now expect an order in three to four days." With the new labeling system in place, Turtle Wax expected to save $85,000 annually, and still recoup the cost of equipment and labor within a year.

In 1992 Turtle Wax put full marketing support behind a line of colored waxes it had produced for years, but not advertised heavily. Television "infomercials" stirred interest in the product, which was developed to hide minor scratches and enhance the color of a vehicle. Color Magic sported a label with a rainbow, and was bottled in plastic containers of the eight available shades. The product breathed new life into "a market that doesn't change much, year to year,'' according to a 1992 survey in *Household and Personal Products Industry.*

## International Development

Turtle Wax has maintained a strong presence in the Canadian market since its introduction there in the late 1940s. With no manufacturing facilities in Canada, the company produced via contract packaging. The British arm of Turtle Wax, established in the mid-1960s, shipped products worldwide to areas not serviced by the U.S. or local manufacturing plants. Like the Chicago headquarters, which mixed and packaged car polish and shoe polish with many of the same machines in a surprisingly small amount of space, the British plant in Skelmersdale, near Manchester in northern England, ran up to 70 different products through six filling lines in 40,000 square feet of space. In the early 1990s, Turtle Wax expanded into the Japanese market through a joint venture with Autobaachs, Japan's largest automotive retail chain. By year-end 1992 the company sold twenty product-lines through that arrangement.

In the United States, Turtle Wax remained the dominant producer of automobile wax and polish, and was highly competitive in sales of car maintenance products and cleaners in late 1993. A growth area was the Turtle Wax Car Wash division of the company, with thirteen car washes up and running in Chicago.

## Further Reading:

"Auto Polishes: How Much Dazzle Can You Expect?" *Consumer Reports,* July 1981, p. 381.

Blickstead, Mary, "None Lasted as Long as Their Claims Might Have You Believe," *Canadian Consumer,* August 1986, p. 22.

Ceppos, Rich, "Simonizing Poetic," *Car and Driver,* January 1987, p. 22.

Chalmers, Ray, "New Packages Help Propel Turtle Wax to No. 1," *Packaging,* January 1987, p. 9.

Holmgren, Bruce, "Gain Peak Output in Spite of Many Products, Short Runs," *Packaging,* December 1985, p. 34.

Hume, Scott, "Turtle Wax Goes from Car to House," *Advertising Age,* June 22, 1987, p. 86.

Jannot, Mark, "Waxing Creative: Meet the Heirs of Ben Hirsch," *Chicago,* August 1988, p. 63.

"Label Changes Solve Scanning, Market-Positioning Problems," *Packaging,* April 1992, p. 15.

Liesse, Julie, "Chuck Tornabene: Executive Gives New Polish to Turtle Wax," *Advertising Age,* January 14, 1991, p. 28.

"Manufacturers Survey: Wax/Polish," *Automotive Marketing,* January 1983, p. 82.

McGeehan, Pat, "Turtle Wax Emerges from Car-Market Shell," *Advertising Age,* August 26, 1985, p. 4.

Randle, Wilma, "Strong Family Histories Help Turtle Wax Shine," *Chicago Tribune,* April 11, 1993, Sec. 7, p. 5.

Schwartz, Joe, "Turtle Wax Shines Water, Too," *American Demographics,* April 1992, p. 14.

Snyder, David, "Turtle Wax Speeds Up with New Ad Strategy," *Crain's Chicago Business,* August 25, 1986, p. 8.

"Turtle Wax Shines up Its Labeling Act," *Packaging Digest,* April 1991, p. 32.

"Wax Market Shows Slow Growth But Competition Quickens," *Automotive Marketing,* June 1991, p. 14.

"The Wax Market: Clear Coats, Competitors & Growth," *Automotive Marketing,* June 1990, p. 16.

"Will Wax Market Wane in 1988?," *Automotive Marketing,* January 1988, p. 16.

*—Frances E. Norton*

# TYLENOL®

# TYLENOL®

Tylenol is the brand name of the analgesic drug acetaminophen marketed by the McNeil Consumer Products Company, a division of Johnson & Johnson. It is the number one over-the-counter drug in America, out-selling all other pain relievers. Originally a low profile brand marketed primarily to doctors and hospitals, Tylenol enjoyed a precipitous rise in popularity when it began heavy advertising directly to the public in the mid-1970s. Because, unlike aspirin, Tylenol could be dispensed as a liquid, it was long recommended by doctors as a fever reducer for children. Adult Tylenol took hold as a pain relief alternative for people who could not tolerate aspirin. Tylenol now covers a complete line of infant, child, and junior strength pain relievers, regular and extra strength adult formulas, and acetaminophen-based combination medications for colds, flu, upset stomach, and wakefulness. Tylenol was a late-comer to the fiercely competitive analgesic market, where essentially identical aspirin brands battled to prove their superiority over each other. Tylenol's sudden rise in sales reconfigured the entire market and set off a slew of new acetaminophen-based brands. But none of these could catch Tylenol, which has held the top share position since 1977.

## Brand Origins

Tylenol's active ingredient, acetaminophen, was first synthesized in 1878, and its fever- and pain-reducing powers were documented in the ensuing decades. But there was little interest in acetaminophen until the 1950s, when medical researchers found it to be equivalent to aspirin in its analgesic powers. A small Pennsylvania pharmaceutical company, McNeil Laboratories, came across some promising scientific reports on acetaminophen in 1951 and decided to market the drug. The Food and Drug Administration granted McNeil a license for Tylenol in 1955. McNeil sold Tylenol as a pediatric drug in liquid form until 1959, when the FDA granted the company permission to market an adult version as well.

McNeil promoted Tylenol primarily to doctors and avoided direct consumer advertising. Tylenol slowly gained recognition as an alternative to aspirin, and by 1965 was one of the 200 most frequently prescribed drugs. All the while, Tylenol was available without a prescription. But its relatively high cost and lack of advertising made it no competition for the better-known brands of aspirin.

## Commercial Success

McNeil was unwilling to change marketing tactics by advertising its product directly to the public, fearing that consumer ads would alienate the doctors who prescribed Tylenol. But in 1959 McNeil had been bought by the giant health products firm of Johnson & Johnson. Johnson & Johnson realized the potential of Tylenol, and wanted it marketed just like aspirin, that is, with extensive media advertising. Any company could acquire a license to market acetaminophen, and Johnson & Johnson was afraid that it would get scooped by another company if it did not push Tylenol. McNeil managers were reluctant to accept the parent company's advice, and Johnson & Johnson even came out briefly with its own brand of acetaminophen, called Truce.

Then, in 1968, the Bristol-Myers company launched an acetaminophen product. The advertising for its new "Neotrend" harped on the dangers of aspirin's possible side-effects and declared, "We replaced aspirin." Jolted into action at last, McNeil had already decided to spend $700,000 advertising Tylenol by the time Bristol Myers' Neotrend debuted. Tylenol's modest ads ran, "Many doctors have long recommended Tylenol, and your drugstore has it without a prescription." Subsequently, Tylenol sales grew, and Neotrend disappeared from the market.

By 1969, Tylenol had a 2.5 percent share of the non-prescription analgesic market, with annual sales of around $10 million. McNeil continued to advertise, but spent only a fraction of what the major aspirin makers did. Tylenol's market share crept steadily upwards, to stand at slightly over 10 percent by 1974. In 1975 Bristol-Myers decided to take on Tylenol again with another acetaminophen product, this time called Datril. Bristol-Myers had promoted its failed Neotrend as an alternative to aspirin. In contrast, the company marketed Datril as an alternative to Tylenol. The results of this tactic were far from what Bristol-Myers expected.

Since Datril and Tylenol were essentially the same, both consisting of acetaminophen, Datril could not be fairly promoted as being superior to Tylenol. But it was less expensive. Ad copy for Datril stated that Datril cost a dollar less than Tylenol. Consumers in test markets proved happy to save money with Datril, and Tylenol's market share in the test cities plummeted.

## AT A GLANCE

**T**ylenol brand analgesic licensed by the Food & Drug Administration in 1955 to McNeil Laboratories, Fort Washington, PA; McNeil became a division of Johnson & Johnson, 1959.

*Performance:* *Market share*—27% (top share; 1989) of the adult non-prescription analgesic category. *Sales*—$570 million (1990).

*Major competitor:* American Home Product Co.'s Advil brand ibuprofen; also, aspirin brands and brands that come in an acetaminophen formula, such as Bayer, Excedrin, and Anacin.

*Advertising:* *Agency*—Saatchi & Saatchi, New York, NY, 1975—. *Major campaign*—"The pain reliever hospitals use most."

*Addresses:* *Parent company*—McNeil Consumer Products Company, Camp Hill Road, Fort Washington, PA 19034; phone: (215) 233-7000. *Ultimate parent company*—Johnson & Johnson, One Johnson & Johnson Plaza, New Brunswick, NJ 08933; phone (908) 524-0400.

Johnson & Johnson got ready to fight for Tylenol. First off, the company slashed prices on Tylenol to meet Datril. Then Johnson & Johnson lawyers hectored the television networks for carrying Datril's ads, which were now incorrect, as Datril did not cost a dollar less than Tylenol any more. Bristol-Myers was forced to rewrite the ads. The first rewrite claimed that Datril "can cost less. A lot less" than Tylenol. Then further badgering by Johnson & Johnson resulted in the "A lot less" being dropped. Johnson & Johnson continued to cut Tylenol prices, and so a later version of the Datril ad ran, "Datril can cost less depending on where you shop." The final installment merely advised consumers to shop around and "buy the one that costs less." Not only did Bristol-Myers' campaign fail to sell its own product, but the Datril ads presented the Tylenol name to consumers who may never have heard of it.

With Tylenol pushed unexpectedly into the spotlight, Johnson & Johnson decided to launch a major ad campaign of its own. The parent company sent a marketing team headed by Wayne Nelson to subsidiary McNeil, and the team plotted a strategy to bring Tylenol to the top. After spending over $1 million on research and development, Johnson & Johnson came out with "Extra-Strength Tylenol" in May of 1976. The extra-strength tablets were 500 milligrams, up from the regular dose of 325 milligrams. McNeil had long promoted Tylenol as a safe product, gentler than aspirin and recommended by doctors, and the company thought that might give the drug the aura of lesser pain relieving power than aspirin. The extra-strength version of Tylenol was advertised with the slogan, "You can't buy a more potent pain reliever without a prescription." This image of potency coupled with Tylenol's reputation for safety led to blockbuster sales. During the Datril campaign, Tylenol's share of the analgesic market climbed four percentage points; with the introduction of Extra-Strength, Tylenol nosed out Bufferin and Anacin, and took the number one slot.

### Competition with Aspirin

Bristol-Myers' Datril campaign shook Tylenol out of its low-key marketing style, and the brand rose to the top with astonishing speed. But once Tylenol had achieved front-runner status, it was forced to become involved in one hard-hitting campaign after another, as the established brands of pain reliever struggled to regain their former prominence. Bayer aspirin took on Tylenol directly with a 1977 ad centered on a Food and Drug Administration report that Bayer declared "found no basis for the claim that aspirin substitutes are safer than aspirin." The FDA did not appreciate being used in this way, and the agency promptly asked Sterling Drug Inc., makers of Bayer, to drop the ad, saying it was confusing and misleading. The FDA also warned Tylenol to make sure its ads were fair and accurate. Sterling was not ready to give up, and the company sent a variety of scientific reports to the FDA, detailing side-effects of acetaminophen. Sterling demanded that a large warning label be placed on Tylenol bottles, alerting consumers to possible liver damage. Johnson & Johnson responded by providing the FDA with other material affirming the safety of acetaminophen. This material came from the makers of a British brand of acetaminophen called Panadol; the makers of Panadol just happened to be Sterling Drug. Sterling sold only aspirin in the United States and only acetaminophen in the United Kingdom. Its Panadol brand had enjoyed huge success by warning the British public of the dangers of aspirin. Sterling's inconsistency was apparent.

The following year saw Johnson & Johnson in court with American Home Products Co., makers of Anacin brand aspirin. Anacin's advertising had claimed that "Your body knows the difference" between Tylenol and Anacin, and said that Anacin was more effective than Tylenol because it was better at reducing inflammation. A district court judge ruled that this claim was deceptive, but Johnson & Johnson had to take American Home Products back to court to keep a slightly altered ad from running. When American Home released its new "Maximum-Strength Anacin" in 1978, Johnson & Johnson went to court again, alleging an unfair comparison between "Maximum-Strength" and its "Extra-Strength." This kind of lawsuit characterized the analgesic market, because the different brands were presumed by the FDA to be identical in their effects, so none could claim actual superiority. Johnson & Johnson found itself involved in almost continuous lawsuits, and in disputes brokered by the FDA and the Federal Trade Commission, as the aspirin brands kept trying to disparage Tylenol in their ads.

When the aspirin makers were unable to get past Johnson & Johnson in court, they came out with their own acetaminophens. Anacin produced Anacin-3, and Bayer aspirin was now accompanied by Bayer Non-Aspirin. But Tylenol had been there first, and these new brands could not compete. Tylenol continued to gain customers. By 1981, it had garnered almost one-third of the entire analgesic market, and was still rising.

### Tamperings

In 1980 Johnson & Johnson began to market its Extra-Strength Tylenol in capsule form. These capsules were remarkably successful. They sold for more than the regular tablets, so profits for the company were higher. They went over very well with consumers, presumably because capsules looked more like prescription drugs than did tablets, and so seemed more powerful; also, many people found them easier to swallow. Fueled by the success of the new format, Tylenol sales stood at more than $350 million by the end of 1981, and Tylenol's market share reached over 35 percent. Johnson & Johnson executives were predicting that Tylenol would grab 50 percent of the analgesic market in the next five years.

A tragedy dashed these hopeful predictions in September of 1982, when seven people in Chicago died from cyanide poisoning after swallowing tainted Tylenol capsules. Investigators quickly discovered that the Extra-Strength capsules had been tampered with at the retail level. Some one had removed the bottles from the shelves, opened the capsules and added cyanide, then returned the poisoned containers to their places. Johnson & Johnson was clearly not at fault, and the incidents appeared to be confined to the west side of Chicago. Yet the public was understandably alarmed. Executives from McNeil and Johnson & Johnson acted quickly to suspend all Tylenol advertising and recall all 31 million bottles of Extra-Strength capsules from across the country. Sales of all Tylenol products dropped 80 percent, and the cost of the recall was a staggering $100 million. Market analysts widely predicted that Tylenol would never recover.

Johnson & Johnson soon put Tylenol capsules back on the shelf, now in triple sealed, tamper-proof packages. The company placed $2.50 coupons good toward any Tylenol product in newspapers nationwide and began an expensive advertising campaign. Public opinion polls showed that most people believed Johnson & Johnson had acted quickly and responsibly in dealing with the sabotage, and Tylenol customers had strong loyalty to their brand. A year after the poisonings, Tylenol had regained 30 percent of the over-the-counter analgesic market, and the crisis was over for the time being.

The new packages featured three different seals—the flaps of the box glued down, a plastic ring around the mouth and neck of the bottle, and a foil seal under the cap, across the mouth of the bottle. But even with these protective measures in place, a second tampering case occurred in February of 1986, again with cyanide, killing a New York woman. The method of the tampering remained a mystery. Johnson & Johnson's chairman quickly announced another recall. The company promoted its traditional Tylenol tablets, as well as "caplets," a long, smooth, easy to swallow tablet that had been introduced several years before. Then Johnson & Johnson informed the press that the company would no longer sell any over-the-counter drugs in capsule form.

## Brand Development

With the loss of its profitable capsule category, Tylenol went on to face new challenges. The over-the-counter analgesic market had begun to change in 1984, when two drug companies applied to the FDA to be allowed to market a new non-prescription painkiller, ibuprofen. Bristol-Myers soon brought out Nuprin, and American Home Products Co. came out with Advil. These brands threatened to alter the analgesic market the way Tylenol had some ten years earlier, wiping out the established sellers with a new, perhaps improved product. Johnson & Johnson hoped that, if Advil and Nuprin caught on, they would further erode aspirin sales and leave Tylenol alone. In 1985 ibuprofen products took 8 percent of the non-prescription painkiller market; in 1986 their market share had jumped to around 15 percent. Most of this increase did come at the expense of aspirin, and Advil's sales of around $85 million in 1986 were still far below Tylenol's total sales, estimated at $525 million in 1985.

Nevertheless, the makers of Tylenol moved to protect the brand by expanding the Tylenol line. Junior Tylenol, for 6- to 14-year olds, came out in December of 1983. By 1990, the children's category had expanded to include Junior Strength Chewable Tylenol tablets, an infant dosage, and several child dosages differing by the intended user's weight. Tylenol Cold and Tylenol Sinus medicines debuted in the mid-1980s, and Tylenol Extra-Strength Antacid was introduced in 1988. The latter was meant to compete with Alka-Seltzer, and was a stomach medicine and headache painkiller in one. Alka-Seltzer responded by bringing out its own acetaminophen combination product, called Alka-Seltzer Headache Medicine, so the two brands were even. Tylenol Cold Nighttime, a cherry-flavored liquid, came out in 1990, as did Tylenol Cold & Flu, a lemon-flavored powder to be mixed with hot water. These two were similar to existing products, Nyquil nighttime cold medicine and TheraFlu brand flu relief, respectively. A 1991 line extension was apparently too closely modelled on an existing brand, and Johnson & Johnson found itself in court. Tylenol PM, a painkiller/sleep-aid combination, used similar packaging to the 20-year-old Excedrin PM brand, angering Excedrin's maker, Bristol-Myers. Johnson & Johnson prevailed in court, and these line extensions widened Tylenol's presence in the growing cold relief market and seemed a successful strategy to bank against ibuprofen's encroachment in the analgesic market.

## Performance Appraisal

Tylenol's aggressive brand development kept it the top-selling over-the-counter drug, with yearly sales more than twice that of its nearest competitor. Despite the fact that ibuprofen products, particularly Advil, gained rapidly in sales and market share in the 1990s, Tylenol's top position seemed solid. Market share estimates for the early 1990s gave Tylenol around 27 percent of the adult non-prescription painkiller market, or 31 percent including children's products. This was below the 35 percent market share Tylenol had held a decade earlier, but still represented a much bigger share than any other analgesic, as the number two brand, Advil, had only 12 percent. Tylenol had a formidable reputation that had allowed it to vault past all the established analgesic brands when it began to be widely advertised in the 1970s, and the brand had weathered terrible crises in the 1980s with the tampering cases. The over-the-counter drug market was turbulent and still growing in the early 1990s, and competition was as intense as it had ever been. Yet Tylenol evidently has a strong base of consumer trust, and so it may long remain the top-selling painkiller.

## Further Reading:

"A 'Safer' Tylenol Gets a Second Chance," *Newsweek,* November 22, 1982, p. 100.

"After Its Recovery, New Headaches for Tylenol," *Business Week,* May 14, 1984, p. 137.

"An Industry Reaches to the Converted," *Superbrands,* 1991, pp. 108–09.

Christopher, Maureen, "Datril/Tylenol Ad Battle Sparks NBC Policy Move," *Advertising Age,* August 11, 1975, p. 1.

Davidson, Spencer, "A Replay of the Tylenol Scare," *Time,* February 24, 1986, p. 22.

Deveny, Kathleen, "Painkiller Ads Strive to Give Foes Headaches," *Wall Street Journal,* January 23, 1990, p. B1.

"Finally, Tylenol Campaign Set for National Debut," *Advertising Age,* July 12, 1976, p. 3.

Freeman, Laurie, "Alka-Seltzer Fights Move by Tylenol," *Advertising Age,* April 3, 1989, p. 4.

Giges, Nancy, "FDA Bad-Mouths Bayer and Tylenol Advertising," *Advertising Age,* December 19, 1977, p. 2.

"Hard to Swallow," *Time,* March 9, 1992, p. 49.

"J & J Sends Tylenol after Alka-Seltzer," *Advertising Age,* November 21, 1988, p. 2.

"J & J Yanks Ads; Tylenol Reeling," *Advertising Age,* October 4, 1982, p. 1.

"Judge Rules for Tylenol; Anacin Ordered to Halt Inflammation Ad Claims," *Advertising Age,* August 22, 1977, p. 1.

Koepp, Stephen, "A Hard Decision to Swallow," *Time,* March 3, 1986, p. 59.

"Long-Awaited Tylenol Ad Drive Highlights Extra-Strength Tablet," *Advertising Age,* May 17, 1976, p. 2.

Mann, Charles C. and Plummer, Mark L., *The Aspirin Wars: Money, Medicine, and 100 Years of Rampant Competition,* New York: Alfred A. Knopf, 1991.

Moore, Thomas, "The Fight to Save Tylenol," *Fortune,* November 29, 1982, p. 44.

"New Headaches in the Painkiller Market," *Fortune,* September 15, 1986, p. 10.

"One Year Later, Tylenol Faces New Challenge," *Advertising Age,* September 26, 1983, p. 3.

"Prescription for Growth," *Forbes,* June 26, 1978, pp. 97–99.

Sloan, Pat, "Tylenol Launches 'Comeback' Ads," *Advertising Age,* January 3, 1983, p. 1.

"Two-Time Loser," *Advertising Age,* February 17, 1986, p. 1.

"Tylenol Comes Back as Case Grows Cold," *Newsweek,* April 25, 1983, p. 16.

"Tylenol Expands with Cold Remedies," *Advertising Age,* August 27, 1990, p. 3.

"Tylenol Fallout," *Broadcasting,* October 11, 1982, p. 74.

"Tylenol Gains in Court Fight with Anacin," *Advertising Age,* May 8, 1978, p. 2.

"Tylenol Tablets Leading Rebound," *Advertising Age,* December 13, 1982, p. 1.

"Tylenol's 'Miracle' Comeback," *Time,* October 17, 1983, p. 67.

Winters, Patricia, "Excedrin Bangs Tylenol," *Advertising Age,* August 13, 1990, p. 3.

—*A. Woodward*

# VAN HEUSEN®

# VAN HEUSEN®

VAN HEUSEN®

The rise of the Van Heusen brand dress shirt and the growth of the United States apparel industry in the twentieth century are closely intertwined. Van Heusen was the first company to produce collar-attached dress shirts in 1919. In 1920 inventor John M. Van Heusen successfully developed methods for weaving cloth on a curve and for producing a no-wrinkle one-piece collar with a liner insert. These inventions gave birth to the "Van Heusen collar," which "revolutionized the entire dress shirt industry," according to *Time* magazine. Subsequent brand precedents included wash-and-wear shirts in 1956 and the permanent press shirt in 1965. In 1970 specially designed body shirts were followed by the all cotton permanent press shirt in 1978.

Van Heusen shirts held a meager two percent market share to rival Arrow brand's 25 percent in 1967. It was not until 1991, under the forward looking leadership of the Phillips-Van Heusen Corporation, that the brand overtook its principle rival and steadily gained market share as the number one selling dress shirt in the United States. The seeds for the brand's triumph where planted in 1987 when the Phillips-Van Heusen Corporation launched a dramatic internal restructuring which transformed the company into a vertically integrated manufacturer, marketer, and retailer of brand name dress shirts. As part of its overall strategy, the company was a forerunner of retailing through outlet mall shops and remains a dominant force in the field.

The Phillips family has remained at the management helm of Van Heusen's corporation for four generations. Noting the company's union-free record of success in a highly volatile industry, Lawrence Phillips, chairman of Phillips-Van Heusen Corporation, remarked in *Forbes* that "During [the 1987] recession, we have never had to close a factory. In fact, we have expanded capacity."

## Brand Origins

The origins of the Van Heusen dress shirt brand date back to a 1907 merger between the companies of D. Jones and Sons and M. Phillips and Sons, from which the Phillips-Jones Corporation was formed. D. Jones and Sons had been active in the shirt business since 1859 and had operated a string of manufacturing facilities throughout Lebanon County, Pennsylvania. M. Phillips and Sons was founded by Polish immigrant Moses Phillips who arrived in the United States in 1881. Phillips settled in a one-room flat in Pottsville, Pennsylvania, heart of the state's bustling anthracite coal region, and Phillips' wife stitched homemade flannel shirts

which Moses would sell to the Pottsville miners. From the humble proceeds of selling two to three shirts a day with his pushcart—his total sales in 1881 were $250.00—Phillips financed the arrival of other family members, who in turn helped expand the family business. Soon Phillips' pushcart was replaced by a horse and buggy, and he extended his market to neighboring coal towns.

In July, 1957, the Phillips-Jones Corporation changed its name to the Phillips-Van Heusen Corporation. The company was incorporated in 1976. Since its formation, Phillips-Van Heusen has emphasized the high quality of its shirts along with a no-frills corporate philosophy. Company chairman Lawrence Phillips recollected walking through the family's factories as a youth and picking pins off the floor with his father and grandfather. Recent company policy reflects this view as the company neither owns nor leases a plane and all upper-level managers, chairman included, are forbidden to fly first class.

## Early Product Development and Advertising

The success of the Van Heusen dress shirt can be attributed to the company's foresight in being one of the few major shirt producers to recognize that the rising popularity of the collar-attached dress shirt was more than just a passing fad. Ironically, what was to shortly attain the status of the standard men's dress shirt first made its appearance as a working class garment common to factory floors and mills. The white, collar-attached dress shirt became the rage immediately following World War I. The comfortable experience of wearing collar-attached military shirts had left a favorable impression on the five million men who served in the armed forces. Upon their discharge from military duty, the soldiers continued to favor the collar-attached dress shirt, and sales of these shirts, made from imported broadcloth fabric, sky-rocketed. The detachable neck band shirt, long an industry standard, was soon eclipsed by the new fashion. Phillips-Van Heusen was an exception to most of the older clothing companies who refused to accommodate consumers' changing tastes and ceased to be competitive.

Perhaps the most historic moment for Van Heusen shirts, and for the men's shirt industry as a whole, occurred in 1920 when John M. Van Heusen devised a method for weaving cloth on a curve. Van Heusen applied this technique to the production of men's dress shirt collars and scored a stylistic coup. Gone were the irritable wrinkled folds that formed when a straight piece of cloth

## AT A GLANCE

**V**an Heusen brand dress shirts founded in 1907 in Pennsylvania by the Phillips-Jones Corporation, which was formed by the merger of D. Jones and Sons, founded in 1859, and M. Phillips and Sons, founded in 1887; renamed the Phillips-Van Heusen Corporation, 1957.

**Performance:** *Market share*—10.6% (top share) of dress shirt category (1992). *Sales*—$1 billion company-wide (1992).

**Major competitor:** Bidermann Industries' Arrow.

**Advertising:** *Agency*— Lintas, New York, 1988—. *Major campaign*—"Picture Yourself in Van Heusen."

**Addresses:** *Parent company*—Phillips-Van Heusen Corporation, 1290 Avenue of the Americas, New York, NY 10104-0101; phone: (212) 541-5200; fax: (212) 468-7064.

was fitted into a curve. Instead, Van Heusen's process executed a smooth fold line that added to the shirts wearing comfort and further added to the respectable gentlemanly quality ascribed to men's dress shirts.

This weaving process also led to the one-piece collar, which soon became the industry standard—a collar of uniform thickness without any lining that could be wrinkled or buckled. After securing a patent, Van Heusen began to differentiate the dress shirt product line. Each new line of shirts emphasized a collar style and height slightly different from its predecessor, and the name of each different type collar began with the trademark "Van" title. By 1929 a person could purchase the Van Jack, Van Nord, Van Kissel, Van Fame, Van Esty, Van Garde, Van Dort, Van Ince, Van Todd and Van Turo styles of collared shirts from Van Heusen.

The "Van Heusen Collar" was widely promoted via the print media in the 1920s. Full page advertisements placed in general publications like the *Saturday Evening Post* and *Collier's* prominently displayed the large print slogan that Van Heusen dress shirts had "The World's Smartest Collar." Ad copy notified the consumer of the various qualities and comforts associated with the shirt. For instance, the Van Heusen collar shirt was touted as being "correct for all occasions formal and informal" and "laundered entirely without starch." Van Heusen advertisements further asserted that they "save[d] shirts and ties," and were always "perfect in appearance."

### Recent Product Development and Structure

Since 1987 the principle products and line extensions of the Phillips-Van Heusen Corporation have been apparel and footwear. The company's apparel products group is split into five separate brand marketing divisions: Van Heusen, Bass, Designer Group, Private Label—Dress and Sports Shirts, and Private Label—Sweaters and Knitwear. Phillips-Van Heusen markets its apparel lines through its wholesale division and company-owned retail outlets.

The motivation to pursue a growth strategy that transformed the company into a vertically-integrated operation arose from a number of fundamental changes that impacted the retail apparel industry. First, a number of the company's longstanding wholesale customers who operated department and specialty stores had been teetering on the brink of financial ruin for several years. Second, the consolidation of several independent retail chains served to

increase their purchasing power clout. Third, established department stores began merchandising private label brands that would impinge on Van Heusen's profit margins. Finally, Phillips-Van Heusen recognized that a permanent shift in consumer buying habits was underway; consumers were no longer satisfied with the generic approach to traditional retailing and were moving instead to a value-oriented approach in search of specific brand names. To meet these pressures, Phillips-Van Heusen began to directly market their apparel lines through company-owned manufacturers' outlet stores.

A critical component of the brand's new vertically integrated business strategy was a flexible design, manufacturing, and sourcing network. Facilities in the United States, Puerto Rico, and the Caribbean serviced the brand's wholesale marketing division. Coordination between facilities was conducted on a cost-efficient basis which emphasized their state-of-the-art inventory management systems and cost-reducing manufacturing techniques that enhanced brand quality.

The company-owned Van Heusen brand retail outlets were linked to a management system known as PVH International (PVH-I). This system was formed to develop, design, and administer the company's "retail only" line of Van Heusen brand apparel and monitor the brand from conception to in-store delivery. The Van Heusen brand outlet stores carried a full line of products which, other than men's dress shirts and woven and knit sports shirts, were not merchandised to its wholesale customers. The line featured men's classic and traditional dress shirts and neckwear, men's and women's sportswear, active wear, and casual wear.

Although the amount of time from initial design to finished product varies for each Van Heusen shirt type, most shirts fall within a time span of nine months to one year between conception and introduction to the market. Commitments to procure the supply of raw materials are taken four to 12 months in advance of production. In addition, the quick response feature of the brand's PVH Pulse System was designed to monitor information regarding the levels of wholesale and retail sales so that production adjustments could be made to increase or decrease the product's availability.

All of Van Heusen's brand name apparel products were designed in-house by numerous merchandise/product development groups. Members were drawn from fabric designers, product line builders, and retail store merchants who took consumer tastes, fashion, history, and the prevailing economic climate into consideration before the seasonal introduction of a particular product.The concept of ongoing employee empowerment has also figured largely in the company's successful restructuring. Phillips-Van Heusen has pursued a corporate policy whereby both its store and factory workers are given the authority and skills to participate in the decision-making process within their own area of responsibility.

### Recent Marketing Strategies

Another key element of Van Heusen's integrated strategy was the formation and expansion of its own retail operation. The idea was to offer the brand in markets where it had little previous exposure. The targeted customers were value-oriented consumers whose shopping habits did not include frequent visits to the brand's wholesale establishments. Van Heusen's participation in manufacturers' outlet malls proved to be the perfect fit. Most outlet malls were located in tourist/vacation areas or along major thoroughfares leading to these areas. They attracted shopping enthusiasts with significant disposable income and minimized conflict with the brand's wholesale customers. To promote the brand's status as a retail-only concept, store layout, presentation, packaging, sales personnel, product, and price were planned with a product-enhancing effect in mind.

Additional advantages of the brand's retail only format was the opportunity to quickly liquidate excess and out-of-fashion inventory "seconds" which otherwise would be sold to outside discounters at considerably marked down prices. Outlet stores also minimized the potential damage to the brand's image caused by discounters' substandard in-store presentation and advertisements. In 1992 Van Heusen retail outlet stores numbered 234; most were located in the Northeast. The brand's major wholesale customers were May Co., Federated Stores, Dayton Hudson, J.C. Penney, Macy's, and Mercantile Stores.

The Phillips-Van Heusen Corporation also maintained a real estate department which assisted in planning and designing their new stores. The department's role was to locate appropriate sites dependent upon demographics, model store size, estimated volume and operating returns, and available lease arrangements. Prior to construction, the store planning and design department informed landlords, division heads, contractors, and developers of their interior plans. Once construction was underway, a project manager oversaw the installation of fixtures and monitored workmanship to verify that it adhered to company standards.

## Advertising Strategies

Since the 1920s Van Heusen has aimed its advertising efforts at a national audience in order to facilitate brand awareness and recognition among all U.S. consumers. By 1992 adults from 25-54 years of age were the targeted demographic. According to Ron Sok, the apparel group's vice president of communications, Van Heusen's magazine ad campaigns aimed for a 40 percent male and 60 percent female audience. The emphasis on female advertising, Sok explained, was based on research which indicated that 67 percent of Van Heusen shirts were purchased by women.

Van Heusen's ads are concentrated in the national print media. Magazine ads typically run in publications that specialize in fashion, entertainment, business, and sports. To a lesser extent, Van Heusen undertakes joint advertising efforts with individual retailers to locally promote the brand and share the cost of store radio, television, newspaper, and in-store advertisements and promotional events. Local outlet mall advertising is conducted through multiple formats such as highway billboards and brochures and travel magazines, as well as direct marketing aimed at tour bus companies and travel agencies. Ever since the brand has gained an international presence, advertising campaigns, like those in South America, target and carry themes meant to appeal to the growing numbers of the educated population.

## International Growth

By 1992 Van Heusen had secured agreements with 19 international licensees to manufacture and market the brand's products in 24 countries throughout North, Central, and South America. Prior to this, the brand's international growth through licensing arrangements had been its only option given the longstanding problems posed by trade barriers and restrictions. One licensing partner, Van Heusen de Mexico, had been in existence for over 50 years. As reported in the *Daily Record News,* Phillips-Van Heusen reached a 1992 licensing agreement with the John Forsyth Co., Inc. to manufacture and distribute a line of dress shirts carrying the Van Heusen trademark in Canada. These are retailed through Eatons, one of Canada's largest department stores.

Although trade legislation provoked a storm of controversy within the U.S. apparel industry, Phillips-Van Heusen looked favorably upon the enactment of the North American Free Trade Agreement (NAFTA). The company believed that the passage of NAFTA would open up new opportunities which would allow Van Heusen to sell its finished products to its licensees and, in turn, the licensees could engage in the trade of finished products with one another. Bruce Klatsky, president of Phillips-Van Heusen, praised the NAFTA pact in the *Daily News Record* as legislation that would enable the corporation "to further our prime corporate objective of expanding U.S. employment by exporting products to Mexico." To facilitate these trade flows, Van Heusen organized a trading company to assist licensees in the purchase of company-based textiles and products.

## Future Trends

Through the years Van Heusen brand dress shirts have continued to prosper despite the country's economic climate. The company has demonstrated a willingness to invest in its own people, systems, support groups, and retail concepts in spite of the industry's fad-driven nature. An investment report prepared by Stephens Inc., suggests that the brand's aggressive foray into its own retail outlet store format should continue to bolster its market share leadership position. It also looked favorably upon wholesale division sales, which have made a significant rebound since 1991 when J.C. Penney, the brand's largest customer, introduced Van Heusen shirts. By 1993 approximately 1000 J.C. Penney stores were merchandising the Van Heusen brand. Should the expected forecasts surrounding the implementation of NAFTA prove accurate, the Van Heusen shirt should retain its strong market share and position within the apparel industry.

## Further Reading:

Arnold, Pauline, *Clothes and Cloth: America's Apparel Business,* New York: Holiday House Press, 1961.

Hart, Elena, "Van Heusen Canada," *Daily News Record,* October 9, 1992, p. 4.

Lloyd, Brenda, "Outlook Favorable For U.S. Dress Shirts," *Daily News Record,* August 7, 1992, p. 2.

Morgenson, Gretchen, "We're Still Hungry," *Forbes,* October 14, 1991, pp. 60–62.

Ostroff, Jim, "NAFTA Draws Mixed Reviews," *Daily News Record,* August 13, 1992, p. 1.

Phillips-Van Heusen Annual Report, New York: Phillips-Van Heusen Corporation, 1992.

Ryan, Thomas J., "P-VH Sees Its Outlets Surpassing 1,400 Units," *Daily News Record,* May 15, 1993, p. 1.

—*Daniel E. King*

# VASELINE®

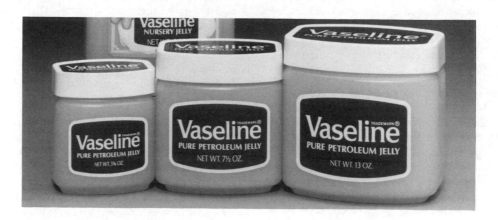

Vaseline brand petroleum jelly, discovered as a byproduct of the oil refinery process in the 19th century, became the top-selling brand of petroleum jelly in the United States. Highly credible as a medicinal product for relief for dry skin, the Vaseline name was extended to a line of other skin care products, such as Vaseline Intensive Care Lotion and Vaseline Intensive Care Hand and Nail Formula Lotion.

## Brand Origins

In 1859 a young chemist named Robert A. Chesebrough was busy in his lab, working on a distilling process that would turn "rod wax," the waxy substance found on the rods of oil pumps, into the present-day Vaseline petroleum jelly. Chesebrough was already in the business of refining crude oil from cannel coal in Brooklyn and manufacturing kerosene and other lubricating oils.

At age 22, he had accidentally found the wax while investigating the first oil strike in the United States in Titusville, Pennsylvania. Workers in the field raved about how this paraffin-like rod wax worked as a salve for burns and cuts. The only down side was that rod wax would gum up the machinery and bring work to a halt.

Bringing it back to his lab in Brooklyn, Chesebrough slaved for months, often acting as a human guinea pig to see if it would work. According to *Getting It Right the Second Time,* Chesebrough knew the Egyptians used oil as a healing balm. So he extracted rod wax into the form of a clear jelly. To test each sample, he would cut, burn, and otherwise injure himself. Chesebrough's efforts finally paid off with the invention of Vaseline brand petroleum jelly in 1870. The word Vaseline comes from the German word "wasser" for water and the Greek "elaion" for olive oil.

## Early Marketing Strategy

Chesebrough then began producing Vaseline petroleum jelly in quantity. To market it, he sent free samples to doctors and apothecaries hoping to drum up enough interest for drugstore distribution. When the medical community panned its health benefits, Chesebrough took to the streets of upper New York State with horse and buggy and handed out free jars of Vaseline to every person he met. Chesebrough had to sell the product's benefits and convince skeptics to try something that "came from underneath the ground." According to *Getting It Right the Second Time,*

"some were afraid it might explode; however, such fears disappeared once Chesebrough showed them how useful the jelly could be for soothing cuts and burns."

Newly won consumers would ask their local druggists to reorder the Vaseline brand and soon Chesebrough's "direct marketing" efforts paid off. With the help of a horse-and-buggy sales force, Vaseline petroleum jelly sold around the New York, New Jersey, and Connecticut areas at a rate of about a jar a minute. Favorable reviews appeared in the *Lancet,* Great Britain's medical journal. The Vaseline brand's international reputation was given more impetus when it was displayed at the Paris Exposition of 1878, according to the company's 100th anniversary report.

Chesebrough incorporated the Chesebrough Manufacturing Company in 1880 and a year later sold out to his source of supply, the Standard Oil Company. The Chesebrough Manufacturing Company functioned independently of its parent and grew in size and prestige with Chesebrough himself at the helm as president and operating head. When the Standard Oil Trust was dissolved in 1911, Chesebrough was free to operate entirely as an independent company.

In 1955 the company merged with the Pond's Extract Company of Clinton, Connecticut, to form Chesebrough-Pond's. Wall Street hailed the merger as "the marriage of Aristocrats." Chesebrough, however, did not live to see the day. He died September 8, 1933, and left to his company several tracts of land in Manhattan. In the early 1970s Chesebrough-Pond's moved its corporate headquarters from New York to its current location in Greenwich, Connecticut. In 1987 Chesebrough-Pond's was acquired by British/Netherlands-based Unilever, Inc., which promoted the Vaseline brand and its extended product line and helped make it a top-selling name globally.

## Early Successes

Vaseline proved to be a versatile product beyond Chesebrough's dreams, thanks to consumers who thought up many ways to use it. In 1916 the brand spun off as Vaseline hair tonic. For his own health, Chesebrough dutifully swallowed a spoonful of Vaseline every day for 35 years. When in his late 50s and seriously ill with pleurisy, Chesebrough reportedly was rubbed head to toe with Vaseline and recovered to live until age 96.

## AT A GLANCE

**V**aseline brand originated when Vaseline petroleum jelly was invented by Robert Chesebrough, a chemist and founder of Chesebrough Manufacturing Company of Brooklyn, NY, in 1859; Vaseline became a registered trademark in 1905; the Vaseline product line expanded to include hand and body lotions and bath beads called Vaseline Intensive Care (launched in 1970), Vaseline Lip Therapy (1984), Vaseline Ultra-Therapeutic Lotion, Vaseline Intensive Care Moisturizing SunCare Lotion, and Vaseline Intensive Care Hand and Nail Formula Lotion (1989); the company was briefly bought and sold by the Standard Oil Company and eventually merged with Pond's Extract Company in 1955 to form Chesebrough-Pond's; in 1987, Chesebrough-Pond's was acquired by the Netherlands-based Unilever, Inc.

**Performance:** *Market share*—23.6% of hand and body lotion category in units sold.

**Major competitor:** Private label or generic petroleum jelly brands; also KAO's Jergens, Warner-Lambert's Lubriderm, S.C. Johnson's Soft Sense.

**Advertising:** *Agency*—McCann-Erickson Worldwide, New York, NY, 1989—. *Major campaign*—*Good Morning America*'s Joan Lunden delivering "Skin Science Updates" in a news-style campaign."

**Addresses:** *Parent company*—Chesebrough-Pond's USA, 33 Benedict Place, Greenwich, CT 06836-6000; phone: (203) 661-2000; fax: (203) 625-1602. *Ultimate parent company*—Unilever USA, 390 Park Ave., New York, NY 10022-4698; phone: (212) 888-1260; fax: (212) 906-4411.

Vaseline petroleum jelly was successfully used to treat burn victims after the 1912 Equitable Life Assurance Society's New York building fire and similarly after Boston's Coconut Grove fire in 1942. The company also had been commissioned to develop a gauze burn pad loaded with Vaseline for use on the battlefields in Europe and Asia during World War II.

Gobs of Vaseline petroleum jelly placed on fisherman's hooks were said to lure trout. Smeared on the face of movie stars, Vaseline often simulated tears. Commander Perry's Arctic explorers took it with them to the North Pole because it resisted freezing even at 40 degrees below zero. The Vaseline brand could also be used in hot weather because it would not turn rancid. There were even reports that Vaseline petroleum jelly was used to butter bread in India. The Vaseline name became synonymous with petroleum jelly. In the 1990s, Vaseline petroleum jelly was available to consumers in sizes ranging from 1.75-ounce to 13-ounce jars and one to two-ounce tubes. Vaseline also came in a special nursery pack in baby powder scent.

### Brand Development

Vaseline petroleum jelly remained Chesebrough-Pond's tried and true product until 1970, when the company launched Vaseline Intensive Care Lotion as "an effective, caring, dependable moisturizing lotion," according to *World's Greatest Brands*. From 1968 to 1987 Chesebrough-Pond's underwent massive diversification, buying Ragu Packing Co. (makers of Ragu spaghetti sauce) and repositioning its health and beauty lines, which also included Aziza eye makeup, Cutex nail care products, Q-Tips cotton swabs, and Pond's Cold Cream.

Vaseline Intensive Care met with competition from Procter & Gamble's Wondra skin lotion. "Two-for-the-price-of-one" Vaseline Intensive Care bottles of lotion were sold in Wondra's test market. The debut of an "enriched" Vaseline Intensive Care lotion helped Chesebrough-Pond's gain 25 percent of the hand lotion market by the end of 1981. At the same time, Vaseline Intensive Care Bath Beads and Vaseline Intensive Care baby products (baby powder, lotion, and shampoo) were introduced. Another significant change in product packaging occurred at this time when plastic containers were produced for Vaseline and other Chesebrough-Pond's products.

In 1984 the Vaseline petroleum jelly line expanded to include Vaseline Lip Therapy, packaged in small, pocket-sized, convenient tubes, which met with immediate success, according to the company's 100th anniversary report. The lip balm product line included Vaseline Medicated Lip Therapy and Vaseline Lip Therapy with sun screen. In 1989 Vaseline Dermacare Ultra-Therapeutic Lotion and Vaseline Intensive Care Hand and Nail Formula Lotion both came to the market. In the same year, the company entered into the sun protection market by extending the Vaseline Intensive Care line to include new sun protection lotions and sun screens.

### Advertising Innovations

Robert A. Chesebrough not only was a marketing whiz—he was credited with starting the first "giveaway" campaign when he canvassed the New York State area with horse and buggy—but he also heavily invested in advertising his product from the start. In 1874 he contracted the Kellog Newspaper Company to run 25,000 ads in a small-town paper publicizing Vaseline petroleum jelly and a popular song, "Ballad of the Vaseline Brigade." Chesebrough also used other forms of advertising: bus and tram car advertising cards, sky writing, huge kites, and radio.

The merger of Chesebrough-Pond's with Unilever, already one of the world's largest consumer products manufacturers, improved marketing and advertising for the Vaseline name worldwide. Unilever's main advertising agencies were J. Walter Thompson Co., Lintas: Worldwide, Ogilvy & Mather, and McCann Erickson Worldwide. McCann Erickson supervised advertising for the Vaseline product lines beginning in the early 1990s.

Vaseline petroleum jelly was described as "pure petroleum jelly, with 100 percent purity and no additives to irritate sensitive skin." The brand's unique properties formed an occlusive barrier on skin, sealing in the skin's natural moisture. Vaseline petroleum jelly was a "unique, multi-use product that is unsurpassed for moisturizing, healing and protecting skin all over," company documents stated. However, most of the advertising focus shifted to the extensions of the Vaseline brand into hand and body lotion lines. In fact, advertising expenditures for Vaseline petroleum jelly in the early 1990s were a mere $2.6 to $4.9 million, compared to advertising spending for Vaseline Intensive Care products, which ranged from $15 to $25 million. "The Vaseline brand has shown that even when there is a close association with one particular product, opportunities exist to extend a well established brand," according to *World's Greatest Brands*.

McCann's advertising campaign in the early 1990s for the Vaseline Intensive Care line of lotions used *Good Morning America* co-host Joan Lunden in informational television commercials to discuss Vaseline Intensive Care "Skin Science Updates." This $45 million advertising campaign featured Lunden reinforcing

Vaseline Intensive Care's leadership position by communicating interesting skin care facts with information about the brand's usefulness. *Advertising Age* in a 1992 article reported that Chesebrough-Pond's planned to continue the Joan Lunden spots even though they initially attracted criticism for potentially confusing customers.

Chesebrough-Pond's attributed its success in building leading brands like Vaseline to continuous investment in research and development. Unilever established major skin care laboratories in the United States, India, England, and the Netherlands, and maintained satellite facilities in 35 other countries.

Chesebrough-Pond's in 1992 launched a "Master Brand" strategy for its Vaseline Intensive Care and Pond's brand lines to capitalize on the reputation of these trusted brands while strengthening them with new products and a unified marketing strategy. According to a 1992 *Advertising Age* article, Vaseline Intensive Care in 1992 was to be supported by $38 million in ad spending and $21 million in promotions.

To develop better programs at the customer level, Chesebrough-Pond's told *Discount Store News* that it was developing a comprehensive category management program to enhance shelf management and create incremental sales and higher profits for retailers. In addition to the Joan Lunden campaign, Vaseline Intensive Care was featured in promotional events such as Skin Awareness Month in March of 1992. At that time, the company featured a 1-800 phone line and offered an advice booklet and special refund offer to make it easier for consumers with skin care questions to visit their dermatologist.

Future advertising plans called for spending another $1 million to promote Vaseline Intensive Care in the editorial pages of popular women's magazines and in key dermatologist journals, and another $3 million to promote visits and offer rebates to dermatologists, according to *Discount Store News*. The company also would develop a "Vaseline Journal" and launch a direct mail and sampling campaign to 12,000 dermatologists and family physicians, in addition to bonus pack and store rebate promotions.

## Performance Appraisal

*Discount Store News* reported that in the hand and body lotion segment in the drug store trade, Vaseline Intensive Care Lotion had more than twice the unit share of its closest competitor and delivered almost triple the gross profit dollars. Three years after the introduction of Vaseline Intensive Care lotions and related products, the brand line ranked number one in all its market categories. Vaseline Intensive Care was also credited with the following innovations: it was the first hand and body lotion positioned as "therapeutic"; the first to launch extra strength, herbal/aloe, sensitive skin, and hand and nail formulas; the first to launch a full sun care line; and the first to advertise protection from ultraviolet rays. Chesebrough-Pond's became the leader in hand and body lotion brands, and ranked second in the category of facial moisturizers and cleansers.

## Future Growth

Consumer concerns about protecting their skin from sun damage and aging were the key drivers making skin care one of the fastest growing categories in mass-market retail stores. Facial creams and lotions, hand and body lotions, and sun care alone accounted for 85 percent of the skin care category volume and 96 percent of the category's growth.

Rising to the occasion, Chesebrough-Pond's, as part of its 1992 Master Brand marketing strategy, launched an Overnight Moisture Treatment Cream to deliver active moisture therapy for especially rough and dry skin, and an Extra Defense UV Protection Lotion for Fair Skin. Five new products were also launched in the sun care line and were completely repackaged, according to *Discount Store News*.

Chesebrough-Pond's in 1992 also planned to relaunch Vaseline Intensive Care Moisturizing Sunscreen lotions, which were repackaged to resemble the base lotion brand, supported by $12 million in advertising and promotion. As part of this line, Chesebrough was to add No Burn No Bite sunblock containing an insect repellent. The sun screens had an estimated 6.1 percent share of the estimated $475 million sun skin care market, *Advertising Age* reported. Nail care also received a boost in late 1992. Chesebrough-Pond's placed this line under the Vaseline Intensive Care umbrella with new packaging and an $11 million ad campaign featuring a nail tearing on a soda can.

What began as a one-brand company and became a household name, also added a line of related products that continued to evolve to meet market and consumer demands. Vaseline petroleum jelly developed a name and consumer brand loyalty that spelled success for its extended line of Vaseline Intensive Care products well into the 1990s.

## Further Reading:

"Chesebrough-Pond's the Experts in Skin Care," *Discount Store News*, May 18, 1992, pp. 62–64.

Gershman, Michael, *Getting It Right the Second Time,* Reading: Addison-Wesley, 1990, pp. 183–85.

"The Global Brand Age," *Management Today,* September 1991, pp. 78–80.

Maljers, Floris A., "Inside Unilever: The Evolving Transnational Company," *Harvard Business Review,* September/October 1992, pp. 46–52.

O'Leary, Noreen, "The Hand on the Lever," *Adweek (Western Advertising News),* December 14, 1992, pp. 22–27.

"Poor Countries Rich in Wealthy People," *Economist,* August 15, 1992, pp. 56–57.

Sambrook, Clare, "The Top 500 Brands," *Marketing,* March 7, 1991, pp. 27–33.

van Mesdag, Martin, "What Needs Changing in Brand Strategies? The Maintenance and Stretching of Brands," *Marketing Intelligence & Planning,* vol. 9, issue 7, 1991, pp. 14–16.

Wentz, Laurel, "Unilever Adopts Agency Incentives," *Advertising Age,* September 28, 1992, pp. 45–46.

Wilson, Mitchell, *American Science and Invention,* New York: Simon & Schuster, 1954.

*—Evelyn S. Dorman*

# VELCRO®

Within less than 50 years, Velcro brand hook and loop fastener, manufactured by Velcro USA Inc., has grown from an invention based on one of nature's seed dispersal devices to a ubiquitous fastener found everywhere from hospitals to spacecraft. In the late 1980s and early 1990s, the Velcro companies, held by Velcro Industries BV of the Netherlands, shifted their sales emphasis from consumer product markets to more stable industrial markets. In the early 1990s, the Velcro companies offered over 40 branded hook and loop products made from materials ranging from nylon to stainless steel and in formats varying from tape to washers, screws and studs. Velcro fasteners have also given rise to other innovative items, including toys, games and athletic equipment. The uses for Velcro hook-and-loop fasteners appear to be limited only by imagination: Late-night talk-show host David Letterman started a trend when he attached himself to a wall using only Velcro. The stunt was later adapted as a carnival attraction.

## Brand Origins

The idea for the Velcro product and brand originated in the 1940s when George de Mestral, a Swiss inventor, became curious about the cockleburs that clung persistently to his pants and his dog's coat after a walk in the woods. Upon examining the burs under a microscope, de Mestral noted that minuscule hooks on the burs attached themselves to equally small loops in the fabric of his clothing. Envisioning a strong, reusable clothing fastener, the inventor set out to develop a product that imitated the cocklebur's hooks and the fabric's loops.

The logistics of attaching hundreds of tiny hooks to cloth tape held up de Mestral's work for eight years, and mechanizing the production process of weaving 300 hooks and loops per square inch was another hurdle for the inventor. De Mestral used a combination of French words to trademark his invention: "vel" from *velour,* the French word for velvet, and "cro" from *crochet,* the French word for hook. De Mestral created a company to manufacture Velcro, and earned about $55 per week in the early years of the business. He later sold the company and worldwide patent rights to Velcro SA, a Swiss company organized by Jean Revaud, a French-born naturalized American, and has since made millions of dollars in royalties.

## International Expansion

In 1957, Montreal, Canada's Velok Ltd. purchased an exclusive license to produce Velcro fasteners in Canada, the United States, Latin America, the Caribbean, Australia, New Zealand, and parts of Asia. Velcro SA, the Swiss holding company that held the world patent rights received royalties on any sales made by Velok (later Velcro Industries Ltd.) and stipulated that any patentable innovations made by the Canadian company and its subsidiaries would automatically become the property of the Swiss company. By the mid-1960s, however, Velcro Industries Ltd. had become the pre-eminent member of the Velcro family. The Canadian company had two wholly owned subsidiaries, American Velcro Inc. (later Velcro USA Inc.) and Canadian Velcro Ltd. (later Velcro Canada Ltd.), and dominated Velcro SA in terms of sales and product development. By the early 1990s, there were Velcro operations in North America, Europe, Asia, and the Pacific Rim.

## Product Development

Although de Mestral had originally planned to use Velcro as a clothing fastener, the product's promoters found that the garment industry was not initially interested in it. In the early 1960s, Velcro company officials turned to alternative applications of their fastener, and found many uses for strong, yet lightweight, Velcro fasteners in the aerospace industry. By the mid-1960s, all jet aircraft built in the United States utilized Velcro to attach fuselage insulation. Velcro was also used in space on astronauts' suits and in spacecraft equipment.

Crafted of nylon, Velcro tape was eventually accepted by the garment industry and soon replaced more conventional fasteners on shoes, wallets, jackets and other apparel and accessories. Since fastening Velcro didn't require the coordination that buttons, ties, or zippers demanded, it was an especially convenient fastener for toddler's clothing. By the mid-1970s, a variety of home sewing and scuba and marine gear products were also being marketed by the Velcro companies.

Over the years, the company's research and development group introduced varieties of hook and loop fasteners made from polyester, glass fiber, stainless steel, silver-coated nylon and Teflon, among other materials. These unusual materials offered features for varying environments and applications, including ultraviolet and chemical resistance, flame retardancy and electrical

## AT A GLANCE

**V**elcro brand of fasteners created in the 1940s by Swiss inventor George de Mestral; product and name sold to Velcro SA, a Swiss holding company; in the late 1960s, Velcro North America of Montreal, Canada (formerly Velcro Industries, Ltd., which was formerly Velok Ltd.) purchased patent rights, which expired in 1978.

*Advertising:* Agency—Bozell & Jacobs. *Major campaign—* "The First, The Best."

*Addresses: Parent company*—Velcro USA Inc., 406 Brown Ave., Manchester, NH 03108; phone: (603) 669-4892; fax: (603) 669-1728. *Ultimate parent company*—Velcro Industries BV, Hoekenrode 6, NL-1000 BL, Amsterdam Zuidoost, Netherlands.

conduction. Velcro brand fastening products included tapes up to 12 inches wide, cut pieces, straps, studs, washers and clips and custom forms. The methods of attaching Velcro hook and loop products were also dramatically expanded. Originally limited to sewn-on applications, new Velcro fasteners could be secured by screws, bolts, rivets, lamination, and self-adhesives. Once available only in black, Velcro brand fasteners were later available in a wide variety of stock and custom colors. These developments helped vastly extend Velcro's markets into industrial, medical, and automotive markets. For example, Velcro is used in the medical field for surgical gowns, blood pressure cuffs, and orthopedic appliances. Velcro fasteners are also used to attach access panels, air filters and wire and cable harnesses to computer and electronics products.

## Competition

Velcro stood virtually alone in the industry it created until its patents expired in 1978. For the first time, the Velcro companies faced competition, especially from low-cost manufacturers in Taiwan and South Korea. Manufacturers of children's and athletic footwear began to demand Velcro closures, bringing the company more business than it could handle and throwing it into a heavily competitive market. When Velcro lost control of the market, prices fell 40 percent within two years.

Once the shoe fastener fad subsided, Velcro USA Inc. looked for markets that were less susceptible to price competition. Velcro managers were attracted to industrial markets, especially automotive manufacturing. Velcro fasteners had advantages car companies could appreciate—they were lighter than metal and didn't rattle or rust. Automotive products included tape for headliners, door panels, seat covers, carpets, and mats.

## Brand Promotion

By the time the Velcro product patents expired in 1978, the companies had done such a good job of promoting their brand that the trademark had become essentially a synonym for the hook and loop tape product. The Velcro companies were forced to move from vigilance against patent infringement to strict control of the Velcro trademark and its use. Employees and others were reminded that Velcro was not a generic term, and should not be used as such. In 1991, the company even published a brochure outlining the proper use of the brand name and acceptable terminology for competitors' products. Although often copied, the branded product was, as one of its trademarks proclaims, "The First, The Best."

## Further Reading:

Giges, Nancy, "Velcro Faces Patent Problems by Diversifying Line," *Advertising Age,* November 7, 1977, p. 24.

Krantz, K. Theodor, "How Velcro Got Hooked on Quality," *Harvard Business Review,* September/October 1989, pp. 34–36, 38, 40.

Marcial, Gene, "Sticking with Velcro," *Business Week,* January 18, 1993, p. 74.

"Velcro: A Success Story," *The Magazine of Wall Street,* June 10, 1967, pp. 31–32, 40.

*—April S. Dougal*

# VICKS®

The average person might suffer from as many as 200 colds in a lifetime. For more than 100 years, Vicks VapoRub was there to help relieve cold symptoms and make people feel better. Recognized by its cobalt blue jar with the red "V" and menthol-eucalyptus fragrance, Vicks VapoRub proved to be an effective externally applied remedy that was innovative for its time. The brand's success spawned a line of Vicks cough and cold medicines, throat lozenges and inhalers, and Vicks remained a top seller in the 1990s.

## Brand Origins

Vicks VapoRub was invented in 1890 by Lunsford Richardson, a pharmacist from Greensboro, North Carolina. Together with partner John Fariss, Richardson bought the Porter and Tate Drugstore in Greensboro, where they conducted experiments and developed remedies for colds, coughs, and other ailments. Particularly troubling to Richardson was his older son Smith's "croupy" cough. In the late 19th century, colds were often treated two ways: with poultices made of flour or muster plasters, or with vapor lamps. Each remedy gave off nose-clearing fumes, but one caused painful blisters and the other was too expensive and difficult to use. Richardson tried to take the best of both worlds. By using petroleum jelly as a base—it had been discovered and refined by Robert A. Chesebrough of Vaseline fame in the 1880s— Richardson combined camphor, nutmeg, eucalyptus oil, and, according to *Getting It Right the Second Time,* "made a lucky guess" by adding menthol, then a new drug from Japan. This concoction would be rubbed onto a patient's chest, and when the patient's body heat melted it, the ointment, initially called Richardson's Croup and Pneumonia Salve, emitted vapors that opened the nasal passages. As an external rub, it did not upset the stomach.

Richardson was 51 years old when he sold his drug business in 1898 and used his life savings of $8,000 to establish the Vick Family Remedies Company to manufacture and sell his line of 21 home remedies. His mentholated chest rub was then dubbed Vicks Magic Croup Salve, and later Vicks Croup and Pneumonia Salve, using the trade name Vick in honor of his brother-in-law and friend Dr. Joshua Vick. The name Vick was shorter than using his own name and, under the advice of son Smith, the salve was renamed Vicks VapoRub in 1908. Smith Richardson, instrumental in directing the company's successful marketing campaigns, also advised his father to focus the company's time and energy on VapoRub, which led to dropping the other 21 remedies.

## Early Marketing Strategy

The Vick Family Remedies Company consisted of a laboratory where petrolatum was heated in kettles on stoves and medication was mixed by hand and later stirred with big wooden paddles. Women would pour the warm salves into jars from large coffee pots. Richardson originally promoted Vicks VapoRub with the slogan, "Rub it on, sniff it in, it's good for you, it's made by Presbyterians," according to *Everybody's Business.* He emphasized the fact that using Vicks would avoid stomach upset and potential overdosing. But the brand initially did not sell well to druggists because Richardson had a one-product company. *Getting It Right the Second Time* attributed their disinterest to preferring to "spend their time with salespeople from major companies whose sample cases bulged with dozens of familiar items." This forced Richardson to come up with a way to demonstrate his product's effectiveness, since it wasn't being distributed by drugstores.

A top-selling Vicks salesman named Herbert Ray was credited with devising a unique product demonstration that would be emulated by others—the "spoon test." A spoonful of Vicks VapoRub would be heated with a match to release its vapors, which convinced many a skeptic to reconsider the product. In fact, one merchant was so impressed that he bought an unusually large order, and soon all Vicks salesmen were using the method to sell VapoRub in their regions.

In the South, satisfied customers in a 20-county area around Greensboro advertised the brand by word-of-mouth. Unique product sampling helped push the brand. Merchants buying 12-dozen jars received double that amount free to give away to women customers who would give the product a full trial and report the results.

Up North, Richardson placed ads and coupons in newspapers offering free samples to the public, according to *Getting It Right the Second Time.* Vick company salesmen would then visit druggists and offer them a case of 12-dozen jars providing that the druggist promised to give 72 jars away to good customers and obtain signed agreements from them to try Vicks and report their results to the company. Richardson then reimbursed the druggist at

## AT A GLANCE

**V**icks brand cold remedies originated in 1890 in Greensboro, NC, when pharmacist Lunsford Richardson combined a petroleum jelly base with camphor, nutmeg, eucalyptus oil, and menthol to invent the product which became Vicks VapoRub; the Vicks line extended to include Vicks Formula 44 Cough Medication, Vicks Formula 44-D Decongestant Cough Medicine, and Vicks Throat Lozenges; in 1898, Richardson sold his medical business and invested in the Vick Family Remedies Company, which became the Vick Chemical Company, Inc., in 1933 and eventually Richardson-Vicks, Inc., in 1981; Procter & Gamble purchased Richardson-Vicks in 1985.

**Performance:** *Sales*—$260 million in wholesale sales overall; $90 million in cough/cold preparation category.

**Major competitor:** Warner-Lambert's Halls brand of cough drops; also A. H. Robins' Robitussin cough/cold preparations, McNeil Consumer Products' Tylenol, American Home Products Corporation's Advil.

**Advertising:** *Agency*—D'Arcy Masius Benton & Bowles, New York, NY; *Major campaign*—Brand celebrated its centennial with the slogan: "Over a Century of Care: Vicks VapoRub."

**Addresses:** *Parent company*—Richardson-Vicks, Inc., P.O. Box 854, One Far Mill Crossing, Shelton, CT; phone: (203) 925-6000. *Ultimate parent company*—Procter & Gamble Company, One Procter & Gamble Plaza, Cincinnati, OH 45202; phone: (513) 983-1100; fax: (513) 562-2062.

the full retail price of 25 cents a jar. Participating druggists were then listed in local newspapers to drum up sales. "Reader-style" ads were placed in the local newspaper resembling news articles chronicling customer testimonials.

To conquer the Western market, Richardson resorted to hiring sales representatives, which lasted until 1917 when the U.S. Post Office first allowed deliveries to "resident." Another marketing technique called the "mark-up" ad was used in 1919 by stating, "Over 17 Million Vick Jars Used Yearly." The slogan was designed to demonstrate annual sales growth with the old figure crossed out and the new one placed above it.

### First Commercial Successes

By 1910, annual sales had increased to about $50,000, enabling the company to advertise directly to the public. According to company press materials, Richardson's company became one of America's first outdoor advertisers. Vicks VapoRub began appearing on road signs everywhere. Vicks also became the first company to offer its salesmen company cars when it purchased a fleet of Model T Fords. Each car came with ladders so that salesmen could erect road signs on their runs.

Success with sampling made Richardson the first mail order direct marketer on a national basis. Interested customers on both coasts would then request their druggists to stock Vicks VapoRub. By the end of World War I, it was estimated that nearly every American household had received a free sample of Vicks VapoRub and every pharmacist knew the brand by name, according to *Getting It Right the Second Time*. Sales increased eight-fold in five years to $613,000 in 1917.

The true test came during 1918 and 1919, when an epidemic of the Spanish Flu bombarded the country. "Reader-style" advertis-

ing suggested that Vicks VapoRub would relieve coughs and congestion. The demand for Vicks VapoRub reportedly increased so rapidly that salesmen were brought back from the field to supervise extra shifts of workers as the plant operated overtime to keep up. Demand was so great that the brand had to be rationed by druggists. By the end of the epidemic, sales of Vicks had reached $2.9 million.

Vicks VapoRub also became one of the earliest television advertisers, sponsoring live ads on the *Gary Moore Show* in the 1950s. Actress/comedienne Lily Tomlin also advertised VapoRub. At one time, the "voice of Vicks" belonged to actor Burgess Meredith.

### Foreign Expansion

Vicks also became one of the first American companies to expand into foreign markets in the 1920s when the brand was introduced in England, Mexico, and Canada. In England, however, the company had to forfeit trademark rights in order to sell VapoRub without paying taxes. Heavy import duties also priced Vicks VapoRub out of reach for most Mexican families. In 1924 Vicks set up a small manufacturing facility in Mexico to keep retail prices down. Vicks products were sold worldwide through New York-based export facilities by 1930. Vicks VapoRub became one of the most widely distributed products in the world, sold in more than 100 countries. The formula remained virtually the same one that Richardson created in 1890.

### Product Changes

The Vick Family Remedies Company officially incorporated in 1933 as the Vick Chemical Company and by 1981 was renamed Richardson-Vicks. Procter & Gamble purchased the $1 billion Richardson-Vicks in 1985. The key to the company's continued success was the introduction of several franchise-extension product categories of the brand name it established in the 1930s. Thus, Vicks VapoRub extensions centered around cold care, including cough drops, medicines, inhalers, and nasal sprays. Vicks cough and nose drops were introduced in the 1930s and cough medicines such as Vicks Formula 44 and 44D and NyQuil followed in the late 1960s to mid-1970s, making the Vicks brand of cough and cold medicines the top-selling products at this time. However, the recession of the early 1980s and a low incidence of colds and flu in the United States and worldwide contributed to an erosion of market share, according to Richardson-Vicks annual reports. Internationally, Vicks cough drops were top sellers from Germany to Japan. Consequently, while Richardson-Vicks pushed Vicks VapoRub and Vicks Formula 44 and 44D cough syrups, it also marketed similar but differently named products such as Viscoat cough syrup and Victors cough drops in foreign markets.

By 1984, the company reported double-digit gains in sales and a recovery of previously eroded earnings. The strongest performer in the Vicks line was NyQuil, and company reports also attributed a gain in market share in the cough medicine category to better performance by Vicks Formula 44D and the launch of a Cremacoat cough medicine line. Yet at the same time, Richardson-Vicks made a decision it termed "difficult and emotional" to move the production of Vicks VapoRub decongestant ointment to Puerto Rico as a way of consolidating production of its Vidal Sassoon and Pantene hair care products at the Greensboro, North Carolina, plant. "The result was lower costs, higher productivity and an improvement in our tax rate and at the same time, more jobs at both of these facilities,'' stated the 1984 Richardson-Vicks Annual Report.

## Performance Appraisal

Nearly four out of five Americans reported having used Vicks VapoRub to treat their colds. The brand's success was attributed to innovative marketing techniques that continued to be used by companies worldwide.

The brand's tradition of effectiveness, coupled with the boom in inexpensive over-the-counter nonprescription drugs, helped to revive sales for the Vicks brands of cold and cough medicines. According to David Kiley in a 1992 *Adweek Superbrands* supplement, the Vicks line experienced a 30 percent jump in sales in 1990. Ultimate parent company Procter & Gamble had been building its over-the-counter brands ten years prior by acquiring such firms as Richardson-Vicks and competitor G. D. Searle. Emphasis on family branding vaulted Vicks brand of cough and cold remedies into the number three spot among over-the-counter drugs in 1991. The Vicks brand earned the number one ranking in sales of $260 million, beating out A. H. Robins' Robitussin and Warner-Lambert's Halls with $125 million among them respectively. *Adweek*'s Kiley attributed the brand's growth more to trade promotion than advertising and noted that ad spending for Vicks declined to $32 million from the $53 million spent in 1990.

As Vicks VapoRub entered its centennial in the 1990s, it remained a remedy as modern and effective as it was 100 years ago. With so many nonprescription medications on the market, there was growing concern about the problem of adverse reactions and drug interactions. Because VapoRub was applied externally, it was advertised as a safe and effective alternative to internal decongestants because it would not interact or interfere with other medicines the way pills could. The Vicks name became well established as a key cold and cough medicine, but its future growth depended on how well it could beat the competition by continued "leveraging" of the brand name.

## Further Reading:

Frankenstein, Diane, *Brandnames: Who Owns What,* Facts on File, 1986, pp. 312–313.

Freeman, Laurie, and Patricia Winters, "Cold Season Starts Heating Up," *Advertising Age,* October 2, 1989, p. 3.

Gershman, Michael, *Getting It Right the Second Time,* Reading: Addison-Wesley, 1990, pp. 185–88.

Kiley, David, "Vicks, Baker Cummins Test OTC Innovations," *Adweek's Marketing Week,* November 26, 1990, p. 25.

Kiley, David, "Lessons in the Art of Leveraging," *Adweek Special Supplement (Superbrands 1992),* pp. 94–96.

McMath, Robert, "Twenty-four Brand Loyalty," *Adweek's Marketing Week,* January 20, 1992, p. 40.

"OTC Market Shows Steady Growth," *Standard & Poor's Industry Surveys,* August 20, 1992, pp. H30–H31.

*—Evelyn S. Dorman*

# WD-40®

WD-40 is a petroleum based lubricant, moisture retardant, and rust preventative, which has a wide variety of applications. Originally created by the Rocket Chemical Company for the aerospace industry in the 1950s, today WD-40 can be found in millions of homes and workshops around the world. The lubricant was the sole product manufactured by the WD-40 Company as of 1993. Primarily sold through retail chain stores, hardware stores, and automotive parts outlets, WD-40 is used in 75 percent of American households. Consumers are continually finding new ways to use the lubricant and passing the word on to friends and co-workers. With a product ranked in the top three percent of consumer awareness by Landor Associates, WD-40 Company celebrated its 40th year in 1993 as the leader in multipurpose lubricant market.

## Brand Origins

With the financial support of three investors, Norm Larsen founded the Rocket Chemical Company in San Diego, California, in 1952. Working out of one room, the company consisted of Larsen and two employees. Rocket Chemical Company's line of products consisted of rust resistors and removers for metal parts and tools, devised especially for utilization in the aerospace industry.

WD-40 was developed a year after the company was founded. The name is derived from the "Water Displacement" formula experiment that was deemed successful on the 40th test. Created for Convair, the aerospace and defense contractor, WD-40 was first used for removing moisture from metals and protecting them from rust and corrosion. In addition, WD-40 was used to protect missile coverings from corrosion and moisture damage on electrical circuitry and was eventually designated for use on NASA's Atlas missiles.

Larsen soon determined the product would also have potential in consumer markets as a lubricant and solvent. Apparently, employees of the young company were sneaking the product out of the plant for use at home on squeaky doors and stuck drawers. Two years after it was developed, attempts were made to put WD-40 into aerosol cans, and in 1958 the Rocket Chemical Company contracted an aerosol packager to package the product for consumer markets. In 1961 a small amount of mineral spirits was added to the original formula, providing a light scent to cover the smell of the petroleum in WD-40. Thus far, this has been the only adjustment made to the original formula.

By this time the company had expanded to include 7 employees, and sales were averaging 45 cases a day. WD-40 was sold and distributed out of the trunks of salesmen's cars to local sporting and hardware stores in the San Diego area. When hurricane "Carla" hit the Florida coast in 1961, the demand for WD-40 increased dramatically. Additional amounts of WD-40 were produced for the hurricane victims who needed to recondition water-damaged vehicles and machinery. In 1965 the company phased out the other items in its line of industrial chemicals, and when John Barry joined the business as the new president in 1969, he renamed it after its only product: WD-40.

## Early Marketing Strategy

Discussing his successful marketing approach in a *Communication World* interview, Chairman of the Board John Barry said "our best salesman has always been a free sample." Barry, who stepped down as CEO in 1992, is remembered for sending thousands of free samples a month to soldiers stationed overseas during the Vietnam War. The GIs used the spray to help keep their weapons dry in the stifling weather of Southeast Asia and subsequently became customers after the war. He also conceived a distribution plan that has given WD-40 extensive exposure to consumers at a low cost to the company. Under Barry's tutelage, WD-40 was sold exclusively through distributors and retail suppliers with numerous accounts and outlets. The strategy has been simple and successful; continuous mailings of samples to prospective accounts, several trade shows each month, and advertising in selected magazines, including *Readers Digest* and *Sports Illustrated*.

The uncomplicated marketing approach has paid large dividends for the WD-40 company. In 1969, when Barry joined WD-40, sales were at the two million dollar level. The company went public in 1973, and on its 25th anniversary in 1978, sales had reached $26 million. Without the cost of research and development, or debt to repay, WD-40 continued to pay an average of five percent back to investors during the 1980s. Between 1969 and 1981 the wholesale price of the product rose only 43 percent, compared to a 132 percent increase in the U.S. wholesale price index during the same time period. The growth and success of WD-40 can be credited to two factors: tight management controls by Barry and a marketing plan that highlights the versatility of the product for use at home, factory, garage, or office.

## AT A GLANCE

**W**D-40 brand of petroleum based lubricant founded in 1953 by Norm Larsen, president of the Rocket Chemical Company; became a registered trademark, 1953; initially produced for use by the aerospace industry, WD-40 was made for commercial sale beginning in 1958; company name changed to WD-40 Company, 1969.

**Performance:** *Market share*—83% (top share) of multipurpose lubricant category. *Sales*—$99.9 million (1992)

**Major competitor:** 3M's Q4; also Valvoline 1-2-99 and Borden's Ten*4.

**Advertising:** *Agency*—Phillips-Ramsey, San Diego, CA.

**Addresses:** *Parent company*—WD-40 Company, 1061 Cudahy Place, San Diego, CA; phone: (619) 275-1400; fax: (619) 275-5823.

## Brand Versatility

WD-40 employs under 150 people at its headquarters in San Diego with additional offices in Canada, the United Kingdom, and Australia. The petroleum based concentrate used in North America is produced at the San Diego facilities. Independent contractors package the product to specifications set out by WD-40 company. "They add the solvent and propellant," explained president Gerald Schleif in *USA Today*, "but we make well over a million gallons of the secret sauce [in San Diego]."

Market research conducted by the Nielsen Scantrack Household Panel from May of 1989 to May of 1992 found that 83 percent of consumers who bought an all-purpose lubricant during the three-year period purchased WD-40. Capitalizing on impulse purchasing by the consumer, the key to success for WD-40 has been versatility. It began with engineers from the company taking the product home with them during the early years of Rocket Chemical Company. That trend has continued as industrial workers and their supervisors discovered the product through the workplace, eventually buying WD-40 for use at home. Beyond protection from moisture, the lubricant has many household uses. Sewing machines were found to work better when treated with WD-40. Rusted nuts and bolts loosen up when sprayed with WD-40. The lubricant spray helps keep lawn mower and outboard engines running in wet weather. It is now customary to use WD-40 on frozen locks and door handles. The lock application may be the origin of the infamous little red tube that accompanies each spray can of WD-40 to be attached to the nozzle of the can so the spray can go directly into the lock opening.

While the consumer uses for WD-40 vary—squeaky hinges and rusted garden tools are also customary uses for the product—many consumers report unconventional ways to use WD-40. Certain fisherman swear by it, not only to protect their rod and reel, but to use on their bait and lures. A coating of WD-40 on a lure or piece of bait will attract fish who are dependent upon their sense of smell to find food. The company has received letters from all over the United States confirming the fish stories. Another novel use for WD-40 came from a senior citizen in Texas who wrote the company about the way in which he uses the lubricant spray to keep his hips and knees limber, so he can continue to go out dancing. The distinctive blue and yellow can describes itself as an all-purpose lubricant that "stops squeaks," but consumers have found more and more uses for the product.

## Sales and Earnings

Sales of WD-40 have grown continually since 1969; this growth in demand for the product confirms customer satisfaction with its performance. In 1987 net sales reached $71 million and by 1992 had hit a record $99.9 million, marking an 11.3 percent increase in sales over the previous year's $89.8 million. These figures are especially notable when considering the WD-40 Company did not increase the price of the product between 1981 and 1990, at which time it was raised by nine percent. Profits have grown with sales, reaching an impressive 18 million in 1992. Earnings per share grew 17.8 percent to $2.38 in 1992 versus $2.02 in 1991, while cash dividends rose to $2.16 per share in 1992, up from $1.72 in 1991.

Beginning in 1988, the company adopted a change in sales policy that was financially feasible, but has proved to be troublesome. WD-40 Company wanted to do more business with the large retailers upon whom they had become dependent for a significant amount of sales—40 percent of the company's sales came from 50 of its 12,000 accounts. Large accounts like Wal-Mart had expressed a desire to keep costs down by removing the intermediary distributor. "Because of mergers and acquisitions, there are fewer and fewer big accounts, and they want and deserve company attention," asserted Chairman John Barry in a *Forbes* interview.

In November of 1988 the company used a clause in its contract with 60 independent distributors that allowed either side to end the agreement on 90 days notice. Instead, WD-40 hired their own sales people to cater to the larger accounts. "Their objective was to make calls that produce commissions," stated WD-40 President and Chief Financial Officer Gerald Schleif in the *New York Times*, adding, "Our objective was to build a business." The company's success is due in part to the new sales policies and marketing staff.

After being let go, 8 of the 12 independent sales distributors sued the WD-40 Company. They claimed the company management had assured them job security in exchange for loyalty to the company. The group asked for $19 million in damages for lost profits. In 1992 a Sonoma County (California) Superior Court jury was persuaded and granted the eight distributors a $10.3 million settlement, an average of $1.30 million each. By the middle of 1993, the suit was still in the appeal process.

Two former sales representatives that were not part of the initial action against WD-40, filed a separate suit in April of 1992. Using the same lawyers and claiming the same facts, the suit was settled for $2.5 million the following year. The settlement reached in this case may indicate the company's willingness to settle the initial suit, though as of August 1993 the matter was still in the courts.

## International Growth

The overseas market presents the largest potential sales growth opportunity for the WD-40 Company. In 1986 the company did not renew its contract with its licensed distributor in the United Kingdom, having instead decided to build their own plant in Milton Keyes, outside of London. WD-40 Company Ltd. (United Kingdom) was created a year later in order to manufacture the product and oversee distribution in Europe, the Middle East, and Africa. WD-40 concentrate is made in Milton Keyes and turned around for sale by three independent British packagers. Labeling is done in a dozen different languages, and the product is standardized for each country.

Sales for the United Kingdom and Europe have grown steadily since 1987, when sales of $10 million were recorded. An aggressive marketing plan for France, Spain, and the Middle East had raised net sales to $17.5 million by 1992, which also marked increases over 1991 figures of 10 percent in England, 50 percent in Europe, and 35 percent in the Middle East. In 1992 the company continued to expand it's sales force in Europe, adding three new sales representatives in France and two sales representatives in Spain and Italy respectively.

The San Diego facility handles the distribution and licensing of WD-40 in Mexico, Central America, the Caribbean, and South America. A subsidiary, WD-40 Ltd. (Australia), was set up in 1990 for marketing the product in that country as well as New Zealand, Southeast Asia, and the Far East. Planning an aggressive marketing campaign for mainland China, a sales manager was added to the company's staff in Hong Kong in 1992.

With a myriad of applications and competition virtually nonexistent, WD-40 has become a household word in the past 25 years. However, it may be difficult for the WD-40 Company to sustain its growth in the future. The overseas markets holds the most promise for continued sales growth. Encouraged by the acceptance of WD-40 overseas, the company has implemented creative marketing practices and sought to bring prices down. In fiscal year 1992, sales were on a ratio of two-thirds domestic to one-third international. WD-40 Company has set a goal to make that ratio 50-50. If the success achieved by the direct marketing staff is any indication, the international sales goal is entirely attainable.

## Further Reading:

Cowan, Alison Leigh, "Terminating Outside Sales Staff Proves Costly to WD-40," *New York Times,* July 23, 1993, p. C4.

Edgerton, Jerry, "Rustproofing Your Portfolio," *Money,* May 1988, p. 12.

Lockwood, Herbert, "WD-40 Executive Lubes His Brain for New Product," *San Diego Daily Transcript,* May 8, 1991, p. A1.

Meeks, Fleming, "Hull Speed Ahead," *Forbes,* September 5, 1988, pp. 64–68.

Murray, Thomas, "The Five Best Managed Companies," *Business Month,* December 1989, pp. 42–43.

Patnode, Randall, "Proposal Would Convert WD-40 to Partnership," *San Diego Business Journal,* September 28, 1987, p. 3.

Taylor, Anne Marie, "PR Pros Find Room at the Top," *Communications World,* April 1990, pp. 19–22.

WD-40 Company Annual Report, San Diego: WD-40 Company, 1992.

"WD-40 Company History," San Diego: WD-40 Company, 1993.

Wilson, Craig, "Slippery Business," *The Detroit News,* February 27, 1993, pp. 13D–14D.

*—William Tivenan*

# WINDEX®

Developed in 1935 by the Ohio-based Drackett Co., the blue spray Windex has become virtually synonymous with glass cleaning. Windex was introduced in the 1930s as a simplified approach to cleaning windows in the absence of domestic servants, who had traditionally borne the responsibility for window cleaning in American homes. The Drackett Co. was bought in 1965 by Bristol-Myers Squibb but continued to produce and distribute Windex under the Drackett name until December 31, 1992, when the company was bought by S.C. Johnson & Son, Inc. Because Windex was the first major glass cleaner on the market and its brand name so effectively communicated its main purpose, it has enjoyed widespread product recognition and has dominated the marketplace despite aggressive challenges from other glass cleaning products. The advantage that Windex has enjoyed in being the brand name most closely associated with window and glass cleaning has also presented some marketing problems for the company over the years. It has been difficult for marketers and advertisers to convince consumers that Windex can be used on surfaces other than the glass with which it is so closely associated. As a result, competitors have been able to gnaw at Windex's market share with less specific multi-surface cleaners while the growth of Windex into the all-purpose sector has not balanced these incursions.

## Brand Origins

The Drackett Co., the originator of Windex, was incorporated in 1915 as a small chemical company producing a variety of chemicals, including lye and ammonia, for industrial use. In 1924 Drackett scored a tremendous commercial success with the introduction of Drāno, a lye-based drain cleaner. Encouraged by the success of Drāno, the Drackett Co. proceeded to experiment with a variety of cleaning products for home use. The timing couldn't have been more ripe for the introduction of home care products. The early part of the twentieth century had seen a virtual revolution in housekeeping, as technological innovations and social upheaval had torn apart nineteenth-century traditions of domestic chores. The most important feature of this shift away from traditional cleaning patterns for Drackett's Windex was the dramatic reduction in the availability of domestic servants.

Traditionally, cleaning windows involved lugging a large bucket of water and ammonia to the window, washing the window with a sponge, and using a squeegee to remove the water and prevent streaking. This task was normally performed on all windows only once or twice a year during the intensive periods of spring and fall cleaning. While no cleaning fluid would be able to greatly reduce the labor involved in this annual cleaning ritual, Drackett realized that some windows and all mirrors and interior glass surfaces needed to be cleaned on a more regular basis. It was towards this more frequent maintenance that Drackett aimed its new product.

As discussed in Susan Strasser's book on American housework, *Never Done,* routine cleaning in middle- and upper-class households had traditionally been the responsibility of domestic servants. But shifting social and economic patterns in the early twentieth century had made it increasingly difficult to hire such help. With the loss of the domestic servant went the specialized equipment and skills required to clean the home efficiently. The housewife was expected to pick up the slack. In order to accomplish the many tasks formerly expected of the domestic servant, the housewife was transformed from a household "manager," as she was usually referred to in late nineteenth century housekeeping manuals, to a household laborer, personally responsible for cooking and cleaning. By 1918 *The Ladies Home Journal* illustrated no fewer than 19 different brushes necessary for women to "perform that dreaded bit of housework . . . when help is scarce." Four of these were described as being needed in window and glass cleaning. The marketplace seized the opportunity of alleviating the difficulties that the housewife faced in accomplishing the expanded duties of matrimony. Windex was a perfect example of a product that promised the same results as those achieved by paid help but in less time and without specialized equipment.

The formula of Windex was a fairly simple combination of water, ammonia as a cleansing agent, and chemicals to speed evaporation. Although the presence of ammonia in Windex (or the Drackett Co.'s trademark Ammonia-D) became a selling point in later years, this was not, in fact, an important innovation of the product. Other than regular soaps, ammonia had been the only major commercial cleaning agent for over a century. Widely available to housewives, ammonia mixed with water was used for everything from laundry to dishes. It was not the superior cleaning ability of Windex that led to its success but the fact that it could be used without additional water or a squeegee. Previously, only a squeegee could ensure that all water was completely removed from the glass so that the water would not leave streaks as it

## AT A GLANCE

**W**index brand of window and glass cleaner founded in 1935 in Cincinnati, Ohio, by Drackett Co.; Drackett Co. sold as subsidiary to Bristol-Myers Squibb, 1965; Drackett Co., including Windex brand, sold to S.C. Johnson & Son, Inc., 1992.

**Performance:** *Market share*—40% (top share) of window and glass cleaner category, *Sales*—$79 million.

**Major competitor:** DowBrands L.P.'s Glass Plus, Miles Inc.'s S.O.S. Glass Works, Procter & Gamble's Cinch.

**Advertising:** *Agency*—DDB Needham, Chicago, IL, 1993.

**Addresses:** *Parent company*—S.C. Johnson & Son, Inc., 1525 Howe St., Racine, WI 53403; phone: (414) 631-2000; fax: (414) 631-2000.

evaporated. Windex was designed to eliminate this step by allowing the user to wipe the product off the glass with the same cloth with which it was applied. This was accomplished by adding ingredients that decreased evaporation time, allowing one or two wipes of the cloth to remove all liquid and thereby reduce streaking. The elimination of the squeegee also meant that much less liquid was needed so that instead of a heavy bucket of water, brushes, and a squeegee, the homemaker needed only to carry a cloth and a small bottle of the new Windex. This system was ideal for the routine light cleaning that had become such a major part of the daily chores of most women.

### Product Development

The blue-colored, ammonia-based Windex was an immediate and soaring success. By the 1950s Windex had strengthened its position still further by introducing the plastic sprayer and bottle that allowed much easier and efficient application of the product. Based in large part on the Windex model, the plastic spray dispenser would become the dominant format for glass and all-purpose cleaners to the end of the century. Drackett also brought out a new formula Windex in an aerosol format during the first aerosol boom in the late 1950s. The new Blue Mist Aerosol Windex claimed to be a more efficient cleaner and to be easier to use than the original formula. Although Windex was still being produced in an aerosol format through the 1990s, this version of the brand never captured consumer attention the way the spray formula had, perhaps because of its higher price on the supermarket shelf.

The 1960s saw the growth of a new sector in the home cleaning market, that of the all-purpose detergent cleaner. Led by such brands as Adell Chemical's Lestoil and Texize's Fantastik, this new series of products did not pose a direct threat to Windex because their harsh detergents were ruinous to glass surfaces. Nevertheless, the Drackett Co., by this time a subsidiary of Bristol-Myers, attempted to capitalize on the booming market in all-purpose cleaners by introducing an all-purpose cleaning version of Windex. Composed of ammonia and "seven other cleansing ingredients," the new Windex cleaner had the advantage of being effective on glass as well as other surfaces, foreshadowing the successful glass and surface cleaners of the 1970s and 1980s. This product extension was not successful, however, and was dropped from the Windex line. Ironically, the first major threat to Windex's complete dominance of the glasscleaning sector came

less than a decade later from Texize's Glass Plus, also marketed as an all-purpose cleaner.

Glass Plus and other Windex competitors essentially copied the format of the successful Windex brand. Windex responded to these new threats by expanding the Windex line. Although the ammonia base of Windex had been one of the keys to its success, the strong smell of ammonia became undesirable to a certain group of increasingly environmentally-conscious consumers. What had once been the acceptable odor of an efficient cleaner became an unpleasant smell associated with chemicals. In response to this perception, in 1985 Drackett introduced Lemon Windex, a yellow-tinted, lemon-scented version of its traditional ammonia formula.

The first serious threat to Windex's market share by a product claiming to offer a substantially different approach to glass cleaning did not appear until 1986, some 50 years after Windex first appeared on the market. As part of the 1980s trend towards "natural" products, Miles Laboratories introduced a vinegar based product called S.O.S. Glass Works. This product was developed after consumer focus groups had indicated that many people believed that vinegar was a very effective yet "natural" glass cleaner. It is unclear how this tradition had developed but it is possible that it derived from the restaurant industry, which had long used vinegar to clean glass containers in order to avoid both possible contamination of food and the strong smell of ammonia. Although it can be demonstrated that vinegar is in fact a relatively inefficient cleaning aid in comparison to ammonia, or even regular tap water, vinegar-based Glass Works quickly picked up 15 percent of the glass cleaning market. Drackett responded quickly. Within a year they had introduced Vinegar Windex, a product that combined vinegar, surfactants, and solvents and was tinted green in clear imitation of Miles' Glass Works. The new Vinegar Windex regained much of the market share lost to Glass Works but it and all other vinegar-based glass cleaners have received consistently poor ratings in *Consumer Reports* tests when compared to ammonia-based products, and none have retained a sizable share of the glass cleaner sector.

The negative association that developed around the ammonia smell of Windex was a small symptom of a larger phenomenon concerning the consumer's awareness of and sensitivity to environmental issues that developed in the 1980s and 1990s. Although ammonia itself is readily biodegradable and presents no threat to the environment, there was nonetheless a perceived association amongst consumers between the distinctive ammonia scent and dangerous household chemicals. This association was addressed by the launch of Windex Clear. Introduced by S.C. Johnson & Son in 1993 soon after their purchase of Drackett, Windex Clear dropped the ammonia along with the color blue that had become so closely associated with window cleaning. When this product was introduced it was promoted as having all of the cleaning power of the traditional blue ammonia formula but without the ammonia odor. This marketing strategy was soon changed, however, to one that stressed the superior cleaning ability of the product rather than its appearance and scent.

### Advertising and Marketing

When Windex was introduced in 1935 the Drackett Co. already had an effective marketing and distribution network in place thanks to its already very successful Drāno brand. The early success of Windex was in part due to the Drackett Co.'s ability to distribute and advertise the product nationally at a time when most manufacturers of cleaning products were operating at a regional level. By the 1950s Drackett had established a strong national production and distribution network with plants in Ohio, California, and Pennsylvania. While newspaper advertising represented the bulk of Drackett's advertising expenditures in the early years, by the late 1950s television had assumed a major role in the company's campaigns. Drackett was able to reach a huge national audience as sponsors of the extremely popular *Jackie Gleason Show*. Gleason delivered comical lead-ins to the Drackett commercials, posing with a shopping cart full of oversized versions of Drackett products, including a three-foot-high bottle of Windex.

Drackett switched to a more diversified approach in the mid-1960s, as the sponsoring of television shows by one dominant company or brand became less feasible. The Ogilvy & Mather agency ran a series of highly produced ads that relied to a great extent on Windex's already well-established reputation. As the overwhelming market leader, Drackett could afford to emphasize Windex's equivalence with clean sun-drenched windows and shiny mirrors. It was the beauty and allure of clean glass and its natural association in the consumer's mind with Windex that was emphasized rather than Windex's superior performance to other glass cleaners. This approach to advertising persisted through the 1980s under the direction of Grey Advertising and into the early 1990s under Laurence, Charles, Free and Lawson.

Windex, although still the overwhelming market leader, was faced with a dwindling market share when S.C. Johnson & Son, Inc., bought the Drackett Co. in late 1992. The new line extension, Windex Clear, was ready to be launched as an ammonia-free, fresh-scented, glass cleaner. S C Johnson Wax put together an initial package of promotional materials stressing the fresh scent of the product. Over the summer of 1993, however, it was apparently decided that, in order to counter the major threat to Windex from a number of newly launched multi-surface cleaners, Windex Clear should be promoted, instead, as a multi-surface cleaner with superior grease cutting abilities. The label on the package was changed from "works like ammonia with no ammonia odor . . . glass cleaner" to "unique degreasing formula . . . glass and surface cleaner." A series of television ads were also launched by DDB Needham showing the new Windex Clear cleaning a clear glass stove top, apparently in an attempt to capitalize on Windex's traditional association with glass cleaning while extending this association to kitchen surfaces.

The highly successful Drackett Co. began to expand its international operations in the late 1950s and early 1960s. Its first move outside the USA involved the founding of a wholly-owned subsidiary, Drackett Canada, which handled distribution in that area of North America. By 1964 Drackett was distributing Windex in Germany, Australia, and England and test marketing the product in other common market countries. The acquisition of the company by Bristol-Myers Squibb in 1965 further expanded the distribution of Windex, as Bristol-Myers established distribution networks in the Middle and Far East. By 1992, when it was purchased by S.C. Johnson & Son, Drackett had facilities in Taiwan, Great Britain, Australia, New Zealand, and Canada. S.C. Johnson & Son also maintained a very strong overseas presence that conveniently meshed with the already established distribution system for Windex.

## Performance and Major Competitors

When Windex was first introduced in 1935 a number of other more regionally-based window cleaners were on the market, but Windex soon eclipsed them in the national ratings. Through the next 40 years a myriad of glass cleaning products were introduced, including some with bizarre claims or formats. These ranged from Brand "X," a window cleaning cream that claimed to end window washing forever, to Open Sky, a product that came with an extra "tablet" to be dissolved in the liquid before cleaning. None of these products made any significant impact on Windex, which in 1959 could claim 75 percent of the glass cleaning market.

The first real threat to Windex's complete dominance of the market came from Texize's Glass Plus, introduced in the mid-1970s and since acquired by Dow Chemical's DowBrands L.P. Essentially imitating the successful elements of Windex—including its ammonia base and blue color—Glass Plus was marketed as a multi-surface cleaner at a time when increasingly busy householders were switching from specialized to all-purpose products. Although Windex itself had been unsuccessful in its launch of a similar product a decade earlier, Glass Plus managed to gain some 20 percent of the market, mostly at the expense of Windex. By the early 1980s Windex had dropped to a 60 percent market share of the then-expanding $127 million glass cleaning sector. Surprisingly, Windex did not respond directly to this significant new threat. Although Glass Plus's success was in large part due to its marketing as an all-purpose surface cleaner, Drackett did not make any major attempts to try to reposition Windex as a multi-surface cleaner. Some ads and packaging did suggest that Windex was effective at cleaning a variety of surfaces but Windex packaging continued to label the product as a glass cleaner even when most competitors had switched to a multi-surface cleaner label. It was only in 1993, after its acquisition by S.C. Johnson & Son, that Windex labeling was finally converted to read "glass and multi-surface cleaner."

Following the success of Glass Plus, the 1980s saw a rash of new glass and surface cleaners enter the market, many piggy-backing on already established brands. This included Colgate-Palmolive Company's Ajax glass cleaner, Miles Inc.'s S.O.S. Glass Works and Clorox's Formula 409 glass and surface cleaner. While Miles Inc.'s. vinegar-based Glass Works initially did very well, capturing some 15 percent of the market at Windex's expense, Windex's counter-product—Vinegar Windex—recaptured much of this share. Procter & Gamble's sweetly scented Cinch, one of the first glass cleaners to drop the format (blue, ammonia-based) established by Windex, made major inroads into the glass and all-purpose cleaner market in the early 1990s. By 1993 the total market share of Windex products, which included Regular, Vinegar, Lemon and Clear versions of the product, had dropped to below 50 percent of the window cleaning sector. Compounding Windex's problems in 1993, the glass and window cleaning sector as a whole, after expanding steadily for the almost 60 years since Windex was introduced, underwent a relatively abrupt drop of more than 10 percent from its 1991 peak of $237 million. Given both the overall decline in sales in the sector and Windex's diminished share of this market, the new owners of Windex, S.C. Johnson & Son, will have to develop new marketing strategies for Windex if the brand is to maintain its historically dominant position.

## Further Reading:

Battaglio, Stephen, "Cleaners Shine Up to 'Lemon Law'," *Adweek's Marketing Week,* May 18, 1987, p. 1.

Bird, Laura, "Cleanser Free-for-all," *The Wall Street Journal,* April 9, 1993, p. B3.

Deveny, Kathleen, "As More Americans Declare War on Dirt, Cleaning-Product Firms Make Tidy Sums," *The Wall Street Journal,* April 6, 1993, p. B1.

"Drackett Earnings Gleam on Research, Promotion," *Barron's,* February 9, 1959, pp. 34–6.

Fitzgerald, Kate, "How Johnson will Gain with Drackett," *Advertising Age,* November 3, 1992, p. 5.

Freeman, Laurie, "New Household Products Bow," *Advertising Age,* November 25, 1985, p. 3; "Drackett Fights to Keep Household Edge," *Advertising Age,* February 27, 1989, p. 35.

"Glass Cleaner War Gets Bitter," *Adweek's Marketing Week,* January 12, 1987, p. 41.

"Glass Cleaners: Cleaner Windows Cheaper," *Consumer Reports,* January 1992, pp. 22–24.

Lazarus, George, "Windex: Vim with Vinegar," *Adweek's Marketing Week,* January 26, 1987, p. 24.

Mathews, Carol, "Stick-To-It-iveness Pays Off For Drackett Co.," *Investment Dealers' Digest,* February 24, 1964, pp. 30–31.

"Now There's a Real Brand X," *Broadcasting,* October 10, 1960, p. 50.

Strasser, Susan, *Never Done,* New York: Pantheon Books, 1982.

"Windex Tests TV Ad Showing How It Cleans Up Grand Central Terminal," *Advertising Age,* January 29, 1968, p. 39.

*—Hilary Gopnik and Donald McManus*

# WISK®

Industry giant Procter & Gamble forever changed U.S. laundry habits in 1946 when it introduced Tide, the first synthetic detergent powerful enough to get dirty clothes really clean. Tide almost overnight became the country's best-selling laundry product, and other soap makers, such as Lever Brothers, a subsidiary of Unilever, were left scrambling to catch up. The first synthetic detergent from Lever Brothers was Surf, initially marketed in the early 1950s. Then in 1956 Lever Brothers introduced Wisk, the first heavy-duty liquid detergent.

Wisk eventually became the second-leading brand of laundry detergent in the United States, holding an 8.5 percent share of the market compared to 38.5 percent for Procter & Gamble's Tide brand. It was available as a liquid or as a superconcentrated powder.

## Ring around the Collar

Marketed as the "liquid miracle for family wash," liquid Wisk initially attracted consumer attention as the latest innovation in laundry detergents. Despite costing almost twice as much as powdered detergents, sales of Wisk grew steadily over the first few years until it had captured a modest but significant share of the market, estimated at about 4.2 percent. But as the novelty of a liquid detergent wore off, the share of the market held by the Wisk brand began to fade. By 1967 it had fallen to less than three percent, and it was obvious that Wisk needed help if the brand was to continue.

James Jordan, then a copywriter with the advertising agency of Batten, Barton, Durstine & Osborne, suggested a new marketing strategy that focused attention on one particular wash-day challenge. Jordan had read consumer research suggesting that housewives considered their husbands' dirty shirt collars to be their single biggest laundry problem. Jordan proposed an advertising campaign that touted the Wisk brand's effectiveness on "ring around the collar." The result was one of the most effective, longest-running, and well-remembered advertising campaigns in history.

Dirty collars became almost a national hysteria, according to television commercials showing housewives reduced to tears by unrelenting chants of "ring around the collar." In *Getting It Right the Second Time*, author Michael Gershman stated that the ad campaign made dirty collars into "an all-purpose villain that

could create tension with neighbors, produce migraine headaches, prevent promotions for hubby, [and] upset stable marriages." According to the commercials, only Wisk brand detergent could save housewives from such humiliation. Sales of Wisk tripled over the next seven years.

Years later, Jordan, then a principal in his own agency, told *Advertising Age* that the famous ring-around-the-collar campaign "has dogged me a little bit." While it was enormously effective, many viewers also found the commercials among the most irritating to ever appear on television. But Jordan added, "I'm proud of Wisk, and I'm a devout believer in the campaign. It sold the bejesus out of Wisk." The ring-around-the-collar campaign was finally abandoned in 1987.

Ironically, when Lever Brothers changed advertising agencies and awarded the Wisk account to J. Walter Thompson in 1989, the copywriter on the account was Jordan's son, J.J. Jordan. After clinging to the ring-around-the-collar slogan for 20 years, Lever Brothers had become concerned that consumers were associating the Wisk brand with the "obnoxious" commercials while the message about the detergent's effectiveness as a stain fighter was getting lost. Lever Brothers wanted a new image. However, the new campaign clearly reflected its lineage. The first commercial from J. Walter Thompson retained the idea of public humiliation by showing people in various embarrassing situations, such as being splashed with mud. Bystanders scolded them with "tisk, tisk, tisk," which was then answered by an off-stage announcer with "Wisk, Wisk, Wisk."

## Rise of Liquid Detergents

Wisk also benefitted in the late 1960s from environmental concerns over phosphates. In 1967 Stewart L. Udall, then Secretary of the Interior, called upon U.S. detergent makers to eliminate the use of phosphates, which studies showed contributed to eutrophication (the process by which freshwater lakes eventually become clogged with organic material, especially algae, causing fish and other marine life to die). Phosphates were used in almost all powdered detergents to boost cleaning power. However, because phosphates would not stay suspended in solution, they were not used in liquid detergents. Initially, this was a major drawback, since liquid detergents were generally less effective than powdered detergents. But as concern over phosphates grew, more people began using liquid detergents. In addition, as communities

## AT A GLANCE

**W**isk brand of laundry detergent was introduced in 1956 by Lever Brothers, New York-based subsidiary of the Unilever Group.

*Performance:* *Market share*—8.5% of laundry detergent category. *Sales*—$69 million.

*Major competitor:* Procter & Gamble's Tide.

*Advertising:* *Agency*—J. Walter Thompson, 1989—. *Major campaign*—"Tisk, Tisk, Tisk."

*Addresses:* *Parent company*—Lever Brothers Company, 390 Park Avenue, New York, NY 10022; phone: (212) 688-6000; fax: (212) 906-4411. *Ultimate parent company*—Unilever Group, Unilever PLC, Unilever House, London, UK; Unilever NV, P.O. Box 760-3000, Rotterdam, Netherlands.

and entire states began to ban phosphates, powdered detergent makers began to eliminate phosphates, which put liquids on a more comparable basis.

The uproar over phosphates eventually died down as the detergent industry developed effective substitutes and environmental scientists came to agree that sewage and other chemicals were probably more to blame for eutrophication than phosphates. But the switch to liquids had begun. Wisk was the sole major brand of liquid laundry detergent until the late 1960s, but liquid detergents proliferated over the next 15 years and eventually captured almost 60 percent of the total market for laundry detergents. In 1987, Michael Angus, then Lever Brothers' vice president for technical development, told *Soap/Cosmetics/Chemical Specialties* magazine that legislative action to reduce phosphates "without question" gave rise to the market for liquid detergents.

Although the Tide brand continued to dominate the market, by the mid 1980s Wisk had grown to hold about eight percent and replaced Procter & Gamble's Cheer as the number two detergent in the United States. Unfortunately for Lever Brothers, Wisk's reign as number two was short lived. Procter & Gamble entered the market for liquid laundry detergents in the 1970s with Era and Solo. Neither of those brands ever gained much popularity, but in 1985, Procter & Gamble introduced Liquid Tide. By 1987 Liquid Tide had moved into the number two spot, ending Wisk's 30-year run as the leading brand of liquid detergent. Lever Brothers responded by introducing Advanced Action Wisk; however, the Tide name kept the new Liquid Tide brand in first place among liquids.

## Super Concentrates

In the 1990s liquid detergents, including Wisk, also began losing ground to new superconcentrated powders, which also nearly eliminated regular powdered detergents altogether. As the *Wall Street Journal* reported in 1993, "In the past two years, U.S. consumers have fundamentally changed the way they go about performing one of life's perpetual chores: washing their clothes. For four decades, people spilled powdery soap out of giant-sized boxes into their washing machines. In recent years, many consumers switched to liquid detergents. But now, most are flipping up the top of a small cardboard cube and measuring out a dose of concentrated granules with a recyclable scoop."

Colgate-Palmolive introduced the first concentrated powder, Fresh Start, in 1980 but it not well received. However, ten years later, wash-day habits had changed significantly. Consumers were washing bigger loads and washing less often. In addition, environmental concerns had shifted from phosphates to wasteful packaging. In 1990 Lever Brothers responded by introducing two new superconcentrated powdered detergents under the Wisk brand name, Wisk Power Scoop and Unscented Wisk Power Scoop.

George Yuen, then Lever Brothers' senior product manager, called the Wisk Power Scoop brand "the first real innovation [in laundry detergents] in more than 30 years." According to the company's press releases, Wisk Power Scoop was "concentrated to the theoretical limit of density." Wisk Power Scoop was also "bio-engineered" with "an entirely new class of enzymes specifically designed to dislodge and dissolve oily dirt and stains." Advertising also stressed that Wisk Power Scoop was "environmentally friendly" because of the smaller package size. David F. Webb, then president of Lever Brothers, told *Advertising Age* in 1990 that Wisk Power Scoop was "more concentrated than any other detergent [in the United States] at the moment. Small is beautiful."

## Future

In the early 1990s, superconcentrated powders accounted for more than half the market for laundry detergents. Liquid detergents accounted for another 38 percent, while regular-strength

*Wisk detergent as it looked upon its introduction in 1956.*

powders had fallen to about seven percent. Another category, superconcentrated liquids, was just beginning to emerge. In 1993, Lever Brothers launched Double Power Wisk, a thick blue liquid "packed with double the cleaning power, so consumers need to use only half the liquid to clean more kinds of stains better than ever before.''

## Further Reading:

Bird, Laura, ''Detergent Industry Spins Into New Cycle,'' *Wall Street Journal,* January 5, 1993, p. B1.

Brown, Andrew C., ''Unilever Fights Back in the U.S.,'' *Fortune,* May 26, 1986, pp. 32–8.

Dagnoli, Judann, and Jennifer Lawrence, ''Lever, Colgate Chase P&G,'' *Advertising Age,* May 13, 1991, p. 16.

Donohue, Janet, ''Lever's Hockey Talks about Changes in Household Products,'' *Soap/Cosmetics/Chemical Specialties,* August, 1987.

Elliot, Stuart, ''An Enthusiastic Pitchman at the Helm of Lever Bros.,'' *New York Times,* August 20, 1992.

Freeman, Laurie, ''Wisk Rings in New Ad Generation,'' *Advertising Age,* September 18, 1989, p. 1.

Gershman, Michael, *Getting It Right the Second Time,* New York: Addison-Wesley, 1990, pp. 3–4.

Levin, Gary, ''Peopleworks: James Jordan, On Wisk Acount It's Like Father, Like Son,'' *Advertising Age,* October 2, 1989, p. 48.

*—Dean Boyer*

# WRANGLER®

**Wrangler**

Wrangler, the leader in the jeans market since 1992, claims that in 1947 it gave the world the first fully proportioned denim jeans that were designed to fit the body. Prior to this new design, jeans were merely a modified version of loose-fitting bib overalls, a standard form of work apparel. While jeans enjoyed tremendous popularity in the 1960s and 1970s, the jeans market experienced a slump in the 1980s. Wrangler rallied in the early 1990s as the company began capitalizing on its Western cache and the country music craze that swept the country. In 1992 Wrangler wrested leadership in the jeans market from Levi Strauss & Co. Along with it companion brand, Lee, Wrangler is part of the jeanswear division of VF Corporation, the world's largest publicly-held apparel company.

## Brand Origins

The Wrangler brand was launched circa 1947 when Blue Bell, Inc., a major producer of work clothing, decided to expand its line to include Western wear and recreational clothes. In the mid-1930s the Greensboro, North Carolina, company had pioneered such processes as sanforizing, proportioned fit and informative labeling for its work clothing. During World War II, the company developed new production methods while making over 24 million military garments for the U.S. Armed Services. With its production facilities and manufacturing processes well established by the end of the war, Blue Bell was transformed from the "world's largest producer of work clothes to the world's largest producer of work and play clothes," according to company-published literature. With the birth of its national brand name, Wrangler, an uninterrupted period of growth began.

By 1949 there were 21 Blue Bell plants across the country. Later plants were established in Indiana, Georgia, Alabama, Mississippi, North Carolina, Oklahoma, and Texas. While the company that eventually became Blue Bell had experienced several mergers before the birth of Wrangler, the merger with VF Corporation in 1986 was the most significant. Financial analysts estimated the value of the transaction at $775 million, according to *Wall Street Journal*. The newspaper reported that the merger gave VF the "opportunity to double its sales and diversify its product lines." Today Wrangler operates as a separate division of VF Corporation.

## Early Marketing Strategy

To secure a foothold in the Western wear market, Wrangler forged a powerful relationship with the Professional Rodeo Cowboy Association (PRCA) in 1947—a relationship it continues to nurture. Wrangler consulted some of the association's top rodeo riders to develop a pair of jeans that would fit their needs. The riders said they wanted a snug fit for a better grip in the saddle, leg bottoms that were wide enough to fit over boots and ample pockets. Wrangler developed 13 versions before it got the jeans right, and consequently named the jeans 13MWZ (men's with zipper) Cowboy Cut jeans. The company became the exclusive apparel sponsor of the PRCA and helped make rodeo a professional sport by working to establish standardized rules and increase prize money.

To enhance its association with the PRCA, Wrangler began displaying promotional signs in rodeo arenas and placing ads in the PRCA's annual guide and program booklets. Print ads with a rodeo theme appeared in such publications as *Western Horseman, Horse Illustrated, Quarter Horse Journal* and *Pro Rodeo Sports News*. "Wrangler, country music and the rodeo are inextricably connected," Mervyn Rozet, the senior vice president of The Martin Agency, Wrangler's ad agency, was quoted as saying in *Advertising Age*. "Wrangler's big strength is its Western authenticity. Wrangler jeans are standard equipment for the rodeo cowboy, just like the rope, saddle and boots. It's the brand of the working cowboy. People want to emulate that."

## Advertising Innovations

In response to the sagging jeans market in the mid-1980s, Wrangler began developing a new ad campaign that stressed the jeans' Western flavor and all-American appeal. Wrangler's target audience was blue collar workers who had been buying fewer jeans as the result of the economic slowdown. The new Wrangler commercials were "compelling and uniquely photographed vignettes of real blue-collar working men on and off the job, wearing jeans at both work and play," according to *New York Times*. The 60-, 30-, and 15-second spots were designed to capture a feeling rather than discuss product benefits. Each spot had the same minimal copy: "There's a new stone-washed jeans from Wrangler, made for a man after his work is done."

## AT A GLANCE

**T**he Wrangler brand of jeanswear established c. 1947 by the organizational leadership of Blue Bell Inc., a manufacturer of work and recreational clothing located in Greensboro, NC; Blue Bell and the Wrangler brand were acquired by VF Corporation in 1986.

**Performance:** *Market share*—19% of the jeanswear category. *Sales*—$1.9 billion (VF Corporation's jeanswear division, which includes Wrangler, Lee and Girbaud).

**Major competitor:** Levi Strauss & Co.'s Levi's.

**Advertising:** *Agency*—The Martin Agency, 1988—. *Major campaign*—"A Western original wears a Western original," featuring sports figures, celebrities and country music singers wearing Wrangler jeans.

**Addresses:** *Parent company*—VF Corporation, 1047 North Park Road, Wyomissing, PA 19610; phone: (215) 378-1151; fax: (215) 375-9371.

Wrangler and its ad agency at the time, Saatchi & Saatchi DFS Compton, described them as the "American Hero" spots. The vignettes pictured groups of muscular, jeans-wearing men on the job in steel mills, fighting forest fires, and on tugboats; and then showed them at leisure. The featured men moved in slow motion, and the film's gritty quality served "to enhance the image of the working man," Terry Gallo, a creative director at Saatchi, commented in the *New York Times*. The music for the spots had a hymn-like quality that Gallo saw as "heroic and uplifting" with a tone of "strong masculine purity."

The "American Hero" campaign helped Wrangler solve a marketing problem in the East, where Wrangler jeans were perceived as work clothing that was inappropriate for social settings. Wrangler ran the ads primarily in the East and in a few large Western markets. The commercial that ran in the West, where Wrangler was already a widely respected name in both work and casualwear, featured five rodeo stars and a musical score by country music star Willie Nelson, who had a long association with the Wrangler brand.

In 1988 Wrangler hired The Martin Agency of Richmond, Virginia, to run its ad campaigns. The agency hired Cleo award-winning director Peter Smillie to direct two new TV spots, each of which was available in 60- and 30-second formats. Again, Wrangler was targeting blue-collar males, particularly those who buy large numbers of jeans. Wrangler had surveyed men who bought at least 12 pairs a year and had redesigned its jeans accordingly. "The man we want to reach lives in and around small towns," Mike Hughes, creative director at The Martin Agency, explained in *Back Stage*. "He is comfortable with himself and the way he lives. These spots address that way of life."

As in the previous ad campaign, the spots were primarily mood pieces designed to capture a laid-back feeling. In the spot entitled "Driving Lesson," a man takes his son out in a pickup to give him his first driving lesson. The kid runs into a mailbox, causing mail to scatter along the dusty road. At first the father and son are taken aback, then Dad sees the humor in the situation and they both end up laughing. In "Old Dog," a man gets out of bed, puts on his jeans, shaves and goes out to the fishing pond with his faithful dog. They fish all day and return home empty-handed. "The quietude

of the images is truly striking: a cup of hot coffee steaming in the morning light, a slightly paunchy guy regarding himself in the mirror, the interior of a rough-hewn country house," *Back Stage* magazine commented. "The stories draw their power from the simplicity and clarity of Smillie's images."

Wrangler continued to focus on its Western wear niche in its 1990 print ad campaign, "A Western original wears a Western original." Wrangler CEO Mackey McDonald explained in *Business North Carolina* that the company decided to expand its line of western apparel to appeal to would-be cowboys. "We decided rather than be the brand that 80 percent of the people in the United States liked, we'd be the brand that 20 percent of the people has to have." This strategy helped Wrangler maintain an edge in the fiercely competitive jeans market.

The "Western Original" campaign, developed with The Martin Agency, was designed to "celebrate the role Wrangler plays in the authentic Western lifestyle." Some of the notables featured in the campaign were country music star George Strait, football hero Earl Campbell, rodeo legend Jim Shoulders and Miss American 1990/cattle broker, Gretchen Polhemus. The ads ran in general interest magazines and Western-oriented publications. "The beauty of this campaign was that we didn't have to find Western heroes and put them in our jeans," Craig Veazey, Wrangler's director of advertising, was quoted as saying in *Marketing News*. "They've always worn Wrangler."

In 1992 Wrangler marketed the official George Strait concert tour jacket, underscoring its association with country music. "The rodeo circuit is what catapulted Wrangler into country music, Rozet of The Martin Agency explained in *Advertising Age*. "All [country stars] want to be rooted in authenticity in the West." Wrangler further extended its country music connections by regularly providing new acts in Nashville with complementary clothes. Capitalizing on the popularity of country music, Wrangler increased its advertising spending by 15 percent in 1992, said Veazey in *Advertising Age*. LNA/Arbitron Multi-Media estimated that Wrangler spent about $6.9 million on measured media in 1991. Wrangler placed more ads on network and cable country programming, including cable's Nashville Network in 1992. In the Western United States, it aired a spot that saluted "rodeo cowboys and the women who love them."

### International Growth

VF International, VF Corporation's international operations division, posted increased sales in its jeanswear division in 1992, although overall operating profit declined slightly, according to the company's 1992 annual report. This decline resulted from startup expenses in newly acquired divisions and additional advertising and structuring costs in existing divisions. VF International continued to pursue opportunities for long-term growth in Europe. To support the growth of Wrangler and other jeanswear brands in Central Europe, a new factory in Poland was opened in 1993. VF International's jeanswear unit continued to implement programs with major retailers across Europe and the United Kingdom. "Wrangler has provided European retailers with a well-established, quality brand that satisfied key consumer groups and distribution channels—backed up world class capabilities," Barry Brennan, director of business development for Wrangler Europe, commented in VF Corporation's 1992 annual report.

## Brand Development

Since Wrangler's first attempt to develop the perfect rodeo riding jeans, the company has been receptive to the needs of the marketplace. Wrangler offers a wide variety of jeans and jeans-related products, from its basic jeans to Western-style shirts and blouses. In 1991 Wrangler launched a men's clothing line called Timber Creek to compete with Levi Strauss and Co.'s Dockers line. Aimed at males in the 20 to 40 age group, Timber Creek featured four pre-washed cotton long-sleeve shirts. Unlike the Dockers line, which was sold primarily through department stores, Timber Creek was marketed through discount stores, such as Kmart and Wal-Mart. "We feel that the [discount] market is totally untapped" for men's casual wear," said Angelo LeGrega, vice president of Wrangler, in *Advertising Age*. Wrangler also introduced Riata, a Western line that is dressier and more fashionable than its basic Wrangler Western line. The Riata 75 pant, for example, is made from lightweight twill and has a pleated front and two dress back pockets.

A year before Timber Creek and Riata were introduced, Wrangler had launched Wrangler Rugged Wear, a collection of casual rugged apparel targeted to male consumers aged 25 and older who engage in outdoor activities such as hunting and fishing. Although the majority of Rugged Wear products have basic features, the line includes a series of specialty products that combine denim with high-tech attributes such as 3M Thinsulate quilted linings for warmth or Cordura nylon covering for water resistance.

Earth Wash Jeans, produced using fewer environmentally hazardous chemicals, were incorporated into the Rugged Wear line in 1993. The jeans were produced through the use of specially engineered dyes that reduce the amount of sulfides emitted in chemical plants and fabric mills. The dying process also uses significantly less water to help in the conservation of rivers, lakes, and streams. Additionally, all Earth Wash Jeans are laundered by prewashing or with natural protein enzymes, thus reducing or eliminating stonewashing (which produces sediment, harsh bleaches, and harmful chemicals). "Our objective with Earth Wash was to find a manufacturing process that is environmentally responsible yet allows us to continue to offer high-quality products at the right price," Juan Munoz, vice president of Wrangler Rugged Wear said in a Wrangler press release.

## Performance Appraisal

Since VF Corporation acquired the Wrangler brand in 1986, it has been one of the company's major brands. Like other jeanswear manufacturers, Wrangler was affected when consumer demand for jeans tumbled in the 1980s. Market-wide sales of jeans shrank from 510 million pairs sold in 1981 to 385 million in 1992. The entire jeans market generated about $6.5 billion in sales in 1987, and Wrangler enjoyed a nine percent market share that year. Wrangler's market share grew to 14.7 percent by 1991, making the company the number two jeanswear manufacturer in the country. By February of 1992 Wrangler had a 15.4 percent market share, second still to Levi Strauss and Co.'s 20.2 percent share, according to MRCA Information Services.

Although Wrangler placed second to Levi's national market share, it was still number one with rodeo fans. "Wrangler is by far the dominant brand in Western wear," according to John Wilcox, vice president of sales promotion for Sheplers, the largest Western wear retail and catalog company, in *Advertising Age*. Wrangler

had always been popular in the West and Southwest but sales in the Midwest and Southeast grew by 40 percent in 1991.

VF Corporation's sales rose 13 percent to $3 billion in 1991 and by more than 30 percent in the first half of 1992, according to *Forbes*. Half of the company's total business was in jeans, which accounted for 60 percent of 1992's sales increase. By the end of the first eight months of 1992, Wrangler, with a 19 percent market share, had taken the leadership position in the jeans market from Levi Strauss, which had a 18 percent market share. *Forbes* states that the craze for country music—and the fact that many top country music performers wear Wrangler—has contributed to Wrangler's outstanding performance.

## Future Predictions

Wrangler has remained true to its Western connections since the brand's inception and has enjoyed consistently positive results in terms of sales and brand loyalty. To keep pace with the division's rapid growth, VF Corporation made substantial capital investments in 1992 to expand Wrangler's production and distribution facilities. These additions were expected to improve service and reduce costs, according to VF Corporation's 1992 annual report.

VF International's jeanswear unit was planning for growth in worldwide business, and was in the process of implementing programs with major retailers across Europe and in the United Kingdom. The unit was also expanding its Market Response System, a sophisticated system of electronic links between the selling floor and VF divisions that helps bring products more quickly to market and gives real-time feedback about how customers are responding to products.

## Further Reading:

Beamon, Todd, "Wrangler Closings to Lay Off 1,200," *New York Times*, January 14, 1987, p. D5.

"Cleo Plans Green Cards, Gift Wrap," *Advertising Age*, February 25, 1991, p. 47.

Dale, Arden, "Peter Smillie Directs Wrangler Spots for The Martin Agency," *Back Stage*, July 14, 1989, p. 14.

Dougherty, Philip H., "Blue Collar Images for Wrangler," *New York Times*, August 3, 1987, p. D9.

"The Downtown Strips Fashion of All Pretense," *Superbrands 1991*, p. 44.

Fisher, Christy, "Timber Creek Set to Take on Dockers," *Advertising Age*, July 29, 1991, pp. 3; "Wrangler Makes Brand Imprint Via Rodeo Scene," *Advertising Age*, May 25, 1992, pp. 33–38.

Gerrie, Anthea, "Ad Battle Hots Up in Jeans Sector," *Marketing*, April 3, 1986, p. 6.

Interbrand, *World's Greatest Brands*, New York: Wiley & Sons, 1992, p. 69.

"Jeans Bottom Out, But He Tightens Up," *Business North Carolina*, August, 1991, pp. 56–57.

Miller, Cyndee, "Jeans Marketers Look for Good Fit with Older Men and Women," *Marketing News*, September 16, 1991, pp. 1(2).

Poushine, Tatiana, "Ridin' High," *Forbes*, November 9, 1992, pp. 78–80.

Sloan, Pat, and Magiera, Marcy, "Rustlin Up Jeans Ads," *Advertising Age*, July 29, 1991, pp. 3(2).

VF Corporation 1992 Annual Report, Wyomissing, Pennsylvania: VF Corporation, 1992.

"Wrangler Replaces Leased Lines with Circuit-Switched Data," *Telecommunications*, July, 1990, p. 37.

*—Pam Berry*

# ZEST®

The Zest brand of soap, in its original deodorant formula, is one of the most enduring lines of soap in the United States. Packaged in both trademarked aqua-green and white boxes, each with a burst composed of pink and yellow lines, Zest soap has been offering performance and value to consumers for more than 30 years. Just one line of products put out by the Procter & Gamble Company (P&G), which also manufactures such popular brands as Luvs diapers, Downy fabric softener, and Duncan Hines cake mixes, Zest soap has remained a market share leader due to years of innovative reformulation and astute advertising.

## Brand Origins and First Commercial Success

The year was 1952, Harry S. Truman was president of the United States, and at the research laboratories of the Procter & Gamble Company in Cincinnati, Ohio, Zest soap was born. Company scientists felt that at last they actually had a bar that amalgamated all the advantages of a detergent. The advertising campaign blared: ''For the first time in your life, really feel clean!'' Indeed, within months, the brand rose to sales leadership. *Consumer Reports*, after running its own tests, wrote: ''Zest was the only product that lathered well in hard water; it lathered well even in salt water and left no curd; and it left no bathtub ring.''

In spite of all the kudos, however, something went wrong. When cold weather arrived, sales began to slip. The reason, researchers discovered, was that Zest worked *too* well, removing so many natural bodily oils that winter-cold skin became itchy and chapped. Apparently, the technical difficulties of putting synthetic properties into a toilet soap proved more onerous than anyone had thought, and Zest suffered a periodic setback.

## Early Marketing Strategy

Not to be deterred, P&G scientists began a concentrated effort to find a soap formula that retained the advantages of detergents. Product after product, each with a new feature, was tested. At last a bacteria-fighting ingredient was added to provide deodorant protection, and the color was changed from white to blue-green. ''We tried everything we could think of,'' commented a brand manager. ''I used to rub various formulas of Zest into my own arms on the coldest winter days to see the effects. Nothing was altogether satisfactory—at least, not for four long years.''

While P&G was working hard to improve its product, several competitors (particularly Lever Brothers—the maker of Dove soap) were introducing their own variations of what became known as a ''synthetic bar.'' At P&G laboratories, whenever some of the researchers' tests appeared encouraging, the urge arose to expand Zest's formulation. However, the view at executive conferences was that the perfect new Zest formula had not yet been discovered.

Finally, four years after the first marketing effort, a formula satisfactory to executives was found, and in 1957 ''new, improved'' Zest became a sudsy sales clincher, surpassing Camay as a leading soap, second only to the long-lived Ivory. Thereafter, testing of Zest would persist until a product was considered unequivocally ''right.''

At the time Zest was climbing in popularity, another soap, called Dial, marketed by Armour, was gaining sales momentum. Dial was advertised as a deodorant soap, promising the reduction of odor-causing bacteria because of a new ingredient—hexachlorophene. In the beginning, Dial had only Lever's Lifebuoy as competition in the deodorant soap market, but soon it started building sales in that portion of the soap sector dominated by complexion bars Lux and Camay.

Because consumer interest was stimulated by heavy advertising of such toiletry items as underarm deodorants and anti-perspirants, Dial capitalized on the toiletry trend of the times by promoting its deodorant bar. Although P&G moved too slowly to recognize this widening deodorant market, once the company perceived it, Zest was able to quickly establish its own tenable position in the soap sector.

## Advertising Innovations

In addition to having Zest sponsor wholesome TV programs fostering family values, Procter & Gamble took full advantage of all types of media to market the soap. P&G advertising dated back to 1882, when Harley Procter, son of the cofounder of the Company, formulated the first promotional campaign for Ivory Soap. Many of his marketing concepts proved so intrinsically well thought out, so logically planned, and so consumer-oriented that they continued into the next century. By 1993 health and beauty aids sections of retail stores regularly received large cardboard displays of Zest featuring refund tear-off forms; color inserts,

## AT A GLANCE

**Z**est brand of soap founded in 1952 in Cincinnati, OH, by Procter & Gamble Company; improved formula introduced in 1957.

**Performance:** *Market share*—6.5% of toilet soap category.

**Major competitor:** Lever Brothers' Dove and Lever 2000; also Greystone/Dial's Dial.

**Advertising:** *Agency*—Jordan, McGrath, Case & Taylor, New York, NY. *Major campaign*—"You're not fully clean until you're Zest-fully clean!"

**Addresses:** *Parent company*—Procter & Gamble Company, One Procter & Gamble Plaza, Cincinnati, OH 45202; phone: (513) 983-1100; fax: (513) 983-7847.

exemplified by exquisite artwork, and vendor coupons appeared in Sunday newspapers; and consumers could receive premiums in exchange for proofs-of-purchase from Zest.

### Brand Development and Product Changes

As times and styles changed, so did Zest. Having premiered as a white bar in 1952—then reformulated in 1957—it was improved upon again in 1986. The new Zest rinsed and lathered better and was less drying to the skin. In September of 1987, Zest Free, a white, unscented bar with a masking fragrance, was introduced in a limited area—St. Louis—but was eventually discontinued because of a lack of consumer interest. In June of 1992, trichlocarbon, an additive commonly found in deodorants and deodorant soaps, was removed from Zest for health reasons. Also that year, the Zest line was expanded with the addition of Whitewater Fresh Zest with fragrance.

The restive guardians of Zest's future always made certain the soap received new packaging from time to time. In 1981 the swirl on the wrapper was changed from chartreuse to gold, and in 1992 the paper wrapper was dropped in favor of a box. The following year the two varieties available were Original, in the aqua-green box, and Whitewater Fresh, in the white box.

### International Growth

Procter & Gamble had long vended its products abroad, so the marketing framework was already in place when the company decided to expand Zest's availability. In 1897 Ivory Soap had been introduced in England. Even as far back as the 1930s, P&G had acquired Sabates, S.A., a soap, perfume, and candle factory in Havana, Cuba, to debut its own brands, and the Philippines Manufacturing Company in Manila, which brought with it an existing business in soap and vegetable products. By 1993, Zest was sold in Mexico and Europe.

### Performance Appraisal

Zest was developed in direct response to the post-World War II proliferation of malls that attracted an affluent clientele and spurred the trend toward self-service. Prior to the war, most toiletries had been retailed through department stores, beauty shops, and full-service drugstores. By the mid-1950s, however, grocery supermarkets had added departments to handle toilet articles, and

a new breed of discount self-service outlet had come on the scene. These large-volume stores were rapidly capturing a mushrooming portion of toiletry sales and would go on to handle more than 16 percent of all toiletries by the early 1970s.

Unfortunately, P&G failed to recognize quickly enough the hygiene-improvement movement and marketed Zest too slowly to capsize Armour's lead, for Armour not only touted a soap— Dial—it introduced an accompanying anti-perspirant/deodorant as well. Thereafter, Dial always maintained a sizable market share, even though Zest was an excellent product and performed superlatively. If any single factor could be blamed for Zest's inability to capture the lead in the toilet soap category, it would have to be the lack of deodorant market savvy on the part of P&G executives. Despite this sluggish start, Zest remained in the marketplace while other soaps slipped away. Through the years, Zest might not have been number one, but it did garner a loyal following of deodorant soap users and kept pace with progress in both formulation and packaging.

### Future Predictions

Zest is a soap that was born of Procter & Gamble's belief that consumers counted and deserved the best. For more than 40 years it has remained an enduring brand in the United States and later internationally. Zest grew up on these marketing foundations of performance and value. In addition, P&G chemists and marketers were always thinking of the future by querying consumers, sampling and advertising, creating new technologies, and updating Zest Soap—improving, but not deviating from, the basic formula. As a P&G researcher once remarked: "It isn't enough to invent a new product. Through constant improvement, we must manage every existing brand so that it can flourish year after year in an ever-changing and intensely competitive marketplace. . . . At P&G, we create the future."

### Further Reading:

*Answers About Marketing,* Cincinnati: Procter & Gamble Company, 1993.

Cleary, David Powers, *Great American Brands,* New York: Fairchild Publications, 1981.

Diamano, Nancy, "Soaping Up," *Canadian Consumer,* March 1991, p. 15.

*Facts About Procter & Gamble,* Cincinnati: Procter & Gamble Company, 1993.

Editors of *Advertising Age, Procter & Gamble: The House That Ivory Built,* Lincolnwood, IL: NTC Business Books, 1988.

"Hand and Bath Soaps," *Consumer Reports 1991 Buying Guide,* December 1990, pp. 328–330.

"Ivorydale—A Procter & Gamble Landmark," Cincinnati: Procter & Gamble Company, 1993.

Lawrence, Jennifer, "Will P&G's Pricing Policy Pull Retailers Over to Its Side?" *Advertising Age,* April 19, 1991, pp. 1, 42–43; "P&G Hooks Up Interactive Product-Sampling Hot Line," *Advertising Age,* November 23, 1992, p. 12; "P&G Customizes Ads to Plug Retailers," *Advertising Age,* February 8, 1993, p. 38.

Lief, Alfred, *"It Floats"; The Story of Procter & Gamble,* New York: Rinehart, 1958.

*Procter & Gamble Company 1992 Annual Report,* Cincinnati: Procter & Gamble Company, 1993.

Schisgall, Oscar, *Eyes on Tomorrow: The Evolution of Procter & Gamble,* Chicago: J. G. Ferguson Publishing Company, 1981.

*—Virginia Barnstorff*

# ZIPLOC®

Ziploc brand of storage bags are the nation's top-selling zippered bags. When DowBrands introduced its patented zipper closure on its storage bag in 1970, it revolutionized the plastic bag market. The company was also the first introduce a heavy duty bag specially designed to meet harsh freezer conditions and protect against freezer burn. Ziploc storage, freezer, and sandwich bags are recommended for refrigerated storage and pantry/counter-top storage, but not for use in conventional or microwave ovens or ranges, or submersion in hot or boiling water.

## Brand Origins

The plastic storage bag was developed in response to consumer requests for a convenient, disposable food protector. Before the advent of plastic bags, consumers stored food in glass or plastic containers, or wrapped food in aluminum foil, wax paper, or plastic wraps. Various companies manufactured plastic bags specifically for holding sandwiches. Some general plastic storage bags existed in the market, but required twist ties. DowBrands introduced its own sandwich bag, but test marketing deemed it unsuccessful. DowBrands was interested in marketing a bag with a different type of closure that could provide the company with a competitive edge.

In 1966 company officials noticed a plastic bag with a zipper while attending a packaging trade show. Researchers at DowBrands saw widespread applications for the zipper closure, but realized that the innovative product would be more expensive to produce than existing plastic storage bags. In 1970 DowBrands introduced the Ziploc storage bag, with a patented, tongue-in-groove "zipper" closure designed to provide an airtight, watertight seal to keep moisture out and ensure food freshness. By 1972 the company was distributing Ziploc storage bags nationally.

The company then educated consumers about the bag's unique closure system. To help consumers make the association with the company, the Handi-Wrap name—another of Dowbrands' products—was cited on packages and advertisements. Within a year, sales of Ziploc bags were strong because consumers recognized its quality and did not mind paying the premium price.

## Brand Development

The success of the Ziploc storage bag led Dowbrands to look for other types of zipper bags to market. In 1975 the Ziploc sandwich bag made its debut because it represented a major market and had strong growth potential. After learning that about 30 percent of consumers buying storage bags used them for freezer storage, the company introduced the heavyweight Ziploc freezer bag in 1979. The bag could be used in conventional or frost-free freezers. In 1983 Dowbrands offered a new and improved closure, wide track seal that was an easier to close. In 1984 marketed pint-sized freezer bags for holding single servings of food. The following year the company introduced jumbo storage bags, realizing that consumers used Ziploc bags for non-food storage. The wide track zipper seal was added to all freezer bags.

A grip strip closure that made the bags easier to open was added to the entire Ziploc line in 1986. The same year, jumbo storage bags went into national distribution, and pint size storage bags went into regional distribution in the southeast. The company briefly marketed a microwaveable bag called Microfreez, but later discontinued it due to disappointing sales. In 1988 Dowbrands introduced a pleated half-gallon storage bag. In 1989 the company added a write-on label to storage, freezer, and sandwich bags for easy identification of contents. In 1991 DowBrands made yet

---

## AT A GLANCE

**Z**iploc brand of storage bags introduced in 1970 by DowBrands, the consumer products affiliate of the Dow Chemical Co. Dow was founded by Herbert Dow, 1897. DowBrands formed in 1953 and introduced its first product in 1960.

**Performance:** *Market share*—43% (top share) of food storage bags. *Sales*—$190.3 million (1991).

**Major competitor:** First Brands Glad bags.

**Advertising:** *Agency*—CME-KHBB, Minneapolis, MN 1991—. *Major campaign*—Fingerman, the finger with a smiling face on its tip, focusing on the different types of bags having the ability to keep food fresh. Ad accompanied by the tag line, "Ziploc Has The Lock On Freshness."

**Addresses:** *Parent company*—DowBrands, 9550 North Zionsville Rd., Indianapolis, IN 46268; phone: (317) 873-7000; fax: (317) 873-7316. *Ultimate parent company*—Dow Chemical Co., 2030 Willard H. Dow Center, Midland, MI, 48674; phone: (517) 636-1000; fax: (517) 636-0922.

another improvement in its zipper feature, the Gripper zipper feature. The locking strip felt like little plastic teeth when touched. According to a product manager for Ziploc bags, the feature "gives the consumer a definite tactile sensation when the bag is closed."

## Advertising Innovations

Early advertising campaigns for Ziploc bags focused on the benefits of the zipper seal. From 1981 to 1983, the country was experiencing high inflation and high food costs. DowBrands sought to show consumers that costs could be saved if there was less food spoilage, and this could be achieved by using high quality protection products. By 1984, the focus had shifted to how the bags could ensure that foods would stay fresh and good tasting. From 1986 to 1988, Dom DeLuise was used as a spokesperson because he was perceived as a lover of good food. The concept of food protection was emphasized with the tag line, "We've Got The Lock On Food Protection."

From 1989 to 1990, an advertising campaign had the tag line was "Put Your Trust In A Ziploc Bag." One humorous spot showed a woman jumping up and down on a Ziploc bag full of food. Despite her punishment, the bag did not break. A new spokesman was introduced in 1991 when the new Gripper zipper feature was introduced. Fingerman, a finger with a face painted on it, talked about the convenience of Ziploc bags and demonstrated how easy the bags were to seal—it only took one finger. The next campaign used Fingerman to point out how fresh food would stay in the bags. Sporting ear muffs, Fingerman also touted Ziploc freezer bags. In 1992 the advertising tag line was "There's Only One Ziploc," and in 1993 the tag line was, "Ziploc Has The Lock On Freshness."

## Performance Appraisal

In 1973, just one year after Ziploc storage bags went into national distribution, demand had outstripped supply and the company had to expand its manufacturing plant. By 1977 Ziploc had become the market leader with a 33 percent share, surpassing competitors that had introduced their plastic bags before Ziploc was introduced. In spite of the nation being gripped in a lingering recession during the late 1980s and early 1990s, sales increased. (Industry wisdom was that during recessions people eat more leftovers during tough economic times, thus increasing their use of food storage bags.) Twenty years later, in 1993, the market share for Ziploc bags had grown to 43 percent.

## Future Predictions

The Ziploc brand of storage bags was built on the premise that consumers will show loyalty to a well-made, dependable, and convenient product. DowBrands should continue its pattern of determining consumer preferences and needs, and consequently improve existing products or develop new products to satisfy them. Dowbrands envisions itself as a company that markets products that are "Consumers' First Choice Around the World." The company will continue its international market expansion as nations become more affluent and look for convenience items to enhance their lives.

### Further Reading:

*The Dow Chemical Company Annual Report,* Midland, MI: Dow Chemical Company, 1992.
"Leading National Advertisers," *Advertising Age,* September 23, 1992, p. 28.
McMurray, Scott, "Ziploc No Longer Has Its Market in the Bag," *Wall Street Journal,* December 24, 1991, p. 8.

*—Dorothy Kroll*

# ZIPPO®

The originators of the Zippo brand of lighters have long endeavored to make the name synonymous with old fashioned reliability and long-lasting dependability. Almost every GI had one during World War II. As a dependable source of flame and light, Zippo lighters were used to light campfires, cook soups, send fire signals, and simply to shed light when needed; the famed World War II correspondent Ernie Pyle once scratched a crucial message on the side of a Zippo: the destination of an attacking U.S. carrier: "TO-KYO." Zippo lighters, equipped with free repair service over the course of their lifetime guarantee and offering the option of personalized engravings, have become personal mementos as well as reliable windproof lighters. In the early 1990s, Zippo lighters were sold in four major styles—regular, slim, souvenir, and collectible—each available in a number of colors and more subtle style variations. While the Zippo Manufacturing Company has diversified into many similar products, including "writing instruments," knives, and keyholders, the Zippo lighter remains their central item.

## Brand Origins: An Entrepreneurial Man

As the force behind the success of the Zippo lighter, George Grant Blaisdell proved insightful and persistent. When in 1932 he failed to clear any profits on a shipment of cheap imported Austrian lighters, Blaisdell decided to redesign them, rename them, and manufacture them himself. Before the Zippo, Blaisdell had already struggled for a break in the business arena. At the age of 16, he went to work in his father's machinery factory in his hometown of Bradford, Pennsylvania. He became a salesman and took over the ailing business at the age of 20. Nursing it through the World War I on government contracts, Blaisdell sold the business in 1920 and went to New York to play the stock market. Unsuccessful, he returned to Bradford, invested his money in a few local oil wells, and lived modestly from these holdings over the next ten years. He was waiting for an opportunity to start a business himself when he discovered the opportunity in lighters.

On a muggy summer night in 1932 at the Bradford Pennhill Country Club, Blaisdell and a friend stepped out onto the Club terrace. Blaisdell's friend lit a cigarette with an Austrian lighter. Struck by the cumbersome look of the removable brass top, Blaisdell chided his friend: "You're all dressed up. Why don't you get a lighter that looks decent?" "Well, George," his friend replied, "it works!"

Impressed by his friend's loyalty to what seemed a reliable product, Blaisdell decided to begin selling them. He imported them for twelve cents each and tried to sell them for $1, but apparently their quality was not as high as he originally thought. The venture quickly failed. Not one to give up so easily, however, Blaisdell upgraded the quality and adapted the look for the U.S. market. He completely redesigned the case, making it rectangular and easier to hold in the hand. He attached the top to the main case with a hinge and added a wind hood to protect the wick. Inspired by the name of another recent invention, the zipper, Blaisdell named the new lighter a "Zippo."

Blaisdell struggled for years to develop the market for his windproof lighters. He began production in 1932 from a $10-per-month room over a Bradford gas station with $260 of equipment and two employees. Each Zippo sold for $1.95 at retail. Blaisdell's first major sales break came five years later in 1937 when he began selling Zippos via the use of punchboards, small-time gambling board games ruled illegal in 1940. He sold 65,000 lighters in 1937 through punchboards and for the first time cleared a small profit. Between 1934 and 1940, Blaisdell sold 300,000 lighters through punchboards.

Before his punchboard success, Blaisdell attempted to market Zippo lighters through free samples and gifts to long distance bus drivers, jewelers, and tobacconists. When he discovered that retailers were reluctant to stock an item unsupported by advertising, Blaisdell in 1937 spent $3,000 of mostly borrowed funds to place a full page advertisement in *Esquire* magazine. The ad, however, failed to bring the watershed of orders Blaisdell had hoped for. Still, Blaisdell continued to explore different marketing venues and began to witness the steady growth of his business. In 1936 Blaisdell first broke in to the specialty advertising market. In that year, an Iowa life insurance company ordered 200 engraved Zippo lighters to present to its salesman as contest prizes; similarly, the Kendall Oil Company in Bradford ordered 500 engraved Zippo lighters for its customers and employees. By 1938 Blaisdell had achieved a level of sales that could support a significant expansion of his production facilities. The sales staff moved into new office space while Zippo production expanded to occupy the entire floor of the original building. In 1938 the factory and offices were moved together into one building, a former garage.

## AT A GLANCE

**Z**ippo brand lighters established in 1932 in Bradford, PA, by the Zippo Manufacturing Company owner, George G. Blaisdell; brand became popular in World War II and has since grown internationally; known for its unconditional life-time guarantee: "It works always, or we fix it free!"; eventually sold in 80 countries.

*Performance:* Market share—Only U.S. manufacturer of non-disposable lighters.

*Major competitor:* None in U.S. non-disposable lighter market.

*Advertising:* Agency—Zadco (in-house), Bradford, PA, 1971—. *Major campaign*—"American Classics" series, a print and point-of-purchase set of advertisements featuring a Zippo next to such monuments as the Statue of Liberty and the Golden Gate Bridge, with the slogan, "American Classics."

*Addresses: Parent company*—Zippo Manufacturing Company, 33 Barbour St., Bradford, PA 16701; phone: (814) 368-2700; fax: (814) 362-3598.

## Zippo Development

Zippo Manufacturing Company began reshaping what was then its sole product, the Zippo lighter, in 1938. While Zippo construction remained solid and the Zippo quality pledge—that each will "work always or Zippo will fix it free"—remained unaltered, the design of the Zippo changed for peak performance and style. Zippo's first maturation culminated in the replacement of the soldered, square-cornered original with a single-unit rounded design in 1938. Following the 1938 change, Zippo introduced what was in 1939 its most sophisticated style yet—a plain or engine-turned 14-Karat solid gold Zippo.

World War II necessitated some changes in the Zippo design and precipitated Zippo's rise to international fame. The U.S. government ceased production of many consumer goods with their entry into the war. While Zippo production continued, it was entirely directed to fulfilling the demand of the U.S. military. Brass became unavailable for non-military uses, so Zippo lighters were then made out of low grade steel, sprayed with black paint, and baked to a dull black crackle finish. Virtually every serviceman owned one and Zippo lighters became famous. Blaisdell became known as "Mr. Zippo" through the daily column of World War II correspondent Ernie Pyle. This fame fueled Zippo's post-war sales growth and future international marketing efforts.

Immediately after the war, the Zippo Manufacturing Company noticed that the most frequent need for their free Zippo repairs arose from worn flint wheels. Blaisdell halted shipments of subsequent Zippo lighters and embarked on a $300,000 research program to design a better wheel. After consulting leading metallurgists, testing a number of types and combinations of steel, and experimenting with a variety of manufacturing operations, Zippo engineers developed what was considered to be the most reliable striking wheel in the world.

The Zippo brand continued to be recognized through the 1950s and beyond as the top quality lighter. In December 1956, *Consumers' Research Bulletin* rated Zippo's guarantee as the best among all lighter manufacturers of the time. Zippo's competitors at the time, the Evans Case Co. and Ronson Corp., also guaranteed

their lighters, but these guarantees offered repairs which were neither as cost-free to the consumer nor as comprehensive as Zippo's. In addition, the Zippo brand's flint wheel design was considered superior. "The Zippo is a non-automatic lighter operated by a flick of the thumb on the sparkling wheel; on that account there is little to get out of order; the most probable point of failure is the hinge on the case," stated *Consumers' Research Bulletin.* In contrast, the more complicated automatic design was more likely to break down or create a fire hazard, the chief danger associated with lighter use.

Meanwhile, the Zippo look continued to change with the times. In 1946 Zippo materials changed from low grade steel to nickel silver only. In 1947 Town and Country designs were introduced that featured portraits of pheasants, mallards, geese, and sailboats, among others. Full cover leather lighters and sterling silver lighters first became available in 1950. During the Korean War in the early 1950s, Zippo lighters switched once again to a steel case. After 1953, Zippo lighters switched back to chrome-plated brass. Silver and gold filled Zippo lighters were designed and introduced in 1955. The line of slim Zippo lighters—still available today—debuted in 1956. With the completion of a new etching and color filling process in 1957, still more intricate designs in any number of colors became available. Manufacturing date markings also began in 1957. Since then, Zippo has introduced a number of specialty series, including the Moon Landing series in 1969, the Zodiac series in the early 1970s, the founder edition, the Venetian design series in 1974, the Bicentennial series in 1976, the presidential election series in 1980, and the Wild West series in 1990.

*Featured on both sides of this 1947 Chrysler were Zippo lighters with removable flames and lids that closed. The car was commissioned by founder George G. Blaisdell for use in special events from 1948 to the 1960s.*

Table Zippo lighters were first introduced in 1949 and were available in the early 1990s in the Handilite style. Finally, in 1985 Zippo entered the refillable butane market with its "Contempo" lighter, protected under the same famous guarantee but targeted at the "upwardly mobile."

## Increased Production and International Distribution

All the while, the sales force supporting Zippo lighters matured. From 1939 to 1950, Zippo relied on two cigar salesmen who also sold Zippo lighters, mainly to tobacco wholesalers. In 1950, Zippo Manufacturing organized its own sales force, hiring district managers for specific areas of the country. Not restricted to tobacco wholesalers, the Zippo sales force called on jewelry, drug store, and grocery wholesalers as well.

International sales had begun in World War II, when U.S. GIs introduced Zippo lighters in Japan, the Middle East, and Europe. Impressed by their quality and life-time guarantee, consumers overseas just kept on buying. "I don't think we developed the market. The market [overseas] developed itself," the Zippo company president, Robert D. Galey, was quoted as saying in *Global Trade Executive*. In January of 1886, the same periodical reported that Zippo international sales were up during a time of generally decreased U.S. exports. For instance, in the Japanese market—generally tough for U.S. exporters—Zippo sold more than any other non-disposable lighter. In Tokyo, enthusiasts even developed a Zippo fan club and newsletter. In 1984, 40 percent of Zippo Manufacturing's $30 million to $40 million total sales derived from exports.

Corresponding with steadily growing Zippo sales, Zippo production and distribution has also increased, achieving notable international levels. A new building for chrome-plating and fabricating was opened in 1954 on Congress Street in Bradford, Pennsylvania. In 1950 Zippo Manufacturing opened a small plant in Niagara Falls, Ontario, Canada, which continued to grow in the early 1990s. New corporate offices were built in 1955 in Bradford. During the 1960s the Congress Street complex grew to become the primary location for the fabrication and assembly of Zippo lighters.

## The Diversification Highwire

Despite its international success, some marketing consultants deemed a decline inevitable within the U.S. market if Zippo Manufacturing failed to diversify. Clive Chajet, chairman of the identity and image management consultants Lippincott & Margulies, Inc., was quoted as saying in 1989 in *USA Today* that "Zippo is frozen in time. If all Zippo wants is nostalgia, that's terrific. But their image will eventually die as their audience ages." In contrast, Bill Jones, Zippo vice president for advertising in 1989, pointed out in *USA Today* the necessity of maintaining the unique integrity of the Zippo brand name—a name developed from the Zippo lighter.

The solution: diversification into related specialty advertising items. Zippo Manufacturing began this approach in 1962 when it

unveiled a six-foot flexible steel pocket rule, protected under the same lifetime guarantee. By the early 1990s, Zippo offered a large line of similar specialty items, including pen-and-pencil sets, money clips, knives, key holders, and even golf balls (each guaranteed playable for 180 holes). All products are covered by the famous Zippo guarantee and may be engraved for Zippo clients.

In the early 1990s Zippo lighters remained a mainstay of the expanded Zippo product line. In 1992 Zippo introduced their catalog as follows: "Welcome to the world of Zippo! We are proud to present the most comprehensive look at Zippo products we have ever produced. In this one catalog are more than 600 products beautifully illustrated in full-color. Starting with our world-famous Zippo windproof lighter."

The Zippo lighter still provided the force in the Zippo brand name. In 1989 the Zippo lighter was selling worldwide at the rate of 9 million annually. Zippo Manufacturing then installed manufacturing equipment worth $1.5 million to boost Zippo lighter production from 45,000 to 80,000 per day. The Zippo brand appears fit to retain its position for some time among *Interbrand*'s list of the "world's greatest brands."

## Further Reading:

"An American Classic: Zippo, 1932," Zippo, October 1992.

Collins, Lisa, "Keeping Zippo's Flame Name Is Hot, Marketing Lacks Spark," *USA Today*, August 11, 1989, p. 1B.

*Consumers' Research Bulletin*, December 1956, pp. 15–16.

*Global Trade Executive*, January 1986, p. 54.

"The History of Zippo Table Lighters," Zippo Manufacturing Company, 1993.

McGrath, Molly Wade, *Top Sellers, U.S.A.: Success Stories Behind America's Best-Selling Products from Alka-Seltzer to Zippo*, William Morrow and Company, 1983, p. 157.

"Mr. Zippo," *Fortune*, October 1952, p. 220.

"A New Zippo Lighter," *New York Times*, August 7, 1985, p. 33 (N).

"Safer Lighters," *Fortune*, June 29, 1992.

*World's Greatest Brands: An International Review by Interbrand*, John Wiley & Sons, p. 143.

"The Zippo Lighter and How It Grew . . . ," Zippo Manufacturing Company, 1993.

"The Zippo Lighter Collectors' Guide," Zippo Manufacturing Company, 1992.

"Zippo: The Name That Sells," Zippo Manufacturing Company, 1992.

*—Nicholas Patti*

# INDEX TO BRAND NAMES

Listings are arranged in alphabetical order under brand name. Brand names appearing in bold type have historical essays on the page numbers appearing in bold. The index is cumulative with volume numbers printed in bold type.

# INDEX TO COMPANIES AND PERSONS

Listings are arranged in alphabetical order under the company name; thus Philip Morris Companies Inc. will be found under the letter P. Definite articles (The) that precede the name are ignored for alphabetical purposes. The index is cumulative with volume numbers printed in bold type.

# INDEX TO ADVERTISING AGENCIES

# INDEX TO BRAND CATEGORIES

Brand categories are arranged alphabetically; listings beneath each category in turn are arranged alphabetically. This index contains only brand names that have individual historical essays in the series. The index is cumulative with volume numbers following the brand category.

## CIGARETTES
See TOBACCO

## CLEANING AGENTS   II
Ajax
Bon Ami
Borax
Brillo
Clorox
Comet
Drāno
Formula 409
Ivory
Johnson's Wax
Lava
Lysol
Mr. Clean
Palmolive
Pine-Sol
Pledge
S.O.S
Spic and Span
Windex

## CLOTHING
See APPAREL

## COFFEE   I
Folgers
Maxwell House
Nescafé
Sanka
Taster's Choice

## COLD CARE (also see ANALGESICS)   II
Alka-Seltzer
Contac
Dristan
Robitussin
Smith Brothers
Sucrets
Vicks

## COLOGNE
See FRAGRANCE

## CONDIMENTS, JAMS, AND SAUCES   I
French's
Grey Poupon
Heinz Ketchup
Hellmann's
Lea & Perrins
Miracle Whip
Ragú
Smucker's
Tabasco

## CONTRACEPTIVES   II
Trojan Condoms

## COSMETICS   II
Avon

Chanel
Cover Girl
Estée Lauder
L'Oréal
Max Factor
Maybelline
Revlon

## COTTON SWABS   II
Q-tips

## COUGH REMEDIES
See COLD CARE

## CRAYONS   II
Crayola

## DAIRY   I
Borden Dairy
Breyers
Carnation
Dannon
Kraft Cheese
Häagen-Dazs
Land O Lakes
Philadelphia Brand Cream Cheese
Velveeta
Yoplait

## DEODORANTS
See ANTIPERSPIRANTS AND DEODORANTS

## DESSERTS
See SNACK FOOD: SWEET

## DETERGENT
See DISHWASHING DETERGENT or LAUNDRY PRODUCTS

## DIAPERS   II
Huggies
Pampers

## DIET AIDS
See WEIGHT LOSS PROGRAMS

## DISHWASHING DETERGENT   II
Ajax
Ivory
Palmolive

## DOG FOOD
See PET FOOD

## DRUGS
See ANALGESICS or COLD CARE

## EYE CARE AND EYE WEAR   II
Bausch & Lomb
Ray-Ban

## FACIAL TISSUE   II
Kleenex
Puffs
Scott

## FASTENERS   II
Velcro

## FEMININE HYGIENE   II
Kotex
Playtex
Stayfree
Tampax

## FIRST AID
See BANDAGES

## FOOT CARE   II
Dr. Scholl's

## FRAGRANCE   II
Aramis
Calvin Klein
Chanel
Estée Lauder
Giorgio Beverly Hills
Liz Claiborne
Old Spice
Polo/Ralph Lauren

## FROZEN FOOD   I
Banquet
Birds Eye
Green Giant
Healthy Choice
Ore-Ida
Sara Lee
Stouffer's
Swanson
Van de Kamp's
Weight Watchers

## FRUITS AND VEGETABLES   I
Birds Eye
Chiquita
Del Monte
Dole Pineapple
Green Giant
Ore-Ida
Sunkist
Sun-Maid

## GRAINS: BREAD, PASTA, RICE I

Chef Boyardee
Rice-A-Roni
Uncle Ben's
Wonder Bread

## GREETING CARDS II

Hallmark

## HAIR COLOR II

Clairol
L'Oréal

## HOSIERY II

Hanes
Jockey
L'eggs

## IBUPROFIN

See ANALGESICS

## INSECT KILLER AND REPELLENT II

Off!
Raid

## JEWELRY

See WATCHES AND JEWELRY

## JUICE AND FRUIT-FLAVORED BEVERAGES I

Gatorade
Hawaiian Punch
Hi-C
Kool-Aid
Minute Maid
Ocean Spray
Tropicana
V-8
Welch's Grape Juice
Wyler's

## LAUNDRY PRODUCTS II

Ajax
all
Cheer
Clorox
Downey
Tide
Wisk

## LAXATIVES II

Ex-Lax
Phillips' Milk of Magnesia

## LEATHER II

Coach
Gucci

## LIGHTERS II

Bic
Zippo

## LIP BALM II

Chap Stick
Vaseline

## LIQUOR (also see BEER and WINE AND CHAMPAGNE) I

Absolut
Bacardi Rum
Baileys
Canadian Mist
Dewar's
Di Saronno Amaretto
Gordon's
Grand Marnier
J&B
Jack Daniel's
Jim Beam
Johnnie Walker
Jose Cuervo
Kahlua
Seagram's
Smirnoff
Southern Comfort
Tanqueray

## LUBRICANTS II

WD-40

## MAKEUP

See COSMETICS

## MARGARINE AND COOKING OIL I

Crisco
Fleischmann's
Land O Lakes
Mazola
Parkay

## MEAT I

Butterball
Healthy Choice
Louis Rich
Oscar Mayer
Perdue
Spam
StarKist
Tyson
Underwood
Van de Kamp's

## MOISTURIZERS

See SKIN CARE PRODUCTS

## MOUTHWASH II

Listerine
Scope

## OFFICE SUPPLY

See SCHOOL AND OFFICE SUPPLY

## OVER-THE-COUNTER DRUGS

See ANALGESICS or COLD CARE

## PAPER PLATES AND CUPS II

Chinet
Dixie Cups

## PAPER TOWELS II

Bounty
Scott

## PASTA

See GRAINS

## PEANUT BUTTER I

Jif
Skippy

## PENCILS

See WRITING INSTRUMENTS

## PENS

See WRITING INSTRUMENTS

## PERFUME

See FRAGRANCE

## PET FOOD I

Alpo
Friskies
Kal Kan
Mighty Dog
Milk-Bone
9-Lives
Purina Pet Chow
Whiskas

## PLASTIC BAGS II

Glad
Hefty
Ziplock

## PLASTIC WRAPS

See WRAPS

## RICE

See GRAINS

## SANITARY NAPKINS

See FEMININE HYGIENE

## SCHOOL AND OFFICE SUPPLY (also see WRITING INSTRUMENTS) II

Elmer's Glue
Mead
Post-It
Scotch Tape

## SCOURING PADS
### See CLEANING AGENTS

## SHAMPOO  II

Breck
Head & Shoulders
Ivory
Prell
Suave

## SHAVING  II

Bic
Burma Shave
Gillette
Mennen

## SHIRTS
### See APPAREL

## SHOE CARE  II

Kiwi

## SHOES (also see SHOES: ATHLETIC and SHOES: CHILDREN)  II

Bass
Florsheim
Hush Puppies
Keds
Red Wing Shoes

## SHOES: ATHLETIC  II

Adidas
ASICS
Avia
British Knights
Converse
K-Swiss
L.A. Gear
Nike
Reebok

## SHOES: CHILDREN  II

Buster Brown
Keds
Stride Rite

## SKIN CARE PRODUCTS (also see SUN CARE PRODUCTS)  II

Chap Stick
Jergens
Neutrogena
Nivea
Noxzema
Oil of Olay
Pond's
Vaseline

## SNACK FOOD: SALTY  I

Doritos
Fritos
Keebler

Lay's
Orville Redenbacher's
Pepperidge Farm
Planters
Ritz
Rold Gold
Ruffles
Wise

## SNACK FOOD: SWEET  I

Barnum's Animals Crackers
Breyers
Cracker Jack
Entenmann's
Fig Newtons
Häagen-Dazs
Jell-O
Keebler
Little Debbie
Oreo
Pepperidge Farm
Sara Lee
Twinkies

## SOAP
### See BATH AND HAND SOAP; CLEANING AGENTS; DISHWASHING DETERGENT; or LAUNDRY PRODUCTS

## SOFT DRINKS  I

A&W
Canada Dry
Coca-Cola
Dr Pepper
Hires
Mountain Dew
Pepsi-Cola
RC Cola
Schweppes
7UP
Shasta
Slice
Sprite

## SOUP  I

Campbell's Soup
Progresso Soup

## SPORTSWEAR (also see APPAREL)  II

Champion
Danskin
Jantzen
Speedo

## STATIONERY
### See GREETING CARDS or SCHOOL AND OFFICE SUPPLY

## SUGAR AND SWEETENER  I

Domino Sugar
NutraSweet

## SUN CARE PRODUCTS  II

Bain de Soleil
Coppertone
Hawaiian Tropic

## TAMPONS
### See FEMININE HYGIENE

## TEA  I

Lipton
Nestea
Salada
Tetley

## TISSUE
### See FACIAL TISSUE or TOILET TISSUE

## TOBACCO  I

Benson & Hedges
Camel
Kool
Lucky Strike
Marlboro
Newport
Salem
Virginia Slims
Winston

## TOILET TISSUE  II

Charmin
Northern
Scott

## TOOTHPASTE  II

Aquafresh
Close-Up
Colgate
Crest
Pepsodent

## UNDERGARMENTS (also see HOSIERY)  II

BVD
Calvin Klein
Carter's
Fruit of the Loom
Hanes
Jockey
Maidenform

## VEGETABLES
### See FRUITS AND VEGETABLES

## VITAMINS  II

Geritol

## WATCHES AND JEWELRY  II

Citizen
Monet
Rolex

# NOTES ON CONTRIBUTORS

**ARMSTRONG, Robin.** Free-lance writer. Contributor to *Contemporary Musicians, Contemporary Black Biography,* and *International Dictionary of Opera.*

**AVIZIENIS, Audra.** Free-lance writer.

**BARNSTORFF, Virginia.** Free-lance writer. Special assignment writer and mathematics correlator for Silver Burdett Ginn (Simon & Schuster), 1989–91. Contributing writer, *HSPT Success: Work-A-Text Study Program for Writing,* 1991.

**BERRY, Pam.** Free-lance writer and editor.

**BILAS, Wendy Johnson.** Free-lance writer with 8 years of professional marketing experience; MBA in marketing, Wake Forest University; director of marketing for the Charlotte Symphony Orchestra.

**BOYER, Dean.** Former newspaper reporter; free-lance writer in Seattle area.

**BROWN, Susan Windisch.** Free-lance writer and editor.

**COHEN, Kerstan.** Free-lance writer and French translator; editor for *Letter-Ex* poetry review, Chicago.

**DORMAN, Evelyn.** Free-lance journalist, public relations, French teacher, tutor, and graduate student. Contributor to *Brides Today,* the *Chicago Sun-Times, Lerner-Pulitzer* newspapers, and *International Directory of Company Histories.*

**DOUGAL, April S.** Archivist and free-lance writer specializing in business and social history.

**DUBOVOJ, Sina.** History contractor and free-lance writer; adjunct professor of history, Montgomery College, Rockville, Maryland.

**FINN, Michael.** Free-lance writer; consultant to the International Trademark Association. Former newspaper reporter and speechwriter.

**GOPNIK, Hilary.** Free-lance writer.

**INGRAM, Frederick.** Free-lance writer.

**KIELTYKA, Carol.** Free-lance writer.

**KING, Daniel E.** Free-lance writer working on doctorate in economics at the New School for Social Research.

**KROLL, Dorothy.** Free-lance business writer, journalist, and industry analyst.

**MASH, Jeffrey E.** Free-lance writer.

**MAXFIELD, Doris Morris.** Owner of Written Expressions, an editorial services business. Contributor to numerous reference publications. Editor of *Online Database Search Services Directory,* 1983–84

and 1988, and of *Charitable Organizations of the U.S.,* 1991–92 and 1992–93.

**McMANUS, Donald.** Free-lance writer.

**MOGELONSKY, Marcia K.** Free-lance editor and writer; contributor to *American Demographics,* the *Numbers News, Modern Women,* and other magazines.

**NEWMAN, Laura.** Free-lance business and medical journalist; correspondent for medical trade press and news publications.

**NORTON, Frances E.** Free-lance writer; contributor to *Evanston Arts Review* and *Helicon.*

**PATTI, Nicholas.** Free-lance writer. Master's degree in English from the University of Michigan, Ann Arbor.

**PEDERSON, Jay P.** Free-lance writer and editor.

**PENDERGAST, Sara.** Free-lance writer and editor.

**PENDERGAST, Tom.** Free-lance writer and graduate student in business administration at Purdue University.

**RIGGS, Thomas.** Free-lance writer and editor.

**SALTER, Susan.** Writer/contributor to several reference series, including *Contemporary Authors, Newsmakers,* and *Major Authors and Illustrators for Children and Young Adults.*

**SHEEHAN, Kate.** Free-lance writer in Chicago.

**SHERMAN, Francine Shonfeld.** Free-lance writer and editor. Assistant editor, *Compton's Encyclopedia,* 1986–92. Contributing editor, *Britannica Book of the Year,* annual.

**SIMLEY, John.** Professional researcher and corporate issues analyst. Former research editor for *International Directory of Company Histories.*

**TIVENAN, William.** Free-lance writer.

**TROESTER, Maura.** Chicago-based free-lance writer.

**TUDAHL, Kim.** Executive assistant/travel consultant, Oriental Tours & Travel, Cambridge, Massachusetts. Free-lance writer; contributor to the *Harbus News,* Harvard Business School, and the *Rochester Post-Bulletin.*

**WOLF, Gillian.** Free-lance writer. Author of ''The Ultimate Slingshot,'' 1989, and ''Akh, Odessa!'' 1990, both for *Jewish Affairs.*

**WOODWARD, Angela.** Free-lance writer.

**YOUNG, Shannon.** Ph.D. student in education at the University of Michigan. Free-lance writer and editor.